NEW HAMPSHIRE PLANNING AND LAND USE REGULATION

2017-2018 EDITION

Reprinted from LEXIS New Hampshire Revised Statutes
Annotated and 2017 Cumulative Supplement

 LexisNexis®

QUESTIONS ABOUT THIS PUBLICATION?

For CUSTOMER SERVICE ASSISTANCE concerning replacement pages,
shipments, billing, reprint permission, or other matters,

please contact Customer Support at our self-service portal
available 24/7 at *support.lexisnexis.com/print*
or call us at 800-833-9844

For EDITORIAL **content questions** concerning this publication,

please email: *LLP.CLP@lexisnexis.com*

For **information on other LEXISNEXIS MATTHEW BENDER publications**,

please call us at 800-223-1940
or visit our online bookstore at *www.lexisnexis.com/bookstore*

ISBN: 978-1-5221-4801-2

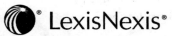 LexisNexis®

Matthew Bender & Company, Inc.
Editorial Offices
701 E. Water Street
Charlottesville, VA 22902
800-446-3410
www.lexisnexis.com

(Pub. 28821)

Preface

This publication is designed to provide a compilation of statutes relating to the performance of planning and land use regulation by municipalities in New Hampshire. It includes the full text of the statutes most frequently employed by local officials, including Title LXIV, "Planning and Zoning", accompanied by statutory notes and annotations, and an appendix listing and summarizing the content of other statutes relating to planning and land use regulation, and an Index. We have included a convenient listing of "Sections Affected by 2017 Legislation."

The statutes included in this publication include new legislation and amendments enacted through Chapter 258 of the 2017 Session of the General Court.

This publication contains annotations taken from decisions of the New Hampshire Supreme Court, and from decisions of the appropriate federal courts posted on *lexis.com* with decisions dates up through September 19, 2017. These cases will be printed in the following reports:

New Hampshire Reports
Atlantic Reporter, 3rd Series
Federal Supplement, 2nd Series
Bankruptcy Reporter
Federal Rules Decisions
Federal Reporter, 3rd Series
United States Supreme Court Reports, Lawyers' Edition, 2nd Series

December 2017

 LexisNexis·

Table of Contents

Sections Affected by 2017 Legislation

NOTE: In addition to the sections listed below, users of this edition should be aware that additional section and case note annotations have also been appropriately incorporated throughout this publication. The sections with new and/or revised annotations do *not* appear in this listing.

RSA	Effect	Bill No.	Act No.	Act Sec.
RSA 4-C:1	Amended	HB 517	156	63
RSA 4-C:2	Amended	HB 517	156	64
RSA 4-C:3	Amended	HB 517	156	64
RSA 4-C:5	Amended	HB 517	156	64
RSA 4-C:6	Amended	HB 517	156	64
RSA 4-C:7	Amended	HB 517	156	64
RSA 4-C:8	Amended	HB 517	156	64
RSA 4-C:9	Amended	HB 517	156	64
RSA 4-C:9-a	Amended	HB 517	156	64
RSA 4-C:10	Amended	HB 517	156	64
RSA 4-C:31	Enacted	HB 517	156	108
RSA 4-C:32	Enacted	HB 517	156	108
RSA 4-C:33	Enacted	HB 517	156	108
RSA 4-C:34	Enacted	HB 517	156	108
RSA 4-C:35	Enacted	HB 517	156	108
RSA 4-E:1	Amended	HB 517	156	64
RSA 9-A:1	Amended	HB 517	156	58
RSA 9-A:2	Amended	HB 517	156	64
RSA 9-A:4	Amended	HB 517	156	64
RSA 10:5	Enacted	HB 340	240	1
RSA 10:6	Enacted	HB 340	240	1
RSA 10:7	Enacted	HB 340	240	1
RSA 10:8	Enacted	HB 340	240	1
RSA 10:9	Enacted	HB 340	240	1
RSA 10:10	Enacted	HB 340	240	1
RSA 12-K:2	Amended	HB 517	156	64
RSA 12-K:3	Amended	HB 517	156	64
RSA 12-K:6	Amended	HB 517	156	64
RSA 12-K:8	Amended	HB 517	156	64
RSA 12-K:9	Amended	HB 517	156	64
RSA 31:95-h	Amended	HB 89	95	1
RSA 36:45	Amended	HB 517	156	64
RSA 36:46	Amended	HB 517	156	64
RSA 36:47	Amended	HB 517	156	64
RSA 36-A:2	Amended	HB 526	156	14
RSA 36-A:6	Amended	HB 527	156	14
RSA 79-E:2	Amended	SB 185	203	2
RSA 79-E:4-a	Enacted	SB 185	203	3
RSA 91-A:2	Amended	HB 460	165	1
RSA 91-A:2	Amended	HB 164	234	1
RSA 91-A:8-a	Enacted	HB 178	126	1
RSA 91-A:8-a	Repealed	HB 178	126	2
RSA 155-A:1	Amended	SB 135	201	3
RSA 155-A:2	Amended	SB 135	201	6
RSA 155-A:3-c	Enacted	HB 85	157	1
RSA 162-C:1	Amended	HB 517	156	43
RSA 162-C:1	Amended	HB 517	156	44
RSA 162-C:1	Amended	HB 517	156	64
RSA 162-C:2	Amended	HB 517	156	59

RSA	Effect	Bill No.	Act No.	Act Sec.
RSA 162-N:1	Amended	HB 517	156	14
RSA 162-N:2	Amended	HB 517	156	14
RSA 162-N:3	Amended	HB 517	156	14
RSA 162-N:4	Amended	HB 517	156	14
RSA 162-N:5	Amended	HB 517	156	14
RSA 162-N:7	Amended	HB 517	156	14
RSA 162-N:8	Amended	HB 517	156	14
RSA 162-N:9	Amended	HB 517	156	14
RSA 215-A:15	Amended	HB 163	56	1
RSA 215-C:32	Amended	HB 517	156	14
RSA 229:1	Amended	HB 517	156	123
RSA 482-A:3	Amended	HB 517	156	14
RSA 482-A:14-a	Amended	HB 517	156	14
RSA 482-A:32	Amended	HB 517	156	14
RSA 482-A:32	Amended	HB 517	156	64
RSA 483:8	Amended	HB 517	156	14
RSA 483:8	Amended	HB 517	156	64
RSA 483:10	Amended	HB 517	156	14
RSA 483:10	Amended	HB 517	156	64
RSA 483-A:6	Amended	HB 517	156	14
RSA 483-A:6	Amended	HB 517	156	64
RSA 483-A:7	Amended	HB 517	156	64
RSA 483-B:4	Amended	SB 118	38	1
RSA 483-B:4	Amended	SB 30	225	1
RSA 483-B:4	Amended	SB 30	225	2
RSA 483-B:5	Amended	HB 517	156	14
RSA 483-B:5	Amended	HB 517	156	64
RSA 483-B:5-b	Amended	SB 30	225	3
RSA 483-B:5-b	Amended	SB 30	225	4
RSA 483-B:7-a	Enacted	SB 121	256	1
RSA 483-B:7-a	Repealed	SB 121	256	2
RSA 483-B:9	Amended	HB 517	156	14
RSA 483-B:9	Amended	HB 517	156	14
RSA 483-B:9	Amended	SB 30	225	5
RSA 483-B:9	Amended	SB 30	225	6
RSA 483-B:9	Amended	SB 30	225	7
RSA 483-B:9	Amended	SB 30	225	8
RSA 483-B:9	Amended	SB 30	225	9
RSA 483-B:12	Amended	HB 517	156	64
RSA 483-B:15	Amended	HB 517	156	14
RSA 483-B:16	Amended	HB 517	156	64
RSA 483-B:22	Amended	HB 517	156	64
RSA 485-A:2	Amended	SB 127	211	1
RSA 485-A:4	Amended	HB 517	156	64
RSA 485-A:6	Amended	SB 127	211	3
RSA 485-A:8	Amended	SB 127	211	2
RSA 485-A:17	Amended	HB 517	156	14
RSA 485-A:22-a	Amended	HB 517	156	14
RSA 485-A:29	Amended	HB 258	238	1
RSA 485-A:32	Amended	HB 258	238	2
RSA 485-A:38	Amended	HB 258	238	3
RSA 489:6	Amended	HB 517	156	14
RSA 673:3-a	Amended	HB 517	156	64
RSA 673:6	Amended	HB 514	143	1
RSA 674:3	Amended	HB 517	156	64
RSA 674:27	Amended	HB 299	59	1
RSA 674:66	Amended	HB 299	59	2
RSA 674:72	Amended	HB 265	89	1

RSA	Effect	Bill No.	Act No.	Act Sec.
RSA 674:72	Amended	HB 258	238	4
RSA 675:7	Amended	HB 131	231	1
RSA 675:9	Amended	HB 517	156	64
RSA 676:4	Amended	HB 299	59	3
RSA 676:4-a	Amended	HB 299	59	4
RSA 676:7	Amended	HB 123	4	1
RSA 676:7	Amended	HB 299	59	5

TITLE I

THE STATE AND ITS GOVERNMENT

RESEARCH REFERENCES AND PRACTICE AIDS

Cross References.
Abuse of office, see RSA 643.
Administrative Procedure Act, see RSA 541-A.
Claims against the state, see RSA 541-B.
Construction and inspection of public buildings, see RSA 155-A.
Corrupt practices, see RSA 640.
Courts, see RSA 490 et seq.
Form of government generally, see New Hampshire Constitution, Part 2.
Liens on public work for labor and materials, see RSA 447:15– 18.

CHAPTER 4-C

OFFICE OF STRATEGIC INITIATIVES

HISTORY:
2017, 156:62, eff. July 1, 2017.

Amendment Notes

—2004.
2004, 257:44, eff. July 1, 2004, substituted "office of energy and planning" for "office of state planning and energy programs" in the chapter heading.

—2003.
2003, 319:8, eff. July 1, 2003, added "and energy programs" following "planning" in the chapter heading.

RESEARCH REFERENCES AND PRACTICE AIDS

Cross References.
Council on resources and development, see RSA 162-C.
Interstate Regional Planning Compact, see RSA 36-B.
Lakes management and protection program, see RSA 483-A.
Planning and zoning generally, see RSA 672 et seq.
Rivers management and protection program, see RSA 483.

4-C:1. Establishment; General Duties and Responsibilities.

I. There is established the office of strategic initiatives within the office of the governor. The office of strategic initiatives shall be under the supervision and direction of the governor or the governor's designee. The governor's designee shall be known as the director of the office of strategic initiatives. The office of strategic initiatives shall include the division of energy and the division of planning.

II. The office of strategic initiatives shall:

(a) Plan for the orderly development of the state and the wise management of the state's resources.

(b) Compile, analyze, and disseminate data, information, and research services as necessary to advance the welfare of the state.

(c) Encourage and assist planning, growth management, and development activities of cities and towns and groups of cities and towns with the purpose of encouraging smart growth.

(d) Encourage the coordination and correlation of state planning by agencies of state government.

(e) Participate in interstate, regional, and national planning efforts.

(f) Administer federal and state grant-in-aid programs assigned to the office by statute or executive order.

(g) Participate and advise in matters of land use planning regarding water resources and floodplain management.

(h) Take a leadership role in encouraging smart growth and preserving farmland, open space land, and traditional village centers.

(i) Administer the following programs: the statewide comprehensive outdoor recreation plan, the national flood insurance program, the land conservation investment program, fuel assistance contracts, and weatherization contracts. The office shall employ necessary personnel to administer these programs. In administering fuel assistance and weatherization contracts, the office shall ensure that when an individual applies for fuel assistance or weatherization, the individual shall be provided with application forms and information about the Link-Up New Hampshire and Lifeline Telephone Assistance programs, and shall be provided assistance in applying for these programs.

(j) Perform such other duties as the governor may assign.

HISTORY:
1987, 283:3. 1989, 263:10. 1990, 118:1, eff. June 18, 1990. 1996, 251:4, eff. Aug. 9, 1996. 2000, 292:1, 2, eff. Aug. 20, 2000. 2003, 319:10, eff. July 1, 2003. 2004, 257:44, eff. July 1, 2004. 2005, 20:3, eff. May 10, 2005. 2007, 263:173, eff. July 1, 2007. 2011, 224:110, eff. July 1, 2011. 2017, 156:63, eff. July 1, 2017.

Amendment Notes
The 2017 amendments to this section by Ch. 156, in the introductory paragraph of I, substituted "office of the strategic initiatives" for "office of energy and planning" in the first through third sentences, and added the last sentence; and substituted "office of the strategic initiatives" for "office of energy and planning" in the introductory language of II.

—2011.
The 2011 amendment substituted "water resources and floodplain management" for "lakes and rivers management programs" in II(g) and deleted "the scenic and cultural byways system" following "investment program" in the first sentence of II(i).

—2007.
Paragraph II(i): Added the third sentence.

—2005.
Paragraph II(i): Deleted "the coastal zone management program, the New Hampshire estuaries project, the saltmarsh restorability program, the southeast New Hampshire groundwater sustainability program" preceding "the statewide comprehensive".

—2004.
Substituted "office of energy and planning" for "office of state planning and energy programs" in par. I and in the introductory paragraph of par. II.

—2003.
Rewritten to the extent that a detailed comparison would be impracticable.

—2000.
Paragraph II: Added "with the purpose of encouraging smart growth" following "groups of cities and towns" in subpar. (c), added a new subpar. (j) and redesignated former subpar. (j) as present subpar. (i).

—1996.
Paragraph II(h): Deleted "under RSA 149-M:13-a, II" following "towns".

—1990.
Paragraph II: Added a new subpar. (i) and redesignated former subpar. (i) as subpar. (j).

—1989.
Paragraph II: Added new subpars. (g) and (h) and redesignated former subpar. (g) as subpar. (i).

Transfer of Estuaries Project From Department of Environmental Services to University of New Hampshire.
2005, 20:1, eff. May 10, 2005, provides:
"I. Notwithstanding any provision of law to the contrary, all of the functions, powers, duties, and responsibilities of the department of environmental services relating to the New Hampshire estuaries project shall be transferred to the university of New Hampshire. The transfer provided for in this section shall include, but not be limited to, the following personnel from the estuaries project: position numbers 9T003, 9T005, and 8Temp. The transfer provided in this section shall include all of the equipment, books, papers, records, unexpended appropriations, and other available funds in any account or subdivision of an account of the department of environmental services related to the above function and authorized for use by the department of environmental services for said project.

"II. All existing rules, statutory responsibilities, regulations, and procedures in effect, in operation, or adopted in or by the New Hampshire estuaries project are transferred to the university of New Hampshire, and are declared in effect and shall continue in effect until rescinded, revised, or amended in accordance with applicable law."

RESEARCH REFERENCES AND PRACTICE AIDS

Cross References.
Administrative attachment of Connecticut River Valley resource commission to office, see RSA 227-E:3.

4-C:2. State Development Plan.

I. The office of strategic initiatives, under the direction of the governor, shall:

(a) Assist the governor in preparing, publishing, and revising the comprehensive development plan required under RSA 9-A.

(b) Coordinate and monitor the planning efforts of various state agencies and departments to ensure that program plans published by such agencies are consistent with the policies and priorities established in the comprehensive development plan.

(c) Coordinate and monitor the planning efforts of the regional planning commissions to ensure that the plans published by the commissions are consistent, to the extent practical, with the policies and priorities established in the state development plan.

II. In preparing the state development plan, the office of strategic initiatives shall consult with the chief executive officers of the various departments and agencies of state government. The office shall also consult with officials of regional planning commissions and regional and local planning and development agencies, local officials, representatives of the business and environmental community, and the general public.

III. All state agencies and departments shall provide the office of strategic initiatives with information and assistance as required by the office to fulfill its responsibilities under RSA 4-C:2, I. The office shall maintain the confidentiality of any information which is protected by law.

HISTORY:
1987, 283:3, eff. May 25, 1987. 2002, 229:2, 3, eff. July 1, 2002. 2003, 319:9, eff. July 1, 2003. 2004, 257:44, eff. July 1, 2004. 2011, 224:111, eff. July 1, 2011. 2017, 156:64, eff. July 1, 2017.

Amendment Notes
The 2017 amendments to this section by Ch. 156 substituted "office of strategic initiatives" for "office of energy and planning" in the introductory language of I and in II and III.

—2011.
The 2011 amendment deleted former I(b), which read: "Develop and maintain a technical data base of information to support statewide policy development and planning" and redesignated former I(c) and I(d) as I(b) and I(c).

—2004.
Substituted "office of energy and planning" for "office of state planning and energy programs" wherever it appeared throughout the section.

—2003.
Substituted "office of state planning and energy programs" for "office of state planning" in the introductory paragraph of par. I, and in pars. II and III.

—2002.
Paragraph I(d): Added.
Paragraph II: Deleted "with responsibilities which are relevant to economic development" following "state government" in the first sentence, and substituted "shall" for "may" following "office", and "local officials, representatives of the business and environmental community, and the general public" for "and representatives of business and industry" in the second sentence.

RESEARCH REFERENCES AND PRACTICE AIDS

Cross References.
Coordination of state resources and development activities, see RSA 4-C:6.

4-C:3. Data and Information Services.

The office of strategic initiatives shall:
I. Gather, tabulate, and periodically publish information on the location and pace of development throughout the state, including, but not limited to, population, housing, and building permit data.
II. Initiate data coordination procedures as the state agency responsible for coordinating data collection and dissemination among the state, the private sector, and the various political subdivisions.
III. Gather information for storage in a data bank concerning the data which is currently available within all state agencies. This data shall be used to provide information which is useful in measuring growth and its impact and for statewide planning purposes in general. The data available for dissemination shall include, but shall not be limited to, information for determining future demands for state services and demographic and economic statistics. Any other state agency or department which initiates a data collection program shall inform the office of strategic initiatives of its efforts so that the office may utilize that information for planning purposes in its dissemination program.
IV. Cooperate with the department of environmental services in identifying potential sites for hazardous waste facilities.
V. Develop and maintain a computerized geographic information system in support of state, regional, or local planning and management activities.
VI. Cooperate with the Bureau of the Census and other federal agencies with the objective of improving access to the statistical products, data, and information of the federal government.
VII. Annually estimate the resident population for all cities and towns of the state pursuant to RSA 78-A:25.

HISTORY:
1987, 283:3, eff. May 25, 1987. 1996, 228:108, eff. July 1, 1996. 2003, 319:9, eff. July 1, 2003. 2004, 257:44, eff. July 1, 2004. 2017, 156:64, eff. July 1, 2017.

Amendment Notes
The 2017 amendments to this section by Ch. 156 substituted "office of strategic initiatives" for "office of energy and planning" in the introductory language and in the last sentence of III.

—2004.
Substituted "office of energy and planning" for "office of state planning and energy programs" in the introductory paragraph and in par. III.

—2003.
Substituted "office of state planning and energy programs" for "office of state planning" in the introductory paragraph and in paragraph III.

—1996.
Paragraph IV: Substituted "department of environmental services" for "division of waste management".

RESEARCH REFERENCES AND PRACTICE AIDS

Cross References.
Hazardous waste facility review generally, see RSA 147-C.

4-C:4. Coordinator of Federal Funds. [Repealed.]

[Repealed 2011, 224:112, eff. July 1, 2011.]

Former section(s).
Former RSA 4-C:4, which was derived from 1987, 283:3; 1992, 242:5; 2003, 319:9; and 2004, 257:44, related to the coordination of federal funds in the office of energy and planning.

4-C:5. Rulemaking Authority.

The director of the office of strategic initiatives shall adopt rules, as necessary, under RSA 541-A, establishing procedures for grant programs administered by the office. These rules shall be adopted for all state grant programs administered by the office in which the office has authority to establish requirements or procedures or interpret state statutes. These rules shall include, as appropriate:

I. Application or grant distribution procedures.

II. Criteria and procedures for evaluating applications.

III. Procedures for administration of funds by grantees.

IV. Monitoring and report procedures.

V. Appeal procedures for parties dissatisfied with grant decisions.

HISTORY:

1987, 283:3, eff. May 25, 1987. 2003, 319:9, eff. July 1, 2003. 2004, 257:44, eff. July 1, 2004. 2011, 224:114, eff. July 1, 2011. 2017, 156:64, eff. July 1, 2017.

Amendment Notes

The 2017 amendments to this section by Ch. 156 substituted "office of strategic initiatives" for "office of energy and planning" in the first sentence of the introductory language.

—2011.

The 2011 amendment, in the introductory language, in the first sentence, added "as necessary" and deleted the I designation following " RSA 541-A" and in the second sentence, deleted "federal or" following "adopted for all" and "federal requirements and" following "or interpret"; redesignated former I(a) through I(e) as I through V; and deleted former II, which read: "As provided by RSA 4-C:16, I(a)."

—2004.

Substituted "office of energy and planning" for "office of state planning and energy programs" in the introductory paragraph.

—2003.

Substituted "office of state planning and energy programs" for "office of state planning" in the introductory paragraph.

4-C:5-a. Model Ordinance. [Repealed.]

[Repealed 2011, 224:115, I, eff. July 1, 2011.]

Former section(s).

Former RSA 4-C:5-a, which was derived from 2008, 357:4, related to model ordinances.

4-C:6. Coordination.

I. The office of strategic initiatives shall formulate policies and plans for consideration by the governor which serve to integrate and coordinate resource and development activities affecting more than one state agency, level of government, or governmental function. Nothing in this paragraph shall be construed to grant the governor any additional authority to implement such plans beyond that which has been granted to him under the constitution and other laws of this state. Such activities may include, but shall not be limited to, the following subject areas:

(a) Water resources.

(b) Transportation.

(c) Recreation and natural resources.

(d) Solid waste and hazardous waste management.

(e) Off-shore, coastal, and estuarine resources.

(f) Housing.

(g) Economic development.

(h) Energy.

(i) Shoreland protection.

(j) Smart growth.

II. The director of the office of strategic initiatives or his designee shall promote coordination of state agency planning and management activities through participation in the deliberations of the following statutory bodies:

(a) Council on resources and development as established in RSA 162-C:1;

(b) [Repealed.]

(c) Wetlands council as established in RSA 21-O:5-a;

(d) Site evaluation committee as established in RSA 162-H:3;

(e) [Repealed.]

(f) Agricultural lands preservation committee as established in RSA 432:19.

HISTORY:

1987, 283:3. 1989, 339:3. 1991, 303:2, eff. July 1, 1994. 1996, 228:2, eff. July 1, 1996. 296:2, eff. Aug. 9, 1996. 1998, 264:5, eff. June 26, 1998. 2000, 292:3, eff. Aug. 20, 2000. 2003, 319:9, eff. July 1, 2003. 2004, 257:44, eff. July 1, 2004. 2014, 217:28(I), eff. July 1, 2014. 2015, 67:3, eff. August 1, 2015. 2017, 156:64, eff. July 1, 2017.

Effective date of 1991 amendment

1991, 303:10, I, as amended by 1994, 383:25, eff. July 1, 1994, provided that the amendment to this section by 1991, 303:2, shall take effect on July 1, 1994.

Amendment Notes

The 2017 amendments to this section by Ch. 156 substituted "office of strategic initiatives" for "office of energy and planning" in the introductory languages of I and II.

—2015.

The 2015 amendment deleted II(b), which read: "Water council as established in RSA 21-O:7."

—2014.

The 2014 amendment deleted II(e).

—2004.

Paragraphs I and II: Substituted "office of energy and planning" for "office of state planning and energy programs" in the introductory paragraphs.

—2003.

Substituted "office of state planning and energy programs" for "office of state planning" in pars. I and II.

—2000.

Paragraph I(j): Added.

—1998.

Paragraph II: Deleted "Bulk power supply facility" preceding "Site" and substituted "162-H:3" for "162-F:3".

—1996.

Paragraph II(b): Chapter 228 deleted "supply and pollution control" following "water".

Paragraph II(c): Chapter 296 substituted "council" for "board" following "wetlands" and " RSA 21-O:5-a" for " RSA 482-A:5".

—1991.
Paragraph I(i): Added.

—1989.
Paragraph II(c): Substituted " RSA 482-A:5" for " RSA 483-A:1-c".

Reports on Economic Development Loans and Grants

4-C:6-a. Reports on Economic Development Program Loans and Grants. [Repealed.]

[Repealed 2011, 224:115, II, eff. July 1, 2011.]

Former section(s).
Former RSA 4-C:6-a, which was derived from 1996, 189:1; 2000, 292:4; 2003, 319:9; and 2004, 257:44, related to reports on economic development loans and grants.

Regional and Municipal Assistance

RESEARCH REFERENCES AND PRACTICE AIDS

Cross References.
Planning and zoning generally, see RSA 672 et seq.
Regional planning commissions, see RSA 36:45– 35:50, RSA 36:53.

4-C:7. Program Established.

The director shall establish a program of regional and municipal assistance within the office of strategic initiatives. This program shall coordinate state, regional, and local planning efforts with the goal of assuring delivery of efficient and effective assistance to local governments in areas related to growth management and resource protection.

HISTORY:
1987, 283:3, eff. May 25, 1987. 2003, 319:9, eff. July 1, 2003. 2004, 257:44, eff. July 1, 2004. 2017, 156:64, eff. July 1, 2017.

Amendment Notes
The 2017 amendments to this section by Ch. 156 substituted "office of strategic initiatives" for "office of energy and planning" in the first sentence.

—2004.
Substituted "office of energy and planning" for "office of state planning and energy programs" in the first sentence.

—2003.
Substituted "office of state planning and energy programs" for "office of state planning".

4-C:8. Responsibilities for Assistance.

The office of strategic initiatives shall:
I. Provide technical assistance and, within the limits of biennial legislative appropriations, financial grants to regional planning commissions established under RSA 36:45–36:53 in support of:
(a) Planning assistance to local units of government.
(b) Preparation of regional plans.
(c) Contributions to and coordination with statewide planning and management activities, including the formulation and updating of the comprehensive state development plan prepared pursuant to RSA 4-C:2.
II. As requested and in cooperation with regional planning commissions, provide technical assistance and information in support of the planning and growth management efforts of local units of government, including training requested under RSA 673:3-a. The office shall encourage municipalities to first seek assistance from established regional planning commissions.
III. Provide computer interface capability among and between each regional planning commission, the office of strategic initiatives, and state data collection and storage sources. The computer interface capability shall be used by regional planning commissions to respond to municipal requests for assistance in the preparation and amending of master plans and in the evaluation of municipal infrastructure needs. The computer interface capability shall also be used by regional planning commissions to develop and update regional master plans, as provided in RSA 36:47. The computer equipment used for the purposes of this paragraph shall be compatible and able to interface with the office of strategic initiatives's geographic information system, as well as with other similar state computerized data collection and storage sources.
IV. Provide technical assistance and information to municipalities with the cooperation of other state and regional planning agencies in the following areas:
(a) Use and application of geographic data available in the state's geographic information system (GIS) for local planning and growth management purposes.
(b) Recommending standard procedures for the establishment of accurate, large-scale base mapping to support municipal administrative functions such as tax assessment, public facility management and engineering.

HISTORY:
1987, 283:3. 1988, 102:1. 1989, 366:2, eff. July 1, 1989. 2003, 319:11, eff. July 1, 2003. 2004, 257:44, 45, eff. July 1, 2004. 2017, 156:64, eff. July 1, 2017.

Amendment Notes
The 2017 amendments to this section by Ch. 156 substituted "office of strategic initiatives" for "office of energy and planning" in the introductory language and in the first and last sentences of III.

—2004.
Substituted "office of energy and planning" for "office of state planning and energy programs" in the introductory paragraph.

Paragraph III: Substituted "office of energy and planning" for "office of state planning and energy programs" in the first sentence and "office of energy and planning's" for "office of state planning and energy program's" in the fourth sentence.

—2003.

Inserted "and energy programs" following "planning" in the introductory paragraph; substituted " RSA 36:45– 36:53" for " RSA 36:45 et seq." in the introductory paragraph of par. I, "statewide" for "state-wide" in par. I(c); inserted "and energy programs" following "planning" in the first sentence and substituted "planning and energy program's" for "planning's" in the fourth sentence of par. III.

—1989.

Paragraph IV: Added.

—1988.

Paragraph III: Added.

RESEARCH REFERENCES AND PRACTICE AIDS

References in text.

RSA 36:51 and 52, contained in RSA 36:45– 36:53 in par. I, were repealed by 2000, 200:8, I, II, respectively, eff. July 29, 2000.

4-C:9. Coordination at State Level.

The office of strategic initiatives shall coordinate efforts by state agencies to provide technical assistance to municipal governments in areas related to growth management and resource protection.

HISTORY:

1987, 283:3, eff. May 25, 1987. 2003, 319:9, eff. July 1, 2003. 2004, 257:44, eff. July 1, 2004. 2017, 156:64, eff. July 1, 2017.

Amendment Notes

The 2017 amendments to this section by Ch. 156 substituted "office of strategic initiatives" for "office of energy and planning."

—2004.

Substituted "office of energy and planning" for "office of state planning and energy programs".

—2003.

Substituted "office of state planning and energy programs" for "office of state planning".

4-C:9-a. Revolving Funds.

In order to enhance its ability to provide education and training assistance to municipalities and regional agencies, the following nonlapsing revolving funds, which shall not exceed $20,000 on June 30 of each year, shall be established in the office of strategic initiatives:

I. A revolving fund known as the publications revolving fund.

(a) The moneys in this fund shall be used for the purposes of printing materials for distribution. A reasonable charge shall be established for each copy of a document. This charge shall be only in the amount necessary to pay the cost of producing such document.

(b) The amount in the nonlapsing publications revolving fund shall not exceed $20,000, on June 30 of each year and any amounts in excess of $20,000 on June 30 of each year shall

be deposited in the general fund as unrestricted revenue.

II. A revolving fund known as the municipal and regional training fund.

(a) The moneys in this fund shall be used for the purpose of providing training to local and regional officials. A reasonable charge shall be established for such training. This charge shall be fixed to reflect the cost of payments to experts to provide the training, the cost of written training material, rental of facilities, advertising and other associated costs. Such training shall be conducted in a geographically dispersed manner and scheduled with the convenience of part-time officials in mind.

(b) The amount in the nonlapsing municipal and regional training revolving fund shall not exceed $20,000 on June 30 of each year and any amounts in excess of $20,000 on June 30 of each year shall be deposited in the general fund as unrestricted revenue.

HISTORY:

1989, 245:1, eff. July 25, 1989. 2003, 319:9, eff. July 1, 2003. 2004, 257:44, eff. July 1, 2004. 2017, 156:64, eff. July 1, 2017.

Amendment Notes

The 2017 amendments to this section by Ch. 156 substituted "office of strategic initiatives" for "office of energy and planning" in the introductory language.

—2004.

Substituted "office of energy and planning" for "office of state planning and energy programs" in the introductory paragraph.

—2003.

Substituted "office of state planning and energy programs" for "office of state planning" in the introductory paragraph.

4-C:10. Contact Point.

The office of strategic initiatives shall serve as the state's point of contact for local and regional officials seeking assistance from the state on growth management and resource protection matters.

HISTORY:

1987, 283:3, eff. May 25, 1987. 2003, 319:9, eff. July 1, 2003. 2004, 257:44, eff. July 1, 2004. 2017, 156:64, eff. July 1, 2017.

Amendment Notes

The 2017 amendments to this section by Ch. 156 substituted "office of strategic initiatives" for "office of energy and planning."

—2004.

Substituted "office of energy and planning" for "office of state planning and energy programs".

—2003.

Substituted "office of state planning and energy programs" for "office of state planning".

Community Development Block Grants

4-C:11–4-C:18. [Repealed.]

[Repealed 2003, 319:15, eff. July 1, 2003.]

III. A person shall not have been adjudicated delinquent or convicted or pled guilty or nolo contendere to any felonies or any second or subsequent alcohol or drug-related offenses under the laws of this or any other state, or under the laws of the United States, except that an otherwise eligible person who has been adjudicated delinquent or has been convicted or pled guilty or nolo contendere to a second or subsequent alcohol or drug-related misdemeanor offense shall be eligible or continue to be eligible for a scholarship after the expiration of one academic year from the date of adjudication, conviction, or plea.

HISTORY:
  2017, 156:108, eff. July 1, 2017.

4-C:34. Governor's Scholarship Fund Established.

I. There is hereby established in the office of the state treasurer the governor's scholarship fund which shall be kept distinct and separate from all other funds. The fund shall provide scholarships for the benefit of eligible residents of the state pursuing programs of study or training at a postsecondary educational institution or training program within the state.

II. The state treasurer shall credit to the fund any appropriation relating to the governor's scholarship program made to the department of education, division of higher education for each fiscal year. The state treasurer shall invest the fund in accordance with RSA 6:8. Any earnings on trust fund moneys shall be added to the fund.

III. All moneys in the fund shall be nonlapsing.

IV. The office may institute promotional programs and solicit and receive gifts or donations of any kind for the purpose of supporting educational scholarships from the fund. The office may accept gifts to the fund including, but not limited to, cash gifts, and real or personal property, without the approval of the governor and council.

V. All gifts, grants, and donations of any kind shall be credited to the fund.

HISTORY:
  2017, 156:108, eff. July 1, 2017.

4-C:35. Procedures.

I. All scholarship funds shall be distributed by the postsecondary educational institution. The institution shall include the scholarship in the student's financial aid package and may seek subsequent reimbursement. The state shall provide the reimbursements twice per year to each institution for the number of eligible students enrolled in the current semester or term who are receiving a scholarship in the amount of $1,000. An institution shall submit the list of scholarship students to the office or its designee no later than November 30 and April 30 of each academic year, and shall be reimbursed within 30 days of those submittal dates.

II. An eligible person may receive a scholarship in the amount of $1,000 per year provided he or she maintains at least a 2.0 grade point average. An eligible person who earned the New Hampshire scholar designation at the time of high school graduation shall be eligible to receive a scholarship in the amount of $2,000 per year provided he or she maintains at least a 2.5 grade point average. In all cases the postsecondary educational institution shall agree to not reduce any merit or need based grant aid that would have otherwise been provided to the eligible person. An eligible person may receive an annual scholarship for a maximum of 4 years.

III. In the event the state does not reimburse a postsecondary educational institution for scholarship amounts paid to an eligible person receiving an award, the institution shall agree not to seek additional payments from the eligible person and to absorb the loss of funds without any consequence to the student.

IV. The office shall determine procedures for distributing scholarship funds to an eligible person enrolled in an approved training program.

HISTORY:
  2017, 156:108, eff. July 1, 2017.

CHAPTER 4-E
STATE ENERGY STRATEGY

Section

State Energy Strategy; Purpose.
  2013, 276:1, eff. July 24, 2013, provided: "Development of a state energy strategy is necessary to ensure that the state's energy policies and programs support the state's economic, environmental, and public health goals."

State Energy Strategy; Findings.
  2013, 276:2, eff. July 24, 2013, provided:
  "**I.** The general court finds that a comprehensive energy strategy will:
  "**(a)** Provide forward-looking guidance on electric, gas, and thermal energy strategies.
  "**(b)** Optimize the ready availability of energy supply, energy affordability, the retention in-state of energy expenditures, the retention of jobs, and the use of renewable energy sources and energy efficiency policies, including demand-side policies.
  "**(c)** Minimize negative impacts to the economy, the environment, and the natural beauty of our state.
  "**II.** The general court further finds that the use of funding sources under the jurisdiction of the public utilities commission, notwithstanding requirements under other provisions of law, to fund the development of a state energy strategy is in the public interest."

4-E:1. State Energy Strategy.

I. The office of energy planning, in consultation with the state energy advisory council established in

RSA 4-E:2, with assistance from an independent consultant and with input from the public and interested parties, shall prepare a 10-year energy strategy for the state. The office shall review the strategy and consider any necessary updates in consultation with the senate energy and natural resources committee and the house science, technology and energy committee, after opportunity for public comment, at least every 3 years starting in 2017. The state energy strategy shall include, but not be limited to, sections on the following:

(a) The projected demand for consumption of electricity, natural gas, and other fuels for heating and other related uses.

(b) Existing and proposed electricity and natural gas generation and transmission facilities, the effects of future retirements and new resources, and consideration of possible alternatives.

(c) Renewable energy and fuel diversity.

(d) Small-scale and distributed energy resources, energy storage technologies, and their potential in the state.

(e) The role of energy efficiency, demand response, and other demand-side resources in meeting the state's energy needs.

(f) The processes for siting energy facilities in the state and the criteria used by the site evaluation committee in giving adequate consideration to the protection of the state's ecosystems and visual, historic, and aesthetic resources in siting processes.

(g) The relationship between land use and transportation policies and programs on electricity and thermal energy needs in the state.

(h) New Hampshire's role in the regional electric markets, how the regional market affects the state's energy policy goals, and how the state can most effectively participate at the regional level.

II. The strategy shall include a review of all state policies related to energy, including the issues in paragraph I, and recommendations for policy changes and priorities necessary to ensure the reliability, safety, fuel diversity, and affordability of New Hampshire's energy sources, while protecting natural, historic, and aesthetic resources and encouraging local and renewable energy resources. The strategy shall also include consideration of the extent to which demand-side measures including efficiency, conservation, demand response, and load management can cost-effectively meet the state's energy needs, and proposals to increase the use of such demand resources to reduce energy costs and increase economic benefits to the state.

III. The strategy development process shall include review and consideration of relevant studies and plans, including but not limited to those developed by the independent system operator of New England (ISO-NE), the public utilities commission, the energy efficiency and sustainable energy board, legislative study committees and commissions, and other state and regional organizations as appropriate. The strategy shall also include consideration of new technologies and their potential impact on the state's energy future.

HISTORY:
2013, 276:3, eff. July 24, 2013. 2017, 156:64, eff. July 1, 2017.

Editor's Notes
2017, 156:64 provided for the amendment of this section by replacing "office of energy and planning" with "office of strategic initiatives"; however, that language was not in the current version of this section.

4-E:2. New Hampshire State Energy Advisory Council. [Repealed]

HISTORY:
2013, 276:3, eff. July 24, 2013.

4-E:3. Public Participation. [Repealed]

HISTORY:
2013, 276:3, eff. July 24, 2013.

4-E:4. Costs. [Repealed]

HISTORY:
2013, 276:3, eff. July 24, 2013.

4-E:5. Reports. [Repealed]

HISTORY:
2013, 276:3, eff. July 24, 2013.

CHAPTER 9-A
STATE DEVELOPMENT PLAN

Rescinded 1987 amendments.
1987, 76:1, eff. July 1, 1987, provided for amendment of this chapter by the addition of a subdivision, entitled "Regional and Municipal Assistance," and comprised of RSA 9-A:5– 9-A:8. However, under the terms of 1987, 283:14, eff. May 25, 1987, the provisions of 1987, 76:1 did not take effect. Provisions similar to those which appeared in 1987, 76:1, were included in RSA 4-C, as added by 1987, 283:3, See RSA 4-C:7– 4-C:10.

RESEARCH REFERENCES AND PRACTICE AIDS

Cross References.
Council on resources and developement, see RSA 162-C.
Office of state planning, see RSA 4-C.

9-A:1. Comprehensive Plan.

I. There shall be a comprehensive state development plan which establishes state policy on development related issues and proposes new or expanded programs to implement such policies. The plan shall provide a basis for identifying critical issues facing the state, determining state priorities, allocating limited state resources, and taking into account the plans of various state, regional, and local governmental units.

II. The comprehensive development plan shall establish policies in areas related to the orderly physical, social, and economic growth and development of the state.

III. The comprehensive development plan shall include:

(a) State policies to provide for the orderly growth and development of the state and to maximize smart growth.

(b) Goals and policies which are relevant to the topical areas included in the plan, including but not limited to:

(1) An overall vision section that serves as the direction for the other sections of the plan. This section shall contain a set of statements which articulates the desires of the public relative to the future. It shall contain a set of guiding principles and priorities to implement that vision, with special emphasis on maximizing the smart growth principles in RSA 9-B.

(2) A land use section which examines the state's role in land development and in funding projects and programs which affect land uses.

(3) A transportation section which considers all pertinent modes of transportation and provides a framework of policies and actions which will provide for a safe and adequate transportation system to serve the needs of the state.

(4) A public facilities section which examines the projected needs of state institutions and coordinates with other governmental units, whether federal, county, local, special districts, or school districts, as to their needs as well.

(5) A housing section which sets forth approaches to meeting the need for affordable housing.

(6) An economic development section which proposes actions and policies to suit the state's economic goals and needs, based on the current and projected economic strengths and weaknesses. The section shall reference the economic development strategy and operating plan and process developed by the division of economic development under RSA 12-O:24 through 12-O:28.

(7) A natural resources section which identifies trends in land protection, open space, farm land preservation and protection, and proposes policies and actions necessary at the state level to protect those resources which are perceived to be of statewide significance.

(8) A natural hazards section which identifies actions to improve the ability of the state to minimize damages from future disasters that affect land and property subject to such disasters.

(9) A recreation section which assesses current and future recreation needs within the foreseeable future and identifies policies and a plan of action to support them at the state level.

(10) A utility and public service section which details state level policies and actions necessary to assure adequate service to the citizens of the state.

(11) A regional concerns section which describes specific areas of the state with potentially unique concerns and identifies policies and actions which may reasonably be undertaken to assist in addressing those issues.

(12) A section which identifies state policies and actions necessary to protect cultural and historic resources of statewide significance and assist in their rehabilitation or preservation, and generally assure their availability for future generations of state citizens.

(13) An implementation section, which is a long range action program for assessing the effectiveness of each section of the plan.

IV. The comprehensive development plan shall serve as the basis for policy and program development by the various departments of state government. State agencies shall develop and regional planning commissions and local planning boards are encouraged to develop plans which are consistent with the policies and priorities established in the comprehensive development plan.

V. The comprehensive development plan shall be renewed or revised every 4 years, beginning on October 1, 2003, and the plan transmitted to the general court.

HISTORY:

1985, 270:4, eff. June 10, 1985. 2000, 292:5, eff. Aug. 20, 2000. 2002, 229:4, eff. July 1, 2002. 2008, 248:2, eff. June 24, 2008. 2014, 275:4, eff. July 28, 2014. 2017, 156:58, eff. July 1, 2017.

Amendment Notes

The 2017 amendments to this section by Ch. 156, in the second sentence III(b)(6), substituted "economic development strategy and operating plan" for "economic development operating plan" and "RSA 12-O:24 through 12-O:28" for "RSA 12-A:62."

—2014.
The 2014 amendment added the second sentence of III(b)(6).

—2008.
The 2008 amendment added "and the plan transmitted to the general court" at the end of V.

—2002.
Paragraph I: Added the second sentence.
Paragraph II: Inserted "physical, social, and economic growth" following "orderly".
Paragraph III: Rewritten to the extent that a detailed comparison would be impracticable.
Paragraph IV: Substituted "and regional planning commissions and local planning boards are encouraged to develop" for "program" in the second sentence.
Paragraph V: Added.

—2000.
Paragraph III: Added subpar. (d) and made stylistic changes in subpars. (b) and (c).

Cross References.
Preparation of plan generally, see RSA 4-C:2.

9-A:2. Office of Strategic Initiatives.

The office of strategic initiatives, under the direction of the governor, shall:

I. Assist the governor in preparing, publishing and revising the comprehensive development plan.

II. Develop and maintain a technical data base of information to support statewide policy development and planning.

III. Coordinate and monitor the planning efforts of various state agencies and departments to ensure that program plans published by such agencies are consistent with the policies and priorities established in the comprehensive development plan.

IV. Coordinate and monitor the planning efforts of the regional planning commissions.

HISTORY:
1985, 270:4, eff. June 10, 1985. 2002, 229:5, eff. July 1, 2002. 2003, 319:9, eff. July 1, 2003. 2004, 257:44, eff. July 1, 2004. 2017, 156:64, eff. July 1, 2017.

Amendment Notes
The 2017 amendments to this section by Ch. 156 substituted "Office of Strategic Initiatives" for "Office of Energy and Planning" in the section heading; and substituted "office of strategic initiatives" for "office of energy and planning" in the introductory language.

—2004.
Substituted "office of energy and planning" for "office of state planning and energy programs" in the section heading and introductory paragraph.

—2003.
Substituted "office of state planning and energy programs" for "office of state planning" in the section catchline and in the introductory paragraph.

—2002.
Paragraph IV: Added.

Cross References.
Powers and duties of office of state planning generally, see RSA 4-C:1.

9-A:3. Transmittal of Plan. [Repealed.]

[Repealed 2008, 248:1, eff. June 24, 2008.]

Former section(s).
Former RSA 9-A:3, which was derived from 1985, 270:4, related to transmitting the comprehensive development plan to the general court.

9-A:4. Consultation With Other Agencies.

I. In preparing the state development plan, the office of strategic initiatives shall consult with the chief executive officers of the various departments and agencies of state government with responsibilities which are relevant to economic development.

II. The office may also consult with officials of regional and local planning and development agencies and representatives of business and industry.

III. All state agencies and departments shall provide the office of strategic initiatives with such information and assistance required by the office to fulfill its responsibilities under RSA 9-A:2. The office shall maintain the confidentiality of any information which is protected by law.

HISTORY:
1985, 270:4, eff. June 10, 1985. 2003, 319:9, eff. July 1, 2003. 2004, 257:44, eff. July 1, 2004. 2017, 156:64, eff. July 1, 2017.

Amendment Notes
The 2017 amendments to this section by Ch. 156 substituted "office of strategic initiatives" for "office of energy and planning" in I and in the first sentence of III.

—2004.
Paragraphs I and III: Substituted "office of energy and planning" for "office of state planning and energy programs".

—2003.
Substituted "office of state planning and energy programs" for "office of state planning" in pars. I and III.

Cross References.
Preparation of plan generally, see RSA 4-C:2.

9-A:5. Commission on Rural Affairs Established.

There is established a commission to study and make recommendations relating to public policy that specifically affects rural areas and rural people.

I. The members of the commission shall be as follows:

(a) One member of the senate, appointed by the president of the senate.

(b) One member of the house of representatives, appointed by the speaker of the house of representatives.

(c) Eight public members drawn from, respectively, the areas of health care, agriculture, natural resources, business, public safety, telecommunications, youth services, and local government, appointed by the governor.

(d) Two members appointed by the chancellor of the university system of New Hampshire, one of whom shall be an employee of the UNH cooperative extension.

(e) One member appointed by the chancellor of the community college system of New Hampshire.

II. Members of the commission shall serve without compensation. Legislative members of the commission shall serve a term coterminous with their term in office. Non-legislative members appointed under subparagraphs I(c), (d), and (e) shall serve for a term of 3 years, except that the initial appointment of such members shall be for staggered terms of one, 2, and 3 years. No member shall serve more than 3 consecutive terms.

III. The commission shall study and recommend actions:

(a) To expand economic and social opportunities for rural communities and their residents.

(b) To promote equal treatment of and effective delivery to rural areas by government agencies and the private sector.

(c) To assess the effectiveness of programs designed to promote rural viability.

(d) To provide a collective voice for rural areas.

IV. The commission shall have the authority to accept and expend funds from any public or private source, including private gifts, grants, and donations. The funds shall be used exclusively to further the purposes of the commission, which may include the payment of mileage to members of the commission.

V. The members of the commission shall elect a chairperson from among the members. The first meeting of the commission shall be called by the first-named senate member. The first meeting of the commission shall be held within 45 days of the effective date of this section. Four members of the commission shall constitute a quorum.

VI. Beginning September 15, 2015, and each September 15 thereafter, the commission shall submit an annual report of its findings and any recommendations for proposed legislation to at least the president of the senate, the speaker of the house of representatives, the senate clerk, the house clerk, the governor, and the state library.

HISTORY:
2014, 209:1, eff. July 11, 2014.

CHAPTER 9-B

STATE ECONOMIC GROWTH, RESOURCE PROTECTION, AND PLANNING POLICY

9-B:1. Findings.

The general court finds that:

I. In addition to clean water and air, productive mountain, forest, and agricultural open space land is one of the state's most valuable assets, and is necessary for the economy and health and welfare of the citizens. The maintenance of this asset is vital if the state is to provide future generations with the same quality of life and environment that we have traditionally enjoyed.

II. Economic development is essential to the well-being and prosperity of our citizens. However, when haphazard development sprawls across the state's landscape, our collective well-being suffers. Fortunately, economic development can take place in a form that maximizes smart growth.

III. The state can encourage development in accordance with this chapter by regularly reviewing its operating procedures, granting policies, and regulatory framework.

IV. A coordinated and comprehensive planning effort by state agencies on future development in the state is needed, which will not only improve our economy, but also encourages smart growth by locating development in appropriate growth areas and thus retaining as much open space land as possible for the long-term.

HISTORY:
2000, 292:6, eff. Aug. 20, 2000.

9-B:2. Policy.

It shall be the policy of the state of New Hampshire that state agencies act in ways that encourage smart growth.

HISTORY:
2000, 292:6, eff. Aug. 20, 2000.

9-B:3. Definition.

In this chapter, "smart growth" means the control of haphazard and unplanned development and the use of land which results over time, in the inflation of the amount of land used per unit of human development, and of the degree of dispersal between such land areas. "Smart growth" also means the development and use of land in such a manner that its physical, visual, or audible consequences are appropriate to the traditional and historic New Hampshire landscape. Smart growth may include denser development of existing communities, encouragement of mixed uses in such communities, the protection of villages, and planning so as to create ease of movement within and among communities. Smart growth preserves the integrity of open space in agricultural, forested, and undeveloped areas. The results of smart growth may include, but shall not be limited to:

I. Vibrant commercial activity within cities and towns.

II. Strong sense of community identity.

III. Adherence to traditional settlement patterns when siting municipal and public buildings and services.

IV. Ample alternate transportation modes.

V. Uncongested roads.

VI. Decreased water and air pollution.

VII. Clean aquifer recharge areas.

VIII.　Viable wildlife habitat.
IX.　Attractive views of the landscape.
X.　Preservation of historic village centers.

HISTORY:
2000, 292:6, eff. Aug. 20, 2000.

9-B:4.　Expenditure of State or Federal Funds.

All state agencies shall give due consideration to the state's policy on smart growth under RSA 9-B:2 when providing advice or expending state or federal funds, for their own use or as pass-through grants, for public works, transportation, or major capital improvement projects, and for the construction, rental, or lease of facilities. The intent of this action is that new investments and grants for existing sites and buildings in existing community centers will be given preference over investments in outlying areas where that is a practical solution for the use and community in question.

HISTORY:
2000, 292:6, eff. Aug. 20, 2000.

9-B:5.　Procedures for Review.

The governor shall review actions taken by state agencies relative to the provisions of RSA 9-B:4 to ensure compliance with this chapter. The governor shall establish procedures for review no later than December 1, 2000.

HISTORY:
2000, 292:6, eff. Aug. 20, 2000.

9-B:6.　Report to the General Court and the Governor.

By October 1 of 2001, and every 4 years thereafter, the council on resources and development, established in RSA 162-C, shall report to the general court and the governor on the following:
I.　Progress by state agencies in complying with the expenditure requirements under RSA 9-B:4.
II.　Progress by the state agencies represented on the council in coordinating the activities to encourage smart growth.
III.　Efforts made to encourage development in accordance with this chapter by regular review of state operating procedures, granting policies, and regulatory framework.
IV.　Suggested policy changes or legislation that the council believes would strengthen the state's ability to achieve the smart growth goal of RSA 9-B:2.
V.　An assessment of how state agencies are complying with the goals and objectives established in the statewide development plan, under RSA 9-A, and an identification of any suggested changes.

HISTORY:
2000, 292:6, eff. Aug. 20, 2000. 2002, 229:6, 7, eff. July 1, 2002.

Amendments

—2002.
Substituted "2001, and every 4 years thereafter" for "each year, beginning in the year 2000" in the introductory paragraph and added par. V.

CHAPTER 10
STATE INSTITUTIONS

Lakeshore Redevelopment Planning Commission

Lakeshore Redevelopment Planning Commission

10:5.　Lakeshore Redevelopment Planning Commission.

I.　There is hereby established the lakeshore redevelopment planning commission to study the former Laconia state school land and buildings and training center property to identify potential development alternatives, including but not limited to potential public private partnerships, for the purpose of developing the state-owned property for self-sustaining economic development and job creation for the benefit of the city of Laconia, Belknap county, and the state of New Hampshire.
II.　In this subdivision, "commission" means the lakeshore redevelopment planning commission, and "lakes region facility" means the former Laconia state school land and buildings and training center property.
III.　The provisions of this subdivision shall be liberally construed in order to effect its purpose. Nothing in this subdivision shall be construed to waive the state's sovereign immunity.

HISTORY:
2017, 240:1, eff. July 18, 2017.

10:6.　Membership; Meetings; Compensation.

I.　The commission shall be comprised of the following members:
　(a)　Three members who shall have experience as real estate developers or have business experience, appointed by the governor and council.
　(b)　One member with business experience who is a resident of Belknap county, appointed by the governor and council.
　(c)　One member appointed by the mayor and city council of the city of Laconia.

(d) One member with business experience, appointed by the speaker of the house of representatives.

(e) One member with business experience, appointed by the senate president.

II. The governor shall appoint a member of the commission to be the chairperson.

III. Appointments to the commission shall be made within 20 days of the effective date of this section. The first meeting shall be not later than 30 days after the effective date of this section. The commission shall hold meetings at the call of the chairperson. Meetings shall be held at least quarterly. Four members of the commission shall constitute a quorum. An affirmative vote by 4 members is necessary for any action by the commission.

IV. Members shall serve without compensation from the commission, except for reimbursement of such incidental expenses determined by the commission to be necessary which are incurred while performing commission business.

HISTORY:
2017, 240:1, eff. July 18, 2017.

10:7. Duties of the Commission.

The commission shall:

I. Conduct a comprehensive evaluation and study of the physical and environmental condition of the lakes region facility, including the land and buildings. This study shall have as a primary concern collecting information to assess the potential of the lakes region facility for economic development benefitting the city of Laconia, Belknap county, and the state. This study may include undertaking environmental reviews and assessments necessary to evaluate opportunities and alternatives for future site reuse and development.

II. Formulate a comprehensive plan, including potential alternative uses which may also include change of ownership, for the reuse and redevelopment of the lakes region facility. This plan shall include an evaluation and recommendation regarding each existing building at the lakes region facility, assessing its potential for short-term and long-term reuse and redevelopment. Such recommendations shall be consistent with the purposes of this subdivision. This plan shall also include an evaluation of proposed financing mechanisms for implementing any recommended action proposed by the commission.

III. Solicit input from relevant parties to identify potential reuse and redevelopment opportunities from a broad range of public and private sources, not limited to, developers, planners, and state, county, and municipal officials.

IV. Identify potential opportunities for integrating future reuse and redevelopment of the lakes region facility with Ahern state park that will mutually benefit both locations, and make recommendations based upon the findings.

V. Explore different partnership models and agency structures, including a state authority similar to the Pease development authority, and recommend a governing structure to implement the comprehensive plan for reuse and redevelopment prepared by the commission.

VI. Identify opportunities to fund the elimination of barriers to reuse and redevelopment, including, but not limited to, the receipt of grants, awards, tax credits, and other similar public or private funds.

VII. Develop recommendations for infrastructure needs related to the lakes region facility for consideration in the state capital budget for fiscal years 2020 and 2021. Recommendations may include but not be limited to any transportation, water, or redevelopment needs based on the comprehensive evaluation of the lakes region facility prepared by the commission.

VIII. Make recommendations, in consultation with the planning board and the city council in the city of Laconia, for any local planning or zoning changes needed to further reuse and redevelopment of the lakes region facility, including, without limitation, integrating such reuse and redevelopment with Ahern state park.

IX. Make recommendations for any legislative changes necessary to implement the recommendations by the commission.

X. Make recommendations for administrative rule changes necessary to implement the recommendations of the commission.

HISTORY:
2017, 240:1, eff. July 18, 2017.

10:8. Powers of the Commission.

I. The commission may appoint a coordinator and establish committees and subcommittees of the commission. The commission, or the coordinator subject to the direction of the commission, may hire agents and employees, without regard to any personnel or civil service law or rule of the state, prescribe their duties and qualifications, and fix and pay their compensation and expenses. Any person hired by the commission as an employee shall be a nonclassified employee of the state, an employee at will, and serve at the pleasure of the commission.

II. Notwithstanding any other provision of law, the commission may:

(a) Request, accept, and expend any federal funds available to the commission to carry out the purposes of this subdivision or the duties of the commission, provided that state funds available to be expended by the commission shall not exceed $365,000 in capital and general fund appropriations.

(b) Make purchases and enter into contracts on behalf of the commission without regard to any provision of law relating to public purchases or contracts.

(c) Enter into leases or rental agreements with terms not to exceed 3 years for office space or equipment deemed necessary by the commission to carry out its duties under this subdivision.

III. Notwithstanding any other provision of law, public employees and officials, both elected or appointed, of the state and any of its political subdivisions may serve, if appointed in accordance with the provisions of this subdivision, as commission members or members of any committee or subcommittee of the commission. Any such public employee or official shall serve without compensation, except that such officials and employees may be reimbursed by the commission for such incidental expenses determined by the commission to be necessary and incurred while performing commission business.

HISTORY:
2017, 240:1, eff. July 18, 2017.

10:9. Coordinator Authorized.

I. The coordinator, if one is appointed by the commission, shall be the chief executive and administrative officer of the commission and shall have general and active supervision and direction over the day-to-day business and affairs of the commission and its committees, subcommittees, employees, and consultants, subject, however, to the direction and control of the commission.

II. The coordinator shall perform all such other duties as from time to time may be assigned to him or her by the commission.

III. The coordinator shall be entitled to:

(a) Such compensation as established by the commission subject to approval by the fiscal committee of the general court; and

(b) Payment for such other necessary expenses incurred while actually engaged in the performance of her or his duties under this subdivision.

IV. Once appointed, the coordinator shall serve in such capacity until he or she resigns or is removed by vote of the commission. The commission may remove the coordinator without cause and for any reason.

HISTORY:
2017, 240:1, eff. July 18, 2017.

10:10. Reports.

The commission shall make its first report no later than September 1, 2018, and every 6 months thereafter or more frequently as deemed necessary by the commission, to each of the appointing authorities under RSA 10:5 and to the capital budget overview committee under RSA 17-J. The initial report shall include a progress report of the commission's work and any proposals for legislation deemed necessary by the commission.

HISTORY:
2017, 240:1, eff. July 18, 2017.

CHAPTER 12-K

DEPLOYMENT OF PERSONAL WIRELESS SERVICE FACILITIES

Redesignation of chapter; revision of internal references.
RSA 12-K was originally enacted as RSA 12-J by 2000, 240:1, but was redesignated, pursuant to 2000, 240:7, in light of the enactment of RSA 12-J by 2000, 204:2. All internal references to RSA 12-J appearing in this chapter have been revised to refer to RSA 12-K pursuant to 2000, 240:7.

12-K:1. Goals; Purpose.

I. The federal Telecommunications Act of 1996 regulates the deployment of wireless services in the United States. Its purpose is to make these services available to the American people quickly and in a very competitive manner. Nothing in this chapter is intended to preempt the federal Telecommunications Act of 1996.

II. The visual effects of tall antenna mounts or towers may go well beyond the physical borders between municipalities, and should be addressed so as to require that all affected parties have the opportunity to be heard.

III. Carriers wishing to build personal wireless service facilities (PWSFs) in New Hampshire should consider commercially available alternative PWSFs to tall cellular towers, which may include the use of the following:

(a) Lower antenna mounts which do not protrude as far above the surrounding tree canopies.

(b) Disguised PWSFs such as flagpoles, artificial tree poles, light poles, and traffic lights, which blend in with their surroundings.

(c) Camouflaged PWSFs mounted on existing structures and buildings.

(d) Custom designed PWSFs to minimize the visual impact of a PWSF on its surroundings.

(e) Other available technology.

IV. A PWSF map is necessary to allow for the orderly and efficient deployment of wireless communication services in New Hampshire, and so that local communities have adequate information with which to consider appropriate siting and options to mitigate the visual effects of PWSFs.

V. Municipalities will benefit from state guidance regarding provisions to be considered in zoning ordinances relative to the deployment of wireless communications facilities, including one or more model ordinances.

V-a. It is the policy of this state to facilitate the provision of broadband and other advanced personal wireless services across the state; and to promote access to broadband and advanced personal wireless services for all residents, students, government agencies, and businesses to ensure the availability of educational opportunities, economic development, and public safety services throughout New Hampshire. Deployment of personal wireless service facilities infrastructure is also critical to ensuring that first responders can provide for the health and safety of all residents of New Hampshire. Consistent with the federal Middle Class Tax Relief and Job Creation Act of 2012, Public Law 112-96, section 6409, which creates a national wireless emergency communications network for use by first responders that will be dependent on facilities placed on existing antenna mounts or towers, it is the policy of this state to facilitate the collocation of personal wireless services facilities on existing antenna mounts or towers in all areas of New Hampshire, while also allowing for expeditious modification of existing personal wireless service facilities to keep pace with technological improvements.

VI. Except as provided in RSA 12-K:10 and RSA 12-K:11, nothing in this chapter shall be construed as altering any municipal zoning ordinance, and this chapter itself shall not be construed as a zoning ordinance.

HISTORY:
   2000, 240:1, eff. Aug. 7, 2000. 2013, 267:1, 2, eff. September 22, 2013.

Amendments

—2013.
   The 2013 amendment added V-a and added "Except as provided in RSA 12-K:10 and RSA 12-K:11" in VI.

Severability of 2013 amendment
   2013, 267:12, eff. September 22, 2013, provided: "If any provision of this chapter or the application thereof to any person or circumstance is held invalid, such invalidity shall not affect other provisions or applications of the chapter which can be given effect without the invalid provision or application, and to that end the provisions of this chapter are declared to be severable."

RESEARCH REFERENCES AND PRACTICE AIDS

References in text.
   The Telecommunication Act of 1996, referred to in par. I, is classified as 47 U.S.C.S. §§ 151 et seq.

12-K:2. Definitions.

In this chapter:

I. "Accessory equipment" means any equipment serving or being used in conjunction with a PWSF or mount. The term includes utility or transmission equipment, power supplies, generators, batteries, cables, equipment buildings, cabinets and storage sheds, shelters, or similar structures.

II. "Antenna" means the equipment from which wireless radio signals are sent and received by a PWSF.

III. "Applicant" means a carrier or any person engaged in the business of providing the infrastructure required for a PWSF who submits a collocation application or a modification application.

IV. "Authority" means each state, county, and each governing body, board, agency, office, or commission of a municipality authorized by law to make legislative, quasi judicial, or administrative decisions relative to the construction, installation, modification, or siting of PWSFs and mounts. The term shall not include state courts having jurisdiction over land use, planning, or zoning decisions made by an authority.

V. "Average tree canopy height" means the average height found by inventorying the height above ground level of all trees over a specified height within a specified radius.

VI. "Base station" means a station at the base of a mount or in the area near the PWSF that is authorized to communicate with mobile stations, generally consisting of radio transceivers, antennas, coaxial cables, power supplies, and other associated electronics.

VII. "Building permit" means a permit issued pursuant to RSA 676 by an authority prior to the collocation or modification of PWSFs, solely to ensure that the work to be performed by the applicant satisfies the applicable building code.

VIII. "Camouflaged" means for a personal wireless service facility one that is disguised, hidden, part of an existing or proposed structure, or placed within an existing or proposed structure.

IX. "Carrier" means a person that provides personal wireless services.

X. "Collocation" means the placement or installation of new PWSFs on existing towers or mounts, including electrical transmission towers and water towers, as well as existing buildings and other structures capable of structurally supporting the attachment of PWSFs in compliance with applicable codes. "Collocation" does not include a "substantial modification."

XI. "Collocation application" shall mean a request submitted by an applicant to an authority for collocation on a tower or mount.

XII. "Director" means the director of the office of strategic initiatives.

XIII. "Disguised" means, for a PWSF, designed to look like a structure which may commonly be found in the area surrounding a proposed PWSF such as, but not limited to, flagpoles, light poles, traffic lights, or artificial tree poles.

XIV. "Electrical transmission tower" means an electrical transmission structure used to support high voltage overhead power lines. The term shall not include any utility pole.

XV. "Equipment compound" means an area surrounding or near the base of a tower or mount supporting a PWSF, and encompassing all equipment shelters, cabinets, generators, and appurtenances primarily associated with the PWSF.

XVI. "Equipment shelter" means an enclosed structure, cabinet, shed vault, or box near the base of a mount within which are housed equipment for PWSFs, such as batteries and electrical equipment.

XVII. "Height" means the height above ground level from the natural grade of a site to the highest point of a structure.

XVIII. "Modification" means the replacement or alteration of an existing PWSF within a previously approved equipment compound or upon a previously approved mount. Routine maintenance of an approved PWSF shall not be considered a modification.

XIX. "Modification application" means a request submitted by an applicant to an authority for modification of a PWSF.

XX. "Mount" means the structure or surface upon which antennas are mounted and includes roof-mounted, side-mounted, ground-mounted, and structure-mounted antennas on an existing building, as well as an electrical transmission tower and water tower, and excluding utility poles.

XXI. "Municipality" means any city, town, unincorporated town, or unorganized place within the state.

XXII. "Personal wireless service facility" or "PWSF" or "facility" means any "PWSF" as defined in the federal Telecommunications Act of 1996, 47 U.S.C. section 332(c)(7)(C)(ii), including facilities used or to be used by a licensed provider of personal wireless services. A PWSF includes the set of equipment and network components, exclusive of the underlying tower or mount, including, but not limited to, antennas, accessory equipment, transmitters, receivers, base stations, power supplies, cabling, and associated equipment necessary to provide personal wireless services.

XXIII. "Radio frequency emissions" means the emissions from personal wireless service facilities, as described in the federal Telecommunications Act of 1996, 47 U.S.C. section 332(c)(7)(B)(iv).

XXIV. "Tower" shall mean a freestanding or guyed structure, such as a monopole, monopine, or lattice tower, designed to support PWSFs.

XXV. "Substantial modification" means the mounting of a proposed PWSF on a tower or mount which, as a result of single or successive modification applications:

(a) Increases or results in the increase of the permitted vertical height of a tower, or the existing vertical height of a mount, by either more than 10 percent or the height of one additional antenna array with separation from the nearest existing antenna not to exceed 20 feet, whichever is greater; or

(b) Involves adding an appurtenance to the body of a tower or mount that protrudes horizontally from the edge of the tower or mount more than 20 feet, or more than the width of the tower or mount at the level of the appurtenance, whichever is greater, except where necessary to shelter the antenna from inclement weather or to connect the antenna to the tower or mount via cable; or

(c) Increases or results in the increase of the permitted square footage of the existing equipment compound by more than 2,500 square feet; or

(d) Adds to or modifies a camouflaged PWSF in a way that would defeat the effect of the camouflage.

XXVI. "Utility pole" means a structure owned and/or operated by a public utility, municipality, electric membership corporation, or rural electric cooperative that is designed specifically for and used to carry lines, cables, or wires for telephony, cable television, or electricity, or to provide lighting.

XXVII. "Water tower" means a water storage tank, or a standpipe or an elevated tank situated on a support structure, originally constructed for use as a reservoir or facility to store or deliver water.

HISTORY:
2000, 240:1, eff. Aug. 7, 2000. 2003, 319:9, eff. July 1, 2003. 2004, 257:44, eff. July 1, 2004. 2013, 267:3, eff. September 22, 2013. 2017, 156:64, eff. July 1, 2017.

Amendment Notes
The 2017 amendments to this section by Ch. 156 substituted "office of strategic initiatives" for "office of energy and planning" in XII.

—2013.
The 2013 amendment rewrote the section to the extent that a detailed comparison would be impracticable.

—2004.
Paragraph V: Substituted "office of energy and planning" for "office of state planning and energy programs".

—2003.
Paragraph V: Substituted "office of state planning and energy programs" for "office of state planning".

Severability of 2013 amendment
2013, 267:12, eff. September 22, 2013, provided: "If any provision of this chapter or the application thereof to any person or circumstance is held invalid, such invalidity shall not affect other provisions or applications of the chapter which can be given effect without the invalid provision or application, and to that end the provisions of this chapter are declared to be severable."

12-K:3. Wireless Carriers Doing Business in this State.

Each carrier or its appointed agent doing business, or seeking to do business, in this state shall:

I. Be allowed to construct new towers, provided that these towers comply with municipal regulations for maximum height or maximum allowed height above the average tree canopy height, subject to any exceptions, waivers, or variances allowed or granted by the municipality.

II. Comply with all applicable state and municipal land use regulations laws.

III. Comply with all federal, state, and municipal statutes, rules, and regulations, including federal radio frequency radiation emission regulations and the National Environmental Policy Act of 1969, as amended.

IV. Provide information at the time of application to construct an externally visible tower or to make a substantial modification to an existing tower, mount, or PWSF, or prior to construction if no approval is required, to the municipality in which the tower, mount, or PWSF is to be constructed and to the office of strategic initiatives as follows:

(a) A copy of its license from the Federal Communications Commission (FCC) demonstrating its authority to provide personal wireless services in the geographical area where the PWSF is located, or where a person is seeking to construct a new tower or make a substantial modification to a tower, mount, or PWSF on behalf of a carrier, a signed authorization from a representative of the carrier, and a copy of the carrier's license.

(b) Upon request, maps showing all of the carrier's current externally visible tower and monopole PWSF locations in the state within a 20-mile radius of the proposed externally visible new ground-mounted PWSF, including permanent, temporary or to-be-decommissioned sites, if any.

(c) Upon request, a description of why less visually intrusive alternatives for this tower or mount were not proposed.

HISTORY:
2000, 240:1, eff. Aug. 7, 2000. 2003, 319:9, eff. July 1, 2003. 2004, 257:44, eff. July 1, 2004. 2013, 267:4, eff. September 22, 2013. 2017, 156:64, eff. July 1, 2017.

Amendment Notes
The 2017 amendments to this section by Ch. 156 substituted "office of strategic initiatives" for "office of energy and planning" in the introductory language of IV.

—2013.
The 2013 amendment rewrote the section to the extent that a detailed comparison would be impracticable.

—2004.
Paragraph IV: Substituted "office of energy and planning" for "office of state planning and energy programs" in the introductory paragraph.

—2003.
Paragraph IV: Substituted "office of state planning and energy programs" for "office of state planning".

Severability of 2013 amendment
2013, 267:12, eff. September 22, 2013, provided: "If any provision of this chapter or the application thereof to any person or circumstance is held invalid, such invalidity shall not affect other provi-

sions or applications of the chapter which can be given effect without the invalid provision or application, and to that end the provisions of this chapter are declared to be severable."

RESEARCH REFERENCES AND PRACTICE AIDS

References in text.
The National Environmental Policy Act of 1969, referred to in par. III, is classified as 42 U.S.C.S. §§ 4321 et seq.
The Telecommunication Act of 1996, referred to in par. IV(a), is classified as 47 U.S.C.S. §§ 151 et seq.

12-K:4. Payment of Costs.

A wireless carrier seeking approval to deploy a wireless communication facility may be required to pay reasonable fees, including regional notification costs, imposed by the municipality in accordance with RSA 676:4, I(g).

HISTORY:
2000, 240:1, eff. Aug. 7, 2000.

12-K:5. Fall Zones.

Zoning ordinances may include provisions for fall zones for new towers and substantial modifications to the extent necessary to protect public safety.

HISTORY:
2000, 240:1, eff. Aug. 7, 2000. 2013, 267:5, eff. September 22, 2013.

Amendments

—2013.
The 2013 amendment rewrote the section to the extent that a detailed comparison would be impracticable.

Severability of 2013 amendment
2013, 267:12, eff. September 22, 2013, provided: "If any provision of this chapter or the application thereof to any person or circumstance is held invalid, such invalidity shall not affect other provisions or applications of the chapter which can be given effect without the invalid provision or application, and to that end the provisions of this chapter are declared to be severable."

12-K:6. Personal Wireless Services Facilities Map.

The director of the office of strategic initiatives shall develop a personal wireless service facilities map for the state. This map shall include all externally visible tower and monopole PWSF locations in the state, both active and inactive, for all carriers. This map shall also include for each of the above locations a site description. Upon request of the director, any wireless carrier or its appointed agent doing business in this state shall provide a map of all of its existing externally visible tower and monopole PWSF locations in the state and a site description of each.

HISTORY:
2000, 240:1, eff. Aug. 7, 2000. 2003, 319:9, eff. July 1, 2003. 2004, 257:44, eff. July 1, 2004. 2013, 267:6, eff. September 22, 2013. 2017, 156:64, eff. July 1, 2017.

Amendment Notes
   The 2017 amendments to this section by Ch. 156 substituted "office of strategic initiatives" for "office of energy and planning" in the first sentence.

—2013.
   The 2013 amendment deleted "as described in RSA 12-K:3, IV(c)" at the end of the last two sentences.

—2004.
   Substituted "office of energy and planning" for "office of state planning and energy programs" in the first sentence.

—2003.
   Substituted "office of state planning and energy programs" for "office of state planning" in the first sentence.

Severability of 2013 amendment
   2013, 267:12, eff. September 22, 2013, provided: "If any provision of this chapter or the application thereof to any person or circumstance is held invalid, such invalidity shall not affect other provisions or applications of the chapter which can be given effect without the invalid provision or application, and to that end the provisions of this chapter are declared to be severable."

12-K:7. Regional Notification.

I.(a) Any municipality or other authority which receives an application to construct a new tower or to complete a substantial modification to an existing tower or mount which will be visible from any other New Hampshire municipality within a 20-mile radius shall provide written notification of such application and pending action to such other municipality within the 20-mile radius.

(b) This notification shall include sending a letter to the governing body of the municipality within the 20-mile radius detailing the pending action on the application and shall also include publishing a notice in a newspaper customarily used for legal notices by such municipality within the 20-mile radius, presenting a synopsis of the application, providing relevant information concerning the applicable permits required and the date of the next public hearing on the application. Where a public hearing is scheduled by the local governing body, such notice shall be published not less than 7 days nor more than 21 days prior to the public hearing date.

II.(a) Any person, prior to constructing a new tower in any location where no approval is required but which will be visible from any other New Hampshire municipality within a 20-mile radius, shall provide written notification of such planned construction to such other municipality within the 20-mile radius.

(b) This notification shall include sending a letter to the governing body of the municipality within the 20-mile radius detailing the planned construction and shall also include publishing a notice in a newspaper customarily used for legal notices by such municipality within a 20-mile radius, presenting a synopsis of the planned construction.

III. Municipalities within the 20 mile radius described in paragraphs I or II and their residents

shall be allowed to comment at any public hearing related to the application. Regional notification and comments from other municipalities or their residents shall not be construed to imply legal standing to challenge any decision.

HISTORY:
   2000, 240:1, eff. Aug. 7, 2000. 2013, 267:7, eff. September 22, 2013.

Amendments

—2013.
   The 2013 amendment, in I(a), substituted "other authority" for "state authority or agency" and "new tower or to complete a substantial modification to an existing tower or mount" for "PWSF"; in I(b), in the first sentence, substituted "presenting a synopsis of" for "stating the specifics of" and "providing relevant information concerning the applicable permits required and" for "the pending action, and" and added "Where a public hearing is scheduled by the local governing body" in the second sentence; substituted "tower" for "PWSF" in II(a); and substituted "presenting a synopsis of" for "outlining" in II(b).

Severability of 2013 amendment
   2013, 267:12, eff. September 22, 2013, provided: "If any provision of this chapter or the application thereof to any person or circumstance is held invalid, such invalidity shall not affect other provisions or applications of the chapter which can be given effect without the invalid provision or application, and to that end the provisions of this chapter are declared to be severable."

12-K:8. Model Ordinances and Guidance.

The director of the office of strategic initiatives shall develop a set of model municipal ordinances relative to the deployment of personal wireless communications facilities. Prior to development, the director shall hold one or more public hearings and solicit comments from interested parties. The office of strategic initiatives shall provide a copy of the set of model ordinances to any New Hampshire municipality that requests it.

HISTORY:
   2000, 240:1, eff. Aug. 7, 2000. 2003, 319:9, eff. July 1, 2003. 2004, 257:44, eff. July 1, 2004. 2017, 156:64, eff. July 1, 2017.

Amendment Notes
   The 2017 amendments to this section by Ch. 156 substituted "office of strategic initiatives" for "office of energy and planning" in the first and third sentences.

—2004.
   Substituted "office of energy and planning" for "office of state planning and energy programs" in the first and third sentences.

—2003.
   Substituted "office of state planning and energy programs" for "office of state planning".

12-K:9. Rulemaking.

The director of the office of strategic initiatives, after holding a public hearing, shall adopt rules under RSA 541-A to provide sufficient information to municipalities, other state agencies, wireless companies doing business or seeking to do business in this state, and the public.

timely when the 30-day deadline fell on Saturday, February 5, because the deadline was extended until Monday, February 7. Trefethen v. Town of Derry, 164 N.H. 754, 64 A.3d 959, 2013 N.H. LEXIS 39 (N.H. 2013).

RSA 508:4 does not contain a specific directive stating a day or date to begin computing the time period; therefore, the general rule in RSA 21:35 does apply, and the day upon which the incident occurred in computing the three-year period of time is excluded from the time limit. Accordingly, a writ had been timely filed because the statute of limitations did not begin to run until the day after the incident. Chesley v. Harvey Indus., 157 N.H. 211, 949 A.2d 728, 2008 N.H. LEXIS 51 (N.H. 2008).

Because RSA 21:35 provides that the general rule for computing a time period does not apply if the statute in question specifically states a contrary rule, the general rule of computing a time period by excluding the first day from which a period is to be determined does not apply to RSA 677:2, which specifically states that the time period for filing a motion for a rehearing of a zoning board's decision begins to run on the date of a zoning board's vote. Pelletier v. City of Manchester, 150 N.H. 687, 844 A.2d 484, 2004 N.H. LEXIS 54 (N.H. 2004).

The fact that this section provides that the day from which time is to be reckoned is to be excluded in computing the time within which an act must be done tends to the conclusion that that is the only day to be excluded in making the computation. Clough v. Wilton, 79 N.H. 66, 104 A. 453, 1918 N.H. LEXIS 24 (N.H. 1918).

The terms of this section are general, and apply equally whether the time is to be reckoned backward or forward from the specified day or act. Bernard v. Martel, 68 N.H. 466, 41 A. 183, 1896 N.H. LEXIS 28 (N.H. 1896).

Cited:
   Cited in Osgood v. Blake, 21 N.H. 550, 1850 N.H. LEXIS 89 (1850); Opinion declaring the soldiers' voting bill a valid & binding statute of the state, 45 N.H. 607, 1864 N.H. LEXIS 87 (1864); Fairgraves v. Stark Mills, 77 N.H. 215, 90 A. 510, 1914 N.H. LEXIS 16 (1914); Drowne v. Lovering, 93 N.H. 195, 37 A.2d 190, 1944 N.H. LEXIS 122 (1944); Larochelle v. Birch, 98 N.H. 190, 96 A.2d 573, 1953 N.H. LEXIS 46 (1953); Ware v. Champagne's Super Mkt., 99 N.H. 19, 104 A.2d 736, 1954 N.H. LEXIS 6 (1954); Opinion of Justices, 101 N.H. 536, 133 A.2d 506, 1957 N.H. LEXIS 59 (1957); H I K Corp. v. Manchester, 103 N.H. 378, 172 A.2d 368, 1961 N.H. LEXIS 55 (1961); Hunter v. Department of Employment Sec., 107 N.H. 365, 222 A.2d 214, 1966 N.H. LEXIS 192 (1966); Rafferty v. State, 107 N.H. 387, 222 A.2d 823, 1966 N.H. LEXIS 197 (1966); Bridgham v. Keene, 112 N.H. 84, 289 A.2d 392, 1972 N.H. LEXIS 148 (1972); Ayotte v. Department of Employment Sec., 114 N.H. 147, 317 A.2d 16, 1974 N.H. LEXIS 226 (1974); Dustin v. Cruise Craft, Inc., 487 F. Supp. 67, 1980 U.S. Dist. LEXIS 10668 (D.N.H. 1980); Brent v. Paquette, 132 N.H. 415, 567 A.2d 976, 1989 N.H. LEXIS 123 (1989).

RESEARCH REFERENCES AND PRACTICE AIDS

New Hampshire Practice.
   8-13 N.H.P. Personal Injury-Tort & Insurance Practice § 13.13.
   13-2 N.H.P. Local Government Law § 21.
   13-10 N.H.P. Local Government Law § 230.
   14-31 N.H.P. Local Government Law § 1266.

21:45. "Bylaw" or "Ordinance".

The term "bylaw" when used in reference to legislative action taken by a city, town, county or village district shall have the same meaning as an ordinance and shall be subject to the same procedures for enactment.

HISTORY:
   1975, 300:1, eff. Aug. 6, 1975.

RESEARCH REFERENCES AND PRACTICE AIDS

New Hampshire Practice.
   13-15 N.H.P. Local Government Law § 492.
   14-24 N.H.P. Local Government Law § 891.

21:46. Mobile Homes.

The words "mobile home" shall mean manufactured housing as defined by RSA 674:31.

HISTORY:
   1983, 230:2, eff. Aug. 17, 1983.

Revision note.
   Substituted " RSA 674:31" for " RSA 31:118". RSA 31:118 was repealed by 1983, 447:5, III.

21:47. Legislative Body.

When used to refer to a municipality, and in the absence of applicable chapter or subdivision definitions, the term "legislative body" shall mean a town meeting, school district meeting, village district meeting, city or town council, mayor and council, mayor and board of aldermen, or, when used to refer to unincorporated towns or unorganized places, or both, the county convention.

HISTORY:
   1989, 205:1, eff. July 21, 1989.

NOTES TO DECISIONS

Construction
   Trial court properly granted the two school districts' cross-motion for summary judgment and properly denied the taxpayers summary judgment motion on the taxpayers' claim that voters were required to approve the three-year agreement for the one school district to educate the other school district's students in return for a specified per pupil payment, as the taxpayers did not show anything in the relevant statute, RSA 194:22, that required a school district to obtain prior approval from the district's voters to enter a contract; furthermore, the taxpayers' argument overlooked the fact that school districts were authorized to make necessary contracts through its governing body, the school board, and that it was authorized to raise and appropriate money necessary to fund the approved contracts through its legislative body, the school district meeting. Foote v. Manchester Sch. Dist., 152 N.H. 599, 883 A.2d 283, 2005 N.H. LEXIS 145 (N.H. 2005).

RESEARCH REFERENCES AND PRACTICE AIDS

New Hampshire Practice.
   13-2 N.H.P. Local Government Law § 14.

21:48. Governing Body.

When used to refer to a municipality, and in the absence of applicable chapter or subdivision definitions, the term "governing body" shall mean the board of selectmen in a town, the board of aldermen or council in a city or town with a town council, the school board in a school district or the village district commissioners in a village district, or when used to refer to unincorporated towns or unorganized places, or both, the county commissioners.

HISTORY:
   1989, 205:1, eff. July 21, 1989.

NOTES TO DECISIONS

Construction
   Trial court properly granted the two school districts' cross-motion for summary judgment and properly denied the taxpayers sum-

mary judgment motion on the taxpayers' claim that voters were required to approve the three-year agreement for the one school district to educate the other school district's students in return for a specified per pupil payment, as the taxpayers did not show anything in the relevant statute, RSA 194:22, that required a school district to obtain prior approval from the district's voters to enter a contract; furthermore, the taxpayers' argument overlooked the fact that school districts were authorized to make necessary contracts through its governing body, the school board, and that it was authorized to raise and appropriate money necessary to fund the approved contracts through its legislative body, the school district meeting. Foote v. Manchester Sch. Dist., 152 N.H. 599, 883 A.2d 283, 2005 N.H. LEXIS 145 (N.H. 2005).

RESEARCH REFERENCES AND PRACTICE AIDS

New Hampshire Practice.
13-2 N.H.P. Local Government Law § 14.

TITLE II
COUNTIES

Chapter
28. County Commissioners

CHAPTER 28
COUNTY COMMISSIONERS

Section
28:7-b. Planning and Zoning in Unincorporated Towns and Unorganized Places.

NOTES TO DECISIONS

The office of county commissioner is purely of statutory origin. Opinion of Justices, 99 N.H. 540, 114 A.2d 879, 1955 N.H. LEXIS 72 (N.H. 1955).

RESEARCH REFERENCES AND PRACTICE AIDS

Cross References.
Annual reports, see RSA 30.
Bonds of county commissioners, see RSA 27.
Districts for election of county commissioner, see RSA 655:9.
Term and number of county commissioners, see RSA 653:1.

Vacancy in office of county commissioner, see RSA 661:9.

28:7-b. Planning and Zoning in Unincorporated Towns and Unorganized Places.

For each unincorporated town or unorganized place, the county in which it is located and its commissioners shall have the same responsibilities and powers to exercise planning, zoning, subdivision and related regulations as city and local land use boards. Regulations shall be exercised in accordance with the provisions of RSA 672-677 to the extent practical, in order to ensure reasonable development and planning in the unincorporated town or unorganized place.

HISTORY:
1983, 161:1. 1986, 31:1. 1989, 266:2, eff. July 1, 1989.

Amendments

—1989.
Rewritten to the extent that a detailed comparison would be impracticable.

—1986.
Rewritten to the extent that a detailed comparison would be impracticable.

2. Garbage and waste disposal

Although a dump ordinance may incidentally affect the use of land, such incidental effect is not comprehensive enough to require that the ordinance be adopted pursuant to the zoning statutes rather than pursuant to this section. Derry Sand & Gravel v. Londonderry, 121 N.H. 501, 431 A.2d 139, 1981 N.H. LEXIS 358 (N.H. 1981).

Regulation of the disposal of garbage and waste by local dump ordinance was valid. Derry Sand & Gravel v. Londonderry, 121 N.H. 501, 431 A.2d 139, 1981 N.H. LEXIS 358 (N.H. 1981).

3. Traffic control

Where record suggested that town fathers were acting to relieve traffic congestion, not to impinge upon rights of private entrepreneurs, when they adopted ordinance to keep certain street vendors out of certain high traffic areas, challenged ordinance was valid as a traffic control ordinance, a proper exercise of the police power delegated to the town by the legislature. Piane v. Conway, 118 N.H. 883, 395 A.2d 517, 1978 N.H. LEXIS 312 (N.H. 1978).

4. Prudential affairs

The term "prudential affairs" should not be used as substitute means of granting authority when express grants of power are more desirable to attain that end. Girard v. Allenstown, 121 N.H. 268, 428 A.2d 488, 1981 N.H. LEXIS 295 (N.H. 1981).

The language of the "prudential affairs" clause of this section does not constitute a separate and distinct grant of legislative authority; rather, it is more suggestive of merely granting those powers that are "necessary and proper" in the execution of the powers that have been specifically granted to towns. Girard v. Allenstown, 121 N.H. 268, 428 A.2d 488, 1981 N.H. LEXIS 295 (N.H. 1981).

5. Surfing

Although the regulation of surfing is not specifically authorized by this section, an ordinance prohibiting surfing in the ocean in a certain area and at certain times is implicitly permitted by the grant of authority to make by-laws for the use of the public parks, commons and other public institutions to the town. State v. Zetterberg, 109 N.H. 126, 244 A.2d 188, 1968 N.H. LEXIS 135 (N.H. 1968).

6. Buildings

Ordinances regulating setback, space between buildings and height of buildings are valid exercises of the police power granted by this section. Piper v. Meredith, 110 N.H. 291, 266 A.2d 103, 1970 N.H. LEXIS 156 (N.H. 1970).

An ordinance establishing a height and setback limitation for buildings in a portion of a town came within the police powers of this section and did not have to be adopted as a zoning ordinance. Piper v. Meredith, 110 N.H. 291, 266 A.2d 103, 1970 N.H. LEXIS 156 (N.H. 1970).

A municipal ordinance prohibiting the erection of any building or trailer within one-fourth mile of the town common unless the selectmen approve the plans for construction and location "in order that the atmosphere of the Town ... may be maintained" was a valid exercise of the police power granted by this section, and the fact that no zoning ordinance of general application had been adopted by the town and that the regulation applied to a limited area of town does not invalidate the ordinance. Deering ex rel. Bittenbender v. Tibbetts, 105 N.H. 481, 202 A.2d 232, 1964 N.H. LEXIS 106 (N.H. 1964).

An ordinance requiring approval by the selectmen of plans for construction and location of proposed building sought to be erected in the regulated area "in order that the atmosphere of the Town ... may be maintained" furnished a sufficient guide for determination of whether a building was compatible and appropriate in the typical environment and characteristic setting of the town common. Deering ex rel. Bittenbender v. Tibbetts, 105 N.H. 481, 202 A.2d 232, 1964 N.H. LEXIS 106 (N.H. 1964).

7. Mobile homes

The regulation of mobile homes is a proper exercise of a town's police power. Village House v. Loudon, 114 N.H. 76, 314 A.2d 635, 1974 N.H. LEXIS 211 (N.H. 1974).

A town may properly seek to regulate and restrict the location of mobile homes under the police power provisions of this section. Weare v. Stone, 114 N.H. 80, 314 A.2d 638, 1974 N.H. LEXIS 212 (N.H. 1974).

Where town building code regulated setback, minimum floor size and lot size, required sanitary facilities to conform to state regulations and required a building permit, the code, together with mobile home ordinance did not have to be enacted in compliance with the zoning statutes, and mobile home ordinance could be enacted under the police power. Village House v. Loudon, 114 N.H. 76, 314 A.2d 635, 1974 N.H. LEXIS 211 (N.H. 1974).

A town may, under the police power, restrict the total number of trailer units to be located within the town. Riverview Park v. Hinsdale, 113 N.H. 693, 313 A.2d 733, 1973 N.H. LEXIS 353 (N.H. 1973).

This section furnished adequate authorization for town ordinance regulating the location of a mobile home within the town, under which selectmen would decide whether permit would be issued, after notice to abutters and by publication, and after hearing, and under which no permit would issue unless selectmen found that the mobile home's location and maintenance, inter alia, would advance public health, safety and morals, conserve private property values, encourage appropriate land use and preserve general attractiveness and welfare of town. New Boston v. Coombs, 111 N.H. 359, 284 A.2d 920, 1971 N.H. LEXIS 201 (N.H. 1971).

Town ordinance requiring permit by selectmen after notice and hearing in order to locate mobile home within town could properly require selectmen to consider opinions of all persons taking a position at the hearing and give particular significance to the consent or objections of owners of neighboring property. New Boston v. Coombs, 111 N.H. 359, 284 A.2d 920, 1971 N.H. LEXIS 201 (N.H. 1971).

8. Rent control

This section does not convey to towns authority to adopt and enforce a rent control ordinance. Girard v. Allenstown, 121 N.H. 268, 428 A.2d 488, 1981 N.H. LEXIS 295 (N.H. 1981).

9. Setback

Town setback ordinance, requiring septic systems to be placed at least 125 feet from edge of water, was enacted in order to prevent further pollution of lake and such ordinance was reasonable exercise of the general police power granted to municipalities by this section. Freedom v. Gillespie, 120 N.H. 576, 419 A.2d 1090, 1980 N.H. LEXIS 361 (N.H. 1980).

10. Zoning

General police power delegated to a municipality pursuant to this section may not be used as a usual and expedient mechanism for effecting zoning regulations which would otherwise fall within the zoning enabling statutes. Beck v. Raymond, 118 N.H. 793, 394 A.2d 847, 1978 N.H. LEXIS 296 (N.H. 1978).

When legislation attempts to control population growth through definite and detailed control of land development, it must be enacted in accordance with the zoning statutes, rather than pursuant to this section. Beck v. Raymond, 118 N.H. 793, 394 A.2d 847, 1978 N.H. LEXIS 296 (N.H. 1978).

A town ordinance containing comprehensive regulations which sought to restrict the use of three areas of a town to single and two-family residential buildings, to regulate the use of buildings, the size and percentage of lots and indirectly to regulate the size of yards and other open spaces and the density of population, and which contemplated that permits would be granted for nonconforming uses, was a zoning ordinance which could not be legally enacted except in compliance with the statute authorizing zoning regulations and could not be justified under this section. Bisson v. Milford, 109 N.H. 287, 249 A.2d 688, 1969 N.H. LEXIS 136 (N.H. 1969).

11. Subdivisions

Town's "slow growth" subdivision ordinance, providing that no owner of land of record could subdivide his land into more than five building lots in any one calendar year, was an impermissible and invalid attempt to exercise its police power under this section to regulate a subject matter that requires compliance with statutes governing zoning regulation. Stoney-Brook Dev. Corp. v. Pembroke, 118 N.H. 791, 394 A.2d 853, 1978 N.H. LEXIS 295 (N.H. 1978).

12. Growth control

A growth control ordinance, enacted as a general ordinance, was not a valid exercise of the police power delegated to a municipality pursuant to this section. Stoney-Brook Dev. Corp. v. Fremont, 124 N.H. 583, 474 A.2d 561, 1984 N.H. LEXIS 348 (N.H. 1984).

13. Enforcement

Town could delegate enforcement of ordinance to its planning board. Freedom v. Gillespie, 120 N.H. 576, 419 A.2d 1090, 1980 N.H. LEXIS 361 (N.H. 1980).

14. Penalties

Penalty of $10 for each day a mobile home was located within town in violation of ordinance was specifically authorized by this section and not unconstitutional on its face. New Boston v. Coombs, 111 N.H. 359, 284 A.2d 920, 1971 N.H. LEXIS 201 (N.H. 1971).

Town may not enact bylaws to provide for penalties in excess of its statutory authority. State v. Jenkins, 102 N.H. 545, 162 A.2d 613, 1960 N.H. LEXIS 76 (N.H. 1960).

Cited:

Cited in State v. Wimpfheimer, 69 N.H. 166, 38 A. 786, 1897 N.H. LEXIS 9 (1897); Chung Mee Restaurant Co. v. Healy, 86 N.H. 483, 171 A. 263, 1934 N.H. LEXIS 89 (1934); State v. Guertin, 89 N.H. 126, 193 A. 237, 1937 N.H. LEXIS 25 (1937); McMahon v. Salem, 104 N.H. 219, 182 A.2d 463, 1962 N.H. LEXIS 54 (1962); Robbins Auto Parts v. Laconia, 117 N.H. 235, 371 A.2d 1167, 1977 N.H. LEXIS 308 (1977); Garofoli v. Henniker, 121 N.H. 153, 427 A.2d 35, 1981 N.H. LEXIS 270 (1981); Grondin v. Hinsdale, 122 N.H. 882, 451 A.2d 1299, 1982 N.H. LEXIS 485 (1982); Stablex Corp. v. Hooksett, 122 N.H. 1091, 456 A.2d 94, 1982 N.H. LEXIS 539 (1982).

OPINIONS OF THE ATTORNEY GENERAL

Prudential affairs

Provision in this section allowing municipalities to enact bylaws for "making and ordering their prudential affairs" is not a general grant of authority giving municipalities any significant independent legislative authority; language is more properly construed to grant powers that are necessary and proper in execution of powers that have been specifically granted. Op. Atty. Gen. #0-93-6.

RESEARCH REFERENCES AND PRACTICE AIDS

Cross References.

Animals running at large, see RSA 467.
Cemeteries generally, see RSA 289.
Establishment and discontinuance of parks, see RSA 50.
Fire hazard regulations, see RSA 154:18 et seq.
Motorboat noise levels, see RSA 270:36 et seq.
Muffling devices on boats, see RSA 270:25.
Muzzling and restraining dogs, see RSA 466:29 et seq.
Police attendance at public dances, see RSA 105:9.
Power to regulate registration, sale, transportation or use of pesticides as exception, see RSA 430:49.
Public libraries generally, see RSA 202-A.
Solid waste management generally, see RSA 149-M.
State food service licenses, see RSA 143-A.
Traffic rules and regulations, see RSA 265.

New Hampshire Bar Journal.

Slow growth zoning ordinances, 20 N.H. B.J. 257 (July 1979).

New Hampshire Practice.

14-24 N.H.P. Local Government Law § 920.

31:39-a.   Conflict of Interest Ordinances.

The legislative body of a town or city may adopt an ordinance defining and regulating conflicts of interest for local officers and employees, whether elected or appointed. Any such ordinance may include provisions requiring disclosure of financial interests for

specified officers and employees, establishing incompatibility of office requirements stricter than those specified by state law or establishing conditions under which prohibited conflicts of interest shall require removal from office. Any such ordinance shall include provisions to exempt affected officers and employees who are in office or employed at the time the ordinance is adopted for a period not to exceed one year from the date of adoption. The superior court shall have jurisdiction over any removal proceedings instituted under an ordinance adopted under this section.

HISTORY:

1981, 221:1, eff. Aug. 10, 1981.

Contingent 1999 repeal.

1999, 278:16, eff. July 14, 1999, provided:

"If a constitutional amendment to the New Hampshire constitution providing that municipalities shall have home rule authority to exercise any powers not specifically prohibited by the state or federal constitutions is adopted by the voters in the 2000 general election, then sections 1– 15 of this act [which repealed this section and RSA 31:40– 43 and amended RSA 31:39; 41: 11; 47: 17; 143-A:5, I, III; 149-M:17, II(b); 179:19, V; 231:132-a, Intro. par.; 266:24, I; 466:30-b, V; and 502-A:8, and enacted RSA 31:39-b and 47:17-a], shall take effect January 1, 2001. If such a constitutional amendment is not adopted, then sections 1– 15 of this act shall not take effect."

Contingent 1999 repeal; outcome of 2000 general election.

In the 2000 general election, the voters of New Hampshire rejected the constitutional amendment, referred to above, which would have provided that municipalities would have home rule authority to exercise any powers not specifically prohibited by the state or federal constitutions. Consequently, sections 1– 15 of 1999, 278:16 [which repealed this section and RSA 31:40– 43 and amended RSA 31:39; 41: 11; 47: 17; 143-A:5, I, III; 149-M:17, II(b); 179:19, V; 231:132-a, Intro. par.; 266:24, I; 466:30-b, V; and 502-A:8, and enacted RSA 31:39-b and 47:17-a] did not take effect.

31:41.   Open-Air Motion Picture Theatres.

Towns shall have the power to make bylaws relating to the regulation and licensing of open-air motion picture theatres within the limits of the town, and may fix reasonable fees for the operation of said theatres, and failure to conform to such bylaws shall constitute a violation and any fines collected hereunder shall inure to such uses as said towns may direct.

HISTORY:

1949, 252:1, par. 32-b. RSA 31:41. 1973, 531:5, eff. at 11:59 p.m., Oct. 31, 1973.

Amendments

—1973.

Substituted "failure to conform to such by-laws shall constitute a violation and any fines collected hereunder shall" for "may enforce the observance of such by-laws by suitable penalties not exceeding twenty-five dollars for each offense, to" preceding "inure".

Contingent 1999 repeal.

1999, 278:16, eff. July 14, 1999, provided:

"If a constitutional amendment to the New Hampshire constitution providing that municipalities shall have home rule authority to exercise any powers not specifically prohibited by the state or federal constitutions is adopted by the voters in the 2000 general election, then sections 1– 15 of this act [which repealed this section and RSA 31:39-a, 40, 41-a–43 and amended RSA 31:39; 41: 11; 47: 17; 143-A:5, I, III; 149-M:17, II(b); 179:19, V; 231:132-a, Intro. par.; 266:24, I; 466:30-b, V; and 502-A:8, and enacted RSA 31:39-b and 47:17-a], shall take effect January 1, 2001. If such a constitutional amendment is not adopted, then sections 1– 15 of this act shall not take effect."

Contingent 1999 repeal; outcome of 2000 general election.

In the 2000 general election, the voters of New Hampshire rejected the constitutional amendment referred to above, which would have provided that municipalities would have home rule authority to exercise any powers not specifically prohibited by the state or federal constitutions. Consequently, sections 1– 15 of 1999, 278:16 [which repealed this section and RSA 31:39-a, 40, 41-a–43 and amended RSA 31:39; 41: 11; 47: 17; 143-A:5, I, III; II(b); 179:19, V; 231:132-a, Intro. par.; 266:24, I; 466:30-b, V; and 502-A:8, and enacted RSA 31:39-b and 47:17-a] did not take effect.

NOTES TO DECISIONS

Analysis

1. Purpose
2. Fees

1. Purpose

In enacting this section the legislature intended to grant towns merely a police power to regulate and license open-air motion picture theatres in the interest of the public good. Hooksett Drive-in Theatre v. Hooksett, 110 N.H. 287, 266 A.2d 124, 1970 N.H. LEXIS 155 (N.H. 1970).

2. Fees

A fee of $500 for each showing of a picture rated "X" bore no reasonable relationship to the cost of administering and enforcing an ordinance adopted under this section and was therefore confiscatory and rendered the ordinance invalid and unenforceable. Hooksett Drive-in Theatre v. Hooksett, 110 N.H. 287, 266 A.2d 124, 1970 N.H. LEXIS 155 (N.H. 1970).

Cited:

Cited in Mason v. Salem, 103 N.H. 166, 167 A.2d 433, 1961 N.H. LEXIS 7 (1961); State v. Sukoff, 105 N.H. 70, 192 A.2d 622, 1963 N.H. LEXIS 19 (1963).

RESEARCH REFERENCES AND PRACTICE AIDS

Cross References.

Classification of crimes, see RSA 625:9.

Regulation by selectmen prior to adoption of bylaws, see RSA 31:42.

Sentences, see RSA 651.

31:41-a. Motor Vehicle Race Tracks.

Towns shall have the power to make bylaws relating to the regulation and licensing of motor vehicle race tracks within the limits of the town, and may fix fees not to exceed $100 annually for the operation of such race tracks, and failure to observe such bylaws shall constitute a violation and any fines collected hereunder shall inure to such uses as said towns may direct. For the purposes of this section, a motor vehicle shall be defined as any self-propelled vehicle, except tractors, activated by an internal combustion engine and not operated exclusively on stationary tracks.

HISTORY:

1967, 149:1. 1973, 531:6, eff. at 11:59 p.m., Oct. 31, 1973.

Amendments

—1973.

Substituted "failure to observe such by-laws shall constitute a violation and any fines collected hereunder shall" for "may enforce the observance of such by-laws by suitable penalties not exceeding twenty-five dollars for each offense, to" preceding "inure" in the first sentence.

Contingent 1999 repeal.

1999, 278:16, eff. July 14, 1999, provided:

"If a constitutional amendment to the New Hampshire constitution providing that municipalities shall have home rule authority to exercise any powers not specifically prohibited by the state or federal constitutions is adopted by the voters in the 2000 general election, then sections 1– 15 of this act [which repealed this section and RSA 31:39-a, 40, 41, 41-b–43 and amended RSA 31:39; 41: 11; 47: 17; 143-A:5, I, III; 149-M:17, II(b); 179:19, V; 231:132-a, Intro. par.; 266:24, I; 466:30-b, V; and 502-A:8, and enacted RSA 31:39-b and 47:17-a], shall take effect January 1, 2001. If such a constitutional amendment is not adopted, then sections 1– 15 of this act shall not take effect."

Contingent 1999 repeal; outcome of 2000 general election.

In the 2000 general election, the voters of New Hampshire rejected the constitutional amendment, referred to above, which would have provided that municipalities would have home rule authority to exercise any powers not specifically prohibited by the state or federal constitutions. Consequently, sections 1– 15 of 1999, 278:16 [which repealed this section and RSA 31:39-a, 40, 41, 41-b–43 and amended RSA 31:39; 41: 11; 47: 17; 143-A:5, I, III; 149-M:17, II(b); 179:19, V; 231:132-a, Intro. par.; 266:24, I; 466:30-b, V; and 502-A:8, and enacted RSA 31:39-b and 47:17-a] did not take effect.

RESEARCH REFERENCES AND PRACTICE AIDS

Cross References.

Classification of crimes, see RSA 625:9.

Regulation by selectmen prior to adoption of by-laws, see RSA 31:42.

Sentences, see RSA 651.

31:41-b. Hazardous Embankments.

Towns shall have the power to make bylaws regulating hazardous embankments, including the removal, stabilization, or fencing thereof, for the protection of the health and safety of the public. Whoever violates any such bylaw shall be guilty of a violation for each offense and the penalty therefor shall inure to such uses as the town may direct. Regulation of "excavation" as defined in RSA 155-E:1, II shall be in accordance with RSA 155-E, but any hazardous embankment resulting from excavation, whether undertaken prior to, on, or after August 4, 1989, may be subject to bylaws made under the authority of this section.

HISTORY:

1971, 212:1. 1973, 531:7. 1989, 363:16. 1991, 310:2, eff. Aug. 23, 1991.

Amendments

—1991.

Added "but any hazardous embankment resulting from excavation, whether undertaken prior to, on, or after August 4, 1989, may be subject to bylaws made under the authority of this section" following "with RSA 155-E" in the third sentence.

—1989.

Substituted "Embankments" for "Pits" in the section catchline, "hazardous embankments, including the removal, stabilization, or fencing thereof" for "land excavation" following "regulating" in the first sentence, and "the" for "said" preceding "town" in the second sentence, and added the third sentence.

—1973.

Rewritten to the extent that a detailed comparison would be impracticable.

Contingent 1999 repeal.

1999, 278:16, eff. July 14, 1999, provided:

"If a constitutional amendment to the New Hampshire constitution providing that municipalities shall have home rule authority to exercise any powers not specifically prohibited by the state or federal constitutions is adopted by the voters in the 2000 general election, then sections 1– 15 of this act [which repealed this section and RSA 31:39-a, 40–41-a, 41-c–43 and amended RSA 31:39; 41: 11; 47: 17; 143-A:5, I, III; 149-M:17, II(b); 179:19, V; 231:132-a, Intro. par.; 266:24, I; 466:30-b, V; and 502-A:8, and enacted RSA 31:39-b and 47:17-a], shall take effect January 1, 2001. If such a constitutional amendment is not adopted, then sections 1– 15 of this act shall not take effect."

Contingent 1999 repeal; outcome of 2000 general election.

In the 2000 general election, the voters of New Hampshire rejected the constitutional amendment, referred to above, which would have provided that municipalities would have home rule authority to exercise any powers not specifically prohibited by the state or federal constitutions. Consequently, sections 1– 15 of 1999, 278:16 [which amended this section and RSA 31:39; 41: 11; 47: 17; 143-A:5, I, III; 149-M:17, II(b); 170:19, V; 231:132-a, Intro par.; 266:24, I; 466:30-b, V; 502:14; 502-A:8; enacted RSA 31:39-b and 47:17-a, and repealed RSA 31:39-a; 31: 40– 43] did not take effect.

NOTES TO DECISIONS

Construction with other laws

This section and RSA ch. 155-E, granting authority to local governing bodies to regulate a specific land use, namely earth excavation, exist as grants of authority independent of the zoning enabling legislation. Goffstown v. Thibeault, 129 N.H. 454, 529 A.2d 930, 1987 N.H. LEXIS 184 (N.H. 1987).

Cited:

Cited in Flanagan v. Hollis, 112 N.H. 222, 293 A.2d 328, 1972 N.H. LEXIS 181 (1972); Surry v. Starkey, 115 N.H. 31, 332 A.2d 172, 1975 N.H. LEXIS 215 (1975).

RESEARCH REFERENCES AND PRACTICE AIDS

Cross References.

Classification of crimes, see RSA 625:9.
Sentences, see RSA 651.

Miscellaneous

31:95-a. Tax Maps.

I. Every city and town shall, prior to January 1, 1980, have a tax map, so-called, drawn. Each tax map shall:

(a) Show the boundary lines of each parcel of land in the city or town and shall be properly indexed.

(b) Accurately represent the physical location of each parcel of land in the city or town.

(c) Show on each parcel of land the road or water frontage thereof.

II.(a) The scale on a tax map shall be meaningful and adequately represent the land contained on the map, taking into consideration the urban or rural character of the land. The scale shall be sufficient to allow the naming and numbering of, and the placement of dimensions within, if possible, the parcel represented in the individual plat.

(b) Nothing in this paragraph shall apply to any city or town which, prior to the imposition of such scale requirements, has drawn a tax map, appropriated funds or contracted with any person or firm to prepare a tax map or expended funds in the initial phase of preparing a tax map.

III. Each parcel shall be identified by a map and parcel number and shall be indexed alphabetically by owner's name and numerically by parcel number.

IV. Tax maps shall be updated at least annually to indicate ownership and parcel size changes.

V. Each tax map shall be open to public inspection in a city or town office during regular business hours.

HISTORY:

1971, 426:1. 1975, 402:1, eff. Aug. 15, 1975. 2004, 203:10, eff. June 11, 2004.

Amendments

—2004.

Paragraph II(a): Inserted "if possible" following "dimensions within" in the second sentence.
Paragraph III: Amended without change.
Paragraph IV: Deleted "continually" preceding "updated" and inserted "at least annually" thereafter.

—1975.

Rewritten to the extent that a detailed comparison would be impracticable.

RESEARCH REFERENCES AND PRACTICE AIDS

New Hampshire Practice.

16-16 N.H.P. Municipal Law & Taxation § 16.07.

31:95-h. Revolving Funds.

I. A town may, by vote of the legislative body, establish a revolving fund. Each revolving fund shall be limited to one of the following purposes:

(a) Facilitating, maintaining, or encouraging recycling as defined in RSA 149-M:4;

(b) Providing ambulance services;

(c) Providing public safety services by municipal employees or volunteers outside of the ordinary detail of such persons, including but not limited to public safety services in connection with special events, highway construction, and other construction projects, or for any other public safety purpose deemed appropriate by the municipality;

(d) Creating affordable housing and facilitating transactions relative thereto;

(e) Providing cable access for public, educational, or governmental use; or

Validity of Municipal Legislation

31:126. Presumption of Procedural Validity.

Municipal legislation, after 5 years following its enactment, shall, without further curative act of the legislature, be entitled to a conclusive presumption of compliance with statutory enactment procedure. Any claim that municipal legislation is invalid for failure to follow statutory enactment procedure, whether that claim is asserted as part of a cause of action or as a defense to any action, may be asserted within 5 years of the enactment of the legislation and not afterward.

HISTORY:
1988, 33:1, eff. May 23, 1988.

31:127. Definitions.

In this subdivision:

I. "Enactment procedure" includes any required notice, copying, filing, service, reporting, publication, posting, public hearing, voting procedure, vote count, ballots, or the form or timing of any of these.

II. "Municipal legislation" means any charter, ordinance, code, bylaw, vote, resolution or regulation enacted by, or any condition or requirement imposed by, a properly authorized official, board, governing body or legislative body of any city, town or village district. It shall not include an "election" as defined in RSA 652:1.

HISTORY:
1988, 33:1, eff. May 23, 1988.

31:128. Certified Copy of Legislation Prima Facie Evidence of Enactment.

A certified copy of the municipal legislation, or a certified code, codification or compilation which includes the legislation, shall constitute prima facie evidence that the legislation was enacted on or prior to the date of certification. Certification shall be by the town or city clerk, or by the official enacting the legislation, or by the chairman, secretary or clerk of the board or body enacting the municipal legislation. The copy or code shall specify, by name or title, which officer, board or body of the municipality enacted the legislation. This method of proving municipal legislation shall not be exclusive.

HISTORY:
1988, 33:1, eff. May 23, 1988.

31:129. Limitation.

This subdivision shall not affect any claim of invalidity which is founded upon the substance of the municipal legislation, or upon the lack of authority of the municipality or its officials, under the federal and state constitutions and laws, to enact such legislation.

HISTORY:
1988, 33:1, eff. May 23, 1988.

31:130. Conformity With Enabling Statute.

The forms of questions prescribed by municipal enabling statutes shall be deemed advisory only, and municipal legislation shall not be declared invalid for failure to conform to the precise wording of any question prescribed for submission to voters, so long as the action taken is within the scope of, and consistent with the intent of, the enabling statute or statutes.

HISTORY:
1991, 113:2, eff. July 13, 1991.

31:131. Origin of Warrant Articles.

Any question which an enabling statute authorizes to be placed in the warrant for a town meeting by petition may also be inserted by the selectmen, even in the absence of any petition. So long as the subject matter of an action taken at a town meeting was distinctly stated in the warrant, no defect in the process by which such subject matter came to appear in the warrant shall affect the validity of such action.

HISTORY:
1991, 113:2, eff. July 13, 1991.

Records Storage and Management

31:132. Records Storage.

A municipality may offer storage space for paper records or other storage media formats, such as electronic records, and associated records management services to any agency of the United States government, political subdivisions of the state, and qualified non-profit organizations operating under Internal Revenue Code section 501(c). A municipality, by written agreement, shall establish a rate for service that is no higher than the actual expense of operation and associated capital costs.

HISTORY:
2004, 62:1, eff. May 3, 2004. 2015, 6:1, eff. July 4, 2015.

Amendment Notes

—2015.
The 2015 amendment inserted "or other storage media formats, such as electronic records" in the first sentence.

RESEARCH REFERENCES AND PRACTICE AIDS

References in text.
Internal Revenue Code section 501(c), referred to in this section, is classified to 26 U.S.C.S. § 501(c).

31:133. Liability Limitation.

A municipality shall employ the highest standards in record management practices. However, a municipality's liability for loss, damage, delay, improper delivery, or non-delivery shall be limited to the actual value of the storage container and the value of the paper contained within the storage container.

HISTORY:
2004, 62:1, eff. May 3, 2004.

Water and/or Sewer Utility Districts

31:134. Statement of Purpose.

The establishment of water and/or sewer utility districts will enable municipalities to provide property services at a more intensive level than is provided in the balance of the municipality; provide funds for capital expenditures towards constructing and maintaining those utilities; provide funds for the operation and maintenance of those utilities; and authorize the establishment of charges to owners and users of property within such water and/or sewer utility districts in an amount not to exceed the costs to the municipality of providing such utility services at levels over and above those provided in the balance of the municipality.

HISTORY:
2013, 214:1, eff. September 8, 2013.

31:135. Definition.

In this subdivision, "water and/or sewer utility" means an entity established for the acquisition, operation, and management of water and sewer infrastructure.

HISTORY:
2013, 214:1, eff. September 8, 2013.

31:136. Water and/or Sewer Utility Authorized; Intermunicipal Agreement.

I. For the purposes of this subdivision, the legislative body of any city or town shall have the authority by a majority vote to establish one or more water and/or sewer utility districts and designate a water and/or sewer utility commission to be the governing body to manage the activities of the district.

II. In the case where a utility district encompasses land within more than one municipality, the district may be authorized by majority vote of the legislative bodies within each affected jurisdiction in accordance with the terms of an intermunicipal agreement under RSA 53-A:3. Such agreement shall be contingent upon approval of the legislative bodies of each of the parties to the agreement, and shall, in addition to the requirements of RSA 53-A:3, II, specify the following:

(a) The source of the water.

(b) The disposition of sewage.

III. For a water and/or sewer utility that encompasses more than one municipality, the intermunicipal agreement shall create the water and/or sewer utility commission and representation on such commission shall be proportional to the number of the owners or users, or both, of properties in the water and/or sewer utility district as defined by the intermunicipal agreement.

HISTORY:
2013, 214:1, eff. September 8, 2013.

31:137. Commissioners.

For the convenient management of any water and/or sewer utility district, a municipality shall vest the construction, management, control, and direction of such district in a board of commissioners to consist of 3, 5, or 7 citizens of each municipality, the commissioners to have such powers and duties as the municipality may prescribe. Their term of office shall be for 3 years and until their successors are elected and qualified. The first board of commissioners may be chosen for terms of one, 2, and 3 years, respectively.

HISTORY:
2013, 214:1, eff. September 8, 2013.

31:138. Election or Appointment.

I. The board of commissioners may be elected by the legal voters of the municipality at any meeting or election at which the provisions of this subdivision are accepted, or at any special meeting or election thereafter called for that purpose, and their successors shall be elected at each annual meeting or election thereafter in the manner or form as the municipality may determine.

II. The board of commissioners may be appointed by the mayor and board of aldermen or city council or by the selectmen of the town in the manner or form as the municipality may determine.

HISTORY:
2013, 214:1, eff. September 8, 2013.

31:139. Services Provided; Cost.

I. The services provided by a water and/or sewer utility district under this subdivision may include property-related services, including but not limited to providing public drinking water and water for domestic uses; water for fire suppression; and wastewater management; related construction, operation, and maintenance of capital facilities needed in the performance of these services; and other business development services and activities related to the maintenance of an attractive, useful, and economically viable business environment within the district. These services and activities may be either those of a routine nature provided for all properties, or may be particular to those in the water and/or sewer utility district.

II. The legislative body of each municipality shall define the water and/or sewer utility district, select specific services and levels of services to be provided, and, subject to RSA 31:137, authorize the department, agency, or other party that is to undertake the work.

III. The costs of providing services in the water and/or sewer utility district shall be those accruing to the municipality, which result exclusively from the provision of services in the district, and which exceed those being provided in the balance of the municipality.

HISTORY:
2013, 214:1, eff. September 8, 2013.

31:140. Method of Appropriation.

Each municipality shall adopt a budgetary appropriation for capital and operating expenditures including replacement and upgrades, or services to be performed in a water and/or sewer utility district as part of its budget process. The expense of constructing and maintaining the facilities needed to perform the authorized services to the district, or paying off any capital debt or interest incurred in constructing or maintaining the district on an annual basis shall be included in the budgetary appropriation. At the end of each fiscal year, a full accounting of expenditures shall be made.

HISTORY:
2013, 214:1, eff. September 8, 2013.

31:141. Assessments and Fees.

Upon adoption of the budgetary appropriation, the municipality may levy assessments or fees, or both, in an amount not greater than the net appropriation to a water and/or sewer utility district fund. The assessments and fees shall be made against the owners or users, or both, of properties in the water and/or sewer utility district and shall be based upon a formula determined by the municipality to be in relative proportion to benefits received by each property owner or user, or both, in the water and/or sewer utility district. Assessments and fees shall be billed and collected as specified by ordinance adopted by majority vote of the governing body of the municipality after a public hearing or in accordance with the terms of the intermunicipal agreement. Government property and non-profit organizations within the district shall be subject to the assessment and fees. Interest and other collection procedures shall be made by the tax collector or other official responsible for property tax collection. Enforcement powers for nonpayment shall be the same as those provided under RSA 80 relative to property tax collection.

HISTORY:
2013, 214:1, eff. September 8, 2013.

31:142. Limit on Liability.

The provisions of RSA 507-B relative to bodily injury actions against governmental units shall apply to all municipal activities performed in connection with a water and/or sewer utility district.

HISTORY:
2013, 214:1, eff. September 8, 2013.

31:143. Authority to Incur Capital Debt.

The commission shall have the authority to issue bonds under RSA 33 or RSA 33-B, as approved by the governing body of the municipality or, if intermunicipal, in accordance with the terms of the intermunicipal agreement.

HISTORY:
2013, 214:1, eff. September 8, 2013.

31:144. Assessment Funds.

I. The funds received from the collection of water and/or sewer assessments and fees shall be kept as separate and distinct funds to be known as the water assessment fund and the sewer assessment fund respectively. Such funds shall be allowed to accumulate from year to year, shall not be commingled with municipal tax revenues, and shall not be deemed part of the municipality's general fund accumulated surplus. Such funds shall be expended only for the purposes of this subdivision as it relates to public drinking water and domestic supplies or the previous expansion or replacement of water lines or water treatment facilities; or for wastewater or the previous expansion or replacement of sewage lines or sewage treatment facilities.

II. Except when a capital reserve fund is established pursuant to paragraph III, all assessment funds shall be held in the custody of the municipal treasurer. Estimates of anticipated assessments or fees and anticipated expenditures from the assessment funds shall be submitted to the governing body under RSA 32:6 if applicable, and shall be included as part of the municipal budget submitted to the legislative body for approval. Notwithstanding RSA 41:29 or RSA 48:16, the treasurer shall pay out amounts from the assessment funds only upon order of the governing body of the district. Expenditures shall be within amounts appropriated by the legislative body.

III. At the option of the governing body of the district, all or part of any surplus in the assessment funds may be placed in one or more capital reserve funds under RSA 35:7 and placed in the custody of the trustees of trust funds. If such a reserve fund is created, then the governing body of the district may expend such funds pursuant to RSA 35:15 without prior approval or appropriation by the local legislative body, but all such expenditures shall be reported to the municipality pursuant to RSA 31:148. This section shall not be construed to prohibit the establishment of other capital reserve funds for any lawful purpose relating to municipal water.

HISTORY:
2013, 214:1, eff. September 8, 2013.

31:145. District Utility Fund.

Notwithstanding RSA 31:144, the local legislative body upon establishing a utility district may vote to establish a separate and distinct fund to be known as the district utility fund to serve as a collective operating fund for the district, or to administer funds common to the district that are not directly attributable to water or wastewater services. Such fund shall be allowed to accumulate from year to year, shall not be commingled with town or city tax revenues, and shall not be deemed part of the municipality's general fund accumulated surplus. Such fund shall function as a collective water and sewer fund and shall be authorized to be managed in the same ways as water or sewer funds are used under RSA 31:144.

HISTORY:
2013, 214:1, eff. September 8, 2013.

31:146. Abatement and Appeal of Assessments and Fees.

I. Any person aggrieved by an assessment or fee made under this subdivision may, within 2 months of the notice of assessment, apply in writing to the governing body of the district for an abatement of such assessment or fee.

II. Upon receipt of an application under paragraph I, the governing body of the district shall review the application and shall, in writing, grant or deny the application in whole or in part to correct any error in the assessment or fee within 6 months after the notice of assessment or imposition of the fee.

III. If the governing body of the district neglects or refuses to abate the assessment or fee, any person aggrieved may petition the superior court in the county where the property is located within 8 months of the notice of assessment or imposition of the fee.

IV. For purposes of this section, "notice of assessment" means the date shown on the assessment bill.

V. Each assessment bill or fee shall require a separate request and appeal.

VI. For good cause shown, the governing body of the district may abate any such assessment or fee made by them or by their predecessors.

HISTORY:
2013, 214:1, eff. September 8, 2013.

31:147. Liens and Collection of Assessments.

In the collection of assessments and fees under RSA 31:141, municipalities shall have the same liens and use the same collection procedures as authorized by RSA 38:22. Interest on overdue charges shall be assessed in accordance with RSA 76:13.

HISTORY:
2013, 214:1, eff. September 8, 2013.

31:148. Reports.

In municipalities adopting this subdivision, the governing body of the district shall annually, at the time other municipal officers report, make a report to the municipality of the condition of the plant financially and otherwise, showing the funds of the district, the expenses and income thereof, and all other material facts. This report shall be published in the annual report of the municipality.

HISTORY:
2013, 214:1, eff. September 8, 2013.

31:149. Local Option.

Any city or town may adopt this subdivision and shall thereafter have all the authority, powers, duties, and responsibilities set forth in this subdivision.

I. A city may adopt this subdivision by majority vote of the legislative body of the city after notice and hearing.

II. A town may adopt this subdivision by majority vote of the voters present and voting at any legal town meeting under a proper article after notice and hearing.

HISTORY:
2013, 214:1, eff. September 8, 2013.

CHAPTER 36

REGIONAL PLANNING COMMISSIONS

Regional Planning Commissions

Amendments

—2000.
2000, 200:1, eff. July 29, 2000, rewrote the chapter heading.

Regional Planning Commissions

RESEARCH REFERENCES AND PRACTICE AIDS

Cross References.
Review of developments of regional impact, see RSA 36:54 et seq.

New Hampshire Bar Journal.
For article, "Regional Economic Desegregation: *Britton v. Town of Chester*," see 33 N.H. B.J. 486 (1992).

36:45. Purposes.

The purpose of this subdivision shall be to enable municipalities and counties to join in the formation of regional planning commissions whose duty it shall be to prepare a coordinated plan for the development of a region, taking into account present and future needs with a view toward encouraging the most appropriate use of land, such as for agriculture, forestry, industry, commerce, and housing; the facilitation of transportation and communication; the proper and economic location of public utilities and services; the development of adequate recreational areas; the promotion of good civic design; and the wise and efficient expenditure of public funds. The aforesaid plan shall be made in order to promote the health, safety, morals and general welfare of the region and its inhabitants. To promote these purposes the office of strategic initiatives shall delineate planning regions for the state so that each municipality of the state will fall within a delineated region and shall have the opportunity of forming or joining the regional planning commission for that planning region. In determining these regions the office shall consider such factors as community of interest and homogeneity, existing metropolitan and regional planning agencies, patterns of communication and transportation, geographic features and natural boundaries, extent of urban development, relevancy of the region for provision of governmental services and functions and its use for administering state and federal programs, the existence of physical, social and economic problems of a regional character, and other related characteristics. To accommodate changing conditions, the office may adjust the boundaries of the planning regions, after consultation with the respective regional planning commissions.

HISTORY:
1969, 324:1, eff. Aug. 29, 1969. 2000, 200:2, eff. July 29, 2000. 2003, 319:9, eff. July 1, 2003. 2004, 257:44, eff. July 1, 2004. 2017, 156:64, eff. July 1, 2017.

Amendment Notes
The 2017 amendments to this section by Ch. 156 substituted "office of strategic initiatives" for "office of energy and planning" in the third sentence.

—2004.
Substituted "office of energy and planning" for "office of state planning and energy programs" in the third sentence.

—2003.
Substituted "office of state planning and energy programs" for "office of state planning" in the third sentence.

—2000.
Added "after consultation with the respective regional planning commissions" at the end of the fifth sentence.

36:46. Formation of Regional Planning Commissions.

I. If no regional planning commission exists in any specific planning region as delineated by the office of strategic initiatives, then 2 or more municipalities in said planning region and having planning boards may, by ordinance or resolution adopted by the respective legislative bodies of said municipalities, form a regional planning commission.

II. If a regional planning commission already exists in any specific planning region as delineated by the office of strategic initiatives, then any municipality in said planning region and having a planning board may, by ordinance or resolution adopted by the respective legislative body of said municipality, become a member of the regional planning commission. A regional planning commission may also include municipalities located in an adjacent state.

III. Each municipality which shall become a member of a regional planning commission shall be entitled to 2 representatives on said commission. A municipality with a population of over 10,000 but less than 25,000 shall be entitled to have 3 representatives on said commission and a municipality with a population of over 25,000 shall be entitled to have 4 representatives on said commission. Population as set forth in this section shall be deemed to be determined by the last federal census. Representatives to a regional planning commission shall be nominated by the planning board of each municipality from the residents thereof and shall be appointed by the municipal officers of each municipality. Representatives may be elected or appointed officials of the municipality or county. In any county or counties in which a regional planning commission has been formed, the county may, by resolution of its county commissioners, become a member of said regional planning commission and shall be entitled to appoint 2 representatives on said commission. The terms of office of members of a regional planning commission shall be for 4 years, but initial appointments shall be for 2 and 4 years. In municipalities entitled to 3 or more representatives, initial appointment shall be for 2, 3 and 4 years. Vacancies shall be filled for the remainder of the unexpired term in the same manner as original appointments. Municipalities and counties may also appoint alternate representatives. A representative to a regional planning commission shall, when acting within the scope of his official duties and authority, be deemed to be acting as an agent of both the regional planning commission and of the municipality or county which he represents. In addition, regional planning commissions are encouraged to consult, at their discretion, with agencies and institutions operating within the region whose activities influence planning and development in that region.

HISTORY:
1969, 324:1. 1991, 72:4, eff. July 12, 1991. 2000, 200:3, eff. July 29, 2000. 2003, 319:9, eff. July 1, 2003. 2004, 257:44, eff. July 1, 2004. 2017, 156:64, eff. July 1, 2017.

Amendment Notes
The 2017 amendments to this section by Ch. 156 substituted "office of strategic initiatives" for "office of energy and planning" in I and II.

—2004.
Paragraphs II and II: Substituted "office of energy and planning" for "office of state planning and energy programs".

—2003.
Substituted "office of state planning and energy programs" for "office of state planning" in pars. I and II.

—2000.
Paragraph III: Added the twelfth sentence.

—1991.
Paragraph III: Added the eleventh sentence.

RESEARCH REFERENCES AND PRACTICE AIDS

Cross References.
Liability and indemnification for damages of regional planning commissioners, see RSA 31:104-106.

36:47. General Powers and Duties.

I. A regional planning commission's powers shall be advisory, and shall generally pertain to the development of the region within its jurisdiction as a whole. Nothing in this subdivision shall be deemed to reduce or limit any of the powers, duties or obligations of planning boards in individual municipalities. The area of jurisdiction of a regional planning commission shall include the areas of the respective municipalities within the delineated planning region. It shall be the duty of a regional planning commission to prepare a comprehensive master plan for the development of the region within its jurisdiction, including the commission's recommendations, among other things, for the use of land within the region; for the general location, extent, type of use, and character of highways, major streets, intersections, parking lots, railroads, aircraft landing areas, waterways and bridges, and other means of transportation, communication, and other purposes; for the development, extent, and general location of parks, playgrounds, shore front developments, parkways, and other public reservations and recreation areas; for the location, type, and character of public buildings, schools, community centers, and other public property; and for the improvement, redevelopment, rehabilitation, or conservation of residential, business, industrial and other areas; including the development of programs for the modernization and coordination of buildings, housing, zoning and subdivision regulations of municipalities and their enforcement on a coordinated and unified basis. A regional planning commission may authorize its employees or consultants to render assistance on local planning problems to any municipality or county which is not a member of said regional planning commission. The cost of such assistance shall be paid entirely by the municipality or county to which the service is rendered or partly by said municipality or county and partly by any gift, grant, or contribution which may be available for such work or by combination thereof. Said commission shall keep a strict account of the cost of such assistance and shall provide such municipality or county with an itemized statement.

II. For the purpose of assisting municipalities in complying with RSA 674:2, III(m), each regional planning commission shall compile a regional housing needs assessment, which shall include an assessment of the regional need for housing for persons and families of all levels of income. The regional housing needs assessment shall be updated every 5 years and made available to all municipalities in the planning region.

III. In preparing a comprehensive plan for the development of the region within its jurisdiction, each regional planning commission may use the framework for the state's comprehensive development plan in RSA 9-A:1, III as the basis for its plan. Such plan shall be updated every 5 years or sooner if desired by the regional planning commission. Prior to its adoption, the plan shall be distributed to every library, planning board, and board of selectmen/aldermen/city council in each of the communities within the region, and to the office of strategic initiatives. The regional planning commission shall address in writing all comments received prior to the publication of a final draft. A public hearing shall be held by the regional planning commission with 30 days' notice published in all newspapers of general circulation in the region, and shall state where the document can be viewed, the time and place of the public hearing, and shall allow for written comments. For each regional plan, the office of strategic initiatives shall offer comments as to its consistency with the state plan. The first regional development plans affected by this statute shall be adopted within 5 years of the effective date of this paragraph and renewed at least every 5 years thereafter.

IV. Regional planning commissions shall make a good faith effort to inform and respond to their local communities regarding the purposes and progress of their work in developing the regional development plan.

HISTORY:
1969, 324:1. 1988, 270:2, eff. July 1, 1988. 2002, 178:6, eff. July 14, 2002. 229:8, eff. July 1, 2002. 2003, 319:9, eff. July 1, 2003. 2004, 257:44, eff. July 1, 2004. 2017, 156:64, eff. July 1, 2017.

Amendment Notes
The 2017 amendments to this section by Ch. 156 substituted "office of strategic initiatives" for "office of energy and planning" in the third and second to the last sentences.

—2004.
Paragraph III: Substituted "office of energy and planning" for "office of state planning and energy programs" in the second and fifth sentences.

—2003.
Paragraph III: Substituted "office of state planning and energy programs" for "office of state planning" in the second and fifth sentences.

—2002.
Paragraph II: Chapter 178 inserted "(m)" following "RSA 674:2, III" and substituted "an assessment" for "as assessment" in the first sentence.
Paragraphs III and IV: Added by ch. 229.

—1988.
Designated existing provisions of section as par. I and added par. II.

36:48.　Organization, Officers, and Bylaws.

A regional planning commission shall elect annually from among its members a chairman, vice-chairman, and such other officers as it deems necessary. Meetings shall be held at the call of the chairman and at such other time as the commission may determine. A commission shall keep minutes of its proceedings and such minutes shall be filed in the office of the commission and shall be a public record. A commission may adopt such bylaws as it deems necessary to the conduct of its business.

HISTORY:
1969, 324:1, eff. Aug. 29, 1969.

RESEARCH REFERENCES AND PRACTICE AIDS

Cross References.
Access to public records, see RSA 91-A.

36:49.　Finances.

A regional planning commission shall determine on a reasonable and equitable basis the proportion of its costs to be borne respectively by each municipality or county which is a member of said commission. A commission may accept and receive in furtherance of its functions, funds, grants, and services from the federal government or its agencies, from departments, agencies and instrumentalities of state, municipal or local government or from private and civic sources. Such funds may be used in conjunction with other funds from federal or state governments or from gifts, grants or contributions available for such work. Municipalities or counties are hereby authorized to appropriate funds to the use of a regional planning commission and to furnish a regional planning commission legal or other services which it may deem reasonable. Failure upon the part of any municipality or county to pay its proportionate annual share of the cost as determined by a regional planning commission shall constitute a termination of such municipality's or county's vote in the commission's affairs until such annual share is paid. Municipalities or counties are hereby authorized to enter into contracts with a regional planning commission for the furnishing of funds or services in connection with the preparation of a comprehensive regional master plan and any special planning work to be done by a regional planning commission for any member municipality or county. Within the amounts appropriated to it or placed at its disposal by gift, grant, or contribution, a regional planning commission may engage employees, contract with professional consultants, rent offices, and obtain such other goods, or services and incur short-term operating debt, not to exceed a term of one year and/or a line of credit secured by the assets of the commission, as are necessary to it in the carrying out of its proper function. Member municipalities and counties shall not be liable for any debt or line of credit incurred by a regional planning commission. Any private gifts or funds when received shall be deemed a contribution to the regional planning commission for a public purpose within the meaning of any federal or state laws relative to tax exemptions.

HISTORY:
   1969, 324:1, eff. Aug. 29, 1969. 2000, 200:4, eff. July 29, 2000.

Amendments

—2000.
   In the seventh sentence, inserted "and incur short-term operating debt, not to exceed a term of one year and/or a line of credit secured by the assets of the commission" preceding "as are necessary to it" and added the eighth sentence.

36:49-a. Status as a Political Subdivision.

Regional planning commissions are political subdivisions of the state. However, regional planning commissions have only that power and authority expressly provided for in RSA 36.

HISTORY:
   2000, 200:6, eff. July 29, 2000.

36:50. Relationship To Local Planning Boards.

A regional planning commission may assist the planning board of any municipality within the delineated region to carry out any regional plan or plans developed by said commission. A regional planning commission may also render assistance on local planning problems. A regional planning commission may make recommendations on the basis of its plans and studies to any planning board, to the legislative body of any city and to the selectmen of any town within its region, to the county commissioners of the county or counties in which said region is located and to any state or federal authorities. Upon completion of a comprehensive master plan for the region or any portion of said comprehensive master plan, a regional planning commission may file certified copies of said comprehensive master plan or portion thereof with the planning board of any member municipality. Such planning boards may adopt all or any part of such comprehensive master plan which pertains to the areas within its jurisdiction as its own master plan, subject to the requirements of RSA 674:1-4.

HISTORY:
   1969, 324:1, eff. Aug. 29, 1969. 2000, 200:5, eff. July 29, 2000.

Amendments

—2000.
   Substituted "RSA 674:1-4" for "sections 13, 14, and 15, chapter 36 of the Revised Statutes Annotated" at the end of the fifth sentence.

36:51. Assistance to Urban Renewal by Municipalities and Other Public Bodies. [Repealed.]

[Repealed 2000, 200:8, I, eff. July 29, 2000.]

Former section(s).
   Former RSA 36:51, relating to assistance to urban renewal by municipalities and other public bodies, was derived from 1969, 324:1.

36:53. Additional Powers and Duties of Regional Planning Commissions.

In order to implement any of the provisions of a regional plan, which has been adopted or is in preparation, a regional planning commission may, in addition to its powers and duties under RSA 36:47 undertake studies and make specific recommendations on economic, industrial and commercial development within the region and carry out, with the cooperation of municipalities and/or counties within the region, economic development programs for the full development, improvement, protection and preservation of the region's physical and human resources.

HISTORY:
   1969, 324:1, eff. Aug. 29, 1969.

Revision note.
   Substituted "RSA 36:47" for "section 47" to conform reference to citation style of LEXIS New Hampshire Revised Statutes Annotated.

Review of Developments of Regional Impact

RESEARCH REFERENCES AND PRACTICE AIDS

Cross References.
   Planning and zoning generally, see RSA 672 et seq.
   Regional planning commissions, see RSA 36:45– 36:50, 36:53.

36:54. Purpose.

The purpose of this subdivision is to:
   I. Provide timely notice to potentially affected municipalities concerning proposed developments which are likely to have impacts beyond the boundaries of a single municipality.
   II. Provide opportunities for the regional planning commission and the potentially affected municipalities to furnish timely input to the municipality having jurisdiction.
   III. Encourage the municipality having jurisdiction to consider the interests of other potentially affected municipalities.

HISTORY:
   1991, 300:1, eff. Jan. 1, 1992.

36:55. Definition.

In this subdivision "development of regional impact" means any proposal before a local land use board which in the determination of such local land use board could reasonably be expected to impact on a neighboring municipality, because of factors such as, but not limited to, the following:
   I. Relative size or number of dwelling units as compared with existing stock.
   II. Proximity to the borders of a neighboring community.
   III. Transportation networks.

IV. Anticipated emissions such as light, noise, smoke, odors, or particles.

V. Proximity to aquifers or surface waters which transcend municipal boundaries.

VI. Shared facilities such as schools and solid waste disposal facilities.

HISTORY:
1991, 300:1, eff. Jan. 1, 1992.

36:56. Review Required.

I. A local land use board, as defined in RSA 672:7, upon receipt of an application for development, shall review it promptly and determine whether or not the development, if approved, reasonably could be construed as having the potential for regional impact. Doubt concerning regional impact shall be resolved in a determination that the development has a potential regional impact.

II. Each regional planning commission may, with public participation following the public posting of notice of the intent to develop guidelines, including notice published in a newspaper of general circulation in the planning region, develop guidelines to assist the local land use boards in its planning region in their determinations whether or not a development has a potential regional impact. The regional planning commission may update the guidelines as needed and provide them, as voted by the regional planning commissioners, to all municipalities in the planning region.

HISTORY:
1991, 300:1, eff. Jan. 1, 1992. 2009, 194:1, eff. September 11, 2009.

Amendments

—2009.
The 2009 amendment added the I designation and added II.

36:57. Procedure.

I. Upon determination that a proposed development has a potential regional impact, the local land use board having jurisdiction shall afford the regional planning commission and the affected municipalities the status of abutters as defined in RSA 672:3 for the limited purpose of providing notice and giving testimony.

II. Not more than 5 business days after reaching a decision regarding a development of regional impact, the local land use board having jurisdiction shall, by certified mail, furnish the regional planning commission and the affected municipalities with copies of the minutes of the meeting at which the decision was made. The local land use board shall, at the same time, submit an initial set of plans to the regional planning commission, the cost of which shall be borne by the applicant.

III. At least 14 days prior to public hearing, the local land use board shall notify, by certified mail, all affected municipalities and the regional planning commission of the date, time, and place of the hearing and their right to testify concerning the development.

IV. Notwithstanding the foregoing, when the building inspector determines that a use or structure proposed in a building permit application will have the potential for regional impact and no such determination has previously been made by another local land use board, he or she shall notify the local governing body. The building inspector shall also notify by certified mail the regional planning commission and the affected municipalities, who shall be provided 30 days to submit comment to the local governing body and the building inspector prior to the issuance of the building permit.

HISTORY:
1991, 300:1, eff. Jan. 1, 1992. 2003, 220:1, eff. Aug. 30, 2003. 2005, 39:1, eff. July 16, 2005. 2008, 357:5, eff. July 11, 2008. 2009, 49:1, eff. January 1, 2010.

Amendments

—2009.
The 2009 amendment substituted "Not more than 5 business days after" for "Within 144 hours of" at the beginning of the first sentence of II.

—2008.
The 2008 amendment added IV.

—2005.
Paragraph II: Substituted "144 hours" for "72 hours" in the first sentence.

—2003.
Paragraph II: Added the second sentence.

NOTES TO DECISIONS

Construction
Town notified abutting towns of pending public hearings on retail mall, and notice specifically informed abutter towns that it served as notice with respect to potential regional impact and that abutter towns were legally entitled to attend hearing and offer input; abutter towns thus received proper statutory notice of potential regional impact, notwithstanding fact that town failed to mail minutes of hearing to abutter towns. Mountain Valley Mall Assocs. v. Municipality of Conway, 144 N.H. 642, 745 A.2d 481, 2000 N.H. LEXIS 1 (N.H. 2000).

36:58. Applicability.

The provisions of this subdivision shall supersede any contrary or inconsistent provisions of local land use regulations enacted under RSA 155-E and RSA 674.

HISTORY:
1991, 300:1, eff. Jan. 1, 1992.

CHAPTER 36-A

CONSERVATION COMMISSIONS

NOTES TO DECISIONS

Cited:
 Cited in Claridge v. New Hampshire Wetlands Bd., 125 N.H. 745, 485 A.2d 287, 1984 N.H. LEXIS 307 (1984).

RESEARCH REFERENCES AND PRACTICE AIDS

Cross References.
 Connecticut River Valley resource commission, see RSA 227-E.
 Land conservation investment program, see RSA 162-C:6 et seq.
 Soil conservation and farmland preservation, see RSA 432.

36-A:1. Method of Adoption.

Any city by vote of its city council, and any town at any duly warned meeting, may adopt or rescind the provisions of this chapter.

HISTORY:
 1963, 168:1, eff. Aug. 20, 1963. 2008, 317:1, eff. January 1, 2009.

Amendments

—2008.
The 2008 amendment added "or rescind" following "may adopt".

36-A:2. Conservation Commission.

A city or town which accepts the provisions of this chapter may establish a conservation commission, hereinafter called the commission, for the proper utilization and protection of the natural resources and for the protection of watershed resources of said city or town. Such commission shall conduct researches into its local land and water areas and shall seek to coordinate the activities of unofficial bodies organized for similar purposes, and may advertise, prepare, print and distribute books, maps, charts, plans and pamphlets which in its judgment it deems necessary for its work. It shall keep an index of all open space and natural, aesthetic or ecological areas within the city or town, as the case may be, with the plan of obtaining information pertinent to proper utilization of such areas, including lands owned by the state or lands owned by a town or city. It shall keep an index of all marshlands, swamps and all other wet lands in a like manner, and may recommend to the city council or selectmen or to the department of natural and cultural resources a program for the protection, development or better utilization of all such areas. It shall keep accurate records of its meetings and actions and shall file an annual report which shall be printed in the annual town or municipal report. The commission may appoint such clerks and other employees or subcommittees as it may from time to time require.

HISTORY:
 1963, 168:1. 1973, 550:1, eff. Sept. 3, 1973. 2017, 156:14, eff. July 1, 2017.

Amendment Notes
 The 2017 amendments to this section by Ch. 156 substituted "natural and cultural resources" for "resources and economic development" in the fourth sentence.

—1973.
 Rewritten to the extent that a detailed comparison would be impracticable.

Purpose of 2012 amendment.
 2012, 202:1, eff. June 13, 2012, provided: "The purpose of this act is to set guidelines for entry by conservation commissions or their designees onto private property for data gathering for conservation and natural resource inventory purposes and for the publication of such data, and to ensure that property owners are informed of data gathering on their property. These guidelines do not supercede guidelines already established by state agencies as they may be modified from time to time, but establish guidelines for conservation projects at the regional, local, and individual level."

36-A:3. Composition of Commission.

The commission shall consist of not less than 3 nor more than 7 members. In a town which has a planning board, one member of the commission may also be on the planning board. In a city which has a planning board, one member of the commission may be on the planning board. In cities, the members of the commission shall be appointed by the mayor subject to the provisions of the city charter, and in towns the members of the commission shall be appointed by the selectmen. Alternate members may be appointed in a like manner and when the alternate serves in the absence or disqualification of a regular member, the alternate shall have full voting powers. When a commission is first established, terms of the members shall be for one, 2, or 3 years, and so arranged that the terms of approximately ⅓ of the members will expire each year, and their successors shall be appointed for terms of 3 years each. Any member of a commission so appointed may, after a public hearing, if requested, be removed for cause by the appointing authority. A vacancy occurring otherwise than by expiration of a term shall be filled for the unexpired term in the same manner as an original appointment. Members of a conservation commission shall be residents of the city or town which they represent. Members of a conservation commission also may serve on other municipal boards and commissions, including, but not limited to a historic district commission established under RSA 673:4, and a heritage commission established under RSA 673:4-a.

HISTORY:
 1963, 168:1. 1973, 550:2. 1974, 44:2. 1987, 318:1. 1995, 138:1, eff. July 23, 1995. 1997, 31:1, eff. June 27, 1997.

Amendments

—1997.
 Added the next to last sentence.

—1995.

Substituted "the alternate" for "his" following "regular member" in the fifth sentence and added the last sentence.

—1987.

Inserted the fifth sentence and made other minor stylistic changes.

—1974.

Rewrote the second sentence, inserted the third sentence, deleted "remaining" following "cities, the" and following "towns the" in the fourth sentence and inserted "of the commission" preceding "shall be appointed by the selectmen" at the end of that sentence.

—1973.

Inserted the second sentence and "remaining" following "cities, the" in the third sentence and following "terms of the" in the fourth sentence and substituted "the remaining members" for "they" following "towns" in the third sentence.

RESEARCH REFERENCES AND PRACTICE AIDS

New Hampshire Practice.

13-15 N.H.P. Local Government Law § 530.

36-A:4. Powers.

I. Said commission may receive gifts of money, personal property, real property, and water rights, either within or outside the boundaries of the municipality, by gift, grant, bequest, or devise, subject to the approval of the local governing body, such gifts to be managed and controlled by the commission for the purposes of this section. Said commission may acquire in the name of the city or town, subject to the approval of the local governing body, by purchase, the fee in such land or water rights within the boundaries of the municipality, or any lesser interest, development right, easement, covenant, or other contractual right including conveyances with conditions, limitations, or reversions, as may be necessary to acquire, maintain, improve, protect, or limit the future use of or otherwise conserve and properly utilize open spaces and other land and water areas within their city or town, and shall manage and control the same, but the city or town or commission shall not have the right to condemn property for these purposes.

II. No commission, its members, or designee shall enter private property to gather data about the property for use in a wetlands designation, prime wetlands designation, natural resource inventory report or map, or natural heritage map without first obtaining permission of the property owner or agent, or a lawfully issued warrant. Such permission may be oral or written, provided that record is made of oral authorization. If consent for entry is denied, the conservation commission, or designee, may obtain an administrative inspection warrant under RSA 595-B.

III. Prior to requesting permission, the commission, its members, or designee shall notify the landowner of the purpose of the data gathering, the specific features that will be evaluated, the manner in which the data collected will be recorded and distributed, and possible known consequences of the data collection.

IV. No data gathered by entering property without the permission of the landowner or an administrative warrant shall be used for any purpose other than law enforcement purposes authorized by statute.

V. The conservation commission, in reviewing an application to provide input to any other municipal board, shall not require submission of an application for or receipt of a permit or permits from other state or federal governmental bodies prior to accepting a submission for its review or providing such input.

HISTORY:

1963, 168:1. 1973, 550:3. 1995, 138:2, eff. July 23, 1995. 2008, 317:2, eff. January 1, 2009. 2012, 202:2, eff. June 13, 2012. 2013, 270:4, eff. September 22, 2013.

Amendment Notes

—2013.

The 2013 amendment added V.

—2012.

The 2012 amendment added the I designation and added II through IV.

—2008.

The 2008 amendment rewrote the section to the extent that a detailed comparison would be impracticable.

—1995.

Substituted "local governing body" for "city council in a city or the selectmen in a town" in the first sentence and inserted "subject to the approval of the local governing body" preceding "by gift" in the second sentence.

—1973.

Inserted "in the name of the town or city" following "acquire" in the second sentence.

RESEARCH REFERENCES AND PRACTICE AIDS

Cross References.

Acquisition of trails by conservation commission, see RSA 231-A:5.

36-A:4-a. Optional Powers.

I. The legislative body of a city or town may vote at an annual meeting to authorize the conservation commission to:

(a) Expend funds for the purchase of interests in land outside the boundaries of the municipality, subject to the approval of the local governing body; and

(b) Expend funds for contributions to "qualified organizations," as defined in section 170(h)(3) of the Internal Revenue Code of 1986, for the purchase of property interests or facilitating transactions relative thereto to be held by the qualified organization, when such purchase carries out the purposes of this chapter. Because such contributions further the protection of the state's natural resources, they are hereby declared to be a public purpose.

II. A vote under this section may be taken simultaneously with the adoption of this chapter or any time thereafter. If the vote is taken simultaneously with the adoption of this chapter, a separate question shall be placed on the warrant.

(a) The wording of the question under subparagraph I(a) shall be: "Shall the town vote to adopt the provisions of RSA 36-A:4-a, I(a) to authorize the conservation commission to expend funds to purchase interests in land outside the boundaries of our municipality, subject to the approval of the local governing body?"

(b) The wording of the question under subparagraph I(b) shall be: "Shall the town vote to adopt the provisions of RSA 36-A:4-a, I(b) to authorize the conservation commission to expend funds for contributions to 'qualified organizations' for the purchase of property interests, or facilitating transactions related thereto, where the property interest is to be held by the qualified organization and the town will retain no interest in the property?"

III. The provisions of this section may be rescinded by vote of the legislative body.

HISTORY:
2008, 317:3, eff. January 1, 2009.

36-A:5. Appropriations Authorized.

I. A town or city, having established a conservation commission as authorized by RSA 36-A:2, may appropriate money as deemed necessary for the purpose of this chapter. The whole or any part of money so appropriated in any year and any gifts of money received pursuant to RSA 36-A:4 may be placed in a conservation fund and allowed to accumulate from year to year. Money may be expended from said fund by the conservation commission for the purposes of this chapter without further approval of the town meeting.

II. The town treasurer, pursuant to RSA 41:29, shall have custody of all moneys in the conservation fund and shall pay out the same only upon order of the conservation commission. The disbursement of conservation funds shall be authorized by a majority of the conservation commission. Prior to the use of such funds for the purchase of any interest in real property or for a contribution to a qualified organization for the purchase of property interests under RSA 36-A:4-a, I(b), the conservation commission shall hold a public hearing with notice in accordance with RSA 675:7.

III. In the municipality that has adopted the provisions of RSA 79-A:25, II, the specified percentage of the revenues received pursuant to RSA 79-A shall be placed in the conservation fund.

HISTORY:
1963, 168:1. 1973, 550:4. 1987, 318:2. 1988, 120:1, eff. June 18, 1988. 2008, 317:4, eff. January 1, 2009.

Amendments

—2008.
The 2008 amendment added "or for a contribution to a qualified organization for the purchase of property interests under RSA 36-A:4-a, I(b)" in the third sentence of II.

—1988.
Paragraph III: Added.

—1987.
Designated the existing provisions of the section as par. I, in that paragraph rewrote the first sentence, inserted "and any gifts of money received pursuant to RSA 36-A:4" preceding "may be placed" in the second sentence and "by the conservation commission" preceding "for the purposes of this chapter" and "without further approval of the town meeting" thereafter in the third sentence, and added par. II.

—1973.
Deleted "development and" preceding "better utilization" in the first sentence.

36-A:6. Commissioner of Natural and Cultural Resources.

The commissioner of the department of natural and cultural resources may establish a program to assist, at their request, the cities and towns which have adopted the provisions of this chapter, in acquiring land and in planning of use and structures as described in RSA 36-A:2.

HISTORY:
1963, 168:1, eff. Aug. 20, 1963. 2017, 156:14, eff. July 1, 2017.

Revision note.
At the end of the section, substituted "RSA 36-A:2" for "section 2" to conform reference to citation style of LEXIS New Hampshire Revised Statutes Annotated.

Amendment Notes
The 2017 amendments to this section by Ch. 156 substituted "Natural and Cultural Resources" for "Resources and Economic Development" in the section heading; and substituted "natural and cultural resources" for "resources and economic development."

CHAPTER 39

TIME FOR HOLDING TOWN MEETINGS AND WARNING THEREOF

NOTES TO DECISIONS

Cited:
Cited in Piper v. Meredith, 110 N.H. 291, 266 A.2d 103, 1970 N.H. LEXIS 156 (1970).

RESEARCH REFERENCES AND PRACTICE AIDS

Cross References.
Government of town meeting, see RSA 40.
School district meetings, see RSA 197.

Town elections, see RSA 669.
Village district meetings, see RSA 52:11-a– 14.

39:3. Articles.

Upon the written application of 25 or more registered voters or 2 percent of the registered voters in town, whichever is less, although in no event shall fewer than 10 registered voters be sufficient, presented to the selectmen or one of them not later than the fifth Tuesday before the day prescribed for an annual meeting, the selectmen shall insert in their warrant for such meeting the petitioned article with only such minor textual changes as may be required. For the purposes of this section, the number of registered voters in a town shall be the number of voters registered prior to the last state general election. The right to have an article inserted in the warrant conferred by this section shall not be invalidated by the provisions of RSA 32. In towns with fewer than 10,000 inhabitants upon the written application of 50 or more voters or ¼ of the voters in town, whichever is fewer, and in towns with 10,000 or more inhabitants upon the written application of 5 percent of the registered voters in the town, so presented not less than 60 days before the next annual meeting, the selectmen shall warn a special meeting to act upon any question specified in such application. The checklist for an annual or special town meeting shall be corrected by the supervisors of the checklist as provided in RSA 654:25–31. Those persons qualified to vote whose names are on the corrected checklist shall be entitled to vote at the meeting. The same checklist used at a recessed town meeting shall be used at any reconvened session of the same town meeting. In no event shall a special town meeting be held on the biennial election day.

HISTORY:
RS 32:3. CS 34:3. GS 35:3. GL 38:3. PS 41:3. PL 45:3. 1937, 40:1. RL 57:3. 1947, 21:1. RSA 39:3. 1969, 59:1. 1971, 79:1. 1975, 160:1. 1981, 454:1. 1987, 299:1. 1990, 192:1. 1991, 223:1. 370:5. 1994, 197:1, eff. July 23, 1994. 1998, 194:1, eff. Aug. 17, 1998.

Amendments

—1998.
Deleted "except that the session 3 weeks before the meeting shall not be required" following "RSA 654:25-31" in the fifth sentence.

—1994.
In the fourth sentence, added "in towns with fewer than 10,000 inhabitants" preceding "upon" at the beginning of the sentence and inserted "and in towns with 10,000 or more inhabitants upon the written application of 5 percent of the registered voters in the town" preceding "so presented".

—1991.
Chapter 223 inserted "although in no event shall fewer than 10 registered voters be sufficient" preceding "presented" in the first sentence.
Chapter 370 deleted "or biennial" following "annual" in the first sentence and added the eighth sentence.

—1990.
Substituted "25" for "10", inserted "registered" preceding "voters" in two places, and substituted "2 percent" for "⅙" and "less" for

"fewer" preceding "presented" in the first sentence and added the second sentence.

—1987.
Substituted "not later than the fifth Tuesday" for "at least 35 days" preceding "before the day" in the first sentence.

—1981.
Rewritten to the extent that a detailed comparison would be impracticable.

—1975.
Substituted "the petitioned article with only such minor textual changes as may be required" for "any subject specified in such application" following "such meeting" at the end of the first sentence.

—1971.
Added the fourth sentence.

—1969.
Substituted "thirty-five" for "twenty-five" preceding "days" in the first sentence.

NOTES TO DECISIONS

Analysis

1. Insertion of articles
2. Subject of articles
3. Special meetings
4. Recommendations by selectboard

1. Insertion of articles
Selectmen have no discretion whether to insert in a warrant an article presented to them in compliance with this section. Woodside v. Selectmen of Derry, 116 N.H. 606, 366 A.2d 210, 1976 N.H. LEXIS 424 (N.H. 1976).

2. Subject of articles
Petitioner residents asserted unsuccessfully that a deliberative session, by law, could amend articles but could not deprive the voters or take final action on the same. Nothing in RSA 40:13, IV, or RSA 39:3 prevented voters at the deliberative session from effectively removing a subject from consideration at the second session by amending an article to delete the entire subject thereof. Grant v. Town of Barrington, 156 N.H. 807, 943 A.2d 829, 2008 N.H. LEXIS 29 (N.H. 2008), superseded by statute as stated in Cady v. Town of Deerfield, 169 N.H. 575, 154 A.3d 157, 2017 N.H. LEXIS 3 (N.H. 2017).

This section is of general but not all-inclusive application and is not applicable where the legislature has treated a subject specified in an application in a special, exclusive and different manner. Seabrook v. Perkins, 112 N.H. 37, 288 A.2d 688, 1972 N.H. LEXIS 138 (N.H. 1972).

3. Special meetings
Town selectmen may exercise a certain amount of judgment in determining whether to schedule a special town meeting when petitioned to do so by voters, but selectmen do not have unbridled discretion to frustrate the voters' attempts to call a special town meeting. Winchester Taxpayers' Ass'n v. Board of Selectmen, 118 N.H. 144, 383 A.2d 1125, 1978 N.H. LEXIS 361 (N.H. 1978).

Town selectmen are under no obligation to warn a special meeting if the issue to be considered is prohibited or limited in scope by statute. Winchester Taxpayers' Ass'n v. Board of Selectmen, 118 N.H. 144, 383 A.2d 1125, 1978 N.H. LEXIS 361 (N.H. 1978).

Where selectmen of town had been empowered to sell and convey certain town land and had advertised sale by public auction to be held on specified date, there was no requirement as matter of law that selectmen postpone the sale and call special town meeting to see if town would vote to retain such land where petition by requisite number of voters under provisions of this section was filed within four days of date of sale and sufficient time did not permit compliance with the notice requirements of RSA 39:4 and 39:5. Preston v. Gillam, 104 N.H. 279, 184 A.2d 462, 1962 N.H. LEXIS 68 (N.H. 1962).

4. Recommendations by selectboard

Selectboard did not lack authority under RSA 39:3 to insert its recommendations as to plaintiffs' warrant articles on the official ballot below each of the articles, as the recommendations, which appeared in bolded, italicized text below each of the warrant articles, did not constitute textual changes to the articles themselves. Olson v. Town of Grafton, 168 N.H. 563, 133 A.3d 270, 2016 N.H. LEXIS 11 (N.H. 2016).

Cited:

Cited in Curtis v. Berry, 68 N.H. 18, 40 A. 393, 1894 N.H. LEXIS 9 (1894); Moulton v. Beals, 98 N.H. 461, 102 A.2d 489, 1954 N.H. LEXIS 88 (1954); McDonnell v. Derry, 116 N.H. 3, 350 A.2d 620, 1976 N.H. LEXIS 247 (1976); Levasseur v. Board of Selectmen, 116 N.H. 340, 358 A.2d 665, 1976 N.H. LEXIS 349 (1976).

RESEARCH REFERENCES AND PRACTICE AIDS

Cross References.

Abolition of planning board or zoning commission, see RSA 39:3-c.

Application to court for insertion of article in warrant, see RSA 39:9.

Consideration of warrant articles in towns with 10,000 or more inhabitants, see RSA 40:11.

Penalty for refusal to insert article in warrant, see RSA 39:3-b.

Publication of warrant for special town meeting, see RSA 39:4.

New Hampshire Bar Journal.

For article, "The Attorney General's Role in Overseeing Municipal Governance," see 48 N.H. B.J. 46 (Autumn 2007).

New Hampshire Practice.

13-9 N.H.P. Local Government Law § 200.
13-10 N.H.P. Local Government Law § 226.
13-10 N.H.P. Local Government Law § 229.
13-13 N.H.P. Local Government Law § 352.
13-15 N.H.P. Local Government Law § 479.
13-15 N.H.P. Local Government Law § 481.
13-15 N.H.P. Local Government Law § 494.
14-23 N.H.P. Local Government Law § 872.
14-31 N.H.P. Local Government Law § 1282.
16-1 N.H.P. Municipal Law & Taxation § 1.07.
16-2 N.H.P. Municipal Law & Taxation § 2.21.
16-31 N.H.P. Municipal Law & Taxation § 31.12.
16-38 N.H.P. Municipal Law & Taxation § 38.07.

39:3-b. Penalty.

A board of selectmen is guilty of a violation if it refuses to insert an article in the warrant, after being petitioned to do so in accordance with RSA 39:3.

HISTORY:

1971, 79:4. 1977, 588:26, eff. Sept. 16, 1977.

Amendments

—1977.

Rewritten to the extent that a detailed comparison would be impracticable.

NOTES TO DECISIONS

Cited:

Cited in Seabrook v. Perkins, 112 N.H. 37, 288 A.2d 688, 1972 N.H. LEXIS 138 (1972); Woodside v. Selectmen of Derry, 116 N.H. 606, 366 A.2d 210, 1976 N.H. LEXIS 424 (1976); Winchester

Taxpayers' Ass'n v. Board of Selectmen, 118 N.H. 144, 383 A.2d 1125, 1978 N.H. LEXIS 361 (1978).

RESEARCH REFERENCES AND PRACTICE AIDS

Cross References.

Classification of crimes, see RSA 625:9.

Penalty for failure to give notice of meeting or election, see RSA 39:13.

Sentences, see RSA 651.

39:3-c. Limitation.

Any petitioned article, which if adopted, would abolish a planning board, or zoning commission shall not be included in the warrant, unless such petition meets the requirements established by RSA 673:18, II.

HISTORY:

1971, 396:1. 1985, 103:1, eff. Jan. 1, 1986.

Amendments

—1985.

Substituted "RSA 673:18, II" for "RSA 31:63-c" following "established by".

CHAPTER 40

GOVERNMENT OF TOWN MEETING

Optional Form of Meeting—Official Ballot Referenda

NOTES TO DECISIONS

Cited:

Cited in State v. Boisvert, 117 N.H. 291, 371 A.2d 1182, 1977 N.H. LEXIS 323 (1977).

RESEARCH REFERENCES AND PRACTICE AIDS

Cross References.

Time for holding town meetings and warning thereof, see RSA 39.

Optional Form of Meeting—Official Ballot Referenda

40:13. Use of Official Ballot.

I. Notwithstanding RSA 39:3-d, RSA 40:4-e, or any other provision of law, any local political subdivision as defined in RSA 40:12 which has adopted this subdivision shall utilize the official ballot for voting on all issues before the voters.

II. The warrant for any annual meeting shall prescribe the place, day and hour for each of 2 separate sessions of the meeting, and notice shall be given as otherwise provided in this section. Final budgets and ballot questions shall be printed in the annual report made available to the legislative body at least one week before the date of the second session of the annual meeting.

II-a. Notwithstanding any other provision of law, all local political subdivisions which adopt this subdivision, who have not adopted an April or May election date under RSA 40:14, X, shall comply with the following schedule pertaining to notice, petitioned articles, hearings, and warrants for the annual meeting:

(a) The final date for posting notice of budget hearings under RSA 32:5 and RSA 195:12 and hearings under RSA 33:8-a shall be the second Tuesday in January.

(b) The "budget submission date" as defined in RSA 273-A:1, III and the final date for submission of petitioned articles under RSA 39:3 and RSA 197:6 shall be the second Tuesday in January, provided however, that if a petitioned article proposes a bond governed by RSA 33:8-a, the deadline shall be the preceding Friday.

(c) Budget hearings under RSA 32:5 and RSA 195:12 and hearings under RSA 33:8-a shall be held on or before the third Tuesday in January. One or more supplemental budget hearings may be held at any time before the first session of the annual meeting, subject to the 7-day notice requirement in RSA 32:5. If the first hearing or any supplemental hearing is recessed to a later date or time, additional notice shall not be required for a supplemental session if the date, time, and place of the supplemental session are made known at the original hearing. In a political subdivision that has adopted a municipal budget committee pursuant to RSA 32:14, the last day for the budget committee to deliver copies of the final budget and recommendations to the governing body pursuant to RSA 32:16, IV shall be the Thursday before the last Monday in January.

(d) Warrants under RSA 39:5 and RSA 197:7 and budgets shall be posted and copies available to the general public on or before the last Monday in January.

II-b. Notwithstanding any other provision of law, all political subdivisions which hold their annual meetings in April shall comply with the following schedule pertaining to notice, petitioned articles, hearings, and warrants for the annual meeting.

(a) The final date for posting notice of budget hearings under RSA 32:5 and RSA 195:12 and hearings under RSA 33:8-a shall be the second Tuesday in February.

(b) The "budget submission date" as defined in RSA 273-A:1, III and the final date for submission of petitioned articles under RSA 39:3 and RSA 197:6 shall be the second Tuesday in February, provided however, that if a petitioned article proposes a bond governed by RSA 33:8-a, the deadline shall be the preceding Friday.

(c) Budget hearings under RSA 32:5 and RSA 195:12 and hearings under RSA 33:8-a shall be held on or before the third Tuesday in February. One or more supplemental budget hearings may be held at any time before the first session of the annual meeting, subject to the 7-day notice requirement in RSA 32:5. If the first hearing or any supplemental hearing is recessed to a later date or time, additional notice shall not be required for a supplemental session if the date, time, and place of the supplemental session are made known at the original hearing. In a political subdivision that has adopted a municipal budget committee pursuant to RSA 32:14, the last day for the budget committee to deliver copies of the final budget and recommendations to the governing body pursuant to RSA 32:16, IV shall be the Thursday before the last Monday in February.

(d) Warrants under RSA 39:5 and RSA 197:7 and budgets shall be posted and copies available to the general public on or before the last Monday in February.

II-c. Notwithstanding any other provision of law, all political subdivisions which hold their annual meetings in May shall comply with the following schedule pertaining to notice, petitioned articles, hearings, and warrants for the annual meeting:

(a) The final date for posting notice of budget hearings under RSA 32:5 and RSA 195:12 and hearings under RSA 33:8-a shall be the second Tuesday in March.

(b) The "budget submission date" as defined in RSA 273-A:1, III and the final date for submission of petitioned articles under RSA 39:3 and RSA 197:6 shall be the second Tuesday in March, provided however, that if a petitioned article proposes a bond governed by RSA 33:8-a, the deadline shall be the preceding Friday.

(c) Budget hearings under RSA 32:5 and RSA 195:12 and hearings under RSA 33:8-a shall be held on or before the third Tuesday in March. One or more supplemental budget hearings may be held at any time before the first session of the annual meeting, subject to the 7-day notice requirement in RSA 32:5. If the first hearing or any supplemental hearing is recessed to a later date or time, additional notice shall not be required for a supplemental session if the date, time, and place of the supplemental session are made known at the original hearing. In a political subdivision that has adopted a municipal budget committee pursuant to RSA 32:14, the last day for the budget committee to deliver copies of the final budget and recommendations to the governing body pursuant to RSA 32:16, IV shall be the Thursday before the last Monday in March.

(d) Warrants under RSA 39:5 and RSA 197:7 and budgets shall be posted and copies available to the general public on or before the last Monday in March.

II-d. The voter checklist shall be updated in accordance with RSA 669:5 for each session of the annual meeting.

III. The first session of the annual meeting, which shall be for the transaction of all business other than voting by official ballot, shall be held between the first and second Saturdays following the last Monday in January, inclusive of those Saturdays; between the first and second Saturdays following the last Monday in February, inclusive of those Saturdays; or between the first and second Saturdays following the last Monday in March, inclusive of those Saturdays at a time prescribed by the local political subdivision's governing body.

IV. The first session of the meeting, governed by the provisions of RSA 40:4, 40:4-a, 40:4-b, 40:4-f, and 40:6–40:10, shall consist of explanation, discussion, and debate of each warrant article. A vote to restrict reconsideration shall be deemed to prohibit any further action on the restricted article until the second session, and RSA 40:10, II shall not apply. Warrant articles may be amended at the first session, subject to the following limitations:

(a) Warrant articles whose wording is prescribed by law shall not be amended.

(b) Warrant articles that are amended shall be placed on the official ballot for a final vote on the main motion, as amended.

(c) No warrant article shall be amended to eliminate the subject matter of the article. An amendment that changes the dollar amount of an appropriation in a warrant article shall not be deemed to violate this subparagraph.

V. [Repealed.]

V-a. The legislative body of any town, school district, or village district may vote to require that all votes by an advisory budget committee, a town, school district, or village district budget committee, and the governing body or, in towns, school districts, or village districts without a budget committee, all votes of the governing body relative to budget items or any warrant articles or ballot questions shall be recorded votes and the numerical tally of any such vote shall be printed in the town, school district, or village district warrant next to the affected warrant article or on the ballot next to the affected ballot question. Unless the legislative body has voted otherwise, if a town or school district has not voted to require such tallies to be printed in the town or school district warrant next to the affected warrant article or on the ballot next to the affected ballot question, the governing body may do so on its own initiative.

VI. All warrant articles shall be placed on the official ballot for a final vote, including warrant articles as amended by the first session. All special warrant articles shall be accompanied on the ballot by recommendations as required by RSA 32:5, V, concerning any appropriation or appropriation as amended. For any article that proposes the adoption or amendment of an ordinance, a topical description of the substance of the ordinance or amendment, which shall be neutral in its language, may be placed on the official ballot instead of the full text of the ordinance or amendment, subject to the provisions of paragraphs VII-a and VIII-a. With respect to the adoption or amendment of a zoning ordinance, historic district ordinance, or building code, the provisions of RSA 675:3 shall govern to the extent they are inconsistent with anything contained in this paragraph or in paragraph VII-a or VIII-a.

VII. The second session of the annual meeting, to elect officers of the local political subdivision by official ballot, to vote on questions required by law to be inserted on said official ballot, and to vote on all warrant articles from the first session on official ballot, shall be held on the second Tuesday in March, the second Tuesday in April, or the second Tuesday in May, as applicable. Notwithstanding RSA 669:1, 670:1, or 671:2, the second session shall be deemed the annual election date for purposes of all applicable election statutes including, but not limited to, RSA 669:5, 669:19, 669:30, 670:3, 670:4, 670:11, 671:15, 671:19, and 671:30 through 32; and votes on zoning ordinances, historic district ordinances, and building codes under RSA 675.

VII-a. When a topical description of the substance of a proposed ordinance or amendment to an ordinance is to be placed on the official ballot, an official copy of the proposed ordinance or amendment, including any amendment to the proposal adopted the first session, shall be placed on file and made available to the public at the office of the clerk of the political subdivision not later than one week prior to the date of the second session of the annual meeting. An official copy of the proposed ordinance or amendment shall be on display for the voters at the meeting place on the date of the meeting.

VIII. The clerk of the local political subdivision shall prepare an official ballot, which may be separate from the official ballot used to elect officers, for all warrant articles. Wording shall be substantively the same as the main motion, as it was made or amended at the first session, with only such minor textual changes as may be required to cast the motion in the form of a question to the voters.

VIII-a. A question as to the adoption or amendment of an ordinance shall be in substantially the following form:

"Are you in favor of the adoption of (amendment to) the ordinance as proposed by the selectmen as follows: (here insert text or topical description of proposed ordinance or amendment)?" In the event that there shall be more than a single proposed amendment to an ordinance to be submitted to the voters at any given meeting, the issue as to the several amendments shall be put in the following manner: "Are you in favor of the adoption of Amendment No.__ to the ordinance as proposed by the selectmen as follows: (here insert text or topical description of proposed amendment)?"

IX.(a) "Operating budget" as used in this subdivision means "budget," as defined in RSA 32:3, III, exclusive of "special warrant articles," as defined in RSA 32:3, VI, and exclusive of other appropriations voted separately.

"I. The governing body of any town, village district, or school district that has adopted the provisions of RSA 40:13 may elect to hold and conduct the meeting in accordance with the provisions of RSA 39 and RSA 40 and other applicable law without regard to RSA 40:13. If the governing body elects to follow the provisions of RSA 40:13, it shall provide at least a 15-day period between the deliberative session and the official ballot vote for the purposes of proceedings under this section.

"II. The governing body of such town, village district, or school district shall post a notice, which shall include the warrant, in at least 2 public places within the political subdivision, one of which shall be on the political subdivision's website, if such exists, at least 7 days prior to the meeting. Additional notice shall be published in a newspaper of general circulation in the political subdivision, provided that if there is no newspaper of general circulation in which notice can be published at least 7 days before the date of the meeting, public notice shall be posted in at least one additional place within the political subdivision.

"III. The governing body shall hold a public hearing on the proposed warrant articles at the town meeting. In the event that the special meeting includes a warrant article for a bond, note, or other financing agreement subject to RSA 33:8-a, a public hearing held pursuant to this paragraph shall satisfy the public hearing requirement of RSA 33:8-a.

"IV. In towns that have adopted the provisions of RSA 40:13, even if the governing body has elected to hold the meeting without regard to RSA 40:13, the issuance of notes or bonds shall be authorized by a vote of ⅗ of all ballots cast. In all other towns, the issuance of notes or bonds shall be authorized by a ballot vote of ⅔ of all voters present and voting, unless the town has adopted a charter provision specifically stating an alternate vote requirement.

"V. The meeting shall be conducted in accordance with RSA 40:1 through RSA 40:11. The most recently updated checklist shall be used.

"VI. Except as provided in this section, the special meetings provisions for the legislative bodies of towns, school districts, and village districts in the following chapters shall not be required for special meetings held under this section: RSA 31, RSA 32, RSA 33, RSA 39, RSA 49-D, RSA 52, RSA 197, RSA 654, RSA 669, RSA 670, and RSA 671."

Ratification of Greenland School District Meeting.

2013, 117:6, eff. June 25, 2013, provided: "All acts, notices, hearings, proceedings, and votes of the annual Greenland school district meeting and election held on March 11, 2013 and March 12, 2013, concerning warrant article 9 to adopt the provisions of RSA 40:13 to allow official ballot voting, which passed by the required ³/₅ vote, are hereby legalized, ratified, and confirmed."

NOTES TO DECISIONS

Analysis

1. Amendment
2. Transfer of funds in default budget proper

1. Amendment

RSA 40:13, IV(c) prohibits only amendments that eliminate a warrant article's textual subject matter, not amendments that may change the intent or purpose sought to be achieved by the article's drafters. Cady v. Town of Deerfield, 169 N.H. 575, 154 A.3d 157, 2017 N.H. LEXIS 3 (N.H. 2017).

Although the proposed warrant articles here posed the question of whether two municipal positions should be elected, the subject matter of the amended articles encompassed the broader question of how the town should fill those two municipal positions, i.e., by election or appointment, and therefore the amended warrant articles did not entirely eliminate the subject matter of the proposed warrant articles and thus did not violate RSA 40:13, IV(c). Cady v. Town of Deerfield, 169 N.H. 575, 154 A.3d 157, 2017 N.H. LEXIS 3 (N.H. 2017).

Petitioner residents asserted unsuccessfully that a deliberative session, by law, could amend articles but could not deprive the voters or take final action on the same. Nothing in RSA 40:13, IV, or

RSA 39:3 prevented voters at the deliberative session from effectively removing a subject from consideration at the second session by amending an article to delete the entire subject thereof. Grant v. Town of Barrington, 156 N.H. 807, 943 A.2d 829, 2008 N.H. LEXIS 29 (N.H. 2008), superseded by statute as stated in Cady v. Town of Deerfield, 169 N.H. 575, 154 A.3d 157, 2017 N.H. LEXIS 3 (N.H. 2017).

2. Transfer of funds in default budget proper

When voters failed to pass an operating budget, selectmen in implementing a default budget had the discretionary authority under RSA 32:10, I to transfer funds within a previously adopted budget, and the 2004 amendment to RSA 40:13 did not restrict this authority. Failure to pass an operating budget was a sufficient change in circumstances to justify the use of the authority, and the transfers, which had not increased the bottom line, did not amount to a revised operating budget under RSA 40:13. Sullivan v. Town of Hampton Bd. of Selectmen, 153 N.H. 690, 917 A.2d 188, 2006 N.H. LEXIS 93 (N.H. 2006).

Cited:

Cited in Opinion of the Justices (Municipal Bonds), 145 N.H. 680, 765 A.2d 706, 2001 N.H. LEXIS 6 (2001).

RESEARCH REFERENCES AND PRACTICE AIDS

New Hampshire Practice.
13-9 N.H.P. Local Government Law § 200.
13-10 N.H.P. Local Government Law § 213.
13-10 N.H.P. Local Government Law § 222.
13-10 N.H.P. Local Government Law § 223.
13-10 N.H.P. Local Government Law § 232.
13-10 N.H.P. Local Government Law § 255.
14-31 N.H.P. Local Government Law § 1283.
14-31 N.H.P. Local Government Law § 1284.
16-2 N.H.P. Municipal Law & Taxation § 2.26.
16-3 N.H.P. Municipal Law & Taxation § 3.02.
16-3 N.H.P. Municipal Law & Taxation § 3.16.
16-4 N.H.P. Municipal Law & Taxation § 4.26.

CHAPTER 43

HEARINGS BEFORE TOWN OR CERTAIN OTHER LOCAL OFFICERS

Section

NOTES TO DECISIONS

Analysis

1. School boards
2. Police officers
3. Board of selectmen

1. School boards

This chapter did not apply to hearings, under RSA 189:14-a, before school board on teacher's failure to be renominated to teach the coming year. Farrelly v. Timberlane Regional Sch. Dist., 114 N.H. 560, 324 A.2d 723, 1974 N.H. LEXIS 323 (N.H. 1974); Hawthorne v. Dresden Sch. Dist., 114 N.H. 567, 324 A.2d 728, 1974 N.H. LEXIS 324 (N.H. 1974).

2. Police officers

RSA 43:7 did not apply to a police officer's termination hearing. Had the legislature intended RSA ch. 43 to apply to police officers, it would have explicitly stated so within the text of RSA 41:48, as it did for the removal of other town officials; moreover, the language of RSA 43:1 did not encompass police officer termination hearings. Correia v. Town of Alton, 157 N.H. 716, 958 A.2d 992, 2008 N.H. LEXIS 110 (N.H. 2008).

3. Board of selectmen

Board of selectmen did not have subject matter jurisdiction under RSA 43:1 to determine whether the disputed section of a road became public by prescription, as no statute conferred such jurisdiction. RSA ch. 43 did not establish jurisdiction in the board over a matter it was not otherwise statutorily authorized to hear. Gordon v. Town of Rye, 162 N.H. 144, 27 A.3d 644, 2011 N.H. LEXIS 80 (N.H. 2011).

Cited:

Cited in Merrill v. Manchester, 124 N.H. 8, 466 A.2d 923, 1983 N.H. LEXIS 352 (1983).

RESEARCH REFERENCES AND PRACTICE AIDS

New Hampshire Practice.
13-16 N.H.P. Local Government Law § 553.

43:1. Hearings by Selectmen.

On petition to the selectmen for the laying out or altering of highways, or for laying out lands for any public use, and generally for the purpose of deciding any question affecting the conflicting rights or claims of different persons, their proceedings shall be governed by the following rules.

HISTORY:
GS 233:1. GL 43:1. PS 45:1. PL 49:1. RL 61:1.

NOTES TO DECISIONS

Analysis

1. Applicability
2. Subject matter jurisdiction of board

1. Applicability

RSA 43:7 did not apply to a police officer's termination hearing. Had the legislature intended RSA ch. 43 to apply to police officers, it would have explicitly stated so within the text of RSA 41:48, as it did for the removal of other town officials; moreover, the language of RSA 43:1 did not encompass police officer termination hearings. Correia v. Town of Alton, 157 N.H. 716, 958 A.2d 992, 2008 N.H. LEXIS 110 (N.H. 2008).

Legislature did not intend the language of RSA 43:1 to encompass the termination hearings of public officials in general, nor police officers in particular. Correia v. Town of Alton, 157 N.H. 716, 958 A.2d 992, 2008 N.H. LEXIS 110 (N.H. 2008).

2. Subject matter jurisdiction of board

Board of selectmen did not have subject matter jurisdiction under RSA 43:1 to determine whether the disputed section of a road became public by prescription, as no statute conferred such jurisdiction. RSA ch. 43 did not establish jurisdiction in the board over a matter it was not otherwise statutorily authorized to hear. Gordon v. Town of Rye, 162 N.H. 144, 27 A.3d 644, 2011 N.H. LEXIS 80 (N.H. 2011).

Cited:

Cited in Lenoix v. Dover, S. & R. S. R.R., 72 N.H. 58, 54 A. 1022, 1903 N.H. LEXIS 11 (1903).

43:2. Notice of Hearing.

They shall appoint a time and place of hearing, and order notice thereof to be given to all persons whose property or rights may be directly affected by the proceeding, by giving to them or leaving at their abode an attested copy of the petition and order 14 days at least before such hearing, or, if such persons are nonresidents, by publication. If the owner is under guardianship such notice shall be given to his guardian. If the owner is a minor, or under any legal disability, the judge of probate may appoint a guardian for such person, to whom notice shall be given.

HISTORY:
RS 49:3. CS 52:3. GS 233:2. 1870, 28:1. GL 43:2. PS 45:2. PL 49:2. RL 61:2.

NOTES TO DECISIONS

Analysis

1. Failure to notify
2. Waiver

1. Failure to notify

One to whom notice of hearing was not given and who did not appear is not bound by the determination of fence viewers. Davis v. Hazen, 61 N.H. 383, 1881 N.H. LEXIS 84 (N.H. 1881), overruled in part, Sherry v. Rochester, 62 N.H. 346, 1882 N.H. LEXIS 68 (N.H. 1882), overruled, Horne v. Rochester, 62 N.H. 347, 1882 N.H. LEXIS 69 (N.H. 1882).

2. Waiver

Appearance without objection to the sufficiency of notice is a waiver of all right to notice and of all exceptions to the regularity of issuing it. School Dist. v. Carr, 55 N.H. 452, 1875 N.H. LEXIS 109 (N.H. 1875).

Cited:

Cited in Lyford v. Laconia, 75 N.H. 220, 72 A. 1085, 1909 N.H. LEXIS 20 (N.H. 1909); Worthen v. Kingsbury, 84 N.H. 304, 149 A. 869, 1930 N.H. LEXIS 83 (N.H. 1930).

43:3. Posting of Notice.

Notice shall be given to all other persons interested by posting a like copy in one of the most public places in the town or district affected by the petition, and by leaving a like copy at the abode of the clerk of such town or district a like time before the hearing.

HISTORY:
GS 233:3. 1878, 7:1. GL 43:3. PS 45:3. PL 49:3. RL 61:3.

NOTES TO DECISIONS

1. Failure to post notice

The laying out of a highway by selectmen, upon petition and a hearing before them, is a judgment which cannot be attacked collaterally on account of a failure to order notice by posting a copy of the petition and order of notice, and serving a like copy on the town clerk, as required by this section. Horne v. Rochester, 62 N.H. 347, 1882 N.H. LEXIS 69 (N.H. 1882).

Cited:

Cited in Lenoix v. Dover, S. & R. S. R.R., 72 N.H. 58, 54 A. 1022, 1903 N.H. LEXIS 11 (1903); Worthen v. Kingsbury, 84 N.H. 304, 149 A. 869, 1930 N.H. LEXIS 83 (1930).

RESEARCH REFERENCES AND PRACTICE AIDS

New Hampshire Practice.
13-16 N.H.P. Local Government Law § 553.

43:4. Hearing; Record.

They shall hear all parties who desire to be heard, and examine them and their witnesses under oath, which either of the selectmen may administer; they may adjourn when they deem it necessary; and they shall make their decision in writing, and cause the petition, order of notice, evidence of service and their decision to be filed in the town clerk's office and recorded at length upon the town records; and their decision shall be of no force or effect until the same is done.

HISTORY:
GS 233:4. GL 43:4. PS 45:4. PL 49:4. RL 61:4.

NOTES TO DECISIONS

Analysis

1. Construction with other laws
2. Street railways

1. Construction with other laws
Without compliance with this section and RSA 234:13 there can be no taking of land, but if petition for layout of public parking lot, order of notice and evidence of service have not been filed and recorded, board inaugurated after filing of petition can file and record such documents. Rogers v. Concord, 104 N.H. 47, 178 A.2d 509, 1962 N.H. LEXIS 14 (N.H. 1962).

2. Street railways
Proceedings for the location of a street railway are subject to this provision. Lenoix v. Dover, S. & R. S. R.R., 72 N.H. 58, 54 A. 1022, 1903 N.H. LEXIS 11 (N.H. 1903).

43:5. Hearings by Other Officers.

The same rules shall apply to and govern the proceedings of fence-viewers, school boards, village commissioners, committees appointed by the selectmen and all town officers when they are applied to or appointed to decide any question affecting the rights or claims of individuals, saving that other or shorter notice, when required or allowed by statute, shall be sufficient.

HISTORY:
RS 136:13. CS 77:3. 142:13. GS 233:5. GL 43:5. PS 45:5. PL 49:5. RL 61:5.

NOTES TO DECISIONS

Cited:
Cited in School Dist. v. Carr, 55 N.H. 452, 1875 N.H. LEXIS 109 (1875); Hawthorne v. Dresden Sch. Dist., 114 N.H. 567, 324 A.2d 728, 1974 N.H. LEXIS 324 (1974).

43:6. Disqualification.

No selectman or other officer shall act, in the decision of any such case, who would be disqualified to sit as a juror for any cause, except exemption from service, in the trial of a civil action in which any of the parties interested in such case was a party.

HISTORY:
GS 233:7. GL 43:7. PS 45:6. PL 49:6. RL 61:6.

NOTES TO DECISIONS

Analysis

1. Construction with other laws
2. Prejudice
3. Effect of disqualification

1. Construction with other laws
In proceedings for condemnation of land required for county uses, legislature did not intend application of juror disqualification standard of this section to selectmen or any other official participating in hearings before county commissioners mandated by RSA 26:1. Brouillard v. Atwood, 116 N.H. 842, 367 A.2d 596, 1976 N.H. LEXIS 484 (N.H. 1976).

2. Prejudice
Selectmen are disqualified by prejudice from further consideration of a petition for the establishment of boundaries for a village district where the report has been set aside on the ground that they have not acted in good faith. Attorney Gen. v. Littlefield, 78 N.H. 185, 98 A. 38, 1916 N.H. LEXIS 33 (N.H. 1916).

3. Effect of disqualification
The fact that one of the selectmen before whom a highway petition was brought was disqualified by interest is not a jurisdictional defect which operates to quash the proceedings, but is a voidable irregularity for which appeal furnishes an adequate remedy. Bickford v. Franconia, 73 N.H. 194, 60 A. 98, 1905 N.H. LEXIS 14 (N.H. 1905).
The fact that one of the three selectmen signing a notice for a hearing upon a petition for the changing of the lines of a school district is disqualified by interest to act upon the petition does not invalidate the notice. Fifield v. Swett, 56 N.H. 432, 1876 N.H. LEXIS 166 (N.H. 1876).

Cited:
Cited in Farrelly v. Timberlane Regional Sch. Dist., 114 N.H. 560, 324 A.2d 723, 1974 N.H. LEXIS 323 (1974); Hawthorne v. Dresden Sch. Dist., 114 N.H. 567, 324 A.2d 728, 1974 N.H. LEXIS 324 (1974).

43:7. Appointment by Board to Fill Place of Disqualified Officer.

The place of a selectman or other officer so disqualified shall be supplied by appointment, by the other members of the board, of a qualified person who has theretofore holden the same office in the town, or, in the case of committees, by a new appointment.

HISTORY:
GS 233:8. GL 43:8. 1881, 16:1. 1883, 103:1. PS 45:7. PL 49:7. RL 61:7.

NOTES TO DECISIONS

Analysis

1. Generally
2. Applicability
3. Duration of office

1. Generally

If there remains one of the board who is qualified, he must appoint. Northern Railroad v. Enfield, 57 N.H. 508, 1876 N.H. LEXIS 126 (N.H. 1876).

2. Applicability

RSA 43:7 did not apply to a police officer's termination hearing. Had the legislature intended RSA ch. 43 to apply to police officers, it would have explicitly stated so within the text of RSA 41:48, as it did for the removal of other town officials; moreover, the language of RSA 43:1 did not encompass police officer termination hearings. Correia v. Town of Alton, 157 N.H. 716, 958 A.2d 992, 2008 N.H. LEXIS 110 (N.H. 2008).

3. Duration of office

An appointment under this section is good only for the special occasion. Hartshorn v. Schoff, 51 N.H. 316, 1871 N.H. LEXIS 34 (N.H. 1871).

43:8. Appointment by Court Where Whole Board is Disqualified.

If in any case the whole board is disqualified the selectmen shall, in writing, so inform some justice of the superior court, who shall thereupon, with or without notice, appoint a new board for that case from qualified persons who have before holden the same office in the town, if such there be, otherwise from qualified persons, residents of another town, who have holden the same office.

HISTORY:

GL 46:8. 1881, 16:1. 1883, 103:1. PS 45:8. PL 49:8. RL 61:8.

NOTES TO DECISIONS

Cited:

Cited in Attorney Gen. v. Littlefield, 78 N.H. 185, 98 A. 38, 1916 N.H. LEXIS 33 (1916).

CHAPTER 47
POWERS OF CITY COUNCILS

NOTES TO DECISIONS

Analysis

1. Charter amendment
2. Budgetary approval

1. Charter amendment

Where the proper procedures for amending a charter are followed, a charter providing for citizen initiative or referendum can exist in a municipality with a city councilmanager form of government as long as the initiative petition neither intrudes into matters reserved for the city council under this chapter, setting forth powers of city councils, not contravenes the general laws or constitution. Harriman v. Lebanon, 122 N.H. 477, 446 A.2d 1158, 1982 N.H. LEXIS 382 (N.H. 1982).

2. Budgetary approval

Proposed changes in city charter to require voter approval of city budget would create a impermissible form of government. Claremont v. Craigue, 135 N.H. 528, 608 A.2d 866, 1992 N.H. LEXIS 72 (N.H. 1992).

Statutory duties imposed upon city council are fundamentally incompatible with vote approval of annual budget. Claremont v. Craigue, 135 N.H. 528, 608 A.2d 866, 1992 N.H. LEXIS 72 (N.H. 1992).

Cited:

Cited in Attorney Gen. ex rel. Quinn v. Hunter, 92 N.H. 206, 29 A.2d 116, 1942 N.H. LEXIS 58 (1942).

RESEARCH REFERENCES AND PRACTICE AIDS

Cross References.

Composition of city councils, see RSA 44:3.

Bylaws and Ordinances

Editor's note.

1999, 278:16, eff. July 14, 1999, provided for the contingent enactment of RSA 47:17-a. This section was to take effect if a home rule constitutional amendment was adopted in the 2000 general election. This amendment to the NH constitution was not adopted in the 2000 general election, and, therefore, RSA 47:17-a never took effect.

47:17. Bylaws and Ordinances.

The city councils shall have power to make all such salutary and needful bylaws as towns and the police officers of towns and engineers or firewards by law have power to make and to annex penalties, not exceeding $1,000, for the breach thereof; and may make, establish, publish, alter, modify, amend and repeal ordinances, rules, regulations, and bylaws for the purposes stated in this section. Provisions in this section granting authority to establish and collect fines for certain violations shall not be interpreted to limit the authority hereunder to establish and collect fines for any other violations:

I. IN GENERAL. To carry into effect all the powers by law vested in the city.

II. ORDER AND POLICE DUTY. To regulate the police of the city; to prevent any riot, noise, disturbance, or disorderly assemblages; to regulate the ringing of bells, blowing of horns or bugles, and crying goods and other things; and to prescribe the powers and duties of police officers and watchmen.

III. DISORDERLY HOUSES AND GAMING. To suppress and restrain disorderly houses and houses of ill-fame, gambling houses and places, billiard tables, nine or ten pin alleys or tables and ball alleys, and all playing of cards, dice or other games of chance; to restrain and prohibit all descriptions of gaming and

—1986.

Paragraph XVI: Added.

—1983.

Substituted "$1,000" for "one hundred dollars" in the introductory paragraph.

—1981.

Paragraph XIV-a: Added.

—1971.

Substituted "one hundred" for "twenty" preceding "dollars" in the introductory paragraph.

—1961.

Paragraph VII: Inserted "public telephones, telephone booths, and other appurtenances thereto" following "steps".

Contingent 1999 amendment.

1999, 278:16, eff. July 14, 1999, provided:

"If a constitutional amendment to the New Hampshire constitution providing that municipalities shall have home rule authority to exercise any powers not specifically prohibited by the state or federal constitutions is adopted by the voters in the 2000 general election, then sections 1– 15 of this act [which amended this section and RSA 31:39; 41: 11; 143-A:5, I, III; 149-M:17, II(b); 179:19, V; 231:132-a, Intro. par.; 266:24, I; 466:30-b; 502:14; and 502-A:8, enacted RSA 31:39-b and 47:17-a, and repealed RSA 31:39-a; 31: 40– 43], shall take effect January 1, 2001. If such a constitutional amendment is not adopted, then sections 1– 15 of this act shall not take effect."

Contingent 1999 amendment; outcome of 2000 general election.

In the 2000 general election, the voters of New Hampshire rejected the constitutional amendment referred to above. Consequently, sections 1– 15 of 1999, 278:16 did not take effect.

NOTES TO DECISIONS

Analysis

1. Bowling alleys
2. Sale of liquor
3. Vehicles—Parking
4. —Taxicabs
5. Use of public ways—Moving buildings
6. —Sale or display of merchandise
7. —Snow removal
8. —Discontinuance of highways
9. —State preemption
10. Traffic devices and signals
11. Combustibles
12. Dogs
13. Obscene conduct
14. Adult books and magazines
15. Nuisances
16. Grade of sidewalks
17. Commons
18. Licensing hawkers and peddlers
19. Noise
20. Housing standards
21. Sewers and sewage
22. Terms of officers
23. Limitations
24. Employee matters

1. Bowling alleys

The power to make ordinances includes the power to adopt a statute restricting the operation of bowling alleys. State v. Noyes, 30 N.H. 279, 1855 N.H. LEXIS 261 (N.H. 1855).

2. Sale of liquor

The legislature may constitutionally authorize a city to enact an ordinance that no intoxicating liquor shall be used or kept in any refreshment saloon or restaurant within the city. State v. Clark, 28 N.H. 176, 1854 N.H. LEXIS 56 (N.H. 1854).

3. Vehicles—Parking

The power to enact ordinances regulating vehicles authorizes an ordinance limiting the time and places for parking. State v. Sweeney, 90 N.H. 127, 5 A.2d 41, 1939 N.H. LEXIS 28 (N.H. 1939).

4. —Taxicabs

Such powers as a city has to regulate the wages of common carriers by cab, hack or taxicab within it limits spring from paragraph VI of this section, rather than from the provision giving them the same right to enact bylaws as is conferred upon towns. State v. Guertin, 89 N.H. 126, 193 A. 237, 1937 N.H. LEXIS 25 (N.H. 1937).

A city has a power to establish rates of fares for taxicabs, operating within the city limits, and as an incident thereof to require their equipment with taximeters. State v. Guertin, 89 N.H. 126, 193 A. 237, 1937 N.H. LEXIS 25 (N.H. 1937).

An ordinance requiring taxicabs to be equipped with taximeters is not discriminatory or unreasonable because it excepts from such requirements cars for hire used in conveying passengers for attendance at marriages or funerals or christenings, or for use in ceremonial parades, and excludes entirely from the provision fixing rates for the transportation of passengers cars used for sightseeing purposes. State v. Guertin, 89 N.H. 126, 193 A. 237, 1937 N.H. LEXIS 25 (N.H. 1937).

5. Use of public ways—Moving buildings

An ordinance forbidding the moving of a building through any street without first obtaining a license is within the authority granted in paragraph VII of this section. Concord v. Burleigh, 67 N.H. 106, 36 A. 606, 1891 N.H. LEXIS 13 (N.H. 1892).

6. —Sale or display of merchandise

Although selectmen referred to wrong source of their power to enact ordinance forbidding use of certain streets for sale or display of merchandise, ordinance was still valid because power to enact such an ordinance was contained in paragraph VII of this section. Stamper v. Selectmen, Hanover, 118 N.H. 241, 385 A.2d 1213, 1978 N.H. LEXIS 388 (N.H. 1978).

7. —Snow removal

Where the highway law makes it the duty of municipalities to keep their highways in repair and free from obstruction by snow or other things that impede travel or render the highway dangerous, and empowers them to raise money for such purposes, a municipal ordinance requiring owners or occupants of abutting property to keep the sidewalks free of snow is valid as making an unequal distribution of a public burden. State v. Jackman, 69 N.H. 318, 41 A. 347, 1898 N.H. LEXIS 7 (N.H. 1898).

8. —Discontinuance of highways

Selectmen are given broad statutory authority to regulate the use of public highways and sidewalks, but the discontinuance of an established town highway is not favored, and may be accomplished only by vote of the town. Marrone v. Hampton, 123 N.H. 729, 466 A.2d 907, 1983 N.H. LEXIS 363 (N.H. 1983).

9. —State preemption

RSA 47:17, VII grants towns only the authority to regulate public docks, and consistent with well-established rules of statutory interpretation, the New Hampshire Supreme Court does not find within RSA 47:17, VII, implied local authority to regulate the use of private docks for personal boating or boat docking on public waters. Accordingly, the trial court erred in relying on the statute to find that local regulation of private dock use for boat storage on the lake in question was not preempted by state laws. Lakeside Lodge, Inc. v. Town of New London, 158 N.H. 164, 960 A.2d 1268, 2008 N.H. LEXIS 140 (2008).

Where statute specifically provides that commissioner of public works and highways "may" regulate highways, and where legislature has specifically empowered municipalities to regulate use of vehicles on particular highways within their limits, which includes power to exclude such vehicles from certain highways, legislature has not clearly manifested intent to preempt field of highway regulation. State v. Hutchins, 117 N.H. 924, 380 A.2d 257, 1977 N.H. LEXIS 462 (N.H. 1977).

Where general court gave commissioner of public works and highways authority to regulate use of class I highways in cities outside compact portions thereof, if commissioner to promulgated regulations under the grant, any conflicting municipal ordinance would be voided. State v. Hutchins, 117 N.H. 924, 380 A.2d 257, 1977 N.H. LEXIS 462 (N.H. 1977).

10. Traffic devices and signals

Under paragraph VIII of this section the authority to provide for the control of traffic by stop signs and to regulate the use of highways in a city resides exclusively with the city council. Beaule v. Weeks, 95 N.H. 453, 66 A.2d 148, 1949 N.H. LEXIS 196 (N.H. 1949).

In the absence of municipal regulation with respect to a stop sign legally erected at intersecting city streets, the conduct of a motorist after having brought his vehicle to a stop is to be governed by the statute relating to the right of way of intersections where his vehicle arrives at the intersection at approximately the same instant as another. Beaule v. Weeks, 95 N.H. 453, 66 A.2d 148, 1949 N.H. LEXIS 196 (N.H. 1949).

A stop sign not shown to have conformed to standards set by the highway commissioner or to have been approved by him, is not legally erected and maintained and failure to stop is therefore not negligence per se but only evidence of negligence. Legere v. Buinicky, 93 N.H. 71, 35 A.2d 508, 1943 N.H. LEXIS 51 (N.H. 1943).

11. Combustibles

A city ordinance may require one proposing to erect a steam mill or garage to obtain a license therefor. Page v. Brooks, 79 N.H. 70, 104 A. 786, 1918 N.H. LEXIS 27 (N.H. 1918), overruled, Johnson v. Boston & M. R.R., 83 N.H. 350, 143 A. 516, 1928 N.H. LEXIS 29 (N.H. 1928).

An ordinance enacted in exercise of the power to regulate the keeping of combustibles, which prohibited the use as a blacksmith's shop or other thing or business which shall more immediately expose the precinct to destruction by fire, of any building, within the limits of the precinct, without consent of the commissioners, is void as reserving to the commissioners the right to decide the question of fire risk in each individual case, guided by no general rule or regulation. Village Precinct of Hanover v. Atkins, 78 N.H. 308, 99 A. 293, 1916 N.H. LEXIS 61 (N.H. 1916).

12. Dogs

Paragraph XI of this section and RSA 466:39 authorized city to enact ordinance allowing chief of police to issue a complaint against one who violates the ordinance by allowing his dog to run at large, and the chief of police is not thereby unlawfully delegated legislative authority. State v. Merski, 115 N.H. 48, 333 A.2d 159, 1975 N.H. LEXIS 220 (N.H. 1975).

13. Obscene conduct

The authority to restrain all kinds of immoral and obscene conduct extends to an ordinance governing the operation and licensing of centralized music systems and coin-operated music-producing instruments. Marine Corps League v. Benoit, 96 N.H. 423, 78 A.2d 513, 1951 N.H. LEXIS 179 (N.H. 1951).

14. Adult books and magazines

Although there exists no express authority for city to enact ordinance regulating display of adult books and magazines, paragraph XV of this section, providing that cities may make regulations which may seem for well-being of city and which are not repugnant to state constitution or laws, authorized city to enact type of ordinance in question, in which display of adult books and magazines, defined as being harmful to minors, was regulated. Dover News v. City of Dover, 117 N.H. 1066, 381 A.2d 752, 1977 N.H. LEXIS 500 (N.H. 1977).

Legislature has not seen fit to enter field of controlling display of adult material, and therefore until it does, it leaves it open for cities and towns to do so. Dover News v. City of Dover, 117 N.H. 1066, 381 A.2d 752, 1977 N.H. LEXIS 500 (N.H. 1977).

Where state sought to deal with general problem of sexually explicit materials by enacting RSA 650, relating to obscene matter, and RSA 571-B, generally providing that it shall be unlawful to expose harmful materials to minors, and where legislature failed to enact bill which would have amended RSA 571-B:2 to prohibit person from "openly display[ing] where a minor is present any picture, photograph [etc.] ...", state had not preempted city from acting and city was not precluded from enacting ordinance regulating display of adult books and magazines. Dover News v. City of Dover, 117 N.H. 1066, 381 A.2d 752, 1977 N.H. LEXIS 500 (N.H. 1977).

15. Nuisances

The statutory authority to prohibit any person from bringing, depositing or leaving within the city any dead carcass or unwholesome substance applies only to those substances which cause injury to health. Lane v. Concord, 70 N.H. 485, 49 A. 687, 1900 N.H. LEXIS 51 (N.H. 1901), overruled, Johnson v. Boston & M. R.R., 83 N.H. 350, 143 A. 516, 1928 N.H. LEXIS 29 (N.H. 1928).

16. Grade of sidewalks

Sidewalks are parts of highways concerning which grades may be established which differ from that of the portion used for vehicular traffic. Hinckley v. Franklin, 69 N.H. 614, 45 A. 643, 1899 N.H. LEXIS 24 (N.H. 1899).

17. Commons

City councils may permit one to occupy a public common for the purpose of furnishing the public with recreation and, as an incident, to erect the structures necessary to carry on the business, if that would be a reasonable use of the premises. Sherburne v. Portsmouth, 72 N.H. 539, 58 A. 38, 1904 N.H. LEXIS 53 (N.H. 1904).

18. Licensing hawkers and peddlers

The power to make ordinances relative to licensing hawkers and peddlers is suspended in operation by an act of the legislature upon the same subject. State v. Angelo, 71 N.H. 224, 51 A. 905, 1902 N.H. LEXIS 8 (N.H. 1902).

19. Noise

Ample statutory authority exists for city to abate noise by emergency vehicles when those vehicles are not responding to emergency calls. State by Rochester v. Driscoll, 118 N.H. 222, 385 A.2d 218, 1978 N.H. LEXIS 384 (N.H. 1978).

20. Housing standards

Inclusion in housing standards ordinance of provision that violations shall be punished by a fine not to exceed twenty dollars per day and that each day's failure to comply with the ordinance constitutes a separate violation was consistent with this section and RSA 48-A:8. Davy v. Dover, 111 N.H. 1, 273 A.2d 849, 1971 N.H. LEXIS 108 (N.H. 1971).

21. Sewers and sewage

Chapter of city ordinances imposing sewer rents on industrial users before their sewage facilities were connected to the city sewer system exceeded its source of authority and was therefore invalid. Seal Tanning Co. v. Manchester, 118 N.H. 693, 393 A.2d 1382, 1978 N.H. LEXIS 272 (N.H. 1978).

22. Terms of officers

A city may establish by ordinance the term of office, within reasonable limits, of those of its officers and agents whose terms are not fixed by law. State v. Wimpfheimer, 69 N.H. 166, 38 A. 786, 1897 N.H. LEXIS 9 (N.H. 1897).

23. Limitations

Where the state has enacted a comprehensive regulatory scheme, paragraph XV of this section provides that no actions or ordinances will be permitted to contravene it. Wasserman v. Lebanon, 124 N.H. 538, 474 A.2d 994, 1984 N.H. LEXIS 242 (N.H. 1984).

Power given to city councils to enact bylaws and ordinances for well being of their cities is not unlimited; local legislation must not be inconsistent with state law. State by Rochester v. Driscoll, 118 N.H. 222, 385 A.2d 218, 1978 N.H. LEXIS 384 (N.H. 1978).

The constitutional limits of local legislation are not enlarged by the provision of paragraph XV of this section empowering cities to make bylaws and regulations which "may seem for the well being of the city" and declaring that "no bylaw or ordinance may be repugnant to the constitution or laws of the state". State v. Paille, 90 N.H. 347, 9 A.2d 663, 1939 N.H. LEXIS 74 (N.H. 1939).

24. Employee matters

In a declaratory judgment action wherein a city employee sought restoration of his sick leave credit pursuant to a city ordinance and the city counterclaimed for repayment of the sick leave credit given, a trial court erred by adding language to the ordinance creating a repayment obligation that did not exist; the wording of the ordinance was clear on its face and did not impose upon the employee any obligation to repay the sick leave credit received. Stankiewicz v. City of Manchester, 156 N.H. 587, 938 A.2d 873, 2007 N.H. LEXIS 232 (N.H. 2007).

Cited:

Cited in State v. Hogan, 30 N.H. 268, 1855 N.H. LEXIS 259 (1855); Mayor of Manchester v. Smyth, 64 N.H. 380, 10 A. 700, 1887 N.H. LEXIS 21 (1887); Eaton v. Burke, 66 N.H. 306, 22 A. 452, 1890 N.H. LEXIS 25 (1890); State v. Scott, 82 N.H. 278, 132 A. 685, 1926 N.H. LEXIS 21 (1926); Warren Kay Vantine Studio v. Portsmouth, 95 N.H. 171, 59 A.2d 475, 1948 N.H. LEXIS 207 (1948); Appeal of McKenney, 120 N.H. 77, 412 A.2d 116, 1980 N.H. LEXIS 232 (1980); State v. Yee, 129 N.H. 155, 523 A.2d 116, 1987 N.H. LEXIS 164 (1987); Appeal of Coastal Materials Corp., 130 N.H. 98, 534 A.2d 398, 1987 N.H. LEXIS 280 (1987); State v. Hodgkiss, 132 N.H. 376, 565 A.2d 1059, 1989 N.H. LEXIS 114 (1989); Chouinard v. New Hampshire Speedway, 829 F. Supp. 495, 1993 U.S. Dist. LEXIS 11154 (D.N.H. 1993).

OPINIONS OF THE ATTORNEY GENERAL

1. Limitations

Paragraph XV of this section provides that where the legislature has enacted a comprehensive regulatory scheme, no actions or ordinances will be permitted to contravene it. Op. Atty. Gen. #0-93-6.

Proposed reserve fund provision in city's voter initiative petition would be inconsistent with general laws of the State, since legislature had enacted specific procedures for adoption, management and use of such appropriated funds. Op. Atty. Gen. #0-93-6.

RESEARCH REFERENCES AND PRACTICE AIDS

Cross References.

Animals running at large, see RSA 467.
Burials and disinterments, see RSA 290.
Cemeteries, see RSA 289.
Criminal trespass, see RSA 635:2.
Distributing campaign materials at polling place, see RSA 659:43.
Fire hazard regulations, see RSA 154:18 et seq.
Food service licensure, see RSA 143-A.
Hawkers and peddlers, see RSA 320.
Interfering with voters, see RSA 659:37.
Licensing dogs, see RSA 466:1 et seq.
Licensing pawnbrokers, see RSA 398:4 et seq.
Licensing shows, open-air meetings, billiard tables and bowling alleys, see RSA 286.
Liquor licenses, see RSA 178.
Muzzling and restraining dogs, see RSA 466:29 et seq.
Nuisances, see RSA 147.
Obscene matter, see RSA 650.
Parking enforcement provisions for municipalities, see RSA 231:132-a.
Power to regulate registration, sale, transportation or use of pesticides as exception, see RSA 430:49.
Public indecency, see RSA 645.
Solid waste management generally, see RSA 149-M.
Town bylaws, see RSA 31:39 et seq.
Traffic rules and regulations, see RSA 265.

New Hampshire Practice.

13-15 N.H.P. Local Government Law § 479.
14-24 N.H.P. Local Government Law § 920.

14-25 N.H.P. Local Government Law § 953.

47:18. Notice and Publication of Ordinances.

All proposed city bylaws and ordinances and all adopted city bylaws and ordinances shall be kept on file at the office of the city clerk and at such other public place as the city council may designate. Notice of proposal and of adoption of a bylaw or an ordinance shall be made by publishing the title and brief description of the bylaw or ordinance in such newspaper or newspapers as the city council shall direct. The sufficiency of the published notice shall not affect the validity of the ordinance.

HISTORY:

1846, 384:17. GS 44:12. 1877, 72:1. GL 48:11. PS 50:11. 1925, 41:1. PL 54:13. RL 66:14. RSA 47:18. 1985, 183:1, eff. July 26, 1985.

Amendments

—1985.

Rewritten to the extent that a detailed comparison would be impracticable.

NOTES TO DECISIONS

Analysis

1. Construction
2. Failure to publish

1. Construction

This provision is directory, and a failure to comply with it does not render an ordinance invalid. State v. Wimpfheimer, 69 N.H. 166, 38 A. 786, 1897 N.H. LEXIS 9 (N.H. 1897).

2. Failure to publish

The failure of the city councils to publish a city ordinance as required by this section does not render the ordinance invalid in the absence of a provision in this section that the ordinance shall not be effective until such publication. Dover Hous. Bd. v. Colbath, 106 N.H. 481, 213 A.2d 923, 1965 N.H. LEXIS 195 (N.H. 1965).

Cited:

Cited in State v. Sweeney, 90 N.H. 127, 5 A.2d 41, 1939 N.H. LEXIS 28 (1939).

Building Codes

Severability of enactment.

1945, 105:1 was subject to a severability clause. See 1945, 105:1, par. 23.

RESEARCH REFERENCES AND PRACTICE AIDS

Cross References.

Appointment and terms of members of building code boards of appeals, see RSA 673:3 et seq.
Building codes to provide for building inspector and building code board of appeals, see RSA 673:1.
Building permits, see RSA 676:11 et seq.
Enactment procedures, see RSA 675.
Energy conservation in new building construction, see RSA 155-D.
Hazardous and dilapidated buildings, see RSA 155-B.
Housing standards, see RSA 48-A.
Powers of building code boards of appeals, see RSA 674:34.

47:22. Grant of Power.

The board of mayor and aldermen, or the corresponding governmental body of any city, is hereby empowered and authorized in the passing and adopting of ordinances, establishing codes, rules and regulations for the construction of buildings, relating to the installation of plumbing, the use of concrete, masonry, metal, iron and wood, and other building material, the installation of electric wiring, and fire protection incident thereto or for the prevention of fires to adopt any additional regulations provided that the regulations are not less stringent than the requirements of the state building code under RSA 155-A or the state fire code under RSA 153; provided, that upon adoption of such ordinance wherein such code, rules and regulations or portions thereof have been incorporated by reference, there shall be filed 3 copies of such codes, rules and regulations in the main office of the municipal department or agency administering the same and 3 copies in the office of the city clerk. All copies of any code, rules and regulations filed as provided herein, shall be for use and examination by the public.

HISTORY:
1945, 105:1, par. 18. RSA 47:22. 1963, 232:1. 1965, 255:1, eff. Aug. 31, 1965. 2002, 8:2, eff. Sept. 14, 2002.

Amendments

—2002.
Substituted "additional regulations provided that the regulations are not less stringent than the requirements of the state building code under RSA 155-A or the state fire code under RSA 153" for "nationally recognized code, rules and regulations to develop good engineering practice or safety that have been printed as a code in book form or such portions thereof by reference thereto in such ordinance" in the first sentence.

—1965.
Substituted "in the main office of the municipal department or agency administering the same and three copies in the office of the city clerk" for "in the office of the city clerk, and in the case of a fire prevention code or portions thereof, three copies in the main office of the fire department" at the end of the first sentence.

—1963.
Substituted "city clerk, and, in the case of a fire prevention code or portion thereof, three copies in the main office of the fire department" for "building inspector and three copies in the office of the city clerk" at the end of the first sentence.

47:22-a. Manufactured Housing.

The board of mayor and aldermen, or the corresponding governmental body of any city or the local legislative body of any town is hereby empowered and authorized to establish minimum construction standards for manufactured housing used as dwellings in the city or town, by adopting by reference any nationally recognized code for manufactured housing that has been printed as a code or any portions thereof, or any amendments to such code, to apply to all manufactured housing manufactured on or after January 1, 1964; provided that upon adoption of such ordinance wherein such code or portions

thereof have been incorporated by reference, there shall be filed 3 copies of such code in the office of the building inspector, if any, and 3 copies in the office of the city or town clerk. All copies of any code filed as provided herein shall be for the use and examination by the public.

HISTORY:
1963, 137:1. 1983, 230:18, eff. Aug. 17, 1983.

Amendments

—1983.
Substituted "manufactured housing" for "mobile homes and travel trailers" and "mobile homes or travel trailers" in the catchline and in the first sentence of the section.

NOTES TO DECISIONS

1. Constitutionality
The regulation of mobile homes is a proper exercise of the police power of a town. Plainfield v. Hood, 108 N.H. 502, 240 A.2d 60, 1968 N.H. LEXIS 200 (N.H. 1968).

RESEARCH REFERENCES AND PRACTICE AIDS

Cross References.
Zoning of manufactured housing, see RSA 674:32.

47:22-b. Manufactured Housing Foundations.

The authority granted under RSA 47:22-a to establish minimum construction standards for manufactured housing, as defined by RSA 674:31, shall not extend to imposing requirements that manufactured housing which is located in parks be placed on other than the structural carriers designed for that purpose.

HISTORY:
1977, 481:2. 1983, 230:6, eff. Aug. 17, 1983.

Revision note.
Reference to "RSA 31:118" was changed to "RSA 674:31". RSA 31:118 was repealed by 1983, 447:5, III.

Amendments

—1983.
Substituted "Manufactured Housing" for "Mobile Homes" in the section catchline, "manufactured housing, as defined in RSA 31:118" for "mobile homes" following "standards for" and "manufactured housing which is located in parks" for "mobile homes" following "requirements that".

RESEARCH REFERENCES AND PRACTICE AIDS

Cross References.
Manufactured housing parks generally, see RSA 205-A.

47:23. Amendment.

Any such ordinance may be amended or supplemented in like manner, provided, that 3 copies of such ordinance, as amended or supplemented, shall be filed, as provided in RSA 47:22, in the office of the building inspector and 3 copies filed in the office of the city clerk for use and examination by the public.

HISTORY:
1945, 105:1, par. 19, eff. April 10, 1945.

Revision note.
Substituted "RSA 47:22" for "section 22" to conform reference to style employed in LEXIS New Hampshire Revised Statutes Annotated.

47:24. Exception.

The provisions of this subdivision shall not be construed to permit the adoption by reference of penalty clauses which may be part of any nationally recognized code, rules and regulations. The said city councils shall have power to annex penalties deemed necessary, not exceeding $1000, for the breach of any violation of any such ordinance.

HISTORY:
1945, 105:1, par. 20, eff. April 10, 1945.

47:25. Examination by Public.

At least 30 days prior to the adoption of any such ordinance or any amendment or supplement thereto, not less than 3 copies of such code or regulation referred to shall have been filed in the office of the building inspector, and 3 copies in the office of the city clerk for the use and examination of the public.

HISTORY:
1945, 105:1, par. 21, eff. April 10, 1945.

47:26. Public Hearing; Notice.

No such ordinance or amendments or supplements thereto, as hereinbefore set forth, shall become effective or be altered until after a public hearing in relation thereto, at which parties in interest and citizens shall have an opportunity to be heard. Notice of the time and place of such hearing shall be published in a paper of general circulation in the state at least 15 days before the holding of said hearing.

HISTORY:
1945, 105:1, par. 22, eff. April 10, 1945.

Oil Refinery Siting

47:27. Local Option for Oil Refinery Siting in Cities.

Notwithstanding the provisions of any other law, an oil refinery shall not be located in any city without a vote of approval by one of the procedures specified in paragraphs I, II or III.

I. A site plan for an oil refinery may be approved by a ⅔ vote of the entire governing body of any city.

II. If the governing body of a city should vote to place the question of whether or not to approve the location of an oil refinery in said city on the ballot for referendum, it may place said question on the ballot to be voted upon at any regular municipal or biennial election, or at a special election called for the purpose of voting on said question. Such special election shall be held at the usual ward polling places by the regular city election officers. Should a referendum be held, the following question shall be placed on the ballot: "Shall an oil refinery be permitted within the city of (-)?" Said question shall be printed in the form prescribed by RSA 59:12-a. If a majority of those voting on the question shall vote in the affirmative, then such approval shall be deemed granted and the governing body of the city shall be bound by the outcome. If a majority of those voting on the question shall vote in the negative, such approval shall be deemed not granted and no oil refinery may be located in such city unless approval is subsequently granted in accordance with this paragraph or paragraph III.

III. Upon submission to the governing body of a city of a petition signed by at least 10 percent of the registered voters of said city requesting a referendum on the question of whether or not an oil refinery should be located in said city, the governing body shall direct that such question appear on the ballot at the next regular municipal or biennial election. If said petition is submitted at any time prior to 2 months before the next regular municipal or biennial election, the governing body shall direct that a special election be called. The election procedure and the form of the question shall be as provided in paragraph II. If a majority of those voting on the question shall vote in the affirmative, then such approval shall be deemed granted and the governing body of the city shall be bound by the outcome. If a majority of those voting on the question shall vote in the negative, such approval shall be deemed not granted and no oil refinery may be located in such city unless approval is subsequently granted in accordance with this paragraph or paragraph II.

IV. Nothing in this section shall be construed as changing, modifying or affecting in any way the provisions of RSA 31 and RSA 36 relating to zoning regulations.

HISTORY:
1974, 36:2, eff. April 5, 1974.

RESEARCH REFERENCES AND PRACTICE AIDS

References in text.
RSA 59:12-a, referred to in par. II, was repealed by 1979, 436:7, I, eff. July 1, 1979. For present provisions relating to form of questions on ballots, see RSA 656:13, 663:1.
RSA 36 relating to zoning, referred to in par. IV, was repealed by 1983, 447:5. For present provisions, see RSA 672 et seq.

CHAPTER 52
VILLAGE DISTRICTS

NOTES TO DECISIONS

Analysis

1. Constitutionality
2. Power of legislature
3. Reorganization

1. Constitutionality

This chapter, governing formation and operation of village districts, is not contrary either to democratic values or the state constitution. Chasan v. Village Dist. of Eastman, 128 N.H. 807, 523 A.2d 16, 1986 N.H. LEXIS 393 (N.H. 1986).

2. Power of legislature

Action of legislature in separating certain area from town, unless village district identical with former district was in existence on specific date and thereafter maintained, which was designed to prevent dissolution of such district except by legislative permission was not unconstitutionally arbitrary. Lisbon v. Lisbon Village Dist., 104 N.H. 255, 183 A.2d 250, 1962 N.H. LEXIS 62 (N.H. 1962), superseded by statute as stated in Opinion of Justices, 134 N.H. 711, 598 A.2d 864, 1991 N.H. LEXIS 127 (N.H. 1991).

3. Reorganization

Where village district was established by special act of legislature with power to maintain highways and such district dissolved itself and organized itself into a new district under the provisions of this chapter which does not grant power to village districts to maintain highways, such new district was held not to be a district "identical so far as possible to the" former district within the meaning of special act which established original district. Lisbon v. Lisbon Village Dist., 104 N.H. 255, 183 A.2d 250, 1962 N.H. LEXIS 62 (N.H. 1962), superseded by statute as stated in Opinion of

Justices, 134 N.H. 711, 598 A.2d 864, 1991 N.H. LEXIS 127 (N.H. 1991).

Cited:

Cited in Lebanon v. Lebanon Water Works, 98 N.H. 328, 100 A.2d 167, 1953 N.H. LEXIS 74 (1953).

RESEARCH REFERENCES AND PRACTICE AIDS

Cross References.

Applicability of provisions relating to reconsideration of school district meeting votes, see RSA 40:10.

Village district elections, see RSA 670.

Village district managers, see RSA 37.

New Hampshire Code of Administrative Rules

Rules of the Department of Revenue Administration, Rev 2001.01 et seq., New Hampshire Code of Administrative Rules Annotated.

52:1. Establishment.

I. Upon the petition of 10 or more voters, persons domiciled in any village situated in one or more towns, the selectmen of the town or towns shall fix, by suitable boundaries, a district including such parts of the town or towns as may seem convenient, for any of the following purposes:

(a) The extinguishment of fires;

(b) The lighting or sprinkling of streets;

(c) The planting and care for shade and ornamental trees;

(d) The supply of water for domestic and fire purposes, which may include the protection of sources of supply;

(e) The construction and maintenance of sidewalks and main drains or common sewers;

(f) The construction, operation, and maintenance of sewage and waste treatment plants;

(g) The construction, maintenance, and care of parks or commons;

(h) The maintenance of activities for recreational promotion;

(i) The construction or purchase and maintenance of a municipal lighting plant;

(j) The control of pollen, insects, and pests;

(k) The impoundment of water;

(*l*) The appointing and employment of watchmen and police officers;

(m) The layout, acceptance, construction, and maintenance of roads; and

(n) The maintenance of ambulance services.

II. The voters who are domiciled in any village shall cause a record of the petition, pursuant to paragraph I, and their proceedings thereon to be recorded in the records of the towns in which the district is situate.

HISTORY:

1849, 852:1. CS 116:1. GS 97:1. GL 107:1. 1889, 82:1. PS 53:1. 1909, 27:1. 1911, 5:1. PL 57:1. 1939, 108:1. RL 70:1. RSA 52:1. 1957, 179:1. 1961, 120:3. 1975, 13:1. 455:1. 1977, 154:1. 1981, 375:1, eff. Aug. 22, 1981. 2003, 289:14, eff. Sept. 1, 2003.

Amendments

—2003.

Paragraph I: Deleted "legal" preceding "voters" and substituted "persons domiciled in" for "inhabitants of" thereafter in the introductory paragraph.

Paragraph II: Deleted "legal" preceding "voters" and substituted "who are domiciled in" for "and inhabitants of".

—1981.

Paragraph I: Substituted "situated" for "situate"; deleted "or all" preceding "of the following purposes" and added "which may include the protection of sources of supply" following "purposes" in subpar. (d).

—1977.

Paragraph I: Deleted "and" following "officers" in subpar. (*l*), added "and" following "roads" in subpar. (m), added subpar. (n) and made minor changes in punctuation.

—1975.

Chapter 13 added "the impoundment of water" following "pests" in the second sentence.

Chapter 455 rewrote section to the extent that a detailed comparison would be impracticable.

—1961.

Inserted "the construction, operation and maintenance of sewage and waste treatment plants" following "common sewers" in the second sentence.

—1957.

Inserted "the control of pollen, insects and pests" following "plant" in the second sentence.

NOTES TO DECISIONS

Analysis

1. Residence of petitioners
2. Contents of petition
3. Subsequent petition
4. Additional powers
5. Change of boundaries

1. Residence of petitioners

This section does not require that a petition to form a village district partly in a town, presented to the selectmen of that town, be signed by ten registered voters in the same town; the section clearly provides that the voters of any village in one or more towns may petition the selectmen. Chasan v. Village Dist. of Eastman, 128 N.H. 807, 523 A.2d 16, 1986 N.H. LEXIS 393 (N.H. 1986).

This section does not require that the selectmen be served with a petition signed by ten voters from their own town before they act. Chasan v. Village Dist. of Eastman, 128 N.H. 807, 523 A.2d 16, 1986 N.H. LEXIS 393 (N.H. 1986).

2. Contents of petition

A petition for the laying out of a village district which states that the layout is desired for "any or either of the following purposes" enumerating the purposes mentioned in the statute, is sufficiently definite without specifying the particular purpose for which the district is desired. Attorney Gen. v. Littlefield, 78 N.H. 185, 98 A. 38, 1916 N.H. LEXIS 33 (N.H. 1916).

3. Subsequent petition

A vote against the establishment of a district does not preclude a subsequent petition for the organization of a district with other boundaries. Attorney Gen. v. Littlefield, 78 N.H. 185, 98 A. 38, 1916 N.H. LEXIS 33 (N.H. 1916).

4. Additional powers

The inclusion of the construction of sewers among the purposes for which a village district was organized is not necessary to authorize the district to adopt a statute conferring upon municipal corporations power to construct and maintain sewers. Granite State Land Co. v. Hampton, 76 N.H. 1, 79 A. 25, 1911 N.H. LEXIS 137 (N.H. 1911).

5. Change of boundaries

Unanimous vote at village district meeting that selectmen be petitioned to change boundaries of water district and ensuing detailed description of such boundaries could be construed as a petition by 10 or more voters to form new district. Sugar Hill Improvement Ass'n v. Lisbon, 104 N.H. 40, 178 A.2d 512, 1962 N.H. LEXIS 13 (N.H. 1962).

Cited:

Cited in Goodrich Falls Elec. Co. v. Howard, 86 N.H. 512, 171 A. 761, 1934 N.H. LEXIS 92 (1934); Welch v. Read, 100 N.H. 174, 121 A.2d 569, 1956 N.H. LEXIS 24 (1956); Chasan v. Village Dist. of Eastman, 572 F. Supp. 578, 1983 U.S. Dist. LEXIS 13323 (D.N.H. 1983); Rockhouse Mountain Property Owners Ass'n v. Conway, 127 N.H. 593, 503 A.2d 1385, 1986 N.H. LEXIS 207 (1986); Durgin v. Pillsbury Lake Water Dist., 153 N.H. 818, 903 A.2d 1003, 2006 N.H. LEXIS 110 (2006).

RESEARCH REFERENCES AND PRACTICE AIDS

Cross References.

Establishment and discontinuance of parks and commons, see RSA 50.

Firewards, firefighters, and fire hazards, see RSA 154.

Insect pests and plant diseases, see RSA 430.

Licensing of emergency medical service vehicles, see RSA 153-A:10.

Municipal electric, gas, or water systems, see RSA 38.

Police officers and watchmen, see RSA 105.

Public recreation and parks, see RSA 35-B.

Roads and sidewalks, see RSA 231.

Sewage and wastewater treatment, see RSA 485-A.

Sewers, see RSA 149-I.

52:1-a. Flood Control Projects.

Any village district organized under the provisions of this chapter may at a regular or special village district meeting vote to cooperate or act jointly with other village districts or with towns to defray expenses and take other appropriate action necessary to protect its interest in connection with federal or interstate flood control projects. Such village district may enter into agreements with other districts or towns for the purposes hereof and in such case the agreement shall be governed by the conditions set.

HISTORY:

1957, 287:3, eff. Oct. 1, 1957.

RESEARCH REFERENCES AND PRACTICE AIDS

Cross References.

Agreements between government units generally, see RSA 53-A.

State guarantee, see RSA 31:97.

Taxation of municipal flood control property, see RSA 72:11, 11-a.

52:2. Meeting to Consider.

Such selectmen shall also forthwith call a meeting of the voters domiciled in the district to see if they will vote to establish the district, and if so to choose necessary officers therefor. They shall call the meeting and give notice thereof as town meetings are called and warned, excepting that the warrant shall be posted at 2 or more public places in the district.

HISTORY:

1849, 852:2, 3, 4. CS 116:2–4. GS 97:2. GL 107:2. PS 53:2. PL 57:2. RL 70:2. 2003, 289:15, eff. Sept. 1, 2003.

Amendments

—2003.

Deleted "legal" preceding "voters" and substituted "domiciled" for "residing" thereafter in the first sentence.

NOTES TO DECISIONS

Cited:

Cited in Attorney Gen. v. Littlefield, 78 N.H. 185, 98 A. 38, 1916 N.H. LEXIS 33 (1916); Chasan v. Village Dist. of Eastman, 128 N.H. 807, 523 A.2d 16, 1986 N.H. LEXIS 393 (1986).

RESEARCH REFERENCES AND PRACTICE AIDS

Cross References.

Warning of town meetings, see RSA 39.

52:2-a. Budgetary Official Ballot.

Notwithstanding any other provision of law, any village district may vote to raise and appropriate money for the support of the district by official ballot as provided for in RSA 49-D:3, II-a, by following the procedures set forth in RSA 49-B. The village district may also include within its charter a plan for voting by official ballot, pursuant to RSA 49-B and RSA 49-D, on such other warrant articles as the village district may determine. For the purposes of this section, all references in RSA 49-B and RSA 49-D to "municipal," "municipality," "city," and "town" shall mean and include "village district," and all references to "elected body" and "governing body" shall mean and include "district commissioners."

HISTORY:

1995, 53:5, eff. July 8, 1995. 1997, 319:8, eff. Aug. 22, 1997.

Amendments

—1997.

Added the second sentence and inserted "and RSA 49-D" following "RSA 49-B" in the third sentence.

RESEARCH REFERENCES AND PRACTICE AIDS

New Hampshire Practice.

13-3 N.H.P. Local Government Law § 35.

16-39 N.H.P. Municipal Law & Taxation § 39.05.

52:3. Procedure and Powers.

I. At such meeting the legal voters may by vote establish the district, give to it a name, and choose necessary officers therefor to hold office until the first annual meeting of the district.

II. The district shall thereupon be a body corporate and politic, and shall have all the powers in relation to the objects for which it was established that towns have or may have in relation to like objects, and all that are necessary for the accomplishment of its purposes.

III. The district may at an annual meeting vote to raise such sums of money as the voters judge necessary for the purpose of reducing an accumulated general fund deficit.

HISTORY:

1849, 852:2–4, 7. CS 116:2–4, 7. GS 97:2, 4. 1874, 11:1. GL 107:2, 4. 1887, 42:1. 1889, 11:1. PS 53:3. PL 57:3. RL 70:3. RSA 52:3. 1994, 147:3, eff. Sept. 22, 1994.

Amendments

—1994.

Rewritten to the extent that a detailed comparison would be impracticable.

NOTES TO DECISIONS

Cited:

Cited in Granite State Land Co. v. Hampton, 76 N.H. 1, 79 A. 25, 1911 N.H. LEXIS 137 (1911); Chasan v. Village Dist. of Eastman, 128 N.H. 807, 523 A.2d 16, 1986 N.H. LEXIS 393 (1986).

52:3-a. Commissioners Duties; Acceptance by Municipalities of Roads.

I. In addition to the general powers provided in RSA 52:3, the commissioners of a village district formed for the purposes of RSA 52:1, I(m), shall have the same powers, duties and responsibilities of selectmen of towns which are granted or required pursuant to RSA Title XX; and, where appropriate, selectmen of towns shall be construed to mean commissioners of village districts.

I-a. The commissioners shall publish in the next annual report, or post at the annual meeting, the general fund balance sheet from the most recently completed audited financial statements or from the financial report filed pursuant to RSA 21-J:34, V.

I-b. In the case of an accumulated general fund deficit, the commissioners shall insert an article in the warrant recommending such action as they deem appropriate, which may include, but is not limited to, raising a sum of money for the purpose of reducing that deficit.

II. No town or city shall be required to accept, lay out or maintain any road solely because the road was established or maintained by a village district. Dissolution of a village district under RSA 52:21 shall not affect the powers, duties and responsibilities of a city or town to accept, lay out, maintain or otherwise assume responsibility for any road established by that village district.

III. No town or city shall levy any fee or collect any tax for the use by any utility of roads maintained by a village district under RSA 52:1, I(m), except on the vote of the village district commissioners for remittance to the village district.

HISTORY:

1975, 455:2. 1979, 72:1. 1994, 147:4, eff. July 22, 1994. 2015, 83:1, eff. August 4, 2015.

Amendments

—2015.

The 2015 amendment added paragraph III.

—1994.

Added pars. I-a and I-b.

—1979.

Designated the existing provisions of the section as par. I and added par. II.

RESEARCH REFERENCES AND PRACTICE AIDS

References in text.

RSA Title XX, referred to in par. I, is classified to Title 20 of LEXIS New Hampshire Revised Statutes Annotated, which is comprised of chapters 228–240.

52:4. Appropriations.

I. No village district shall raise or appropriate money, or reduce or rescind any appropriation of money previously authorized, at any special meeting of the voters thereof except by vote by ballot, nor unless the ballots cast at such meeting shall be equal in number to at least ½ of the number of voters of such district at the regular meeting next preceding such special meeting; and if a checklist was used at the last preceding regular meeting the same shall be used to ascertain the number of voters in the district; and such checklist, corrected according to law, shall be used at such special meeting upon request of 10 voters. In case of an emergency arising in a district for which immediate expenditure of money is necessary, the district through its commissioners may appeal to the superior court for permission to hold a special district meeting which, if granted, shall give said meeting the same authority as the annual district meeting.

II. Ten days prior to petitioning the superior court, the district commissioners shall notify, by certified mail, the commissioner of the department of revenue administration that an emergency exists by providing the commissioner with a copy of the explanation of the emergency, the warrant article or articles and the petition to be submitted to the superior court. The petition to the superior court shall include a certification that the commissioner of the department of revenue administration has been notified pursuant to this paragraph.

HISTORY:

1907, 121:1. PL 57:4. 1931, 103:1. RL 70:4. 1943, 88:1. RSA 52:4. 1989, 172:2, eff. July 16, 1989. 2003, 289:16, eff. Sept. 1, 2003.

Amendments

—2003.

Paragraph I: Substituted "voters" for "inhabitants" following "special meeting of the" and deleted "legal" preceding "voters" wherever it appeared throughout the first sentence.

Paragraph II: Substituted "the commissioner" for "him" preceding "with a copy" in the first sentence.

—1989.

Designated the existing provisions of the section as par. I and added par. II.

NOTES TO DECISIONS

1. Number voting

A district may vote an issue of bonds regardless of the total number present and voting, if two-thirds of those participating vote for the issue. In re Opinion of Justices, 86 N.H. 604, 171 A. 443, 1934 N.H. LEXIS 105 (N.H. 1934).

Cited:

Cited in Frost v. Hoar, 85 N.H. 442, 160 A. 51, 1932 N.H. LEXIS 100 (1932); Laconia Water Co. v. Laconia, 99 N.H. 409, 112 A.2d 58, 1955 N.H. LEXIS 37 (1955); Welch v. Read, 100 N.H. 174, 121 A.2d 569, 1956 N.H. LEXIS 24 (1956).

RESEARCH REFERENCES AND PRACTICE AIDS

Cross References.

Municipal Finance Act, see RSA 33.

52:4-a. Contingency Fund.

Every village district annually by an article in the warrant may establish a contingency fund to meet the cost of unanticipated expenses that may arise during the year. Such fund shall not exceed one percent of the amount appropriated exclusive of capital expenditures and amortization of debt by such village district during the preceding year. A detailed report of all expenditures from the contingency fund shall be made annually by the commissioners and published with their report.

HISTORY:

1965, 123:3, eff. July 27, 1965.

52:5. Changing Boundaries.

I. The selectmen of towns in which any such district has been established upon petition, after notice to parties interested and a hearing, may change the boundaries thereof; and the district shall cause the petition and the return of the selectmen's proceedings and decision thereon to be recorded in the records of the district, and of the towns in which it is situated, within 60 days after the decision.

II. In the case of any district formed for the purpose of impoundment of water, any such change of boundaries shall be ratified before taking effect by the voters domiciled in the district and in any area proposed to be added to the district in the same manner as is required for the initial establishment of the district.

III. In the case of any district formed for the purpose of the supply of water for domestic and fire purposes, which may include the protection of sources of supply, any such change of boundaries shall be ratified before taking effect by the voters domiciled in the district and in any area proposed to be added to the district in the same manner as is required for the initial establishment of the district.

HISTORY:

1853, 1421. GS 97:6. GL 107:6. 1887, 28:1. PS 53:4. PL 57:5. RL 70:5. RSA 52:5. 1975, 13:2, eff. April 25, 1975. 2002, 174:2, eff. May 15, 2002. 2003, 289:17, eff. Sept. 1, 2003.

Amendments

—2003.

Substituted "domiciled" for "residing" following "voters" in pars. II and III.

designated time, the time for such annual meeting so designated in such special act shall govern the holding of such annual meeting unless said village district or precinct shall otherwise vote in adopting the provisions of this chapter.

HISTORY:
  GS 97:7 GL 107:7. PS 53:16. PL 57:21. RL 70:21. 1943, 88:2, eff. March 25, 1943.

52:23. Public Water.

Upon the written application of 10 percent of the registered voters in any village water district, presented to the commissioners or one of them at least 15 days before the day prescribed for an annual meeting of the district, the commissioners shall insert in their warrant for such meeting an article relative to the use of fluoride in the water system for said district, and the district clerk shall prepare a ballot for said meeting with the following question: "Shall fluoride be used in the district water system?" Beside the question shall be printed the word "yes" and the word "no" with the proper boxes for the voter to indicate his or her choice. If a majority of those voting in a water system that serves only one municipality does not approve the use of fluoride in the district water system, no fluoride shall be introduced into the district water system; or if fluoride has, prior to said vote, been so introduced, such use shall be discontinued until such time as the majority of those voting in the town approve of the use of fluoride. After such popular referendum, the commissioners shall not insert an article relative to the use of fluoride in the district water system in the warrant nor shall the district clerk prepare such a ballot for a minimum period of 3 years from the date of the last popular referendum of the district and only upon written application at that time of not less than 10 percent of the registered voters of said district. The procedure for a referendum on the use of fluoride in a village district that is part of a water system serving more than one municipality shall be the procedure in RSA 485:14-a.

HISTORY:
  1959, 273:3. 1979, 335:3, eff. Aug 21, 1979. 2004, 225:5, eff. July 1, 2004. 2008, 230:8, eff. August 19, 2008.

Amendments

—2008.
  The 2008 amendment substituted "those voting" for "the registered voters" and "majority of those voting in the town" for "registered voters of the town shall, by majority vote" in the third sentence.

—2004.
  Rewritten to the extent that a detailed comparison would be impracticable.

—1979.
  Provided for a voter petition of 10 percent to place article relative to the use of fluorides in the public water system for an annual meeting of the village water district and limited resubmission of such article.

RESEARCH REFERENCES AND PRACTICE AIDS

Cross References.
  Aid to municipalities for water pollution control, see RSA 486.
  Public hearing on introduction of fluorine into public water supply, see RSA 485:14.

52:24. Filing with Secretary of State.

The selectmen of every town, and the councilors or aldermen of every city, which have a village district established under the provisions of this chapter lying in whole or in part within said town or city, shall file with the secretary of state the following information concerning the village district or districts within their respective municipalities.
  I. Within one year of the enactment of this section there shall be filed:
    (a) The name of the village district;
    (b) The powers granted to said district; and
    (c) The territorial boundaries of the district.
  II. Thereafter, within one year of any change in the above, there shall be filed:
    (a) Any change in the name, powers or territorial limits of the district; and
    (b) Any notice of dissolution of the district.

HISTORY:
  1969, 25:1, eff. May 3, 1969.

52:25. Authorized to Contract with the Department of Environmental Services. [Repealed.]

[Repealed 2010, 22:2, eff. July 6, 2010.]

Former section(s).
  Former RSA 52:25, which was derived from 1975,13:4; 1989, 138:1, 339:15; and 1996, 228:108, related to authorization to contract with the department of environmental services.

52:26. Contracts with the Department of Environmental Services.

Any contract between a district formed for the purpose of impoundment of water, organized pursuant to this chapter, and the department of environmental services for the construction, operation, and maintenance of any dam located within the district's boundaries that is in effect on the effective date of this act shall continue in effect for the remaining term of the contract or until terminated in accordance with the terms of the contract. If the district terminates the contract, any obligations and liabilities outstanding at the time of such termination shall be outstanding obligations and liabilities of the district and, if the district is terminated, such obligations shall be treated in the same manner as under RSA 52:21.

HISTORY:
  2010, 22:1, eff. July 6, 2010.

CHAPTER 52-A

SPECIAL ASSESSMENT DISTRICTS

52-A:1.   Definitions.

In this chapter:

I. "Improvement plan" means the plan for the special assessment district which sets forth the supplemental public services and facilities to be provided in the district and a plan for providing such services and facilities, including a budget and fee structure, which is approved by the municipal governing body as part of the creation of the special assessment district. An improvement plan shall be updated at least once every 3 years by the governing body.

II. "Proportionate share of the benefits" means that share, or portion, of the value of the total public facilities and service which specially and peculiarly benefits the property upon which they are imposed, as determined under RSA 52-A:3, III.

III. "Public facilities" means capital improvements, including but not limited to transportation, sanitary sewer, solid waste, drainage, potable water, communication infrastructure, and parks and recreational facilities that have a life expectancy of 3 or more years.

IV. "Public services" means the performance by employees, consultants, or agents of functions, operations, design, engineering, planning and maintenance, and repair activities in order to provide public facilities.

V. "Special assessment" means a charge imposed upon properties located within a designated special assessment district by a town or city to pay for public facilities and services which specially benefit the properties upon which they are imposed.

VI. "Special assessment district" means the district in which public facilities and services are to be provided and in which special assessments and charges may be levied and collected pursuant to this chapter to pay for those public facilities and services.

HISTORY:
2015, 240:2, eff. September 11, 2015.

52-A:2.   Authority.

I. Consistent with the provisions of this chapter, any town or city may establish special assessment districts for a part of the area of the town or city, within which may be provided public facilities and services from funds derived from service charges, special assessments, or other charges within the special assessment district.

II. For the purpose of providing public facilities and services within any special assessment district, the town or city may levy and collect service charges, special assessments, or other charges within the district, and borrow and expend money, and issue bonds, notes, and other obligations of indebtedness, which powers shall be exercised in the manner and subject to the limitations provided by this chapter and by the general laws of the state.

III. The provisions of this chapter shall not affect or limit any other provisions of law authorizing or providing for the furnishing of public facilities and services or the raising of revenue for these purposes. A town or city may use the provisions of this chapter instead of, or in conjunction with, any other method of financing part or all of the cost of providing the public facilities and services authorized under this chapter.

HISTORY:
2015, 240:2, eff. September 11, 2015.

52-A:3.   Requirements for Special Assessment Districts.

A special assessment district shall meet the following requirements:

I. Public facilities and services for which special assessments are levied and collected must peculiarly and specially benefit the properties upon which the special assessments are imposed.

II. Special assessments levied and collected pursuant to a designated special assessment district shall not exceed a proportionate share of the benefits received by the property upon which the special assessments are imposed.

III. The proportionate share of the benefits received by the properties upon which a special assessment is imposed shall be calculated and apportioned by using any equitable means of assessment and apportionment which the governing body of the municipality may prescribe, including but not limited to square footage, front-footage, increased value, number of dwelling units, distance from the public facility, traffic generation, or other impact generation factors, or any combination thereof.

HISTORY:
2015, 240:2, eff. September 11, 2015.

52-A:4.   Procedures for Initiation of Special Assessment Districts.

I. Proceedings for the establishment of a special

assessment district may be instituted by a petition filed with the governing body. The petition shall:

(a) Describe the boundaries of the territory which is proposed for inclusion in the special assessment district and include a map clearly delineating the boundaries.

(b) Contain a proposed improvement plan, as defined in RSA 52-A:1, I, for the special assessment district.

(c) Be signed by the owners of at least 50 percent of the lots within the proposed district, representing at least 65 percent of the assessed valuation within the proposed district. The name of each property owner signing the petition shall be indicated clearly on the petition, along with a listing by street address or lot number of all properties owned. In the case of any property that is owned jointly or in the name of a corporation, partnership, trust, or other legal entity, the signature and authority of any person purporting to represent the owner or owners shall be presumed valid for that purpose, subject to challenge. In the event of any dispute about the validity of such a signature or the authority of the person purporting to represent the entity, the decision of the governing body shall be conclusive.

(d) Designate a representative of the petitioners solely for the purpose of payment of mailing costs under RSA 52-A:5, I.

II. If the governing body finds that the petition is signed by the requisite number of petitioners under subparagraph I(c), that finding shall be final and conclusive.

HISTORY:
2015, 240:2, eff. September 11, 2015.

52-A:5. Establishment of District.

I. Within 15 days after receipt of a petition that satisfies the requirements of RSA 52-A:4, the governing body shall notify the petitioners" representative that it has determined the petition to be sufficient and shall request payment of the cost of mailing notice under paragraph II.

II. Within 60 days after receipt of payment under paragraph I, the governing body shall hold a hearing on the establishment of the special assessment district. Written notice of the date, time, and location of the hearing, together with a copy of the proposed improvement plan, or a summary of the plan, and a description of the proposed boundaries of the district, shall be posted in 2 public places in the municipality, one of which may be on the municipality's Internet website. Written notice shall also be sent by first-class mail at least 30 days before the hearing to the owner of each property within the boundary of the proposed district. For each property, notice shall be sent to the person and address listed in the municipality's property tax records. In the case of property under a condominium or similar form of collective ownership, notice shall be sent to

the officers of the collective or association, as defined in RSA 356-B:3, XXIII. In the case of property under a manufactured housing park form of ownership as defined in RSA 205-A:1, II, notice shall be sent to the manufactured housing park owner. In the case of 2 or more properties owned by the same person or persons, a single notice shall be sufficient.

III. At the public hearing, the proposed improvement plan shall be presented in writing. The governing body shall obtain public comment regarding the plan and the effect that creation of the proposed special assessment will have on the property owners, tenants, and others within the district. Any proposed changes to the improvement plan shall be submitted in writing at the hearing. The hearing may be continued one or more times, and additional notice shall not be required if the date, time, and location of the continued hearing are announced at the hearing and are included in the minutes of the hearing.

IV. Within 45 days after the conclusion of the public hearing, the governing body, in its sole discretion, shall either approve or disapprove establishment of the special assessment district. Approval shall be based upon the improvement plan presented at the hearing, subject only to changes that were presented in writing at the hearing and other minor technical changes. If the governing body approves establishment of the district, it shall declare the district organized and describe the boundaries and service area of the district. Upon such declaration, the district may commence operations and the municipality may impose and collect special assessments as provided in the improvement plan and in this chapter.

V. In establishing the boundaries of a special assessment district, the governing body may alter the exterior boundaries of a special assessment district to include less territory than that described in the notice of the public hearing, but it may not include any territory not described in the notice of the public hearing.

VI. In designating the types of public facilities and services to be provided in a special assessment district, the governing body may eliminate one or more of the types of public facilities or services specified in the improvement plan, but it may not include any types of public facilities or services not specified in the improvement plan.

HISTORY:
2015, 240:2, eff. September 11, 2015.

52-A:6. Method of Appropriation.

The municipality shall adopt a budgetary appropriation for capital and operating expenditures in a special assessment district as part of its budget process. The expense of constructing and maintaining the public facilities and performing public services described in the improvement plan, or paying off any capital debt or interest incurred in constructing or maintaining the public facilities on an annual basis, shall be included in the budgetary appropriation. At the end of each fiscal year, a full accounting of expenditures shall be made.

HISTORY:
2015, 240:2, eff. September 11, 2015.

52-A:7. Assessment and Collection of Special Assessments.

Upon adoption of the budgetary appropriation, the municipality may levy assessments in an amount necessary to fund the appropriation, net of other revenues applied to the appropriation. The assessments shall be made against the owners of properties in the special assessment district based on their proportionate shares of the benefits as determined by the governing body. Government property and nonprofit organizations within the district shall be subject to the assessments. The special assessments shall be assessed and collected in the same manner as property taxes under RSA 76 and RSA 80 and be subject to the same penalties and the same procedure and sale in case of delinquency. The town or city shall commit a special assessment to the tax collector with a warrant signed by the appropriate municipal officials requiring the tax collector to collect them. The tax collector shall have the same rights and remedies, including a lien on the real estate, and be subject to the same liabilities in relation thereto as in the collection of taxes as provided in RSA 80.

HISTORY:
2015, 240:2, eff. September 11, 2015.

52-A:8. Use of Proceeds.

Any special assessments collected pursuant to this chapter shall be used, in whole or in part, only for public facilities and services authorized by this chapter or for the payment of the principal and interest of bonds and other obligations of indebtedness for such public facilities and services.

HISTORY:
2015, 240:2, eff. September 11, 2015.

52-A:9. Issuance of Bonds and Other Indebtedness.

I. A municipality may borrow money and issue bonds or notes to finance the public facilities and services of a special assessment district, provided that bonds or notes may be issued only for the purposes authorized under RSA 33:3 or RSA 33:3-c. All bonds or notes authorized in accordance with this section shall be issued under the procedures in RSA 33, provided that the payments on the bond and note shall be made only from special assessment district revenues.

II. Any such debt shall at no time be included in the net indebtedness of the municipality for the purpose of ascertaining its borrowing capacity under RSA 33.

HISTORY:
2015, 240:2, eff. September 11, 2015.

52-A:10. Priority of Lien.

A special assessment shall be payable at the same time and in the same manner as property taxes assessed under RSA 76 and shall remain a lien, co-equal with the lien of all state, county, district, and municipal taxes, superior in dignity to all other liens, titles, and claims until paid.

HISTORY:
2015, 240:2, eff. September 11, 2015.

52-A:11. Assessment Funds.

I. The funds received from the collection of special assessments shall be kept as a separate fund to be known as the special assessment fund. The fund shall be allowed to accumulate from year to year, shall not be commingled with municipal tax revenues, and shall not be deemed part of the municipality's general fund accumulated surplus. The fund shall be expended only for the purposes of this chapter.

II. Except when a capital reserve fund is established pursuant to paragraph III, all special assessment funds shall be held in the custody of the municipal treasurer. Estimates of anticipated assessments and anticipated expenditures from the assessment funds shall be submitted to the governing body under RSA 32:6 if applicable, and shall be included as part of the municipal budget submitted to the legislative body for approval. The treasurer shall pay out amounts from the assessment funds only upon order of the governing body. Expenditures shall be within amounts appropriated by the legislative body.

III. All or part of any surplus in the special assessment fund may be placed in one or more capital reserve funds under RSA 35 and placed in the custody of the trustees of trust funds. If such a reserve fund is created, the governing body may expend such funds pursuant to RSA 35:15 without prior approval or appropriation by the local legislative body.

HISTORY:
2015, 240:2, eff. September 11, 2015.

52-A:12. Dissolution of District.

A special assessment district created under this chapter may not be dissolved until all debt incurred with respect to the district is finally discharged and all special assessments levied for the purpose of paying the debt have been paid or otherwise satisfied. Upon satisfaction of those conditions, the municipality's governing body may dissolve the district, and it shall dissolve the district upon receipt of a petition signed by the number of property owners specified in RSA 52-A:4, I(c). Upon dissolution of the district, all amounts remaining in the special assessment fund shall become part of the municipality's general fund accumulated surplus.

HISTORY:

2015, 240:2, eff. September 11, 2015.

CHAPTER 53-F

ENERGY EFFICIENCY AND CLEAN ENERGY DISTRICTS

Section
53-F:1. Definitions.
53-F:2. Adoption By Municipality.
53-F:3. Authority.
53-F:4. Agreements with Property Owners.
53-F:5. Eligibility of Property Owners.
53-F:6. Qualifying Improvements.
53-F:7. Financing Terms.
53-F:8. Priority; Collection and Enforcement.

Findings and Purpose.

2010, 215:1, eff. August 27, 2010, provided:

"The general court finds that:

"I. Energy conservation and efficiency and clean energy improvements to residential, commercial, industrial, and other buildings and facilities are necessary to:

"(a) Protect the economic and social well-being of New Hampshire communities by reducing the cost of fuel oil, electricity, natural gas, propane, and other forms of energy, and the risks associated with future escalation in energy prices;

"(b) Protect the economic and social well-being of New Hampshire communities by encouraging investment in the development and implementation of energy conservation and efficiency and clean energy improvements; and

"(c) Address the threat of global climate change.

"II. The upfront cost of energy conservation and efficiency and clean energy improvements prevents many property owners from making such improvements.

"III. To achieve the public benefits of reducing the cost of energy use and the risks associated with future escalation in energy prices, encouraging investment in the development and implementation of energy conservation and efficiency and clean energy improvements, and addressing the threat of global climate change, it is necessary to authorize a procedure for enabling property owners, on a voluntary basis, to finance such improvements and make repayments in the form of special assessments on their property tax bills or municipal service bills.

"IV. The purposes of this chapter are to authorize municipalities to establish such a procedure and to set forth requirements to ensure that its use will achieve the intended purposes of improving the social and economic well-being of New Hampshire communities and reducing greenhouse gas emissions."

53-F:1. Definitions.

In this chapter:

I. "Clean energy improvement" means the installation of any system on the property for producing electricity for, or meeting heating, cooling, or water heating needs of the property, using either renewable energy sources, combined heat and power systems, or district energy systems using wood biomass (but not construction and demolition waste), waste heat, or natural gas. Such improvements include but are not limited to solar photovoltaic, solar thermal, wood biomass, wind, and geothermal systems, provided that, to be covered by an agreement with a property owner and financed under this chapter, such improvements shall be qualifying improvements under RSA 53-F:6.

II. "District" means an energy efficiency and clean energy district established under this chapter.

II-a. "Eligible property" means real property located within the boundaries of the district, whether zoned or used for residential, commercial, industrial, or other uses, excluding residential property containing less than 5 dwelling units.

III. "Energy conservation and efficiency improvements" means measures to reduce consumption, through conservation or more efficient use, of electricity, fuel oil, natural gas, propane, or other forms of energy on or off the property, including but not limited to air sealing, installation of insulation, installation of heating, cooling, or ventilation systems meeting or exceeding ENERGY STAR standards, building modifications to increase the use of daylighting, replacement of windows with units meeting or exceeding ENERGY STAR standards, installation of energy controls or energy recovery systems, and installation of efficient lighting equipment, provided that, to be covered by an agreement with a property owner and financed under this chapter, all such improvements must be permanently affixed to a building or facility that is part of the property and shall be qualifying improvements under RSA 53-F:6.

IV. "Municipality" means any city, town, or village district, or the designated representative of the city, town, or village district.

V. [Repealed.]

VI. "Special assessment" means a special assessment within the meaning and subject to the provisions of RSA 80:19, except as provided in RSA 53-F:8.

HISTORY:

2010, 215:2, eff. August 27, 2010. 2011, 68:4, eff. July 15, 2011. 2014, 294:1, eff. September 30, 2014. 2015, 121:1, 8, eff. June 8, 2015.

Amendments

—2015.

The 2015 amendment by chapter 121, §§ 1 and 8, added paragraph II-a; and deleted paragraph V, which read: "'Property owner' means the owner of record of real property within the boundaries of the district, whether zoned or used for residential, commercial, industrial, or other uses, excluding residential property containing less than 5 dwelling units."

—2014.

The 2014 amendment added "waste heat" in the first sentence of I; added "or off" in III; added "or the designated representative of the city, town, or village district" in IV; and added "excluding residential property containing less than 5 dwelling units" in V.

—2011.

The 2011 amendment added "except as provide in RSA 53-F:8" in VI.

53-F:2. Adoption By Municipality.

A city, town, or village district may adopt the provisions of this chapter in the following manner:

I. In a town, other than a town that has adopted a charter pursuant to RSA 49-D, the question shall be placed on the warrant of an annual meeting only by the governing body, and not pursuant to RSA 39:3.

II. In a city or a town that has adopted a charter pursuant to RSA 49-C or RSA 49-D, the legislative body may consider and act upon the question in accordance with its normal procedures for passage of resolutions, ordinances, and other legislation. In the alternative, the legislative body of any such municipality may vote to place the question on the official ballot for any regular municipal election.

III. In a village district, the question may be considered and acted upon by any means authorized by RSA 52.

IV. The language of the question shall designate an energy efficiency and clean energy district, which may cover all or a portion of the area within the municipality, or may designate all or a portion of the area within the municipality as part of an energy efficiency and clean energy district that encompasses all or portions of multiple municipalities.

V. A municipality may vote to rescind its action in the same manner as it may vote to adopt, provided that all agreements entered into with property owners and related legal obligations created prior to its vote to rescind shall remain in effect.

HISTORY:
2010, 215:2, eff. August 27, 2010.

53-F:3. Authority.

To achieve the public benefits of protecting the economic and social well-being by reducing energy costs in the community and risks to the community associated with future escalation in energy prices, and addressing the threat of global climate change, any municipality which has adopted the provisions of this chapter and established an energy efficiency and clean energy district may, upon a finding by the governing body of the municipality, after notice and hearing, that the energy conservation and efficiency and clean energy improvements will serve the public purposes as set forth in this chapter and not primarily be for the benefit of private persons or uses even though such private benefits and uses may incidentally result, do the following:

I. A municipality which adopts this chapter shall thereafter be authorized to establish one or more energy efficiency and clean energy districts.

II. Encourage private financing from individuals or institutions for qualifying improvements to eligible properties within the district and enter into agreements with those private lenders to administer the energy conservation and efficiency improvements or clean energy improvements program on their behalf, including evaluating eligible properties, supervising the improvements, arranging for the closing of the loans, collecting the special assessments, and assisting them with the exercise of their lienholder rights, provided that anticipated expenses for the administration of the program shall be borne by the owners of eligible properties participating in the program.

III. Participate in state or federal programs providing support for municipal energy efficiency and clean energy finance programs such as those authorized by this chapter.

IV. Enter into agreements with owners of eligible property in which the owners consent to make energy conservation and efficiency improvements or clean energy improvements to their properties and to have the municipality include a special assessment to pay for such improvements on their property tax bills, their bills for water or sewer service or another municipal service, or separate bills, provided that such agreements shall not affect the tax liability or municipal services charges of other participating or nonparticipating property owners in the district.

V. Collect charges from participating owners of eligible properties to cover the cost of administration for the district.

VI. Otherwise administer a program for promoting and financing energy efficiency and clean energy improvements within a district in accordance with this chapter, enter into an agreement with a public or private entity to administer such a program on its behalf in accordance with this chapter, and enter into an agreement with one or more other municipalities to share services and otherwise cooperate in the administration of a district or districts in accordance with this chapter.

HISTORY:
2010, 215:2, eff. August 27, 2010. 2011, 68:2, eff. July 15, 2011. 2014, 294:2, eff. September 30, 2014. 2015, 121:2, eff. June 8, 2015.

Amendments

—2015.

The 2015 amendment inserted "or physician assistant" following "APRN" throughout the section; and made related changes.

—2014.

The 2014 amendment, in the first sentence of I, substituted "but not limited to the" for "through" and added "or funds from private individuals or institutions."

—2011.

The 2011 amendment, in I, added "revenue" in the first sentence and in the second sentence, substituted "may be secured by a pledge of revenues, moneys, rights, and proceeds under this chapter" for "shall constitute a pledge of the municipality's full faith and credit" and added "and RSA 33-B" and in II, deleted "general municipal revenues, bond funds" following "RSA 31:95-h using" and "provided that the use of general municipal revenues shall be pursuant to an appropriation by special warrant article in accordance with RSA 32 and the municipality's appropriation procedures" at the end.

53-F:4. Agreements with Property Owners.

I.(a) A municipality may make an assessment under this chapter only pursuant to an agreement entered into with the free and willing consent of the owner of an eligible property to which the assessment applies. In the case of any eligible property with multiple owners, an agreement under this chapter shall be signed by all owners.

(b) An agreement with an owner of eligible property shall provide that the owner shall contract for qualifying improvements with one or more qualified contractors, purchase materials to be used in making qualified improvements, or both, and that, upon submission of documentation required by the municipality, the municipality shall disburse funds to those contractors and vendors in payment for the qualifying improvements or materials used in making qualified improvements. An agreement with a property owner shall require that the property owner report post-installation energy use data for program evaluation purposes over a period determined by the municipality.

(c) The agreement shall stipulate that all funding for the qualifying improvements shall be made by private lenders and that the loan will be evidenced by a note and secured by a mortgage on the eligible property. The agreement shall include a payment schedule showing the term over which payments will be due on the assessment, the frequency with which payments will be billed and the amount of each payment, and the annual amount due on the assessment. The obligations of the agreement and loan will run with the eligible property. If the property is sold, the new owner shall automatically assume the obligations of the agreement, note, and mortgage and shall be subject to all liability related to such obligations. Upon full payment of the amount of the special assessments, including all outstanding interest and charges and any penalties that may become due, the municipality shall provide the then participating property owner with a written statement certifying that the obligations of the agreement and the loan have been satisfied and the special assessments have been paid in full and shall record a discharge of the mortgage from the private lender.

II. The municipality shall disclose to the owners of eligible property participating in the program the risks associated with their participation, including risks related to their failure to make payments and the risk of enforcement of property tax or special assessment liens under RSA 53-F:8.

III. At least 30 days prior to entering into an agreement with a municipality under this chapter, the owner of eligible property shall provide to the holders of any existing mortgages on the property notice of his or her intent to enter into the agreement.

IV. The municipality shall file a notice of the assessment under this chapter for recording in the county registry of deeds. The notice shall consist of the following statement or its substantial equivalent: "This property is subject to a special assessment related to the installation of qualifying cost-effective energy conservation and efficiency improvements or clean energy improvements under RSA 53-F."

V. Any personal or business financial information provided to a municipality or an entity administering a program under this chapter on behalf of a municipality by a participating property owner or potential participating property owner shall be confidential and shall not be disclosed to any person except as required to administer the program and only on a need-to-know basis.

HISTORY:
2010, 215:2, eff. August 27, 2010. 2011, 68:5, eff. July 15, 2011. 2014, 294:3, eff. September 30, 2014. 2015, 121:3, eff. June 8, 2015.

Amendments

—2015.
The 2015 amendment in I(a), substituted "an eligible property" for "the property" in the first sentence, and substituted "any eligible property" for "any property" in the second sentence; substituted "an owner of eligible property" for "a property owner" in I(b); rewrote I(c); substituted "the owners of eligible property participating in the program the risks associated with their participation" for "participating property owner participating in the program" in paragraph II; substituted "the owner of eligible property" for "the property owner" in paragraph III; and deleted paragraphs IV and V.

—2014.
The 2014 amendment added "or business" in V.

—2011.
The 2011 amendment substituted "RSA 53-F:8" for "RSA 80:19" in II.

53-F:5. Eligibility of Property Owners.

I. A municipality may enter into an agreement under this chapter only with the legal owner of eligible property.

II. Prior to entering into an agreement with an owner of eligible property, the municipality shall determine that all property taxes and any other assessments levied with property taxes are current and have been current for 3 years or the owner's period of ownership, whichever is less; that there are no involuntary liens such as mechanic's liens on the property; and that no notices of default or other evidence of property-based debt delinquency have been recorded during the past 3 years or the property owner's period of ownership, whichever is less. The municipality shall adopt additional criteria, appropriate to property-assessed clean energy finance programs. The municipality shall determine whether any mortgages or liens of record exist in the registry of deeds on the property, whether they are current in the obligations, and whether the total debt to equity ratio specified by the private lender will be met. If any such mortgage or lien exists, the municipality shall notify each such mortgagee or lienholder in writing that a private lender is considering making a loan secured by a municipal lien pursuant to the provisions of this chapter and request the consent of each such mortgagee or lienholder to the making of such loan. Each mortgagee or lienholder shall have the right to determine in its sole discretion whether or not it will consent to such loan. If all of the mortgagees or lienholders of record elect to consent, the consents shall be in writing and recorded with the municipal lien in the registry of deeds. The legal effect of having all consents shall be that the municipal lien shall not be extinguished in the event of a foreclosure or sheriff's sale by the mortgagee or lienholder as provided in RSA 53-F:8. If all of the mortgagees or lienholders of record do not consent, but the private lender determines that it will proceed in making such loan, then in the event of a foreclosure or sheriff's sale by a mortgagee or lienholder, the municipal lien shall be extinguished.

HISTORY:
2010, 215:2, eff. August 27, 2010. 2014, 294:4, eff. September 30, 2014. 2015, 121:4, eff. June 8, 2015.

Amendments

—2015.
—2015.The 2015 amendment amended generally.

—2014.
The 2014 amendment, in II, deleted "and that the property owner is current on all mortgage debt on the property" at the end of the first sentence and added the third through last sentences.

53-F:6. Qualifying Improvements.

I. Improvements financed pursuant to an agreement under this chapter shall be based upon an audit performed by a person who has been certified as a building analyst by the Building Performance Institute or who has obtained other appropriate certification as determined by the public utilities commission or another appropriate New Hampshire-based entity. The audit shall identify recommended energy conservation and efficiency and clean energy improvements; provide the estimated energy cost savings, useful life, benefit-cost ratio, and simple payback or return on investment for each improvement; and provide the estimated overall difference in annual energy costs with and without recommended improvements. Financed improvements shall be consistent with the audit recommendations. The cost of the audit may be included in the total amount financed under this chapter.

II. Improvements shall be permanently affixed to an existing building or facility that is part of the eligible property. The owner of the property may not finance projects in buildings or facilities under new construction.

III. Improvements shall be made by a contractor or contractors, which may include a cooperative or not-for-profit organization, determined by the municipality to be qualified to make the energy efficiency or clean energy improvements in the agreement. Contractors may be designated as qualified by an electric or gas utility program or another appropriate New Hampshire-based entity. Any work requiring a license under any applicable law shall be performed by an individual holding such license. A municipality may elect to permit the financing pursuant to an agreement under this chapter of improvements made by the owner of the property, but shall not permit the value of the owner's labor to be included in the amount financed.

IV. Prior to disbursement of final payments to any contractor or vendor pursuant to an agreement with a property owner, submission is required by the property owner in a form acceptable to the municipality of:

(a) A post-installation report, based on an independent inspection acceptable to the municipality, certifying that improvements have been installed properly and verifying that they are performing satisfactorily; and

(b) Documentation of all costs to be financed and copies of any required permits.

HISTORY:
2010, 215:2, eff. August 27, 2010. 2015, 121:5, eff. June 8, 2015.

Amendments

—2015.
The 2015 amendment, in paragraph II, substituted "the eligible property" for "the property" at the end of the first sentence, and substituted "The owner of the property may not finance projects" for "An agreement between a municipality and a qualifying property owner may not cover projects" at the beginning of the last sentence; substituted "Contractors may be designated as qualified" for "A municipality may accept a designation of contractors as qualified made" in the beginning of the third sentence of paragraph III; in the introductory language of paragraph IV, deleted "A municipality shall require," and substituted "submission is required by the property owner" for "submission by the property owner."

53-F:7. Financing Terms.

I. Improvements shall be financed pursuant to an agreement under this chapter only on terms such that the total energy cost savings realized by the property owner and the property owner's successors during the useful lives of the improvements are expected to exceed the total cost to the property owner and the property owner's successors of the improvements.

II. A property owner who escrows property taxes with the holder of a mortgage on a property subject to an agreement under this chapter may be required by the holder to escrow amounts due on the special assessment under this chapter and the mortgage holder shall remit such amounts to the municipality in the manner that property taxes are escrowed and remitted.

III. The maximum term of finance provided pursuant to an agreement under this chapter shall be 30 years.

HISTORY:

2010, 215:2, eff. August 27, 2010. 2011, 68:3, eff. July 15, 2011. 2014, 294:5, eff. September 30, 2014. 2015, 121:6, eff. June 8, 2015.

Amendments

—2015.

The 2015 amendment deleted former paragraph II, which read: "A municipality that provides financing to participating property owners shall establish a loss reserve account and maintain funds in such account at a level that meets generally accepted standards for property-assessed clean energy finance programs. Funds in a loss reserve account shall not be provided from general municipal revenues"; redesignated former paragraph III as paragraph II; and redesignated former paragraph IV as paragraph III.

—2014.

The 2014 amendment rewrote the section to the extent that a detailed comparison would be impractical.

—2011.

The 2011 amendment added the second sentence of II.

53-F:8. Priority; Collection and Enforcement.

Collection of special assessments under this chapter shall be made by the tax collector or other official responsible for property tax or municipal service charge collection. A municipality shall commit bills for amounts due on the special assessments, including interest and any charges, to the tax collector with a warrant signed by the appropriate municipal officials requiring the tax collector to collect them. Each year bills for amounts due on the special assessments shall coincide with bills for property taxes or municipal service charges. Each special assessment on the property of a participating property owner shall create a lien on the property pursuant to RSA 80:19, except that the lien shall be junior to existing liens of record at the time the bill for the assessment is mailed to the participating property owner. Enforcement powers for nonpayment shall be those provided under RSA 80 relative to property tax collection, including RSA 80:19; provided, however, a tax sale of the property shall not extinguish prior liens of record. At the time of enforcement, only the past due balances of the special assessment under this chapter, including all interest, charges, and penalties, shall be due for

payment. Notwithstanding any other provision of law, in the event of a transfer of property ownership through foreclosure or a sheriff's sale by a senior mortgagee or lienholder which has consented to the making of a loan by a private lender under the provisions of this chapter, the lien of the municipality shall not be extinguished, and the net proceeds of the sale, if any, after payment of all prior obligations to mortgagees and lienholders, costs and expenses of foreclosure or sheriff's sale, shall be first applied to the payment of any past due balances of the loan and then any excess shall be applied against the remaining balance of the loan. If a senior mortgagee or lienholder has not given its consent to the loan, a foreclosure or sheriff's sale by the mortgagee or lienholder shall extinguish all junior mortgages and liens.

HISTORY:

2010, 215:2, eff. August 27, 2010. 2011, 68:6, eff. July 15, 2011. 2014, 294:6, eff. September 30, 2014. 2015, 121:7, eff. June 8, 2015.

Amendments

—2015.

The 2015 amendment inserted "special" preceding "assessments" or variants throughout the section; in the second to the last sentence, substituted "private lender" for "municipality" preceding "under the provisions of this chapter," and substituted "balances of the loan" for "balances of the municipal loan" following "payment of any past due," and deleted the former last sentence, which read: "Payment of a past due balance from the loss reserve established under this chapter shall not relieve a participating property owner from the obligation to pay that amount."

—2014.

The 2014 amendment substituted "mortgagee or lienholder which has consented to the making of a loan by a municipality under the provisions of this chapter, the lien of the municipality shall not be extinguished, and the net proceeds of the sale, if any, after payment of all prior obligations to mortgagees and lienholders, costs and expenses of foreclosure or sheriff's sale, shall be first applied to the payment of any past due balances of the municipal loan and then any excess shall be applied against the remaining balance of the loan" for "lienor, the lien of the municipality shall be extinguished" in the seventh sentence and added the eighth sentence.

—2011.

The 2011 amendment added "Priority" in the section heading; added "Each year" in the third sentence; in the fourth sentence, added "Each assessment on the property of a participating property owner" and "except that the lien shall be junior to existing liens of record at the time the bill for the assessment is mailed to the participating property owner"; added "provided, however, a tax sale of the property shall not extinguish prior liens of record" in the fifth sentence; substituted "or a sheriff's sale by a senior lienor, the lien of the municipality shall be extinguished" for "collection by the municipality shall be limited to any past due balances and future payments shall neither be accelerated nor extinguished by foreclosure" in the next to last sentence; and made a related change.

TITLE V
TAXATION

RESEARCH REFERENCES AND PRACTICE AIDS

Cross References.
Assignments for creditors not valid against unpaid taxes, see RSA 569:2.
County taxes, see RSA 24:20, RSA 29.
Department of revenue administration, see RSA 21-J.
Highway taxes by towns, see RSA 231:57 et seq.
Motor fuel tax, see RSA 260:30 et seq.
Religious society's power to tax members, see RSA 306:2.
School taxes, see RSA 194:5– 8, 198: 4-7.
Tax to satisfy execution against town or district, see RSA 530:5–7.
Taxation of health maintenance organizations, see RSA 420-B:17.
Taxation of insurers, see RSA 400-A:31– 34.
Taxation of motor vehicles prohibited, see RSA 261:162.
Taxation of pari-mutuel pools, see RSA 284:23, 24.

CHAPTER 79-E

COMMUNITY REVITALIZATION TAX RELIEF INCENTIVE

79-E:1. Declaration of Public Benefit.

I. It is declared to be a public benefit to enhance downtowns and town centers with respect to economic activity, cultural and historic character, sense of community, and in-town residential uses that contribute to economic and social vitality.

II. It is further declared to be a public benefit to encourage the rehabilitation of the many underutilized structures in urban and town centers as a means of encouraging growth of economic, residential, and municipal uses in a more compact pattern, in accordance with RSA 9-B.

II-a. In instances where a qualifying structure is determined to possess no significant historical, cultural, or architectural value and for which the governing body makes a specific finding that rehabilitation would not achieve one or more of the public benefits established in RSA 79-E:7 to the same degree as the replacement of the underutilized structure with a new structure, the tax relief incentives provided under this chapter may be extended to the replacement of an underutilized structure in accordance with the provisions of this chapter.

II-b. It is further declared to be a public benefit to encourage the rehabilitation of historic structures in a municipality by increasing energy efficiency in the preservation and reuse of existing building stock.

III. Short-term property assessment tax relief and a related covenant to protect public benefit as provided under this chapter are considered to provide a demonstrated public benefit if they encourage substantial rehabilitation and use of qualifying structures, or in certain cases, the replacement of a qualifying structure, as defined in this chapter.

HISTORY:
2006, 167:1, eff. April 1, 2006. 2009, 200:3, 4, eff. July 15, 2009. 2013, 78:1, eff. April 1, 2013.

Amendments

—2013.
The 2013 amendment added II-b.

—2009.
The 2009 amendment added II-a and added "or in certain cases, the replacement of a qualifying structure" in III.

79-E:2. Definitions.

In this chapter:

I. "Historic structure" means a building that is listed on or determined eligible for listing on the National Register of Historic Places or the state register of historic places.

II. "Qualifying structure'" means a building located in a district officially designated in a municipality's master plan, or by zoning ordinance, as a downtown, town center, central business district, or village center, or, where no such designation has been made, in a geographic area which, as a result of its compact development patterns and uses, is identified by the governing body as the downtown, town center, or village center for purposes of this chapter. Qualifying structure shall also mean historic structures in a municipality whose preservation and reuse would conserve the embodied energy in existing building stock. Cities or towns may further limit "qualifying structure'" according to the procedure in RSA 79-E:3 as meaning only a structure located within such districts that meet certain age, occupancy, condition, size, or other similar criteria consistent with local economic conditions, community character, and local planning and development goals. Cities or towns may further modify "qualifying structure"' to include buildings that have been destroyed by fire or act of nature, including where such destruction occurred within 15 years prior to the adoption of the provisions of this chapter by the city or town. In a city or town that has adopted the provisions of RSA 79-E:4-a, "qualifying structure" also means potentially impacted structures identified by the municipality within the coastal resilience incentive zone established under RSA 79-E:4-a.

III. "Replacement" means the demolition or removal of a qualifying structure and the construction of a new structure on the same lot.

IV. "Substantial rehabilitation" means rehabilitation of a qualifying structure which costs at least 15 percent of the pre-rehabilitation assessed valuation or at least $75,000, whichever is less. In addition, in the case of historic structures, substantial rehabilitation means devoting a portion of the total cost, in the amount of at least 10 percent of the pre-rehabilitation assessed valuation or at least $5,000, whichever is less, to energy efficiency in accordance with the U.S. Secretary of the Interior's Standards for Rehabilitation. Cities or towns may further limit "substantial rehabilitation" according to the procedure in RSA 79-E:3 as meaning rehabilitation which costs a percentage greater than 15 percent of pre-rehabilitation assessed valuation or an amount greater than $75,000 based on local economic conditions, community character, and local planning and development goals.

V. "Tax increment finance district" means any district established in accordance with the provisions of RSA 162-K.

VI. "Tax relief" means:

(a) For a qualifying structure, that for a period of time determined by a local governing body in accordance with this chapter, the property tax on a qualifying structure shall not increase as a result of the substantial rehabilitation thereof.

(b) For the replacement of a qualifying structure, that for a period of time determined by a local governing body in accordance with this chapter, the property tax on a replacement structure shall not exceed the property tax on the replaced qualifying structure as a result of the replacement thereof.

(c) For a qualifying structure which is a building destroyed by fire or act of nature, that for a period of time determined by a local governing body in accordance with this chapter, the property tax on such qualifying structure shall not exceed the tax on the assessed value of the structure that would have existed had the structure not been destroyed.

VII. "Tax relief period" means the finite period of time during which the tax relief will be effec-

tive, as determined by a local governing body pursuant to RSA 79-E:5.

HISTORY:
2006, 167:1, eff. April 1, 2006. 2009, 200:5–7, eff. July 15, 2009. 2010, 329:1, 2, eff. July 20, 2010. 2011, 237:1, 2, eff. July 5, 2011. 2013, 78:2, eff. April 1, 2013. 2017, 203:2, eff. September 3, 2017.

Amendment Notes
The 2017 amendments to this section by Ch. 203 added the last sentence of II.

—2013.
The 2013 amendment added I; redesignated former I, I-a, II, II-a, III, and IV as II through VII; and added the second sentence of IV.

—2011.
The 2011 amendment added the last sentence of I and added III(c).

—2010.
The 2010 amendment added the second sentence of I and II.

—2009.
The 2009 amendment added I-a and II-a; added the III(a) designation; added "For a qualifying structure" in III(a); and added III(b).

Applicability of 2011 amendment.
2011, 237:4, eff. July 5, 2011, provided: "The authority conferred by this act shall apply retroactively to cities and towns that adopted the provisions of RSA 79-E in effect prior to the effective date of this act."

79-E:3. Adoption of Community Revitalization Tax Relief Incentive Program.

I. Any city or town may adopt or modify the provisions of this chapter by voting whether to accept for consideration or modify requirements for requests for community revitalization tax relief incentives. Any city or town may do so by following the procedures in this section.

II. In a town, other than a town that has adopted a charter pursuant to RSA 49-D, the question shall be placed on the warrant of a special or annual town meeting, by the governing body or by petition under RSA 39:3.

III. In a city or town that has adopted a charter under RSA 49-C or RSA 49-D, the legislative body may consider and act upon the question in accordance with its normal procedures for passage of resolutions, ordinances, and other legislation. In the alternative, the legislative body of such municipality may vote to place the question on the official ballot for any regular municipal election.

IV. If a majority of those voting on the question vote "yes," applications for community revitalization tax relief incentives may be accepted and considered by the local governing body at any time thereafter, subject to the provisions of paragraph VI of this section.

V. If the question is not approved, the question may later be voted on according to the provisions of paragraph II or III of this section, whichever applies.

VI. The local governing body of any town or city that has adopted this program may consider rescinding its action in the manner described in paragraph II or III of this section, whichever applies. A vote terminating the acceptance and consideration of such applications shall have no effect on incentives previously granted by the city or town, nor shall it terminate consideration of applications submitted prior to the date of such vote.

HISTORY:

2006, 167:1, eff. April 1, 2006. 2010, 329:3, eff. July 20, 2010.

Amendments

—2010.

The 2010 amendment, in the first sentence of I, added "or modify" following "adopt" and added "or modify requirements for."

Applicability of act.

2013, 78:4, eff. April 1, 2013, provided: "The provisions of this act shall not be applied in any city or town until the amendments to RSA 79-E made in sections 1– 3 of this act have been adopted according to the procedures in RSA 79-E:3."

Early Adoption by Municipalities.

2009, 200:16, eff. July 15, 2009, provided: "Any city or town that has adopted the provisions of RSA 79-E prior to the effective date of this section may adopt the provisions of this act relating to the extension of tax relief to the replacement of qualifying structures in accordance with the provisions of RSA 79-E:3. If a city or town that has adopted RSA 79-E prior to the effective date of this act desires to extend the tax relief benefits for replacement structures provided herein, such city or town must readopt RSA 79-E in its entirety or all of the provisions of this act pertaining to tax relief for replacement structures."

79-E:4. Community Revitalization Tax Relief Incentive.

I. An owner of a qualifying structure who intends to substantially rehabilitate or replace such structure may apply to the governing body of the municipality in which the property is located for tax relief. The applicant shall include the address of the property, a description of the intended rehabilitation or replacement, any changes in use of the property resulting from the rehabilitation or replacement, and an application fee.

I-a. In order to assist the governing body with the review and evaluation of an application for replacement of a qualifying structure, an owner shall submit to the governing body as part of the application, a New Hampshire division of historical resources individual resource inventory form, prepared by a qualified architectural historian and a letter issued by the local heritage commission and if the qualifying structure is located within a designated historic district established in accordance with RSA 674:46, a letter from the historic district commission or, if such local commissions are not established, a letter issued by the New Hampshire division of historical resources that identifies any and all historical, cultural, and architectural value of the structure or structures that are proposed to be replaced and the property on which those structures are located. The application for tax relief shall not be deemed to be complete and the governing body shall not schedule the public hearing on the application for replacement of a qualifying structure as required under RSA 79-E:4, II until the inventory form and the letter, as well as all other required information, have been submitted.

II. Upon receipt of an application, the governing body shall hold a duly noticed public hearing to take place no later than 60 days from receipt of the application, to determine whether the structure at issue is a qualifying structure; whether any proposed rehabilitation qualifies as substantial rehabilitation; and whether there is a public benefit to granting the requested tax relief and, if so, for what duration.

III. No later than 45 days after the public hearing, the governing body shall render a decision granting or denying the requested tax relief and, if so granting, establishing the tax relief period.

IV.(a) The governing body may grant the tax relief, provided:

(1) The governing body finds a public benefit under RSA 79-E:7; and

(2) The specific public benefit is preserved through a covenant under RSA 79-E:8; and

(3) The governing body finds that the proposed use is consistent with the municipality's master plan or development regulations; and

(4) In the case of a replacement, the governing body specifically finds that the local heritage commission or historic district commission or, if such local commissions are not established, the New Hampshire division of historical resources has determined that the replaced qualifying structure does not possess significant historical, cultural, or architectural value, the replacement of the qualifying structure will achieve one or more of the public benefits identified in RSA 79-E:7 to a greater degree than the renovation of the underutilized structure, and the historical, cultural, or architectural resources in the community will not be adversely affected by the replacement. In connection with these findings, the governing body may request that the division of historical resources conduct a technical evaluation in order to satisfy the governing body that historical resources will not be adversely affected.

(b) If the governing body grants the tax relief, the governing body shall identify the specific public benefit achieved under RSA 79-E:7, and shall determine the precise terms and duration of the covenant to preserve the public benefit under RSA 79-E:8.

V. If the governing body, in its discretion, denies the application for tax relief, such denial shall be accompanied by a written explanation. The governing body's decision may be appealed either to the board of tax and land appeals or the superior court in the same manner as provided for appeals of current use classification pursuant to RSA 79-A:9 or 79-A:11 provided, however, that such denial shall be deemed discretionary and shall not be set aside by the board of tax and land appeals or the superior court except for bad faith or discrimination.

VI. Municipalities shall have no obligation to grant an application for tax relief for properties located within tax increment finance districts when the governing body determines, in its sole discretion, that the granting of tax relief will impede, reduce, or negatively affect:

(a) The development program or financing plans for such tax increment finance districts; or

(b) The ability to satisfy or expedite repayment of debt service obligations incurred for a tax increment financing district; or

(c) The ability to satisfy program administration, operating, or maintenance expenses within a tax increment financing district.

HISTORY:
2006, 167:1, eff. April 1, 2006. 2009, 200:8–11, eff. July 15, 2009.

Amendments

—2009.
The 2009 amendment added "or replace" following "rehabilitate" or variants in I; added I-a, IV(a)(4), and VI; and made related and stylistic changes.

79-E:4-a.   Coastal Resilience Incentive Zone.

I. A city or town may adopt the provisions of this section by vote of its legislative body, according to the procedures described in RSA 79-E:3, to establish a coastal resilience incentive zone (CRIZ). Municipalities may use storm surge, sea-level rise, and extreme precipitation projections in the 2016 report of the New Hampshire Coastal Risk and Hazards Commission, "Preparing New Hampshire for Projected Storm Surge, Sea-Level Rise, and Extreme Precipitation," and its successor projections, to identify potentially impacted structures.

II. The municipality implementing a CRIZ shall determine the resilience measures it deems qualifying, such as, but not limited to, elevation and freeboard renovations, elevation of mechanicals, construction of resilient natural features, enhancement or creation of tidal marshes, elevation of private driveways and sidewalks, construction or enlargement of private culverts and other structures to enable increased water flow and storm-surge, and movement of property to higher elevation on the property or to a newly acquired property at a higher elevation within the municipality. Municipalities may grant tax relief to the qualifying structure and property as described in RSA 79-E:4.

III. Municipalities may provide other relief to properties in a coastal resilience incentive zone that are subject to repeated inundation, by acquiring preservation or water control easements or establishing tax increment financing districts.

IV. Municipalities may create a nonlapsing CRIZ fund as a capital reserve fund under RSA 34 or RSA 35, or a town-created trust fund under RSA 31:19-a, to provide funding for projected municipal costs associated with projected storm surge, sea-level rise, and extreme precipitation, and such funds may be used to support the coastal resilience incentive zone purpose established in this section.

HISTORY:
2017, 203:3, eff. September 3, 2017.

79-E:5.   Duration of Tax Relief Period.

I. The governing body may grant such tax assessment relief for a period of up to 5 years, beginning with the completion of the substantial rehabilitation.

I-a. For the approval of a replacement of a qualifying structure, the governing body may grant such tax assessment relief for a period of up to 5 years, beginning only upon the completion of construction of the replacement structure. The governing body may, in its discretion, extend such additional years of tax relief as provided for under this section, provided that no such additional years of tax relief may be provided prior to the completion of construction of the replacement structure. The municipal tax assessment of the replacement structure and the property on which it is located shall not increase or decrease in the period between the approval by the governing body of tax relief for the replacement structure and the time the owner completes construction of the replacement structure and grants to the municipality the covenant to protect the public benefit as required by this chapter. The governing body may not grant any tax assessment relief under this chapter with respect to property and structures for which an election has been made for property appraisal under RSA 75:1-a.

II. The governing body may, in its discretion, add up to an additional 2 years of tax relief for a project that results in new residential units and up to 4 years for a project that includes affordable housing.

III. The governing body may, in its discretion, add up to an additional 4 years of tax relief for the substantial rehabilitation of a qualifying structure that is listed on or determined eligible for listing on the National Register of Historic Places, state register of historic places, or is located within and important to a locally designated historic district, provided that the substantial rehabilitation is conducted in accordance with the U.S. Secretary of Interior's Standards for Rehabilitation.

IV. The governing body may adopt local guidelines to assist it in determining the appropriate duration of the tax assessment relief period.

HISTORY:
2006, 167:1, eff. April 1, 2006. 2009, 200:12, eff. July 15, 2009. 2010, 329:4, eff. July 20, 2010.

Amendments

—2010.
The 2010 amendment added IV.

—2009.
The 2009 amendment added I-a.

79-E:6.　Resumption of Full Tax Liability.

Upon expiration of the tax relief period, the property shall be taxed at its market value in accordance with RSA 75:1.

HISTORY:
2006, 167:1, eff. April 1, 2006.

79-E:7.　Public Benefit.

In order to qualify for tax relief under this chapter, the proposed substantial rehabilitation must provide at least one of the public benefits, and the proposed replacement must provide one or more of the public benefits to a greater degree than would a substantial rehabilitation of the same qualifying structure, as follows:

I. It enhances the economic vitality of the downtown;

II. It enhances and improves a structure that is culturally or historically important on a local, regional, state, or national level, either independently or within the context of an historic district, town center, or village center in which the building is located;

II-a. It promotes the preservation and reuse of existing building stock throughout a municipality by the rehabilitation of historic structures, thereby conserving the embodied energy in accordance with energy efficiency guidelines established by the U.S. Secretary of the Interior's Standards for Rehabilitation.

III. It promotes development of municipal centers, providing for efficiency, safety, and a greater sense of community, consistent with RSA 9-B; or

IV. It increases residential housing in urban or town centers.

HISTORY:
2006, 167:1, eff. April 1, 2006. 2009, 200:13, eff. July 15, 2009. 2013, 78:3, eff. April 1, 2013.

Amendments

—2013.
The 2013 amendment added II-a.

—2009.
The 2009 amendment rewrote the introductory paragraph to the extent that a detailed comparison would be impracticable.

79-E:7-a.　Public Benefit Determinations.

Cities or towns may adopt according to the procedure in RSA 79-E:3 provisions that further define the public benefits enumerated in RSA 79-E:7 to assist the governing body in evaluating applications made under this chapter based on local economic conditions, community character, and local planning and development goals.

HISTORY:
2010, 329:5, eff. July 20, 2010.

79-E:8.　Covenant to Protect Public Benefit.

I. Tax relief for the substantial rehabilitation or replacement of a qualifying structure shall be effective only after a property owner grants to the municipality a covenant ensuring that the structure shall be maintained and used in a manner that furthers the public benefits for which the tax relief was granted and as otherwise provided in this chapter.

II. The covenant shall be coextensive with the tax relief period. The covenant may, if required by the governing body, be effective for a period of time up to twice the duration of the tax relief period.

III. The covenant shall include provisions requiring the property owner to obtain casualty insurance, and flood insurance if appropriate. The covenant may include, at the governing body's sole discretion, a lien against proceeds from casualty and flood insurance claims for the purpose of ensuring proper restoration or demolition or damaged structures and property. If the property owner has not begun the process of restoration, rebuilding, or demolition of such structure within one year following damage or destruction, the property owner shall be subject to the termination of provisions set forth in RSA 79-E:9, I.

IV. The local governing body shall provide for the recording of the covenant to protect public benefit with the registry of deeds. It shall be a burden upon the property and shall bind all transferees and assignees of such property.

V. The applicant shall pay any reasonable expenses incurred by the municipality in the drafting, review, and/or execution of the covenant. The applicant also shall be responsible for the cost of recording the covenant.

HISTORY:
2006, 167:1, eff. April 1, 2006. 2009, 200:14, eff. July 15, 2009.

Amendments

—2009.
The 2009 amendment, in I, added "or replacement" following "rehabilitation" and added "and as otherwise provided in this chapter" at the end.

79-E:9.　Termination of Covenant; Reduction of Tax Relief; Penalty.

I. If the owner fails to maintain or utilize the building according to the terms of the covenant, or fails to restore, rebuild, or demolish the structure following damage or destruction as provided in RSA 79-E:8, III, the governing body shall, after a duly noticed public hearing, determine whether and to

II. Upon receipt of an application under paragraph I, the selectmen or assessors shall review the application and shall grant or deny the application in writing within 6 months after the notice of tax date.

III.(a) If the selectmen or assessors neglect or refuse to abate the use change tax, any person aggrieved may either:

(1) Apply in writing to the board of tax and land appeals accompanied with a $65 filing fee; or

(2) Petition the superior court in the county.

(b) The appeal to either the board of tax and land appeals or superior court shall be filed within 8 months of the notice of tax date and not afterwards.

IV. For purposes of this section, "notice of tax date" means the date the taxing jurisdiction mails the use change tax bill.

V. Each use change tax bill shall require a separate abatement request and appeal.

HISTORY:
2008, 390:1, eff. July 17, 2008.

79-F:9. Lien for Unpaid Taxes.

The real estate of every person shall be held liable for the taxes levied pursuant to RSA 79-F:5.

HISTORY:
2008, 390:1, eff. July 17, 2008.

79-F:10. Enforcement.

All taxes levied pursuant to RSA 79-F:5 which are not paid when due shall be collected in the same manner as provided in RSA 80.

HISTORY:
2008, 390:1, eff. July 17, 2008.

79-F:11. Disposition of Revenues.

All money received by the tax collector pursuant to the provisions of this chapter shall be for the use of the town or city.

HISTORY:
2008, 390:1, eff. July 17, 2008.

79-F:12. Location of Contiguous Land in More Than One Taxing District.

Where contiguous land which could be classified as land under qualifying farm structures is located in more than one town, compliance with any minimum area requirement pursuant to RSA 79-F:4 shall be determined on the basis of the total area of such land, and not the area which is located in any particular town.

HISTORY:
2008, 390:1, eff. July 17, 2008.

TITLE VI
PUBLIC OFFICERS AND EMPLOYEES

NOTES TO DECISIONS

Strikes

Public employees have no right to strike unless such right is conferred by legislative action. Manchester v. Manchester Teachers Guild, 100 N.H. 507, 131 A.2d 59, 1957 N.H. LEXIS 86 (N.H. 1957).

RESEARCH REFERENCES AND PRACTICE AIDS

Cross References.

Abuse of office, see RSA 643.

Certification of bills rendered by state officers and employees, see RSA 9:23.

Corrupt practices, see RSA 640.

Military leave, see RSA 112.

Public employee labor relations, see RSA 273-A.

CHAPTER 91-A
ACCESS TO GOVERNMENTAL RECORDS AND MEETINGS

Amendment Notes

—2008.

The 2008 amendment by 2008, 303:2, eff. July 1, 2008, substituted "Governmental" for "Public" in the chapter heading.

—1986.

1986, 83:1, eff. Jan. 1, 1987, added "and meetings" following "records" in the chapter heading.

Purpose.

2003, 287:1, eff. July 18, 2003, provided:

"The general court hereby establishes a commission to study clarifying the right-to-know law in light of the supreme court's December 31, 2001 decision in *Hawkins v. N.H. Department of Health and Human Services* and increasing use of electronic communication in the transaction of governmental business. The general court recognizes that guidance is needed for all government officials as well as for members of the public regarding what meetings and what documentation are considered subject to RSA 91-A, the right-to-know law."

NOTES TO DECISIONS

Analysis

1. Purpose
2. Appointments
3. Unofficial tape recording
4. Confidentiality of information
5. Burden of proof
6. Attorney-client privilege
7. Tests
8. Surveillance equipment
9. Procedure

1. Purpose

This chapter was intended to increase public access to governmental proceedings in order to augment popular control of government and encourage administrative agency responsibility. Society for Protection of N.H. Forests v. Water Supply & Pollution Control Comm'n, 115 N.H. 192, 337 A.2d 788, 1975 N.H. LEXIS 257 (N.H. 1975).

Main purpose of this chapter is based upon theory that public knowledge of the considerations upon which governmental action is based and of the decisions taken is essential to the democratic process. Carter v. Nashua, 113 N.H. 407, 308 A.2d 847, 1973 N.H. LEXIS 285 (N.H. 1973).

2. Appointments

Trial court properly ruled that a government official does not necessarily violate this chapter whenever he or she requests a citizen to make an appointment before reviewing a public record. Brent v. Paquette, 132 N.H. 415, 567 A.2d 976, 1989 N.H. LEXIS 123 (N.H. 1989).

3. Unofficial tape recording

Trial court properly found that tape recording made by school superintendent during a public meeting was not a public record subject to this chapter, where the tape was unofficial and made solely for the superintendent's personal use. Brent v. Paquette, 132 N.H. 415, 567 A.2d 976, 1989 N.H. LEXIS 123 (N.H. 1989).

4. Confidentiality of information

The determination of whether information is confidential for purposes of Right-to-Know Law is assessed objectively, not based upon the subjective expectations of the party generating that information. Goode v. N.H. Office of the Legislative Budget Assistant, 148 N.H. 551, 813 A.2d 381, 2002 N.H. LEXIS 168 (N.H. 2002).

5. Burden of proof

The burden of proving whether information is confidential rests with the party seeking non-disclosure. Goode v. N.H. Office of the Legislative Budget Assistant, 148 N.H. 551, 813 A.2d 381, 2002 N.H. LEXIS 168 (N.H. 2002).

6. Attorney-client privilege

Under the Right-to-Know Law, Department of Transportation (DOT) documents were properly redacted as subject to the attorney-client privilege. The redacted language revealed the substance of a communication from DOT to its attorney that was made for the purpose of facilitating the rendition of professional legal services to the client; moreover, under the circumstances, in which two state agencies, both represented by the attorney general's office, were jointly working on a single policy issue, the court could not say the privileged communication was shared with someone outside the privileged relationship. ATV Watch v. N.H. Dep't of Transp., 161 N.H. 746, 20 A.3d 919, 2011 N.H. LEXIS 56 (N.H. 2011).

Under the Right-to-Know Law, the Department of Transportation (DOT) properly redacted certain e-mails based on the attorney-client privilege. The DOT's redaction of the e-mails in their entirety was equivalent to withholding a letter sent through the post office to its attorney as an entire document, which was common practice, rather than disclosing the letter with everything but the letterhead and addressee's name and address redacted; furthermore, the DOT identified the senders and recipients of the e-mails in its Vaughn index, thus providing the functional equivalent of the information petitioners claimed was denied them. ATV Watch v. N.H. Dep't of Transp., 161 N.H. 746, 20 A.3d 919, 2011 N.H. LEXIS 56 (N.H. 2011).

7. Tests

Trial court had not applied the Freedom of Information Act (FOIA) to petitioner's request under the Right-to-Know Law. While the Murray test employed by the trial court was one the present court had adopted from the FOIA, use of the test did not constitute an application of federal law. Montenegro v. City of Dover, 162 N.H. 641, 34 A.3d 717, 2011 N.H. LEXIS 150 (N.H. 2011).

In Murray, the New Hampshire Supreme Court intended to adopt the amended test set out in 5 U.S.C.S. § 552(b)(7) (2006); thus, to withhold materials under the modified test adopted in Murray, an agency need not establish that the materials are investigatory, but need only establish that the records at issue were compiled for law enforcement purposes, and that the material satisfies the requirements of one of the subparts of the test. Accordingly, even accepting petitioner's assertion that his request did not encompass investigatory files, the trial court did not err in applying the Murray test. Montenegro v. City of Dover, 162 N.H. 641, 34 A.3d 717, 2011 N.H. LEXIS 150 (N.H. 2011).

8. Surveillance equipment

Under the Murray test, precise locations of a city's surveillance equipment, the recording capabilities for each piece of equipment, the specific time periods each piece of equipment was expected to be operational, and the retention time for any recordings were exempt from disclosure, as this information was of such substantive detail that it could reasonably be expected to risk circumvention of the law by providing those who wished to engage in criminal activity with the ability to adjust their behaviors in an effort to avoid detection. Because this was not an unreasonable restriction on public access, there was no conflict between the exemption and N.H. Const. pt. I, art. 8. Montenegro v. City of Dover, 162 N.H. 641, 34 A.3d 717, 2011 N.H. LEXIS 150 (N.H. 2011).

9. Procedure

Because a fire investigator in his affidavit broke the sought-after records down into 12 categories, explained each category, and explained how disclosure would interfere with law enforcement proceedings, the trial court did not err in not conducting an in camera review or requiring a Vaughn index. 38 Endicott St. N., LLC v. State Fire Marshal, 163 N.H. 656, 44 A.3d 571, 2012 N.H. LEXIS 69 (N.H. 2012).

Cited:

Cited in State v. LaFrance, 124 N.H. 171, 471 A.2d 340, 1983 N.H. LEXIS 377 (1983); Gomez v. Nashua, 126 F.R.D. 432, 1989 U.S. Dist. LEXIS 7406 (D.N.H. 1989); Appeal of Salem Regional Medical Ctr., 134 N.H. 207, 590 A.2d 602, 1991 N.H. LEXIS 47 (1991); Chambers v. Gregg, 135 N.H. 478, 606 A.2d 811, 1992 N.H. LEXIS 62 (1992); Appeal of Atlantic Connections, 135 N.H. 510, 608 A.2d 861, 1992 N.H. LEXIS 69 (1992); In re Keene Sentinel, 136 N.H. 121, 612 A.2d 911, 1992 N.H. LEXIS 146 (1992); Union Leader Corp. v. Fenniman, 136 N.H. 624, 620 A.2d 1039, 1993 N.H. LEXIS 4 (1993).

OPINIONS OF THE ATTORNEY GENERAL

Analysis

1. Generally
2. Tax Returns
3. Veterans' needs committee

1. Generally

This chapter does not necessarily require the state to be placed at a disadvantage when bargaining with the private sector. 1987 Op. Att'y Gen. 122.

2. Tax Returns

Bank tax returns are not subject to public disclosure under this chapter. 1986 Op. Att'y Gen. 198.

3. Veterans' needs committee

State veterans' needs committee is subject to this chapter. 1986 Op. Att'y Gen. 231.

RESEARCH REFERENCES AND PRACTICE AIDS

Cross References.
Accountability of government officers; public's right to know, see New Hampshire Constitution, Part 1, Article 8.

New Hampshire Bar Journal.
New Hampshire Right to Know Law, 20 N.H. B.J. 98 (March 1979).
The New Hampshire Right to Know Law—An analysis, 16 N.H. B.J. 227 (March 1975).
For article, "The Right to Know Your Privacy: An Analysis of *Petition of Keene Sentinel*," see 34 N.H. B.J. 5 (Sept. 1993).

New Hampshire Trial Bar News.
For article, "How to Acquire Information Under the New Hampshire Right-to-Know Law," see 7 N.H. Trial Bar News 57, 57-61 (Winter 1987).

New Hampshire Practice.
13-11 N.H.P. Local Government Law § 296.
13-15 N.H.P. Local Government Law § 514.
13-18 N.H.P. Local Government Law §§ 651, 653.
13-19 N.H.P. Local Government Law § 711.

91-A:1. Preamble.

Openness in the conduct of public business is essential to a democratic society. The purpose of this chapter is to ensure both the greatest possible public access to the actions, discussions and records of all public bodies, and their accountability to the people.

HISTORY:
1967, 251:1. 1971, 327:1. 1977, 540:1, eff. Sept. 13, 1977.

Amendment Notes

—1977.
Rewritten to the extent that a detailed comparison would be impracticable.

—1971.

Rewritten to the extent that a detailed comparison would be impracticable.

NOTES TO DECISIONS

Analysis

1. Investigatory records
2. Photographs taken by police

1. Investigatory records

Law enforcement representatives did not meet their burden of justifying their withholding of requested documents that the father sought regarding the disappearance of the father's daughter following reports that the daughter had been involved in a traffic accident; since police investigative reports were not mentioned in the state law concerning the disclosure of government records, the state supreme court determined that the six-part test under the corresponding federal law applied and required the law enforcement representatives on remand of the case to the trial court to show how disclosure of the requested records could interfere with an ongoing investigation or law enforcement proceeding. Murray v. N.H. Div. of State Police, 154 N.H. 579, 913 A.2d 737, 2006 N.H. LEXIS 201 (N.H. 2006).

2. Photographs taken by police

Photographs which police took with the consent of people who were stopped by police but not arrested were public records, and the trial court's judgment ordering the City of Manchester to provide a civil liberties union with access to consensual photographs which police officers took over a five-year period was upheld. N.H. Civ. Liberties Union v. City of Manchester, 149 N.H. 437, 821 A.2d 1014, 2003 N.H. LEXIS 61 (N.H. 2003).

Cited:

Cited in Orford Teachers Ass'n v. Watson, 121 N.H. 118, 427 A.2d 21, 1981 N.H. LEXIS 255 (1981); Brent v. Paquette, 132 N.H. 415, 567 A.2d 976, 1989 N.H. LEXIS 123 (1989); Union Leader Corp. v. City of Nashua, 141 N.H. 473, 686 A.2d 310, 1996 N.H. LEXIS 127 (1996); Lambert v. Belknap Cty. Convention, 157 N.H. 375, 949 A.2d 709, 2008 N.H. LEXIS 75 (2008).

OPINIONS OF THE ATTORNEY GENERAL

Cited:

Cited in 1986 Op. Att'y Gen. 220; 1986 Op. Att'y Gen. 231.

RESEARCH REFERENCES AND PRACTICE AIDS

New Hampshire Bar Journal.

For annual survey article by Pierce law students, "Murray v. N.H. State Police: The Right to Access Police Investigatory Files," see 48 N.H. B.J. 34 (Summer 2007).

91-A:1-a. Definition of Public Proceedings.

In this chapter:

I. "Advisory committee" means any committee, council, commission, or other like body whose primary purpose is to consider an issue or issues designated by the appointing authority so as to provide such authority with advice or recommendations concerning the formulation of any public policy or legislation that may be promoted, modified, or opposed by such authority.

II. "Governmental proceedings" means the transaction of any functions affecting any or all citizens of the state by a public body.

III. "Governmental records" means any information created, accepted, or obtained by, or on behalf of, any public body, or a quorum or majority thereof, or any public agency in furtherance of its official function. Without limiting the foregoing, the term "governmental records" includes any written communication or other information, whether in paper, electronic, or other physical form, received by a quorum or majority of a public body in furtherance of its official function, whether at a meeting or outside a meeting of the body. The term "governmental records" shall also include the term "public records."

IV. "Information" means knowledge, opinions, facts, or data of any kind and in whatever physical form kept or maintained, including, but not limited to, written, aural, visual, electronic, or other physical form.

V. "Public agency" means any agency, authority, department, or office of the state or of any county, town, municipal corporation, school district, school administrative unit, chartered public school, or other political subdivision.

VI. "Public body" means any of the following:

(a) The general court including executive sessions of committees; and including any advisory committee established by the general court.

(b) The executive council and the governor with the executive council; including any advisory committee established by the governor by executive order or by the executive council.

(c) Any board or commission of any state agency or authority, including the board of trustees of the university system of New Hampshire and any committee, advisory or otherwise, established by such entities.

(d) Any legislative body, governing body, board, commission, committee, agency, or authority of any county, town, municipal corporation, school district, school administrative unit, chartered public school, or other political subdivision, or any committee, subcommittee, or subordinate body thereof, or advisory committee thereto.

(e) Any corporation that has as its sole member the state of New Hampshire, any county, town, municipal corporation, school district, school administrative unit, village district, or other political subdivision, and that is determined by the Internal Revenue Service to be a tax exempt organization pursuant to section 501(c)(3) of the Internal Revenue Code.

HISTORY:

1977, 540:2. 1986, 83:2. 1989, 274:1. 1995, 260:4, eff. July 1, 1995. 2001, 223:1, eff. Jan. 1, 2002. 2008, 278:3, eff. at 12:01 a.m., July 1, 2008. 303:3, eff. July 1, 2008. 303:8, eff. at 12:01 a.m., September 5, 2008. 354:1, eff. September 5, 2008.

Amendment Notes

—2008.

The 2008 amendment by Chapter 278 added VI(e).

The 2008 amendment by Chapter 303:3, effective July 1, 2008, rewrote the section to the extent that a detailed comparison would be impracticable.

The 2008 amendment by Chapter 303:8, effective September 5, 2008 at 12:01 a.m., substituted "chartered public" for "charter" in V.

The 2008 amendment by Chapter 354:1 substituted "chartered public school" for "charter school" in I(d) (now VI(d) as amended by Chapter 303:3).

—2001.

Redesignated the former introductory paragraph as par. I, redesignated former pars. I through IV as pars. I(a) through I(d), and in par. I(a), inserted "and including any advisory committee established by the general court", in par. I(b), inserted "including any advisory committee established by the governor by executive order or by the governor's council", and in par. I(c), inserted "and including any advisory committee established by such entities", and added new par. II.

—1995.

Paragraph IV: Inserted "school administrative unit, charter school" following "school district".

—1989.

Paragraph II: Added "and the governor with the governor's council" at the end of the paragraph.

—1986.

Paragraph III: Added "including the board of trustees of the university system of New Hampshire" following "authority".

Contingent 2008, ch. 278 amendment.

2008, 278:4, II, eff. August 26, 2008, provided in part: "If HB 1408-LOCAL [ch. 303] of the 2008 legislative session becomes law, section 3 of this act shall take effect July 1, 2008 at 12:01 a.m. and section 1 of this act shall not take effect." Pursuant to the terms of this provision par. II is set out above as amended by Ch. 278:3, eff. July 1, 2008 at 12:01 a.m. and the amendment by Ch. 278:1 did not take effect.

Contingent 2008, ch. 303 amendment.

2008, 303:9, eff. July 1, 2008, provided in part: "If SB 418 [ch. 354] of the 2008 regular legislative session becomes law, section 8 of this act shall take effect at 12:01 a.m. on the day SB 418 takes effect." Pursuant to the terms of this provision par. V is set out above as amended by Ch. 303:8, eff. September 5, 2008 at 12:01 a.m.

NOTES TO DECISIONS

Analysis

1. Organizations
2. Special legislative session

1. Organizations

The New Hampshire Housing Finance Authority is subject to the Right-to-Know Law as the authority performs the essential government function of providing safe and affordable housing to the elderly and low income residents of the state. Union Leader Corp. v. New Hampshire Hous. Fin. Auth., 142 N.H. 540, 705 A.2d 725, 1997 N.H. LEXIS 132 (N.H. 1997).

Not all organizations that work for or with the government are subject to the right-to-know law. Bradbury v. Shaw, 116 N.H. 388, 360 A.2d 123, 1976 N.H. LEXIS 361 (N.H. 1976).

Where there was no statute or ordinance establishing mayor's industrial advisory committee consisting of prominent businessmen, newspapermen, and city council members, which met monthly on call of mayor and performed variety of functions including contacting concerns which might locate in city, gathering information which might be useful to potential concerns, discussing of sale of city-owned land to commercial developers and extension of city water and sewer lines and construction of new streets, advisory committee's involvement in governmental programs brought it

within scope of right-to-know law. Bradbury v. Shaw, 116 N.H. 388, 360 A.2d 123, 1976 N.H. LEXIS 361 (N.H. 1976).

Municipal finance committee was an agency of municipal corporation so that its meetings were included in the term "public proceedings" as defined by former RSA 91-A:1. Selkowe v. Bean, 109 N.H. 247, 249 A.2d 35, 1968 N.H. LEXIS 171 (N.H. 1968).

2. Special legislative session

Assuming arguendo that the due process protections applied to the passage of legislation, an inmate's due process rights were not violated by the enactment of RSA 651:2, II-e, as the session during which this occurred was open to the public, as required by RSA 91-A:1-a, VI(a) and RSA 91-A:2, II. Starr v. Governor, 154 N.H. 174, 910 A.2d 1247, 2006 N.H. LEXIS 140 (N.H. 2006).

Cited:

Cited in Lodge v. Knowlton, 118 N.H. 574, 391 A.2d 893, 1978 N.H. LEXIS 246 (1978); Appeal of Plantier, 126 N.H. 500, 494 A.2d 270, 1985 N.H. LEXIS 341, 51 A.L.R.4th 1129 (1985).

OPINIONS OF THE ATTORNEY GENERAL

Analysis

Construction
Cited:

Construction

Public informational meetings conducted by Department of Transportation were "public proceedings" for purposes of this chapter, and department was required to give notice to public and to keep brief minutes. Op. Atty. Gen. #0-93-1.

Cited:

Cited in 1986 Op. Att'y Gen. 220; 1986 Op. Att'y Gen. 231; 1987 Op. Att'y Gen. 122.

RESEARCH REFERENCES AND PRACTICE AIDS

References in text.

Section 501(c)(3) of the Internal Revenue Code, referred to in par. VI(e), is classified to 26 U.S.C.S. § 501(c)(3).

91-A:2. Meetings Open to Public. [Effective until January 1, 2018]

I. For the purpose of this chapter, a "meeting" means the convening of a quorum of the membership of a public body, as defined in RSA 91-A:1-a, VI, or the majority of the members of such public body if the rules of that body define "quorum" as more than a majority of its members, whether in person, by means of telephone or electronic communication, or in any other manner such that all participating members are able to communicate with each other contemporaneously, subject to the provisions set forth in RSA 91-A:2, III, for the purpose of discussing or acting upon a matter or matters over which the public body has supervision, control, jurisdiction, or advisory power. A chance, social, or other encounter not convened for the purpose of discussing or acting upon such matters shall not constitute a meeting if no decisions are made regarding such matters. "Meeting" shall also not include:

(a) Strategy or negotiations with respect to collective bargaining;

(b) Consultation with legal counsel;

(c) A caucus consisting of elected members of a public body of the same political party who were elected on a partisan basis at a state general election or elected on a partisan basis by a town or city which has adopted a partisan ballot system pursuant to RSA 669:12 or RSA 44:2; or

(d) Circulation of draft documents which, when finalized, are intended only to formalize decisions previously made in a meeting; provided, that nothing in this subparagraph shall be construed to alter or affect the application of any other section of RSA 91-A to such documents or related communications.

II. Subject to the provisions of RSA 91-A:3, all meetings, whether held in person, by means of telephone or electronic communication, or in any other manner, shall be open to the public. Except for town meetings, school district meetings, and elections, no vote while in open session may be taken by secret ballot. Any person shall be permitted to use recording devices, including, but not limited to, tape recorders, cameras, and videotape equipment, at such meetings. Minutes of all such meetings, including nonpublic sessions, shall include the names of members, persons appearing before the public bodies, and a brief description of the subject matter discussed and final decisions. Subject to the provisions of RSA 91-A:3, minutes shall be promptly recorded and open to public inspection not more than 5 business days after the meeting, except as provided in RSA 91-A:6, and shall be treated as permanent records of any public body, or any subordinate body thereof, without exception. Except in an emergency or when there is a meeting of a legislative committee, a notice of the time and place of each such meeting, including a nonpublic session, shall be posted in 2 appropriate places one of which may be the public body's Internet website, if such exists, or shall be printed in a newspaper of general circulation in the city or town at least 24 hours, excluding Sundays and legal holidays, prior to such meetings. An emergency shall mean a situation where immediate undelayed action is deemed to be imperative by the chairman or presiding officer of the public body, who shall post a notice of the time and place of such meeting as soon as practicable, and shall employ whatever further means are reasonably available to inform the public that a meeting is to be held. The minutes of the meeting shall clearly spell out the need for the emergency meeting. When a meeting of a legislative committee is held, publication made pursuant to the rules of the house of representatives or the senate, whichever rules are appropriate, shall be sufficient notice. If the charter of any city or town or guidelines or rules of order of any public body require a broader public access to official meetings and records than herein described, such charter provisions or guidelines or rules of order shall take precedence over the requirements of this chapter. For the purposes of this paragraph, a business day means the hours of 8 a.m. to 5 p.m. on Monday through Friday, excluding national and state holidays.

III. A public body may, but is not required to, allow one or more members of the body to participate in a meeting by electronic or other means of communication for the benefit of the public and the governing body, subject to the provisions of this paragraph.

(a) A member of the public body may participate in a meeting other than by attendance in person at the location of the meeting only when such attendance is not reasonably practical. Any reason that such attendance is not reasonably practical shall be stated in the minutes of the meeting.

(b) Except in an emergency, a quorum of the public body shall be physically present at the location specified in the meeting notice as the location of the meeting. For purposes of this subparagraph, an "emergency" means that immediate action is imperative and the physical presence of a quorum is not reasonably practical within the period of time requiring action. The determination that an emergency exists shall be made by the chairman or presiding officer of the public body, and the facts upon which that determination is based shall be included in the minutes of the meeting.

(c) Each part of a meeting required to be open to the public shall be audible or otherwise discernable to the public at the location specified in the meeting notice as the location of the meeting. Each member participating electronically or otherwise must be able to simultaneously hear each other and speak to each other during the meeting, and shall be audible or otherwise discernable to the public in attendance at the meeting's location. Any member participating in such fashion shall identify the persons present in the location from which the member is participating. No meeting shall be conducted by electronic mail or any other form of communication that does not permit the public to hear, read, or otherwise discern meeting discussion contemporaneously at the meeting location specified in the meeting notice.

(d) Any meeting held pursuant to the terms of this paragraph shall comply with all of the requirements of this chapter relating to public meetings, and shall not circumvent the spirit and purpose of this chapter as expressed in RSA 91-A:1.

(e) A member participating in a meeting by the means described in this paragraph is deemed to be present at the meeting for purposes of voting. All votes taken during such a meeting shall be by roll call vote.

HISTORY:

1967, 251:1. 1969, 482:1. 1971, 327:2. 1975, 383:1. 1977, 540:3. 1983, 279:1. 1986, 83:3. 1991, 217:2, eff. Jan. 1, 1992. 2003, 287:7, eff. July 18, 2003. 2007, 59:2, eff. July 31, 2007. 2008, 278:2, eff. at

12:01 a.m., July 1, 2008. 303:4, eff. July 1, 2008. 2016, 29:1, eff. January 1, 2017.

Amendment Notes

The 2016 amendments to this section by Ch. 29 rewrote the former fourth sentence as the fourth and fifth sentences of paragraph II, which read: "Minutes of all such meetings, including names of members, persons appearing before the public bodies, and a brief description of the subject matter discussed and final decisions, shall be promptly recorded and open to public inspection not more than 5 business days after the meeting, except as provided in RSA 91-A:6, and shall be treated as permanent records of any public body, or any subordinate body thereof, without exception."

—2008.

The 2008 amendment by Chapter 278, in I, added "subject to the provisions set forth in RSA 91-A:2, III" in the first sentence.

The 2008 amendment by Chapter 303 rewrote the section to the extent that a detailed comparison would be impracticable.

—2007.

Paragraph II: Substituted "not more than 5 business days after" for "within 144 hours of" preceding "the public meeting" in the fourth sentence and added the tenth sentence.

—2003.

Paragraph I: Made minor stylistic changes in subpars. (b) and (c) and added subpar. (d).

—1991.

Paragraph II: Substituted "a nonpublic" for "an executive" preceding "session" in the fifth sentence.

—1986.

Paragraph I: Added the second sentence.

Paragraph II: Inserted "or the senate, whichever rules are appropriate" following "house of representatives" in the eighth sentence and made other minor stylistic changes.

—1983.

Paragraph II: Substituted "144" for "72" following "inspection within" and deleted "of this chapter" following "91-A:6" in the fourth sentence.

—1977.

Deleted "the" preceding "public" in the section catchline, designated existing provisions of the section as par. II, added the second sentence of that paragraph, and added par. I.

—1975.

Added the second sentence.

—1971.

Inserted "or when there is a meeting of a legislative committee" following "emergency" and substituted "Sundays" for "Sunday" following "excluding" in the third sentence and added the fifth sentence.

—1969.

Rewritten to the extent that a detailed comparison would be impracticable.

Contingent 2008 amendment.

2008, 278:4, I, eff. August 26, 2008, provided in part: "If HB 1408-LOCAL [ch. 303] of the 2008 legislative session becomes law, section 2 of this act shall take effect July 1, 2008 at 12:01 a.m." Pursuant to the terms of this provision par. I is set out above as amended by Ch. 278:2, eff. July 1, 2008 at 12:01 a.m.

NOTES TO DECISIONS

Analysis

1. Construction
2. Availability of records
3. Public dissemination
4. Notice—Generally
5. —Personal notice
6. —Subsequent meetings
7. Collective bargaining
8. Public proceedings
9. Attorney-client privilege

1. Construction

Based on the definition of a "consultation," and when read with the phrase "with legal counsel," the "consultation with legal counsel" exclusion did not encompass a situation in which the public body convened a quorum of its membership only to discuss a legal memorandum prepared by, or at the direction of, the public body's attorney where that attorney was unavailable at the time of the discussion pursuant to RSA 91-A:2, I. Ettinger v. Town of Madison Planning Bd., 162 N.H. 785, 35 A.3d 562, 2011 N.H. LEXIS 178 (N.H. 2011).

Right-to-know law applies only to meetings of a quorum of members of a public body, not to conversations among individual members outside of such meetings. Webster v. Town of Candia, 146 N.H. 430, 778 A.2d 402, 2001 N.H. LEXIS 91 (N.H. 2001), amended, 2001 N.H. LEXIS 154 (N.H. Aug. 20, 2001).

2. Availability of records

Where newspaper sought to compel clerk of New Hampshire House of Representatives to turn over to it under Right-to-Know Law a certain tape recording of the proceedings of the house, for the purpose of duplicating and using it for a so-called voice stress analysis, case would not be viewed as a true Right-to-Know Law case because the legislative session in question was open to the public and press, an official journal was prepared of the proceedings, and written transcripts were available if the newspaper or anyone else wished to obtain them. Union Leader Corp. v. Chandler, 119 N.H. 442, 402 A.2d 914, 1979 N.H. LEXIS 336 (N.H. 1979).

Where newspaper sought to compel clerk of New Hampshire House of Representatives to turn over to it under Right-to-Know Law a certain tape recording of the proceedings of the house, for the purpose of duplicating and using it for a so-called voice stress analysis, house could properly decide, consistent with the right of reasonable public access, that its official tape should not be duplicated or subjected to a voice stress analysis. Union Leader Corp. v. Chandler, 119 N.H. 442, 402 A.2d 914, 1979 N.H. LEXIS 336 (N.H. 1979).

Verbatim stenographic records of testimony at zoning hearing are not required, nor are they commonly made, unless by the parties themselves. Dipietro v. Nashua, 109 N.H. 174, 246 A.2d 695, 1968 N.H. LEXIS 149 (N.H. 1968).

3. Public dissemination

This chapter does not mandate that a negotiating party may not be restricted from issuing press releases regarding the status of closed public sector collective bargaining sessions. Appeal of Exeter, 126 N.H. 685, 495 A.2d 1288, 1985 N.H. LEXIS 352 (N.H. 1985).

This section and RSA 365:8 empower the Public Utilities Commission to regulate all private recordings of its hearings and to deny a news media request to broadcast a recording. 1590 Broadcasting Corp. v. Public Utils. Comm'n, 113 N.H. 258, 306 A.2d 49, 1973 N.H. LEXIS 248 (N.H. 1973).

Radio broadcasting corporation had no unrestrained right to gather information through the taping of Public Utilities Commission public hearing on rate increase request, and public's right to be informed was satisfied where the commission, which validly denied radio broadcasting corporation's request that it be allowed to broadcast tapes the commission had allowed it to make for litigation purposes, allowed other reasonable methods of recording and reporting the hearing. 1590 Broadcasting Corp. v. Public Utils. Comm'n, 113 N.H. 258, 306 A.2d 49, 1973 N.H. LEXIS 248 (N.H. 1973).

4. Notice—Generally

Fact that a meeting of a county convention where salaries for elected officials were voted upon did not comply with the notice requirements of RSA 91-A:2, II or RSA 24:9-d did not render the vote a nullity. The plain language of RSA 23:7 did not reflect a legislative intent that defective notice automatically rendered a vote a nullity. Hull v. Grafton County, 160 N.H. 818, 10 A.3d 1193, 2010 N.H. LEXIS 114 (N.H. 2010).

Where principal's contract was improperly terminated because school board meeting was not preceded by proper notice, trial court would have power, if principal was interested in continuing his position, to order school board to hold a new and open meeting on the question whether the contract should be renewed. Stoneman v. Tamworth Sch. Dist., 114 N.H. 371, 320 A.2d 657, 1974 N.H. LEXIS 281 (N.H. 1974).

Fundamental purpose of requirements for notice and hearing is to advise all affected parties of their opportunity to be heard in public meeting and to be apprised of the relief sought. Carter v. Nashua, 113 N.H. 407, 308 A.2d 847, 1973 N.H. LEXIS 285 (N.H. 1973).

Lack of compliance with requirements that hearings be upon notice and open to the public would deprive a zoning board of adjustment of jurisdiction to grant a variance. Carter v. Nashua, 113 N.H. 407, 308 A.2d 847, 1973 N.H. LEXIS 285 (N.H. 1973).

Where counsel for applicant for zoning variance posted the notices required by this section, this ministerial act was properly permitted and complied with statutory requirements. Carter v. Nashua, 113 N.H. 407, 308 A.2d 847, 1973 N.H. LEXIS 285 (N.H. 1973).

5. —Personal notice

Where two probationary teachers employed pursuant to individual written contracts were not offered contracts for the upcoming school year after a regularly scheduled school board meeting, the provisions of this section governing meetings open to the public did not require personal notice to be given for the teachers' nominations; the school board had not agreed to provide such personal notice pursuant to a collective bargaining agreement and the teachers' association was the exclusive representative of the two teachers. Brown v. Bedford Sch. Bd., 122 N.H. 627, 448 A.2d 1375, 1982 N.H. LEXIS 414 (N.H. 1982).

School board which decided not to renew principal's contract would not successfully meet fact it had not given posted or published notice of the meeting with fact principal received notice prior to the meeting. Stoneman v. Tamworth Sch. Dist., 114 N.H. 371, 320 A.2d 657, 1974 N.H. LEXIS 281 (N.H. 1974).

6. —Subsequent meetings

Where notice was published in a newspaper of general circulation that town planning board would consider adoption of subdivision regulations on January 5, and at such time only one-half of the proposed regulations were discussed and the hearing was recessed until January 12, recess of hearing without posting of additional notice was not violative of any of defendant's rights under this chapter or under RSA 36:23. Nottingham v. Harvey, 120 N.H. 889, 424 A.2d 1125, 1980 N.H. LEXIS 428 (N.H. 1980).

Where notice of second meeting of zoning board of adjustment in the matter of a variance application was given 24 hours before the meeting instead of the 72-hour notice required by city ordinance, such failure was not sufficient to affect board's jurisdiction over the matter, which it acquired by its compliance with all notice requirements for the first meeting. Carter v. Nashua, 113 N.H. 407, 308 A.2d 847, 1973 N.H. LEXIS 285 (N.H. 1973).

7. Collective bargaining

This chapter does not mandate that public sector collective bargaining sessions be open to the public when one of the negotiating parties insists upon such a format. Appeal of Exeter, 126 N.H. 685, 495 A.2d 1288, 1985 N.H. LEXIS 352 (N.H. 1985).

Negotiation sessions between school board and teachers' representative were not within the ambit of this chapter, though any board approval of recommendations arrived at during the negotiations must be given at an open meeting in accordance with this chapter. Talbot v. Concord Union Sch. Dist., 114 N.H. 532, 323 A.2d 912, 1974 N.H. LEXIS 318 (N.H. 1974).

8. Public proceedings

Where a town planning board met in a private session not only to read a memorandum prepared at the direction of an attorney, but also to discuss and consider the memorandum without counsel present, the clear legislative mandate of the Right-to-Know Law

required that they should have done so in the open, as there were no applicable exceptions pursuant to RSA 91-A:2, I(b) and II. Ettinger v. Town of Madison Planning Bd., 162 N.H. 785, 35 A.3d 562, 2011 N.H. LEXIS 178 (N.H. 2011).

Although written communications from a town planning board's counsel could have been protected from disclosure under RSA 91-A:5, a meeting of the board still had to be held in the open pursuant to RSA 91-A:2; an exemption from disclosure was allowed under RSA 91-A:4 and 91-A:5 for confidential information. Ettinger v. Town of Madison Planning Bd., 162 N.H. 785, 35 A.3d 562, 2011 N.H. LEXIS 178 (N.H. 2011).

Although abutting property owners were refused access to a public proceeding of a town planning board when it went into a private session for a period of time, they were not entitled to attorney's fees under RSA 91-A:8, I, as the issue of statutory construction as to whether the board's actions were legally within the "consultation with legal counsel" exclusion of RSA 91-A:2, I(b) were a matter of first impression. Ettinger v. Town of Madison Planning Bd., 162 N.H. 785, 35 A.3d 562, 2011 N.H. LEXIS 178 (N.H. 2011).

New Hampshire Department of Fish and Game violated RSA 91-A:2, II by excluding a television station's cameras from a hunting license hearing on grounds that the commotion they would cause would deprive the license applicant of his right to a fair hearing. The Department failed to identify what constitutional interest was at stake; a hunting license had never been found to be a constitutionally protected right. WMUR Channel Nine v. N.H. Dep't of Fish & Game, 154 N.H. 46, 908 A.2d 146, 2006 N.H. LEXIS 113 (N.H. 2006).

Executive Director of the New Hampshire Department of Fish and Game violated RSA 91-A:2, II by excluding a television station's cameras from a hunting license hearing. Even if N.H. Code Admin. R. Ann. Fis. 203.01(b) could be read as authorizing the Director to take such action, a Department regulation could not override the clear directive of RSA 91-A:2, II. WMUR Channel Nine v. N.H. Dep't of Fish & Game, 154 N.H. 46, 908 A.2d 146, 2006 N.H. LEXIS 113 (N.H. 2006).

Though the Executive Director of the New Hampshire Department of Fish and Game violated RSA 91-A:2, II by excluding a television station's cameras from a hunting license hearing on grounds that the commotion they would cause would deprive the license applicant of his right to a fair hearing, the station was properly denied attorney's fees under RSA 91-A:8. The trial court properly found, given the state of the case law, that the Director neither knew nor should have known that his conduct violated RSA 91-A:2, II. WMUR Channel Nine v. N.H. Dep't of Fish & Game, 154 N.H. 46, 908 A.2d 146, 2006 N.H. LEXIS 113 (N.H. 2006).

Assuming arguendo that the due process protections applied to the passage of legislation, an inmate's due process rights were not violated by the enactment of RSA 651:2, II-e, as the session during which this occurred was open to the public, as required by RSA 91-A:1-a, VI(a) and RSA 91-A:2, II. Starr v. Governor, 154 N.H. 174, 910 A.2d 1247, 2006 N.H. LEXIS 140 (N.H. 2006).

9. Attorney-client privilege

Redacted portions of meeting minutes were protected by the attorney-client privilege of N.H. R. Evid. 502 and thus were exempt from disclosure under RSA 91-A:5, IV. Because no members of the public were actually present at the meetings, the fact that the meetings were technically open to the public under RSA 91-A:2 was of no import. Prof. Fire Fighters of N.H. v. N.H. Local Gov't Ctr., 163 N.H. 613, 44 A.3d 542, 2012 N.H. LEXIS 66 (N.H. 2012).

Cited:

Cited in Stoneman v. Tamworth Sch. Dist., 114 N.H. 371, 320 A.2d 657, 1974 N.H. LEXIS 281 (1974); Orford Teachers Ass'n v. Watson, 121 N.H. 118, 427 A.2d 21, 1981 N.H. LEXIS 255 (1981); Lambert v. Belknap Cty. Convention, 157 N.H. 375, 949 A.2d 709, 2008 N.H. LEXIS 75 (2008).

OPINIONS OF THE ATTORNEY GENERAL

Analysis

Construction
Cited:

v. Watson, 121 N.H. 118, 427 A.2d 21, 1981 N.H. LEXIS 255 (N.H. 1981).

8. Termination of employee

Governmental body may not move to go into executive session for the purpose of considering termination of a public employee unless it has previously put that employee on notice that such a motion would be made. Johnson v. Nash, 135 N.H. 534, 608 A.2d 200, 1992 N.H. LEXIS 73 (N.H. 1992).

9. Appointment to fill vacant office

The "hiring of a public employee" under RSA 91-A:3, II(b) does not include the appointment of an interim sheriff. Accordingly, when a sheriff's office became vacant during the sheriff's term of office, a county convention was required to fill the vacancy in the office of the sheriff in public session. Lambert v. Belknap Cty. Convention, 157 N.H. 375, 949 A.2d 709, 2008 N.H. LEXIS 75 (N.H. 2008).

Cited:

Cited in Appeal of Exeter, 126 N.H. 685, 495 A.2d 1288, 1985 N.H. LEXIS 352 (1985); Perras v. Clements, 127 N.H. 603, 503 A.2d 843, 1986 N.H. LEXIS 208 (1986).

OPINIONS OF THE ATTORNEY GENERAL

Cited:

Cited in 1986 Op. Att'y Gen. 220; 1986 Op. Att'y Gen. 231.

RESEARCH REFERENCES AND PRACTICE AIDS

Cross References.

Dismissal of town officer for breach of confidentiality, see RSA 42:1-a.

New Hampshire Bar Journal.

For article, "The New Practitioner's Guide to Representing Municipal Boards," see 48 N.H. B.J. 56 (Autumn 2007).

New Hampshire Practice.

13-18 N.H.P. Local Government Law §§ 675, 677.

91-A:4. Minutes and Records Available for Public Inspection.

I. Every citizen during the regular or business hours of all public bodies or agencies, and on the regular business premises of such public bodies or agencies, has the right to inspect all governmental records in the possession, custody, or control of such public bodies or agencies, including minutes of meetings of the public bodies, and to copy and make memoranda or abstracts of the records or minutes so inspected, except as otherwise prohibited by statute or RSA 91-A:5. In this section, "to copy" means the reproduction of original records by whatever method, including but not limited to photography, photostatic copy, printing, or electronic or tape recording.

I-a. Records of any payment made to an employee of any public body or agency listed in RSA 91-A:1-a, VI(a)–(d), or to the employee's agent or designee, upon the resignation, discharge, or retirement of the employee, paid in addition to regular salary and accrued vacation, sick, or other leave, shall immediately be made available without alteration for public inspection. All records of payments shall be available for public inspection notwithstanding that the matter may have been considered or acted upon in nonpublic session pursuant to RSA 91-A:3.

II. After the completion of a meeting of a public body, every citizen, during the regular or business hours of such public body, and on the regular business premises of such public body, has the right to inspect all notes, materials, tapes, or other sources used for compiling the minutes of such meetings, and to make memoranda or abstracts or to copy such notes, materials, tapes, or sources inspected, except as otherwise prohibited by statute or RSA 91-A:5.

III. Each public body or agency shall keep and maintain all governmental records in its custody at its regular office or place of business in an accessible place and, if there is no such office or place of business, the governmental records pertaining to such public body or agency shall be kept in an office of the political subdivision in which such public body or agency is located or, in the case of a state agency, in an office designated by the secretary of state.

III-a. Governmental records created or maintained in electronic form shall be kept and maintained for the same retention or archival periods as their paper counterparts. Governmental records in electronic form kept and maintained beyond the applicable retention or archival period shall remain accessible and available in accordance with RSA 91-A:4, III. Methods that may be used to keep and maintain governmental records in electronic form may include, but are not limited to, copying to microfilm or paper or to durable electronic media using standard or common file formats.

III-b. A governmental record in electronic form shall no longer be subject to disclosure pursuant to this section after it has been initially and legally deleted. For purposes of this paragraph, a record in electronic form shall be considered to have been deleted only if it is no longer readily accessible to the public body or agency itself. The mere transfer of an electronic record to a readily accessible "deleted items" folder or similar location on a computer shall not constitute deletion of the record.

IV. Each public body or agency shall, upon request for any governmental record reasonably described, make available for inspection and copying any such governmental record within its files when such records are immediately available for such release. If a public body or agency is unable to make a governmental record available for immediate inspection and copying, it shall, within 5 business days of request, make such record available, deny the request in writing with reasons, or furnish written acknowledgment of the receipt of the request and a statement of the time reasonably necessary to determine whether the request shall be granted or denied. If a computer, photocopying machine, or other device maintained for use by a public body or agency is used by the public body or agency to copy the governmental record requested, the person requesting the copy may be charged the actual cost of providing the copy, which cost may be collected by the public body or agency. No fee shall be charged for the inspection or delivery, without copying, of governmental records, whether in paper, electronic, or other form. Nothing in this section shall exempt any person from paying fees otherwise established by law for obtaining copies of governmental records or documents, but if such fee is established for the copy, no additional costs or fees shall be charged.

V. In the same manner as set forth in RSA 91-A:4, IV, any public body or agency which maintains governmental records in electronic format may, in lieu of providing original records, copy governmental records requested to electronic media using standard or common file formats in a manner that does not reveal information which is confidential under this chapter or any other law. If copying to electronic media is not reasonably practicable, or if the person or entity requesting access requests a different method, the public body or agency may provide a printout of governmental records requested, or may use any other means reasonably calculated to comply with the request in light of the purpose of this chapter as expressed in RSA 91-A:1. Access to work papers, personnel data, and other confidential information under RSA 91-A:5, IV shall not be provided.

VI. Every agreement to settle a lawsuit against a governmental unit, threatened lawsuit, or other claim, entered into by any political subdivision or its insurer, shall be kept on file at the municipal clerk's office and made available for public inspection for a period of no less than 10 years from the date of settlement.

VII. Nothing in this chapter shall be construed to require a public body or agency to compile, cross-reference, or assemble information into a form in which it is not already kept or reported by that body or agency.

HISTORY:
1967, 251:1. 1983, 279:2. 1986, 83:5, eff. Jan. 1, 1987. 1997, 90:2, eff. Aug. 2, 1997. 2001, 223:2, eff. Jan. 1, 2002. 2004, 246:2, eff. Aug. 14, 2004. 2008, 303:4, eff. July 1, 2008. 2009, 299:1, eff. September 29, 2009. 2016, 283:1, eff. June 21, 2016.

Amendment Notes
The 2016 amendments to this section by Ch. 283 added the second to the last sentence of paragraph IV.

—2009.
The 2009 amendment, in III-a, substituted "be kept and maintained" for "remain accessible" in the first sentence, added the second sentence, and substituted "keep and maintain governmental records in electronic form may" for "accomplish this requirement" in the third sentence.

—2008.
The 2008 amendment rewrote the section to the extent that a detailed comparison would be impracticable.

—2004.
Paragraph VI: Added.

—2001.
Paragraph I-a: Substituted "I(a)–(d)" for "I–IV" in the first sentence.

—1997.
Paragraph I-a: Added.

—1986.
Paragraphs III–IV: Added.

—1983.
Designated the existing provisions of the section as par. I, made minor stylistic changes in that paragraph, and added par. II.

NOTES TO DECISIONS

Analysis

1. Right to inspect generally
2. Temporarily unavailable records
3. Furnishing of copies
4. Minutes of executive sessions
5. Employment records
6. Real estate records
7. Public utilities
8. Destruction of tapes and notes used to prepare minutes
9. Agency budget materials
10. Records not in final form
11. Work Papers
12. Mootness
13. Adequacy of search
14. Timeliness
15. Vaughn index
16. Disclosure exemption
17. Electronic format
18. Annulled criminal records
19. Place of delivery.

1. Right to inspect generally
Trial court erred in considering whether the New Hampshire Department of Resources and Economic Development's (DRED's) conduct in withholding certain requested documents by an organization was reasonable or whether it committed a knowing violation when rejecting the organization's request for costs, which required the trial court's denial of costs to the organization to be vacated. Since the organization's request for costs remained viable only if DRED violated the Right-to-Know Law, the case was remanded to the trial court to consider costs and the lawfulness of the DRED's conduct in its delayed disclosure and retention of documents. ATV Watch v. N.H. Dep't of Res. & Econ. Dev., 155 N.H. 434, 923 A.2d 1061, 2007 N.H. LEXIS 72 (N.H. 2007).

Photographs which police took with the consent of people who were stopped by police but not arrested were public records, and the trial court's judgment ordering the City of Manchester to provide a civil liberties union with access to consensual photographs which police officers took over a five-year period was upheld. N.H. Civ. Liberties Union v. City of Manchester, 149 N.H. 437, 821 A.2d 1014, 2003 N.H. LEXIS 61 (N.H. 2003).

Right to inspect does not depend upon a need, or demonstration of a need, for the information. Mans v. Lebanon Sch. Bd., 112 N.H. 160, 290 A.2d 866, 1972 N.H. LEXIS 166 (N.H. 1972).

2. Temporarily unavailable records
Trial court properly concluded that official did not violate this section by failing to provide requested documents immediately on the basis that the official was "too busy," where documents were sent to citizen two days later. Brent v. Paquette, 132 N.H. 415, 567 A.2d 976, 1989 N.H. LEXIS 123 (N.H. 1989).

Where the only school official with the authority to respond to request for information was on vacation when the request was made, trial court properly concluded that computation of 5-day period within which official had to respond began on the day this official returned from vacation. Brent v. Paquette, 132 N.H. 415, 567 A.2d 976, 1989 N.H. LEXIS 123 (N.H. 1989).

Where town resident asked town building inspector for plans for proposed industrial park, the latter said the chairman of the planning board had them out for the day on official business, and town otherwise at all times provided resident with access to the plans, town did not deny resident access to the plans in violation of this section. Gallagher v. Windham, 121 N.H. 156, 427 A.2d 37, 1981 N.H. LEXIS 271 (N.H. 1981).

3. Furnishing of copies

This section does not contain language imposing an absolute duty on towns or agencies to provide copies of public records to citizens; it contemplates that the records be made available for inspection and reproduction. Gallagher v. Windham, 121 N.H. 156, 427 A.2d 37, 1981 N.H. LEXIS 271 (N.H. 1981).

Where record did not demonstrate that plaintiff offered to pay town for copies of town records were they provided to her by photocopying them on town's photocopier, and the parties' briefs were silent on the issue, finding below that town did not violate this section when town did not provide copies of the record to plaintiff was amply supported by the evidence. Gallagher v. Windham, 121 N.H. 156, 427 A.2d 37, 1981 N.H. LEXIS 271 (N.H. 1981).

4. Minutes of executive sessions

Construing the provisions of the right-to-know law for withholding minutes narrowly, supreme court concluded that there is no blanket exemption for minutes of executive sessions, and that they are public records covered by this section. Orford Teachers Ass'n v. Watson, 121 N.H. 118, 427 A.2d 21, 1981 N.H. LEXIS 255 (N.H. 1981).

5. Employment records

Where public employee labor relations board's orders were within its jurisdiction and were supported by ample evidence in the record, superior court properly ordered enforcement of board's order that school board produce specific salary information for school year so that public employee labor relations board could determine which teachers were entitled to back pay and amount owing to each one under master agreement, because this information was contained in records which any citizen had a right to examine. Rochester Sch. Bd. v. Public Employee Labor Relations Bd., 119 N.H. 45, 398 A.2d 823, 1979 N.H. LEXIS 240 (N.H. 1979).

Order that school district administrator supply educational association representing striking teacher with the names and addresses of substitute teachers hired during the strike was proper. Timberlane Regional Educ. Ass'n v. Crompton, 114 N.H. 315, 319 A.2d 632, 1974 N.H. LEXIS 267 (N.H. 1974).

Teachers' contracts with school board were public records under this section. Mans v. Lebanon Sch. Bd., 112 N.H. 160, 290 A.2d 866, 1972 N.H. LEXIS 166 (N.H. 1972).

6. Real estate records

Computer tape containing information contained on approximately 35,000 field record cards made out when city had all its real estate revaluated, each card containing, inter alia, details of land, buildings, owners, use, topography, improvements, area trends, construction, value and a sketch of the property, was a public record under this section, and was not exempt from disclosure under RSA 91-A:5; and disclosure to the public would not constitute an unconstitutional invasion of privacy. Menge v. Manchester, 113 N.H. 533, 311 A.2d 116, 1973 N.H. LEXIS 311 (N.H. 1973).

7. Public utilities

Intervenors opposing permit to company planning to build nuclear generating electrical units had right to examine all the evidence relied upon by the commission involved in making its final determination. Society for Protection of N.H. Forests v. Water Supply & Pollution Control Comm'n, 115 N.H. 192, 337 A.2d 788, 1975 N.H. LEXIS 257 (N.H. 1975).

8. Destruction of tapes and notes used to prepare minutes

School official's practice of routinely destroying tapes and notes used to prepare minutes of public meetings did not violate this section, where the tapes and notes were destroyed only after the minutes of the meetings were approved. Brent v. Paquette, 132 N.H. 415, 567 A.2d 976, 1989 N.H. LEXIS 123 (N.H. 1989).

9. Agency budget materials

State agency budget requests and income estimates are subject to public scrutiny on October 1, the statutory deadline for their submission to the commissioner of administrative services, unless they are exempt from the provisions of the Right-to-Know Law.

Chambers v. Gregg, 135 N.H. 478, 606 A.2d 811, 1992 N.H. LEXIS 62 (N.H. 1992).

10. Records not in final form

Trial court erred in failing to order disclosure of preliminary materials prepared for, but not expressly incorporated in, agency's final audit report, since Right-to-Know Law did not exempt public records from disclosure simply because they were not in their final form. Goode v. New Hampshire Office of the Legislative Budget Assistant, 145 N.H. 451, 767 A.2d 393, 2000 N.H. LEXIS 92 (N.H. 2000).

11. Work Papers

Even if certain interview materials from an audit by the New Hampshire Legislative Budget Assistant constituted work papers within the meaning of this section, a balancing test for exemption from disclosure applied, just as with other confidential materials, and the materials were not exempt from disclosure under that test, as the government's interest in nondisclosure did not outweigh the public's interest in disclosure, especially where there was no evidence that requiring disclosure of such materials would have caused future auditors to be less honest or complete in recording information. Goode v. N.H. Office of the Legislative Budget Assistant, 148 N.H. 551, 813 A.2d 381, 2002 N.H. LEXIS 168 (N.H. 2002).

Fact that records are "work papers" within the meaning of RSA 91-A:4, V does not render them categorically exempt from disclosure; rather, as with other asserted confidential information under RSA 91-A:5, IV, a court must balance the competing interests regarding disclosure and non-disclosure. Goode v. N.H. Office of the Legislative Budget Assistant, 148 N.H. 551, 813 A.2d 381, 2002 N.H. LEXIS 168 (N.H. 2002).

12. Mootness

Trial court erred by dismissing, as moot, the remainder of an organization's Right-to-Know Law petition requesting all terrain vehicle trail documentation from the New Hampshire Department of Resources and Economic Development as the trial court was required to determine if the state agency's conduct in withholding the documents was unlawful despite the ultimate release of the documents since the organization may have been entitled to a remedy despite the ultimate release of the documents. ATV Watch v. N.H. Dep't of Res. & Econ. Dev., 155 N.H. 434, 923 A.2d 1061, 2007 N.H. LEXIS 72 (N.H. 2007).

13. Adequacy of search

Department of Transportation had not conducted an inadequate search under RSA 91-A:4. The search had not been limited to e-mails or to documents after a certain date, as claimed by petitioners. ATV Watch v. N.H. Dep't of Transp., 161 N.H. 746, 20 A.3d 919, 2011 N.H. LEXIS 56 (N.H. 2011).

Trial court violated RSA 91-A:4, I, in requiring a town, through outside counsel, to create a revised invoice that would provide an association with the requested information. The Right-to-Know Law did not require public officials to retrieve and compile into a list random information gathered from numerous documents, if a list of this information did not already exist. Hampton Police Assoc. v. Town of Hampton, 162 N.H. 7, 20 A.3d 994, 2011 N.H. LEXIS 59 (N.H. 2011).

14. Timeliness

Department of Transportation did not respond untimely to petitioners' request for documents. Petitioners did not identify those documents that they claimed were immediately available or elaborate as to why they were "probably" available for immediate release. ATV Watch v. N.H. Dep't of Transp., 161 N.H. 746, 20 A.3d 919, 2011 N.H. LEXIS 56 (N.H. 2011).

15. Vaughn index

State's written responses to plaintiffs' Right-to-Know requests satisfied the requirements of RSA 91-A:4, IV. In response to each request, the State cited statutory provisions, case law, or applicable privileges; it was not required to provide a Vaughan index. N.H. Right to Life v. Dir., N.H. Charitable Trusts Unit, 169 N.H. 95, 143 A.3d 829, 2016 N.H. LEXIS 55 (N.H. 2016).

Initial agency denial of a Right-to-Know request need not contain the detail of a Vaughn index. Thus, the Department of Transportation was not required to provide petitioners with such an index when responding to their initial request. ATV Watch v. N.H. Dep't of Transp., 161 N.H. 746, 20 A.3d 919, 2011 N.H. LEXIS 56 (N.H. 2011).

16. Disclosure exemption

Trade secrets misappropriated under the Uniform Trade Secrets Act fall squarely within the exemption in the Right-to-Know Law for information the disclosure of which is "otherwise prohibited by statute." Accordingly, information designated by petitioner as confidential in its proposal for a government contract was exempt from disclosure under the Right-to-Know Law. CaremarkPCS Health, LLC v. N.H. Dep't of Admin. Servs., 167 N.H. 583, 116 A.3d 1054, 2015 N.H. LEXIS 35 (N.H. 2015).

Legislative history clearly supported the argument that RSA 91-A:4, I-a, which was ambiguous, was intended to apply only to incentive payments made to employees to bring about their retirement, not to regular retirement annuities. Accordingly, the statute did not mandate disclosure to a newspaper publisher of the names of the 500 state retirement system members who received the highest pension payments in 2009 as well as the amounts each received that year. Union Leader Corp. v. N.H. Retirement Sys., 162 N.H. 673, 34 A.3d 725, 2011 N.H. LEXIS 153 (N.H. 2011).

Newspaper was entitled under the Right-to-Know Law to the names of the 500 state retirement system members who received the highest pension payments in 2009 as well as the amounts each received that year. The members' privacy interest in their names and benefit amounts was outweighed by the public interest in knowing where and how tax dollars were spent; thus, disclosure would not constitute an invasion of privacy under RSA 91-A:5, IV. Union Leader Corp. v. N.H. Ret. Sys., 162 N.H. 673, 34 A.3d 725, 2011 N.H. LEXIS 153 (N.H. 2011).

Although written communications from a town planning board's counsel could have been protected from disclosure under RSA 91-A:5, a meeting of the board still had to be held in the open pursuant to RSA 91-A:2; an exemption from disclosure was allowed under RSA 91-A:4 and 91-A:5 for confidential information. Ettinger v. Town of Madison Planning Bd., 162 N.H. 785, 35 A.3d 562, 2011 N.H. LEXIS 178 (N.H. 2011).

17. Electronic format

Because a thumb drive falls into the catch-all category of some "other device . . . used by the public body or agency to copy the governmental record requested," an agency's policy of providing records on a thumb drive at the actual cost of the thumb drive complied with RSA 91-A:4. Taylor v. Sch. Admin. Unit #55, — N.H. —, — A.3d —, 2017 N.H. LEXIS 170 (N.H. Sept. 21, 2017).

Nothing in the text of RSA 91-A:4, IV or V imposes a requirement that the agency deliver records in the electronic format requested. So long as the manner of electronic production chosen does not diminish the ease of use of the information produced or the public's access to the information sought, the New Hampshire Supreme Court's decision in Green does not counsel in favor of one method over another. Taylor v. Sch. Admin. Unit #55, — N.H. —, — A.3d —, 2017 N.H. LEXIS 170 (N.H. Sept. 21, 2017).

Plaintiff was entitled to the requested documents in electronic format because there was no evidence in the record that the paper documents made available constituted original records, and there was no evidence that it was not reasonably practicable to copy the requested documents to electronic media using standard or common file formats. Green v. School Administrative Unit #55, 168 N.H. 796, 138 A.3d 1278, 2016 N.H. LEXIS 39 (N.H. 2016).

18. Annulled criminal records

Records maintained by arresting and prosecuting agencies pertaining to an annulled arrest and the related prosecution do not fall under the exemption in RSA 91-A:4, I, for records that are "otherwise prohibited by statute" from public inspection; thus, the trial court properly held that records related to defendant's annulled arrest and prosecution were not categorically exempt from public inspection. Grafton County Attorney's Office v. Canner, 169 N.H. 319, 147 A.3d 410, 2016 N.H. LEXIS 185 (N.H. 2016).

19 Place of delivery.

RSA 91-A:4, I, provides that the right of access for purposes of inspection and copying of governmental records exists during the regular or business hours and on the regular business premises of all public bodies or agencies. There is no provision of RSA ch. 91-A that requires a governmental body to "deliver" records to any location other than its regular place of business; thus, requiring that a requester appear in person at the agency offices in order to obtain copies of the records on a thumb drive was consistent with RSA 91-A:4, I. Taylor v. Sch. Admin. Unit #55, — N.H. —, — A.3d —, 2017 N.H. LEXIS 170 (N.H. Sept. 21, 2017).

Cited:

Cited in New Hampshire Challenge v. Commissioner, New Hampshire Dept. of Educ., 142 N.H. 246, 698 A.2d 1252, 1997 N.H. LEXIS 85 (1997).

OPINIONS OF THE ATTORNEY GENERAL

Cited:

Cited in 1986 Op. Att'y Gen. 198.

RESEARCH REFERENCES AND PRACTICE AIDS

Cross References.

Access to analysis and compilations of data prepared by cancer registry, see RSA 141-B:9.

Disposition of municipal records, see RSA 33-A.

State records management and archives, see RSA 5:25 et seq.

New Hampshire Code of Administrative Rules

Rules of the Commission for Human Rights, Hum 103.02, New Hampshire Code of Administrative Rules Annotated.

New Hampshire Bar Journal.

For article, "Electronic Records and Communications under New Hampshire's Right-to-Know Law," see 48 N.H. B.J. 38 (Autumn 2007).

For annual survey article by Pierce law students, "Murray v. N.H. State Police: The Right to Access Police Investigatory Files," see 48 N.H. B.J. 34 (Summer 2007).

For Article, "What Do You Have the Right to Know," see 43 N.H. B.J. 1 (March 2002).

New Hampshire Practice.

13-18 N.H.P. Local Government Law § 653.

13-19 N.H.P. Local Government Law § 711.

91-A:5. Exemptions.

The following governmental records are exempted from the provisions of this chapter:

I. Records of grand and petit juries.

I-a. The master jury list as defined in RSA 500-A:1, IV.

II. Records of parole and pardon boards.

III. Personal school records of pupils.

IV. Records pertaining to internal personnel practices; confidential, commercial, or financial information; test questions, scoring keys, and other examination data used to administer a licensing examination, examination for employment, or academic examinations; and personnel, medical, welfare, library user, videotape sale or rental, and other files whose disclosure would constitute invasion of privacy. Without otherwise compromising the confidentiality of the files, nothing in this paragraph shall prohibit a public body or agency from releasing information relative to health or safety from investigative files on a limited basis to persons whose health or safety may be affected.

V. Teacher certification records in the department of education, provided that the department shall make available teacher certification status information.

VI. Records pertaining to matters relating to the preparation for and the carrying out of all emergency functions, including training to carry out such functions, developed by local or state safety officials that are directly intended to thwart a deliberate act that is intended to result in widespread or severe damage to property or widespread injury or loss of life.

VII. Unique pupil identification information collected in accordance with RSA 193-E:5.

VIII. Any notes or other materials made for personal use that do not have an official purpose, including but not limited to, notes and materials made prior to, during, or after a governmental proceeding.

IX. Preliminary drafts, notes, and memoranda and other documents not in their final form and not disclosed, circulated, or available to a quorum or a majority of the members of a public body.

X. Video and audio recordings made by a law enforcement officer using a body-worn camera pursuant to RSA 105-D except where such recordings depict any of the following:

(a) Any restraint or use of force by a law enforcement officer; provided, however, that this exemption shall not include those portions of recordings which constitute an invasion of privacy of any person or which are otherwise exempt from disclosure.

(b) The discharge of a firearm, provided that this exemption shall not include those portions of recordings which constitute an invasion of privacy of any person or which are otherwise exempt from disclosure.

(c) An encounter that results in an arrest for a felony-level offense, provided, however, that this exemption shall not apply to recordings or portions thereof that constitute an invasion of privacy or which are otherwise exempt from disclosure.

HISTORY:
1967, 251:1. 1986, 83:6. 1989, 184:2. 1990, 134:1. 1993, 79:1, eff. June 22, 1993. 2002, 222:4, eff. Jan. 1, 2003. 2004, 147:5, eff. Aug. 1, 2004. 246:3, 4, eff. Aug. 14, 2004. 2008, 303:4, eff. July 1, 2008. 2013, 261:9, eff. July 1, 2013. 2016, 322:3, eff. January 1, 2017.

Amendment Notes
  The 2016 amendments to this section by Ch. 322 added paragraph X.

—2013.
  The 2013 amendment added I-a.

—2008.
  The 2008 amendment in the introductory language, added "governmental" preceding "records"; in IV, in the second sentence,

added "public" preceding "body or agency"; in V, deleted "both hard copies and computer files" following "certification records"; in VIII, added "but not limited to" and substituted "governmental" for "public"; and in IX, substituted "the members of a public body" for "those entities defined in RSA 91-A:1-a".

—2004.
  Chapter 147 added par. VII.
  Chapter 246 inserted "following" preceding "records" and deleted "of the following bodies" thereafter in the introductory paragraph, added "records of" in pars. I and II, and added pars. VIII and IX.

—2002.
  Paragraph VI: Added.

—1993.
  Paragraph V: Added.

—1990.
  Paragraph IV: Inserted "videotape sale or rental" following "library user" in the first sentence.

—1989.
  Paragraph IV: Inserted "library user" following "welfare" in the first sentence.

—1986.
  Paragraph IV: Rewritten to the extent that a detailed comparison would be impracticable.

Purpose of 1989 amendment.
  1989, 184:1, eff. July 21, 1989, provided:
  "The Access to Public Records and Meetings Law, RSA 91-A, or Right-to-Know Law, does not include a definition of what constitutes a public record. The New Hampshire supreme court has applied a balancing test to determine whether a record is public by weighing the benefits of disclosure to the public versus the benefits of nondisclosure. By weighing the benefits of allowing disclosure of library user records against the benefits of denial of disclosure, the general court has determined that the benefits of nondisclosure clearly prevail. This act, therefore, exempts library user records from RSA 91-A to ensure that the individual's right to privacy regarding the nature of the library materials used by the individual is not invaded. To protect the right to privacy of all New Hampshire citizens, both public and other than public library records are protected."

NOTES TO DECISIONS

Analysis

1. Construction
2. Factors considered
3. Grand juries
4. Salaries
5. Real estate records
6. Names and addresses of pupils
7. Agency budget materials
8. Internal personnel practices
9. Market analysis
10. Audit interview materials
11. Police records
12. Mootness
13. Candidates for office
14. Drafts
15. Materials made for personal use
16. Disclosure exemption
17. Law enforcement exemption
18. Work product
19. Privacy exemption
20. Personnel files

1. Construction
  The statute requires an analysis of both whether the information sought is "confidential, commercial, or financial information," and

whether disclosure would constitute an invasion of privacy. Union Leader Corp. v. New Hampshire Hous. Fin. Auth., 142 N.H. 540, 705 A.2d 725, 1997 N.H. LEXIS 132 (N.H. 1997).

In determining whether information is sufficiently "confidential" to justify nondisclosure, the emphasis should be placed on the potential harm that will result from disclosure, rather than simply promises of confidentiality, or whether the information has customarily been regarded as confidential. Union Leader Corp. v. New Hampshire Hous. Fin. Auth., 142 N.H. 540, 705 A.2d 725, 1997 N.H. LEXIS 132 (N.H. 1997).

When a public entity seeks to avoid disclosure of material under Right-to-Know Law, that entity bears a heavy burden to shift balance toward nondisclosure. Union Leader Corp. v. City of Nashua, 141 N.H. 473, 686 A.2d 310, 1996 N.H. LEXIS 127 (N.H. 1996).

2. Factors considered

When reviewing exemptions from Right-to-Know Law, court balances public interest in disclosure of requested information against government interest in nondisclosure, and in privacy exemption cases, the individual's privacy interest in nondisclosure. Union Leader Corp. v. City of Nashua, 141 N.H. 473, 686 A.2d 310, 1996 N.H. LEXIS 127 (N.H. 1996).

Although trial court's ex parte, in camera review of records whose release could cause invasion of privacy was plainly appropriate, court erred in considering plaintiff's motives in seeking disclosure of information. Union Leader Corp. v. City of Nashua, 141 N.H. 473, 686 A.2d 310, 1996 N.H. LEXIS 127 (N.H. 1996).

3. Grand juries

The legislature has protected the secrecy of grand jury proceedings by specifically exempting them from the purview of this otherwise expansive statute. State v. Purrington, 122 N.H. 458, 446 A.2d 451, 1982 N.H. LEXIS 377 (N.H. 1982).

4. Salaries

In determining whether teachers' salaries are exempted from the provisions of this chapter as being financial or private information, the benefits of disclosure to the public are to be balanced against the benefits of non-disclosure to the school administration and teachers. Mans v. Lebanon Sch. Bd., 112 N.H. 160, 290 A.2d 866, 1972 N.H. LEXIS 166 (N.H. 1972).

Teachers' salaries are not exempt from inspection. Mans v. Lebanon Sch. Bd., 112 N.H. 160, 290 A.2d 866, 1972 N.H. LEXIS 166 (N.H. 1972).

5. Real estate records

A property owner was not entitled to copies of appraisal reports prepared in connection with condemnation proceedings under the provisions of this chapter since disclosure of information regarding the range of offers of compensation available to the state would put the property owner in an unfair bargaining position. Perras v. Clements, 127 N.H. 603, 503 A.2d 843, 1986 N.H. LEXIS 208 (N.H. 1986).

Computer tape containing information contained on approximately 35,000 field record cards made out when city had all its real estate revaluated, each card containing, inter alia, details of land, buildings, owners, use, topography, improvements, area trends, construction, value and a sketch of the property, was a public record under RSA 91-A:4, and was not exempt from disclosure under this section; and disclosure to the public would not constitute an unconstitutional invasion of privacy. Menge v. Manchester, 113 N.H. 533, 311 A.2d 116, 1973 N.H. LEXIS 311 (N.H. 1973).

6. Names and addresses of pupils

Names and addresses of children of a public school district are part of the personal school records of the pupils and therefore exempt from public inspection under paragraph III of this section. Brent v. Paquette, 132 N.H. 415, 567 A.2d 976, 1989 N.H. LEXIS 123 (N.H. 1989).

Providing access to records pertaining to names and addresses of public school students would constitute an invasion of the students' and their parents' privacy under paragraph IV of this section. Brent v. Paquette, 132 N.H. 415, 567 A.2d 976, 1989 N.H. LEXIS 123 (N.H. 1989).

7. Agency budget materials

State agency budget requests and income estimates are subject to public scrutiny on October 1, the statutory deadline for their submission to the commissioner of administrative services, unless they are exempt from the provisions of the Right-to-Know Law. Chambers v. Gregg, 135 N.H. 478, 606 A.2d 811, 1992 N.H. LEXIS 62 (N.H. 1992).

To determine whether state agency budget requests and income estimates are exempt from the Right-to-Know Law as confidential, the benefits of disclosure to the public must be weighed against the benefits of nondisclosure to the government. Chambers v. Gregg, 135 N.H. 478, 606 A.2d 811, 1992 N.H. LEXIS 62 (N.H. 1992).

8. Internal personnel practices

Completed rubric forms used to evaluate applicants for the position of school superintendent pertained to "internal personnel practices" and thus were exempt from disclosure under the Right-to-Know Law, as the completed forms related to hiring, a personnel practice, and were gathered through a process that was internal to the search committee and conducted on behalf of the superintendent's employer. As the forms were categorically exempt, the court did not need to perform a balancing test. Clay v. City of Dover, 169 N.H. 681, 156 A.3d 156, 2017 N.H. LEXIS 15 (N.H. 2017).

Because defendant New Hampshire Attorney General was not the employer of a county attorney in that their relationship did not have the attributes of an employer-employee relationship such as to ability to set a salary and to hire and fire, and because defendant's supervisory authority over criminal law enforcement by the county attorney was not sufficient to warrant treating defendant as the employer, the trial court erred in applying the "internal personnel practices" exemption from the Right-to-Know Law to records of defendant's investigation into the county attorney's alleged wrongdoing. Reid v. N.H. AG, 169 N.H. 509, 152 A.3d 860, 2016 N.H. LEXIS 238 (N.H. 2016).

New Hampshire Supreme Court construes "internal personnel practices" to mean practices that exist or are situated within the limits of employment. Accordingly, while the court follows Fenniman and Hounsell in treating an investigation into employee misconduct as a personnel practice, the investigation must take place within the limits of an employment relationship; in other words, the investigation must be conducted by, or on behalf of, the employer of the investigation's target. Reid v. N.H. AG, 169 N.H. 509, 152 A.3d 860, 2016 N.H. LEXIS 238 (N.H. 2016).

Trial court erred in exempting from disclosure under RSA 91-A:5, IV, the job titles of any persons who monitored a city's surveillance equipment. The titles were not an "internal personnel practice," as they were not related to internal personnel discipline or akin to such matters as hiring and firing, work rules, and discipline. Montenegro v. City of Dover, 162 N.H. 641, 34 A.3d 717, 2011 N.H. LEXIS 150 (N.H. 2011).

Trial court properly held that an investigatory report was exempt from disclosure under RSA 91-A:5, IV; the report, which resulted from allegations that one water precinct employee was harassing another, could have resulted in disciplinary action and was thus a record pertaining to internal personnel practices. Furthermore, there was no merit to petitioners' argument that the exemption applied only to internal police investigations, and the precinct's release of another report did not create an estoppel because that report related to precinct mismanagement, not internal personnel practices. Hounsell v. North Conway Water Precinct, 154 N.H. 1, 903 A.2d 987, 2006 N.H. LEXIS 108 (N.H. 2006), limited, Reid v. N.H. AG, 169 N.H. 509, 152 A.3d 860, 2016 N.H. LEXIS 238 (N.H. 2016).

Certain investigatory documents under the control of the defendants, a police department and the department's chief, were exempt from disclosure as records pertaining to internal personnel practices; the documents in question were compiled during an internal investigation of a department lieutenant accused of making harassing phone calls. Union Leader Corp. v. Fenniman, 136 N.H. 624, 620 A.2d 1039, 1993 N.H. LEXIS 4 (N.H. 1993), limited, Reid v. N.H. AG, 169 N.H. 509, 152 A.3d 860, 2016 N.H. LEXIS 238 (N.H. 2016).

9. Market analysis

A market analysis of potential condominium sales at a certain location was not exempt as commercial information since the negative competitive impact of disclosing market information regarding potential condominium sales that was gathered in 1987 was blunted by time, and did not, on balance, outweigh the public interest in understanding the market conditions that gave rise to the housing finance authority's role in the project. Union Leader Corp. v. New Hampshire Hous. Fin. Auth., 142 N.H. 540, 705 A.2d 725, 1997 N.H. LEXIS 132 (N.H. 1997).

10. Audit interview materials

Even if certain interview materials from an audit by the New Hampshire Legislative Budget Assistant constituted confidential information under RSA 91-A:5, IV, the trial court erred in determining that the materials were exempt from disclosure, as the government's interest in nondisclosure did not outweigh the public's interest in disclosure, especially where there was no evidence that requiring disclosure of such materials would have caused future auditors to be less honest or complete in recording information. Goode v. N.H. Office of the Legislative Budget Assistant, 148 N.H. 551, 813 A.2d 381, 2002 N.H. LEXIS 168 (N.H. 2002).

11. Police records

Law enforcement representatives did not meet their burden of justifying their withholding of requested documents that the father sought regarding the disappearance of the father's daughter following reports that the daughter had been involved in a traffic accident; since police investigative reports were not mentioned in the state law concerning the disclosure of government records, the state supreme court determined that the six-part test under the corresponding federal law applied and required the law enforcement representatives on remand of the case to the trial court to show how disclosure of the requested records could interfere with an ongoing investigation or law enforcement proceeding. Murray v. N.H. Div. of State Police, 154 N.H. 579, 913 A.2d 737, 2006 N.H. LEXIS 201 (N.H. 2006).

Photographs which police took with the consent of people who were stopped by police but not arrested were public records, and the trial court's judgment ordering the City of Manchester to provide a civil liberties union with access to consensual photographs which police officers took over a five-year period was upheld. N.H. Civ. Liberties Union v. City of Manchester, 149 N.H. 437, 821 A.2d 1014, 2003 N.H. LEXIS 61 (N.H. 2003).

12. Mootness

Trial court erred by dismissing, as moot, the remainder of an organization's Right-to-Know Law petition requesting all terrain vehicle trail documentation from the New Hampshire Department of Resources and Economic Development as the trial court was required to determine if the state agency's conduct in withholding the documents was unlawful despite the ultimate release of the documents since the organization may have been entitled to a remedy despite the ultimate release of the documents. ATV Watch v. N.H. Dep't of Res. & Econ. Dev., 155 N.H. 434, 923 A.2d 1061, 2007 N.H. LEXIS 72 (N.H. 2007).

13. Candidates for office

It was error to deny petitioners access to documents relating to the application of candidates for a vacant sheriff's office on the ground that disclosure would constitute invasion of privacy under RSA 91-A:5, IV. A candidate voluntarily seeking to fill an elected public office had a diminished privacy expectation in personal information relevant to that office, which was significantly outweighed by the public's interest in disclosure. Lambert v. Belknap Cty. Convention, 157 N.H. 375, 949 A.2d 709, 2008 N.H. LEXIS 75 (N.H. 2008).

14. Drafts

Department of Transpiration did not violate RSA 91-A:5, IX, by withholding certain documents as "drafts" because the documents were too far along in development, were circulated to or created by an entity outside DOT, or contained facts. ATV Watch v. N.H. Dep't of Transp., 161 N.H. 746, 20 A.3d 919, 2011 N.H. LEXIS 56 (N.H. 2011).

"Preliminary draft" exemption in right-to-know or freedom of information acts was designed to protect pre-decisional, deliberative communications that are part of an agency's decision-making process. ATV Watch v. N.H. Dep't of Transp., 161 N.H. 746, 20 A.3d 919, 2011 N.H. LEXIS 56 (N.H. 2011).

There is no conflict between N.H. Const. pt. I, art. 8 and a construction of RSA ch. 91-A that exempts pre-decisional agency documents. The object of preliminary draft exemptions is to strike a balance between the public's right to know and the government's need to function effectively. ATV Watch v. N.H. Dep't of Transp., 161 N.H. 746, 20 A.3d 919, 2011 N.H. LEXIS 56 (N.H. 2011).

Having concluded that RSA 91-A:5, IX is intended to protect pre-decisional agency communications, the New Hampshire Supreme Court rejects a construction of "preliminary" as denoting an early stage in the drafting process. The distinction between preliminary and final documents does not consist of the extent to which the person or persons from whom they originate expect to alter them. ATV Watch v. N.H. Dep't of Transp., 161 N.H. 746, 20 A.3d 919, 2011 N.H. LEXIS 56 (N.H. 2011).

New Hampshire Supreme Court rejects the proposition that under the Right-to Know Law, when a document contains facts, rather than contemporaneous opinions or suggestions not based on fact, it is public, regardless of its stage in policy development as inconsistent with the premise that the focus of the exemption is on the pre-decisional posture of the document. ATV Watch v. N.H. Dep't of Transp., 161 N.H. 746, 20 A.3d 919, 2011 N.H. LEXIS 56 (N.H. 2011).

Nothing in the plain language of RSA 91-A:5, IX, specifically invalidates the exemption when a document is circulated outside the agency. Rather, the statute exempts documents not in their final form and not disclosed, circulated, or available to a quorum or a majority of the members of a public body. ATV Watch v. N.H. Dep't of Transp., 161 N.H. 746, 20 A.3d 919, 2011 N.H. LEXIS 56 (N.H. 2011).

Last part of RSA 91-A:5, IX, indicates that the exemption was intended to distinguish between pre-decisional documents, on the one hand, and those that are available for policy-making consideration or have been already acted upon, on the other. Describing documents as "available to a quorum or a majority of the members of a public body" delineates a point at which documents become subject to agency deliberation and action; taking that as the point at which the legislature intended to make agency documents subject to disclosure, the New Hampshire Supreme Court reads the terms "disclosed" and "circulated" as also being modified by "to a quorum or a majority of the members of a public body." ATV Watch v. N.H. Dep't of Transp., 161 N.H. 746, 20 A.3d 919, 2011 N.H. LEXIS 56 (N.H. 2011).

The New Hampshire Supreme Court rejects the assumption that disclosure to another agency invalidates the exemption under RSA 91-A:5, IX. ATV Watch v. N.H. Dep't of Transp., 161 N.H. 746, 20 A.3d 919, 2011 N.H. LEXIS 56 (N.H. 2011).

Town failed to prove that narrative descriptions in billing statements of the work its outside counsel performed were privileged under N.H. R. Evid. 502 and thus exempt from disclosure under RSA 91-A:5, IV. The town had urged the trial court to find that all of the narratives were privileged, and the court declined to adopt such a per se rule. Hampton Police Assoc. v. Town of Hampton, 162 N.H. 7, 20 A.3d 994, 2011 N.H. LEXIS 59 (N.H. 2011).

15. Materials made for personal use

Nothing in the language of RSA 91-A:5, VIII, supports the premise that when a "note" is circulated within or without the agency it is by definition agency business. Accordingly, material containing handwritten personal notes was exempt despite being circulated. ATV Watch v. N.H. Dep't of Transp., 161 N.H. 746, 20 A.3d 919, 2011 N.H. LEXIS 56 (N.H. 2011).

RSA 91-A:5, VIII, clearly contemplates that notes made "on government time" may be exempt, as it applies to notes made "during . . . a governmental proceeding"; in addition, having "an official purpose" under the statute is narrower than "bearing on the agency's business." Accordingly, the fact that notes were made on government time did not mean that they were not exempt from disclosure. ATV Watch v. N.H. Dep't of Transp., 161 N.H. 746, 20 A.3d 919, 2011 N.H. LEXIS 56 (N.H. 2011).

16. Disclosure exemption

Newspaper was entitled under the Right-to-Know Law to the names of the 500 state retirement system members who received the highest pension payments in 2009 as well as the amounts each received that year. The members' privacy interest in their names and benefit amounts was outweighed by the public interest in knowing where and how tax dollars were spent; thus, disclosure would not constitute an invasion of privacy under RSA 91-A:5, IV. Union Leader Corp. v. N.H. Ret. Sys., 162 N.H. 673, 34 A.3d 725, 2011 N.H. LEXIS 153 (2011).

Although written communications from a town planning board's counsel could have been protected from disclosure under RSA 91-A:5, a meeting of the board still had to be held in the open pursuant to RSA 91-A:2; an exemption from disclosure was allowed under RSA 91-A:4 and 91-A:5 for confidential information. Ettinger v. Town of Madison Planning Bd., 162 N.H. 785, 35 A.3d 562, 2011 N.H. LEXIS 178 (N.H. 2011).

17. Law enforcement exemption

State Fire Marshal's Office clearly has some law enforcement functions and thus is a mixed-function agency for purposes of the Murray exemption to the Right-to-Know Law. Accordingly, as the head of a mixed-function agency, the Fire Marshal can satisfy the threshold requirement for the exemption by showing that the pertinent records were compiled pursuant to the agency's law enforcement functions, as opposed to administrative functions. 38 Endicott St. N., LLC v. State Fire Marshal, 163 N.H. 656, 44 A.3d 571, 2012 N.H. LEXIS 69 (N.H. 2012).

Fire investigation records held by the Fire Marshal's Office were exempt from the Right-to-Know Law. The records were compiled during an investigation into potential criminal wrongdoing and were thus compiled for law enforcement purposes, and the Fire Marshal showed through an affidavit that disclosure would interfere with enforcement proceedings in that the investigation was ongoing and was expected to lead to criminal charges. 38 Endicott St. N., LLC v. State Fire Marshal, 163 N.H. 656, 44 A.3d 571, 2012 N.H. LEXIS 69 (N.H. 2012).

18. Work product

Declaration by an official of a group that provided abortions was exempt from the Right-to-Know Law as attorney work product pursuant to RSA 91-A:5, IV, as it was prepared at the direction of attorneys for use in buffer-zone litigation. Furthermore, the entire declaration was exempt even though it arguably contained some purely factual information; the Right-to-Know Law did not mandate disclosure even if the declaration constituted only "ordinary" work product; and there was no waiver of the doctrine as the declaration was prepared at the request of the attorney general, who was one of the defendants in the buffer litigation. N.H. Right to Life v. Dir., N.H. Charitable Trusts Unit, 169 N.H. 95, 143 A.3d 829, 2016 N.H. LEXIS 55 (N.H. 2016).

E-mail messages were exempt from the Right-to-Know Law as attorney work product when they were created for abortion clinic buzzer zone litigation either by attorneys at the Attorney General's Office or at their direction, and the subject of the messages was the preparation of pleadings for that litigation. N.H. Right to Life v. Dir., N.H. Charitable Trusts Unit, 169 N.H. 95, 143 A.3d 829, 2016 N.H. LEXIS 55 (N.H. 2016).

E-mail messages exchanged between the state attorney general (AG) and offices of attorneys general in other states were exempt from the Right-to-Know Law as attorney work product. They were created in connection with a case then pending before the United States Supreme Court and included draft amicus briefs and concerned the process by which the AG decided whether to join or file amicus briefs in that case; the fact that New Hampshire did not ultimately file such briefs did not mean that the work product protection was waived. N.H. Right to Life v. Dir., N.H. Charitable Trusts Unit, 169 N.H. 95, 143 A.3d 829, 2016 N.H. LEXIS 55 (N.H. 2016).

19. Privacy exemption

Although non-protesting individuals shown in DVD footage of a public sidewalk by an abortion clinic, or whose vehicles were shown, had at least some privacy interest under the Right-to-Know Law in controlling the dissemination of the footage, remand for additional fact-finding was necessary to determine whether the DVDs implicated heightened privacy concerns. N.H. Right to Life v. Dir., N.H. Charitable Trusts Unit, 169 N.H. 95, 143 A.3d 829, 2016 N.H. LEXIS 55 (N.H. 2016).

Correspondence consisting of an undated envelope and pieces of mostly blank paper demonstrating that the envelope contained certain DVDs was improperly withheld under the Right-to-Know Law on privacy grounds, as the State did not argue that the correspondence implicated any privacy concerns. N.H. Right to Life v. Dir., N.H. Charitable Trusts Unit, 169 N.H. 95, 143 A.3d 829, 2016 N.H. LEXIS 55 (N.H. 2016).

State properly withheld on privacy grounds under RSA 91-A:5, IV the names of individuals listed in an abortion provider's applications for renewed licenses to distribute medication without a pharmacist on site, given the evidence of protests in New Hampshire against abortion clinics and the history nationally of harassment and violence associated with the provision of abortion services and the attenuated public interest in the names of those individuals. Even if the names of the individuals at issue had been previously made available to the public, prior revelations of exempt information did not destroy an individual's privacy interest. N.H. Right to Life v. Dir., N.H. Charitable Trusts Unit, 169 N.H. 95, 143 A.3d 829, 2016 N.H. LEXIS 55 (N.H. 2016).

State properly redacted monetary amounts contained in financial documents of a women's health center under the Right-to-Know Law, as plaintiffs failed to sufficiently develop their argument that the center had little or no privacy interest in the documents and there was a relatively weak public interest in disclosure in that the documents did not demonstrate how state grant money was spent. N.H. Right to Life v. Dir., N.H. Charitable Trusts Unit, 169 N.H. 95, 143 A.3d 829, 2016 N.H. LEXIS 55 (N.H. 2016).

State properly redacted names from documents from a women's health center, as the individuals had a cognizable privacy interest in controlling the dissemination of their names and their connection to the center and the only public interest, enabling the public to scrutinize whether the individuals had contributed to political campaigns, was derivative. N.H. Right to Life v. Dir., N.H. Charitable Trusts Unit, 169 N.H. 95, 143 A.3d 829, 2016 N.H. LEXIS 55 (N.H. 2016).

20. Personnel files

Determination of whether material is subject to the exemption for personnel files whose disclosure would constitute invasion of privacy requires a two-part analysis of: (1) whether the material can be considered a "personnel file" or part of a "personnel file"; and (2) whether disclosure of the material would constitute an invasion of privacy. Accordingly, in analyzing the "personnel files" exemption, the trial court must first determine whether any of the disputed material is, or is contained in, a personnel file. If not, the "personnel files" exemption does not apply. Reid v. N.H. AG, 169 N.H. 509, 152 A.3d 860, 2016 N.H. LEXIS 238 (N.H. 2016).

Cited:

Cited in Hampton Nat'l Bank v. State, 114 N.H. 38, 314 A.2d 668, 1974 N.H. LEXIS 203 (1974); Orford Teachers Ass'n v. Watson, 121 N.H. 118, 427 A.2d 21, 1981 N.H. LEXIS 255 (1981); Gallagher v. Windham, 121 N.H. 156, 427 A.2d 37, 1981 N.H. LEXIS 271 (1981); Hansen v. Lamontagne, 808 F. Supp. 89, 1992 U.S. Dist. LEXIS 19301 (D.N.H. 1992); Pivero v. Largy, 143 N.H. 187, 722 A.2d 461, 1998 N.H. LEXIS 91 (1998); Goode v. New Hampshire Office of the Legislative Budget Assistant, 145 N.H. 451, 767 A.2d 393, 2000 N.H. LEXIS 92 (2000).

RESEARCH REFERENCES AND PRACTICE AIDS

Cross References.

Access to information relating to location of archeological sites, see RSA 227-C:11.

Confidentiality and disclosure of library user records, see RSA 201-D:11.

Confidentiality of information compiled for statewide and enhanced 911 system, see RSA 106-H:14.

Confidentiality of videotape rental and sales records, see RSA 351-A:1.

Dismissal of town officer for breach of confidentiality, see RSA 42:1-a.

New Hampshire Code of Administrative Rules

Rules of the Commission for Human Rights, Hum 102.01, 102.02 and 219.01, New Hampshire Code of Administrative Rules Annotated.

New Hampshire Bar Journal.

For article, "Electronic Records and Communications under New Hampshire's Right-to-Know Law," see 48 N.H. B.J. 38 (Autumn 2007).

For annual survey article by Pierce law students, "Murray v. N.H. State Police: The Right to Access Police Investigatory Files," see 48 N.H. B.J. 34 (Summer 2007).

For Article, "What Do You Have the Right to Know," see 43 N.H. B.J. 1 (March 2002).

New Hampshire Practice.

13-17 N.H.P. Local Government Law § 619.

13-18 N.H.P. Local Government Law §§ 653, 682.

13-19 N.H.P. Local Government Law §§ 711, 714, 717.

91-A:5-a. Limited Purpose Release.

Records from non-public sessions under RSA 91-A:3, II(i) or that are exempt under RSA 91-A:5, VI may be released to local or state safety officials. Records released under this section shall be marked "limited purpose release" and shall not be redisclosed by the recipient.

HISTORY:

2002, 222:5, eff. Jan. 1, 2003.

91-A:6. Employment Security.

This chapter shall apply to RSA 282-A, relative to employment security; however, in addition to the exemptions under RSA 91-A:5, the provisions of RSA 282-A:117–123 shall also apply; this provision shall be administered and construed in the spirit of that section, and the exemptions from the provisions of this chapter shall include anything exempt from public inspection under RSA 282-A:117–123 together with all records and data developed from RSA 282-A:117–123.

HISTORY:

1967, 251:1. 1981, 576:5, eff. July 1, 1981.

Revision note.

Pursuant to 1981, 408:9, substituted " RSA 282-A" for " RSA 282" and " RSA 282-A:117– 123" for " RSA 282:9(M)".

Substituted a semicolon for a comma following "shall also apply" to correct a grammatical error.

Amendment Notes

—1981.

Rewritten to the extent that a detailed comparison would be impracticable.

OPINIONS OF THE ATTORNEY GENERAL

Cited:

Cited in 1986 Op. Att'y Gen. 220.

91-A:7. Violation.

Any person aggrieved by a violation of this chapter may petition the superior court for injunctive relief. In order to satisfy the purposes of this chapter, the courts shall give proceedings under this chapter high priority on the court calendar. Such a petitioner may appear with or without counsel. The petition shall be deemed sufficient if it states facts constituting a violation of this chapter, and may be filed by the petitioner or his or her counsel with the clerk of court or any justice thereof. Thereupon the clerk of court or any justice shall order service by copy of the petition on the person or persons charged. When any justice shall find that time probably is of the essence, he or she may order notice by any reasonable means, and he or she shall have authority to issue an order ex parte when he or she shall reasonably deem such an order necessary to insure compliance with the provisions of this chapter.

HISTORY:

1967, 251:1. 1977, 540:5, eff. Sept. 13, 1977. 2008, 303:5, eff. July 1, 2008.

Amendment Notes

—2008.

The 2008 amendment in the second sentence added "In order to satisfy the purposes of this chapter" and "high" and made stylistic changes throughout.

—1977.

Added the third through sixth sentences.

NOTES TO DECISIONS

Review

In order to be heard in supreme court, issue of violation of this chapter must be promptly and properly raised below, especially where it does not appear that the alleged violation was obvious, intentional or prejudicial. Hardiman v. Dover, 111 N.H. 377, 284 A.2d 905, 1971 N.H. LEXIS 206 (N.H. 1971).

Cited:

Cited in Perras v. Clements, 127 N.H. 603, 503 A.2d 843, 1986 N.H. LEXIS 208 (1986).

RESEARCH REFERENCES AND PRACTICE AIDS

New Hampshire Bar Journal.

For annual survey article by Pierce law students, "Murray v. N.H. State Police: The Right to Access Police Investigatory Files," see 48 N.H. B.J. 34 (Summer 2007).

91-A:8. Remedies.

I. If any public body or public agency or officer, employee, or other official thereof, violates any provisions of this chapter, such public body or public agency shall be liable for reasonable attorney's fees and costs incurred in a lawsuit under this chapter, provided that the court finds that such lawsuit was necessary in order to enforce compliance with the provisions of this chapter or to address a purposeful violation of this chapter. Fees shall not be awarded unless the court finds that the public body, public agency, or person knew or should have known that the conduct engaged in was in violation of this chapter or if the parties, by agreement, provide that no such fees shall be paid.

II. The court may award attorney's fees to a public body or public agency or employee or member thereof, for having to defend against a lawsuit under the provisions of this chapter, when the court finds that the lawsuit is in bad faith, frivolous, unjust, vexatious, wanton, or oppressive.

III. The court may invalidate an action of a public body or public agency taken at a meeting held in violation of the provisions of this chapter, if the circumstances justify such invalidation.

IV. If the court finds that an officer, employee, or other official of a public body or public agency has violated any provision of this chapter in bad faith, the court shall impose against such person a civil penalty of not less than $250 and not more than $2,000. Upon such finding, such person or persons may also be required to reimburse the public body or public agency for any attorney's fees or costs it paid pursuant to paragraph I. If the person is an officer, employee, or official of the state or of an agency or body of the state, the penalty shall be deposited in the general fund. If the person is an officer, employee, or official of a political subdivision of the state or of an agency or body of a political subdivision of the state, the penalty shall be payable to the political subdivision.

V. The court may also enjoin future violations of this chapter, and may require any officer, employee, or other official of a public body or public agency found to have violated the provisions of this chapter to undergo appropriate remedial training, at such person or person's expense.

HISTORY:
1973, 113:1. 1977, 540:6. 1986, 83:7, eff. Jan. 1, 1987. 2001, 289:3, eff. July 17, 2001. 2008, 303:6, eff. July 1, 2008. 2012, 206:1, eff. January 1, 2013.

Amendment Notes

—2012.
The 2012 amendment rewrote the section to the extent that a detailed comparison would be impracticable.

—2008.
The 2008 amendment in I, added "public" in several places and substituted "governmental" for "public" throughout the paragraph; and in I-a, substituted "public body or public agency" for "board, agency" and made a stylistic change.

—2001.
Paragraph I-a: Added.

—1986.
Designated the existing provisions of the section as par. I, rewrote that paragraph, and added pars. II and III.

—1977.
Rewritten to the extent that a detailed comparison would be impracticable.

NOTES TO DECISIONS

Analysis

1. Attorney's fees—Purpose
2. —Liability
3. —Review
4. Injunctive relief
5. Costs
6. Invalidation of action

1. Attorney's fees—Purpose
The word "shall" in the statute acts as a mandate if the necessary findings to support an award of attorney's fees are made. New Hampshire Challenge v. Commissioner, New Hampshire Dept. of Educ., 142 N.H. 246, 698 A.2d 1252, 1997 N.H. LEXIS 85 (N.H. 1997).

Provision for award of attorney's fees is critical to securing rights guaranteed by this section; attorney fee provision was enacted so that public's right-to-know law would not depend upon individual's ability to finance litigation. Bradbury v. Shaw, 116 N.H. 388, 360 A.2d 123, 1976 N.H. LEXIS 361 (N.H. 1976).

2. —Liability
Trial court did not err by denying plaintiffs attorney's fees when it found that the lawsuit was not necessary to enforce one agency's compliance with the law, when the State sufficiently justified its exemptions and withholdings with regard to certain documents, and when the trial court found that certain redactions and withholdings were not so unreasonable under current New Hampshire case law that the State knew or should have known that disclosure was required. N.H. Right to Life v. Dir., N.H. Charitable Trusts Unit, 169 N.H. 95, 143 A.3d 829, 2016 N.H. LEXIS 55 (N.H. 2016).

Because a petitioner's proceedings under the Right-to-Know Law were not necessary to make the information available, the trial court properly denied attorney's fees and costs. 38 Endicott St. N., LLC v. State Fire Marshal, 163 N.H. 656, 44 A.3d 571, 2012 N.H. LEXIS 69 (N.H. 2012).

Petitioners were properly denied attorney fees under RSA 91-A:8, I, as the documents they did receive were released before they retained an attorney. ATV Watch v. N.H. Dep't of Transp., 161 N.H. 746, 20 A.3d 919, 2011 N.H. LEXIS 56 (N.H. 2011).

Although abutting property owners were refused access to a public proceeding of a town planning board when it went into a private session for a period of time, they were not entitled to attorney's fees under RSA 91-A:8, I, as the issue of statutory construction as to whether the board's actions were legally within the "consultation with legal counsel" exclusion of RSA 91-A:2, I(b) were a matter of first impression. Ettinger v. Town of Madison Planning Bd., 162 N.H. 785, 35 A.3d 562, 2011 N.H. LEXIS 178 (N.H. 2011).

Trial court did not err in not awarding attorney's fees under RSA 91-A:8, I, after respondents failed to give proper notice of a county convention meeting. Petitioners had failed to show that they were either refused access to the meeting or denied access to any records concerning the meeting. Hull v. Grafton County, 160 N.H. 818, 10 A.3d 1193, 2010 N.H. LEXIS 114 (N.H. 2010).

Though the Executive Director of the New Hampshire Department of Fish and Game violated RSA 91-A:2, II by excluding a television station's cameras from a hunting license hearing on grounds that the commotion they would cause would deprive the license applicant of his right to a fair hearing, the station was properly denied attorney's fees under RSA 91-A:8. The trial court properly found, given the state of the case law, that the Director neither knew nor should have known that his conduct violated RSA 91-A:2, II. WMUR Channel Nine v. N.H. Dep't of Fish & Game, 154 N.H. 46, 908 A.2d 146, 2006 N.H. LEXIS 113 (N.H. 2006).

Where it was clear that a lawsuit by petitioner, the risk management administrator for the New Hampshire Property and Casualty Loss Program, was necessary to make the New Hampshire Legislative Budget Assistant (LBA) disclose certain materials related to an audit of the New Hampshire Property and Casualty Loss Program, the trial court erred in denying the administrator's request for attorney's fees under RSA 91-A:8, simply because the LBA voluntarily disclosed some of the materials after the supreme court found that the materials were not exempt from disclosure; instead, the trial court should have considered whether the LBA knew or should have known that its withholding of the information violated the Right-to-Know Law. Goode v. N.H. Office of the Legislative Budget Assistant, 148 N.H. 551, 813 A.2d 381, 2002 N.H. LEXIS 168 (N.H. 2002).

The superior court utilized an incorrect legal standard in resolving the plaintiffs' request for attorney's fees when it denied such an award on the basis that the defendants' conduct was not a "knowing violation"; on remand, the court would be required to determine whether the defendants "should have known" that their conduct was improper. New Hampshire Challenge v. Commissioner, New

Hampshire Dept. of Educ., 142 N.H. 246, 698 A.2d 1252, 1997 N.H. LEXIS 85 (N.H. 1997).

In a proceeding arising from the dismissal of the plaintiff police chief by a town, attorney's fees were improperly awarded against the town where: (1) the town selectmen consulted with town counsel about what procedure should be followed before dismissing the plaintiff and followed that advice, (2) at the time of the plaintiff's dismissal, it was not generally understood among municipal law practitioners that advance notice was required to an employee that his or her dismissal would be considered in executive session, and (3) the town acted in good faith and the violation of the Right-To-Know Law was not obvious, deliberate, or willful. Voelbel v. Town of Bridgewater, 140 N.H. 446, 667 A.2d 1028, 1995 N.H. LEXIS 168 (N.H. 1995).

Where defendants did not knowingly violate, or have reason to believe that their refusal to provide documents would violate, the Right-to-Know Law, plaintiff's request for attorney's fees was denied. Chambers v. Gregg, 135 N.H. 478, 606 A.2d 811, 1992 N.H. LEXIS 62 (N.H. 1992).

Where mayor was sued in his official capacity, award of attorney's fees was properly chargeable to city. Bradbury v. Shaw, 116 N.H. 388, 360 A.2d 123, 1976 N.H. LEXIS 361 (N.H. 1976).

Where plaintiff petitioned to secure access to records of mayor's industrial advisory committee under this section, and trial court ruled that committee was subject to right-to-know law although certain records of its meetings were exempt from disclosure, plaintiff was substantially successful and thus entitled to recover his counsel fees. Bradbury v. Shaw, 116 N.H. 388, 360 A.2d 123, 1976 N.H. LEXIS 361 (N.H. 1976).

3. —Review

As the trial court properly denied petitioners' request for documents concerning internal personnel practices, there was no need for the appellate court to consider its denial of petitioners' request for attorney's fees. Hounsell v. North Conway Water Precinct, 154 N.H. 1, 903 A.2d 987, 2006 N.H. LEXIS 108 (N.H. 2006), limited, Reid v. N.H. AG, 169 N.H. 509, 152 A.3d 860, 2016 N.H. LEXIS 238 (N.H. 2016).

Plaintiff's request for attorney's fees under Right-to-Know Law was properly denied, since agency neither knew nor should have known that its refusal to disclose materials was in violation of statute. Goode v. New Hampshire Office of the Legislative Budget Assistant, 145 N.H. 451, 767 A.2d 393, 2000 N.H. LEXIS 92 (N.H. 2000).

Because no abuse of discretion on the part of the trial court appeared on the record, its decision denying plaintiffs' petition for an award of attorney's fees under this section was affirmed. Orford Teachers Ass'n v. Watson, 122 N.H. 803, 451 A.2d 378, 1982 N.H. LEXIS 467 (N.H. 1982).

4. Injunctive relief

Trial court did not err under RSA 91-A:8, III, in declining to enjoin respondents from future violations of RSA 24:9-d and RSA ch. 91-A and in declining to appoint a monitor after respondents failed to give proper notice of a May county convention meeting. The May meeting was neither closed to the public nor secret, and the county had provided one petitioner with the documents relative to the meeting; furthermore, the convention cured the defects in notice by promptly and properly noticing a July meeting. Hull v. Grafton County, 160 N.H. 818, 10 A.3d 1193, 2010 N.H. LEXIS 114 (N.H. 2010).

Trial court did not err by denying injunctive relief to an organization requesting information relating to the New Hampshire Department of Resources and Economic Development's intended purchase of a large tract of land as well as its plan to develop all terrain vehicle and other trails once the land was purchased, because at the time of the organization's Right-to-Know petition, the State did not own the land at issue, the property was not state land and, thus, the provisions of RSA 215-A:41, II(f) did not apply. ATV Watch v. N.H. Dep't of Res. & Econ. Dev., 155 N.H. 434, 923 A.2d 1061, 2007 N.H. LEXIS 72 (N.H. 2007).

5. Costs

Because the trial court found, and the record supported its finding, that plaintiffs' lawsuit was not necessary to enforce compliance with the Right-to-Know Law, it properly denied plaintiffs'

request for costs. N.H. Right to Life v. Dir., N.H. Charitable Trusts Unit, 169 N.H. 95, 143 A.3d 829, 2016 N.H. LEXIS 55 (N.H. 2016).

Trial court erred in considering whether the New Hampshire Department of Resources and Economic Development's (DRED's) conduct in withholding certain requested documents by an organization was reasonable or whether it committed a knowing violation when rejecting the organization's request for costs, which required the trial court's denial of costs to the organization to be vacated. Since the organization's request for costs remained viable only if DRED violated the Right-to-Know Law, the case was remanded to the trial court to consider costs and the lawfulness of the DRED's conduct in its delayed disclosure and retention of documents. ATV Watch v. N.H. Dep't of Res. & Econ. Dev., 155 N.H. 434, 923 A.2d 1061, 2007 N.H. LEXIS 72 (N.H. 2007).

6. Invalidation of action

Trial court erred in declining to invalidate a county convention's selection of a sheriff by secret ballot. The decision to fill a vacancy in the office by secret ballot contravened not only the explicit legislative mandate against such votes, but also the fundamental purpose of the Right-to-Know Law; furthermore, the public's need for scrutiny was critical since there was no other manner in which members of the public could determine how their representatives voted so that they could then hold the representatives accountable. Lambert v. Belknap Cty. Convention, 157 N.H. 375, 949 A.2d 709, 2008 N.H. LEXIS 75 (N.H. 2008).

Cited:

Cited in Johnson v. Nash, 135 N.H. 534, 608 A.2d 200, 1992 N.H. LEXIS 73 (1992); Disabilities Rights Ctr., Inc. v. Commissioner, N.H. Dep't of Corrections, 143 N.H. 674, 732 A.2d 1021, 1999 N.H. LEXIS 56 (1999).

RESEARCH REFERENCES AND PRACTICE AIDS

New Hampshire Trial Bar News.
For article, "Contingent Fees Attacked," see 16 N.H. Trial Bar News 52 (Summer 1994).

New Hampshire Practice.
13-18 N.H.P. Local Government Law § 680.

91-A:8-a. Commission to Study Processes to Resolve Right-to-Know Complaints.

I. There is established a commission to study processes to resolve right-to-know complaints.

(a) The members of the commission shall be as follows:

(1) Three members of the house of representatives, appointed by the speaker of the house of representatives.

(2) One member of the senate, appointed by the president of the senate.

(3) The attorney general, or designee.

(4) One municipal official, appointed by the New Hampshire Municipal Association.

(5) One school board member, appointed by the New Hampshire School Boards Association.

(6) One county official, appointed by the New Hampshire Association of Counties.

(7) One member who shall have brought suit pro se under RSA 91-A:7, appointed by the governor.

(8) One member representing the New Hampshire Press Association, appointed by that association.

(9) One member representing Right To Know New Hampshire, appointed by that organization.

(10) One member of the New Hampshire Civil Liberties Union, appointed by that organization.

(11) One citizen member, appointed by the governor.

(b) Legislative members of the commission shall receive mileage at the legislative rate when attending to the duties of the commission.

II.(a) The commission shall study alternative processes to resolve right-to-know complaints consistent with the following:

(1) Encouraging resolution of right-to-know complaints directly between citizens and public agencies and bodies.

(2) Reducing the burden and costs of right-to-know complaints on the courts.

(3) Reducing the burden and costs of right-to-know complaints on public agencies and bodies.

(4) Reducing the burden and costs of right-to-know complaints on citizens aggrieved by violations of RSA 91-A.

(5) Increasing awareness and compliance with the right-to-know law to minimize violations.

(b) The commission may solicit information from any person or entity the commission deems relevant to its study.

III. The members of the commission shall elect a chairperson from among the members. The first meeting of the commission shall be called by the first-named house member. The first meeting of the commission shall be held within 30 days of the effective date of this section. Seven members of the commission shall constitute a quorum.

IV. The commission shall report its findings and any recommendations for proposed legislation to the speaker of the house of representatives, the president of the senate, the house clerk, the senate clerk, the governor, and the state library on or before November 1, 2017.

HISTORY:
2017, 126:1, eff. June 16, 2017.

91-A:8-a. Commission to Study Processes to Resolve Right-to-Know Complaints. [Repealed]

HISTORY:
2017, 126:1, eff. June 16, 2017. Repealed by 2017, 126:2, eff. November 1, 2017.

91-A:9. Destruction of Certain Information Prohibited.

A person is guilty of a misdemeanor who knowingly destroys any information with the purpose to prevent such information from being inspected or disclosed in response to a request under this chapter. If a request for inspection is denied on the grounds that the information is exempt under this chapter, the requested material shall be preserved for 90 days or while any lawsuit pursuant to RSA 91-A:7–8 is pending.

HISTORY:
2002, 175:1, eff. Jan. 1, 2003.

RESEARCH REFERENCES AND PRACTICE AIDS

Cross References.
Classification of crimes, see RSA 625:9
Sentences, see RSA 651.

Procedure for Release of Personal Information for Research Purposes

91-A:10. Release of Statistical Tables and Limited Data Sets for Research.

I. In this subdivision:

(a) "Agency" means each state board, commission, department, institution, officer or other state official or group.

(b) "Agency head" means the head of any governmental agency which is responsible for the collection and use of any data on persons or summary data.

(c) "Cell size" means the count of individuals that share a set of characteristics contained in a statistical table.

(d) "Data set" means a collection of personal information on one or more individuals, whether in electronic or manual files.

(e) "Direct identifiers" means:

(1) Names.

(2) Postal address information other than town or city, state, and zip code.

(3) Telephone and fax numbers.

(4) Electronic mail addresses.

(5) Social security numbers.

(6) Certificate and license numbers.

(7) Vehicle identifiers and serial numbers, including license plate numbers.

(8) Personal Internet IP addresses and URLs.

(9) Biometric identifiers, including finger and voice prints.

(10) Personal photographic images.

(f) "Individual" means a human being, alive or dead, who is the subject of personal information and includes the individual's legal or other authorized representative.

(g) "Limited data set" means a data set from which all direct identifiers have been removed or blanked.

(h) "Personal information" means information relating to an individual that is reported to the state or is derived from any interaction between the state and an individual and which:

   (1) Contains direct identifiers.

   (2) Is under the control of the state.

  (i) "Provided by law" means use and disclosure as permitted or required by New Hampshire state law governing programs or activities undertaken by the state or its agencies, or required by federal law.

  (j) "Public record" means records available to any person without restriction.

  (k) "State" means the state of New Hampshire, its agencies or instrumentalities.

  (*l*) "Statistical table" means single or multivariate counts based on the personal information contained in a data set and which does not include any direct identifiers.

II. Except as otherwise provided by law, upon request an agency shall release limited data sets and statistical tables with any cell size more than 0 and less than 5 contained in agency files to requestors for the purposes of research under the following conditions:

  (a) The requestor submits a written application that contains:

   (1) The following information about the principal investigator in charge of the research:

    (A) name, address, and phone number;

    (B) organizational affiliation;

    (C) professional qualification; and

    (D) name and phone number of principal investigator's contact person, if any.

   (2) The names and qualifications of additional research staff, if any, who will have access to the data.

   (3) A research protocol which shall contain:

    (A) a summary of background, purposes, and origin of the research;

    (B) a statement of the general problem or issue to be addressed by the research;

    (C) the research design and methodology including either the topics of exploratory research or the specific research hypotheses to be tested;

    (D) the procedures that will be followed to maintain the confidentiality of any data or copies of records provided to the investigator; and

    (E) the intended research completion date.

   (4) The following information about the data or statistical tables being requested:

    (A) general types of information;

    (B) time period of the data or statistical tables;

    (C) specific data items or fields of information required, if applicable;

    (D) medium in which the data or statistical tables are to be supplied; and

    (E) any special format or layout of data requested by the principal investigator.

  (b) The requestor signs a "Data Use Agreement" signed by the principal investigator that contains the following:

   (1) Agreement not to use or further disclose the information to any person or organization other than as described in the application and as permitted by the Data Use Agreement without the written consent of the agency.

   (2) Agreement not to use or further disclose the information as otherwise required by law.

   (3) Agreement not to seek to ascertain the identity of individuals revealed in the limited data set and/or statistical tables.

   (4) Agreement not to publish or make public the content of cells in statistical tables in which the cell size is more than 0 and less than 5 unless:

    (A) otherwise provided by law; or

    (B) the information is a public record.

   (5) Agreement to report to the agency any use or disclosure of the information contrary to the agreement of which the principal investigator becomes aware.

   (6) A date on which the data set and/or statistical tables will be returned to the agency and/or all copies in the possession of the requestor will be destroyed.

III. The agency head shall release limited data sets and statistical tables and sign the Data Use Agreement on behalf of the state when:

  (a) The application submitted is complete.

  (b) Adequate measures to ensure the confidentiality of any person are documented.

  (c) The investigator and research staff are qualified as indicated by:

   (1) Documentation of training and previous research, including prior publications; and

   (2) Affiliation with a university, private research organization, medical center, state agency, or other institution which will provide sufficient research resources.

  (d) There is no other state law, federal law, or federal regulation prohibiting release of the requested information.

IV. Within 10 days of a receipt of written application, the agency head, or designee, shall respond to the request. Whenever the agency head denies release of requested information, the agency head shall send the requestor a letter identifying the specific criteria which are the basis of the denial. Should release be denied due to other law, the letter shall identify the specific state law, federal law, or federal regulation prohibiting the release. Otherwise the agency head shall provide the requested data or set a date on which the data shall be provided.

V. Any person violating any provision of a signed Data Use Agreement shall be guilty of a violation.

VI. Nothing in this section shall exempt any requestor from paying fees otherwise established by law for obtaining copies of limited data sets or statistical tables. Such fees shall be based on the cost of providing the copy in the format requested. The agency head shall provide the requestor with a written description of the basis for the fee.

HISTORY:
2003, 292:2, eff. July 18, 2003.

Right-to-Know Oversight Commission

91-A:11. Oversight Commission Established. [Repealed.]

[Repealed 2005, 3:2, eff. Nov. 1, 2010.]

Former section(s).
Former RSA 91-A:11, which was derived from 2005, 3:1, related to oversight commission established.

91-A:12. Membership and Compensation. [Repealed.]

[Repealed 2005, 3:2, eff. Nov. 1, 2010.]

Former section(s).
Former RSA 91-A:12, which was derived from 2005, 3:1, related to membership and compensation.

91-A:13. Duties. [Repealed.]

[Repealed 2005, 3:2, eff. Nov. 1, 2010.]

Former section(s).
Former RSA 91-A:13, which was derived from 2005, 3:1, related to duties.

91-A:14. Chairperson; Quorum. [Repealed.]

[Repealed 2005, 3:2, eff. Nov. 1, 2010.]

Former section(s).
Former RSA 91-A:14, which was derived from 2005, 3:1, related to chairperson; quorum.

91-A:15. Report. [Repealed.]

[Repealed 2005, 3:2, eff. Nov. 1, 2010.]

Former section(s).
Former RSA 91-A:15, which was derived from 2005, 3:1, related to report.

TITLE X
PUBLIC HEALTH

CHAPTER 149-P

LANDOWNER'S RIGHT OF ACTION

HISTORY:
2016, 278:1, eff. January 1, 2017.

149-P:1. Landowner's Right of Action.

I. It is hereby declared to be in the public interest to encourage the preservation and conservation of the land, water, forest, agricultural, and wildlife resources of this state. It is also declared to be in the public interest to discourage and provide means for preventing the spoliation of such resources from the effects of illegal dumping, and to create rights in landowners to provide the means for obtaining such objectives. It is the intention of this chapter to create a landowner's right of action in support of these purposes.

II. Notwithstanding any rules adopted by the department of environmental services, any ordinance adopted by a municipality, or any provision of law, any person, as defined in RSA 147-A:2, XII, who without authorization, intentionally, recklessly, or negligently discharges, spills, releases, pollutes, disposes, dumps, leaks, injects, or places oil, gasoline, diesel fuel, fuel oil, motor oil, automotive oil, gasoline ethers, offensive matter, hazardous waste, waste, refuse, or solid waste as those terms are defined in RSA 146-A through RSA 149-O, upon the land of another, shall be liable to the owner of the land.

III. Upon such discharge occurring, the owner of the land may:

(a) Commence an action for the cost of cleanup and any such damages as may result from the discharge;

(b) Seek injunctive relief enjoining any activity described in paragraph II, if such activity is imminent or likely;

(c) Obtain a court order requiring the person causing the discharge to contain, clean up, and remediate the discharge at such person's expense;

(d) Obtain multiple damages against the person causing the discharge of up to 3 times actual damages, based upon the degree of culpability, as determined by the trier of fact;

(e) Obtain reasonable attorneys' fees and professional fees associated with the containment, cleanup, and remediation, and the seeking and obtaining relief and damages;

(f) Require the person causing the discharge to provide a bond, or other assurances sufficient to cover the costs of containment, cleanup, and remediation, upon a showing by the owner that there is a reasonable likelihood of a judgment; and

(g) Obtain an attachment, prejudgment attachment, or trustee process in accordance with RSA 511, RSA 511-A and RSA 512.

IV.(a) This chapter shall only apply to discharges that are made directly upon the landowner's land and shall not apply to those discharges that originate from the land of another, including without limitation, discharges from any above ground or underground storage tank. However, this chapter shall not otherwise limit any other rights afforded a landowner for such discharges originating from the land of another.

(b) For the purposes of this chapter, a landowner shall include any owner holding an entire, joint, fractional, mortgage, or other ownership interest in the land, but any separate claims made by more than one such owner shall be consolidated into a single action.

(c) This chapter shall not apply to or benefit any owner holding an interest in the land making claim against any other owner holding an interest in the same land.

(d) This chapter shall not apply to a discharge on a landowner's land, when the discharge results from a motor vehicle involved in a motor vehicle accident not originating on the landowner's land.

(e) The rights and benefits conferred upon a landowner under this chapter shall not apply to any claim or claims against the state and its subdivisions.

HISTORY:
2016, 278:1, eff. January 1, 2017.

TITLE XII
PUBLIC SAFETY AND WELFARE

RESEARCH REFERENCES AND PRACTICE AIDS

Cross References.
Department of safety, see RSA 21-P.
Hazardous waste management, see RSA 147-A.
Housing standards, see RSA 48-A.
Labeling of hazardous substances, see RSA 339-A.
Liability for expenses of patients and residents of public institutions, see RSA 126-A:46– 57.
Nuclear planning and response program,see RSA 107-B.
Safety and health of employees, see RSA 277.
Solid waste management, see RSA 149-M.
Transportation of hazardous materials and waste, see RSA 21-P:16 et seq.
Vocational rehabilitation programs, see RSA 200-C.

CHAPTER 155-A
NEW HAMPSHIRE BUILDING CODE

Repeal and reenactment of chapter.
2002, 8:3, eff. Sept. 14, 2002, provided for the repeal and reenactment of RSA 155-A. Original RSA 155-A, consisting of RSA 155-A:1– 155-A:4 was derived from 1955, 191:1, 2, 4; 1973, 107:3; 1975, 235:1, 387:1, 2; 1979, 398:2; 1981, 233:1, 2; 1990, 140:2; 1991, 290:3; and 1997, 44.

RESEARCH REFERENCES AND PRACTICE AIDS

Cross References.
Building requirements for accommodation of physically disabled persons, see RSA 155:39-c, 39-d.

Double door safety in buildings open to public, see RSA 155:2-a.
Energy conservation in new building construction, see RSA 155-D.
Energy cost reduction in state facilities, see RSA 21-I:19-a et seq.

155-A:1. Definitions. [Effective until January 1, 2018]

In this chapter:

I. "Building" means building as defined and interpreted by the International Code Council's International Building Code 2009, as amended by the state building code review board and ratified by the legislature in accordance with RSA 155-A:10.

II. "County" means the local legislative body of a county in which there are unincorporated towns or unorganized places.

III. "Local enforcement agency" means for a municipality that has adopted enforcement provisions or additional regulations under RSA 674:51 or RSA 47:22, the building inspector, code official, or other local government official qualified and authorized to make inspections and to enforce the laws, ordinances, and rules enacted by the state and by local government that establish standards and requirements applicable to the construction, alteration, or repair of buildings. For the purpose of enforcement of the state fire code for buildings and structures not owned by the state, the local enforcement agency means the municipal fire chief or his or her representative, pursuant to RSA 154:2, II.

IV. "New Hampshire building code" or "state building code" means the adoption by reference of the International Building Code 2009, the International Existing Building Code 2009, the International Plumbing Code 2009, the International Mechanical Code 2009, the International Energy Conservation Code 2009, and the International Residential Code 2009, as published by the International Code Council, and the National Electrical Code 2014, as amended by the state building code review board and ratified by the legislature in accordance with RSA 155-A:10. The provisions of any other national code or model code referred to within a code listed in this definition shall not be included in the state building code unless specifically included in the codes listed in this definition.

IV-a. "New Hampshire fire code" or "state fire code" means the state fire code as defined in RSA 153:1 and as amended by rules adopted pursuant to RSA 153:5.

V. "Person" means any individual or organized group of any kind, including partnerships, corporations, limited liability partnerships, limited liability companies, and other forms of association, as well as federal, state or local instrumentalities, political subdivisions, or officers.

VI. "Structure" means structure as defined and interpreted by the International Code Council's International Building Code 2009, as amended by the state building code review board and ratified by the legislature in accordance with RSA 155-A:10.

HISTORY:

2002, 8:3, eff. Sept. 14, 2002. 2003, 245:1, eff. July 14, 2003. 2006, 112:1, eff. July 8, 2006. 2007, 187:1–3, eff. August 17, 2007. 2009, 41:2, eff. July 14, 2009. 2012, 242:7–10, eff. June 18, 2012. 2014, 314:4, eff. January 1, 2015.

Amendment Notes

—2014.

The 2014 amendment substituted "National Electrical Code 2014" for "National Electric Code 2011" in the first sentence of IV.

—2012.

The 2012 amendment substituted "International Code Council's International Building Code 2009, as amended by the state building code review board and ratified by the legislature in accordance with RSA 155-A:10" for "International Code Council's International Building Code 2006" in I and VI; in III, in the first sentence, added "or RSA 47:22," added "code official," and substituted "qualified and authorized" for "with authority" and added the second sentence; in the first sentence of IV, substituted "International Building Code 2009, the International Existing Building Code 2009" for "International Building Code 2006," "International Plumbing Code 2009" for "International Plumbing Code 2006," "International Mechanical Code 2009" for "International Mechanical Code 2006," "International Energy Conservation Code 2009" for "International Energy Conservation Code 2006," "International Residential Code 2009" for "International Residential Code 2006," and "National Electric Code 2011, as amended by the state building code review board and ratified by the legislature in accordance with RSA 155-A:10" for "National Electric Code 2008"; added IV-a; and made a stylistic change.

—2009.

The 2009 amendment substituted "the National Electric Code 2008" for "the National Electric Code 2005" in the first sentence of IV.

—2007.

Paragraphs I and VI: Substituted "2006" for "2000" following "International Building Code".

Paragraph IV: Substituted "2006" for "2000" following "Code" throughout the paragraph and "2005" for "2002" following "National Electric Code".

—2006.

Paragraph IV: Inserted "and the International Residential Code 2000" following "Conservation Code 2000" in the first sentence.

—2003.

Paragraph IV: Substituted "National Electric Code 2002" for "National Electric Code 1999" in the first sentence.

RESEARCH REFERENCES AND PRACTICE AIDS

New Hampshire Practice.

14-24 N.H.P. Local Government Law § 900.

155-A:1. Definitions. [Effective January 1, 2018]

In this chapter:

I. "Building" means building as defined and interpreted by the International Code Council's International Building Code 2009, as amended by the state building code review board and ratified by the legislature in accordance with RSA 155-A:10.

II. "County" means the local legislative body of a county in which there are unincorporated towns or unorganized places.

III. "Local enforcement agency" means for a municipality that has adopted enforcement provisions or additional regulations under RSA 674:51 or RSA 47:22, the building inspector, code official, or other local government official qualified and authorized to make inspections and to enforce the laws, ordinances, and rules enacted by the state and by local government that establish standards and requirements applicable to the construction, alteration, or repair of buildings. For the purpose of enforcement of the state fire code for buildings and structures not owned by the state, the local enforcement agency means the municipal fire chief or his or her representative, pursuant to RSA 154:2, II.

IV. "New Hampshire building code" or "state building code" means the adoption by reference of the International Building Code 2009, the International Existing Building Code 2009, the International Plumbing Code 2009, the International Mechanical Code 2009, the International Energy Conservation Code 2009, and the International Residential Code 2009, as published by the International Code Council, and the National Electrical Code 2017, as amended by the state building code review board and ratified by the legislature in accordance with RSA 155-A:10. The provisions of any other national code or model code referred to within a code listed in this definition shall not be included in the state building code unless specifically included in the codes listed in this definition.

IV-a. "New Hampshire fire code" or "state fire code" means the state fire code as defined in RSA 153:1 and as amended by rules adopted pursuant to RSA 153:5.

V. "Person" means any individual or organized group of any kind, including partnerships, corporations, limited liability partnerships, limited liability companies, and other forms of association, as well as federal, state or local instrumentalities, political subdivisions, or officers.

VI. "Structure" means structure as defined and interpreted by the International Code Council's International Building Code 2009, as amended by the state building code review board and ratified by the legislature in accordance with RSA 155-A:10.

HISTORY:

2002, 8:3, eff. Sept. 14, 2002. 2003, 245:1, eff. July 14, 2003. 2006, 112:1, eff. July 8, 2006. 2007, 187:1–3, eff. August 17, 2007. 2009, 41:2, eff. July 14, 2009. 2012, 242:7–10, eff. June 18, 2012. 2014, 314:4, eff. January 1, 2015. 2017, 201:3, eff. January 1, 2018.

Amendment Notes

The 2017 amendment to this section by Ch. 201 substituted "National Electrical Code 2017" for "National Electrical Code 2014" in the first sentence of IV.

155-A:2. State Building Code.

I. All buildings, building components, and structures constructed in New Hampshire shall comply with the state building code and state fire code. The construction, design, structure, maintenance, and use of all buildings or structures to be erected and the alteration, renovation, rehabilitation, repair, removal, or demolition of all buildings and structures previously erected shall be governed by the provisions of the state building code.

II. To the extent that there is any conflict between the state building code and the state fire code, the code creating the greater degree of life safety shall take precedence, subject to the review provisions contained in RSA 155-A:10. If the municipal building and fire code officials cannot agree which code creates the greater degree of life safety, the property owner may notify the 2 officials in writing that if agreement is not reached within 2 business days of delivery of said notification, that the decision shall be made by the property owner to comply with either the applicable building code or fire code. Such decision by the property owner after proper notification shall not be grounds for the denial of a certificate of occupancy.

III. To the extent that it does not conflict with any other provision of law, and except as otherwise provided in this paragraph, the issuance of permits and the collection of fees pursuant to the state building code is expressly reserved for counties, towns, cities, and village districts where such activities have been authorized in accordance with RSA 674:51 and RSA 47:22. Pursuant to the state fire marshal's authority to enforce the state building code under RSA 155-A:7, I, the fire marshal may establish for municipalities that do not have a building inspector or other enforcement mechanism authorized in RSA 155-A:4, with approval of the commissioner of safety and by rules adopted under RSA 541-A, fees to defray the cost of issuing building permits in accordance with the state building code. Such fees shall be deposited in the fire standards and training and emergency medical services fund established in RSA 21-P:12-d.

IV. Except for buildings owned by the state, the community college system of New Hampshire, or the university system, the issuance of permits and certificates of occupancy pursuant to the state building code is expressly reserved for counties, towns, cities, and village districts. The state fire marshal shall issue permits and conduct inspections for buildings owned by the state, the community college system of New Hampshire, and the university system. Nothing in this section shall prohibit the state fire marshal from contracting with or authorizing a local enforcement agency or other qualified third party for these services.

V. Counties, towns, cities, and village districts may adopt by ordinance pursuant to RSA 674:51 or RSA 47:22 any additional regulations provided that such regulations are not less stringent than the requirements of the state building code and the state fire code.

VI. For any municipality which has not adopted an enforcement mechanism under RSA 674:51, the contractor of the building, building component, or structure shall notify the state fire marshal concerning the type of construction before construction begins excluding one- and 2-family dwellings. Any municipality that has adopted an enforcement mechanism under RSA 674:51 may contract with a local enforcement agency or a qualified third party for these services as an alternative to establishing the position of building inspector under RSA 674:51, III(c), and such agency or third party shall have the same authority as a building inspector as provided in that section.

VII. The contractor of a building, building component, or structure shall be responsible for meeting the minimum requirements of the state building code and state fire code. No municipality shall be held liable for any failure on the part of a contractor to comply with the provisions of the state building code.

VIII. Nothing in this chapter shall be construed as amending, repealing, or superseding any local law, ordinance, code, or regulation, except local code requirements that are less stringent than the state building code or state fire code, and all buildings, building components, and structures shall comply with all applicable state or local building and fire code requirements, land use restrictions including but not limited to subdivision regulations, use and location restrictions, density and dimensional limitations, or historic district laws or ordinances.

IX. Nothing in this chapter shall be construed to permit or encourage the state to initiate or assume an independent role in the administration and enforcement of the New Hampshire building code for a building or structure that is not owned by the state unless otherwise authorized by law.

X. No state agency, authority, board, or commission shall vary, modify, or waive the requirements of the state building code or state fire code, unless approved by the state building code review board pursuant to RSA 155-A relative to the state building code or the state fire marshal pursuant to RSA 153:8-a, I(c) for the state fire code. Nothing in this chapter shall affect the statutory authority of the commissioner of labor, the state board for the licensing and regulation of plumbers, or the state electricians' board to administer their respective programs, provided that any changes to codes proposed under the rulemaking authority of these agencies shall not be enforced until approved by the state building code review board.

XI. Notwithstanding the inclusion of the National Electrical Code 2017 in the state building code under RSA 155-A:1, IV, the amended provisions of section 210.12 of the National Electrical Code, which modify the National Electrical Code 2014 version to add arc-fault circuit interrupter requirements for dormitory unit devices and bathrooms, guest rooms and guest suites, and branch circuit extensions or modifications for dormitory units shall not be enforced under the state building code or this chapter.

HISTORY:

2002, 8:3, eff. Sept. 14, 2002. 2003, 245:2, eff. July 14, 2003. 2009, 175:1, eff. July 13, 2009. 2010, 326:2, eff. September 18, 2010. 2012, 242:11, eff. June 18, 2012. 2017, 201:6, eff. September 3, 2017.

Amendment Notes

The 2017 amendments to this section by Ch. 201 added XI.

—2012.

The 2012 amendment rewrote the section to the extent that a detailed comparison would be impracticable.

—2010.

The 2010 amendment added "the commissioner of labor" in the second sentence of XI.

—2009.

The 2009 amendment, in IV, added "and except as otherwise provided in this paragraph" in the first sentence and added the last two sentences.

—2003.

Paragraph VII: Deleted "for the state building code" preceding "under RSA 674:51".

Legislative Declaration of Purpose.

2012, 242:1, eff. June 18, 2012, provided:

"The general court declares that the purpose of this act is the following:

"**I.** The general court finds that a clearer distinction between codes that apply to new construction and codes that apply to existing buildings and their uses is in the best interest of the citizens of New Hampshire.

"**II.** The state building code and the state fire code both govern the construction and renovation of buildings. Additionally, the state fire code governs the fire safety requirements of existing buildings. Amendments to these 2 codes currently follow separate processes, the building code requiring action by the legislature and the fire code requiring approval by the joint legislative committee on administrative rules. When overlap of these 2 codes creates a conflict with differing requirements, property owners with building projects may suffer undue expense and/or delay.

"**III.** The purpose of this act is to reduce the number of conflicts between the building code and the fire code, create a less burdensome regulatory process when conflicts arise, promote a more parallel adoption process for the building and fire codes, clearly define the authority of the state fire marshal and the building code review board to amend adopted codes, reserve the authority for code adoption and changes to code editions to the general court, ratify updates and changes to the state building code already adopted by the building code review board, and adopt by reference the 2009 editions of the Life Safety Code 2009 edition and the Uniform Fire Code NFPA 1, as published by the National Fire Protection Association."

RESEARCH REFERENCES AND PRACTICE AIDS

New Hampshire Practice.

14-24 N.H.P. Local Government Law § 900.

155-A:3. Local Amendments; Application.

For a municipality which has adopted an enforcement mechanism or additional regulations to the state building code pursuant to RSA 674:51:

I. The municipality may adopt local amendments to the state building code which do not prohibit minimum implementation and enforcement of the state building code.

II. The procedure for amendment shall be in accordance with applicable statutes and local regulations.

III. At a minimum, the municipality shall ensure that implementation and enforcement includes:

(a) Review and acceptance of appropriate plans.

(b) Issuance of building permits.

(c) Inspection of the work authorized by the building permits.

(d) Issuance of appropriate use and occupancy certificates.

IV.(a) The provisions of this chapter and any local amendments under this section shall not be construed to restrict or encumber the local governing body's authority relative to the appointment, removal, or duties of municipal employees and the organization of municipal departments.

(b) Any provision of the state building code that conflicts with existing or amended local ordinances, regulations, policies, practices, or procedures regarding the appointment, removal, or duties of municipal employees and the organization of municipal departments, shall not apply provided that the ordinances, regulations, policies, practices, or procedures do not prevent effective enforcement of the state building code or state fire code.

HISTORY:

2002, 8:3, eff. Sept. 14, 2002. 2012, 242:12, eff. June 18, 2012.

Amendment Notes

—2012.

The 2012 amendment added "provided that the ordinances, regulations, policies, practices, or procedures do not prevent effective enforcement of the state building code or state fire code" in IV(b).

RESEARCH REFERENCES AND PRACTICE AIDS

New Hampshire Practice.

14-24 N.H.P. Local Government Law § 900.

155-A:3-a. Code Requirements; Biomass Burning Boilers.

I. Notwithstanding any provisions of the state building code or state fire code, the board shall adopt a code and amendments thereto which shall regulate the installation and operation of biomass burning boilers. The code adopted shall include the 1999 EN 303-5 standard established by the European Committee for Standardization, and shall include requirements for the safe installation, operation, and repair of such boilers, and for data plates and warning labels written in English, limits on temperature and pressure with associated relief valves, and the filing of construction and emissions specifications written in English.

II. The inspection procedures and enforcement requirements for the commissioner of labor in RSA 157-A shall apply to boilers installed according to the code and amendments adopted by the board under this section.

III. The code and amendments thereto adopted under paragraph I shall be ratified by appropriate legislation within 2 years of their adoption. If such code and amendments are not ratified, then the code and amendments shall expire at the end of the 2-year period.

HISTORY:
2010, 326:1, eff. September 18, 2010.

155-A:3-b. Code Requirements; Log Structures.

I. Notwithstanding any provisions of the state building code or state fire code, the state building code review board shall adopt amendments to the state building code regulating the design and construction of log structures. The adopted amendments shall include ICC 400 Standard on the Design and Construction of Log Structures.

II. The amendments adopted under paragraph I shall be ratified by appropriate legislation within 2 years of their adoption. If such amendments are not ratified, then the amendments shall expire at the end of the 2-year period.

HISTORY:
2012, 189:1, eff. June 11, 2012.

155-A:3-c. Installation of Arc-Fault Circuit Interrupters (AFCI); Exception.

I. Notwithstanding any provision of the state building code or state fire code requiring the installation of arc-fault circuit interrupters, after repeated tripping of an AFCI device and determination the branch circuit is not causing the AFCI to trip, an AFCI device may be replaced with one without AFCI protection in accordance with this section.

II. All receptacle outlets supplied by the branch circuit without AFCI protection shall prior to occupancy either be:

    (a) Marked "No AFCI Protection;" or

    (b) Identified in a notice given by the property owner to all occupants.

III. If an electrician installs a device without AFCI protection, within 5 working days the electrician shall file an AFCI unwanted tripping report with the National Electrical Manufacturers Association on the association's webpage for arc fault breaker safety, and shall submit a copy of the report to the property owner and the electricians' board.

IV. The device without AFCI protection shall be permitted to remain in place for the period of time it takes for the manufacturer to resolve the matter.

V. Nothing in this section shall prevent a homeowner from making electrical installations in or about a single family residence owned and occupied by him or her or to be occupied by him or her as his or her bona fide personal abode.

HISTORY:
2017, 157:1, eff. June 28, 2017.

155-A:4. Permit Required.

I. Before starting new construction or renovation of buildings and structures as described in RSA 155-A:2, I, the person responsible for such construction shall obtain a permit.

II. In municipalities that have adopted an enforcement mechanism pursuant to RSA 674:51 and RSA 47:22, the permit under this section shall conform to the locally adopted process. No permit shall be issued that would not result in compliance with the state building code and state fire code.

III. For buildings and structures owned by the state, the community college system of New Hampshire, or the university system, the person responsible for such activities shall obtain a permit from the state fire marshal. Before issuing the permit, the state fire marshal shall give due consideration to any written recommendations of the municipal fire chief, building official, or designee in the community where the state building is located.

HISTORY:
2002, 8:3, eff. Sept. 14, 2002. 2012, 242:13, eff. June 18, 2012.

Amendment Notes

—2012.
The 2012 amendment rewrote the section to the extent that a detailed comparison would be impracticable.

RESEARCH REFERENCES AND PRACTICE AIDS

New Hampshire Practice.
14-24 N.H.P. Local Government Law § 900.

155-A:5. Accessibility Standards for Public Buildings; Purpose and Intent.

The requirements of this section and RSA 155-A:5-a and RSA 155-A:5-b are intended to establish a system of certification and enforcement for the accessibility standards in the state building code for public buildings. For purposes of this section, public building means any building that is regulated by the accessibility standards contained in the state building code. This section is not intended to enlarge upon or expand any substantive standard of the state building code. This section is intended to apply solely to the new construction, addition, or alteration of a public building that is commenced on or after July 1, 2010 and only to the extent that the new construction, addition, or alteration is regulated by the accessibility standards in the state building code.

HISTORY:
2002, 8:3, eff. Sept. 14, 2002. 2009, 285:1, eff. January 1, 2010.

Amendments

—2009.
The 2009 amendment rewrote the section to the extent that a detailed comparison would be impracticable.

Applicability of 2009 amendment.
2009, 285:3, eff. January 1, 2010, provided: "Nothing in RSA 155-A:5, 155-A:5-a, or 155-A:5-b as inserted by sections 1 and 2 of this act shall require the owner of a public building to obtain an inspection or certification for the new construction, addition, or alteration of a public building commenced before the effective date of this act."

RESEARCH REFERENCES AND PRACTICE AIDS

New Hampshire Practice.
14-24 N.H.P. Local Government Law § 900.

155-A:5-a. Accessibility Standards for Public Buildings.

I. The new construction, addition, or alteration of a public building as described in RSA 155-A:5 and as governed under RSA 155-A:2, I shall be subject to the requirements of this section and RSA 155-A:5-b.

II. Except as provided in paragraph III, the contractor shall obtain and submit to the owner of the public building a written certification from a person qualified under RSA 155-A:5-b that:

(a) The design drawings or construction drawings for the proposed new construction, addition, or alteration meets the accessibility standards of the state building code; and

(b) Upon the completion and after inspection, the new construction, addition, or alteration meets the accessibility standards of the state building code.

III. The requirements of paragraph II shall not apply to a public building for which the review of design drawings or construction drawings and inspection of completed work is performed by a municipal building inspector who:

(a) Satisfies the qualifications under RSA 155-A:5-b;

(b) Examines the design drawings or construction drawings prior to the commencement of work and inspects the building upon completion of work for compliance with the accessibility standards in the state building code; and

(c) Provides the governing body of the municipality with a written certification that the design and construction of the building upon completion of work comply with the accessibility standards of the state building code.

IV. Nothing in this section shall be construed as requiring municipalities to inspect and certify public buildings for compliance with accessibility standards. Public buildings located in a municipality that has chosen to authorize its municipal building inspector to inspect and certify shall remain subject to all other provisions of this section.

V. In addition to other enforcement authority granted in this chapter, the protection and advocacy system for New Hampshire, as designated by the governor pursuant to 42 U.S.C. section 15043, shall have standing to enforce the accessibility standards required by this section. If the protection and advocacy system determines that probable cause exists that a public building violates the accessibility certification or inspection requirements of this section, it shall issue a letter to the owner of the building specifically identifying the deficiencies and requesting that the building be brought into compliance. The owner shall have 30 days to respond to the letter and 270 days to bring the building into compliance. If the owner does not respond, does not agree that there are some or all of the deficiencies asserted, or does not agree to bring the building into compliance within the specified time periods, or any other dispute remains as to compliance, either the owner or the protection and advocacy system may file an action in the superior court to determine compliance with this section. The protection and advocacy system may bring the action in its name or in the name of any individual with a physical impairment who is adversely affected by the alleged failure to adhere to the accessibility standards of the state building code, or both. If it is determined by the superior court that the building is not in compliance with the accessibility standards in the state building code, the court shall order that the responsible party bring the building into compliance. The court may award reasonable attorney's fees and costs to the prevailing party. For purposes of this section, a party prevails only if it receives either an enforceable judgment on the merits or a consent decree.

VI. Any individual with a physical impairment who is adversely affected by the failure to adhere to the requirements of this section shall have a private right of action against the owner pursuant to the procedure established in paragraph V, including the right to court costs and reasonable attorney's fees as the prevailing party.

VII. Any owner of a public building or contractor who is found by a preponderance of the evidence in a proceeding under this section to have knowingly violated the accessibility standards of the state building code shall be subject to a civil penalty. The penalties shall be the same as those established by RSA 155-A:8. All civil penalties shall be deposited into the general fund. The party bringing the action shall be entitled to reasonable attorney's fees and costs if it is determined by the court to be the prevailing party.

HISTORY:
2009, 285:2, eff. January 1, 2010. 2012, 197:1, eff. August 12, 2012.

Amendment Notes

—2012.
The 2012 amendment, in V, substituted "responsible party" for "owner" in the sixth sentence and rewrote the last two sentences,

which formerly read: "If the protection and advocacy system prevails in such action, it shall be awarded court costs and reasonable attorney's fees from the owner. For purposes of this section, 'prevailing' is defined to include a judgment by the court, a consent decree, or instances where the owner agrees to make or makes some or all of the requested changes after the filing date of the action" and made a stylistic change.

Applicability of enactment.
2009, 285:3, eff. January 1, 2010, provided: "Nothing in RSA 155-A:5, 155-A:5-a, or 155-A:5-b as inserted by sections 1 and 2 of this act shall require the owner of a public building to obtain an inspection or certification for the new construction, addition, or alteration of a public building commenced before the effective date of this act."

155-A:5-b. Accessibility Certifiers and Inspectors; Penalty.

I. New Hampshire licensed architects, professional engineers, certified building officials, and master code officials may certify building plans and/or inspect public buildings for compliance with the accessibility standards in RSA 155-A:5 and RSA 155-A:5-a without further examination. Any other person engaged in the business of certifying building plans and/or inspecting public buildings for compliance with accessibility standards required by RSA 155-A:5 and RSA 155-A:5-a shall successfully pass an International Code Council examination that covers the accessibility standards contained in the state building code prior to certifying that a building complies with RSA 155-A:5 and RSA 155-A:5-a. All accessibility certifiers and inspectors shall complete 2 hours of continuing education related to accessibility codes every 3 years and be able to produce proof of continuing education upon request.

II. Whoever falsely claims to be certified under this section through advertising, signage, or other written or oral representation shall be guilty of a violation if a natural person, or guilty of a class B misdemeanor if any other person.

HISTORY:
2009, 285:2, eff. January 1, 2010.

Applicability of enactment.
2009, 285:3, eff. January 1, 2010, provided: "Nothing in RSA 155-A:5, 155-A:5-a, or 155-A:5-b as inserted by sections 1 and 2 of this act shall require the owner of a public building to obtain an inspection or certification for the new construction, addition, or alteration of a public building commenced before the effective date of this act."

RESEARCH REFERENCES AND PRACTICE AIDS

Cross References.
Classification of crimes, see RSA 625:9.
Sentences, see RSA 651.

155-A:6. Inspection of State Buildings. [Repealed.]

[Repealed 2012, 242:22, eff. June 18, 2012.]

Former section(s).
Former RSA 155-A:6, which was derived from 2002, 8:3, related to the inspection of state buildings.

155-A:7. Enforcement Authority.

I. The local enforcement agency appointed pursuant to RSA 674:51 or RSA 47:22 shall have the authority to enforce the provisions of the state building code and the local fire chief shall have the authority to enforce the provisions of the state fire code, provided that where there is no local enforcement agency or contract with a qualified third party pursuant to RSA 155-A:2, VI, the state fire marshal or the state fire marshal's designee may enforce the provisions of the state building code and the state fire code, subject to the review provisions in RSA 155-A:10, upon written request of the municipality.

II. Upon the request of a local enforcement agency, state agencies, boards, and commissions may provide advisory services and technical assistance concerning any building or any construction project in the local enforcement agent's jurisdiction.

III. The local enforcement agency appointed to enforce the state building code shall have the authority to inspect all buildings, structures, construction sites, and other places in the jurisdiction. If consent for such inspection is denied or not reasonably obtainable, the local enforcement agency may obtain an administrative inspection warrant under RSA 595-B.

IV. All local enforcement agencies and selectmen and the state fire marshal in those communities without a local enforcement agency shall provide information on the local and state appeals process when issuing a building permit or notice of violation.

HISTORY:
2002, 8:3, eff. Sept. 14, 2002. 2012, 225:1, eff. August 14, 2012. 242:14, eff. June 18, 2012.

Amendment Notes

—2012.
The 2012 amendment by Chapter 225 added IV.
The 2012 amendment by Chapter 242 rewrote I to the extent that a detailed comparison would be impracticable.

RESEARCH REFERENCES AND PRACTICE AIDS

New Hampshire Practice.
14-24 N.H.P. Local Government Law § 900.

155-A:8. Penalty.

Fines, penalties, and remedies for violations of this chapter shall be the same as for violations of title LXIV, as stated in RSA 676:15 and 676:17.

HISTORY:
2002, 8:3, eff. Sept. 14, 2002.

RESEARCH REFERENCES AND PRACTICE AIDS

New Hampshire Practice.
14-24 N.H.P. Local Government Law § 900.

References in text.
Title LXIV, referred to in this section, is Title 64 of LEXIS New Hampshire Revised Statutes Annotated, which is comprised of chapters 672–678.

155-A:9. Fees.

The municipality may establish fees to defray the costs of administration, implementation, and enforcement of the state building code and any local amendments. Such fees shall be for the general use of the municipality having responsibility over the local enforcement agency.

HISTORY:
2002, 8:3, eff. Sept. 14, 2002.

RESEARCH REFERENCES AND PRACTICE AIDS

New Hampshire Practice.
14-24 N.H.P. Local Government Law § 900.

155-A:10. State Building Code Review Board.

I. There is established a state building code review board consisting of the commissioner of safety or the commissioner's designee, and the following members, appointed by the commissioner of safety:

(a) One architect licensed in this state for a minimum of 5 years, nominated by the board of architects established in RSA 310-A:29.

(b) One structural engineer licensed in this state for a minimum of 5 years, nominated by the board of professional engineers established in RSA 310-A:3.

(c) One mechanical engineer licensed in this state for a minimum of 5 years, nominated by the board of professional engineers established in RSA 310-A:3.

(d) One electrical engineer licensed in this state for a minimum of 5 years, nominated by the board of professional engineers established in RSA 310-A:3.

(e) One representative of the state's municipalities, nominated by the New Hampshire Municipal Association.

(f) One municipal building official, nominated by the New Hampshire Building Officials Association.

(g) One municipal fire chief, nominated by the New Hampshire Association of Fire Chiefs.

(h) One active fire prevention officer, nominated by the New Hampshire Association of Fire Chiefs.

(i) One building contractor, primarily engaged in the business of constructing nonresidential buildings, nominated by the Associated General Contractors of New Hampshire.

(j) One building contractor primarily engaged in the business of constructing residential buildings, nominated by the New Hampshire Home Builders Association.

(k) One representative from the state energy conservation code office under RSA 155-D, nominated by the New Hampshire public utilities commission.

(*l*) One master plumber licensed in this state for a minimum of 5 years, nominated by the mechanical licensing board established in RSA 153:27-a.

(m) One mechanical contractor, primarily engaged in the business of mechanical construction, nominated by the Plumbers, Fuel Gas Fitters, and HVAC Association of New Hampshire.

(n) One master electrician licensed in this state for a minimum of 5 years, nominated by the electricians' board established in RSA 319-C.

(*o*) One representative of the Committee on Architectural Barrier-Free Design nominated by the governor's commission on disability.

(p) One electrical contractor, nominated by Electrical Contractors Business Association.

II. The term of each member shall be 3 years. The chair of the board shall be appointed by the commissioner of safety after meeting with the board. Board members shall be appointed for no more than 2 consecutive 3-year terms. The board shall elect from among the members a vice-chair, who shall assume the responsibilities of the chair in the event of the chair's absence.

III. The board shall be administratively attached to the department of safety under RSA 21-G:10.

IV. The board shall meet to review and assess the application of the state building code and shall recommend legislation, as the board deems necessary, to amend the requirements of the state building code in order to provide consistency with the application of other laws, rules, or regulations, to avoid undue economic impacts on the public by considering the cost of such amendments, and to promote public safety and best practices.

V. The board may adopt rules to amend the state building code for the codes described in RSA 155-A:1, IV and IV-a, to the extent the board deems that such amendments are necessary, provided that any such amendments are ratified by the adoption of appropriate legislation within 2 years of their adoption. If such amendments are not ratified, then the rules shall expire, notwithstanding RSA 541-A:17, I, at the end of the 2-year period. With the approval of the commissioner of safety, the board shall be authorized, pursuant to RSA 541-A, to adopt rules relative to procedures of its operation and appeals to the board.

VI. The state building code review board shall not adopt or enforce any rule requiring the installation of fire sprinkler systems in any new or existing detached one- or 2-family dwelling unit in a structure used only for residential purposes. This paragraph shall not prohibit a duly adopted requirement mandating that fire sprinkler systems be offered to the owners of dwellings for a reasonable fee.

VII. Members of the board shall receive mileage at the rate established in the United States Internal Revenue Code and Regulations when attending meetings of the board for the round trip distance from their residences to the location of the board meeting.

HISTORY:
2002, 8:3, eff. April 17, 2002. 270:4, eff. at 12:01 a.m., April 17,

2002. 2003, 245:3, 4, 6, eff. July 14, 2003. 2007, 11:1, 2, eff. July 1, 2007. 2010, 282:3, eff. July 8, 2010. 2012, 242:15, eff. June 18, 2012. 2013, 64:1, eff. June 6, 2013. 275:10, eff. July 1, 2013. 2015, 276:197, eff. July 1, 2015.

Amendment Notes

—2015.

The 2015 amendment added paragraph VII.

—2013.

The 2013 amendment by Chapter 64 substituted "Plumbers, Fuel Gas Fitters, and HVAC Association of New Hampshire" for "New Hampshire Plumbing and Mechanical Contractors Association" in I(m).

The 2013 amendment by Chapter 275 substituted "mechanical licensing board established in RSA 153:27-a" for "state board for the licensing and regulation of plumbers established in RSA 329-A" in I(l).

—2012.

The 2012 amendment, in the introductory language of I, substituted "the following members" for "additional members" and deleted "as follows" at the end; added "professional" in I(b) through I(d); deleted "with a minimum of 5 years experience" following "One mechanical contractor" in I(m); substituted "One electrical contractor" for "One master electrician licensed in this state for a minimum of 5 years" in I(p); in II, in the second sentence, added "of the board" and "after meeting with the board" and added the last sentence; in IV, substituted "amend" for "modify," deleted "and the state fire code" preceding "in order to," and added "to avoid undue economic impacts on the public by considering the cost of such amendments"; in the first sentence of V, substituted "amend" for "update or change" and substituted "RSA 155-A:1, IV and IV-a" for "RSA 155-A:1, IV"; substituted "amendments" for "updates or changes" wherever it appears in the first and second sentences of V; deleted former VI; redesignated former VII as VI; and made a stylistic change.

—2010.

The 2010 amendment added VII.

—2007.

Paragraph I(h): Substituted "active fire prevention officer" for "municipal volunteer fire chief".

Paragraph II: Deleted "except that persons initially appointed under subparagraphs I(a), (d), (g), (j), and (m) shall serve one-year terms, and persons initially appointed under subparagraphs I(b), (e), (h), (k), and (n) shall serve 2-year terms" following "3 years" in the first sentence.

—2003.

Paragraph I: Deleted "15" preceding "additional members" in the introductory paragraph.

Paragraph I(p): Added.

Paragraph V: Deleted "manuals" following "building code" in the first sentence.

—2002.

Paragraph I(n): Substituted "electricians' board established in RSA 319-C" for "New Hampshire Electrical Contractors Business Association".

State Building Code; Ratification of Amendments by the State Building Code Review Board.

2012, 242:18, eff. June 18, 2012, provided: "Pursuant to RSA 155-A:10, V, the general court hereby ratifies the amendments to the state building codes, as defined in RSA 155-A:1, adopted by the state building code review board between January 1, 2010 and February 29, 2012, in administrative rules Bcr 300."

Working Group Formed.

2012, 242:19, eff. June 18, 2012, provided: "There is established a working group to study the egress provisions in the International Building Code and the egress provisions in the Life Safety Code in an effort to harmonize the codes and make them applicable to the needs of New Hampshire citizens balancing life safety considerations and economic concerns. The working group shall consist of the commissioner of safety or designee, a representative of the board of architects chosen by the board, a representative of the New Hampshire Home Builders and Remodelers Association chosen by the association, a representative of the New Hampshire Building Officials Association chosen by the association, a representative of the New Hampshire Association of Fire Chiefs chosen by the association, and the state fire marshal or designee. The commissioner of safety or designee shall serve as the chair and shall convene the meetings of the group. The group shall file a report with the chairs of the house and senate executive departments and administration committees not later than April 1, 2013, recommending any legislative changes."

Initial term of new member.

2003, 245:5, eff. July 14, 2003, provided:

"The initial term of the master electrician appointed under RSA 155-A:10, I(p) as inserted by this act shall coincide with the remaining term for the master electrician appointed under RSA 155-A:10, I(n). Subsequent terms shall be for 3 years".

RESEARCH REFERENCES AND PRACTICE AIDS

New Hampshire Practice.

14-24 N.H.P. Local Government Law § 900.

155-A:11. Appeals of Decisions of the State Fire Marshal.

I. Any person aggrieved by a decision of the state fire marshal relative to the application and enforcement of the state building code pursuant to RSA 153:8-a, I(a), or the state fire code, may appeal the decision to the board.

II. The board shall hold a hearing within 40 days of receipt of a complaint, unless an extension of time has been granted by the board at the written request of one of the parties and shall render a decision within 30 days of the conclusion of a hearing.

HISTORY:

2002, 8:3, eff. Sept. 14, 2002. 2012, 242:16, eff. June 18, 2012.

Amendment Notes

—2012.

The 2012 amendment rewrote I to the extent that a detailed comparison would be impracticable.

NOTES TO DECISIONS

Proper review

Property owner's due process rights were not violated by the procedures used by the fire marshal in reclassifying his property for fire code purposes because N.H. Code Admin. R. Ann. Saf.-C 6006.02 was preempted by the adoption of RSA 155-A:11, which provided that appeals from the marshal's decision would be heard by a board and not by a hearing in front of the fire marshal. Fischer v. N.H. State Bldg. Code Review Bd., 154 N.H. 585, 914 A.2d 1234, 2006 N.H. LEXIS 198 (N.H. 2006).

RESEARCH REFERENCES AND PRACTICE AIDS

New Hampshire Practice.

14-24 N.H.P. Local Government Law § 900.

155-A:11-a. Appeal of Decisions of the Electricians' Board and the Board of Home Inspectors.

I. The board shall hear appeals of final decisions of the board established under RSA 319-C:4 and the board established under RSA 310-A:186.

II. The board shall hold a hearing within 40 days of the receipt of an appeal, unless an extension of time has been granted by the board at the written request of one of the parties and shall render a decision within 30 days of the conclusion of the hearing.

HISTORY:

2004, 257:55, eff. June 15, 2004. 2008, 339:3, eff. July 1, 2008. 2013, 275:11, eff. July 1, 2013.

Amendment Notes

—2013.

The 2013 amendment substituted "Board of Home Inspectors" for "State Board for the Licensing and Regulation of Plumbers" in the section heading and deleted "the board established under RSA 329-A:3" following "RSA 319-C:4" in I.

—2008.

The 2008 amendment in I added "and the board established under RSA 310-A:186" and made a related change.

155-A:12. Appeal From Board's Decision.

I. A party to the proceeding shall have the right to file a petition in the superior court of the county in which the building or structure is located to review the final order of the board within 30 days of the date of the final order.

II. At the earliest practical time, the court shall review the record as developed before the board, together with any written legal argument presented to the court. Based on that review, the court may affirm or reverse the decision of the board or order that oral argument be held. As justice may require, the court may remand the case to the board for further findings and rulings. The petition for appeal shall set forth all the grounds upon which the final order is sought to be overturned. Issues not raised by the appellant before the board shall not be raised before the superior court. The burden of proof shall be on the appellant to show that the decision of the board was clearly unreasonable or unlawful.

III. No new or additional evidence shall be introduced in the superior court, but the case shall be determined upon the record and evidence transferred, except that in any case, if justice requires the review of evidence which by reason of accident, mistake, or misfortune could not have been offered before the board, the superior court shall remand the case to the board to receive and consider such additional evidence.

HISTORY:

2002, 8:3, eff. Sept. 14, 2002.

Decision upheld

Under RSA 155-A:12, II, state building code review board properly determined that owner's property no longer qualified as two-family dwellings under state fire code as adopted under N.H. Code Admin. R. Ann. Saf.-C 6008.01, 6008.03 because the regulations were not unconstitutionally retrospective under N.H. Const. pt. I, art. 23, the owner did not have a vested right to continued classification under N.H. Const. pt. I, art. 12, the interpretation fit the purpose of RSA 153:5, and the regulation did not impermissibly discriminate between related and unrelated individuals under the Fourteenth Amendment to the United States Constitution in that there was a rational basis for the classification. Fischer v. N.H. State Bldg. Code Review Bd., 154 N.H. 585, 914 A.2d 1234, 2006 N.H. LEXIS 198 (N.H. 2006).

RESEARCH REFERENCES AND PRACTICE AIDS

New Hampshire Practice.

14-24 N.H.P. Local Government Law § 900.

155-A:13. Building Requirements for State Funded Buildings.

I. Any new construction, reconstruction, alteration, or maintenance in any state owned building, plant, fixture, or facility, meeting the definition of "project" in RSA 21-I:78, considered a major project under RSA 21-I:80, and constructed using any state funding, shall meet a high performance, energy efficient, sustainable design standard determined by the commissioners of the department of environmental services and the department of administrative services, in consultation with the division of historic resources and the community college system, that shows the building or structure can recoup the incremental costs of implementing the requirements of this section as measured by reduced energy costs over a 10-year period of time.

II. The following construction or renovation projects shall be exempt from the requirements of paragraphs I:

(a) A building or structure that is less than 25,000 square feet.

(b) A building or structure that does not consume energy for heating, ventilating, or air conditioning.

(c) A renovation or modification that is estimated to cost less than $1,000,000.

(d) Temporary structures.

(e) Public school facilities that are subject to RSA 198:15-c.

(f) The university system of New Hampshire.

(g) Projects employing new, innovative, or experimental energy efficient technology that may not recoup their incremental costs within 10 years, as may be determined by the commissioner of the department of administrative services to be in the best interest of the state.

HISTORY:

2010, 347:1, eff. July 1, 2011.

CHAPTER 155-E
LOCAL REGULATION EXCAVATIONS

Codification.

This chapter was enacted as RSA 155-D and renumbered as 155-E to avoid conflict with pre-existing RSA 155-D which was added by 1979, 460:1.

State and municipal roles relating to regulation of mining and excavation.

1988, 285:2, eff. May 2, 1988, provided:

"It is hereby declared to be the intent of the legislature to clarify the respective roles of state and local governments concerning the regulation of mining and excavation activities in light of the recent Supreme Court decision in Appeal of Coastal Materials Corporation [(1987) 130 NH 98, 534 A2d 398]. The state shall have the power to regulate the extraction of minerals including the removal of dimension stone. The municipalities shall have the power to regulate the removal of earth to be used as construction aggregate."

NOTES TO DECISIONS

Analysis

1. Purpose
2. Construction
3. Construction with other laws
4. Preemption

1. Purpose

Legislature's purpose in enacting this chapter was, in part, to increase supply of construction materials and decrease cost of roads and other governmental infrastructure to the public by curtailing simultaneous state and local regulations of the same activity. Arthur Whitcomb, Inc. v. Town of Carroll, 141 N.H. 402, 686 A.2d 743, 1996 N.H. LEXIS 117 (N.H. 1996), limited, Guildhall Sand & Gravel, LLC v. Town of Goshen, 155 N.H. 762, 929 A.2d 199, 2007 N.H. LEXIS 128 (N.H. 2007).

2. Construction

This chapter expresses a clear intention that the crushing of granite not be regulated by local authorities. Appeal of Coastal Materials Corp., 130 N.H. 98, 534 A.2d 398, 1987 N.H. LEXIS 280 (N.H. 1987).

3. Construction with other laws

This chapter and RSA 31:41-b, granting authority to local governing bodies to regulate a specific land use, namely earth excavation, exist as grants of authority independent of the zoning enabling legislation. Goffstown v. Thibeault, 129 N.H. 454, 529 A.2d 930, 1987 N.H. LEXIS 184 (N.H. 1987).

4. Preemption

RSA ch. 155-E did not impliedly preempt a town's variance requirement for an excavation. The plain language of RSA 155-E:2, IV(b) evinced the legislature's intent to preempt local regulation of excavation undertaken exclusively for highway construction purposes only with respect to the statutory operational and reclamation standards. Town of Carroll v. Rines, 164 N.H. 523, 62 A.3d 733, 2013 N.H. LEXIS 4 (N.H. 2012).

Ordinance requiring a property owner to obtain a local use variance before excavating was preempted by RSA ch. 155-E. It provided no exceptions for excavations for highway purposes or excavations incidental to building construction and thus purported to regulate excavations that were permit-exempt under RSA ch. 155-E; furthermore, it imposed substantive requirements on such excavations and thus frustrated state authority. Town of Carroll v. Rines, 2012 N.H. LEXIS 150 (N.H. Nov. 9, 2012), op. withdrawn, 2012 N.H. LEXIS 175 (N.H. Dec. 7, 2012), sub. op., 164 N.H. 523, 62 A.3d 733, 2013 N.H. LEXIS 4 (N.H. 2012).

This chapter's exhaustive treatment of the field of excavation manifested a legislative intent to preempt it, although not all local legislation applicable to excavation was therefore void; rather, this chapter preempted only local ordinances and regulations that would have the effect or intent of frustrating state authority. Arthur Whitcomb, Inc. v. Town of Carroll, 141 N.H. 402, 686 A.2d 743, 1996 N.H. LEXIS 117 (N.H. 1996), limited, Guildhall Sand & Gravel, LLC v. Town of Goshen, 155 N.H. 762, 929 A.2d 199, 2007 N.H. LEXIS 128 (N.H. 2007).

Cited:

Cited in Lorette v. Peter-Sam Inv. Props., 142 N.H. 207, 697 A.2d 1386, 1997 N.H. LEXIS 78 (1997).

RESEARCH REFERENCES AND PRACTICE AIDS

Cross References.

Hazardous excavations, see RSA 155-B:13.
Mining and reclamation, see RSA 12-E.

New Hampshire Practice.

13-4 N.H.P. Local Government Law § 66.
14-20 N.H.P. Local Government Law § 745.
16-20 N.H.P. Municipal Law & Taxation § 20.03A.

155-E:1. Definitions.

In this chapter:

I. "Earth" means sand, gravel, rock, soil or construction aggregate produced by quarrying, crushing or any other mining activity or such other naturally-occurring unconsolidated materials that normally mask the bedrock.

II. "Excavation" means a land area which is used, or has been used, for the commercial taking of earth, including all slopes.

III. "Regulator" means:

(a) The planning board of a city or town, or if a town at an annual or special meeting duly warned for the purpose so provides, the selectmen of the town or the board of adjustment; or

(b) If there is no planning board, the selectmen of the town or the legislative body of the city; or

(c) The county commissioners if the land area is in an unincorporated place.

IV. "Dimension stone" means rock that is cut, shaped, or selected for use in blocks, slabs, sheets, or other construction units of specified shapes or sizes and used for external or interior parts of buildings, foundations, curbing, paving, flagging, bridges, revetments, or for other architectural or engineering purposes. Dimension stone includes quarry blocks from which sections of dimension stone are to be produced. Dimension stone does not include earth as defined in RSA 155-E:1, I.

V. "Excavation site" means any area of contiguous land in common ownership upon which excavation takes place.

VI. "Excavation area" means the surface area within an excavation site where excavation has occurred or is eligible to occur under the provisions of this chapter.

HISTORY:

1979, 481:2. 1988, 285:6, 7. 1989, 363:2. 1991, 310:3, eff. Aug. 23, 1991. 2002, 103:9, eff. April 1, 2002.

Amendments

—2002.

Paragraph VI: Inserted "surface" preceding "area within".

—1991.

Paragraph VI: Added.

—1989.

Paragraph V: Added.

—1988.

Paragraph I: Added "produced by quarrying, crushing or any other mining activity or such other naturally-occurring unconsolidated materials that normally mask the bedrock" following "construction aggregate".

Paragraph IV: Added.

NOTES TO DECISIONS

Analysis

1. Construction
2. Slopes

1. Construction

Statutory definition of "excavation" in RSA 155-E:1, II includes "all slopes" in the land area used for the commercial taking of earth and includes no exception for slopes created as part of reclamation; thus, the argument that the slope is separate from the excavation activity is contrary to the plain language of RSA 155-E:1, II. Moreover, permitting disruption of the soil in the setback area as part of reclamation would contravene the express statutory provisions protecting the setback area; the requirement in RSA 155-E:5, III that slopes be "graded to natural repose" does not vitiate the prohibition against excavation within 50 feet of the boundary of a disapproving abutter under RSA 155-E:4-a, II. Bedard v. Town of Alexandria, 159 N.H. 740, 992 A.2d 607, 2010 N.H. LEXIS 13 (N.H. 2010).

2. Slopes

There was no merit to the argument that the creation of a 45-degree slope in a setback area did not constitute "excavation." The definition of "excavation" in RSA 155-E:1 included "all slopes" in the land area used for the commercial taking of earth; the definition included no exception for slopes created as part of reclamation under RSA 155-E:5. Bedard v. Town of Alexandria, 159 N.H. 740, 992 A.2d 607, 2010 N.H. LEXIS 13 (N.H. 2010).

Cited:

Cited in Appeal of Coastal Materials Corp., 130 N.H. 98, 534 A.2d 398, 1987 N.H. LEXIS 280 (1987); Wolfeboro (Planning Bd.) v. Smith, 131 N.H. 449, 556 A.2d 755, 1989 N.H. LEXIS 17 (1989); Barrington v. Gadd, 132 N.H. 650, 569 A.2d 231, 1990 N.H. LEXIS 6 (1990); Arthur Whitcomb, Inc. v. Town of Carroll, 141 N.H. 402, 686 A.2d 743, 1996 N.H. LEXIS 117 (1996).

OPINIONS OF THE ATTORNEY GENERAL

Cited:

Cited in 1986 Op. Att'y Gen. 193.

155-E:2. Permit Required.

No owner shall permit any excavation of earth on his premises without first obtaining a permit therefor, except as follows:

I. EXISTING EXCAVATIONS. The owner of an excavation which lawfully existed as of August 24, 1979, from which earth material of sufficient weight or volume to be commercially useful has been removed during the 2-year period before August 24, 1979, may continue such existing excavation on the excavation site without a permit, subject to the following:

(a) Such an excavation site shall be exempt from the provisions of local zoning or similar ordinances regulating the location of the excavation site, provided that at the time the excavation was first begun, it was in compliance with such local ordinances and regulations, if any, as were then in effect.

(b) Such an excavation area may not be expanded, without a permit under this chapter, beyond the limits of the town in which it is situated and the area which, on August 24, 1979, and at all times subsequent thereto has been contiguous to and in common ownership with the excavation site as of that date, and has been appraised and inventoried for property tax purposes as part of the same tract as the excavation site of that date, as modified by the limitations of RSA 155-E:4-a, I, II, and II-a. In this paragraph the term "contiguous" means land whose perimeter can be circumscribed without interruption in common ownership except for roads or other easements, in a single town. It is further provided that when such excavation is not allowed in that location by local zoning or similar ordinances in effect on August 4, 1989, or when such ordinances allow such excavation only by special exception, expansion may be restricted or modified with conditions by order of the regulator if after notice to the owner and a hearing, the regulator finds that such expansion will have a substantially different and adverse impact on the neighborhood.

(c) Such an excavation shall be performed in compliance with the express operational standards of RSA 155-E:4-a and the express reclamation standards of RSA 155-E:5 and 155-E:5-a. Any violations of those standards shall be enforceable pursuant to RSA 155-E:10.

(d) The owners or operators of any existing excavation area for which no permit has been obtained under this chapter shall file a report with the local regulator within one year after receiving written notice of this requirement from the regulator and in no case later than 2 years following August 4, 1989. The report shall include:

(1) The location of the excavation and the date the excavation first began;

(2) A description of the limits of permissible expansion, as described in subparagraph (b), which are claimed to apply to the excavation;

(3) An estimate of the area which has been excavated at the time of the report; and

(4) An estimate of the amount of commercially viable earth materials still available on the parcel.

(e) The exemption from local zoning or site location regulations as stated in subparagraph (a) shall include the quarrying or crushing of bedrock for the production of construction aggregate; provided, however, that no owner shall, after August 4, 1989, permit any such quarrying or crushing of bedrock to occur for the first time on any excavation site without first obtaining a permit therefor under this chapter.

II. **ABANDONED EXCAVATIONS.** The permit and zoning exemptions under RSA 155-E:2, I shall not apply to any abandoned excavation, as defined in subparagraph (a).

(a) For purposes of this section, any excavation, except for excavations or excavation sites described in RSA 155-E:2, III, whether subject to a permit under this chapter or not, for which the affected area has not yet been brought into complete compliance with the reclamation standards of RSA 115-E:5 shall be deemed "abandoned" if:

(1) No earth material of sufficient weight or volume to be commercially useful has been removed from that excavation site during any 2-year period, either before, on, or after August 4, 1989; provided, however, that before the end of such 2-year period, the owner or operator may extend the period by submitting to the regulator a reclamation timetable to be approved by the regulator, and posting a bond or other security with the municipal treasurer in a form and amount prescribed by the regulator, sufficient to secure the reclamation of the entire excavation site in accordance with the standards of RSA 155-E:5; or

(2) The excavation site is in use and is not an excavation or excavation site as described in RSA 155-E:2, III, but does not conform with the incremental reclamation requirement of RSA 155-E:5-a, or the owner or operator has not posted a bond or other security and submitted a reclamation timetable to be approved by the regulator as described in subparagraph (a)(1); or

(3) The owner or operator of the excavation has neither secured a permit pursuant to this chapter nor filed a report of an existing excavation pursuant to subparagraph I(d) within the prescribed period.

(b) In addition to the enforcement remedies of RSA 155-E:10, the regulator may order the owner of any land upon which an abandoned excavation is located to either file a reclamation timetable, to be approved by the regulator, and bond or other security as described in subparagraph II(a)(1), or to complete reclamation in accordance with this chapter within a stated reasonable time. Such an order shall only be made following a hearing for which notice has been given in accordance with RSA 155-E:7, if the regulator finds that the public health, safety, or welfare requires such reclamation. If the owner fails to complete reclamation within the time prescribed in the order, the regulator may request the governing body to cause reclamation to be completed at the expense of the municipality. The municipality's costs shall constitute an assessment against the owner, and shall create a lien against the real estate on which the excavation is located. Such assessment and lien may be enforced and collected in the same manner as provided for real estate taxes.

(c) The site of an excavation which ceased commercially useful operation prior to August 24, 1977, but for which the affected area has not been brought into compliance with the reclamation standards of RSA 155-E:5, may be made subject to the remedy prescribed in RSA 155-E:2, II(b) only if the regulator finds in writing that specified reclamation measures are necessary to eliminate or mitigate an identified hazard to public health or safety.

III. **Stationary Manufacturing Plants.**

(a) No permit shall be required under this chapter for excavation from an excavation site which on August 4, 1989, was contiguous to or was contiguous land in common ownership with stationary manufacturing and processing plants which were in operation as of August 24, 1979, and which use earth obtained from such excavation site. Such excavation shall be performed in compliance with the operational standards as expressly set forth in RSA 155-E:4-a and the reclamation standards as expressly set forth in RSA 155-E:5 and 155-E:5-a, which express standards shall be the sole standards with which such excavations must comply in order to retain their non-permit status as provided under this paragraph. Loss of such non-permit status shall be preceded by written notice from the regulator that the excavation is not in compliance and the owner shall have failed to bring such excavation into compliance within 30 days of receipt of such notice. Such excavation may be expanded without a permit under this chapter to any contiguous lands which were in common ownership with the site of the plant on August 4, 1989, except as limited by RSA 155-E:4-a, I, II, and III.

(b) No further permit shall be required under this chapter for excavation from a site which on August 4, 1989, was contiguous to or was contiguous land in common ownership with stationary manufacturing and processing plants for which local or state permits have been granted since

August 24, 1979, and before August 4, 1989, which use earth obtained from such site. It is further provided that their operation and reclamation shall continue to be regulated by such local or state permits and any renewals or extensions thereof by the permitting authority or authorities.

IV. HIGHWAY EXCAVATIONS. No permit shall be required under this chapter for excavation which is performed exclusively for the lawful construction, reconstruction, or maintenance of a class I, II, III, IV or V highway by a unit of government having jurisdiction for the highway or an agent of the unit of government which has a contract for the construction, reconstruction, or maintenance of the highway, subject, however, to the following:

(a) A copy of the pit agreement executed by the owner, the agent, and the governmental unit shall be filed with the regulator prior to the start of excavation. The failure to file such agreement, or the failure of the excavator to comply with the terms of such agreement, shall be deemed a violation of this chapter, and may be enforced pursuant to RSA 155-E:10.

(b) Such excavation shall not be exempt from local zoning or other applicable ordinances, unless such an exemption is granted pursuant to subparagraph (c), or from the operational and reclamation standards as expressly set forth in RSA 155-E:4-a, 155-E:5 and 155-E:5-a, which express standards shall be the sole standards with which such excavations must comply in order to retain their non-permit status as provided under this paragraph. Before beginning such excavation, the governmental unit or its agents shall certify to the regulator that:

(1) The excavation shall comply with the operational and reclamation standards of RSA 155-E:4-a, RSA 155-E:5, and 155-E:5-a.

(2) The excavation shall not be within 50 feet of the boundary of a disapproving abutter or within 10 feet of the boundary of an approving abutter, unless requested by said approving abutter.

(3) The excavation shall not be unduly hazardous or injurious to the public welfare.

(4) Existing visual barriers in the areas specified in RSA 155-E:3, III shall not be removed, except to provide access to the excavation.

(5) The excavation shall not substantially damage a known aquifer, so designated by the United States Geological Survey.

(6) All required permits for the excavation from state or federal agencies have been obtained.

(c) The department of transportation or its agent may apply directly to the appeals board created under RSA 21-L to be exempted from the provisions of local zoning or other ordinances or regulations, with respect to the excavation or transportation of materials being used exclusively for the lawful construction, reconstruction, or maintenance of a class I, II, or III highway.

(1) The application shall state whether the applicant has requested any exceptions or variances which may be available at the local level, and shall describe the outcome of such requests.

(2) Prior to acting on the application, the board shall hold a hearing in the municipality whose ordinance or regulation is at issue. At least 7 days prior to such hearing, notice shall be published in a newspaper of general circulation in the municipality, and shall be sent by certified mail to the applicant, the municipality's chief executive officer as defined in RSA 672:9, the chairman of its governing board as defined in RSA 672:6, the chairman of the local regulator as defined in RSA 155-E:1, the chairman of its conservation commission, if any, and, if the proposed exemption concerns an excavation site, to the abutters of that site as defined in RSA 672:3.

(3) Following the hearing, the board shall issue a written decision, copies of which shall be mailed to the applicant and the parties to whom notice was sent. If an exemption is granted, the written decisions shall include:

(A) A statement of the precise section of the ordinance or regulation from which the applicant is exempted. The applicant shall not be exempt from any section or provisions not so listed.

(B) An identification of the public interest being protected by the ordinance or regulation.

(C) A statement of the state interest involved, and of why, in the opinion of the board, that state interest overrides the interest protected by the ordinance or regulation.

(D) Any conditions to be imposed on the applicant, to protect the public health, safety, or welfare.

(4) The decision of the board may be appealed in the manner provided for zoning decisions in RSA 677:4–14; provided, however, that a decision under this section shall be considered a rehearing under RSA 677, and no further motion for rehearing shall be required.

HISTORY:
  1979, 481:2. 1985, 88:2. 1988, 285:8. 1989, 363:3. 1991, 310:4–9, eff. Aug. 23, 1991.

Revision note.
  Substituted "August 4 1989" for "the effective date of this subparagraph" in subpar. I(e) for purposes of clarity.

Amendments

—1991.
  Rewritten to the extent that a detailed comparison would be impracticable.

—1989.
  Rewritten to the extent that a detailed comparison would be impracticable.

—**1988.**
Paragraph IV: Added "for the purpose of producing dimension stone" following "quarry".

—**1985.**
Paragraph VI: Added.

NOTES TO DECISIONS

Analysis

1. Existing excavation exemption
2. Stationary plant exemption
3. Scope of exemption
4. Municipal ordinance not preempted

1. Existing excavation exemption

Where town established that excavations were ongoing and that no permit had been granted, burden was on defendant to prove that their mining activities satisfied requirements for invocation of statutory "grandfather clause." Barrington v. Gadd, 132 N.H. 650, 569 A.2d 231, 1990 N.H. LEXIS 6 (N.H. 1990).

Party claiming exemption from excavation permit requirement under grandfather clause has burden of proving the "intent" to excavate an area larger than that already excavated prior to effective date of this section. Wolfeboro (Planning Bd.) v. Smith, 131 N.H. 449, 556 A.2d 755, 1989 N.H. LEXIS 17 (N.H. 1989).

Superior court order based on finding that defendants were entitled to additional excavation on their property without a permit under grandfather clause exemption was reversed and remanded, where evidence was inadequate to manifest the necessary objective "intent" to excavate the acreage in question prior to the effective date of this section. Wolfeboro (Planning Bd.) v. Smith, 131 N.H. 449, 556 A.2d 755, 1989 N.H. LEXIS 17 (N.H. 1989).

Party who desires to continue excavation operations without a permit under grandfather clause exemption must meet a three-pronged test: first, he must prove that excavation activities were actively being pursued when the law became effective; second, he must prove that the area he desires to excavate was clearly intended to be excavated, as measured by objective manifestations and not by subjective intent; and, third, he must prove that the continued operations do not, and/or will not, have a substantially different and adverse impact on the neighborhood. Wolfeboro (Planning Bd.) v. Smith, 131 N.H. 449, 556 A.2d 755, 1989 N.H. LEXIS 17 (N.H. 1989).

Municipality requesting that an excavation permit be obtained need only prove that excavations are ongoing and that no permit has been granted; upon this showing, burden of proof shifts to a party desiring to continue excavation operations without a permit under grandfather clause exemption to meet three-pronged test. Wolfeboro (Planning Bd.) v. Smith, 131 N.H. 449, 556 A.2d 755, 1989 N.H. LEXIS 17 (N.H. 1989).

2. Stationary plant exemption

Assuming compliance with other requirements of subdivision III(a) of this section, contiguity provision allowed new excavation in any area bordering an excavation. Arthur Whitcomb, Inc. v. Town of Carroll, 141 N.H. 402, 686 A.2d 743, 1996 N.H. LEXIS 117 (N.H. 1996), limited, Guildhall Sand & Gravel, LLC v. Town of Goshen, 155 N.H. 762, 929 A.2d 199, 2007 N.H. LEXIS 128 (N.H. 2007).

3. Scope of exemption

Under plain reading of statutory language, exemption in subdivision III(a) of this section applied to plaintiff's blasting operation. Arthur Whitcomb, Inc. v. Town of Carroll, 141 N.H. 402, 686 A.2d 743, 1996 N.H. LEXIS 117 (N.H. 1996), limited, Guildhall Sand & Gravel, LLC v. Town of Goshen, 155 N.H. 762, 929 A.2d 199, 2007 N.H. LEXIS 128 (N.H. 2007).

Permitting exception found in subdivision III(a) of this section has limited applicability, and blasting operations must comply with State and federal strictures relating to explosives. Arthur Whitcomb, Inc. v. Town of Carroll, 141 N.H. 402, 686 A.2d 743, 1996 N.H. LEXIS 117 (N.H. 1996), limited, Guildhall Sand & Gravel, LLC v.

Town of Goshen, 155 N.H. 762, 929 A.2d 199, 2007 N.H. LEXIS 128 (N.H. 2007).

4. Municipal ordinance not preempted

RSA 155-E:2, IV evinces the legislature's intent to preempt local regulation of excavation undertaken exclusively for highway construction purposes only with respect to the statutory operational and reclamation standards. All other local regulations applicable to highway excavation are not preempted, unless an exemption from those regulations is granted. Town of Carroll v. Rines, 164 N.H. 523, 62 A.3d 733, 2013 N.H. LEXIS 4 (N.H. 2012).

RSA ch. 155-E did not impliedly preempt a town's variance requirement for an excavation. The plain language of RSA 155-E:2, IV(b) evinced the legislature's intent to preempt local regulation of excavation undertaken exclusively for highway construction purposes only with respect to the statutory operational and reclamation standards. Town of Carroll v. Rines, 164 N.H. 523, 62 A.3d 733, 2013 N.H. LEXIS 4 (N.H. 2012).

Goshen, N.H., Zoning Ordinance fit within the scope of permissible municipal regulation under RSA ch. 155-E because, by its terms, it applied only to excavations requiring a permit; it followed that the more stringent requirements set forth in the ordinance were not preempted. Guildhall Sand & Gravel, LLC v. Town of Goshen, 155 N.H. 762, 929 A.2d 199, 2007 N.H. LEXIS 128 (N.H. 2007).

Cited:

Cited in Small v. Zoning Bd. of Adjustment, 121 N.H. 226, 427 A.2d 520, 1981 N.H. LEXIS 284 (1981); Appeal of Coastal Materials Corp., 130 N.H. 98, 534 A.2d 398, 1987 N.H. LEXIS 280 (1987); North Hampton v. Sanderson, 131 N.H. 614, 557 A.2d 643, 1989 N.H. LEXIS 32 (1989).

RESEARCH REFERENCES AND PRACTICE AIDS

New Hampshire Practice.
13-4 N.H.P. Local Government Law § 66.

References in text.
The reference to "RSA 115-E:5" in subpar. II(a) appears to be incorrect and should probably be RSA 155-E:5.

155-E:2-a. Other Exceptions.

I. No permit shall be required for the following types of excavations:

(a) Excavation that is exclusively incidental to the construction or alteration of a building or structure or the construction or alteration of a parking lot or way including a driveway on a portion of the premises where the removal occurs; provided, however, that no such excavation shall be commenced without a permit under this chapter unless all state and local permits required for the construction or alteration of the building, structure, parking lot, or way have been issued.

(b) Excavation that is incidental to agricultural or silvicultural activities, normal landscaping, or minor topographical adjustment.

(c) Excavation from a granite quarry for the purpose of producing dimension stone, if such excavation requires a permit under RSA 12-E.

II. A person owning land abutting a site which was taken by eminent domain or by any other governmental taking upon which construction is taking place may stockpile earth taken from the construction site and may remove the earth at a later date after written notification to the appropriate local official.

HISTORY:

1989, 363:4, eff. Aug. 4, 1989.

155-E:3. Application for Permit.

Any owner or owner's designee subject to this chapter shall, prior to excavation of his land, apply to the regulator in each city or town involved for a permit for excavation. If the area subject to this chapter is situated in an unincorporated place application shall be made to the county commissioners. The applicant shall also send a copy of the application to the conservation commission, if any, of the city or town. Such application shall be signed and dated by the applicant and shall contain at least the following information:

I. The name and address of the owner of the land to be excavated, the person who will actually do the excavating and all abutters to the premises on which the excavation is proposed;

II. A sketch and description of the location and boundaries of the proposed excavation, the number of acres to be involved in the project and the municipalities and counties in which the project lies;

III. A sketch and description of the access and visual barriers to public highways to be utilized in the proposed excavation;

IV. The breadth, depth and slope of the proposed excavation and the estimated duration of the project;

V. The elevation of the highest annual average groundwater table within or next to the proposed excavation;

VI. A plan for the reclamation of the area affected by the excavation at least in compliance with RSA 155-E:5 and RSA 155-E:5-a. Such plan shall address the effects of the proposed excavation on soil, surface water and groundwater, vegetation, overburden, topography, and fill material, and may address future land use consistent with the approved master plan, and shall include a timetable for reclamation of fully depleted areas within the excavation site during said project;

VI-a. Specific actions to be taken by the applicant on the excavation site relative to fuel and chemical handling and storage, dust control, traffic, noise control and abatement, and comprehensive site safety of unauthorized persons; and

VII. Such other information or other special investigative studies as the regulator may reasonably deem necessary.

HISTORY:

1979, 481:2. 1989, 363:5. 1991, 310:10, 11, eff. Aug. 23, 1991. 1996, 141:2, eff. Jan. 1, 1997.

Revision note.

In par. V, substituted "groundwater" for "ground water" to conform to proper grammatical usage.

Amendments

—1996.

Paragraph VII: Inserted "or other special investigative studies" following "information," and substituted "deem necessary" for "require."

—1991.

Paragraph VI: Rewritten to the extent that a detailed comparison would be impracticable.

Paragraph VI-a: Added.

—1989.

Paragraph VI: Substituted "reclamation" for "restoration" following "plan for the".

NOTES TO DECISIONS

Cited:

Cited in Wolfeboro (Planning Bd.) v. Smith, 131 N.H. 449, 556 A.2d 755, 1989 N.H. LEXIS 17 (1989).

155-E:4. Prohibited Projects.

The regulator shall not grant a permit:

I. Where the excavation would violate the operational standards of RSA 155-E:4-a;

II. For excavation within 50 feet of the boundary of a disapproving abutter or within 10 feet of the boundary of an approving abutter unless approval is requested by said abutter;

III. When the excavation is not permitted by zoning or other applicable ordinance, provided, however, that in municipalities which have commercial earth resources on unimproved land within their boundaries, and which do not provide for opportunities for excavation of some of these resources in at least some, but not necessarily all areas within the municipality, or in municipalities which have zoning ordinances which do not address the subject of excavations, excavation shall be deemed to be a use allowed by special exception as provided in RSA 674:33, IV, in any non-residential area of the municipality, and the zoning board of adjustment shall grant such a special exception upon a finding that:

(a) The excavation will not cause a diminution in area property value or unreasonably change the character of the neighborhood;

(b) The excavation will not unreasonably accelerate the deterioration of highways or create safety hazards in the use thereof;

(c) The excavation will not create any nuisance or create health or safety hazards; and

(d) The excavation complies with such other special exception criteria as may be set out in applicable local ordinances.

IV. When the issuance of the permit would be unduly hazardous or injurious to the public welfare;

V. Where existing visual barriers in the areas specified in RSA 155-E:3, III would be removed, except to provide access to the excavation;

VI. Where the excavation would substantially damage a known aquifer, so designated by the United States Geological Survey;

VII. When the excavation requires land use permits from state or federal agencies; but the regulator may approve the application when all necessary land use permits have been obtained; or

VIII. Where the project cannot comply with the reclamation provisions of RSA 155-E:5 and 155-E:5-a.

HISTORY:

1979, 481:2. 1989, 138:5. 363:6–8. 1991, 310:12, 13, eff. Aug. 23, 1991.

Amendments

—1991.

Paragraph III: Deleted "reasonable" preceding "opportunities", substituted "these" for "those" preceding "resources", and inserted "in at least some, but not necessarily all areas within the municipality" thereafter and "in any non-residential area of the municipality" following "RSA 674:33, IV" in the introductory paragraph, substituted "a" for "an unreasonable" following "cause" in subpar. (a), deleted "and" following "thereof" in subpar. (b), deleted "unreasonable" preceding "nuisance" and added "and" following "hazards" in subpar. (c) and added subpar. (d).

Paragraph VII: Rewritten to the extent that a detailed comparison would be impracticable.

—1989.

Paragraphs I and III: Rewritten by ch. 363 to the extent that a detailed comparison would be impracticable.

Paragraph VII: Chapter 138 substituted "division of water supply and pollution control, the division of water resources, the wetlands board" for "water supply and pollution control commission, the water resources board, the special board on dredge and fill" following "required from the".

Chapter 363 substituted "department of environmental services" for "division of water supply and pollution control, the division of water resources, the wetlands board or other state" following "required from the".

Paragraph VIII: Chapter 363 substituted "reclamation" for "restoration" following "comply with the" and added "and 155-E:5-a" following "RSA 155-E:5".

NOTES TO DECISIONS

Cited:

Cited in North Hampton v. Sanderson, 131 N.H. 614, 557 A.2d 643, 1989 N.H. LEXIS 32 (1989).

155-E:4-a. Minimum and Express Operational Standards.

It shall be a violation of this chapter for any person to excavate, or for any owner to permit excavation on his excavation site, when such excavation is subject to a permit under this chapter, without complying with the following minimum standards or when such excavation is not subject to a permit under this chapter pursuant to RSA 155-E:2 without complying with the following express standards:

I. No excavation shall be permitted below road level within 50 feet of the right of way of any public highway as defined in RSA 229:1 unless such excavation is for the purpose of said highway.

II. No excavation shall be permitted within 50 feet of the boundary of a disapproving abutter, within 150 feet of any dwelling which either existed or for which a building permit has been issued at the time the excavation is commenced.

II-a. No excavation shall be permitted within 75 feet of any great pond, navigable river, or any other standing body of water 10 acres or more in area or within 25 feet of any other stream, river or brook which normally flows throughout the year, or any naturally occurring standing body of water less than 10 acres, prime wetland as designated in accordance with RSA 482-A:15, I or any other wetland greater than 5 acres in area as defined by the department of environmental services.

III. Vegetation shall be maintained or provided within the peripheral areas required by paragraphs I and II.

IV. Drainage shall be maintained so as to prevent the accumulation of free-standing water for prolonged periods. Excavation practices which result in continued siltation of surface waters or any degradation of water quality of any public or private water supplies are prohibited.

V. No fuels, lubricants, or other toxic or polluting materials shall be stored on-site unless in compliance with state laws or rules pertaining to such materials.

VI. Where temporary slopes will exceed a grade of 1:1, a fence or other suitable barricade shall be erected to warn of danger or limit access to the site.

VII. Prior to the removal of topsoil or other overburden material from any land area that has not yet been excavated, the excavator shall file a reclamation bond or other security as prescribed by the regulator, sufficient to secure the reclamation of the land area to be excavated.

VIII. Nothing in this chapter shall be deemed to supersede or preempt applicable environmental standards or permit requirements contained in other state laws, and no exemption under this chapter shall be construed as an exemption from any other state statute.

HISTORY:

1989, 363:9. 1991, 310:14–17, eff. Aug. 23, 1991. 1996, 296:36, eff. Aug. 9, 1996.

Amendments

—1996.

Paragraph II-a: Substituted "department of environmental services" for "wetlands board" at the end of the paragraph.

—1991.

Added "Minimum and Express" preceding "Operational" in the section catchline and rewrote the introductory paragraph.

Paragraph II-a: Added.

Paragraph IV: Inserted "continued" preceding "siltation of" and substituted "surface waters or any" for "streams or" thereafter and "water quality of any public or private" for "any" following "degradation of" in the second sentence and deleted the former third and fourth sentences of par. IV.

Paragraph VII: Inserted "overburden" preceding "material from" and substituted "any land area that has not yet been excavated" for "a new excavation area" thereafter and "land area to be excavated" for "site" following "secure the reclamation of the".

Contingent 1996 amendment.

1996, 296:8, provided for amendment of this section. However, under the terms of 1996, 296:54, eff. Aug. 9, 1996, the amendment did not become effective.

NOTES TO DECISIONS

Analysis

1. Municipal ordinance not preempted
2. Abutters

1. Municipal ordinance not preempted

Goshen, N.H., Zoning Ordinance fit within the scope of permissible municipal regulation under RSA ch. 155-E because, by its terms, it applied only to excavations requiring a permit; it followed that the more stringent requirements set forth in the ordinance were not preempted. Guildhall Sand & Gravel, LLC v. Town of Goshen, 155 N.H. 762, 929 A.2d 199, 2007 N.H. LEXIS 128 (N.H. 2007).

2. Abutters

Statutory definition of "excavation" in RSA 155-E:1, II includes "all slopes" in the land area used for the commercial taking of earth and includes no exception for slopes created as part of reclamation; thus, the argument that the slope is separate from the excavation activity is contrary to the plain language of RSA 155-E:1, II. Moreover, permitting disruption of the soil in the setback area as part of reclamation would contravene the express statutory provisions protecting the setback area; the requirement in RSA 155-E:5, III that slopes be "graded to natural repose" does not vitiate the prohibition against excavation within 50 feet of the boundary of a disapproving abutter under RSA 155-E:4-a, II. Bedard v. Town of Alexandria, 159 N.H. 740, 992 A.2d 607, 2010 N.H. LEXIS 13 (N.H. 2010).

Cited:

Cited in NBAC Corp. v. Town of Weare, 147 N.H. 328, 786 A.2d 867, 2001 N.H. LEXIS 219 (2001).

RESEARCH REFERENCES AND PRACTICE AIDS

Cross References.
Exceptions, see RSA 155-E:5-b.

155-E:5. Minimum and Express Reclamation Standards.

Within 12 months after the expiration date in a permit issued under this chapter, or of the completion of any excavation, whichever occurs first, the owner of the excavated land shall have completed the reclamation of the areas affected by the excavation to meet each of the following minimum standards or when such excavation is not subject to a permit under this chapter pursuant to RSA 155-E:2, to meet each of the following express standards:

I. Except for exposed rock ledge, all areas which have been affected by the excavation or otherwise stripped of vegetation shall be spread with topsoil or strippings, if any, but in any case covered by soil capable of sustaining vegetation, and shall be planted with seedlings or grass suitable to prevent erosion. Areas visible from a public way, from which trees have been removed, shall be replanted with tree seedlings, wet out in accordance with acceptable horticultural practices.

II. Earth and vegetative debris resulting from the excavation shall be removed or otherwise lawfully disposed of.

III. All slopes, except for exposed ledge, shall be graded to natural response for the type of soil of which they are composed so as to control erosion or at a ratio of horizontal to vertical proposed by the owner and approved by the regulator. Changes of slope shall not be abrupt, but shall blend with the surrounding terrain.

IV. The elimination of any standing bodies of water created in the excavation project as may constitute a hazard to health and safety.

V. The topography of the land shall be left so that water draining from the site leaves the property at the original, natural drainage points and in the natural proportions of flow. For excavation projects which require a permit from the department of environmental services pursuant to RSA 485-A:17, the provisions of that statute, and rules adopted under it, shall supersede this paragraph as to areas of excavation sites covered thereby. The excavator shall file a copy of permits issued under RSA 485-A:17 with the regulator.

HISTORY:

1979, 481:2. 1989, 363:10. 1991, 310:18–20, eff. Aug. 23, 1991. 1996, 228:108, eff. July 1, 1996.

Amendments

—1996.

Paragraph V: Substituted "department of environmental services" for "division of water supply and pollution control" in the second sentence.

—1991.

Added "Minimum and Express" preceding "Reclamation" in the section catchline and deleted "whether subject to permit or not" preceding "whichever" and substituted "standards or when such excavation is not subject to a permit under this chapter pursuant to RSA 155-E:2, to meet each of the following express standards" for "conditions" following "minimum" in the introductory paragraph.

Paragraph III: Inserted "for" preceding "exposed" and substituted "so as to control erosion or at a ratio of horizontal or vertical proposed by the owner and approved by the regulator" for "but shall not in any case be left steeper than 2:1 without an exception under RSA 155-E:5-a" following "composed" in the first sentence.

Paragraph V: Substituted "RSA 485-A:17" for "RSA 149:8-a" in the second and third sentences.

—1989.

Rewritten to the extent that a detailed comparison would be impracticable.

NOTES TO DECISIONS

Analysis

1. Municipal ordinance not preempted
2. Slopes

1. Municipal ordinance not preempted

Goshen, N.H., Zoning Ordinance fit within the scope of permissible municipal regulation under RSA ch. 155-E because, by its terms, it applied only to excavations requiring a permit; it followed that the more stringent requirements set forth in the ordinance were not preempted. Guildhall Sand & Gravel, LLC v. Town of Goshen, 155 N.H. 762, 929 A.2d 199, 2007 N.H. LEXIS 128 (N.H. 2007).

2. Slopes

Statutory definition of "excavation" in RSA 155-E:1, II includes "all slopes" in the land area used for the commercial taking of earth and includes no exception for slopes created as part of reclamation; thus, the argument that the slope is separate from the excavation activity is contrary to the plain language of RSA 155-E:1, II. Moreover, permitting disruption of the soil in the setback area as part of reclamation would contravene the express statutory provisions protecting the setback area; the requirement in RSA 155-E:5, III that slopes be "graded to natural repose" does not vitiate the prohibition against excavation within 50 feet of the boundary of a disapproving abutter under RSA 155-E:4-a, II. Bedard v. Town of Alexandria, 159 N.H. 740, 992 A.2d 607, 2010 N.H. LEXIS 13 (N.H. 2010).

There was no merit to the argument that the creation of a 45-degree slope in a setback area did not constitute "excavation." The definition of "excavation" in RSA 155-E:1 included "all slopes" in the land area used for the commercial taking of earth; the definition included no exception for slopes created as part of reclamation under RSA 155-E:5. Bedard v. Town of Alexandria, 159 N.H. 740, 992 A.2d 607, 2010 N.H. LEXIS 13 (N.H. 2010).

Cited:
Cited in North Hampton v. Sanderson, 131 N.H. 614, 557 A.2d 643, 1989 N.H. LEXIS 32 (1989).

RESEARCH REFERENCES AND PRACTICE AIDS

Cross References.
Exceptions, see RSA 155-E:5-b.

155-E:5-a. Incremental Reclamation.

Except for excavation sites of operating stationary manufacturing plants, any excavated area of 5 contiguous acres or more, which is depleted of commercial earth materials, excluding bedrock, or any excavation from which earth materials of sufficient weight or volume to be commercially useful have not been removed for a 2-year period, shall be reclaimed in accordance with RSA 155-E:5, within 12 months following such depletion or 2-year non-use, regardless of whether other excavation is occurring on adjacent land in contiguous ownership. Each operator, other than the operator of stationary manufacturing plants which are exempt from permit requirements pursuant to RSA 155-E:2, III, shall prepare and submit for the regulator's record a reclamation plan for the affected land, including a timetable for reclamation of the depleted areas within the reclamation site.

HISTORY:
1989, 363:11. 1991, 310:21, eff. Aug. 23, 1991.

Amendments

—1991.
Added "Except for excavation sites of operating stationary manufacturing plants" preceding "any excavated area", deleted "either" preceding "is depleted", and substituted "any excavation from which" for "from which no" following "bedrock, or" and "of sufficient weight or volume to be commercially useful have not" for "have" preceding "been removed" in the first sentence and added the second sentence.

RESEARCH REFERENCES AND PRACTICE AIDS

Cross References.
Exceptions, see RSA 155-E:5-b.

155-E:5-b. Exceptions.

The regulator, upon application and following a hearing held in accordance with RSA 155-E:7, may grant an exception in writing to the standards contained in RSA 155-E:4-a, 155-E:5 and 155-E:5-a for good cause shown. The written decision shall state specifically what standards, if any, are being relaxed, and include reasonable alternative conditions or standards. The regulator's decision on any

request for such exception may be appealed in accordance with RSA 155-E:9.

HISTORY:
1989, 363:11, eff. Aug. 4, 1989.

155-E:6. Application for Amendment.

When the scope of a project for which an excavation permit has been issued is proposed to be altered so as to affect either the size or location of the excavation, the rate of removal or the plan for reclamation, the owner shall submit an application for amendment of his excavation permit which application shall be subject to approval in the same manner as provided for an excavation permit.

HISTORY:
1979, 481:2. 1989, 363:12, eff. Aug. 4, 1989.

Amendments

—1989.
Substituted "reclamation" for "restoration" following "plan for".

155-E:7. Hearing.

Prior to the regulator approving an application for an excavation permit or an application for an amended excavation permit, a public hearing shall be held within 30 days on such application. A notice of said hearing shall be sent to all abutters and shall specify the grounds for the hearing as well as the date, time and place and at least 10 days' notice of the time and place of such hearing shall be published in a paper of general circulation in the city, town or unincorporated place wherein the proposed excavation is to be located and a legal notice thereof shall also be posted in at least 3 public places in such city, town or unincorporated place; the 10 days shall not include the day of publications nor the day of the meeting, but shall include any Saturdays, Sundays and legal holidays within said period. Within 20 days of said hearing or any continuation thereof, the regulator shall render a decision approving or disapproving the application, giving reasons for disapproval.

HISTORY:
1979, 481:2, eff. Aug. 24, 1979. 2002, 89:1, eff. July 2, 2002.

Amendments

—2002.
Substituted "10 days" for "14 days" twice in the second sentence.

NOTES TO DECISIONS

Burden of proof
Because the owner failed to prove that the evidence lacked credibility, the trial court found a sufficient evidentiary basis for the town's denial of the owner's excavation permit application on the ground that it would be injurious to public welfare. NBAC Corp. v. Town of Weare, 147 N.H. 328, 786 A.2d 867, 2001 N.H. LEXIS 219 (N.H. 2001).

155-E:8. Issuance of Permit.

If the regulator after the public hearing approves the application for a permit and determines it is not prohibited by RSA 155-E:4 it shall, upon receipt of an excavation fee determined by the regulator not to exceed $50 and the posting of a bond or other such surety with the municipal treasurer in an amount, as it requires, reasonably sufficient to guarantee compliance with the permit, grant a permit to the applicant for an excavation. A copy of the permit shall be prominently posted at the excavation site or the principal access thereto. A permit shall not be assignable or transferable without the prior written consent of the regulator. A permit shall specify the date upon which it expires. The regulator may include in a permit such reasonable conditions as are consistent with the purpose of this chapter and may include requirements for a permit for excavation which are more stringent than the standards set forth in this chapter including the provision of visual barriers to the excavation.

HISTORY:
1979, 481:2. 1991, 310:22, eff. Aug. 23, 1991.

Amendments

—1991.
Inserted "and may include requirements for a permit for excavation which are more stringent than the standards set forth in this chapter" preceding "including the provision" in the fifth sentence.

NOTES TO DECISIONS

Municipal ordinance not preempted
Goshen, N.H., Zoning Ordinance fit within the scope of permissible municipal regulation under RSA ch. 155-E because, by its terms, it applied only to excavations requiring a permit; it followed that the more stringent requirements set forth in the ordinance were not preempted. Guildhall Sand & Gravel, LLC v. Town of Goshen, 155 N.H. 762, 929 A.2d 199, 2007 N.H. LEXIS 128 (N.H. 2007).

155-E:9. Appeal.

If the regulator disapproves or approves an application for an excavation permit or an application for an amended permit, any interested person affected by such decision may appeal to the regulator for a rehearing on such decision or any matter determined thereby. The motion for rehearing shall fully specify every ground upon which it is alleged that the decision or order complained of is unlawful or unreasonable and said appeal shall be filed within 10 days of the date of the decision appealed from. The regulator shall either grant or deny the request for rehearing within 10 days, and if the request is granted a rehearing shall be scheduled within 30 days. Any person affected by the regulator's decision on a motion for rehearing to the regulator may appeal in conformity with the procedures specified in RSA 677:4–15.

HISTORY:
1979, 481:2. 1985, 103:2, eff. Jan. 1, 1986.

Amendments

—1985.
Substituted "RSA 677:4– 15" for "RSA 31:77– 87" following "specified in" at the end of the fourth sentence.

155-E:10. Enforcement.

I. The regulator or its duly authorized agent may suspend or revoke the permit of any person who has violated any provision of his permit or this chapter or made a material misstatement in the application upon which his permit was granted. Such suspension or revocation shall be subject to a motion for rehearing thereon and appeal in accordance with RSA 155-E:9

II. Fines, penalties, and remedies for violations of this chapter shall be the same as for violations of RSA title LXIV, as stated in RSA 676:15, 676:17, 676:17-a, and 676:17-b. In addition, the regulator or a person directly affected by such violation may seek an order from the superior court requiring the violator to cease and desist from violating any provision of a permit or this chapter and to take such action as may be necessary to comply with the permit and this chapter. If the superior court issues such an order, the superior court in its discretion may award all costs and attorneys' fees incurred in seeking such an order to the regulator or person directly affected by such violation.

III. To ascertain if there is compliance with this chapter, a permit issued hereunder or an order issued hereunder, the regulator or its duly authorized agent may enter upon any land on which there is reason to believe an excavation is being conducted or has been conducted since August 24, 1979.

IV. [Repealed.]

HISTORY:
1979, 481:2. 1989, 363:13, 18, eff. Aug. 4, 1989. 1996, 141:1, eff. Jan. 1, 1997.

Revision note.
In par. II, substituted "RSA title LXIV" for "RSA title LX" to correct an error in the reference.
At the end of par. III, substituted "August 24, 1979" for "the effective date of this chapter" for purposes of clarity.

Amendments

—1996.
Paragraph II: Inserted "676:17-a, and 676:17-b" following "676:17" in the first sentence, added the second and third sentences, and made a minor stylistic change.

—1989.
Paragraph II: Rewritten to the extent that a detailed comparison would be impracticable.
Paragraph IV: Repealed.

NOTES TO DECISIONS

Analysis

1. Municipal ordinance not preempted
2. Attorney fees

162-C:2. Responsibilities.

The council shall:

I. Consult upon common problems in the fields of environmental protection, natural resources, and growth management including the encouragement of smart growth;

II. Consult with, negotiate with, and obtain information from, any federal or state agency concerned with any of the council's problems, reports, recommendations or studies;

III. Make biennial reports and recommendations, as may be desirable, to the governor and council;

IV. Make studies and recommendations concerning changes to effectively coordinate the work of the agencies which have membership in the council;

V. Resolve differences or conflicts concerning development, resource management, or the encouragement of smart growth which result from the work of any agency represented on the council in developing policies, plans, or programs. The council shall investigate; if possible, resolve the problem; and if appropriate, submit its recommendations to the governor and council or to the general court. If investigation by the council shows that the laws and rules of an agency represented on the council are in conflict with those of another agency, the council shall submit a report with recommendations to the governor and council or to the general court;

VI. Resolve differences and conflicts among the agencies and departments of the state in the implementation of the tourism policy under RSA 12-O:14;

VII. Review the disposal of state owned real property pursuant to RSA 4:40;

VIII. Provide oversight relative to the statewide public boat access program, work with the public water access advisory board and provide recommendations to the governor and executive council regarding public access;

IX. Complete the smart growth report required under RSA 9-B:6;

X. Review and coordinate the distribution of funds by state agencies to local and regional entities to encourage consistency with and provide support for New Hampshire's smart growth policies under RSA 9-B:4;

XI. Review the following actions by state agencies and ensure, in consultation with the long range capital planning and utilization committee established by RSA 17-M:1–3, that these actions are taken into consideration in the long range capital improvement program that is updated every 2 years in conjunction with the capital budget process, and provide recommendations to the governor regarding whether the actions are consistent with New Hampshire's smart growth policies under RSA 9-B:5:

(a) Capital budget requests;

(b) Building operation and maintenance plans; and

(c) Facility location and planning; and

XII. Facilitate coordination of state agencies to support local, regional, and state planning efforts consistent with RSA 9-A:1–4.

HISTORY:

1963, 301:2. 1965, 212:2. 1973, 140:7. 1981, 364:1. 1986, 165:3. 224:5. 1987, 283:6, 7. 1992, 265:6, eff. Jan. 1, 1993. 2000, 292:7–9, eff. Aug. 20, 2000. 2001, 249:3, eff. Sept. 11, 2001. 2006, 307:2, eff. July 1, 2006. 2008, 150:2, eff. June 6, 2008.

Amendment Notes

The 2017 amendments to this section by Ch. 156 substituted "RSA 12-O:14" for "RSA 12-A:23" in VI.

—2008.

The 2008 amendment deleted "annual" preceding "smart growth" in IX.

—2006.

Paragraph IV: Deleted the former second sentence.

—2001.

Made a minor stylistic change in par. VIII, made a minor change in punctuation in par. IX, and added pars. X-XII.

—2000.

Paragraph I: Added "including the encouragement of smart growth" following "management".

Paragraph V: Inserted "or the encouragement of smart growth" following "management" and made a stylistic change in the first sentence.

Paragraphs VII and VIII: Made minor stylistic changes.

Paragraph IX: Added.

—1992.

Paragraph VIII: Added.

—1987.

Paragraph I: Rewritten to the extent that a detailed comparison would be impracticable.

Paragraph V: Substituted "development or resource management" for "water management and supply" following "concerning" and "policies, plans, or programs" for "a plan or program affecting water allocation" following "developing" in the first sentence.

—1986.

Paragraph IV: Chapter 224 deleted "and" following "rules" at the end of the paragraph.

Paragraph V: Chapter 224 made minor stylistic changes.

Paragraph VI: Added by ch. 165.

Chapter 224 added "and" following "RSA 12-A:23".

Paragraph VII: Added by ch. 224.

—1981.

Rewritten to the extent that a detailed comparison would be impracticable.

—1973.

Substituted "biennial" for "such" following "studies; make" in the first sentence.

—1965.

Added "or state" after federal in the first sentence.

Contingent 1986 amendment.

1986, 224:2, provided for amendment of this section. However, under the terms of 1986, 224:6, eff. Aug. 5, 1986, the amendment did not become effective.

RESEARCH REFERENCES AND PRACTICE AIDS

References in text.
RSA 9-A:3, contained in RSA 9-A:1– 4 in par. XII, was repealed by 2008, 248:1, eff. June 24, 2008.

162-C:3. Tenure of Members.

Members shall serve without compensation, and any member's term of office shall terminate when he ceases to be a member of the state agency he represents.

HISTORY:
1963, 301:3. 1965, 212:3, eff. July 1, 1965.

Amendments

—1965.
Rewritten to the extent that a detailed comparison would be impracticable.

162-C:4. Meetings.

The council shall meet at least once every 3 months, but may meet more often as it shall determine. The chairman shall prepare and deliver an agenda to all members at least 7 days in advance of each meeting. The council shall provide a copy of the minutes from each meeting to the senate president, the speaker of the house of representatives, the long range capital planning and utilization committee, and the governor and council.

HISTORY:
1963, 301:4. 1965, 212:4. 1987, 283:8, eff. May 25, 1987. 2006, 307:3, eff. July 1, 2006.

Amendments

—2006.
Added the third sentence.

—1987.
Rewritten to the extent that a detailed comparison would be impracticable.

—1965.
Deleted "and who shall prepare and have delivered at least seven days before every meeting of the council an agenda for said meeting" at the end of the first sentence, rewrote the third sentence and deleted the fourth sentence.

162-C:5. Staff.

The council may employ staff needed to carry out its responsibilities.

HISTORY:
1981, 364:2, eff. Aug. 22, 1981.

Land Conservation Investment Program

162-C:6. Purpose; Management.

I. The general court recognizes that in order to maintain New Hampshire's distinctive quality of life, strong economic growth must be balanced with responsible conservation initiatives, and that the history of conservation in New Hampshire has been marked by cooperation among government, business, individuals, and conservation organizations. The general court further recognizes the strong traditions of both public and private land ownership and use, and the need to respect investments in the conservation of natural resource lands in the state for the perpetual use of the people of New Hampshire. In addition, the general court recognizes that the land conservation investment program was undertaken, in part, with significant donations of cash and land value by citizens of the state who intended that the conservation value of these lands be protected in perpetuity.

II. In addition to its other responsibilities, the council shall manage and administer the lands acquired and funds established under the land conservation investment program under the former RSA 221-A, according to the provisions of this subdivision and consistent with agreements entered into with persons with ownership interests in such lands.

III. The council shall manage the lands acquired under the former RSA 221-A so as to preserve the natural beauty, landscape, rural character, natural resources, and high quality of life in New Hampshire. The council shall maintain and protect benefits derived from such lands and maintain public access to such lands, where appropriate. On state-owned lands, whenever the council shall deem it in the best interest of conservation and protection of the values outlined in this section, it may, with the consent of the governor, authorize the exchange of any interest in the property when the conservation values of the property would be degraded if no action were taken. Prior to submitting a request to the governor to exchange any interest in the property, the council shall provide at least 30 calendar days advance notice to the local governing body and conservation commission. Such exchanges shall be reviewed and approved by the council, shall involve lands contiguous to the original acquisition which have equal or greater conservation value, and shall convey only those interests necessary to compensate for the potential degradation.

IV. Notwithstanding paragraphs I-III, the council shall recognize that the interest of public safety and welfare may, from time to time, require minor expansion, minor modification, or minor alteration of existing roads within the state highway system. After review and approval by the council, and notwithstanding RSA 162-C:10, the department of transportation may obtain interests in lands acquired under the former RSA 221-A adjacent to state highways. Permissible expansion, modification, or alterations under this section shall include drainage easements, slope easements, lane widening, the addition of a passing, climbing, or turning lane, or similar adjustments, but shall not include construction of a new highway or portion thereof, construction of a bypass for an existing highway, or similar major alterations. Approval shall not be granted if reasonable and prudent alternatives exist nor if individual or cumulative approvals are likely to materially impair the conservation purposes for which the parcel was originally protected. Projects determined by the council to be outside of the scope permitted by this subdivision shall require approval from the general court.

V. The review and approval process required by paragraph IV shall give full consideration to the management provisions contained in paragraphs I-III. The department of transportation shall submit a written request to the council with plans and supporting documentation to demonstrate compliance with the provisions of this chapter. A quorum of the council, consisting of at least 6 members, shall hold a public hearing within 90 days of receipt of a complete request to release land conservation investment program interests. The council shall provide at least 10 calendar days notice in advance of such hearing. Notification shall be made, at the expense of the department, to the landowner, local governing body and conservation commission, abutters, the Society for the Protection of New Hampshire Forests, The Nature Conservancy, the Audubon Society of New Hampshire, the New Hampshire Wildlife Federation, and the county conservation district, or their successors. Notification of the public hearing shall be published, by the department, in a paper of general circulation in the municipality and shall be posted, by the department, in at least 2 public places. At the hearing or within 15 days after the hearing, a majority of the council members attending the hearing shall vote to approve or deny the application, unless a time extension is requested by the department. Aggrieved parties, which include all parties who must be notified under this paragraph, may appeal the council's decision to the superior court in the same manner as planning board decisions are appealed under RSA 677:15.

VI. Compensation for any interest in land obtained by the state department of transportation under this section shall be at the appraised full fair market value of those property interests at the time of the department's acquisition. Alternative forms of compensation such as replacement land with comparable conservation value, or a combination of monetary compensation and replacement land may be considered in appropriate circumstances provided all parties owning an interest in the property agree to such terms.

VII. Compensation due to the state under this section shall be deposited in the trust fund of the New Hampshire land and community heritage investment program established under RSA 227-M and used for the purposes of that program. Compensation due to municipalities shall be dedicated to the acquisition or monitoring of protected lands consistent with the purposes of this chapter. Compensation due to landowners of conservation easement lands shall be as specified in the conservation easement, deed, or as otherwise negotiated. Any party aggrieved by the amount of compensation may file a petition with the superior court in the same manner as damage appeals are filed from the board of tax and land appeals under RSA 498-A:27.

HISTORY:
1995, 10:4, eff. April 12, 1995. 1998, 364:1, eff. Jan. 1, 1999. 2000, 245:2, eff. June 8, 2000.

Amendments

—2000.
Paragraph VII: Rewrote the former first through third sentences as the present first sentence.

—1998.
Rewritten to the extent that a detailed comparison would be impracticable.

NOTES TO DECISIONS

Analysis

1. Application
2. Particular cases

1. Application
RSA 162-C:6, IV, applies only when the Department of Transportation seeks to obtain interests in Land Conservation Investment Program lands, thereby removing such interests from the public trust. Town of Newbury v. N.H. Fish & Game Dep't, 165 N.H. 142, 70 A.3d 461, 2013 N.H. LEXIS 73 (N.H. 2013).

New Hampshire Council on Resources and Development must seek approval from the general court under RSA 162-C:6, IV only when it concludes that a project is outside the scope of RSA 162-C:6. Town of Newbury v. N.H. Fish & Game Dep't, 165 N.H. 142, 70 A.3d 461, 2013 N.H. LEXIS 73 (N.H. 2013).

2. Particular cases
Trial court erred in holding that under RSA 162-C:6, IV, the Council on Resources and Development (CORD) lacked authority to approve a boat launch because it was a public highway. The interest in land was not being removed from the public trust, and CORD had not found that the project fell outside the scope of RSA 162-C:6. Town of Newbury v. N.H. Fish & Game Dep't, 165 N.H. 142, 70 A.3d 461, 2013 N.H. LEXIS 73 (N.H. 2013).

RESEARCH REFERENCES AND PRACTICE AIDS

References in text.
RSA 221-A, referred to in pars. II–IV, was repealed by 1995, 10:16, VII, eff. April 12, 1995.

162-C:7. Powers and Duties.

The council shall oversee, direct, and expend funds in the monitoring endowment of the former New Hampshire land conservation investment program in accordance with the purposes of this subdivision and RSA 227-M:12. This includes, but is not limited to, the authority to draw upon funds for the administrative costs of the endowment.

HISTORY:
1995, 10:4, eff. April 12, 1995. 2000, 245:3, eff. June 8, 2000.

Amendments

—2000.
Inserted "and RSA 227-M:12" following "subdivision" in the first sentence.

162-C:8. Monitoring Endowment.

I. The monitoring endowment established by the board of directors pursuant to former RSA 221-A:5, III shall be maintained in perpetuity and shall be utilized by the council only for the purposes of monitoring and enforcing the property rights of persons with ownership interests in property acquired through the former land conservation investment program. Additional contributions to the endowment pursuant to RSA 227-M:12, I shall be accounted for separately and shall be utilized only for the purposes of RSA 227-M:12, II. Additional gifts, donations, and grants to the endowment may be utilized for monitoring and enforcing other land conservation interests that may be acquired by the state of New Hampshire.

II. The principal of the endowment shall be managed by the state treasurer for the sole purpose of providing a perpetual source of income, as defined by the state treasurer, for the purposes set forth in this subdivision and RSA 227-M:12.

III. Any income earned on the endowment principal which is not used for the purposes set forth in this subdivision and RSA 227-M:12 within the fiscal year in which it is earned shall be nonlapsing. The state treasurer is authorized to accept gifts, donations, and grants, including federal gifts, donations, and grants, for the purposes set forth in this chapter, and such gifts, donations and grants shall be added to the principal amount.

IV. The council shall, pursuant to the monitoring endowment established under former RSA 221-A:5, III, and the provisions of RSA 162-C:8, I, prepare an annual report to be presented no later than December 1 of each year to the speaker of the house, the president of the senate, the governor, the house clerk, the senate clerk, and the state library. The report shall include a listing of all lands and interests in lands subject to the monitoring provisions of RSA 162-C:7, I and a complete financial accounting of the funds in the monitoring endowment including expenditures for the most recent full fiscal year. The report shall also summarize monitoring activities and findings for each property, as conducted in the most recent full fiscal year.

HISTORY:
1995, 10:4, eff. April 12, 1995. 2000, 245:4, eff. June 8, 2000. 2002, 86:2, eff. July 2, 2002. 2004, 257:47, eff. July 1, 2004. 2007, 151:1, eff. August 17, 2007.

Amendments

—2007.
Paragraph I: Deleted "any interest generated thereon" following "in perpetuity and" the first sentence and substituted "shall be

accounted for separately and" for "and any interest generated thereon" in the second sentence.
Paragraph II: Rewritten to the extent that a detailed comparison would be impracticable.
Paragraph III: Substituted "any income earned" for "any interest earned" in the first sentence.

—2004.
Paragraph I: Inserted "any interest generated thereon" following "perpetuity and" and deleted "and for the purposes of RSA 227-M:12" at the end of the first sentence and added the second and third sentences.

—2002.
Paragraph III: Substituted "nonlapsing" for "added to the principal amount" following "shall be" in the first sentence.

—2000.
Paragraph I: Added "and for the purposes of RSA 227-M:12" following "investment program".
Paragraph II: Inserted "and RSA 227-M:12" following "in this subdivision".
Paragraph III: Inserted "and RSA 227-M:12" following "subdivision" in the first sentence.

RESEARCH REFERENCES AND PRACTICE AIDS

References in text.
RSA 221-A:5, referred to in pars. I and IV, was repealed by 1995, 10:16, VII, eff. April 12, 1995.

162-C:9. Management.

I. Each assignment of land under this subdivision to a state agency or a municipality shall be subject to review and reassignment if the council deems it advisable.

II. No lands purchased in fee for permanent state ownership under the former RSA 221-A shall be posted to prohibit hunting or fishing, unless the council, by a majority vote of the voting members, deems such posting to be necessary to protect the interests of the state and the safety of its citizens, or upon recommendation of the fish and game commission or the division of forests and lands.

HISTORY:
1995, 10:4, eff. April 12, 1995. 2006, 307:4, eff. July 1, 2006.

Amendments

—2006.
Paragraph I: Inserted "under this subdivision" following "of land".

RESEARCH REFERENCES AND PRACTICE AIDS

References in text.
RSA 221-A, referred to in par. II, was repealed by 1995, 10:16, VII, eff. April 12, 1995.

162-C:10. Public Trust.

The lands and interests in lands acquired under the former RSA 221-A through the use of the trust fund for the program shall be held in public trust and used and applied for the purposes of this subdivision. Notwithstanding any other provision of law relating to the disposal of publicly-owned real estate, no deviation in the uses of any land or interest in land so acquired to uses or purposes not consistent with the purposes of this subdivision shall be permitted. The sale, transfer, conveyance, or release of any such land or interest in land from public trust is prohibited.

HISTORY:
1995, 10:4, eff. April 12, 1995.

RESEARCH REFERENCES AND PRACTICE AIDS

References in text.
RSA 221-A, referred to in the first sentence, was repealed by 1995, 10:16, VII, eff. April 12, 1995.

162-C:11. Public Access; Liability.

No person, or the person's successor in title, who has granted or sold rights of public access by virtue of an easement, right-of-way, development right, or other means in accordance with the purposes of this subdivision shall be liable to a user of that right of access for injuries suffered on that portion of the access way unless those injuries are caused by the willful or wanton misconduct of the grantor or successor in title.

HISTORY:
1995, 10:4, eff. April 12, 1995.

Commission to Develop a Land Conservation Plan

HISTORY:
2015, 174:1, eff. June 26, 2015.

162-C:12. Commission Established. [Repealed]

HISTORY:
2015, 174:1, eff. June 26, 2015. Repealed by 2015, 174:2, eff. December 31, 2016.

CHAPTER 162-K

MUNICIPAL ECONOMIC DEVELOPMENT AND REVITALIZATION DISTRICTS

Purpose.
1979, 175:1, eff. Aug. 5, 1979, provided:
"It is hereby declared that there is a need for new development in areas of municipalities which are already built up in order to provide employment opportunities, to improve the tax base and to improve the general economy of the state. Therefore, municipalities are authorized to develop a program for improving a district of the municipality to provide: impetus for commercial development; increased employment; off-street parking to serve the shoppers and employees of the district; open space relief within the district; and other facilities as are outlined in the development program adopted by the municipality. It is hereby declared that the actions required to assist the implementation of these development programs are a public purpose and that the execution and financing of such programs are a public purpose."

162-K:1. Local Option.

Any city or town may adopt this chapter and shall thereafter have all the authority, powers, duties and responsibilities set forth in this chapter.

I. A city may adopt this chapter by majority vote of the legislative body of the city after notice and hearing as set forth in RSA 162-K:4.

II. A town may adopt this chapter by majority vote of the voters present and voting at any legal town meeting under a proper article and after notice and hearing as set forth in RSA 162-K:4.

HISTORY:
1979, 175:2, eff. Aug. 5, 1979.

162-K:2. Definitions.

In this chapter:

I. "Budget submission date" has the meaning set forth under RSA 273-A:1, III.

II. "Development district" means a specific area within the corporate limits of any municipality which has been so designated and separately numbered by the legislative body of said municipality acting under this chapter.

III. "Development program" means a statement of objectives of the municipality for improvement of a development district established under RSA 162-K:6.

IV. "District administrator" means the head of the department, office agency, municipal housing and redevelopment authority or corporation designated under RSA 162-K:13.

V. "Governing body" means the board of aldermen or city council in the case of a city and the board of selectmen in the case of a town.

VI. "Legislative body" means the board of aldermen or city council in the case of a city and the town meeting in the case of a town.

VII. "Maintenance and operation" means all activities necessary to maintain facilities after they have been developed and all activities necessary to operate the facilities including but not limited to informational and educational programs, and safety and surveillance activities.

VIII. "Municipality" means a city or town.

IX. "Parking structure" means any building the principal use of which is designed for and intended for parking of motor vehicles, and includes open air parking on parking lots.

IX-a. "Public use" means:

(a)(1) The possession, occupation, and enjoyment of real property by the general public or governmental entities;

(2) The acquisition of any interest in real property necessary to the function of a public or private utility or common carrier either through deed of sale or lease;

(3) The acquisition of real property to remove structures beyond repair, public nuisances, structures unfit for human habitation or use, and abandoned property when such structures or property constitute a menace to health and safety; and

(4) Private use that occupies an incidental area within a public use; provided, that no real property shall be condemned solely for the purpose of facilitating such incidental private use.

(b) Except as provided in subparagraphs (a)(2) and (4) of this paragraph, public use shall not include the public benefits resulting from private economic development and private commercial enterprise, including increased tax revenues and increased employment opportunities.

X. "Substantially residential development district" means any development district in which 40 percent or more of the land area, exclusive of streets and open space, is used for residential purposes at the time the district is designated.

XI. "Tax increment" means the amount of taxes raised in a development district due to increases in assessed value over the assessed value of the district at the time of its establishment.

HISTORY:
1979, 175:2, eff. Aug. 5, 1979. 2006, 324:1, eff. January 1, 2007.

Amendments

—2006.
Paragraph IX-a: Added.

162-K:3. Authorization; Initial Adoption.

A municipality which adopts this chapter shall thereafter be authorized to establish one or more development districts. For each such district, the municipality shall establish a development program and a tax increment financing plan. A municipality that has not previously adopted this chapter may carry out the planning and hearing procedures for establishment of one or more development districts at the same time it is conducting the planning and hearing procedures on initial adoption of this chapter; provided that any vote on establishing a particular development district shall not be taken until after the legislative body shall have voted on the question of adopting this chapter.

HISTORY:
1979, 175:2, eff. Aug. 5, 1979.

162-K:4. Hearing.

Prior to adopting this chapter or designating any development district, a hearing on the subject shall be conducted in the municipality. The hearing shall be conducted by the governing body. The hearing shall be held at least 15 days prior to the date on which action on the proposal is scheduled to take place. Notice of the hearing, including a description of any proposed district, shall be posted in 2 appropriate places in the municipality or published in a newspaper of general circulation in the municipality at least 7 days prior to the hearing.

HISTORY:
1979, 175:2, eff. Aug. 5, 1979.

162-K:5. Establishment of Districts; Limitations.

Upon a finding that such action will serve public purposes, the legislative body of the municipality may create, within its jurisdiction, development districts. The area of a district may be enlarged following the date of designation of the district. Municipalities establishing development districts shall comply with one of the following limitations:

I. The total acreage included in any one development district when designated shall not exceed 5 percent of the total acreage of the municipality, and when added to the total current acreage within the development districts for which bonds remain outstanding shall not exceed 10 percent of the total acreage of the municipality.

II. The total assessed value of taxable real property of any one development district when designated shall not exceed 8 percent of the most recent total assessed value of taxable real property in the municipality, and when added to the current total assessed value of taxable real property within development districts for which bonds remain outstanding, shall not exceed 16 percent of the most recent total assessed value of taxable real property in the municipality.

HISTORY:
1979, 175:2. 1985, 135:1. 1991, 362:10, eff. July 2, 1991. 1998, 9:1, eff. May 29, 1998. 2004, 181:1, eff. July 31, 2004.

Amendments

—2004.
Substituted "district may be enlarged following" for "district shall not be enlarged after 5 years following" in the second sentence of the introductory paragraph; "5 percent" for "1-½ percent" and "10 percent" for "3 percent" in par. I; and "8 percent" for "5 percent" and "16 percent" for "10 percent" in par. II.

—1998.
Deleted the second sentence of the introductory paragraph.

—1991.
Added the first sentence, rewrote the fourth sentence and deleted the fifth sentence of the introductory paragraph, substituted "1-½" for "one" in par. I and deleted par. III.

—1985.
Paragraph III: Substituted "10" for "6" preceding "acres".

162-K:6. District Establishment and Development Programs.

A municipality which has adopted this chapter and which intends to establish a development district shall, in addition to establishing the district, establish a development program under this section and a tax increment financing plan under RSA 162-K:9 and 10.

I. The development program shall contain a complete statement as to the public facilities to be constructed within the district, the open space to be created, the environmental controls to be applied, the proposed reuse of private property, and the proposed operations of the district after the capital improvements within the district have been completed.

II. The development program shall also provide for carrying out relocation of persons, families, business concerns, and others displaced by the project, pursuant to a relocation plan, including the method for the relocation of residents in decent, safe and sanitary dwelling accommodations, and reasonable moving costs, determined to be feasible by the municipality.

III. In conformity with the development program, within the district, the municipality may:

(a) Acquire, construct, reconstruct, improve, alter, extend, operate, maintain or promote developments aimed at improving the physical facilities, quality of life and quality of transportation;

(b) Acquire real property or easements through negotiation or through powers of eminent domain, except that property acquired through powers of eminent domain shall be put to public use, as defined in RSA 162-K:2, IX-a;

(c) Adopt ordinances regulating the use of public parking structures and other facilities constructed within the development district and access to them and the conditions under which such access is allowed. Traffic regulations may include, but shall not be limited to, direction and speed of traffic, kinds of service activities that will be allowed in arcades, parking structures and plazas, and rates to be charged in the parking structures;

(d) Require construction of buildings within the district so as to accommodate and support pedestrian systems which are part of the program for the development district. When the municipality requires for the public benefit the construction of columns, beams or girders with greater strength than required for normal building purposes, the municipality shall reimburse the owner for the added expense from development district funds;

(e) Install lighting systems, street signs and street furniture, landscaping of street and public property, and snow removal systems compatible with the character of the district;

(f) Acquire property for the district;

(g) Lease air rights over public property and spend public funds for constructing the foundations and columns in the public buildings strong enough to support the buildings to be constructed on air rights;

(h) Lease all or portions of basements, ground and second floors of the public buildings constructed in the district; and

(i) Negotiate the sale or lease of property for private development if the development is consistent with the development program for the district.

HISTORY:
1979, 175:2, eff. Aug. 5, 1979. 2006, 324:2, eff. January 1, 2007.

Amendments

—2006.
Paragraph III(b): Substituted "real property" for "land" and added the end of the sentence following "eminent domain".

162-K:7. Grants.

A municipality may accept grants or other financial assistance from the government of the United States, the state of New Hampshire or any other entity to do studies and to construct and operate the public improvements authorized by this chapter.

HISTORY:
1979, 175:2, eff. Aug. 5, 1979.

RESEARCH REFERENCES AND PRACTICE AIDS

Cross References.
Economic development matching grants program, see RSA 12-A:32.

162-K:8. Issuance of Bonds.

The municipality may authorize, issue and sell general obligation bonds, which shall mature within 30 years from the date of issue, to finance the acquisition and betterment of real and personal property needed to carry out the development program within the development district together with all relocation costs incidental thereto. Bonds issued under authority of this chapter shall be payable in annual payments which shall be so arranged that the amount of annual payment of principal and interest in any year on account of any bond shall not be less than the amount of principal and interest payable in any subsequent year by more than 5 percent of the principal of the entire bond. The total amount of such payments shall be sufficient to extinguish the entire bond on account of which they are made at maturity. The first payment of principal on any bond shall be made no later than 5 years and the last payment not later than 30 years after the date thereof. Each authorized issue of bonds shall be a separate loan. All dedicated tax increments received by the municipality pursuant to RSA 162-K:10 shall be pledged for the payment of these bonds and used to reduce or cancel the taxes otherwise required to be extended for that purpose, and the bonds shall not be included when computing the municipality's net debt under RSA 33.

HISTORY:
1979, 175:2, eff. Aug. 5, 1979. 2000, 280:1, eff. Aug. 20, 2000.

Amendments

—2000.
Added the second through fifth sentences.

RESEARCH REFERENCES AND PRACTICE AIDS

Cross References.
Notification of office of investment and debt management of proposed bond issues, see RSA 6-B:3.

162-K:9. Tax Increment Financing Plan.

The municipality shall adopt a tax increment financing plan for any development district established under this chapter. The plan shall allocate use of tax increments for retirement of bonds and notes, operation, maintenance and improvements in the district and for general municipal purposes.

I. A tax increment financing plan shall contain a statement of objectives of a municipality for improvement of a development district. Such plan shall be incorporated into the development program for the district. It shall contain estimates of the following: cost of the development program; sources of revenues to finance those costs including estimates of tax increments; amount of bonded indebtedness to be incurred; and the duration of the program's existence. The plan shall also contain a statement of the estimated impact of tax increment financing on the assessed values of all taxing jurisdictions in which the district is located.

II. Before approving any tax increment financing plan, a public hearing shall be held as part of the hearing on the development district under RSA 162-K:4.

III. Before formation of a development district, the municipality shall provide a reasonable opportunity to the county commissioners of any county in which any portion of the development district is located and to the members of the school board of any school district in which any portion of the development district is located to meet with the governing body. The governing body shall fully inform the county commissioners and the school boards of the fiscal and economic implications of the proposed development district. The county commissioners and the school boards may present their recommendations at the public hearing. A municipality's tax increment financing plan may include agreements with the county commissioners and the school boards in which the district is located to share a portion of the captured tax increments of the district.

IV. A tax increment financing plan may be modified provided such modification shall be approved by the legislative body upon such notice and hearing and agreements as are required for approval of the original plan. In a case where the financing plan calls for the appropriation of a specific sum of money, the sum of money appropriated thereunder may be decreased or increased by the vote of the legislative body, provided that in a town under the municipal budget act no increase shall be valid which would violate the provisions of RSA 32:18, except as provided in RSA 32:18-a. Any modification shall maintain use of dedicated tax increments for retirement of bonds and notes as required.

HISTORY:
1979, 175:2, eff. Aug. 5, 1979. 2015, 167:1, eff. August 25, 2015.

Amendment Notes

—2015.
The 2015 amendment added the second sentence of paragraph IV.

162-K:10. Computation of Tax Increments.

I. Upon formation of a development district, the assessors of the municipality in which it is situated shall determine the current assessed value of the real property within the boundaries of the development district. The current assessed value so determined shall be known as the "original assessed value." Property exempt from taxation at the time of the determination shall be included at zero, unless it later becomes taxable, in which case its most recently determined assessed valuation shall be included. Each year thereafter, the assessors shall determine the amount by which the assessed value has increased or decreased from the original assessed value. The assessors shall also determine the proportion which any increase or decrease bears to the total assessed value of the real property in that district for that year.

II. Any amount by which the current assessed value of a development district exceeds the original assessed value is referred to as the captured assessed value. The assessors shall determine the amount of the captured assessed value each year.

(a) The tax increment financing plan shall designate the portion of captured assessed value which will be dedicated for retirement of bonds and notes and the portion of captured assessed value which will be dedicated to the operation and further development of the tax increment financing district.

(b) The portion of captured assessed value which is not used either for the purpose of retirement of bonds and notes or for the purpose of the operation and development of the tax increment financing district shall be deemed excess captured assessed value. Excess captured assessed value shall be returned to the tax lists.

III.(a) Each subsequent year the assessors shall determine current assessed valuation, and tax increments and shall report them to the commissioner of the department of revenue administration according to the following method:

(1) If the municipality retains the full captured assessed value for the development district the assessors shall certify to the commissioner of revenue administration, for the purposes of the report required by RSA 41:15, the current assessed value, as the basis to equalize annually the valuation of property throughout the state, and the full captured assessed value, to be deducted from the current assessed valuation for the calculation of the property tax rate. The assessors shall extend all rates as established by the commissioner of revenue administration under the provisions of RSA 41:15 against the current assessed value, including all captured assessed value. In each year for which the current assessed value exceeds the original assessed value, the municipal tax collector shall remit to the municipality that proportion of all taxes paid that year on real property in the district which the captured assessed value bears to the total current assessed value. The amount so remitted each year is referred to in this section as the tax increment for that year.

(2) If the municipality retains only a portion of the captured assessed value for the development district and returns the remaining portion to the tax lists, the assessors shall include the current assessed value, to be used as a basis to equalize annually the valuation of property throughout the state, and that portion of the captured assessed value which the municipality does retain, to be deducted from the current assessed valuation for the calculation of the property tax rate. The assessors shall extend all rates against the total current assessed value. In each year for which the current assessed value exceeds the original assessed value, the municipal tax collector shall remit to the municipality that proportion of all taxes billed on real property in the district that the retained captured assessed value bears to the total current assessed value in the district. The amount so remitted each year is referred to as the tax increment.

(b) The general court finds that municipalities that have adopted a tax increment financing plan and issued tax increment financing plan bonds under this chapter before April 29, 1999, or which have adopted a tax increment financing plan and entered into contracts and incurred liabilities in reliance upon the tax increment plans under this chapter before April 29, 1999, have incurred obligations which must be honored. The general court recognizes also that in accordance with the intent of this chapter, such obligations were entered into in order to accomplish a public purpose and for the improvement of development in municipalities.

Accordingly, the provisions of subparagraph III(a) shall not apply to tax increment financing plan districts which authorized and issued tax increment bonds under this chapter before April 29, 1999 or which adopted a tax increment financing plan under this chapter and entered into contracts and incurred financial liabilities in reliance upon such tax increment plan before April 29, 1999. This subparagraph shall only apply to tax development districts as they existed as of April 29, 1999. To the extent such tax increment financing plan is amended to increase the amount of bonded indebtedness, to increase the cost of the development program, or to extend the duration of the program's existence, this subparagraph shall not apply. The assessors shall determine assessed valuation and tax increments according to the following method:

(1) If the municipality retains the full captured assessed value for the development district, the assessors shall certify to the commissioner of revenue administration for the purposes of the report required by RSA 21-J:34, no more than the original assessed value of the real property in the development district. The assessors shall extend all rates as established by the commissioner of revenue administration under the provisions of RSA 21-J:35 against the current assessed value, including all captured assessed value. In each year for which the current assessed value exceeds the original assessed value, the municipal tax collector shall remit to the municipality that proportion of all taxes billed that year on real property in the district which the captured assessed value bears to the total current assessed value. That amount is referred to in this section as the tax increment for that year.

(2) If the municipality retains only a portion of the captured assessed value for the development district and returns the excess to the tax lists, the assessors shall certify to the commissioner of revenue administration for the purposes of the report required by RSA 21-J:34 the original assessed value and that portion of the captured assessed value which is shared with all the affected taxing districts for the purposes of determining the assessed value for computing property tax rates. The commissioner of revenue administration shall compute the rates of all taxes levied by the state, county, municipality, school district and every other taxing district in which the district is located on this aforementioned assessed value. The assessors shall extend all rates against the total current assessed value, including that portion of the captured assessed value which the municipality is retaining for the development district only. In each year for which the current assessed value exceeds that original assessed value, the municipal tax collector shall remit to the munici-

pality that proportion of all taxes paid on real property in the district that the retained captured value bears to the total current assessed value in the district. That amount is referred to as the tax increment for that year.

(c) In any year in which the current assessed value of the development district is equal to or less than the original assessed value, the assessors shall compute and extend taxes against the current value. Taxes shall be distributed from the affected property to each of the taxing authorities as determined by the current levy and there is no tax increment.

IV. The municipality shall expend the tax increments received for any development program only in accordance with the tax increment financing plan. Tax increments shall be used only to pay off costs and administrative expenses incurred in developing the district.

HISTORY:

1979, 175:2, eff. Aug. 5, 1979. 1999, 303:13, eff. July 16, 1999. 2000, 222:1–3, eff. April 1, 2000.

Editor's note.

RSA 41:15, as amended by 1987, 285:3, eff. July 1, 1987, no longer requires reports or authorizes the commissioner of revenue administration to establish tax rates. For present provisions governing municipal tax reports and authority to establish tax rates, see RSA 21-J:34, 35.

Amendments

—2000.

Paragraph II: Inserted "and the portion of captured assessed value which will be dedicated to the operation and further development of the tax increment financing district" following "bonds and notes" in subpar. (a) and rewrote subpar. (b).

Paragraph III(a): Deleted "excess" following "full" and "portion of the" in subpars. (1) and (2), deleted "not" preceding "retain" and added "rate" following "tax" in the first sentence, deleted "including that portion of the captured assessed value which the municipality is retaining for the development district only" following "current assessed value" in the second sentence and substituted "billed" for "paid" in the third sentence of subpar. (2).

Paragraph III(b): Added the last sentence in the introductory paragraph and added subpars. (1) and (2).

—1999.

Paragraph III: Rewritten to the extent that a detailed comparison would be impracticable.

162-K:11. Annual Report.

The municipality's annual report shall contain a financial report for any development district in the municipality. The report shall include at least the following information: the amount and source of revenue of the district; the amount and purpose of expenditures, the amount of principal and interest on any outstanding bonded indebtedness, the original assessed value of the district, the captured assessed value retained by the district, the tax increments received and any additional information necessary to demonstrate compliance with the tax increment financing plan.

HISTORY:

1979, 175:2, eff. Aug. 5, 1979.

162-K:12. Maintenance and Operation.

Maintenance and operation of the systems and improvements constructed under this chapter shall be under the supervision of the district administrator. The cost of maintenance and operation of the non-revenue-producing facilities together with excess of costs of operation and maintenance of revenue-producing facilities, if any, shall be charged against the development district in which it is located. The charges against each property within the district shall be in proportion to the benefit to the properties within the district 60 days before the budget submission date. The district administrator shall submit to the governing body of the municipality the maintenance and operating budget for the following year, and the prorated share of the budget to be charged to each property in the district. The budget for the district as approved by the municipality, and pursuant to RSA 32, shall contain necessary appropriations and provisions for collecting charges against affected properties in the district.

HISTORY:

1979, 175:2, eff. Aug. 5, 1979. 2012, 186:5, eff. June 11, 2012.

Amendment Notes

—2012.

The 2012 amendment added "and pursuant to RSA 32" in the last sentence.

162-K:13. Administration.

The municipality may create a department or designate an existing department or office or agency or municipal housing and redevelopment authority, or form a corporation under RSA 292, to administer development districts. The district administrator may, subject to such rules and limitations as may be adopted by the governing or legislative body, be granted the power to:

I. Acquire property or easements through negotiations;

II. Enter into operating contracts on behalf of the municipality for operation of any of the facilities authorized to be constructed under this chapter;

III. Lease space to private individuals or corporations within the buildings constructed under this chapter;

IV. Lease or sell land and lease or sell air rights over structures constructed under this chapter;

V. Enter into contracts for construction of several facilities or portions thereof authorized under this chapter;

VI. Contract with the housing and redevelopment authority of the municipality for the administration of any or all of the provisions of this chapter;

VII. Certify to the governing body of the municipality, for acquisition through eminent domain, property that cannot be acquired by negotiation, but is required for implementation of the development program;

VIII. Certify to the governing body of the municipality the amount of funds, if any, which must be raised through sale of bonds to finance the program for development districts;

IX. Apply for grants from the government of the United States or other source.

HISTORY:

1979, 175:2, eff. Aug. 5, 1979.

162-K:14. Advisory Board.

I. The legislative body of the municipality shall create an advisory board for each development district. The board shall consist of such number of members appointed or elected as determined by the legislative body. A majority of members shall be owners or occupants of real property within or adjacent to the development district. In a substantially residential development district, however, the board shall consist solely of owners or occupants of real property within or adjacent to the district.

II. The advisory board shall advise the governing body and district administrator on planning, construction and implementation of the development program and on maintenance and operation of the district after the program has been completed.

III. The governing body shall by resolution delineate the respective powers and duties of the advisory board and the planning staff or agency. The resolution shall establish reasonable time limits for consultation by the advisory board on the phases of the development program, and provide a mechanism for appealing to the governing body for a final decision when conflicts arise between the advisory board and the planning staff or agency, regarding the development program in its initial and subsequent stages.

HISTORY:

1979, 175:2, eff. Aug. 5, 1979.

162-K:15. Relocation.

Unless they desire otherwise, provision shall be made for relocation of all persons who would be displaced by a proposed development district prior to displacement in accordance with the provisions of RSA 162-K:6. Prior to undertaking any relocation of displaced persons, the municipality shall insure that housing and other facilities of at least comparable quality be made available to the persons to be displaced.

HISTORY:

1979, 175:2, eff. Aug. 5, 1979.

CHAPTER 162-N

ECONOMIC REVITALIZATION ZONE TAX CREDITS [EFFECTIVE UNTIL JULY 1, 2020; SEE PROSPECTIVE REPEAL NOTE BELOW.]

Repeal and reenactment of chapter.

2007, 263:120, eff. July 1, 2007, provided for the repeal and reenactment of RSA 162-N. Original RSA 162-N, consisting of RSA 162-N:1– 162-N:9, was derived from 2003, 301:2, eff. July 1, 2003.

Prospective repeal of chapter.

2007, 263:123, I, as amended by 2010, 311:1, eff. July 13, 2010, as amended by 2014, 139:1, eff. August 15, 2014, provided for the repeal of this chapter on July 1, 2020.

Applicability of 2010 amendment.

2010, 311:6, eff. July 13, 2010, provided: "This act shall apply for taxable periods ending on or after January 1, 2010."

162-N:1. Definitions. [Repealed effective July 1, 2020; see prospective repeal note preceding RSA 162-N:1]

In this chapter:

I. "Economic revitalization zone" means a zone designated by the commissioner of business and economic affairs as an economic revitalization zone in accordance with the provisions of this chapter.

II. "Full-time job" means a job that is at least 35 hours per week and is a permanent, year-round position.

HISTORY:

2007, 263:120, eff. July 1, 2007. 2015, 265:8, eff. July 1, 2015. 2017, 156:14, eff. July 1, 2017.

Amendment Notes
   The 2017 amendments to this section by Ch. 156 substituted "business and economic affairs" for "resources and economic development" in I.

—2015.
   The 2015 amendment added the I designation; added paragraph II; and made related changes.
   Prospective repeal of chapter.See Prospective Repeal note set out preceding this section.

162-N:2. Designation of Economic Revitalization Zone. [Repealed effective July 1, 2020; see prospective repeal note preceding RSA 162-N:1]

I. .Economic revitalization zone. means a zone with a single continuous boundary, designated in accordance with the rules adopted under RSA 162-N:8, and having at least one of the following characteristics:

   (a) Unused or underutilized industrial parks; or

   (b) Vacant land or structures previously used for industrial, commercial, or retail purposes but currently not so used due to demolition, age, obsolescence, deterioration, brownfields, relocation of the former occupant.s operations, or cessation of operation resulting from unfavorable economic conditions either generally or in a specific economic sector.

II. Economic revitalization zones shall be designated by the commissioner of business and economic affairs only upon petition by the local governing body, as defined by RSA 672:6, or the town council. The commissioner of business and economic affairs shall certify that the economic revitalization zone meets the criteria required in paragraph I.

HISTORY:
   2007, 263:120, eff. July 1, 2007. 2010, 311:2, eff. July 13, 2010. 2015, 265:1, eff. July 1, 2015. 2017, 156:14, eff. July 1, 2017.

Amendment Notes
   The 2017 amendments to this section by Ch. 156 substituted "resources and economic development" for "business and economic affairs" twice in II.

—2015.
   The 2015 amendment rewrote the section.

—2010.
   The 2010 amendment rewrote I(b), which formerly read: "The median household income in the census tract or tracts in which the zone is located is less than $40,500 according to the most recent federal decennial census."
   Prospective repeal of chapter.See Prospective Repeal note set out preceding RSA 162-N:1.

162-N:2-a. Reevaluation of Economic Revitalization Zone. [Repealed effective July 1, 2020; see note below.]

Each economic revitalization zone shall be evaluated every 5 years to determine if it meets the criteria required in RSA 162-N:2. If an economic revitalization zone fails to meet the criteria in RSA

162-N:2, its designation as an economic revitalization zone shall be removed.

HISTORY:
   2015, 265:2, eff. July 1, 2015.

Prospective repeal of section.
   2015, 265:7 provides for the repeal of this section on July 1, 2020.

162-N:3. Eligibility Requirements for Business Tax Credits. [Repealed effective July 1, 2020; see prospective repeal note preceding RSA 162-N:1]

No economic revitalization zone tax credits shall be allowed to any taxpayer unless the taxpayer.s project receives written certification in accordance with RSA 162-N:4, I from the commissioner of business and economic affairs that it will expand the commercial or industrial base in a designated economic revitalization zone and will create new jobs in the state.

HISTORY:
   2007, 263:120, eff. July 1, 2007. 2015, 265:3, eff. July 1, 2015. 2017, 156:14, eff. July 1, 2017.

Amendment Notes
   The 2017 amendments to this section by Ch. 156 substituted "resources and economic development" for "business and economic affairs."

—2015.
   The 2015 amendment inserted "in accordance with RSA 162-N:4, I."
   Prospective repeal of chapter.See Prospective Repeal note set out preceding RSA 162-N:1.

162-N:4. Economic Revitalization Zone Tax Credit Agreement. [Repealed effective July 1, 2020; see prospective repeal note preceding RSA 162-N:1]

I. The commissioner of business and economic affairs shall enter into a written economic revitalization zone tax credit agreement with each taxpayer; such agreement to be certified by the commissioner of business and economic affairs under this section. The agreement shall contain such provisions as the commissioner of business and economic affairs determines to be in the public interest, which shall include, but not be limited to:

   (a) Quality and quantity of full-time jobs to be created.

   (b) Duration of the taxpayer.s commitments with respect to the economic revitalization zone.

   (c) The amount of the taxpayer.s investment in the project.

   (d) A precise definition of the location of the facility eligible for the credit.

   (e) The maximum amount of the economic revitalization zone tax credit that will be allowed to the business under this agreement for jobs created and for construction or reconstruction expenses.

II. The agreement shall contain a determination of the final amount of the credit awarded and shall be provided to the commissioner of revenue administration and the taxpayer claiming the credit no later than March 10 of each year.

HISTORY:
2007, 263:120, eff. July 1, 2007. 2010, 311:3, eff. July 13, 2010. 2015, 265:4, eff. July 1, 2015. 2017, 156:14, eff. July 1, 2017.

Amendment Notes
The 2017 amendments to this section by Ch. 156 substituted "resources and economic development" for "business and economic affairs" three times in the introductory language of I.

—2015.
The 2015 amendment inserted "full-time" in I(a); and substituted "The agreement shall contain a determination of the final amount of the credit awarded and shall be provided" for "A certified copy of each agreement signed by the commissioner of resources and economic development and the taxpayer and a certified copy of each determination of the final amount of the credit awarded under the agreement shall be provided" in paragraph II.

—2010.
The 2010 amendment, in II, added "and a certified copy of each determination of the final amount of the credit awarded under the agreement" and "and the taxpayer claiming the credit no later than March 10 of each year."
Prospective repeal of chapter.See Prospective Repeal note set out preceding RSA 162-N:1.

162-N:5. Limit on Total Economic Revitalization Zone Credits. [Repealed effective July 1, 2020; see prospective repeal note preceding RSA 162-N:1]

The aggregate of tax credits issued by the commissioner of business and economic affairs to all taxpayers claiming the credit shall not exceed $825,000 for any calendar year, except that any amount of the credit less than $825,000 that is not claimed in the calendar year may be issued in the next calendar year and in following years. Amounts carried forward pursuant to RSA 162-N:7 shall not be counted against this limit in any year in which they are applied. Notwithstanding RSA 162-N:6, the maximum credit which may be utilized by a taxpayer in any calendar year shall not exceed $40,000. In the case in which the aggregate credits requested during the calendar year exceed the amount available, each taxpayer shall receive a credit for the proportional share of the maximum aggregate credit amount.

HISTORY:
2007, 263:120, eff. July 1, 2007. 2008, 58:1, eff. July 1, 2008. 2010, 311:4, eff. July 13, 2010. 2017, 156:14, eff. July 1, 2017.

Amendment Notes
The 2017 amendments to this section by Ch. 156 substituted "resources and economic development" for "business and economic affairs" in the first sentence.

—2014.
The 2014 amendment added "except that any amount of the credit less than $825,000 that is not claimed in the calendar year

may be issued in the next calendar year and in following years" in the first sentence and substituted "the amount available" for "$825,000" in the last sentence.

—2010.
The 2010 amendment rewrote the section to the extent that a detailed comparison would be impracticable.

—2008.
The 2008 amendment added the second sentence and in the last sentence, substituted "which may be utilized by a taxpayer" for "awarded to a taxpayer".
Prospective repeal of chapter.See Prospective Repeal note set out preceding RSA 162-N:1.

Applicability of 2008 amendment.
2008, 58:3, eff. July 1, 2008, provided: "Notwithstanding any other provision of law, all agreements made by the commissioner of resources and economic development under 2003, 301:2 prior to July 1, 2007, shall be honored, according to the provisions of 2003, 301:2."

162-N:6. Determination of Economic Revitalization Zone Tax Credits Eligible Amount. [Repealed effective July 1, 2020; see prospective repeal note preceding RSA 162-N:1]

For the purpose of determining the economic revitalization zone tax credit that the taxpayer is eligible to receive, the amount of the credit to be taken shall be the lesser of the following:

I. The maximum amount of the economic revitalization zone tax credit as stated in the agreement as specified by RSA 162-N:4, I(e); or

II. The sum of the following:

(a) 4 percent of the salary for each new full-time job created in the calendar year with a wage less than or equal to 1.75 times the then current state minimum wage.

(b) 5 percent of the salary for each new full-time job created in the calendar year with a wage greater than 1.75 times the then current state minimum wage and less than or equal to 2.5 times the then current state minimum wage.

(c) 6 percent of the salary for each new full-time job created in the calendar year with a wage greater than 2.5 times the then current state minimum wage.

(d) 4 percent of the lesser of the following:

(1) The actual cost incurred in the calendar year of creating a new facility or renovating an existing facility, and expenditures for machinery, equipment, or other materials, except inventory.

(2) $20,000 for each new full-time job created in the calendar year.

HISTORY:
2007, 263:120, eff. July 1, 2007. 2010, 311:5, eff. July 13, 2010. 2015, 265:5, eff. July 1, 2015.

Amendment Notes

—2015.
The 2015 amendment substituted "each new full-time job created" for "each new job created" in II(a), II(b), II(c), and II(d)(2).

—2010.
The 2010 amendment rewrote II to the extent that a detailed comparison would be impracticable.
Prospective repeal of chapter.See Prospective Repeal note set out preceding RSA 162-N:1.

162-N:7.   Application of Economic Revitalization Zone Tax Credit. [Repealed effective July 1, 2020; see prospective repeal note preceding RSA 162-N:1]

The economic revitalization zone tax credit shall be applied against the business profits tax under RSA 77-A, and any unused portion thereof may be applied against the business enterprise tax under RSA 77-E. Any unused portion of the credit allowed under this chapter or any eligible credit in excess of $40,000 allowed under this chapter, may be carried forward and allowed against taxes due under RSA 77-A or RSA 77-E for 5 taxable periods from the taxable period in which the tax was paid. For the purpose of the credit allowed under RSA 77-A:5, X, the economic revitalization zone credit shall be considered taxes paid under RSA 77-E.

HISTORY:
2007, 263:120, eff. July 1, 2007. 2008, 58:2, eff. July 1, 2008. 2017, 156:14, eff. July 1, 2017.

Editor's Notes
2017, 156:14 provided for the amendment of this section by replacing "resources and economic development" with "natural and cultural resources"; however, that language was not in the current version of this section.

Amendment Notes

—2008.
The 2008 amendment in the second sentence, added "or any eligible credit in excess of $40,000 allowed under this chapter" and added the last sentence.
Prospective repeal of chapter.See Prospective Repeal note set out preceding RSA 162-N:1.

Applicability of 2008 amendment.
2008, 58:3, eff. July 1, 2008, provided: "Notwithstanding any other provision of law, all agreements made by the commissioner of resources and economic development under 2003, 301:2 prior to July 1, 2007, shall be honored, according to the provisions of 2003, 301:2."

162-N:8.   Rules. [Repealed effective July 1, 2020; see prospective repeal note preceding RSA 162-N:1]

The commissioner of revenue administration shall adopt rules, under RSA 541-A, relative to documentation of the credits claimed under this chapter. The commissioner of business and economic affairs shall, in consultation with the executive director of the community development finance authority, adopt rules, under RSA 541-A, relative to the administration and implementation of this chapter. The rules adopted by the commissioner of business and economic affairs shall include provisions relative to:
I. Establishment and certification of economic revitalization zones.
II. Criteria for and approval of projects in economic revitalization zones, including jobs per dollar thresholds.
III. Fees which the commissioner of business and economic affairs may charge to each applicant to cover the reasonable costs of the state.s administration of the applicant.s participation in the economic revitalization zone tax credit program.
IV. Criteria for evaluation of the effectiveness of the tax credit program and whether existing economic revitalization zones continue to meet the criteria of RSA 162-N:2.

HISTORY:
2007, 263:120, eff. July 1, 2007. 2015, 265:6, eff. July 1, 2015. 2017, 156:14, eff. July 1, 2017.

Amendment Notes
The 2017 amendments to this section by Ch. 156 substituted "resources and economic development" for "business and economic affairs" twice in the introductory language and in III.

—2015.
The 2015 amendment added paragraph IV.
Prospective repeal of chapter.See Prospective Repeal note set out preceding RSA 162-N:1.

162-N:9.   Reports. [Repealed effective July 1, 2020; see prospective repeal note preceding RSA 162-N:1]

The commissioner of business and economic affairs shall file an annual report 60 days after the close of each fiscal year with the governor, the senate president, the speaker of the house of representatives, and the fiscal committee of the general court. The report shall describe the results of the economic revitalization zone tax credit program and shall include any recommendations for further legislation regarding the economic revitalization zone tax credit program.

HISTORY:
2007, 263:120, eff. July 1, 2007. 2012, 247:19, eff. August 17, 2012. 2017, 156:14, eff. July 1, 2017.

Amendment Notes
The 2017 amendments to this section by Ch. 156 substituted "resources and economic development" for "business and economic affairs" in the first sentence.

—2012.
The 2012 amendment, in the first sentence, added "60 days after the close of each fiscal year" and "of the general court."
Prospective repeal of chapter.See Prospective Repeal note set out preceding RSA 162-N:1.

TITLE XVII
HOUSING AND REDEVELOPMENT

RESEARCH REFERENCES AND PRACTICE AIDS

Cross References.
Actions against tenants, see RSA 540.
Automatic fire warning devices and carbon monoxide detection devices in dwellings, see RSA 153:10-a.
Condominium Act, see RSA 356-B.
Emergency shelter program, see RSA 126-A:25 et seq.
Housing standards, see RSA 48-A.
Prohibited rental practices and security deposits, see RSA 540-A.
Protection of tenants in conversion of rental units, see RSA 356-C.

CHAPTER 205-A

REGULATION OF MANUFACTURED HOUSING PARKS

Revision note.
Substituted "Manufactured Housing" for "Mobile Home" in the chapter heading in light of changes made by 1983, 230:18.

Moratorium on conversion of existing manufactured housing parks into condominiums.
1991, 143:1, eff. May 20, 1991, provided:
"Notwithstanding RSA 356-B, there is hereby established a 1-year moratorium, which shall be in effect upon the effective date of this act [May 20, 1991] on converting existing manufactured housing parks, as defined in RSA 205-A:1, II, into condominiums."

NOTES TO DECISIONS

Analysis

1. Constitutionality
2. Construction

1. Constitutionality
Legislation establishing the board of manufactured housing does not conflict with the separation of powers doctrine of the New Hampshire Constitution because its dispute resolution function is inextricably linked to its regulatory function, and the board is empowered only to decide claims arising under statutes governing manufactured housing park rules. Hynes v. Hale, 146 N.H. 533, 776 A.2d 722, 2001 N.H. LEXIS 111 (N.H. 2001).

2. Construction
Although a renter lived on an owner's property, which was not considered a "campground" under RSA 216-I:1, VII, the trial court did not reach the issue of whether the renter's camper/trailer was a "manufactured housing" unit within the meaning of RSA 205-A:1 and RSA 674:31 before determining if the owner was a "landlord";

therefore, the owner's conviction under RSA 540-A:3, III had to be reversed and remanded for further proceedings. Comeau v. Vergato, 149 N.H. 508, 823 A.2d 764, 2003 N.H. LEXIS 74 (N.H. 2003).
Neither the implied warranty of habitability recognized in a prior case nor the statutory language of this chapter or RSA 540:13-d immunizes a manufactured housing park tenant who withholds rent without a court order from an action for possession. Penrich, Inc. v. Sullivan, 140 N.H. 583, 669 A.2d 1363, 1995 N.H. LEXIS 193 (N.H. 1995).

OPINIONS OF THE ATTORNEY GENERAL

Cited:
Cited in 1986 Op. Att'y Gen. 189.

RESEARCH REFERENCES AND PRACTICE AIDS

Cross References.
Licensing requirements for sale of manufactured housing by park owners generally, see RSA 331-A:10.
Zoning of manufactured housing, see RSA 674:32.

205-A:1. Definitions.

As used solely in this chapter unless the context specifically requires otherwise:

I. "Manufactured housing" includes, but is not limited to, manufactured housing as defined by RSA 674:31, and also includes any prefabricated dwelling unit which:

(a) Is designed for long term and continuous residential occupancy;

(b) Is designed to be moved on wheels, as a whole or in sections; and

(c) On arrival on the site, is complete and ready for occupancy, except for incidental unpacking, assembly, connection with utilities, and placing on support or permanent structure.

Nothing herein shall be construed to include campers or recreational vehicles within the definition of "manufactured housing".

II. "Manufactured housing park" means any parcel of land under single or common ownership or control which contains, or is designed, laid out or adapted to accommodate 2 or more manufactured houses. Nothing herein shall be construed to apply to premises used solely for storage or display of manufactured housing.

III. "Person" means any natural person, corporation, partnership, or sole proprietorship.

IV. "Tenant" means any person who owns or occupies manufactured housing and pays rent or other consideration to place said manufactured housing in a manufactured housing park.

V. "Manufactured housing park owner" means the person holding title to the manufactured housing park to be sold.

VI. "Family member" includes the owner's spouse, son, daughter, mother, father, brother, sister, grandson, granddaughter, stepchildren, stepgrandchildren, or first cousins.

VII. "Final unconditional offer" means a fully executed agreement for the sale of a manufactured housing park.

HISTORY:
1973, 291:1. 1983, 230:10, 18. 1985, 333:1. 1987, 383:1, eff. May 26, 1987.

Amendments

—1987.
Paragraphs V–VII: Added.

—1985.
Paragraphs I–III: Rewritten to the extent that a detailed comparison would be impracticable.

—1983.
Paragraph I: Rewritten to the extent that a detailed comparison would be impracticable.
Paragraph II: Substituted "manufactured housing" for "mobile home" preceding "park" at the beginning of the first sentence and for "mobile homes" following "display of" at the end of the second sentence and "manufactured houses" for "mobile homes" following "2 or more" at the end of the first sentence.
Paragraph IV: Substituted "manufactured housing" for "a mobile home" following "occupies" and for "mobile home" following "place said" and preceding "park".

NOTES TO DECISIONS

Cited:
Cited in Whispering Springs Tenant Ass'n v. Barrett, 137 N.H. 203, 624 A.2d 1345, 1993 N.H. LEXIS 65 (1993).

CHAPTER 205-B

WARRANTIES ON PRESITE BUILT AND PREFABRICATED HOMES

Section

RESEARCH REFERENCES AND PRACTICE AIDS

Cross References.
Manufacturer's right to indemnification from purchaser or lessee, see RSA 359-F.
Warranties generally, see RSA 382-A:2-312– 2-318.

205-B:1. Definitions.

In this chapter:
I. "New" shall include any unit not previously sold or occupied as a dwelling unit.
II. "Prefabricated" shall mean construction materials or assembled units fabricated prior to erection or installation in a building or structure, but shall not include manufactured housing as defined in RSA 674:31.
III. "Presite built housing" means "presite built housing" as defined by RSA 674:31-a.

HISTORY:
1988, 231:4, eff. June 29, 1988.

205-B:2. Manufacturer's Warranty.

No person shall sell at retail a new prefabricated or presite built home in this state without a written manufacturer's warranty to the buyer which shall include the following terms:
I. That such home is free from any substantial defects in materials or workmanship in the structure, plumbing, heating, and electrical systems and in all appliances and other equipment installed or included in such home by the manufacturer.
II. That the seller or manufacturer shall take appropriate corrective action at the site of such home in instances of substantial defects in materials or workmanship which become evident within one year from the date of delivery of such home to the buyer, provided the buyer gives written notice of the defects to the seller, manufacturer, or dealer at his business address as soon as such defects become evident.

HISTORY:
1988, 231:4, eff. June 29, 1988.

NOTES TO DECISIONS

"Substantial defect"
"Substantial defect" encompasses, at a minimum, the absence of something necessary to adequately perform an important or essential function. McNeal v. Lebel, 157 N.H. 458, 953 A.2d 396, 2008 N.H. LEXIS 86 (N.H. 2008).
Modular home manufacturer's failure to deliver stairs constituted a "substantial defect" under RSA 205-B:2. The lack of stairs made it impossible for the occupants to access the second floor, rendering the second floor unusable, and the provision of access to the second floor was an essential function which the stairs were necessary to accomplish. McNeal v. Lebel, 157 N.H. 458, 953 A.2d 396, 2008 N.H. LEXIS 86 (N.H. 2008).

205-B:3. Waiver Prohibited.

The warranty provided in RSA 205-B:2 shall be in addition to and not in derogation of any other right or privilege which the buyer may have as otherwise provided by law. The seller or manufacturer shall not require the buyer to waive his rights under this chapter and any waiver shall be deemed contrary to public policy and shall be void and unenforceable.

HISTORY:
1988, 231:4, eff. June 29, 1988.

205-B:4. Attorney's Fees.

Any action instituted by a buyer for failure of a manufacturer to comply with the provisions of this chapter shall allow for the recovery of court costs and reasonable attorney's fees.

HISTORY:
1988, 231:4, eff. June 29, 1988.

CHAPTER 205-C

MODULAR BUILDING STANDARDS

RESEARCH REFERENCES AND PRACTICE AIDS

Cross References.
Adoption of building codes generally, see RSA 674:51, 51-a.
Department of safety generally, see RSA 21-P.

205-C:1. Definitions.

In this chapter:

I. "Approved third party inspection agency" means an entity or organization, public or private, determined by the department to be qualified by reason of facilities, personnel, experience, and demonstrated reliability and independence of judgment, to evaluate and certify building manufacturers and factory assembled modular construction.

II. "Modular building code" means the state building code as defined in and adopted in RSA 155-A.

III. "Building component" means any system, subsystem, or subassembly of closed construction designed for use in or as part of a modular building, which may include structural, electrical, mechanical, plumbing, and fire protection systems and other systems affecting health and safety.

IV. "Certification" means the process by which modular building manufacturers or modular construction has been evaluated to ensure conformity with the state modular construction standard and applicable rules of the department.

V. "Closed construction" means a method of manufacturing in which parts or processes are concealed and cannot be inspected at the building site without disassembly, damage, or destruction.

V-a. "Commissioner" means the commissioner of safety.

VI. "Department" means the department of safety.

VII. "Installation" means the assembly of modular buildings on site and the process of affixing modular buildings or building components to land, a foundation, footings, utilities, or an existing building.

VIII. "Label" means the approved insignia or seal including the name of the approved third party inspection agency that shall be affixed to a modular building or building component certified in accordance with the provisions of this chapter.

IX. "Local enforcement agency" means the agency or agencies of local government with authority to make inspections and to enforce the laws, ordinances and rules enacted by the state and by local government that establish standards and requirements applicable to the construction, alteration, or repair of buildings.

X. "Manufacturing facilities" means the place at which machinery, equipment and other capital goods are assembled and operated for the purpose of making, fabricating, constructing, forming or assembling modular buildings.

XI. "Modular building" means any building of closed construction, which is made or assembled in manufacturing facilities off the building site, for installation, or assembly and installation, on the building site. This definition shall not be construed to include any structure labeled in accordance with the Federal Manufactured Housing Construction and Safety Standards Act of 1974, nor shall it include single-wide structures under 750 square feet, provided that they are not for residential or classroom use, nor shall it include any recreational vehicle or park trailer as defined in American National Standards Institute A119.2, Standard for Recreational Vehicles, or A119.5, Standard for Park Trailers, or any building type not subject to the requirements of nationally recognized model building codes.

XII. [Repealed.]

XIII. "Person" means any individual or organized group of any kind, including partnerships, corporations and other forms of association, as well as federal, state or local instrumentalities, political subdivisions, or officers.

HISTORY:
1990, 169:2, eff. June 26, 1990. 1997, 44:2–4, eff. July 11, 1997. 2002, 8:5, 12, I, eff. Sept. 14, 2002. 270:2, eff. at 12:01 a.m., Sept. 14, 2002. 2007, 108:1, eff. August 10, 2007. 2011, 197:4, eff. June 14, 2011.

Amendment Notes

—2011.
The 2011 amendment added "nor shall it include single-wide structures under 750 square feet, provided that they are not for residential or classroom use" in the second sentence of XI.

—2007.
Paragraph II: Deleted "and the International Residential Code 2000 as published by the International Code Council" at the end.

—2002.
Paragraph II: Chapter 8, eff. Sept. 14, 2002, substituted the definition of "state building code" for the definition of "BOCA National Building Code".
Chapter 270, eff. at 12:01 a.m., Sept. 14, 2002, substituted the definition of "modular building code" for the definition of "state building code".
Paragraph XII: Repealed by ch. 8.

—1997.
Rewrote pars. II and XII and added par. V-a.

References in text.

The Federal Manufactured Housing Construction and Safety Standards Act of 1974, referred to in the second sentence of par. XI, is principally classified to 42 U.S.C.S. §§ 5401 et seq.

205-C:2. Modular Building Standard.

I. All modular buildings and building components ordered on or after the date one year after the effective date of RSA 155-A:2 shall comply with the modular building code and the state fire code.

II. All modular buildings and building components bearing a label of certification pursuant to the requirements of this chapter shall be deemed by local enforcement agencies as meeting the modular building code, however, such certification shall not be deemed to preempt enforcement of any state or local standards governing installation or work performed on the building site, including but not limited to site grading, foundations, driveways, on-site water and sewer systems or connections to off-site systems, and electrical line connections to the power source.

III. Nothing in this chapter shall be construed as amending, repealing or superseding any local law, ordinance, code or regulation, and all modular buildings and building components shall comply with all applicable state or local building requirements that exceed the modular building code, in addition to any land use restrictions including but not limited to subdivision regulations, use and location restrictions, density and dimensional limitations, or historic district laws or ordinances.

HISTORY:

1990, 169:2, eff. June 26, 1990. 1997, 44:5, eff. July 11, 1997. 2002, 8:6, eff. at 12:01 a.m., Sept. 14, 2002. 270:3, eff. at 12:01 a.m., Sept. 14, 2002.

Amendments

—2002.

Chapter 8, eff. Sept. 14, 2002, rewrote pars. I and II, and deleted "other state or" preceding "local law" and substituted "state building code, in addition to any" for "BOCA National Building Code or the National Electrical Code" preceding "land use restrictions" in par. III.

Chapter 270, eff. at 12:01 a.m., September 14, 2002, substituted "modular" for "state" preceding "building code" in pars. I–III.

—1997.

Substituted "national" for "basic" following "BOCA" wherever it appeared throughout the section, and "July 24, 1992" for "the effective date of the rules adopted by the department pursuant to RSA 541-A" in par. I.

Cross References.

Requirement that all new public buildings conform to standards not lower than those in the state building code, see RSA 155-A:1.

205-C:3. Certification Required.

No person shall sell, lease, or install for use in this state any modular building or building component manufactured after July 24, 1992, unless such building or building component bears a label of certification issued by the department.

HISTORY:

1990, 169:2, eff. June 26, 1990. 1997, 44:6, eff. July 11, 1997.

Amendments

—1997.

Substituted "July 24, 1992" for "the effective date of the rules adopted by the department pursuant to this chapter".

205-C:4. Rulemaking.

The commissioner shall adopt rules under RSA 541-A relative to:

I. Requirements for approval of third party inspection agencies by the department.

II. Requirements for approved third party inspection agency certification of the manufacturing facilities of any person who engages in the business of manufacturing modular buildings or building components for installation in this state.

III. Requirements for approved third party inspection agency certification and labeling or modular buildings and building components for sale, lease or installation in this state.

IV. Investigation of complaints of noncompliance.

V. Enforcement procedures, including standards for revocation and suspension of certification.

VI. Imposition and collection of fees, administrative fines, and penalties.

VII. Standards and requirements in interagency agreements.

HISTORY:

1990, 169:2, eff. June 26, 1990. 1997, 44:7, eff. July 11, 1997.

Amendments

—1997.

Substituted "commissioner" for "department" in the introductory paragraph.

205-C:5. Interagency Coordination.

I. The department may issue a label of certification to modular buildings or building components that have been certified by an agency of the federal government or component authority within another state, if the department finds that such certification is granted on the basis of a standard which is equivalent or more stringent than required under RSA 205-C:2.

II. The department may enter into interagency agreements with any other department or agency of state government necessary or appropriate for administration of this chapter.

HISTORY:

1990, 169:2, eff. June 26, 1990.

Cross References.
Powers and duties of building inspectors generally, see RSA 676:11– 13.

205-C:6. Fees.

The commissioner shall by rule establish fees to defray the costs of administering this chapter. Such rules shall specify fees for the certification of third party inspection agencies by the department; certification of manufacturing facilities by approved third party inspection agencies; and certification of modular buildings and building components by approved third party inspection agencies. Fees established by the commissioner shall be sufficient to produce estimated revenues equal to 125 percent of the direct operating expenses for administering this chapter budgeted for the biennium in which they will apply. All fees collected by the department shall be deposited into the general fund.

HISTORY:
1990, 169:2. 1993, 358:2, eff. July 1, 1993. 1997, 44:8, eff. July 11, 1997. 2014, 269:2, eff. July 1, 2014.

Amendment Notes

—2014.
The 2014 amendment added the third sentence.

—1997.
Substituted "commissioner" for "department" in the first sentence.

—1993.
Added the third sentence.

Severability of 1993 amendment.
1993, 358 was subject to a severability clause. See 1993, 358:106.

205-C:7. Enforcement.

I. The department shall investigate or cause to be investigated all complaints made to it alleging noncompliance with the requirements of this chapter.

II. Where the department finds that a manufacturer, modular building, or building component does not conform to the requirements of this chapter or applicable rules, the department may obtain injunctive relief from a court of competent jurisdiction to enjoin the sale, lease, delivery or installation in this state of any or all modular buildings or building components manufactured by the person in violation.

III. Where the department finds that an approved third party inspection agency, manufacturer, modular building, or building component does not conform to the requirements of this chapter or applicable rules, the department may suspend or revoke its certification, including any certification granted through an approved third party inspection agency acting on behalf of the department. Under no circumstances shall the offender be eligible for reinstatement until the department has confirmed that the agency, manufacturer, system, building or component in question is in full compliance with the requirements of this chapter and applicable rules.

IV. Additional fines, penalties, and remedies for violations of this chapter shall be the same as for violations of RSA title LXIV, as stated in RSA 676:15 and 676:17.

V. The building inspector or other local official with the authority to enforce building or land use regulations or codes may enforce the provisions of this chapter. A copy of the complaint or petition shall be sent, by certified mail, to the department on or before the date upon which it is filed.

HISTORY:
1990, 169:2, eff. June 26, 1990.

Cross References.
Powers of building code board of appeals, see RSA 674:34.

References in text.
RSA title LXIV, referred to in par. IV, is classified to Title 64 of LEXIS New Hampshire Revised Statutes Annotated, which is comprised of chapters 672–678.

TITLE XVIII
FISH AND GAME

NOTES TO DECISIONS

Cited:
Cited in State v. Jenkins, 102 N.H. 545, 162 A.2d 613, 1960 N.H. LEXIS 76 (1960).

RESEARCH REFERENCES AND PRACTICE AIDS

Cross References.
Council on resources and development, see RSA 162-C.
Exposing poisons for the destruction of animals, see RSA 644:16.

CHAPTER 215-A

OFF HIGHWAY RECREATIONAL VEHICLES AND TRAILS

Amendments

—1993.
1993, 53:1, eff. June 15, 1993, added "and trails" following "vehicles" in the chapter heading.

NOTES TO DECISIONS

Construction with other laws
Trial court erred when it concluded that RSA ch. 215-A preempted the Town's attempt to regulate the owners' use of their land, where RSA ch. 215-A created a different set of procedures for regulating the operation of OHRVs on public land and private land, and it did not constitute a detailed and comprehensive regulatory scheme with respect to OHRV trails on private property. Town of Lyndeborough v. Boisvert Props., LLC, 150 N.H. 814, 846 A.2d 1187, 2004 N.H. LEXIS 74 (N.H. 2004).

RESEARCH REFERENCES AND PRACTICE AIDS

New Hampshire Practice.
16-50 N.H.P. Municipal Law & Taxation § 50.25.

215-A:15. Regulations of Political Subdivisions.

I. With bylaws or ordinances city or town councils and boards of selectmen may regulate the operation of OHRVs within city or town limits, providing they do not conflict with provisions of this chapter.

I-a.(a) Any municipality that enacts an ordinance or bylaw under paragraph I relating to this chapter shall be responsible for the enforcement of such ordinance or bylaw.

(b) Any person who is guilty of a violation of an ordinance or bylaw under subparagraph (a) shall be subject to all other provisions of this chapter.

II. [Repealed.]

III. [Repealed.]

IV. Speed limits for OHRVs traveling on the frozen surface of Turtle Pond, also known as Turtle Town Pond, in the city of Concord shall not exceed 55 miles per hour.

V. Enforcement of paragraph IV shall be the joint responsibility of the city of Concord and the state of New Hampshire.

VI. [Repealed.]

HISTORY:
1981, 538:3, eff. June 30, 1981. 1996, 41:1, eff. June 30, 1996. 41:2, eff. June 30, 1998. 1999, 48:1, eff. July 20, 1999. 2004, 47:2, eff. July 2, 2004. 243:5, eff. June 15, 2004. 2005, 210:64, VIII, eff. July 1, 2006. 2017, 56:1, eff. August 1, 2017.

Amendment Notes
The 2017 amendment to this section by Ch. 56 added I-a.

—2005.
Paragraph VI: Repealed.

—2004.
Paragraph I: Substituted "city or town councils and boards of selectmen" for "any town or city" following "ordinances" and "city or town" for "its" preceding "limits".
Paragraph VI: Added.

—1999.
Paragraphs IV, V: Added.

—1996.
Chapter 41:1, designated the existing text of the section as par. I and added pars. II and III.
Chapter 41:2 repealed pars. II and III.

RESEARCH REFERENCES AND PRACTICE AIDS

New Hampshire Practice.
16-50 N.H.P. Municipal Law & Taxation § 50.25.

CHAPTER 215-C

SNOWMOBILES

Continuation of rules.
2005, 210:63, eff. July 1, 2006, provided: "All existing rules adopted by the commissioner of resources and economic development and the executive director of fish and game relative to snowmobiles pursuant to authority in RSA 215-A, shall continue in effect until such rules are amended, repealed, or expire under RSA 541-A."

215-C:32. Enforcement.

I. The provisions of this chapter shall be enforced by all duly authorized representatives of the department of fish and game and by every police and law enforcement officer including, but not limited to, members of the state police, sheriffs, deputy sheriffs, policemen, and constables and all persons empowered to make arrests in criminal cases.

II. The commissioner of the department of natural and cultural resources shall appoint a chief supervisor of the bureau of trails, who shall have additional duties as state parks and forest security officer with authority under RSA 594. The commissioner of the department of natural and cultural resources shall, at his or her discretion, also appoint bureau of trail area supervisors and foremen, who shall be peace officers for the purposes of RSA 594.

III. The commissioner of the department of natural and cultural resources may designate employees of the bureau as forest and park patrol officers. The chief supervisors appointed under paragraph II and RSA 215-A:16, II and the forest and park patrol officers shall have the authority of peace officers, as defined under RSA 594:1, to enforce the provisions of this chapter anywhere in the state and all rules of the department of natural and cultural resources on lands owned by, leased to, or under control of the department of natural and cultural resources. Forest and park patrol officers shall also have authority as peace officers under RSA 594:1 to enforce laws dealing with trespass, litter, breaking and entering, larceny, and vandalism on lands owned by, leased to, or otherwise being used by the state in connection with official recreational or snowmobile trails.

HISTORY:
  2005, 210:1, eff. July 1, 2006. 2017, 156:14, eff. July 1, 2017.

Amendment Notes
  The 2017 amendments to this section by Ch. 156 substituted "natural and cultural resources" for "resources and economic development" throughout the section.

NOTES TO DECISIONS

Exculpatory clause
  Even if RSA ch. 215-C applied to the operation of snowmobiles on privately owned land in a ski area, a snowboarder's execution of exculpatory clauses that waived negligence claims had no effect upon the State's ability to enforce the snowmobile operation rules pursuant to RSA 215-C:32 and RSA 215-C:34, such that there was no public policy violation by enforcement of the clauses as a defense to the snowboarder's negligence action, arising from a collision with a snowmobile that was operated by a ski area employee. McGrath v. SNH Dev., Inc., 158 N.H. 540, 969 A.2d 392, 2009 N.H. LEXIS 43 (N.H. 2009).

TITLE XX

TRANSPORTATION

Revision note.

1985, 402:1, eff. July 1, 1985, provided for the enactment of RSA 21-L, relating to the department of transportation. 1985, 402:2 provided for the abolition of the department of public works and highways and for the transfer of all powers, functions, duties, responsibilities and officials of the department of the commissioner of transportation appointed pursuant to RSA 21-L:3. Other provisions in 1985, 402, amended chapters 228–238 of Title XX to provide for administration by the commissioner of transportation and added provisions to RSA 228– 238 relating to modes of transportation not previously covered by the chapters.

In order to provide for a logical and comprehensible integration into the LEXIS Revised Statutes Annotated of the changes effected by 1985, 185 and 402, Title XX, formerly entitled "Highways, Bridges and Turnpike System," has been retitled "Transportation," RSA 228, formerly entitled "Department of Public Works and Highways," has been retitled "Administration of Transportation Laws," the designation for Title XX-A has been omitted as no longer necessary in light of the changes in the name of Title XX, and RSA 239 has been incorporated in Title XX.

RESEARCH REFERENCES AND PRACTICE AIDS

Cross References.
Aeronautics, see RSA 422 et seq.
Carriage of household goods for hire by motor vehicle, see RSA 375-A.
Common carriers by water, see RSA 270.
Motor carriers of passengers, see RSA 376.
Motor carriers of property for hire, see RSA 375-B.
Motor vehicles, see RSA 259 et seq.
Railroad transportation of passengers, baggage and freight, see RSA 377.
Regulation of railroads generally, see RSA 367:50 et seq.

CHAPTER 228

ADMINISTRATION OF TRANSPORTATION LAWS

Commissioner, Deputy and Assistant Commissioners

Revision note.

In the chapter heading, substituted "Administration of Transportation Laws," for "Department of Public Works and Highways" in view of the abolition of the department of public works and highways and the transfer of its function, powers, duties, personnel, records, equipment, etc., to the department of transportation created by RSA 21-L by 1985, 402:2, and in view of the modification of the provisions of this chapter by 1985, 402, for purposes of implementation of the reorganization provided for in that act.

Effective date of 1985 amendments, additions and repeals

1985, 402:41, II, eff. July 1, 1985, provided that the provisions of 1985, 402 which affected this chapter would take effect when the department of transportation became operational on the date set according to 1983, 372:5, II. Pursuant to 1983, 372:5, II, the joint committee on implementation of reorganization and the governor determined the effective date upon which the department became operational to be Feb. 28, 1986.

Abolition of department of public works and highways; transfer of powers, functions, duties and officials to commissioner of transportation.

1985, 402:2, I, eff. July 1, 1985, provided for the abolition of the department of public works and highways and for the transfer of all powers, functions, duties, responsibilities and officials of the department to the commissioner of transportation appointed pursuant to RSA 21-L:3. 1985, 402:2, VII, eff. July 1, 1985, provided that the transfer of powers, functions, duties and officials of the department of public works and highways to the commissioner of transportation would take effect when the department of transportation became operational on the date set according to 1983, 372:5, II. Pursuant to 1983, 372:5, II, the joint committee on implementation of reorganization and the governor determined the effective date upon which the department became operational to be Feb. 28, 1986.

RESEARCH REFERENCES AND PRACTICE AIDS

Cross References.
Department of transportation, see RSA 21-L.

Commissioner, Deputy and Assistant Commissioners

228:31-a. Agreements for Telecommunications-Related Uses of the State Highway System and State-Owned Railroad Rights-of-Way.

The commissioner may, with the approval of the governor and council, execute contracts, leases, licenses, and other agreements relating to the use or occupation of state-owned rights-of-way, whether easement or fee-owned, for purposes of allowing the installation and maintenance of commercial mobile radio service devices. Such agreements, which shall be for commercially reasonable value, shall not extend for a period of more than 10 years. Any leases executed pursuant to this section shall be subject to the requirements of RSA 72:23 with regard to properly assessed real estate taxes and subject to local zoning and planning requirements. Said devices shall take into consideration the scenic beauty of the landscape. There shall be no advertising signs on these devices. The provisions of RSA 4:40 shall not apply to this section.

HISTORY:
1998, 337:2, eff. June 26, 1998.

CHAPTER 229

HIGHWAY SYSTEM IN THE STATE

NOTES TO DECISIONS

Historical

Since 1905, New Hampshire has had two highway systems, one including state highways and state-aided highways, and the other consisting of those which were not. Attorney Gen. ex rel. Highway Agents v. Brooks, 80 N.H. 70, 113 A. 216, 1921 N.H. LEXIS 23 (N.H. 1921).

RESEARCH REFERENCES AND PRACTICE AIDS

Cross References.

State 10-year transportation improvement program, see RSA 240.

229:1. Highways Defined.

Highways are only such as are laid out in the mode prescribed therefor by statute, or roads which have been constructed for or are currently used for motor vehicle, bicycle, or pedestrian public travel over land which has been conveyed to a city or town or to the state by deed of a fee or easement interest, or roads which have been dedicated to the public use and accepted by the city or town in which such roads are located, or roads which have been used as such for public travel, other than travel to and from a toll bridge or ferry, for 20 years prior to January 1, 1968, and shall include the bridges thereon. Highway does not include any bridge, trail, or path intended for use by off highway recreational vehicles, as defined in RSA 215-A:1, or snowmobiles, as defined in RSA 215-C:1.

HISTORY:

RS 53:7. CS 57:7. GS 68:8. GL 74:8. PS 67:1. PL 74:1. RL 90:1. 1943, 57:1. 1945, 188:1, part 1:1. RSA 230:1. 1967, 283:1. 1981, 87:1, eff. April 20, 1981. 2017, 156:123, eff. July 1, 2017.

Amendment Notes

The 2017 amendments to this section by Ch. 156 added "or are currently used for motor vehicle, bicycle, or pedestrian" preceding "public travel over land" and added the last sentence.

NOTES TO DECISIONS

Analysis

1. Construction with other laws
2. Creation of highways
3. Establishment under statutory authority—Application for laying out
4. —Authority of selectmen
5. —Private roads
6. —Sidewalks
7. —Presumption
8. —Estoppel
9. Dedication and acceptance
10. Establishment under prescription—Generally
11. —Public use
12. —Adverse use
13. —Permissive use
14. —Toll bridge or ferry road
15. —Access road to public property
16. —Sidewalks
17. —Extent of right acquired
18. —Responsibility for maintenance and repair
19. —Estoppel
20. —Burden of proof
21. —Evidence
22. Bridges

1. Construction with other laws

Under former RSA 234:23, authorizing selectmen to reestablish a highway according to the boundaries which, in their opinion, were those by which that highway had been originally established, precise location of restored boundaries could be determined according to opinion of selectmen, but question whether lost, uncertain, or doubtful boundaries had ever been established remained an issue to be determined not by opinion or reasonable belief in prior establishment but by proof pursuant to this section. Nute v. Wakefield, 117 N.H. 602, 376 A.2d 134, 1977 N.H. LEXIS 391 (N.H. 1977). (Decided under prior law.)

Where town initiated proceedings under former RSA 234:23 to "reestablish" boundary lines of a certain road involving an extension across plaintiffs' property, and plaintiffs sought temporary and permanent injunctive relief and decree to quiet title, finding of referee denying establishment of highway town sought to "reestablish" would not be disturbed on appeal, since road had never been originally established in accordance with this section. Nute v. Wakefield, 117 N.H. 602, 376 A.2d 134, 1977 N.H. LEXIS 391 (N.H. 1977). (Decided under prior law.)

The provisions of former RSA 36:26(a) that no building permit shall be issued unless the street shall have been accepted or received the status of a public street contemplates streets and highways as defined in this section. Blevens v. Manchester, 103 N.H. 284, 170 A.2d 121, 1961 N.H. LEXIS 33 (N.H. 1961). (Decided under prior law.)

2. Creation of highways

Public highway may be created in any one of four ways: (1) through taking of land by eminent domain and laying out of a highway by some governmental authority; (2) through construction of a road on public land; (3) through twenty years of use by public; or (4) by dedication and acceptance. Polizzo v. Hampton, 126 N.H. 398, 494 A.2d 254, 1985 N.H. LEXIS 342 (N.H. 1985).

3. Establishment under statutory authority—Application for laying out

Laying out of a highway by selectmen with out an application for it was invalid. State v. Morse, 50 N.H. 9, 1870 N.H. LEXIS 54 (N.H. 1870). (Decided under prior law.)

4. —Authority of selectmen

Laying out of a highway by selectmen in the exercise of a judicial power conferred on them could not be impeached or set aside in a collateral proceeding. Bryant v. Tamworth, 68 N.H. 483, 39 A. 431, 1896 N.H. LEXIS 38 (N.H. 1896). (Decided under prior law.)

Upon a petition to the selectmen for a highway between two fixed bounds, their laying out of a way beginning at one of the bounds but not extending to the other might be valid. Spaulding v. Groton, 68 N.H. 77, 44 A. 88, 1894 N.H. LEXIS 36 (N.H. 1894). (Decided under prior law.)

Road constructed on courses other than those described in judgment laying it out was not a legal highway. Spaulding v. Groton, 68 N.H. 77, 44 A. 88, 1894 N.H. LEXIS 36 (N.H. 1894). (Decided under prior law.)

Upon a petition to selectmen to lay out a new highway, they had no jurisdiction to lay out a highway with termini substantially different from those set out in the petition. Eames v. Northumberland, 44 N.H. 67, 1862 N.H. LEXIS 19 (N.H. 1862). (Decided under prior law.)

5. —Private roads

Laying out of roads in manner prescribed was not limited to creation of new roads, but also included making into public highways of private roads already in existence. Locke Dev. Corp. v. Barnstead, 115 N.H. 642, 349 A.2d 598, 1975 N.H. LEXIS 385 (N.H. 1975). (Decided under prior law.)

6. —Sidewalks

Sidewalks could legally be a part of the highway. Hall v. Manchester, 40 N.H. 410, 1860 N.H. LEXIS 167 (N.H. 1860). (Decided under prior law.)

7. —Presumption

Twenty years of continuous and uninterrupted use gave rise to conclusive presumption that highway had at some previous time been established pursuant to law by the proper authority. Windham v. Jubinville, 92 N.H. 102, 25 A.2d 415, 1942 N.H. LEXIS 31 (N.H. 1942). (Decided under prior law.)

Presumption that a highway had been laid out agreeably to law did not arise from mere use of it by the public for any period less than 20 years. State v. Morse, 50 N.H. 9, 1870 N.H. LEXIS 54 (N.H. 1870). (Decided under prior law.)

Compliance with necessary conditions for laying out of a road could be presumed after lapse of nearly 40 years although not shown by the record. State v. Alstead, 18 N.H. 59, 1846 N.H. LEXIS 69 (N.H. 1846). (Decided under prior law.)

8. —Estoppel

Where a road had not been used for twenty years as a public highway, town was not estopped to show that it had not been legally laid out as a highway. Eames v. Northumberland, 44 N.H. 67, 1862 N.H. LEXIS 19 (N.H. 1862). (Decided under prior law.)

Town which had acquiesced for more than twenty years in doings of selectmen in laying out a highway was estopped from saying that the road was not legally laid out. State v. Boscawen, 32 N.H. 331, 1855 N.H. LEXIS 214 (N.H. 1855). (Decided under prior law.)

9. Dedication and acceptance

In an action to quiet title to a subdivision plan's proposed road that was never constructed, this "paper street" never became a public highway by dedication and acceptance because: (1) the town never formally or impliedly accepted the paper street for public use by 1971 since the use of the land underneath the paper street for recreational purposes or for "parking" was insufficient to establish acceptance; and (2) subsequent subdivision plans did not rededicate the paper street. Hersh v. Plonski, 156 N.H. 511, 938 A.2d 98, 2007 N.H. LEXIS 219 (N.H. 2007).

Town meeting article did not lack a vote of acceptance of relocated road and did not merely constitute an exchange of deeds; when liberally construed, article expressed an intent to both discontinue a portion of road and then accept a new portion, and portion to be discontinued was sufficiently defined in article for voters to make a rational decision. Neville v. Highfields Farm, Inc., 144 N.H. 419, 744 A.2d 89, 1999 N.H. LEXIS 135 (N.H. 1999).

Dedication and acceptance by the proper authority was sufficient to establish a highway. Perrotto v. Claremont, 101 N.H. 267, 140 A.2d 576, 1958 N.H. LEXIS 15 (N.H. 1958). (Decided under prior law.)

Where claim of dedication rested upon implication, subsequent use, to constitute an acceptance and ripen it into a title, must have been adverse. Wason v. Nashua, 85 N.H. 192, 155 A. 681, 1931 N.H. LEXIS 99 (N.H. 1931). (Decided under prior law.)

Twenty years' use of a dedicated highway was conclusive evidence of an acceptance. Stevens v. Nashua, 46 N.H. 192, 1865 N.H. LEXIS 55 (N.H. 1865); State v. Atherton, 16 N.H. 203, 1844 N.H. LEXIS 43 (N.H. 1844). (Decided under prior law.)

To constitute acts of selectmen an acceptance or recognition of dedicated highway so as to bind a town, there must have been either an express vote of the town, concurrence of a majority of the selectmen, or such circumstances that actual concurrence could be inferred. State v. Atherton, 16 N.H. 203, 1844 N.H. LEXIS 43 (N.H. 1844). (Decided under prior law.)

Dedication could be accepted by substituting dedicated way for an ancient highway. State v. Atherton, 16 N.H. 203, 1844 N.H. LEXIS 43 (N.H. 1844). (Decided under prior law.)

10. Establishment under prescription—Generally

The legislature added the language "prior to January 1, 1968" to allow any roads already acquired by prescription to stand, but restricted any further establishment of public highways by prescription; the legislature did not intend to redefine public roads that had already been acquired by prescription. Mahoney v. Town of Canterbury, 150 N.H. 148, 834 A.2d 227, 2003 N.H. LEXIS 153 (N.H. 2003).

Highway could be established by prescription when it appeared that the public had used it continuously and uninterruptedly for a period of twenty years. Windham v. Jubinville, 92 N.H. 102, 25 A.2d 415, 1942 N.H. LEXIS 31 (N.H. 1942). (Decided under prior law.)

11. —Public use

In a zoning appeal and quiet title case, a trial court's determination that an old road was a public road, not acquired by plaintiff through adverse possession, was upheld because the evidence presented at trial showed that the road had been used for public travel since the early 1800s and no evidence that the local municipality ever discontinued the public use of the road was shown. Blagbrough Family Realty Trust v. A & T Forest Prods., 155 N.H. 29, 917 A.2d 1221, 2007 N.H. LEXIS 25 (N.H. 2007).

One cannot acquire rights in a public highway by adverse possession. Blagbrough Family Realty Trust v. A & T Forest Prods., 155 N.H. 29, 917 A.2d 1221, 2007 N.H. LEXIS 25 (N.H. 2007).

Where plaintiff lot owners seeking declaratory judgment that roads over which they held easements were public highways, plaintiffs were required to prove the "public," not just the lot owners and guests, acquired adverse possession. Catalano v. Windham, 133 N.H. 504, 578 A.2d 858, 1990 N.H. LEXIS 95 (N.H. 1990).

12. —Adverse use

Evidence did not support trial court's finding that public use of gravel road was adverse and of such a character as to put landowner on notice of an adverse claim. Town of Warren v. Shortt, 139 N.H. 240, 652 A.2d 140, 1994 N.H. LEXIS 136 (N.H. 1994).

Criterion designating as public highways "roads which have been used as such for public travel ... for 20 years ..." requires more than a showing of public use for 20 years; the use must additionally be shown to have been adverse. Catalano v. Windham, 133 N.H. 504, 578 A.2d 858, 1990 N.H. LEXIS 95 (N.H. 1990).

13. —Permissive use

In determining whether a road has become a public highway by prescription, once plaintiffs prove public used road openly and under claim of right for statutory period, burden shifts to the defendant to show permissive use. Catalano v. Windham, 133 N.H. 504, 578 A.2d 858, 1990 N.H. LEXIS 95 (N.H. 1990).

To establish that a public use was adverse or under a claim of right, either color or title in the public must have been shown or the public use must have been of the character to apprise the owner that it was under a claim of right and not permissive. Wason v. Nashua, 85 N.H. 192, 155 A. 681, 1931 N.H. LEXIS 99 (N.H. 1931). (Decided under prior law.)

Way by prescription could not be established by permissive use. Burnham v. McQuesten, 48 N.H. 446, 1869 N.H. LEXIS 58 (N.H. 1869). (Decided under prior law.)

14. —Toll bridge or ferry road

Land thrown open or dedicated to the public would not become a public highway, however long it might be used, if the travel upon it was limited to travel to or from a toll bridge or ferry. Harriman v. Moore & Co., 74 N.H. 277, 67 A. 225, 1907 N.H. LEXIS 42 (N.H. 1907). (Decided under prior law.)

15. —Access road to public property

Fact that access road which school district intended to construct on land taken by eminent domain, so as to have access to school, would be used by the public to reach the school did not make it a public highway. Wilton-Lyndeboro Coop. Sch. Dist. v. Gregg, 111 N.H. 60, 274 A.2d 787, 1971 N.H. LEXIS 123 (N.H. 1971). (Decided under prior law.)

16. —Sidewalks

Right to a sidewalk for foot passengers as part of a highway could be acquired by 20 years' use. Stevens v. Nashua, 46 N.H. 192, 1865 N.H. LEXIS 55 (N.H. 1865). (Decided under prior law.)

17. —Extent of right acquired

If during alleged period of prescription owner continued to make a use of space above highway, by maintaining overhanging eaves discharging water thereon, public could acquire no title thereto.

Woodsville Fire Dist. v. Stahl, 80 N.H. 502, 119 A. 123, 1922 N.H. LEXIS 60 (N.H. 1922). (Decided under prior law.)

Right acquired by prescriptive use did not extend to space above highway occupied by a bay window, since as to such space public's use was not adverse and owner's continued occupancy of it amounted to denial of public's claim. Exeter v. Meras, 80 N.H. 132, 114 A. 24, 1921 N.H. LEXIS 44 (N.H. 1921). (Decided under prior law.)

When highway was established by use alone, it was not necessarily limited to travelled track and ditches on each side, but jury could find that easement extended over whole space marked by fences which had been maintained more than 20 years and which gave about the usual width of a highway. State v. Morse, 50 N.H. 9, 1870 N.H. LEXIS 54 (N.H. 1870). (Decided under prior law.)

18. —Responsibility for maintenance and repair

Twenty years' use was conclusive evidence of a right to use a highway not only as against the landowner, but also as against the city or town to be charged with its maintenance and repair. Stevens v. Nashua, 46 N.H. 192, 1865 N.H. LEXIS 55 (N.H. 1865). (Decided under prior law.)

19. —Estoppel

After 20 years' use by the public, city could be estopped to deny that a street was a highway for the defects and insufficiency of which it was liable. Gilbert v. Manchester, 55 N.H. 298, 1875 N.H. LEXIS 76 (N.H. 1875). (Decided under prior law.)

20. —Burden of proof

When a prescriptive easement is claimed and a landowner's defense to it is that use of property was permissive, burden of proof remains on claimant to prove absence of permission by a preponderance of evidence. Town of Warren v. Shortt, 139 N.H. 240, 652 A.2d 140, 1994 N.H. LEXIS 136 (N.H. 1994).

Plaintiffs who sought declaratory judgment that roads qualified as public highway under provision of this section designating as such a road held by the public adversely for 20 years, bore burden of proving by a balance of the probabilities that the public used the roads for twenty years under a claim of right without the owner's permission. Catalano v. Windham, 133 N.H. 504, 578 A.2d 858, 1990 N.H. LEXIS 95 (N.H. 1990).

21. —Evidence

Road was properly deemed a highway established by prescription based on adverse public use for 20 continuous years during either the 1800's or the early 1900's as the public use of the road was without interruption for 20 years prior to January 1, 1968 as required by RSA 229:1 as amended. Mahoney v. Town of Canterbury, 150 N.H. 148, 834 A.2d 227, 2003 N.H. LEXIS 153 (N.H. 2003).

Evidence was insufficient to support a finding that plaintiffs' driveway had become public through prescription, since photographs and historical documents failed to support an inference that public used driveway and bridge for a continuous twenty-year period and that such use was adverse. Blagbrough v. Town of Wilton, 145 N.H. 118, 755 A.2d 1141, 2000 N.H. LEXIS 28 (N.H. 2000).

Plaintiffs made out a prima facie case that roads had become public highways by prescription where public used them under a claim of right for statutory period, there was no evidence in the record that members of the public had ever asked permission, and where no "Private Road" sign had ever been erected; owner knew or ought to have known the road was being used without regard to his consent. Catalano v. Windham, 133 N.H. 504, 578 A.2d 858, 1990 N.H. LEXIS 95 (N.H. 1990).

Testimony that road had been used by the public as a public highway for at least thirty or forty years and that it was generally used by the public during that time to look for a place to swim showed a use which, while it may have been intermittent and of slight volume, was sufficient to sustain finding that road was established by prescription. Leo Found. v. State, 117 N.H. 209, 372 A.2d 1311, 1977 N.H. LEXIS 303 (N.H. 1977), cert. denied, Leo Foundation v. New Hampshire, 434 U.S. 890, 98 S. Ct. 264, 54 L. Ed. 2d 176, 1977 U.S. LEXIS 3545 (1977). (Decided under prior law.)

Evidence that stretches of road were discontinued by town meeting vote was evidence that road was a public highway. Leo Found. v. State, 117 N.H. 209, 372 A.2d 1311, 1977 N.H. LEXIS 303 (1977), cert. denied, Leo Foundation v. New Hampshire, 434 U.S. 890, 98 S. Ct. 264, 54 L. Ed. 2d 176, 1977 U.S. LEXIS 3545 (1977). (Decided under prior law.)

Uninterrupted use of a road by those who had occasion to use it as members of the general public under a claim of right and without permission of the owner for more than twenty years, although intermittent and of slight volume, was sufficient to sustain a finding that a highway had been established by prescription. Blake v. Hickey, 93 N.H. 318, 41 A.2d 707, 1945 N.H. LEXIS 122 (N.H. 1945). (Decided under prior law.)

Evidence that a highway of record became a public highway by reason of 20 years' use was not objectionable on the ground that it was secondary proof. Harriman v. Moore & Co., 74 N.H. 277, 67 A. 225, 1907 N.H. LEXIS 42 (N.H. 1907). (Decided under prior law.)

Proof that part of an entire highway, the laying out of which was defective, had been used by the public for twenty years, was evidence of a legal highway as to the part so used, although no distinct act of acceptance by the town was shown. State v. Morse, 50 N.H. 9, 1870 N.H. LEXIS 54 (N.H. 1870). (Decided under prior law.)

22. Bridges

A bridge is public if the road it services is public, and private if the road it services is private. Blagbrough v. Town of Wilton, 145 N.H. 118, 755 A.2d 1141, 2000 N.H. LEXIS 28 (N.H. 2000).

Cited:

Cited in Marrone v. Hampton, 123 N.H. 729, 466 A.2d 907, 1983 N.H. LEXIS 363 (1983); Morin v. Somersworth, 131 N.H. 253, 551 A.2d 527, 1988 N.H. LEXIS 109 (1988); Town of Warren v. Shortt, 139 N.H. 240, 652 A.2d 140, 1994 N.H. LEXIS 136 (1994).

RESEARCH REFERENCES AND PRACTICE AIDS

Cross References.
Classification of highways, see RSA229:5.
Laying out of city, town and village district highways, see RSA 231:1 et seq.
Laying out of state highways, see RSA 230:8 et seq.

New Hampshire Bar Journal.
For article, "Creation and Termination of Highways in New Hampshire," see 31 N.H. B.J. 33 (1990).

New Hampshire Practice.
16-45 N.H.P. Municipal Law & Taxation § 45.01.
16-45 N.H.P. Municipal Law & Taxation § 45.02.
16-45 N.H.P. Municipal Law & Taxation § 45.03.
16-55 N.H.P. Municipal Law & Taxation § 55.08.

229:5. Classification.

Highways of the state shall be divided into 7 classes as follows:

I. Class I highways shall consist of all existing or proposed highways on the primary state highway system, excepting all portions of such highways within the compact sections of the cities and towns listed in RSA 229:5, V, provided that the portions of the turnpikes and the national system of interstate and defense highways within the compact sections of these cities and towns shall be class I highways.

II. Class II highways shall consist of all existing or proposed highways on the secondary state highway system, excepting all portions of such highways within the compact sections of the cities and towns listed in RSA 229:5, V.

III. Class III highways shall consist of all recreational roads leading to, and within, state reservations designated by the legislature.

III-a. Class III-a highways shall consist of new boating access highways from any existing highway to any public water in this state. All class III-a highways shall be limited access facilities as defined in RSA 230:44. Class III-a highways shall be subject to the layout, design, construction, and maintenance provisions of RSA 230:45–47 and all other provisions relative to limited access facilities, except that the executive director of the fish and game department shall have the same authority for class III-a highways that is delegated to the commissioner of the department of transportation for limited access facilities. A class III-a highway may be laid out subject to the condition that it shall not be maintained during the winter months. A class III-a highway may be laid out subject to gates and bars or restricted to the accommodation of persons on foot, or certain vehicles, or both, if federal funds are not used. The executive director of fish and game may petition the governor and council to discontinue any class III-a highway.

IV. Class IV highways shall consist of all highways within the compact sections of cities and towns listed in RSA 229:5, V. The compact section of any such city or town shall be the territory within such city or town where the frontage on any highway, in the opinion of the commissioner of transportation, is mainly occupied by dwellings or buildings in which people live or business is conducted, throughout the year and not for a season only. Whenever the commissioner reclassifies a section of a class I or class II highway as a class IV highway, the commissioner shall prepare a statement of rehabilitation work which shall be performed by the state in connection with the turnback. No highway reclassification from class I or II to class IV shall take effect until all rehabilitation needed to return the highway surface to reputable condition has been completed by the state. Rehabilitation shall be completed during the calendar year preceding the effective date of the reclassification. A copy of the commissioner's statement of work to be performed by the state shall be attached to the notification of reclassification to class IV, and receipt of said statement shall be acknowledged, in writing, by the selectmen of the town, or the mayor of the city, affected by the reclassification.

V. The commissioner of transportation may establish compact sections in the following cities and towns:

Amherst	Keene
Bedford	Laconia
Berlin	Lebanon
Claremont	Londonderry
Concord	Manchester
Derry	Merrimack
Dover	Milford
Durham	Nashua
Exeter	Pelham
Franklin	Portsmouth
Goffstown	Rochester
Hampton	Salem
Hanover	Somersworth
Hudson	

VI. Class V highways shall consist of all other traveled highways which the town has the duty to maintain regularly and shall be known as town roads. Any public highway which at one time lapsed to Class VI status due to 5-years' nonmaintenance, as set forth in RSA 229:5, VII, but which subsequently has been regularly maintained and repaired by the town on more than a seasonal basis and in suitable condition for year-round travel thereon for at least 5 successive years without being declared an emergency lane pursuant to RSA 231:59-a, shall be deemed a Class V highway.

VII. Class VI highways shall consist of all other existing public ways, and shall include all highways discontinued as open highways and made subject to gates and bars, except as provided in paragraph III-a, and all highways which have not been maintained and repaired by the town in suitable condition for travel thereon for 5 successive years or more except as restricted by RSA 231:3, II.

HISTORY:
1925, 110:1. PL 83:22. RL 99:24. 1943, 123:1. 1945, 188:1, part 1:4. 1951, 30:1. RSA 230:4. 1955, 333:2. 1957, 181:1–3. 1961, 4:2. 1973, 418:1–3. 1975, 249:1–3. 1979, 216:1. 1981, 87:1. 443:1. 1983, 131:1. 1985, 235:1–4. 402:6, I(b)(1). 1992, 265:8–10. 1995, 77:1, eff. June 8, 1995. 1999, 109:1, eff. Aug. 9, 1999. 2000, 24:1, eff. May 28, 2000.

Effective date of 1985 amendment
1985, 402:41, II, provided that 1985, 402:6, I, would take effect when the department of transportation became operational on the date set according to 1983, 372:5, II. Pursuant to 1983, 372:5, II, the joint committee on implementation of reorganization and the governor determined the effective date upon which the department became operational to be Feb. 28, 1986.

Amendments

—2000.
Paragraph III-a: Rewrote the fourth sentence.

—1999.
Paragraph VI: Added the second sentence.

—1995.
Paragraph VII: Added "except as restricted by RSA 231:3, II" following "more".

—1992.
Substituted "7" for "6" preceding "classes" in the introductory paragraph, added par. III-a, and inserted "except as provided in paragraph III-a" following "bars" in par. VII.

—1985.
Paragraph I: Chapter 235 inserted "the" preceding "cities or towns" and substituted "listed in RSA 229:5, V" for "of 7,500 inhabitants and over" thereafter and inserted "these" preceding "cities and towns" and deleted "of 7,500 inhabitants and over" thereafter.

Paragraph II: Chapter 235 substituted "the cities and towns listed in RSA 229:5, V" for "cities or towns of 7,500 inhabitants and over" following "sections of".

Paragraph IV: Chapter 235 substituted "and" for "or" preceding "towns" in the first sentence and "listed in RSA 229:5, V" for "of 7,500 inhabitants and over" thereafter.

Chapter 402 substituted "commissioner of transportation" for "highway commissioner" in the second sentence.

Paragraph V: Rewritten by ch. 235 to the extent that a detailed comparison would be impractical.

Chapter 402 substituted "commissioner of transportation" for "commissioner of public works and highways" in the introductory paragraph.

—1983.

Paragraph V: Substituted "the annual city or town population estimate reported by the office of state planning; and, in a case in which" for "those shown by the latest available federal census and where" preceding "the classification" and "in said annual population estimate" for language beginning "by said census; provided" and continuing to the end of the paragraph following "as reported".

NOTES TO DECISIONS

Analysis

1. Reclassification
2. Maintenance and repair
3. Public use

1. Reclassification

There is no statutory requirement that a highway be reclassified by means of a formal procedure that includes a town meeting. Glick v. Ossipee, 130 N.H. 643, 547 A.2d 231, 1988 N.H. LEXIS 79 (N.H. 1988).

2. Maintenance and repair

In a property owner's action against a harvester who trespassed onto the owner's land and felled 5000 trees, the owner was properly awarded damages to repair a road that the harvester had damaged because the road had been rendered virtually impassable and because it was a Class VI road, the town had no obligation to maintain it. Berliner v. Clukay, 150 N.H. 80, 834 A.2d 297, 2003 N.H. LEXIS 140 (N.H. 2003).

Road is not "maintained" or "repaired" for purposes of this section's classification scheme if the only work done consists of snowplowing; other work to protect against yearly erosion by the elements is required. Catalano v. Windham, 133 N.H. 504, 578 A.2d 858, 1990 N.H. LEXIS 95 (N.H. 1990).

Finding of trial court that defendant town maintained road during applicable time period, and therefore road met standard required for Class V status, would not be overturned where record supported findings of maintenance, even though there was conflicting testimony. Catalano v. Windham, 133 N.H. 504, 578 A.2d 858, 1990 N.H. LEXIS 95 (N.H. 1990).

Road which had been traveled continuously and was not subject to gates and bars, but which had not been maintained for more than five years, was determined to be a class VI highway. Glick v. Ossipee, 130 N.H. 643, 547 A.2d 231, 1988 N.H. LEXIS 79 (N.H. 1988).

Trial court erroneously concluded that traveled road was a class V highway that a town had a duty to maintain, where town did not maintain it for travel for more than five successive years. Glick v. Ossipee, 130 N.H. 643, 547 A.2d 231, 1988 N.H. LEXIS 79 (N.H. 1988).

3. Public use

On summary judgment in a 42 U.S.C.S. § 1983 suit against a town and its selectmen, a federal district court dismissed a landowner's constitutional claims because he failed to show that the town's denial of a building permit and delay of utility access and its permitting the public use of snowmobiles on the landowner's unpaved access road, which was a Class VI public road under RSA 229:5, VI, were motivated by personal animosity or the result of a conspiracy against the landowner; the selectmen were also quali-

fiedly immune from liability because there was no clearly established constitutional right to be free from official corruption. Bourne v. Town of Madison, 2007 DNH 84, 494 F. Supp. 2d 80, 2007 U.S. Dist. LEXIS 47625 (D.N.H. 2007), aff'd, 2011 U.S. App. LEXIS 12404 (1st Cir. N.H. May 31, 2011).

Cited:

Cited in Orcutt v. Richmond, 128 N.H. 552, 517 A.2d 1160, 1986 N.H. LEXIS 346 (1986); Vachon v. New Durham Zoning Bd. of Adjustment, 131 N.H. 623, 557 A.2d 649, 1989 N.H. LEXIS 29 (1989); Turco v. Barnstead, 136 N.H. 256, 615 A.2d 1237, 1992 N.H. LEXIS 164 (1992); Stevens v. Town of Goshen, 141 N.H. 219, 683 A.2d 814, 1996 N.H. LEXIS 74 (1996); Gill v. Gerrato, 154 N.H. 36, 904 A.2d 576, 2006 N.H. LEXIS 117 (2006).

RESEARCH REFERENCES AND PRACTICE AIDS

Cross References.

Classification of highways between military reservations or defense industries and transportation facilities, see RSA 228:51.

Definition of highways, see RSA 229:1.

Scenic roads, see RSA 231:157 et seq.

New Hampshire Practice.

16-44 N.H.P. Municipal Law & Taxation § 44.04.

16-44 N.H.P. Municipal Law & Taxation § 44.10.

16-55 N.H.P. Municipal Law & Taxation § 55.04.

16-55 N.H.P. Municipal Law & Taxation § 55.09.

229:6. Roads Laid Out by Courts of Common Pleas or County Commissioners.

All roads laid out by the courts of common pleas or the county commissioners, which have not been maintained by them for at least 20 years, are town-owned rights-of-way and are legally subject to the actions of the town's legislative body.

HISTORY:

1997, 78:1, eff. Aug. 2, 1997.

RESEARCH REFERENCES AND PRACTICE AIDS

New Hampshire Practice.

16-44 N.H.P. Municipal Law & Taxation § 44.04.

CHAPTER 230
STATE HIGHWAYS

Duty to Construct and Maintain Highways

Section
230:6. Construction and Reconstruction; Limitation.

Effective date of 1985 amendment

1985, 402:41, II, eff. July 1, 1985, provided that the provisions of 1985, 402 which affected this chapter would take effect when the department of transportation became operational on the date set according to 1983, 372:5, II. pursuant to 1983, 372:5, II, the joint committee on implementation of reorganization and the governor determined the effective date upon which the department became operational to be Feb. 28, 1986.

Reimbursement of public utilities for cost of replacement or relocation of facilities.

1985, 305:2, eff. Aug. 13, 1985, provided:

"Notwithstanding any provision of law to the contrary, whenever any highway or public way construction or maintenance project undertaken by the department of public works and highways [department of transportation] requires the replacement or relocation of facilities of a public utility company and a portion of the cost of said project is to be reimbursed from federal funds, such utility shall be reimbursed for the cost of replacing or relocating its facilities in direct proportion to such federal funding of the project."

RESEARCH REFERENCES AND PRACTICE AIDS

Cross References.
  Classification of highways, see RSA229:5.
  Lines of telegraph and other companies in highways, see RSA 231:161 et seq.
  Removal of wires and poles, see RSA 231:177.
  State supervision, planning, maintaining and removal of trees, see RSA 231:155.
  Turnpike system, see RSA 237.

Duty to Construct and Maintain Highways

RESEARCH REFERENCES AND PRACTICE AIDS

Cross References.
  Departmental liability for failure to maintain highways or highway bridges, see RSA 230:78 et seq.

230:6.   Construction and Reconstruction; Limitation.

Notwithstanding any other provision of law to the contrary, the state shall not perform any new construction or major reconstruction of any class I, II or III highway, except highways laid out under the provisions of RSA 230:44–54 unless the city or town in which the highway is located has adopted a zoning ordinance pursuant to RSA 675:2 or 3 or a master plan pursuant to RSA 675:6. This limitation shall not apply to new construction or major reconstruction of bridges on class I, II or III highways.

HISTORY:
  RSA 231:10. 1979, 216:2. 1981, 87:1. 363:2. 1985, 103:3, eff. Jan. 1, 1986.

Amendments

—1985.
  Substituted " RSA 675:2 or 3" for " RSA 31:63 or 63-a" preceding "or a master plan pursuant to" in the first sentence and " RSA 675:6" for " RSA 36:15" thereafter and made other minor stylistic changes throughout that sentence.

CHAPTER 230-A

CORRIDOR PROTECTION

RESEARCH REFERENCES AND PRACTICE AIDS

Cross References.
  Classification of highways, see RSA229:5.
  Laying out of city, town and village district highways, see RSA 231.
  Laying out of state highways, see RSA 230:8 et seq.

230-A:1. Definitions.

In this chapter:
  I. "Corridor protection restriction" means a deeded conservation restriction, as defined by RSA 477:45, I, which conveys to a unit of government having power to lay out highways the right to wholly or partially prohibit development on a described tract of land within a highway planning corridor for a limited time period stated in the restriction, not exceeding 10 years.
  II. "Development" means the subdivision of land or erection or construction of any structures or improvements on such land, or expansions or additions to such land, or any other action which will appreciably increase the future cost of acquiring such land, if such acquisition is required for highway purposes.
  III. "Development permit" includes subdivision or site plan approval, building or zoning permit, or any other permit required by a unit of government as a prerequisite to development.
  IV. "Layout authority" means the governor and council or a commission appointed by the governor in the case of class I and II highways, or the mayor and aldermen of a city, selectmen of a town, or village district commissioners of a village district in the case of class IV or V highways.
  V. "Highway planning corridor" means an area of land which has been designated as such under this chapter.
  VI. "Return" means a written report of the highway planning corridor designation proceedings, including the findings of occasion, and a detailed map showing the boundaries of such corridor. Such return need not include a full metes and bounds description of the corridor boundary.

HISTORY:
  1991, 309:2, eff. Jan. 1, 1992.

230-A:2. Occasion for Layout.

A layout authority may determine upon hearing whether there is occasion for the designation of one or more highway planning corridors. For class I or II highways, the location shall be proposed by the commissioner of the department of transportation.

In making such determination the layout authority shall:

I.   Identify public transportation needs for the present and foreseeable future.

II.   Determine whether the public interest requires development restriction along proposed planning corridors.

III.   Allow flexibility in planning the design of the highway.

IV.   Consider methods to prevent disruption and relocation of residential neighborhoods, residences, and businesses and interference with utility facilities.

V.   Determine the acquisition costs of subsequently developed property if a highway planning corridor is not established.

VI.   Establish the termini and width of the proposed highway planning corridor.

HISTORY:
    1991, 309:2, eff. Jan. 1, 1992.

230-A:3.   Notice of Hearing.

Notice of the hearing, together with a description of the proposed corridor, shall be given to the same parties with respect to such corridor, and in the same manner, as in the case of a highway layout hearing, pursuant to RSA 230:17–18 or 231:9–10, as the case may be, including every owner of land or other property within the proposed planning corridor.

HISTORY:
    1991, 309:2, eff. Jan. 1, 1992.

230-A:4.   Hearing.

The layout authority, at the time and place appointed for hearing, shall make a personal examination of the proposed corridors, shall hear all parties interested who may attend, and may adjourn as it sees cause.

HISTORY:
    1991, 309:2, eff. Jan. 1, 1992.

230-A:5.   Appeal.

Any owner of land or other property aggrieved by a finding of the layout authority on the matter of occasion for the layout of a highway planning corridor or alteration thereof, may appeal to the superior court, for the county in which such land or other property is situated, by petition within 60 days after the filing of the return with the secretary of state as provided in RSA 230-A:6. The burden of proof shall be upon the party seeking to set aside any finding of the layout authority to show that such decision is unlawful or unreasonable. All findings of the layout authority upon all questions of fact properly before the court shall be prima facie lawful and reasonable. The decision appealed from shall not be set aside or

vacated, except for errors of law, unless the court is persuaded by the balance of probabilities, on the evidence before it, that said finding is unreasonable or unlawful.

HISTORY:
    1991, 309:2, eff. Jan. 1, 1992.

230-A:6.   Return.

The layout authority shall make a return of the highway planning corridor, including a detailed map identifying the boundaries of such corridor, and file the return with the secretary of state, with every unit of government having the authority to issue development permits for the property located within such corridor and with the registry of deeds for each county in which such corridor is located.

HISTORY:
    1991, 309:2, eff. Jan. 1, 1992.

230-A:7.   Effect of Corridor.

After the highway planning corridor return has been filed, no person shall subdivide any land, begin any development, or alter or expand any structure or use of land within such corridor, without first obtaining a corridor permit from the layout authority or its designated agent. The layout authority shall adopt by rules pursuant to RSA 541-A the form for corridor permits, and what constitutes submission of a completed application. No existing structure or established use of property within the corridor shall be affected.

HISTORY:
    1991, 309:2, eff. Jan. 1, 1992.

230-A:8.   Relationship to Other Land Use Permits.

The corridor permit requirement shall be in addition to other federal, state or local permits which may be required for such development, and no development shall be exempt from a corridor permit by reason of any other permit, any grandfather clause, or any other exemption. Authorities issuing other development permits should inform applicants of the corridor permit requirement, but the corridor designation shall not interfere with or delay other development permit procedure, unless agreed to by the applicant. No zoning or other land use ordinance or regulation shall be deemed or required to be altered or modified by the creation of the corridor, but any permits issued under any such ordinance or regulation shall be deemed conditional upon the corridor permit.

HISTORY:
    1991, 309:2, eff. Jan. 1, 1992.

230-A:9.   Action on Application.

Within 60 days after receipt of a completed corridor permit application, the layout authority or its designated agent shall:

I.   Determine that the impact of the proposed development on highway design planning and impact on the cost of possible acquisition is not substantial, and issue the permit;

II.   Notify the applicant of its intent to take an interest in all or part of the land or other property, in which case, the date of notification shall constitute the date of valuation for taking purposes; or

III.   Reach agreement with the applicant on some alternative action.

HISTORY:
1991, 309:2, eff. Jan. 1, 1992.

230-A:10.   Payment or Tender of Damages.

Within 180 days after notice of intent to take an interest in property has been delivered under this chapter, the layout authority or its designated agent shall pay or tender damages for a specified interest in the applicant's property. The procedure for the payment or tender, and any appeals of assessments, shall be as set forth in RSA 498-A. If the layout authority fails to make a payment or tender within 180 days, the corridor permit shall be deemed to be granted.

HISTORY:
1991, 309:2, eff. Jan. 1, 1992.

230-A:11.   Corridor Protection Restriction.

All property interests taken under this chapter shall be in the form of a corridor protection restriction, unless the layout authority or its designated agent makes a written finding that the public interest requires taking a greater property interest in the property. Reasons for such a finding may include, but are not limited to, a probable likelihood that the layout will eventually require a taking of greater property interest, or a substantial similarity between the appraised value of the greater property interest and the corridor protection restriction. The layout authority may amend the terms and duration of any corridor protection restriction to meet the needs of its planning process, but the duration of any term thereof shall not exceed 10 years, unless renewed.

HISTORY:
1991, 309:2, eff. Jan. 1, 1992.

230-A:12.   Other Acquisitions.

The layout authority may acquire corridor protection restrictions or other property interests within the highway planning corridor, absent the submission of a corridor permit application, provided, that, in its discretion, the layout authority determines that such acquisitions are consistent with the purposes of this chapter.

HISTORY:
1991, 309:2, eff. Jan. 1, 1992.

230-A:13.   Corridor Amendments.

The layout authority may add to the land area of any highway planning corridor, provided, however, that written notice shall be given to each owner of land or other property affected by the amendment, and no determination of whether there is occasion for the designation shall be made unless the amendment is based on new or revised findings of transportation needs.

HISTORY:
1991, 309:2, eff. Jan. 1, 1992.

230-A:14.   Termination of Corridor.

The highway planning corridor shall terminate:

I.   Upon the filing of a return of highway layout and the acquisition of the property necessary for the highway for which the planning corridor was created; or

II.   Upon a declaration by the layout authority that the corridor, or any portion thereof, is discontinued. The discontinuance of a highway planning corridor shall not be subject to appeal, and shall not entitle any person to damages.

HISTORY:
1991, 309:2, eff. Jan. 1, 1992.

230-A:15.   Notice of Termination of Corridor.

Notice of the corridor termination shall be given by first class mail to all owners of land or other property or their successors in interest, and governmental units to whom notice was sent under RSA 230-A:3.

HISTORY:
1991, 309:2, eff. Jan. 1, 1992.

230-A:16.   Remedies.

Penalties and remedies for violations of this chapter shall be the same as for violations of title LXIV, as stated in RSA 676:15 and 676:17; and, if any development occurs on any land within a designated highway planning corridor, without a corridor permit, the layout authority shall be entitled to exclude the value of such development from any compensation otherwise due upon the subsequent layout of a highway.

HISTORY:
1991, 309:2, eff. Jan. 1, 1992.

RESEARCH REFERENCES AND PRACTICE AIDS

References in text.
Title LXIV, referred to in this section, is classified to Title 64 of LEXIS New Hampshire Revised Statutes Annotated, which is comprised of chapters 672–678.

230-A:17. Municipalities.

The powers granted by this chapter may be exercised by a municipality either independently of, or concurrently with, the creation of an official map pursuant to RSA 674:9–15. The designation of a highway planning corridor by a municipal layout authority shall require the approval of the planning board or local legislative body, under RSA 674:40, III, but such corridor shall not be deemed as a "street" for purposes of title LXIV.

HISTORY:
1991, 309:2, eff. Jan. 1, 1992.

RESEARCH REFERENCES AND PRACTICE AIDS

References in text.
Title LXIV, referred to in this section, is classified to Title 64 of LEXIS New Hampshire Revised Statutes Annotated, which is comprised of chapters 672–678.

230-A:18. Intergovernmental Agreements.

The powers described in this chapter may be exercised jointly by the state and any municipality, or by 2 or more municipalities, utilizing RSA 53-A or any other lawful means of agreement.

HISTORY:
1991, 309:2, eff. Jan. 1, 1992.

230-A:19. Other Laws.

Nothing in this chapter shall preclude the necessity to comply with the provisions of any other applicable federal, state or local law or regulation.

HISTORY:
1991, 309:2, eff. Jan. 1, 1992.

CHAPTER 231

CITIES, TOWNS AND VILLAGE DISTRICT HIGHWAYS

Laying Out Highways

Effective date of 1985 amendment
1985, 402:41, II, eff. July 1, 1985, provided that the provisions of 1985, 402 which affected this chapter would take effect when the department of transportation became operational on the date set according to 1983, 372:5, II. Pursuant to 1983, 372:5, II, the joint committee on implementation of reorganization and the governor determined the effective date upon which the department became operational to be Feb. 28, 1986.

Reimbursement of public utilities for cost of replacement or relocation of facilities.
1985, 305:2, eff. Aug. 13, 1985, provided:
"Notwithstanding any provision of law to the contrary, whenever any highway or public way construction or maintenance project undertaken by the department of public works and highways [department of transportation] requires the replacement or relocation of facilities of a public utility company and a portion of the cost of said project is to be reimbursed from federal funds, such utility shall be reimbursed for the cost of replacing or relocating its facilities in direct proportion to such federal funding of the project."

NOTES TO DECISIONS

Analysis

1. Construction with other law
2. Historical
3. Failure to conform
4. Curbing
5. Imposition of duty

1. Construction with other law
By its express terms, RSA 507-B:2 does not alone govern a town's liability with respect to its sidewalks, streets, and highways; rather, RSA 507-B:2 has to be read in conjunction with the limits on governmental liability set forth in RSA ch. 231. Accordingly, RSA 507-B:2 did not in and of itself impose a duty upon a town to warn motorists that due to an ice storm, lights were out at the intersection of two class I and II highways. Ford v. N.H. Dep't of Transp., 163 N.H. 284, 37 A.3d 436, 2012 N.H. LEXIS 23 (N.H. 2012).

2. Historical
Procedure prescribed for laying out of highways by Highway Law of 1945 differed in no material respect from procedure long followed here. Waisman v. Board of Mayor & Aldermen of Manchester, 96 N.H. 50, 69 A.2d 871, 1949 N.H. LEXIS 14 (N.H. 1949). (Decided under prior law.)

3. Failure to conform
Town which had not conformed to statutory requirements in laying out a highway was guilty of trespass and answerable in damages to landowner therefor in a suit at law, and if trespass was established and town threatened to continue trespass, bill in equity could be brought in aid of the action at law to enjoin further trespasses. Perley v. Effingham, 94 N.H. 120, 48 A.2d 484, 1946 N.H. LEXIS 160 (N.H. 1946). (Decided under prior law.)

4. Curbing
Action of city in leveling, surfacing and installing curbing on highway constructed by real estate developer and dedicated to public use was not laying out of a highway within meaning of this chapter. Perrotto v. Claremont, 101 N.H. 267, 140 A.2d 576, 1958 N.H. LEXIS 15 (N.H. 1958). (Decided under prior law.)

5. Imposition of duty
Nothing in RSA ch. 231 imposed a duty upon a town to warn motorists that traffic lights at an intersection of class I and class II highways were inoperable because of an ice storm. Ford v. N.H. Dep't of Transp., 163 N.H. 284, 37 A.3d 436, 2012 N.H. LEXIS 23 (N.H. 2012).

Cited:
Cited in Goslin v. Farmington, 132 N.H. 48, 561 A.2d 507, 1989 N.H. LEXIS 68 (1989).

RESEARCH REFERENCES AND PRACTICE AIDS

Cross References.

Bridge inspections, see RSA 234:21 et seq.

Bridge regulations, see RSA 234:32 et seq.

Classification of highways, see RSA229:5.

Commissioner may regulate use of class I, II, and III highways in certain towns and cities under specified conditions, see RSA 236:1.

Duty to maintain certain bridges on class II highways, see RSA 234:1.

Federal and state highway aid, see RSA 235.

Highways defined, see RSA 229:1.

Lights along highways, see RSA 236:55.

Local highway safety programs, see RSA 238:6.

Maintenance of class V road to recreational area, see RSA 233:10.

Roads in 2 or more towns, see RSA 232:18.

School bus shelters, see RSA 236:87.

State planning aid and inspection service, see RSA 228:46.

State 10-year transportation improvement program, see RSA 240.

Town or city conveyance to state for highway construction, see RSA 230:5.

New Hampshire Bar Journal.

For article, "Creation and Termination of Highways in New Hampshire," see 31 N.H. B.J. 33 (1990).

New Hampshire Practice.

13-15 N.H.P. Local Government Law § 533.

16-48 N.H.P. Municipal Law & Taxation § 48.01.

Laying Out Highways

231:22. Previously Discontinued Highway.

Notwithstanding any other provisions of this chapter to the contrary, any owner who has no access to his land by public highway may petition the selectmen to layout, subject to gates and bars, a highway located where any previously discontinued highway was located. Upon receipt of such a petition, the selectmen shall immediately post notice thereof in 2 public places in the town in which the land is situated and shall mail like notices to the owners of the land over which such highway may pass, postage prepaid, at their last known mail addresses. Unless written objection to such layout is filed with the selectmen within 60 days after the posting and mailing of such notice, the highway shall be laid out, subject to gates and bars, in the location in which it previously existed if the selectmen find that the petitioner in fact has no other access to his land by public highway. The selectmen shall assess the damages sustained by each owner of land or other property taken for such highway, which damages shall be paid by the petitioner. They shall take and cause to be recorded by the town clerk a return as required by RSA 231:16. The petitioner and all those succeeding him in title shall be required to maintain the gates and bars and to maintain the highway so laid out at their own expense. In the event written objection to such layout is filed with the selectmen prior to the expiration of said 60-day period, the petition shall be deemed to be a petition filed for the layout of a new class IV, V or VI highway in accordance with RSA 231:8, and all the

provisions of this chapter shall be applicable thereto.

HISTORY:

RSA 234:18-a. 1963, 274:1. 1981, 87:1, eff. April 20, 1981.

NOTES TO DECISIONS

Nature of remedy

Petitioning selectmen to layout, subject to gates and bars, a highway located "where any previously discontinued highway was located", was an administrative remedy requiring appeal to another body and was not a judicial remedy. Williams v. Babcock, 116 N.H. 819, 368 A.2d 1166, 1976 N.H. LEXIS 477 (N.H. 1976). (Decided under prior law.)

Plaintiff's remedy to seek right-of-way in a purportedly discontinued highway running through defendant's property and past her property was not an adequate and complete remedy under this section and plaintiff's petition for declaratory judgment and injunctive relief should not have been dismissed. Williams v. Babcock, 116 N.H. 819, 368 A.2d 1166, 1976 N.H. LEXIS 477 (N.H. 1976). (Decided under prior law.)

Cited:

Cited in Caouette v. New Ipswich, 125 N.H. 547, 484 A.2d 1106, 1984 N.H. LEXIS 396 (1984); Green Crow Corp. v. Town of New Ipswich, 157 N.H. 344, 950 A.2d 163, 2008 N.H. LEXIS 68 (2008).

RESEARCH REFERENCES AND PRACTICE AIDS

Cross References.

Liability for expenses for proceedings to reopen highways subject to gates and bars, see RSA 231:10-a.

231:22-a. Reclassifying a Class VI Highway.

I. A class VI highway or portion thereof may be reclassified by vote of the town as a class V highway, or as a class IV highway if located within the compact sections of cities and towns as set forth in RSA 229:5, IV and V.

II. The warrant article for such a reclassification may be inserted either by the selectmen pursuant to RSA 39:2, or by petition pursuant to RSA 39:3. The reclassification shall become effective upon a majority vote of the registered voters present and voting at any annual or special meeting, or at such later time as may be specified by vote of the meeting.

III. Any class VI highway may be made subject to reclassification under this section, regardless of whether such class VI status resulted from a layout pursuant to RSA 231:21, a discontinuance subject to gates and bars pursuant to RSA 231:45, or by the failure of the town to maintain and repair such highway in suitable condition for travel thereon for 5 successive years or more as set forth in RSA 229:5, VII.

IV. A town meeting vote to reclassify a class VI highway under this section may provide that the highway be conditionally reclassified upon compliance with betterment assessments, as provided in RSA 231:28–33, even if such condition was not stated as part of the warrant article. The public hearing required by RSA 231:28 shall be held within 90 days of such a vote, or within such longer period as the vote may specify. The owners of property abutting or served by the highway shall have the same rights and remedies as provided in RSA 231:28–33, including the right to submit, within 10 days following the public hearing, a petition not to conditionally reclassify the highway. The costs assessed against the owners by the selectmen shall not reflect construction standards any higher or more stringent than those reflected in the best town highway giving access to the highway or portion thereof being reclassified. However, this paragraph shall not be deemed to limit the authority of the planning board to impose more stringent construction standards as a condition of approving new development.

V. This section shall not be deemed to limit the authority of the selectmen to layout an existing class VI highway as a class IV or V highway upon petition pursuant to RSA 231:8. This section shall not affect the classification of any highway which has been reclassified by other means prior to June 18, 1990.

HISTORY:

1990, 155:1, eff. June 18, 1990.

Revision note.

Substituted "June 18, 1990" for "the effective date of this section" at the end of par. V for purposes of clarity.

RESEARCH REFERENCES AND PRACTICE AIDS

Cross References.

Reclassification of class V or VI highways as class A or B trails, see RSA 231-A:2, 3.

231:23.   Conditional Layout.

Whenever a highway will be of special advantage to any individual the selectmen may require him to bear such portion of land damages and expenses of constructing and maintaining it, and the gates and bars across it, if any, or any of the same, as they may deem just; and the highway may be laid out subject to such condition.

HISTORY:

1850, 957:1. 1871, 20:1. GL 67:16. 78:4. PS 67:16. PL 74:16. RL 90:17. 1945, 188:1, part 5:19. RSA 234:19. 1981, 87:1, eff. April 20, 1981.

NOTES TO DECISIONS

Analysis

1. Amendment of return
2. Illegal condition
3. Damages

1. Amendment of return

Amendment of return of layout which contained such condition, on the ground that it was not intended at time of laying out highway but was found in form used in making return, was not permissible. Brown's Petition, 51 N.H. 367, 1871 N.H. LEXIS 39 (N.H. 1871). (Decided under prior law.)

2. Illegal condition

Where permissible condition was illegally imposed, any person appealing from layout could take advantage of the illegality, not-

withstanding individual for whose benefit highway was laid out was willing to assent to the imposition. Underwood v. Bailey, 56 N.H. 187, 1855 N.H. LEXIS 237 (N.H. 1875). (Decided under prior law.)

3. Damages

Commissioners' finding of damages was required to be accepted unless it was such as no reasonable person could make. Tracy v. Surry, 101 N.H. 438, 146 A.2d 268, 1958 N.H. LEXIS 58 (N.H. 1958). (Decided under prior law.)

231:28.   Conditional Layout for Existing Private Rights-of-Way or Class VI Highways.

Whenever, pursuant to the provisions of this chapter, the selectmen receive a petition to lay out roads over existing private rights-of-way or to lay out a class V highway over an existing class VI highway and such private right-of-way or class VI highway does not conform to construction standards and requirements currently in effect in the town, the selectmen may conditionally lay out roads upon compliance with betterment assessments as provided in this section and in RSA 231:29–33. Prior to commencement of conditional layout, however, a public hearing shall be held, written notice of which shall be given by the appropriate governing board to all owners of property abutting or served by the private right-of-way or class VI highway, at least 14 days before the hearing, at which hearing details of the proposed construction, reconstruction or repairs, and the estimated costs thereof shall be presented by the selectmen. Conditional layout proceedings may commence 10 days following the public hearing unless within that period a petition not to conditionally lay out said thoroughfare signed by a majority of the owners of property abutting or served by the existing private right-of-way or class VI highway is received by the selectmen. If a highway is so laid out, the selectmen may construct, reconstruct, repair or cause to be constructed, reconstructed or repaired such highways, streets, roads, or traveled ways to conform in every way with the highway or street construction standards and regulations previously established by the town. The betterment assessments shall be assessed under the provisions of RSA 231:29.

HISTORY:

RSA 234:23-a. 1979, 166:1. 1981, 87:1. 1989, 134:1, eff. July 16, 1989.

Amendments

—1989.

Added "or class VI highways" following "rights-of-way" in the section catchline, inserted "or to lay out a class V highway over an existing class VI highway" preceding "and such private" and substituted "right-of-way or class VI highway does" for "rights-of-way do" thereafter in the first sentence, inserted "or class VI highway" following "right-of-way" in the second and third sentences and made other minor stylistic changes.

NOTES TO DECISIONS

Analysis

1. Public benefit

2. Requirement that occasion for layout exist

1. Public benefit

Superior court erred in ruling that occasion existed for town to lay out roadway system in housing development, where it was clear that burden to town of laying out roads far outweighed any benefit public could receive. Rockhouse Mountain Property Owners Ass'n v. Conway, 133 N.H. 130, 574 A.2d 380, 1990 N.H. LEXIS 41 (N.H. 1990).

2. Requirement that occasion for layout exist

RSA 231:28 incorporates the requirement of RSA 231:8 that occasion exist for the layout of a road. Accordingly, petitioner requesting permission from a board of selectmen to upgrade a class VI road to a class V road must show that occasion exists for the layout of that road. Green Crow Corp. v. Town of New Ipswich, 157 N.H. 344, 950 A.2d 163, 2008 N.H. LEXIS 68 (N.H. 2008).

Cited:

Cited in Rockhouse Mountain Property Owners Ass'n v. Conway, 127 N.H. 593, 503 A.2d 1385, 1986 N.H. LEXIS 207 (1986).

Liability of Municipalities

Amendments

—1991.

1991, 385:2, eff. Jan. 1, 1992, added the subdivision heading preceding RSA 231:90 and 1991, 385: 10, III, eff. Jan. 1, 1992, deleted the subdivision heading preceding RSA 231:92.

Legislative findings and purpose.

1991, 385:1, eff. Jan. 1, 1992, provided:

"The New Hampshire Supreme Court, in the case of *City of Dover v. Imperial Casualty Indemnity Company* (April 30, 1990), declared unconstitutional existing RSA 507-B:2, I, insofar as it provides immunity to municipalities in the ownership, occupation, maintenance or operation of public sidewalks, streets and highways. The purpose of this act [which amended RSA 231:90, 91, 92, 93, 412: 3 and 507-B:2, enacted RSA 231:92-a, and repealed RSA 231:82– 89, 96–104, and 507-B:2-a], in light of that decision, is to provide municipalities with the greatest possible protection from highway and sidewalk liability, consistent with the constitution. The general court hereby recognizes that municipal highways and sidewalks, unlike other property interests, are open to constant unsupervised public use, subject to interruption only in limited circumstances; that their condition for public use is subject to the ever-changing, unpredictable effects of sun, rain, wind, ice, snow and frost; that the number, length, and degree of use of highways and sidewalks in a community is not necessarily related to that community's population or financial resources; and that the existing construction standard or state of repair of any highway or sidewalk is a product of its unique history of capital investments, made at different times, in response to differing and evolving needs of the traveling public. It is, therefore, unreasonable to expect that all highways and sidewalks will be routinely patrolled or subject to regular preventive maintenance, or that all such highways and sidewalks should be constructed and maintained to any uniform standards. The general court finds, therefore, that municipalities, in the exercise of their statutory duty to maintain certain highway and sidewalks, should not be held as guarantors of the safety of the traveling public, nor guarantors of any particular condition or standard of construction or maintenance, nor should they be held liable under a standard of ordinary negligence."

RESEARCH REFERENCES AND PRACTICE AIDS

Cross References.

Liability for damages caused by grade change, see RSA 231:75–78.

Liability for damages where highways or bridges closed by commissioner of transportation, see RSA 228:37.

Liability of person causing defect or insufficiency of highway for damages paid by town to injured person, see RSA 236:39.

New Hampshire Bar Journal.

For article, "Masked Immunity?—Analysis of Functional and Constitutional Implications of Municipal Liability Under RSA 231:90– 92," see 33 N.H. B.J. 466 (1992).

231:90. Duty of Town After Notice of Insufficiency.

I. Whenever any class IV or class V highway or bridge or sidewalk thereon in any municipality shall be insufficient, any person may give written notice of such insufficiency to one of the selectmen or highway agents of the town, or the mayor or street commissioners of the city, and a copy of said notice to the town or city clerk. The notice shall be signed and shall set forth in general terms the location of such highway, bridge, or sidewalk and the nature of such insufficiency.

II. For purposes of this subdivision, a highway or sidewalk shall be considered "insufficient" only if:

(a) It is not passable in any safe manner by those persons or vehicles permitted on such sidewalk or highway by state law or by any more stringent local ordinance or regulation; or

(b) There exists a safety hazard which is not reasonably discoverable or reasonably avoidable by a person who is traveling upon such highway at posted speeds or upon such sidewalk, in obedience to all posted regulations, and in a manner which is reasonable and prudent as determined by the condition and state of repair of the highway or sidewalk, including any warning signs, and prevailing visibility and weather conditions.

III. A highway or sidewalk shall not, in the absence of impassability or hidden hazard as set forth in paragraph II, be considered "insufficient" merely by reason of the municipality's failure to construct, maintain or repair it to the same standard as some other highway or sidewalk, or to a level of service commensurate with its current level of public use.

HISTORY:

1893, 59:2. PL 82:8. RL 98:8. 1945, 188:1, part 18:9. RSA 247:9. 1981, 87:1. 1991, 385:3, eff. Jan. 1, 1992.

Amendments

—1991.

Rewritten to the extent that a detailed comparison would be impracticable.

NOTES TO DECISIONS

Analysis

1. Constitutionality
2. Construction
3. Requirement of notice
4. Effect of notice
5. Traveling
6. Jury instructions

1. Constitutionality

Proposed amendment of this section precluding municipal liability for injury or damage arising out of construction, maintenance or repair of public highways and sidewalks unless such injury or damage was caused by an "insufficiency" was not constitutionally inadequate merely because statute provided that a finding of insufficiency could not be made solely on basis that a highway or sidewalk was not maintained at same level of repair as other highways or sidewalks. Opinion of Justices, 134 N.H. 266, 592 A.2d 180, 1991 N.H. LEXIS 53 (N.H. 1991).

2. Construction

In RSA 231:91, the reference to "such insufficiency" and, in RSA 231:92, to "an insufficiency" are references to the insufficiencies described in RSA 231:90, which apply only to insufficiencies in class IV and V highways. Similarly, the reference in RSA 231:91 to "such highway" is a reference to the highways which are "insufficient, as defined by RSA 231:90, II." Ford v. N.H. Dep't of Transp., 163 N.H. 284, 37 A.3d 436, 2012 N.H. LEXIS 23 (N.H. 2012).

3. Requirement of notice

Where it was clear that the grassy area where a school visitor tripped and fell was actually a part of the curb, the issue was one of alleged failure to maintain a sidewalk, and the visitor could not prevail in a personal injury action because there was no showing of gross negligence, intentional actions, or failure to respond after receiving notice of a dangerous condition; therefore, summary judgment was properly entered for the school district. Richard v. Pembroke Sch. Dist., 151 N.H. 455, 859 A.2d 1157, 2004 N.H. LEXIS 176 (N.H. 2004).

Notice of want of repair was necessary to town's liability. Wilder v. Concord, 72 N.H. 259, 56 A. 193, 1903 N.H. LEXIS 61 (N.H. 1903). (Decided under prior law.)

4. Effect of notice

Notice to town that highway was out of repair or unsafe rendered town liable for accidents which happened subsequent to such notice and prior to repairs by town. Beer v. North Conway Lighting Precinct, 108 N.H. 465, 238 A.2d 8, 1968 N.H. LEXIS 189 (N.H. 1968). (Decided under prior law.)

5. Traveling

Words "traveling upon a highway or bridge" were added to the statute in 1867 apparently for purpose of showing that it was the object of the statute to give a remedy to persons harmlessly and properly using highway or bridge which town was bound to maintain and keep in suitable repair. Wilder v. Concord, 72 N.H. 259, 56 A. 193, 1903 N.H. LEXIS 61 (N.H. 1903). (Decided under prior law.)

Person was traveling upon a highway when he was making a reasonable use of the highway as a way, and while this included motion from one place to another more or less distant, continuous movement was not necessary. Varney v. Manchester, 58 N.H. 430, 1878 N.H. LEXIS 125 (N.H. 1878). (Decided under prior law.)

One could not be said to have been traveling on highway so as to be entitled to recover for loss of a horse, which fell over an unrailed embankment while running away, where he had left horse hitched in the highway and gone elsewhere. Cummings v. Center Harbor, 57 N.H. 17, 1876 N.H. LEXIS 45 (N.H. 1876). (Decided under prior law.)

Whether a person was a traveler on the highway depended upon the use which he was making of it. Hardy v. Keene, 52 N.H. 370, 1872 N.H. LEXIS 54 (N.H. 1872). (Decided under prior law.)

6. Jury instructions

RSA 231:90, I, II, and III, standing alone, did not provide a standard of care to be imparted on the city and did not provide immunity to the city, but merely defined "insufficiency," and "written notice." As such, it was not error for the trial court to provide the jury with instructions related to their meaning when the driver claimed that the city was liable to her because of an accident allegedly caused by poor road conditions. Cloutier v. City of Berlin, 154 N.H. 13, 907 A.2d 955, 2006 N.H. LEXIS 118 (N.H. 2006).

Cited:

Cited in Glick v. Ossipee, 130 N.H. 643, 547 A.2d 231, 1988 N.H. LEXIS 79 (1988); Dover v. Imperial Casualty & Indem. Co., 133 N.H. 109, 575 A.2d 1280, 1990 N.H. LEXIS 39 (1990); Boston & Me. Corp. v. Hampton, 987 F.2d 855, 1993 U.S. App. LEXIS 4159 (1st Cir. N.H. 1993); Schoff v. City of Somersworth, 137 N.H. 583, 630 A.2d 783, 1993 N.H. LEXIS 124 (1993).

RESEARCH REFERENCES AND PRACTICE AIDS

New Hampshire Practice.
8-9 N.H.P. Personal Injury-Tort & Insurance Practice § 9.14.
8-9 N.H.P. Personal Injury-Tort & Insurance Practice § 9.24.
14-27 N.H.P. Local Government Law § 1057.
14-27 N.H.P. Local Government Law § 1058.

231:91. Municipality to Act; Liability.

I. Upon receipt of such notice of insufficiency, and unless the highway agents or street commissioners determine in good faith that no such insufficiency exists, the municipality shall immediately cause proper danger signals to be placed to warn persons by day or night of such insufficiency, and shall, within 72 hours thereafter, develop a plan for repairing such highway, bridge, or sidewalk and shall implement such plan in good faith and with reasonable dispatch until the highway, bridge, or sidewalk is no longer insufficient, as defined by RSA 231:90, II.

II. If the municipality fails to act as set forth in paragraph I, it shall be liable in damages for all personal injury or property damage proximately caused by the insufficiency identified in the notice, subject to the liability limits under RSA 507-B:4.

HISTORY:

1893, 59:2. PL 82:9. RL 98:9. 1945, 188:1, part 18:10. RSA 247:10. 1981, 87:1. 1991, 385:4, eff. Jan. 1, 1992.

Amendments

—1991.

Rewritten to the extent that a detailed comparison would be impracticable.

NOTES TO DECISIONS

Analysis

1. Construction
2. Effect of notice
3. Sidewalks

1. Construction

In RSA 231:91, the reference to "such insufficiency" and, in RSA 231:92, to "an insufficiency" are references to the insufficiencies described in RSA 231:90, which apply only to insufficiencies in class IV and V highways. Similarly, the reference in RSA 231:91 to "such highway" is a reference to the highways which are "insufficient, as defined by RSA 231:90, II." Ford v. N.H. Dep't of Transp., 163 N.H. 284, 37 A.3d 436, 2012 N.H. LEXIS 23 (N.H. 2012).

RSA 231:91, by itself, did not confer any sort of immunity on a municipality because it did not limit the liability of a municipality, but instead, required a municipality to respond to any written notice of an insufficiency or to risk being liable for any such insufficiency. Cloutier v. City of Berlin, 154 N.H. 13, 907 A.2d 955, 2006 N.H. LEXIS 118 (N.H. 2006).

2. Effect of notice

Notice to town that highway was out of repair or unsafe rendered town liable for accidents which happened subsequent to such notice and prior to repairs by town. Beer v. North Conway Lighting Precinct, 108 N.H. 465, 238 A.2d 8, 1968 N.H. LEXIS 189 (N.H. 1968). (Decided under prior law.)

3. Sidewalks

Duty to repair, maintain and reconstruct sidewalks which are component parts of highways rested with municipalities. Gossler v.

Miller, 107 N.H. 303, 221 A.2d 249, 1966 N.H. LEXIS 180 (N.H. 1966). (Decided under prior law.)

Cited:

Cited in Glick v. Ossipee, 130 N.H. 643, 547 A.2d 231, 1988 N.H. LEXIS 79 (1988); Dover v. Imperial Casualty & Indem. Co., 133 N.H. 109, 575 A.2d 1280, 1990 N.H. LEXIS 39 (1990); Schoff v. City of Somersworth, 137 N.H. 583, 630 A.2d 783, 1993 N.H. LEXIS 124 (1993).

RESEARCH REFERENCES AND PRACTICE AIDS

New Hampshire Practice.

14-27 N.H.P. Local Government Law § 1057.
14-27 N.H.P. Local Government Law § 1058.

231:92. Liability of Municipalities; Standard of Care.

I. A municipality shall not be held liable for damages in an action to recover for personal injury or property damage arising out of its construction, maintenance, or repair of public highways and sidewalks constructed thereupon unless such injury or damage was caused by an insufficiency, as defined by RSA 231:90, and:

(a) The municipality received a written notice of such insufficiency as set forth in RSA 231:90, but failed to act as provided by RSA 231:91; or

(b) The selectmen, mayor or other chief executive official of the municipality, the town or city clerk, any on-duty police or fire personnel, or municipal officers responsible for maintenance and repair of highways, bridges, or sidewalks thereon had actual notice or knowledge of such insufficiency, by means other than written notice pursuant to RSA 231:90, and were grossly negligent or exercised bad faith in responding or failing to respond to such actual knowledge; or

(c) The condition constituting the insufficiency was created by an intentional act of a municipal officer or employee acting in the scope of his official duty while in the course of his employment, acting with gross negligence, or with reckless disregard of the hazard.

II. Any action to recover damages for bodily injury, personal injury or property damage arising out of municipal construction, repair or maintenance of its public highways or sidewalks constructed on such highways shall be dismissed unless the complaint describes with particularity the means by which the municipality received actual notice of the alleged insufficiency, or the intentional act which created the alleged insufficiency.

III. The acceptance or layout of a private road as a public highway shall not be construed to confer upon the municipality any notice of, or liability for, insufficiencies or defects which arose or were created prior to such layout or acceptance.

IV. The setting of construction, repair, or maintenance standards of levels of service for highways and sidewalks by municipal officials with responsibility therefor, whether accomplished formally or informally, shall be deemed a discretionary, policy function for which the municipality shall not be held liable in the absence of malice or bad faith.

HISTORY:

RS 57:1. CS 61:1, 7. GS 69:1, 2. GL 75:1, 2. PS 76:1. 1893, 59:1. 1915, 48:1. 1921, 107:1. 1925, 52:2, 4. PL 89:1. 1935, 118:1. RL 105:1. 1945, 188:1, part 18:17. RSA 247:17. 1981, 87:1. 1991, 385:5, eff. Jan. 1, 1992.

Amendments

—1991.

Rewritten to the extent that a detailed comparison would be impracticable.

NOTES TO DECISIONS

Analysis

1. Constitutionality
2. Construction
3. Application
4. Standard of care—Municipalities
5. —Travelers
6. Bridges
7. Ice
8. Lowered grade
9. Railings and embankments
10. Turnouts
11. Widened highways
12. Bars
13. Standing to sue
14. Defenses
15. Evidence
16. Questions of jury
17. Damages—Generally
18. —Property
19. —Exemplary
20. Effect of insurance policy
21. Former law

1. Constitutionality

Provision of proposed amendment of this section that labeled setting of road maintenance standards a discretionary policy function for which immunity was extended in absence of malice or bad faith was constitutional, even though determination of whether acts are discretionary was for court, not legislature, to make, where supreme court agreed with legislative designation. Opinion of Justices, 134 N.H. 266, 592 A.2d 180, 1991 N.H. LEXIS 53 (N.H. 1991).

Provision of proposed amendment of this section which required plaintiffs claiming municipality had actual notice of statutorily actionable "insufficiency" to specify means by which municipality learned of insufficiency was constitutional, as it did no more than admonish a plaintiff to properly plead case. Opinion of Justices, 134 N.H. 266, 592 A.2d 180, 1991 N.H. LEXIS 53 (N.H. 1991).

Where proposed amendment of this section provided municipalities with immunity for injury or damage arising out of construction, maintenance or repair of highways and sidewalks except for statutorily delimited "insufficiencies" of which municipality has actual notice, provision that municipality's acceptance or layout of a road does not give it actual notice was constitutional, as one cannot assume municipal officials carefully inspect every foot of a road before the road is made public. Opinion of Justices, 134 N.H. 266, 592 A.2d 180, 1991 N.H. LEXIS 53 (N.H. 1991).

2. Construction

In RSA 231:91, the reference to "such insufficiency" and, in RSA 231:92, to "an insufficiency" are references to the insufficiencies described in RSA 231:90, which apply only to insufficiencies in class IV and V highways. Similarly, the reference in RSA 231:91 to "such highway" is a reference to the highways which are "insufficient, as defined by RSA 231:90, II." Ford v. N.H. Dep't of Transp., 163 N.H. 284, 37 A.3d 436, 2012 N.H. LEXIS 23 (N.H. 2012).

3. Application

Where it was clear that the grassy area where a school visitor tripped and fell was actually a part of the curb, the issue was one of alleged failure to maintain a sidewalk, and the visitor could not prevail in a personal injury action because there was no showing of gross negligence, intentional actions, or failure to respond after receiving notice of a dangerous condition; therefore, summary judgment was properly entered for the school district. Richard v. Pembroke Sch. Dist., 151 N.H. 455, 859 A.2d 1157, 2004 N.H. LEXIS 176 (N.H. 2004).

The former version of this section did not apply to an action against a town arising from the failure of a police officer to warn of an icy road condition because the road was not a highway which the town had the duty to maintain. Trull v. Town of Conway, 140 N.H. 579, 669 A.2d 807, 1995 N.H. LEXIS 196 (N.H. 1995).

Municipal liability for personal injuries resulting from hazards in a road flows from control of the road and a duty to maintain them; where there is no duty to correct a condition there is no actionable duty to warn users of a highway that the condition has not been corrected. Trull v. Town of Conway, 140 N.H. 579, 669 A.2d 807, 1995 N.H. LEXIS 196 (N.H. 1995).

This section applied only to open bridges and highways, not to discontinued bridges. Bancroft v. Canterbury, 118 N.H. 453, 388 A.2d 199, 1978 N.H. LEXIS 437 (N.H. 1978). (Decided under prior law.)

Operation of this section was limited to defects in structures specified. Bernier v. Whitefield, 80 N.H. 245, 116 A. 133, 1921 N.H. LEXIS 72 (N.H. 1921). (Decided under prior law.)

Obligation of this section did not extend to fire district. Henry v. Haverhill, 67 N.H. 172, 37 A. 1039, 1891 N.H. LEXIS 35 (N.H. 1892). (Decided under prior law.)

4. Standard of care—Municipalities

Beyond requirement imposed by this section and within the limits of reason at the least, it was for municipality to determine how fine or perfect its highway should be. Langley v. Brown, 86 N.H. 382, 169 A. 477, 1933 N.H. LEXIS 80 (N.H. 1933). (Decided under prior law.)

Duty of repairing and maintaining highways included performance of any act reasonably necessary to put and keep them in a condition suitable for travel thereon. Connor v. Manchester, 73 N.H. 233, 60 A. 436, 1905 N.H. LEXIS 24 (N.H. 1905). (Decided under prior law.)

This section, which imposed liability upon towns, was required to be understood with the qualification that obstructions or want of repairs causing injury existed by some fault or neglect of town. Palmer v. Portsmouth, 43 N.H. 265, 1861 N.H. LEXIS 65 (N.H. 1861). (Decided under prior law.)

Question of negligence on part of town did not arise except incidentally as it was involved in question whether obstruction, insufficiency or want of repair existed, and this question could depend upon manner in which defect originated and circumstances of its continuance. Johnson v. Haverhill, 35 N.H. 74, 1857 N.H. LEXIS 46 (N.H. 1857). (Decided under prior law.)

5. —Travelers

Traveler on highway was bound to use ordinary care to avoid any danger which he had reason to apprehend. Cullen v. Littleton, 84 N.H. 373, 150 A. 809, 1930 N.H. LEXIS 94 (N.H. 1930). (Decided under prior law.)

One was required to use ordinary care and prudence in obtaining treatment of injuries sustained by him. Boynton v. Somersworth, 58 N.H. 321, 1878 N.H. LEXIS 52 (N.H. 1878). (Decided under prior law.)

Traveler was required to use ordinary care and prudence in selection of a reasonably safe horse, wagon and harness, and was bound to exercise only ordinary care and prudence in their management. Tuttle v. Farmington, 58 N.H. 13, 1876 N.H. LEXIS 10 (N.H. 1876). (Decided under prior law.)

One injured by reason of defect in highway was not precluded from recovery by proof that defect in his carriage contributed to injury, provided that defect was not known to him and he was in no fault for not knowing it. Clark v. Barrington, 41 N.H. 44, 1860 N.H. LEXIS 38 (N.H. 1860). (Decided under prior law.)

6. Bridges

Laying of planks lengthwise on a bridge having a substantial slope upon which a pedestrian fell could be found to render city

liable for injuries sustained on an icy morning. Leonard v. Manchester, 96 N.H. 115, 70 A.2d 915, 1950 N.H. LEXIS 8 (N.H. 1950). (Decided under prior law.)

Approach to bridge could be regarded as part of bridge for purpose of determining liability of towns for injuries to highway travelers under this section. Saloshin v. Houle, 86 N.H. 132, 164 A. 767, 1933 N.H. LEXIS 10 (N.H. 1933); Wilson v. Barnstead, 74 N.H. 78, 65 A. 298, 1906 N.H. LEXIS 71 (N.H. 1906). (Decided under prior law.)

7. Ice

Temporary accumulation of ice was not within this section. Bernier v. Whitefield, 80 N.H. 245, 116 A. 133, 1921 N.H. LEXIS 72 (N.H. 1921). (Decided under prior law.)

8. Lowered grade

Town was not liable for injury due to lowering of grade where driveway entered highway. Robertson v. Hillsborough, 78 N.H. 603, 99 A. 1069, 1916 N.H. LEXIS 81 (N.H. 1916). (Decided under prior law.)

9. Railings and embankments

The 1982 version of the statute provided the plaintiffs with a private cause of action where they alleged that they drove off the end of road which ends in a "cliff-like precipitous drop" within approximately 750 feet of its entrance and that they were unable to see the "No Thru Street" sign intended to alert travelers that the street was a dead end because the sign was small and facing directly opposite the direction in which they were traveling. Schoff v. City of Somersworth, 137 N.H. 583, 630 A.2d 783, 1993 N.H. LEXIS 124 (N.H. 1993). (Decided under prior law.)

Although some of the acts or omissions for which municipalities may be liable under the 1982 version of the statute, including failure to provide warning signs or guardrails for dangerous embankments, may implicate discretionary functions, the statute permits suit for injuries resulting from such acts or omissions. Schoff v. City of Somersworth, 137 N.H. 583, 630 A.2d 783, 1993 N.H. LEXIS 124 (N.H. 1993). (Decided under prior law.)

Defective railing was not in legal effect the same thing as none, since it could serve as a guide and warning. Bridgham v. Effingham, 87 N.H. 103, 174 A. 769, 1934 N.H. LEXIS 24 (N.H. 1934). (Decided under prior law.)

Unrailed embankment could be found to be proximate cause of injury to one who fell over it in consequence of slipping on ice. Prichard v. Boscawen, 78 N.H. 131, 97 A. 563, 1916 N.H. LEXIS 13 (N.H. 1916). (Decided under prior law.)

Town was liable to traveler for injuries resulting from defective railing of dangerous highway embankment. Seeton v. Dunbarton, 72 N.H. 269, 56 A. 197, 1903 N.H. LEXIS 63 (N.H. 1903). (Decided under prior law.)

Among facts material to be considered in determining whether an embankment should have been railed were the character and amount of travel, the character of the road itself, its width and general construction, the character and extent of the slope or descent of the bank, the direction of the road at the place, the length of the portion claimed to require a rail, whether the danger was concealed or obvious, and the extent of injury liable to occur therefrom. Seeton v. Dunbarton, 72 N.H. 269, 56 A. 197, 1903 N.H. LEXIS 63 (N.H. 1903). (Decided under prior law.)

Want of sufficient railing when necessary for security of traveler constituted defect for which town in case of accident could be held liable. Whipple v. Walpole, 10 N.H. 130, 1839 N.H. LEXIS 63 (1839), overruled in part, Woodman v. Nottingham, 49 N.H. 387, 1870 N.H. LEXIS 30 (1870). (Decided under prior law.)

10. Turnouts

Failure to fence off an unsafe private way in the general direction of public travel on highway was not an actionable defect. Knowlton v. Pittsfield, 62 N.H. 535, 1883 N.H. LEXIS 52 (N.H. 1883). (Decided under prior law.)

Duty of town to keep highway in repair extended to that part of turnout which it permitted to exist from traveled part of its highway to private way as was within limits of highway. Stark v. Lancaster, 57 N.H. 88, 1876 N.H. LEXIS 55 (N.H. 1876). (Decided under prior law.)

11. Widened highways

If town suffered traveled part of highway to become widened so as to hold out to travelers that whole width was equally suitable for travel it was answerable for damages growing out of defects in part so widened. Saltmarsh v. Bow, 56 N.H. 428, 1876 N.H. LEXIS 165 (N.H. 1876). (Decided under prior law.)

12. Bars

Bars across road for purpose of turning water from road into gutters could be so constructed as to constitute an actionable defect. Clark v. Barrington, 41 N.H. 44, 1860 N.H. LEXIS 38 (N.H. 1860). (Decided under prior law.)

13. Standing to sue

Fireman of city in which he lived had no such relation to it as to prevent his maintaining an action under this section to recover for injuries occasioned by defects in highway while he was hastening to a fire. Palmer v. Portsmouth, 43 N.H. 265, 1861 N.H. LEXIS 65 (N.H. 1861). (Decided under prior law.)

14. Defenses

Failure to perform statutory duty to keep highways in good repair was not excused by the poverty of town. Winship v. Enfield, 42 N.H. 197, 1860 N.H. LEXIS 23 (N.H. 1860). (Decided under prior law.)

15. Evidence

Verdict for plaintiff in action based upon defective condition of culvert was vitiated by plaintiff's failure to produce evidence that a standard railing would have prevented the accident. Bridgham v. Effingham, 87 N.H. 103, 174 A. 769, 1934 N.H. LEXIS 24 (N.H. 1934). (Decided under prior law.)

In an action under this section for failure to rail an embankment, evidence that slope was concealed by bushes and that ground gave way beneath wheels of plaintiff's car warranted conclusion that embankment constituted danger making road unsuitable for travel. Bridgham v. Effingham, 87 N.H. 103, 174 A. 769, 1934 N.H. LEXIS 24 (N.H. 1934). (Decided under prior law.)

In determining whether traveler exercised sufficient care, evidence of traveler's knowledge or ignorance of condition of road and his choice of tracks thereon could be considered. Griffin v. Auburn, 58 N.H. 121, 1877 N.H. LEXIS 39 (N.H. 1877). (Decided under prior law.)

In an action under this section it was competent to show that town had paid claim for damages to owner of wagon in which plaintiff was riding at time of accident, even though payment was made with a disclaimer of liability. Coffin v. Plymouth, 49 N.H. 173, 1870 N.H. LEXIS 3 (N.H. 1870). (Decided under prior law.)

16. Questions of jury

Whether condition complained of rendered highway unsuitable for public travel was for jury. Seeton v. Dunbarton, 72 N.H. 269, 56 A. 197, 1903 N.H. LEXIS 63 (N.H. 1903). (Decided under prior law.)

Whether plaintiff exercised ordinary care and diligence in traveling upon highway at time and in manner he did, and if not, whether want of such care and diligence contributed to injury, were questions of fact to be found by jury under proper instructions. Palmer v. Portsmouth, 43 N.H. 265, 1861 N.H. LEXIS 65 (N.H. 1861); Whipple v. Walpole, 10 N.H. 130, 1839 N.H. LEXIS 63 (N.H. 1839), overruled, Woodman v. Nottingham, 49 N.H. 387, 1870 N.H. LEXIS 30 (N.H. 1870), overruled as stated in Newport v. Fact Concerts, Inc., 453 U.S. 247, 101 S. Ct. 2748, 69 L. Ed. 2d 616, 1981 U.S. LEXIS 129 (U.S. 1981); Norris v. Litchfield, 35 N.H. 271, 1857 N.H. LEXIS 69 (N.H. 1857); Stack v. Portsmouth, 52 N.H. 221, 1872 N.H. LEXIS 34 (N.H. 1872); Sleeper v. Sandown, 52 N.H. 244, 1872 N.H. LEXIS 38 (N.H. 1872); State v. Manchester & L. R.R., 52 N.H. 528, 1873 N.H. LEXIS 73 (N.H. 1873); Daniels v. Lebanon, 58 N.H. 284, 1878 N.H. LEXIS 29 (N.H. 1878). (Decided under prior law.)

Question whether highway was obstructed, insufficient, or out of repair within meaning of those terms as used in this section was for jury under proper instructions from court as to the meaning of the terms, and in view of all the circumstances of the case in reference to nature and extent of defect, character, ground, amounts and kind of travel, ability and means of town, and other like circumstances tending to show whether highway was or was not reasonably safe and convenient for customary travel and whether or not it ought to

have been repaired before accident. Johnson v. Haverhill, 35 N.H. 74, 1857 N.H. LEXIS 46 (N.H. 1857). (Decided under prior law.)

17. Damages—Generally

Under this section damages were recoverable for probable, proximate or direct consequences of a defect. Whipple v. Walpole, 10 N.H. 130, 1839 N.H. LEXIS 63 (1839), overruled in part, Woodman v. Nottingham, 49 N.H. 387, 1870 N.H. LEXIS 30 (1870). (Decided under prior law.)

Damages for which private person could maintain suit against town were limited to such as happened in use of highway as such and which were direct and not consequential results of defect complained of. Ball v. Winchester, 32 N.H. 435, 1855 N.H. LEXIS 230 (N.H. 1855). (Decided under prior law.)

18. —Property

Damages recoverable included those for injury to property as well as to the person. Whipple v. Walpole, 10 N.H. 130, 1839 N.H. LEXIS 63 (1839), overruled in part, Woodman v. Nottingham, 49 N.H. 387, 1870 N.H. LEXIS 30 (1870). (Decided under prior law.)

19. —Exemplary

This section did not contemplate exemplary or vindictive damages to suffering party. Whipple v. Walpole, 10 N.H. 130, 1839 N.H. LEXIS 63 (1839), overruled in part, Woodman v. Nottingham, 49 N.H. 387, 1870 N.H. LEXIS 30 (1870). (Decided under prior law.)

20. Effect of insurance policy

It was not error for the trial court to instruct the jury concerning the notice and liability requirements of the municipality as set forth in RSA 231:92 even though the municipality had obtained an insurance policy. RSA 231:90 through 231:92 establish "a [statutory] standard of care differing from that of [a] private corporation," within the meaning of former RSA 412:3 (see now RSA 507-B:7-a). The presence or absence of liability insurance does not change the legal duty owed to users of highways, or change the type of conduct that constitutes a breach of such duty. Cloutier v. City of Berlin, 154 N.H. 13, 907 A.2d 955, 2006 N.H. LEXIS 118 (N.H. 2006).

21. Former law

Provision having effect of making towns liable for damages happening from snow encumbering highway as from any other defect was repealed by act of 1893. Miner v. Hopkinton, 73 N.H. 232, 60 A. 433, 1905 N.H. LEXIS 23 (N.H. 1905). (Decided under prior law.)

Prior to amendment of 1893, towns and cities were liable for injuries suffered by travelers upon their highways due to their obstruction, insufficiency, or want of repair, provided the defect or insufficiency was one that town or city ought to have remedied and it knew or in the exercise of due care could have known of the defect or insufficiency and remedied it; and this was so whether creation of the defect or insufficiency was due to the act or acts of their agents, public officers, strangers, or to some natural cause. Clair v. Manchester, 72 N.H. 231, 55 A. 935, 1903 N.H. LEXIS 53 (N.H. 1903). (Decided under prior law.)

While under this section prior to its amendment in 1867, when using any part of highway traveler might have an action, under new language no action was given except to one injured when using parts of the highway enumerated, namely, a bridge, culvert, sluiceway, or embankment. Wilder v. Concord, 72 N.H. 259, 56 A. 193, 1903 N.H. LEXIS 61 (N.H. 1903). (Decided under prior law.)

Changes introduced in this section in 1867 indicated a purpose to strictly limit liability arising in this way, but not to entirely remove it; for no liability could arise at any portion of highway other than those enumerated and not then because obstruction rendered highway unsuitable unless the matter complained of constituted an obstruction, defect, insufficiency, or want of repair in a structure the defect in which was made a ground of liability. Wilder v. Concord, 72 N.H. 259, 56 A. 193, 1903 N.H. LEXIS 61 (N.H. 1903). (Decided under prior law.)

Prior to restrictive 1867 amendment, location or character of defect or insufficiency in highway complained of as cause of injury was immaterial; by such amendment liability of towns was limited to damages resulting by reason of any obstruction, defect, insufficiency, or want of repair of a bridge, culvert or sluiceway or from a dangerous embankment and defective railing which rendered highway unsuitable. Owen v. Derry, 71 N.H. 405, 52 A. 926, 1902 N.H. LEXIS 48 (N.H. 1902). (Decided under prior law.)

Cited:

Cited in Dover v. Imperial Casualty & Indem. Co., 133 N.H. 109, 575 A.2d 1280, 1990 N.H. LEXIS 39 (1990); Doucette v. Town of Bristol, 138 N.H. 205, 635 A.2d 1387, 1993 N.H. LEXIS 182 (1993); Boston & Me. Corp. v. Hampton, 987 F.2d 855, 1993 U.S. App. LEXIS 4159 (1st Cir. N.H. 1993).

RESEARCH REFERENCES AND PRACTICE AIDS

Cross References.

Liability of two or more towns, see RSA 231:105 et seq.
Venue of actions, see RSA 231:110.

New Hampshire Practice.

8-9 N.H.P. Personal Injury-Tort & Insurance Practice § 9.14.
14-27 N.H.P. Local Government Law § 1057.
14-27 N.H.P. Local Government Law § 1058.
16-48 N.H.P. Municipal Law & Taxation § 48.01.
16-48 N.H.P. Municipal Law & Taxation § 48.07.
16-48 N.H.P. Municipal Law & Taxation § 48.10.

231:93. When Municipalities not Liable.

Municipalities shall not be deemed to have any duty of care whatsoever with respect to the construction, maintenance or repair of class I, III, III-a or VI highways, or state maintained portions of class II highways. Upon any highway or other way with respect to which a municipality is found to have a duty of care of any kind, its liability shall be limited as set forth in this subdivision.

HISTORY:

RS 105:4. 1945, 188:1, part 18:18. RSA 247:18. 1981, 87:1. 1991, 385:7. 1992, 265:14, eff. July 1, 1992.

Amendments

—1992.

Inserted "III-a" preceding "or VI" and deleted "or highways to public waters laid out by a commission appointed by the governor and council" following "class II highways" in the first sentence.

—1991.

Rewritten to the extent that a detailed comparison would be impracticable.

NOTES TO DECISIONS

Analysis

1. Constitutionality
2. Reason for immunity
3. Extent of immunity
4. State control
5. Duty to warn

1. Constitutionality

Provision of proposed amendment of this section granting immunity for injuries suffered on classes of highways either maintained solely by the state or not required to be maintained by a municipality did not create unconstitutional classification between private and public tortfeasors; municipalities should not be held responsible for insufficiencies on these classes of highways. Opinion of Justices, 134 N.H. 266, 592 A.2d 180, 1991 N.H. LEXIS 53 (N.H. 1991).

2. Reason for immunity

Reason for immunity afforded by this section was that control had been taken from town either in whole or in part. Bridgham v. Effingham, 87 N.H. 103, 174 A. 769, 1934 N.H. LEXIS 24 (N.H. 1934); Hanover v. Burroughs, 215 F. 817, 1914 U.S. App. LEXIS 1293 (1st Cir. N.H. 1914). (Decided under prior law.)

3. Extent of immunity

Immunity under this section was effective only for that portion of highway which received benefit of state aid. Bridgham v. Effingham, 87 N.H. 103, 174 A. 769, 1934 N.H. LEXIS 24 (N.H. 1934). (Decided under prior law.)

Grant of state aid upon application of town affected its liability only as to portions of highways to which aid was so granted, or those as to which at least some official action seeking grant had been taken. Bridgham v. Effingham, 86 N.H. 332, 168 A. 904, 1933 N.H. LEXIS 57 (N.H. 1933). (Decided under prior law.)

4. State control

Mere formulation of plan that designated road should become state-aided over its entire length did not amount to designation in the legal sense, even if approved by highway commissioner. Bridgham v. Effingham, 87 N.H. 103, 174 A. 769, 1934 N.H. LEXIS 24 (N.H. 1934). (Decided under prior law.)

Until improvement had begun, or at least a definite portion of highway had been concurrently designated for improvement, there was no state control, and town's liability to travelers continued. Bridgham v. Effingham, 87 N.H. 103, 174 A. 769, 1934 N.H. LEXIS 24 (N.H. 1934). (Decided under prior law.)

5. Duty to warn

To the extent the two statutes conflict, the more specific statute, RSA 231:93, controls over the general statute, RSA 21-P:44. RSA 231:93 specifically provides that a municipality owes no duty of care with respect to class I and state-maintained portions of class II state highways; thus, a town did not have a duty under RSA 21-P:44 to warn motorists that due to an ice storm, lights were out at the intersection of two class I and II highways. Ford v. N.H. Dep't of Transp., 163 N.H. 284, 37 A.3d 436, 2012 N.H. LEXIS 23 (N.H. 2012).

In a negligence suit, because the intersecting roads where an accident occurred were class I and II state highways, a town had no duty to maintain them under RSA 231:93 and thus had no duty to warn motorists that the lights at the intersection were inoperable due to an ice storm. Ford v. N.H. Dep't of Transp., 163 N.H. 284, 37 A.3d 436, 2012 N.H. LEXIS 23 (N.H. 2012).

Cited:

Cited in Schoff v. City of Somersworth, 137 N.H. 583, 630 A.2d 783, 1993 N.H. LEXIS 124 (1993); Trull v. Town of Conway, 140 N.H. 579, 669 A.2d 807, 1995 N.H. LEXIS 196 (1995); Berliner v. Clukay, 150 N.H. 80, 834 A.2d 297, 2003 N.H. LEXIS 140 (2003).

RESEARCH REFERENCES AND PRACTICE AIDS

Cross References.

Classification of highways, see RSA229:5.
Town not liable for damages or injuries caused by use of closed highway or bridge, see RSA 228:37.

New Hampshire Practice.

8-9 N.H.P. Personal Injury-Tort & Insurance Practice § 9.14.
16-48 N.H.P. Municipal Law & Taxation § 48.07.

Street Names and Markers

231:133. Names; Changes; Signs.

I. In all towns, cities, and those village districts which maintain public highways, every highway and street under the control of the town, city, or village district shall have a name which shall be given it by the governing body. Said name shall be legibly marked on a suitable signboard or other marker and placed in at least 2 conspicuous places on said street. The governing body may change the name of any such street or highway at any time when in its judgment there is occasion for so doing. The governing body may change the name of a private street or highway when the name change is necessary to conform to the requirements of the enhanced 911 telecommunications system. In towns and village districts the governing body may at its discretion provide for public hearing and submit such names for approval at any meeting of the legislative body, and voters may submit a petitioned warrant article for such a name change under the procedure of RSA 39:3.

II. The naming of any new street or highway shall form a part of the return of the layout of the street or highway, or of the acceptance of any dedicated way. The municipality shall not be bound by any name previously assigned to the street or highway by any private owner, developer, or dedicator. No name for a highway or street shall be selected which is already in use, or which is confusingly similar to any such existing name, or which otherwise might delay the locating of any address in an emergency.

III. Whenever a name is assigned to any new street or highway, or a change is made in the name of any street or highway, the governing body shall make a return of the same to the town, city, or village district clerk, who shall make a record of the new name or name change, and shall forward a copy of such record to the commissioner of transportation.

HISTORY:

1911, 79:1. PL 93:5. RL 109:5. 1945, 188:1, part 21:1. RSA 251:1. 1981, 87:1. 1991, 53:1, eff. July 5, 1991. 2005, 113:1, eff. August 14, 2005.

Amendments

—2005.

Paragraph I: Added the fourth sentence.

—1991.

Rewritten to the extent that a detailed comparison would be impracticable.

NOTES TO DECISIONS

Historical

Similar provision requiring town under penalty to maintain guide posts at highway intersections was held not to make failure to maintain guide posts at each intersection a separate offense in Clark v. Lisbon, 19 N.H. 286, 1848 N.H. LEXIS 43 (N.H. 1848). (Decided under prior law.)

RESEARCH REFERENCES AND PRACTICE AIDS

New Hampshire Practice.

16-49 N.H.P. Municipal Law & Taxation § 49.03.

Scenic Roads

RESEARCH REFERENCES AND PRACTICE AIDS

Cross References.

Scenic and cultural byways system, see RSA 238:19 et seq.

231:157. Scenic Roads; Designation.

Any road in a town, other than a class I or class II highway, may be designated as a scenic road in the following manner. Upon petition of 10 persons who are either voters of the town or who own land which abuts a road mentioned in the petition (even though not voters of the town), the voters of such town at any annual or special meeting may designate such road as a scenic road. Such petitioners shall be responsible for providing the town clerk with a list of known property owners whose land abuts any of the roads mentioned in the petition. The town clerk shall notify by regular mail within 10 days of the filing all abutters along the road that lies within the town that a scenic road petition has been filed for and that an article to designate such road as a scenic road will appear in the warrant at the next town meeting. The voters at a regular town meeting may rescind in like manner their designation of a scenic road upon petition as provided above. Notice to the abutting landowners shall also be given as provided above. Each town shall maintain and make available to the public a list of all roads or highways or portions thereof within the town which have been designated as scenic roads. Such list shall be kept current by updating not less than annually and shall contain sufficient information to permit ready identification of the location and extent of each scenic road or portion thereof, by reference to a town map or otherwise.

HISTORY:

RSA 253:17. 1971, 455:1. 1973, 586:1. 1981, 87:1. 1992, 160:3, eff. July 5, 1992.

Amendments

—1992.

Added the seventh and eighth sentences.

NOTES TO DECISIONS

Analysis

1. Constitutionality
2. Construction

1. Constitutionality

Scenic road statute is not an impermissible delegation of legislative power because the legislature has deemed scenic roads to be a matter of local concern and has delegated the authority to designate scenic roads to local voters, and the authority to regulate tree and stone wall removal from these roads to the local planning board or other "official municipal body" selected by the voters. Webster v. Town of Candia, 146 N.H. 430, 778 A.2d 402, 2001 N.H. LEXIS 91 (N.H. 2001), amended, 2001 N.H. LEXIS 154 (N.H. Aug. 20, 2001).

2. Construction

Trial court erred in finding that removal of scenic road designation, accomplished by vote at town meeting, amounted to a circumvention of planning board's earlier decision denying relocation of portion of road; decisions made by voters and by planning board were not the same, and only entity with jurisdiction to designate or undesignate a road as scenic was the town, through its vote. Neville v. Highfields Farm, Inc., 144 N.H. 419, 744 A.2d 89, 1999 N.H. LEXIS 135 (N.H. 1999).

Cited:
Cited in Cormier v. Town of Danville Zoning Bd. of Adjustment, 142 N.H. 775, 710 A.2d 401, 1998 N.H. LEXIS 35 (1998).

RESEARCH REFERENCES AND PRACTICE AIDS

New Hampshire Practice.
16-49 N.H.P. Municipal Law & Taxation § 49.13.

231:158. Effect of Designation as Scenic Roads.

I. As used in this subdivision, "tree" means any woody plant which has a circumference of 15 inches or more at a point 4 feet from the ground.

II. Upon a road being designated as a scenic road as provided in RSA 231:157, any repair, maintenance, reconstruction, or paving work done with respect thereto by the state or municipality, or any action taken by any utility or other person acting to erect, install or maintain poles, conduits, cables, wires, pipes or other structures pursuant to RSA 231:159–189 shall not involve the cutting, damage or removal of trees, or the tearing down or destruction of stone walls, or portions thereof, except with the prior written consent of the planning board, or any other official municipal body designated by the meeting to implement the provisions of this subdivision, after a public hearing duly advertised as to time, date, place and purpose, 2 times in a newspaper of general circulation in the area, the last publication to occur at least 7 days prior to such hearing, provided, however, that a road agent or his designee may, without such hearing, but only with the written permission of the selectmen, remove trees or portions of trees which have been declared a public nuisance pursuant to RSA 231:145 and 231:146, when such trees or portions of such trees pose an imminent threat to safety or property, and provided, further, that a public utility when involved in the emergency restoration of service, may without such hearing or permission of the selectmen, perform such work as is necessary for the prompt restoration of utility service which has been interrupted by facility damage and when requested, shall thereafter inform the selectmen of the nature of the emergency and the work performed, in such manner as the selectmen may require.

III. Designation of a road as scenic shall not affect the eligibility of the town to receive construction, maintenance or reconstruction aid pursuant to the provisions of RSA 235 for such road.

IV. Designation of a road as a scenic road shall not affect the rights of any landowner with respect to work on his own property, except to the extent that trees have been acquired by the municipality as shade or ornamental trees pursuant to RSA 231:139–156, and except that RSA 472:6 limits the removal or alteration of boundary markers including stone walls.

V. A town may, as part of a scenic road designation under RSA 231:157 or as an amendment to such designation adopted in the same manner, impose provisions with respect to such road which are different from or in addition to those set forth in this section. Such provisions may include, but are not limited to, decisional criteria for the granting of consent by the planning board or other designated municipal body under paragraph II, or protections for trees smaller than those described in paragraph I, designated for the purpose of establishing regenerative growth along the scenic road.

VI. Any person who violates this section or any local provision adopted under this section shall be guilty of a violation and shall be liable for all damages resulting therefrom.

HISTORY:
RSA 253:18. 1971, 455:1. 1973, 586:2. 1981, 87:1. 1983, 122:2. 1991, 134:3, 4. 1992, 160:2, eff. July 5, 1992.

Amendments

—1992.
Paragraph II: Rewritten to the extent that a detailed comparison would be impracticable.

—1991.
Paragraph II: Rewritten to the extent that a detailed comparison would be impracticable.
Paragraph IV: Added "except to the extent that trees have been acquired by the municipality as shade or ornamental trees pursuant to RSA 231:139– 156, and except that RSA 472:6 limits the removal or alteration of boundary markers including stone walls" following "property".
Paragraphs V, VI: Added.

—1983.
Paragraph III: Inserted "maintenance" following "construction" in the first sentence and deleted the second sentence.

NOTES TO DECISIONS

Analysis

1. Constitutionality
2. Planning board procedures

1. Constitutionality
This section is not unconstitutionally vague because it is sufficiently clear to warn the average person of the prohibited conduct (cutting trees of a specific circumference or destroying stone walls on designated scenic roads) and that if he or she wishes to engage in the prohibited activity, he or she must first obtain written planning board consent. Webster v. Town of Candia, 146 N.H. 430, 778 A.2d 402, 2001 N.H. LEXIS 91 (N.H. 2001), amended, 2001 N.H. LEXIS 154 (N.H. Aug. 20, 2001).
This section is not void on the basis that it does not apprise an applicant of the standards that planning board, or other official municipal body, will use when reviewing plans to cut trees or destroy stone walls on scenic roads; a law is not necessarily vague because it does not precisely apprise an applicant of the standards by which an administrative board will make its decision. Webster v. Town of Candia, 146 N.H. 430, 778 A.2d 402, 2001 N.H. LEXIS 91 (N.H. 2001), amended, 2001 N.H. LEXIS 154 (N.H. Aug. 20, 2001).
This section is not vague on the basis that it does not specify standards planning board will use when reviewing plans for tree cutting or stone wall destruction on designated scenic roads because it is implied that the board will exercise its discretion consistent with the purpose of the road's scenic designation. Webster v. Town of Candia, 146 N.H. 430, 778 A.2d 402, 2001 N.H. LEXIS 91 (N.H. 2001), amended, 2001 N.H. LEXIS 154 (N.H. Aug. 20, 2001).

Warrant articles by which a town voted to designate a road as scenic specifying that the purpose of so doing was to "protect and enhance ... the scenic beauty of [the town]" was sufficient notice to developers of relevant standards planning board would use when reviewing plans for tree cutting or stone wall destruction. Webster v. Town of Candia, 146 N.H. 430, 778 A.2d 402, 2001 N.H. LEXIS 91 (N.H. 2001), amended, 2001 N.H. LEXIS 154 (N.H. Aug. 20, 2001).

This section was not impermissibly vague as applied to plaintiffs because, under the facts of the case, it gave them adequate warning that they could not cut certain kinds of trees absent planning board consent. Webster v. Town of Candia, 146 N.H. 430, 778 A.2d 402, 2001 N.H. LEXIS 91 (N.H. 2001), amended, 2001 N.H. LEXIS 154 (N.H. Aug. 20, 2001).

Scenic road statute is not an impermissible delegation of legislative power because the legislature has deemed scenic roads to be a matter of local concern and has delegated the authority to designate scenic roads to local voters, and the authority to regulate tree and stone wall removal from these roads to the local planning board or other "official municipal body" selected by the voters. Webster v. Town of Candia, 146 N.H. 430, 778 A.2d 402, 2001 N.H. LEXIS 91 (N.H. 2001), amended, 2001 N.H. LEXIS 154 (N.H. Aug. 20, 2001).

2. Planning board procedures

In denying plaintiffs' applications to remove trees from a designated scenic road, it was reasonable for planning board to have considered whether there was alternative access to plaintiffs' property since the roads constituting alternative means of access were not designated scenic roads. Webster v. Town of Candia, 146 N.H. 430, 778 A.2d 402, 2001 N.H. LEXIS 91 (N.H. 2001), amended, 2001 N.H. LEXIS 154 (N.H. Aug. 20, 2001).

In denying plaintiffs' applications to remove trees from a designated scenic road, planning board's consideration of alternative access did not violate their constitutional rights to due process on the basis that they never received notice that the board would consider the possibility of alternative accesses because they received both adequate notice and an opportunity to be heard on their request to cut trees from the scenic road and this is all the procedure due process requires. Webster v. Town of Candia, 146 N.H. 430, 778 A.2d 402, 2001 N.H. LEXIS 91 (N.H. 2001), amended, 2001 N.H. LEXIS 154 (N.H. Aug. 20, 2001).

Notice of planning board's decision denying plaintiffs' applications to remove trees from a designated scenic road was not unreasonable and unlawful on the basis that it did not include reasons for the denial where evidence before the trial court, including approved and unapproved minutes of the meeting, reasonably supported a finding that reasons for the denial were adequately set forth. Webster v. Town of Candia, 146 N.H. 430, 778 A.2d 402, 2001 N.H. LEXIS 91 (N.H. 2001), amended, 2001 N.H. LEXIS 154 (N.H. Aug. 20, 2001).

Planning board's reasons for its denial of plaintiffs' request to cut trees on designated scenic road were valid based on its finding that the proposed tree cutting "would lead to the deterioration of the scenic quality of the road," and because the request failed to mark all of the trees to be removed and failed to present a study or documentation about how removing the trees would affect drainage for other trees on the road. Webster v. Town of Candia, 146 N.H. 430, 778 A.2d 402, 2001 N.H. LEXIS 91 (N.H. 2001), amended, 2001 N.H. LEXIS 154 (N.H. Aug. 20, 2001).

Cited:

Cited in Cormier v. Town of Danville Zoning Bd. of Adjustment, 142 N.H. 775, 710 A.2d 401, 1998 N.H. LEXIS 35 (1998); Neville v. Highfields Farm, Inc., 144 N.H. 419, 744 A.2d 89, 1999 N.H. LEXIS 135 (1999).

RESEARCH REFERENCES AND PRACTICE AIDS

New Hampshire Practice.
16-49 N.H.P. Municipal Law & Taxation § 49.13.
16-49 N.H.P. Municipal Law & Taxation § 49.14.

CHAPTER 236

HIGHWAY REGULATION, PROTECTION AND CONTROL REGULATIONS

Excavations and Driveways

EFFECTIVE DATE OF 1985 AMENDMENT

1985, 402:41, II, eff. July 1, 1985, provided that the provisions of 1985, 402 which affected this chapter would take effect when the department of transportation became operational on the date set according to 1983, 372:5, II. Pursuant to 1983, 372:5, II, the joint committee on implementation of reorganization and the governor determined the effective date upon which the department became operational to be Feb. 28, 1986.

RESEARCH REFERENCES AND PRACTICE AIDS

New Hampshire Practice.
16-50 N.H.P. Municipal Law & Taxation § 50.06.
16-50 N.H.P. Municipal Law & Taxation § 50.13.

Excavations and Driveways

236:13. Driveways and Other Accesses to the Public Way.

I. It shall be unlawful to construct, or alter in any way that substantially affects the size or grade of, any driveway, entrance, exit, or approach within the limits of the right-of-way of any class I or class III highway or the state-maintained portion of a class II highway that does not conform to the terms and specifications of a written permit issued by the commissioner of transportation.

II. Pursuant to this section, a written construction permit application must be obtained from and filed with the department of transportation by any abutter affected by the provisions of paragraph I. Before any construction or alteration work is commenced, said permit application shall have been reviewed, and a construction permit issued by said department. Said permit shall:

(a) Describe the location of the driveway, entrance, exit, or approach. The location shall be selected to most adequately protect the safety of the traveling public.

(b) Describe any drainage structures, traffic control devices, and channelization islands to be installed by the abutter.

(c) Establish grades that adequately protect and promote highway drainage and permit a safe and controlled approach to the highway in all seasons of the year.

(d) Include any other terms and specifications necessary for the safety of the traveling public.

III. For access to a proposed commercial or industrial enterprise, or to a subdivision, all of which for the purposes of this section shall be considered a single parcel of land, even though acquired by more than one conveyance or held nominally by more than one owner:

(a) Said permit application shall be accompanied by engineering drawings showing information as set forth in paragraph II.

(b) Unless all season safe sight distance of 400 feet in both directions along the highway can be obtained, the commissioner shall not permit more than one access to a single parcel of land, and this access shall be at that location which the commissioner determines to be safest. The commissioner shall not give final approval for use of any additional access until it has been proven to him that the 400-foot all season safe sight distance has been provided.

(c) For the purposes of this section, all season safe sight distance is defined as a line which encounters no visual obstruction between 2 points, each at a height of 3 feet 9 inches above the pavement, and so located as to represent the critical line of sight between the operator of a vehicle using the access and the operator of a vehicle approaching from either direction.

IV. No construction permit shall allow:

(a) A driveway, entrance, exit, or approach to be constructed more than 50 feet in width, except that a driveway, entrance, exit, or approach may be flared beyond a width of 50 feet at its junction with the highway to accommodate the turning radius of vehicles expected to use the particular driveway, entrance, exit or approach.

(b) More than 2 driveways, entrances, exits or approaches from any one highway to any one parcel of land unless the frontage along that highway exceeds 500 feet.

V. The same powers concerning highways under their jurisdiction as are conferred upon the commissioner of transportation by paragraphs I, II, III, and IV shall be conferred upon the planning board or governing body in cities and towns in which the planning board or governing body has been granted the power to regulate the grading and improvement of streets within a subdivision as provided in RSA 674:35, and they shall adopt such regulations as are necessary to carry out the provisions of this section. Such regulations may delegate administrative duties, including actual issuance of permits, to a highway agent, board of selectmen, or other qualified official or body. Such regulations, or any permit issued under them, may contain provisions governing the breach, removal, and reconstruction of stone walls or fences within, or at the boundary of, the public right of way, and any landowner or landowner's agent altering a boundary in accordance with such provisions shall be deemed to be acting under a mutual agreement with the city or town pursuant to RSA 472:6, II(a).

VI. The commissioner of transportation or planning board shall retain continuing jurisdiction over the adequacy and safety of every existing driveway, entrance, exit, and approach to a highway, whether or not such access was constructed or installed pursuant to a permit under this section, and, unless the access is a public highway, the owners of property to which the access is appurtenant shall have continuing responsibility for the adequacy of the access and any grades, culverts, or other structures pertaining to such access, whether or not located within the public right of way. If any such access is or becomes a potential threat to the integrity of the highway or its surface, ditches, embankments, bridges, or other structures, or a hazard to the safety of the traveling public, by reason of siltation, flooding, erosion, frost action, vegetative growth, improper grade, or the failure of any culvert, traffic control device, drainage structure, or any other feature, the commissioner of transportation or planning board or their designee may issue an order to the landowner or other party responsible for such access to repair or remove such hazardous condition and to obtain any and all permits required therefor. The order shall describe the hazard, prescribe what corrective action or alteration in the location or configuration of such access shall be required, and set a reasonable time within which the action shall be completed. Such an order shall be sent by certified mail, and shall be enforceable to the same extent as a permit issued under this section. If the order is not complied with within the time prescribed, the commissioner or planning board or their designee may cause to be taken whatever action is necessary to protect the highway and the traveling public, and the owner or other responsible party shall be civilly liable to the state or municipality for its costs in taking such action.

HISTORY:
1939, 109:1. RL 107:4. 1945, 188:1, part 19:12. 1950, 5:1, part 9:1,

par. 2. RSA 249:17. 1969, 254:1. 1971, 302:1. 1981, 87:1. 1985, 103:4, eff. Jan. 1, 1986. 402:6, I(a)(7), (b)(7). 1997, 52:1, 2, eff. July 18, 1997. 2014, 125:1, eff. August 15, 2014.

Revision note.
Substituted a comma for a semicolon following "commenced" in the second sentence of par. II to correct a grammatical error.

Effective date of 1985 amendment
See note preceding RSA 236:1 regarding effective date of 1985, 402:6, I.

Amendment Notes

—2014.
The 2014 amendment, in the first sentence of V, added "or governing body" twice and substituted "grading and improvement of streets within a subdivision" for "subdivision of land" and made a stylistic change.

—1997.
Paragraph V: Substituted "in which" for "wherein" following "cities and towns" in the first sentence and added the second and third sentences.
Paragraph VI: Added.

—1985.
Paragraph I: Chapter 402 substituted "commissioner of transportation" for "commissioner of public works and highways" at the end of the paragraph.
Paragraph II: Chapter 402 substituted "department of transportation" for "department of public works and highways" in the first sentence of the introductory paragraph.
Paragraph V: Chapter 103 substituted " RSA 674:35" for " RSA 36:19" following "provided in" and "adopt" for "promulgate" preceding "such" and deleted "rules and" thereafter and made other minor stylistic changes throughout the paragraph.
Chapter 402 substituted "commissioner of transportation" for "commissioner of public works and highways".

NOTES TO DECISIONS

Analysis

1. State preemption
2. Powers of commissioner
3. Safe sight distance
4. Damages
5. Exceptions

1. State preemption
Since New Hampshire legislature had given commissioner of public works and highways broad powers to regulate driveways and other means of access to state highways and had made it unlawful for anyone to construct or alter any entrance onto a state highway without complying with the terms of a permit obtained from the commissioner, state had preempted control of access to state highways. J. E. D. Assocs. v. Sandown, 121 N.H. 317, 430 A.2d 129, 1981 N.H. LEXIS 332 (N.H. 1981). (Decided under prior law.)

2. Powers of commissioner
New Hampshire Department of Transportation's (DOT's) three driveway rule neither conflicts with the standards in the driveway statute, RSA 236:13, nor oversteps the limited discretion granted to the DOT concerning driveway permits. In re Appeal of N.H. DOT, 152 N.H. 565, 883 A.2d 272, 2005 N.H. LEXIS 139 (N.H. 2005).
Basic design and function of limited access highway was to allow for optimum mobility of through traffic by permitting owners and occupants of abutting land to have only restricted right of physical access to and from roadway and only at points planned and controlled by official highway plan, but such control must have been exercised in a reasonable and nonarbitrary manner in any action by commissioner of public works and highways. Treat v. State, 117 N.H. 6, 369 A.2d 214, 1977 N.H. LEXIS 253 (N.H. 1977). (Decided under prior law.)

3. Safe sight distance
Four-hundred-foot safe sight distance at a highway intersection required by subparagraph III(b) of this section applied when more than one access to a single parcel of land was involved. J. E. D. Assocs. v. Sandown, 121 N.H. 317, 430 A.2d 129, 1981 N.H. LEXIS 332 (N.H. 1981). (Decided under prior law.)

4. Damages
Subjecting 50-foot wide right of access to limited access highway reserved to abutting landowners to reasonable control of commissioner of public works and highways was regulation under police power of state to promote public safety and general welfare and was not taking by eminent domain of private property, because it was useful to public and was not compensable. Treat v. State, 117 N.H. 6, 369 A.2d 214, 1977 N.H. LEXIS 253 (N.H. 1977). (Decided under prior law.)
Power to regulate access to highways conferred upon commissioner applied to all abutters on limited access highways and to abutters on certain other highways; thus, abutting landowners shared hardship resulting from regulation with all other abutters, and damages, not being peculiar to them, constituted general damages and were not compensable. Treat v. State, 117 N.H. 6, 369 A.2d 214, 1977 N.H. LEXIS 253 (N.H. 1977). (Decided under prior law.)

5. Exceptions
New Hampshire Transportation Appeals Board erred by requiring the New Hampshire Department of Transportation (DOT) to present evidence that respondent's proposed driveway would create a specific safety issue. It was the owner who sought an exception from the DOT's three driveway rule, and the burden remained with him to establish all requirements to warrant the grant of an exception. In re Appeal of N.H. DOT, 152 N.H. 565, 883 A.2d 272, 2005 N.H. LEXIS 139 (N.H. 2005).

Cited:
Cited in Diversified Properties v. Hopkinton Planning Bd., 125 N.H. 419, 480 A.2d 194, 1984 N.H. LEXIS 262 (1984); Collier v. Redbones Tavern & Restaurant, Inc., 601 F. Supp. 927, 1985 U.S. Dist. LEXIS 22951 (D.N.H. 1985); Dumont v. Town of Wolfeboro, 137 N.H. 1, 622 A.2d 1238, 1993 N.H. LEXIS 28 (1993).

RESEARCH REFERENCES AND PRACTICE AIDS

Cross References.
Classification of highways, see RSA229:5.
Exemption of rules adopted under this section from provisions of Administrative Procedure Act, see RSA 541-A:21.

New Hampshire Practice.
16-50 N.H.P. Municipal Law & Taxation § 50.06.
16-55 N.H.P. Municipal Law & Taxation § 55.10.

236:14. Penalty.

Any person who violates any provision of this subdivision or the rules and regulations made under authority thereof shall be guilty of a violation if a natural person, or guilty of a misdemeanor if any other person; and, in addition, shall be liable for the cost of restoration of the highway to a condition satisfactory to the person empowered to give such written permission.

HISTORY:
1917, 96:3. PL 91:3. 1939, 109:2. RL 107:5. 1945, 188:1, part 19:13. RSA 249:18. 1973, 530:26. 1981, 87:1, eff. April 20, 1981.

RESEARCH REFERENCES AND PRACTICE AIDS

Cross References.
Classification of crimes, see RSA 625:9.
Sentences, see RSA 651.

Outdoor Advertising

NOTES TO DECISIONS

Analysis

1. Constitutionality
2. Purpose
3. Construction

1. Constitutionality

Proposed legislation (enacted as former RSA 249-A) restricting outdoor advertising signs beside interstate highways which was induced in part by the consideration that federal funds would be available to assist in furthering the policies of the legislation was not a delegation of state's sovereign police power and violated no provision of the constitution of this state. Opinion of Justices, 103 N.H. 268, 169 A.2d 762, 1961 N.H. LEXIS 29 (N.H. 1961). (Decided under prior law.)

Proposed legislation (enacted as former RSA 249-A) which would restrict outdoor advertising signs beside interstate highways of this state for declared purpose of decreasing dangers of motor vehicle accidents and promotion of attractiveness of roadside scenery for visiting tourists related to benefit and welfare of state and would be a valid exercise of police powers. Opinion of Justices, 103 N.H. 268, 169 A.2d 762, 1961 N.H. LEXIS 29 (N.H. 1961). (Decided under prior law.)

2. Purpose

This subdivision was intended as a comprehensive scheme to regulate billboards on federal aid primary highways. Appeal of Clement, 124 N.H. 503, 471 A.2d 1193, 1984 N.H. LEXIS 224 (N.H. 1984).

3. Construction

The Outdoor Advertising Law was entitled to broad interpretation to accomplish its purpose for making highway safe and devoid of distracting devices. David v. Whitaker, 116 N.H. 266, 358 A.2d 404, 1976 N.H. LEXIS 328 (N.H. 1976). (Decided under prior law.)

Cited:

Cited in National Advertising Co. v. Stickney, 129 N.H. 402, 529 A.2d 380, 1987 N.H. LEXIS 210 (1987).

RESEARCH REFERENCES AND PRACTICE AIDS

Cross References.

Location of roadside advertising, see RSA 236:54.

Motorist service signs on limited access highways, see RSA 230:49.

Rental of advertising space and traveler information services on limited access highways, see RSA 230:52.

236:73-a. "RV Friendly" Markers.

I. Subject to the prior approval of the Federal Highway Administration, the department of transportation shall incorporate the use of "RV friendly" markers on specific business directional signs for business establishments that cater to the needs of persons driving recreational vehicles. A business establishment that qualifies for a business directional sign and that also qualifies as "RV friendly" may request that an "RV friendly" marker be displayed immediately adjacent to such establishment's business logo sign on the appropriate background sign panel. The business applicant shall pay all costs of the "RV friendly" marker. For purposes of this section, the "RV friendly" marker to be displayed shall be such marker as may be approved by the Federal Highway Administration in the Manual on Uniform Traffic Control Devices.

II. In accordance with the provisions of RSA 21-L:12, and subject to the approval of the Federal Highway Administration, the department shall adopt rules, pursuant to RSA 541-A, necessary to implement the provisions of this section, including rules setting forth the minimum requirements for business establishments to qualify as "RV friendly." Such requirements shall include, but shall not be limited to:

(a) Roadways shall be hard surface, such as gravel, compacted stone dust, pavement, or other firm surface, and at least 12 feet wide with a minimum swing radius of 50 feet for entering and exiting the facility.

(b) Roadway access and parking facilities shall be free of any obstructions up to 14 feet above the surface.

(c) Facilities requiring short-term parking shall have 2 or more spaces that are 12 feet wide and 65 feet long with a swing radius of 50 feet to enter and exit the spaces.

(d) Fueling facilities with canopies shall have a 14-foot clearance and facilities selling diesel fuel shall have pumps with non-commercial nozzles.

(e) Fueling facilities shall allow for pull-through with a swing radius of 50 feet.

(f) Campgrounds shall have 2 or more spaces that are 18 feet wide and 45 feet long.

HISTORY:

2007, 87:1, eff. August 10, 2007.

Motor Vehicle Recycling Yards and Junk Yards

Amendments

—1992.

1992, 88:11, eff. Jan. 1, 1993, substituted "Recycling" for "Junk" following "Vehicle" in the subdivision heading.

RESEARCH REFERENCES AND PRACTICE AIDS

Cross References.

Control of junk yards and automotive recycling yards adjacent to interstate highways, and turnpikes, see RSA 236:90 et seq.

Junk and scrap metal dealers, see RSA 322.

Motor vehicle junk dealers, see RSA 261:123 et seq.

Prohibition against siting of junk yards under Groundwater Protection Act, see RSA 485-C:12.

Transporting of junk motor vehicles, see RSA 266:69.

236:111. Purposes.

This subdivision is adopted under the police power of the state to conserve and safeguard the public safety, health, morals, and welfare, and to further the economic growth and stability of the people of the state through encouragement to the development of the tourist industry within the state. A clean, wholesome, attractive environment is declared to be of importance to the health and safety of the inhabitants and the safeguarding of their material rights against unwarrantable invasion. In addition, such an environment is considered essential to the maintenance and continued development of the tourist and recreational industry which is hereby declared to be of significant and proven importance to the economy of the state and the general welfare of its citizens. At the same time, it is recognized that the maintenance of junk yards as defined in this subdivision, is a useful and necessary business and ought to be encouraged when not in conflict with the express purposes of this subdivision.

HISTORY:
RSA 267-A:1. 1965, 372:1. 1981, 87:1, eff. April 20, 1981. 1999, 288:2, eff. Sept. 14, 1999. 2002, 27:1, eff. July 1, 2002.

Amendments

—2002.
Deleted the fifth sentence.

—1999.
Rewrote the last sentence.

NOTES TO DECISIONS

Analysis

1. Applicability
2. Construction with other law
3. Preemption

1. Applicability
The local licensing provisions of RSA 236:111– 236:129 did not apply to a junkyard located adjacent to an interstate highway. Corey v. Town of Merrimack, 140 N.H. 426, 666 A.2d 1359, 1995 N.H. LEXIS 164 (N.H. 1995).

2. Construction with other law
Law governing the licensing of established junkyards is a pure licensing scheme because it is concerned with the proper operation of junkyards, not uniformity of land use and stability of community growth. Therefore, because licensing and zoning were distinct, an applicant's failure to obtain a junkyard license did not divest his junkyard of its status as a nonconforming use. Guy v. Town of Temple, 157 N.H. 642, 956 A.2d 272, 2008 N.H. LEXIS 106 (N.H. 2008).

3. Preemption
The trial court erred by ruling that the town's licensing requirements were per se arbitrary and unreasonable because the town lacked authority to license the junkyard under the legislature's bifurcated scheme; the statutory scheme was concerned with the location and effective control of junkyards near certain highways, but did not purport to be a comprehensive regulatory scheme. Corey v. Town of Merrimack, 140 N.H. 426, 666 A.2d 1359, 1995 N.H. LEXIS 164 (N.H. 1995).

236:111-a. Scope.

I. Except as provided by paragraphs II and III, the provisions of this subdivision shall apply to all junk yards, as defined by RSA 236:112, I, including those approved under RSA 149-M and those subject to regulation under RSA 236:90–110.

II. The provisions of this subdivision shall not apply to any junk yard that is also a type of solid waste management facility listed below and approved under RSA 149-M, including any such solid waste management facility approved prior to May 1, 1989:

(a) Landfills;

(b) Incinerators and other processing or treatment facilities, not including automotive recycling yards; and

(c) Transfer stations that collect, store, and transfer municipal solid waste, whether or not they also collect:

(1) Source separated waste derived from motor vehicles, such as tires, lead acid batteries, or used oil; and/or

(2) Common household or commercial machinery, such as appliances, office equipment, or lawn mowers.

III. The provisions of this subdivision shall not apply to any noncommercial antique motor vehicle restoration activities involving antique motor vehicles over 25 years old, where the owner or lessee demonstrates that each of the following requirements are met:

(a) All antique motor vehicles kept on the premises are owned by the property owner or lessee; and

(b) All antique motor vehicles and parts of antique motor vehicles are kept out of view of the public and abutters by means of storage inside a permanent structure, or by suitable fencing which complies with the fencing requirements of RSA 236:123, or by trees or shrubbery sufficient to block visual access year round; and

(c) Any combination of antique motor vehicles or parts of antique motor vehicles that are not stored inside a permanent structure shall otherwise comply with the requirements of this section and shall not exceed a total amount of 5 vehicles. For purposes of this section, the sum of the parts of antique motor vehicles that equal in bulk to one antique motor vehicle shall be counted as one antique motor vehicle; and

(d) All mechanical repairs and modifications are performed out of view of the public and abutters; and

(e) Not more than one unregistered and uninspected motor vehicle that is not over 25 years old shall be kept on the premises; and

(f) The use of the premises is in compliance with all municipal land use ordinances and regulations.

HISTORY:
1989, 95:1, eff. May 1, 1989. 2002, 27:2, eff. July 1, 2002. 228:1, 2, eff. at 12:01 a.m, July 1, 2002.

Revision note.
Substituted "May 1, 1989" for "the effective date of this section" in par. II for purposes of clarity.

Amendments

—2002.
Chapter 27:2 rewrote the section to the extent that a detailed comparison would be impracticable.

Chapter 228:1 substituted "paragraphs II and III" for "paragraph II" in par. I.

Chapter 228:2 added par. III.

RESEARCH REFERENCES AND PRACTICE AIDS

New Hampshire Practice.

16-50 N.H.P. Municipal Law & Taxation § 50.13.

236:112. Definitions.

For the purposes of this subdivision:

I. "Junk yard" means a place used for storing and keeping, or storing and selling, trading, or otherwise transferring old or scrap copper, brass, rope, rags, batteries, paper, trash, rubber debris, waste, or junked, dismantled, or wrecked motor vehicles, or parts thereof, iron, steel, or other old or scrap ferrous or nonferrous material. As used in this subdivision, the term includes, but is not limited to, the following types of junk yards:

(a) Automotive recycling yards, meaning a motor vehicle junk yard, as identified in subparagraph (c), the primary purpose of which is to salvage multiple motor vehicle parts and materials for recycling or reuse;

(b) Machinery junk yards, as defined in paragraph III; and

(c) Motor vehicle junk yards, meaning any place, not including the principal place of business of any motor vehicle dealer registered with the director of motor vehicles under RSA 261:104 and controlled under RSA 236:126, where the following are stored or deposited in a quantity equal in bulk to 2 or more motor vehicles:

(1) Motor vehicles which are no longer intended or in condition for legal use according to their original purpose including motor vehicles purchased for the purpose of dismantling the vehicles for parts or for use of the metal for scrap; and/or

(2) Used parts of motor vehicles or old iron, metal, glass, paper, cordage, or other waste or discarded or secondhand material which has been a part, or intended to be a part, of any motor vehicle.

II. "Local governing body" means the mayor and board of aldermen or the council of a city, the selectmen of a town, or the commissioners of a village district.

III. "Machinery junk yard" means any yard or field used as a place of storage in which there is displayed to the public view, junk machinery or scrap metal that occupies an area of 500 square feet.

IV. "Motor vehicle" means "motor vehicle" as defined by RSA 259:60, I, namely, any self-propelled vehicle not operated exclusively upon stationary tracks, including ski area vehicles.

V. "Motor vehicle dealer."

(a) "New motor vehicle dealer" means every person principally engaged in the business of buying, selling or exchanging new and second-hand motor vehicles, or tractors on commission or otherwise who maintains in operating condition, and in operation, and at which the dealer does a major portion of his business a place of business capable of housing indoors in one building in an area of 1200 square feet, 5 average-sized automobiles, devoted to the motor vehicle, or tractor business and gives mechanical service on the same and who holds a written contract with a manufacturer giving such person selling rights for new motor vehicles, or tractors, or with a distributor of such vehicles who, as such distributor, holds a manufacturer's franchise or contract giving selling rights on new motor vehicles, or tractors.

(b) "Used motor vehicle dealer" means every person or firm principally engaged in the business of buying, selling and exchanging secondhand motor vehicles or tractors, who maintains in operating condition and in operation and at which the dealer does the major portion of his business a place of business capable of housing indoors in one building, in an area of at least 1200 square feet, 5 average-sized motor vehicles devoted to the used motor vehicles, or tractor business, and gives mechanical service on the same and at which the repair of used motor vehicles, or tractors is subordinate or incidental to the business of buying, selling and exchanging the same.

(c) "Junk motor vehicle dealer" means any person or firm who has an established place of business at which he is engaged in the business of buying secondhand motor vehicles for the purpose of taking the same apart, or buying, and selling parts of secondhand motor vehicles, or tires, for the assembling of secondhand motor vehicle parts.

HISTORY:

1939, 50:1. RL 165:22. RSA 267:1(b). 267-A:2. 1955, 275:1, par. 22. 1965, 372:1. 1967, 372:2. 1981, 87:1. 1985, 103:7, eff. Jan. 1, 1986. 2002, 27:3, 4, eff. July 1, 2002.

Amendments

—2002.

Paragraph I: Rewritten to the extent that a detailed comparison would be impracticable.

Paragraph IV: Inserted "'motor vehicle' as defined by RSA 259:60, I, namely" following "means" and substituted "including ski area vehicles" for "originally intended for the use on public highways".

—1985.

Paragraph II: Substituted "local governing" for "legislative" preceding "body" at the beginning of the paragraph.

NOTES TO DECISIONS

Analysis

1. Relation to other laws
2. Used motor vehicle dealers

1. Relation to other laws

In order to qualify as a motor vehicle junkyard under a city ordinance, the property had to contain two or more vehicles that were both unregistered and no longer intended for legal use on the public highways, and thus, a city ordinance effectively made it more difficult for a property to be classified as a motor vehicle junkyard because it contained an extra requirement not present in RSA 236:112, I(c)(1). Therefore, there was an actual conflict between RSA 236:112, I(c)(1) and the city ordinance, and since the express language of RSA 236:124 provided that state statutes in that particular field were intended to aid local ordinances, the city's ordinance controlled over the conflicting statutory provision set forth in RSA 236:112, I(c)(1). City of Rochester v. Corpening, 153 N.H. 571, 907 A.2d 383, 2006 N.H. LEXIS 73 (N.H. 2006).

2. Used motor vehicle dealers

On petition for mandatory injunction ordering defendants to remove all junk from their property so as to comply with provisions relative to junk yards along federally funded highways, trial court erred in finding that defendants were entitled to exemption for used motor vehicle dealers; in order to qualify for such exception under RSA 236:91, IV, used vehicle dealer must satisfy definition set forth in subparagraph V(b) of this section in order to be controlled under RSA 236:126. State v. Autoware, Inc., 133 N.H. 465, 578 A.2d 351, 1990 N.H. LEXIS 85 (N.H. 1990).

RESEARCH REFERENCES AND PRACTICE AIDS

New Hampshire Practice.
16-50 N.H.P. Municipal Law & Taxation § 50.13.

236:113. Minimum Area Waiver Authorized.

The director of motor vehicles may in his discretion and after a public hearing waive the minimum 1200 square foot requirement specified in RSA 236:112, V(a) and (b).

HISTORY:
RSA 267-A:2-a. 1975, 121:2. 1981, 87:1, eff. April 20, 1981.

236:114. Requirement for Operation or Maintenance.

A person shall not operate, establish, or maintain a junk yard or machinery junk yard until he (1) has obtained a license to operate a junk yard business and (2) has obtained a certificate of approval for the location of the junk yard.

HISTORY:
RSA 267-A:3. 1965, 372:1. 1981, 87:1, eff. April 20, 1981.

NOTES TO DECISIONS

Cited:
Cited in Town of Henniker v. Homo, 136 N.H. 88, 612 A.2d 360, 1992 N.H. LEXIS 132 (1992).

236:115. Application for License and Certificate of Approval.

Application for the license and the certificate of approved location shall be made in writing to the local governing body of the municipality where it is proposed to locate the junk yard or automotive recycling yard. In municipalities having a zoning ordinance and a zoning board of adjustment, the application must be accompanied by a certificate from the board of adjustment that the proposed location is not within an established district restricted against such uses or otherwise contrary to

the prohibitions of the zoning ordinance. The application shall include:

I. A description of the land to be included within the junk yard or automotive recycling yard, by reference to so-called permanent boundary markers.

II. Certification of compliance with best management practices established by the department of environmental services, for applications to establish automotive recycling yards and motor vehicle junk yards.

HISTORY:
RSA 267-A:4. 1965, 372:1. 1981, 87:1. 1985, 103:8. 1992, 88:12, eff. Jan. 1, 1993. 2006, 100:1, eff. January 1, 2007.

Amendments

—2006.
Rewritten to the extent that a detailed comparison would be impracticable.

—1992.
Added "or automotive recycling yard" following "junk yard" in the first and third sentences.

—1985.
Substituted "local governing" for "legislative" preceding "body" in the first sentence.

236:116. Time of Hearing.

A hearing on the application shall be held within the municipality not less than 2 nor more than 4 weeks from the date of the receipt of the application by the local governing body. Notice of the hearing shall be given to the applicant by mail, postage prepaid, to the address given in the application and the notice shall be published once in a newspaper having a circulation within the municipality, which publication shall be not less than 7 days before the date of the hearing.

HISTORY:
RSA 267-A:5. 1965, 372:1. 1981, 87:1. 1985, 103:9, eff. Jan. 1, 1986.

Amendments

—1985.
Substituted "local governing" for "legislative" preceding "body" at the end of the first sentence.

236:117. License Requirements.

At the time and place set for hearing, the local governing body shall hear the applicant and all other persons wishing to be heard on the application for a license to operate, establish, or maintain the junk yard or automotive recycling yard. In passing upon the application, it shall take into account the suitability of the applicant with reference to his ability to comply with the fencing requirements or other reasonable regulations concerning the proposed junk yard or automotive recycling yard, to any record of convictions for any type of larceny or receiving of stolen goods, and to any other matter within the purposes of this subdivision.

HISTORY:
RSA 267-A:6. 1965, 372:1. 1981, 87:1. 1985, 103:10. 1992, 88:13, eff. Jan. 1, 1993.

Amendments

—1992.
Added "or automotive recycling yard" following "junk yard" in the first and second sentences.

—1985.
Substituted "local governing" for "legislative" preceding "body" in the first sentence.

236:118. Location Requirements.

I. At the time and place set for hearing, the local governing body shall hear the applicant and all other persons wishing to be heard on the application for certificate of approval for the location of the junk yard or automotive recycling yard. In passing upon the application, after proof of legal ownership or right to the use of the property by the applicant for the license period, it shall take into account the nature and development of surrounding property, such as the proximity of churches, schools, hospitals, public buildings or other places of public gatherings; and whether or not the use of that proposed location can be reasonably prevented from affecting the public health, safety, or morals by reason of offensive or unhealthy odors or smoke, or of other causes.

II. In no case may a license be granted for a new junk yard or automotive recycling yard located less than 1,000 feet from the right-of-way lines of an interstate highway.

III. Unless a lesser setback is allowed by local zoning ordinance, or an ordinance adopted pursuant to paragraph IV, in no case may a license be granted for a new junk yard or automotive recycling yard located:

(a) Less than 660 feet from the right-of-way lines of a non-interstate class I, class II, class III, or class III-a highway; or

(b) Less than 300 feet from the right-of-way lines of class IV, class V, and class VI highways.

IV. In a municipality that has not enacted a zoning ordinance, the local governing body may adopt an ordinance establishing lesser setback requirements than those established in paragraph III.

HISTORY:
RSA 267-A:7. 1965, 372:1. 1981, 87:1. 1985, 103:11. 1992, 265:18, eff. July 1, 1992. 265:21, eff. Jan. 1, 1993. 2008, 164:7, eff. August 5, 2008. 2012, 108:1, eff. July 28, 2012.

Amendment Notes

—2012.
The 2012 amendment added "or an ordinance adopted pursuant to paragraph IV" in the introductory language of III and added IV.

—2008.
The 2008 amendment added designations I and II; in II, substituted "1,000 feet" for "660 feet" and "an interstate highway" for

"class I, class II, class III or class III-a highways or located less than 300 feet from the right-of-way lines of class IV, class V and class VI highways"; and added III.

—1992.
Chapter 265:18 deleted "and" preceding "class III" and inserted "or class III-a" thereafter in the third sentence.
Chapter 265:21 inserted "or automotive recycling yard" following "junk yard" in the first and third sentences.

—1985.
Substituted "local governing" for "legislative" preceding "body" in the first sentence and made other minor stylistic changes throughout the section.

Nullification of 1992 amendment.
1992, 88:14, provided for the amendment of this section; however, under the terms of 1992, 265:22, the amendment did not take effect.

RESEARCH REFERENCES AND PRACTICE AIDS

Cross References.
Classification of highways, see RSA229:5.

New Hampshire Practice.
16-50 N.H.P. Municipal Law & Taxation § 50.13.

236:119. Nuisance.

Any junk yard or machinery junk yard located or maintained in violation of the provisions of this subdivision is hereby declared a nuisance, and the same may be abated on complaint of any prosecuting officer as provided in RSA 236:128.

HISTORY:
1939, 50:3. RL 165:24. RSA 267:3. 1955, 275:1, par. 24. 1981, 87:1, eff. April 20, 1981. 2003, 118:1, eff. Jan. 1, 2004.

Amendments

—2003.
Added "as provided in RSA 236:128" following "prosecuting officer".

236:120. Aesthetic Considerations.

At the hearing regarding location of the junk yard or automotive recycling yard, the local governing body may also take into account the clean, wholesome, and attractive environment which has been declared to be of vital importance to the continued stability and development of the tourist and recreational industry of the state and the general welfare of its citizens by considering whether or not the use of the proposed location can be reasonably prevented from having an unfavorable effect thereon. In this connection the local governing body may consider collectively the type of road servicing the junk yard or automotive recycling yard or from which the junk yard or automotive recycling yard may be seen, the natural or artificial barriers protecting the junk yard or automotive recycling yard from view, the proximity of the proposed junk yard or automotive recycling yard to established tourist and recreational areas or main access routes thereto, as well as the reasonable availability of other suitable sites for the junk yard or automotive recycling yard.

HISTORY:
    RSA 267-A:8. 1965, 372:1. 1981, 87:1. 1985, 103:12. 1992, 88:15, eff. Jan. 1, 1993.

Amendments

—1992.
    Inserted "or automotive recycling yard" following "junk yard" wherever it appeared.

—1985.
    Substituted "local governing" for "legislative" preceding "body" in the first and second sentences.

236:121.   Grant or Denial of Application; Renewal; Appeal.

I. After the hearing the local governing body shall, within 2 weeks, make a finding as to whether or not the application should be granted, giving notice of their finding to the applicant by mail, postage prepaid, to the address given on the application. If approved, the license, including the certificate of approved location, shall be forthwith issued to remain in effect until the following July 1. Approval is personal to the applicant and is not assignable.

II. Licenses shall be renewed thereafter upon payment of the annual license fee without a hearing, if all provisions of this subdivision are complied with during the license period, if the junk yard does not become a public nuisance under the common law or is not a nuisance under RSA 236:119, and if the applicant is not convicted of any type of larceny or of receiving stolen goods. In addition, applications to renew a license to operate an automotive recycling yard or motor vehicle junk yard shall include certification of compliance with best management practices established by the department of environmental services for the automobile salvage industry.

III. A writ of certiorari lies from the denial of the application to the superior court of the county in which the proposed location is situated.

HISTORY:
    RSA 267-A:9. 1965, 372:1. 1981, 87:1. 1985, 103:13, eff. Jan. 1, 1986. 2006, 100:2, eff. January 1, 2007. 2009, 120:1, eff. July 1, 2009.

Amendment Notes

—2009.
    The 2009 amendment substituted "July 1" for "April 1" at the end of the second sentence of I.

—2006.
    Rewritten to the extent that a detailed comparison would be impracticable.

—1985.
    Substituted "local governing" for "legislative" preceding "body" in the first sentence.

Licenses Issued Prior to Effective Date.
    2009, 120:2, eff. July 1, 2009, provided: "All licenses issued pursuant to RSA 236:121 before the effective date of this act [July 1, 2009] shall remain effective until July 1, 2010."

236:122.   License Fees.

The annual license fee is not more than $250 to be paid at the time the application is made and annually thereafter in the event of renewal. If the application is not granted, the fee shall be returned to the applicant.

HISTORY:
    RSA 267-A:10. 1965, 372:1. 1981, 87:1, eff. April 20, 1981. 2006, 71:1, eff. April 25, 2006.

Amendments

—2006.
    Substituted "fee is not more than $250" for "fee is $25".

236:123.   Fencing.

Before use, a new junk yard or automotive recycling yard shall be completely surrounded with a solidly constructed fence at least 6 feet in height which substantially screens the area and with a suitable gate which shall be closed and locked except during the working hours of the junk yard or automotive recycling yard or when the applicant or his agent is within. All motor vehicles and parts stored or deposited by the applicant shall be kept within the enclosure of the junk yard or automotive recycling yard except as removal is necessary for its transportation in the reasonable course of the business. All wrecking or other work on such motor vehicles and parts and all burning of vehicles shall be accomplished within the enclosure. Where the topography, natural growth of timber, a natural barrier, or other considerations accomplish the purposes of this subdivision in whole or in part, the fencing requirements hereunder may be reduced by the local governing body, upon granting the license. Any citizen of the municipality may apply for writ of certiorari to the superior court for the county in which the new junk yard or automotive recycling yard is located to review the action of the local governing body.

HISTORY:
    RSA 267-A:11. 1965, 372:1. 1981, 87:1. 1985, 103:14. 1992, 88:16, eff. Jan. 1, 1993.

Amendments

—1992.
    Inserted "or automotive recycling yard" following "junk yard" in two places in the first sentence and in the second and fifth sentences.

—1985.
    Substituted "local governing" for "legislative" preceding "body" wherever it appeared in the second paragraph.

236:124.   Effect of Local Ordinances.

This subdivision is not in derogation of zoning ordinances or ordinances for the control of junk yards now or hereafter established within the proper exercise of the police power granted to municipalities, but rather is in aid thereof. Specific local ordinances shall control when in conflict with this subdivision.

HISTORY:
RSA 267-A:12. 1965, 372:1. 1981, 87:1, eff. April 20, 1981.

NOTES TO DECISIONS

Cited:
Cited in Town of Henniker v. Homo, 136 N.H. 88, 612 A.2d 360, 1992 N.H. LEXIS 132 (1992).

236:125. Established Junk Yards or Automotive Recycling Yards.

For the purposes of this subdivision the location of junk yards or automotive recycling yards already established are considered approved by the local governing body of the municipality where located and the owner of the yard considered suitable for the issuance of a license. Within 60 days from the passage of this subdivision, however, the owner shall furnish the local governing body the information as to location which is required in an application, together with the license fee, and the local governing body shall issue him a license valid until April 1, 1966, at which time the owner may apply for a renewal. The owner shall comply with all other provisions of this subdivision including the fencing requirements set forth in RSA 236:123.

HISTORY:
RSA 267-A:13. 1965, 372:1. 1981, 87:1. 1985, 103:15. 1992, 88:17, eff. Jan. 1, 1993.

Amendments

—1992.
Added "or automotive recycling yards" following "junk yards" in the section catchline and in the first sentence.

—1985.
Substituted "local governing" for "legislative" preceding "body" throughout the first and second sentences.

NOTES TO DECISIONS

Analysis

1. Applicability
2. Licensing requirements

1. Applicability
Nothing in the language of RSA 236:125, which requires furnishing information as to location which is required in an application, suggests that the remedy for failure to submit such an application is to subject established junkyards to the licensing process for new junkyards. Thus, because RSA 236:125 applied to an applicant's case, and because licensing was distinct from zoning, his failure to obtain a license did not divest his junkyard of its status as a nonconforming use. Guy v. Town of Temple, 157 N.H. 642, 956 A.2d 272, 2008 N.H. LEXIS 106 (N.H. 2008).

2. Licensing requirements
RSA 236:125 did not require a town to issue an applicant a junkyard license. He had to comply with all of the requirements in the licensing statute in order to obtain a license to operate his junkyard, as well as a renewal of such license. Guy v. Town of

Temple, 157 N.H. 642, 956 A.2d 272, 2008 N.H. LEXIS 106 (N.H. 2008).

RESEARCH REFERENCES AND PRACTICE AIDS

References in text.
The date of passage of this subdivision, referred to in the second sentence, was April 20, 1981.

236:126. Motor Vehicle Dealers.

Both new and used car dealers are hereby required to remove from their premises registered with the director of motor vehicles as their principal place of business any motor vehicle which is of the type referred to in RSA 236:112, I, under the definition of junk yard, within at least 160 days from the date of its original entrance thereon. Any other location within the same community used by such dealer shall be subject to the terms of this subdivision if in its operation it falls within the confines of the definition of the term junk yard as defined in this subdivision.

HISTORY:
RSA 267-A:14. 1965, 372:1. 1969, 189:1. 1981, 87:1, eff. April 20, 1981.

NOTES TO DECISIONS

Used motor vehicle dealers
On petition for mandatory injunction ordering defendants to remove all junk from their property so as to comply with provisions relative to junk yards along federally funded highways, trial court erred in finding that defendants were entitled to exemption for used motor vehicle dealers; in order to qualify for such exception under RSA 236:91, IV, used vehicle dealer must satisfy definition set forth in RSA 236:112, V(b) in order to be controlled under this section. State v. Autoware, Inc., 133 N.H. 465, 578 A.2d 351, 1990 N.H. LEXIS 85 (N.H. 1990).

236:127. Penalty.

Any person who is in violation of any provisions of this subdivision shall be guilty of a violation and each day or fraction thereof shall constitute a separate offense.

HISTORY:
RSA 267-A:15. 1965, 372:1. 1973, 531:89. 1981, 87:1, eff. April 20, 1981.

NOTES TO DECISIONS

Jury trial
Defendants were not entitled to jury trial despite imposition of $6,060 in fines where defendants had committed 606 separate violations of local ordinance against maintaining unlicensed junk yard, since maximum fine for any single violation was $100. Town of Henniker v. Homo, 136 N.H. 88, 612 A.2d 360, 1992 N.H. LEXIS 132 (N.H. 1992), cert. denied, 516 U.S. 949, 116 S. Ct. 392, 133 L. Ed. 2d 313, 1995 U.S. LEXIS 7307 (U.S. 1995).

RESEARCH REFERENCES AND PRACTICE AIDS

Cross References.
Classification of crimes, see RSA 625:9.
Sentences, see RSA 651.

236:128. Local Enforcement; Injunction; Civil Penalties.

The governing body, elected or appointed officers or other appointed agents of a town, city, or unincorporated place, or a private person pursuant to RSA 236:129 may initiate proceedings for the enforcement of the provisions of this subdivision. In addition to the criminal penalty in RSA 236:127, enforcement may be by the following:

I. The local governing body may obtain a mandatory injunction to end the violation.

II. If the local governing body does not obtain such an injunction the attorney general may obtain an injunction in the name of the state.

III. The local governing body or other enforcement official of the town, city, or unincorporated place, after providing notice, may impose a civil penalty of up to $50 for each day upon any person whose land is deemed a nuisance pursuant to RSA 236:119 until such time as the nuisance is removed or abated to the satisfaction of the governing body, or until the owner of the land acquires a license and is in compliance with the provisions of this subdivision. The building inspector or other local official with the authority to enforce the provisions of this section may commence an action to collect the civil penalty in the district court. Imposition of a civil penalty under this paragraph shall not relieve the owner of any requirement to comply with the provisions of this subdivision, nor shall it preclude the imposition of further actions or remedies under this chapter. The proceeds from the assessment of civil penalties under this section shall be for the use of the town, city, or unincorporated place. This paragraph shall not apply to automotive recycling yards and junkyards properly licensed or pending license renewal under this subdivision.

HISTORY:
RSA 267-A:16. 1965, 372:1. 1981, 87:1. 1985, 103:16, eff. Jan. 1, 1986. 2003, 118:2, eff. Jan. 1, 2004.

Amendments

—2003.
Rewritten to the extent that a detailed comparison would be impracticable.

—1985.
Substituted "local governing" for "legislative" preceding "body" throughout the section.

NOTES TO DECISIONS

Cited:
Cited in Town of Henniker v. Homo, 136 N.H. 88, 612 A.2d 360, 1992 N.H. LEXIS 132 (1992).

236:129. Private Persons.

Any person owning real property whose property is directly affected by the site of a junk yard or automotive recycling yard maintained in violation of the provisions of this subdivision may in writing addressed to the local governing body request the local governing body to take appropriate action under this subdivision. A copy of the written communication to the local governing body shall be mailed to the person complained of. If the local governing body shall not, within 30 days thereafter, make a determination that a junk yard or automotive recycling yard does exist and issue the appropriate order, such person may, in his own name and in his own right, seek appropriate injunctive relief for the enforcement of this subdivision in the superior court.

HISTORY:
RSA 267-A:17. 1967, 372:1. 1969, 415:1. 1981, 87:1. 1985, 103:17. 1992, 88:18, eff. Jan. 1, 1993.

Amendments

—1992.
Inserted "or automotive recycling yard" following "junk yard" in the first and third sentences.

—1985.
Substituted "local governing" for "legislative" preceding "body" throughout the section.

TITLE XXXI
TRADE AND COMMERCE

Chapter
356-B. Condominium Act

RESEARCH REFERENCES AND PRACTICE AIDS

Cross References.
Banks and other financial institutions generally, see RSA 383.
Board of accountancy, see RSA 309-B.
Business profits tax, see RSA 77-A.
Certification of nursery stock, plants and seeds, see RSA 433.
Commercial bribery, see RSA 638:7.
Conveyances and mortgages of realty, see RSA 477.
Deceptive business practices, see RSA 638:6.
Disclosure of finance charges for extensions of credit, see RSA 399-B.
Dispensing of generic drugs, see RSA 318.
Fraud on creditors, see RSA 638:9.
Fraudulent use of credit card, see RSA 638:5.
Grading, marking and sale of agricultural and vegetable seeds, see RSA 434.
Hawkers and peddlers, see RSA 320.
Issuing bad checks, see RSA 638:4.
Itinerant vendors, see RSA 321.
Liens generally, see RSA 444.
Meals and rooms tax, see RSA 78-A.
Pawnbrokers, see RSA 398.
Refined petroleum products tax, see RSA 78-C.
Registration, labeling and sale of commercial feed, see RSA 435.
Registration, labeling and sale of economic poisons, see RSA 430.
Registration, labeling and sale of fertilizers, see RSA 431.
Regulation of business corporations generally, see RSA 293-A.
Regulation of consumer cooperative associations, see RSA 301-A.
Regulation of debt adjusters, see RSA 399-D.
Regulation of lenders of money generally, see RSA 399-C.
Regulation of professional corporations, see RSA 294-A.
Regulation of revolving credit plans, see RSA 384-G.
Regulation of small loans, title loans, and payday loans, see RSA 399-A.
Regulation of water well contractors and well pump installers, see RSA 482-B:5.
Retail installment sales generally, see RSA 361-A.
Sale of animals and birds generally, see RSA 437.
Secured transactions, see RSA 382-A:9-101 et seq.
Securities generally, see RSA 421-B.
Sunday business activities, see RSA 332-D.
Taxation of interest and dividend income, see RSA 77.
Timber harvesting, see RSA 227-J.
Uniform Commercial Code, see RSA 382-A.
Water treatment plant operators and water distribution system personnel, see RSA 332-E.

CHAPTER 356-B
CONDOMINIUM ACT

I. General Principles

Section
356-B:3. Definitions.

NOTES TO DECISIONS

Piercing corporate veil
Setting up a corporation with insufficient assets or plan for assets to meet its expected debts and obligations under this chapter can justify the remedy of piercing the corporate veil. Terren v. Butler, 134 N.H. 635, 597 A.2d 69, 1991 N.H. LEXIS 117 (N.H. 1991).

Cited:
Cited in Davis v. Barrington, 127 N.H. 202, 497 A.2d 1232, 1985 N.H. LEXIS 387 (1985); Aranson v. Schroeder, 140 N.H. 359, 671 A.2d 1023, 1995 N.H. LEXIS 157 (1995); LSP Ass'n v. Town of Gilford, 142 N.H. 369, 702 A.2d 795, 1997 N.H. LEXIS 106 (1997).

RESEARCH REFERENCES AND PRACTICE AIDS

Cross References.
Land sales full disclosure generally, see RSA 356-A.
Protection of tenants in conversion of rental units, see RSA 356-C.
Unit ownership of real property generally, see RSA 479-A.

I. General Principles

356-B:3. Definitions.

In this chapter:

I. "Board of directors" means an executive and administrative entity, by whatever name denominated, designated in the condominium instruments as the governing body of the unit owners' association.

II. "Common area" or "common areas" means all portions of the condominium other than the units.

III. "Common expenses" means all expenditures lawfully made or incurred by or on behalf of the unit owners' association, together with all funds lawfully assessed for the creation and/or maintenance of reserves pursuant to the provisions of the condominium instruments; "future common expenses" shall mean common expenses for which assessments are not yet due and payable.

IV. "Common profits" means all income collected or accrued by or on behalf of the unit owners' association, other than income derived from assessments pursuant to RSA 356-B:45.

V. "Condominium" means real property, and any interests therein, lawfully submitted to this chapter by the recordation of condominium instruments pursuant to the provisions of this chapter. No project shall be deemed a condominium within the meaning of this chapter unless the undivided interests in the common area are vested in the unit owners.

VI. "Condominium instruments" is a collective term referring to the declaration, bylaws, and site plans and floor plans, recorded pursuant to the provisions of this chapter. Any exhibit, schedule, or certification accompanying a condominium instrument and recorded simultaneously therewith shall be deemed an integral part of that condominium instrument. Any amendment or certification of any condominium instrument shall, from the time of the recordation of such amendment or certification, be deemed an integral part of the affected condominium instrument, so long as such amendment or certification was made in accordance with the provisions of this chapter.

VII. "Condominium unit" means a unit together with the undivided interest in the common area appertaining to that unit.

VIII. "Contractable condominium" means a condominium from which one or more portions of the submitted land may be withdrawn in accordance with the provisions of the declaration and of this chapter. If such withdrawal can occur only by the expiration or termination of one or more leases, then the condominium shall not be deemed a contractable condominium within the meaning of this chapter.

IX. "Conversion condominium" means a condominium containing structures which before the recording of the declaration were wholly or partially occupied by someone other than the declarant or those who have contracted for the purchase of condominium units and those who occupy with the consent of such purchasers.

X. "Convertible land" means a building site which is a portion of the common area, within which additional units and/or a limited common area may be created in accordance with this chapter.

XI. "Convertible space" means a portion of a structure within the condominium which portion may be converted into one or more units and/or common area, including but not limited to limited common area, in accordance with this chapter.

XII. "Days" mean calendar days, unless modified by the word "business", in which case said term shall include all days except Saturdays, Sundays and legal holidays in the state of New Hampshire.

XIII. "Declarant" means all persons who execute or propose to execute the declaration or on whose behalf the declaration is executed or proposed to be executed. From the time of the recordation of any amendment to the declaration expanding an expandable condominium, all persons who execute that amendment or on whose behalf that amendment is executed shall also come within this definition. Any successors of the persons referred to in this paragraph who come to stand in the same relation to the condominium as their predecessors did shall also come within this definition; provided, however, this definition shall not include any homeowners association which is not controlled by a declarant or any mortgage holder that forecloses on a declarant's interest in the condominium, provided that the foreclosing mortgagee refrains from exercising any of the rights reserved to the declarant by this chapter. A foreclosing mortgagee may transfer all such rights to a successor builder or developer without registration or exemption, provided that prior to such intended transfer, the mortgagee files an affidavit

or with the attorney general identifying the intended transferee by name, address, and telephone number, and listing the number of units or interests remaining in the condominium, and the number of units or interests so transferred.

XIV. "Dispose" or "disposition" refers to any sale, contract, assignment, or any other voluntary transfer of a legal or equitable interest in a condominium unit, except as security for a debt.

XV. "Expandable condominium" means a condominium to which additional land may be added in accordance with the provisions of the declaration and of this chapter.

XVI. "Identifying number" means one or more letters and/or numbers that identify only one unit in the condominium.

XVII. "Institutional lender" means one or more commercial or savings banks, savings and loan associations, trust companies, credit unions, industrial loan associations, insurance companies, pension funds, or business trusts including but not limited to real estate investment trusts, any other lender regularly engaged in financing the purchase, construction, or improvement of real estate, or any assignee of loans made by such a lender, or any combination of any of the foregoing entities.

XVIII. "Interest in a unit" and "interest in a condominium unit", when not modified by the word "undivided," include without limitation any fee simple interest, leasehold interest for a term of more than 5 years, life estate and, for the purposes of this subdivision and subdivision IV, Administration and Enforcement, time sharing interest.

XIX. "Leasehold condominium" means a condominium in all or any portion of which each unit owner owns an estate for years in his unit, or in the land within which or on which that unit is situated, or both, with all such leasehold interests due to expire naturally at the same time. A condominium including leased land, or an interest therein, within which or on which no units are situated or to be situated shall not be deemed a leasehold condominium within the meaning of this chapter, nor shall a condominium be deemed to be a leasehold condominium solely because of the offering or disposition of time sharing interests therein.

XX. "Limited common area" means a portion of the common area reserved for the exclusive use of those entitled to the use of one or more, but less than all, of the units.

XXI. "Nonbinding reservation agreement" means an agreement between the declarant and a prospective purchaser which is in no way binding on the prospective purchaser and which may be cancelled without penalty at the sole discretion of the prospective purchaser by written notice, hand delivered or sent by United States mail, return receipt requested, to the declarant or to any agent of the declarant at any time prior to the formation of a contract for the sale or lease of any interest in a condominium unit. Such agreement shall not contain any provision for waiver or any other provision in derogation of the rights of the prospective purchaser as contemplated by this paragraph, nor shall any such provision be a part of any ancillary agreement.

XXII. "Offer" means any inducement, solicitation, or attempt to encourage any person or persons to acquire any legal or equitable interest in a condominium unit, except as security for a debt.

XXIII. "Officer" means any member of the board of directors or official of the unit owners' association.

XXIV. "Person" means a natural person, corporation, partnership, association, trust, or other entity capable of holding title to real property, or any combination thereof.

XXV. "Publicly held corporation," "subsidiary corporation," "closely held corporation," "hearing" and "broker" have the same meaning as set forth in the respective definitions of such terms in RSA 356-A:1; and "agent" and "blanket encumbrance" have the same meaning as set forth in the respective definitions of such terms in RSA 356-A:1, except that within such definitions references to "developer" or "subdivider" shall mean "declarant," references to "lot" or "lots" shall mean "unit" or "units" and references to "subdivision" shall mean "condominium project."

XXVI. "Purchaser" means any person or persons who acquires by means of a voluntary transfer a legal or equitable interest in a condominium unit, except as security for a debt.

XXVII. "Size" means the number of cubic feet, or the number of square feet of ground and/or floor space, within each unit as computed by reference to the floor plans and rounded off to a whole number. Certain spaces within the units including, without limitation, attic, basement, and/or garage space may but need not be omitted from such calculation or partially discounted by the use of a ratio, so long as the same basis of calculation is employed for all units in the condominium, and so long as that basis is described in the declaration.

XXVIII. "Time sharing interest" means the exclusive right to occupy one or more units for less than 60 days each year for a period of more than 5 years from the date of execution of an instrument for the disposition of such right, regardless of whether such right is accompanied by a fee simple interest or a leasehold interest, or neither of them, in a condominium unit. Time sharing interest shall include "interval ownership interest," "vacation license" or any other similar term.

XXIX. "Unit" shall mean a portion of the condominium designed and intended for individual ownership and use. For the purposes of this chapter, a convertible space shall be treated as a unit in accordance with RSA 356-B:24, IV.

XXX. "Unit owner" means one or more persons who owns a condominium unit, or, in the case of a leasehold condominium, whose leasehold interest or interests in the condominium extend for the entire balance of the unexpired term or terms.

XXXI. "Value" means a number of dollars or points assigned to each unit by the declaration. Substantially identical units shall be assigned the same value, but units located at substantially different heights above the ground, or having substantially different views, or having substantially different amenities or other characteristics that might result in differences in market value, may, but need not, be considered substantially identical within the meaning of this paragraph. If value is stated in terms of dollars, that statement shall not be deemed to reflect or control the sales price or fair market value of any unit, and no opinion, appraisal, or fair market transaction at a different figure shall affect the value of any unit, or any undivided interest in the common area, voting rights in the unit owners' association, liability for common expenses, or rights to common profits, assigned on the basis thereof.

HISTORY:

1977, 468:1. 1992, 278:5, eff. July 17, 1992. 2011, 156:1, eff. August 7, 2011.

Amendment Notes

—2011.

The 2011 amendment, in XIII, added "or any mortgage holder that forecloses on a declarant's interest in the condominium, provided that the foreclosing mortgagee refrains from exercising any of the rights reserved to the declarant by this chapter" in the third sentence and added the last sentence.

—1992.

Paragraph XIII: Added "provided, however, this definition shall not include any homeowners association which is not controlled by a declarant" following "definition" in the third sentence.

NOTES TO DECISIONS

1. Common area

Trial court properly granted summary judgment to a developer in an action by a condominium unit owners' association, arising from a dispute over further development of condominium land, as pursuant to the plain language of the Condominium Act, there was no need to convert the common area into units because no units were built on any portion of the condominium previously identified as "common area," the developer did not plan to do so in the future, and the units were always identified as units. Condominiums at Lilac Lane Unit Owners' Association v. Monument Garden, 170 N.H. 124, 166 A.3d 221, 2017 N.H. LEXIS 105 (N.H. 2017).

Trial court properly granted summary judgment to a developer in an action by a condominium unit owners' association, arising from a dispute over further development of condominium land, as pursuant to the plain language of the Condominium Act, there was no need to convert the common area into units because no units were built on any portion of the condominium previously identified as "common area," the developer did not plan to do so in the future, and the units were always identified as units. Condominiums at Lilac Lane Unit Owners' Association v. Monument Garden, 170 N.H. 124, 166 A.3d 221, 2017 N.H. LEXIS 105 (N.H. 2017).

Under a condominium declaration and the New Hampshire Condominium Act, RSA 356-B:3, XX, limited common area was a subset of the common area; the upper surface of the attic spaces in which mold was discovered did not have an inside lining of finished or unfinished material that comprised a ceiling, and since the beams, supports, and roof were defined to be limited common area, they could not also be part of a unit, and could not constitute a ceiling in a unit. Carleton v. Edgewood Heights Condo. Owners' Ass'n, 156 N.H. 407, 938 A.2d 120, 2007 N.H. LEXIS 200 (N.H. 2007).

Trial court properly granted summary judgment to a developer in an action by a condominium unit owners' association, arising from a dispute over further development of condominium land, as pursuant to the plain language of the Condominium Act, there was no need to convert the common area into units because no units were built on any portion of the condominium previously identified as "common area," the developer did not plan to do so in the future, and the units were always identified as units. Condominiums at Lilac Lane Unit Owners' Association v. Monument Garden, 170 N.H. 124, 166 A.3d 221, 2017 N.H. LEXIS 105 (N.H. 2017).

Cited:

Cited in Appeal of New Eng. Mktg. Assocs., 128 N.H. 750, 519 A.2d 303, 1986 N.H. LEXIS 359 (1986).

TITLE XXXIX
AERONAUTICS

RESEARCH REFERENCES AND PRACTICE AIDS

Cross References.
Airboats, see RSA 270:25-a.
Filing of aircraft insurance policies, see RSA 412-A.
Leasing of air rights, see RSA 48-B.
Liens on aircraft, see RSA 450.

CHAPTER 424
AIRPORT ZONING

Effective date of 1985 amendment.
1985, 402:41, II, provided that the provisions of 1985, 402:6 which affected this chapter would take effect when the department of transportation became operational on the date set according to 1983, 372:5, II. Pursuant to 1983, 372:5, II, the joint committee on implementation of reorganization and the govern determined the effective date upon which the department became operational to be Feb. 28, 1986.

Separability clause.
1941, 145:1–9 were subject to a separability clause. See 1945, 145:10.

RESEARCH REFERENCES AND PRACTICE AIDS

Cross References.
Control of tall structures, see RSA 422-B.
Zoning generally, see RSA 672 et seq.

424:1. Definitions.

As used in this chapter unless the context otherwise requires:

I. "Airport" means any area of land or water, whether constructed or not, which has been approved by the commissioner as a site for the landing and taking-off of aircraft or utilized or to be utilized by the public as a point of arrival or departure by air.

II. "Airport hazard" means any structure, tree, smoke, steam, dust or other substance which obstructs the aerial approaches of a publicly owned airport or impairs the reasonable visibility in the vicinity thereof, electrical impulses and distur-bances which interfere with radio aids or communi-cations and lights which might result in glare in the vision of pilots of aircraft or be confused with airport lights.

III. An airport is "publicly-owned" if the portion thereof used for the landing and taking-off of air-craft is owned by a governmental body, political subdivision, public agency, or other public corpora-tion.

IV. "Department" means the department of trans-portation.

V. "Person" means any individual, firm, co-part-nership, corporation, company, association, joint stock association or body politic, and includes any trustee, receiver, assignee, or other similar repre-sentative thereof.

VI. "Structure" means any object constructed or installed by man, including such objects although regulated or licensed by other provisions of law.

VII. "Tree" means any object of natural growth.

HISTORY:
1941, 145:1. 199:40. RL 51:78. RSA 424:1. 1955, 58:1. 1985, 402:6, I(c)(3), 32.

Effective date of 1985 amendment.
See note preceding RSA 424:1 regarding effective date of 1985, 402:6.

Amendments

—1985.
Paragraph I: Substituted "commissioner" for "director of aero-nautics" preceding "as a site".
Paragraph IV: Rewritten to the extent that a detailed comparison would be impracticable.

—1955.
Paragraphs I, II: Rewritten to the extent that a detailed compari-son would be impracticable.

RESEARCH REFERENCES AND PRACTICE AIDS

References in text.
The commissioner referred to in this section is the commissioner of transportation. For provisions relating to the department of transportation, see RSA 21-L.

424:2. Airport Hazards Not in Public Interest.

It is hereby found and declared that an airport hazard endangers the lives and property of users of the airport and of occupants of land in its vicinity, and also, if of the obstruction type, in effect reduces the size of the area available for the landing, taking-off and maneuvering of aircraft, thus tending to destroy or impair the utility of the airport and the public investment therein, and is therefore not in the interest of the public health, public safety, or general welfare.

HISTORY:
1941, 145:2. RL 51:79.

424:3. Preparation of Airport-Approach Plans.

The department of transportation is hereby empowered and directed to formulate and adopt, and from time to time as may be necessary revise, an airport-approach plan for each publicly-owned airport in the state. Each such plan shall indicate the circumstances in which structures and trees are or would be airport hazards, the area within which measures for the protection of the airport's aerial approaches should be taken, and what the height limits and other objectives of such measures should be. In adopting or revising any such plan, the department shall consider, among other things, the character of the flying operations expected to be conducted at the airport, the nature of the terrain, the height of existing structures and trees above the level of the airport, and the practicability of lowering or removing existing obstructions, and all other material matters, and the department may obtain and consider the views of the agency of the federal government charged with the fostering of civil aeronautics as to the aerial approaches necessary to safe flying operations at the airport.

HISTORY:
    1941, 145:3. RL 51:80. RSA 424:3. 1985, 402:6, I(c)(3)

Effective date of 1985 amendment.
    See note preceding RSA 424:1 regarding effective date of 1985, 402:6.

Amendments

—1985.
    Substituted "department of transportation" for "aeronautics commission" at the beginning of the first sentence, "department" for "commission" in two places in the third sentence.

NOTES TO DECISIONS

Cited:
    Cited in Treisman v. Bedford, 132 N.H. 54, 563 A.2d 786, 1989 N.H. LEXIS 75 (1989).

RESEARCH REFERENCES AND PRACTICE AIDS

Cross References.
    Fees of department of transportation for rendition of services under section, see RSA 422:37.

424:4. Privately-owned Airports.

The department of transportation is hereby empowered and directed to formulate and adopt, and from time to time as may be necessary revise, an airport-approach plan for such airports as are privately owned but which have been licensed for commercial operation, have facilities available for public use and are necessary in the opinion of the department for the maintenance of an effective airway system in the state. Every privately-owned airport so designated by the department is hereby declared to be eligible for zoning protection and for the purposes hereof shall be deemed to be a publicly-owned airport for the purposes of airport zoning as provided in this chapter.

HISTORY:
    1949, 53:2. RSA 424:4. 1985, 402:6, I(c)(3)

Effective date of 1985 amendment.
    See note preceding RSA 424:1 regarding effective date of 1985, 402:6.

Amendments

—1985.
    Substituted "department of transportation" for "aeronautics commission" preceding "is hereby" and "department" for "commission" preceding "for the maintenance" in the first sentence and following "designated by the" in the second sentence.

NOTES TO DECISIONS

Noncommercial heliports
    This section did not invalidate town zoning amendment allowing the storage and operation of helicopters, since helicopter amendment applied only to private, noncommercial heliports. Treisman v. Bedford, 132 N.H. 54, 563 A.2d 786, 1989 N.H. LEXIS 75 (N.H. 1989).

Cited:
    Cited in In re Opinion of Justices, 95 N.H. 548, 65 A.2d 700, 1949 N.H. LEXIS 221 (1949).

RESEARCH REFERENCES AND PRACTICE AIDS

Cross References.
    State airways system, see RSA 422:15.

424:5. Adoption of Airport Zoning Regulations.

I. Every town having within its territorial limits an airport, or an area approved as an airport site by the commissioner, shall adopt, administer and enforce, under the police power and in the manner and upon the conditions hereinafter prescribed, airport zoning regulations applicable to such area, which regulations shall divide the area into zones, and, within such zones, specify the land uses permitted, regulate and restrict the height to which structures or trees may be erected or allowed to grow, and regulate and restrict the creation and discharge of smoke, steam, dust or other obstructions to visibility, electrical impulses and disturbances which interfere with radio aids or communication and regulate and restrict lighting as may be necessary to effectuate the safe approach to the airport.

II. In the event that a town has adopted, or hereafter adopts, a general zoning ordinance regulating, among other things, the height of buildings, any airport zoning regulations adopted for the same area or portion thereof under this chapter, may be incorporated in and made a part of such general zoning regulations, and be administered and enforced in connection therewith, but such general zoning regulations shall not limit the effectiveness or scope of the regulations adopted hereunder.

III. Any zoning or other regulations applicable to any area within which, according to an airport-approach plan adopted by the department, measures should be taken for the protection of airport approaches, including not only any airport zoning regulations adopted under this chapter but any zoning or other regulations dealing with the same or similar matters that have been or may be adopted under authority other than that conferred by this chapter, shall be consistent with, and conform to, the department's approach plan for such area, and shall be amended from time to time as may be necessary to conform to any revision of the plan that may be made by the department.

IV. All airport zoning regulations adopted hereunder shall be reasonable, and none shall require the removal, lowering, or other change or alteration of any structure or tree not conforming to the regulations when adopted or amended, or otherwise interfere with the continuance of any nonconforming use, except as provided in RSA 424:6, I.

V. If any city or town fails to adopt within a reasonable time airport zoning regulations, the department may, for the protection of the public safety, adopt and from time to time as may be necessary amend or repeal such regulations for such city or town until airport zoning regulations herein provided for are adopted by such city or town.

HISTORY:

1941, 145:4. RL 51:81. RSA 424:5. 1955, 58:2. 1985, 402:6, I(c)(3)

Effective date of 1985 amendment.

See note preceding RSA 424:1 regarding effective date of 1985, 402:6.

Amendments

—1985.

Paragraph I: Substituted "commissioner" for "director" following "site by the".

Paragraph III: Substituted "department" for "commission" preceding "measures", "department's" for "commission's" following "conform to, the" and "department" for "commission" following "may be made by the".

Paragraph V: Substituted "department" for "commission" preceding "may, for the protection".

—1955.

Paragraph I: Rewritten to the extent that a detailed comparison would be impracticable.

NOTES TO DECISIONS

Analysis

1. Construction with other laws
2. Noncommercial heliports

1. Construction with other laws

The fact that a town, in adopting a zoning ordinance, had complied with the requirements of this chapter, relating to airport zoning, did not render compliance with former RSA 31:60–89 unnecessary, and zoning ordinance which did not provide for board of adjustment required by former RSA 31:66 was, therefore, invalid. Jaffrey v. Heffernan, 104 N.H. 249, 183 A.2d 246, 1962 N.H. LEXIS 61 (N.H. 1962).

2. Noncommercial heliports

This section did not invalidate town zoning amendment allowing the storage and operation of helicopters, since helicopter amendment applied only to private, noncommercial heliports. Treisman v. Bedford, 132 N.H. 54, 563 A.2d 786, 1989 N.H. LEXIS 75 (N.H. 1989).

Cited:

Cited in Manchester Airport Auth. v. Romano, 120 N.H. 166, 412 A.2d 1020, 1980 N.H. LEXIS 255 (1980).

RESEARCH REFERENCES AND PRACTICE AIDS

References in text.

The commissioner referred to in this section is the commissioner of transportation. For provisions relating to the department of transportation, see RSA 21-L.

424:6. Permits and Variances.

I. **PERMITS.** Where advisable to facilitate the enforcement of zoning regulations adopted pursuant to this chapter, a system may be established for granting permits to establish or construct new structures and other uses and to replace existing structures and other uses or make substantial changes therein or substantial repairs thereof. In any event, before any nonconforming structure or tree may be replaced, substantially altered or repaired, rebuilt, allowed to grow higher, or replanted, a permit must be secured from the administrative agency authorized to administer and enforce the regulations, authorizing such replacement, change or repair. No such permit shall be granted that would allow the structure or tree in question to be made higher or become a greater hazard to air navigation than it was when the applicable regulation was adopted; and whenever the administrative agency determines that a nonconforming structure or tree has been abandoned or more than 80 percent torn down, destroyed, deteriorated, or decayed: (a) no permit shall be granted that would allow said structure or tree to exceed the applicable height limit or otherwise deviate from the zoning regulations, but a permit shall be issued as of right if the structure as erected or altered is in conformance with the regulations or will not constitute a greater hazard than the structure that is replaced or altered; and (b) whether application is made for a permit under this paragraph or not, the said agency may by appropriate action compel the owner of the nonconforming structure or tree to lower, remove, reconstruct, or equip such object as may be necessary to conform to the regulations. Except as indicated, all applications for permits for replacement, change or repair of nonconforming uses shall be granted.

II. **VARIANCES.** Any person desiring to erect any structure, or increase the height of any structure, or permit the growth of any tree, or otherwise use his property in violation of airport zoning regulations adopted hereunder may apply to the zoning board of adjustment for a variance from the zoning regulations in question. Such variances shall be allowed where a literal application or enforcement of the regulations would result in practical difficulty or unnecessary hardship and the relief granted would not be contrary to the public interest but do substantial justice and be in accordance with the spirit of the regulations.

III. OBSTRUCTION MARKING AND LIGHTING. In granting any permit or variance under this section, the administrative agency or zoning board of adjustment may, if it deems such action advisable to effectuate the purposes hereof and reasonable in the circumstances, so condition such permit or variance as to require the owner of the structure or tree in question to permit the political subdivision, at its own expense, to install, operate, and maintain suitable obstruction markers and obstruction lights thereon.

HISTORY:
   1941, 145:5. RL 51:82. 2001, 40:1, eff. Aug. 7, 2001.

Amendments

—2001.
   Paragraph II: Substituted "zoning board of adjustment" for "board of appeals, as provided herein" in the first sentence.
   Paragraph III: Inserted "zoning board of adjustment" for "board of appeals".

424:6-a. Application of Zoning and Planning Laws.

The provisions of title LXIV shall apply to procedures for adoption of local airport zoning regulations, the administration and enforcement of the requirements of local airport zoning regulations, and procedures for rehearing and appeal from any action taken by a local land use board, building inspector, or the local legislative body with respect to airport zoning regulations.

HISTORY:
   2001, 40:2, eff. Aug. 7, 2001.

RESEARCH REFERENCES AND PRACTICE AIDS

References in text.
   Title LXIV, referred to in this section, is Title 64 of LEXIS New Hampshire Revised Statutes Annotated, which is comprised of chapters 672–678.

424:7. Procedure. [Repealed.]

[Repealed 2001, 40:3, I, eff. Aug. 7, 2001.]

Former section(s).
   Former RSA 424:7, which was derived from 1941, 145:6 and RL 51:83, related to procedure for adoption and administration of airport zoning regulations and board of appeals.

424:8. Applications of Laws. [Repealed.]

[Repealed 2001, 40:3, II, eff. Aug. 7, 2001.]

Former section(s).
   Former RSA 424:8, which was derived from 1941, 145:7 and RL 51:84, related to applications of laws.

424:9.   Enforcement and Remedies. [Repealed.]

[Repealed 2001, 40:3, III, eff. Aug. 7, 2001.]

Former section(s).
   Former RSA 424:9, which was derived from 1941, 145:8; RL 51:85; RSA 424:9; and 1973, 528:291, related to enforcement and remedies.

424:10. Acquisition of Air Rights.

In any case in which: (1) it is desired to remove, lower, or otherwise terminate a nonconforming use; or (2) the approach protection necessary according to the department's airport-approach plan cannot, because of constitutional limitations, be provided by airport zoning regulations hereunder; or (3) it appears advisable that the necessary approach protection be provided by acquisition of property rights rather than by airport zoning regulations, the town within which the property or nonconforming use is located, the town owning the airport or served by it, or the governor and council, upon recommendation of the department, may acquire, by purchase, grant, or condemnation in the manner provided by law by which towns or the governor and council are authorized to acquire real property for public purposes, such an air right, easement, or other estate or interest in the property or nonconforming use in question, and so may acquire a substitute property, structure and easement and convey the same to anyone whose structures, easements and property are or may be a nonconforming use, as may be necessary to effectuate the purposes hereof.

HISTORY:
   1941, 145:9. RL 51:86. RSA 424:10. 1985, 402:6, I(c)(3)

Effective date of 1985 amendment.
   See note preceding RSA 424:1 regarding effective date of 1985, 402:6.

Amendments

—1985.
   Substituted "department's" for "commission's" following "according to the" and "department" for "commission" following "recommendation of the".

RESEARCH REFERENCES AND PRACTICE AIDS

Cross References.
   Eminent domain procedure generally, see RSA 498-A.
   Leasing of air rights, see RSA 48-B.

TITLE XL

AGRICULTURE, HORTICULTURE AND ANIMAL HUSBANDRY

Chapter
432. Soil Conservation and Farmland Preservation

Recodification of title.
1985, 72:1, eff. July 1, 1985, provided for the recodification of Title XL. All relevant notes and annotations appearing under statutory provisions which have been incorporated in new Title XL have been included under the corresponding modifications.

Table of comparative sections.
See table set out following this title for present disposition of recodified sections.

Effect of recodification of title upon existence and term of or appropriations to state officials or agencies.
1985, 72:7, eff. July 1, 1985, provided:
"The provisions of this act, recodifying the agriculture, horticulture and animal husbandry laws, shall not be deemed to affect the term or legal existence of any official or agency of the state of New Hampshire, nor shall it be deemed to increase, lapse or in any way affect appropriations to any entities contained in this act."

Effect of recodification of title upon references in notices, documents, contracts, etc.
1985, 72:6, eff. July 1, 1985, provided:
"On the effective date of this act, any of the existing references to the chapters, sections, paragraphs and subparagraphs in Title XL of the Revised Statutes Annotated as published in the 1983 replacement volume 4-A and 1983 supplement thereto and the other chapters, sections and paragraphs references which are repealed or amended by this act shall remain valid wherever they may appear in publications, notices, documents, contracts or in or on any other matter for a period of time not to exceed 2 years or until such references are revised to conform to the recodification cites as they appear in section 1 of this act, whichever occurs first."

Repeal of provisions of former Title XL.
1985, 112:1, I–III, eff. July 1, 1985, provided for the repeal of RSA 437-A:1– 437-A:3 of former Title Xl, relating to mosquito control. Former RSA 437-A:1, which was derived from 1965, 349:1, related to the declaration of the purpose of mosquito control. Former RSA 437-A:2, which was derived from 1965, 349:1, 267:4 1967, 147:14; and 1975, 171:1, related to establishment, composition and compensation of the state committee on mosquito control. Former RSA 437-A:3, which was derived from 1965, 349:1, related to the duties from 1965, 349:1, related to the duties of the committee on mosquito control.
1985, 33:2, eff. July 1, 1985, provided for the repeal of RSA ch. 436 of former Title XL. Former RSA ch. 436, comprising RSA 436:1–436:9, which was derived from 1903, 43:1–3, 5–6; 1915, 71:1, 2; PL 183:1–3, 8, 9, 11; 1937, 32:1; RL 225:1–9; and 1973, 530:56, related to nurseries and nursery stock. See now RSA 433:21 et seq.
1985, 111:2, VI, eff. July 9, 1985, provided for the repeal of RSA ch. 429-A of former Title XL. Former RSA ch. 429-A, comprising RSA 429-A:1– 429-A:4, which was derived from 1973, 64:1, related to the new Hampshire fruit marketing committee. Prior to repeal, the chapter had terminated pursuant to RSA 17-G:5.

RESEARCH REFERENCES AND PRACTICE AIDS

Cross References.
Cold storage of foods, see RSA 145.
Cooperative marketing and rural electrification associations, see RSA 301.

Exemption of agricultural producers from antitrust laws, see RSA 356:8.
Inspection and sale of dairy products, see RSA 184.
Purity and branding of foods and drugs,see RSA 146.
Sale of milk or cream in containers, see RSA 351.
Sale of raw cotton, see RSA 339:19 et seq.
Sanitary production and distribution of foods, see RSA 143.

CHAPTER 432

SOIL CONSERVATION AND FARMLAND PRESERVATION

Nuisance Liability of Agricultural Operations

Nuisance Liability of Agricultural Operations

RESEARCH REFERENCES AND PRACTICE AIDS

Cross References.
Regulation of nuisances generally, see RSA 147:1 et seq.

432:32. Agricultural Operation.

"Agricultural operation" when used in this subdivision includes any farm, agricultural or farming activity as defined in RSA 21:34-a.

HISTORY:
1985, 72:1, eff. July 1, 1985.

432:33. Immunity from Suit.

No agricultural operation shall be found a public or private nuisance as a result of changed conditions in or around the locality of the agricultural operation, if such agricultural operation has been in operation for one year or more and if it was not a nuisance at the time it began operation. This section shall not apply when any aspect of the agricultural operation is determined to be injurious to public health or safety under RSA 147:1 or RSA 147:2.

HISTORY:
1985, 72:1, eff. July 1, 1985.

432:34. Negligent or Improper Operations.

The provisions of this subdivision shall not apply if a nuisance results from the negligent or improper operation of an agricultural operation. Agricultural operations shall not be found to be negligent or improper when they conform to federal, state and local laws, rules and regulations.

HISTORY:
1985, 72:1, eff. July 1, 1985.

432:35. Limits.

Nothing contained in this subdivision shall be construed to modify or limit the duties and authority conferred upon the department of environmental services under RSA 485 or RSA 485-A or the commissioner of agriculture, markets, and food under any of the chapters in this title.

HISTORY:
1985, 72:1. 1989, 339:27. 1995, 130:5, eff. July 23, 1995. 1996, 228:108, eff. July 1, 1996.

Revision note.
Pursuant to 1986, 202:6, II, substituted "division of water supply and pollution control" for "water supply and pollution control commission".

Amendments

—1996.
Substituted "department of environmental services" for "division of water supply and pollution control".

—1995.
Substituted "commissioner of agriculture, markets, and food" for "commissioner of agriculture".

—1989.
Substituted " RSA 485 or RSA 485-A" for " RSA 148 or RSA 149".

TITLE XLVIII

CONVEYANCES AND MORTGAGES OF REALTY

CHAPTER 477

CONVEYANCES OF REALTY AND INTERESTS THEREIN

Solar Skyspace Easements

NOTES TO DECISIONS

Cited:
Cited in State v. Marion, 122 N.H. 20, 440 A.2d 448, 1982 N.H. LEXIS 277 (1982); Ouellette v. Butler, 125 N.H. 184, 480 A.2d 76, 1984 N.H. LEXIS 357 (1984).

RESEARCH REFERENCES AND PRACTICE AIDS

Cross References.
Actions against tenants, see RSA 540.
Chattel mortgages generally, see RSA 382-A:9-101 et seq.
Condominiums generally, see RSA 356-B.
Conveyances involving married persons generally, see RSA 460:2 et seq.
Forfeiture of grants, see RSA 535.
Fraudulent transfers, see RSA 545-A.
"Grantee" and "Grantor" defined, see RSA 21:16.
Homestead right, see RSA 480.
"Land" and "Real estate" defined, see RSA 21:21.
Land Sales Full Disclosure Act, see RSA 356-A.
Levy of executions on real estate, see RSA 529.
Limitation period for actions for recovery of real estate, see RSA 508:2.
"Mortgagee" and "Mortgagor" defined, see RSA 21:17.
Prohibited practices by landlords and tenants, see RSA 540-A:1 et seq.
Protection of tenants in conversion of rental units, see RSA 356-C.
Registers of deeds, see RSA 478.
Sale of real estate by administrators or executors generally, see RSA 559.
Tax on transfer of real property, see RSA 78-B.
Uniform Law on Notarial Acts, see RSA 456-B.

New Hampshire Bar Journal.
For article, "Breach of the Warranty Covenants in Deeds and Allowable Measure of Damages," see 17 N.H. B.J. 1 (Sept. 1975).

Solar Skyspace Easements

477:49. Definitions.

As used in this subdivision:

I. "Solar energy" means radiant energy, whether direct, diffuse, or reflected, received from the sun at wavelengths suitable for conversion into thermal, chemical, or electrical energy.

II. "Solar energy collector" means part or all of a device or structure used to transform solar energy into thermal, chemical, or electrical energy and any space or structural components of a building specifically designed to retain heat derived from solar energy.

III. "Solar skyspace" means the space between a solar energy collector and the sun which must remain unobstructed in order to permit sufficient solar energy to the collector for thermally efficient operation.

IV. "Solar skyspace easement" means a limitation, whether or not stated in the form of a restrictive easement, covenant, or condition, in any deed or other instrument executed by or on behalf of the landowner described in the deed or instrument creating and preserving a right to unobstructed access to solar energy; provided, however, the easement shall be exempt from the frontage and area requirements of local zoning ordinances.

HISTORY:
1985, 369:3, eff. Aug. 17, 1985.

RESEARCH REFERENCES AND PRACTICE AIDS

Cross References.
Zoning and land use regulation generally, see RSA 672 et seq.

477:50. Creation of a Solar Skyspace Easement.

I. A solar skyspace easement may be acquired and transferred and shall be recorded in the same manner as any other conveyance of an interest in real property. The easement shall run with the land benefited and burdened and shall terminate upon the conditions stated in the instrument creating the easement or upon court decree based upon abandonment or changed conditions or as provided in RSA 477:26; provided, however, that no planning board may require a landowner to grant an easement.

II. An instrument creating a solar skyspace easement shall include, but not be limited to:

(a) A description of the vertical and horizontal angles, expressed in degrees and measured from the site of the solar energy system, at which the solar skyspace easement extends over the real property subject to the solar skyspace easement, or any other description which describes the 3-dimensional space, or the place and times of day in which an obstruction to solar energy is prohibited or limited;

(b) Terms or conditions under which the easement is granted or shall be terminated;

(c) Provisions for compensation of the benefited landowner in the event of interference with the enjoyment of the easement or compensation of the burdened landowner for maintaining the easement; and

(d) A description of the real property subject to the solar skyspace easement and a description of the real property benefiting from the solar skyspace easement.

III. A solar skyspace easement shall not terminate within 10 years after its creation unless an earlier termination is expressly stated in the instrument or is otherwise negotiated by the owners of the benefited and burdened land. The easement may be enforced by proceedings in equity and by actions at law for damages.

HISTORY:
1985, 369:3, eff. Aug. 17, 1985.

RESEARCH REFERENCES AND PRACTICE AIDS

Cross References.
Recording of conveyances generally, see RSA 477:3-a.

477:51. Statutory Form of Solar Skyspace Easement.

A recorded instrument in the following form shall be sufficient to create a solar skyspace easement. The authorization of this form shall not preclude the use of other forms for the creation of a solar skyspace easement.

(Form for solar skyspace easement)
, of county, state of ,
for consideration paid, hereby conveys, grants and warrants to

of ,
county, state of a
negative easement to restrict, in accordance with the following terms, the future use and development of the real property of grantor recorded in registry of deeds, vol. , page . The solar energy collector for which solar skyspace is to be protected is on the real property of grantee, which is recorded in registry of deeds, vol. , page , at the

following locations:

The boundaries of the solar skyspace for the solar collector of grantee are as follows: (Description of boundaries with reference to applicable survey map, if any.)

(Alternative A)

No structure, vegetation, activity, or land use of grantor except utility lines, antennas, wires, and poles shall cast a shadow on a solar energy collector of grantee during the times specified unless such structure, vegetation, activity, or land use exists on the effective date of this easement and is not required to be removed or is excepted by the terms of this instrument. A shadow shall not be cast from 3 hours before noon to 3 hours after noon from September 22 through March 21 and from 4 hours before noon to 4 hours after noon from March 22 to September 21, all times being eastern standard time.

(or)—(Alternative B)

No structure, vegetation, activity, or land use other than those which exist on the effective date of this easement and which are not required to be removed or are excepted by the terms of this instrument shall penetrate the airspace at a height greater than over the real property of grantor.

Burdens and benefits of this easement are transferable and run with the land to subsequent grantees of the grantor and the grantee. This solar skyspace easement shall remain in effect until use of the solar energy collector is abandoned, provided it shall remain in effect for a period of at least 10 years, or until the grantee and grantor or their successors in interest terminate it. The solar energy terms used in this instrument are defined in RSA 477:49. The survey map depicting the affected properties and the boundaries of the protected areas of solar skyspace is incorporated by reference as part of this instrument.

Witness hand this day
of , 19
Witness:

(Here add acknowledgment)

HISTORY:
1985, 369:3, eff. Aug. 17, 1985.

TITLE L

WATER MANAGEMENT AND PROTECTION

Amendments

—1989.

1989, 339:31, eff. Jan. 1, 1990, substituted "Management and Protection" for "Resources" following "Water" in the Title L heading.

Recodification of RSA 481-A–489-B and certain other water laws as RSA 482–487.

1989, 339:1, eff. Jan. 1, 1990, provided for the repeal and reenactment of RSA 481-A— 489-B as RSA 482— 487. 1989, 339:35, eff. Jan. 1, 1990, provided for the repeal of various provisions of Title X, RSA 227-F, RSA 355 and various provisions of RSA 481, from which the substance of certain provisions contained in recodified RSA 482 and the provisions of recodified RSA 483, 485, 495-A, 486 and 487 were derived. Tables of comparative provisions are set out following this title.

RESEARCH REFERENCES AND PRACTICE AIDS

Cross References.
Boats and boating generally, see RSA 270– 270-B, 270-D, 270-E.
Fencing waterways, see RSA 475.
Hampton harbor channel and beach erosion control, see RSA 216-B.
Hazardous waste cleanup fund, see RSA 147-B.
Hazardous waste fee, see RSA 147-D.
Hazardous waste management generally, see RSA 147-A.
Improvement of back channels of Portsmouth harbor, see RSA 216-C.
Incurring of debt by municipalities for construction or improvement of waterworks, see RSA 33:5-a.
Mercury emissions reduction and control program, see RSA 125-M.
Municipal water systems, see RSA 38.
Navigable waters defined, see RSA 271:9.
New Hampshire-Massachusetts Interstate Sewage and Waste Disposal Facilities Compact, see RSA 149-J.
New Hampshire-Vermont Interstate Sewage and Waste Disposal Facilities Compact, see RSA 149-K.
Oil discharge or spillage in surface water or groundwater, see RSA 146-A.
Protection of state water rights by governor, see RSA 4:10.
Public waters defined, see RSA 271:20.
Saco Watershed Compact, see RSA 226-A.
Sewers, see RSA 149-I.
Shore and beach preservation and development, see RSA 217.
Solid waste management generally, see RSA 149-M.
Sufficiency of waters as fences, see RSA 473:7.
Testing of water supplies, see RSA 131:3, 3-a.

New Hampshire Code of Administrative Rules
Rules of the Water Resources Division, Env-Wr 100 et seq., New Hampshire Code of Administrative Rules.
Rules of the Water Supply and Pollution Control Division, Env-Ws 300 et seq., New Hampshire Code of Administrative Rules.

Rules of the Wetlands Board, Wt 100 et seq., New Hampshire Code of Administrative Rules.

New Hampshire Bar Journal.
For article, "A Survey of New Hampshire Water Law," see 13 N.H. B.J. 3 (Fall 1970).

CHAPTER 482-A

FILL AND DREDGE IN WETLANDS

NOTES TO DECISIONS

Analysis

1. Constitutionality
2. Construction
3. Application
4. Jurisdiction
5. Statute of limitations

1. Constitutionality

Controlling and restricting the filling of wetlands is clearly within the scope of the police power of the state. Sibson v. State, 115 N.H. 124, 336 A.2d 239, 1975 N.H. LEXIS 240 (1975), overruled in part, Burrows v. Keene, 121 N.H. 590, 432 A.2d 15, 1981 N.H. LEXIS 369 (1981). (Decided under prior law.)

The denial of a permit to fill a salt marsh is valid exercise of the police power proscribing future activities which would be harmful to the public and, thus, there is no taking of private property for public purposes without compensation in violation of the state and federal constitutions. Sibson v. State, 115 N.H. 124, 336 A.2d 239, 1975 N.H. LEXIS 240 (N.H. 1975), overruled, Burrows v. Keene, 121 N.H. 590, 432 A.2d 15, 1981 N.H. LEXIS 369 (N.H. 1981); Burrows v. Keene, 121 N.H. 590, 432 A.2d 15, 1981 N.H. LEXIS 369 (N.H. 1981). (Decided under prior law.)

Regulations such as prescribed by this chapter to prevent fill runoff back into tidal waters and to protect marine fisheries and wildlife are in the public good. Sibson v. State, 110 N.H. 8, 259 A.2d 397, 1969 N.H. LEXIS 110 (N.H. 1969). (Decided under prior law.)

The rights of littoral owners n public waters are always subject to the paramount right of the state to control them reasonably and in the interests of navigation, fishing, and other public purposes, and the rights of those owners are burdened with a servitude in favor of the state which comes onto operation when the state properly exercises its power to control, regulate, and utilize such waters; it is only where the legislative action amounts to an actual taking of the the property rights of those owners that compensation is constitutionally required. Sibson v. State, 110 N.H. 8, 259 A.2d 397, 1969 N.H. LEXIS 110 (N.H. 1969). (Decided under prior law.)

2. Construction

The legislature, by enacting the regulatory scheme created by provisions of this chapter, did not intend to vest exclusive jurisdiction over state waters in the water resources board, and to eliminate the right of property owners to bring an action for a violation of their riparian rights when the board has not authorized the filling or dredging in state waters. Wisniewski v. Gemmill, 123 N.H. 701, 465 A.2d 875, 1983 N.H. LEXIS 337 (N.H. 1983). (Decided under prior law.)

3. Application

Reference to RSA ch. 482-A in the deeds granting former Air Force base property to the Pease Development Authority, without more, did not confer standing upon a town to challenge compliance with the deed restrictions. Town of Newington v. State, 162 N.H. 745, 34 A.3d 1206, 2011 N.H. LEXIS 173 (2011).

This chapter was intended by the legislature to be an exercise of its dominant servitude over tidal waters and to apply only to land in or contiguous to tidewaters, that is, to land of littoral owners. Sibson v. State, 110 N.H. 8, 259 A.2d 397, 1969 N.H. LEXIS 110 (N.H. 1969). (Decided under prior law.)

4. Jurisdiction

Property which is part of an area contiguous to tidal water may not be removed from the jurisdiction of the wetlands board by property owner's subdivision of the property so as to create a "buffer zone" where a subdivided lot consequently would not border tidal water, since such a manufactured artificial boundary would contravene the legislature's intent and purpose of this chapter. State Wetlands Bd. v. Marshall, 127 N.H. 240, 500 A.2d 685, 1985 N.H. LEXIS 435 (N.H. 1985). (Decided under prior law.)

5. Statute of limitations

In an action by the State for violations of RSA ch. 482-A and RSA ch. 485-A, the doctrine of "nullum tempus occurrit regi" precluded a statute of limitations defense. The doctrine endured in New Hampshire, and the three-year general statute of limitations, RSA 508:4, I, did not expressly waive nullum tempus by making a limitations period applicable to the State. State v. Lake Winnipesaukee Resort, 159 N.H. 42, 977 A.2d 472, 2009 N.H. LEXIS 82 (N.H. 2009).

Cited:

Cited in Allen v. Wetlands Bd., 133 N.H. 379, 577 A.2d 92, 1990 N.H. LEXIS 71 (1990).

OPINIONS OF THE ATTORNEY GENERAL

Jurisdiction

Wetlands board had jurisdiction over proposed development which would excavate portions of the bank of Lake Sunapee, dredge lake bed below the mean high water mark, and construct piers for boats which will use the lake. 1987 Op. Att'y Gen. 67. (Decided under prior law.)

RESEARCH REFERENCES AND PRACTICE AIDS

New Hampshire Code of Administrative Rules

Rules of the Wetlands Board, Wt 202.03, 303.03-303.04, 501.01 et seq., New Hampshire Code of Administrative Rules Annotated.

Rules of the Wetlands Board, Wt 100 et seq., New Hampshire Code of Administrative Rules Annotated.

New Hampshire Bar Journal.

For article, "Land Use Controls, Takings, and the Police Power—A Discussion of the Myth," see 15 N.H. B.J. 149 (Spring 1974).

For article, "State Regulation of Marshlands: Sibson v. State," see 17 N.H. B.J. 68 (Dec. 1975).

For article, "Wetlands Legislation in New Hampshire," see 18 N.H. B.J. 265 (June 1977).

For article, "Recent Developments in Land Use Regulation," see 19 N.H. B.J. 257 (June 1978).

482-A:1. Finding of Public Purpose.

It is found to be for the public good and welfare of this state to protect and preserve its submerged lands under tidal and fresh waters and its wetlands, (both salt water and fresh-water), as herein defined, from despoliation and unregulated alteration, because such despoliation or unregulated alteration will adversely affect the value of such areas as sources of nutrients for finfish, crustacea, shellfish and wildlife of significant value, will damage or destroy habitats and reproduction areas for plants, fish and wildlife of importance, will eliminate, depreciate or obstruct the commerce, recreation and aesthetic enjoyment of the public, will be detrimental to adequate groundwater levels, will adversely affect stream channels and their ability to handle the runoff of waters, will disturb and reduce the natural ability of wetlands to absorb flood waters and silt, thus increasing general flood damage and the silting of open water channels, and will otherwise adversely affect the interests of the general public.

HISTORY:

1989, 339:1, eff. Jan. 1, 1990.

NOTES TO DECISIONS

Analysis

1. Construction

2. Agency findings

1. Construction

Trial court did not err by ruling that the New Hampshire Department of Environmental Services (DES) review authority of a wetlands permit was limited to assessing the impacts of construction activities in the protected wetlands, as DES' authority did not extend to assessing the effects of upland construction activities upon such wetlands. An appellate court did not further review the appeal because the trial court determined, as a matter of law, based upon its review of the certified record, that an environmental council's decision granting a developer the permit was legally correct and the appellate court, having reviewed the certified record itself, found that the evidence was sufficient for the trial court to have reached that conclusion. Greenland Conservation Comm'n v. N.H. Wetlands Council, 154 N.H. 529, 913 A.2d 776, 2006 N.H. LEXIS 195 (N.H. 2006).

Although defendants satisfactorily complied with a remediation plan approved by the New Hampshire Department of Environmental Services Wetlands Bureau, a nuisance finding and injunctive relief ordered by a trial court were upheld on appeal, as defendants' neighboring landowners were not bound by the administrative decision, under either the doctrine of res judicata or collateral estoppel; the focus of the Wetlands Bureau was to investigate and enforce the wetlands regulations under RSA ch. 482-A to ensure compliance, not to protect plaintiffs' rights, and the authority of the Wetlands Board to regulate did not include the power to determine the relative rights of property owners. Cook v. Sullivan, 149 N.H. 774, 829 A.2d 1059, 2003 N.H. LEXIS 123 (N.H. 2003).

2. Agency findings

It was error for the Wetlands Council to reverse an award of a wetlands permit. The Department of Environmental Services found that adverse impacts should not result in the significant loss of wetlands values because the monitoring devices themselves, in addition to mitigation requirements, assured that groundwater withdrawal would be reduced or halted before any significant loss of RSA 482-A:1 values occurred; these were precisely the type of findings that were entitled to deference under RSA 482-A:10, V. Appeal of Garrison Place Real Estate Inv. Trust, 159 N.H. 539, 986 A.2d 670, 2009 N.H. LEXIS 145 (N.H. 2009).

OPINIONS OF THE ATTORNEY GENERAL

Review of project proposals

In its review of project proposals, the wetlands board must be guided by the legislature's stated finding that it is for the public good and welfare of the state to protect and preserve its submerged lands and wetlands. 1987 Op. Att'y Gen. 67. (Decided under prior law.)

RESEARCH REFERENCES AND PRACTICE AIDS

New Hampshire Code of Administrative Rules

Rules of the Department of Environmental Services—Wetlands Board, Env-Wt 501.02 and 501.05–.07, New Hampshire Code of Administrative Rules Annotated.

New Hampshire Bar Journal.

For article, "Lex Loci: A Survey of New Hampshire Supreme Court Decisions," see 44 N.H. B.J. 50 (Dec. 2003).

482-A:2. Definitions.

In this chapter:

I. "Commissioner" means the commissioner of environmental services.

I-a. "Council" means the wetlands council established in RSA 21-O:5-a.

I-b. "Department" means the department of environmental services.

II. "Division" means the division of water resources, department of environmental services.

II-a. "Local governing body" means "local governing body" as defined in RSA 672:6.

III. "Local legislative body" means "local legislative body" as defined in RSA 672:8.

IV. "Mean high tide" shall be determined according to the published tables and standards of the United States Coast and Geodetic Survey, adjusted to the locality from such tables.

V. "Municipality" shall include cities, towns, and village districts.

VI. "Person" shall mean any natural person, firm, partnership, association, corporation, company, organization or legal entity of any kind including municipal corporations, governmental departments and agencies, or their subdivisions.

VII. "Sand dune" shall mean a hill or ridge of sand piled up by the wind and commonly found on the seacoast.

VIII. "Boat slip" means:

(a) On water bodies over 10,000 acres, means a volume of water 25 feet long, 8 feet wide, and 3 feet deep as measured at normal high water and located adjacent to a structure to which a watercraft may be secured.

(b) On water bodies of 10,000 acres or less, a volume of water 20 feet long, 6 feet wide, and 3 feet deep as measured at normal high water mark and located adjacent to a structure to which a watercraft may be secured.

IX. "Structure" means, notwithstanding any other provision of law, something installed, erected, or constructed, but shall not include a bench, landing with dimensions no larger than 10 feet wide by 10 feet long, or stairs with a width not exceeding 6 feet, provided that such benches, landings, or stairs are installed, erected, or constructed without regrading or recontouring of the shoreline and are not over water. Structures include, but are not limited to, the following: fence, dock, breakwater, post, pile, building, bridge, culvert, and wall.

X. "Wetlands" means an area that is inundated or saturated by surface water or groundwater at a frequency and duration sufficient to support, and that under normal conditions does support, a prevalence of vegetation typically adapted for life in saturated soil conditions.

XI. "Wetland functions" means the practical measurable values of wetlands. The 12 primary wetland functions are ecological integrity, wetland-dependent wildlife habitat, fish and aquatic life habitat, scenic quality, educational potential, wetland-based recreation, flood storage, groundwater recharge, sediment trapping, nutrient trapping/retention/transformation, shoreline anchoring, and noteworthiness.

HISTORY:

1989, 225:2. 339:1. 1991, 20:1, 2, eff. Jan. 1, 1992. 1996, 296:12, 39, eff. Aug. 9, 1996. 2002, 272:14, eff. May 18, 2002. 2004, 243:1, eff. July 1, 2004. 2012, 235:4, eff. August 17, 2012.

Codification.
Pursuant to 1989, 339:34, former RSA 483-A:1-a, IV, as added by 1989, 225:2, eff. July 23, 1989, was redesignated as par. VII of this section. For purposes of conformity with the language of the remainder of this section, the language "as used in this chapter" was deleted in par. VII.

Amendments

—2012.
The 2012 amendment added XI.

—2004.
Paragraph X: Added.

—2002.
Paragraphs VIII and IX: Added.

—1996.
Paragraph I: Rewritten to the extent that a detailed comparison would be impracticable.
Paragraphs I-a and I-b: Added.

—1991.
Paragraph II-a: Added.
Paragraph III: Rewritten to the extent that a detailed comparison would be impracticable.

Contingent 1996 amendment.
1996, 296:13, provided for amendment of this section. However, under the terms of 1996, 296:54, eff. Aug. 9, 1996, the amendment did not become effective.

NOTES TO DECISIONS

Wetlands
Statutory definition of "wetlands" does not, by itself, suggest local authority to regulate personal boating and boat docking on waters held in trust for the public. The legislature could have defined "wetlands" either to facilitate wetland setbacks or for local wetland regulation outside the sphere of any exclusive State wetland regulation. Lakeside Lodge, Inc. v. Town of New London, 158 N.H. 164, 960 A.2d 1268, 2008 N.H. LEXIS 140 (2008).

RESEARCH REFERENCES AND PRACTICE AIDS

References in text.
The reference to the United States Coast and Geodetic Survey in par. IV. is obsolete. Reorganization Plan No. 2 of 1965, eff. July 13, 1965, 79 Stat. 1318, abolished the Coast and Geodetic Survey and transferred its functions to the Secretary of Commerce. See 33 U.S.C.S. §§ 851 et seq.

482-A:3. Excavating and Dredging Permit; Certain Exemptions.

I.(a) No person shall excavate, remove, fill, dredge, or construct any structures in or on any bank, flat, marsh, or swamp in and adjacent to any waters of the state without a permit from the department. Unless otherwise specified in rules adopted by the commissioner pursuant to RSA 482-A:11, any person seeking to obtain a permit shall submit to the department:

(1) A complete application form that has been signed by the town or city clerk of the municipality in which the property is located or, if the property is located in more than one municipality, by the city or town clerk of each such municipality, certifying that the municipality

has received 4 copies of the form and attachments as provided in subparagraph (a)(2). The town or city clerk shall send a copy of the form and attachments to the local governing body, the municipal planning board, if any, and the municipal conservation commission, if any, and shall retain one copy to be made reasonably accessible to the public. Applications and fees for projects by agencies of the state may be filed directly with the department, with 4 copies of the application, plan, and map filed at the same time with the town or city clerk.

(2) Such other information as required by rules adopted by the commissioner pursuant to RSA 482-A:11, which may include maps and plans.

(3) A nonrefundable application fee as specified in subparagraphs (b) or (c), as applicable.

(b) The application fee for shoreline structure projects shall be $200 plus an amount based on the area of dredge, fill, or dock surface area proposed, or a combination thereof, which shall be $2 per square foot for permanent dock surface area; $1 per square foot for seasonal dock surface area; and $.20 per square foot for dredge or fill surface area or both. For projects involving only the repair, reconstruction, or reconfiguration of an existing docking structure, the application fee shall be $200.

(c) The application fee shall be $200 for minimum impact dredge and fill projects under this chapter. The application fee for all projects under this chapter which are not covered by subparagraph (b) or (c) or paragraphs IV-a, V, X through XII, XV, XVI, or XVII through XIX shall be $.20 per square foot of proposed impact, with a minimum fee of $200 for all such projects that impact fewer than 1,000 square feet.

(d) At the time the applicant files the application with the department, the applicant shall provide written notice of the proposed project to:

(1) All abutters, as defined in the rules of the department, unless exempted in such rules, which shall be provided by certified mail or other delivery method that provides proof of receipt. The applicant shall retain such receipts and provide copies to the department upon request. The department shall have no obligation to verify the identity of abutters or their receipt of notice. Any abutter who has actual notice of the filing of an application shall have no cause to challenge the application based on failure to receive written notice. Nothing in this subparagraph shall prevent the department from taking appropriate action in the event an applicant fails to provide the required notice or provides false information.

(2) The local river management advisory committee if the project is within a river corridor as defined in RSA 483:4, XVIII, or a river segment designated in RSA 483:15. Such notice

shall be sent by certified mail or other delivery method that provides proof of receipt. The applicant shall retain such receipts and provide copies to the department upon request. The local river management advisory committee shall, under RSA 483:8-a, III(a)-(b), advise the commissioner and consider and comment on the permit application.

(e) Beginning October 1, 2007, the department shall submit an annual report to the house and senate finance committees, the house resources, recreation and development committee, and the senate energy and natural resources committee relative to administration of the wetlands fees permit process established by this section.

I-a. Notwithstanding any law or rule to the contrary, in reviewing requests proposed, sponsored, or administered by the department of transportation, there shall be a rebuttable presumption that there is a public need for the requested project, and that the department of transportation has exercised appropriate engineering judgment in the project's design.

II.(a) The department shall submit to the governor and council all requests for permits approved by the department which meet the definition of major projects located in great ponds or public-owned water bodies under the rules of the department which have been approved by the department.

(b) The governor and council shall consider the request for permit transmitted by the department. The governor and council may approve as transmitted or deny the submitted request. Following action by the governor and council the requests shall be returned to the department for permitting, if approved, or filing, if denied.

III. The filing fees collected pursuant to paragraphs I, V(c), XI(h), and XII(c), are continually appropriated to and shall be expended by the department for paying per diem and expenses of the public members of the council, hiring additional staff, reviewing applications and activities relative to the wetlands of the state and protected shorelands under RSA 483-B, conducting field investigations, and holding public hearings. Such fees shall be held by the treasurer in a nonlapsing fund identified as the wetlands and shorelands review fund.

IV.(a) The replacement or repair of existing structures in or adjacent to any waters of the state which does not involve excavation, removal, filling, or dredging in any waters or of any bank, flat, marsh, or swamp is exempt from the provisions of this chapter.

(b) Man-made nontidal drainage ditches, roadside and railroad ditches, detention basins, ponds, and wetlands that have been legally constructed to collect, convey, treat, or control storm water and spring run-off, legally constructed ponds on active farms, erosional features caused by proximate human activity, fire ponds and intake areas of dry

hydrants that have been legally constructed to provide water for municipal firefighting purposes as approved by a local fire chief, and aggregate wash ponds, sluiceways, and other legally constructed man-made water conveyance systems that are used for the commercial or industrial purpose of collecting, conveying, storing, and recycling water, may be maintained, repaired, replaced, or modified as necessary to preserve their usefulness without a permit under this chapter; provided, that the exempted facility, area, or feature is not extended into any area of wetlands jurisdiction of the department of environmental services, dredged spoils are deposited in areas outside wetlands jurisdiction of the department of environmental services, wetlands or surface waters outside the limits of the exempted facility, area, or feature are neither disturbed nor degraded, the exempted facility, area, or feature was not constructed as mitigation under a wetlands permit or as part of a settlement agreement, best management practices are followed, and the work does not infringe on the property rights or unreasonably affect the value or enjoyment of property of abutting owners.

(c) Legally constructed culverts may be cleaned as necessary to preserve their usefulness without a permit under this chapter provided the conditions of subparagraph (b) are met, however any repair, replacement or modification of a culvert must be made in accordance with RSA 482-A:3, XVI.

IV-a. Temporary seasonal docks installed on any lake or pond shall be exempt from the permitting requirements of this section, provided that a notification is sent to the department by the owner of property that includes the name and address of the property owner, the municipality, the waterbody, and tax map and lot number on which the proposed dock will be located. To qualify for an exemption under this paragraph, a temporary seasonal dock shall be:

(a) The only docking structure on the frontage;

(b) Constructed to be removed during the non-boating season;

(c) Removed from the lake bed for a minimum of 5 months of each year;

(d) Configured to be narrow, rectangular, and erected perpendicular to the shoreline;

(e) No more than 6 feet wide and no more than 40 feet long if the water body is 1,000 acres or larger, or no more than 30 feet long if the water body is less than 1,000 acres;

(f) Located on a parcel of land that has 75 feet or more of shoreline frontage;

(g) Located at least 20 feet from an abutting property line or the imaginary extension of the property line over the water;

(h) Installed in a manner which requires no modification, regrading, or recontouring of the shoreline, such as installation of a concrete pad for construction of a hinged dock;

(i) Installed in a manner which complies with RSA 483-B; and

(j) Installed in a location that is not in, or adjacent to, an area that has been designated as a prime wetland in accordance with RSA 482-A:15.

V.(a) Persons who have complied with notice of intent to cut wood requirements under RSA 79:10, and who have filed an appropriate notice of intent with the department and the department of natural and cultural resources, shall have satisfied the permitting requirements of this section for minimum impact activities only as defined by rules adopted by the commissioner. Minimum impact notifications issued by the department shall be valid for 2 years.

(b) Appropriate notice to the department and the department of natural and cultural resources shall include the following information:

(1) Name and address of property owner;

(2) Name and address of logger or forester;

(3) Town, tax map, number and lot number of job site; and

(4) A copy of the appropriate United States Geological Survey topographic map, or a copy of the appropriate United States Natural Resources Conservation Service soils map, with the type and location of all wetland and waterbody crossings clearly indicated.

(c) A $25 filing fee shall accompany the notice to the department. Such fees shall be held in accordance with paragraph III.

(d) The filing of an intent to cut form under RSA 79:10 shall be considered as permission to the department or the department of natural and cultural resources, or their agents, to enter the property for determining compliance with this chapter.

(e) The certificate issued under RSA 79:10 shall be posted upon receipt. Prior to receipt of such certificate, a copy of the intent to cut form, signed by the appropriate municipal official, shall be available on the job site, and shall be shown to any person who asks to see it.

VI. The permittee shall record, in the registry of deeds for the county or counties in which the real estate is located, each permit granted under this chapter for the installation, construction, or repair of a dock, docking facility, or marina, or for alteration of wetlands associated with a subdivision of 4 or more lots. The permit shall not be effective until so recorded.

VII. No person shall destroy, raze, deface, reduce, alter, build upon or remove any sand or vegetation from any sand dune in this state without a permit from the department; provided, however, that any person may remove sand which blows or drifts onto any lawn, driveway, walkway, parking or storage area, or boat ramp, or which blows or drifts in, on, or around buildings or other structures owned by the person. Upon request of the property owner, the department shall provide a preapplication assessment of any lot of record located in sand dunes.

VIII. Except as set forth in paragraph IX, no person shall operate or ride any mechanized or off highway recreational vehicle on any sand dune in the state of New Hampshire.

IX. This section shall not apply to:

(a) Police vehicles or fire vehicles.

(b) Vehicles used in cases of emergency.

(c) Authorized maintenance vehicles when performing maintenance duties.

(d) Vehicles used by commercial fishermen or commercial lobstermen when engaged in activities related to fishing or lobstering.

X.(a) The maximum cash application fee for the New Hampshire department of transportation shall be $10,000 per application plus provisions for technical or consulting services or a combination of such services as necessary to meet the needs of the department. The department may enter into a memorandum of agreement with the New Hampshire department of transportation to accept equivalent technical or consulting services or a combination of such services in lieu of a portion of their standard application fees.

(b) For tidal dredging projects with the primary purpose to improve navigation for a municipality, the maximum application fee for a municipality shall be $10,000 per application plus provisions for technical or consulting services or a combination of such services as necessary to meet the needs of the department. The department may enter into a memorandum of agreement with a municipality to accept equivalent technical or consulting services or a combination of such services in lieu of a portion of their standard application fees.

(c) For municipal dredging projects with the primary purpose to restore or reclaim a lake or pond, the maximum application fee for a municipality shall be $10,000 per application plus provisions for technical or consulting services or a combination of such services as necessary to meet the needs of the department. The department may enter into a memorandum of agreement with a municipality to accept equivalent technical or consulting services or a combination of such services in lieu of a portion of the standard application fees.

XI.(a) Small motor mineral dredging shall be limited to activities which are classified as minimum impact under rules adopted by the commissioner under RSA 482-A:11 and which do not exceed the following limits:

(1) Power equipment shall be limited to 5 horsepower.

(2) Suction dredges shall be limited to a single 4-inch diameter intake nozzle.

(3) Sluice and rocker boxes shall be limited to 10 square feet.

(b) Any person who wishes to engage in small motor mineral dredging shall obtain a permit from the department. A permit application shall be filed directly with the department, and the procedural requirements of RSA 482-A:3, I and RSA 482-A:11, III shall not apply. Any permit issued by the department under this paragraph shall expire at the end of the calendar year in which it is issued. Any person who engages in panning only shall not be required to obtain a permit but shall be subject to rules of the department. Panning shall include those activities associated with the manual search for minerals in a river bed without the use of motorized equipment.

(c) Any person wishing to engage in mineral dredging which in any way exceeds the limits of small motor mineral dredging shall first obtain, in addition to a wetlands permit, a mining permit from the department of natural and cultural resources pursuant to RSA 12-E.

(d) The commissioner shall adopt rules, under RSA 541-A, relative to:

(1) Small motor mineral dredging and panning.

(2) The issuance of statewide small motor mineral dredging permits.

(3) Any other matters relative to small motor mineral dredging and panning.

(e) The state shall retain the right to prohibit panning and mineral dredging activity at certain times or in certain locations when such activity would be detrimental to the public interest for reasons including, but not limited to, environmental and wildlife protection.

(f) Any person who has obtained a small motor mineral dredging permit from the department pursuant to this paragraph, or any person who intends to engage in any panning activity shall, prior to engaging in any small motor mineral dredging or panning activity, obtain the written permission to engage in such activity from the riverbed landowner on whose property the activity is to be conducted.

(g) The department may enter into a cooperative agreement with the fish and game department relative to enforcement of the provisions of this paragraph.

(h) Application fees shall be $25 for residents of the state of New Hampshire and $50 for out-of-state applicants. Fees shall be collected by the department and held in accordance with paragraph III.

XII.(a) Persons who construct and maintain recreational trails in accordance with the Best Management Practices for Erosion Control During Trail Maintenance and Construction published by the department of natural and cultural resources and who have filed an appropriate notice, as described in subparagraph (b), to construct or maintain such trails with the department and the department of natural and cultural resources shall have satisfied the permitting requirements of this section for minimum impact activities, as defined by rules adopted by the commissioner.

(b) Appropriate notice to the department and the department of natural and cultural resources shall include the following information:

(1) Name and address of organization constructing or maintaining the recreational trail.

(2) Name and address of property owner.

(3) Town, tax map number, and lot number of property.

(4) A copy of the appropriate United States Geological Survey topographic map with the type and location of all wetland and waterbody crossings clearly indicated.

(c) A $25 filing fee shall accompany the notice to the department. Such fees shall be held in accordance with paragraph III.

XIII.(a) All boat docking facilities shall be at least 20 feet from an abutting property line in non-tidal waters, and at least 20 feet in tidal waters.

(b) Boat docking facilities may be perpendicular or parallel to the shoreline or extend at some other angle into a water body, depending on the needs of the landowners, factors related to safe navigation, and the difficulty of construction. However, any boat secured to such a dock shall not extend beyond the extension of the abutter's property line.

(c) Notwithstanding the provisions of subparagraph (a), boat docking facilities may be located closer than 20 feet from an abutter's property line in non-tidal waters and 20 feet in tidal waters, if the owner of the boat docking facility obtains the written consent of the abutting property owner. Such consent shall be signed by all parties, notarized and filed with the dock application with the department of environmental services.

(d) Abutters may apply for a common dock on or near their common property line. Any application for a common dock shall be accompanied by a notarized written agreement which shall be signed by all property owners. Such agreement shall be filed at the registry of deeds and attached to the deed of each property owner.

XIV.(a) In processing an application for permits under this chapter, except for a permit by notification, the department shall:

(1) Within 14 days of receipt by the department, issue a notice of administrative completeness or send notice to the applicant, at the address provided on the application, identifying any additional information required to make the application administratively complete and providing the applicant with the name and telephone number of the department employee to whom all correspondence shall be directed by the designated department employee regarding incompleteness of the application. Each receipt of additional information in response to any notice shall re-commence the 14-day period until the department issues a notice of administrative completeness. Any notice of incompleteness sent under this subparagraph shall specify that

the applicant or authorized agent shall submit such information as soon as practicable and shall notify the applicant or authorized agent that if the requested information is not received within 60 days of the notice, the department shall deny the application.

(2) Within 75 days of the issuance of a notice of administrative completeness for projects where the applicant proposes under one acre of jurisdictional impact and 105 days for all other projects, request any additional information that the department is permitted by law to require to complete its evaluation of the application, together with any written technical comments the department deems necessary. Such request and technical comments may be sent by electronic means if the applicant or authorized agent has indicated an agreement to accept communications by electronic means, either by so indicating on the application or by a signed statement from the applicant or authorized agent that communicating by electronic means is acceptable. Any request for additional information under this subparagraph shall specify that the applicant submit such information as soon as practicable and shall notify the applicant that if the requested information is not received within 60 days of the request, the department shall deny the application. The department may grant an extension of this 60 day time period upon request of the applicant.

(3) Where the department requests additional information pursuant to subparagraph (a)(2), within 30 days of the department's receipt of a complete response to the department's information request:

(A) Approve the application, in whole or in part, and issue a permit; or

(B) Deny the application and issue written findings in support of the denial; or

(C) Schedule a public hearing in accordance with this chapter and rules adopted by the commissioner; or

(D) Extend the time for rendering a decision on the application for good cause and with the written agreement of the applicant; or

(4) Where no request for additional information is made pursuant to subparagraph (a)(2), within 75 days from the issuance of the notice of administrative completeness for proposed projects under one acre of jurisdictional impact, or 105 days for all others:

(A) Approve the application, in whole or in part, and issue a permit; or

(B) Deny the application and issue written findings in support of the denial; or

(C) Schedule a public hearing in accordance with this chapter and rules adopted by the commissioner; or

(D) Extend the time for rendering a decision on the application for good cause and with the written agreement of the applicant.

(5) Where the department has held a public hearing on an application filed under this chapter, within 60 days following the closure of the hearing record, approve the application in whole or in part, and issue a permit or deny the application and issue written findings in support of the denial.

(b)(1) The time limits prescribed by this paragraph shall supersede any time limits provided in any other provision of law. If the department fails to act within the applicable time frame established in subparagraphs (a)(3), (a)(4), and (a)(5), the applicant may ask the department to issue the permit by submitting a written request. If the applicant has previously agreed to accept communications from the department by electronic means, a request submitted electronically by the applicant shall constitute a written request.

(2) Within 14 days of the date of receipt of a written request from the applicant to issue the permit, the department shall:

(A) Approve the application, in whole or in part, and issue a permit; or

(B) Deny the application and issue written findings in support of the denial.

(3) If the department does not issue either a permit or a written denial within the 14-day period, the applicant shall be deemed to have a permit by default and may proceed with the project as presented in the application. The authorization provided by this subparagraph shall not relieve the applicant of complying with all requirements applicable to the project, including but not limited to requirements established in or under this chapter, RSA 485-A relating to water quality, and federal requirements.

(4) Upon receipt of a written request from an applicant, the department shall issue written confirmation that the applicant has a permit by default pursuant to subparagraph (b)(3), which authorizes the applicant to proceed with the project as presented in the application and requires the work to comply with all requirements applicable to the project, including but not limited to requirements established in or under this chapter, and RSA 485-A relating to water quality, and federal requirements.

(c) If extraordinary circumstances prevent the department from conducting its normal function, time frames prescribed by this paragraph shall be suspended until such condition has ended, as determined by the commissioner.

(d) The time limits prescribed by this paragraph shall not apply to an application filed after the applicant has already undertaken some or all of the work covered by the application, or where the applicant has been adjudicated after final appeal, or otherwise does not contest, the department's designation as a chronic non-complier in accordance with rules adopted pursuant to this chapter.

(e) Any request for a significant amendment to a pending application or an existing permit which changes the footprint of the permitted fill or dredge area shall be deemed a new application subject to the provisions of RSA 482-A:3, I and the time limits prescribed by this paragraph. "Significant amendment" means an amendment which changes the proposed or previously approved acreage of the permitted fill or dredge area by 20 percent or more, relocates the proposed footprint of the permitted fill or dredge area, includes a prime wetland or surface waters of the state, includes a wetland of a different classification as classified by the department, or includes non-wetland areas requiring permits for filling and dredging. This meaning of "significant amendment" shall not apply to an application amendment that is in response to a request from the department.

(f) The department may extend the time for rendering a decision under subparagraphs (a)(3)(D) and (a)(4)(D), without the applicant's agreement, on an application from an applicant who previously has been determined, after the exhaustion of available appellate remedies, to have failed to comply with this chapter or any rule adopted or permit or approval issued under this chapter, or to have misrepresented any material fact made in connection with any activity regulated or prohibited by this chapter, pursuant to an action initiated under RSA 482-A:13, RSA 482-A:14, or RSA 482-A:14-b. The length of such an extension shall be no longer than reasonably necessary to complete the review of the application, but shall not exceed 30 days unless the applicant agrees to a longer extension. The department shall notify the applicant of the length of the extension.

(g) The department may suspend review of an application for a proposed project on a property with respect to which the department has commenced an enforcement action against the applicant for any violation of this chapter, RSA 483-B, RSA 485-A:17, or RSA 485-A:29–44, or of any rule adopted or permit or approval issued pursuant to this chapter, RSA 483-B, RSA 485-A:17, or RSA 485-A:29–44. Any such suspension shall expire upon conclusion of the enforcement action and completion of any remedial actions the department may require to address the violation; provided, however, that the department may resume its review of the application sooner if doing so will facilitate resolution of the violation. The department shall resume its review of the application at the point the review was suspended, except that the department may extend any of the time limits under this paragraph and its rules up to a total of 30 days for all such extensions. For purposes of this subparagraph, "enforcement action" means

an action under RSA 482-A:13, RSA 482-A:14, RSA 482-A:14-b, RSA 483-B:18, RSA 485-A:22, RSA 485-A:42, or RSA 485-A:43.

XIV-a.(a) With the exception of permits issued under subparagraph (b), all permits issued pursuant to this chapter shall be valid for a period of 5 years. Requests for extensions of such permits may be made to the department. The department shall grant one extension of up to 5 additional years, provided the applicant demonstrates all of the following:

(1) The permit for which extension is sought has not been revoked or suspended without reinstatement.

(2) Extension would not violate a condition of law or rule.

(3) The project is proceeding towards completion in accordance with plans and other documentation referenced by the permit.

(4) The applicant proposes reasonable mitigation measures to protect the public waters of the state from deterioration during the period of extension.

(b) Any permit issued to repair or replace shoreline structures to maintain the integrity and safety of such structures including, but not limited to docks, sea walls, breakwaters, riprap, access ramps and stairs, that are damaged by storms or ice, shall expire 10 years from the date the permit was issued as long as any work performed after the initial permitted work complies with the following:

(1) The work is not in violation of the original permit or subparagraphs (a)(1)–(4).

(2) All structures are repaired or replaced to the original permitted location and configuration.

(3) All significant work is reported to the department in accordance with the reporting requirements for the original permit.

XIV-b. A permit issued under this chapter that is associated with the excavation or mining of construction aggregate materials and quarry stone from the earth shall not expire for the life of the project identified in the permit application, provided that the permit holder submits revised project plans and a written update of the project's status every 5 years from the date of the permit issuance using a form obtained from the department as specified in department rules. Permitted impacts to aquatic resources shall be postponed until such impacts become necessary for the operation of the excavation or mining area. If there has not been excavation or mining of construction aggregate materials and quarry stone during any 5 year period, the project shall be deemed abandoned and the permit deemed expired. When or if a new proposal to develop the property for a different use is proposed, a new application shall be submitted.

XV.(a) Utility providers who maintain and repair existing utility services within existing rights of way under the Best Management Practices Manual for Utility Maintenance in and Adjacent to Wetlands and Waterbodies in New Hampshire published by the department of natural and cultural resources, and who have complied with subparagraphs (b)–(e) shall satisfy the permitting requirements of this section, including any portion located in or adjacent to a prime wetland, for minimum impact activities as defined by rules adopted by the commissioner.

(b) Appropriate notice to the department shall include the following information:

(1) The name and address of the person, employed by the utility provider responsible for overseeing the maintenance.

(2) A brief written description of the nature of the work to be conducted.

(3) A copy of the appropriate United States Geological Survey topographic map with the locations of the projects indicated.

(c) Appropriate notice to the town clerk of each municipality in which work will occur shall include the name of a utility provider contact and a brief description of the work to be conducted.

(d) A one-time annual filing fee of $200 per town, not to exceed a maximum of $10,000, shall accompany the notice to the department. Such fees shall be held in accordance with paragraph III.

(e) No additional fee shall be required for amendments to the notification as long as additional towns are not included in the amendment. Additional towns included in the amendment shall be subject to an additional fee of $200 per town, not to exceed the annual maximum under subparagraph (d).

XVI.(a) Except as provided in paragraph XVII, any person or political subdivision that repairs or replaces culverts or stream crossing structures in accordance with the best management practices for routine roadway maintenance in New Hampshire published by the department of transportation, including culverts up to and including 48 inches in diameter or the functional hydraulic equivalent, and files an appropriate notice under subparagraph (b), shall satisfy the permitting requirements of this section for minimum impact activities, as defined by rules adopted by the commissioner.

(b) Appropriate notice to the department shall include a completed routine roadway notification form as outlined in rules adopted by the commissioner pursuant to RSA 541-A including, at a minimum, the following information:

(1) Name and mailing address of the applicant or authorized person.

(2) Name and mailing address of the applicant or authorized agent, if any, representing the political subdivision.

(3) Telephone number, and email address and fax number if available.

(4) A copy of the appropriate United States Geological Survey topographic map at its original scale on 8-½ x 11 sheets with the project locations clearly labeled.

(5) Town tax map, number, and lot number, if any, of the project sites.

(6) Project location including street name and address or distance from the nearest intersection to the project.

(7) Information regarding the existing and proposed structure shown on plan sheets or equivalent plans as shown in the best management practices for routine roadway manual and a listing of the best management practices to be used during construction.

(8) Color photographs depicting the proposed work sites showing existing structures, surrounding land, and jurisdictional areas in and adjacent to the work location.

(9) A signed certification that information is accurate and correct and that work will conform to the best management practices for routine roadway maintenance.

(c) Appropriate notice to the department under subparagraphs (a) and (b) shall be mailed and received by department at least 5 days prior to the start of construction.

XVII. State and municipal public works employees who have fulfilled the requirements of a certification program developed by the department may maintain, repair, replace, or modify culverts up to a maximum diameter of 48 inches, or the hydraulic equivalent, as long as the structure can pass flows from the contributing watershed without causing damage to upstream or downstream properties, and in accordance with best management practices to protect water quality, without prior notification to the department. Federal employees who otherwise meet the requirements of the program developed by the department may maintain, repair, replace, or modify culverts as specified in this paragraph on any land within the state that is owned or managed by the federal government.

XVIII. The department shall develop an installer's certification program, in accordance with paragraph XVII, and shall determine the educational requirements for certification, including continuing education requirements. Professional engineers who are duly licensed by the New Hampshire board of professional engineers are exempt from the program requirements of this section. All certified individuals who perform such work shall submit a quarterly report to the department fully identifying work that they performed during each quarter and documentation of continuing education requirements.

XIX. The department shall issue an installer's permit to any individual who submits an application provided by the department, and has satisfactorily completed the program in accordance with paragraphs XVII and XVIII. Permits shall be issued from January 1 and shall expire December 31 of every other year. Permits shall be renewable upon proper application, and documentation of compliance with the continuing education requirement of paragraph XVIII. The installer's permit may be suspended, revoked, or not renewed for just cause, including, but not limited to, the installation of culverts in violation of this chapter or the refusal by a permit holder to correct defective work. The department shall not suspend, revoke, or refuse to renew a permit except for just cause until the permit holder has had an opportunity to be heard by the department. An appeal from such decision to revoke, suspend, or not renew a permit may be taken pursuant to RSA 21-O:14.

HISTORY:

1989, 339:1. 1990, 3:84, 85. 83:2. 1991, 20:3. 273:1. 1992, 37:2, 3. 278:3, 6. 1994, 26:1, eff. April 22, 1994. 1995, 206:2, eff. Aug. 11, 1995. 236:1, 2, eff. Aug. 18, 1995. 1996, 250:3, eff. at 12:01 a.m., Aug. 9, 1996. 296:40–42, eff. Aug. 9, 1996. 1997, 212:1–3, eff. July 1, 1997. 1998, 224:1, eff. Aug. 23, 1998. 2001, 144:1, eff. July 1, 2001. 2002, 272:15, eff. May 18, 2002. 2003, 224:1, 2, eff. July 1, 2003. 224:3, eff. July 1, 2006. 2004, 2:1, eff. March 5, 2004. 116:4, eff. May 17, 2004. 2005, 29:1, eff. May 10, 2005. 2007, 211:1, eff. August 24, 2007. 263:32, eff. July 1, 2007. 263:33, eff. July 1, 2010. 269:3, eff. July 1, 2007. 269:7, eff. July 1, 2011. 2008, 5:24, eff. July 1, 2008. 363:1, eff. September 9, 2008. 2009, 185:1, eff. September 11, 2009. 201:1, eff. July 15, 2009. 201:2, eff. at 12:01 a.m., July 1, 2010. 2010, 295:1–3, eff. September 11, 2010. 2011, 114:1, 2, eff. May 31, 2011. 143:1, eff. August 6, 2011. 195:1, eff. August 13, 2011. 195:2, eff. at 12:01 a.m., August 13, 2011. 195:3, eff. at 12:01 a.m., May 31, 2011. 2012, 145:1, eff. August 6, 2012. 273:1, 2, eff. June 19, 2012. 2013, 151:1, eff. July 1, 2013. 2014, 124:1–3, eff. June 16, 2014. 2015, 236:4, eff. September 11, 2015. 2017, 156:14, eff. July 1, 2017.

Revision note.

In the last sentence of paragraph XIX, substituted "RSA 21-O:14" for "RSA 21- 0: 14" to correct an error in the reference.

Codification.

Pursuant to 1989, 339:34, the amendments to former RSA 483-A:1, I by 1989, 408:75, eff. July 5, 1989 and 1989, 408:120, eff. July 23, 1989, were incorporated in par. I of this section; former RSA 483-A:1, V, as added by 1989, 215:2 eff. July 23, 1989, was redesignated as par. V of this section; and former RSA 483-A:1, VI, as added by 1989, 249:1, 2, eff. July 25, 1989, was redesignated as par. VI of this section. For purposes of conformity with the recodification of former RSA 483-A:1, III as par. III of this section, substituted "paragraph III" for "RSA 483-A:1, III" in the second sentence of par. V(c).

Contingent 2011, 195:4, I amendment.

2011, 195:4, I eff. August 13, 2011, provided in part, that if HB 621-FN-LOCAL [ch. 114] of the 2011 legislative session becomes law before the effective date of section 1 of this act, section 2 shall take effect at 12:01 a.m. 60 days after passage of this act. Pursuant to the terms of this provision RSA 482-A:3 is set out above as amended by Ch. 195:2, eff. August 13, 2011 at 12:01 a.m.

Contingent 2011, 195:4, II amendment.

2011, 195:4, II eff. August 13, 2011, provided in part, that if HB 621-FN-LOCAL [ch. 114] of the 2011 legislative session becomes law, then section 3 of this act shall take effect at 12:01 a.m. on the effective date of HB 621-FN-LOCAL. Pursuant to the terms of this provision RSA 482-A:3 is set out above as amended by Ch. 195:3, eff. May 31, 2011 at 12:01 a.m.

Amendment Notes

The 2017 amendments to this section by Ch. 156 substituted "natural and cultural resources" for "resources and economic development" throughout the section.

—2015.

The 2015 amendment rewrote paragraph II(b).

—2014.

The 2014 amendment rewrote I to the extent that a detailed comparison would be impracticable; added XIV-b; and added the second sentence of XVII.

—2013.

The 2013 amendment added X(c).

—2012.

The 2012 amendment by Chapter 145, added the XIV-a(a) designation; added "With the exception of permits issued under subparagraph (b)" in the first sentence of the introductory language of XIV-a(a); redesignated former XIV-a(a) through XIV-a(d) as XIV-a(a)(1) through XIV-a(a)(4); and added XIV-a(b).

The 2012 amendment by Chapter 273, added "Except as provided in paragraph XVII" in XVI(a) and added XVII through XIX.

—2011.

The 2011 amendment by Chapter 114, added "Notwithstanding any law or rule to the contrary" in (I-a) and added XVI.

The 2011 amendment by Chapter 143 added XIV-a.

The 2011 amendment by Chapter 195:1, effective August 13, 2011, rewrote IV(b) and added IV(c).

The 2011 amendment by Chapter 195:2, effective August 13, 2011 at 12:01 a.m., added "however any repair, replacement or modification of a culvert must be made in accordance with RSA 482-A:3, XVI" in IV(c).

The 2011 amendment by Chapter 195:3 effective May 31, 2011 at 12:01 a.m., substituted in XVI(a), "culverts or stream crossing" for "or maintains" and added "and including" and made a related change.

—2010.

The 2010 amendment, in XIV(a)(3)(A) and XIV(a)(4)(A), deleted "or deny" following "Approve" and added "and issue a permit"; added XIV(a)(3)(B), XIV(a)(4)(B), XIV(a)(4)(D), XIV(b)(2) through XIV(b)(4), XIV(f), and XIV(g); redesignated former XIV(a)(3)(B), XIV(a)(3)(C), and XIV(a)(4)(B) as XIV(a)(3)(C), XIV(a)(3)(D), and XIV(a)(4)(C); substituted "Schedule a public hearing" for "Commence a non-adjudicative proceeding" in XIV(a)(3)(C) and XIV(a)(4)(C); substituted "rendering a decision on the application" for "response" in XIV(a)(3)(D); in the introductory language of XIV(a)(4), substituted "subparagraph (a)(2)" for "subparagraph (b)," added "for proposed projects under one acre of jurisdictional impact," and substituted "for all others" for "if the application proposes more than one acre of jurisdictional impact"; in XIV(a)(5), substituted "held a public" for "commenced a non-adjudicative," added "the application in whole or in part, and issue a permit," and substituted "and issue written findings in support of the denial" for "either in whole or in part"; added the XIV(b)(1) designation; rewrote XIV(b)(1); and made related and stylistic changes.

—2009.

The 2009 amendment by Chapter 185 added XV.

The 2009 amendment by Chapter 201:1, effective July 15, 2009, rewrote I(d) to the extent that a detailed comparison would be impracticable.

The 2009 amendment by Chapter 201:2, effective July 1, 2010 at 12:01 a.m., rewrote I(d) to the extent that a detailed comparison would be impracticable.

—2008.

The 2008 amendment by Chapter 5 substituted "RSA 483-B:5-b" for "RSA 483-B:5-a" in III.

The 2008 amendment by Chapter 363 rewrote XIV to the extent that a detailed comparison would be impracticable.

—2007.

Paragraph I: Rewritten by chapter 263:32 to the extent that a detailed comparison would be impracticable.

Rewritten by chapter 263:33 to the extent that a detailed comparison would be impracticable.

Paragraph III: Ch. 269:3 inserted "and RSA 483-B:5-a" following "XII(c)" and "continually" preceding "appropriated to" and "and protected shorelands under RSA 483-B" following "of the state" in the first sentence and inserted "and shorelands" following "the wetlands" in the second sentence.

Ch. 269:7 deleted "and RSA 483-B:5-a" preceding "are continually" in the first sentence

Paragraph IV-a: Chapter 211 substituted "installed" for "constructed" preceding "on any lake" and inserted "by the owner of property" preceding "that includes" and deleted "the owner of" following "address of" and inserted "owner" preceding "the municipality" and "from the lake bed" following "Removed" in subpar. (c) and added subpar. (j) and made some related changes.

—2005.

Paragraph IV(b): Rewritten to the extent that a detailed comparison would be impracticable.

—2004.

Paragraph I-a: Added by ch. 2.

Paragraph V(a): Chapter 116 added the second sentence.

—2003.

Paragraph I: Rewritten by ch. 224:2 to the extent that a detailed comparison would be impracticable.

Chapter 224:3, eff. July 1, 2006, substituted "$.06 per square foot" for "$.10 per square foot" in the sixth sentence.

Paragraph XIV: Added.

—2002.

Paragraph IV-a: Added.

—2001.

Paragraph X: Designated the existing provisions as subpar. (a) and added subpar. (b).

—1998.

Paragraph XIII: Added.

—1997.

Paragraph I: Substituted "dredge, fill, or construction" for "dredge or fill" preceding "proposed" in the fourth sentence and "$0.04 per square foot for all proposed projects under this chapter" for "$0.025 per square foot" in the fifth sentence.

Paragraph III: Inserted "hiring additional staff" preceding "reviewing applications" in the first sentence.

Paragraph IV(b): Rewritten to the extent that a detailed comparison would be impracticable.

—1996.

Paragraph I: Chapter 296 substituted "department" for "wetlands board" in the first, fifth, seventh, and tenth sentences and inserted "state of" preceding "New Hampshire" and deleted "wetlands board" thereafter in the second sentence.

Paragraph II(a): Chapter 296 substituted "department" for "wetlands board" and "board" throughout the paragraph.

Paragraph II(b): Chapter 296 substituted "department" for "board" in the first and third sentences, and inserted "governor and" preceding "council may approve" in the second sentence.

Paragraph III: Chapter 296 substituted "department" for "wetlands board" and inserted "of the council" following "members" in the first sentence, and deleted "board" preceding "review fund" in the second sentence.

Paragraph IV(b): Chapter 296 substituted "department" for "wetlands board" in the first sentence, deleted "board" preceding "jurisdiction" and inserted "of the department of environmental services" thereafter in two places in the second sentence.

Paragraph V(a): Chapter 296 substituted "department" for "wetlands board" following "intent with the" and "commissioner" for "wetlands board" following "adopted by the".

Paragraphs V(b)–(d): Chapter 296 substituted "department" for "wetlands board" wherever it appeared.

Paragraphs VII, X, XI(b), and XII(b), (c): Chapter 296 substituted "department" for "wetlands board" wherever it appeared.

Paragraphs XI(a), XI(d): Chapter 296 substituted "commissioner" for "wetlands board" in the introductory paragraph.

Paragraph XI(c): Chapter 296 deleted "board" following "wetlands".

Paragraphs XI(f), (g): Chapter 296 substituted "department" for "wetlands board".

Paragraph XI(h): Chapter 296 substituted "department" for "wetlands board" in the second sentence and deleted the third sentence.

Paragraph XII(a): Chapter 296 substituted "department" for "wetlands board" following "trails with the" and "commissioner" for "wetlands board" following "adopted by the" at the end of the sentence.

Chapter 250 substituted "Best Management Practices for Erosion Control During Trail Maintenance and Construction" for "Trail Administrators Manual" and "department" for "division" following "trails with the".

—1995.

Paragraph III: Chapter 236 deleted "and" preceding "XI(h)" and inserted "and XII(c)" thereafter in the first sentence.

Paragraph V(b)(4): Chapter 206 substituted "Natural Resources" for "Soil" preceding "Conservation".

Paragraph XII: Added by ch. 236.

—1994.

Paragraph VII: Inserted "without a permit from the wetlands board" following "state" in the first sentence and added the second sentence.

—1992.

Paragraph III: Rewritten by ch. 37 to the extent that a detailed comparison would be impracticable.

Paragraph IV: Chapter 278 designated existing provisions of the paragraph as subpar. (a) and added subpar. (b).

Paragraph XI: Added by ch. 37.

Chapter 278 added the second sentence of subpar. (b).

—1991.

Paragraph I: Rewritten by ch. 20 to the extent that a detailed comparison would be impracticable.

Paragraph X: Added by ch. 273.

—1990.

Paragraph I: Chapter 3 substituted "$50" for "$25" preceding "for minimum impact projects" and deleted "$100 for minor projects, and $300 for major projects" thereafter in the third sentence and added the fourth and fifth sentences.

Paragraph V(c): Chapter 3 substituted "$25" for "$10" in the first sentence.

Paragraphs VII–IX: Added by ch. 83.

Contingent 1996 amendments.

1996, 296:14–16, provided for amendment of this section. However, under the terms of 1996, 296:54, eff. Aug 9, 1996, the amendments did not become effective.

1996, 250:1, 3, provided for amendment of this section. However, under the terms of 1996, 250:4, eff. Aug. 9, 1996, the amendments did not become effective.

NOTES TO DECISIONS

Analysis

1. Applicability
2. Groundwater withdrawal
3. Judicial review of permit approval
4. Trenching
5. Total wetlands impact

1. Applicability

Dock permit did not adversely affect the value and enjoyment of petitioners' property because even if the Environmental Council erred in treating petitioners as "abutting owners" under RSA 482-A:11, II, this afforded them more protection than that to which they were entitled under the statute because petitioners had granted respondents an easement; the findings that the small, seasonal dock did not unreasonably affect their use and enjoyment were supported by the record; petitioners retained the right to seek relief should respondents make unreasonable use of their easement; and RSA 482-A:3, XIII(a), concerning abutting property owners, did not apply. Appeal of Michele (New Hampshire Wetlands Council), 168 N.H. 98, 123 A.3d 255, 2015 N.H. LEXIS 80 (N.H. 2015).

Once a boathouse project was relocated landward of a bank, it lost its status as a water dependent structure because it was no longer located over, on, or in the waters of the State of New Hampshire. It was then located over a dredged inlet, and no longer required a dredge and fill permit so that there was no legal basis for imposing the N.H. Code Admin. R. Ann., Env-Wt 302.03 requirements on the boathouse. Cayten v. N.H. Dep't of Envtl. Servs., 155 N.H. 647, 927 A.2d 494, 2007 N.H. LEXIS 113 (N.H. 2007).

2. Groundwater withdrawal

As a proposed groundwater withdrawal is not subject to the permitting requirements of RSA 482-A:3, I, the Department of Environmental Services did not err in not holding a public hearing on the withdrawal under RSA 482-A:11, IV. Appeal of Town of Nottingham (N.H. Dep't of Envtl. Servs.), 153 N.H. 539, 904 A.2d 582, 2006 N.H. LEXIS 71 (N.H. 2006).

3. Judicial review of permit approval

Trial court did not err by ruling that the New Hampshire Department of Environmental Services (DES) review authority of a wetlands permit was limited to assessing the impacts of construction activities in the protected wetlands, as DES' authority did not extend to assessing the effects of upland construction activities upon such wetlands. An appellate court did not further review the appeal because the trial court determined, as a matter of law, based upon its review of the certified record, that an environmental council's decision granting a developer the permit was legally correct and the appellate court, having reviewed the certified record itself, found that the evidence was sufficient for the trial court to have reached that conclusion. Greenland Conservation Comm'n v. N.H. Wetlands Council, 154 N.H. 529, 913 A.2d 776, 2006 N.H. LEXIS 195 (N.H. 2006).

4. Trenching

Trial court properly determined that respondents violated the Wetlands Act, RSA 482-A:3, I in building their home, as digging a trench and refilling it after it was dug constituted excavating, removing, filling, or dredging as those terms were used in the Wetlands Act. N.H. Dep't of Envtl. Servs. v. Marino, 155 N.H. 709, 928 A.2d 818, 2007 N.H. LEXIS 120 (N.H. 2007).

5. Total wetlands impact

Pursuant to N.H. Code Admin. R. Ann. Env.-Wt 302.04(a)(4), (17), to obtain a permit under RSA 482-A:3, I(a), an applicant must demonstrate — and consequently, the Department of Environmental Services (DES) cannot decline to address — the total wetlands impact of the proposed project. Thus, when the DES evaluates a permit application involving an activity that falls within the scope of RSA 482-A:3, it may not decline to consider a related activity that itself may not require a wetlands permit but has a bearing on the total wetlands impact of the proposed project. Appeal of Morrissey, 165 N.H. 87, 70 A.3d 465, 2013 N.H. LEXIS 66 (N.H. 2013).

To obtain a permit under RSA 482-A:3, I(a), an applicant had to demonstrate the total wetlands impact of a proposed project. Accordingly, the Department of Environmental Services erred in declining to consider a town's activity relative to the water level in a pond on the ground that the activity did not itself require a wetlands permit. Appeal of Morrissey, 165 N.H. 87, 70 A.3d 465, 2013 N.H. LEXIS 66 (N.H. 2013).

Cited:

Cited in Gray v. Seidel, 143 N.H. 327, 726 A.2d 1283, 1999 N.H. LEXIS 5 (1999).

RESEARCH REFERENCES AND PRACTICE AIDS

Cross References.

Conduct of hearings and filing of reports as to projects by municipal conservation commissions, see RSA 482-A:8, 11.

New Hampshire Code of Administrative Rules

Rules of the Department of Environmental Services—Wetlands Board, Env-Wt 501.02 and 501.05–.07, New Hampshire Code of Administrative Rules Annotated.

482-A:4. Definition.

Without limiting RSA 482-A:3, the waters and adjacent areas within this state to which this chapter applies are defined as follows:

I. Wherever the tide ebbs and flows, this chapter shall apply to all lands submerged or flowed by mean high tide as locally determined, any sand dune or vegetation thereon in the state of New Hampshire, and, in addition, to those areas within 100 feet of the highest observable tide line which border on tidal waters, such as, but not limited to, banks, upland areas, bogs, salt marsh, swamps, meadows, flats or other lowlands subject to tidal action.

II. Wherever fresh water flows or stands and in all areas above tidal waters not included in paragraph I of this section, it shall apply (in addition to great ponds or lakes of 10 acres or more in natural area as provided for in RSA 482-A:16–20 and RSA 482-A:21–25) to those portions of great ponds or lakes created by the raising of the water level of the same, whether by public or private structure, and to all surface waters of the state as defined in RSA 485-A:2 which contain fresh water, including the portion of any bank or shore which borders such surface waters, and to any swamp or bog subject to periodical flooding by fresh water including the surrounding shore.

HISTORY:

1989, 339:1. 1990, 83:3, eff. April 10, 1990.

Codification.

Pursuant to 1989, 339:34, the amendment to former RSA 483-A:1-a, I by 1989, 225:1, eff. July 23, 1989, was incorporated in par. I of this section.

Amendments

—1990.

Paragraph I: Inserted "any sand dune or vegetation thereon in the state of New Hampshire" following "determined".

NOTES TO DECISIONS

Analysis

1. Constitutionality
2. Permit

1. Constitutionality

The definitions contained in this section are not unconstitutionally vague and over broad because they set forth imprecise or incalculable scientific requirements, since expert witnesses at trial had little difficulty in determining whether property met these definitions. State Wetlands Bd. v. Marshall, 127 N.H. 240, 500 A.2d 685, 1985 N.H. LEXIS 435 (N.H. 1985). (Decided under prior law.)

2. Permit

Once a boathouse project was relocated landward of a bank, it lost its status as a water dependent structure because it was no longer located over, on, or in the waters of the State of New Hampshire. It was then located over a dredged inlet, and no longer required a dredge and fill permit so that there was no legal basis for imposing the N.H. Code Admin. R. Ann., Env-Wt 302.03 requirements on the boathouse. Cayten v. N.H. Dep't of Envtl. Servs., 155 N.H. 647, 927 A.2d 494, 2007 N.H. LEXIS 113 (N.H. 2007).

Cited:
Cited in Greenland Conservation Comm'n v. N.H. Wetlands Council, 154 N.H. 529, 913 A.2d 776, 2006 N.H. LEXIS 195 (2006).

482-A:5. Establishment of Wetlands Board. [Repealed.]

[Repealed 1996, 296:33, eff. Aug. 9, 1996.]

Former section(s).
Former RSA 482-A:5, which was derived from 1989, 339:1; 1991, 238:1; 1992, 292:5; and 1996, 228:105, related to the establishment of the Wetlands Board.

Abolition of wetlands board; transfer of functions, etc. to commissioner of environmental services; effect on board members.
1996, 296:32, eff. Aug. 9, 1996, provided:
"**I.** The wetlands board is hereby abolished and all of the functions, duties, powers, responsibilities, and unexpended appropriations are hereby transferred to and vested in the commissioner of environmental services.
"**II.** The transfer and termination provided for in this section shall become effective upon the effective date of this section. Prior to that date the wetlands board, and the officials of the wetlands board shall retain their full power and authority.
"**III.** The incumbent public members of the wetlands board in office on the effective date of the transfers provided for in this section shall become the first public members of the wetlands council established by RSA 21-O:5-a for the remainder of the terms to which they were originally appointed. Upon expiration of their terms, the governor and council shall appoint their successors in accordance with RSA 21-O:5-a, so as to provide for a staggering of the 3-year terms to which those successors are appointed so that those terms shall expire at one-year intervals."

482-A:6. Powers of Department.

I. The department may deny the petition or may require the installation of bulkheads, barriers, proper retention or containment structures, or both, to prevent subsequent fill runoff back into waters or other protective measures.

II. To perform its duties under this chapter, it shall be lawful for the department, its agents or employees to enter upon any lands in the state.

III. Whenever it is found that a wetlands is at immediate risk from dredging, filling, or other activity in violation of this chapter, the department may issue an emergency order in writing requiring the immediate cessation of such activity. Any person to whom such an order is directed shall comply immediately, but may appeal as provided in RSA 482-A:10.

IV. The department may issue an order to any person in violation of this chapter, a rule adopted under this chapter or any condition in a permit issued under this chapter to comply with this chapter, the rule or the permit, and require such remedial measures as may be necessary. Any person to whom such an order is directed may appeal as provided in RSA 482-A:10.

HISTORY:
1989, 339:1, eff. Jan. 1, 1990. 1996, 296:43, eff. Aug. 9, 1996. 2012, 246:7, eff. June 18, 2012.

Codification.
Pursuant to 1989, 339:34, former RSA 483-A:3, III and IV, as added by 1989, 99:1, eff. June 30, 1989, were redesignated as pars. III and IV of this section, respectively.

Abolition of wetlands board; transfer of functions, duties, powers and responsibilities from wetlands board to commissioner of environmental services.
1996, 296:32, I, II, eff. Aug. 9, 1996, provided:
"I. The wetlands board is hereby abolished and all of the functions, duties, powers, responsibilities, and unexpended appropriations are hereby transferred to and vested in the commissioner of environmental services.
"II. The transfer and termination provided for in this section shall become effective upon the effective date of this section. Prior to that date the wetlands board, and the officials of the wetlands board shall retain their full power and authority."

Amendments

—2012.
The 2012 amendment deleted "request reconsideration and then" preceding "appeal as provided" in the second sentence of III and IV.

—1996.
Rewritten to the extent that a detailed comparison would be impracticable.

Contingent 1996 amendments.
1996, 296:17, provided for amendment of this section. However, under the terms of 1996, 296:54, eff. Aug. 9, 1996, the amendments did not become effective.

RESEARCH REFERENCES AND PRACTICE AIDS

Cross References.
Administrative inspection warrants, see RSA 595-B.
Granting of permits for projects, see RSA 482-A:12.
Requirements as to decision by board, see RSA 482-A:11.

482-A:7. Gifts, Grants or Donations.

The department is authorized to solicit and receive any gifts, grants or donations made for the efforts of the department under the provisions of this chapter and to disburse and administer the same through the department.

HISTORY:
1989, 339:1, eff. Jan. 1, 1990. 1996, 296:44, eff. Aug. 9, 1996.

Editor's note.
1989, 138:7 amended former RSA 483-A:1-d by substituting "division of water resources" for "water resources board". This change was also made in 1989, 339:1, which recodified former RSA 483-A:1-d as this section.

Amendments

—1996.
Rewritten to the extent that a detailed comparison would be impracticable.

Contingent 1996 amendment.
1996, 296:18, provided for the amendment of this section. However, under the terms of 1996, 296:54, eff. Aug. 9, 1996, the amendments did not become effective.

482-A:8. Public Comment and Hearing.

The department shall provide a reasonable opportunity for public comment on proposals under RSA 482-A:3 and shall hold a public hearing for projects with significant impact on the resources protected by this chapter or of substantial public interest. The department shall notify by mail, the applicant and the property owner if different, the local governing body of the municipality involved, the planning board, if any, and the municipal conservation commission, if any, of the hearing. The department shall maintain a chronological file of all applications received under RSA 482-A:3, which shall be available for public review during normal business hours. The hearing requirement in this section may not apply to such minor projects and to such minor improvements of the shoreline of those waters subject to the jurisdiction of this chapter as the department may by reasonable rule provide.

HISTORY:

1989, 339:1. 1991, 20:4, eff. Jan. 1, 1992. 1996, 296:44, eff. Aug. 9, 1996. 2013, 43:1, eff. August 3, 2013.

Amendment Notes

—2013.

The 2013 amendment deleted the former last sentence, which read: "The hearing requirements of RSA 541-A:30 shall be satisfied by a hearing on reconsideration in accordance with RSA 482-A:10, III."

—1996.

Rewritten to the extent that a detailed comparison would be impractical.

—1991.

Substituted "governing" for "legislative" preceding "body" in the first sentence.

Contingent 1996 amendment.

1996, 296:18, provided for the amendment of this section. However, under the terms of 1996, 296:54, eff. Aug. 9, 1996, the amendment did not become effective.

NOTES TO DECISIONS

Cited:

Cited in Cayten v. N.H. Dep't of Envtl. Servs., 155 N.H. 647, 927 A.2d 494, 2007 N.H. LEXIS 113 (2007).

RESEARCH REFERENCES AND PRACTICE AIDS

Cross References.

Suspension of action by board pending investigations and reports by municipal conservation commissions, see RSA 482-A:11.

482-A:9. Notice to Abutters.

Like notice shall be mailed to all known abutting landowners, supplemented by reasonable notice by newspaper publications to those unknown, as may be ordered by the department.

HISTORY:

1989, 339:1, eff. Jan. 1, 1990. 1996, 296:44, eff. Aug. 9, 1996.

Amendments

—1996.

Substituted "department" for "wetlands board".

Contingent 1996 amendment.

1996, 296:18, provided for the amendment of this section. However, under the terms of 1996, 296:54, eff. Aug. 9, 1996, the amendment did not become effective.

NOTES TO DECISIONS

Cited:

Cited in Cayten v. N.H. Dep't of Envtl. Servs., 155 N.H. 647, 927 A.2d 494, 2007 N.H. LEXIS 113 (2007).

RESEARCH REFERENCES AND PRACTICE AIDS

Cross References.

Notice generally, see RSA 482-A:8.

482-A:10. Appeals.

I. Any person aggrieved by a decision made by the department under RSA 482-A:3 may appeal to the wetlands council and to the supreme court as provided in RSA 21-O:14, including the provisions relative to requesting mediated or unmediated settlement discussions. A person aggrieved under this section shall mean the applicant and any person required to be noticed by mail in accordance with RSA 482-A:8 and RSA 482-A:9.

II. Any person subject to an order of the department under RSA 482-A:6 may appeal to the wetlands council and to the supreme court as provided in RSA 21-O:14, including the provisions relative to requesting mediated or unmediated settlement discussions.

III. An appeal from a decision of the department under RSA 482-A:3 or an appeal from an order issued by the department under RSA 482-A:6, shall be filed in accordance with the applicable provisions of RSA 21-O:14 and rules adopted by the council pursuant to RSA 541-A regarding the number of copies to be filed, the address to which the notice of appeal must be sent or delivered, and the method of delivery.

IV. A notice of appeal to the council shall contain a detailed description of the land involved in the department's decision and shall set forth fully every ground upon which it is claimed that the decision complained of is unlawful or unreasonable. Only those grounds set forth in the notice of appeal shall be considered by the council.

V. Any appeal hearing held by the council shall be an adjudicative hearing as provided in RSA 541-A and the council's rules. The hearing shall be noticed in accordance with RSA 541-A:31, III. For appeals of department decisions under RSA 482-A:3, the notice shall also be sent to all persons entitled to notice of applications under RSA 482-A:8 and RSA 482-A:9. The burden of proof shall be on the party seeking to set aside the department's decision to show that the decision is unlawful or unreasonable. On appeal of requests proposed, sponsored, or administered by the department of transportation, there shall be a rebuttable presumption that there is a public need for the requested project, and that the department of transportation has exercised appropriate engineering judgment in the project's design. All findings of the department upon all questions of fact properly before it shall be prima facie lawful and reasonable.

V-a. Any person whose rights will be directly affected by the outcome of the appeal may appear and become a party to the appeal. Any person whose rights may be directly affected by the outcome of the appeal may file a request to intervene as provided in RSA 541-A:32.

VI. On appeal, the council may affirm the decision of the department or may remand to the department with a determination that the decision complained of is unlawful or unreasonable. The council shall specify the factual and legal basis for its determination and shall identify the evidence in the record created before the council that supports its decision.

VII. Any party aggrieved by a decision of the council may apply to the council for reconsideration as specified in RSA 541.

VIII. Any party aggrieved by a decision of the council after reconsideration may appeal to the supreme court as specified in RSA 541.

IX. In the case of a remand to the department by the council, the department may accept the council's determination and reissue a decision or order, imposing such conditions as are necessary and consistent with the purposes of this chapter, or may appeal as provided in paragraphs VII and VIII.

X–XVII. [Repealed.]

XVIII. If a permit is granted with respect to any activity proposed to be undertaken in or adjacent to a prime wetland as mapped, designated, and filed pursuant to RSA 482-A:15, the conservation commission or local governing body may appeal said decision to the wetlands council and the supreme court in the manner prescribed in this section. The filing of a request for reconsideration under paragraph VII shall automatically stay the effectiveness of the council's decision relating to said prime wetland. Said stay shall remain in force until the council has issued its decision after reconsideration.

HISTORY:

1989, 339:1. 1991, 20:5, eff. Jan. 1, 1992. 1996, 296:45, eff. Aug. 9, 1996. 2004, 2:2, 3, eff. March 5, 2004. 243:3, eff. July 1, 2004. 2008, 171:6, 7, 16, eff. July 1, 2008. 363:5, eff. September 9, 2008. 2012, 246:8, 9. eff. June 18, 2012. 2013, 43:2, eff. August 3, 2013.

Contingent 2008 ch. 171, amendment.

2008, 171:21, I, eff. June 6, 2008, provided in part, that if HB 1601-FN-A [ch. 5] of the 2008 legislative session becomes law, sections 6, 7 and 16 of this act shall take effect July 1, 2008. Pursuant to the terms of this provision pars. I through VIII, XVIII and X–XVII are set out above as amended by Ch. 171:6, 7 and 16, eff. July 1, 2008.

Amendment Notes

—2013.

The 2013 amendment, in the first sentence of I, deleted "apply for reconsideration by the department, and then may" following "RSA

482-A:3 may" and substituted "RSA 21-O:14, including the provisions relative to requesting mediated or unmediated settlement discussions" for "this section"; redesignated former I-a, IV, and IV-a as II through IV; in II, substituted "RSA 21-O:14, including the provisions relative to requesting mediated or unmediated settlement discussions" for "this section" and deleted the former second sentence; deleted former II and III; deleted "after reconsideration" following "RSA 482-A:3" in III; substituted "Any appeal hearing held by the council shall be" for "The council on appeal shall hold" in the first sentence of V; and in XVIII, deleted "request reconsideration by the department and, if aggrieved by the decision or reconsideration" following "body may" in the first sentence, added "under paragraph VII" in the second sentence, and substituted "council" for "department" or variants in the last two sentences.

—2012.

The 2012 amendment rewrote IV to the extent that a detailed comparison would be impracticable and added IV-a.

—2008.

The 2008 amendment by Chapter 171, rewrote I–VIII to the extent that a detailed comparison would be impracticable; added I-a and V-a; deleted X through XVII; in XVIII, added "request reconsideration by the department and, if aggrieved by the decision or reconsideration" and substituted "wetlands council and the supreme court" for "superior court" in the first sentence.

The 2008 amendment by Chapter 363, rewrote II and III to the extent that a detailed comparison would be impracticable.

—2004.

Paragraph IV: Chapter 243 added the third sentence and inserted "or hand delivery" following "certified mail" and substituted "wetlands" for "chairperson of the" preceding "council" in the fourth sentence.

Paragraph V: Chapter 2 added the fifth sentence.

Paragraph XI: Chapter 2 added the second sentence.

—1996.

Rewritten to the extent that a detailed comparison would be impracticable.

—1991.

Paragraph IV: Substituted "local governing" for "municipal executive" preceding "body" in the first sentence and "RSA 677:2" for "RSA 31:74" in the second sentence.

Contingent 2008 ch. 363, amendment.

2008, 363:6, eff. July 11, 2008, provided in part, that if SB 352-FN [ch. 171] of the 2008 legislative session becomes law, section 5 of this act shall take effect 60 days after its passage and section 2 of this act shall not take effect." Pursuant to the terms of this provision pars. II–III are set out above as amended by Ch. 363:5, eff. September 9, 2008.

Contingent 1996 amendment.

1996, 296:19, provided for the amendment of this section. However, under the terms of 1996, 296:54, eff. Aug. 9, 1996, the amendment did not become effective.

NOTES TO DECISIONS

Analysis

1. Evidence
2. Illustrative cases
3. Parties to appeal
4. Standard of review

1. Evidence

It was not an abuse of discretion for a trial court to supplement the record in an appeal from the grant of a wetlands permit with the opinion testimony of an expert who discovered vernal and seasonal pools at a wetlands site for which the permit had been requested. Conservation Law Found. v. N.H. Wetlands Council, 150 N.H. 1, 834 A.2d 193, 2003 N.H. LEXIS 130 (N.H. 2003).

2. Illustrative cases

Petitioners' argument that a town should have procured a wetlands permit in order to remove beaver dams had not been preserved because petitioners failed to raise it in their appeal to the Wetlands Council under RSA 482-A:10, IV-a and in their motion for reconsideration. Appeal of Morrissey, 165 N.H. 87, 70 A.3d 465, 2013 N.H. LEXIS 66 (N.H. 2013).

It was error for the Wetlands Council to reverse an award of a wetlands permit. The Department of Environmental Services found that adverse impacts should not result in the significant loss of wetlands values because the monitoring devices themselves, in addition to mitigation requirements, assured that groundwater withdrawal would be reduced or halted before any significant loss of RSA 482-A:1 values occurred; these were precisely the type of findings that were entitled to deference under RSA 482-A:10, V. Appeal of Garrison Place Real Estate Inv. Trust, 159 N.H. 539, 986 A.2d 670, 2009 N.H. LEXIS 145 (N.H. 2009).

Trial court did not err by ruling that the New Hampshire Department of Environmental Services (DES) review authority of a wetlands permit was limited to assessing the impacts of construction activities in the protected wetlands, as DES' authority did not extend to assessing the effects of upland construction activities upon such wetlands. An appellate court did not further review the appeal because the trial court determined, as a matter of law, based upon its review of the certified record, that an environmental council's decision granting a developer the permit was legally correct and the appellate court, having reviewed the certified record itself, found that the evidence was sufficient for the trial court to have reached that conclusion. Greenland Conservation Comm'n v. N.H. Wetlands Council, 154 N.H. 529, 913 A.2d 776, 2006 N.H. LEXIS 195 (N.H. 2006).

Trial court erred in vacating a wetlands permit because the documentation of seasonal and vernal pools was not required under N.H. Code Admin. R. Ann. Env-Wt 302.04(a)(7) and the New Hampshire Department of Transportation adequately addressed whether a roundabout was a practicable alternative to the proposed trumpet interchange that required filling in several acres of wetlands. Conservation Law Found. v. N.H. Wetlands Council, 150 N.H. 1, 834 A.2d 193, 2003 N.H. LEXIS 130 (N.H. 2003).

3. Parties to appeal

Trial court erred by permitting supporting individuals who did not sign an appeal to be parties in the appeal after they were dismissed from the administrative proceedings under review and did not file for reconsideration of their dismissal. RSA 482-A:10, XII was not meant to provide a bypass around the statutory reconsideration and appeal process. Cayten v. N.H. Dep't of Envtl. Servs., 155 N.H. 647, 927 A.2d 494, 2007 N.H. LEXIS 113 (N.H. 2007).

4. Standard of review

Under the plain language of RSA 482-A:10, V, the Wetlands Council's review of New Hampshire Department of Environmental Services (DES) decisions is deferential; the party appealing to the council bears the burden of presenting the council with a preponderance of clear and concise evidence that otherwise persuades the council such a decision was unreasonable and/or unlawful. The council cannot substitute its independent judgment of the facts and circumstances of a decision for that used by DES in its own deliberations. Appeal of Garrison Place Real Estate Inv. Trust, 159 N.H. 539, 986 A.2d 670, 2009 N.H. LEXIS 145 (N.H. 2009).

RESEARCH REFERENCES AND PRACTICE AIDS

Cross References.

Fish and game fund, see RSA 206:33 et seq.

Rehearings and appeals from state agencies, departments or officials, see RSA 541.

482-A:10-a. Damages.

I. If, upon appeal of the landowner, the superior court determines that the decision appealed from so exceeds the bounds of the police power as to constitute the equivalent of taking without compensation and that the land as so regulated meets the public purpose standards of this chapter, and if such ruling is affirmed on appeal or becomes the law of the trial by failure of the state to appeal, the superior court shall then proceed to the assessment of the landowner's damages. Unless the department, at this stage, consents to the reversal or modification of its decision by the superior court, that court shall first determine all questions of land title, after notice to all persons interested in the land, including notice by publication to any unknown owners, and then shall assess the damages of the landowner or landowners proceeding as provided in RSA 482:35-38, inclusive, and RSA 498-A:27, and may enter judgment against the state accordingly. The interest acquired by the state by virtue of such proceedings shall be a perpetual negative easement that the privately-ownedland or interest in the land described in the proceedings shall not thereafter be excavated, removed, filled, dredged, canalized or ditched, subject to any such reasonable reservations to the landowner as the department may have stipulated to prior to the assessment of damages. The state may, in the alternative, purchase the land or interest in the land in fee simple or other acceptable title, or subject to acceptable reservations and exceptions, by agreement with the landowner. To satisfy any judgment or purchase agreement under this section, the governor and council, in their discretion, may draw their warrant on the marine fisheries fund, the fish and game fund, any other available appropriation for such purpose, or on any money in the treasury not otherwise appropriated, or any combination of such funds, as they may determine to be just and reasonable, or, in the alternative, they may certify a judgment to the next session of the general court for the passage of an appropriation of money sufficient to satisfy the same. The department may, in the name of the state, accept gifts of land or interests in land for the purposes of this chapter.

II. The use of the marine fisheries fund or the fish and game fund under paragraph I shall require a finding that the expenditure will be of substantial benefit to marine fisheries or to fish and wildlife, as the case may be, and the governor and council shall request the prior opinion of the fish and game commission in each such case.

HISTORY:

1996, 296:46, eff. Aug. 9, 1996.

Contingent enactment of section.

1996, 296:19, provided for the enactment of this section. However, under the terms of 1996, 296:54, eff. Aug. 9, 1996, the enactment did not become effective.

482-A:11. Administrative Provisions.

I. The commissioner shall adopt reasonable rules, pursuant to the rulemaking provisions of RSA 541-A, to implement the purposes of this chapter.

II. Decisions of the department or council under this chapter shall be consistent with the purposes of this chapter as set forth in RSA 482-A:1. Before granting a permit under this chapter, the department may require reasonable proof of ownership by a private landowner-applicant. If a permit is granted, the decision of the department may contain reasonable conditions designed to protect the public good. No permit to dredge or fill shall be granted if it shall infringe on the property rights or unreasonably affect the value or enjoyment of property of abutting owners.

III.(a) Upon written notification to the department by a municipal conservation commission that it intends to investigate any notice received by it pursuant to RSA 482-A:3, the department shall not make its decision on the application that is the subject of the notice until it has received and acknowledged receipt of a written report from such commission, or until 40 days from the date of filing with the municipal clerk of such notice, whichever occurs earlier, subject to an extension as permitted by the department. In connection with any local investigation, a conservation commission may hold a public informational meeting or a public hearing, the record of which shall be made a part of the record of the department. Where the department grants an extension, the time limits prescribed by RSA 482-A:3, XIV(b) shall be suspended until a date agreed to by the applicant and the department. If a conservation commission makes a recommendation to the department in its report, the department shall specifically consider such recommendation and shall make written findings with respect to each issue raised in such report which is contrary to the decision of the department. If notification by a local conservation commission pursuant to this paragraph is not received by the department within 14 days following the date the notice is filed with the municipal clerk, the department shall not suspend its normal action, but shall proceed as if no notification has been made.

(b) Relative to any expedited permit under paragraph VI, the provisions of subparagraph (a) shall be modified as follows:

(1) The 40-day suspended action limit is reduced to 21 days; and

(2) The notification by a municipal conservation commission of intended investigation shall be assumed unless the application filed under RSA 482-A:3 was signed by the conservation commission, or, if one has not been established in the municipality, by the local governing body, in which case the provisions of subparagraph (a) shall not apply.

IV.(a) The department shall not grant a permit with respect to any project to be undertaken in an area mapped, designated, and filed as a prime wetland pursuant to RSA 482-A:15, or within 100 feet of any prime wetland where a 100 foot buffer was required at the time of designation, unless the department first notifies the local governing body, the planning board, if any, and the conservation commission, if any, in the municipality within which the wetlands lie, either in whole or in part, of its decision. Any such permit shall not be issued unless the department is able, specifically, to find clear and convincing evidence on the basis of all information considered by the department, and after a public hearing, if a public hearing is deemed necessary under RSA 482-A:8, that the proposed project, either alone or in conjunction with other human activity, will not result in the significant net loss of any of the values set forth in RSA 482-A:1. This paragraph shall not be construed so as to relieve the department of its statutory obligations under this chapter to protect wetlands not so mapped and designated.

(b)(1) A property owner may request from the department a waiver from subparagraph (a), under rules adopted by the department, to perform forest management work and related activities in the forested portion of a prime wetland or its 100-foot buffer, where such buffer was required at the time of designation, that do not qualify under the notification of forest management or timber harvest activities having minimum wetlands impact process. The request for the waiver shall include, but not be limited to:

(A) A sketch of the property depicting the best approximate location of each prime wetland and its 100-foot buffer, where such buffer was required at the time of designation, in which work is proposed and the location of proposed work, including access roads;

(B) A written description of the work to be performed and a copy of the notice of intent to cut, if applicable; and

(C) A list of the prime wetland values as identified by the municipality in designating each prime wetland under RSA 482-A:15.

(c) A property owner may request a waiver from the department, under rules adopted by the department under RSA 541-A, from the provisions of this chapter to perform work not addressed under subparagraph (b) within a portion of any 100-foot buffer of a prime wetland on his or her property as provided in subparagraph (a). At the time of the waiver request, the property owner shall notify, by certified mail, the local governing body, the planning board, if any, and the conservation commission, if any, of the municipalities in which the waiver is being sought that a waiver is being sought from the department. Where a buffer associated with the application extends into an abutting property, the property owner requesting the waiver shall provide notice to the owner of that abutting property.

V. Notwithstanding any rules adopted by the commissioner defining minor projects, a series of minor projects undertaken by a single developer or several developers over a period of 5 years or less may, when considered in the aggregate, amount to a major project in the opinion of the department; all such related projects shall be subject to a public hearing as provided in RSA 482-A:8. A series of minor projects shall be considered in the aggregate if they abut or if they are a part of an overall scheme of development or are otherwise consistent parts of an eventual whole.

VI. The commissioner shall adopt rules pursuant to RSA 541-A establishing an expedited application and permitting process for certain minimum impact projects. The provisions of RSA 482-A:3, I and paragraph III of this section shall apply.

VI-a. The commissioner shall adopt rules pursuant to RSA 541-A establishing a permit by notification process for certain minimum impact projects. The provisions of RSA 482-A:3, I(a) and (c) shall apply.

VII. The commissioner shall adopt rules, pursuant to RSA 541-A, identifying those activities within the jurisdiction of RSA 482-A that may be conducted without obtaining a permit and those that may be conducted without a permit if the project is registered with the department, consistent with the provisions of this chapter.

VIII. The commissioner shall adopt rules pursuant to RSA 541-A relative to the waiver of existing standards provided for in RSA 482-A:26, III(b). Such rules shall list the specific criteria to be used by the commissioner in determining whether a waiver will be granted.

IX. The commissioner shall adopt rules, pursuant to RSA 541-A, relative to the circumstances under which the commissioner may grant a waiver of rules adopted pursuant to this chapter. Such rules shall list the specific criteria to be used by the commissioner in determining whether a waiver will be granted.

X. The department shall have the authority to grant permits, in accordance with the rules adopted under RSA 482-A:11, VI for expedited application and permitting, for any projects funded through the Emergency Watershed Protection Program of the Natural Resources Conservation Service, United States Department of Agriculture, when such projects are necessary to safeguard lives and property from floods and the products of erosion when a natural disaster is causing or has caused a sudden impairment of the watershed.

HISTORY:

1989, 339:1. 1991, 20:6. 28:1. 1993, 30:1, eff. June 7, 1993. 1996, 296:47, eff. Aug. 9, 1996. 2002, 272:17, 18, eff. May 18, 2002. 2004, 116:5, eff. May 17, 2004. 2007, 211:2, eff. August 24, 2007. 278:1, eff. September 1, 2007. 2008, 363:3, eff. September 9, 2008. 2009, 185:2, eff. September 11, 2009. 2012, 235:1, 3, eff. August 17, 2012. 2015, 236:5, 6, eff. September 11, 2015.

Revision note.

Substituted "RSA 482-A:8" for "RSA 482-A:2" in par. V to correct an error in the reference.

Codification.

Pursuant to 1989, 339:34, the amendment to former RSA 483-A:4-a, VI by 1989, 225:4, eff. July 23, 1989, was incorporated in par. V of this section.

Amendment Notes

—2015.

The 2015 amendment by chapter 236, §§ 5 and 6, substituted "expedited permit" for "permit by notification" in the introductory paragraph of III(b); deleted "or permit by notification process" following "process" in the first sentence of paragraph VI; added paragraph VI-a; and inserted "and those that may be conducted without a permit if the project is registered with the department" in paragraph VII.

—2012.

The 2012 amendment, in the first sentence of IV(a), deleted "or within 100 feet of" following "undertaken in" and added "or within 100 feet of any prime wetland where a 100 foot buffer was required at the time of designation"; added "where such buffer was required at the time of designation, that do not qualify under the notification of forest management or timber harvest activities having minimum wetlands impact process" in the first sentence of the introductory language of IV(b)(1); added "where such buffer was required at the time of designation" in IV(b)(1)(A); added "as provided in subparagraph (a)" in the first sentence of IV(c); and made a stylistic change.

—2009.

The 2009 amendment added the IV(a) designation; in IV(a), substituted "any project" for "any activity proposed" in the first sentence and in the second sentence, added "if a public hearing is deemed necessary under RSA 482-A:8" and substituted "proposed project" for "proposed activity"; added IV(b) and IV(c); and made stylistic changes.

—2008.

The 2008 amendment in III(a), in the first sentence, deleted "suspend action upon such notice and shall" following "department shall" and substituted "application that is the subject of the notice" for "notice of a minor or minimum impact project nor hold a hearing on it if a major project" and added the third sentence.

—2007.

Paragraph IV: Chapter 211 substituted "within 100 feet of" for "adjacent to" in the first sentence.

Paragraph X: Added by Chapter 278.

—2004.

Paragraph IX: Added.

—2002.

Paragraph III: Designated the existing provisions of the paragraph as subpar. (a), and in that subparagraph inserted "or minimum impact" following "a minor" in the first sentence, and added subpar. (b).

Paragraph VI: Substituted "shall" for "may" preceding "adopt", inserted "or permit by notification process" following "permitting process", and deleted "and minor" following "minimum" in the first sentence.

Paragraphs VII and VIII: Added.

—1996.

Rewritten to the extent that a detailed comparison would be impracticable.

—1993.

Paragraph VII: Added.

—1991.

Paragraph III: Chapter 28 substituted "14" for "10" in the fourth sentence.

Paragraph V: Chapter 20 substituted "governing" for "legislative" preceding "body" in the first sentence.

Contingent 1996 amendment.

1996, 296:21, provided for the amendment of this section. However, under the terms of 1996, 296:54, eff. Aug. 9, 1996, the amendment did not become effective.

Continuation of wetlands board rules; transfer of rulemaking authority to commissioner.

1996, 296:30, eff. Aug. 9, 1996, provided:

"Existing rules adopted by the wetlands board shall continue in full force and effect until such rules expire or are amended or repealed by the commissioner of environmental services. Rulemaking proceedings of the wetlands board in progress on the effective date of this section [Aug. 9, 1996] shall be taken over by the commissioner of environmental services. The commissioner may continue the proceedings or may begin a new rulemaking proceeding."

NOTES TO DECISIONS

Analysis

1. Groundwater withdrawal
2. Judicial review of permit approval
3. Ownership
4. Dock permit

1. Groundwater withdrawal

As a proposed groundwater withdrawal is not subject to the permitting requirements of RSA 482-A:3, I, the Department of Environmental Services did not err in not holding a public hearing on the withdrawal under RSA 482-A:11, IV. Appeal of Town of Nottingham (N.H. Dep't of Envtl. Servs.), 153 N.H. 539, 904 A.2d 582, 2006 N.H. LEXIS 71 (N.H. 2006).

2. Judicial review of permit approval

Trial court did not err by ruling that the New Hampshire Department of Environmental Services (DES) review authority of a wetlands permit was limited to assessing the impacts of construction activities in the protected wetlands, as DES' authority did not extend to assessing the effects of upland construction activities upon such wetlands. An appellate court did not further review the appeal because the trial court determined, as a matter of law, based upon its review of the certified record, that an environmental council's decision granting a developer the permit was legally correct and the appellate court, having reviewed the certified record itself, found that the evidence was sufficient for the trial court to have reached that conclusion. Greenland Conservation Comm'n v. N.H. Wetlands Council, 154 N.H. 529, 913 A.2d 776, 2006 N.H. LEXIS 195 (N.H. 2006).

3. Ownership

Based upon the common meaning of the term, "ownership," as used in RSA 482-A:11, II, neither is limited to fee ownership nor requires possession; parties who hold title to a shoreline easement are "owners" under the statute. Accordingly, given the broad grant of respondents' easement, they had a sufficient ownership interest to apply for a dock permit. Appeal of Michele (New Hampshire Wetlands Council), 168 N.H. 98, 123 A.3d 255, 2015 N.H. LEXIS 80 (N.H. 2015).

4. Dock permit

Dock permit did not adversely affect the value and enjoyment of petitioners' property because even if the Environmental Council erred in treating petitioners as "abutting owners" under RSA 482-A:11, II, this afforded them more protection than that to which they were entitled under the statute because petitioners had granted respondents an easement; the findings that the small, seasonal dock did not unreasonably affect their use and enjoyment were supported by the record; petitioners retained the right to seek relief should respondents make unreasonable use of their easement; and RSA 482-A:3, XIII(a), concerning abutting property owners, did not apply. Appeal of Michele (New Hampshire Wetlands Council), 168 N.H. 98, 123 A.3d 255, 2015 N.H. LEXIS 80 (N.H. 2015).

RESEARCH REFERENCES AND PRACTICE AIDS

New Hampshire Code of Administrative Rules

Rules of the Department of Environmental Services—Wetlands Board, Env-Wt 501.02 and 501.05–.07, New Hampshire Code of Administrative Rules Annotated.

482-A:12. Posting of Permits and Reports of Violations.

Project approval by the department shall be in the form of a permit, a copy of which the applicant shall post in a secured manner in a prominent place at the site of the approved project. The department shall mail a copy of such permit to the local governing body of the municipality where the project is located. Any person proceeding without a posted permit shall be in violation of this chapter. All state, county and local law enforcement officers are directed to be watchful for violations of the provisions of this chapter and to report all suspected violations to the department.

HISTORY:

1989, 339:1. 1991, 20:7, eff. Jan. 1, 1992. 1996, 296:47, eff. Aug. 9, 1996.

Amendments

—1996.

Substituted "department" for "board" throughout the section.

—1991.

Substituted "governing" for "legislative" preceding "body" in the second sentence.

Contingent 1996 amendment.

1996, 296:21, provided for the amendment of this section. However, under the terms of 1996, 296:54, eff. Aug. 9, 1996, the amendments did not become effective.

RESEARCH REFERENCES AND PRACTICE AIDS

Cross References.

Administrative fine for violation of chapter, see RSA 482-A:13.

Penalties for violation of chapter, see RSA 482-A:14.

482-A:13. Administrative Fine.

The commissioner, after notice and hearing in accordance with the procedures set forth in RSA 541-A, is empowered to impose an administrative fine of up to $5,000 for each violation, irrespective of the duration of violation, upon any person who violates any provision of this chapter. This fine is appealable under RSA 541. Any administrative fine imposed under this section will not preclude the imposition of further penalties under this chapter. The proceeds of administrative fines levied pursuant to this section shall be placed in the nonlapsing fund authorized in RSA 482-A:14, III.

HISTORY:

1989, 339:1, eff. Jan. 1, 1990. 1996, 296:47, eff. Aug. 9, 1996. 2010, 295:4, eff. September 11, 2010.

Revision note.

Substituted "RSA 482-A:14, III" for "RSA 482:14, III" in the fourth sentence to correct an error in the reference.

Amendments

—2010.

The 2010 amendment substituted "$5,000 for each violation, irrespective of the duration of violation" for "$2,000 for each offense" in the first sentence.

—1996.

Substituted "commissioner" for "wetlands board" in the first sentence and "section" for "paragraph" in the fourth sentence.

Contingent 1996 amendment.

1996, 296:21, provided for the amendment of this section. However, under the terms of 1996, 296:54, eff. Aug. 9, 1996, the amendments did not become effective.

NOTES TO DECISIONS

Appeal

An appeal to the supreme court of an administrative fine imposed by the wetlands board was not timely filed when not made either within 30 days of the board's decision denying petition for rehearing or of date of notification of same, even though appeal to the superior court, which did not have jurisdiction, was filed within 30 days of the board's denial decision. Allen v. Wetlands Bd., 133 N.H. 379, 577 A.2d 92, 1990 N.H. LEXIS 71 (N.H. 1990). (Decided under prior law.)

482-A:14. Penalties.

I. Whoever recklessly or knowingly fails, neglects or refuses to comply with this chapter, rules adopted under this chapter, or an order or condition of a permit issued under this chapter, or recklessly or knowingly misrepresents any material fact in connection with any activities regulated or prohibited by this chapter, whether or not the owner of the land in question, shall be guilty of a misdemeanor if a natural person and guilty of a felony if any other person.

II. State and local law enforcement officials may prosecute any violation of this chapter as a violation. This provision shall not limit the state's enforcement authority under this chapter.

III. Failure, neglect or refusal to comply with this chapter or rules adopted under this chapter, or an order or condition of a permit issued under this chapter, and the misrepresentation by any person of a material fact made in connection with any activities regulated or prohibited by this chapter shall be deemed violations of this chapter. The court may, upon separate petition of the attorney general, or in connection with a petition for equity relief, levy upon any person who violates this chapter, whether or not the owner of the land in question, a civil penalty in an amount not to exceed $10,000 per violation. Each day of a continuing violation shall constitute a separate violation. The proceeds of any civil penalty levied pursuant to this chapter shall be placed in a nonlapsing fund held by the treasurer, which may be expended by the department, subject to the approval of the governor and council, for the purpose of restoration, research, investigation and enforcement relative to wetlands.

HISTORY:

1989, 339:1, eff. Jan. 1, 1990. 1996, 296:22, eff. Aug. 9, 1996.

Codification.

Pursuant to 1989, 339:34, the amendment to former RSA 483-A:5 by 1989, 225:5, eff. July 23, 1989, was incorporated in par. I of this section and the amendment to former RSA 483-A:6 by 1989, 225:6, eff. July 23, 1989, was incorporated in par. III of this section.

Amendments

—1996.

Paragraph III: Substituted "department" for "board" in the fourth sentence.

NOTES TO DECISIONS

Analysis

1. Construction
2. Jurisdiction
3. Order
4. Bad faith
5. Defenses
6. Party liable for penalty
7. Maximum penalty
8. Propriety of penalty

1. Construction

Issuance of an administrative order by the wetlands board is not a precondition to the imposition of a civil penalty when a person acts in violation of this chapter. State Wetlands Bd. v. Marshall, 127 N.H. 240, 500 A.2d 685, 1985 N.H. LEXIS 435 (N.H. 1985). (Decided under prior law.)

2. Jurisdiction

The superior court had jurisdiction to hear board of wetlands claim for a civil penalty and for removal of a retaining wall built in violation of a board permit. Allen v. Wetlands Bd., 133 N.H. 379, 577 A.2d 92, 1990 N.H. LEXIS 71 (N.H. 1990). (Decided under prior law.)

3. Order

For purposes of this section, denial of a fill permit application meets the requirement of a board order. State Wetlands Bd. v. Marshall, 127 N.H. 240, 500 A.2d 685, 1985 N.H. LEXIS 435 (N.H. 1985). (Decided under prior law.)

4. Bad faith

Presence or absence of bad faith is not the proper standard to apply in determining the appropriateness of a civil penalty in connection with failure, neglect or refusal to obey a lawful order of the wetlands board. Allen v. Wetlands Bd., 133 N.H. 379, 577 A.2d 92, 1990 N.H. LEXIS 71 (N.H. 1990). (Decided under prior law.)

5. Defenses

Where defendants were assessed civil penalties for disobeying an order of the wetlands board, the defense that they relied on their attorney's advice was properly rejected, where the order in question could only have been overturned on appeal to the superior court, and where the attorney did advise them that action could be taken against them for not obeying the order. State Wetlands Bd. v. Marshall, 127 N.H. 240, 500 A.2d 685, 1985 N.H. LEXIS 435 (N.H. 1985). (Decided under prior law.)

6. Party liable for penalty

Trust as an entity could properly be fined for disobeying an order of the wetlands board, where the specific prayer requesting a penalty against the trustee did not indicate whether the request was directed at her individually or as trustee, and therefore the court could properly find, taking the petition as a whole, that the request was directed at her in her fiduciary role, and therefore at the trust itself. State Wetlands Bd. v. Marshall, 127 N.H. 240, 500 A.2d 685, 1985 N.H. LEXIS 435 (N.H. 1985). (Decided under prior law.)

7. Maximum penalty

Total of $7,000 in penalties assessed against a trust and its agent for disobeying an order of the wetlands board did not exceed this section's limit of $5,000, since the maximum penalty is aimed at each violator, not each violation, so that it was not error to impose two fines even though their total exceeded $5,000. State Wetlands Bd. v. Marshall, 127 N.H. 240, 500 A.2d 685, 1985 N.H. LEXIS 435 (N.H. 1985). (Decided under prior law.)

8. Propriety of penalty

Trial court properly imposed a civil penalty of $10,000 upon respondents under the Wetlands Act, RSA 482-A:14, III, based on respondents' construction of a home without a permit from the Department of Environmental Services, because nothing in the statute required the trial court to find that a person's failure to obtain a permit before excavating, removing, filling, or dredging damaged the wetlands. N.H. Dep't of Envtl. Servs. v. Marino, 155 N.H. 709, 928 A.2d 818, 2007 N.H. LEXIS 120 (N.H. 2007).

RESEARCH REFERENCES AND PRACTICE AIDS

Cross References.
Administrative fine for violation of chapter, see RSA 482-A:13.
Classification of crimes, see RSA 625:9.
Sentences, see RSA 651.

482-A:14-a. Cease and Desist Orders; Penalty.

The director of the division of forests and lands, department of natural and cultural resources, or his authorized agents, may issue a written cease and desist order against any timber operation in violation of this chapter. Any such violation may be enjoined by the superior court, upon application of the attorney general. A person failing to comply with the cease and desist order shall be guilty of a violation.

HISTORY:
1989, 214:20. 1990, 29:3, eff. May 22, 1990. 2017, 156:14, eff. July 1, 2017.

Codification.
This section was originally enacted as RSA 483-A:5-c and was redesignated pursuant to 1989, 339:34 in order to incorporate the provision in the recodification of RSA 481-A– 489-B as RSA 482–487.

Amendment Notes
The 2017 amendments to this section by Ch. 156 substituted "natural and cultural resources" for "resources and economic development" in the first sentence.

—1990.
Substituted "may" for "shall" preceding "issue", "timber operation" for "act" preceding "in violation" and deleted "not specifically covered by other penalty provisions" following "chapter" in the first sentence and substituted "violation" for "act" preceding "may be enjoined" in the second sentence.

RESEARCH REFERENCES AND PRACTICE AIDS

Cross References.
Classification of crimes, see RSA 625:9.
Sentences, see RSA 651.

482-A:14-b. Removal; Restoration; Equity Relief.

I. Whoever fails, neglects or refuses to comply with this chapter or rules adopted under this chapter, or an order or condition of a permit issued under this chapter, or misrepresents any material fact made in connection with any activity regulated or prohibited by this chapter, whether or not the owner of the land in question, shall be liable for the removal of fill, spoil or structure placed pursuant to such a violation and the restoration of any wetlands disturbed in connection with the violation. The superior court shall have jurisdiction to order such relief and such additional relief in equity as may be appropriate.

II. Municipalities may apply to a justice of the superior court for injunctive relief against existing or impending violations of this chapter, or any rule or order issued under this chapter. The municipality shall give notice of any such action to the attorney general and the commissioner of environmental services, who may take such steps as they deem necessary to ensure uniform statewide enforcement, including but not limited to joining the action, assuming sole prosecution of the action, or, as of right, dismissing the action without prejudice. Such notice shall be given at least 30 days prior to the commencement of any such action, unless more immediate action is necessary to prevent irreparable environmental damage or other serious public harm, in which case such notice shall be given as soon as practicable, but in no event later than the date of commencement of the action. This paragraph shall not be construed to affect, in any manner, existing authority of municipalities to act based upon the provisions of other statutes or local ordinances.

III. A landowner shall not be liable for violations of this chapter caused by persons operating OHRVs, as defined in RSA 215-A:1, V, or snowmobiles, as defined in RSA 215-C:1, in a location or in a manner not authorized by the landowner.

HISTORY:
1989, 225:7. 1991, 340:2, eff. Jan. 1, 1992. 2004, 122:1, eff. May 17, 2004. 2005, 210:62, eff. July 1, 2006.

Codification.
This section was originally enacted as RSA 483-A:6-a and was redesignated pursuant to 1989, 339:34 in order to incorporate the provision in the recodification of RSA 481-A– 489-B as RSA 482–487.

Amendments

—2005.
Paragraph III: Inserted "or snowmobiles, as defined in RSA 215-C:1".

—2004.
Paragraph III: Added.

—1991.
Designated the existing provisions of the section as par. I and added par. II.

482-A:14-c. Limitation on Enforcement Action.

No person who acquires property, by any means, more than 5 years after an activity constituting a violation of this chapter has been completed, shall be subject to an enforcement action under this chapter for such violation, provided such person allows restoration of impacted areas, unless the person knew of the existence of the violation at the time that the person acquired the property. Nothing in this section shall limit any enforcement action for violation of this chapter, including injunctive relief requiring restoration of impacted areas, against the person who committed the violation. Nothing in this section shall limit any enforcement action with respect to any violation of this chapter, including injunctive relief requiring restoration of impacted areas, for which written notice of the violation has been provided to the owner by the department prior to January 1, 2013. In addition to any common law remedy, any person who suffers damages as a result of a violation of this chapter committed by another may seek compensation from the person who committed the violation, including diminution in property value and reasonable attorney's fees.

HISTORY:
2012, 55:1, eff. January 1, 2013.

482-A:15. Local Option; Prime Wetlands.

I.(a) Any municipality, by its conservation commission, or, in the absence of a conservation commission, the planning board, or, in the absence of a planning board, the local governing body, may undertake to designate, map, and document prime wetlands lying within its boundaries, or if such areas lie only partly within its boundaries, then that portion lying within its boundaries. The conservation commission, planning board, or governing body shall give written notice to the owner of the affected land and all abutters 30 days prior to the public hearing, before designating any property as prime wetlands.

(b) Prior to municipal vote under paragraph II, maps that depict wetland boundaries shall be prepared and landowners having proposed prime wetlands on their property shall be informed of the boundary delineation. The acceptance of any prime wetland designation by the department prior to the effective date of this paragraph shall remain in effect; however, any revision to the boundary shall be delineated using wetland delineation methods as adopted by the department and by the standards of this section.

I-a. For the purposes of this chapter, "prime wetlands" shall mean any contiguous areas falling within the jurisdictional definitions of RSA 482-A:2, X and RSA 482-A:4 that, because of their size, unspoiled character, fragile condition, or other relevant factors, make them of substantial significance. A prime wetland shall be at least 2 acres in size, shall not consist of a water body only, shall have at least 4 primary wetland functions, one of which shall be wildlife habitat, and shall have a width of at least 50 feet at its narrowest point. The boundary of a prime wetland shall coincide, where present, with the upland edge of any wetland, as defined in RSA 482-A:2, X, that is part of the prime wetland. On-site verification of proposed prime wetland boundaries shall be performed where landowner permission is provided.

I-b. The commissioner shall adopt rules under RSA 541-A relative to the form, criteria, and methods that shall be used to designate, map, and document prime wetlands, determine boundaries in the field, and amend maps and designations once filed and accepted by the department under paragraph II.

II. Any municipal conservation commission or that local body which has mapped and designated prime wetlands in accordance with paragraph I may, after approval by any town or city council meeting, file such maps and designations with the department, which shall accept and maintain them and provide public access to such maps during regular business hours. The procedure for acceptance by the local legislative body of any prime wetland designations as provided in paragraph I shall be the same as set forth in RSA 675:2 or RSA 675:3, as applicable.

HISTORY:
1989, 339:1. 1991, 20:8, eff. Jan. 1, 1992. 1996, 296:48, eff. Aug. 9, 1996. 2009, 185:3, eff. September 11, 2009. 2012, 235:2, eff. August 17, 2012.

Amendments

—2012.
The 2012 amendment added the I(a), I-a, and I-b designations; added the second sentence of I(a); added I(b); and in I-a, in the first sentence, added "contiguous" and substituted "RSA 482-A:2, X and RSA 482-A:4" for "RSA 482-A:3 and RSA 482-A:4 that possess one or more of the values set forth in RSA 482-A:1 and" and added the second through last sentences.

—2009.
The 2009 amendment rewrote the last sentence of I, which formerly read: "Such maps or designations, or both, shall be in such form and to such scale, and shall be based upon such criteria, as are established by the commissioner through rules adopted pursuant to RSA 541-A" and made stylistic changes.

—1996.
Paragraph I: Substituted "commissioner" for "board" and "541-A" for "482-A:11" in the third sentence.
Paragraph II: Substituted "department" for "board" in the first sentence, and inserted "675:3" following "RSA 675:2 or" in the second sentence.

—1991.
Paragraph I: Substituted "governing" for "legislative" preceding "body" in the first sentence.

Contingent 1996 amendment.
1996, 296:23, provided for the amendment of this section. However, under the terms of 1996, 296:54, eff. Aug. 9, 1996, the amendments did not become effective.

NOTES TO DECISIONS

Application
Designation of prime wetlands under RSA 482-A:15 is a "land use

control" under RSA 12-G:13, I and RSA 12-G:2, XVI. Therefore, RSA 482-A:15 could not be applied by a town to control development of any property owned by the Pease Development Authority. Town of Newington v. State of N.H., 162 N.H. 745, 34 A.3d 1206, 2011 N.H. LEXIS 173 (N.H. 2011).

482-A:15-a. Wetlands Program Annual Report.

The department shall report annually to the wetlands council on the wetlands program. The report shall include, but not be limited to, the status of the wetlands program including program performance, rules, and funding and the status of the Clean Water Act section 404 program in New Hampshire.

HISTORY:
2003, 224:4, eff. July 1, 2003.

RESEARCH REFERENCES AND PRACTICE AIDS

References in text.
Section 404 of the Clean Water Act, referred to in this section, is classified to 33 U.S.C.S. § 1344.

Placing Fill in Public Waters

RESEARCH REFERENCES AND PRACTICE AIDS

Cross References.
Excavating and dredging in public waters, see RSA 482-A:21 et seq.

482-A:16. Artificial Fill; Exemptions.

No person shall place or cause to be placed any fill in any area below the mean high water level of any public waters or below the artificially-created high water level of publicly-owned bodies of water in this state with the intent or with the effect of creating or forming filled land adjacent to such bodies of water, except as provided in this subdivision. For the purposes of this subdivision, "public waters" means all natural ponds of more than 10 acres, and "publicly-owned bodies of water" or "public-owned water bodies" means those bodies of water whose artificial high water level is maintained by the state's exercise of its flowage rights on these ponds. The provisions of this subdivision shall not apply to such minor improvements of shorelines as the department, by rules adopted by the commissioner under RSA 541-A, may allow.

HISTORY:
1989, 339:1, eff. Jan. 1, 1990. 1996, 296:48, eff. Aug. 9, 1996.

Amendments

—1996.
Substituted "department" for "board" preceding "by rules adopted" and inserted "by the commissioner" thereafter in the third sentence.

Contingent 1996 amendment.
1996, 296:23, provided for the amendment of this section. However, under the terms of 1996, 296:54, eff. Aug. 9, 1996, the amendments did not become effective.

RESEARCH REFERENCES AND PRACTICE AIDS

New Hampshire Bar Journal.
For article, "Wetlands Legislation in New Hampshire," see 18 N.H. B.J. 265 (June 1977).

482-A:17. Grant of Right.

The governor and council, upon petition and only upon the recommendation of the department, may, for just consideration, grant to an owner of shoreline on public waters the right to place fill in the bed of such pond before the owner's shoreline. Every petition to place fill in the bed of public waters shall be filed with the department. The department, after 30 days' notice to abutters, to the local governing body of the municipality in which the property is situated, and to the department of health and human services, shall hold a public hearing. Notice of the hearing shall be published twice in 2 different weeks, the last publication to be 7 days before the hearing, in one newspaper of general circulation throughout the state and another newspaper of general circulation in the municipality, and notice posted in 2 public places in the municipality, and upon appropriate investigation shall make its recommendations to the governor and council with regard to such petition. If the department recommends that the petition be granted, in whole or in part, such recommendation shall include appropriate specifications and conditions necessary to the protection of public rights and to the protection of the rights and privileges of persons owning land in the vicinity of the area to be filled by the petitioner. The grant of the governor and council shall be evidenced by an instrument in writing, executed by the governor and council, attested by the secretary of state, and recorded in the county where the right is to be exercised. Land created by fill in accordance with the grant of the governor and council shall belong to the owner of the natural shoreline as if it were formed by natural accretion. The owner of a shoreline on a public-owned water body may petition the department for the right to place fill below the artificially-created high water level of a public-owned water body to the extent that the flowage rights owned by the state allow.

HISTORY:
1989, 339:1. 1991, 20:9. 1995, 310:181, eff. Nov. 1, 1995. 1996, 296:48, eff. Aug. 9, 1996.

Amendments

—1996.
Rewritten to the extent that a detailed comparison would be impracticable.

—1995.
Deleted "division of public health services of the" preceding "department of health and human services" in the third sentence.

—1991.
Substituted "governing" for "legislative" preceding "body" in the third sentence and inserted "newspaper of general circulation

throughout the state and another" following "in one" in the fourth sentence.

Contingent 1996 amendment.
1996, 296:23, provided for the amendment of this section. However, under the terms of 1996, 296:54, eff. Aug. 9, 1996, the amendments did not become effective.

Severability of 1995 amendment.
1995, 310, which amended this section, was subject to a severability clause. See 1995, 310:186.

Construction of 1995 amendment.
1995, 310:187, eff. Nov. 1, 1995, provided:
"Nothing in this act is intended to, nor shall it be construed as, mandating or assigning any new, expanded, or modified program or responsibility for any political subdivision in violation of part I, article 28-a of the constitution of the state of New Hampshire."

OPINIONS OF THE ATTORNEY GENERAL

Private property
Proposal contemplating construction of piers on privately-owned property was not subject to statutory grant-of-right of governor and executive council for wharves or piers on public land. 1987 Op. Att'y Gen. 67. (Decided under prior law.)

RESEARCH REFERENCES AND PRACTICE AIDS

Cross References.
Filing of deposit with petition, see RSA 482-A:20.

482-A:18. Procedure for Removal of Fill.

If any person places fill in the bed of public waters or below the artificially-created high water level of public-owned water bodies except as provided in this subdivision, such person shall be guilty of a misdemeanor if a natural person, or guilty of a felony if any other person. Any person may be compelled to remove the same by the superior court upon a petition brought by the attorney general.

HISTORY:
1989, 339:1, eff. Jan. 1, 1990. 1996, 296:48, eff. Aug. 9, 1996.

Amendments

—1996.
Substituted "such person" for "he" preceding "shall be guilty" in the first sentence, and deleted "at the request of the wetlands board" following "attorney general" in the second sentence.

Contingent 1996 amendment.
1996, 296:23, provided for the amendment of this section. However, under the terms of 1996, 296:54, eff. Aug. 9, 1996, the amendments did not become effective.

RESEARCH REFERENCES AND PRACTICE AIDS

Cross References.
Classification of crimes, see RSA 625:9.
Sentences, see RSA 651.

482-A:19. Fees.

Any payment received by the state as determined by the governor and council under the provisions of RSA 482-A:17 for the grant of the right to place fill in the bed of a great pond shall be paid over to the state treasurer and shall be available for general revenue of the state.

HISTORY:
1989, 339:1, eff. Jan. 1, 1990.

482-A:20. Costs for Hearing.

The petitioner for a right to place fill in public waters shall make a deposit to the department of $50 with each such petition. This payment shall be for expenses of publication, mailing and posting of notices by the department and for the expenses of hiring a hearing site, if a hearing outside of Concord is necessary. If the expenses amount to more than $50, the department shall require the petitioner to pay the additional amount before it sends its recommendations to the governor and council with regard to the petition.

HISTORY:
1989, 339:1, eff. Jan. 1, 1990. 1996, 296:49, eff. Aug. 9, 1996.

Amendments

—1996.
Substituted "department" for "wetlands board" in the first sentence and for "board" in the second and third sentences and "the" for "such" preceding "expenses" in the third sentence.

Contingent 1996 amendment.
1996, 296:24, provided for the amendment of this section. However, under the terms of 1996, 296:54, eff. Aug. 9, 1996, the amendment did not become effective.

RESEARCH REFERENCES AND PRACTICE AIDS

Cross References.
Notice and hearing, see RSA 482-A:17.

Excavating and Dredging in Public Waters

OPINIONS OF THE ATTORNEY GENERAL

Review by governor and council
Wetlands board's practice of separating out the dredging portion of a project for purposes of determining whether it is exempt from governor and executive council review conflicts with express language of applicable statute. 1987 Op. Att'y Gen. 67. (Decided under prior law.)

RESEARCH REFERENCES AND PRACTICE AIDS

Cross References.
Placing fill in public waters, see RSA 482-A:16 et seq.

New Hampshire Bar Journal.
For article, "Wetlands Legislation in New Hampshire," see 18 N.H. B.J. 265 (June 1977).

482-A:21. Excavating and Dredging.

I. No person shall excavate, remove, or dredge any bank, flat, marsh, swamp, or lake bed that lies below the natural mean high water level of any public waters of this state, except as provided in this subdivision. For the purposes of this subdivision, "public waters" are defined as all natural ponds of more than 10 acres. Upon the request of the owner of land abutting any public waters, the division shall determine the natural mean high water level of the abutting public water.

II. The provisions of this subdivision shall not apply to:

(a) Any land above the natural mean high water level of public waters.

(b) Any land below any artificially created high water level of any body of water.

(c) Projects classified as minor or minimum impact under rules adopted by the commissioner under RSA 482-A:11 which exclusively involve excavation or dredging within a great pond, and no other associated major project activities requiring a permit pursuant to RSA 482-A.

HISTORY:
1989, 339:1, eff. Jan. 1, 1990. 1996, 296:25, eff. Aug. 9, 1996.

Amendments

—1996.
Subparagraph II(c): Substituted "commissioner" for "wetlands board".

NOTES TO DECISIONS

Permit
Once a boathouse project was relocated landward of a bank, it lost its status as a water dependent structure because it was no longer located over, on, or in the waters of the State of New Hampshire. It was then located over a dredged inlet, and no longer required a dredge and fill permit so that there was no legal basis for imposing the N.H. Code Admin. R. Ann., Env-Wt 302.03 requirements on the boathouse. Cayten v. N.H. Dep't of Envtl. Servs., 155 N.H. 647, 927 A.2d 494, 2007 N.H. LEXIS 113 (N.H. 2007).

RESEARCH REFERENCES AND PRACTICE AIDS

Cross References.
Limitations on excavations near certain waters and prime wetlands, see RSA 155-E:4-a.

482-A:22. Grant of Right.

The governor and council, upon petition and upon the recommendation of the department, may, for just consideration, grant to an owner of a shoreline on public waters the right to excavate, remove, or dredge any bank, flat, marsh, swamp or lake bed before the owner's shoreline. Every petition to excavate or dredge said areas shall be filed with the department. The department, after 30 days' notice to abutters, the local governing body of the municipality in which the property is situate, and the department of health and human services shall hold a public hearing. Notice of the hearing shall be published twice in 2 different weeks, the last publication to be 7 days before the hearing, in one newspaper of general circulation throughout the state and another newspaper of general circulation in the municipality. The notice shall also be posted

in 2 public places in the municipality. Upon appropriate investigation the department shall make its recommendations to the governor and council with regard to such petition. If the department recommends that the petition be granted, in whole or in part, such recommendation shall include appropriate specifications and conditions necessary to the protection of public rights and to the protection of the rights and privileges of persons owning land in the vicinity of the area to be excavated or dredged by the petitioner.

HISTORY:
1989, 339:1. 1991, 20:10. 1995, 310:181, eff. Nov. 1, 1995. 1996, 296:50, eff. Aug. 9, 1996.

Amendments

—1996.
Rewritten to the extent that a detailed comparison would be impracticable.

—1995.
Deleted "division of public health services of the" preceding "department of health and human services" in the third sentence.

—1991.
Substituted "governing" for "legislative" preceding "body" in the third sentence and made other minor stylistic changes.

Contingent 1996 amendment.
1996, 296:26, provided for the amendment of this section. However, under the terms of 1996, 296:54, eff. Aug. 9, 1996, the amendment did not become effective.

Severability of 1995 amendment.
1995, 310, which amended this section, was subject to a severability clause. See 1995, 310:186.

Construction of 1995 amendment.
1995, 310:187, eff. Nov. 1, 1995, provided:
"Nothing in this act is intended to, nor shall it be construed as, mandating or assigning any new, expanded, or modified program or responsibility for any political subdivision in violation of part I, article 28-a of the constitution of the state of New Hampshire."

RESEARCH REFERENCES AND PRACTICE AIDS

Cross References.
Filing of deposit with petition, see RSA 482-A:25.

482-A:22-a. Grant in Right for Submerged Logs; Exemption.

I. The governor and council, upon petition and upon the recommendation of the department, may grant to the governing body of a municipality the right to remove submerged logs from the portion of the bed of any great pond that is located within the municipality's boundaries as delineated in the NH Granit database, Complex Systems Research Center, University of New Hampshire.

II. Every petition to remove such submerged logs shall be filed by the governing body of the municipality with the department as an application under RSA 482-A:3, I, and shall demonstrate that:

(a) Removing the submerged logs will have minimal or no adverse environmental impact, based on considerations including whether the logs were treated with hazardous or toxic chemicals and whether the logs are providing important aquatic habitat as determined by the department of fish and game; or

(b) The submerged logs to be removed are interfering with navigation or otherwise adversely affecting public safety or the environment.

III. The application filed pursuant to paragraph II shall:

(a) Identify the manner in which the logs will be removed, the measures to be taken to minimize any adverse environmental impact, and the formula by which the net proceeds of the use or sale of the removed logs will be determined; and

(b) Include the results of such testing as the department may require to determine the environmental impact of the logs in place and of removing the logs.

IV. A municipality that receives a permit under this section may enter into a commercially reasonable private contract to undertake the log removal after publicly requesting bids for such work.

V. The net proceeds of any use or sale of the removed logs shall accrue directly to the benefit of the municipality.

VI. The municipality shall hold a public hearing on the application in conjunction with the department. The municipality shall send direct notice of the application and the public hearing to the department of fish and game and to each person owning land within 150 feet of the area from which the logs will be removed. The municipality also shall post notice of the hearing in 2 public places in the municipality, one of which may be the municipality's website, and shall publish notice of the hearing twice in 2 different weeks, the last publication to be 7 days before the hearing, in one newspaper of general circulation throughout the state and another newspaper of general circulation in the municipality. The department shall post notice of the hearing and of the deadline for submission of written comments on the department's website, which deadline shall be not less than 10 days following the public hearing.

VII. After appropriate consideration of the application and any comments received, the department shall make its recommendations to the governor and council with regard to such petition. If the department recommends that the petition be granted, in whole or in part, such recommendation shall include appropriate specifications and conditions necessary to protect public rights and the rights and privileges of persons owning land within 150 feet of the area from which the logs will be removed, which shall include requirements for testing the submerged logs prior to and during removal to determine proper handling and disposal.

VIII. Notwithstanding the provisions of this section, if a submerged log presents a safety hazard, the state police may remove the submerged log or logs.

HISTORY:
2013, 96:1, eff. August 19, 2013.

482-A:23. Penalty.

Any person who violates any provision of this subdivision shall be guilty of a misdemeanor if a natural person, or guilty of a felony if any other person. Any person may be compelled to return said land to its original condition by the superior court upon a petition brought by the attorney general.

HISTORY:
1989, 339:1, eff. Jan. 1, 1990. 1996, 296:50, eff. Aug. 9, 1996.

Amendments

—1996.
Deleted "at the request of the wetlands board" following "attorney general" in the second sentence.

Contingent 1996 amendment.
1996, 296:26, provided for the amendment of this section. However, under the terms of 1996, 296:54, eff. Aug. 9, 1996, the amendment did not become effective.

RESEARCH REFERENCES AND PRACTICE AIDS

Cross References.
Classification of crimes, see RSA 625:9.
Sentences, see RSA 651.

482-A:24. Fees.

Any payment received by the state as determined by the governor and council under the provisions of this subdivision shall be paid over to the state treasurer and shall be deposited in the general funds of the state.

HISTORY:
1989, 339:1, eff. Jan. 1, 1990.

482-A:25. Hearing Costs.

The petitioner shall make a deposit of $50 with each petition to pay for the expenses of publication, mailing, and posting of notices, and for the expenses of hiring a hearing site, if a hearing outside of Concord is necessary. If these expenses are more than $50, the department shall require the petitioner to pay the additional expenses before it sends its recommendations to the governor and council with regard to the petition.

HISTORY:
1989, 339:1, eff. Jan. 1, 1990. 1996, 296:51, eff. Aug. 9, 1996.

Amendments

—1996.
Substituted "department" for "board" preceding "shall require" in the second sentence.

Contingent 1996 amendment.
1996, 296:27, provided for the amendment of this section. However, under the terms of 1996, 296:54, eff. Aug. 9, 1996, the amendment did not become effective.

Restrictions on Use of Structures Built over the Waters of the State

482-A:26. Dwellings Over Water.

I. No person shall construct any structure suitable for use as a dwelling if the structure or any part of the structure extends beyond the shoreline of any public water or publicly-owned water body.

II. No person shall convert or modify any existing structure in order to make the structure suitable as a dwelling if the structure or any part of the structure extends beyond the shoreline of any public water or publicly-owned water body.

III.(a) Existing dwellings over water which were constructed or converted to be made suitable for use as a dwelling in accordance with the law in effect at the time of construction or conversion, may be repaired or reconstructed, for maintenance purposes only, using any modern technologies, provided the result is a functionally equivalent use. Such repair or reconstruction may alter the interior design or existing cribwork, but no expansion of the existing footprint or outside dimensions shall be permitted. A condition of RSA 482-A:3 approval shall be the existence or installation of a sewage disposal system which has been approved pursuant to RSA 485-A:29–44. No permit shall be required for routine maintenance that does not involve work in the water.

(b) Without otherwise limiting the provisions of this section, where the effect of repair or reconstruction of a structure subject to the provisions of this section represents greater protection of public water or the environment and where such repair or reconstruction does not change a recreational, water-based activity to a land-based, residential or commercial activity, the commissioner may waive the existing standards, provided that there shall be no expansion of the existing footprint, outside dimensions, and square footage of floor space; and there shall be a net reduction in the total square footage of kitchen, bathroom, shower, and toilet facilities.

IV. For the purpose of this section:

(a) "Dwelling over water" means any structure suitable for use as a dwelling which extends in any part beyond the shoreline of any public water or public-owned water body.

(b) "Shoreline" means that shoreline which exists when the surface of the water is at the mean high water level.

(c) "Suitable for use as a dwelling" means any structure which is used for residential purposes by one or more persons, or which contains kitchen, bathroom, shower, or toilet facilities.

V. The provisions of RSA 482-A:10, relative to appeals, and RSA 482-A:10-a, relative to takings without compensation, shall apply to all decisions of the department made under paragraph III.

HISTORY:
1989, 339:1, eff. Jan. 1, 1990. 1998, 23:1, 2, eff. Jan. 1, 1999. 2002, 272:16, eff. May 18, 2002. 2013, 43:3, eff. August 3, 2013.

Amendment Notes

—2013.
The 2013 amendment deleted "reconsideration and" preceding "appeals" in V.

—2002.
Paragraph III: Designated the existing provisions of the paragraph as subpar. (a), and added subpar. (b).

—1998.
Rewrote the section catchline and pars. I and II and added pars. III–V.

482-A:27. Penalty.

Any person who violates any provision of RSA 482-A:26 shall be required to remove the structure or portion of the structure constructed, reconstructed, repaired, converted, or modified in violation of said section and shall be subject to the civil, criminal, and other penalties set forth in RSA 482-A:13, 14, and 14-b. Any criminal fine collected for a violation of RSA 482-A:26 shall accrue to the use of the municipality in which the structure is located.

HISTORY:
1989, 339:1, eff. Jan. 1, 1990. 1998, 23:3, eff. Jan. 1, 1999.

Amendments

—1998.
Rewritten to the extent that a detailed comparison would be impracticable.

RESEARCH REFERENCES AND PRACTICE AIDS

Cross References.
Classification of crimes, see RSA 625:9.
Sentences, see RSA 651.

Aquatic Resource Compensatory Mitigation

482-A:28. Aquatic Resource Compensatory Mitigation.

In lieu of other forms of compensatory mitigation, the department may accept payment for an unavoidable loss of aquatic resource functions and values from impacts to resources protected under this chapter.

HISTORY:
2006, 313:1, eff. August 18, 2006. 2009, 303:1, eff. September 29, 2009.

Amendments

—2009.
The 2009 amendment substituted "impacts to resources protected under this chapter" for "a proposed activity which at a minimum" and deleted former I and II, which read: "I. Impacts less than one acre of wetlands and meets the criteria for a United States

Army Corps of Engineers state programmatic general permit. II. Exceeds one acre of impact for a public roadway or a public utility project and meets the criteria for a United States Army Corps of Engineers state programmatic general permit."

RESEARCH REFERENCES AND PRACTICE AIDS

New Hampshire Code of Administrative Rules

Rules of the Department of Environmental Services—Wetlands Board, Env-Wt 501.02 and 501.05–.07, New Hampshire Code of Administrative Rules Annotated.

482-A:29. Fund Established.

I. There is hereby established the aquatic resource compensatory mitigation fund into which payments made under this subdivision shall be deposited. The fund shall be a separate, nonlapsing fund continually appropriated to the department to be used only as specified in this subdivision for costs related to wetlands creation or restoration, stream and river restoration, stream and river enhancement, preservation of upland areas adjacent to wetlands and riparian areas, and the subsequent monitoring and maintenance of such areas.

II. A separate, non-lapsing account shall be established within the fund into which all administrative assessments collected under RSA 482-A:30, III and RSA 482-A:30-a, II shall be placed. Such account moneys shall only be used to support up to 2 full-time positions for administration of the fund and related projects. No other fund moneys shall be used for state personnel costs.

III. The state treasurer shall invest the fund as provided by law. Interest received on such investment shall be credited to the fund.

IV. The wetlands council, established by RSA 21-O:5-a, shall approve disbursements of the aquatic resource compensatory mitigation fund based on recommendations provided by the site selection committee established under RSA 482-A:32, and in accordance with rules adopted by the commissioner.

HISTORY:

2006, 313:1, eff. August 18, 2006. 2009, 303:2, eff. September 29, 2009. 303:5, eff. July 31, 2009. 303:6, eff. July 1, 2010. 2010, 16:1, eff. at 12:01 a.m., July 1, 2010.

Amendments

—2010.

The 2010 amendment rewrote II to the extent that a detailed comparison would be impracticable.

—2009.

The 2009 amendment by Chapter 303:2, effective September 29, 2009, in the second sentence of I, substituted "stream and river restoration, stream and river enhancement" for "stream restoration" and added "and riparian areas."

The 2009 amendment by Chapter 303:5, effective July 31, 2009, rewrote II, which formerly read: "The fund may not be used to pay state personnel costs except, upon approval of the fiscal committee, to support up to one full-time position for administration of the fund and related projects. Only money from the 5 percent administrative assessment collected under RSA 482-A:30, III shall be used for this purpose."

The 2009 amendment by Chapter 303:6, effective July 1, 2010, rewrote II to the extent that a detailed comparison would be impracticable.

RESEARCH REFERENCES AND PRACTICE AIDS

New Hampshire Code of Administrative Rules

Rules of the Department of Environmental Services—Wetlands Board, Env-Wt 501.02 and 501.05–.07, New Hampshire Code of Administrative Rules Annotated.

482-A:30. Payment for Freshwater and Tidal Wetlands Losses.

For freshwater and tidal wetlands losses, the in lieu payment shall be the sum of:

I. The cost that would have been incurred if a wetland of the same type was constructed at the ratios adopted by the department based on a price of $65,000 per acre of wetland created, to be adjusted at the beginning of the calendar year according to the annual simple rate of interest on judgments established by RSA 336:1;

II. The area of wetlands, as used in the calculation performed under paragraph I, times the cost of land in the municipality where the impact is occurring as calculated by the total assessed land values in the municipality, as determined by the department of revenue administration, which are equalized, divided by the number of acres in the municipality to yield a per acre equalized land value; and

III. An administrative assessment which equals 20 percent of the sum of paragraphs I and II.

HISTORY:

2006, 313:1, eff. August 18, 2006. 2010, 16:2, eff. July 1, 2010. 16:3, eff. July 1, 2012. 2011, 171:1, eff. July 1, 2011. 171:2, eff. July 1, 2015.

Amendments

—2011.

The 2011 amendment by Chapter 171:1, effective July 1, 2011, substituted "10 percent" for "20 percent" in III.

The 2011 amendment by Chapter 171:2, effective July 1, 2015, substituted "20 percent" for "10 percent" in III.

—2010.

The 2010 amendment by Chapter 16:2, effective July 1, 2010, substituted "20 percent" for "5 percent" in III.

The 2010 amendment by Chapter 16:3, effective July 1, 2012, substituted "5 percent" for "20 percent" in III.

Repeal of 2010, 16:3 amendment.

2011, 171:7, eff. July 1, 2011, provided for the repeal of the amendment to par. III by 2010, 16:3.

RESEARCH REFERENCES AND PRACTICE AIDS

New Hampshire Code of Administrative Rules

Rules of the Department of Environmental Services—Wetlands Board, Env-Wt 501.02 and 501.05–.07, New Hampshire Code of Administrative Rules Annotated.

482-A:30-a. Payment for Stream or Shoreline Losses.

For stream or shoreline resource losses, the in lieu payment shall be the sum of:

I. The cost that would have been incurred if a stream of the same type was restored at the ratios adopted by the department, based on a price of $200 per linear foot of channel or bank impacts or both, to be adjusted at the beginning of the calendar year according to the annual simple rate of interest on judgments established by RSA 336:1; and

II. **[Paragraph II effective until July 1, 2015; see also paragraph II set out below.]** An administrative assessment equal to 10 percent of the amount in paragraph I.

II. **[Paragraph II effective July 1, 2015; see also paragraph II set out above.]** An administrative assessment equal to 20 percent of the amount in paragraph I.

HISTORY:
2009, 303:3, eff. September 29, 2009. 2010, 16:4, eff. July 1, 2010. 16:5, eff. July 1, 2012. 2011, 171:3, eff. July 1, 2011. 171:4, eff. July 1, 2015.

Amendments

—2011.
The 2011 amendment by Chapter 171:3, effective July 1, 2011, substituted "10 percent" for "20 percent" in II.
The 2011 amendment by Chapter 171:4, effective July 1, 2015, substituted "20 percent" for "10 percent" in II.

—2010.
The 2010 amendment by Chapter 16:4, effective July 1, 2010, substituted "20 percent" for "5 percent" in II.
The 2010 amendment by Chapter 16:5, effective July 1, 2012, substituted "5 percent" for "20 percent" in II.

Repeal of 2010, 16:5 amendment.
2011, 171:7, eff. July 1, 2011, provided for the repeal of the amendment to par. II by 2010, 16:5.

482-A:31. Rulemaking.

The commissioner shall adopt rules under RSA 541-A relative to:

I. Identification of appropriate situations under which in lieu payments may be made. The criteria in RSA 482-A:28 shall be the minimum requirements for projects eligible for in lieu payments.

II. **[Paragraph II effective until July 1, 2015; see also paragraph II set out below.]** The method of calculating the amount of in lieu payments under RSA 482-A:30 and RSA 482-A:30-a which shall approximate the total cost of wetlands construction, stream and river construction, or such other mitigation actions as would have been required by the department and incurred by the applicant in the absence of making such payments. An administrative assessment of 10 percent of the total cost shall be added as part of the calculation method.

II. **[Paragraph II effective July 1, 2015; see also paragraph II set out above.]** The method of calculating the amount of in lieu payments under RSA 482-A:30 and RSA 482-A:30-a which shall approximate the total cost of wetlands construction, stream and river construction, or such other mitigation actions as would have been required by the department and incurred by the applicant in the absence of making such payments. An administrative assessment of 20 percent of the total cost shall be added as part of the calculation method.

III. Criteria to use in selecting projects that would compensate for the lost aquatic resource functions or values.

(a) Tidal aquatic resources shall be compensated by the selection of qualifying tidal projects.

(b) An emphasis shall be given to selecting from among the qualifying projects those that are nearer to the site of the lost aquatic resource.

(c) No project shall be funded with in lieu payments from losses that occurred outside the service area in which the project is located. A service area may be a hydrologic unit code 8 watershed, as developed by the United States Geological Survey, or a modification of a hydrologic unit code 8 watershed by the department as approved by the United States Army Corps of Engineers.

(d) Such criteria shall be adopted in consultation with the site selection committee established under RSA 482-A:32.

IV. Requests for extensions of excavating and dredging permits.

V. The certification program for municipal culvert installers under RSA 482-A:3, XVIII.

HISTORY:
2006, 313:1, eff. August 18, 2006. 2009, 303:4, eff. September 29, 2009. 2010, 16:6, eff. July 1, 2010. 16:7, eff. July 1, 2012. 2011, 143:2, eff. August 6, 2011. 171:5, eff. July 1, 2011. 171:6, eff. July 1, 2015. 2012, 74:2, eff. July 22, 2012. 273:3, eff. June 19, 2012.

Amendments

—2012.
The 2012 amendment by Chapter 74, in III(c), substituted "service area" for "hydrologic unit code 8 watershed, as developed by the United States Geological Survey" in the first sentence and added the second sentence.
The 2012 amendment by Chapter 273 added V.

—2011.
The 2011 amendment by Chapter 143 added IV.
The 2011 amendment by Chapter 171:5, effective July 1, 2011, substituted "10 percent" for "20 percent" in the second sentence of II.
The 2011 amendment by Chapter 171:6, effective July 1, 2015, substituted "20 percent" for "10 percent" in the second sentence of II.

—2010.
The 2010 amendment by Chapter 16:6, effective July 1, 2010, substituted "20 percent" for "5 percent" in the second sentence of II.

The 2010 amendment by Chapter 16:7, effective July 1, 2012, substituted "5 percent" for "20 percent" in the second sentence of II.

—2009.

The 2009 amendment, in the first sentence of II, added "and RSA 482-A:30-a" and "stream and river construction."

Repeal of 2010, 16:7 amendment.

2011, 171:7, eff. July 1, 2011, provided for the repeal of the amendment to par. II by 2010, 16:7.

RESEARCH REFERENCES AND PRACTICE AIDS

New Hampshire Code of Administrative Rules

Rules of the Department of Environmental Services—Wetlands Board, Env-Wt 501.02 and 501.05–.07, New Hampshire Code of Administrative Rules Annotated.

482-A:32.   Site Selection Committee Established.

I. There is established a site selection committee for the purpose of identifying projects to be funded from the aquatic resource compensatory mitigation fund.

II. The committee shall consist of the following members:

(a) The commissioner of the department of environmental services, or designee.

(b) The executive director of the fish and game department, or designee.

(c) The director of the office of strategic initiatives, or designee.

(d) The commissioner of the department of natural and cultural resources, or designee.

(e) Five members of the public, appointed by the governor and council for a term of 3 years or until a successor is chosen. The members of the public shall be as follows:

(1) A member of a municipal conservation commission at the time of appointment, who shall be one of 3 nominees submitted by the New Hampshire Association of Conservation Commissions.

(2) A natural resource scientist, who shall be one of 3 nominees submitted by the New Hampshire Association of Natural Resource Scientists.

(3) A person with experience in environmental protection and resource management at the time of appointment, who shall be one of 3 nominees submitted by the Nature Conservancy.

(4) A person with experience in environmental protection and resource management at the time of appointment, who shall be one of 3 nominees submitted by the Society for the Protection of New Hampshire Forests.

(5) A person with experience in stream restoration work, who shall be nominated jointly by the Northeast Region of American Rivers and the New Hampshire Rivers Council.

III. The members of the committee shall elect a chairperson annually.

IV. Each public member of the committee shall receive $50 per meeting. The other members of the site selection committee shall receive no compensation other than their regular state salaries but shall receive mileage paid at the rate set for state employees.

HISTORY:

2006, 313:1, eff. August 18, 2006. 2016, 68:1, eff. May 5, 2016. 2017, 156:14, 64, eff. July 1, 2017.

Amendment Notes

The **2017 amendments to this section by Ch. 156** substituted "natural and cultural resources" for "resources and economic development" in II(d); and substituted "office of strategic initiatives" for "office of energy and planning" in II(c).

The **2016 amendments to this section by Ch. 68**, in II(e), substituted "Five members" for "Four members" in the first sentence of the introductory paragraph and added (5).

RESEARCH REFERENCES AND PRACTICE AIDS

New Hampshire Code of Administrative Rules

Rules of the Department of Environmental Services—Wetlands Board, Env-Wt 501.02 and 501.05–.07, New Hampshire Code of Administrative Rules Annotated.

482-A:33.   Report.

The department shall submit a biennial report 60 days after the close of each odd-numbered fiscal year, to the fiscal committee of the general court, the chairperson of the house resources, recreation and development committee, and the chairperson of the senate environment and wildlife committee summarizing all receipts and disbursements of the aquatic resource compensatory mitigation fund, including a description of all projects undertaken and the status of the administrative assessment account. Each report shall be in such detail with sufficient information to be fully understood by the general court and the public. After submission to the general court, the report shall be available to the public.

HISTORY:

2006, 313:1, eff. August 18, 2006. 2010, 16:8, eff. July 1, 2010. 2012, 247:30, eff. August 17, 2012. 2015, 259:11, eff. July 1, 2015.

Amendment Notes

—2015.

The 2015 amendment, in the first sentence, substituted "a biennial report" for "an annual report" and inserted "odd-numbered."

—2012.

The 2012 amendment, in the first sentence, substituted "60 days after the close of each fiscal year" for "by October 1 beginning with fiscal year 2006" and added "of the general court."

—2010.

The 2010 amendment added "and the status of the administrative assessment account" at the end of the first sentence.

Department Investigation.

2010, 16:9, eff. July 1, 2010, provided: "The department of environmental services shall investigate ways of compiling and providing information on known compensatory mitigation opportunities to applicants who need to compensate for unavoidable impacts by their proposed projects, as part of the wetlands permitting process. The department shall report on the results of this investigation on October 1, 2011 as part of its annual report under RSA 482-A:33."

Wetland Mitigation Banks

482-A:34. Wetland Mitigation Banks Authorized.

Any individual or public or private entity may establish a wetland mitigation bank, provided such bank complies with all federal and state regulations and all requirements of the Army Corps of Engineers.

HISTORY:
2012, 74:1, eff. July 22, 2012.

CHAPTER 483

NEW HAMPSHIRE RIVERS MANAGEMENT AND PROTECTION PROGRAM

483:1. Statement of Policy.

New Hampshire's rivers and streams comprise one of its most important natural resources, historically vital to New Hampshire's commerce, industry, and tourism, and the quality of life of New Hampshire people. It is the policy of the state to ensure the continued viability of New Hampshire rivers as valued ecologic, economic, public health and safety, and social assets for the benefit of present and future generations. The state shall encourage and assist in the development of river corridor management plans and regulate the quantity and quality of instream flow along certain protected rivers or segments of rivers to conserve and protect outstanding characteristics including recreational, fisheries, wildlife, environmental, hydropower, cultural, historical, archaeological, scientific, ecological, aesthetic, community significance, agricultural, and public water supply so that these valued characteristics shall endure as part of the river uses to be enjoyed by New Hampshire people. If conflicts arise in the attempt to protect all valued characteristics within a river or stream, priority shall be given to those characteristics that are necessary to meet state water quality standards.

HISTORY:
1989, 339:1. 1990, 233:21, eff. June 26, 1990. 2009, 201:3, eff. July 15, 2009.

Amendments

—2009.
The 2009 amendment substituted "ecologic, economic, public health and safety" for "economic" in the second sentence; added "hydropower" following "environmental" in the third sentence; added the last sentence; and made a stylistic change.

—1990.
Deleted "and" preceding "community significance" and added "agricultural, and public water supply" thereafter in the third sentence.

483:2. Program Established; Intent.

There is established within the department of environmental services the New Hampshire rivers management and protection program. It is the intent of the legislature that the New Hampshire rivers management and protection program shall complement and reinforce existing state and federal water quality laws, and that in-stream flows are maintained along protected rivers, or segments thereof, in a manner that will enhance or not diminish the enjoyment of outstanding river characteristics pursuant to RSA 483:1. It is also the intent of the legislature that, through said program, the outstanding characteristics including recreational, fisheries, wildlife, environmental, hydropower, cultural, historical, archaeological, scientific, ecological, aesthetic, community significance, agricultural, public water supply, instream public uses, and riparian rights of such rivers shall be restored, protected, and maintained, and notwithstanding the provisions of

RSA 483-B, that nothing in this chapter shall be interpreted to preempt any land and zoning authority granted to municipal bodies under RSA title LXIV.

HISTORY:
1989, 339:1. 1990, 233:1, eff. June 26, 1990. 2016, 287:1, eff. August 20, 2016.

Amendment Notes
The 2016 amendments to this section by Ch. 287 substituted "outstanding characteristics including recreational, fisheries, wildlife, environmental, hydropower, cultural, historical, archaeological, scientific, ecological, aesthetic, community significance, agricultural, public water supply, instream public uses, and riparian rights of such rivers shall be restored, protected, and maintained, and notwithstanding the provisions of RSA 483-B" for "scenic beauty and recreational potential of such rivers shall be restored and maintained, that riparian interests shall be respected and" in the last sentence.

—1990.
Deleted "and" preceding "that riparian" and added "and that nothing in this chapter shall be interpreted to preempt any land and zoning authority granted to municipal bodies under RSA title LXIV" following "respected" in the third sentence.

RESEARCH REFERENCES AND PRACTICE AIDS

References in text.
RSA title LXIV, referred to in the section, is classified to Title 64 of LEXIS New Hampshire Revised Statutes Annotated, which is comprised of chapters 672–678.

483:3. Rivers Coordinator.

There is established in the department of environmental services, a state rivers coordinator, who shall be a classified employee qualified by reason of education and experience, and who shall administer the New Hampshire rivers management and protection program.

HISTORY:
1989, 339:1, eff. Jan. 1, 1990. 2007, 285:1, eff. September 1, 2007.

Amendments

—2007.
Deleted "office of planning" preceding "department".

483:4. Definitions.

In this chapter:
I. "Advisory committee" means the rivers management advisory committee established in RSA 483:8.
II. "Agriculture" means agriculture as defined in RSA 21:34-a.
II-a. "Aquatic connectivity" means the ability of aquatic organisms to move naturally within and among water bodies, riparian areas, and floodplains freely without barriers.
III. "Breached dam" means any dam which impounds water at less than 80 percent of its original design level at seasonal high flows and for which the original configuration of the dam can still be determined.

IV. "Channel alteration" means any human activity which changes the character of a river or stream channel including, but not limited to, filling, dredging, relocating, excavating, cleaning, deepening, widening, straightening or riprapping.
V. "Commissioner" means the commissioner, department of environmental services.
VI. "Dam" means any artificial barrier, including appurtenant works, across a river which impounds or diverts water.
VII. "Department" means the department of environmental services.
VIII. "Designated river" means that portion of a perennial river which has been specifically designated by the general court pursuant to RSA 483:15.
IX. "Existing dam" means any dam which has not deteriorated or been breached or modified to the point where it no longer impounds water at 80 percent or more of its original design level at seasonal high flows.
IX-a. "Flowage right" means an easement to flow water over the land of others.
IX-b. "Fluvial geomorphology" means a description of the physical forms and processes of a river or stream, including but not limited to bank erosion, bed scour, sediment aggradation, channel constrictions, and modifications, based on historical and field data, that may be used to evaluate the impact of riverine hazards, and improve management of associated risks.
X. "Free-flowing," as applied to any designated river or river segment, means existing or flowing without artificial impoundment, diversion, channel alterations, or other modifications excluding upstream flow management.
XI. "Instream public uses" means those uses which comprise the state's interests in surface waters including, but not limited to: navigation; recreation; fishing; storage; conservation; maintenance and enhancement of aquatic and fish life; fish and wildlife habitat; wildlife; the protection of water quality and public health; pollution abatement; aesthetic beauty; and hydroelectric energy production.
XII. "Interbasin transfer" means any transfer of water for use from one river drainage basin to another.
XII-a. "Meander belt" means the width on either side of a river channel which the river can occupy through time as a result of migration.
XIII. "New dam" means any dam which requires the construction or enlargement of any impoundment or diversion structure.
XIV. "New hydroelectric power facilities" means the construction, operation, or installation of electric generating units at dams where no hydroelectric power generation has occurred for a period of 6 years or more.
XV. [Repealed.]
XVI. "Protected instream flow" means a stream flow pattern which is established to maintain water for present and future instream public uses.

XVI-a. "Restore" means to return an ecosystem to a close approximation of its natural condition.

XVII. "River" means a flowing body of water including the tidal mouth of rivers whose salinity, flow, or level is influenced by the tides, or a segment or tributary of such water body.

XVIII. "River corridor" means the river and the land area located within a distance of 1,320 feet of the normal high water mark or to the landward extent of the 100 year floodplain as designated by the Federal Emergency Management Agency, whichever distance is larger.

XIX. "River drainage basin" means the New Hampshire portions of USGS Hydrologic Unit Codes 0104 (Androscoggin), 0108 (Connecticut), 0107 (Merrimack), 01060003 (Piscataqua), and 01060002 (Saco) river basins as delineated on a map compiled by the department.

HISTORY:
1989, 339:1. 1990, 233:2. 1992, 261:8, eff. July 14, 1992. 2007, 285:10, eff. September 1, 2007. 2009, 201:4, 5, eff. July 15, 2009. 2016, 286:1, eff. August 20, 2016. 2016, 287:2, 3, 4, 5, 6, 7, 36, eff. August 20, 2016.

Revision note.
Substituted "RSA 483:15" for "RSA 483:14" at the end of par. VIII in light of the redesignation of RSA 483:14 as RSA 483:15.

Amendment Notes
The 2016 amendments to this section by Ch. 286 substituted "stream flow pattern which is established" for "constant minimum stream flow level established" in paragraph XVI.

The 2016 amendments to this section by Ch. 287 added paragraph II-a; substituted "a perennial river" for "a river" in paragraph VIII; added paragraph IX-b; in paragraph X, substituted "any designated river" for "any river," deleted "in a natural condition" following "flowing," and substituted "excluding" for "and without consideration of"; added paragraph XII-a; substituted "stream flow pattern which is established" for "constant minimum stream flow level" in paragraph XVI; and repealed and reenacted paragraph XIX, which formerly read: "'River drainage basin' means the Androscoggin, Coastal, Connecticut, Merrimack, Piscataqua, and Saco river basins as delineated on a map compiled by the department."

—2009.
The 2009 amendment added XVI-a and added "including the tidal mouth of rivers whose salinity, flow, or level is influenced by the tides" in XVII.

—2007.
Paragraph XV: Repealed.

—1992.
Paragraph IX-a: Added.

—1990.
Rewritten to the extent that a detailed comparison would be impracticable.

483:5. Coordination With Federal Statutes.

For the purposes of section 10(a)(2)(A) of the Federal Power Act, those rivers or segments designated under this chapter and any state or local river corridor management plans developed pursuant to this chapter shall constitute one element of the state comprehensive plan for river conservation and de-velopment. Designated rivers or segments shall constitute protected waterways under the provisions of the Public Utilities Regulatory Policies Act, section 210(j)(2), 16 U.S.C. section 824a-3(j)(2).

HISTORY:
1989, 339:1. 1990, 233:3, eff. June 26, 1990. 2016, 287:8, eff. August 20, 2016.

Amendment Notes
The 2016 amendments to this section by Ch. 287 substituted "local river corridor management" for "local management" in the first sentence.

—1990.
Rewrote the first sentence, substituted "designated" for "protected" preceding "rivers or segments" and deleted "of such rivers so designated" thereafter and substituted "under" for "with respect to" preceding "the provisions" in the second sentence and deleted the third sentence.

New dams.
1990, 233:17, II, as amended by 1991, 338:5, eff. June 28, 1991, provided:
"Notwithstanding the provisions of RSA 483, but for the purposes of RSA 483:5, no new dams shall be permitted, between June 29, 1988 and July 1, 1993, on the main stem of the Connecticut River, excepting that segment north of the confluence of the Israel River in the town of Lancaster."

RESEARCH REFERENCES AND PRACTICE AIDS

References in text.
Section 10(a)(2)(A) of the Federal Power Act, referred to in this section, is classified to 16 U.S.C.S. § 803(a)(2)(A).

483:6. Nominations; Criteria.

I. Any New Hampshire organization or resident may nominate a perennial river or any segment or segments of such river for protection by submitting to the commissioner a description of the river or segment or segments of such river and its values and characteristics. The completed nomination shall be submitted to the rivers coordinator on or before June 1 in order for it to be considered in the next legislative session. This nomination shall include, but not be limited to, an assessment of fisheries; geologic and hydrologic features; vegetation; wildlife; historical and archaeological features; open space and recreation features and potential; water quality and quantity; dams, hydropower generation, buildings, and other manmade structures; riparian interests and public water supply, including flowage rights known by the nominating individual or group, and other pertinent instream and riverbank and tributary drainage area information. The nominating party shall hold at least one public meeting on the information prior to final submittal to the commissioner. The department shall encourage the nominating party to include tributary drainage area information in the nomination. Nominations shall include identification of the stream order of each river or river segment proposed for designation and the provisions of RSA 483-B that apply to each segment. The nominating party shall advertise the meeting publicly in cooperation with the rivers coordinator and shall give written notice to riparian landowners and the governing body of any municipality where segments of the river are located. The rivers coordinator shall provide assistance to the nominating party in the presentation of the nomination at the public meeting.

II. The rivers coordinator shall assist and cooperate with the nominator or nominating organization and shall, within 120 days of receipt of a nomination, review the nomination and prepare a recommendation for review by the commissioner under the criteria established in paragraph IV and adopted by rules under RSA 483:11, II.

III. The rivers coordinator, in cooperation with the advisory committee, shall hold at least one public hearing in a community along the nominated river or segment of such river to receive public comment on the nomination. Public hearing comments on the nomination, comments on the nomination from local boards and commissions, factors listed in RSA 483:6, IV(a) as further defined in rules adopted under RSA 483:11, II, and other public comments on the nomination submitted to the rivers coordinator shall be considered by the rivers coordinator and the advisory committee when preparing a recommendation for review by the commissioner.

IV. The commissioner shall review the nomination within 45 days. The commissioner shall, in reviewing a nomination under this chapter, consider the following factors:

(a) Whether the river, or segment or segments of such river, contain or represent either a significant statewide, regional, or local example of one or more of the following:

(1) Geologic resources.

(2) Wildlife resources.

(3) Vegetation and natural communities.

(4) Fish resources.

(5) Water quality.

(6) Water quantity.

(7) Riparian interests.

(8) Existing and potential withdrawals and discharges.

(9) Existing and potential hydroelectric resources.

(10) Hydrologic resources, including natural flow characteristics.

(11) Existing and potential recreational resources.

(12) Public access.

(13) Scenic characteristics.

(14) Cultural, historical, and archaeological resources.

(15) Open space.

(16) Community resources.

(17) Current land use and land use controls.

(18) Scientific resources.

(b) Public hearing comments on the nomination and other public comments submitted to the rivers coordinator.

(c) The recommendation of the rivers coordinator.

(d) The recommendation of the advisory committee.

V. If the commissioner, after reviewing a nomination and considering the factors in RSA 483:6, IV, determines that designation of the river, or segment or segments of such river, would be consistent with the purpose of this chapter, the commissioner shall forward the nomination to the general court for review and legislative approval according to RSA 483:7.

HISTORY:
1989, 339:1. 1991, 338:6–8. 1992, 261:4. 1995, 219:1, eff. Aug. 11, 1995. 2009, 201:6, eff. July 15, 2009. 2011, 32:1, eff. May 9, 2011. 2016, 287:9, 10, eff. August 20, 2016.

Revision note.
In par. II, substituted "paragraph IV" for "paragraph V" following "criteria established in" in light of changes made by 1991, 338:7, 8.

Amendment Notes
The 2016 amendments to this section by Ch. 287, in paragraph I, substituted "nominate a perennial river" for "nominate a river" in the first sentence, added the sixth sentence, and substituted "meeting publicly in cooperation" for "meeting in cooperation" in the second to the last sentence; and rewrote IV(a).

—2011.
The 2011 amendment added "riparian landowners and" in the next to last sentence of I.

—2009.
The 2009 amendment, in I, in the third sentence, added "hydropower generation," "and public water supply," and "and tributary drainage area" and added the fifth sentence.

—1995.
Paragraph I: Substituted "June 1" for "July 15" in the second sentence.

—1992.
Paragraph I: Inserted "including flowage rights known by the nominating individual or group" following "interests" in the third sentence, and rewrote the former fifth sentence as the fifth and sixth sentences.

—1991.
Paragraph I: Added the second, fourth and fifth sentences.
Paragraph III: Added the second sentence.
Paragraphs IV and V: Rewritten to the extent that a detailed comparison would be impractical.

New dams.
1990, 233:17, II, as amended by 1991, 338:5, eff. June 28, 1991, provided:
"Notwithstanding the provisions of RSA 483, but for the purposes of RSA 483:5, no new dams shall be permitted, between June 29, 1988 and July 1, 1993, on the main stem of the Connecticut River, excepting that segment north of the confluence of the Israel River in the town of Lancaster."

483:7. Legislative Designation.

I. Any nomination approved by the commissioner shall require review and approval by the general court prior to inclusion in the program. Such action shall be filed as a bill in the next legislative session following the nomination.

II. Any nomination which is forwarded to the general court for review and approval shall include:

(a) A map showing the boundaries of the river or segment;

(b) A report which specifies the values and characteristics which qualify the river or segment for designation; and

(c) The classifications of the proposed designation pursuant to RSA 483:7-a.

HISTORY:

1989, 339:1. 1990, 233:4, eff. June 26, 1990.

Amendments

—1990.

Designated the existing provisions of the section as par. I and added par. II.

483:7-a. River Classification Criteria; Management.

I. Those rivers or segments designated for inclusion in the program shall be classified as one or more of the following:

(a) Natural rivers are free-flowing rivers or segments characterized by the high quality of natural and scenic resources. River shorelines are in primarily natural vegetation and river corridors are generally undeveloped. Development, if any, is limited to forest management and scattered housing. For natural rivers, the following criteria and management objectives shall apply:

(1) The minimum length of any segment shall be 3 miles.

(2) Existing water quality shall be not lower than Class B level pursuant to the water quality standards established under RSA 485-A:8.

(3) Any paved road open to the public for motor vehicle use shall be screened by the river bank or a vegetative or other natural barrier to effectively conceal the sight and sound of motor vehicles for a majority of the length of the river or segment.

(4) Management of natural rivers and segments shall perpetuate their natural condition as defined in this chapter and shall consider, protect, and ensure the rights of riparian owners to use the river for forest management, agricultural, public water supply, and other purposes which are compatible with instream public uses of the river and the management and protection of the resources for which the river or segment is designated.

(b) Rural rivers are those rivers or segments adjacent to lands which are partially or predominantly used for agriculture, forest management and dispersed or clustered residential development. Some instream structures may exist, including low dams, diversion works and other minor modifications. The following criteria and management objectives shall apply to rural rivers:

(1) The minimum length of any segment shall be 3 miles.

(2) Existing water quality shall be at least Class B level pursuant to the water quality standards established under RSA 485-A:8 or have the potential for restoration to that level.

(3) There shall be no minimum distance from the shoreline to an existing road. Roads may parallel the river shoreline with regular bridge crossings and public access sites.

(4) Management of rural rivers and segments shall maintain and enhance the natural, scenic, and recreational values of the river and shall consider, protect and ensure the rights of riparian owners to use the river for agricultural, forest management, public water supply, and other purposes which are compatible with the instream public uses of the river and the management and protection of the resources for which the river or segment is designated.

(c) Rural-community rivers are those rivers or segments which flow through developed or populated areas of the state and which possess existing or potential community resource values such as those defined in official municipal plans or land use controls. Such rivers have mixed land uses in the corridor reflecting some combination of open space, agricultural, residential, commercial and industrial land uses. Such rivers are readily accessible by road or railroad and may include impoundments or diversions. The following criteria and management objectives shall apply to rural-community rivers:

(1) The minimum length of any segment shall be 3 miles.

(2) Existing water quality shall be at least Class B level pursuant to the water quality standards established under RSA 485-A:8, or have the potential for restoration to that level.

(3) Management of rural-community rivers and segments shall maintain and enhance the natural, scenic, recreational and community values of the river and shall consider, protect, and ensure the rights of riparian owners to use the river for such uses as agricultural, forest management, public water supply, residential, recreational, commercial, industrial, flood control, and other community uses which are compatible with the instream public uses of the river and the management and protection of the resources for which the river or segment is designated.

(d) Community rivers are those rivers or segments which flow through developed or populated areas of the state and which possess existing or potential community resource values, such as those identified in official municipal plans or land use controls. Such rivers have mixed land uses in the corridor reflecting some combination of open space, agricultural, residential, commercial and industrial land uses. Such rivers are readily accessible by road or railroad, may include existing impoundments or diversions, or potential sites for new impoundments or diversions for hydropower, flood control or water supply purposes, and may include the urban centers of municipalities. The following criteria and management objectives shall apply to community rivers:

(1) The minimum length of any segment shall be one half mile.

(2) Existing water quality shall be at least Class B level pursuant to the water quality standards established under RSA 485-A:8, or have the potential for restoration to that level.

(3) Management of community rivers and segments shall maintain and enhance the natural, scenic, recreational and community values of the river and shall consider, protect, and ensure the rights of riparian owners to use the river for such uses as agricultural, forest management, public water supply, residential, recreational, commercial, industrial, flood control and hydroelectric energy production purposes which are compatible with the instream public uses of the river and the management and protection of the resources for which the river or segment is designated.

II. The existence of limited exceptions to the criteria for a certain classification under this section shall not necessarily exclude a river or segment from that classification. The river or segment shall be examined as a whole, and the classification of such river or segment shall be based on the overall values and characteristics of such river or segment.

III. A designated river and its tributary drainage area rivers that are subsequently designated shall be listed in the same paragraph in RSA 483:15. Each tributary river shall be named in a subparagraph under the main stem, and designated segments of each tributary shall be listed as further subparagraphs under each tributary.

HISTORY:
1990, 233:5. 1991, 338:10, 11, eff. June 28, 1991. 2011, 32:2, eff. May 9, 2011. 2016, 287:11, 12, 13, eff. August 20, 2016.

Revision note.
Redesignated par. (bb), as added by 1991, 338:10, as par. (c) and former par. (c) as par. (d) for purposes of conformity with the numbering scheme generally employed in LEXIS New Hampshire Revised Statutes Annotated.

Amendment Notes
The 2016 amendments to this section by Ch. 287 substituted "3 miles" for "5 miles" in I(a)(1); in I(a)(3), substituted "Any" for "The minimum distance from the river shoreline to a," "screened by the river bank or" for "250 feet, except where," and "to effectively conceal" for "exists which effectively screens"; and substituted "one half mile" for "one mile" in I(d)(1).

—2011.
The 2011 amendment added III.

—1991.
Paragraph I(bb): Added.
Paragraph I(c): Rewrote the introductory paragraph and inserted "such uses as" preceding "agricultural", deleted "and" preceding "industrial" and inserted "flood control and hydroelectric energy production" thereafter in subpar. (3).

483:8. Rivers Management Advisory Committee; Establishment.

There is established a rivers management advisory committee appointed by the governor and council. All members shall be New Hampshire residents and the department shall request that nominating organizations select nominees representing diverse geographic areas of the state.

I. The advisory committee shall include:

(a) A representative of public water suppliers who shall be an officer or employee of any municipal or privately owned water works in the state nominated by the New Hampshire Water Works Association.

(b) A municipal officer nominated by the New Hampshire Municipal Association.

(c) A member of the fish and game commission.

(d) A representative nominated by the Business and Industry Association.

(e) A representative of the hydropower industry nominated by the Granite State Hydropower Association in consultation with the New Hampshire hydropower industry.

(f) A conservation commission member nominated by the New Hampshire Association of Conservation Commissions.

(g) A representative of the conservation community nominated by the Society for the Protection of New Hampshire Forests, the Audubon Society of New Hampshire, and the New Hampshire Council of Trout Unlimited.

(h) A representative of recreational interests nominated by the New Hampshire Rivers Council and the Appalachian Mountain Club.

(i) A representative of historic/archaeological interests nominated by the New Hampshire Historical Society.

(j) A representative of the agricultural community nominated by the New Hampshire Farm Bureau Federation, the Northeast Organic Farming Association, and the New Hampshire Association of Conservation Districts.

(k) A representative of local river management advisory committees nominated by the commissioner from a list of members submitted by the local river management advisory committees.

II. The director of the office of strategic initiatives, the executive director of the fish and game department, the commissioner of natural and cultural resources, the commissioner of the department of transportation, the commissioner of the department of safety, and the commissioner of the department of agriculture, markets, and food or their designees shall serve as nonvoting members of the committee.

III. The terms of state agency members shall be the same as their terms in office. The members shall serve 3-year terms.

IV. Any vacancy shall be filled in the same manner as the original appointment for the remainder of the unexpired term. Members may hold office until their successors are appointed and confirmed.

V. The committee shall elect a chairperson and vice chairperson. Meetings shall be at the call of the chairperson, or at the request of 5 or more committee members. The rivers coordinator under RSA 483:3 shall serve as secretary and staff to the committee.

VI. The advisory committee shall report biennially and advise the commissioner, the rivers coordinator, state agencies, municipalities, and the general court in implementing the purposes of this chapter.

VI-a. The advisory committee, at its discretion, may provide testimony and advice on legislation and rules relevant to the management and protection of New Hampshire's rivers.

VII. No state-owned property adjacent to or providing access to a river or river segment shall be recommended for disposal by the council on resources and development or the long range capital planning and utilization committee, whichever is the first point of review, except upon the review and recommendation of the advisory committee established under this section.

VIII. When attending to the duties of the committee, appointed members of the committee shall be eligible to receive mileage at the state employee rate, within the limits of the department's appropriations.

HISTORY:

1989, 339:1. 1990, 233:7, 8. 1995, 130:4, eff. July 23, 1995. 1999, 14:1, eff. June 25, 1999. 2003, 319:9, eff. July 1, 2003. 2004, 257:44, eff. July 1, 2004. 2007, 285:2–4 eff. September 1, 2007. 2009, 201:7, 8, eff. July 15, 2009. 2017, 156:14, 64, eff. July 1, 2017.

Amendment Notes

The 2017 amendments to this section by Ch. 156, in II, substituted "office of strategic initiatives" for "office of energy and planning" and "natural and cultural resources" for "resources and economic development."

The 2016 amendments to this section by Ch. 287 rewrote paragraph I; substituted "the rivers coordinator, state agencies, municipalities" for "rivers coordinator, state agencies" in paragraph VI; added paragraph VI-a; and made stylistic changes.

—2009.

The 2009 amendment, in the second sentence of the introductory paragraph, deleted "At least 3 committee members shall represent the North Country and" at the beginning and added "and the department shall request that nominating organizations select nominees representing diverse geographic areas of the state" at the end; added "the commissioner of the department of safety" in II; deleted "except that the terms of the initial members appointed under subparagraphs I(a), (d), and (g) shall be one year, and those appointed under subparagraphs I(b), (e), and (h) shall be 2 years" at the end of the second sentence of III; added IV and VIII; redesignated former IV through VI as V through VII; deleted the former first sentence of V, which read: "The commissioner shall convene the first meeting no later than September 15, 1988"; in VI, added "report biennially and" and "state agencies, and the general court"; added "or the long range capital planning and utilization committee, whichever is the first point of review" in VII; and made related and stylistic changes.

—2007.

Paragraph I(b): Substituted "a" for "an elected" preceding "municipal".

Paragraph I(k): Added.
Paragraph II: Inserted "the commissioner of the department of transportation" following "economic development".

—2004.

Paragraph II: Substituted "office of energy and planning" for "office of state planning and energy programs".

—2003.

Paragraph II: Substituted "office of state planning and energy programs" for "office of state planning".

—1999.

Paragraph I(j): Added.

—1995.

Paragraph II: Substituted "department of agriculture, markets, and food" for "department of agriculture".

—1990.

Added "and all members shall be New Hampshire residents" following "North Country" in the second sentence of the introductory paragraph, deleted "and" following "game department" and inserted "and the commissioner of the department of agriculture" following "economic development" in par. II and added par. VI.

483:8-a. Local River Management Advisory Committees; Establishment; Duties.

I. The commissioner shall appoint a local river management advisory committee for each designated river or segment. Committee members shall be chosen from lists of nominees submitted by the local governing bodies of the municipalities through which the designated river or segment flows. All members of such committees shall be New Hampshire residents.

II. Each committee shall be composed of at least 3 members who represent a broad range of interests in the vicinity of the designated river or segment. These interests shall include, but not be limited to, local government, business, conservation interests, recreation, agriculture, and riparian landowners. If an interest is not represented by the local governing bodies' nominations, the commissioner may appoint a member from the vicinity of the designated river or segment, to the local river management advisory committee who will represent that interest. County commissioners shall be permitted to nominate members to the local river management advisory committee in unincorporated towns or unorganized places. Upon the request of the committee, local governing bodies or county commissioners within tributary drainage areas may submit nominees for appointment. Each member shall serve a term of 3 years, except when the committee is first established. When the committee is first established the commissioner shall appoint members to one, 2, or 3 year terms to create staggered terms.

III. The duties of such committees shall be:

(a) To advise the commissioner, the advisory committee, the municipalities through which the designated river or segment flows, and municipalities within tributary drainage areas on matters pertaining to the management of the river or segment, tributary drainage areas, and disposal of state-owned lands. Municipal officials, boards, and agencies shall inform such committees of actions which they are considering in managing and regulating activities within designated river corridors.

(b) To consider and comment on any federal, state, or local governmental plans to approve, license, fund, or construct facilities or applications for permits, certificates, or licenses, that may alter the resource values and characteristics for which the river or segment is designated.

(c) To develop or assist in the development and adoption of local river corridor management plans under RSA 483:10. The local planning board, or, in the absence of a planning board, the local governing body, may adopt such plans pursuant to RSA 675:6 as an adjunct to the local master plan adopted under RSA 674:4. No such plan shall have any regulatory effect unless implemented through properly adopted ordinances.

(d) To report biennially to the advisory committee and the commissioner, and annually to municipalities on the status of compliance with federal and state laws and regulations, local ordinances, and plans relevant to the designated river or segment, its corridor, tributary drainage areas, and the activities of the local river management advisory committee including, but not limited to, committee volunteer hours, permit applications reviewed, corridor management plans and their implementation, and education and outreach efforts.

III-a. Local river management advisory committees may apply for and accept, from any source, gifts, grants, and other donations of money or services that directly assist the committee in meeting its duties, programs, and projects. The committees may, without further authorization, expend any funds so received to carry out their duties under this section.

III-b. Local river management advisory committees may, with the approval and consensus of the local governing bodies, merge with other local river management advisory committees for a designated river or segment or re-establish individual committees from previously merged committees.

IV. In the case of the Connecticut River, the commissioner shall appoint the New Hampshire Connecticut River Valley resource commission as the local river management advisory committee to work with the Vermont Connecticut River Watershed Advisory Commission as provided in RSA 227-E. A minimum of 5 subcommittees shall be established by the Connecticut River Valley resource commission along the river between Vermont and New Hampshire as provided in RSA 483:8-a, II. Vermont residents may be appointed in an advisory capacity to the local river management advisory committee, except where the Connecticut River is exclusively intrastate.

V. In order to establish the tax exempt status of local river management advisory committees established under this section, such advisory committees are deemed to be governmental instrumentalities having a distinct legal existence separate from the state and shall not be considered as departments of state government. The exercise by a local river management advisory committee of any authority granted by this section shall be deemed to be the performance of public and essential governmental functions not otherwise fulfilled by state government.

HISTORY:

1990, 233:6. 1991, 338:9. 1992, 261:2. 1995, 219:2, eff. Aug. 11, 1995. 1997, 7:1, eff. June 20, 1997. 267:3, eff. Aug. 18, 1997. 2007, 285:5, eff. September 1, 2007. 2009, 201:9, eff. July 15, 2009. 2016, 287:17, 18, eff. August 20, 2016.

Amendment Notes

The 2016 amendments to this section by Ch. 287 deleted the former next to last sentence of paragraph I, which read: "The commissioner shall appoint at least one person from each municipality to the local river management advisory committee"; in paragraph II, substituted "at least 3 members" for "at least 7 members" in the first sentence, added "except when the committee is first established" in the next to last sentence, and added the last sentence; added "disposal of state-owned lands" in the first sentence of III(a); substituted "or applications for permits, certificates, or licenses, that may alter" for "that would alter" in III(b); added "the activities of the local river management advisory committee including, but not limited to, committee volunteer hours, permit applications reviewed, corridor management plans and their implementation, and education and outreach efforts" in III(d); added paragraph III-b; and made related changes.

—2009.

The 2009 amendment added the fifth sentence of II; in the first sentence of III(a), added "and municipalities within tributary drainage areas" and added "and tributary drainage areas" at the end; in III(d), substituted "biennially" for "annually," added "and annually to municipalities," and added "and tributary drainage areas"; added III-a; and made related and stylistic changes.

—2007.

Paragraph III(a): Substituted "river" for "rivers" following "designated" in the second sentence.

—1997.

Paragraph III(c): Chapter 7 rewrote the second sentence and added the third sentence.

Paragraph V: Chapter 267 added.

—1995.

Paragraph III(a): Added the second sentence.

—1992.

Paragraph IV: Added.

—1991.

Paragraph I: Rewrote the third sentence.

Paragraph II: Added the third and fourth sentences.

483:9. Natural Rivers Protection.

The following protection measures shall apply to a river or segment designated as a natural river:

I. No dam or other structure or improvement that impedes or significantly alters the free-flowing condition or natural character of the river or segment shall be permitted, certified, constructed, or operated in such river or segment.

II. No interbasin transfers of water from a designated natural river or segment shall be permitted.

III. No channel alteration activities shall be permitted. The commissioner may approve channel alterations as follows:

(a) Temporary channel alterations in conjunction with the repair or maintenance of a bridge, road, or riprap which is in place at the time a river or segment is designated; or

(b) Permanent alterations in conjunction with the repair or maintenance of a bridge, road, or riprap which is in place at the time a river or segment is designated which have only de minimis impact to or restore the channel's geomorphic characteristics.

IV. A protected instream flow shall be established by the commissioner for each designated natural river or segment and any upstream impoundment or diversion facility which may affect the free-flowing condition or natural character of the designated river or segment pursuant to RSA 483:9-c.

V. Water quality shall be maintained at, or restored to the Class A level, or maintained at the Class B level. Each designated natural river or segment shall constitute an outstanding natural resource water pursuant to the standards adopted under RSA 485-A:8. The department shall review and consider adopted local river corridor management plans prior to issuing any permit under RSA 485-A:13 or RSA 485-A:17.

VI. Any new solid waste storage or treatment facility, as defined in RSA 149-M:4, IX shall be set back a minimum of 250 feet from the normal high water mark of a designated natural river or segment and screened with a vegetative or other natural barrier to minimize visual impact, except:

(a) New solid waste landfills shall not be permitted within the corridor of a designated natural river or segment, or less than 100 feet from the landward extent of the 500 year floodplain, whichever distance is greater, and shall be screened from the river with a vegetative or other natural barrier to minimize visual impact;

(b) Expansion of existing solid waste landfills shall not occur within the 500 year floodplain of a designated natural river or segment and any expansion of such a landfill located within the corridor of a designated natural river or segment shall be set back a minimum of 100 feet from the landward extent of the 500 year floodplain and screened from the river with a vegetative or other natural barrier to minimize visual impact;

(c) Any land application within the river corridor of septage, sludge, or solid waste, as defined in RSA 149-M:4, XXII, shall be set back a minimum of 250 feet from the normal high water mark and shall be immediately incorporated into the soil. The provisions of this subparagraph shall not apply to manure, lime, or wood ash when used for agricultural purposes and that follow established state or federal best management practices for the protection of water quality.

VII. No new hazardous waste facilities as defined in RSA 147-A:2 which store hazardous waste for more than 90 days, shall be permitted within the corridor of a designated natural river or segment.

VIII. No motorized watercraft shall be permitted to operate on a designated natural river or segment, except for emergency purposes.

HISTORY:
1989, 339:1. 1990, 233:10. 1991, 58:1, eff. May 6, 1991. 338:2, eff. June 28, 1991. 1996, 251:14, 15, eff. Aug. 9, 1996. 1998, 56:2, eff. May 7, 1998. 2007, 308:1, eff. September 11, 2007. 2009, 201:10, eff. July 15, 2009. 2011, 32:3, eff. May 9, 2011. 2016, 286:2, eff. August 20, 2016. 2016, 287:19, 20, eff. August 20, 2016.

Amendment Notes
The 2016 amendments to this section by Ch. 286 deleted "level" following "protected instream flow" in paragraph IV.

The 2016 amendments to this section by Ch. 287 deleted "level" following "protected instream flow" in paragraph IV; and added "and that follow established state or federal best management practices for the protection of water quality" in the second sentence of VI(c).

—2011.
The 2011 amendment rewrote III(b) to the extent that a detailed comparison would be impracticable.

—2009.
The 2009 amendment, in the introductory language of III, deleted "except that" at the end of the first sentence and substituted "channel alterations as follows" for "temporary channel alterations in conjunction with the repair or maintenance of a bridge, road, or riprap which is in place at the time a river or segment is designated"; and added III(a) and III(b).

—2007.
Paragraph VI: Substituted "IX" for "XI" following "RSA 149-M:4" in the introductory par., added the language beginning with "or less than 100 feet" at the end of subpar. (a), added "Expansion of" in the beginning, deleted "permitted and secure" preceding "solid waste" and substituted "occur" for "be expanded" preceding "within the 500" in subpar. (b).

—1998.
Paragraph VI(c): Rewritten to the extent that a detailed comparison would be impracticable.

—1996.
Paragraph VI: Substituted "RSA 149-M:4, XI" for "RSA 149-M:1, VIII" in the introductory paragraph and "RSA 149-M:4, XXIV" for "RSA 149-M:1, XIX" in subpar. (c).

—1991.
Paragraph VI(c): Chapter 58 inserted "or lime or wood ash" following "fertilizer".
Chapter 338 inserted "lime and wood ash" preceding "used for fertilizer" and substituted "and sludge and septage" for "or lime or wood ash" thereafter.

—1990.
Rewritten to the extent that a detailed comparison would be impracticable.

Applicability of 1998 amendment.
1998, 56:6, eff. May 7, 1998, as amended by 2003, 43:14, eff. May 6, 2003, 302:3, eff. July 18, 2003, by 2005, 141:2, eff. June 30, 2005, by 2007, 287:1, eff. July 1, 2007, and 2011, 32:5, eff. May 9, 2011, provided: "The septage and sludge land application restrictions contained in RSA 483:9, VI(c), RSA 483:9-a, VII(b), RSA 483:9-aa, VII(b), and RSA 483:9-b, VII(b) shall not apply until January 1, 2017 to any land upon which septage or sludge has been spread in accordance with all applicable rules adopted by the federal Envi-

ronmental Protection Agency and the New Hampshire department of environmental services, during any portion of the 3-year period prior to January 1, 1998. In addition, there shall be no termination of this restriction exemption for qualifying land that is used for scientific research on septage or sludge. Any continued application of septage and sludge pursuant to this section shall comply with all applicable federal and state laws and any best management practices published by the university of New Hampshire cooperative extension."

NOTES TO DECISIONS

1. Setback

Construction of accessory structures does not violate the requirement that a solid waste facility not be located within the 250-foot setback. Appeal of Old Dutch Mustard Co., 166 N.H. 501, 99 A.3d 290, 2014 N.H. LEXIS 78 (N.H. 2014).

Because accessory structures are not included in the definition of a "facility" and their construction within the setback does not violate the Rivers Management and Protection Act or the Comprehensive Shoreland Protection Act, petitioner had failed to show that the council acted improperly in allowing an applicant for a solid waste permit to build the accessory structures within the setback. Appeal of Old Dutch Mustard Co., 166 N.H. 501, 99 A.3d 290, 2014 N.H. LEXIS 78 (N.H. 2014).

Construction of accessory structures does not violate the requirement of the Rivers Management and Protection Act that a facility not be located within the 250-foot setback, when that provision is construed together with the Comprehensive Shoreland Protection Act, and thus the Waste Management Council did not err in allowing the applicant for a solid waste permit to build accessory structures within the setback. Appeal of Old Dutch Mustard Co., 166 N.H. 501, 99 A.3d 290, 2014 N.H. LEXIS 78 (N.H. 2014).

RESEARCH REFERENCES AND PRACTICE AIDS

New Hampshire Bar Journal.

For article, "State Preemption of Environmental Regulation: Do Municipalities Still Have a Role in Protecting the Environment?," see 48 N.H. B.J. 28 (Autumn 2007).

483:9-a. Rural River Protection.

The following protection measures shall apply to a river or segment designated as a rural river:

I. No new dams shall be permitted, certified, constructed, operated or maintained in such river or segment. The repair of a structural failure of a dam which is in place at the time a river or segment is designated shall not be considered to be a new dam if such dam is repaired or reconstructed at the same location and with the same impoundment level within 6 years of the date of failure.

II. Notwithstanding paragraph I, the department may approve permits and certificates for the construction, operation, or maintenance of new hydroelectric power facilities at existing dams provided that:

(a) The operational mode of any proposed facility shall be run-of-the-river, with project outflow equal to project inflow on an instantaneous basis and the project does not significantly alter the natural flow characteristics of the river; and

(b) The proposed facility does not provide for diversion of the river above or below the existing dam for a significant distance; and

(c) The height of the impoundment is constant and is not raised above the maximum historic level of impoundment at that site; and

(d) The proposed facility provides adequate fish passage as determined by the fish and game department.

III. No interbasin transfers of water from a designated rural river or segment shall be permitted.

IV. No new channel alteration activities shall be permitted which interfere with or alter the natural flow characteristics of the river or segment or which adversely affect the resources for which the river or segment is designated. However, the commissioner may approve such channel alterations as may be necessary for the construction, repair, or maintenance of a project, including public water supply intake facilities in the river or river corridor. The department shall encourage the use of native vegetation to stabilize streambanks of designated rural rivers.

V. A protected instream flow shall be established by the commissioner for each designated rural river or segment and any upstream impoundment or diversion facility which may affect the natural flow characteristics or natural character of the designated river or segment pursuant to RSA 483:9-c.

VI. Water quality shall be restored to or maintained at least at the Class B level. Significant adverse impacts on water quality or other instream public uses shall not be permitted. The department shall review and consider adopted local river corridor management plans prior to issuing any permit under RSA 485-A:13, RSA 485-A:17, or RSA 482-A.

VII. Any new solid waste storage or treatment facility, as defined in RSA 149-M:4, IX shall be set back a minimum of 250 feet from the normal high water mark of a designated rural river or segment and shall be screened with a vegetative or other natural barrier to minimize visual impact, except:

(a) New solid waste landfills shall not be permitted within the corridor of a designated rural river or segment or less than 100 feet from the landward extent of the 500 year floodplain, whichever distance is greater, and shall be screened from the river with a vegetative or other natural barrier to minimize visual impact;

(b) New solid waste landfills may be permitted within the city of Rochester within the corridor of the segment defined in RSA 483:15, XIV(c), and if located in the river corridor shall be set back a minimum of 100 feet from the landward extent of the 500 year floodplain and shall be screened from the river with a vegetative or other natural barrier to minimize visual impact;

(c) Expansion of existing solid waste landfills shall not occur within the 500 year floodplain of a designated rural river or segment, and any expansion of such a landfill shall be set back a minimum of 100 feet from the landward extent of the 500 year floodplain and shall be screened from the river with a vegetative or other natural barrier to minimize visual impact;

(d) Any land application within the river corridor of septage, sludge, or solid waste, as defined in RSA 149-M:4, XXII, shall be set back a minimum of 250 feet from the normal high water mark and shall be immediately incorporated into the soil. The provisions of this subparagraph shall not apply to manure, lime, or wood ash when used for agricultural purposes and that follow established state or federal best management practices for the protection of water quality;

(e) An existing solid waste facility which is located within 250 feet of the normal high water mark of a designated rural river or segment may continue to operate under an existing permit provided it does not cause degradation to an area in excess of that area under permit at the time of designation; and

(f) The department may permit a resource recovery operation at an existing landfill located within 250 feet of the normal high water mark of a designated rural river or segment.

VIII. Any motorized watercraft operating within 150 feet of the shoreline of a designated rural river or segment shall travel at the slowest possible speed necessary to maintain steerage way, but at no time shall exceed 6 miles per hour.

HISTORY:

1990, 233:11. 1991, 58:2, eff. May 6, 1991. 338:3, eff. June 28, 1991. 1996, 251:16, eff. June 10, 1996. 251:17, eff. Aug. 9, 1996. 1998, 56:3, eff. May 7, 1998. 2007, 308:2, eff. September 11, 2007. 2016, 286:3, eff. August 20, 2016. 2016, 287:21, 22, 23, eff. August 20, 2016.

Revision note.

In par. VII, substituted "RSA 149-M:4, IX" for "RSA 149-M:4, XI" in the introductory paragraph and "RSA 149-M:4, XXII" for "RSA 149-M:4, XXIV" in subpar. (b) to correct the references pursuant to 1996, 251:28. See RSA 149-M:4.

Amendment Notes

 The 2016 amendments to this section by Ch. 286 deleted "level" following "protected instream flow" in paragraph V.

 The 2016 amendments to this section by Ch. 287 added "and" at the end of II(c); added II(d); deleted "level" following "protected instream flow" in paragraph V; and added "and that follow established state or federal best management practices for the protection of water quality" in the second sentence of VII(d).

—2007.

Paragraph VII: Inserted "shall be" preceding "screened with a vegetative" in the introductory par., rewrote subparagraph (a), added present subparas. (b) and (c), and redesignated former subparas. (b) through (d) as subparas. (d) through (f).

—1998.

Paragraph VII(b): Rewritten to the extent that a detailed comparison would be impracticable.

—1996.

Paragraph VII: Substituted "RSA 149-M:4, XI" for "RSA 149-M:1, VIII" in the introductory paragraph and "RSA 149-M:4, XXIV" for "RSA 149-M:1, XIX" in subpar. (b).

—1991.

Paragraph VII(b): Chapter 58 inserted "or lime or wood ash" following "fertilizer".

Chapter 338 inserted "lime and wood ash" preceding "used for fertilizer" and substituted "and sludge and septage" for "or lime or wood ash" thereafter.

Applicability of 1998 amendment.

1998, 56:6, eff. May 7, 1998, as amended by 2003, 43:14, eff. May 6, 2003, 302:3, eff. July 18, 2003, by 2005, 141:2, eff. June 30, 2005, by 2007, 287:1, eff. July 1, 2007, and 2011, 32:5, eff. May 9, 2011, provided: "The septage and sludge land application restrictions contained in RSA 483:9, VI(c), RSA 483:9-a, VII(b), RSA 483:9-aa, VII(b), and RSA 483:9-b, VII(b) shall not apply until July 1, 2017 to any land upon which septage or sludge has been spread in accordance with all applicable rules adopted by the federal Environmental Protection Agency and the New Hampshire department of environmental services, during any portion of the 3-year period prior to January 1, 1998. In addition, there shall be no termination of this restriction exemption for qualifying land that is used for scientific research on septage or sludge. Any continued application of septage and sludge pursuant to this section shall comply with all applicable federal and state laws and any best management practices published by the university of New Hampshire cooperative extension."

Emergency repair of stream banks.

1990, 233:23, eff. June 26, 1990, provided:

"Nothing in this act [which added this section and RSA 483:7-a, 483:8-a, 483:9-b, 483:9-c, 483:10-a, 483:10-b, 483:12-a and 483:15 and amended RSA 4:40, 227-E:7, 483:1, 483:2, 483:4, 483:5, 483:7, 483:8, 483:9 and 483:11] shall be construed to prohibit emergency repair of streambanks made necessary by flood damage or stream bank stabilization by riprapping or other means in rivers or segments designated as rural or community rivers, subject to applicable state and federal laws and regulations."

483:9-aa. Rural-Community Rivers Protection.

The following protection measures shall apply to rivers or segments designated as a rural-community river:

I. No new dams shall be permitted, certified, constructed, operated or maintained in such river or segment. The repair of a structural failure of a dam which is in place at the time a river or segment is designated shall not be considered to be a new dam if repaired or reconstructed at the same location and with the same impoundment level within 6 years of the date of failure.

II. Notwithstanding paragraph I, the department may approve permits and certificates for the construction, operation, or maintenance of new hydroelectric power facilities at existing dams provided that:

(a) The operational mode of any proposed facility shall be run-of-the-river, with project outflow equal to project inflow on an instantaneous basis and the project does not significantly alter the natural flow characteristics of the river; and

(b) The proposed facility does not provide for diversion of the river or segment above or below the existing dam for a significant distance; and

(c) The height of the impoundment is constant and is not raised above the maximum historic level of impoundment at that site; and

(d) The proposed facility provides adequate fish passage as determined by the fish and game department.

III. No interbasin transfers of water from a designated rural-community river or segment shall be permitted.

IV. No new channel alteration activities shall be permitted which interfere with or alter the natural flow characteristics of the river or segment or which adversely affect the resources for which the river or segment is designated. However, the commissioner may approve such channel alterations as may be necessary for the construction, repair, or maintenance of a project including public water supply intake facilities in the river or river corridor. The department shall encourage the use of native vegetation to stabilize streambanks of designated rural-community rivers.

V. A protected instream flow shall be established by the commissioner for each designated rural-community river or segment and any upstream impoundment or diversion facility which may affect the natural flow characteristics of such river or segment pursuant to RSA 483:9-c.

VI. Water quality shall be restored or maintained at least at the Class B level. Significant adverse impacts on water quality or other instream public uses shall not be permitted. The department shall review and consider adopted local river corridor management plans prior to issuing any permit under RSA 485-A:13, RSA 485-A:17 or RSA 482-A.

VII. Any new solid waste storage or treatment facility, as defined in RSA 149-M:4, IX shall be set back a minimum of 250 feet from the normal high water mark of a designated rural-community river or segment and screened with a vegetative or other natural barrier to minimize visual impact, except:

(a) New solid waste landfills shall not be permitted within the 500 year floodplain of a designated rural-community river or segment and any new solid waste landfill located within the corridor of a designated rural-community river or segment shall be set back a minimum of 100 feet from the landward extent of the 500 year floodplain and screened from the river with a vegetative or other natural barrier to minimize visual impact;

(b) Any land application within the river corridor of septage, sludge, or solid waste, as defined in RSA 149-M:4, XXII, shall be set back a minimum of 250 feet from the normal high water mark and shall be immediately incorporated into the soil. The provisions of this subparagraph shall not apply to manure, lime, or wood ash when used for agricultural purposes and that follow established state or federal best management practices for the protection of water quality;

(c) An existing solid waste facility which is located within 250 feet of the normal high water

mark of a designated rural-community river or segment may continue to operate under an existing permit provided it does not cause degradation to an area in excess of that area under permit at the time of designation; and

(d) The department may permit a resource recovery operation at an existing landfill located within 250 feet of the normal high water mark of a designated rural-community river or segment.

VIII. Any motorized watercraft operating within 150 feet of the shoreline of a designated rural-community river or segment shall travel at the slowest possible speed necessary to maintain steerage way, but at no time shall exceed 6 miles per hour.

HISTORY:
1991, 338:12, eff. June 28, 1991. 1996, 251:18, 19, eff. Aug. 9, 1996. 1998, 56:4, eff. May 7, 1998. 2016, 286:4, eff. August 20, 2016. 2016, 287:24, 25, 26, eff. August 20, 2016.

Revision note.
In par. VII, substituted "RSA 149-M:4, IX" for "RSA 149-M:4, XI" in the introductory paragraph and "RSA 149-M:4, XXII" for "RSA 149-M:4, XXIV" in subpar. (b) to correct the references pursuant to 1996, 251:28. See RSA 149-M:4.

Amendment Notes
The 2016 amendments to this section by Ch. 286 deleted "level" following "protected instream flow" in paragraph V.
The 2016 amendments to this section by Ch. 287 added "and" at the end of II(c); added II(d); deleted "level" following "protected instream flow" in paragraph V; and added "and that follow established state or federal best management practices for the protection of water quality" in the second sentence of VII(b).

—1998.
Paragraph VII(b): Rewritten to the extent that a detailed comparison would be impracticable.

—1996.
Paragraph VII: Substituted "RSA 149-M:4, XI" for "RSA 149-M:1, VIII" in the introductory paragraph and "RSA 149-M:4, XXIV" for "RSA 149-M:1, XIX" in subpar. (b).

Applicability of 1998 amendment.
1998, 56:6, eff. May 7, 1998, as amended by 2003, 43:14, eff. May 6, 2003, 302:3, eff. July 18, 2003, by 2005, 141:2, eff. June 30, 2005, by 2007, 287:1, eff. July 1, 2007, and 2011, 32:5, eff. May 9, 2011, provided: "The septage and sludge land application restrictions contained in RSA 483:9, VI(c), RSA 483:9-a, VII(b), RSA 483:9-aa, VII(b), and RSA 483:9-b, VII(b) shall not apply until July 1, 2017 to any land upon which septage or sludge has been spread in accordance with all applicable rules adopted by the federal Environmental Protection Agency and the New Hampshire department of environmental services, during any portion of the 3-year period prior to January 1, 1998. In addition, there shall be no termination of this restriction exemption for qualifying land that is used for scientific research on septage or sludge. Any continued application of septage and sludge pursuant to this section shall comply with all applicable federal and state laws and any best management practices published by the university of New Hampshire cooperative extension."

483:9-b. Community Rivers Protection.

The following protection measures shall apply to rivers or segments designated as a community river:

I. The department may approve permits for the construction of new dams for public water supply, flood control or hydroelectric energy production purposes if such construction is consistent with management and protection of the resources for which the river or segment is designated.

II. The department may approve permits and certificates for the construction, operation, or maintenance of new hydroelectric power facilities at existing or breached dams provided that:

(a) The operational mode of any proposed facility shall be run-of-the-river, with project outflow equal to project inflow on an instantaneous basis and the project does not significantly alter the natural flow characteristics of the river; and

(b) The proposed facility does not provide for diversion of the river or segment above or below the existing dam for a significant distance; and

(c) The height of the impoundment is constant and, for existing or breached dams, is not raised above the maximum historic level of impoundment at that site; and

(d) The proposed facility provides adequate fish passage as determined by the fish and game department.

III. No interbasin transfers of water from a designated community river or segment shall be permitted.

IV. No new channel alteration activities shall be permitted which interfere with or alter the natural flow characteristics of the river or segment or which adversely affect the resources for which the river or segment is designated. However, the commissioner may approve such channel alterations as may be necessary for the construction, repair, or maintenance of a project including public water supply intake facilities in the river or river corridor. The department shall encourage the use of native vegetation to stabilize streambanks of designated community rivers.

V. A protected instream flow shall be established by the commissioner for each designated community river or segment and any upstream impoundment or diversion facility which may affect the natural flow characteristics of such river or segment pursuant to RSA 483-A:9-c.

VI. Water quality shall be restored or maintained at least at the Class B level. Significant adverse impacts on water quality or other instream public uses shall not be permitted. The department shall review and consider adopted local river corridor management plans prior to issuing any permit under RSA 485-A:13, RSA 485-A:17 or RSA 482-A.

VII. Any new solid waste storage or treatment facility, as defined in RSA 149-M:4, IX shall be set back a minimum of 250 feet from the normal high water mark of a designated community river or segment and screened with a vegetative or other natural barrier to minimize visual impact, except:

(a) New solid waste landfills shall not be permitted within the 500 year floodplain of a designated community river or segment and any new solid waste landfill located within the corridor of a designated community river or segment shall be set back a minimum of 100 feet from the landward extent of the 500 year floodplain and screened from the river with a vegetative or other natural barrier to minimize visual impact;

(b) Any land application within the river corridor of septage, sludge, or solid waste, as defined in RSA 149-M:4, XXII, shall be set back a minimum of 250 feet from the normal high water mark and shall be immediately incorporated into the soil. The provisions of this subparagraph shall not apply to manure, lime, or wood ash when used for agricultural purposes and that follow established state or federal best management practices for the protection of water quality;

(c) An existing solid waste facility which is located within 250 feet of the normal high water mark of a designated community river or segment may continue to operate under an existing permit provided it does not cause degradation to an area in excess of that area under permit at the time of designation; and

(d) The department may permit a resource recovery operation at an existing landfill located within 250 feet of the normal high water mark of a designated community river or segment.

VIII. Any motorized watercraft operating within 150 feet of the shoreline of a designated community river or segment shall travel at the slowest possible speed necessary to maintain steerage way, but at no time shall exceed 6 miles per hour.

HISTORY:

    1990, 233:11. 1991, 58:3, eff. May 6, 1991. 338:4, 13, 14, eff. June 28, 1991. 1996, 251:20, 21, eff. Aug. 9, 1996. 1998, 56:5, eff. May 7, 1998. 2016, 286:5, eff. August 20, 2016. 2016, 287:27, 28, 29, eff. August 20, 2016.

Revision note.

    In par. VII, substituted "RSA 149-M:4, IX" for "RSA 149-M:4, XI" in the introductory paragraph and "RSA 149-M:4, XXII" for "RSA 149-M:4, XXIV" in subpar. (b) to correct the references pursuant to 1996, 251:28. See RSA 149-M:4.

Amendment Notes

    The 2016 amendments to this section by Ch. 286 deleted "level" following "protected instream flow" in paragraph V.

    The 2016 amendments to this section by Ch. 287 added "and" at the end of II(c); added II(d); deleted "level" following "protected instream flow" in paragraph V; and added "and that follow established state or federal best management practices for the protection of water quality" in the second sentence of VII(b).

—1998.

    Paragraph VII(b): Rewritten to the extent that a detailed comparison would be impracticable.

—1996.

    Paragraph VII: Substituted "RSA 149-M:4, XI" for "RSA 149-M:1, VIII" in the introductory paragraph and "RSA 149-M:4, XXIV" for "RSA 149-M:1, XIX" in subpar. (b).

—1991.

Paragraph I: Rewritten by ch. 338 to the extent that a detailed comparison would be impracticable.

Paragraph II: Chapter 338 deleted "notwithstanding paragraph I" preceding "the department" in the introductory paragraph, deleted "or breached" following "existing" in subpar. (b), and inserted "for existing or breached dams" following "constant and" in subpar. (c).

Paragraph IV: Chapter 338 substituted "community" for "rural" following "designated" in the third sentence.

Paragraph VII(b): Chapter 58 inserted "or lime or wood ash" following "fertilizer".

Chapter 338 inserted "lime and wood ash" preceding "used for fertilizer" and substituted "and sludge and septage" for "or lime or wood ash" thereafter.

Applicability of 1998 amendment.

1998, 56:6, eff. May 7, 1998, as amended by 2003, 43:14, eff. May 6, 2003, 302:3, eff. July 18, 2003, by 2005, 141:2, eff. June 30, 2005, by 2007, 287:1, eff. July 1, 2007, and 2011, 32:5, eff. May 9, 2011, provided: "The septage and sludge land application restrictions contained in RSA 483:9, VI(c), RSA 483:9-a, VII(b), RSA 483:9-aa, VII(b), and RSA 483:9-b, VII(b) shall not apply until July 1, 2017 to any land upon which septage or sludge has been spread in accordance with all applicable rules adopted by the federal Environmental Protection Agency and the New Hampshire department of environmental services, during any portion of the 3-year period prior to January 1, 1998. In addition, there shall be no termination of this restriction exemption for qualifying land that is used for scientific research on septage or sludge. Any continued application of septage and sludge pursuant to this section shall comply with all applicable federal and state laws and any best management practices published by the university of New Hampshire cooperative extension."

Emergency repair of stream banks.

1990, 233:23, eff. June 26, 1990, provided:

"Nothing in this act [which added this section and RSA 483:7-a, 483:8-a, 483:9-a, 483:9-c, 483:10-a, 483:10-b, 483:12-a and 483:15 and amended RSA 4:40, 227-E:7, 483:1, 483:2, 483:4, 483:5, 483:7, 483:8, 483:9 and 483:11] shall be construed to prohibit emergency repair of streambanks made necessary by flood damage or stream bank stabilization by riprapping or other means in rivers or segments designated as rural or community rivers, subject to applicable state and federal laws and regulations."

RESEARCH REFERENCES AND PRACTICE AIDS

References in text.

The reference to RSA 483-A:9-c at the end of par. V is incorrect. The reference should be to RSA 483:9-c.

483:9-c. Establishment of Protected Instream Flows.

I. The commissioner, in consultation with the advisory committee, shall adopt rules under RSA 541-A specifying the standards, criteria, and procedures by which protected instream flows shall be established and enforced for each designated river or segment. The department shall determine the protected instream flow criteria based on the requirements of flow-dependent instream public uses. Each protected instream flow shall be established and enforced to maintain water for instream public uses and to protect characteristics, including recreational, fisheries, wildlife, environmental, hydropower, cultural, historical, archaeological, scientific, ecological, aesthetic, community significance, agricultural, public water supply, riparian rights, and the resources for which the river or segment is

designated. The department shall determine the protected instream flow criteria based on the requirements of flow-dependent, instream public uses.

II. No less than 60 days prior to commencing a protected instream flow study on any designated river, the department shall hold a public hearing jointly with the senate committee with jurisdiction over river management issues and the house committee with jurisdiction over river management issues and provide a public comment period of 30 days. The department shall consider the public comments received before commencing the study.

III. One public hearing shall be held in at least one municipality along the designated river or segment to receive public comment on the establishment of a proposed protected instream flow.

IV. One public hearing shall be held in at least one municipality along the designated river or segment to receive public comment on the establishment of a proposed water management plan intended to implement the protected instream flow.

V. The procedure adopted under this section shall include an assessment of the effect of a protected instream flow upon existing hydroelectric power generation, water supply, flood control, and other riparian users.

VI. Water management plans implementing instream flow protections shall be effective and enforceable upon adoption. The department shall allow a period of up to 5 years for any party subject to the instream flow program to implement the provisions of their water management plan. The department shall adopt rules, pursuant to RSA 541-A, to allow for one 5-year extension for any party who files ongoing progress reports for and is working in good faith on their water management plan but is unable to implement the provisions of their water management plan due to financial or other hardship.

VII. The department shall adopt rules, pursuant to RSA 541-A, to allow for waivers from the provisions of a water management plan. Such rules shall specify the waiver criteria based on negative impacts to public health or safety or an undue financial hardship on a party subject to a water management plan. Should a party meet the criteria for a waiver, and notwithstanding paragraph VI, the department shall waive, in whole or in part, the enforceability of those components of the party's water management plan until the department amends such plan to alleviate the negative impacts to public health or safety or undue financial hardship.

VIII. The protected instream flows established under this section shall be maintained at all times, except when inflow is less than the protected instream flow level as a result of natural causes or when the commissioner determines that a public water supply emergency exists which affects public health and safety.

IX. Only those permits issued by the department that affect stream flow within a designated river shall be required to meet protected instream flows.

X. Any party who is aggrieved by a determination establishing such protected instream flows may petition the commissioner for a hearing to review such determination within 30 days of the date the determination is issued. The filing of such petition shall stay the implementation of the determination until a final decision has been rendered on the petition or an appeal taken pursuant to RSA 541.

HISTORY:
1990, 233:11, eff. June 26, 1990. 2009, 208:2, eff. September 13, 2009. 2011, 32:4, eff. May 9, 2011. 2016, 286:6, eff. August 20, 2016.

Amendment Notes
The 2016 amendments to this section by Ch. 286 rewrote the section.

—2011.
The 2011 amendment added "outstanding characteristics, including recreational, fisheries, wildlife, environmental, hydropower, cultural, historical, archaeological, scientific, ecological, aesthetic, community significance, agricultural, public water supply, and" in the second sentence of I.

—2009.
The 2009 amendment added "and shall respect riparian interests on each designated river or segment consistent with the purposes of this chapter" at the end of the second sentence of I.

Rulemaking.
2000, 242:6, eff. Aug. 7, 2000, provided that notwithstanding any other provision of law, no rules relative to instream flows under par. I of this section shall take effect prior to July 1, 2001.

483:10. River Corridor Management Plans.

I. The rivers coordinator shall provide technical assistance to local river management advisory committees, regional planning commissions, and municipalities, and shall encourage the development and implementation of local river corridor management plans pursuant to RSA 483:8-a, III(c). In developing these plans, the department shall coordinate with the department of natural and cultural resources, the department of fish and game, the office of strategic initiatives, the department of agriculture, markets, and food, the department of transportation, the department of safety, and the division of historical resources.

II. River corridor management plans developed pursuant to paragraph I shall include, but not be limited to, the following:

(a) Permitted recreational uses and activities.

(b) Permitted non-recreational uses and activities.

(c) Existing land uses.

(cc) Aquatic connectivity.

(d) Protection of flood plains, meander belts, wetlands, wildlife and fish habitat, and other significant open space and natural areas.

(e) Dams, bridges, and other water structures.

(f) Access by foot and vehicles.

(g) Setbacks and other location requirements.

(h) Dredging, filling, mining, and earth moving.

(i) Prohibited uses.

(j) State-owned lands within the corridor and tributary drainage areas thereof. The plan shall include a description of the importance of those lands to the characteristics for which the river was designated.

(k) Fluvial geomorphology and risk reduction.

III. River corridor management plans developed according to this section may include tributary drainage areas as determined by the local river management advisory committee.

IV. State agencies shall collaborate with and assist the rivers coordinator and the local river management advisory committee with the implementation of river corridor management plans.

HISTORY:
1989, 339:1, eff. Jan. 1, 1990. 2003, 319:9, eff. July 1, 2003. 2004, 257:44, eff. July 1, 2004. 2007, 285:6, eff. September 1, 2007. 2009, 201:11, 12, eff. July 15, 2009. 2016, 287:31, eff. August 20, 2016. 2017, 156:14, 64, eff. July 1, 2017.

Amendment Notes
The 2017 amendments to this section by Ch. 156, in the second sentence of I, substituted "office of strategic initiatives" for "office of energy and planning" and "natural and cultural resources" for "resources and economic development."
The 2016 amendments to this section by Ch. 287 substituted "River" for "Rivers" in the section heading; rewrote paragraph I, which formerly read: "The rivers coordinator, with the cooperation and assistance of the office of energy and planning, shall develop detailed guidelines for river corridor management plans. The rivers coordinator shall provide technical assistance to regional planning commissions, municipalities, and local river management advisory committees and shall encourage the development and implementation of river corridor management plans"; added II(cc), II(j), and II(k); added "meander belts" in II(d); and substituted "with the implementation" for "in the development and implementation" in paragraph IV.

—2009.
The 2009 amendment, in I, deleted "including but not limited to model shoreline protection ordinances" at the end of the first sentence, deleted the former second sentence, which read: "The rivers coordinator shall hold a public hearing regarding the proposed guidelines and model ordinances," and substituted "local river management advisory committees" for "river corridor commissions" in the second sentence; and added IV.

—2007.
Paragraph III: Added.

—2004.
Paragraph I: Substituted "office of energy and planning" for "office of state planning and energy programs" in the first sentence.

—2003.
Paragraph I: Substituted "office of state planning and energy programs" for "office of state planning".

483:10-a.   Long-Range River Management Plans. [Repealed]

HISTORY:
1990, 233:12. 1995, 130:4, eff. July 23, 1995. 2003, 319:9, eff. July 1, 2003. 2004, 257:44, eff. July 1, 2004. 2007, 285:7, eff. September 1, 2007. Repealed by 2016, 287:38(I), eff. August 20, 2016.

483:10-b. Withholding of Section 401 Certification.

The general court finds that the development of any dam or channel alteration activities within a natural river or segment or the development of any new dam within a rural, rural-community, or community river or segment, except as provided in RSA 483:9-a, II, RSA 483:9-aa, II, and RSA 483:9-b, II, will alter the physical and chemical characteristics of that river and will constitute violation of the water quality standards established under RSA 485-A:8. The commissioner shall deny certification of any federally licensed or permitted activity on such designated rivers or segments under section 401 of the Federal Water Pollution Control Act, P.L. 92-500, as amended.

HISTORY:
1990, 233:12, eff. June 26, 1990. 2016, 287:32, eff. August 20, 2016.

Amendment Notes
The 2016 amendments to this section by Ch. 287 in the first sentence, added "rural community" and "RSA 483:9-aa, II."

RESEARCH REFERENCES AND PRACTICE AIDS

References in text.
Section 401 of the Federal Water Pollution Control Act, P.L.92-500, referred to in this section, is classified to 33 U.S.C.S. § 1341.

483:11. Rulemaking.

The commissioner, with the advice of the advisory committee, shall adopt rules, pursuant to RSA 541-A, relative to the following:

I. Content and submission of nominations, including requirements and criteria for river segments whose salinity, flow, or level is influenced by tides at its tidal mouth, under RSA 483:6, I.

I-a. Determination of the downstream extent for river segments whose salinity, flow, or level is influenced by tides at their tidal mouths.

II. Criteria for acceptance of nominations by the commissioner, including criteria listed in RSA 483:6, IV(a).

III. Preparation for legislative designation of nominated rivers or segments of such rivers under RSA 483:7.

IV. Development of standards, criteria, and procedures for establishment and enforcement of protected instream flow levels for designated rivers and segments under RSA 483:9-c.

HISTORY:
1989, 339:1. 1990, 233:13. 1991, 338:15, eff. June 28, 1991. 2009, 201:17, eff. July 15, 2009.

Amendments

—2009.
The 2009 amendment added "including requirements and criteria for river segments whose salinity, flow, or level is influenced by tides at its tidal mouth" in I and added I-a.

—1991.
Paragraph II: Substituted "IV(a)" for "V" following "RSA 483:6".

—1990.
Paragraph IV: Added.

483:12. Consistency of State Action.

Upon enactment of this chapter, all state agency actions affecting rivers or segments of such rivers which may be designated for protection under this chapter shall conform to the provisions of this chapter.

HISTORY:
1989, 339:1, eff. Jan. 1, 1990.

483:12-a. State Action; Notification of Rivers Coordinator; Petition for Review.

I. Any state agency considering any action affecting any river or segment designated under this chapter shall notify the rivers coordinator and the local river management advisory committee prior to taking any such action. Such agency shall forward to the rivers coordinator and the local river management advisory committee for review and comment copies of all notices of public hearings, or, where a public hearing is not required, a copy of the application for issuance of a permit, certificate, or license within the designated river or corridor under RSA 485-C, RSA 485-A, RSA 483-B, RSA 12-E, RSA 270:12, RSA 482, RSA 482-A, except notifications for minimum impact activities under RSA 482-A:3, V and XII and for routine roadway maintenance under RSA 482-A:3, XVI on land used for agricultural purposes, RSA 149-M, RSA 430, or RSA 147-A. If an agency is notified by the rivers coordinator that a proposed activity would violate a protection measure under RSA 483:9, 483:9-a, 483:9-aa, or 483:9-b, such agency shall deny the application.

I-a. State agencies shall develop, in conjunction with the rivers coordinator and the local river management advisory committees, the procedure by which the state shall notify the appropriate local river management advisory committee when state action is being considered which affects a designated river.

II. If an application is denied solely because the proposed activity would violate a protection measure under RSA 483:9, 483:9-a, 483:9-aa, or 483:9-b, the applicant may petition the commissioner for a review. Within 30 days of receiving such a petition, the commissioner, in consultation with the advisory committee and the appropriate local rivers management advisory committee, shall review the application. If the commissioner determines that the proposed activity is consistent with the character of the designated river or segment or that the proposed activity would provide a public benefit sufficient to outweigh the public benefit of a protection measure under this chapter, the commissioner shall submit to the speaker of the house and the president of the senate a recommendation that the proposed activity be allowed to proceed. Such recommendation shall require review and approval by the general court and shall be filed as a bill in the next legislative session following the petition.

HISTORY:
1990, 233:14. 1995, 219:3, eff. Aug. 11, 1995. 2007, 285:8, eff. September 1, 2007. 2009, 201:13, eff. July 15, 2009. 2016, 287:33, eff. August 20, 2016.

Amendment Notes
The 2016 amendments to this section by Ch. 287, in paragraph I, added "and the local river management advisory committee" in the first and second sentences and added "except notifications for minimum impact activities under RSA 482-A:3, V and XII and for routine roadway maintenance under RSA 482-A:3, XVI on land used for agricultural purpose" in the second sentence; and substituted "State agencies shall develop, in conjunction with the rivers coordinator and the local river management advisory committees" for "The rivers coordinator shall develop, in conjunction with affected state agencies and local river management advisory committees" in paragraph I-a.

—2009.
The 2009 amendment added "RSA 430" in the second sentence of I.

—2007.
Paragraph I: Inserted "RSA 485-C" preceding "RSA 485-A" and "RSA 483-B" thereafter in the second sentence and "483:9-aa" following "483:9-a" in the third sentence.
Paragraph II: Inserted "483:9-aa" following "483:9-a" in the first sentence.

—1995.
Paragraph I-a: Added.

483:12-b. Subject to Other Laws; Existing Hydroelectric Facilities.

I. Any activities permitted under this chapter shall be subject to all applicable state and federal laws and regulations.

II. Nothing in this chapter shall prohibit the continued operation, repair and maintenance of hydroelectric storage and generation facilities existing on the effective date of this paragraph.

HISTORY:
1990, 233:24. 1992, 261:3, eff. July 14, 1992.

Amendments

—1992.
Added "Existing Hydroelectric Facilities" following "laws" in the section catchline, designated the existing provisions of the section as par. I and added par. II.

483:13. Acceptance and Expenditure of Funds.

I. The commissioner may apply for and accept, from any source, gifts; donations of money; grants; federal, local, private, and other matching funds and incentives; and interests in land for the purposes of this chapter. The moneys collected under this paragraph shall be deposited in the fund established under paragraph II.

II. There is hereby established in the office of the state treasurer a fund to be known as the rivers management and protection fund. The fund shall be nonlapsing and continually appropriated to the commissioner for the purposes of this chapter, RSA 487:38 through RSA 487:42, and RSA 483-A.

III. The commissioner may expend any funds deposited in the rivers management and protection fund for the purposes of this chapter, RSA 487:38 through RSA 487:42, and RSA 483-A, and such funds are hereby continually appropriated.

IV. [Repealed.]

HISTORY:
1989, 339:1. 1995, 219:4, eff. Aug. 11, 1995. 2009, 201:14, eff. July 15, 2009. 2010, 269:1, eff. July 6, 2010. 2015, 259:31(II), eff. July 1, 2015.

Amendment Notes

—2015.
The 2015 amendment deleted paragraph IV, which read: "(a) The board shall elect annually from its membership a chairperson and vice-chairperson. (b) The board shall hold 2 or more meetings each year. At any meeting a majority shall constitute a quorum."

—2010.
The 2010 amendment added "and RSA 483-A" at the end of II and in III and made related changes.

—2009.
The 2009 amendment added the second sentence of I; rewrote II, which formerly read: "The rivers coordinator, with the approval of the commissioner and the advisory committee, may expend any funds received under paragraph I for the purposes of this chapter, and such funds are hereby appropriated"; rewrote III, which formerly read: "Local river management advisory committees may apply for and accept, from any source, gifts, grants, and donations of money. The committees may, without further authorization, expend any funds so received to carry out their duties pursuant to RSA 483:8-a"; and added IV.

—1995.
Paragraph III: Added.

483:14. Disposition of State Property.

I. No state-owned property adjacent to or providing access to a river shall be disposed of by the state except upon the review and recommendation of the advisory committee.

II. [Repealed.]

HISTORY:
1990, 118:4, eff. June 18, 1990. 2009, 201:15, eff. July 15, 2009. 2016, 287:38(II), eff. August 20, 2016.

Amendment Notes
The 2016 amendments to this section by Ch. 287 deleted paragraph II, which read: "No state-owned property included in a long-range river management plan shall be disposed of by the state except upon the review and recommendation of the advisory committee."

—2009.
The 2009 amendment added the I designation and added II.

483:15. Rivers Designated for Protection.

The following rivers and river segments are designated as protected:

I. Lamprey River and the watershed tributaries: North Branch, Pawtuckaway, North, Little, and Piscassic Rivers.

(a)(1) Lamprey River:

(A) As a rural river from immediately downstream of Meadow Lake Dam in Northwood to the confluence with the North Branch River in Raymond.

(B) As a rural-community river from the confluence with the North Branch River in Raymond to 0.9 miles downstream of the Langford Road crossing in Raymond.

(C) As a community river from 0.9 miles downstream of the Langford Road crossing in Raymond to 0.3 miles downstream of the Epping Street crossing in Raymond.

(D) As a rural-community river from 0.3 miles downstream of the Epping Street crossing in Raymond to the confluence with the Pawtuckaway River in Epping.

(E) As a community river from the confluence with the Pawtuckaway River in Epping to the downstream side of the New Hampshire Route 125 bridge in Epping.

(F) As a rural river from the downstream side of the New Hampshire Route 125 bridge in Epping to the Epping-Lee town line.

(G) As a rural river from the Epping-Lee town line to the Durham-Newmarket town line. Notwithstanding any other provisions of this chapter, the department of environmental services shall not approve the use of flashboards under RSA 482:29 to increase the height of any existing dam within this segment of the Lamprey River.

(H) As a community river from the Durham-Newmarket town line to 1.8 miles downstream of the MacCallen Dam in Newmarket.

(2) North Branch River-as a natural river from immediately downstream of the Beaver Pond Dam in Deerfield to the confluence with the Lamprey River in Raymond.

(3) Pawtuckaway River-as a rural river from immediately downstream of the Pawtuckaway Lake Dam in Nottingham to the confluence with the Lamprey River in Epping.

(4) North River-as a rural river from immediately downstream of the North River Pond Dam in Nottingham to the confluence with the Lamprey River in Epping.

(5) Little River-as a rural river from immediately downstream of the Mendum's Pond Dam in Nottingham to the confluence with the Lamprey River in Lee.

(6) Piscassic River:

(A) As a natural river from the headwaters 0.5 miles upstream of the Fremont-Brentwood town line to the upstream side of the Piscassic Ice Pond Dam in Newfields.

(B) As a rural-community river from the upstream side of the Piscassic Ice Pond Dam in Newfields to the downstream side of the Grant Road crossing in Newmarket.

(C) As a community river from the downstream side of the Grant Road crossing in Newmarket to the confluence with the Lamprey River in Newmarket.

(b) All 1st, 2nd, and 3rd order portions of the Lamprey River and its tributary rivers shall be exempt from the provisions of the shoreland water quality protection act, RSA 483-B.

II. Merrimack River—main stem from the Bedford-Merrimack town line to the New Hampshire-Massachusetts state line as a "community river." Nothing in this chapter shall be construed to limit complete capacity utilization, not to exceed 30 million gallons per day, or any construction or repairs required to achieve such utilization of the existing intake facilities of Pennichuck Water Works situated on the western bank of the Merrimack River in the vicinity of Chase Brook, so-called. This paragraph shall not affect any private right in the Merrimack River and shall not relieve Pennichuck Water Works, or its successors and assigns, from compliance with other laws or rules under the state's police power.

III. Merrimack River—main stem from the confluence of the Winnipesaukee and Pemigewasset Rivers in the city of Franklin to Garvins Falls in the town of Bow as a "rural river."

IV. Saco River—main stem from the base of Saco Lake dam to the southern boundary of Crawford Notch State Park as a "natural river" and from the southern boundary of Crawford Notch State Park to the New Hampshire-Maine state line as a "rural river." Nothing in this chapter shall prohibit the normal repair or maintenance of the Willey House dam in Crawford Notch State Park.

V. Swift River—main stem from its headwaters to the Albany-Conway town line as a "natural river" and from the Albany-Conway town line to its confluence with the Saco River in Conway as a "rural river."

VI. Pemigewasset River:

(a) As a natural river from the outlet of Profile Lake in Franconia to the southern boundary of Franconia Notch State Park.

(b) As a rural river from the Holderness-Ashland town line to the Franklin Falls flood control dam.

(c) As a rural-community river from the northernmost Thornton town line to the I-93 bridge in Plymouth.

(d) As a community river:

(1) From the I-93 bridge in Plymouth to the Holderness-Ashland town line.

(2) From the Franklin Falls flood control dam to its confluence with the Merrimack River.

VII.(a) Contoocook River—main stem:

(1) As a "rural river":

(A) From the Old Sharon Road bridge in Jaffrey to Noone Falls dam in Peterborough.

(B) From the North Peterborough dam to the monument on the Peterborough-Hancock town line.

(C) From the North Bennington Road bridge in Antrim and Bennington to the confluence of the north branch of the Contoocook River in Hillsborough.

(D) From the Hosiery Mill dam in Hillsborough to the twin iron bridges in West Henniker.

(E) From the Henniker-Hopkinton town line to the Riverhill bridge in Penacook.

(2) As a "community river":

(A) From the outlet of Poole Pond in Rindge to Old Sharon Road bridge in Jaffrey.

(B) From the Noone Falls dam in Peterborough to North Peterborough dam.

(C) From the monument on the Peterborough-Hancock town line to the North Bennington Road bridge in Antrim and Bennington.

(D) From the confluence of the north branch of the Contoocook River in Hillsborough to the Hosiery Mill dam in Hillsborough.

(E) From the twin iron bridges in West Henniker to the Henniker-Hopkinton town line.

(F) From the Riverhill bridge in Penacook to the confluence with the Merrimack River.

(b) Contoocook River—north branch:

(1) As a "rural river," from the outlet of Rye Pond in Stoddard to the outlet of Franklin Pierce Lake.

(2) As a "community river," from the outlet of Franklin Pierce Lake to the confluence of the Contoocook River.

VIII. Connecticut River:

(a) As a rural river from the outlet of the Fourth Connecticut Lake to a point .3 miles above the Second Connecticut Lake Dam.

(b) As a community river from the point above the Second Connecticut Lake Dam to a point .3 miles below the Second Connecticut Lake Dam.

(c) As a rural river from the point below the Second Connecticut Lake Dam to a point .3 miles above the First Connecticut Lake Dam.

(d) As a community river from the point above the First Connecticut Lake Dam to a point .3 miles below the First Connecticut Lake Dam.

(e) As a rural river from the point below the First Connecticut Lake Dam to a point .3 miles above Murphy Dam.

(f) As a community river from the point above the Murphy Dam to a point 2 miles below the Murphy Dam.

(g) As a rural river from the point 2 miles below the Murphy Dam to Bishop Brook in Stewartstown.

(h) As a community river from Bishop Brook to Leach Creek in Canaan, Vermont.

(i) As a rural river from Leach Creek to the confluence with the Mohawk River.

(j) As a rural community river from the confluence with the Mohawk River to the Columbia-Colebrook town line.

(k) As a rural river from the Columbia-Colebrook town line to Wheeler Stream in Brunswick, Vermont.

(l) As a natural river from Wheeler Stream to the Maidstone-Stratford Bridge.

(m) As a rural river from the Maidstone-Stratford Bridge to a point one mile above the breached Wyoming Valley Dam in Northumberland.

(n) As a community river from one mile above the breached Wyoming Valley Dam site to a point one mile below the Wyoming Valley Dam Site.

(o) As a rural river from one mile below the breached Wyoming Valley Dam site to a point .3 miles above the Simpson Paper Company Dam.

(p) As a community river from the point above the Simpson Paper Company Dam to .3 miles below the Simpson Paper Company.

(q) As a rural river from the point below the Simpson Paper Company Dam to .4 miles above the Moore Dam.

(r) As a community river from the point above the Moore Dam to a point .6 miles below the Moore Dam.

(s) As a rural river from the point below Moore Dam to a point .3 miles above the Comerford Dam.

(t) As a community river from the point above the Comerford Dam to a point .2 miles below McIndoes Falls Dam.

(u) As a rural river from the point below the McIndoes Falls Dam to a point .3 miles above the Ryegate Dam.

(v) As a community river from the point above the Ryegate Dam to a point .2 miles below the Ryegate Dam.

(w) As a rural river from the point below the Ryegate Dam to the Ammonoosuc River in Bath.

(x) As a community river from the Ammonoosuc River to the point where routes 135 and 10 meet in Haverhill.

(y) As a rural river from the intersection of routes 135 and 10 to Storrs Pond Brook in Hanover.

(z) As a rural-community river from Storrs Pond Brook to Dothan Brook outlet in Hartford, Vermont.

(aa) As a community river from the Dothan Brook to .3 miles below the Wilder Dam.

(bb) As a rural-community river from the point below the Wilder Dam to the Lebanon-Plainfield town line.

(cc) As a rural river from the Lebanon-Plainfield town line to the Blow-Me-Down Brook in Cornish.

(dd) As a rural-community river from the Blow-Me-Down Brook to the northern end of Chase Island in Cornish.

(ee) As a rural river from the north end of Chase Island to the southern side of the Williams River in Bellows Falls, Vermont.

(ff) As a community river from the southern side of the Williams River to the Saxtons River in Westminster, Vermont.

(gg) As a rural-community river from the Saxtons River to the bridge between Westminster Station and Walpole.

(hh) As a rural river from the bridge at Westminster Station to the Brattleboro-Dummerston, Vermont town line.

(ii) As a rural-community river from the Brattleboro-Dummerston, Vermont town line to Sprague Brook.

(jj) As a community river from Sprague Brook to a point .3 miles below the Vernon Dam.

(kk) As a rural river from the point below the Vernon Dam to the Massachusetts border.

IX. Ashuelot River:

(a) As a natural river from the dam at Butterfield Pond to and including the falls above Ashuelot Pond.

(b) As a rural river from the falls above Ashuelot Pond to Symondsville Road in Marlow.

(c) As a community river from Symondsville Road in Marlow to the Audio Accessories dam.

(d) As a rural river from below the Audio Accessories dam in Marlow up to the breached Blackstock dam located above the town of Gilsum.

(e) As a community river from the breached Blackstock dam above the town of Gilsum to the stone arch bridge in Gilsum.

(f) As a rural river from the stone arch bridge in Gilsum to the Court Street bridge in Keene.

(g) As a community river from the Court Street bridge in Keene to the Branch River in Keene.

(h) As a rural river from the Branch River in Keene to the unnamed brook entering on the west bank near the intersection of Winchester Street and route 10 in West Swanzey.

(i) As a community river from the unnamed brook on the west bank near the intersection of Winchester Street and route 10 in West Swanzey to the Denman Thompson Bridge.

(j) As a rural river from the Denman Thompson Bridge in West Swanzey to and including the oxbow on the west bank before the A.C. Lawrence building in Winchester.

(k) As a community river from the oxbow on the west bank before the A.C. Lawrence building in Winchester to the route 119 bridge.

(l) As a rural river from the route 119 bridge in Winchester to the Winchester dam owned by G.E. Robertson and Company in Hinsdale.

(m) As a community river from the Winchester dam owned by G.E. Robertson and Company in Hinsdale to the route 63 bridge.

(n) As a rural river from the route 63 bridge in Hinsdale to the mouth of the Ashuelot River at the Connecticut River.

X.(a) Piscataquog River—north branch:

(1) As a natural river from the outlet of Deering Lake Dam in Deering, 6.25 miles to the Abijah bridge in Weare.

(2) As a rural river:

(A) From the outlet of Lake Horace Dam in Weare, 8 miles to the Everett Dam flowage in Weare.

(B) From the outlet of Everett Dam in Weare, 8 miles to the river's convergence point with the south branch.

(b) Piscataquog River—middle branch. As a natural river from the natural outlet of Scobie Pond in Francestown to the inlet of the upper cranberry bog at the New Boston town line, approximately 11.5 miles to its mouth in New Boston.

(c) Piscataquog River—south branch:

(1) As a natural river from the outlet of Pleasant Pond in Francestown, 11.5 miles to New Hampshire Route 13 in New Boston.

(2) As a rural river from New Hampshire Route 13 in New Boston, 7 miles to the confluence with the north branch.

(3) As a rural-community river from the confluence with the north branch, 1.7 miles to New Hampshire Route 114 in Goffstown.

(4) As a community river from New Hampshire Route 114 in Goffstown, 1 mile to the Gregg Dam in Goffstown.

(5) As a rural-community river from the Gregg Dam in Goffstown, 6.9 miles to the river's mouth at Bass Island in Manchester.

XI. Exeter/Squamscott River.

(a) As a "rural river" from its headwaters at the route 102 bridge in Chester to its confluence with Great Brook in Exeter;

(b) As a community river from the confluence with Great Brook in Exeter, past the Great Dam and the falls to the head of tide in Exeter;

(c) As a rural river from past the Great Dam and the falls to the head of tide in Exeter, and then the Squamscott River to the boundary of the Great Bay as defined by the upstream side of the railroad trestle in Stratham and Newfields.

XII. Cold River:

(a) As a rural river from the outlet of Crescent Lake Dam in Acworth, 20.3 miles to the most downstream crossing of the Langdon-Walpole town line.

(b) As a community river from the most downstream crossing of the Langdon-Walpole town line, 2.1 miles to its confluence with the Connecticut River in Walpole.

XIII. Souhegan River:

(a) As a rural-community river from the confluence of its south and west branches in New

Ipswich to a point 0.5 miles above the Otis Dam in Greenville.

(b) As a community river from the point 0.5 miles above the Otis Dam in Greenville to a point 0.5 miles below the Otis Dam.

(c) As a rural river from the point 0.5 miles below the Otis Dam to the Label Arts Dam located approximately 0.3 miles above the confluence with Stony Brook in Wilton.

(d) As a community river from the Label Arts Dam to the Wilton Road bridge near the Pine Valley Mill in west Milford.

(e) As a rural-community river from the Wilton Road bridge to a point 0.5 miles above the route 13 bridge in Milford.

(f) As a community river from the point 0.5 miles above the route 13 bridge to a point 0.5 miles below the route 13 bridge.

(g) As a rural river from the point 0.5 miles below the route 13 bridge to the Everett Turnpike bridge in Merrimack.

(h) As a community river from the Everett Turnpike Bridge to the confluence with the Merrimack River in Merrimack.

XIV. Isinglass River:

(a) As a rural river from the outflow of Bow Lake Dam in Strafford, 0.54 miles to immediately downstream of the route 202A bridge.

(b) As a natural river from immediately downstream of the Route 202A bridge in Strafford, 5.75 miles to immediately upstream of the route 126 bridge in Barrington.

(c) As a rural river from immediately upstream of the route 126 bridge in Barrington, 11.64 miles to its confluence with the Cocheco River in Rochester.

XV. Ammonoosuc River:

(a) As a natural river from the Lakes of the Clouds in Sargents Purchase to a point 1.33 miles upstream of Upper Falls in Crawfords Purchase.

(b) As a rural community river from a point 1.33 miles upstream of Upper Falls in Crawfords Purchase to the White Mountain National Forest boundary near Lower Falls in the town of Carroll.

(c) As a rural river from the White Mountain National Forest boundary near Lower Falls in Carroll to the Bethlehem-Littleton town line.

(d) As a community river from the Bethlehem-Littleton town line to the Littleton-Lisbon town line.

(e) As a rural-community river from the Littleton-Lisbon town line to the confluence with Pearl Lake Brook in Lisbon.

(f) As a community river from the confluence with the Pearl Lake Brook in Lisbon to the Lisbon-Landaff-Bath town line.

(g) As a rural-community river from the Lisbon-Landaff-Bath town line to a point 0.9 miles above the covered bridge in Bath.

(h) As a community river from the point 0.9 above the covered bridge in Bath to the confluence with Simonds Brook in Bath.

(i) As a rural-community river from the confluence with Simonds Brook in Bath to the confluence with Burton Brook in Bath.

(j) As a community river from the confluence with Burton Brook in Bath to the confluence with the Connecticut River in Haverhill.

XVI. Cocheco River:

(a) As a natural river from the Cocheco River headwaters south of March's Pond in New Durham to Spring Street crossing in Farmington.

(b) As a community river from Spring Street crossing in Farmington to 0.7 miles south of the Cocheco Road Bridge north of Route 11 in Farmington.

(c) As a rural-community river from 0.7 miles south of the Cocheco Road Bridge north of Route 11 in Farmington to Little Falls Bridge crossing in Rochester.

(d) As a community river from Little Falls Bridge crossing in Rochester to England Road in Rochester.

(e) As a rural-community river from England Road in Rochester to Whittier Street crossing in Dover.

(f) As a community river from Whittier Street crossing in Dover to head of tide at Central Ave dam in Dover.

XVII. Mascoma River:

(a) As a rural river from the downstream side of the confluence of the Mascoma River with the Canaan Street Lake tributary in Canaan to the upstream side of the railroad bridge east of the Baltic Mills Dam in Enfield.

(b) As a community river from the upstream side of the railroad bridge east of the Baltic Mills Dam in Enfield to the downstream side of the railroad bridge south of Main Street in Enfield.

(c) As a rural-community river from the downstream side of the railroad bridge south of Main Street in Enfield, including Mascoma Lake, to the upstream side of the Water Treatment Intake Dam in Lebanon.

(d) As a community river from the upstream side of the Water Treatment Intake Dam in Lebanon to the upstream side of the confluence of the Mascoma River with the Connecticut River in Lebanon.

XVIII. Oyster River:

(a)(1) As a rural-community river immediately downstream of the Hall Road Bridge in Barrington to the upstream side of Old Mill Road in Lee.

(2) As a rural river from the upstream side of Old Mill Road in Lee to the upstream side of Route 155 crossing in Lee.

(3) As a rural-community river from the upstream side of Route 155 crossing in Lee to

the upstream side of the Oyster River Dam in Durham.

(4) As a community river from the upstream side of the Oyster River Dam in Durham to the Mill Pond Dam in Durham.

(b) All 1st, 2nd, and 3rd order portions of the Oyster River shall be exempt from the comprehensive shoreland protection act under RSA 483-B.

HISTORY:

1990, 233:15. 1991, 338:1. 1992, 261:1, 6, 7. 1993, 47:1, eff. June 7, 1993. 132:1, eff. July 16, 1993. 1995, 219:5, eff. Aug. 11, 1995. 1996, 228:108, eff. July 1, 1996. 1999, 64:1, eff. July 20, 1999. 2000, 27:1, eff. May 28, 2000. 2002, 75:1, eff. June 30, 2002. 2007, 66:1, eff. August 10, 2007. 2009, 45:1, eff. July 21, 2009. 208:1, eff. September 13, 2009. 2010, 169:1, 2, eff. June 17, 2010. 2011, 50:1, eff. May 9, 2011. 113:1, eff. May 31, 2011. 118:1, eff. June 2, 2011. 135:1, eff. June 7, 2011. 2016, 287:34, 35, eff. August 20, 2016.

Revision note.

This section was originally enacted as RSA 483:14 and was redesignated pursuant to 1990, 233:25.

Contingent Renumbering.

2011, 118:2, eff. June 2, 2011, provided: "If HB 336 [ch. 50] of the 2011 legislative session becomes law, RSA 483:15, XVII as inserted by section 1 of this act shall be renumbered as RSA 483:15, XVIII." Pursuant to the terms of this provision, RSA 483:15, XVII as added by 2011, 118:1 was renumbered to RSA 483:15, XVIII.

Amendment Notes

The 2016 amendments to this section by Ch. 287, in the introductory paragraph of I, substituted "the watershed tributaries" for "its watershed tributaries including" and "Piscascic Rivers" for "Picassic Rivers"; and substituted "shoreland water quality protection act" for "comprehensive shoreland protection act" in I(b).

—2011.

The 2011 amendment by Chapter 50 added XVII.

The 2011 amendment by Chapter 113, added "Squamscott" in the subsection heading of XI; added the XI(a) designation; added XI(b) and XI(c); and made a related change.

The 2011 amendment by Chapter 118 added XVIII (see contingent renumbering note below).

The 2011 amendment by Chapter 135 rewrote I to the extent that a detailed comparison would be impracticable.

—2010.

The 2010 amendment substituted "south" for "at the outlet" in XVI(a) and added "0.7 miles" in XVI(c).

—2009.

The 2009 amendment by Chapter 45 added XVI.

The 2009 amendment by Chapter 208, added XV(a) and XV(b) and redesignated former XV(a) through XV(h) as XV(c) through XV(j).

—2007.

Paragraph XV: Added.

—2002.

Paragraph XIV: Added.

—2000.

Paragraph XIII: Added.

—1999.

Paragraph XII: Added.

—1996.

Paragraph I: Substituted "department of environmental services" for "division of water resources" in the second sentence.

—1995.

Paragraph XI: Added.

—1993.

Paragraph IX: Added by ch. 47.

Paragraph X: Added by ch. 132.

—1992.

Paragraphs VII(a)(1)(E), VII(a)(2)(F), VIII: Added.

Paragraph VII(a)(2)(E): Substituted "Henniker-Hopkinton town line" for "confluence with the Merrimack River" following "West Henniker to the".

—1991.

Added pars. VI and VII.

Inclusion of Lamprey River, the Swift River and certain portions of the Merrimack River under the shoreland protection act.

1998, 182:1, eff. June 15, 1998, provided:

"Notwithstanding RSA 483-B:20, the provisions of RSA 483-B, relative to comprehensive shoreland protection, shall apply to the Lamprey River, the Swift River and to those portions of the Merrimack River and the Contoocook River designated as protected under RSA 483:15, I–III, V, and VII."

Local approval of additional designation of segment of Exeter River as "rural river".

1995, 219:6, eff. Aug. 11, 1995, as amended by 1998, 182:2, eff. June 15, 1998, provided:

"Notwithstanding RSA 483:7, 483:7-a, I(b)(1), and 483:15, XI, the segment of the Exeter River from its confluence with Great Brook 2.3 miles to the base of the Great Dam in Exeter shall be designated as a rural river provided that the selectmen of the town of Exeter, after a public hearing, vote to approve such designation and notify the commissioner of the department of environmental services of such action."

Designation of Connecticut River segment as natural river and effect of designation on solid waste landfill permit applications filed prior to Jan 1, 1993.

1992, 261:9, eff. July 14, 1992, provided:

"Notwithstanding RSA 483:15, VIII(*l*), the segment of the Connecticut River from Wheeler Stream to Paul Stream shall be designated as a natural river on January 1, 1993. Such natural river designation shall not apply to any entity or person who has filed an application with the department of environmental services for a solid waste landfill permit by December 31, 1992, unless such application is withdrawn or is finally denied and all appeals have been exhausted with respect to the application filed by December 31, 1992."

Management and protection of existing and newly designated community rivers.

1991, 338:16, eff. June 28, 1991, provided:

"**I.** Rivers and river segments designated as community rivers prior to the effective date of this act [June 28, 1991] shall continue to be managed and protected pursuant to the provisions of RSA 483:7-a and RSA 483:9-b under which such rivers and river segments were designated, and pursuant to the values, resources and characteristics addressed in the nomination submitted in support of such designation.

"**II.** Rivers and river segments designated as community rivers under RSA 483:15, VII(a)(2)(A)–(D) as inserted by section 1 of this act shall be managed and protected for the values, resources and characteristics addressed in the nomination submitted in support of such designation."

CHAPTER 483-A

NEW HAMPSHIRE LAKES MANAGEMENT AND PROTECTION PROGRAM

Section

483-A:1. Statement of Policy.

RESEARCH REFERENCES AND PRACTICE AIDS

Cross References.
Clean lakes program, see RSA 487:15 et seq.

483-A:1. Statement of Policy.

New Hampshire's lakes are one of its most important natural resources; vital to wildlife, fisheries, recreation, tourism, and the quality of life of its citizens. It is the policy of the state to insure the continued vitality of New Hampshire lakes as key biological, social, and economic assets, while providing that public health is ensured for the benefit of present and future generations. The state shall encourage and assist in the development of management plans for the waters as well as the shoreland to conserve and protect valued characteristics, including recreational, aesthetic, and those of community significance, so that these valued characteristics shall endure as part of lake uses to be enjoyed by the citizens of New Hampshire. If conflicts arise in the attempt to protect the valued characteristics of a lake, priority shall be given to those characteristics that are necessary to meet state water quality standards.

HISTORY:
1990, 118:2, eff. June 18, 1990. 2010, 269:2, eff. July 6, 2010.

Amendments

—2010.
The 2010 amendment, in the second sentence, substituted "biological" for "environmental" and added "while providing that public health is ensured"; substituted "protect valued" for "protect outstanding" in the third sentence; and added the last sentence.

483-A:2. Definitions.

In this chapter:
I. "Commissioner" means the commissioner, department of environmental services.
II. "Advisory committee" means the lakes management advisory committee established in RSA 483-A:6.
III. "Lake" means the bodies of fresh water as defined in RSA 271:20.
IV. "Valued characteristics" means the uses and values that lakes provide including, but not limited to: passive and active recreational activities such as swimming, fishing, and use of appropriate watercraft; aesthetic values such as scenic beauty, wilderness experiences, and educational opportunities; public uses such as drinking water supplies and flood control; ecosystem values such as providing ecological diversity and wildlife habitat; economic values such as revenue generated for the local, regional, and state economies; and social experiences and the opportunity to use our lakes for public enjoyment.

HISTORY:
1990, 118:2, eff. June 18, 1990. 2010, 269:3, eff. July 6, 2010.

Amendments

—2010.
The 2010 amendment added IV.

483-A:3. Program Established; Intent.

There is established the New Hampshire lakes management and protection program within the department of environmental services. It is the intent of the legislature that the New Hampshire lakes management and protection program shall complement and reinforce existing state and federal water quality laws. It is also the intent of the legislature that, through said program, the scenic beauty and recreational potential of lakes shall be maintained or enhanced, that wildlife habitat shall be protected, that opportunity for public enjoyment of lake uses be ensured, and that littoral interests shall be respected.

HISTORY:
1990, 118:2, eff. June 18, 1990.

483-A:4. Lakes Coordinator.

There is established in the office of the commissioner, department of environmental services, a state lakes coordinator, who shall be a classified employee qualified by reason of education and experience, and who shall administer the New Hampshire lakes management and protection program.

HISTORY:
1990, 118:2, eff. June 18, 1990.

483-A:5. Management.

I. The lakes coordinator, in consultation with the advisory committee, with cooperation and assistance from each of the relevant divisions and bureaus within the department of environmental services, shall prepare every 10 years state level management recommendations for consideration by state agencies in their decision-making regarding lakes management and protection. The purpose of such recommendations shall be to ensure that:
  (a) Water quality shall not be degraded from existing water quality standards established in RSA 485-A.
  (b) Potential sources of pollution, whether point or non-point sources on the land or deriving from activity on the lake, shall be managed in such a way as to minimize their adverse impact on water quality. No significant adverse impact or cumula-

tive adverse impact on water quality shall be permitted.

(c) The environment for wildlife, particularly waterfowl and aquatic life, shall be maintained or improved.

(d) The use of lakes and their drainage areas for flood protection and water supply shall be recognized and protected.

(e) Public access shall be provided and maintained appropriate to suitable uses of the lakes.

(f) Recreational uses of lakes shall be consistent with the carrying capacity and valued characteristics of each lake. Recreational uses shall provide opportunity for the safe enjoyment of a variety of lake experiences within the state as a whole.

II. No state-owned property adjacent to or providing access to a lake shall be disposed of by the state except upon the review and recommendations of the advisory committee.

HISTORY:
1990, 118:2, eff. June 18, 1990. 2010, 269:4, eff. July 6, 2010.

Revision note.
Substituted "Recreational" for "Recreation" preceding "uses" at the beginning of subpar. I(f) to correct a grammatical error.

Amendments

—2010.
The 2010 amendment rewrote the introductory language of I and in I(f), substituted "valued characteristics of each lake" for "character of each lake and shall include, but not be limited to, the use of appropriate watercraft, swimming, and fishing" in the first sentence and "Recreational" for "Permitted" in the second sentence.

483-A:6. Lakes Management Committee; Establishment.

I. There is established a lakes management advisory committee.

II. The advisory committee shall include the following members to be appointed by the governor and council:

(a) A member representing a New Hampshire lake association nominated by the New Hampshire Lakes Association.

(b) A member representing the state conservation committee established in RSA 432:10.

(c) A member of the fish and game commission.

(d) A municipal officer of a lakefront community nominated by the New Hampshire Municipal Association.

(e) A member of a conservation commission from a lakefront community nominated by the New Hampshire Association of Conservation Commissions.

(f) A member representing the scientific community nominated by the university system of New Hampshire.

(g) A member representing the tourism industry nominated by the New Hampshire Travel Council.

(h) A member representing conservation interests nominated jointly by the Loon Preservation Committee, the Society for the Protection of New Hampshire Forests, the Audubon Society of New Hampshire, and the New Hampshire Wildlife Federation.

(i) A member representing the New Hampshire Marine Trades Association.

(j) A member of the New Hampshire Association of Realtors.

(k) A member of a planning board appointed by the New Hampshire Municipal Association.

(l) A member representing the Business and Industry Association of New Hampshire.

(m) A member representing fishing interests nominated jointly by the New Hampshire Wildlife Federation and the New Hampshire Bass Federation.

III. The director of the office of strategic initiatives, the executive director of the fish and game department, the commissioner of natural and cultural resources, the commissioner of the department of safety, the commissioner of the department of agriculture, markets, and food, and the commissioner of the department of transportation, or their designees, shall serve as nonvoting members of the advisory committee.

IV. The terms of state agency members shall be the same as their terms in office. Voting members shall serve 3-year terms.

IV-a. Any vacancy shall be filled in the same manner as the original appointment for the remainder of the unexpired term. Members may hold office until their successors are appointed and confirmed.

V. The advisory committee shall elect a chairperson and vice-chairperson, who shall serve for 3-year terms. Meetings shall be at the call of the chair, or at the request of 3 or more committee members. The lakes coordinator referred to in RSA 483-A:4 shall serve as secretary and staff to the committee.

VI. The advisory committee shall advise the commissioner and lakes coordinator in carrying out the purposes of this chapter and shall report biennially to the commissioner, the state agencies represented on the advisory committee, the house resources, recreation and development committee, and the senate energy, environment and economic development committee regarding the activities carried out for the purposes of this chapter.

HISTORY:
1990, 118:2. 1995, 130:4, eff. July 23, 1995. 2003, 319:9, eff. July 1, 2003. 2004, 257:44, eff. July 1, 2004. 2007, 285:9, eff. September 1, 2007. 2010, 269:5, eff. July 6, 2010. 2017, 156:14, 64, eff. July 1, 2017.

Amendment Notes
The 2017 amendments to this section by Ch. 156, in III, substituted "office of strategic initiatives" for "office of energy and planning" and "natural and cultural resources" for "resources and economic development."

—2010.
The 2010 amendment substituted "New Hampshire Lakes Association" for "New Hampshire Lakes Federation" in II(a); substi-

tuted "nominated by the university system of New Hampshire" for "from the University of New Hampshire" in II(f); rewrote II(h), which formerly read: "A representative of the conservation community chosen from a list of 3 nominees submitted by the Society for Protection of New Hampshire Forests, the Audubon Society, and the New Hampshire Wildlife Federation"; substituted "New Hampshire Marine Trades Association" for "Marine Dealers Association" in II(i); added II(m) and IV-a; added "advisory" near the end of III and in the first sentence of V; deleted "provided, however, that for the initial appointment, persons appointed under subparagraphs" at the end of IV; deleted former IV(a) through IV(c); in V, deleted the former first sentence, which read: "The commissioner shall convene the first meeting no later than September 1, 1990" and deleted "Subsequent" at the beginning of the second sentence; and added the language beginning with "and shall report" at the end of VI.

—2007.
Paragraph II(d): Substituted "a" for "an elected" preceding "municipal".

—2004.
Paragraph III: Substituted "office of energy and planning" for "office of state planning and energy programs".

—2003.
Paragraph III: Substituted "office of state planning and energy programs" for "office of state planning".

—1995.
Paragraph III: Substituted "department of agriculture, markets, and food" for "department of agriculture".

483-A:7. Lakes Management and Protection Plans.

I. The lakes coordinator, in consultation with the advisory committee and the office of strategic initiatives, shall monitor and oversee guidelines for coordinated lake management and shoreland protection plans together with recommendations for implementation, if necessary. Upon acceptance of the guidelines or substantive changes to the guidelines by the advisory committee, the lakes coordinator and members of the advisory committee shall hold public hearings regarding the guidelines or changes to the guidelines. At least one hearing shall be held in each executive council district.

II. The lakes coordinator in consultation with the office of strategic initiatives, with the help of appropriate council on resources and development agencies, shall provide technical assistance and, within the limits of legislative appropriations, award financial grants to regional planning commissions established under RSA 36:45 through RSA 36:53 in support of lake management and shoreland protection planning. The commissioner, with the advice of the lakes coordinator and the advisory committee, shall adopt rules, pursuant to RSA 541-A, relative to awarding financial grants under this paragraph.

III. The lakes coordinator in cooperation with the office of strategic initiatives, regional planning agencies, and appropriate council on resources and development agencies, shall provide technical assistance and information in support of lake management and local shoreland planning consistent with the guidelines established under RSA 483-A:7, I, compatible with the recommendations

under RSA 483-A:5, and consistent with state and federal water quality laws.

IV. Whenever more than one municipality borders a lake, all such municipalities shall be encouraged to cooperate in the development and implementation of a coordinated lake management and shoreland protection plan.

V. Lake management and shoreland protection plans developed pursuant to paragraphs I, II, and III shall address, but not be limited to, the following:

(a) Recreational uses and activities.

(b) Non-recreational uses and activities.

(c) Existing and future land uses.

(d) Protection of wetlands, wildlife, fish habitats, and other significant natural areas.

(e) Dams, bridges, and other water structures.

(f) Public access by foot and vehicle.

(g) Setbacks and other location requirements.

(h) Dredging, filling, mining, and earth moving.

(i) Prohibited uses.

(j) Factors controlling water levels and flowage rights.

(k) Facilities appropriate to support approved lake uses.

(*l*) Water safety.

(m) Other factors affecting water quality.

HISTORY:
1990, 118:2, eff. June 18, 1990. 2003, 319:9, eff. July 1, 2003. 2004, 257:44, eff. July 1, 2004. 2010, 269:6, eff. July 6, 2010. 2017, 156:64, eff. July 1, 2017.

Amendment Notes
The 2017 amendments to this section by Ch. 156 substituted "office of strategic initiatives" for "office of energy and planning" in I through III.

—2010.
The 2010 amendment, in the first sentence of I, deleted "with the cooperation and assistance of" following "committee and," substituted "monitor and oversee" for "develop detailed," and added "if necessary"; in the second sentence of I, added "or substantive changes to the guidelines" and "or changes to the guidelines"; substituted "executive council" for "counselor" in the last sentence of I; in the first sentence of II, added "in consultation with" and substituted "RSA 36:45 through RSA 36:53" for "RSA 36:45– 53"; in III, deleted "efforts" following "shoreland planning," substituted "recommendations" for "criteria established," and added "and consistent with state and federal water quality laws"; added "and implementation" in IV; substituted "Lake management and shoreland protection plans" for "Lake and shoreland management plans" in the introductory language of V; deleted "Permitted" at the beginning of V(a) and V(b); and made related and stylistic changes.

—2004.
Paragraphs I–III: Substituted "office of energy and planning" for "office of state planning and energy programs".

—2003.
Substituted "office of state planning and energy programs" for "office of state planning" in pars. I, II and III.

RESEARCH REFERENCES AND PRACTICE AIDS

References in text.
RSA 36:51 and 52, contained in RSA 36:45– 53 in par. II, was repealed by 2000, 200:8, I, II, respectively, eff. July 29, 2000.

483-A:8. Acceptance and Expenditures of Funds.

I. The commissioner may apply for and accept, from any source, gifts; donations of money; grants; federal, local, private, and other funds and incentives; and interests in land for the purposes of this chapter. The moneys collected under this paragraph shall be deposited in the rivers management and protection fund established under RSA 483:13.

II. The commissioner may expend any funds deposited in the rivers management and protection fund for the purposes of this chapter, in addition to those purposes established under RSA 483:13.

HISTORY:

1990, 118:2, eff. June 18, 1990. 2010, 269:7, eff. July 6, 2010.

Amendments

—2010.

The 2010 amendment added the second sentence of I and rewrote II, which formerly read: "The lakes coordinator, with the approval of the commissioner, may expend any funds received under paragraph I for the purposes of this chapter, and such funds are hereby continually appropriated."

483-A:9. State Agency Cooperation.

Affected state agencies shall cooperate with and assist the lakes coordinator and the advisory committee in the development and implementation of lakes management plans established under RSA 483-A:7.

HISTORY:

1990, 118:2, eff. June 18, 1990.

CHAPTER 483-B

SHORELAND WATER QUALITY PROTECTION ACT

Amendments

—2011.

The 2011 amendment by 2011, 224:382, eff. June 29, 2011, in the chapter heading, deleted "Comprehensive" at the beginning and added "Water Quality."

NOTES TO DECISIONS

Docks

RSA ch. 483-B lacks any provisions regulating the use of docks for boating or boat docking as part of shoreland protection. Had the legislature intended to permit municipalities to enact such regulations, it could have explicitly done so. Lakeside Lodge, Inc. v. Town of New London, 158 N.H. 164, 960 A.2d 1268, 2008 N.H. LEXIS 140 (2008).

Cited:

Cited in Opinion of the Justices (Public Use of Coastal Beaches), 139 N.H. 82, 649 A.2d 604, 1994 N.H. LEXIS 149 (1994).

RESEARCH REFERENCES AND PRACTICE AIDS

Cross References.

Clean lakes program, see RSA 487:15 et seq.
Fill and dredge in wetlands, see RSA 482-A.
Lakes management and protection program, see RSA 483-A.
Rivers management and protection program, see RSA 483.
Shore and beach preservation and development generally, see RSA 217.

483-B:1. Purpose.

The general court finds that:

I. The shorelands of the state are among its most valuable and fragile natural resources and their protection is essential to maintain the integrity of public waters.

I-a. A natural woodland buffer, consisting of trees and other vegetation located in areas adjoining public waters, functions to intercept surface runoff, wastewater, subsurface flow, and deeper groundwater flows from upland sources and to remove or minimize the effects of nutrients, sediment, organic matter, pesticides, and other pollutants and to moderate the temperature of the near-shore waters.

I-b. Scientific evidence has confirmed that even small areas of impervious surface coverage can have deleterious impacts on water quality and the aesthetic beauty of our lakes and rivers if not properly contained or managed within each watershed. These impacts are known to reduce recreational opportunity, reduce property values, and pose human health risks.

II. The public waters of New Hampshire are valuable resources held in trust by the state. The state has an interest in protecting those waters and has the jurisdiction to control the use of the public waters and the adjacent shoreland for the greatest public benefit.

III. There is great concern throughout the state relating to the utilization, protection, restoration and preservation of shorelands because of their effect on state waters.

IV. Under current law the potential exists for uncoordinated, unplanned and piecemeal development along the state's shorelines, which could result in significant negative impacts on the public waters of New Hampshire.

HISTORY:

1991, 303:1. 2002, 263:1, eff. July 17, 2002. 2008, 171:15, eff. July 1, 2008.

Contingent 2008 amendment.

2008, 171:21, I, eff. June 6, 2008, provided in part, that if HB 1601-FN-A [ch. 5] of the 2008 legislative session becomes law, section 15 of this act shall take effect July 1, 2008. Pursuant to the terms of this provision par. I-b is set out above as amended by Ch. 171:15, eff. July 1, 2008.

Effective Date.

1991, 303:8, which was subsequently amended by 1992, 157:1, was repealed by 1994, 383:22, III, eff. July 1, 1994. Pursuant to 1991, 303:10, I, as amended by 1994, 383:25, section 1 of 1991, chapter 303, which added this chapter, shall take effect on July 1, 1994.

1991, 303:8, provided that section 1 of the act, which added this chapter, would take effect only after the general court had approved funding of sections 1, 2 and 5 of this act, which added this chapter, amended RSA 4-C:6 and authorized additional staff in the department of environmental services for the administration of RSA 483-B, respectively, after consideration of the implementation plan required under section 7 of the act.

Amendments

—2008.

The 2008 amendment added I-b.

—2002.

Paragraph I-a: Added.

NOTES TO DECISIONS

Public access to water

Department of Environmental Services was entitled to recreational use immunity under RSA 508:14, I. Because the decedents, who drowned in a lake, used state-owned land for recreational activities, i.e., to access water for swimming, the statute applied here; furthermore, under RSA 271:20 and RSA 483-B:1, II, the state had the authority to control access to public waters, such as the lake here, from public land. Coan v. N.H. Dep't of Env't Servs., 161 N.H. 1, 8 A.3d 109, 2010 N.H. LEXIS 116 (N.H. 2010).

Cited:

Cited in Bacon v. Town of Enfield, 150 N.H. 468, 840 A.2d 788, 2004 N.H. LEXIS 8 (2004).

483-B:2. Minimum Standards Required.

To fulfill the state's role as trustee of its waters and to promote public health, safety, and the general welfare, the general court declares that the public interest requires the establishment of standards for the subdivision, use, and development of the shorelands of the state's public waters. The development standards provided in this chapter shall be the minimum standards necessary to protect the public waters of the state of New Hampshire. These standards shall serve to:

I. Further the maintenance of safe and healthful conditions.

II. Provide for the wise utilization of water and related land resources.

III. Prevent and control water pollution.

IV. Protect fish spawning grounds, aquatic life, and bird and other wildlife habitats.

V. Protect buildings and lands from flooding and accelerated erosion.

VI. Protect archaeological and historical resources.

VII. Protect commercial fishing and maritime industries.

VIII. Protect freshwater and coastal wetlands.

IX. Control building sites, placement of structures, and land uses that may potentially damage the public waters.

X. Conserve shoreline cover and points of access to inland and coastal waters.

XI. Preserve the state's lakes, rivers, estuaries and coastal waters in their natural state.

XII. Promote wildlife habitat, scenic beauty, and scientific study.

XIII. Protect public use of waters, including recreation.

XIV. Conserve natural beauty and open spaces.

XV. Anticipate and respond to the impacts of development in shoreland areas to the extent they may potentially damage the public waters.

XVI. Provide for economic development in proximity to waters.

HISTORY:

1991, 303:1. 1992, 235:1, 2. 1994, 383:1, eff. July 1, 1994. 2011, 224:383, 384, eff. June 29, 2011.

Editor's note.

Although 1992, 235:1, 2 provided for the amendment of par. X and the addition of par XVI effective on Jan. 1, 1993, the amendment did not become effective until July 1, 1994, the date on which this section as originally enacted by 1991, 303:1 became effective under the terms of 1991, 303:10, I, as amended by 1994, 383:25.

Effective Date.

See note under RSA 483-B:1.

Amendments

—2011.

The 2011 amendment added "that may potentially damage the public waters" in IX and added "to the extent they may potentially damage the public waters" in XV.

—1994.

Paragraph XI: Inserted "rivers" following "lakes".

—1992.

Paragraph X: Substituted "shoreline cover and" for "shore cover, and visual as well as actual" preceding "points".
Paragraph XVI: Added.

483-B:3. Consistency Required.

I. All state agencies shall perform their responsibilities in a manner consistent with the intent of this chapter. State and local permits for work within the protected shorelands shall be issued only when consistent with the policies of this chapter.

II. When the standards and practices established in this chapter conflict with other local or state laws and rules, the more stringent standard shall control.

III. All agricultural activities and operations in the state as defined in RSA 21:34-a and as governed by RSA 430, including the use of animal manure, lime, wood ash, irrigation, and the clearing of land for agricultural utilization, and other agricultural technologies, shall be exempt from the provisions of this chapter, provided such activities and operations are in conformance with the most recent best management practices determined by the United States Department of Agriculture Natural Resources Conservation Service, the United States Department of Agriculture Cooperative Extension Service and the department of agriculture, markets, and food. Persons carrying out such agricultural activities and operations in the protected shoreland shall work directly with the local representatives of the above agencies for their particular property.

HISTORY:
    1991, 303:1. 1992, 235:21. 1995, 130:8, eff. July 23, 1995. 206:2, eff. Aug. 11, 1995.

Editor's note.
    Although 1992, 235:21 provided for the amendment of par. III effective on Jan. 1, 1993, the amendment did not become effective until July 1, 1994, the date on which this section as originally enacted by 1991, 303:1 became effective under the terms of 1991, 303:10, I, as amended by 1994, 383:25.

Effective Date.
    See note under RSA 483-B:1.

Amendments

—1995.
    Paragraph III: Chapter 130 substituted "and the department of agriculture, markets, and food" for "and the department of agriculture" following "Extension Service" in the first sentence.
    Chapter 206 substituted "United States Department of Agriculture Natural Resources Conservation Service" for "United States Department of Agriculture Soil Conservation Service" in the first sentence.

—1992.
    Paragraph III: Inserted "and the clearing of land for agricultural utilization" following "irrigation" and "the most recent" following "conformance with" in the first sentence and added the second sentence.

NOTES TO DECISIONS

Permit
    Once a boathouse project was relocated landward of a bank, it lost its status as a water dependent structure because it was no longer located over, on, or in the waters of the State of New Hampshire. It was then located over a dredged inlet, and no longer required a dredge and fill permit so that there was no legal basis for imposing the N.H. Code Admin. R. Ann., Env-Wt 302.03 requirements on the boathouse. Cayten v. N.H. Dep't of Envtl. Servs., 155 N.H. 647, 927 A.2d 494, 2007 N.H. LEXIS 113 (N.H. 2007).

483-B:4. Definitions.

In this chapter:

I. "Abutter" means any person who owns property that is immediately contiguous to the property on which the proposed work will take place, or who owns flowage rights on such property. The term does not include those properties separated by a public road or more than ¼ mile from the limits of the proposed work. If contiguous properties are owned by the person who is proposing the work, then the term includes the person owning the next contiguous property, subject to the ¼ mile limitation.

II. "Accessory structure" means a structure, as defined in paragraph XXII of this section, on the same lot and customarily incidental and subordinate to the primary structure, as defined in paragraph XIV of this section; or a use, including but not limited to paths, driveways, patios, any other improved surface, pump houses, gazebos, woodsheds, garages, or other outbuildings.

III. [Repealed.]

IV. "Commissioner" means the commissioner of the department of environmental services or designee.

V. "Department" means the department of environmental services.

VI. "Disturbed area" means an area in which natural vegetation is removed, exposing the underlying soil.

VII. "Ground cover" means any herbaceous plant or any woody seedling or shrub generally less than 3 feet in height. Ground cover shall not include lawns, landscaped areas, gardens, invasive species as listed by the department of agriculture, markets, and food in accordance with RSA 430:53, III, exotic species as designated by rule of the department of environmental services in accordance with RSA 487:24, VII, imported organic or stone mulches, or other artificial materials.

VII-a. [Repealed.]

VII-b. "Impervious surface" means any modified surface that cannot effectively absorb or infiltrate water. Examples of impervious surfaces include, but are not limited to, roofs, and unless designed to effectively absorb or infiltrate water, decks, patios, and paved, gravel, or crushed stone driveways, parking areas, and walkways.

VII-c. "Horticultural professional" means any arborist, landscape architect, or gardening consultant whose function is that of providing services relative to horticulture.

VIII. "Lot of record" means a legally created parcel, the plat or description of which has been recorded at the registry of deeds for the county in which it is located.

IX. [Repealed.]

X. "Municipality" means a city, town, village district if specifically authorized to zone by the legislature, or county in respect to unincorporated towns or unorganized places or any combination thereof pursuant to RSA 53-A.

X-a, X-b. [Repealed.]

XI. "Natural woodland" means a forested area consisting of various species of trees, saplings, shrubs, and ground covers in any combination and at any stage of growth.

XI-a, XI-b. [Repealed.]

XI-c. "Nonconforming lot of record" means an existing lot which does not conform to the provisions of this chapter.

XI-d. "Nonconforming structure" means a structure that, either individually or when viewed in combination with other structures on the property, does not conform to the provisions of this chapter, including but not limited to the impervious surface limits of RSA 483-B:9, V(g).

XI-e. "Ordinary high water mark" means the line on the shore, running parallel to the main stem of the river, established by the fluctuations of water and indicated by physical characteristics such as a clear, natural line impressed on the immediate bank, shelving, changes in the character of soil, destruction of terrestrial vegetation, the presence of litter and debris, or other appropriate means that consider the characteristics of the surrounding areas. Where the ordinary high water mark is not easily discernable, the ordinary high water mark may be determined by the department of environmental services.

XII. "Person" means a corporation, company, association, society, firm, partnership or joint stock company, as well as an individual, a state, and any political subdivision of a state or any agency or instrumentality thereof.

XII-a. "Pervious surface" means any surface, whether natural, man-made, or modified, that can effectively absorb or infiltrate water including, but not limited to, vegetated surface, such as woodlands, planted beds, and lawns, and those pavements specifically designed and maintained to effectively absorb and infiltrate water.

XIII. "Primary building line" means a setback for primary structures of 50 feet from the reference line.

XIV. "Primary structure" means a structure as defined in paragraph XXII of this section that is central to the fundamental use of the property and is not accessory to the use of another structure on the same premises.

XV. "Protected shoreland" means, for natural, fresh water bodies without artificial impoundments, for artificially impounded fresh water bodies, except private garden water features and ponds of less than 10 acres, and for coastal waters and rivers, all land located within 250 feet of the reference line of public waters. For river segments of third order or lower designated as protected under RSA 483:15 which are either designated after or for which specific exemptions are repealed after December 31, 2015, "protected shoreland" means all land located within 50 feet of the reference line of public water.

XVI. "Public waters" shall include:

(a) All lakes, ponds, and artificial impoundments greater than 10 acres in size.

(b) Coastal waters, being all waters subject to the ebb and flow of the tide, including the Great Bay Estuary and the associated tidal rivers.

(c) Rivers, meaning all year-round flowing waters of fourth order or higher and all rivers and river segments designated as protected under RSA 483:15. Stream order shall be determined using the New Hampshire hydrography dataset archived by the geographically referenced analysis and information transfer system (GRANIT) at the complex systems research center of the university of New Hampshire, and developed by GRANIT in collaboration with the department of environmental services. A listing of the streams of fourth order and higher shall be prepared and periodically updated by the GRANIT at the complex systems research center of the university of New Hampshire and delivered to the commissioner 30 days after the effective date of this subparagraph.

XVII. "Reference line" means:

(a) For all lakes, ponds, and artificial impoundments greater than 10 acres in size, the surface elevation as listed in the Consolidated List of Water Bodies subject to the shoreland water quality protection act as maintained by the department.

(b) For coastal waters, the highest observable tide line, which means a line defining the furthest landward limit of tidal flow, not including storm events, which can be recognized by indicators such as the presence of a strand line of flotsam and debris, the landward margin of salt tolerant vegetation, or a physical barrier that blocks further flow of the tide.

(c) For rivers, the ordinary high water mark.

XVIII. "Removal or removed" means girdled, felled, cut, sawed, pruned, pushed over, buried, burned, or any other activity conducted to the extent that it otherwise kills the vegetation.

XVIII-a. "Repeat violation" means a violation that occurs within 3 years of notification by the department of a prior violation, as defined in RSA 483-B:18, I, whether on the same site or by the same person or entity on a second site. Each day of continuing violation after notification of that violation shall be considered a repeat violation.

XVIII-b. "Repair" means work conducted to restore an existing, legal structure by partial replacement of worn, broken, or unsound parts or to fix a specific defect, during which all of the exterior dimensions are intact and remain so at the conclusion of construction.

XVIII-c. "Replace in kind" means the substitution of a new structure for an existing legal structure, whether in total or in part.

XVIII-d. "Replacement system" means a septic system that is not considered new construction under RSA 485-A:29–44 and rules adopted to implement it.

XIX. "Residential unit" means a structure, or portion thereof, providing complete and independent living facilities, including permanent facilities for living, sleeping, eating, cooking, and sanitation which are used in common by one or more persons.

XX. "Sapling" means any woody plant which normally grows to a mature height greater than 20 feet and has a diameter less than 6 inches at a point 4-½ feet above the ground.

XX-a. "Shoreland frontage" means the actual shoreland frontage along the water front measured at the reference line.

XXI. "Shrub" means any multi-stemmed woody plant which normally grows to a mature height of less than 20 feet.

XXII. "Structure" means anything constructed or erected for the support, shelter or enclosure of persons, animals, goods, or property of any kind, with a fixed permanent location on or in the ground, exclusive of fences.

XXIII. "Subdivision" means subdivision as defined in RSA 672:14.

XXIV. "Tree" means any woody plant which normally grows to a mature height greater than 20 feet and which has a diameter of 6 inches or more at a point 4-½ feet above the ground.

XXIV-a. [Repealed.]

XXIV-b. "Unaltered state" means native vegetation allowed to grow without cutting, limbing, trimming, pruning, mowing, or other similar activities except as needed for renewal or to maintain or improve plant health.

XXV. "Urbanization" means the concentrated development found in the sections of towns or cities where there has been an historic pattern of intensive building for residential, commercial, industrial, or mixed uses such that it contributes to or constitutes the municipality's downtown, community center, or central business district and wherein all vegetative buffers have been depleted, impervious surfaces are in excess of 50 percent, and residential uses are of at least 10 dwelling units per acre.

XXVI. "Water dependent structure" means a structure that is a dock, wharf, pier, breakwater, beach, boathouse, retaining wall, or launching ramp or other similar structure, or any part thereof, built over, on, or in the waters of the state.

XXVII. "Woodland buffer" means all protected shorelands within 150 feet of the reference line including those protected shorelands within 50 feet of the reference line more specifically designated as the waterfront buffer.

HISTORY:
1991, 303:1. 1992, 235:3–7, 22. 1994, 383:2–5, 22, I, eff. July 1, 1994. 1996, 17:1, 2, eff. June 14, 1996. 228:65, eff. July 1, 1996. 2002, 169:1, eff. Jan. 1, 2003. 263:2–7, eff. July 17, 2002. 2003, 319:9, eff. July 1, 2003. 2004, 257:44, eff. July 1, 2004. 2007,

267:1–6, eff. April 1, 2008. 2008, 5:5, III–VI, 6, 7, eff. May 1, 2008. 5:13–18, eff. July 1, 2008. 171:13, eff. July 1, 2008. 171:17, eff. at 12:01 a.m., July 1, 2008. 2009, 218:1–8, 23, I, eff. September 13, 2009. 2011, 224:385–393, 409, eff. June 29, 2011. 2013, 153:1, 2, 9, eff. August 27, 2013. 2016, 287:37, eff. August 20, 2016. 2017, 38:1, eff. May 9, 2017. 2017, 225:1, 2, eff. September 9, 2017.

Editor's note.
Although 1992, 235:3, 5–7, 22 provided for the amendment of pars. IX, XVI, XVII, XIX and XV, respectively, and 1992, 235:4 provided for the addition of par. XI-a effective on Jan. 1, 1993, the amendments to this section did not become effective until July 1, 1994, the date on which this section as originally enacted by 1991, 303:1 became effective under the terms of 1991, 303:10, I, as amended by 1994, 383:25.

Contingent 2008 amendments.
2008, 171:21, I, eff. June 6, 2008, provided in part, that if HB 1601-FN-A [ch. 5] of the 2008 legislative session becomes law, section 13 of this act shall take effect July 1, 2008, section 17 of this act shall take effect July 1, 2008 at 12:01 a.m. and section 8 of this act shall not take effect. Pursuant to the terms of this provision, par. I is set out above as amended by Ch. 171:13, eff. July 1, 2008; par. XXIV-b is set out above as amended by Ch. 171:17, eff. July 1, 2008 at 12:01 a.m.; and the amendment to par. XXIV-a did not take effect.

Effective Date.
See note under RSA 483-B:1.

Amendment Notes
The 2017 amendments by Ch. 38 added XII-a.
The 2017 amendments by Ch. 225 deleted "buffer" after "woodland" in XI; and added XXVII.
The 2016 amendments to this section by Ch. 287 added the second sentence of paragraph XV.

—2013.
The 2013 amendment rewrote VII to the extent that a detailed comparison would be impracticable; deleted X-b; and in XXIV-b, added "native" and substituted "renewal or to maintain or improve plant health" for "plant health, normal maintenance, and renewal."

—2011.
The 2011 amendment, in the second sentence of VII-b, added "and unless designed to effectively absorb or infiltrate water" and deleted "unless designed to effectively absorb or infiltrate water" at the end; added VII-c; deleted the former second sentence of X-b; deleted "at least" following "structures of" in XIII; added "except private garden water features and ponds of less than 10 acres" in XV; substituted "shoreland water quality" for "Comprehensive shoreland" in XVII(a); in XVIII, deleted "killed, or" following "felled" and substituted "kills" for "destructively alters or altered"; deleted "with no change in size, dimensions, footprint, interior square footage, and location, with the exception of changes resulting in an increase in the setback to public waters" at the end of XVIII-c; rewrote XX-a; added "permanent" in XXII; and in XXIV-b, deleted "native" preceding "vegetation" and substituted "for plant health, normal maintenance, and renewal" for "to maintain the health of the plant being trimmed, as allowed by rules of the department."

—2009.
The 2009 amendment deleted III, added "landscaped areas, gardens" in the last sentence of X-b; added "for primary structures of at least 50 feet" in XIII; rewrote XVI(a) and XVII to the extent that a detailed comparison would be impracticable; rewrote XVIII, which formerly read: "'Removal or removed' means cut, sawed, pruned, girdled, felled, pushed over, buried, burned, killed, or otherwise destructively altered"; substituted "at the conclusion of" for "during" in XVIII-b; in XXII, substituted "constructed or erected" for "built" and deleted "as well as anything constructed or erected" preceding "with a fixed"; added "except as needed to maintain the health of the plant being trimmed, as allowed by rules of the department" in XXIV-b; and rewrote XXV, which formerly read: "'Urbanization' means the concentrated development found in

the sections of towns or cities where there has been an historic pattern of intensive building for commercial or industrial use, or mixed residential, commercial, and industrial use."

—2008.

The 2008 amendment by Chapter 5, added VII-b, X-b and XXIV-b, rewrote XI-c to the extent that a detailed comparison would be impracticable, rewrote XVI(c) and XXVI with versions effective May 1, 2008 and July 1, 2008, and deleted VII-a, X-a, XI-a, XI-b, and XXIV-a.

The 2008 amendment by Chapter 171, rewrote I and XXIV-b to the extent that a detailed comparison would be impracticable.

—2007.

Paragraphs VII-a, X-a, XI-a, XI-b, and XXIV-a: Added.

Paragraph XI-c: Redesignated from former par. XI-a.

Paragraphs XVI(c) and XXVI: Rewritten to the extent that a detailed comparison would be impracticable.

—2004.

Paragraph XVI(c): Substituted "office of energy and planning" for "office of state planning and energy programs".

—2003.

Paragraph XVI(c): Substituted "office of state planning and energy programs" for "office of state planning".

—2002.

Paragraph II: Rewritten by ch. 263:2 to the extent that a detailed comparison would be impracticable.

Paragraph VIII: Chapter 263:3 inserted "legally created" preceding "parcel".

Paragraph XIV: Rewritten by ch. 263:4 to the extent that a detailed comparison would be impracticable.

Paragraph XVIII-a: Added by chs. 169 and 263:5.

Paragraphs XVIII-b and XVIII-c: Added by ch. 263:5.

Paragraph XX-a: Added by ch. 263:6.

Paragraph XXVI: Added by ch. 263:7.

—1996.

Paragraph XIII: Chapter 17 substituted "reference" for "public boundary" preceding "line".

Paragraph XVII(a): Chapter 228 substituted "department of environmental services" for "division of water resources of the department".

Paragraph XVII(b): Rewritten by ch. 17 to the extent that a detailed comparison would be impracticable.

—1994.

Paragraph IX: Repealed.

Paragraph X: Added "or any combination thereof pursuant to RSA 53-A" following "places".

Paragraph XV: Substituted "reference" for "public boundary" preceding "line".

Paragraph XVII: Rewrote the introductory clause and amended subpar. (c) generally.

—1992.

Paragraph IX: Inserted "residential" preceding "dwelling".

Paragraphs XI-a, XVI(c), and XVII(d): Added.

Paragraph XV: Inserted "for natural, fresh water bodies without artificial impoundments, for artificially impounded fresh water bodies, and for coastal waters and rivers" following "means".

Paragraph XVII(c): Substituted "mean high tide established by the U.S. Coastal and Geodetic Survey" for "limit of the highest observable tide as determined by the wetlands board" following "waters, the".

Paragraph XIX: Inserted "or portion thereof" preceding "providing", deleted "for one or more persons" preceding "including" and added "which are used in common by one or more persons" following "sanitation".

Redesignation of paragraphs.

Paragraphs XVIII-a–XVIII-c, as added by 2002, 263:5, were redesignated as pars. XVIII-b–XVIII-d pursuant to 2002, 263:13, eff. July 17, 2002.

NOTES TO DECISIONS

Analysis

1. Water dependent structure
2. Setback

1. Water dependent structure

Once a boathouse project was relocated landward of a bank, it lost its status as a water dependent structure because it was no longer located over, on, or in the waters of the State of New Hampshire. It was then located over a dredged inlet, and no longer required a dredge and fill permit so that there was no legal basis for imposing the N.H. Code Admin. R. Ann., Env-Wt 302.03 requirements on the boathouse. Cayten v. N.H. Dep't of Envtl. Servs., 155 N.H. 647, 927 A.2d 494, 2007 N.H. LEXIS 113 (N.H. 2007).

2. Setback

Plain language of the Comprehensive Shoreland Protection Act allows accessory structures such as drains or roads within the setback. Appeal of Old Dutch Mustard Co., 166 N.H. 501, 99 A.3d 290, 2014 N.H. LEXIS 78 (N.H. 2014).

483-B:5. Enforcement by Commissioner; Duties; Woodland Buffer.

I. The commissioner, with the advice and assistance of the office of strategic initiatives, department of natural and cultural resources and department of agriculture, markets, and food, shall enforce the provisions of this chapter.

II. The commissioner or his or her designee may, for cause, enter upon any subject land or parcel at any reasonable time, provided he or she has obtained the oral or written permission of the property owner, attempted to notify the property owner or his or her agent either orally or in writing 24 hours prior to entry, or has observed, or received credible evidence of, the occurrence of activities regulated by this chapter that may impact water quality, to perform oversight and enforcement duties provided for in this chapter.

III. [Repealed.]

IV. To encourage coordination of state and local enforcement measures, the commissioner shall notify, at the time of issuance or filing, the local governing body of enforcement action undertaken by the state in respect to protected shoreland within the municipality by sending it copies of relevant administrative orders issued and pleadings filed.

V. The commissioner may issue an order to any person in violation of this chapter, of rules adopted under this chapter, or of any condition of a permit issued under this chapter.

HISTORY:

1991, 303:1. 1992, 235:8, 9. 1994, 383:6, 22, II, eff. July 1, 1994. 1995, 130:4, eff. July 23, 1995. 2003, 319:9, eff. July 1, 2003. 2004, 257:44, eff. July 1, 2004. 2011, 224:394, eff. June 29, 2011. 2013, 153:3, eff. August 27, 2013. 2017, 156:14, 64, eff. July 1, 2017.

Editor's note.

Although 1992, 235:8, 9 provided for the amendment of pars. II and IV, respectively, effective on Jan. 1, 1993, the amendment did not become effective until July 1, 1994, the date on which this section as originally enacted by 1991, 303:1 became effective under the terms of 1991, 303:10, I, as amended by 1994, 383:25.

Effective Date.
See note under RSA 483-B:1.

Amendment Notes
The 2017 amendments to this section by Ch. 156, in I, substituted "office of strategic initiatives" for "office of energy and planning" and "natural and cultural resources" for "resources and economic development."

—2013.
The 2013 amendment substituted "provided he or she has obtained the oral or written permission of the property owner, attempted to notify the property owner or his or her agent either orally or in writing 24 hours prior to entry, or has observed, or received credible evidence of, the occurrence of activities regulated by this chapter that may impact water quality" for "after written notification" in II.

—2011.
The 2011 amendment, in II, added "subject" and "after written notification" and made a stylistic change.

—2004.
Paragraph I: Substituted "office of energy and planning" for "office of state planning and energy programs".

—2003.
Paragraph I: Substituted "office of state planning and energy programs" for "office of state planning".

—1995.
Paragraph I: Substituted "department of agriculture, markets, and food" for "department of agriculture".

—1994.
Deleted "forest inventory plans" following "buffer" in the section catchline and repealed par. III.

—1992.
Paragraph II: Inserted "for cause" preceding "enter".
Paragraph IV: Inserted "at the time of issuance or filing" following "notify".

483-B:5-a.   Permit Required; Exemption. [Repealed.]

[Repealed 2008, 5:5, I, II, eff. May 1, 2008.]

Former section(s).
Former RSA 483-B:5-a, which was derived from 2007, 269:1, related to the requirement of permit for activities within the protected shoreland. For present provisions, see RSA 483-B:5-b.

Contingent 2008 amendment.
2008, 171:14, provided for amendment of this section. However, under the terms of 2008, 171:21, I, eff. June 6, 2008, the amendment did not take effect.

483-B:5-b.   Permit Required; Exemption.

I.(a) No person shall commence construction, excavation, or filling activities within the protected shoreland without obtaining a permit from the department to ensure compliance with this chapter. Projects which have no impact on water quality and which follow department rules shall qualify for a permit by notification. The owner may proceed with the proposed project immediately upon receipt of written notice from the department that a complete and accepted notification has been received by the department. A notification shall be complete and accepted provided it meets or exceeds all of the minimum standards under RSA 483-B:9, includes a notification form signed by the owner of property, the name and address of the property owner, the address of the site on which the work will occur, the name of the jurisdictional waterbody, the tax map and lot number on which the proposed work will occur, plans clearly and accurately depicting the work to be completed relative to the reference line of the jurisdictional waterbody, photographs of the area to be impacted, and identification of those project criteria listed below that would qualify the project for a permit by notification. Such project criteria shall include:

(1) Construction, excavation, and filing, or other activity that impacts less than 1,500 square feet and adds no more than 900 square feet of impervious area within a protected shoreland area.

(2) Construction, excavation, and filling, directly related to stormwater management improvements and erosion control projects or environmental restoration or enhancement projects.

(3) Maintenance, repairs, and improvements of public utilities, public roads, and public access facilities.

(4) Any similar activities defined as qualified for a permit by notification by rules of the department.

(b) **[Effective until July 1, 2019; see prospective repeal note below.]** The permit application fee shall be $100 plus $.10 per square foot of area affected by the proposed activities and shall be deposited in the wetlands and shorelands review fund established under RSA 482-A:3, III. Such fees shall be capped as follows:

(1) For projects that qualify for permit by notification under this paragraph or RSA 483-B:17, X, $100 for restoration of water quality improvement projects and $250 for all other permit by notification projects.

(2) For projects of 0–9,999 square feet, that do not qualify for a permit by notification, $750.

(3) For projects of 10,000–24,999 square feet, $1,875.

(4) For projects of 25,000 square feet or more, $3,750.

(c) If the application is denied after relying on the recommendations of the department, the application fee shall be refunded to the applicant within 30 days of such denial.

II. Timber harvesting operations permitting requirements shall be in accordance with RSA 485-A:17, IV and therefore shall be exempt from the permitting requirement under paragraph I.

III. **[Effective until July 1, 2019; see prospective repeal note below.]** Applications for the construction of public roads, public utility lines and associated structures, facilities, public water access facilities, and projects solely funded by municipal, county, state, or federal entities shall be exempt from the permitting fees of paragraph I.

IV. Impacts in the protected shoreland that receive a permit in accordance with RSA 482-A and commercial or industrial redevelopment in accordance with RSA 485-A:17 shall not require a permit under this section.

IV-a. At the time of the permit application, the applicant shall provide postal receipts or copies, verifying that the governing body of the municipality or municipalities in which the property is located and the local river management advisory committee, if the project is within a designated river corridor defined in RSA 483:4, XVIII and contains river and river segments designated in RSA 483:15, and all abutters have been notified of the application by certified mail. Applicants for the construction of public roads, public utility lines and associated structures and facilities, and public water access facilities shall only be required to provide postal receipts or copies, verifying that the governing body of the municipality or municipalities in which the property is located, and the local river management advisory committee if the project is within a designated river corridor defined in RSA 483:4, XVIII and contains river and river segments designated in RSA 483:15, have been notified of the application by certified mail.

IV-b. No permits issued by the department pursuant to this chapter that involve private, nonfederal undertakings shall require coordination with or clearance by the New Hampshire division of historical resources.

V.(a) Within 30 days of receipt of an application for a permit or 30 days of receipt of an application for a permit that will require a waiver of the minimum standards of RSA 483-B:9, the department shall request any additional information reasonably required to complete its evaluation of the application, and provide the applicant with any written technical comments the department deems necessary. Any request for additional information shall specify that the applicant submit such information as soon as practicable and notify the applicant that if all of the requested information is not received within 60 days of the request, the department shall deny the application.

(b) When the department requests additional information pursuant to subparagraph (a), the department shall, within 30 days of the department's receipt of the information:

(1) Approve the application and issue a permit; or

(2) Deny the application, and issue written findings in support of the denial; or

(3) Extend the time for rendering a decision on the application for good cause and with the written agreement of the applicant.

(c) Where no request for additional information is made, the department shall, within 30 days of

receipt of the application for a permit or 30 days of receipt of an application for a permit that will require a waiver of the minimum standards of RSA 483-B:9, approve or deny the application with written findings in support of the decision.

(d) Within 5 business days of receipt of a permit by notification filing, the department shall issue a written notice to the property owner or agent stating that the notification has either been accepted or rejected. If the department does not respond within the 5-day period, the property owner or agent may submit to the department a written request for a response. A request submitted electronically by the applicant shall constitute a written request provided that the applicant has previously agreed to accept electronic communication. If the department fails to respond to the written request within an additional 5 days the property owner or agent shall be deemed to have a permit by notification and may proceed with the project as presented in the notification filing. The authorization provided by this subparagraph shall not relieve the applicant of complying with all requirements applicable to the project, including but not limited to requirements established in or under this chapter and RSA 485-A relative to water quality.

(e)(1) The time limits prescribed by this paragraph shall supersede any time limits provided in any other provision of law. If the department fails to act within the applicable time frame established in subparagraphs (b) and (c), the applicant may ask the department to issue the permit by submitting a written request. If the applicant has previously agreed to accept communications from the department by electronic means, a request submitted electronically by the applicant shall constitute a written request.

(2) Within 14 days of the date of receipt of a written request from the applicant to issue the permit, the department shall:

(A) Approve the application, in whole or in part, and issue a permit; or

(B) Deny the application and issue written findings in support of the denial.

(3) If the department does not issue either a permit or a written denial within the 14-day period, the applicant shall be deemed to have a permit by default and may proceed with the project as presented in the application. The authorization provided by this subparagraph shall not relieve the applicant of complying with all requirements applicable to the project, including but not limited to requirements established in or under this chapter and RSA 485-A relating to water quality.

(4) Upon receipt of a written request from an applicant, the department shall issue written confirmation that the applicant has a permit by default pursuant to subparagraph (e)(3), which authorizes the applicant to proceed with the

project as presented in the application and requires the work to comply with all requirements applicable to the project, including but not limited to requirements established in or under this chapter and RSA 485-A relating to water quality.

(f) All applications filed in accordance with the rules adopted by the department under RSA 483-B:17 and which meet the minimum standards of this chapter shall be approved and a permit shall be issued.

(g) The department may extend the time for rendering a decision under subparagraphs (b)(3) and (c)(3), without the applicant's agreement, on an application from an applicant who previously has been determined, after the exhaustion of available appellate remedies, to have failed to comply with this chapter or any rule adopted or permit or approval issued under this chapter, or to have misrepresented any material fact made in connection with any activity regulated or prohibited by this chapter, pursuant to an action initiated under RSA 483-B:18. The length of such an extension shall be no longer than reasonably necessary to complete the review of the application, and shall not exceed 30 days unless the applicant agrees to a longer extension. The department shall notify the applicant of the length of the extension.

(h) The department may suspend review of an application for a proposed project on a property with respect to which the department has commenced an enforcement action against the applicant for any violation of this chapter, RSA 482-A, RSA 485-A:17, or RSA 485-A:29–44, or of any rule adopted or permit or approval issued pursuant to this chapter, RSA 482-A, RSA 485-A:17, or RSA 485-A:29–44. Any such suspension shall expire upon conclusion of the enforcement action and completion of any remedial actions the department may require to address the violation; provided, however, that the department may resume its review of the application sooner if doing so will facilitate resolution of the violation. The department shall resume its review of the application at the point the review was suspended, except that the department may extend any of the time limits under this paragraph and its rules up to a total of 30 days for all such extensions. For purposes of this subparagraph, "enforcement action" means an action initiated under RSA 482-A:13, RSA 482-A:14, RSA 482-A:14-b, RSA 483-B:18, RSA 485-A:22, RSA 485-A:42, or RSA 485-A:43.

VI. All permits issued pursuant to this chapter shall be valid for a period of 5 years. Requests for extensions of such permits may be made to the department. The department shall grant one extension of up to 5 additional years, provided the applicant demonstrates all of the following:

(a) The permit for which extension is sought has not been revoked or suspended without reinstatement.

(b) Extension would not violate a condition of law or rule.

(c) The project is proceeding towards completion in accordance with plans and other documentation referenced by the permit.

(d) The applicant proposes reasonable mitigation measures to protect the shorelands and public waters of the state from deterioration during the period of extension.

HISTORY:
2008, 5:12, eff. July 1, 2008. 5:27, eff. July 1, 2011. 171:18, eff. at 12:01 a.m., July 1, 2008. 2009, 218:9–11, eff. September 13, 2009. 2010, 295:5–7, eff. September 11, 2010. 2011, 141:1, eff. August 6, 2011. 143:3, eff. August 6, 2011. 224:395–397, eff. June 29, 2011. 2017, 225:3, 4, eff. September 9, 2017.

Contingent 2008 amendment.
2008, 171:21, I, eff. June 6, 2008, provided in part, that if HB 1601-FN-A [ch. 5] of the 2008 legislative session becomes law, section 18 of this act shall take effect July 1, 2008 at 12:01 a.m. Pursuant to the terms of this provision par. IV-a is set out above as amended by Ch. 171:18, eff. July 1, 2008 at 12:01 a.m.

Amendment Notes
The 2017 amendments to this section by Ch. 225 rewrote III, which formerly read: "Construction of public roads, public utility lines and associated structures, and facilities, and public water access facilities shall be exempt from the permitting fees of paragraph I"; substituted "60 days" for "120 days" in the second sentence of V(a); and substituted "30 days" for "20 days" in V(b).

—2011.
The 2011 amendment by Chapter 141 added "and commercial or industrial redevelopment in accordance with RSA 485-A:17" in IV.
The 2011 amendment by Chapter 143 added VI.
The 2011 amendment by Chapter 224, added the second through last sentences of the introductory language of I(a); added I(a)(1) through I(a)(4), I(c), IV-b, and V(d); added "this paragraph or" in I(b)(1); added "that do not qualify for a permit by notification" in I(b)(2); in V(a), in the first sentence, substituted "30 days" for "75 days," deleted "variance of the minimum standard of RSA 483-B:9, V or a" following "will require a," and added "reasonably" and substituted "120 days" for "60 days" in the second sentence; substituted "20 days" for "30 days" in the introductory language of V(b); deleted "in whole or in part" following "application" in V(b)(1); rewrote V(c); redesignated former V(d) through V(g) as V(e) through V(h); and updated an internal reference.

—2010.
The 2010 amendment added "in whole or in part" in V(b)(1); in V(b)(2), substituted "and issue" for "with" and "denial" for "decision, in whole or in part"; substituted "rendering a decision on the application" for "response" in V(b)(3); added the V(c)(1) and V(c)(2) designations; in V(c)(1), deleted "or deny" following "Approve" and substituted "in whole or in part, and issue a permit; or" for "with"; in V(c)(2), added "Deny the application, and issue" and substituted "denial; or" for "decision in whole or in part"; added V(c)(3); rewrote V(d) to the extent that a detailed comparison would be impracticable; added V(f) and V(g); and made related changes.

—2009.
The 2009 amendment rewrote I(b)(1) through I(b)(3) to the extent that a detailed comparison would be impracticable; added I(b)(4); added "and the abutter notification requirements of paragraph IV-a" in III; rewrote IV-a, which formerly read: "At the time of the permit application, the applicant shall provide postal receipts or copies, verifying that the governing body of the municipality or municipalities in which the property is located and all abutters have been notified of the application by certified mail"; added "with written findings in support of the decision" in V(b)(2) and V(c); and added V(e).

—2008.

The 2008 amendment added IV-a.

Prospective repeal of par. I(b).

2008, 5:27, I, as amended by 2011, 224:408 and further amended by 2016, 253:1, provides for the repeal of par. I(b) on July 1, 2019.

Prospective repeal of par. III.

2008, 5:27, II, as amended by 2011, 224:408 and further amended by 2016, 253:1, provides for the repeal of par. III on July 1, 2019.

483-B:6. Other Required Permits and Approvals.

I. Within the protected shoreland, any person intending to:

(a) Engage in any earth excavation activity shall obtain all necessary local approvals in compliance with RSA 155-E.

(b) Construct a water-dependent structure, alter the bank, or construct or replenish a beach shall obtain approval and all necessary permits pursuant to RSA 482-A.

(c) Install a septic system as described in RSA 483-B:9, V(c) shall obtain all permits pursuant to RSA 485-A:29.

(d) Conduct an activity resulting in a contiguous disturbed area exceeding 50,000 square feet shall obtain a permit pursuant to RSA 485-A:17.

(e) Subdivide land as described in RSA 483-B:9, V(e) and (f) shall obtain approval pursuant to RSA 485-A:29.

(f) Conduct an activity regulated under a local zoning ordinance shall obtain all necessary local approvals.

II. In applying for approvals and permits, pursuant to paragraph I, applicants shall demonstrate that the proposal meets or exceeds the development standards of this chapter. The department shall develop minimum standards for information to be required on or with all applications under paragraph I. The department or municipality shall grant, deny, or attach reasonable conditions to approvals or permits listed in subparagraphs I(a)–(f), to protect the public waters or the public health, safety, or welfare. Such conditions shall be related to the purposes of this chapter.

III. The commissioner shall have the sole authority to issue variances and waivers of the provisions of this chapter as specifically authorized by this chapter.

IV. No variance, permit, or approval issued by a municipality shall exempt the owner from obtaining any other necessary permit or approval from the department as required by this chapter.

HISTORY:

1991, 303:1. 1992, 235:10, eff. Jan. 1, 1993. 1996, 17:3, eff. June 14, 1996. 2002, 263:8, eff. July 17, 2002. 2007, 267:7, eff. April 1, 2008. 2008, 5:8, eff. May 1, 2008. 5:19, eff. July 1, 2008.

Editor's note.

Although 1992, 235:10 provided for the amendment of this section effective on Jan. 1, 1993, the amendment did not become effective until July 1, 1994, the date on which this section as

originally enacted by 1991, 303:1 became effective under the terms of 1991, 303:10, I, as amended by 1994, 383:25.

Effective Date.

See note under RSA 483-B:1.

Amendments

—2008.

The 2008 amendment by Chapter 5:8, eff. May 1, 2008, rewrote the section to the extent that a detailed comparison would be impracticable.

The 2008 amendment by Chapter 5:19, eff. July 1, 2008, rewrote the section to the extent that a detailed comparison would be impracticable.

—2007.

Rewrote the section heading; substituted "RSA 483-B:9, V(c)" for "RSA 483-B:9, V(b)(1)–(3)" in par. I(c), "RSA 483-B:9, V(e) and (f)" for "RSA 483-B:9, V(d) and (e)" in par. I(e); added par. I(f); rewrote par. II; and added pars. III and IV.

—2002.

Paragraph I(e): Deleted "for residential or non-residential development" following "land".

—1996.

Paragraph I(b): Substituted "alter the bank, or construct or replenish a beach" for "as described in RSA 483-B:9, II(c)" following "structure".

—1992.

Rewritten to the extent that a detailed comparison would be impracticable.

NOTES TO DECISIONS

Cited:

Cited in Cayten v. N.H. Dep't of Envtl. Servs., 155 N.H. 647, 927 A.2d 494, 2007 N.H. LEXIS 113 (2007).

483-B:7. Reporting; On-Site Inspections; Local Participation.

The department may devise a system whereby municipal officials may voluntarily assist with the permitting process under RSA 483-B:6 and the subsequent enforcement of permit conditions, by performing certain reporting functions relative to on-site inspections. Utilization of such reports shall be at the department's discretion, but may, when appropriate, obviate the need for further on-site review by department staff.

HISTORY:

1991, 303:1. 1992, 235:23, eff. Jan. 1, 1993.

Editor's note.

Although 1992, 235:23 provided for the amendment of this section effective on Jan. 1, 1993, the amendment did not become effective until July 1, 1994, the date on which this section as originally enacted by 1991, 303:1 became effective under the terms of 1991, 303:10, I, as amended by 1994, 383:25.

Effective Date.

See note under RSA 483-B:1.

Amendments

—1992.

Substituted "department" for "commissioner" preceding "may devise" in the first sentence and "department's" for "commissioner's" preceding "discretion" in the second sentence.

483-B:7-a. National Pollutant Discharge Elimination System Study Commission. [Repealed]

HISTORY:
2017, 256:1, eff. July 18, 2017. Repealed by 2017, 256:2, eff. November 1, 2017.

483-B:8. Municipal Authority.

I. Municipalities may adopt land use control ordinances relative to all protected shorelands which are more stringent than the minimum standards contained in this chapter.

II. Municipalities are encouraged to adopt land use control ordinances for the shorelands of water bodies and water courses other than public waters.

III. Municipalities in which protected shoreland is situated may enforce the provisions of this chapter by issuing cease and desist orders and by seeking injunctive relief or civil penalties as provided in RSA 483-B:18, III(a) and (b). Civil penalties and fines collected by the court shall be remitted within 14 days to the treasurer of the municipality prosecuting said violations, for the use of the municipality. Any municipality electing to enforce the provisions of this chapter shall send copies of any pleading to the attorney general at the time of filing. Municipalities bordering the same water body are encouraged to employ jointly a single code enforcement officer to monitor compliance.

IV. The authority granted to municipalities under this chapter shall not be interpreted to extend to RSA 430:28–48.

V. Municipalities bordering the same water body are encouraged to employ jointly a single code enforcement officer to monitor compliance.

HISTORY:
1991, 303:1. 1992, 235:11, eff. Jan. 1, 1993.

Editor's note.
Although 1992, 235:11 provided for the addition of par. V effective on Jan. 1, 1993, the amendment did not become effective until July 1, 1994, the date on which this section as originally enacted by 1991, 303:1 became effective under the terms of 1991, 303:10, I, as amended by 1994, 383:25.

Effective Date.
See note under RSA 483-B:1.

Amendments

—1992.
Paragraph V: Added.

RESEARCH REFERENCES AND PRACTICE AIDS

Cross References.
Enforcement of local land use development restrictions generally, see RSA 674:21-a.

References in text.
RSA 430:31-a, contained in RSA 430:28– 48 in par. IV, was repealed by 1997, 101:1, eff. Aug. 3, 1997.

483-B:9. Minimum Shoreland Protection Standards.

I. The standards in this section are designed to minimize shoreland disturbance so as to protect the public waters, while still accommodating reasonable levels of development in the protected shoreland. Development outside the protected shoreland shall conform to local zoning and local ordinances and shall not be subject to standards established in this chapter.

II. Within the protected shoreland the following restrictions shall apply:

(a) The establishment or expansion of salt storage yards, automobile junk yards, and solid or hazardous waste facilities shall be prohibited.

(b) Primary structures shall be set back behind the primary building line which is 50 feet from the reference line.

(c) A water dependent structure, meaning one which is a dock, wharf, pier, breakwater, or other similar structure, or any part thereof, built over, on, or in the waters of the state, shall be constructed only as approved by the department, pursuant to RSA 482-A.

(d) No fertilizer shall be applied to vegetation or soils located within 25 feet of the reference line of any public water. Beyond 25 feet, slow or controlled release fertilizer, as defined by rules adopted by department, may be used.

III. Public water supply facilities, including water supply intakes, pipes, water treatment facilities, pump stations, and disinfection stations shall be permitted by the commissioner as necessary, consistent with the purposes of this chapter and other state law. Private water supply facilities shall not require a permit.

IV. The placement and expansion of public water and sewage treatment facilities shall be permitted by the commissioner as necessary, consistent with the purposes of this chapter and other state law.

IV-a. Hydro electric facilities, including, but not limited to, dams, dikes, penstocks, and powerhouses, shall be recognized as water dependent, and shall be permitted by the commissioner as necessary, consistent with the purposes of this chapter and other state law.

IV-b. Public utility lines and associated structures and facilities, public roads, and public water access facilities including boat ramps shall be permitted by the commissioner as necessary and consistent with the purposes of this chapter and other state law.

IV-c. An existing solid waste facility which is located within 250 feet of the reference line of public waters under this chapter may continue to operate under an existing permit, provided it does not cause degradation to an area in excess of that area under permit.

IV-d. No solid waste facility shall place solid waste within 250 feet of the reference line of public waters under this chapter except as expressly permitted under RSA 483-B:9, IV-c. However, any solid waste facility may be allowed, subject to permitting conditions under RSA 149-M:9, to erect accessory structures and conduct other activities consistent with the operation of the facility within 250 feet of the reference line of public waters under this chapter, such as filling, grading and installing monitoring wells and other drainage structures as is consistent with its solid waste permit as issued by the department of environmental services. Under no circumstances shall the toe of any slope encroach within 150 feet of the reference line.

V. The following minimum standards shall apply to areas and activities within the protected shoreland with the exception of forest management that is not associated with shoreland development or land conversion, and is conducted in compliance with RSA 227-J:9; forestry conducted by or under the direction of a water supplier for the purpose of managing a water supply watershed; and agriculture conducted in accordance with best management practices as required by RSA 483-B:3, III:

(a) **Maintenance of a Waterfront Buffer.**

(1) The waterfront buffer shall be those protected shorelands within 50 feet of the reference line. The purpose of this buffer shall be to protect the quality of public waters while allowing homeowner discretion with regard to water access, safety, viewscape maintenance, and lot design.

(2) Within the waterfront buffer all of the following prohibitions and limitations shall apply:

(A) No chemicals, including pesticides or herbicides of any kind, shall be applied to ground, turf, or established vegetation except if applied by horticultural professionals who have a pesticide application license issued by the department of agriculture or as allowed under special permit issued by the division of pesticide control under rules adopted by the pesticide control board under RSA 541-A, or fertilizers of any kind except those specified in RSA 483-B:9, II(d).

(B) Rocks and stumps and their root systems shall be left intact in the ground unless removal is specifically approved by the department, pursuant to RSA 482-A or RSA 483-B:11, II or unless rocks are removed to improve runoff control or the planting in the waterfront buffer, and stumps that are removed are replaced with pervious surfaces, new trees, or other woody vegetation.

(C) No natural ground cover shall be removed except as necessary for a foot path to water and access ways as provided under RSA 483-B:9, V(a)(2)(D), (viii) and (ix), for normal maintenance, to protect the waterfront buffer, cutting those portions that have grown over 3 feet in height for the purpose of providing a view, to provide access to natural areas or

shoreline, or as specifically approved by the department, pursuant to RSA 482-A or RSA 483-B.

(D) Starting from the northerly or easterly boundary of the property, and working along the shoreline, the waterfront buffer shall be divided into segments measuring 25 feet along the reference line and 50 feet inland. Owners of land within the waterfront buffer shall measure, calculate, and maintain the tree, sapling, shrub, and groundcover point score in each of these segments in accordance with the methods and standards described in subparagraphs (i) through (ix).

(i) Tree and sapling diameters shall be measured at 4 ½ feet above the ground for existing trees and saplings, or by caliper at a height consistent with established nursery industry standards when nursery stock is to be used, and are scored as follows:

Diameter or Caliper – Score

1 to 3 inches – 1

Greater than 3 to and including 6 inches – 5

Greater than 6 to and including 12 inches – 10

Greater than 12 inches – 15

(ii) For the purpose of replanting under RSA 483-B:9, V(g)(3), shrubs and groundcover plants shall be scored as follows:

Four square feet of shrub area—1 point.

Ground cover, not including mowed lawn —one point for every 50 square feet.

Shrub and groundcover shall count for at least 5 points and not more than 10 points in each full segment.

(iii) Dead, diseased, or unsafe trees or saplings shall not be included in scoring.

(iv) If the total tree and sapling score in any 25 foot by 50 foot segment exceeds 25 points, then trees, saplings, and shrubs over 3 feet in height may be removed as long as the sum of the scores for the remaining trees and saplings in that segment does not total less than 25 points. If for any reason there is insufficient area for a full segment, or the segment contains areas naturally incapable of supporting trees and saplings, such as areas of rock, ledge, or beaches, the point score requirement for the remaining vegetation in that partial segment shall be reduced proportionally to that required of a full segment. Vegetation shall not be removed from any segment which fails to meet the minimum point score for that segment. Owners are encouraged to take efforts to plan the maintenance of their waterfront buffer areas including the planting of additional non-invasive vegetation to increase point scores within segments, thus providing sufficient points to allow the future removal of vegetation as may become necessary while still meeting the requirements of this paragraph.

(v) The department shall approve applications pursuant to RSA 482-A or RSA 483-B that include the planting of trees, saplings, shrubs, and groundcover as necessary to at least maintain either the existing point score or the minimum score required. The department shall not approve any application that would result in a combined vegetation score of less than the minimum score required where the segment initially meets the minimum score or would result in any reduction of the point score where the segment does not initially meet the minimum score.

(vi) Owners of lots and holders of easements on lots that were legally developed prior to July 1, 2008 may maintain but not enlarge cleared areas, including but not limited to existing lawns, gardens, landscaped areas, beaches, and rights-of-way for public utilities, public transportation, and public access, and may repair existing utility structures within the waterfront buffer. Conversion to or planting of cleared areas with non-invasive species of ground cover, shrubs, saplings, and trees is encouraged but shall not be required unless it is necessary to meet the requirements of subparagraph (g)(2) or (g)(3), or RSA 483-B:11, II. In addition, the commissioner of the department of natural and cultural resources may order vegetation on lands or properties owned by, leased to, or otherwise under the control of the department of natural and cultural resources within the protected shoreland to be cut when overgrowth of vegetation impairs law enforcement activities and endangers public safety. If such cutting will exceed that which is allowed under subparagraph (iv), the commissioner of the department of natural and cultural resources shall provide written notification to the department of environmental services identifying the areas to be cut and an explanation of the need for the cutting at least 2 weeks prior to the undertaking.

(vii) Normal trimming, pruning, and thinning of branches to the extent necessary to maintain the health of the planted area as well to protect structures, maintain clearances, and provide views is permitted provided such activity does not endanger the health of the plant.

(viii) When necessary for the completion of construction activities permitted in accordance with RSA 483-B:6, a temporary 12-foot wide access path shall be allowed. On those properties accessible only by water, this access path may be maintained provided it is stabilized with a surface that will infiltrate stormwater. On other properties the access path shall be completely restored and replanted with vegetation upon completion of construction except as allowed under subparagraph (ix).

(ix) A permanent 6-foot wide foot path as well as access to any docks, beaches, structures, existing open areas, and the water body, configured in a manner that will not concentrate storm water runoff or contribute to erosion, are allowed.

(b) Maintenance of Vegetation within the Woodland Buffer.

(1) The woodland buffer shall be those protected shorelands within 150 feet of the reference line. The purpose of the woodland buffer shall be to protect the quality of public waters by minimizing erosion, preventing siltation and turbidity, stabilizing soils, preventing excess nutrient and chemical pollution, maintaining natural water temperatures, maintaining a healthy tree canopy and understory, preserving fish and wildlife habitat, and respecting the overall natural condition of the protected shoreland. The first 50 feet of this buffer is designated the waterfront buffer and is subject to the additional requirements of subparagraph (a).

(2)(A) On a given lot, at least 25 percent of the woodland buffer area located between 50 feet and 150 feet from the reference line shall be maintained as natural woodland. The vegetation, exclusive of lawn, within the natural woodland shall be maintained in an unaltered state or improved with additional vegetation. Owners of lots legally developed or landscaped prior to July 1, 2008 that do not comply with this standard are encouraged to, but shall not be required to, increase the percentage of the woodland buffer area to be maintained as natural woodland. The percentage of the woodland buffer area maintained as natural woodland on nonconforming lots shall not be decreased. In addition, the commissioner of the department of natural and cultural resources may order vegetation on lands or properties owned by, leased to, or otherwise under the control of the department of natural and cultural resources within the protected shoreland to be cut when overgrowth of vegetation impairs law enforcement activities and endangers public safety. If such cutting will exceed that which is allowed under this subparagraph, the commissioner of the department of natural and cultural resources shall provide written notification to the department of environmental services identifying the areas to be cut and an explanation of the need for the cutting at least 2 weeks prior to the undertaking.

(B) Any person applying to the department for a septic system construction approval or alteration of terrain permit pursuant to RSA 485-A, or an excavating and dredging permit pursuant to RSA 482-A, within the protected shoreland shall include photographic documentation of any areas of the woodland buffer in which impacts would occur.

(C) Dead, diseased, or unsafe, trees, limbs, saplings, or shrubs that pose a hazard to structures or have the potential to cause personal injury may be removed regardless of any requirements that pertain to the maintenance of vegetation within the woodland buffer under this chapter. Such exemptions shall not be used to contravene the intent of the law.

(D) Maintenance and preservation of dead and living trees that provide dens and nesting places for wildlife is encouraged.

(E) Planting efforts that do not introduce exotic or invasive species and are beneficial to wildlife are encouraged.

(c) **Septic Systems.**

(1) [Repealed.]

(2) The following conditions, based on the characteristics of the receiving soil as they relate to U.S. Department of Agriculture, Natural Resources Conservation Service drainage classes, shall dictate the setback requirements for all new leaching portions of new septic systems, as follows:

(A) Adjacent to ponds, lakes, estuaries, and the open ocean.

(i) Where the receiving soil downgradient of the leaching portions of a septic system is a porous sand and gravel material with a percolation rate equal to or faster than 2 minutes per inch, the setback shall be at least 125 feet from the reference line;

(ii) For soils with restrictive layers within 18 inches of the natural soil surface, the setback shall be at least 100 feet from the reference line; and

(iii) For all other soil conditions, the setback shall be at least 75 feet from the reference line.

(B) Adjacent to rivers the setback shall be no less than 75 feet.

(3) The placement of all septic tanks and leaching portions of septic systems for replacement systems shall comply with the requirements of subparagraph (c)(2), to the maximum extent feasible.

(d) **Erosion and Siltation.**

(1) All new structures, modifications to existing structures, and excavation or earth moving within protected shoreland shall be designed and constructed in a manner that incorporates appropriate protective practices which are substantially equivalent to those required under rules adopted by the department under RSA 541-A for terrain alteration under RSA 485-A:17, to manage stormwater and control erosion and sediment, during and after construction.

(2) New structures and all modifications to existing structures within the protected shoreland shall be designed and constructed to prevent the release of surface runoff across exposed mineral soils.

(3) A permit under RSA 485-A:17, I shall be required for improved, developed, or subdivided land whenever there is a contiguous disturbed area exceeding 50,000 square feet that is either partially or wholly within protected shoreland.

(e) **Minimum Lots and Residential Development.** In the protected shoreland:

(1) The minimum size for new lots in areas dependent upon on-site septic systems shall be determined by soil type lot size determinations, as established by the department of environmental services under RSA 485-A and rules adopted to implement it.

(2) [Repealed.]

(3) No lot having frontage on public waters, shall be created with less than 150 feet of shoreland frontage.

(4) Lots and residential units outside of the protected shoreland shall not be subject to this chapter.

(f) **Minimum Lots and Non-Residential Development.** In the protected shoreland:

(1) The minimum size for new non-residential lots in areas dependent upon on-site septic systems shall be determined by soil type lot size determinations, as set forth under rules adopted under RSA 541-A.

(2) No lot having frontage on public water shall be created with less than 150 feet of shoreland frontage.

(3) Non-residential lots outside of the protected shoreland shall not be subject to this chapter.

(g) **Impervious Surfaces.**

(1) No more than 30 percent of the area of a lot located within the protected shoreland shall be composed of impervious surfaces, unless a stormwater management system designed and certified by a professional engineer is implemented. Such system design shall demonstrate that the post-development volume and peak flow rate based on the 10-year, 24-hour storm event, shall not exceed the pre-development volume and peak flow rate for flow off the property within the protected shoreland.

(2) If the impervious surface area will exceed 20 percent, but is less than 30 percent, a stormwater management system shall be implemented and maintained which is designed to infiltrate increased stormwater from develop-

ment occurring after the effective date of this paragraph in accordance with rules established by the department under RSA 485-A:17.

(3) If the impervious surface area will exceed 30 percent and the tree, sapling, shrub, and groundcover in the waterfront buffer does not meet the point score requirement of RSA 483-B:9, V(a)(2)(D) in any segment, then such segment shall be planted, as determined by rule of the department, with trees, saplings, shrubs, or groundcover in sufficient quantity, type, and location either to meet the minimum score or to provide at least an equivalent level of protection as provided by the minimum score and shall be maintained in accordance with RSA 483-B:9, V(a).

(h) **Common Owners and Residential or Non-Residential Development.** In the protected shoreland, waterfront parcels held in common by one or more owners of contiguous interior parcels may be developed, but only in a manner consistent with the provisions of this chapter. Care shall be taken for the adequate provision of parking, toilet facilities, and related support systems to minimize the project's impact on the public waters.

(i) The commissioner shall have the authority to grant waivers from the minimum standards of this section. Such authority shall be exercised if the commissioner deems that strict compliance with the minimum standards of this section will provide no material benefit to the public and have no material adverse effect on the environment or the natural resources of the state. Waivers shall also be granted to accommodate the reasonable needs of persons with disabilities.

HISTORY:
1991, 303:1. 1992, 235:12–18, 28, I. 1994, 383:7–14, eff. July 1, 1994. 1995, 32:1, eff. April 24, 1995. 206:2, eff. Aug. 11, 1995. 299:16, eff. Jan. 1, 1996. 1996, 17:4, 5, eff. June 14, 1996. 100:1, eff. May 15, 1996. 228:66, 108, eff. July 1, 1996. 251:22, eff. Aug. 9, 1996. 296:52, 53, eff. Aug. 9, 1996. 2002, 114:1, eff. July 2, 2002. 263:9, eff. July 17, 2002. 2007, 267:8, 9 eff. April. 1, 2008. 2008, 5:9, 10, eff. May 1, 2008. 5:20, 21, eff. July 1, 2008. 171:9–12, eff. at 12:01 a.m., July 1, 2008. 2009, 218:12–19, 23, II, eff. September 13, 2009. 2011, 224:398–401, 412, eff. June 29, 2011. 2012, 137:1, 2, eff. August 4, 2012. 2013, 153:4–7, eff. August 27, 2013. 2017, 156:14, eff. July 1, 2017. 2017, 225:5, 6, 7, 8, 9, eff. September 9, 2017.

Editor's Notes
Although 1992, 235:12– 17, 28, I, provided for the amendment of pars. I, II(c), III, IV, V(a)–(d) and added pars. IV-a–IV-d effective on Jan. 1, 1993, the amendment did not become effective until July 1, 1994, the date on which this section as originally enacted by 1991, 303:1 became effective under the terms of 1991, 303:10, I, as amended by 1994, 383:25.

Contingent 2008 amendment.
2008, 171:21, I, eff. June 6, 2008, provided in part, that if HB 1601-FN-A [ch. 5] of the 2008 legislative session becomes law, sections 9– 12 of this act shall take effect July 1, 2008 at 12:01 a.m. Pursuant to the terms of this provision pars. V(b)(2)(A), V(b)(2)(C), V(g)(1)–(4) and V(a)(2)(A) are set out above as amended by Ch. 171:9–12, eff. July 1, 2008 at 12:01 a.m.

Effective Date.
See note under RSA 483-B:1.

1991, 303:8, as amended by 1992, 157:2, eff. Jan. 1, 1993, provided that, excluding par. V(b) and (c) of this section, this section as added by 1991, 303:1, shall take effect only after the general court has approved funding of sections 1, 2 and 5 of this act, which added this chapter, amended RSA 4-C:6 and authorized additional staff in the department of environmental services for the administration of RSA 483-B, respectively, after consideration of the implementation plan required under section 7 of the act.

Pursuant to 1991, 303:10, I-a, as added by 1992, 157:2, eff. Jan. 1, 1993, par. V(b) and (c) of this section shall take effect January 1, 1993.

Amendment Notes.
The 2017 amendments to this section by Ch. 156 substituted "natural and cultural resources" for "resources and economic development" throughout V(a)(2)(D)(vi) and V(b)(2)(A).

The 2017 amendments to this section by Ch. 225 substituted "segments measuring 25 feet along the reference line and 50 feet inland" for "50 by 50 foot segments" in the first sentence of V(a)(2)(D); in V(a)(2)(D)(ii), substituted "replanting" for "planting" in the introductory language and substituted "5 points" for "15 points" and "10 points" for "25 points" in the third paragraph; in V(a)(2)(D)(iv), substituted "25" for "50" three times in the first sentence and added "naturally" in the second sentence;and rewrote V(b).

—2013.
The 2013 amendment deleted "except limestone" following "No fertilizer" in the first sentence of II(d); rewrote V(a)(2)(D)(i) and V(a)(2)(D)(ii); added "state" in the first sentence of V(b)(2)(A); and in V(g)(1), deleted "that will not concentrate stormwater runoff or contribute to erosion" following "a professional engineer" in the first sentence and added the second sentence.

—2012.
The 2012 amendment added the last two sentences of V(a)(2)(D)(vi) and V(b)(2)(A).

—2011.
The 2011 amendment rewrote the second sentence of II(d), which formerly read: "Low phosphate, slow release nitrogen fertilizer or limestone, may be used on areas beyond 25 feet from the reference line"; rewrote V(a) through V(b)(2)(A)(ii) to the extent that a detailed comparison would be impracticable; deleted V(c)(1); in V(g)(1), deleted "Subject to subparagraph (2)" at the beginning and added "unless a stormwater management system designed and certified by a professional engineer that will not concentrate stormwater runoff or contribute to erosion is implemented"; added "but is less than 30 percent" in V(g)(2); in V(g)(3), substituted "30 percent" for "20 percent," "tree, sapling, shrub, and groundcover" for "natural tree and sapling cover," "point score requirement" for "50-point minimum score," and "trees, saplings, shrubs, or groundcover" for "native trees, saplings, or natural groundcover"; and rewrote V(i).

—2009.
The 2009 amendment rewrote II(d); in V(a)(2)(A), deleted "shall be applied" following "No chemicals" and added "shall be applied to ground, turf, or established vegetation"; substituted "RSA 482-A or RSA 483-B" for "RSA 482-A or 483-B:11, II" in V(a)(2)(C); added "or RSA 483-B" in the first sentence of V(a)(2)(D)(iv); in the first sentence of V(a)(2)(D)(v), added "and holders of easements on lots" and "and rights-of-way ... utility structures"; rewrote V(a)(2)(D)(vi); in V(a)(2)(D)(vii), added the second sentence and added "On other properties" in the third sentence; added "provide ... open areas, and" in V(a)(2)(D)(viii); added "or landscaped" in the second sentence of V(b)(2)(A)(i) and V(b)(2)(A)(ii); in V(b)(2)(B), added "any areas of" and "in which impacts would occur"; substituted "a hazard" for "an imminent hazard" in the first sentence of V(b)(2)(C); added "Maintenance and" in V(b)(2)(D); rewrote V(b)(2)(E); substituted "a manner that incorporates ... those required under" for "accordance with" in V(d)(1); deleted V(e)(2); deleted the former second sentence of V(g)(2); and rewrote V(g)(3) to the extent that a detailed comparison would be impracticable.

—2008.

The 2008 amendments by 5:9 and 5:10, effective May 1, 2008 and by 5:20 and 5:21, effective July 1, 2008, rewrote IV-b and V to the extent that a detailed comparison would be impracticable.

The 2008 amendment by Chapter 171, rewrote V(a)(2)(A), V(b)(2)(A), V(b)(2)(C) and V(g)(1)–(4) to the extent that a detailed comparison would be impracticable.

—2007.

Paragraph IV-b: Inserted "public roads, and public water access facilities including boat ramps" following "facilities" and "and" following "as necessary".

Paragraph V: Rewritten to the extent that a detailed comparison would be impracticable.

—2002.

Paragraph II(b): Rewritten by ch. 114 to the extent that a detailed comparison would be impracticable.

Paragraph V: Rewritten by ch. 263 to the extent that a detailed comparison would be impracticable.

—1996.

Paragraph II(c): Chapter 296 substituted "department" for "wetlands board".

Paragraph II(d): Rewritten by ch. 100 to the extent that a detailed comparison would be impracticable.

Paragraph IV-d: Chapter 251 substituted "RSA 149-M:9" for "RSA 149-M:10" in the second sentence.

Paragraph V(a)(2)(D): Chapter 17 deleted "noxious" following "unsafe" in the first sentence.

Paragraph V(a)(2)(E): Chapter 296 substituted "department" for "wetlands board".

Paragraph V(b)(2)(A)(i): Chapter 17 inserted "equal to or" preceding "faster than".

Paragraph V(b)(1): Chapter 228 substituted "department of environmental services" for "division of water supply and pollution control, subsurface systems bureau".

Paragraph V(d)(1): Chapter 228 substituted "department of environmental services" for "water supply and pollution control division".

—1995.

Paragraph V: Chapter 299 inserted "forest management not associated with shoreland development nor land conversion and conducted in compliance with RSA 227-J:9" preceding "forestry" and made a minor change in punctuation in the introductory paragraph.

Chapter 32 added "unless removal is specifically approved by the wetlands board pursuant to RSA 482-A" following "ground" in subpar. (a)(2)(E).

Chapter 206 substituted "Natural Resources Conservation Service" for "soil conservation services" following "Agriculture" in the introductory paragraph in subpar. (b)(2).

—1994.

Paragraph II(b): Substituted "reference" for "public boundary" preceding "line" in the second sentence.

Paragraph II(d): Inserted "lawns or areas with grass on" preceding "residential".

Paragraph IV-c: Substituted "reference" for "public boundary" preceding "line" and "public" for "protected" preceding "waters".

Paragraph IV-d: Substituted "reference" for "public boundary" preceding "line" wherever it appeared in the paragraph and "public" for "protected" preceding "waters" in the first and second sentences.

Paragraph V(a): Substituted "reference" for "public boundary" preceding "line" in the first sentence of subpars. (1) and (2)(E).

Paragraph V(b)(2): Deleted "septic tanks and" preceding "leaching" in the introductory paragraph and substituted "reference" for "public boundary" preceding "line" in subpars. (A)(i)–(iii).

Paragraph V(d)(2): Deleted the second sentence.

Paragraph V(d)(3): Deleted "and" preceding "frontage".

—1992.

Paragraph I: Added the second sentence.

Paragraph II(c): Deleted "The construction of" preceding "a water".

Paragraph III: Added "and other state law" following "chapter" in the first sentence.

Paragraph IV: Added "and other state law" following "chapter".

Paragraphs IV-a–IV-d: Added.

Paragraph V(a)(2)(A): Added the third sentence.

Paragraph V(a)(2)(B): Repealed.

Paragraph V(a)(2)(C): Inserted "accessory" preceding "structures".

Paragraph V(b)(1): Inserted "including those in excess of 5 acres" preceding "created" and deleted "regardless of size" following "RSA 485-A:29".

Paragraph V(b)(2): Rewritten to the extent that a detailed comparison would be impracticable.

Paragraph V(d)(1): Substituted "established by the water supply and pollution control division" for "set forth under rules adopted pursuant to 541-A" following "determinations as".

Paragraph V(d)(2): Substituted "projects" for "new lots" preceding "in areas", inserted "sewage and" preceding "septic", substituted "in the protected shoreland, whether built on individual lots or grouped as" for "including" preceding "cluster" and "or" for "and" thereafter in the first sentence, and added the second sentence.

Contingent 1996 amendments.

1996, 296:28, 29, provided for the amendment of this section. However, under the terms of 1996, 296:54, eff. Aug. 9, 1996, the amendments did not become effective.

Applicability of 2002, ch. 114 amendment.

2002, 114:2, eff. July 2, 2002, provided:

"Municipalities having a setback of less than 50 feet prior to January 1, 2002 may maintain the defined primary building line in that municipality."

Repeal of applicability of 2002, ch. 114 amendment.

2007, 267:14, III, eff. April 1, 2008, provided for the repeal of 2002, 114:2, eff. July 2, 2002, which had provided: "Municipalities having a setback of less than 50 feet prior to January 1, 2002 may maintain the defined primary building line in that municipality."

NOTES TO DECISIONS

Analysis

1. Applicability
2. Minimum setback requirements
3. Construction
4. Particular cases
5. Setback

1. Applicability

Once a boathouse project was relocated landward of a bank, it lost its status as a water dependent structure because it was no longer located over, on, or in the waters of the State of New Hampshire. It was then located over a dredged inlet, and no longer required a dredge and fill permit so that there was no legal basis for imposing the N.H. Code Admin. R. Ann., Env-Wt 302.03 requirements on the boathouse. Cayten v. N.H. Dep't of Envtl. Servs., 155 N.H. 647, 927 A.2d 494, 2007 N.H. LEXIS 113 (N.H. 2007).

2. Minimum setback requirements

Construction of accessory structures does not violate the requirement of the Rivers Management and Protection Act that a facility not be located within the 250-foot setback, when that provision is construed together with the Comprehensive Shoreland Protection Act, and thus the Waste Management Council did not err in allowing the applicant for a solid waste permit to build accessory structures within the setback. Appeal of Old Dutch Mustard Co., 166 N.H. 501, 99 A.3d 290, 2014 N.H. LEXIS 78 (N.H. 2014).

Trial court properly ruled that respondents violated the Comprehensive Shoreland Protection Act, RSA 483-B:9, II(b), by building a home within 50 feet of a lake shore without a permit from the New Hampshire Department of Environmental Services, as RSA 483-B:10, I allowed the Department to impose the condition on the property in question. N.H. Dep't of Envtl. Servs. v. Marino, 155 N.H. 709, 928 A.2d 818, 2007 N.H. LEXIS 120 (N.H. 2007).

3. Construction

Phrase "as necessary" in RSA 483-B:9, III, IV, IV-a, and IV-b cannot mean that the Department of Environmental Services (DES) must determine the necessity or design of facilities over which it lacks authority and expertise, such as hydroelectric plants, public roads, or public utility facilities; rather, the New Hampshire Supreme Court interprets the phrase "as necessary" to mean that a permit is necessary for the project — i.e., that without it, the project cannot be completed. Appeal of Lake Sunapee Protective Ass'n, 165 N.H. 119, 72 A.3d 213, 2013 N.H. LEXIS 74 (N.H. 2013).

No language in RSA ch. 233 makes the Department of Environmental Services (DES) responsible for administering or enforcing the statewide public boat access program. The New Hampshire Supreme Court does not interpret RSA 483-B:9, IV-b as conferring that authority on DES. Appeal of Lake Sunapee Protective Ass'n, 165 N.H. 119, 72 A.3d 213, 2013 N.H. LEXIS 74 (N.H. 2013).

RSA ch. 162-C does not make the Department of Environmental Services (DES) responsible for administering or enforcing the Land Conservation Investment Program, and RSA 483-B:9, IV-b does not confer that authority on DES. Appeal of Lake Sunapee Protective Ass'n, 165 N.H. 119, 72 A.3d 213, 2013 N.H. LEXIS 74 (N.H. 2013).

There is nothing in the plain language of RSA 483-B:9, IV-b that requires the Department of Environmental Services to make specific findings or to refer to specific statutes when it grants a permit application. Appeal of Lake Sunapee Protective Ass'n, 165 N.H. 119, 72 A.3d 213, 2013 N.H. LEXIS 74 (N.H. 2013).

4. Particular cases

Department of Environmental Services (DES) did not violate RSA 483-B:9, IV-b, in issuing a shoreland impact permit for a public boat launch. DES did not have to evaluate whether the boat launch itself was necessary or to consider whether it violated RSA 233-A:6, RSA 162-C:6, or RSA 162-C:10; the evidence supported the Wetland Council's finding that DES reviewed the proposal against the purposes listed in RSA 483-B:1 and the goals listed in RSA 483-B:2; and DES was not required to make specific findings or to refer to specific statutes in granting a permit application. Appeal of Lake Sunapee Protective Ass'n, 165 N.H. 119, 72 A.3d 213, 2013 N.H. LEXIS 74 (N.H. 2013).

5. Setback

Because accessory structures are not included in the definition of a "facility" and their construction within the setback does not violate the Rivers Management and Protection Act or the Comprehensive Shoreland Protection Act, petitioner had failed to show that the council acted improperly in allowing an applicant for a solid waste permit to build the accessory structures within the setback. Appeal of Old Dutch Mustard Co., 166 N.H. 501, 99 A.3d 290, 2014 N.H. LEXIS 78 (N.H. 2014).

Plain language of the Comprehensive Shoreland Protection Act allows accessory structures such as drains or roads within the setback. Appeal of Old Dutch Mustard Co., 166 N.H. 501, 99 A.3d 290, 2014 N.H. LEXIS 78 (N.H. 2014).

Cited:

Cited in Bacon v. Town of Enfield, 150 N.H. 468, 840 A.2d 788, 2004 N.H. LEXIS 8 (2004).

RESEARCH REFERENCES AND PRACTICE AIDS

Cross References.

Fee for division review of terrain alteration plans, see RSA 485-A:17.

483-B:10. Nonconforming Lots of Record.

Nonconforming, undeveloped lots of record that are located within the protected shoreland shall comply with the following restrictions, in addition to any local requirements:

I. Except when otherwise prohibited by law, present and successive owners of an individual undeveloped lot may construct a single family residential dwelling and appurtenant accessory structures on it, notwithstanding the provisions of this chapter. Conditions may be imposed which, in the opinion of the commissioner, more nearly meet the intent of this chapter, while still accommodating the applicant's rights.

II. Building on nonconforming lots of record shall be limited to single family residential structures and related facilities, including, but not limited to, appurtenant accessory structures such as walkways and driveways, and water dependent structures such as docks, piers, and breakwaters consistent with state law.

III. Consistent with RSA 674:39-a, a municipality shall not merge adjacent nonconforming lots in common ownership without the consent of the owner.

HISTORY:

1991, 303:1. 1992, 235:19. 1994, 383:15, eff. July 1, 1994. 2009, 218:20, eff. September 13, 2009. 2011, 224:402, 403, eff. June 29, 2011.

Editor's note.

Although 1992, 235:19 provided for the amendment of par. II effective on Jan. 1, 1993, the amendment did not become effective until July 1, 1994, the date on which this section as originally enacted by 1991, 303:1 became effective under the terms of 1991, 303:10, I, as amended by 1994, 383:25.

Effective Date.

See note under RSA 483-B:1.

Amendments

—2011.

The 2011 amendment added "and appurtenant accessory structures" in the first sentence of I and added III.

—2009.

The 2009 amendment substituted "appurtenant accessory structures such as walkways and driveways, and water dependent structures such as docks, piers, and breakwaters" for "docks, piers, boathouses, boat loading ramps, walkways, and other water dependent structures" in II.

—1994.

Paragraph I: Deleted the second sentence.

—1992.

Paragraph II: Substituted "be limited to" for "not be used for structures other than" following "record shall", inserted "and related facilities" preceding "including", and added "consistent with state law" following "dependent structures".

NOTES TO DECISIONS

Analysis

1. Constitutionality
2. Minimum setback requirements

1. Constitutionality

RSA 483-B:10, I lays down basic standards and a reasonably definite policy and thus does not constitute an impermissible delegation of legislative authority in violation of N.H. Const. pt. I, art. 37. N.H. Dep't of Envtl. Servs. v. Marino, 155 N.H. 709, 928 A.2d 818, 2007 N.H. LEXIS 120 (N.H. 2007).

2. Minimum setback requirements

Trial court properly ruled that respondents violated the Comprehensive Shoreland Protection Act, RSA 483-B:9, II(b), by building a home within 50 feet of a lake shore without a permit from the New Hampshire Department of Environmental Services, as RSA 483-B:10, I allowed the Department to impose the condition on the property in question. The plain meaning of RSA 483-B:10, I allowed the Department to impose conditions on any construction of a single-family home on a nonconforming undeveloped lot of record; the right to build a single-family home on a nonconforming undeveloped lot of record, therefore, was not absolute, but was contingent upon conditions that the DES imposed upon the construction. N.H. Dep't of Envtl. Servs. v. Marino, 155 N.H. 709, 928 A.2d 818, 2007 N.H. LEXIS 120 (N.H. 2007).

483-B:11. Nonconforming Structures.

I. Except as otherwise prohibited by law or applicable municipal ordinance, nonconforming structures located within the protected shoreland may be repaired, replaced in kind, reconstructed in place, altered, or expanded. Repair, replacement-in kind, or reconstruction in place may alter or remodel the interior design or existing foundation of the nonconforming structure, but shall result in no expansion or relocation of the existing footprint within the waterfront buffer. However, alteration or expansion of a nonconforming structure may expand the existing footprint within the waterfront buffer, provided the structure is not extended closer to the reference line and the proposal or property is made more nearly conforming than the existing structure or the existing conditions of the property. This provision shall not allow for the enclosure, or conversion to living space, of any deck or open porch located between the primary structure and the reference line and within the waterfront buffer.

II. For the purposes of this section, a proposal that is "more nearly conforming" means alteration of the location or size of the existing footprints, or redevelopment of the existing conditions of the property, such that the structures or the property are brought into greater conformity with the design standards of this chapter. Methods for achieving greater conformity include, without limitation, reducing the overall square footage of structural footprints, enhancing stormwater management, adding infiltration areas and landscaping, upgrading wastewater treatment, improving traffic management, or other enhancements that improve wildlife habitat or resource protection.

III. An expansion that increases the sewerage load to an on site septic system, or changes or expands the use of a septic system, shall require a subsurface approval issued by the department.

IV. Under paragraph I, and except as otherwise prohibited by law or applicable municipal ordinance, primary nonconforming structures may be entirely demolished and reconstructed, with continued encroachment into the waterfront buffer, provided the replacement structure is located farther back from the reference line than the preexisting nonconforming structure.

V. Notwithstanding paragraphs I and IV, between the primary building line and the reference line, no alteration shall extend the structure closer to the public water, except that a deck or open porch extending a maximum of 12 feet towards the reference line may be added to nonconforming structures erected prior to July 1, 1994.

HISTORY:

1991, 303:1. 1992, 235:20. 1994, 383:16, 17, eff. July 1, 1994. 1996, 17:6, eff. June 14, 1996. 2002, 263:10, eff. July 17, 2002. 2007, 267:10, eff. April 1, 2008. 2008, 5:11, eff. May 1, 2008. 5:22, eff. July 1, 2008. 2011, 224:404, eff. June 29, 2011. 2012, 276:2, 3, eff. June 19, 2012.

Editor's note.

Although 1992, 235:20 provided for the amendment of par. I effective on Jan. 1, 1993, the amendment did not become effective until July 1, 1994, the date on which this section as originally enacted by 1991, 303:1 became effective under the terms of 1991, 303:10, I, as amended by 1994, 383:25.

Effective Date.

See note under RSA 483-B:1.

Amendments

—2012.

The 2012 amendment added the last sentence of I and added V.

—2011.

The 2011 amendment rewrote the section to the extent that a detailed comparison would be impracticable.

—2008.

The 2008 amendment by Chapter 5:11, eff. May 1, 2008, rewrote the section to the extent that a detailed comparison would be impracticable.

The 2008 amendment by Chapter 5:22, eff. July 1, 2008, rewrote the section to the extent that a detailed comparison would be impracticable.

—2007.

Paragraph I: Deleted "erected prior to July 1, 1994" following "structures" in the first sentence, inserted "shall result in" preceding "no expansion", substituted "except as authorized by the department pursuant to paragraph II" for "or outside dimensions shall be permitted" following "footprint" in the second sentence and added "for nonconforming structures erected prior to July 1, 1994" following "reference line" at the end of fourth sentence.

Paragraph II: Substituted "or any expansions of nonconforming structures" for "erected prior to July 1, 1994" preceding "the commissioner" in the first sentence.

—2002.

Rewritten to the extent that a detailed comparison would be impracticable.

—1996.

Paragraph II: Deleted "variances involving" preceding "the redevelopment" and substituted "there is at least the same" for "the net effect represents an improvement in the overall" preceding "degree".

—1994.

Deleted "New Primary Structures" at the end of the section catchline and inserted "nonconforming" following "pre-existing" in the first sentence and "an on-site septic system" following "load to" in the second sentence, and substituted "reference" for "public boundary" preceding "line" in two places in the third sentence.

—1992.
Paragraph I: Substituted "boundary" for "building" preceding "line, no" in the third sentence.

483-B:12. Shoreland Exemptions.

I. The governing body of a municipality may, in its discretion, request the commissioner to exempt all or a portion of the protected shoreland within its boundaries from the provisions of this chapter if the governing body finds that special local urbanization conditions as defined in RSA 483-B:4, XXV, exist in the protected shoreland for which the exemption is sought.

II. If the governing body of a municipality requests such an exemption, it shall submit evidence of existing and historical patterns of building and development in the protected shoreland in demonstration of the special local urbanization conditions. Such evidence shall address:

(a) Current and past building density.

(b) Commercial, industrial, or residential uses.

(c) Municipal or other public utilities.

(d) Current municipal land use regulations which affect the protected shoreland.

(e) Designation as a downtown, community center, central business district, or urbanized area or urban cluster as delineated by the United States Census Bureau.

(f) Any other information which the commissioner may reasonably require.

III. With the advice of the office of strategic initiatives, the commissioner shall approve or deny the request for an exemption and shall issue written findings in support of his decision. A request for an exemption shall be approved only if the municipality demonstrates, using the evidence required under paragraph II, that special conditions of urbanization exist along the portion of shoreland to be exempted.

IV. The Pease development authority, division of ports and harbors may request an exemption under this section for all or a portion of any land purchased, leased, or otherwise acquired by it pursuant to RSA 12-G:39.

HISTORY:
1991, 303:1. 2001, 290:15, eff. July 1, 2001. 2003, 319:9, eff. July 1, 2003. 2004, 257:44, eff. July 1, 2004. 2009, 218:21, eff. September 13, 2009. 2017, 156:64, eff. July 1, 2017.

Effective Date.
See note under RSA 483-B:1.

Amendment Notes
The 2017 amendments to this section by Ch. 156 substituted "office of strategic initiatives" for "office of energy and planning" in III.

—2009.
The 2009 amendment added "as defined in RSA 483-B:4, XXV" in I; added "in demonstration of the special local urbanization conditions" in the first sentence of the introductory language of II; substituted "industrial, or residential uses" for "industrial uses" in II(b); added II(e); redesignated former II(e) as II(f); and made a related change.

—2004.
Paragraph III: Substituted "office of energy and planning" for "office of state planning and energy programs".

—2003.
Paragraph III: Substituted "office of state planning and energy programs" for "office of state planning".

—2001.
Paragraph IV: Substituted "Pease development authority, division of ports and harbors" for "state port authority" and "RSA 12-G:39" for "RSA 271-A".

483-B:13. Public Hearing and Notice to Abutter. [Repealed.]

[Repealed 1992, 235:28, II, eff. Jan. 1, 1993.]

Former section(s).
Former RSA 483-B:13, which was derived from 1991, 303:1, related to notice of public hearing.

Editor's note.
Although 1992, 235:28, II, provided for the repeal of this section effective on Jan. 1, 1993, the repeal did not become effective until July 1, 1994, the date on which this section as originally enacted by 1991, 303:1 became effective under the terms of 1991, 303:10, I, as amended by 1994, 383:25.

483-B:14. Rehearings and Appeals.

Where the requirements of this chapter amend the existing statutory authority of the department or other agencies relative to certain established regulatory programs and shall be enforced under these established regulatory programs, the existing procedures governing contested cases and hearings and appeals regarding these requirements shall apply. Where requirements of this chapter are new and do not amend existing statutory authority relative to any established regulatory programs, the procedures set forth in RSA 541-A:31 for contested cases shall apply.

HISTORY:
1991, 303:1. 1992, 235:24. 1994, 412:51, eff. Aug. 9, 1994.

Editor's note.
Although 1992, 235:24 provided for the amendment of this section effective on Jan. 1, 1993, the amendment did not become effective until July 1, 1994, the date on which this section as originally enacted by 1991, 303:1 became effective under the terms of 1991, 303:10, I, as amended by 1994, 383:25.

Effective Date.
See note under RSA 483-B:1.

Amendments

—1994.
Substituted "RSA 541-A:31" for "RSA 541-A:16" preceding "for contested" in the second sentence.

—1992.
Rewritten to the extent that a detailed comparison would be impracticable.

483-B:15. Gifts, Grants and Donations.

The department is authorized to solicit, receive, and expend any gifts, grants, or donations made for the purposes of this chapter. Gifts of land or easements shall be assigned to the department of natural and cultural resources for management or assignment to another state agency or other public body, as appropriate.

HISTORY:
1991, 303:1, eff. July, 1994. 2017, 156:14, eff. July 1, 2017.

Effective Date.
See note under RSA 483-B:1.

Amendment Notes
The 2017 amendments to this section by Ch. 156 substituted "natural and cultural resources" for "resources and economic development" in the second sentence.

483-B:16. Assistance to Municipalities; Office of State Planning and Energy Programs.

The office of strategic initiatives may assist municipalities with the implementation of local ordinances under this chapter, upon the request of an individual municipality.

HISTORY:
1991, 303:1, eff. July 1, 1994. 2003, 319:9, eff. July 1, 2003. 2004, 257:44, eff. July 1, 2004. 2017, 156:64, eff. July 1, 2017.

Effective Date.
See note under RSA 483-B:1.

Amendment Notes
The 2017 amendments to this section by Ch. 156 substituted "office of strategic initiatives" for "office of energy and planning."

—2004.
Substituted "office of energy and planning" for "office of state planning and energy programs".

—2003.
Substituted "office of state planning and energy programs" for "office of state planning" in the section catchline and in the paragraph.

483-B:17. Rulemaking.

The commissioner shall adopt rules, pursuant to RSA 541-A, relative to:

I. The content and structure of all forms, applications and permits to be received or issued by the department under this chapter, including information and other materials to be submitted by an applicant.

II. Procedures for filing and review of requests for urbanized shoreland exemptions and standards for granting urbanized shoreland exemptions, including time frames for decisions.

III. Implementation and enforcement of the minimum shoreland standards, including methods and timing of inspection and coordination with municipalities.

IV. Procedures and criteria for the size and placement of small accessory structures such as storage sheds and gazebos, which are consistent with the intent of this chapter, between the reference line and the primary building line.

V. Criteria governing the assessment of administrative fines.

VI. Criteria governing low phosphate, slow release nitrogen fertilizer.

VII. A methodology for identifying unsafe trees.

VIII. [Repealed.]

IX. Definitions of terms not defined in this chapter.

X. Procedures and criteria for permitting under RSA 483-B:5-b, including permit by notification and the identification of those activities that may be conducted without obtaining a permit, all consistent with the provisions of this chapter.

XI. Requests for extensions of permits for activities within the protected shoreland.

HISTORY:
1991, 303:1. 1992, 235:25. 1994, 383:18, eff. July 1, 1994. 1996, 100:2, eff. May 15, 1996. 2002, 263:11, eff. July 17, 2002. 2007, 267:11, eff. July 1, 2007. 269:2, eff. July 1, 2007. 2008, 5:23, eff. July 1, 2008. 2009, 218:22, 23, III, eff. September 13, 2009. 2011, 143:4, eff. August 6, 2011. 224:405, eff. June 29, 2011.

Revision note.
Paragraph XI, as added by 269:2, was redesignated as par. X in light of the previous amendments to this section by 2007, 267:11.

Editor's note.
Although 1992, 235:25 provided for the amendment of this section effective on Jan. 1, 1993, the amendment did not become effective until July 1, 1994, the date on which this section as originally enacted by 1991, 303:1 became effective under the terms of 1991, 303:10, I, as amended by 1994, 383:25.

Effective Date.
See note under RSA 483-B:1.

Amendments

—2011.
The 2011 amendment by Chapter 143 added XI.
The 2011 amendment by Chapter 224 deleted "and construction" following "placement" in IV and made a related change.

—2009.
The 2009 amendment, in IV, substituted "size, placement, and construction" for "placement" and deleted "the size, placement, and construction of" following "sheds and gazebos"; deleted VIII; and made a stylistic change.

—2008.
The 2008 amendment substituted "RSA 483-B:5-b" for "RSA 483-B:5-a" in X.

—2007.
Chapter 267 added "implementation and" at the beginning of par. III; deleted former par. VII; and redesignated former pars. VIII–X as present pars. VII–IX.
Chapter 269 added par. X.

—2002.
Paragraphs VII–X: Added.

—1996.
Paragraph VI: Added.

—1994.
Paragraph IV: Substituted "reference" for "public boundary" preceding "line".

—1992.

Deleted former pars. II and III, redesignated former par. IV as par. II and added "including time frames for decisions" at the end of that paragraph, redesignated former pars. V and VI as pars. III and IV respectively, deleted former par. VII, redesignated former par. VIII as par. V, and deleted former par. IX.

Repeal of 2008, 5:26.

2008, 171:19, eff. June 6, 2008, provided: "Section 26 of HB 1601-FN-A [ch. 5] of the 2008 legislative session, relative to repeal and readoption of rules, is repealed." New provisions relative to repeal and readoption of rules were adopted by 2008, 171:20, eff. June 6, 2008.

Repeal and Readoption of Rules.

2008, 171:20, eff. June 6, 2008, provided:

"**I.** Notwithstanding the provisions of RSA 541-A, the commissioner of the department of environmental services shall immediately repeal administrative rules chapter Env-Wq 1400 adopted March 24, 2008 pursuant to RSA 483-B:17.

"**II.** Notwithstanding the provisions of RSA 541-A, the commissioner of the department of environmental services shall immediately readopt the administrative rules that were in effect prior to the effective date of the rules repealed under paragraph I. Such rules shall be effective as rules of the department and shall remain in effect until rules are adopted under paragraph IV, or are otherwise repealed or amended or have expired in accordance with RSA 541-A.

"**III.** The commissioner of the department of environmental services shall notify in writing the director of legislative services of the dates of repeal and readoption of rules under paragraphs I and II.

"**IV.** The commissioner of the department of environmental services may adopt rules to be in effect as of July 1, 2008 that are the same as the rules repealed under paragraph I, except that the commissioner shall modify the date references in the rules to take into account the July 1, 2008 effective date. Such rule adoption shall be exempt from the rulemaking provisions of RSA 541-A, provided the commissioner adopts the rules and files them with the office of legislative services prior to July 1, 2008. The rules shall expire on July 1, 2016 unless readopted, amended, or repealed pursuant to RSA 541-A.

"**V.** The commissioner of the department of environmental services shall prepare, and the director of the office of legislative services shall publish in the rulemaking register, one or more notices, as necessary, to clearly state which rules will be in effect during affected time periods."

Limitation of commencement of rulemaking process.

1991, 303:8, provided:

"The commissioner shall not activate the rulemaking process pursuant to RSA 483-B:17 until the general court has approved funding of sections 1, 2, and 5 of this act [which added this chapter, amended RSA 4-C:6 and authorized additional staff in the department of environmental services for the administration of this chapter, respectively] after consideration of the implementation plan required under section 7 of this act."

483-B:18.　Penalties.

I. The following shall constitute a violation of this chapter:

(a) Failure to comply with the provisions of this chapter.

(b) Failure to obey an order of the commissioner or a municipality issued relative to activities regulated or prohibited by this chapter.

(c) Misrepresentation by any person of a material fact made in connection with any activity regulated or prohibited by this chapter.

II. Any person who violates this chapter and any person who purchases land affected by a violation of this chapter who knew or had reason to know of the violation shall be liable for remediation or restoration of the land affected to bring it into compliance with the provisions of this chapter.

III. Persons violating the provisions of this chapter and damaging the public waterway who, after notification by the department, fail to make a good faith effort at remediation and restoration shall be subject to the following:

(a) Upon petition of the attorney general or of the municipality in which the violation occurred, the superior court may levy upon any person violating this chapter a civil penalty in an amount not to exceed $5,000 for each continuing violation. The superior court shall have jurisdiction to restrain a continuing violation of this chapter, and to require remediation.

(b) The commissioner, after notice and hearing pursuant to RSA 541-A, may impose an administrative fine of up to $5,000 for each offense upon any person who violates this chapter. Rehearings and appeals relating to such fines shall be governed by RSA 541. Imposition of an administrative fine under this section shall not preclude the imposition of further civil penalties under this chapter.

(c) Notwithstanding the $5,000 fine limit in subparagraph (b), the administrative fine for each repeat violation of this chapter may be multiplied by a factor of 2 for every previous violation committed by the person or entity.

HISTORY:

1991, 303:1. 1994, 383:19, eff. July 1, 1994. 2002, 169:2, eff. Jan. 1, 2003. 2011, 224:406, eff. June 29, 2011. 2013, 153:8, eff. August 27, 2013.

Effective Date.

See note under RSA 483-B:1.

Amendment Notes

—2013.

The 2013 amendment added "to bring it into compliance with the provisions of this chapter" in II.

—2011.

The 2011 amendment rewrote III to the extent that a detailed comparison would be impracticable.

—2002.

Paragraph III(c): Substituted "shall impose" for "may impose" in the first sentence.

Paragraph III(d): Added.

—1994.

Paragraph III(a): Inserted "or of the municipality in which the violation occurred" following "attorney general" in the first sentence.

RESEARCH REFERENCES AND PRACTICE AIDS

Cross References.

Classification of crimes, see RSA 625:9.

483-B:19.　Applicability. [Repealed.]

[Repealed 2007, 267:14, I, eff. April 1, 2008.]

Former section(s).

Former RSA 483-B:19, which was derived from 1991, 303:1; 1992, 235:26; 1994, 383:20; 2002, 263:12; 2003, 319:9; and 2004, 257:44, related to applicability.

483-B:20. Designated Rivers. [Repealed.]

[Repealed 2007, 267:14, II, eff. April 1, 2008.]

Former section(s).

Former RSA 483-B:20, which was derived from 1994, 383:21 and 2002, 114:3, related to designated rivers.

483-B:21. Shoreland Advisory Committee. [Repealed]

HISTORY:

2010, 306:1, eff. July 13, 2010. 2011, 224:407, 410, eff. June 29, 2011. Repealed by 2010, 306:2, eff. December 31, 2015.

483-B:22. Coastal and Great Bay Region Reports.

The commissioner of the department of environmental services shall convene representatives of the department of transportation, the division of homeland security and emergency management, the office of strategic initiatives, and other agencies as he or she deems appropriate, at least every 5 years, commencing July 1, 2019 to supervise an updating of storm surge, sea-level rise, precipitation, and other relevant projections recommended in the coastal risks and hazards commission 2014 report "Sea-Level Rise, Storm Surges, and Extreme Precipitation in Coastal New Hampshire: Analysis of Past and Projected Trends." This report shall be distributed to all state agencies, municipalities in the coastal and Great Bay region, the governor, the speaker of the house of representatives, the president of the senate and the chairs of the house and senate committees with jurisdiction over issues related to such projections.

2017, 156:64, eff. July 1, 2017.

Amendment Notes

The 2017 amendments to this section by Ch. 156 substituted "office of strategic initiatives" for "office of energy and planning" in the first sentence.

CHAPTER 485

NEW HAMPSHIRE SAFE DRINKING WATER ACT

RESEARCH REFERENCES AND PRACTICE AIDS

Cross References.
Aid to public water systems for compliance with Federal Safe Drinking Water Act, see RSA 486-A.

Public Water Supply Protection Program

RESEARCH REFERENCES AND PRACTICE AIDS

Cross References.
Municipal water systems, see RSA 38.

New Hampshire Code of Administrative Rules
Rules of the Department of Environmental Services—Water Supply and Pollution Control Division, Env-Ws 301.01 et seq., New Hampshire Code of Administrative Rules Annotated.

485:1. Statement of Purpose.

I. The purpose of this chapter is to provide a comprehensive drinking water protection program for the citizens of New Hampshire. It shall be consistent with and at least as stringent as the Federal Safe Drinking Water Act standards.

II. In order to implement a comprehensive drinking water protection program, the department of environmental services shall:

(a) Monitor the water quality of public water supplies and privately owned redistribution systems.

(b) Provide technical assistance to water operators and the general public.

(c) Review the design of proposed public water systems, privately owned redistribution systems, and alterations for existing systems. Review of the alteration of existing privately owned redistribution systems shall be limited to alterations that involve more than 500 feet of new installation of distribution piping or the addition of new exterior pumping or storage facilities.

(d) Periodically conduct sanitary surveys of public water systems and privately owned redistribution systems to make certain of proper safety and operation.

(e) Require that public water supplies comply with all pertinent federal and state statutes and rules.

(f) Educate citizens for the need and methods of providing safe and adequate drinking water.

(g) Approve sources of water used in the manufacture of bottled water.

(h) Monitor the operation and maintenance of privately owned redistribution systems.

HISTORY:
1989, 339:1. 1990, 163:1, eff. July 1, 1990. 1996, 228:108, eff. July 1, 1996. 1997, 155:4, eff. Aug. 8, 1997. 2008, 279:1, 2, eff. July 1, 2009.

Amendments

—2008.
The 2008 amendment in II(a), in the first sentence of II(c) and II(d), added "and privately owned redistribution systems" or variant; in II(c), added the second sentence; and added II(h).

—1997.
Paragraph II(g): Added.

—1996.
Paragraph II: Substituted "department of environmental services" for "division of water supply and pollution control" in the introductory paragraph.

—1990.
Rewritten to the extent that a detailed comparison would be impracticable.

RESEARCH REFERENCES AND PRACTICE AIDS

References in text.
The Safe Drinking Water Act, referred to in par. I, is classified principally to 42 U.S.C.S. §§ 300f et seq.

485:1-a. Definitions.

As used in this chapter, unless the context clearly indicates otherwise, the following words shall have the following meanings:

I. "Community water system" means a public water system which serves at least 15 service connections used by year-round residents or regularly serves at least 25 year-round residents.

I-a. "Brackish" means a concentration in water of dissolved solids that is between 1,000 and 10,000 milligrams per liter.

I-b. "Closed loop geothermal system" means any heating or cooling system that operates by circulating fluid through a closed loop pipe or loops of pipes installed in the subsurface or surface water for the purpose of utilizing the geothermal properties of the subsurface or surface water as a heat source or sink.

II. "Contaminant" means any physical, chemical, biological, or radiological substance or matter in the water.

III. "Department" means the department of environmental services.

IV. "Commissioner" means the commissioner of the department of environmental services.

V. "Feasible" means capable of being done with the use of the best technology, treatment techniques, and other means which the department finds, after examination for efficacy under field as well as laboratory conditions, is available at reasonable cost.

V-a. "Freshwater" means water with a concentration of total dissolved solids that is less than 1,000 milligrams per liter.

VI. "Household equivalent" means water usage equal to 300 gallons per day.

VII. "Maximum contaminant level" means the maximum permissible level of a contaminant in water which is delivered to the free flowing outlet of the ultimate user of a public water system, except in the case of turbidity where the maximum permissible level is measured at the point of entry to the distribution system. Contaminants added to the water under circumstances controlled by the user, except those resulting from corrosion of piping and plumbing caused by water quality, are excluded from the definition.

VIII. "Maximum contaminant level goal" means that level of a contaminant in water at which no known or anticipated adverse effects on the health of consumers occur and which allows an adequate margin of safety, as determined by federal and state agencies.

IX. "National Drinking Water Regulations" means the drinking water regulations promulgated by the administrator of the U.S. Environmental Protection Agency under the authority of the Safe Drinking Water Act, P.L. 93-523, as amended.

X. "Non-community water system" means a public water system that is not a community water system.

XI. "Non-transient non-community water system" means a system which is not a community water system and which serves the same 25 people, or more, over 6 months per year.

XI-a. "Open loop geothermal system" means any heating or cooling system that operates by withdrawing water from a well and returning the water to the source well or another well for the purpose of utilizing the geothermal properties of the subsurface as a heat source or sink.

XII. "Operator" means the individual who has direct management responsibility for the routine supervision and operation of a public water system or of a water treatment plant or collection, treatment, storage, or distribution facility or structure that is a part of a system.

XIII. "Person" means any individual, partnership, company, public or private corporation, political subdivision or agency of the state, department, agency, or instrumentality of the United States, or any other legal entity.

XIV. "Political subdivision" means any municipality, county, district, or any portion or combination of 2 or more thereof.

XIV-a. "Privately owned redistribution system" means a system for the provision of piped water for human consumption which does not meet the definition of public water system under paragraph XV, and meets all the following criteria: (1) obtains all of its water from, but is not owned or operated by, a public water system; (2) serves a population of at least 25 people, 10 household units, or 15 service connections, whichever is fewest, for at least 60 days per year; and (3) has exterior pumping facilities, not including facilities used to reduce pressure, or exterior storage facilities which are not part of building plumbing.

XV. "Public water system" means a system for the provision to the public of piped water for human consumption, if such system has at least 15 service connections or regularly serves an average of at least 25 individuals daily at least 60 days out of the year. Such term includes (1) any collection, treatment, storage, and distribution facilities under control of the operator of such system and used primarily in connection with such system, and (2) any collection or pretreatment storage facilities not under such control which are used primarily in connection with such system. Any water system which meets all of the following conditions is not a public water system:

XV-a. "Source of water" means a spring, artesian well, spa, geyser, drilled well, public water supply, or other source, of any water used in the manufacture of bottled water, which has been inspected and approved by the department.

(a) Consists only of distribution and storage facilities (and does not have any collection and treatment facilities);

(b) Obtains all of its water from, but is not owned or operated by, a public water system; and

(c) Does not sell water to any person.

XV-b. "Salt water" means water with a concentration of total dissolved solids that exceeds 10,000 milligrams per liter.

XVI. "Supplier of water" means any person who controls, owns or generally manages a public water system.

XVII. "Water treatment plant" means that portion of the public water system which is designed to alter the physical, chemical, biological or radiological quality of the water or to remove any contaminants.

XVIII. "Wellhead protection area" means the surface and subsurface area surrounding a water well or wellfield, supplying a public water system, through which contaminants are reasonably likely to move toward and reach such water well or wellfield.

XIX. "Water conservation" means any beneficial reduction in water losses, waste, or use.

HISTORY:

1990, 163:2, eff. July 1, 1990. 1996, 228:68, 106, eff. July 1, 1996. 1997, 155:5, eff. Aug. 8, 1997. 2002, 142:1, eff. July 12, 2002. 2008, 279:3, eff. July 1, 2009. 2009, 27:2–5, eff. July 7, 2009.

Amendments

—2009.

The 2009 amendment added I-a, I-b, V-a, XI-a, and XV-b.

—2008.
The 2008 amendment added XIV-a.

—2002.
Paragraph XIX: Added.

—1997.
Paragraph XV-a: Added.

—1996.
Paragraph IV: Rewritten to the extent that a detailed comparison would be impracticable.
Paragraph V: Substituted "department" for "division".

RESEARCH REFERENCES AND PRACTICE AIDS

References in text.
The Safe Drinking Water Act, P.L. 93-523, referred to in par. IX, is classified principally to 42 U.S.C.S. §§ 300f et seq.

485:2. Administration.

This chapter shall be administered by the department, which is authorized to:

I. Enter into agreements, contracts or cooperative arrangements under such terms and conditions as it deems appropriate with other state, federal or interstate agencies, municipalities, education institutions, local health departments or other organizations or individuals.

II. Receive financial and technical assistance from the federal government and other public or private agencies.

III. Participate in related programs of the federal government, other states, interstate agencies, or other public agencies or organizations.

IV. Establish adequate fiscal controls and accounting procedures to assure proper disbursement of and accounting for funds.

V. Adopt rules under RSA 541-A to carry out the requirements of this chapter as listed in RSA 485:3.

HISTORY:
1989, 339:1, eff. Jan. 1, 1990. 1996, 228:67, 69, eff. July 1, 1996.

Amendments

—1996.
Deleted "with the exception of RSA 485:44, 45, and 46" preceding "shall be administered by the" and substituted "department" for "division" thereafter in the introductory paragraph.

485:3. Drinking Water Rules.

I. The commissioner shall adopt under RSA 541-A, following public hearing, drinking water rules and primary drinking water standards which are necessary to protect the public health and which shall apply to all public water systems. Such rules shall include:

(a) identification of contaminants which may have an adverse effect on the health of persons;

(b) specification for each contaminant of either:

(1) a maximum contaminant level that is acceptable in water for human consumption, if it is feasible to ascertain the level of such contaminant in water in public water systems; or

(2) one or more treatment techniques or methods which lead to a reduction of the level of such contaminant sufficient to protect the public health, if it is not feasible to ascertain the level of such contaminant in water in the public water system; and

(c) criteria and procedures to assure compliance with the levels or methods determined under subparagraph (b), including quality control monitoring and testing procedures and standards to ensure compliance with such levels or methods; criteria and standards to ensure proper operation and maintenance of the system; requirements as to the minimum quality of water which may be delivered to the consumer; and requirements with respect to siting new facilities. Such rules shall be no less stringent than the most recent national Primary Drinking Water Regulations in effect, as issued or promulgated by the United States Environmental Protection Agency.

II. The commissioner may adopt secondary drinking water rules, which are necessary to protect the public welfare. Such rules may apply to any contaminant in drinking water which may adversely affect the color, odor, taste or appearance of the water and consequently may cause a substantial number of persons to discontinue using a public water system, or which may otherwise adversely affect the public welfare. Such rules may vary according to geographic, economic, technical or other relevant circumstances. Such rules shall reasonably assure the protection of the public welfare and the supply of aesthetically adequate drinking water.

III. The commissioner shall adopt under RSA 541-A all rules necessary to implement the requirements of the following sections of this chapter:

(a) RSA 485:42.

(b) RSA 485:43.

IV. The commissioner may adopt rules specifying criteria and procedures for requiring public water systems to conduct monitoring programs for contaminants which are not identified in the national primary drinking water regulations, but which have been identified by the administrator of the United States Environmental Protection Agency as "unregulated contaminants." Such rules shall require monitoring of drinking water supplied by the system and shall vary the frequency and schedule of monitoring requirements for systems. An unregulated contaminant is one for which no maximum contaminant level or treatment technique has been established under paragraph I or II. In developing such rules, the commissioner shall consider materials submitted by the department of health and human services, pursuant to RSA 125-H:3. Rules adopted under this paragraph shall list unregulated contaminants for which public water systems may be required to monitor. Any list established pursuant to this paragraph shall be consistent with, but not limited by, the list of unregulated contaminants identified in regulations promulgated by the administrator of the United States Environmental Protection Agency.

V. The commissioner may adopt rules specifying the criteria under which filtration, including coagulation and sedimentation, as appropriate, is required as a treatment technique for public water systems supplied by surface water sources. In developing such rules the commissioner shall consider the quality of source waters, protection afforded by watershed management, treatment practices such as disinfection and length of water storage and other factors relevant to protection of health. The commissioner may require any public water supply system to assist in determining the necessity of filtration in that system. The commissioner shall provide an opportunity for notice and public hearing prior to implementation of any filtration requirement. Following such hearing, the commissioner shall prescribe, by rule adopted pursuant to RSA 541-A, a compliance schedule for such filtration requirement.

VI. The commissioner may adopt rules requiring disinfection as a treatment technique for all public water systems.

VII. The commissioner may adopt rules specifying the criteria and procedures to be used to identify and notify persons who may be affected by lead contamination of their drinking water when such contamination results from either the lead content in the construction materials of the public water system or the corrosivity of the water supply, or both. The commissioner may also adopt rules prohibiting the use of lead pipes, solder and flux in the installation or repair of any public water system or any plumbing in a residential or nonresidential facility providing water for human consumption. Such rules shall not prohibit the use of leaded joints necessary for the repair of cast iron pipes.

VIII. The commissioner may adopt rules relative to defining the best available technology, treatment techniques, or other means which are feasible for the purpose of meeting the federal maximum contaminant level. In defining the best available technology, treatment technique or other means, the commissioner may consider the number of persons served by the system, other physical conditions related to engineering feasibility and cost of compliance, and information contained in health risk assessments provided by the department of health and human services pursuant to RSA 125-H:3, II and IV. Such rules shall specify all applicable criteria relative to the commissioner's determination.

IX. The commissioner may adopt rules to implement a wellhead protection program pursuant to RSA 485:48.

X. The commissioner may adopt rules to implement the Underground Injection Control Program of the federal Safe Drinking Water Act, 42 U.S.C. section 300f et seq., as well as rules pertaining to permits for the regulation and remediation of contamination from previous discharges or disposal of waste to the groundwater. The commissioner's rules shall include criteria and procedures to ensure that past and present underground injection will not endanger drinking water sources, and shall provide for consideration of varying geologic, hydrologic, or other conditions in different areas within the state.

XI. The commissioner shall adopt rules, pursuant to RSA 541-A, specifying the water quality standards and other criteria and procedures for obtaining a permit to use a source of water for the manufacture of bottled water.

XII. The commissioner may adopt rules to ensure long-term viability of public drinking water systems as required by section 119 of the federal Safe Drinking Water Act Amendments of 1996, 42 U.S.C. section 300g-9 to qualify for full eligibility for federal and state revolving fund capital grants.

XIII. The commissioner shall adopt rules, pursuant to RSA 541-A, relative to new groundwater withdrawals of 57,600 gallons or more in any 24-hour period by public water systems. Such rules shall include:

(a) Criteria and procedures for requiring public water systems to identify and address impacts of withdrawals on surface waters, subsurface waters, water-related natural resources, and public, private, residential, and farm wells within the anticipated zone of contribution to the withdrawal.

(b) Requirements relative to conservation management plans which demonstrate the need for the proposed withdrawals, to be submitted by the public water system seeking approval for a withdrawal.

(c) Procedures by which the department may deny permission for withdrawals or order the applicant to provide a response policy, as provided by department rules, for provision of alternative water supply at no initial capital cost to persons whose wells are adversely affected by the proposed withdrawal or order reduced withdrawals if hydrogeologic data indicate that water-related resources are being adversely affected by the withdrawals.

XIV. The commissioner may adopt rules to:

(a) Regulate the heat exchange fluids utilized in closed loop geothermal systems. The commissioner's rules shall include criteria and procedures to ensure that these substances when released to the environment will not endanger drinking water sources.

(b) Prohibit the construction of open loop geothermal systems where such process will contaminate freshwater aquifers with brackish or saline groundwater.

HISTORY:

1989, 339:1. 1991, 344:3. 1992, 289:53. 1995, 310:181, eff. Nov. 1, 1995. 1996, 228:110, eff. July 1, 1996. 1997, 155:6, eff. Aug. 8, 1997. 271:1, eff. Aug. 18, 1997. 1998, 124:1, eff. Aug. 1, 1998. 2009, 27:6, eff. July 7, 2009.

Revision note.
Substituted "RSA 485:48" for "RSA 485:50" in par. IX to correct an error in the reference.

Amendments

—2009.
The 2009 amendment added XIV.

—1998.
Paragraph XIII: Added.

—1997.
Paragraph XI: Added by chs. 155 and 271.

—1996.
Substituted "commissioner" for "division" wherever it appeared throughout the section and "commissioner's" for "division's" in the third sentence of par. VIII.

—1995.
Paragraph IV: Deleted "division of public health services" preceding "department of health and human services" in the fourth sentence.
Paragraph VIII: Substituted "department of health and human services" for "division of public health services" in the second sentence.

—1992.
Paragraph V: Deleted the sixth sentence.

—1991.
Paragraph X: Added.

Severability of 1995 amendment.
1995, 310, which amended this section, was subject to a severability clause. See 1995, 310:186.

Construction of 1995 amendment.
1995, 310:187, eff. Nov. 1, 1995, provided:
"Nothing in this act is intended to, nor shall it be construed as, mandating or assigning any new, expanded, or modified program or responsibility for any political subdivision in violation of part I, article 28-a of the constitution of the state of New Hampshire."

Redesignation of paragraph.
Paragraph XI, as added by 1997, 271:1, was redesignated as par. XII pursuant to 1997, 271:2, eff. Aug. 18, 1997.

RESEARCH REFERENCES AND PRACTICE AIDS

New Hampshire Practice.
13-15 N.H.P. Probate Law & Procedure § 510.

485:3-a.   Permit Authority.

The department may grant operational permits for public water systems.

HISTORY:
1990, 163:3, eff. July 1, 1990. 1996, 228:106, eff. July 1, 1996.

Amendments

—1996.
Substituted "department" for "division".

485:3-b.   Site Assessment Review Fee.

I. Any person, except for state and local governments including counties and political subdivisions, that requests an expedited review of environmental site assessment reports by the department shall pay to the department a review fee based on the equalized assessed valuation of the property as determined in rules adopted by the commissioner under RSA 541-A, shall be as follows:

Equalized Assessed Valuation	Fee
$0 to $250,000	$1,800
$250,001 to $500,000	$2,250
$500,001 to $1,000,000	$3,750
greater than $1,000,000	$7,500

II. The department shall provide written comments within 60 days after the date such reports and the required fees are received by the department.

HISTORY:
1993, 289:2, eff. July 1, 1993. 358:93, eff. at 12:01 a.m., July 1, 1993. 2007, 219:9, eff. July 1, 2007.

Amendments

—2007.
Paragraph I: Substituted "that" for "who" preceding "requests" and inserted "as determined in rules adopted by the commissioner under RSA 541-A, shall be" preceding "as follows" and substituted "$1,800" for "$1,200" and substituted "$2,250" for "$1,500" and "$3,750" for "$2,500" and substituted "$7,500" for "$5,000".

—1993.
Paragraph I: Substituted "$250,001" for "$250,000" and "$500,001" for "$500,000".

Severability of 1993 amendment.
1993, 358 was subject to a severability clause. See 1993, 358:106.

485:3-c.   Groundwater Management Permit Fee.

Any person, submitting a permit application under RSA 485:3, X shall pay to the department a groundwater management permit application fee of $2,000. Any person who has paid the environmental site assessment review fee specified in RSA 485:3-b shall be exempt from the groundwater management permit fee. State and local governments including counties and political subdivisions shall be exempt from groundwater management permit application fees, unless eligible for funding under RSA 146-D, RSA 146-E, RSA 146-F, or RSA 146-G.

HISTORY:
1993, 289:2, eff. July 1, 1993. 2007, 219:10, eff. July 1, 2007.

Amendments

—2007.
Rewritten to the extent that a detailed comparison would be impracticable.

485:3-d.   Annual Report Required. [Repealed]

HISTORY:
1993, 289:2, eff. July 1, 1993. Repealed by 2015, 259:31(VI), eff. July 1, 2015.

485:4. Power to Require Improvements.

I. The department is empowered to investigate the sanitary conditions and methods pertaining to the source, treatment, and distribution of all public water supplies for domestic use, and to require the application of any treatment or improvement in conditions and methods as it may deem necessary to insure fitness and safety and adequate protection of the public health. If the department determines that improvements are necessary, the municipality, corporation, or person shall be so notified in writing and the requirements so ordered shall be effected pursuant to RSA 38:25 within a reasonable time to be fixed by the department. Appeals of actions of the department may be made as provided in RSA 485:59. The department may set intermediate goals and time frames to assist municipalities, corporations, or persons to abide by an order of the department under this paragraph.

II. Upon complaint of not less than 10 customers of an existing public water system or not less than 10 residents not currently served by a public water supply, the department shall make an investigation of conditions regarding water quality or quantity problems described in the complaint. If, as a result of any such investigation, the department concludes that a significant public health or safety problem exists due to water supply quality or quantity, it shall perform a preliminary analysis of alternatives which address the problem. The department may request additional information from the complainants and nearby public water supply system owners, such as data on water supply quality and quantity, well characteristics, and water distribution system characteristics, as is necessary to perform its investigation and analysis. If the department determines that an extension of water service from an existing public water supply system to the area of impaired water quality or quantity is the most feasible and cost-effective alternative, that the extension is consistent with municipal master planning, local water system policies and rules, RSA 9-B, and RSA 162-C:2, V, and that the existing public water system has adequate water supply and system capacity to serve the problem area, the municipality, corporation, or person who owns the public water system shall be ordered to allow connection to its water distribution system from the identified area, regardless of existing municipal or public water system service area boundaries. The connection so ordered shall be effected pursuant to RSA 38:25 within a reasonable time to be fixed by the department and may contain limitations on water system connections unrelated to the original petition in order to limit unintended land use impacts. Appeals of actions of the department may be made as provided in RSA 485:59. The department may set intermediate goals and time frames to assist municipalities, corporations, or persons to abide by an order of the department under this paragraph. The provisions of this paragraph or of any order issued under this paragraph shall not delegate any costs associated with a connection to the person receiving the order from the department.

III. The department may investigate the sanitary conditions and methods pertaining to pumper stations, piping, storage, and treatment facilities of privately owned redistribution systems which present a threat to public health and safety. If the department determines that action, such as disinfection, is necessary, the municipality, corporation, or person shall be so notified in writing and the action so ordered shall be effected within a reasonable time to be fixed by the department. Replacement of existing infrastructure shall only be required in response to a specific public health threat. Appeals of actions of the department may be made under RSA 485:59. The department may set intermediate goals and time frames to assist municipalities, corporations, or persons to abide by an order of the department under this paragraph.

HISTORY:

1989, 339:1. 1990, 33:1. 1995, 88:1, eff. Jan. 1, 1996. 1996, 228:106, eff. July 1, 1996. 1997, 206:6, eff. July 1, 1997. 2002, 141:3, eff. May 13, 2002. 2008, 279:4, eff. July 1, 2009.

Amendments

—2008.

The 2008 amendment added III.

—2002.

Designated the existing provisions of the section as par. I and substituted "paragraph" for "section" in the fourth sentence of that paragraph, and added paragraph II.

—1997.

Substituted "RSA 38:25" for "RSA 38:14-a" in the second sentence.

—1996.

Substituted "department" for "division" throughout the section.

—1995.

Deleted the former second sentence, deleted "after such hearing" preceding "if the division determines" in the present second sentence, and added the third sentence.

—1990.

Deleted "Penalty" following "Improvements" in the section catchline and deleted the former fourth sentence.

Severability of enactment.

1997, 206 was subject to a severability clause. See 1997, 206:9.

NOTES TO DECISIONS

Analysis

1. Sewers
2. Reservoirs

1. Sewers

Under this provision the state board of health could require a town to install a sewer in order to preserve a public water supply from contamination. Meredith v. State Bd. of Health, 94 N.H. 123, 48 A.2d 489, 1946 N.H. LEXIS 161 (N.H. 1946). (Decided under prior law.)

2. Reservoirs

Water supply and pollution control commission's order requiring city to cover its high service distribution reservoir because of high bacterial count in the water was not unjust or unreasonable in view of the evidence that for many years city had been urged by the commission to cover the reservoir, which was open to pollution from seagulls, waterfowl and humans and was therefore subject to viral contamination. Concord v. Water Supply & Pollution Control Comm'n, 115 N.H. 614, 347 A.2d 173, 1975 N.H. LEXIS 377 (N.H. 1975). (Decided under prior law.)

485:5. Power to Require Acquisition of Land.

The acquisition of adjacent or marginal lands necessary to provide reasonable sanitary control over the quality of a public water supply shall be deemed an improvement in sanitary conditions which is within the power of the department to require under the provisions of RSA 485:4. Municipalities shall comply with such order pursuant to RSA 38:25.

HISTORY:

1989, 339:1, eff. Jan. 1, 1990. 1996, 228:106, eff. July 1, 1996. 1997, 206:6, eff. July 1, 1997.

Revision note.

Substituted "RSA 485:4" for "RSA 485:2" in the first sentence to correct an error in the reference.

Amendments

—1997.

Substituted "RSA 38:25" for "RSA 38:14-a" in the second sentence.

—1996.

Substituted "department" for "division".

Severability of enactment.

1997, 206 was subject to a severability clause. See 1997, 206:9.

485:6. Disinfection.

Any public water supply system which utilizes any of the surface water of the state, as defined in RSA 485-A, as the source of supply, shall, as a minimum means of treatment, be provided with suitable chlorination or other disinfection facilities installed, operated and maintained in accordance with rules of the department adopted under this chapter.

HISTORY:

1989, 339:1, eff. Jan. 1, 1990. 1996, 228:106, eff. July 1, 1996.

Amendments

—1996.

Substituted "department" for "division".

485:7. Penalty.

Any municipality, corporation or person who shall fail to install or to operate and maintain disinfection facilities in accordance with the foregoing requirements shall be guilty of a violation for each day of failure to so install, operate or maintain such equipment. Said penalty shall not be invoked in the event of a bona fide emergency arising from an unavoidable or unforeseen failure or casualty to such treatment facilities. It shall be the duty of the municipality, corporation or person in responsible charge of said public water supply system to give immediate notice of the emergency condition to the department in order that appropriate action to safeguard the public health may be taken.

HISTORY:

1989, 339:1, eff. Jan. 1, 1990. 1996, 228:106, eff. July 1, 1996.

Amendments

—1996.

Substituted "department" for "division" in the third sentence.

RESEARCH REFERENCES AND PRACTICE AIDS

Cross References.

Classification of crimes, see RSA 625:9.
Sentences, see RSA 651.

485:8. Approval of Construction Plans.

I. No person, proposing to supply water for domestic uses through a public water system or privately owned redistribution system, shall construct any new system, or enlarge any existing system, for supplying water to the public without first submitting detailed plans of the proposed construction to the department and securing its approval of such plans. The department shall examine the topography and the watershed, complete an engineering review of the plans and specifications for said proposed construction, and make chemical and bacteriological analysis of the waters of the proposed supply, before approval is granted. The requirements of this paragraph shall only apply to privately owned redistribution systems if the construction or enlargement of an existing system involves more than 500 feet of new installation of distribution piping or the addition of any new exterior pumping or water storage facility. Any review of plans for a privately owned redistribution system shall be completed within 30 days of the submission of such plans.

II. No new construction, addition, or alteration involving the source, treatment, distribution, or storage of water in any public water system or privately owned redistribution system shall be commenced until the plans and specifications have been submitted to and approved in accordance with rules adopted by the department; except, if such construction, addition, or alteration is exempted by the department because it will have no effect on public health or welfare, then such submission and approval is not required. In granting approval of plans and specifications, the department may require modifications, conditions, or procedures to ensure, as far as feasible, the protection of the public health. The department may require the submission of water samples for analysis to determine the extent of treatment required. Records of construction, including, where possible, plans and descriptions of existing public water systems and privately owned redistribution systems, shall be maintained by such systems and shall be made available to the department upon request. The requirements of this paragraph shall only apply to privately owned redistribution systems if the construction, addition, or alteration of an existing system involves more than 500 feet of new installation of distribution piping or the addition of any new exterior pumping or water storage facility. Any review of plans for a privately owned redistribution system shall be completed within 30 days of the submission of such plans.

III. Any person submitting detailed plans to the department, as provided in this section, for a new public water system, or an existing public water system where conversion from transient use to residential-type use is proposed, shall pay to the department a fee of $45 per residential unit. When usage cannot be apportioned by residential units at new public water systems, the fee shall be based on the flow proportioned equivalent to that of a single family residential unit. The commissioner shall adopt rules pursuant to RSA 541-A defining flow proportioned equivalency.

IV. The fees required under paragraph III shall be for reviewing such detailed plans and making site inspections as may be necessary. The fee shall be paid at the time said detailed plans are submitted and shall be deposited with the state treasurer as unrestricted revenue. The department shall establish by rule, adopted pursuant to RSA 541-A, a minimum threshold below which no fee is required and a maximum level above which the fee will not increase.

V. Any person proposing to install new public sewerage or sewage treatment facilities, or to extend, renovate, replace or substantially repair any such existing facilities, shall submit, at least 30 days in advance of construction, detailed plans and specifications for such facilities to the department and secure its approval of such plans and specifications. The foregoing provisions shall also be applicable to any institution accommodating 30 or more people, which provides its own sewage disposal facilities.

HISTORY:
1989, 339:1, eff. Jan. 1, 1990. 1996, 228:70, 106, eff. July 1, 1996. 2008, 279:5, eff. July 1, 2009.

Amendments

—2008.
The 2008 amendment in I, in the first sentence, added "through a public water system or privately owned redistribution system"; added the third and fourth sentences; in II, in first and fourth sentences, added "or privately owned redistribution system" or variant; and added the fifth and sixth sentences.

—1996.
Paragraphs I, II: Substituted "department" for "division" wherever it appeared in pars. I, II, IV and V and in two places in the first sentence of par. III and "commissioner" for "division" preceding "shall adopt" in the third sentence of par. III.

Codification.
Pursuant to 1989, 339:34, the amendment to former RSA 148:25, I-a by 1989, 408:16, eff. Aug. 4, 1989, was incorporated in par. III of this section.

NOTES TO DECISIONS

Sewers
Whether water supply and pollution control commission had right to approve or disapprove of city's application to extend combination sanitary and storm sewer line, and what general criteria were to determine its decision, were questions of law on supreme court review of denial of application. Roy v. Water Supply & Pollution Control Comm'n, 112 N.H. 87, 289 A.2d 650, 1972 N.H. LEXIS 149 (N.H. 1972). (Decided under prior law.)

Under the plain language of this section, water supply and pollution control commission had authority to deny city's application to extend sewer line. Roy v. Water Supply & Pollution Control Comm'n, 112 N.H. 87, 289 A.2d 650, 1972 N.H. LEXIS 149 (N.H. 1972). (Decided under prior law.)

By the plain language of RSA 125:9 and the commission's history as successor to the state board of health, the water supply and pollution control commission is to judge sewer extension application by the broad criteria of whether extension would be harmful to public health and life. Roy v. Water Supply & Pollution Control Comm'n, 112 N.H. 87, 289 A.2d 650, 1972 N.H. LEXIS 149 (N.H. 1972). (Decided under prior law.)

Finding of water supply and pollution control commission that sanitary and storm sewer extension applied for by city to service apartment complex would endanger public health was reasonable where uncontradicted evidence showed that approximately once a year there was overflowing of the sewer in a low area served by it, flooding the land, that it was getting worse and that the extension would increase the dry weather flow of sewage at three points measured in the area by 14, 16, and 30 percent. Roy v. Water Supply & Pollution Control Comm'n, 112 N.H. 87, 289 A.2d 650, 1972 N.H. LEXIS 149 (N.H. 1972). (Decided under prior law.)

State board of health may require a town to construct sewerage system to prevent contamination of public water supply. Meredith v. State Bd. of Health, 94 N.H. 123, 48 A.2d 489, 1946 N.H. LEXIS 161 (N.H. 1946). (Decided under prior law.)

485:9. Highway Construction.

No public highway, access roads, or private ways of any sort, shall be constructed so as to traverse any watershed tributary to a lake, pond or reservoir used for the storage of public drinking water without first obtaining the approval of the department.

HISTORY:
1989, 339:1, eff. Jan. 1, 1990. 1996, 228:106, eff. July 1, 1996.

Amendments

—1996.
Substituted "department" for "division".

485:10. Approval.

No person supplying water to the public for domestic use shall resort to, hold in reserve, or maintain, a connection through which water may be received from any auxiliary or emergency source of supply, unless such source shall have been duly declared to, registered, and approved by the department.

HISTORY:

1989, 339:1, eff. Jan. 1, 1990. 1996, 228:106, eff. July 1, 1996.

Amendments

—1996.

Substituted "department" for "division".

485:11. Backflow Device Requirements and Tests, Installations, Repairs and Replacements.

There shall be a backflow prevention device installed at every connection to a public water system if the facility connected may pose a hazard to the quality of water supplied by the public water system as determined by the department. Where applicable, the facility receiving water from a public water supply shall be responsible for having such drinking water distribution system protective backflow prevention devices inspected and tested by individuals certified by a third party who has been approved by the department to conduct backflow device inspection and testing certification. The facility shall also have backflow devices installed, maintained, repaired, and replaced by individuals qualified by either a plumbers license or by certification by the department under RSA 332-E:3, III proving competency in distribution system operation. The activities to be conducted by qualified individuals shall be specifically limited to the inspection and testing, maintenance, repair or replacement, and installation of the water meters, meter horns, backflow preventers, and assembly devices directly adjacent to and required as part of the protection for the drinking water distribution system. Testing of drinking water distribution system protective backflow prevention devices, where applicable, shall occur after installation or repair to ensure that new and repaired devices are working properly. There shall be a backflow prevention device installed at every connection to a public water system if the facility connected may pose a hazard to the quality of water supplied by the public water system as determined by the department of environmental services. The facility receiving water from a public water supply shall be responsible for having such backflow prevention devices installed, serviced, and tested by individuals qualified by license or certification to perform these activities. Testing of backflow devices shall occur twice annually unless the public water supplier determines the facility poses a low hazard, in which case testing shall be performed on an annual basis. The facility receiving water from a public water supplier is responsible for ensuring that the backflow prevention device is working properly to prevent backflow into the public water system. Testing shall also occur twice annually for any high hazard devices and facilities. When the public water supplier determines that the facility poses a low hazard, testing shall occur annually. A residential property containing a non-testable device shall not be considered a hazard facility and shall not require annual testing. A residential property may be considered a high hazard facility if it has an irrigation system, private well connection, or other feature that may cause a public health risk. If an outside irrigation system is the sole reason a residential property is considered a hazard to the public water supply distribution system, such irrigation system shall be tested annually during the period when the irrigation system is operated. The facility receiving water from a public water supplier is responsible for ensuring that the backflow prevention device is working properly to prevent backflow into the public water system.

HISTORY:

1989, 339:1, eff. Jan. 1, 1990. 1996, 228:106, eff. July 1, 1996. 2013, 50:1, eff. August 3, 2013. 2014, 304:4, eff. September 30, 2014. 2015, 50:1, eff. August 1, 2015.

Amendment Notes

—2014.

The 2014 amendment rewrote the section to the extent that a detailed comparison would be impracticable.

—2013.

The 2013 amendment rewrote the section to the extent that a detailed comparison would be impracticable.

—1996.

Substituted "department" for "division" in two places in the second sentence.

485:12. Sealed Valves.

All valves or gates used in the connection here described, in the case of sources maintained for public fire protection, shall also be subject to the special seal and inspection of the department. Whenever it shall become necessary to break such seal, or to resort to an unapproved emergency source for public fire protection, notice of such action shall, within 24 hours, be sent to the said department by telephone or telegraph and also by mail.

HISTORY:

1989, 339:1, eff. Jan. 1, 1990. 1996, 228:106, eff. July 1, 1996.

Amendments

—1996.

Substituted "department" for "division" wherever it appeared.

485:13. Control of Intakes.

The department shall have general control and oversight of emergency intakes. It may, when feasible and deemed necessary for the protection of the public health, upon reasonable notice, require the abandonment of any existent emergency source and the adoption of other means of supply.

HISTORY:

1989, 339:1, eff. Jan. 1, 1990. 1996, 228:106, eff. July 1, 1996.

Amendments

—1996.

Substituted "department" for "division" in the first sentence.

485:14. Use of Fluoride.

No fluoride shall be introduced into the public water supply unless and until the municipality or municipalities using said waters have held a public hearing as to the introduction of fluoride into the public water supply of said municipality or municipalities, and the registered voters of such municipality or municipalities have approved such action pursuant to RSA 44:16, RSA 31:17-a, RSA 52:23, or RSA 485:14-a. For purposes of this section "municipality" means a municipality that has 100 or more user connections that are served from the public water supply.

HISTORY:

1989, 339:1, eff. Jan. 1, 1990. 2004, 225:1, eff. July 1, 2004.

Amendments

—2004.

Rewritten to the extent that a detailed comparison would be impracticable.

NOTES TO DECISIONS

Construction

City residents were properly awarded summary judgment in their action against a city and the city was required, under the statute, to gain the approval of voters of each municipality in which residents used water provided by a water works before the water works could provide fluoridated water to any residents of the community. Balke v. City of Manchester, 150 N.H. 69, 834 A.2d 306, 2003 N.H. LEXIS 141 (N.H. 2003).

OPINIONS OF THE ATTORNEY GENERAL

Analysis

1. Construction
2. Application

1. Construction

This section does not require or authorize a city, town or village water district to present a fluoridation proposal to the voters in absence of a petition therefor. N.H. Op. Att'y Gen. No. 99-01.

This section does not require approval of voters in towns and cities who may be using water as contract customers of a water supply located in another city. N.H. Op. Att'y Gen. No. 99-01.

2. Application

This section applies to privately owned as well as municipally owned utilities. N.H. Op. Att'y Gen. No. 99-01.

485:14-a. Referendum Procedure for Public Water Systems Serving More Than One Political Subdivision.

I. Upon the written application of the aggregate of 10 percent of the registered voters in all of the towns served by a water system, presented to the clerk of the town owning the water system at least 90 days before the day prescribed for an annual town meeting or city election, the clerk shall forward a copy of the petition to each town served by the water system. Upon receipt of the petition, the selectmen of the town shall insert on the warrant or the official ballot the following question: "Shall fluo-

ride be used in the public water system?" Beside this question shall be printed the word "yes" and the word "no" with the proper boxes for the voter to indicate his or her choice. If a majority of those voting in a water system that serves multiple towns does not approve the use of fluoride in the public water system, no fluoride shall be introduced into the public water system for said towns. After such popular referendum, the selectmen shall not insert an article relative to the use of fluoride in the public water system in the warrant nor shall such question be inserted on the official ballot for a minimum period of 3 years from the date of the last popular referendum and only upon written application at that time of not less than the aggregate of 10 percent of the registered voters of all of the towns.

II. In this section:

(a) "Town" means town as defined in RSA 21:5.

(b) "Selectmen" means selectmen as defined in RSA 21:28.

HISTORY:

2004, 225:2, eff. July 1, 2004. 2008, 230:5, eff. August 19, 2008.

Effective date of enactment.

2004, 225:6, eff. July 1, 2004, provided:

"Any public water system serving more than one municipality which introduced fluoride into the water supply prior to July 1, 2004 may continue the use of fluoride until a referendum under RSA 485:14-a has taken place."

Amendments

—2008.

The 2008 amendment substituted "those voting" for "the registered voters" in the third sentence of I.

485:14-b. Fluoride Statement Required.

I. If a public water supply is fluoridated, the following notice shall be posted in the water system's consumer confidence report: "Your public water supply is fluoridated. According to the Centers for Disease Control and Prevention, if your child under the age of 6 months is exclusively consuming infant formula reconstituted with fluoridated water, there may be an increased chance of dental fluorosis. Consult your child's health care provider for more information."

II. The notice shall be located in the section of the consumer confidence report dedicated to water quality.

HISTORY:

2012, 122:1, eff. August 4, 2012.

485:15. Appeal.

If the department shall require the abandonment of any such emergency source the person, corporation or association aggrieved by such action shall have an appeal to the superior court, said appeal to be taken within 30 days from the receipt of the order from said department, and said court may make such order on the appeal as justice may require.

HISTORY:
    1989, 339:1, eff. Jan. 1, 1990. 1996, 228:106, eff. July 1, 1996.

Amendments

—1996.
    Substituted "department" for "division" in two places.

485:16. Penalty.

Whoever violates any of the provisions of RSA 485:8–13, but not RSA 485:8, II, or fails to comply with the lawful orders and requirements of the department duly made pursuant to those sections, or whoever hinders or obstructs any inspector in the pursuit of his lawful duty in respect to such sections, shall be guilty of a misdemeanor if a natural person, or guilty of a felony if any other person.

HISTORY:
    1989, 339:1, eff. Jan. 1, 1990. 1996, 228:106, eff. July 1, 1996.

Amendments

—1996.
    Substituted "department" for "division".

RESEARCH REFERENCES AND PRACTICE AIDS

Cross References.
    Classification of crimes, see RSA 625:9.
    Sentences, see RSA 651.

Methyl Tertiary Butyl Ether (MTBE)

485:16-a. Drinking Water Standards and Notification.

I. The commissioner, in consultation with the commissioner of health and human services, shall adopt primary and secondary drinking water standards pursuant to RSA 485:3, and ambient groundwater quality standards pursuant to RSA 485-C:6, applicable to MTBE. The commissioner shall not commence rulemaking for these standards until after the department has reviewed the scientific record on the risks posed by the presence of MTBE in drinking water supplies. Such review shall be completed at the earliest possible date, but no later than January 1, 2000. The commissioner shall commence rulemaking no later than January 1, 2000.

II. Any public water system delivering water with greater than 5 parts per billion of MTBE shall notify each customer of the MTBE content.

HISTORY:
    1999, 313:2, eff. July 16, 1999.

485:16-b. Authority to Limit MTBE in Gasoline; Penalties.

I. Except as provided for in RSA 485:16-d, the commissioner shall seek all necessary authorizations from the Environmental Protection Agency to opt out of the federal reformulated gasoline program as soon as possible, but in no case later than January 1, 2004. The department of environmental services shall prepare and submit to the Environmental Protection Agency as soon as possible, but in no case later than January 1, 2002, all documentation necessary to accomplish this task.

II. In addition to the provisions of paragraph I, the commissioner, after consultation with the commissioner of health and human services, shall limit to the greatest extent practicable, with the approval of the governor and council, the concentration of MTBE allowed in any gasoline sold in all or part of the state after first holding a public hearing on the issue and certifying to the air pollution advisory committee established in RSA 125-J:11 that gasolines which meet such limit are:

(a) Readily available to New Hampshire consumers at a reasonable price;

(b) Less hazardous overall to humans and the environment than gasoline having higher MTBE concentrations taking into account all exposure routes, including air and water; and

(c) Approved for use in New Hampshire by the Environmental Protection Agency without a requirement to substitute additional air emissions reductions beyond those adopted under RSA 485:16-c.

III. Nothing in this section shall prohibit the commissioner from phasing in any limitations approved under paragraph II.

IV. Retail sellers of gasoline and the suppliers to such retail sellers shall comply with the provisions of paragraph II or be subject to the enforcement provisions of RSA 485:58.

V. The limitations on MTBE concentrations established under the provisions of this section shall be exempt from the requirements of RSA 541-A, the administrative procedure act. The department shall file, however, in the office of legislative services a copy of all rules adopted, amended, or repealed under this section by the department.

HISTORY:
    1999, 313:2, eff. July 16, 1999. 2001, 293:2, eff. July 17, 2001.

Amendments

—2001.
    Paragraph I: Rewritten to the extent that a detailed comparison would be impracticable.
    Paragraph II: Substituted "provisions of" for "authority to seek waivers under" preceding "paragraph I" and "services, shall limit to the greatest extent practicable, with" for "services, may limit with" in the introductory paragraph and added "beyond those adopted under RSA 485:16-c" in subpar. (c).

485:16-c. Adoption of Other Air Pollution Control Measures.

In order to reduce air emissions and receive federal credit for such reductions, the commissioner shall be authorized to establish limits on the manufacture, use, or sale of consumer products in accordance with RSA 125-C:6, XVII.

HISTORY:
2001, 293:3, eff. July 17, 2001. 2004, 175:5, eff. May 27, 2004.

Amendments

—2004.
Substituted "to reduce air emissions and receive federal credit for such reductions" for "to fulfill federal air pollutant emission reduction obligations that may be created by opting out of the federal reformulated gasoline program under RSA 485:16-b or by implementing an alternative regional or federal approach under RSA 485:16-d".

485:16-d. Regional and Federal Efforts.

I. The commissioner is authorized to promote such regional or federal efforts as may be required to reduce the ongoing contamination threat posed by MTBE and other gasoline ethers, including but not limited to efforts to eliminate the federal oxygen mandate in the federal Clean Air Act, secure waivers from federal fuel requirements, or implement cleaner, more protective reformulation of gasoline.

II. If an alternative regional or federal approach to cleaner gasoline is developed which provides equal or greater effectiveness in reducing concentrations of MTBE and other gasoline ethers than opting out of the federal reformulated gasoline program under RSA 485:16-b, I, or does so in a manner that requires less costly substitute emission control measures under RSA 485:16-c, then the commissioner may implement such alternative regional or federal approach. Such alternative regional or federal approach may substitute for opting out of the federal reformulated gasoline program under RSA 485:16-b, I if undertaken prior to January 1, 2004.

HISTORY:
2001, 293:3, eff. July 17, 2001.

RESEARCH REFERENCES AND PRACTICE AIDS

References in text.
The Clean Air Act, referred to in par. I, is classified to 42 U.S.C.S. §§ 7401 et seq.

Water Pollution Control

RESEARCH REFERENCES AND PRACTICE AIDS

Cross References.
Household cleaning products containing phosphates prohibited, see RSA 485-A:56.

485:17. Penalty.

I. If a person shall recklessly place, leave, or cause to be placed or left, in or near a lake, pond, reservoir or stream tributary thereto, from which the domestic water supply of a city, town, or village is taken, in whole or in part, any material, substance, or fluid that may cause such water to become impure or unfit for such purposes, such person shall be guilty of a misdemeanor if a natural person or guilty of a felony if any other person.

II. If a person shall purposely or knowingly place, leave, or cause to be placed or left, in or near a lake, pond, reservoir, or stream tributary thereto, from which the domestic water supply of a city, town, or village is taken, in whole or in part, any material, substance, or fluid that may cause such water to become impure or unfit for such purposes, such person shall be guilty of a class B felony.

HISTORY:
1989, 339:1, eff. Jan. 1, 1990. 2009, 210:5, eff. January 1, 2010.

Amendments

—2009.
The 2009 amendment rewrote the section heading, which formerly read: "Pollution"; added the I designation; in I, added "recklessly" near the beginning and "material" preceding "substance"; added II; and made related and stylistic changes.

NOTES TO DECISIONS

Constitutionality
A statute which prohibits the deposit of sawdust in a lake used as a public water supply, and in its tributaries, is not unconstitutional because local in its operation, or as depriving a mill owner of his property without compensation. State v. Griffin, 69 N.H. 1, 39 A. 260, 1896 N.H. LEXIS 1 (N.H. 1897). (Decided under prior law.)

RESEARCH REFERENCES AND PRACTICE AIDS

Cross References.
Classification of crimes, see RSA 625:9.
Sentences, see RSA 651.

485:18. Removal of Polluting Substance.

The health officer of the town, or the water commissioners having charge of the water supply, or the proprietors of the water supply, may remove such material, substance, or fluid and may recover the expense of removal from the person who placed the same, or caused it to be placed, in or near the water, in a court of competent jurisdiction.

HISTORY:
1989, 339:1, eff. Jan. 1, 1990. 2009, 210:6, eff. January 1, 2010.

Amendments

—2009.
The 2009 amendment added "material" following "remove such"; substituted "a court of competent jurisdiction" for "an action on the case" at the end; and made related and stylistic changes.

485:19. Willful Pollution. [Repealed.]

[Repealed 2009, 210:9, eff. January 1, 2010.]

Former section(s).
Former RSA 485:19, which was derived from 1989, 339:1, related to willful pollution.

485:20. Injunctions.

I. The superior court shall have power to issue

injunctions restraining any person from violating the provisions of RSA 485:17.

II. Municipalities may apply to a justice of the superior court for injunctive relief against existing or impending violations of RSA 485:17. The municipality shall give notice of any such action to the attorney general and the commissioner of environmental services, who may take such steps as they deem necessary to ensure uniform statewide enforcement, including but not limited to joining the action, assuming sole prosecution of the action, or, as of right, dismissing the action without prejudice. Such notice shall be given at least 30 days prior to the commencement of any such action, unless more immediate action is necessary to prevent irreparable environmental damage or other serious public harm, in which case such notice shall be given as soon as practicable, but in no event later than the date of commencement of the action. This paragraph shall not be construed to affect, in any manner, existing authority of municipalities to act based upon the provisions of other statutes or local ordinances.

HISTORY:
    1989, 339:1. 1991, 340:3, eff. Jan. 1, 1992. 2009, 210:7, eff. January 1, 2010.

Amendments

—2009.
    The 2009 amendment substituted "RSA 485:17" for "RSA 485:17 or 485:19" in I and in the first sentence of II.

—1991.
    Designated the existing provisions of the section as par. I, substituted "RSA 485:17 or 485:19" for "the preceding section" following "provisions of" in that paragraph, and added par. II.

485:21. Fishing; Ice Racing; Penalty.

Said local legislative bodies and officers may also adopt all reasonable rules regarding fishing and the use of boats in and upon any such lake, pond or reservoir, and regarding racing or speeding horses upon the ice of such water body, which they may deem expedient. Any person who shall violate any of said rules after notice of such rules shall be guilty of a misdemeanor.

HISTORY:
    1989, 339:1, eff. Jan. 1, 1990.

RESEARCH REFERENCES AND PRACTICE AIDS

Cross References.
    Classification of crimes, see RSA 625:9.
    Sentences, see RSA 651.

485:22. Bathing.

If any person shall bathe in such lake, pond or reservoir, within the limits prescribed for the protection of said water supply by the local board of health or health officer or the department, he shall be guilty of a misdemeanor.

HISTORY:
    1989, 339:1, eff. Jan. 1, 1990. 1996, 228:106, eff. July 1, 1996.

Amendments

—1996.
    Substituted "department" for "division".

RESEARCH REFERENCES AND PRACTICE AIDS

Cross References.
    Classification of crimes, see RSA 625:9.
    Sentences, see RSA 651.

485:23. Petition to Protect Water Supplies.

I. Whenever any board of water commissioners, local board of health, local health officer or 10 or more citizens of any town or city have reason to believe that a public water or ice supply is being contaminated or is in danger of contamination, and that the local regulations are not sufficient or effective to prevent such pollution, they may petition the department to investigate the case, and to adopt rules under RSA 541-A as the department may deem necessary for the protection of the said supply against any pollution that in its judgment would endanger the public health. Citizens petitioning under this section shall designate a signatory of the petition as the person to whom the department shall send its response.

II. Whenever any board of water commissioners, local board of health, or other owner of a public water supply has reason to believe that a public water supply is in danger of being contaminated or is otherwise threatened and that an emergency condition exists such that a petition pursuant to paragraph I to the department and the adoption of rules would not adequately protect the water supply, the board or owner may petition the governor to declare a state of emergency for the public water supply. At the request of the governor, the department shall consult with the owner of the water supply and make a recommendation as to emergency protections that may be necessary. If the governor declares a state of emergency for a public water supply, those additional protections that the governor deems necessary shall be effective immediately and for the duration of the emergency. The declaration of a state of emergency for a public water supply shall not exceed 6 months. The governor may renew the declaration one time for up to 6 additional months upon further request by the original petitioner. At such time as any of the emergency protections are to become permanent, the department shall initiate rulemaking in accordance with RSA 485:24. Any protections in the governor's declaration shall be enforced in the same manner as rules adopted pursuant to RSA 485:24 or RSA 485:25 with violations of the protections subject to RSA 485:4 and RSA 485:58.

HISTORY:
    1989, 339:1, eff. Jan. 1, 1990. 1996, 228:106, eff. July 1, 1996. 2002, 141:1, eff. May 13, 2002.

Amendments

—2002.

Designated the existing provisions of the section as par. I and added par. II.

—1996.

Substituted "department" for "division" wherever it appeared.

NOTES TO DECISIONS

Analysis

1. Construction with other laws
2. Procedure

1. Construction with other laws

This and the following section were adopted as a single act and must be read together. Richardson v. Beattie, 98 N.H. 71, 95 A.2d 122, 1953 N.H. LEXIS 17 (N.H. 1953). (Decided under prior law.)

2. Procedure

State board of health may act without a hearing and on its own inspection and knowledge under this section, provided there is contamination or a threat of contamination of a public water supply. Richardson v. Beattie, 98 N.H. 71, 95 A.2d 122, 1953 N.H. LEXIS 17 (N.H. 1953). (Decided under prior law.)

In acting upon such a petition the board, if it sees fit, may adopt a summary procedure, and is not bound to grant requests for findings and rulings of law. Willis v. Wilkins, 92 N.H. 400, 32 A.2d 321, 1943 N.H. LEXIS 101 (N.H. 1943). (Decided under prior law.)

On a petition alleging that a certain source of public water supply was in danger of contamination and asking for regulations "to prohibit swimming or bathing in any part", riparian owners whose rights and privileges would be curtailed thereby are not entitled to a hearing as of right. Willis v. Wilkins, 92 N.H. 400, 32 A.2d 321, 1943 N.H. LEXIS 101 (N.H. 1943). (Decided under prior law.)

In acting upon such a petition the board may properly act on its own inspection and knowledge; hence it is not necessary that members of the board who participated in the final determination did not hear all the testimony. Willis v. Wilkins, 92 N.H. 400, 32 A.2d 321, 1943 N.H. LEXIS 101 (N.H. 1943). (Decided under prior law.)

485:23-a. Review of Private Access Facilities.

No private boat access facility shall be constructed to any public waters which serve as a public water supply for a public or private water utility company, without the approval of the department of environmental services upon consultation with the public water access advisory board and notification to the public utilities commission for any water utility under its jurisdiction.

HISTORY:

1996, 224:2, eff. Aug 9, 1996.

485:24. Investigations; Rules.

I. The department shall respond in writing to a petition filed under RSA 485:23, I, after due investigation, but not later than 30 days after receipt of the petition, informing the petitioners of the department's intended action. In response to a petition, or upon its own motion, the department shall adopt such rules under RSA 541-A as it may deem best to protect the water or ice supply against any dangerous contamination. If requested by the department, the local board of water commissioners, the local board of health, or the local health officer, shall enforce such rules in cooperation with the department.

II. In the case of water supplies any part of which may be outside the town or city concerned, the health officer of such town or city may act as an agent of the department for the enforcement of these rules when so designated by the department. The department may empower the board of water commissioners, local board of health, or local health officer and their agents of the affected municipality to enforce rules adopted under the provisions of this section.

HISTORY:

1989, 339:1, eff. Jan. 1, 1990. 1996, 228:106, eff. July 1, 1996. 2002, 141:2, eff. May 13, 2002.

Amendments

—2002.

Paragraph I: Substituted "RSA 485:23, I" for "RSA 485:23" following "filed under" in the first sentence.

—1996.

Substituted "department" for "division" throughout the section.

NOTES TO DECISIONS

Analysis

1. Constitutionality
2. Construction with other laws
3. Notice of investigation
4. Hearing
5. Reasonableness of regulations
6. Compensation of landowners

1. Constitutionality

The power to make regulations for the protection of the public health does not involve any unconstitutional delegation of legislative power. State v. Normand, 76 N.H. 541, 85 A. 899, 1913 N.H. LEXIS 47 (N.H. 1913). (Decided under prior law.)

2. Construction with other laws

This section and the preceding section were adopted as a single act and must be read together. Richardson v. Beattie, 98 N.H. 71, 95 A.2d 122, 1953 N.H. LEXIS 17 (N.H. 1953). (Decided under prior law.)

3. Notice of investigation

Formal notice of an investigation conducted by the state board of health need not be served upon riparian proprietors, the only provision for notice being posting or publication of regulations. Willis v. Wilkins, 92 N.H. 400, 32 A.2d 321, 1943 N.H. LEXIS 101 (N.H. 1943). (Decided under prior law.)

4. Hearing

Power to make regulations to protect a public water supply from contamination may be exercised without hearing and upon the state health board's own inspection and knowledge even if such action may seriously impair private as well as public rights. Richardson v. Beattie, 98 N.H. 71, 95 A.2d 122, 1953 N.H. LEXIS 17 (N.H. 1953). (Decided under prior law.)

Riparian owners whose rights and privileges will be curtailed by a regulation to prohibit swimming or bathing in waters constituting a public water supply are not entitled to a hearing as of right. Willis v. Wilkins, 92 N.H. 400, 32 A.2d 321, 1943 N.H. LEXIS 101 (N.H. 1943). (Decided under prior law.)

5. Reasonableness of regulations

Regulations adopted must have reasonable connection with protection against dangerous contamination. Richardson v. Beattie, 98 N.H. 71, 95 A.2d 122, 1953 N.H. LEXIS 17 (N.H. 1953). (Decided under prior law.)

In determining reasonableness of a regulation prohibiting human activity on a lake constituting a source of public water supply, court may determine for itself existence of facts necessary to determine whether regulation is clearly unreasonable; and must balance importance of the public benefit sought to be promoted against seriousness of restriction of private right thereby imposed. Richardson v. Beattie, 98 N.H. 71, 95 A.2d 122, 1953 N.H. LEXIS 17 (N.H. 1953). (Decided under prior law.)

A regulation prohibiting all human activity upon a part of a lake used as a public water supply was found unreasonable under the circumstances, in Richardson v. Beattie, 98 N.H. 71, 95 A.2d 122, 1953 N.H. LEXIS 17 (N.H. 1953). (Decided under prior law.)

In determining whether regulations should be adopted prohibiting swimming or bathing in certain waters used as a public supply, and maintenance of any fishing houses on the ice thereof, board should consider the feasibility of a purification system. Willis v. Wilkins, 92 N.H. 400, 32 A.2d 321, 1943 N.H. LEXIS 101 (N.H. 1943). (Decided under prior law.)

6. Compensation of landowners

If the regulations are reasonable, the resulting loss to riparian owners excluded from swimming or bathing in a source of public water supply does not entitle them to compensation. Willis v. Wilkins, 92 N.H. 400, 32 A.2d 321, 1943 N.H. LEXIS 101 (N.H. 1943). (Decided under prior law.)

485:25. Interstate Waters.

To protect the purity of interstate waters used as sources of public drinking water supply by adjoining states, the commissioner is authorized, at the request of the state health department of an adjoining state, to adopt rules under RSA 541-A for the protection of the purity of the waters of any lakes, ponds, streams, and reservoirs within any specified drainage area in this state.

HISTORY:

1989, 339:1, eff. Jan. 1, 1990. 1996, 228:110, eff. July 1, 1996.

Amendments

—1996.

Substituted "commissioner" for "division".

485:26. Penalty for Violation of Rules.

Any person violating rules adopted pursuant to RSA 485:24 or 25 shall be guilty of a misdemeanor if a natural person, or guilty of a felony if any other person.

HISTORY:

1989, 339:1, eff. Jan. 1, 1990.

RESEARCH REFERENCES AND PRACTICE AIDS

Cross References.

Classification of crimes, see RSA 625:9.
Sentences, see RSA 651.

485:27. Power to Require Improvements in Sewage Treatment.

The department is empowered to investigate the conditions and methods pertaining to existing systems of sewerage and sewage treatment works and to require the application of any treatment, improvement or enlargement of such facilities as will insure their proper operation and provide adequate protection of the public health. Issuance of orders requiring changes or improvements in such sewerage systems or treatment works shall be in the manner as prescribed in RSA 485:4.

HISTORY:

1989, 339:1, eff. Jan. 1, 1990. 1996, 228:106, eff. July 1, 1996.

Amendments

—1996.

Substituted "department" for "division" in the first sentence.

NOTES TO DECISIONS

Compliance with regulations

Power of a state board of health to make regulations pertaining to sewage disposal includes the further authority to issue specific orders designed to compel compliance with regulations previously issued but long ignored. Meredith v. State Bd. of Health, 94 N.H. 123, 48 A.2d 489, 1946 N.H. LEXIS 161 (N.H. 1946). (Decided under prior law.)

RESEARCH REFERENCES AND PRACTICE AIDS

Cross References.

Municipal bond issue for sewage system or treatment works, see RSA 33:5, 5-a–5-c.

485:28. Power to Require the Installation of Sewage Facilities.

The department is hereby empowered to investigate the conditions and methods relating to the disposal of sewage in any municipality, as set forth in RSA 486:1, and to require the installation of public sewers, as defined in RSA 147:8, whenever such investigation demonstrates that individual sewage disposal systems are inadequate or incapable of protecting the health and welfare of the citizens of the affected municipality or preventing pollution of the surface waters of the state, as defined in RSA 485-A. Before issuing an order requiring the installation of public sewer facilities, the department shall notify the municipality of its findings and shall give the municipality an opportunity to be heard. After such hearing if it shall be determined that said facilities are necessary, the municipality shall be so notified in writing and the requirements so ordered shall be effected pursuant to RSA 38:25 within a reasonable time to be fixed by the department. If any municipality whose duty it is to act shall fail or refuse for a period of 10 days after the expiration of the time fixed by said order, or, in the case of appeal for a period of 10 days after final judgment shall have been entered, to obey the same or in good faith to begin to make the installation as ordered, such municipality so failing shall be fined not more than $1,000 for each day of failure to comply with the order of the department. Said fine shall be paid to the state and may be recovered in an action of debt brought by the attorney general in the name of the state treasurer.

HISTORY:

1989, 339:1, eff. Jan. 1, 1990. 1996, 228:106, eff. July 1, 1996. 1997, 206:7, eff. July 1, 1997.

Amendments

—1997.

Substituted "RSA 38:25" for "RSA 38:14-a" in the third sentence.

—1996.

Substituted "department" for "division" throughout the section.

Severability of enactment.

1997, 206 was subject to a severability clause. See 1997, 206:9.

NOTES TO DECISIONS

Cited:

Cited in Appeal of Town of Rindge, 158 N.H. 21, 959 A.2d 188, 2008 N.H. LEXIS 123 (2008).

485:29. Appeal.

Any person aggrieved by any decision, regulation, ruling or order made by the department pursuant to the provisions of RSA 485:24, 27, and 28 may appeal such decisions pursuant to RSA 21-O:14.

HISTORY:

1989, 339:1, eff. Jan. 1, 1990. 1996, 228:106, eff. July 1, 1996.

Amendments

—1996.

Substituted "department" for "division".

485:30. Discharge of Sewage; Penalty.

No person, association or corporation shall cause or permit the discharge of sewage or other deleterious waste from any dwelling, camp, factory, hotel, boardinghouse, or other commercial establishment into any stream, lake, pond, or river not previously polluted, without first submitting detailed plans of said proposed discharge to the department and securing the approval of the said department. Any person who violates the provisions of this section shall be guilty of a misdemeanor if a natural person, or guilty of a felony if any other person.

HISTORY:

1989, 339:1, eff. Jan. 1, 1990. 1996, 228:106, eff. July 1, 1996.

Amendments

—1996.

Substituted "department" for "division" in the first sentence.

NOTES TO DECISIONS

Sewers

State board of health could require town to construct sewerage system to prevent contamination of public water supply. Meredith v. State Bd. of Health, 94 N.H. 123, 48 A.2d 489, 1946 N.H. LEXIS 161 (N.H. 1946). (Decided under prior law.)

RESEARCH REFERENCES AND PRACTICE AIDS

Cross References.

Classification of crimes, see RSA 625:9.
Sentences, see RSA 651.

485:31. Tampering With Public Water Systems.

I. Any person who tampers with, attempts to tamper with, or makes a threat to tamper with a public water system shall be guilty of a class B felony if a natural person and guilty of a felony if any other person.

II. Notwithstanding RSA 651:2, a natural person may, in addition to any sentence of imprisonment, probation or conditional discharge, be fined not more than $50,000 if found guilty of tampering with a public water system, and not more than $25,000 if found guilty of an attempt to tamper with or making a threat to tamper with a public water system. Each day of violation shall constitute a separate violation.

III. Any person who tampers, attempts to tamper, or makes a threat to tamper with a public water system shall be liable to the state, upon suit brought by the attorney general, for a civil forfeiture not to exceed $50,000 for such tampering or not to exceed $25,000 for such attempt or threat.

IV. In this section, the term "tamper" means:

(a) To introduce a contaminant into a public water system with the purpose of harming persons; or

(b) To otherwise interfere with the operation of a public water system with the purpose of harming persons.

HISTORY:

1989, 339:1, eff. Jan. 1, 1990.

RESEARCH REFERENCES AND PRACTICE AIDS

Cross References.

Classification of crimes, see RSA 625:9.

485:32. Injuring Property.

Any person who shall willfully injure any of the property of any water company or of any city or town, used by it in supplying water to its inhabitants, shall be guilty of a misdemeanor if a natural person, or guilty of a felony if any other person, and such person shall also forfeit and pay to such water company, city or town 3 times the amount of actual damages sustained, to be recovered in an action on the case.

HISTORY:

1989, 339:1, eff. Jan. 1, 1990.

RESEARCH REFERENCES AND PRACTICE AIDS

Cross References.

Classification of crimes, see RSA 625:9.
Sentences, see RSA 651.

Private Water Sources

485:33. Analyses; Prohibiting Use.

Whenever any well, spring or other water supply is suspected of being polluted by sewage or other matter dangerous to health, the health officer of the town where it is located may cause an analysis of the water to be made by a competent chemist, without expense to the owner. If the analysis shows the water to be unfit for drinking purposes they may, with the approval of the department, prohibit its use, and, if it be from a well, may cause the well to be closed.

HISTORY:

1989, 339:1, eff. Jan. 1, 1990. 1996, 228:106, eff. July 1, 1996.

Amendments

—1996.

Substituted "department" for "division" in the second sentence.

485:34. Enforcement.

The department shall have concurrent jurisdiction with local boards and officers to enforce the provisions of this subdivision.

HISTORY:

1989, 339:1, eff. Jan. 1, 1990. 1996, 228:106, eff. July 1, 1996.

Amendments

—1996.

Substituted "department" for "division".

485:35. Prohibiting Use; Penalty.

Whenever the department, upon investigation, becomes satisfied that a well, spring or other supply of water, used for domestic purposes, has become polluted so as to endanger the public health, it is authorized to prohibit the person or corporation owning or controlling said supply from furnishing such water for domestic purposes, until it becomes satisfied that said water supply has been purified and made fit for domestic use. Any person who knowingly violates the order of the department is guilty of a class B felony for each day he or she continues to furnish water after the order of the department has been served on such person.

HISTORY:

1989, 339:1, eff. Jan. 1, 1990. 1996, 228:106, eff. July 1, 1996. 2008, 161:1, eff. January 1, 2009.

Amendments

—2008.

The 2008 amendment in the second sentence, added "knowingly" preceding "violates", substituted "class B felony" for "misdemeanor", added "such person" at the end and made a stylistic change.

—1996.

Substituted "department" for "division" wherever it appeared.

RESEARCH REFERENCES AND PRACTICE AIDS

Cross References.

Classification of crimes, see RSA 625:9.
Sentences, see RSA 651.

485:35-a. Protective Well Radii. [Repealed.]

[Repealed 1991, 215:3, eff. Aug. 9, 1991.]

Former section(s).

Former RSA 485:35-a, which was derived from 1989, 191:1, related to protective well radii for private water wells. See now RSA 485-A:30-b.

Effect of repeal on existing rules.

1991, 215:1, II, eff. Aug. 9, 1991, provided:

"The rules adopted under former RSA 485:35-a relative to protective well radii shall remain in full force and effect upon enactment of this act [which repealed this section and added RSA 485-A:30-b] to the extent not inconsistent with the provisions of this act. The recodification of the section on protective well radii from RSA 485 to RSA 485-A shall not be construed to affect the validity of such rules otherwise consistent with this act."

485:36. Injunctions to Enforce.

The superior court shall have jurisdiction in equity, upon application of the department, to enforce the orders of the department issued under RSA 485:35.

HISTORY:

1989, 339:1, eff. Jan. 1, 1990. 1996, 228:106, eff. July 1, 1996.

Revision note.

Substituted "RSA 485:35" for "the preceding section" for purposes of clarity in light of the enactment and repeal of RSA 485:35-a.

Amendments

—1996.

Substituted "department" for "division".

485:37. Fencing or Covering.

No person who owns or occupies land shall knowingly allow any well which is within 500 feet of a dwelling or within 200 feet of any highway to remain open on such land, unless there is around such well a substantial fence or protection at least 3 feet high so constructed that no child can crawl through or under it. Any such well shall be deemed to be open unless it is protected by a covering strong enough to hold 1,000 pounds and secured so that it cannot be easily removed by children. The term "well" as used in this subdivision shall mean any artificially made hole in the surface of the earth (a) which is more than 4 feet deep and (b) which is more than 8 inches in diameter and less than 16 square feet in area at the top and (c) the sides of which are steeper than a 60 degree slope.

HISTORY:

1989, 339:1, eff. Jan. 1, 1990.

485:38. Nuisance.

Any open well which is not fenced or protected as provided in RSA 485:37 is declared a nuisance and the same may be ordered abated by any court of competent jurisdiction on complaint of any prosecuting officer.

HISTORY:

  1989, 339:1, eff. Jan. 1, 1990.

485:39. Penalty.

Whoever violates any provision of RSA 485:37 or RSA 485:38 shall be guilty of a misdemeanor if a natural person, or guilty of a felony if any other person.

HISTORY:

  1989, 339:1, eff. Jan. 1, 1990.

RESEARCH REFERENCES AND PRACTICE AIDS

Cross References.

  Classification of crimes, see RSA 625:9.
  Sentences, see RSA 651.

485:40. Emergency Planning.

The department shall develop plans, with the advice and assistance of the division of homeland security and emergency management, and of the public water systems of the state, for emergency conditions and situations that may endanger the public health or welfare by contamination of drinking water. Such plans may include potential sources of contaminants and situations or conditions that could place them in the sources of public drinking water, techniques and methods to be used by public water systems to reduce or eliminate the dangers to public health caused thereby, methods and times for analysis or testing during such emergency conditions or situations, alternate sources of water available to public water systems, and methods of supplying drinking water to consumers if a public water system cannot supply such water.

HISTORY:

  1989, 339:1, eff. Jan. 1, 1990. 1996, 228:71, eff. July 1, 1996. 2002, 257:10, eff. July 1, 2002. 2003, 319:128, eff. Sept. 4, 2003. 2004, 171:20, eff. July 24, 2004. 2008, 361:15, eff. July 11, 2008.

Amendments

—2008.

  The 2008 amendment substituted "division of homeland security and emergency management" for "division of emergency services, communications, and management" in the first sentence.

—2004.

  Substituted "division of emergency services, communications, and management" for "bureau of emergency management" in the first sentence.

—2003.

  Substituted "bureau of emergency management" for "office of emergency management" in the first sentence.

—2002.

  Deleted "governor's" preceding "office of emergency management" in the first sentence.

—1996.

  Deleted "divisions of water resources, water supply and pollution control" preceding "governor's office" in the first sentence.

485:41. Duties of Department.

The department shall:

I. Monitor the operation and maintenance of new and existing public water systems and privately owned redistribution systems.

II. Adopt rules governing the maintenance and operation of public water systems to ensure compliance with drinking water standards and to protect the public health.

III. Adopt rules governing the installation of pipes, fixtures and other apparatus which are used to connect the water system or privately owned redistribution system to a building. Such rules shall be considered minimum standards. The department shall adopt the International Plumbing Code as published by the International Code Council by reference, provided the department specifies which sections of the code are in force in New Hampshire and makes specific any discretionary provisions in the code subject to approval by the state building code review board. The department shall periodically review the rules adopted under this paragraph to assure that they are no less stringent than the requirements of the current code.

IV. Adopt rules establishing recordkeeping, reporting and testing requirements for public water systems.

V. Enter, and authorize its employees and agents to enter, the premises of all public water systems and privately owned redistribution systems for the purpose of carrying out inspection and for the purpose of taking water samples, to determine compliance with the provisions of this chapter or rules adopted under it, and to inspect any and all records and facilities of such public water supply or privately owned redistribution system in order to determine compliance with this chapter and rules adopted under it.

VI. Undertake long-range planning and studies, within available state and federal funding, relating to the purity of drinking water in the state.

VII. Make available to the public the analytical results of all monitoring and testing undertaken pursuant to this chapter.

VIII. Adopt a fee system in recognition of services provided by the water supply engineering bureau including the issuance of an operational permit for public water systems subject to this chapter. The commissioner shall adopt rules establishing the application process for the issuance of operational permits pursuant to RSA 541-A. The fee category for community systems per year shall be $300, but in no case shall the fee exceed $10 per household or household equivalent. The fee category for non-transient and non-community systems shall be $150 per year. All fees shall be paid to the department for deposit in the operational permits account. Moneys in the operational permits account shall be used to pay the salaries, benefits and expenses of the staff in the department's drinking water supply program. Any revenues generated in excess of the costs of funding the drinking water supply program's expenses, shall lapse to the general fund at the close of each fiscal year to be used to offset the future general fund appropriation for the water supply program.

IX. Adopt rules applying to privately owned redistribution systems requiring:

(a) Periodic monitoring of coliform bacteria and public notification, and remedial action in case of violation of bacterial water quality standards, consistent with the rules which apply to public water systems for such bacterial water quality standards.

(b) Retention of a primary water operator who maintains an operating certificate at a minimum grade 1-A level.

(c) Inspection and maintenance of exterior pumping stations, distribution networks, and exterior storage tanks.

(d) Design standards for new and replacement facilities consistent with the rules which apply to public water systems as limited by the provisions of RSA 485 concerning privately owned redistribution systems, and provided that such rules require that any plans review required by RSA 485 shall be completed within 30 days of the submission of such plans.

HISTORY:

1989, 339:1. 1990, 163:4. 1991, 380:3, eff. July 2, 1991. 1996, 228:72, 106, eff. July 1, 1996. 2002, 8:9, eff. Sept. 14, 2002. 2008, 279:6–9, eff. July 1, 2009.

Amendments

—2008.

The 2008 amendment in I, in the first sentence of III and twice in V, added "and privately owned redistribution systems" or variant; and added IX.

—2002.

Paragraph III: Deleted the former third sentence, substituted "shall adopt the International Plumbing Code as published by the International Code Council" for "may adopt the BOCA code" in the present third sentence, and deleted "BOCA" preceding "code" at the end of the present fourth sentence.

—1996.

Substituted "department" for "division" in the section catchline, in the introductory paragraph and throughout par. III, and "commissioner" for "division" in the second sentence, "department" for "division" in the fifth sentence and "department's" for "division's" in the sixth sentence of par. VIII.

—1991.

Paragraph VIII: Substituted "by the water supply engineering bureau including the" for "for the" following "provided" in the first sentence, "$300" for "$600 for all systems serving more than 100 people" following "shall be" in the third sentence and "$150" for "$200" in the fourth sentence, rewrote the sixth sentence, and substituted "drinking water supply program's expenses" for "water supply engineering bureau, operation permits section" preceding "shall lapse" and "water supply program" for "water supply engi-

neering bureau" following "appropriation for the" in the seventh sentence.

—1990.

Paragraph VIII: Added.

Exemptions from fees; refunds.

1991, 380:4, eff. July 2, 1991, provided:

"Any system owned by a state, county, municipality, town, precinct, or district shall be exempt from water system fees as provided in RSA 485:41, VIII. Any state, county, municipality, town, precinct, or district that has been billed and still has an outstanding account, shall have such outstanding account forgiven. In the event that the entity has already paid, then the sum paid shall be refunded to it. The funds necessary to provide the refunds to the state, county, municipality, town, precinct, or district exempted under RSA 485:41, VIII, are hereby appropriated and shall be a charge against the operational permits account."

485:42. Variances and Exemptions.

I. The department may, after notice and opportunity for hearing, grant one or more variances from an applicable state drinking water regulation to a public water system if the variance will not result in an unreasonable risk to the public health, and if:

(a) Because of the characteristics of the raw water sources reasonably available to the system, the system cannot meet the maximum contaminant levels of such drinking water regulation despite application of the best available technology, treatment techniques or other means. The department's finding of the best available technology treatment, treatment technique or other means may vary depending upon the number of persons served by the system or for other physical conditions related to engineering feasibility and cost of compliance with maximum contaminant levels as considered appropriate by the department; or

(b) Where a specified treatment technique for a contaminant is required by the state drinking water regulations, the system demonstrates to the department's satisfaction that such treatment technique is not required to protect the public health because of the nature of the raw water source.

Variances may be conditioned on monitoring, testing, analyzing or other requirements to ensure the protection of the public health, and variances granted under subparagraph (a) shall include a compliance schedule under which the public water system will meet each contaminant level for which a variance is granted as expeditiously as is feasible.

II. The department may, after notice and opportunity for hearing, grant one or more exemptions from an applicable maximum contaminant level or treatment technique in the state drinking water rules to a public water system if:

(a) The exemption will not result in an unreasonable risk to the public health;

(b) The public water system is unable to comply with the rule due to compelling factors, which may include economic factors; and

(c) The public water system was in operation on the earliest effective date, under present or prior law, of the contaminant level or treatment technique requirement. Each exemption shall be conditioned on monitoring, testing, analyzing or other requirements to ensure the protection of the public health, and shall include a compliance schedule under which the public water system will meet each contaminant level or treatment technique for which an exemption is granted as expeditiously as is feasible, but not later than 12 months after the date of issuance of the exemption. The department may extend the final date for compliance provided in any schedule required under this section for a period not to exceed 3 years after the date of the issuance of the exemption if the public water system establishes that:

(1) The system cannot meet the standard without capital improvements which cannot be completed within the period of such exemption;

(2) In the case of a system which needs financial assistance for the necessary improvements, the system has entered into an agreement to obtain such financial assistance; or

(3) The system has entered into an enforceable agreement to become part of a regional public water system; and the system is taking all practicable steps to meet the standards.

If a system serves fewer than 500 service connections and needs financial assistance for necessary improvements, an exemption granted under subparagraph (c)(1) or (c)(2) of this subparagraph may be renewed for one or more additional 2-year periods, if the system establishes that it is taking all practicable steps to meet the requirements of any compliance schedule established under this section.

HISTORY:
1989, 339:1, eff. Jan. 1, 1990. 1996, 228:106, eff. July 1, 1996.

Amendments

—1996.
Substituted "department" for "division" throughout the section.

485:43. Notification of Noncompliance; Water Quality.

I. A public water system shall, upon granting of a variance or exemption or upon determination of its noncompliance with any primary drinking water standard or any rule adopted under this chapter or with any other requirement of this chapter notify the department of such noncompliance within 48 hours and shall notify its users of such noncompliance in accordance with rules adopted by the department under RSA 485:3.

II. Each community public water system shall annually notify each of its users of the results of water quality tests required by RSA 485:41. Such notification shall be in the form prescribed by rule adopted by the commissioner, pursuant to RSA 541-A, under RSA 485:3, VII. Such notification shall include, but not be limited to, a listing of contaminants identified under rules adopted pursuant to RSA 485:3, I, and the results of testing for various bacteriological agents. Where multiple tests have been conducted, a summary or average level of contaminants or biological agents may be provided.

HISTORY:
1989, 339:1, eff. Jan. 1, 1990. 1996, 228:106, 110, eff. July 1, 1996.

Revision note.
Substituted "RSA 485:41" for "RSA 485:42" in the first sentence of par. II to correct an error in the reference.

Amendments

—1996.
Paragraph I: Substituted "department" for "division" in two places.
Paragraph II: Substituted "commissioner" for "division" in the first sentence.

Laboratory Accreditation

Amendments

—1998.
1998, 152:1, eff. Aug. 7, 1998, substituted "Accreditation" for "Certification" in the subdivision heading.

RESEARCH REFERENCES AND PRACTICE AIDS

New Hampshire Code of Administrative Rules
Rules of the Department of Environmental Services—Office of the Commissioner, Env-C 301.01 et seq., New Hampshire Code of Administrative Rules Annotated.

485:44. Water Testing Laboratory Accreditation.

I. Any laboratory conducting water analysis tests for the purpose of determining compliance of a public water supply with the provisions of RSA 485:3 and any laboratory conducting environmental analyses in this state for any other governmental purpose where a requirement of certification or accreditation is specified shall first obtain accreditation.

II. The department shall establish and administer a program to accredit on an annual basis the facilities, equipment, procedures, methods of analysis, analytical assurance and quality control, recordkeeping and traceability, analytical performance, and qualifications of personnel of any laboratory for the purposes of RSA 485:44, I. The program shall be in conformance with and consistent with the national accreditation standards approved by the National Environmental Laboratory Accreditation Conference. The purpose of the accreditation program shall be to ensure that environmental laboratories provide sufficiently accurate, precise, and consistent results of tests, analyses, and measurements.

III. The department shall, upon request of a laboratory accredited pursuant to paragraph II of this section, accredit such laboratory in conformance with and consistent with the national accreditation standards approved by the National Environmental Laboratory Accreditation Conference, provided that such laboratory demonstrates capability to analyze samples with precision and accuracy.

IV. A laboratory may subcontract tests which it is not accredited to perform to another laboratory which is so accredited, provided that the test report clearly indicates which tests were subcontracted and that laboratory test records which specify the name and address of the laboratory which performed the work are maintained and made accessible to the department upon request.

V, VI. [Repealed.]

VII. The department shall accredit laboratories accredited in other states upon request by reciprocity, provided that the accreditation program in such states is in conformance with and consistent with the national accreditation standards approved by the National Environmental Laboratory Accreditation Conference.

VIII. An alternate laboratory test method may be acceptable only if it is in conformance with and consistent with the performance based method requirements set forth in the national accreditation standards approved by the National Environmental Laboratory Accreditation Conference.

IX. Accreditation may be denied, revoked, suspended, or modified as determined by rules of the department. A laboratory which has had accreditation revoked or suspended shall be reaccredited at such time as it again meets criteria for accreditation provided, that such laboratory has not had its accreditation revoked or suspended more than 3 times in the preceding 2 years. Upon notification of the fourth such revocation or suspension, such laboratory shall not be eligible for reaccreditation for one year from the date of such notice, except that, upon appeal by such laboratory, the commissioner may waive such extended period of revocation or suspension if such laboratory can demonstrate to the commissioner good cause for the immediate reaccreditation of such laboratory.

X. Changes in laboratory ownership, location, personnel, methodology, or other factors significantly affecting the performance of analyses for which it was originally accredited shall be reported in writing to the accreditation officer of the department within 5 business days of the change.

XI. The department shall establish by rule, under RSA 541-A, a reasonable time frame for the completion of the accreditation process. The provisions under which any laboratory is certified on January 1, 1990 shall not be affected in any way, except as provided in paragraph IX of this section, before the completion of the accreditation process within the time frame established by the department.

XII. Participation of laboratories in the accreditation program shall be voluntary.

HISTORY:
1989, 339:1. 1992, 191:1, 2, eff. July 11, 1992. 1996, 228:73, eff. July 1, 1996. 1998, 152:3, 4, 8 I, eff. Aug. 7, 1998.

Amendments

—1998.
Rewritten to the extent that a detailed comparison would be impracticable.

—1996.
Paragraph IX: Substituted "commissioner" for "water supply and pollution control council" and for "council" in the third sentence.

—1992.
Paragraph II: In the third sentence inserted "metals by flame AA, metals by furnace AA, metals by ICP" preceding "PCB's, pesticides" and inserted "herbicides" thereafter.
Paragraph VII: Added the third sentence.

485:45. Testing of Water Supplies.

The state laboratory shall make periodic inspections and analyses of the public water supplies of the state and any special investigations of such water supplies that may be called for; also, when requested or as may be deemed by them necessary or expedient in the interests of the public health, make inspections or analyses of sources furnishing water to institutions, schools, hotels, camps, other places of public resort and individuals, and advise in connection with the same.

HISTORY:
1989, 339:1, eff. Jan. 1, 1990.

RESEARCH REFERENCES AND PRACTICE AIDS

Cross References.
Fees for analyses, see RSA 131:3-a.

485:46. Fees; Advertising.

I. The department shall adopt rules under RSA 541-A, after public hearing, establishing a schedule of reasonable fees to be paid by any laboratory applying for accreditation.

II. The schedule of fees shall be designed to recover the costs associated with the accreditation services provided under RSA 485:44, and such fees shall be available to the department to be used to defray the expenses for such services. Funds received shall be deposited in a special revolving fund account maintained by the department which shall be continuously appropriated to the department to offset the costs of the accreditation program. Any balance in excess of $1,000 remaining at the end of the fiscal year shall lapse to the general fund.

III. A laboratory shall provide each prospective New Hampshire client with a list which clearly indicates the specific analytes which the laboratory is accredited to test. In the event that a client has paid a fee to a laboratory in anticipation of testing services before the receipt of said test sampling materials, and the client subsequently determines upon receipt of the test materials that the laboratory is not accredited to provide testing services to meet the client's needs, the client may cancel the order for any testing services which have not yet been performed, and the laboratory shall make full refund to the client. Test reports shall clearly identify those specific analytes for which a laboratory has accreditation and shall specifically identify any analyses which were subcontracted to other laboratories.

HISTORY:
1989, 339:1. 1992, 191:3, eff. July 11, 1992. 1998, 152:5, eff. Aug. 7, 1998.

Amendments

—1998.
Paragraph I: Substituted "accreditation" for "approval and certification" following "applying for".
Paragraph II: Rewritten to the extent that a detailed comparison would be impracticable.
Paragraph III: Substituted "accredited" for "certified" in the first and second sentences, "accreditation" for "certification" in the third sentence, and "the client's" for "his" preceding "needs" and made a minor stylistic change in the second sentence.

—1992.
Paragraph II: In the first sentence inserted "the costs of staff and" following "recover" and "staffing, and the cost of" preceding "travel and associated", in the second sentence inserted "revolving fund" preceding "account", "which shall be continuously appropriated to the department" preceding "to offset" and substituted "certification" for "inspection" preceding "program", in the third sentence inserted "in excess of $1,000" preceding "remaining" and in the fourth sentence "and" preceding "facilities" and deleted "and staff services" thereafter.

485:47. Rulemaking.

The department shall adopt rules, under RSA 541-A, relative to:

I. Procedures and standards for accreditation of laboratories, including but not limited to the form and content of approval and accreditation application forms, analytical techniques to be employed, standard collection and testing procedures, performance on proficiency test samples, as well as qualifications for laboratory personnel. The procedures and standards shall be in conformance with and consistent with the national accreditation standards approved by the National Environmental Laboratory Accreditation Conference.

II. [Repealed.]

III. Procedures and conditions under which accreditation of water testing laboratories may be revoked, suspended, or modified.

IV. Information to be disclosed when tests are subcontracted.

V. Procedures and criteria for laboratory reaccreditation.

VI. Procedures for the accreditation of laboratories which have been accredited by other states.

VII. Procedures for approval of alternate testing methodology.

VIII. Fees for accreditation, including rules for accounting of the fees.

IX. Procedures and standards for testing of water under any expanded accreditation program.

X. A time frame for the completion of the accreditation process.

XI–XIII. [Repealed.]

HISTORY:
1989, 339:1, eff. Jan. 1, 1990. 1998, 152:6, 7, 8 II, 8 III, eff. Aug. 7, 1998.

Amendments

—1998.
Substituted "accreditation" for "certification" in pars. I, III, VI, VIII–X, rewrote the second sentence in par. I, repealed par. II, substituted "reaccreditation" for "recertification" in par. V, and "accredited" for "certified" in par. VI, and repealed pars. XI–XIII.

RESEARCH REFERENCES AND PRACTICE AIDS

Cross References.
Certification of laboratories, see RSA 485:44.
Regulation of laboratory advertising and fees, see RSA 485:46.

Wellhead Protection

485:48. Wellhead Protection.

The department may institute a wellhead protection program as described in section 1428 of the federal Safe Drinking Water Amendments of 1986. The program shall be consistent with the provisions of RSA 485-C and shall include, but not be limited to, the following:

I. Determination of the responsibilities of state and local government units, and those of public drinking water supply systems with respect to wellhead protection.

II. Determination of the extent of the wellhead protection area, based on reasonably available hydrogeologic data, groundwater flow, recharge, discharge, and other data the department deems necessary to such determination.

III. Identify within each wellhead protection area all potential anthropogenic sources of contaminants which may have any adverse effect on human health, through consideration of all potential sources of such contaminants.

IV. Technical assistance, financial assistance, implementation of control measures, education, training, and demonstration projects to protect the water supply within wellhead protection areas from such contaminants.

V. Contingency plans for the location and provision of alternate drinking water supplies for each public water system in the event of well or wellfield contamination by such contaminants.

VI. Procedures, including, but not limited to, the establishment of technical and citizens' advisory committees, to encourage the public to participate in developing the protection program for wellhead areas. Such procedures shall include notice and opportunity for public hearing on the state program before it is submitted to the administrator, United States Environmental Protection Agency, for approval.

HISTORY:
1989, 339:1. 1991, 344:2, eff. June 28, 1991. 1996, 228:106, eff. July 1, 1996.

Amendments

—1996.
Substituted "department" for "division" in the introductory paragraph and in par. II.

—1991.
Rewrote the introductory paragraph.

RESEARCH REFERENCES AND PRACTICE AIDS

References in text.
Section 1428 of the federal Safe Drinking Water Amendments of 1986, referred to in the introductory paragraph, is classified to 42 U.S.C.S. § 300h-7.

Future Supplies of Water for Domestic Use

485:49. Declaration of Need.

It is declared that there is statewide need for long-range planning in order that the health and safety of the people of the state may be protected in respect to adequate water supplies for domestic use.

HISTORY:
1989, 339:1, eff. Jan. 1, 1990.

485:50. Domestic Water Supply Study.

The department of environmental services is authorized and directed to study the probable domestic water supply requirements of groups of towns or cities, or both, which appear likely to have increased industrial and population growths for the next 50 years. In connection with said studies the department shall determine the most feasible and economic sites for sources of water supply for such long-range planning.

HISTORY:
1989, 339:1, eff. Jan. 1, 1990.

485:51. Assistance.

The department of environmental services is authorized, within the limits of the appropriations made therefor, to employ engineers and other assistants to make the studies authorized by this subdivision.

HISTORY:
1989, 339:1, eff. Jan. 1, 1990.

485:52. Reports.

Whenever any study of a group plan for domestic water supply projects is made the department of environmental services shall report the same to the next session of the legislature together with its recommendations to make secure the availability of those sites which the department of environmental services finds will best meet the future needs of the particular locality studied.

HISTORY:
1989, 339:1, eff. Jan. 1, 1990.

485:53. Advice to Municipalities.

Upon request the department of environmental services shall consult with and advise any municipality which is considering a change in its domestic water supply due to an approaching critical situation in the municipality.

HISTORY:
1989, 339:1, eff. Jan. 1, 1990.

Protection of Sources of Ice

485:54. Ice Cutting.

No person shall cut or take ice from any lake, pond or reservoir used as the source of a domestic public water supply, unless he shall first comply in all respects with such reasonable rules regarding the manner and place of such cutting and taking as may be prescribed by the local legislative body, or officers of a water company, who may have charge of the works of any city or town supplying its inhabitants with water from such source.

HISTORY:
1989, 339:1, eff. Jan. 1, 1990.

485:55. Ice; Penalty.

Any person who knowingly or willfully shall cut or take ice for domestic purposes from any waters which are polluted with sewage or other substance deleterious or dangerous to life or health, or from waters which a board of health, local health officer or the department has condemned, shall be guilty of a misdemeanor if a natural person, or guilty of a felony if any other person.

HISTORY:
1989, 339:1, eff. Jan. 1, 1990. 1996, 228:106, eff. July 1, 1996.

Amendments

—1996.
Substituted "department" for "division".

RESEARCH REFERENCES AND PRACTICE AIDS

Cross References.
Classification of crimes, see RSA 625:9.
Sentences, see RSA 651.

485:56. Ice Inspection.

Health officers of the cities and towns of the state, and the department of environmental services, shall examine and inspect the sources from which ice is cut, or is proposed to be cut, for domestic use in such cities and towns, and to employ any necessary means to determine whether the waters of such sources of ice supply have been polluted, or whether ice taken from such sources will be deleterious to the public health.

HISTORY:

1989, 339:1, eff. Jan. 1, 1990. 1996, 228:108, eff. July 1, 1996.

Amendments

—1996.

Substituted "department of environmental services" for "division of water supply and pollution control".

485:57. Ice; Notice of Pollution.

If the waters of the sources of ice supplies shall be found so polluted that the ice taken from those sources will be unsafe for domestic use, the local health officer or the department of environmental services shall immediately notify such person who may have taken, or who proposes to take, ice from such polluted source for domestic use, of the dangerous character of the waters inspected, and that the taking of such ice for domestic use must cease.

HISTORY:

1989, 339:1, eff. Jan. 1, 1990. 1996, 228:108, eff. July 1, 1996.

Amendments

—1996.

Substituted "department of environmental services" for "division of water supply and pollution control".

Enforcement; Appeals

485:58. Enforcement and Penalties.

I. If the department determines that a primary standard has violated, or that, in its judgment, a condition exists in a public water system which will cause a violation of a primary standard and may result in a serious risk to public health, it may issue an order requiring:

(a) The prohibition of transportation, sale, distribution or supplying of water;

(b) The repair, installation or operation of purification equipment or methods;

(c) The notification of all potential users of the system, including travelers, of the nature, extent and possible health effects of the imminent hazard, and precautions to be taken by users; or

(d) The testing, sampling or other analytical operations required to determine the nature, extent, duration or termination of the imminent hazard.

The superior court shall place any action filed by the department to enforce an order under this section at the top of its calendar of cases and shall provide an expeditious hearing on such order.

II. Any reckless violation of any provision of this chapter, any rule adopted under this chapter, any term or condition of an approval, exemption, variance or order issued under this chapter, or any misstatement of a material fact required to be dis-

closed under this chapter shall constitute a misdemeanor for a natural person and a felony for any other person.

III. Unless otherwise provided, any purposeful or knowing violation of any provision of this chapter, any rule adopted under this chapter, any term or condition of an approval, exemption, variance, or order issued under this chapter, or any misstatement of a material fact required to be disclosed under this chapter shall constitute a class B felony.

IV. Any person who violates any provision of this chapter or any rule adopted or any term or condition of an approval, exemption, variance or order issued under this chapter shall be liable to the state, upon suit brought by the attorney general, for a civil forfeiture in an amount not to exceed $25,000 for each day of such violation.

V. The commissioner of environmental services, after notice and hearing pursuant to RSA 541-A, may impose an administrative fine not to exceed $2,000 for each offense upon any person who violates any provision of this chapter including any rule adopted under the provisions of this chapter. Rehearings and appeals from a decision of the commissioner under this paragraph shall be in accordance with RSA 541. Any administrative fine imposed under this section shall not preclude the imposition of further penalties under this chapter. The proceeds of administrative fines levied pursuant to this paragraph shall be deposited by the department in the general fund. The commissioner shall adopt rules, under RSA 541-A, relative to:

(a) A schedule of administrative fines which may be imposed under this paragraph for violations of this chapter as provided above.

(b) Procedures for notice and hearing prior to the imposition of an administrative fine.

VI. Any act or failure to act in violation of RSA 485:8, II; 31; 42; 43; 46; or 48; or any rule adopted under RSA 485:2; 3; 4; 40; 41; 44; or 47 may be enjoined.

VII. Notwithstanding RSA 651:2, any person may, in addition to any sentence of imprisonment, probation or conditional discharge, be fined not more than $25,000 if found guilty of any violation of paragraph II or III of this section. The court may also order the person to pay the costs of remediation. Each day of violation shall constitute a separate offense.

HISTORY:

1989, 339:1. 1990, 33:2. 1995, 88:2, eff. Jan. 1, 1996. 217:6, eff. Jan. 1, 1996. 1996, 228:106, eff. July 1, 1996. 2009, 210:8, eff. January 1, 2010.

Amendments

—2009.

The 2009 amendment, in II, substituted "Any reckless violation" for "Any knowing violation" at the beginning and deleted the former second sentence, which read: "Notwithstanding RSA 651:2, any person, in addition to any sentence of imprisonment, probation, or conditional discharge, may be fined not more than $25,000 for each day of violation"; added III; redesignated former III through VI as

IV through VII; and in VII, in the first sentence, substituted "any person" for "a natural person" and "paragraph II or III" for "paragraph II" and added the second sentence.

—1996.

Substituted "department" for "division" in the introductory and concluding paragraphs of par. I, and in the introductory paragraph of par. IV.

—1995.

Paragraph I: Chapter 88 deleted the first sentence of the concluding paragraph.

Paragraph IV: Chapter 217 added "including any rule adopted under the provisions of this chapter" at the end of the first sentence and substituted "RSA 541" for "RSA 21-O:14" in the second sentence of the introductory paragraph and substituted "violations" for "violation" preceding "of this chapter" and added "as provided above" thereafter in subpar. (a).

—1990.

Paragraph II: Deleted "RSA 485:8, II; 31; 42; 43; 46; or 48 of" following "provision of" and substituted "this chapter" for "RSA 485:2, 3, 40, 41, 44 or 47" following "adopted under", for "RSA 485:5, II; 31; 42; 43; 46; or 48" following "issued under" and for "such sections" following "disclosed under" in the first sentence and added the second sentence.

Paragraph III: Substituted "this chapter or" for "RSA 485:8, II; 31; 42; 43; 46; or 48" preceding "any rule adopted", deleted "under RSA 485:2, 3, 40, 41, 44, or 47" thereafter and substituted "this chapter" for "RSA 485:8, II; 31; 42; 43; 46; or 48" following "issued under".

Paragraph IV: Substituted "of this chapter" for "set forth in paragraph III of this section" following "provision" in the first sentence of the introductory paragraph.

Paragraph V: Inserted "4" following "RSA 485:2; 3".

NOTES TO DECISIONS

Cited:

Cited in Durgin v. Pillsbury Lake Water Dist., 153 N.H. 818, 903 A.2d 1003, 2006 N.H. LEXIS 110 (2006).

RESEARCH REFERENCES AND PRACTICE AIDS

Cross References.

Classification of crimes, see RSA 625:9.

Penalties for tampering with public water system, see RSA 485:31.

485:59. Appeals.

Actions of the department under RSA 485:1–4; 8, II; 31; 41–44; 46–48, or 58, I may be appealed under RSA 21-O:14.

HISTORY:

1989, 339:1. 1995, 88:3, eff. Jan. 1, 1996. 1996, 228:106, eff. July 1, 1996.

Amendments

—1996.

Substituted "department" for "division".

—1995.

Substituted "RSA 485:1– 4" for "RSA 485:1– 3", deleted "or" preceding "46–48" and inserted "or 58, I" thereafter.

485:60. Special Acts.

Nothing in this chapter shall repeal any special act applying to cities and towns.

HISTORY:

1989, 339:1, eff. Jan. 1, 1990.

Rules for Water Conservation

485:61. Rules for Water Conservation.

I. The department shall adopt rules, pursuant to RSA 541-A, for water conservation practices for water users. These rules shall strike a reasonable balance between environmental, energy, and economic impacts and be consistent with current industry standards and practices for different types of water users.

II. The water conservation rules in paragraph I of this section shall apply to all new permit applicants and applications for water withdrawals subject to the provisions of RSA 485:3, RSA 485:48, RSA 485-C:21 and section 401 of the Clean Water Act.

III. Water conservation rules shall be consistent with applicable state or federal rules and regulations.

HISTORY:

2002, 142:2, eff. July 12, 2002.

Applicability of enactment.

2002, 142:3, eff. July 12, 2002, provided:

"Water conservation rules developed under RSA 485:61 shall apply to all new water withdrawal permit applications approved under RSA 485:61, II on or after the effective date of this act [July 12, 2002]."

RESEARCH REFERENCES AND PRACTICE AIDS

References in text.

Section 401 of the Clean Water Act, referred to in par. II, is classified to 33 U.S.C.S. § 1341.

CHAPTER 485-A
WATER POLLUTION AND WASTE DISPOSAL

NOTES TO DECISIONS

Analysis

1. Constitutionality

Necessity and ultimate benefit to be gained by Water Pollution Act, as well as its constitutionality, are firmly established. Plymouth Village Fire Dist. v. Water Pollution Comm'n, 103 N.H. 169, 167 A.2d 677, 1961 N.H. LEXIS 8 (N.H. 1961). (Decided under prior law.)

2. Purpose

This chapter is essentially an act to prohibit the pollution of public waters in the interest of protecting the public health and welfare. Urie v. Franconia Paper Corp., 107 N.H. 131, 218 A.2d 360, 1966 N.H. LEXIS 135 (N.H. 1966). (Decided under prior law.)

3. Due process

To require a town to desist from discharging untreated sewage and wastes into the waters of a certain stream does not involve a taking of the property of its taxpayers without due process, where requirement is justified by fact that waters were used for bathing and recreation by the public. Shirley v. New Hampshire Water Pollution Comm'n, 100 N.H. 294, 124 A.2d 189, 1956 N.H. LEXIS 55 (N.H. 1956). (Decided under prior law.)

4. Police power

Control and elimination of water pollution is a subject clearly within scope of the police power. Shirley v. New Hampshire Water Pollution Comm'n, 100 N.H. 294, 124 A.2d 189, 1956 N.H. LEXIS 55 (N.H. 1956). (Decided under prior law.)

5. Private rights

This chapter was not intended to abrogate or suspend protection of the rights of individual landowners to be free from a private nuisance. Urie v. Franconia Paper Corp., 107 N.H. 131, 218 A.2d 360, 1966 N.H. LEXIS 135 (N.H. 1966). (Decided under prior law.)

There is nothing in this chapter to indicate a legislative intent to take away any private rights of individual landowners, to seek redress in equity to prevent pollution of a river. Urie v. Franconia Paper Corp., 107 N.H. 131, 218 A.2d 360, 1966 N.H. LEXIS 135 (N.H. 1966). (Decided under prior law.)

6. Administration and enforcement

Water supply and pollution control commission is given broad authority over the administration and enforcement of statutes designed to control water pollution and the disposal of wastes. Fenton G. Keyes Assocs. v. Water Supply & Pollution Control Comm'n, 112 N.H. 104, 289 A.2d 655, 1972 N.H. LEXIS 152 (N.H. 1972). (Decided under prior law.)

7. Pollution

When heated water discharged into surface or interstate waters increases the temperature of such water so as to render the water unfit for its normal use or to change unduly its condition, the thermal discharge is a source of "pollution" under both this chapter and RSA 72:12-a, exempting water and air pollution control facilities from taxation. Appeal of Hampton Falls, 126 N.H. 805, 498 A.2d 304, 1985 N.H. LEXIS 410 (N.H. 1985). (Decided under prior law.)

8. Statute of limitations

In an action by the State for violations of RSA ch. 482-A and RSA ch. 485-A, the doctrine of "nullum tempus occurrit regi" precluded a statute of limitations defense. The doctrine endured in New Hampshire, and the three-year general statute of limitations, RSA 508:4, I, did not expressly waive nullum tempus by making a limitations period applicable to the State. State v. Lake Winnipesaukee Resort, 159 N.H. 42, 977 A.2d 472, 2009 N.H. LEXIS 82 (N.H. 2009).

Cited:
Cited in McMullin v. Downing, 135 N.H. 675, 609 A.2d 1226, 1992 N.H. LEXIS 101 (1992).

RESEARCH REFERENCES AND PRACTICE AIDS

Cross References.
Aid to municipalities for water pollution control, see RSA 486.
Aid to public water systems for compliance with Federal Safe Drinking Water Act, see RSA 486-A.
Bond issue for municipal sewage treatment works, see RSA 33:5, 5-a–5-c.
Governmental liability for personal injury, bodily injury or property damage caused by or resulting from pollutant incidents, see RSA 507-B:9, 10.
Groundwater Protection Act, see RSA 485-C.
Local regulation of subsurface sanitary disposal systems, see RSA 147:10.
Mercury Emissions Reduction and Control Program, see RSA 125-M.
Multiple Pollutant Reduction Program, see RSA 125-O.
New Hampshire Safe Drinking Water Act, see RSA 485.
Pesticides controls, see RSA 430:28 et seq.
Water Pollution Control Compact, see RSA 484:17 et seq.

New Hampshire Code of Administrative Rules
Rules of the Department of Environmental Services—Water Supply and Pollution Control Division, Env-Ws 301.01 et seq. New Hampshire Code of Administrative Rules Annotated.
Rules of the Department of Environmental Services—Division of Water Supply and Pollution Control, Env-Ws 301.01 et seq., New Hampshire Code of Administrative Rules Annotated.

485-A:1. Declaration of Purpose.

The purpose of this chapter is to protect water supplies, to prevent pollution in the surface and groundwaters of the state and to prevent nuisances and potential health hazards. In exercising any and all powers conferred upon the department of environmental services under this chapter, the department shall be governed solely by criteria relevant to the declaration of purpose set forth in this section.

HISTORY:
1989, 339:1, eff. Jan. 1, 1990. 1996, 228:106, 108, eff. July 1, 1996.

Amendments

—1996.
Substituted "department of environmental services" for "division of water supply and pollution control" and "department" for "division".

485-A:2. Definitions.

I. "Developed waterfront property" means any parcel of land upon which stands a structure suitable for either seasonal or year-round human occupancy, where such parcel of land is contiguous to or within 200 feet of the reference line, as defined in RSA 483-B:4, XVII, of:

(a) A fresh water body, as defined in RSA 483-B:4, XVI(a);
(b) Coastal waters, as defined in RSA 483-B:4, XVI(b); or
(c) A river, as defined in RSA 483-B:4, XVI(c).

I-a. "Certificate" means a certificate of competency issued by the department stating that the operator has met the particular requirements established by the department for certification at each level of operation.

I-b. "Certification committee" means those persons designated by the commissioner, and those persons elected by the New Hampshire Water Pollution Control Association to serve as the review committee for certification of wastewater treatment plant operators.

I-c. "Commissioner" means the commissioner of the department of environmental services.

II. "Development plan" means the final map, drawing, plat or chart on which the subdivider presents his plan of subdivision to the department of environmental services for approval of planned or proposed sewage or waste disposal systems.

III. "Department" means the department of environmental services.

III-a. "Encroachment waiver" means any waiver of the rules adopted in accordance with this chapter which, if granted, would affect the ability of an owner of abutting property to fully utilize his property.

IV. "Failure" means the condition produced when a subsurface sewage or waste disposal system does not properly contain or treat sewage or causes the discharge of sewage on the ground surface or directly into surface waters, or the effluent disposal area is located in the seasonal high groundwater table.

V. "Groundwaters" shall mean all areas below the top of the water table, including aquifers, wells and other sources of groundwater.

VI. "Industrial waste" means any liquid, gaseous or solid waste substance resulting from any process of industry, manufacturing trade or business or from development of any natural resources.

VII. "Lot" means a part of a subdivision or a parcel of land which can be used as a building site or intended to be used for building purposes, whether immediate or future.

VII-a. "Operator" means:
(a) The individual who has full responsibility for the daily operation of a wastewater treatment plant or a pollution control facility;
(b) The individual normally responsible for the operations shift; or
(c) Individuals who perform important operating functions.

VIII. "Other wastes" means garbage, municipal refuse, decayed wood, sawdust, shavings, bark, lime, ashes, offal, oil, tar, chemicals and other substances other than sewage or industrial wastes, and any other substance harmful to human, animal, fish or aquatic life.

IX. "Person" means any municipality, governmental subdivision, public or private corporation, individual, partnership, or other entity.

IX-a. "Septage" means material removed from septic tanks, cesspools, holding tanks, or other sewage treatment storage units, excluding sewage sludge from public treatment works and industrial waste and any other sludge.

X. "Sewage" means the water-carried waste products from buildings, public or private, together with such groundwater infiltration and surface water as may be present.

XI. "Sewage disposal system" means any private sewage disposal or treatment system, other than a municipally owned and operated system.

XI-a. "Sludge" means the solid or semisolid material produced by water and wastewater treatment processes, excluding domestic septage; provided, however, sludge which is disposed of at solid waste facilities permitted by the department shall be considered solid waste and regulated under RSA 149-M.

XII. "Subdivider" means the legal owner or his authorized agent of a tract or parcel of land being subdivided.

XIII. "Subdivision" means the division of a tract or parcel of land into 2 or more lots, tracts, or parcels for the purpose, whether immediate or future, of sale, rent, lease, building development, or any other reason; provided, however, that sale or other conveyance which involves merely an exchange of land among 2 or more owners and which does not increase the number of owners, and on which no sewage disposal system is to be constructed shall not be deemed a subdivision for the purposes of this chapter. Without limiting the generality of the foregoing, subdivision shall include re-subdivision, and, in the case of a lot, tract or parcel previously rented or leased, the sale, condominium conveyance, or other conveyance thereof; provided however that a re-subdivision of lots in previously approved subdivisions, where lot lines are relocated to conform to necessary changes in the plans because of errors in a survey or new street, access or siting requirements, or errors in building locations, and where the lot sizes are not substantially altered shall not be deemed a subdivision for the purposes of this chapter; and provided further that a re-subdivision in which previously approved lots are grouped together to form larger lots shall not be deemed a subdivision for the purposes of this chapter. The division of a parcel of land held in common and subsequently divided into parts among the several owners shall be deemed a subdivision under this chapter.

XIV. "Surface waters of the state" means perennial and seasonal streams, lakes, ponds, and tidal waters within the jurisdiction of the state, including all streams, lakes, or ponds bordering on the state, marshes, water courses, and other bodies of water, natural or artificial.

XV. "Tract or parcel of land" means an area of land, whether surveyed or not surveyed.

XVI. "Waste" means industrial waste and other wastes.

XVI-a. "Wastewater treatment plant" means the treatment facility or group of treatment devices which treats domestic or combined domestic and industrial wastewater through alteration, alone or in combination, of the physical, chemical, or bacteriological quality of the wastewater and which dewaters and handles sludge removed from the wastewater.

XVII. "Bypass" means the intentional diversion of waste streams from any portion of the wastewater facilities.

XVIII. "Upset" means an exceptional incident in which there is unintentional and temporary noncompliance with permit effluent limitations because of factors beyond the reasonable control of the permittee.

XIX. "Wastewater facilities" means the structures, equipment, and processes required to collect, convey, and treat domestic and industrial wastes, and dispose of the effluent and sludge.

XX. "Bedroom" means a room furnished with a bed and intended primarily for sleeping, unless otherwise specified by local regulations.

XXI. "Innovative/alternative waste treatment" means treatment which differs from standardized and conventional practice, offers an advantage over such practice in a proposed application and satisfies the pollution abatement and treatment requirements for sewerage and sewage or waste treatment systems in such application.

XXII. "Biosolids" means any sludge derived from a sewage wastewater treatment facility that meets the standards for beneficial reuse specified by the department.

XXIII. "Short paper fiber" means any sludge derived from a pulp or papermill wastewater treatment facility that meets the standards for beneficial reuse specified by the department.

XXIV. "7Q10" means the lowest average flow that occurs for 7 consecutive days on an annual basis with a recurrence interval of once in 10 years on average, expressed in terms of volume per time period.

HISTORY:
    1989, 339:1. 1990, 197:1–3. 248:1. 252:9, 10. 1993, 57:1, eff. June 15, 1993. 172:1, eff. July 24, 1993. 1996, 219:1, eff. Aug. 9, 1996. 228:74–76, 105, 106, 108, eff. July 1, 1996. 1998, 102:2, 3, eff. Aug. 1, 1998. 2000, 76:3, eff. June 20, 2000. 121:1, eff. July 7, 2000. 2008, 349:2, 3, eff. January 1, 2009. 2017, 211:1, eff. September 8, 2017.

Revision note.
    Redesignated par. XVII, as added by 1990, 197:3, as par. XVI-a, pursuant to 1990, 197:9.

Codification.
    Pursuant to 1989, 339:34, former RSA 149-E:2, XVI, as added by 1989, 79:1, eff. July 30, 1989, was redesignated as par. III-a of this section.

Amendment Notes
    The 2017 amendments to this section by Ch. 211 added XXIV.

—2008.

The 2008 amendment rewrote I to the extent that a detailed comparison would be impracticable; in IV, deleted "or threatens to cause" following "sewage or causes" and substituted "directly into surface waters, or the effluent disposal area is located in the seasonal high groundwater table" for "into adjacent surface or groundwaters".

—2000.

Paragraph XIV: Chapter 76 inserted "perennial and seasonal" following "means".

Paragraphs XXII and XXIII: Added by ch. 121.

—1998.

Paragraph IX-a: Added "and any other sludge" following "industrial waste".

Paragraph XI-a: Inserted "excluding domestic septage" following "treatment processes".

—1996.

Paragraph I: Chapter 219 inserted "tidal waters or" following "200 feet of".

Paragraph I-a: Chapter 228 substituted "department" for "division".

Paragraph I-b: Chapter 228 substituted "commissioner" for "director, division of water supply and pollution control".

Paragraph I-c: Added by ch. 228.

Paragraph II: Chapter 228 substituted "department of environmental services" for "division of water supply and pollution control".

Paragraph III: Rewritten by ch. 228 to the extent that a detailed comparison would be impracticable.

Paragraph XI-a: Chapter 228 substituted "department" for "waste management division of the department of environmental services".

—1993.

Paragraph XX: Added by ch. 57.

Paragraph XXI: Added by ch. 172.

—1990.

Chapter 197 added pars. I-a, I-b, VII-a and XVII.

Chapter 248 added pars. XVII–XIX.

Chapter 252 added pars. IX-a and XI-a.

NOTES TO DECISIONS

Cited:

Cited in Gray v. First NH Banks, 138 N.H. 279, 640 A.2d 276, 1994 N.H. LEXIS 17 (1994); Cayten v. N.H. Dep't of Envtl. Servs., 155 N.H. 647, 927 A.2d 494, 2007 N.H. LEXIS 113 (2007).

485-A:3. Policies.

It is hereby declared, as a matter of legislative intent, that the department shall, in the administration and enforcement of this chapter, strive to provide that all sources of pollution within the state shall be abated within such times and to such degrees as shall be required to satisfy the provisions of state law or applicable federal law, whichever is more stringent. To the extent not inconsistent with the foregoing nor the aims of any joint state-federal permit program that may from time to time be agreed upon and in force pursuant to this chapter and applicable federal law, the department shall adhere to the following policies:

I. Insofar as practicable, the initial objective of the control program will be to obtain the installation of primary treatment (with adequate disinfection where sewage discharges are involved) for all discharges of sewage and industrial wastes.

II. The second objective will be to require the installation of secondary treatment whenever such additional treatment is necessary to protect the uses assigned to the particular stream classification.

III. The third objective, after all stream classification requirements throughout the state have been satisfied, will be to continue the program of pollution abatement by installing other forms of treatment desirable to maintain all surface waters of the state in as clean a condition as possible, consistent with available assistance funds and technological developments.

IV. Until such time as appropriate methodology and reasonable levels of financial assistance are made available, municipalities with combined sewer systems shall not be required to provide treatment facilities with capacity greater than that necessary to handle anticipated peak dry weather flows.

V. A further objective will be to advance the development and application of innovative/alternative waste treatment systems with guidelines, procedures, pilot projects, demonstration projects, community projects or in any other manner the department may elect.

HISTORY:

1989, 339:1. 1993, 172:2, eff. July 24, 1993. 1996, 228:106, eff. July 1, 1996.

Amendments

—1996.

Substituted "department" for "division" in the introductory paragraph and in par. V.

—1993.

Paragraph V: Added.

485-A:4. Duties of Department.

It shall be the duty of the department and the department is authorized:

I. To exercise general supervision over the administration and enforcement of this chapter.

II. To study and investigate all problems connected with the pollution of the surface waters or groundwaters of the state.

III. To conduct scientific experiments, investigations and research to discover economical and practical methods for the elimination, disposal or treatment of industrial wastes to control pollution of the surface waters or groundwaters of the state.

IV. To cooperate with any other public or private agency in the conduct of such experiments, investigations and research. In order to utilize fully the facilities of the state, it shall be the duty of all other state agencies to cooperate and render such assistance as may be necessary to implement the provisions of this chapter.

V. To do all necessary work relative to the establishment of a proper and reasonable classification pursuant to RSA 485-A:9.

VI. To require the filing with the department of plans and specifications of the installation of systems and devices for handling, treating, or disposing of sewage, industrial and other wastes, at least 30 days prior to the beginning of construction.

VII. To investigate and approve after making such modification as the department deems necessary to conform to the purpose of this chapter and RSA 486, any portions of the applications of those municipalities, industries, or other persons of the state as may request state or federal aid that may at any time be made available in the interest of pollution control. The commissioner of environmental services shall receive or make agreements on behalf of the state for any federal or other moneys as may be allotted for such purposes. Those who have already incurred expense in order to comply with a classification adopted by the legislature or made under RSA 485-A:11 shall be equally eligible to receive any federal or other moneys with those who have not incurred but who are required to incur expense by reason of such classification.

VIII. To confer with responsible authorities of other states relative to methods, means and measures to be employed to control pollution of interstate streams and other waters, and to submit to the legislature recommendations relative to the adoption of interstate compacts pertaining to pollution or its control on all said waters. After said compacts and agreements have been concluded by the necessary legislative and congressional action, the department shall carry out said agreements or compacts by appropriate orders provided for in either the compacts or the provisions of this chapter.

IX. To set standards of design and construction for sewerage and sewage or waste treatment systems and standards or design guidelines as the department determines to be appropriate for innovative/alternative waste treatment systems. Innovative/alternative waste treatment systems shall include solar and such other systems as shall be identified or accepted by the department. To reject, if necessary, or modify and approve as deemed necessary for the purposes of the state water pollution control program all engineering or other documents associated with the design and construction of pollution control projects and perform such other related engineering or inspectional work as will provide for proper design, construction and operation of the facilities involved, and take such other action as the department deems necessary, to maximize the effectiveness of sewerage and other pollution control facilities, both proposed and in construction. The department is authorized to purchase professional liability insurance annually in order to provide coverage in connection with resident construction engineering services which may be made available

to municipalities by the department for projects undertaken with benefit of a federal grant under the provisions of this chapter; provided, however, that no construction engineering services shall be provided to any municipality with a population of greater than 5,000 according to the office of strategic initiatives estimate for that even decade year preceding project application to the department or when the estimated project costs exceed $2,000,000. The purpose of this paragraph is to ensure the planning, construction and operation of publicly owned pollution control facilities which in the judgment of the department will produce maximum benefits with the least expenditure of federal, state and local funds.

IX-a. Any person submitting plans and specifications to the department, as provided for in this section, for the construction of sewerage systems shall pay to the department a fee of $30 for each 300 gallon per day unit of flow for the first 10,000 gallons per day of total flow for which such systems are designed and $15 for each 300 gallon per day unit of flow in excess of such amount. A fee of $200 per plan sheet shall be paid for review of pump stations, force mains, interceptors, and wastewater treatment facilities which are submitted independently of a sewer collection system. This fee shall not apply to municipalities.

IX-b. Any person submitting a request to the department, not accompanied by plans and specifications, for a permit to discharge additional sewage or industrial wastes to a municipal sewer system shall pay to the department a fee of $50. The request, accompanied by the fee, shall be submitted through, and approved by, the affected municipality. This fee shall not apply to municipalities, counties, state agencies, or school districts. These fees shall be deposited with the state treasurer as unrestricted revenue.

IX-c. Any person submitting plans and specifications to the department for the construction or installation of facilities for the pretreatment of industrial wastes shall pay to the department a permit fee of $1,000. The discharge permit request, accompanied by the plans and specifications and the fee, shall be submitted through and approved by the affected municipality. This fee shall not apply to municipalities, state agencies, or school districts. These fees shall be deposited with the state treasurer as unrestricted revenue.

X. To provide such services and technical assistance in the area of sanitary engineering as may be required by the commissioner of the department of health and human services to implement the statutory obligations imposed upon the commissioner of the department of health and human services and the rules adopted by said commissioner.

XI. To scientifically measure and monitor residual pesticides in the waters and in the aquatic resources in the waters of the state.

XII. To review, establish maximum state participation fees and modify in any other way which in the judgment of the department will promote economy and the purposes of this chapter, and following such review or modification, approve and cosign jointly with the municipality or other governmental subdivision concerned any proposed contracts or other proposed agreements or changes in contracts or agreements for engineering services related to sewerage and other pollution control facilities. Further, the department shall prescribe the contract documents to be employed and may provide for the assessment of liquidated damages for failure to complete the work within the time stipulated therefor. Except for the financial assistance available to municipalities under the provisions of RSA 486, nothing in this chapter shall be construed to place any additional financial obligation on the state, the department or its personnel.

XIII. To establish rules governing the prequalification of consulting engineers employed in the planning and construction of public water supply and pollution control projects. Any licensed engineering firm seeking initial prequalification shall pay to the department a fee of $200. Prequalification shall be renewed annually and shall be accompanied by a $50 renewal fee. These fees shall be deposited with the state treasurer as unrestricted revenue. The department is further empowered to prescribe the contract award procedures to be followed in the awarding of construction contracts involving state financial assistance.

XIV. To formulate a policy relating to long-term trends affecting the purity of the surface waters or groundwaters of the state. Insofar as practicable and necessary, a continuing program of sampling and subsequent chemical or biological analysis, or both, shall be conducted to establish patterns and reveal long-term trends to serve as a basis for formulating such policy. In conducting said program of sampling and analysis, the department is authorized to accept any assistance as may be proffered by persons that the department deems to be qualified. The department shall provide proper warning to the public by posting a sign indicating where water quality standards are not being attained as they relate to specified designated uses.

XV. To establish and prescribe physical, chemical and biological pretreatment standards to which waste must conform before discharge into the collection system or the sewage treatment facility of a municipality or other governmental entity being served by or under order to construct a public sewage treatment facility. In establishing and prescribing pretreatment standards, the department shall give consideration to the following:

(a) The treatment capabilities and operating efficiency of the facilities to which they apply.

(b) The discharge criteria applicable to the facility in order for it to conform to established water quality standards for the receiving water, as expressed in the discharge permit or compliance order issued to the municipality.

(c) Toxic effluent standards.

(d) Such standards as will prevent the discharge of any pollutant through the facility that interferes with, passes through without being rendered innocuous or is otherwise incompatible with the effective operation of the facility.

XVI. To enter into, with the consent of the governor and council, cooperative agreements with the United States Environmental Protection Agency or any other federal agency having jurisdiction in the premises relative to any joint state-federal water pollution enforcement abatement and control programs authorized by law, and involving the issuance of discharge permits.

XVI-a. To regulate the removal, transportation, and disposal of septage through administration of a permit system. As a condition of any permit issued under this chapter, the department may require payment of a reasonable fee, established by rules adopted under RSA 485-A:6, X-a. Funds collected under this paragraph shall be deposited with the treasurer as unrestricted revenue.

XVI-b. To regulate the removal, transportation, and disposal of sludge through administration of a permit system. As a condition of any permit issued under this chapter, the department may require payment of a reasonable fee, established by rules adopted under RSA 485-A:6, X-a. Funds collected under this paragraph shall be deposited with the treasurer as unrestricted revenue.

XVI-c.(a) To design and implement a program for state or independent third party sampling and testing of sludge or biosolid materials that are intended for land application. The department shall design the sampling methodology, in consultation with university of New Hampshire statisticians and sludge and biosolid experts, to provide a statistical evaluation of the contaminant levels contained in sludge or biosolids. The department shall concentrate its testing on those contaminants that pose greater risks to public health and the environment due to their toxicity, potential availability, concentration levels, or concentration uncertainty. The department shall maintain a database of testing results and prepare, in consultation with university of New Hampshire statisticians and sludge and biosolid experts, and make available to the public and the general court, a biennial report by November 1 of each year which analyses the compiled test results, including data from prior years, as appropriate. The analysis shall detail contaminant concentrations on both a statewide and generator level and shall indicate the statistical degree of certainty in the results of the analysis. The department shall attempt to present the report in terms that are understandable to the layperson including practical examples such as the probability that any given load of untested sludge exceeds a contaminant standard.

(b) The department shall establish a fee of $500, to be paid by sludge quality certificate holders by January 1 of each year. The fee shall be deposited in a special, nonlapsing sampling and analysis of sludge or biosolids samples fund, for exclusive use by the department to implement the program established in subparagraph (a).

XVI-d. To conduct on-site inspections of sludge or biosolid application sites to monitor adherence to all state and federal requirements for such activity.

XVII. To give notice by first-class mail to the city or town clerk of the municipality in which is located the point of discharge or point of potential discharge, and all adjacent municipalities located on the same receiving water as the water at the point of discharge, when an application is made for a new permit or when a permit is renewed by the department.

XVIII. To establish rules for dental offices relative to the use of environmentally appropriate disposal equipment or methods for amalgam waste to trap and dispose of mercury.

HISTORY:
1989, 339:1. 1990, 3:86, 87. 248:2. 252:11. 1991, 240:1. 371:1. 1993, 172:3, eff. July 24, 1993. 1995, 310:182, 183, eff. Nov. 1, 1995. 1996, 228:106, eff. July 1, 1996. 1998, 102:4, eff. Aug. 1, 1998. 230:2, eff. June 24, 1998. 2000, 326:1, 2, eff. June 30, 2000. 2002, 96:3, eff. Jan. 1, 2003. 240:2, eff. at 12:01 a.m., Jan. 1, 2003. 2003, 319:9, eff. July 1, 2003. 2004, 257:44, eff. July 1, 2004. 2015, 259:9, 10, eff. July 1, 2015. 2017, 156:64, eff. July 1, 2017.

Revision note.
Substituted "division" for "division of water supply and pollution control" in the second sentence of par. IX, in two places in the first sentence of par. IX-a and in the first and second sentences of par. XII in view of RSA 485-A:2, III.

Deleted a comma following "available" in the third sentence of par. IX to correct a grammatical error.

Codification.
Pursuant to 1989, 339:34, the amendment to former RSA 149:4, XIX by 1989, 405:1, eff. Aug. 4, 1989, was incorporated in par. XVII of this section and former RSA 149:4, IX-a, as added by 1989, 408:17, eff. Aug. 4, 1989, was redesignated as par. IX-a of this section.

Amendment Notes
The 2017 amendments to this section by Ch. 156 substituted "office of strategic initiatives" for "office of energy and planning" in the second to the last sentence of IX.

—2015.
The 2015 amendment by chapter 259, §§ 9 and 10, deleted the former fourth sentence of paragraph XIV, which read: "The department shall make a biennial report of its findings to the governor and council, the senate environment committee, and the house resources, recreation, and development committee"; and substituted "a biennial report" for "an annual report" in the fourth sentence of XVI-c(a).

—2004.
Paragraph IX: Substituted "office of energy and planning" for "office of state planning and energy programs".

—2003.
Paragraph IX: Substituted "office of state planning and energy programs" for "office of state planning".

—2002.
Paragraph XVIII: Added by ch. 96.
Chapter 240 inserted "or methods" preceding "for amalgam waste".

—2000.
Paragraph XVI-c: Rewritten to the extent that a detailed comparison would be impracticable.
Paragraph XVI-d: Added.

—1998.
Paragraph XVI-a: Chapter 102 deleted "and sludge" following "disposal of septage" in the middle of the first sentence.
Paragraph XVI-b: Added by ch. 102.
Paragraph XVI-c: Added by ch. 230.

—1996.
Substituted "department" for "division" wherever it appeared.

—1995.
Paragraph X: Substituted "commissioner of the department of health and human services" for "director, division of public health services, department of health and human services" and "director of public health services" respectively and "commissioner" for "director" following "adopted by said".

—1993.
Paragraph IX: Added "and standards or design guidelines as the division determines to be appropriate for innovative/alternative waste treatment systems" following "sewage or waste treatment systems" in the first sentence, added the second sentence, and deleted "1985" preceding "office of state planning" and substituted "estimate for that even decade year preceding project application to the division or" for "estimates, nor" thereafter in the fourth sentence.

—1991.
Paragraph IX-a: Chapter 240 deleted "and sewage or waste treatment" following "sewerage", inserted "the first 10,000 gallons per day of total flow for" preceding "which such systems" and added "and $15 for each 300 gallon per day unit of flow in excess of such amount" following "designed" in the first sentence and added the second sentence.
Paragraph XIV: Chapter 371 rewrote the fourth sentence and added the fifth sentence.

—1990.
Chapter 3 added pars. IX-b and IX-c and the second through fourth sentences in par. XIII.
Chapter 248 amended par. XVII generally.
Chapter 252 added par. XVI-a.

Severability of 1995 amendment.
1995, 310, which amended this section, was subject to a severability clause. See 1995, 310:186.

Construction of 1995 amendment.
1995, 310:187, eff. Nov. 1, 1995, provided:
"Nothing in this act is intended to, nor shall it be construed as, mandating or assigning any new, expanded, or modified program or responsibility for any political subdivision in violation of part I, article 28-a of the constitution of the state of New Hampshire."

Pilot program; random testing of sludge or biosolids.
1997, 209:1, eff. July 18, 1997, provided:
"The commissioner of the department of environmental services shall implement a program of random on-site testing and inspec-

tion of sludge or biosolid samples to be used for any land application by any person obtaining a permit under RSA 485-A:4, XVI-a, provided that inspection shall not be required before the issuance of a permit. The procedures for random inspection and testing of sludge or biosolid samples on a site shall include an inspection for any setback or area requirements of a site for land application and may include testing for such pollutants as heavy metals, toxins, dioxins, and polychlorinated biphenyl, as determined in rules adopted by the commissioner pursuant to RSA 541-A. The department shall develop a database of inspection results and shall monitor adherence to state and federal requirements for the spreading of sludge or biosolids."

Funding of program; fee established.

1997, 209:2, eff. July 18, 1997, provided:

"The program of random inspection and testing of sludge or biosolids established in section 1 of this act shall be funded by a fee of $500 assessed to all sludge quality certification holders as defined in rules adopted by the commissioner. Such fee shall be payable to the department no later than January 1, 1998 by all certification holders as of the effective date of this act and any person certified by the commissioner prior to December 31, 1997. Any person granted sludge quality certification on or after January 1, 1998 shall be assessed the $500 fee upon receipt of certification by the department."

Termination of pilot program.

1997, 209:3, eff. July 18, 1997, provided:

"The pilot program and fee established by this act [which is noted above], shall terminate on June 30, 1998, unless otherwise authorized by the legislature."

NOTES TO DECISIONS

Analysis

1. Scope of authority
2. Fees
3. Contracts
4. Review

1. Scope of authority

Commission is authorized to exercise general supervision over water pollution and the disposal of waste, and this applies to municipalities as well as to individuals and corporations. State v. Goffstown, 100 N.H. 131, 121 A.2d 317, 1956 N.H. LEXIS 13 (N.H. 1956). (Decided under prior law.)

2. Fees

Water supply and pollution control commission was within its authority when it established a maximum fee for design phase of town sewerage and pollution control project beyond which the state would not participate in the project. Fenton G. Keyes Assocs. v. Water Supply & Pollution Control Comm'n, 112 N.H. 104, 289 A.2d 655, 1972 N.H. LEXIS 152 (N.H. 1972). (Decided under prior law.)

The legislature intended that in negotiations between engineers and the water supply and pollution control commission over fees, the competitive forces of the open market are to have full play. Fenton G. Keyes Assocs. v. Water Supply & Pollution Control Comm'n, 112 N.H. 104, 289 A.2d 655, 1972 N.H. LEXIS 152 (N.H. 1972). (Decided under prior law.)

3. Contracts

Engineers prequalified by the water supply and pollution control commission have no right to obtain any particular contract. Fenton G. Keyes Assocs. v. Water Supply & Pollution Control Comm'n, 112 N.H. 104, 289 A.2d 655, 1972 N.H. LEXIS 152 (N.H. 1972). (Decided under prior law.)

4. Review

The executive function by which the water supply and pollution control commission negotiates with an engineer regarding a fee and reaches a conclusion regarding a fee is not reviewable. Fenton G. Keyes Assocs. v. Water Supply & Pollution Control Comm'n, 112

N.H. 104, 289 A.2d 655, 1972 N.H. LEXIS 152 (N.H. 1972). (Decided under prior law.)

Cited:

Cited in Town of Tilton v. State, 137 N.H. 463, 629 A.2d 791, 1993 N.H. LEXIS 101 (1993).

RESEARCH REFERENCES AND PRACTICE AIDS

New Hampshire Code of Administrative Rules

Rules of the Department of Environmental Services—Division of Water, Env-Wr 601–604, New Hampshire Code of Administrative Rules Annotated.

Rules of the Department of Environmental Services—Water Quality and Quantity Programs, Env-Wq 701–714, New Hampshire Code of Administrative Rules Annotated.

485-A:5. Pretreatment Standards.

I. After the effective date of any pretreatment standards established and prescribed by the department pursuant to RSA 485-A:4, XV, no person shall discharge into the collection system or the sewage treatment facility of any municipality or other governmental entity being served by or under orders to construct a public sewage treatment facility, nor discharge to the surface waters of the state if such person will be served by the public sewage treatment facility upon construction of such facility, any waste that does not comply with such pretreatment standards.

II. In setting a date for conformance to pretreatment standards, the department may establish compliance schedules providing a reasonable time for compliance and may give due consideration to expected in-service dates of public sewage and waste treatment facilities not in existence at the time of establishment of pretreatment standards applicable to such facilities. Any such compliance schedule shall be consistent with the purposes and requirements of federal law.

III. No municipality or other governmental entity owning or controlling any public sewage and waste treatment facility shall permit the discharge of any waste to such facility which does not comply with pretreatment standards established by the department.

IV. Pretreatment standards or effluent limits adopted by a municipality as part of its sewer use ordinance or industrial pretreatment program and approved by the department shall be enforceable by the department as pretreatment standards established under RSA 485-A:4, XV and rules adopted under RSA 485-A:6.

V. The department of environmental services may require the installation and operation of monitoring programs by persons subject to pretreatment standards to ensure adherence to such standards.

HISTORY:

1989, 339:1, eff. Jan. 1, 1990. 1996, 228:106, 108, eff. July 1, 1996.

Amendments

—1996.

Paragraphs I–IV: Substituted "department" for "division" wherever it appeared.

Paragraph V: Substituted "department of environmental services" for "division of water supply and pollution control".

485-A:5-a. Operator Certification Required.

The department shall certify operators of wastewater treatment plants. Wastewater treatment plants shall be operated only by certified operators.

HISTORY:

1989, 81:1. 1990, 197:4, eff. June 26, 1990. 1996, 228:106, eff. July 1, 1996.

Codification.

This section, which was originally enacted as RSA 149:4-b, was redesignated pursuant to 1989, 339:34 and "division" was substituted for "division of water supply and pollution control" in view of RSA 485-A:2, III, as added by 1989, 339:1.

Amendments

—1996.

Substituted "department" for "division".

—1990.

Substituted "wastewater treatment plants" for "pollution control facilities" in the first and second sentences.

RESEARCH REFERENCES AND PRACTICE AIDS

Cross References.

Procedure for certification of wastewater treatment plant operators, see RSA 485-A:7-a et seq.

485-A:5-b. Municipal Responsibility.

I. Each municipality shall either provide, or assure access to, a department of environmental services approved septage facility or a department approved alternative option for its residents.

II. For the purposes of paragraph I, "provide, or assure access to" shall mean a written agreement with a recipient facility, or department approved alternative option, indicating that the recipient facility agrees to accept septage generated in that municipality. The municipality shall consider providing sufficient annual capacity equal to the number of households with septic multiplied by the average septic tank capacity of 1,000 gallons divided by the average septage pumpout frequency of 5 years.

HISTORY:

1990, 252:12, eff. April 28, 1990. 1996, 228:108, eff. July 1, 1996. 2005, 98:2, eff. Aug. 14, 2005.

Effective date of 2005 amendment.

2005, 98:4, I, eff. Aug. 14, 2005, provided: "RSA 485-A:5-b, II as inserted by section 2 of this act shall take effect January 1, 2006."

Amendments

—2005.

Rewritten to the extent that a detailed comparison would be impracticable.

—1996.

Substituted "department of environmental services" for "division of water supply and pollution control".

Commissioner's report.

2005, 98:3, eff. August 14, 2005, provided: "The commissioner of the department of environmental services shall report to the legislature on the current compliance status of all municipalities under the revised terms of RSA 485-A:5-b, on November 1, 2006 and November 1 each year thereafter through 2010."

485-A:5-c. Notice of Septage or Sludge Spreading.

I. No person shall spread septage or sludge as defined in RSA 485-A:2 before providing all property owners abutting the spreading site with written notice of the intended date and location of the spreading. Such notice shall be provided by publishing a notice at least 14 days before the intended date of the first spreading of septage or sludge each year in a newspaper of general circulation in the town or city.

II. The notice shall include the names, addresses, and telephone numbers of the following:

(a) The applicant, if applicable.

(b) The generator of the sludge, if applicable.

(c) The person responsible for managing the activities on-site, if different from the applicant under subparagraph (a).

(d) The landowner, if not given under subparagraph (a) or (c).

III. A copy of such notice shall be posted continually on the entrances to the site beginning 3 days prior to the application and ending 3 days after the application.

HISTORY:

1998, 60:1, eff. July 11, 1998.

485-A:5-d. Land Application of Sludge.

Sludge or biosolids which are to be land applied in New Hampshire shall not exceed the maximum concentrations for specific chemical contaminants contained in the rules of the department, or the rules or regulations of the state in which the sludge was generated, whichever are more stringent.

HISTORY:

1998, 230:2, eff. June 24, 1998.

485-A:6. Rulemaking.

The commissioner shall adopt rules, under RSA 541-A, after public hearing, relative to:

I. The classification system required by RSA 485-A:9.

II. Requirements under RSA 485-A:4, VI.

III. Requirements under RSA 485-A:4, IX and establishing the methodology and review process for approval of innovative/alternative wastewater treatment systems.

IV. The fees and contract documents required under RSA 485-A:4, XII.

V. The prequalification and contract award procedures required under RSA 485-A:4, XIII.

VI. The standards required under RSA 485-A:4, XV.

VI-a. Procedures and criteria for requesting, reviewing, and granting certifications under RSA 485-A:12, III and IV.

VII. The required information and prescribed conditions needed to implement the program described in RSA 485-A:13, I(a).

VIII. The requirements for a permit under RSA 485-A:17.

IX. The conditions for a camp license as required by RSA 485-A:24, and the safety standards in camps described in RSA 485-A:25.

X. The safety standards for swimming pools and bathing places required by RSA 485-A:26.

X-a. The requirements for permits under RSA 485-A:4, XVI-a and XVI-b.

XI-a. The contents of the written notification required in RSA 485-A:13, I(c).

XI-b. Certification of operators of wastewater treatment plants and revocation and suspension of such certificates as provided in RSA 485-A:7-d.

XI-c. The location, extent, and duration of the standards specified in RSA 485-A:8, III for the temporary partial use areas provided for in RSA 485-A:8, II.

XII. [Repealed.]

XIII. The disposal of dental office waste under RSA 485-A:4, XVIII.

XIV. Dissolved oxygen concentration water quality standards under RSA 485-A:8, II and II-a.

XV. Water quality standards consistent with RSA 485-A:8 and as required by the Clean Water Act.

HISTORY:
1989, 339:1. 1990, 197:5. 248:4. 252:13. 1991, 371:2. 1993, 172:4, eff. July 24, 1993. 1996, 228:110, eff. July 1, 1996. 1998, 102:5, eff. Aug. 1, 1998. 2002, 96:4, eff. Jan. 1, 2003. 2008, 337:3, eff. September 5, 2008. 2017, 211:3, eff. September 8, 2017.

Revision note.
Redesignated par. XI-a as added by 1990, 197:5 as par. XI-b pursuant to 1990, 197:9.

Codification.
Pursuant to 1989, 339:34, the amendment to former RSA 149:4, XVII by 1989, 81:2, eff. June 30, 1989, was incorporated in the text of this section.

Amendment Notes
The 2017 amendments to this section by Ch. 211 added XIV and XV.

—2008.
The 2008 amendment added VI-a.

—2002.
Paragraph XIII: Added.

—1998.
Paragraph X-a: Added "and XVI-b" following "XVI-a".

—1996.
Substituted "commissioner" for "division" in the introductory paragraph.

—1993.
Paragraph III: Added "and establishing the methodology and review process for approval of innovative/alternative wastewater treatment systems" following "RSA 485-A:4, IX".

—1991.
Paragraph XI-c: Added.

—1990.
Chapter 197 added par. XI-a.
Chapter 248 added par. XI-a.
Chapter 252 added par. X-a.

Repeal of par. XII.
Paragraph XII of this section provided that it would be deemed repealed on July 1, 1987 unless replaced by a later legislative enactment.

485-A:7. State Guarantee.

In view of the general public benefits resulting from the elimination of pollution from the public waters of the state, the governor and council are authorized in the name of the state of New Hampshire to guarantee unconditionally, but at no time in excess of the total aggregate sum for the entire state of $50,000,000, the payment of all or any portion, as they may find to be in the public interest, of the principal of and interest on any bonds or notes issued by any municipality, town, city, county or district for construction of sewerage systems, sewage treatment and disposal plants, or other facilities necessary, required or desirable for pollution control, and the full faith and credit of the state are pledged for any such guarantee. The outstanding amount of principal and interest on such bonds and notes, the payment of which has been guaranteed by the state under the provisions of this section, shall at no time exceed the amount of $50,000,000. The state's guarantee shall be endorsed on such bonds or notes by the state treasurer; and all notes or bonds issued with state guarantee shall be sold at public sealed bidding to the highest bidder. Any and all such bids may be rejected and a sale may be negotiated with the highest bidder. In the event of default in payment of any such notes or bonds, the state may recover any losses suffered by it by action against the municipality, town, city, county or district as provided in RSA 530. Provided, further, that in accordance with RSA 35-A:29, the foregoing requirement for public sealed bidding shall not be applicable to any bonds or notes or both so guaranteed which are sold to the New Hampshire municipal bond bank, and any bonds or notes or both so guaranteed may be sold to the New Hampshire municipal bond bank at private sale in accordance with the provisions of RSA 35-A.

HISTORY:
1989, 339:1. 1991, 179:2, eff. May 27, 1991. 1999, 234:1, eff. Sept. 7, 1999. 2008, 49:1, eff. July 1, 2008.

Amendments

—2008.
The 2008 amendment substituted "$50,000,000" for "$175,000,000" in the first and second sentences.

—1999.
Substituted "$175,000,000" for "$250,000,000" in the first and second sentences.

—1991.
Substituted "$250,000,000" for "$225,000,000" in the first and second sentences.

NOTES TO DECISIONS

Public benefit
This section recognizes that the elimination of pollution from public waters of state results in general public benefits and provides that bonds or note issued for a sewage system or disposal plant may be guaranteed unconditionally by state. State v. Goffstown, 100 N.H. 131, 121 A.2d 317, 1956 N.H. LEXIS 13 (N.H. 1956). (Decided under prior law.)

Wastewater Operator Certification

RESEARCH REFERENCES AND PRACTICE AIDS

New Hampshire Code of Administrative Rules
Rules of the Department of Environmental Services—Water Supply and Pollution Control Division, Env-Ws 901.01 et seq. New Hampshire Code of Administrative Rules Annotated.

485-A:7-a. Application; Special Fund.

I. Any operator of a wastewater treatment plant seeking certification or to increase his level of certification shall file an application with the certification committee at least 6 weeks prior to the next examination date on a form provided by the department.

II. All applications shall be accompanied by a $50 fee to cover department expenses for conducting the certification program. All fees shall be deposited with the state treasurer and deposited in a special nonlapsing wastewater plant operator certification fund to be used by the department for the administration of this subdivision and for the operation of the department-owned Wastewater Plant Operator Training Center.

III. Any applicant failing the examination shall be allowed one retest at the same certification level at no additional cost to the applicant.

HISTORY:
1990, 197:6, eff. June 26, 1990. 1996, 228:106, eff. July 1, 1996.

Amendments

—1996.
Substituted "department" for "division" in par. I and in the second sentence of par. II.

485-A:7-b. Examinations.

The department shall prepare written examinations to determine the knowledge, ability, and judgment of operators. Such examinations shall be administered in accordance with rules adopted by the department pursuant to RSA 485-A:6.

HISTORY:
1990, 197:6, eff. June 26, 1990. 1996, 228:106, eff. July 1, 1996.

Amendments

—1996.
Substituted "department" for "division".

485-A:7-c. Issuance of Certificates.

I. Upon satisfactory completion by an applicant of the established requirements, the department shall issue to the applicant a suitable certificate designating the applicant's competency. The certificate shall indicate the level of operation for which the operator is qualified. The certificate shall remain in effect for 2 years from the date of issuance.

II. Certificates shall be renewed biennially and shall be accompanied by a $50 renewal fee, which shall be deposited pursuant to RSA 485-A:7-a, II. If the renewal fee is not submitted within 90 days of the certificate's expiration date, the certified individual's name shall be removed from the current status and the certificate shall be deemed expired. The department shall charge a late fee of 50 percent of the renewal fee in addition to the renewal fee if the renewal is late.

III. Certificates may be issued, upon payment of the $50 fee, without examination, for a comparable classification to any person actively seeking employment in New Hampshire who holds a certificate issued by the appropriate certification agency of any federal, state, interstate, territorial, or other jurisdiction if, in the judgment of the committee, the certification requirements of the jurisdiction granting such certification do not conflict with the department's rules and are not less stringent than rules adopted under this subdivision. The fee shall be deposited pursuant to RSA 485-A:7-a, II.

HISTORY:
1990, 197:6, eff. June 26, 1990. 1996, 228:106, eff. July 1, 1996. 1997, 261:7, eff. July 1, 1997.

Amendments

—1997.
Paragraph II: Added the second and third sentences.

—1996.
Substituted "department" for "division" in par. I and "department's" for "division's" in par. III.

485-A:7-d. Revocation.

The department may suspend or revoke the certificate of an operator under rules adopted pursuant to RSA 485-A:6.

HISTORY:
1990, 197:6, eff. June 26, 1990. 1996, 228:106, eff. July 1, 1996.

Amendments

—1996.
Substituted "department" for "division".

Classification of Waters

485-A:8. Standards for Classification of Surface Waters of the State.

It shall be the overall goal that all surface waters attain and maintain specified standards of water quality to achieve the purposes of the legislative classification. For purposes of classification there shall be 2 classes or grades of surface waters as follows:

I. Class A waters shall be of the highest quality and shall contain not more than either a geometric mean based on at least 3 samples obtained over a 60-day period of 47 Escherichia coli per 100 milliliters, or greater than 153 Escherichia coli per 100 milliliters in any one sample; and for designated beach areas shall contain not more than a geometric mean based on at least 3 samples obtained over a 60-day period of 47 Escherichia coli per 100 milliliters, or 88 Escherichia coli per 100 milliliters in any one sample; unless naturally occurring. There shall be no discharge of any sewage or wastes into waters of this classification. The waters of this classification shall be considered as being potentially acceptable for water supply uses after adequate treatment.

II. Class B waters shall be of the second highest quality and shall have no objectionable physical characteristics and shall contain not more than either a geometric mean based on at least 3 samples obtained over a 60-day period of 126 Escherichia coli per 100 milliliters, or greater than 406 Escherichia coli per 100 milliliters in any one sample; and for designated beach areas shall contain not more than a geometric mean based on at least 3 samples obtained over a 60-day period of 47 Escherichia coli per 100 milliliters, or 88 Escherichia coli per 100 milliliters in any one sample; unless naturally occurring. There shall be no disposal of sewage or waste into said waters except those which have received adequate treatment to prevent the lowering of the biological, physical, chemical or bacteriological characteristics below those given above, nor shall such disposal of sewage or waste be inimical to aquatic life or to the maintenance of aquatic life in said receiving waters. The pH range for said waters shall be 6.5 to 8.0 except when due to natural causes. The commissioner shall adopt rules, under RSA 541-A, relative to dissolved oxygen water quality standards in a manner consistent with Environmental Protection Agency guidance on dissolved oxygen water criteria published pursuant to section 304(a) of the Clean Water Act, and other relevant scientific information. Any stream temperature increase associated with the discharge of treated sewage, waste or cooling water, water diversions, or releases shall not be such as to appreciably interfere with the uses assigned to this class. The waters of this classification shall be considered as being acceptable for fishing, swimming and other recreational purposes and, after adequate treatment, for use as water supplies. Where it is demonstrated to the satisfaction of the department that the class B criteria cannot reasonably be met in certain surface waters at all times as a result of combined sewer overflow events, temporary partial use areas shall be established by rules adopted under RSA 485-A:6, XI-c, which meet, as a minimum, the standards specified in paragraph III. The commissioner shall not calculate nutrient discharge limits for aquatic life and human health criteria based on 7Q10 flow or such other flow criteria more restrictive than 7Q10.

II-a. The commissioner shall adopt rules, under RSA 541-A, relative to dissolved oxygen water quality standards for tidal and saline waters in a manner consistent with Environmental Protection Agency guidance on dissolved oxygen water criteria published pursuant to section 304(a) of the Clean Water Act, and other relevant scientific information.

III. The waters in temporary partial use areas established under paragraph II shall be free from slick, odors, turbidity, sludge deposits, and surface-floating solids of unreasonable kind or quantity, shall contain not less than 5 parts per million of dissolved oxygen; shall have a hydrogen ion concentration within the range of pH 6.0 to 9.0 except when due to natural causes; and shall be free from chemicals and other materials and conditions inimical to aquatic life or the maintenance of aquatic life. These criteria shall apply during combined sewer overflow discharges and up to 3 days following cessation of said discharge. At all other times the standards and uses specified in paragraph II shall apply.

IV. Notwithstanding anything contained in this chapter, the department in submitting classifications relating to interstate waters to the New England Interstate Water Pollution Control Commission for review and approval, as provided for under the terms of Article V of the compact whereby the interstate commission was created by RSA 484, shall submit such classifications in accordance with the standards of water quality as currently adopted by said interstate water pollution control commission provided, however, that the standards for any classification thus submitted for review and approval shall not be less than, nor exceed the standards of the classification duly adopted by the General Court as provided for in RSA 485-A:9 or 10.

V. Tidal waters utilized for swimming purposes shall contain not more than either a geometric mean based on at least 3 samples obtained over a 60-day period of 35 enterococci per 100 milliliters, or 104 enterococci per 100 milliliters in any one sample, unless naturally occurring. Those tidal waters used for growing or taking of shellfish for human consumption shall, in addition to the foregoing requirements, be in accordance with the criteria recommended under the National Shellfish Program Manual of Operation, United States Department of Food and Drug Administration.

VI. Notwithstanding anything contained in this chapter, the commissioner shall have the authority to adopt such stream classification criteria as may be issued from time to time by the federal Environmental Protection Agency or its successor agency insofar as said criteria may relate to the water uses specified in RSA 485-A:8, I and II, provided, however, that the criteria thus issued shall not result in standards that are less than nor exceed the standards of the classification duly enacted by the general court as provided for in RSA 485-A:9 or 485-A:10.

VII. All tests and sampling for the purposes of examination of waters shall be performed and carried out in a reasonable manner and whenever practicable, in accordance with the commonly accepted scientific method as selected by the department. The waters in each classification shall satisfy all the provisions of all lower classifications. The minimum treatment for the lowest classification shall be as follows:

(a) For sewage, secondary treatment and disinfection as necessary to comply with water quality standards.

(b) For industrial wastes and combined sewer overflows, such treatment as the department shall determine. Appeal from any such determination shall be in the manner provided for in RSA 21-O:14.

VIII. In prescribing minimum treatment provisions for thermal wastes discharged to interstate waters, the department shall adhere to the water quality requirements and recommendations of the New Hampshire fish and game department, the New England Interstate Water Pollution Control Commission, or the United States Environmental Protection Agency, whichever requirements and recommendations provide the most effective level of thermal pollution control.

IX. Subject to the provisions of RSA 485-A:13, I(a), the fish and game department may use rotenone or similar compounds in the conduct of its program to reclaim the public waters of the state for game fishing.

HISTORY:
1989, 339:1. 1991, 371:3–5, eff. Aug. 31, 1991. 1996, 228:77, 106, 110, eff. July 1, 1996. 1998, 63:1, eff. July 11, 1998. 2017, 211:2, eff. September 8, 2017.

Revision note.
Substituted "RSA 485-A:8, I, II, and III" for "RSA 485-A:3, I, II, and III" in the first sentence of par. VI to correct an error in the reference.

Amendment Notes
The **2017 amendments** to this section by **Ch. 211,** in II, deleted "shall contain a dissolved oxygen content of at least 75 percent of saturation" following "physical characteristics" in the

first sentence, added the fourth sentence, and added the last sentence; and added II-a.

—1998.
Deleted the last sentence in par. II and the third sentence in par. III.

—1996.
Substituted "department" for "division" in the sixth sentence of par. II, preceding "in submitting" in par. IV, in the first sentence of the introductory paragraph of par. VII, in the first sentence of par. VII(b) and in par. VIII, "commissioner" for "division" following "chapter, the" in par. VI and "RSA 21-O:14" for "RSA 21-O:7, IV" in the second sentence of par. VII(b).

—1991.
Added the first sentence of the introductory paragraph.
Paragraph I: Rewrote the first sentence and substituted "adequate treatment" for "disinfection" following "after" in third sentence.
Paragraph II: Rewrote the first sentence, inserted "biological" preceding "physical" and substituted "aquatic" for "fish" preceding "life" in two places in the second sentence, inserted "water diversions, or releases" following "cooling water" in the fourth sentence, substituted "fishing, swimming" for "bathing" following "acceptable for" in the fifth sentence, and added the sixth and seventh sentences.
Paragraphs III, V, and VII: Rewritten to the extent that a detailed comparison would be impracticable.
Paragraph VI: Substituted "I and II" for "I, II, and III" following "RSA 485-A:8" and "485-A:10" for "10" following "RSA 485-A:9".

Pleasant Lake in Deerfield, New Hampshire; Classification Changed to Class A.
2010, 44:1, eff. May 18, 2010, provided: "On and after the effective date of this act, the surface waters of Pleasant Lake in Deerfield and its tributaries in New Hampshire shall be classified in accordance with the provisions of RSA 485-A:8, as Class A waters."

NOTES TO DECISIONS

Debt limitation
Legislature has recognized imperative necessity for prevention of water pollution under this section by providing that cost shall not be subject to ordinary limitations upon public debt. State v. Goffstown, 100 N.H. 131, 121 A.2d 317, 1956 N.H. LEXIS 13 (N.H. 1956). (Decided under prior law.)

RESEARCH REFERENCES AND PRACTICE AIDS

Cross References.
Shellfish certificate fees, see RSA 143:22-a.

New Hampshire Bar Journal.
Mechanics of the State certification provisions under the Federal Water Pollution Control Act, 18 N.H. B.J. 142 (Dec. 1976).

485-A:9. Classification Procedure.

The department shall follow the procedures provided in this section and recommend to the legislature a classification for all streams, lakes, ponds, and tidal waters or section of such water.

I. A notice setting forth the contemplated classification of any stream, lake, pond, tidal water or section of such water, shall be published for 3 successive weeks in a newspaper circulated within the county or counties in which the surface water in question is situated. The last notice shall be published at least 7 days before the hearing date. The notice shall stipulate the time and place where a public hearing on the contemplated classification shall be held.

II. A public hearing shall be conducted by the department, at which hearing all interested parties shall be heard relative to their views on classification of the area or areas in question.

III. Following the hearings the department shall review the pertinent evidence and data presented.

IV. After such hearing and review of evidence the department shall determine which classification is for the best interest of the public giving consideration to the health, industrial, economic, geographical and social factors involved.

HISTORY:

1989, 339:1, eff. Jan. 1, 1990. 1996, 228:106, eff. July 1, 1996.

Amendments

—1996.

Substituted "department" for "division" in the introductory paragraph and in pars. II–IV.

NOTES TO DECISIONS

Analysis

1. Public benefit
2. Reasonableness

1. Public benefit

Classification of a stream for the purpose of fixing the limit of pollutability is not unreasonable where its waters are used for bathing and recreation by the public, although some individuals may also be especially benefited. Shirley v. New Hampshire Water Pollution Comm'n, 100 N.H. 294, 124 A.2d 189, 1956 N.H. LEXIS 55 (N.H. 1956). (Decided under prior law.)

2. Reasonableness

Fact that tax rate would be increased does not demonstrate that commission's order is unreasonable or confiscatory. State v. Goffstown, 100 N.H. 131, 121 A.2d 317, 1956 N.H. LEXIS 13 (N.H. 1956). (Decided under prior law.)

485-A:10. Reclassification Procedure.

After adoption of a classification for any surface water or section of such water by the legislature, the department may, by its own motion, or upon the petition of not less than 100 persons, legal inhabitants of the county or counties in which the surface water in question is situated, reinvestigate the conditions of pollution in said surface water or section of such water by following the procedure above outlined, and may at any time make recommendation to the legislature for reclassification.

HISTORY:

1989, 339:1, eff. Jan. 1, 1990. 1996, 228:106, eff. July 1, 1996.

Amendments

—1996.

Substituted "department" for "division".

NOTES TO DECISIONS

Relief from orders

This section provides a method of relief from order of water pollution commission if order works a hardship. Plymouth Village Fire Dist. v. Water Pollution Comm'n, 103 N.H. 169, 167 A.2d 677, 1961 N.H. LEXIS 8 (N.H. 1961); State v. Goffstown, 100 N.H. 131, 121 A.2d 317, 1956 N.H. LEXIS 13 (N.H. 1956); Shirley v. New Hampshire Water Pollution Comm'n, 100 N.H. 294, 124 A.2d 189, 1956 N.H. LEXIS 55 (N.H. 1956). (Decided under prior law.)

485-A:11. Public Waters Classified.

All lakes and ponds defined as public waters of the state by RSA 271:20 shall be classified by the passage of this section as not less than Class B, as set forth in RSA 485-A:8 relating to standards for classification of surface waters of the state.

HISTORY:

1989, 339:1, eff. Jan. 1, 1990. 1999, 232:2, eff. Jan. 1, 2000.

Amendments

—1999.

Deleted "and 21" following "RSA 271:20".

Enforcement

485-A:12. Enforcement of Classification.

I. After adoption of a given classification for a stream, lake, pond, tidal water, or section of such water, the department shall enforce such classification by appropriate action in the courts of the state, and it shall be unlawful for any person or persons to dispose of any sewage, industrial, or other wastes, either alone or in conjunction with any other person or persons, in such a manner as will lower the quality of the waters of the stream, lake, pond, tidal water, or section of such water below the minimum requirements of the adopted classification. If the department shall set a time limit for abatement of pollution under paragraph II, and it becomes apparent at any time during the compliance period that full compliance with the adopted classification will not be attained by the end of such period due to the failure of any person to take action reasonably calculated to secure abatement of the pollution within the time specified, the department shall notify such person or persons in writing. If such person or persons shall fail or neglect to take appropriate steps to comply with the classification requirements within a period of 30 days after such notice, the department shall seek appropriate action in the courts of the state.

II. If, after adoption of a classification of any stream, lake, pond, or tidal water, or section of such water, including those classified by RSA 485-A:11, it is found that there is a source or sources of pollution which lower the quality of the waters in question below the minimum requirements of the classification so established, the person or persons responsible for the discharging of such pollution shall be required to abate such pollution within a time to be fixed by the department. If such pollution is of municipal or industrial origin, the time limit set by the department for such abatement shall be not less than 2 years nor more than 5 years. For good cause shown, the department may from time to time extend any time limit established under this paragraph. Any determination by the department under this paragraph shall be subject to appeal as provided for in RSA 485-A:19.

III. No activity, including construction and operation of facilities, that requires certification under section 401 of the Clean Water Act and that may result in a discharge, as that term is applied under section 401 of the Clean Water Act, to surface waters of the state may commence unless the department certifies that any such discharge complies with the state surface water quality standards applicable to the classification for the receiving surface water body. The department shall provide its response to a request for certification to the federal agency or authority responsible for issuing the license, permit, or registration that requires the certification under section 401 of the Clean Water Act. Certification shall include any conditions on, modifications to, or monitoring of the proposed activity necessary to provide assurance that the proposed discharge complies with applicable surface water quality standards. The department may enforce compliance with any such conditions, modifications, or monitoring requirements as provided in RSA 485-A:22.

IV. No activity that involves surface water withdrawal or diversion of surface water that requires registration under RSA 488:3, that does not otherwise require the certification required under paragraph III, and which was not in active operation as of the effective date of this paragraph, may commence unless the department certifies that the surface water withdrawal or diversion of surface water complies with state surface water quality standards applicable to the classification for the surface water body. The certification shall include any conditions on, modifications to, or monitoring of the proposed activity necessary to provide reasonable assurance that the proposed activity complies with applicable surface water quality standards. The department may enforce compliance with any such conditions, modifications, or monitoring requirements as provided in RSA 485-A:22.

HISTORY:

1989, 339:1, eff. Jan. 1, 1990. 1996, 228:106, eff. July 1, 1996. 2008, 337:2, eff. September 5, 2008. 2009, 26:1, eff. July 7, 2009.

Amendments

—2009.

The 2009 amendment, in the first sentence of IV, added "surface" following "involves" and "surface water" or variants.

—2008.

The 2008 amendment added III and IV.

—1996.

Substituted "department" for "division" throughout the section.

Purpose of 2008 amendment.

2008, 337:1, eff. September 5, 2008, provided: "This act provides for technical review and certification of proposed activities affecting surface waters to ensure that water quality standards appropriate to the legislative classification of the waters are attained. The act makes New Hampshire statutes consistent with section 401 of the Clean Water Act for activities requiring federal permits or licenses, and extends the review to activities requiring registration under RSA 488:3."

NOTES TO DECISIONS

Analysis

1. Postponement of action
2. Private nuisance

1. Postponement of action

Under this section, the commission must enforce the legislative classification of streams by appropriate action, and if every town is permitted to postpone action on commission's orders in hope of something justifying inaction, the purpose of the statute would be defeated. Plymouth Village Fire Dist. v. Water Pollution Comm'n, 103 N.H. 169, 167 A.2d 677, 1961 N.H. LEXIS 8 (N.H. 1961). (Decided under prior law.)

2. Private nuisance

While Laws of 1959, 243:2 provide a 10-year period for abatement of pollution of the Pemigewasset River the language of RSA 149:3, IV was not intended to sanction the continuance of a private nuisance in the meantime, or to suspend injunctive relief calculated to cause abatement of such nuisance. Urie v. Franconia Paper Corp., 107 N.H. 131, 218 A.2d 360, 1966 N.H. LEXIS 135 (N.H. 1966). (Decided under prior law.)

It is doubtful if the Legislature has constitutional power to permit the continuance of a private nuisance in the Pemigewasset River since such legislation would constitute taking private property for a nonpublic purpose. Urie v. Franconia Paper Corp., 107 N.H. 131, 218 A.2d 360, 1966 N.H. LEXIS 135 (N.H. 1966). (Decided under prior law.)

Plaintiffs, not as members of the public, but as landowners specifically damaged by a private nuisance occasioned by the pollution of the Pemigewasset River by discharge of industrial wastes therein, were entitled to injunctive relief. Urie v. Franconia Paper Corp., 107 N.H. 131, 218 A.2d 360, 1966 N.H. LEXIS 135 (N.H. 1966). (Decided under prior law.)

RESEARCH REFERENCES AND PRACTICE AIDS

References in text.

Section 401 of the Clean Water Act, referred to in par. III, is classified to 33 U.S.C.S. § 1341.

485-A:13. Water Discharge Permits.

I.(a) It shall be unlawful for any person or persons to discharge or dispose of any sewage or waste to the surface water or groundwater of the state without first obtaining a written permit from the department of environmental services. Applications for permits shall be made upon forms prescribed by the department of environmental services and shall contain such relevant information as the department of environmental services may require. The department of environmental services shall include in such permits effluent limitations, which may be based upon economic and technological factors, upon the classification enacted by the legislature, upon the projected best use of the surface water downstream or upon the requirements of the Federal Water Pollution Control Act as amended from time to time, and all regulations, guidelines and standards promulgated thereunder, whichever provides the most effective means to abate pollution. The department of environmental services may also prescribe such other reasonable conditions as may be necessary or desirable in order to fulfill the purpose of this chapter or applicable federal law. Such permits may contain, in the case of sources not in compliance with such effluent limitations at the time the permit is issued, compliance schedules, including interim requirements necessary or desirable in order to fulfill the purposes or requirements of this chapter, and any such compliance schedules may be imposed without regard to the time limits for abatement of pollution referred to in RSA 485-A:12, II and shall be consistent with the purposes and requirements of applicable federal law. The department of environmental services may prescribe a monitoring program to be performed by the applicant with periodic reports to the department of environmental services, including, where appropriate in terms of the nature of the effluent, continuous monitoring. Permits shall be issued for a fixed term, not to exceed 5 years. The department of environmental services may revise, modify or suspend in whole or in part or terminate any permit, following hearing, upon a finding that just cause exists for such action. Further, whenever in its judgment the purposes of this chapter will be best served, the department of environmental services may require as a condition to the granting of such permits that either the ownership and operation of the collection and treatment facilities involved be vested in the municipality or any subdivision thereof in which the system is located, if said municipality by legal action agrees thereto, or such other reasonable conditions as will ensure continuous and continuing operation and maintenance of the facilities. No permit shall be granted to utilize the entire assets of the surface water, or in any other case in which the department of environmental services determines that the grant of a permit would be inconsistent with the purposes of this chapter. Any determination by the department of environmental services under this paragraph shall be subject to appeal as provided for in RSA 485-A:19.

(b) Notwithstanding any other provision of law, no permit to discharge sewage or waste shall be issued authorizing any of the following discharges:

(1) The discharge of any radiological, chemical or biological warfare agent or high level radioactive waste.

(2) Any discharge into navigable waters which the secretary of the army of the United States acting through the chief of engineers determines would substantially impair anchorage and navigation.

(3) Any discharge to which the regional administrator of the United States Environmental Protection Agency, or his successor in jurisdiction, has objected in writing pursuant to any right to object each provided such official in section 402(d) of the Federal Water Pollution Control Act, as amended from time to time; provided, that this subparagraph and subparagraph (2) above shall not preclude the department of environmental services or any other person from availing itself of the judicial review of any such objection, or any determination by the secretary of the army, available under applicable federal law.

(4) Any discharge from a point source which is in conflict with a plan or amendment to such plan approved pursuant to section 208(b) of the Federal Water Pollution Control Act, as amended from time to time.

(c) Any person responsible for a bypass or upset at a wastewater facility shall give immediate notice of the bypass or upset to all public or privately owned water systems drawing water from the same receiving water and located within 20 miles downstream of the point of discharge. The permittee shall maintain a list of persons, and their telephone numbers, who are to be notified immediately by telephone. In addition, written notification, which shall be postmarked within 3 days of the bypass or upset, shall be sent to such persons.

II. On application of the department of environmental services, the superior court or any justice of such court, in term time, or in vacation may enjoin any act in violation of any lawful order of the department of environmental services.

III. In the interim between the effective date of classification legislation hereafter enacted affecting any surface water of the state or section of such water, and the time limit for abatement of pollution set thereafter either by the department of environmental services under RSA 485-A:12, II or by the legislature, it shall be unlawful for person or persons to dispose of any sewage or waste into said surface water of the state in excess of the maximum quantity or of a different character, than that being disposed of during the period of one year prior to the effective date of such legislative classification without first obtaining written permission from the department of environmental services.

HISTORY:
1989, 339:1. 1990, 248:3, eff. June 27, 1990. 1996, 228:108, eff. July 1, 1996.

Codification.
Pursuant to 1989, 339:34, former RSA 149:8, III(c), as added by 1989, 405:2, eff. Aug 4, 1989, was redesignated as par. I(c) of this section.

Amendments

—1996.
Substituted "department of environmental services" for "division of water supply and pollution control" throughout par. I(a) and in pars. I(b)(3), II and III.

—1990.

Paragraph I(c): Rewritten to the extent that a detailed comparison would be impracticable.

NOTES TO DECISIONS

Analysis

1. Scope of liability
2. Enforcement of orders

1. Scope of liability

Owner of land leased to another for use as a facility for processing chemical waste who did not participate in the unlicensed discharge of hazardous wastes into the surface water and groundwater of the site was not guilty of violating this section since liability is not extended to mere nonparticipatory landowners. United States v. Ottati & Goss, Inc., 630 F. Supp. 1361, 1985 U.S. Dist. LEXIS 13023 (D.N.H. 1985). (Decided under prior law.)

2. Enforcement of orders

This section authorizes the enforcement of an order of the commission by an injunction, contempt or by fines authorized by RSA 149:19, and superior court may use its equitable powers to enforce the principal provisions of any decree that it may issue. State v. Goffstown, 100 N.H. 131, 121 A.2d 317, 1956 N.H. LEXIS 13 (N.H. 1956). (Decided under prior law.)

Cited:

Cited in N.H. Dep't of Envtl. Servs. v. Mottolo, 155 N.H. 57, 917 A.2d 1277, 2007 N.H. LEXIS 26 (2007).

RESEARCH REFERENCES AND PRACTICE AIDS

New Hampshire Code of Administrative Rules

Rules of the Department of Environmental Services—Water Quality and Quantity Programs, Env-Wq 715, New Hampshire Code of Administrative Rules Annotated.

References in text.

The Federal Water Pollution Control Act, referred to in subpar. I(a), is classified to 33 U.S.C.S. §§ 1251 et seq.

Section 402(d) of the Federal Water Pollution Control Act, referred to in subpar. I(b)(3), is classified to 33 U.S.C.S. § 1342(d).

Section 208(b) of the Federal Water Pollution Control Act, referred to in subpar. I(b)(4), is classified to 33 U.S.C.S. § 1288(b).

485-A:13-a. Groundwater Permit Fee.

Any person, except for state, and local governments, including counties, and political subdivisions, issued a groundwater permit under RSA 485-A:13, I(a) shall pay to the department a fee of $1,000 for the 5-year permit. Said fee shall be for processing such permits, including any necessary inspections and monitoring performed by the department in enforcing the terms and conditions of such permits. The fees shall be deposited with the state treasurer as unrestricted revenue.

HISTORY:

1990, 3:89, eff. Feb. 20, 1990. 1996, 228:106, eff. July 1, 1996.

Amendments

—1996.

Substituted "department" for "division" throughout the section.

485-A:14. Prohibited Acts.

I. The lawful owner of any petroleum-powered vehicle or petroleum container that becomes partially or completely submerged in the surface waters of the state shall remove the vehicle or container from the water within 48 hours or as soon thereafter as safety and weather conditions permit. Petroleum-powered vehicles include, but are not limited to, cars, trucks, motorcycles, snowmobiles, motorized boats, off highway recreational vehicles, all terrain vehicles, construction equipment, trains, and airplanes. Petroleum containers include, but are not limited to, drums, barrels, tanks, pails, cans, jugs, or equipment which contains oil.

II. The lawful owner of the submerged vehicle or container shall notify the department of environmental services in accordance with RSA 146-A, and the department shall investigate any possible contamination and ensure the safe removal of the vehicle or container from the body of water involved. Any partially or completely submerged vehicle or petroleum container shall be presumed to be discharging oil into the surface waters of the state and shall be subject to the reporting, removal, and strict liability requirements of RSA 146-A.

III. The lawful owner of a vehicle shall notify the department of safety, division of state police, if any person is injured or killed in an incident involving a submerged vehicle.

IV. If the owner refuses or fails to remove a submerged vehicle or container as required by paragraph I, or if no owner can be identified, the department of environmental services may contract for the removal of the vehicle or container in question. The owner of the submerged vehicle or container shall be strictly liable for the costs of removing the vehicle or container and the costs of the investigation, containment, cleanup, removal, and corrective measures associated with the discharge. The cost shall be recoverable by the state in an action of debt brought by the attorney general in the name of the state. If the owner of the vehicle or container has been identified, the contractor who removes the vehicle or container shall impound the recovered vehicle or container, at the expense of the owner. No contractor shall release the vehicle or container to the owner until informed by the department that all costs incurred by the state have been paid by the owner of the vehicle or container or that the impounded vehicle or container otherwise may be released. Upon receiving approval from the department to release the impounded vehicle or container, the contractor shall dispose of the impounded vehicle or container in accordance with RSA 262:36-a. If no owner can be identified after reasonable efforts, the contractor who removes the vehicle or container shall deliver the vehicle or container to an appropriate salvage yard. Neither the state nor the contractor shall be liable for such delivery of the vehicle or container to anyone subsequently claiming ownership of the vehicle or container.

V.(a) Any person who fails to remove a submerged or partially submerged vehicle or container, as required by paragraph I, shall be guilty of a violation. Agents of the department of safety, division of state police, or any police officer of the municipality in which the vehicle or container is submerged may issue citations for a violation of this section and issue fines of $500 for each day the vehicle remains in the water. No citation or fine so issued shall preclude the department of environmental services from taking action pursuant to subparagraph (b).

(b) The department of environmental services may take action against any person who fails to remove a submerged or partially submerged vehicle or container, as required by paragraph I, in accordance with RSA 485-A:22. No action initiated by the department of environmental services under RSA 485-A:22 shall preclude the issuance of citations and fines pursuant to subparagraph (a).

VI. Unless otherwise provided in this chapter, any person who knowingly fails to remove a submerged or partially submerged vehicle or container, as required by paragraph I, shall be guilty of a class B felony if the surface water is the source, or a tributary to a source, from which the domestic water supply of a city, town, or village is taken, in whole or in part.

HISTORY:

1989, 339:1, eff. Jan. 1, 1990. 1996, 228:108, eff. July 1, 1996. 2006, 254:4, eff. August 4, 2006. 2009, 190:1, eff. January 1, 2010. 2011, 224:271, 272, eff. July 1, 2011. 2014, 141:1, eff. August 15, 2014.

Amendment Notes

—2014.

The 2014 amendment rewrote IV; added the V(a) designation; in V(a), substituted "of the municipality in which the vehicle or container is submerged" for "having jurisdiction over the water body" in the second sentence and added the last sentence; and added V(b).

—2011.

The 2011 amendment substituted "state police" for "safety services" in III and the second sentence of V.

—2009.

The 2009 amendment added VI.

—2006.

Rewritten to the extent that a detailed comparison would be impracticable.

—1996.

Paragraph II: Substituted "department of environmental services" for "division of water supply and pollution control".

485-A:15. Penalties.

I. It shall be unlawful for any person to put or place, or cause to be put or placed into a surface water of the state or on the ice over such waters, or on the banks of such waters, any solid waste as defined in RSA 149-M or hazardous waste as defined in RSA 147-A, including but not limited to bottles, glass, crockery, cans, scrap metal, junk, paper, garbage, tires, old automobiles or parts thereof, trees or parts thereof, or similar litter.

II. For any violation of this section any authorized member or agent of the department of environmental services shall order the immediate removal of material involved in the violation, by the person responsible for the material in question.

III. If the person or persons responsible for a violation of paragraph I refuse or fail to obey the order of any authorized member or agent of the department of environmental services, the department of environmental services or authorized member or agency may contract for the removal of the material in question and the cost of the removal shall be recoverable by the state in an action of debt brought by the attorney general in the name of the state.

IV. Any person who recklessly violates paragraph I shall be guilty of a misdemeanor if a natural person, or guilty of a felony if any other person.

V. Any person who purposely or knowingly violates paragraph I shall be guilty of a class B felony.

HISTORY:

1989, 339:1, eff. Jan. 1, 1990. 1996, 228:108, eff. July 1, 1996. 2009, 190:2, 3, eff. January 1, 2010.

Amendments

—2009.

The 2009 amendment, in I, added "solid waste as defined in RSA 149-M or hazardous waste as defined in RSA 147-A, including but not limited to" and "or parts thereof" following "trees"; rewrote IV to the extent that a detailed comparison would be impracticable; and added V.

—1996.

Substituted "department of environmental services" for "division of water supply and pollution control" in par. II and in two places in par. III.

485-A:16. Emergency.

If the department finds that an emergency has arisen from failure of or casualty to facilities for the control of pollution, the department may, if it finds that the best interests of the public will not unduly suffer, authorize any person for a reasonable time to discharge sewage or other wastes into surface waters or groundwaters, although such discharge would have the effect of lowering the quality of such waters below the adopted classification.

HISTORY:

1989, 339:1, eff. Jan. 1, 1990. 1996, 228:106, eff. July 1, 1996.

Amendments

—1996.

Substituted "department" for "division" throughout the section.

485-A:17. Terrain Alteration.

I. Any person proposing to dredge, excavate, place fill, mine, transport forest products or undertake construction in or on the border of the surface waters of the state, and any person proposing to significantly alter the characteristics of the terrain, in such a manner as to impede the natural runoff or create an unnatural runoff, shall be directly responsible to submit to the department detailed plans concerning such proposal and any additional relevant information requested by the department, at least 30 days prior to undertaking any such activity. The operations shall not be undertaken unless and until the applicant receives a permit from the department. The department shall have full authority to establish the terms and conditions under which any permit issued may be exercised, giving due consideration to the circumstances involved and the purposes of this chapter, and to adopt such rules as are reasonably related to the efficient administration of this section, and the purposes of this chapter. Nothing contained in this paragraph shall be construed to modify or limit the duties and authority conferred upon the department under RSA 482 and RSA 482-A.

II. The department shall charge a fee for each review of plans, including project inspections, required under this section. The fee shall be based on the extent of contiguous area to be disturbed. Except for RSA 483-B:9, the fee for plans encompassing an area of at least 100,000 square feet but less than 200,000 square feet shall be $1,250. For the purposes of RSA 483-B:9, the fee for plans encompassing an area of at least 50,000 square feet but less than 200,000 square feet shall be $1,250. An additional fee of $500 shall be assessed for each additional area of up to 100,000 square feet to be disturbed. No permit shall be issued by the department until the fee required by this paragraph is paid. All fees required under this paragraph shall be paid when plans are submitted for review and shall be deposited in the terrain alteration fund established in paragraph II-a.

II-a. There is hereby established the terrain alteration fund into which the fees collected under paragraph II shall be deposited. The fund shall be a separate, nonlapsing fund, continually appropriated to the department for the purpose of paying all costs and salaries associated with the terrain alteration program.

II-b. In processing an application for permits under RSA 485-A:17:

(a) Within 50 days of receipt of the application, the department shall request any additional information required to complete its evaluation of the application, together with any written technical comments the department deems necessary. Any request for additional information shall specify that the applicant submit such information as soon as practicable and shall notify the applicant that if all of the requested information is not received within 120 days of the request, the department shall deny the application.

(b) If the department requests additional information pursuant to subparagraph (a), the department shall, within 30 days of the department's receipt of the information:

(1) Approve the application in whole or in part and issue a permit; or

(2) Deny the application and issue written findings in support of the denial; or

(3) Extend the time for rendering a decision on the application for good cause and with the written agreement of the applicant.

(c) If no request for additional information is made pursuant to subparagraph (b), the department shall, within 50 days of receipt of the application:

(1) Approve the application, in whole or in part and issue a permit; or

(2) Deny the application, and issue written findings in support of the denial; or

(3) Extend the time for rendering a decision on the application for good cause and with the written agreement of the applicant.

(d)(1) The time limits prescribed by this paragraph shall supersede any time limits provided in any other provision of law. If the department fails to act within the applicable time frame established in subparagraphs (b) and (c), the applicant may ask the department to issue the permit by submitting a written request. If the applicant has previously agreed to accept communications from the department by electronic means, a request submitted electronically by the applicant shall constitute a written request.

(2) Within 14 days of the date of receipt of a written request from the applicant to issue the permit, the department shall:

(A) Approve the application, in whole or in part, and issue a permit; or

(B) Deny the application and issue written findings in support of the denial.

(3) If the department does not issue either a permit or a written denial within the 14-day period, the applicant shall be deemed to have a permit by default and may proceed with the project as presented in the application. The authorization provided by this subparagraph shall not relieve the applicant of complying with all requirements applicable to the project, including but not limited to requirements established in or under this section and RSA 485-A relating to water quality.

(4) Upon receipt of a written request from an applicant, the department shall issue written

confirmation that the applicant has a permit by default pursuant to subparagraph (d)(3), which authorizes the applicant to proceed with the project as presented in the application and requires the work to comply with all requirements applicable to the project, including but not limited to requirements established in or under this section and RSA 485-A relating to water quality. 295:

(e) The time limits under this paragraph shall not apply to an application from an applicant that has previously been found in violation of this chapter pursuant to RSA 485-A:22-a or an application that does not otherwise comply with the department's rules relative to the permit application process.

(f) The department may extend the time for rendering a decision under subparagraphs (b)(3) and (c)(3), without the applicant's agreement, on an application from an applicant who previously has been determined, after the exhaustion of available appellate remedies, to have failed to comply with this section or any rule adopted or permit or approval issued under this section, or to have misrepresented any material fact made in connection with any activity regulated or prohibited by this section, pursuant to an action initiated under RSA 485-A:22. The length of such an extension shall be no longer than reasonably necessary to complete the review of the application, and shall not exceed 30 days unless the applicant agrees to a longer extension. The department shall notify the applicant of the length of the extension.

(g) The department may suspend review of an application for a proposed project on a property with respect to which the department has commenced an enforcement action against the applicant for any violation of this section, RSA 482-A, RSA 483-B, or RSA 485-A:29–44, or of any rule adopted or permit or approval issued pursuant to this section, RSA 482-A, RSA 483-B, or RSA 485-A:29–44. Any such suspension shall expire upon conclusion of the enforcement action and completion of any remedial actions the department may require to address the violation; provided, however, that the department may resume its review of the application sooner if doing so will facilitate resolution of the violation. The department shall resume its review of the application at the point the review was suspended, except that the department may extend any of the time limits under this paragraph and its rules up to a total of 30 days for all such extensions. For purposes of this subparagraph, "enforcement action" means an action initiated under RSA 482-A:13, RSA 482-A:14, RSA 482-A:14-b, RSA 483-B:18, RSA 485-A:22, RSA 485-A:42, or RSA 485-A:43.

II-c. Beginning October 1, 2007 and each fiscal quarter thereafter, the department shall submit a quarterly report to the house and senate finance committees, the house resources, recreation, and economic development committee, and the senate energy, environment, and economic development committee relative to administration of the terrain alteration review program.

II-d. All permits issued, except for projects covered by paragraph II-e, pursuant to this section shall be valid for a period of 5 years. Requests for extensions of such permits may be made to the department. The department shall grant an extension of up to 5 additional years, provided the applicant demonstrates all of the following:

(a) The permit for which extension is sought has not expired prior to the date on which a written extension request from the permittee is received by the department.

(b) The permit for which extension is sought has not been revoked or suspended without reinstatement.

(c) Extension would not violate a condition of statute or rule.

(d) Surface water quality will continue to be protected as under the original permit.

(e) The project is proceeding towards completion in accordance with plans and other documentation referenced by the permit.

(f) If applicable, any inspection reports have been completed and submitted as required by the permit.

(g) The permit has not previously been extended, unless the subdivision plat or site plan associated with the permit has been deemed substantially complete by the governing municipal planning board in accordance with RSA 674:39, II, in which case subsequent extensions of the permit are allowed.

II-e. A permit issued under this section that is associated with the ongoing excavation or mining of materials from the earth shall not expire for the life of the project identified in the permit application, provided that the permit holder submits a written update of the project's status every 5 years from the date of the permit issuance using a form obtained from the department as specified in department rules.

III. Normal agricultural operations shall be exempt from the provisions of this section. The department may exempt other state agencies from the permit and fee provisions of this section provided that each such agency has incorporated appropriate protective practices in its projects which are substantially equivalent to the requirements established by the department under this chapter.

IV. Timber harvesting operations shall be exempt from the fee provisions of this section. Timber harvesting operations shall be considered in compliance with this section and shall be issued a permit by rule provided such operations are in accordance with procedures prescribed in the Best Management Practices for Erosion Control on Timber Harvesting Operations in New Hampshire, published by the department of natural and cultural resources, and provided that the department of revenue administration's intent to cut form is signed.

V. Trail construction operations for the purposes of modifying existing biking and walking trails shall be exempt from the provisions of this section. Such operations shall be considered in compliance with this section and shall be issued a general permit by rule provided such operations are implemented by a non-profit organization, municipality, or government entity, are limited to a disturbed area no more than 12 feet in width, and are in accordance with procedures prescribed in the Best Management Practices For Erosion Control During Trail Maintenance and Construction, published by the department of natural and cultural resources, bureau of trails in 2004.

HISTORY:
1989, 339:1. 1992, 157:3, eff. Jan. 1, 1993. 1996, 228:106, 109, eff. July 1, 1996. 228:106, 109, eff. July 1, 1996. 2003, 224:5, eff. July 1, 2003. 2005, 32:1, eff. July 9, 2005. 2007, 263:30, eff. July 1, 2007 [see note regarding effective date of par. II-b below]. 2009, 208:3, eff. September 13, 2009. 2010, 295:8–10, eff. September 11, 2010. 2012, 148:1, eff. August 6, 2012. 2017, 156:14, eff. July 1, 2017.

Codification.
Pursuant to 1989, 339:34, the amendment to former RSA 149:8-a by 1989, 190:1, eff. May 22, 1989, was incorporated in the text of this section.

Effective date of 2007 amendment.
2007, 263:176, IV, provided that par. II-b, as added by section 30 of the act shall take effect on January 1, 2008.

Amendment Notes
The 2017 amendments to this section by Ch. 156 substituted "natural and cultural resources" for "resources and economic development" in the second sentences of IV and V.

—2012.
The 2012 amendment added II-d and II-e.

—2010.
The 2010 amendment added "the application in whole or in part" in II-b(b)(1); substituted "and issue written findings in support of the denial" for "in whole or in part" in II-b(b)(2); substituted "rendering a decision on the application" for "response" in II-b(b)(3); rewrote II-b(c), which formerly read: "If no request for additional information is made pursuant to subparagraph (b), the department shall, within 50 days of receipt of the application whole or in part"; rewrote II-b(d) to the extent that a detailed comparison would be impracticable; added II-b(f) and II-b(g); and made a related change.

—2009.
The 2009 amendment added V.

—2007.
Paragraph II: Substituted "$1,250" for "$500" following "feet shall be" in the third and fourth sentences, "$500" for "$200" preceding "shall be" in the fifth sentence and substituted "terrain alteration fund established in paragraph II-a" for "treasury as unrestricted funds" following "deposited in the" at the end of the seventh sentence and added subpars. II-a–II-c.

—2005.
Rewrote former par. III as present pars. III and IV.

—2003.
Paragraph II: Substituted "$500" for "$100" in the first and second sentences, and "$200" for "$100" in the third sentence.

—1996.
Substituted "department" for "division" throughout the section and "department" for "division of water resources" preceding "under RSA 482" in the fourth sentence of par. I.

—1992.
Paragraph II: Added "except for RSA 483-B:9" preceding "the fee" in the third sentence and added the fourth sentence.

NOTES TO DECISIONS

Cited:
Cited in Greenland Conservation Comm'n v. N.H. Wetlands Council, 154 N.H. 529, 913 A.2d 776, 2006 N.H. LEXIS 195 (2006); Cayten v. N.H. Dep't of Envtl. Servs., 155 N.H. 647, 927 A.2d 494, 2007 N.H. LEXIS 113 (2007).

485-A:18. Investigation and Inspection; Records.

I. Any authorized member or agent of the department may enter any land or establishment for the purpose of collecting information that may be necessary to the purposes of this chapter and no owner of such establishment shall refuse to admit any such member or employee.

II. The department, its employees and authorized agents shall at reasonable times have access to any records and monitoring equipment and shall have the authority to sample effluents of any person subject to RSA 485-A:13, I(a) and RSA 485-A:5. Upon written request of the department, such person shall provide to the department such information pertaining to any activities of such person to which this chapter applies as the department may reasonably require. Any information obtained pursuant to this section or under this chapter shall be available to the public at the offices of the department, subject to paragraph III.

III. Any other provisions of law notwithstanding, upon a showing satisfactory to the department by any person that any record, report, or information or any particular part thereof, to which the department has access, if made public would divulge methods or processes entitled to protection as trade secrets of such person, the department shall consider such record, report, information or particular part thereof confidential, and it shall thereafter not be disclosed to the public. All financial information shall be considered confidential for purposes of this chapter. Nothing in this section shall preclude the department from transmitting any such confidential information to any agency of the United States having jurisdiction over water pollution, provided that such agency is authorized by law to maintain the confidentiality of such information and agrees to maintain the confidentiality of any such information. In no case, however, shall effluent data, standards or limitations, names or addresses of permit applicants or permittees, nor permit applications or permits be considered confidential information.

HISTORY:
1989, 339:1, eff. Jan. 1, 1990. 1996, 228:106, eff. July 1, 1996.

Amendments

—1996.
Substituted "department" for "division" throughout the section.

485-A:19. Review of Orders.

The procedure for rehearings and appeal shall be that prescribed by RSA 21-O:14.

HISTORY:
1989, 339:1, eff. Jan. 1, 1990.

485-A:20. Summons; Oath.

The department shall have power to subpoena witnesses and administer oaths in any proceeding or examination instituted before or conducted by it, and to compel the production of any account books, contracts, records, documents, memoranda and papers of any kind necessary to the purposes of this chapter.

HISTORY:
1989, 339:1, eff. Jan. 1, 1990. 1996, 228:106, eff. July 1, 1996.

Amendments

—1996.
Substituted "department" for "division".

485-A:21. Witnesses; Perjury.

Witnesses summoned before the department shall be paid the same fee as witnesses summoned to appear before the superior court, and such summons issued by any justice of the peace shall have the same effects as though issued for appearance in court. No person so testifying shall be exempt from prosecution or punishment for any perjury committed by him in his testimony.

HISTORY:
1989, 339:1, eff. Jan. 1, 1990. 1996, 228:106, eff. July 1, 1996.

Amendments

—1996.
Substituted "department" for "division" in the first sentence.

RESEARCH REFERENCES AND PRACTICE AIDS

Cross References.
Fees of witnesses in superior court, see RSA 516:16.
Perjury, see RSA 641:1.

485-A:22. Penalties and Other Relief; Failure to Provide Facility.

I. Any person who willfully or negligently violates any provision of this subdivision or RSA 485-A:4–6; or any rule of the department adopted pursuant to this subdivision or RSA 485-A:4–6 or any condition or limitation in a permit issued under this subdivision or RSA 485-A:4–6; or who knowingly makes any material false statement, representation, or certifi-cation in any application, record, report, plan, or other document required to be filed or maintained pursuant to this subdivision or RSA 485-A:4–6 or pursuant to a rule adopted by the department under this subdivision or RSA 485-A:4–6 or who knowingly makes any such statement, representation, or certi-fication in connection with any permit issued under this subdivision or RSA 485-A:4–6; or who know-ingly renders inaccurate, falsifies, or tampers with any monitoring device or method required under this subdivision or RSA 485-A:4–6 or rule of the department adopted under this subdivision or RSA 485-A:4–6 or required in connection with any permit issued under this subdivision or RSA 485-A:4–6; or who knowingly fails, neglects, or refuses to obey any lawful order of the department, shall, notwithstand-ing the provisions of RSA title LXII, be punished by a fine of not more than $25,000 for each day of such violation or imprisoned for not more than 6 months or both.

II. Any person who shall violate any provisions of this subdivision or RSA 485-A:4–6, or any lawful regulation of the department issued pursuant to this subdivision or RSA 485-A:4–6, or any condition or limitation in a permit issued under this subdivision or RSA 485-A:4–6, or who shall fail, neglect, or refuse to obey any order lawfully issued pursuant to this subdivision or RSA 485-A:4–6, shall be subject to a civil penalty not to exceed $10,000 per day of such violation.

III. The department shall issue a written cease and desist order against any discharge or act in violation of this subdivision or RSA 485-A:4–6 or lawful regulation of the department made under them or any condition of any permit lawfully issued by the department, and any such discharge or act may be enjoined by the superior court upon applica-tion of the attorney general, whether the court is in term time or vacation. Municipalities shall comply with such orders pursuant to RSA 38:25.

III-a. Municipalities may apply to a justice of the superior court for injunctive relief against existing or impending violations of RSA 485-A:17, or any rule or order issued under that section. The municipality shall give notice of any such action to the attorney general and the commissioner of environmental ser-vices, who may take such steps as they deem neces-sary to ensure uniform statewide enforcement, in-cluding but not limited to joining the action, assuming sole prosecution of the action, or, as of right dismissing the action without prejudice. Such notice shall be given at least 30 days prior to the commencement of any such action, unless more immediate action is necessary to prevent irreparable environmental damage or other serious public harm, in which case such notice shall be given as soon as practicable, but in no event later than the date of commencement of the action. This paragraph shall not be construed to affect, in any manner, existing authority of municipalities to act based upon the provisions of other statutes or local ordinances.

IV. The written cease and desist order issued pursuant to the provisions of paragraph III shall be recorded by the department in the registry of deeds for the county in which the property is situated and, upon recordation, said order shall run with the land; provided, however, that an appropriate description of the land involved including the accurate name of the owner of the land shall be incorporated in the cease and desist order. No fee shall be charged for recording such an administrative order; however, the fee for discharge of any such order shall be the same as for the discharge of a real estate property.

V. The commissioner of environmental services, after notice and hearing pursuant to RSA 541-A, may impose an administrative fine not to exceed $2,000 for each offense upon any person who violates any provision of this subdivision or, RSA 485-A:4–6, any rule adopted under this subdivision or RSA 485-A:4–6, or any permit issued under the authority of this subdivision or RSA 485-A:4–6. Rehearings and appeals from a decision of the commissioner under this paragraph shall be in accordance with RSA 541. Any administrative fine imposed under this section shall not preclude the imposition of further penalties under this chapter. The proceeds of administrative fines levied pursuant to this paragraph shall be deposited by the department in the general fund. The commissioner shall adopt rules, under RSA 541-A, relative to:

(a) A schedule of administrative fines which may be imposed under this paragraph for violations of this chapter, rules adopted under this chapter, and permits issued under this chapter, as provided above.

(b) Procedures for notice and hearing prior to the imposition of an administrative fine.

V-a. Upon receipt of information by the department that a municipality has not complied with RSA 485-A:5-b relative to septage disposal, the department shall issue an order directing said municipality to provide or assure access to an approved septage disposal facility not later than 180 calendar days following issuance of the order. Any municipality to whom such an order is directed may appeal in accordance with RSA 21-O:14.

V-b. If any municipality fails to comply with an order under paragraph V-a, it shall be subject to an administrative fine pursuant to paragraph V. Each day of continuous violation shall constitute a separate offense. The department shall take the following steps:

(a) The department shall conduct an investigation of opportunities for joint action with other municipalities, the availability of private facilities, and possible facility sites within the municipality.

(b) The department shall report findings to the precinct and municipality, and seek local agreement to an acceptable solution to the septage problem.

(c) If no agreement is reached within 60 calendar days after the findings are delivered, the department shall schedule and hold a public hearing in the municipality. The hearing shall be held to solicit alternative septage disposal solutions for the municipality. Notice of the hearing shall be posted in 2 or more public places in the municipality for at least 14 calendar days before it is held, and shall be published in a newspaper of local circulation, at least twice, not less than 10 days prior to the hearing date.

(d) If no agreement is reached within 45 calendar days after the hearing, the department shall either order the municipality to participate in an existing or planned approved facility, or shall recommend that land within the municipality be taken by eminent domain for the establishment of an approved facility.

(e) Before land is taken by eminent domain, the department shall hold a public hearing in the municipality. Such hearing shall be noticed pursuant to the provisions of subparagraph (c).

(f) If the department determines that land shall be taken, the department shall institute eminent domain proceedings.

(g) The department shall be responsible for the facility's design and construction.

V-c. If land is taken for construction of a facility:

(a) The property shall be held in the name of the state and shall not be taxed.

(b) Upon completion, the facility shall be operated by the municipality in accordance with the facility plan.

(c) At the time of the taking, the department shall certify to the commissioner of revenue administration the costs of establishing the facility. The certification shall be revised when the facility is complete to reflect actual costs, including land, buildings, equipment, administration, planning, consultants, and any other necessary costs.

(d) The commissioner of revenue administration shall assess the costs on the municipality over a 20-year period. Each annual assessment shall include the interest on any debt incurred by the state for this purpose. The assessment shall be made as provided in RSA 21-J:15 and RSA 81.

(e) When all costs and interest are paid, the property shall be deeded to the municipality, or in the case of an unincorporated town or unorganized place, to the county.

VI. The provisions of RSA 651:1 shall not apply to offenses under this chapter.

HISTORY:

1989, 339:1. 1990, 252:14, 17. 1991, 340:4. 1995, 217:7, eff. Jan. 1, 1996. 1996, 228:78, 106, eff. July 1, 1996. 1997, 206:8, eff. July 1, 1997. 1999, 232:3, 4, eff. Jan. 1, 2000. 2013, 247:6, eff. see contingent note set out below.

Contingent 2013 amendment.

2013, 247:15, eff. July 24, 2013, provided: "Sections 1–8 of this act shall take effect upon the date when the abolition of position 14455, the transfer of funding and appropriations to the unclassified position established in section 10 of this act, and the initial appointment of the director of the municipal and property division have occurred, as certified by the commissioner of the department of revenue administration to the director of legislative services and the secretary of state." The commissioner certified that sections 1–8 of 2013:47 effective March 24, 2014.

Amendment Notes

—2013.
The 2013 amendment, substituted "RSA 21-J:15" for "RSA 21-J:9" in the third sentence.

—1999.
Paragraphs I–III: Substituted "RSA 485-A:4– 6" for "RSA 485-A:5" wherever it appeared.
Paragraph V: Substituted "RSA 485-A:4– 6" for "RSA 485-A:5 including" preceding "any rule adopted" and "RSA 485-A:4– 6, or any permit issued under the authority of this subdivision or RSA 485-A:4– 6" for "RSA 485-A:5" at the end of the first sentence of the introductory paragraph, and inserted "rules adopted under this chapter, and permits issued under this chapter" preceding "as provided" in subpar. (a).

—1997.
Paragraph III: Substituted "RSA 38:25" for "RSA 38:14-a" at the end of the second sentence.

—1996.
Substituted "department" for "division" throughout the section and "in accordance with RSA 21-O:14" for "to the water supply and pollution council" following "may appeal" in the second sentence of par. V-a.

—1995.
Paragraph V: Added "including any rule adopted under this subdivision or RSA 485-A:5" at the end of the first sentence of the introductory paragraph and substituted "violations" for "violation" preceding "of this chapter" and added "as provided above" thereafter in subpar. (a).

—1991.
Paragraph III-a: Added.

—1990.
Added "Failure to Provide Facility" following "Relief" in the section catchline and added pars. V-a through V-c.

Severability of enactment.
1997, 206 was subject to a severability clause. See 1997, 206:9.

NOTES TO DECISIONS

Enforcement of orders
Order of the commission to enforce the water pollution control act may be enforced by fines authorized by this section, or by injunction or by contempt. State v. Goffstown, 100 N.H. 131, 121 A.2d 317, 1956 N.H. LEXIS 13 (N.H. 1956). (Decided under prior law.)

RESEARCH REFERENCES AND PRACTICE AIDS

Cross References.
Eminent Domain Procedure Act, see RSA 498-A.

References in text.
RSA title LXII, referred to in par. I, is classified to Title 62 of LEXIS New Hampshire Revised Statutes Annotated, which is comprised of chapters 625–651.

485-A:22-a. Cease and Desist Orders; Penalty.

The director of the division of forests and lands, department of natural and cultural resources, or his or her authorized agents, may:

I. Issue a written cease and desist order against any timber operation in violation of this chapter. Any such violation may be enjoined by the superior court, upon application of the attorney general. A person failing to comply with the cease and desist order shall be guilty of a violation.

II. Prosecute any violation of this chapter as a violation. This provision shall not limit the state's enforcement authority under this chapter.

HISTORY:
1989, 214:19. 1990, 29:4, eff. May 22, 1990. 2005, 32:2, eff. July 9, 2005. 2017, 156:14, eff. July 1, 2017.

Codification.
This section was originally enacted as RSA 149:19-a and was redesignated pursuant to 1989, 339:34.

Amendment Notes
The 2017 amendments to this section by Ch. 156 substituted "natural and cultural resources" for "resources and economic development" in the introductory language.

—2005.
Rewritten to the extent that a detailed comparison would be impracticable.

—1990.
Substituted "may" for "shall" preceding "issue", "timber operation" for "act" preceding "in violation" and deleted "not specifically covered by other penalty provisions" following "chapter" in the first sentence and substituted "violation" for "act" preceding "may be enjoined" in the second sentence.

RESEARCH REFERENCES AND PRACTICE AIDS

Cross References.
Classification of crimes, see RSA 625:9.
Sentences, see RSA 651.

Safety Regulations for Camps, Pools, and Bathing Places

Amendment Notes

—2013.
The 2013 amendment by 2013, 250:1, eff. January 1, 2014, added "for Camps, Pools, and Bathing Places" in the subdivision heading.

RESEARCH REFERENCES AND PRACTICE AIDS

New Hampshire Code of Administrative Rules
Rules of the Department of Environmental Services—Water Supply and Pollution Control Division, Env-Ws 1101.01 et seq. New Hampshire Code of Administrative Rules Annotated.

485-A:23. Definitions.

In this subdivision:

I. "Recreation camp" means any place set apart for recreational purposes for boys and girls. It shall not be construed to apply to private camps owned or leased for individual or family use, or to any camp operated for a period of less than 10 days in a year.

II. "Youth skill camp" means a nonprofit or for-profit program that lasts 8 hours total or more in a year for the purpose of teaching a skill to minors. Such camps include, but are not limited to, the teaching of sports, the arts, and scientific inquiry.

HISTORY:
1989, 339:1. 1994, 16:1, eff. June 21, 1994. 2013, 250:2, eff. January 1, 2014.

Amendment Notes

—2013.
The 2013 amendment rewrote the section to the extent that a detailed comparison would be impractical.

—1994.
Substituted "10" for "30" preceding "days" in the second sentence.

485-A:24. Recreation Camp License; Youth Skill Camp Certification of Criminal Background Check.

I. No person shall for profit or for charitable purposes operate any recreation camp, as defined in RSA 485-A:23, I, designed or intended as a vacation or recreation resort, without a license issued by the department. Said license is to be conditioned upon the maintenance of clean, healthful sanitary conditions and methods, as determined and approved by said department, good only for the calendar year in which it is issued and subject to suspension or revocation at any time for cause. The fee for such license shall be $200 which shall be paid into the recreation camp and youth skill camp fund established in RSA 485-A:24-a.

II.(a) No person or entity shall for profit or for charitable purposes operate any youth skill camp, as defined in RSA 485-A:23, II, without maintaining an appropriate policy regarding background checks for camp owners, employees and volunteers who may be left alone with any child or children. Certification of background checks shall be made to the department demonstrating that no individual has a criminal conviction for any offense involving:

(1) Causing or threatening direct physical injury to any individual; or

(2) Causing or threatening harm of any nature to any child or children.

(b) Any person or entity required to perform background checks and provide certification to the department pursuant to subparagraph (a) shall pay a fee of $25 to the department. All such fees collected by the department shall be deposited into the recreation camp and youth skill camp fund established in RSA 485-A:24-a.

(c) Subparagraphs (a) and (b) shall not apply to any person or entity which owns property used to operate a youth skill camp or any buildings or structures on such property used in the operation of a youth skill camp, provided such person or entity obtains written certification signed by the youth skill camp operator stating that background

checks in accordance with this paragraph have been completed.

(d) Nothing in this section shall preclude more stringent requirements for background checks on the part of camp owners, directors, or operators.

(e) Such policies shall be made available to the department and shall include the frequency of the background checks and the sources used to conduct the background checks. The department shall provide information on each youth skill camp's policy on the department's website.

(f) If an employee or volunteer has been the subject of a background check performed by another person or entity within 12 months, the previous background check may, with the signed and written consent of the employee or volunteer, be shared with the operator of the youth skill camp and may be used to satisfy the requirements of this paragraph, notwithstanding any other law providing for the confidentiality of such information.

HISTORY:
1989, 339:1, eff. Jan. 1, 1990. 1996, 228:106, eff. July 1, 1996. 2013, 250:3, eff. January 1, 2014.

Codification.
Pursuant to 1989, 339:34, the amendment to former RSA 149:22 by 1989, 408:18, eff. Aug. 4, 1989, was incorporated in the text of this section.

Amendment Notes

—2013.
The 2013 amendment rewrote the section heading, which formerly read: "License; Fee"; added the I designation; in I, substituted "recreation camp, as defined in RSA 485-A:23, I" for "camp" in the first sentence and in the last sentence, substituted "$200 which shall" for "$50 to" and "recreation camp and youth skill camp fund established in RSA 485-A:24-a" for "state treasury"; and added II.

—1996.
Substituted "department" for "division" throughout the section.

NOTES TO DECISIONS

Failure to comply with licensing requirements
Lessor's failure to make improvements in summer camp, as required by the state board of health in order to get license required by this section, constituted a violation of the lease. Lynch v. Grundy, 97 N.H. 286, 86 A.2d 114, 1952 N.H. LEXIS 12 (N.H. 1952). (Decided under prior law.)

485-A:24-a. Recreation Camp and Youth Skill Camp Fund.

There is established in the office of the state treasurer a nonlapsing fund to be known as the recreation camp and youth skill camp fund to be administered by the commissioner of the department of environmental services, and which shall be kept distinct and separate from all other funds. All moneys in the fund shall be continually appropriated to the commissioner of the department of environmental services for the purpose of paying costs associated with administering the provisions of RSA 485-A:24 and 485-A:25.

HISTORY:
2013, 250:4, eff. January 1, 2014.

485-A:25. Rulemaking.

I. The commissioner shall adopt rules under RSA 541-A relative to:

(a) Issuance of licenses to recreation camp operators under RSA 485-A:24, I.

(b) Requirements for performing criminal background checks at youth skill camps and certifying acceptable results as required under RSA 485-A:24, II(a) and establishing appropriate sanctions and penalties for failing to perform the required background checks.

(c) Water quality-related issues for the protection of persons using recreation camp facilities regulated under RSA 485-A:24, I.

II. The commissioner, in consultation with the department of health and human services, shall adopt all other necessary rules under RSA 541-A, relative to public health and safety issues for the protection of persons attending recreation camps regulated under RSA 485-A:24, I.

HISTORY:
1989, 339:1. 1994, 174:1, eff. July 22, 1994. 1995, 310:181, eff. Nov. 1, 1995. 1996, 228:110, eff. July 1, 1996. 2013, 250:3, eff. August 23, 2013.

Amendment Notes

—2013.

The 2013 amendment added "recreation" in I(a) and I(c); substituted "RSA 485-A:24, I" for "RSA 485-A:24" in I(a); added I(b); redesignated former I(b) as I(c); substituted "RSA 485-A:24, I" for "this subdivision" in I(c); and substituted "attending recreation camps regulated under RSA 485-A:24, I" for "using camp facilities regulated under this subdivision" in II.

—1996.

Substituted "commissioner" for "division" in the introductory paragraph of par. I and in par. II.

—1995.

Paragraph II: Substituted "department of health and human services" for "division of public health services" preceding "shall adopt".

—1994.

Rewritten to the extent that a detailed comparison would be impracticable.

Severability of 1995 amendment.

1995, 310, which amended this section, was subject to a severability clause. See 1995, 310:186.

Construction of 1995 amendment.

1995, 310:187, eff. Nov. 1, 1995, provided:

"Nothing in this act is intended to, nor shall it be construed as, mandating or assigning any new, expanded, or modified program or responsibility for any political subdivision in violation of part I, article 28-a of the constitution of the state of New Hampshire."

RESEARCH REFERENCES AND PRACTICE AIDS

Cross References.

Administrative Procedure Act, see RSA 541-A.

485-A:25-a. Statement of Health for Recreational Camps.

Notwithstanding any law or rule to the contrary, any physical examination which is required before a child may enter a recreational camp may be conducted by a physician, a licensed advanced nurse practitioner or a physician assistant.

HISTORY:
1990, 102:1, eff. April 13, 1990.

485-A:25-b. Possession and Use of Epinephrine Auto-Injectors at Recreation Camps.

A recreation camp shall permit a child with severe, potentially life-threatening allergies to possess and use an epinephrine auto-injector, if the following conditions are satisfied:

I. The child has the written approval of the child's physician and the written approval of the parent or guardian. The camp shall obtain the following information from the child's physician:

(a) The child's name.

(b) The name and signature of the licensed prescriber and business and emergency numbers.

(c) The name, route, and dosage of medication.

(d) The frequency and time of medication administration or assistance.

(e) The date of the order.

(f) A diagnosis and any other medical conditions requiring medications, if not a violation of confidentiality or if not contrary to the request of the parent or guardian to keep confidential.

(g) Specific recommendations for administration.

(h) Any special side effects, contraindications, and adverse reactions to be observed.

(i) The name of each required medication.

(j) Any severe adverse reactions that may occur to another child, for whom the epinephrine auto-injector is not prescribed, should such a pupil receive a dose of the medication.

II. The recreational camp administrator or, if a nurse is assigned to the camp, the nurse shall receive copies of the written approvals required by paragraph I.

III. The child's parent or guardian shall submit written verification from the physician confirming that the child has the knowledge and skills to safely possess and use an epinephrine auto-injector in a camp setting.

IV. If the conditions provided in this section are satisfied, the child may possess and use the epinephrine auto-injector at the camp or at any camp-sponsored activity, event, or program.

V. In this section, "physician" means any physician or health practitioner with the authority to write prescriptions.

HISTORY:
2003, 50:2, eff. Aug. 15, 2003.

Contingent enactment of section.
2003, 51:2, provided for enactment of this section. However, under the terms of 2003, 51:5, eff. May 12, 2003, that enactment did not become effective.

485-A:25-c. Use of Epinephrine Auto-Injector.

Immediately after using the epinephrine auto-injector, the child shall report such use to the nurse or another camp employee to enable the nurse or camp employee to provide appropriate follow-up care.

HISTORY:
2003, 50:2, eff. Aug. 15, 2003.

Contingent enactment of section.
2003, 51:2, provided for enactment of this section. However, under the terms of 2003, 51:5, eff. May 12, 2003, that enactment did not become effective.

485-A:25-d. Availability of Epinephrine Auto-Injector.

The recreational camp nurse or, if a nurse is not assigned to the camp, the recreational camp administrator shall maintain for the use of a child with severe allergies at least one epinephrine auto-injector, provided by the child, in the nurse's office or in a similarly accessible location.

HISTORY:
2003, 50:2, eff. Aug. 15, 2003.

485-A:25-e. Immunity.

No recreational camp or camp employee shall be liable in a suit for damages as a result of any act or omission related to a child's use of an epinephrine auto-injector if the provisions of RSA 485-A:25-b have been met, unless the damages were caused by willful or wanton conduct or disregard of the criteria established in that section for the possession and self-administration of an epinephrine auto-injector by a child.

HISTORY:
2003, 50:2, eff. Aug. 15, 2003.

485-A:25-f. Possession and Use of Asthma Inhalers at Recreation Camps.

A recreation camp shall permit a child to possess and use a metered dose inhaler or a dry powder inhaler to alleviate asthmatic symptoms, or before exercise to prevent the onset of asthmatic symptoms, if the following conditions are satisfied:

I. The child has the written approval of the child's physician and the written approval of the parent or guardian. The camp shall obtain the following information from the child's physician:

(a) The child's name.

(b) The name and signature of the licensed prescriber and business and emergency numbers.

(c) The name, route, and dosage of medication.

(d) The frequency and time of medication administration or assistance.

(e) The date of the order.

(f) A diagnosis and any other medical conditions requiring medications, if not a violation of confidentiality or if not contrary to the request of the parent or guardian to keep confidential.

(g) Specific recommendations for administration.

(h) Any special side effects, contraindications, and adverse reactions to be observed.

(i) The name of each required medication.

(j) At least one emergency telephone number for contacting the parent or guardian.

II. The recreational camp administrator or, if a nurse is assigned to the camp, the nurse shall receive copies of the written approvals required by paragraph I.

III. The child's parent or guardian shall submit written verification from the physician confirming that the child has the knowledge and skills to safely possess and use an asthma inhaler in a camp setting.

IV. If the conditions provided in this section are satisfied, the child may possess and use the inhaler at the camp or at any camp sponsored activity, event, or program.

V. In this section, "physician" includes any physician or health practitioner with the authority to write prescriptions.

HISTORY:
2003, 51:4, eff. Aug. 15, 2003.

485-A:25-g. Immunity.

No recreational camp or camp employee shall be liable in a suit for damages as a result of any act or omission related to a child's use of an inhaler if the provisions of RSA 485-A:25-f have been met, unless the damages were caused by willful or wanton conduct or disregard of the criteria established in that section for the possession and self-administration of an asthma inhaler by a child.

HISTORY:
2003, 51:4, eff. Aug. 15, 2003.

485-A:26. Swimming Pools and Bathing Places.

I. No person shall install, operate or maintain an artificial swimming pool or bathing place open to and used by the public, or as a part of a business venture, unless the construction, design and physical specifications of such pool or bathing place shall have received prior approval by the department. A fee of $100 shall be paid to the department upon submission of such plans for review. Fees collected under this paragraph shall be deposited with the state treasurer as unrestricted revenue. The commissioner shall adopt rules relative to safety standards to protect persons using said facilities. Nothing in this section shall be deemed to affect the powers of local health officers or the department of health and human services, with respect to nuisances.

II. The department may take samples of the water of any such facility for analysis to determine compliance with water quality requirements. The costs of such sampling and analysis shall be paid by the owner or operator of such facility. The costs recovered for such sampling shall be deposited in the general fund as unrestricted revenue. The costs recovered for analysis shall be consistent with the fee structure established in RSA 131:3-a and deposited as provided in RSA 131:3-a. Any municipality which establishes a program of sampling and analysis which is equivalent to the department's program shall not be subject to additional sampling and analysis by the department.

HISTORY:
1989, 339:1. 1990, 3:88. 1995, 310:181, eff. Nov. 1, 1995. 1996, 228:79, eff. July 1, 1996. 1997, 267:1, eff. July 1, 1997.

Amendments

—1997.
Designated the existing provisions of the section as par. I and substituted "paragraph" for "section" in the third sentence of that paragraph, and added par. II.

—1996.
Substituted "department" for "division" in the first and second sentences and "commissioner" for "division" in the fourth sentence.

—1995.
Deleted "division of public health services" preceding "department of health and human services" in the fifth sentence.

—1990.
Added the second and third sentences.

Severability of 1995 amendment.
1995, 310, which amended this section, was subject to a severability clause. See 1995, 310:186.

Construction of 1995 amendment.
1995, 310:187, eff. Nov. 1, 1995, provided:
"Nothing in this act is intended to, nor shall it be construed as, mandating or assigning any new, expanded, or modified program or responsibility for any political subdivision in violation of part I, article 28-a of the constitution of the state of New Hampshire."

485-A:27. Injunction.

Any person operating or maintaining a recreation camp, youth skill camp, public swimming pool, or bathing place without the same having been approved by the department may be enjoined by the superior court or any justice of the court upon petition brought by the attorney general.

HISTORY:
1989, 339:1, eff. Jan. 1, 1990. 1996, 228:106, eff. July 1, 1996. 1997, 267:1, eff. July 1, 1997. 2013, 250:5, eff. January 1, 2014.

Amendment Notes

—2013.
The 2013 amendment substituted "recreation camp, youth skill camp" for "youth camp or" and made a related change.

—1997.
Substituted "a youth camp or public" for "such a" preceding "swimming pool" and deleted "in term time or vacation" preceding "by the superior court".

—1996.
Substituted "department" for "division".

485-A:28. Penalty; Administrative Fines.

I. Whoever violates any of the provisions of this subdivision, or rules adopted under this subdivision shall be guilty of a violation if a natural person, or guilty of a misdemeanor if any other person.

II. The commissioner, after notice and hearing, may impose an administrative fine not to exceed $2,000 for each offense upon any person who violates any provision of this subdivision, any rule adopted under this subdivision, or any license or approval issued under this subdivision. Rehearings and appeals from a decision of the commissioner under this paragraph shall be in accordance with RSA 541. Any administrative fine imposed under this section shall not preclude the imposition of further penalties under this chapter. The proceeds of administrative fines levied pursuant to this paragraph shall be deposited in the general fund. The commissioner shall adopt rules, under RSA 541-A, relative to:

(a) A schedule of administrative fines which may be imposed under this paragraph; and

(b) Procedures for notice and hearing prior to the imposition of an administrative fine.

HISTORY:
1989, 339:1, eff. Jan. 1, 1990. 1997, 267:2, eff. July 1, 1997.

Amendments

—1997.
Added "administrative fines" to the end of the catchline, designated the existing provisions as par. I, and added par. II.

RESEARCH REFERENCES AND PRACTICE AIDS

Cross References.
Classification of crimes, see RSA 625:9.
Sentences, see RSA 651.

Sewage Disposal Systems

RESEARCH REFERENCES AND PRACTICE AIDS

New Hampshire Code of Administrative Rules
Rules of the Department of Environmental Services—Water Supply and Pollution Control Division, Env-Ws 701.01 et seq., 100.01 et seq., New Hampshire Code of Administrative Rules Annotated.

485-A:29. Submission and Approval of Plans and Specifications.

I. Any person proposing either to subdivide land, except as provided in RSA 485-A:33, or to construct a sewage or waste disposal system, shall submit 2 copies of such locally approved plans as are required by the local planning board or other local body having authority for the approval of any such subdivision of land, which is subject to department approval, and 2 copies of plans and specifications for any sewage or waste disposal systems which will be constructed on any subdivision or lot for approval in accordance with the requirements of the department as provided in this paragraph. In the event that such subdivision plans which receive final local approval differ from the plans which are reviewed by the department, the person proposing the subdivision shall resubmit those plans to the department for reapproval. The planning board or other local body having final local approval authority shall submit one copy of such plans which receive final local approval to the department for informational purposes within 30 days of granting such final approval. The department shall adopt rules, pursuant to RSA 541-A, relative to the submission of plans and specifications as necessary to effect the purposes of this subdivision. The rules shall specify when and where the plans and specifications are to be submitted, what details, data and information are to be contained in the plans and specifications, including the location of known burial sites or cemeteries within or adjacent to the property on which the proposed sewage or waste disposal system is to be located, what tests are to be required, what standards, guidelines, procedures, and criteria are to be applied and followed in constructing any sewage or waste disposal system, and other related matters. The rules shall also establish the methodology and review process for approval of innovative/alternative wastewater treatment systems and for approval of a plan for operation, maintenance, and financial responsibility for such operations. For any part or parts of the subdivisions where construction or waste disposal is not contemplated, only the lot lines, property boundaries drawn to scale, and general soil and related data shall be required. The constructed sewage or waste disposal systems shall be in strict accordance with approved plans, and the facilities shall not be covered or placed in operation without final inspection and approval by an authorized agent of the department. All inspections by the department shall be accomplished within 7 business days after receipt of written notification from the builder that the system is ready for inspection. Plans and specifications need not be submitted for subdivision approval for subdivisions consisting of the division of a tract or parcel of land exclusively in lots of 5 or more acres in area. The presence of hydric soils on lots of 5 or more acres in area shall be insufficient, without additional supporting data, to classify these lots as wetlands, or to make such lots unsuitable for sewage or waste disposal systems designed for poorly drained soils. This exemption in no way relieves any person from responsibility for obtaining approval under this chapter for construction of individual or other sewage or waste disposal systems or both in any exempted lots. In such cases, it shall be the responsibility of the subdivider to provide to the lot purchasers satisfactory assurance as the purchasers may require at the time of sale that lots sold shall be adequate to support individual sewage or waste disposal systems or both in accordance with rules adopted by the department and the requirements of this subdivision.

II.   The department shall develop and approve an outline of brief instructions for the periodic maintenance, care and proper usage of waste disposal systems, including a warning of the potential public health hazard and pollution of public and private water supplies and surface water of the state from improperly maintained sewage and waste disposal systems.

III.   The department shall not approve any plan which will cause a violation of the setback requirements in RSA 289:3, III.

HISTORY:
1989, 339:1. 1991, 379:2. 1993, 172:5, eff. July 24, 1993. 1994, 198:1, eff. July 23, 1994. 1995, 93:1, eff. July 1, 1995. 1996, 228:106, eff. July 1, 1996. 233:9, eff. July 1, 2000. 2006, 87:1, 2, eff. July 4, 2006. 2017, 238:1, eff. September 16, 2017.

Amendment Notes
The 2017 amendments to this section by Ch.238 deleted former first sentence, which read: "Permitted designers of subsurface sewage disposal systems shall obtain the registry of deeds volume and page numbers for each lot that relates to the septic system application and provide them to the department." of II.

—2006.
Paragraph I: Inserted "including the location of known burial sites or cemeteries within or adjacent to the property on which the proposed sewage or waste disposal system is to be located" following "and specifications" in the fifth sentence.
Paragraph III: Added.

—1996.
Paragraph I: Chapter 228 substituted "department" for "division" wherever it appeared.
Paragraph II: Chapter 233 deleted the former first sentence.

—1995.
Paragraph I: Inserted "which is subject to division approval" following "subdivision of land" in the first sentence, "subdivision" following "event that such" in the second sentence, and added the eleventh sentence.

—1994.
Paragraph I: Inserted "except as provided in RSA 485-A:33" following "land" and "such" preceding "locally" and substituted "as are required by the local planning board or other local body having authority for the approval of" for "for" following "approved plans" in the first sentence, and added the second sentence.

—1993.
Paragraph I: Inserted "guidelines" preceding "procedures" in the third sentence and added the fourth sentence.

—1991.
Paragraph II: Rewritten to the extent that a detailed comparison would be impracticable.

Contingent 1996 amendment.
1996, 233:4, provided for the amendment of this section. However, under the terms of 1996, 233:10, eff. June 10, 1996, the amendment did not become effective.

NOTES TO DECISIONS

Cited:

Cited in Greenland Conservation Comm'n v. N.H. Wetlands Council, 154 N.H. 529, 913 A.2d 776, 2006 N.H. LEXIS 195 (2006).

RESEARCH REFERENCES AND PRACTICE AIDS

New Hampshire Practice.

13-12 N.H.P. Probate Law & Procedure § 323.

485-A:30. Fees.

I. Any person submitting plans and specifications for a subdivision of land shall pay to the department a fee of $300 per lot. Said fee shall be for reviewing such plans and specifications and making site inspections. Any person submitting plans and specifications or an application for a permit by rule as provided in RSA 485-A:33, IV for sewage or waste disposal systems shall pay to the department a fee of $290 for each system. Said fee shall be for reviewing such plans and specifications or application for permit by rule, making site inspections, the administration of sludge and septage management programs, and establishing a system for electronic permitting for waste disposal systems, subdivision plans, and permits and approvals under the department's land regulation authority. The fees required by this paragraph shall be paid at the time said plans and specifications or application for permit by rule are submitted and shall be deposited in the subsurface systems fund established in paragraph I-b. For the purposes of this paragraph, the term "lot" shall not include tent sites or travel trailer sites in recreational parks which are operated on a seasonal basis for not more than 9 months per year.

I-a. In addition to fees required under paragraph I, any person submitting plans and specifications or an application for a permit by rule as provided in RSA 485-A:33, IV for sewage or waste disposal systems shall pay to the department a fee of $10 for each system for use in the septage handling and treatment facilities grant program to municipalities under RSA 486:3, III. The fees required by this paragraph shall be paid at the time said plans and specifications or application for permit by rule are submitted and shall be deposited in the septage management fund established in paragraph I-c.

I-b. There is hereby established the subsurface systems fund into which the fees collected under paragraph I shall be deposited. The fund shall be a separate, nonlapsing fund, continually appropriated to the department for the purpose of paying all costs and salaries associated with the subsurface systems program.

I-c. There is hereby established the septage management fund into which the fees collected under paragraph I-a shall be deposited. The fund shall be a separate, nonlapsing fund, continually appropriated to the department for the purpose of paying costs associated with the septage handling and treatment facilities grant program or for research,

engineering analysis, or septage sampling and analysis by the department to advance septage management in the state of New Hampshire.

II. [Repealed.]

III. Any person submitting plans and specifications as a resubmission for reapproval of such shall not be required to pay any additional fee under RSA 485-A:30, I or I-a if changes to such plans and specifications would not constitute a new subdivision under the provisions of RSA 485-A:2, XIII.

HISTORY:

1989, 339:1. 1990, 252:15. 1991, 379:3. 1994, 198:2, eff. July 23, 1994. 1996, 228:106, eff. July 1, 1996. 233:5, 7, II, eff. July 1, 2000. 233:8, eff. at 12:01 a.m., July 1, 1996. 2001, 128:2, 3, eff. July 1, 2001. 2003, 246:2, eff. July 1, 2003. 2005, 141:1, eff. Aug. 16, 2005. 2009, 144:43, eff. July 1, 2009. 2012, 174:1, eff. June 11, 2012.

Codification.

Pursuant to 1989, 339:34, the amendment to former RSA 149-E:3, I-b by 1989, 408:19, eff. Aug. 4, 1989, was incorporated in the text of this section.

Amendments

—2012.

The 2012 amendment added "or an application for a permit by rule as provided in RSA 485-A:33, IV" in the third sentence of I and the first sentence of I-a; added "or application for permit by rule" in the fourth and fifth sentences of I and the second sentence of I-a; in I-a, deleted the former second sentence, which read: "Until July 1, 2010, the fees required by this paragraph shall be paid at the time said plans and specifications are submitted and shall be deposited in the subsurface systems fund established in paragraph I-b" and deleted "After July 1, 2010" at the beginning of the second sentence; and made stylistic changes.

—2009.

The 2009 amendment, in I, substituted "$300 per lot" for "$150 per lot" at the end of the first sentence, "$290 for each system" for "$140 for each system" at the end of the third sentence, and "in the subsurface systems fund established in paragraph I-b" for "with the treasurer as unrestricted revenue" at the end of the fifth sentence; rewrote I-a; and added I-b and I-c.

—2005.

Paragraph I-a: Added the third sentence.

—2003.

Paragraph I: Substituted "$150" for "$80" in the first sentence, "$140" for "$80" in the third sentence, and deleted "and for" preceding "the administration of sludge" and added "and for establishing a system for electronic permitting for waste disposal systems, subdivision plans, and for permits and approvals under the department's land regulation authority" in the fourth sentence.

—2001.

Paragraph I-a: Added.

Paragraph III: Inserted "or I-a" preceding "if changes."

—1996.

Paragraph II: Repealed.

Paragraph I: Chapter 228 substituted "department" for "division" wherever it appeared.

Paragraph II: Chapter 228 substituted "department" for "division" in the third sentence.

Chapter 233 inserted "of $5" following "department a fee" in the first sentence and deleted the former second sentence.

Paragraph III: Chapter 333 deleted "and II" following "RSA 485-A:30, I".

—1994.

Paragraph III: Added.

—1991.

Designated the existing provisions of the section as par. I and added par. II.

—1990.

Substituted "$80" for "$75" in the first and third sentences, deleted "and" following "specifications" and added "and for the administration of sludge and septage management programs" following "inspections" in the fourth sentence.

Contingent 1996 amendment.

1996, 233:3, provided for the amendment of this section. However, under the terms of 1996, 233:10, eff. June 10, 1996, the amendment did not become effective.

485-A:30-a.   Notice Requirements; Encroachment Waivers.

I.(a) Any person intending to submit an application for approval of a sewage or waste disposal system, which application will include a request for an encroachment waiver, shall notify the local code enforcement officer or other appropriate designated authority and all abutters as defined in RSA 672:3 that the person intends to file the application. Such notification shall include:

(1) The name and address of the property owner.

(2) Identification of the property for which an encroachment waiver is being requested, including tax map and lot numbers.

(3) Names of abutters, together with applicable tax map and lot numbers.

(4) A description of the specific waivers being requested.

(5) A reasonable facsimile of the plan.

(6) Identification of any local code or ordinance for which a waiver, variance or exception is required, and whether such waiver, variance or exception has been obtained.

(7) Notice that the department is required by law to act on the application within 15 working days of receipt of the application, and that objections to the proposed encroachment waiver may be submitted to the department during the review process or by filing a motion for reconsideration of the decision with the department within 20 days of the department's decision on the application.

(b) Encroachment waiver requests shall appear on the plans. No application which includes any request for an encroachment waiver shall be accepted by the department unless the application includes a copy of the notice, a list of the names and addresses of the abutters to whom the notice was mailed, and a statement signed by the applicant or property owner certifying that the notices were sent by certified mail to the abutters listed.

II. No construction permit shall be issued for a septic system until the department has received a copy of the recorded notice showing that all easements and encroachment waivers associated with the application have been recorded by the property owner in the registry of deeds.

HISTORY:

1989, 79:2, eff. July 30, 1989. 1996, 228:106, eff. July 1, 1996.

Codification.

Pursuant to 1989, 339:34, former RSA 149-E:3, I-c and I-d, as added by 1989, 79:2, eff. July 30, 1989, were redesignated as this section, comprised of pars. I and II, and the section catchline was added.

Amendments

—1996.

Substituted "department" for "division" throughout the section and "department's" for "division's" following "20 days of the" in par. I(a)(7).

485-A:30-b.   Protective Well Radii.

I. All lots on which wastewater is or will be disposed on-site and all lots on which a private well serving a public water system exists or will be installed , including lots created prior to August 20, 1989, shall be subject to the following conditions:

(a) Rules adopted under this section concerning such lots shall include provisions allowing abutting lot owners to overlap their respective well radii for their mutual benefit and provisions allowing well radii to extend over property lines onto state and locally-mandated property line setbacks, recorded easements, or land which is permanently dedicated to a use which precludes development.

(b)(1) For any private well being installed or utilized to serve one or more new commercial buildings or a non-community public water system , the entire protective well radius shall be located on one or more of the following: on-lot, on a recorded easement, on land which is permanently dedicated to a use which precludes development, or on state or locally mandated property line setbacks.

(2) A private well may be installed without being located as required by subparagraph (1) only if it is needed to replace a well serving one or more existing commercial buildings or a public water system, there will be no increase in water use to a level that requires a larger protective well radius under rules adopted by the department, and the lot is not part of a larger parcel that is being subdivided. In such cases, the on-lot protective radius shall be maximized to the extent practicable and the owner of the property shall sign a standard release form prepared by the department, upon which the actual protective radius shall be noted together with a narrative description of the location of the well, to acknowledge the potential loss of the protection of any portion of the radius which extends over the property line. The owner shall record the release form in the registry of deeds and shall file a copy of the recorded release form with the department.

(3) If a private well installed under the provisions of subparagraph (2) is not regulated as a

public water supply well under RSA 485, the department shall require such water quality monitoring, recordkeeping, and reporting as is needed to ensure the water is suitable for its intended uses.

(4) For the purposes of this section, the term "commercial building" means a building that houses a commercial use but shall not include a residence which is also used for commercial purposes unless the total water withdrawal exceeds 600 gallons per day. A new commercial building means a new structure intended for commercial use, an existing residential structure being converted to commercial use, or an increase in water use at an existing commercial building to a level that requires a larger protective well radius under rules adopted by the department.

(c) For private wells serving buildings other than commercial buildings, if the protective well radius cannot be wholly maintained on an existing lot of record due to the size or other physical characteristics of the lot, then the on-lot protective radius shall be maximized to the extent practicable. Subject to the foregoing sentence, the protective well radius shall be maintained on one or more of the following: on-lot, on a recorded easement, on land which is permanently dedicated to a use which precludes development, or on state and locally-mandated property line setbacks.

(d) Any person submitting plans and specifications for a sewage or waste disposal system for a property which is or will be served by an on-lot well, shall show the location or proposed location of the well, or a designated area within which the well will be located, on such plans and shall show the protective radius as specified in the department's rules.

(e) Whenever the department approves a septic plan with an on-lot well radius which is less than the optimum standard, the department shall notify the applicant of the consequences of such reduced radius and advise the applicant whether special precautions should be taken relative to well installation.

(f) If the well is not installed prior to the sewage or waste disposal system being constructed, then the property owner shall provide the water well contractor with a copy of the approved plan showing the location of the well, and the water well contractor shall ensure, to the best of his ability that the well is installed in accordance with the approved plan.

(g) When, for reasons of the condition of the lot or the placement of buildings thereon, the well cannot be installed as shown on the approved plan, the water well contractor shall advise and consult with the property owner, or the property owner's agent, on the best possible alternative location, considering distance to property boundaries and to the sewage or waste disposal system.

Using a standard release form prepared by the department, the water well contractor shall alert the owner to the consequences of the alternate installation, including the potential loss of the protection of any portion of the radius which extends over the property line. The owner, or the owner's agent, may defer to the designer of the sewage or waste disposal system or may allow the water well contractor to proceed in the identified alternative location. Prior to installing the well in the identified alternative location, the well contractor shall, using the standard release form, obtain a written acknowledgment, from the property owner, or the owner's agent, that the consequences are understood. The designer shall prepare an amended plan showing the actual location of the well. The property owner shall forward the amended plan, together with a copy of the signed release form, to the department and the local code enforcement officer or other appropriate designated local official prior to using the well. If the on-lot protective well radius is less than the optimum prescribed standard, the owner shall record the release form, upon which the actual protective radius shall be noted, together with a narrative description of the location of the well in the registry of deeds, and a copy of the recorded release form shall be filed with the department.

II. For lots approved under RSA 485-A:29, the rules adopted under this section concerning such lots shall include provisions allowing abutting lot owners to overlap their respective well radii for their mutual benefit by allowing well radii to extend over property lines, onto state and locally-mandated property line setbacks, recorded easements, or land which is permanently dedicated to a use which precludes development. If after a lot is created pursuant to this section, the well cannot be installed as shown on the subdivision plan, then the provisions of RSA 485-A:30-b, I(d), (e), (f), and (g) shall apply.

III. For the purposes of this paragraph, the term "cluster development" means a form of residential subdivision that permits dwelling units to be grouped on sites or lots with dimensions, frontages, and setbacks reduced from conventional requirements, provided that the remaining land area is permanently designated as open space for cluster development. For cluster developments the following provisions shall apply:

(a) Where the sewage waste disposal systems are located off of the individual home lots or the cluster development is served by municipal sewers, the wells and associated protective radii serving those home lots need not be confined to the individual lot which each well serves so long as all wells and their associated protective radii are confined within the tract of home lots and common land permanently designated as open space, and shall not encumber property situated outside of the cluster development except by recorded easement.

(b) Where the home lots are serviced by on-lot sewage or waste disposal systems, wells and their protective radii may be located wholly or partially on common land permanently designated as open space, and shall not encumber adjacent lots or property situated outside of the cluster development except by recorded easement. The department shall not approve such off-lot wells and radii unless the lot owner or developer demonstrates to the department's satisfaction, by means of recorded easements, land use restrictions or other appropriate mechanisms, that the well owner will be able to maintain and service the well in perpetuity and that the area covered by the protective well radius is permanently dedicated to a use which precludes development.

IV. The commissioner shall adopt rules under RSA 541-A providing for protective well radii for private water wells, and for regulation of land use within the radii boundary.

HISTORY:
   1991, 215:2, eff. Aug. 9, 1991. 1996, 228:106, 110, eff. July 1, 1996. 2015, 236:3, eff. September 11, 2015.

Revision note.
   Substituted "August 20, 1989" for "the effective date of RSA 485:35-a" in the introductory clause of par. I for purposes of clarity.

Amendment Notes

—2015.
   The 2015 amendment rewrote paragraph II(b).

—1996.
   Substituted "department" for "division" throughout pars. I(e) and (g) and III, "department's" for "division's" in pars. I(d) and III(b), and "commissioner" for "department" in par. IV.

Construction; effect on existing rules.
   1991, 215:1, eff. Aug. 9, 1991, provided:
   "I. The provisions of this act [which added this section and repealed RSA 485:35-a] shall not be construed to change in any way the substantive effect of RSA 485:35-a prior to the effective date of this act [Aug. 9, 1991], which required all new subdivisions proposed after August 20, 1989, to confine wells and associated protective well radii to the lot served by the well.
   "II. The rules adopted under former RSA 485:35-a relative to protective well radii shall remain in full force and effect upon enactment of this act to the extent not inconsistent with the provisions of this act. The recodification of the section on protective well radii from RSA 485 to RSA 485-A shall not be construed to affect the validity of such rules otherwise consistent with this act."

RESEARCH REFERENCES AND PRACTICE AIDS

New Hampshire Practice.
   13-12 N.H.P. Probate Law & Procedure § 323.

485-A:31. Action on Applications.

I. Subject to paragraphs II and III, the department shall give notice in writing to the person submitting the plans and specifications for subdivision of land of its approval or disapproval of such plans and specifications within 30 days of the date such plans and specifications and the required fees are received by the department and shall give notice in writing to the person submitting plans and specifications for sewage or waste disposal systems of its approval or disapproval of such plans and specifications within 15 working days of the date such plans and specifications and the required fees are received by the department. Unless such written disapproval shall be mailed to the person submitting plans and specifications within 30 days in the case of plans and specifications for subdivision of land and 15 working days in the case of plans and specifications for sewage or waste disposal systems from the date of receipt with the required fees by the department, the plans and specifications shall be deemed to have been approved. The department shall send a copy of the approval or disapproval of such plans and specifications to the planning board or board of selectmen of the affected municipality.

II. The department may extend the time for rendering a decision under paragraph I, without the applicant's agreement, on an application from an applicant who previously has been determined, after the exhaustion of available appellate remedies, to have failed to comply with RSA 485-A:29–44, or any rule adopted or permit or approval issued pursuant to RSA 485-A:29–44, or to have misrepresented any material fact made in connection with any activity regulated or prohibited by RSA 485-A:29–44, pursuant to an action initiated under RSA 485-A:42 or RSA 485-A:43. The length of such an extension shall be no longer than reasonably necessary to complete the review of the application and shall not exceed 30 days unless the applicant agrees to a longer extension. The department shall notify the applicant of the length of the extension.

III. The department may suspend a review of an application for a proposed project on a property with respect to which the department has commenced an enforcement action against the applicant for any violation of RSA 485-A:29–44; RSA 482-A; RSA 483-B; or RSA 485-A:17, or of any rule adopted or permit or approval issued pursuant to RSA 485-A:29–44; RSA 482-A; RSA 483-B; or RSA 485-A:17. Any such suspension shall expire upon conclusion of the enforcement action and completion of any remedial actions the department may require to address the violation; provided, however, that the department may resume its review of the application sooner if doing so will facilitate resolution of the violation. The department shall resume its review of the application at the point the review was suspended, except that the department may extend any of the time limits under this paragraph and its rules up to a total of 30 days for all such extensions. For purposes of this subparagraph, "enforcement action" means an action initiated under RSA 482-A:13; RSA 482-A:14; RSA 482-A:14-b; RSA 483-B:18; RSA 485-A:22; RSA 485-A:42; or RSA 485-A:43.

HISTORY:
   1989, 339:1, eff. Jan. 1, 1990. 1996, 228:106, eff. July 1, 1996. 2010, 295:11, eff. September 11, 2010.

Codification.

Pursuant to 1989, 339:34, the amendment to former RSA 149-E:3, II by 1989, 79:3, eff. July 30, 1989, was incorporated in the text of this section.

Amendments

—2010.

The 2010 amendment added the I designation; added "Subject to paragraphs II and III" at the beginning of I; and added II and III.

—1996.

Substituted "department" for "division" throughout the section.

485-A:32. Prior Approval; Permits.

I. No person shall construct any building from which sewage or other wastes will discharge or construct a sewage or waste disposal system without prior approval of the plans and specifications of the sewage or waste disposal system by the department. Nothing herein shall be construed to modify or lessen the powers conferred upon local authorities by other statutes; provided, however, that in all instances the requirements contained in this chapter shall be considered as minimum.

II. Any person submitting an application and plans for construction approval shall also certify in writing that he has complied with all local government requirements as relate to water supply and sewage disposal which must be complied with prior to application to the department of environmental services in those municipalities where regulations require prior local approval; and, at the same time, a copy of the certification shall be sent to the board of selectmen of the town or the city council of the city.

II-a. Any person submitting an application and plans for construction approval to replace a subsurface sewage disposal system in failure as defined in RSA 485-A:2, IV shall be exempt from presenting a certification of compliance with local government requirements as required by paragraph II.

III. No person required to submit subdivision plans pursuant to paragraph I shall commence the construction of roads within the lot, tract, or parcel proposed to be subdivided, by clearing the land thereof of natural vegetation, placing any artificial fill thereon, or otherwise altering the land, nor shall he do any other act or acts which will alter the natural state of the land or environment, unless the subdivision plan relating thereto has been submitted and approved in accordance with the requirements of this chapter. Nothing in this paragraph shall be construed to prevent the taking of test borings, the digging of test pits, or any other preliminary testing and inspection necessary to comply with the requirements of the department of environmental services relative to information necessary for review and approval of the subdivision plans.

HISTORY:

1989, 339:1, eff. Jan. 1, 1990. 1996, 228:106, 108, eff. July 1, 1996. 2017, 238:2, eff. September 16, 2017.

Amendment Notes

The 2017 amendments to this section by Ch. 238 added II-a.

—1996.

Substituted "department" for "division" in the first sentence of par. I and "department of environmental services" for "division of water supply and pollution control" in par. II and the second sentence of par. III.

NOTES TO DECISIONS

Cited:

Cited in Smith v. Wolfeboro, 136 N.H. 337, 615 A.2d 1252, 1992 N.H. LEXIS 176 (1992).

485-A:33. Exemptions.

I. No plans and specifications shall be required whenever the proposed sewage or waste disposal system will be connected to any public sewer system operated by any municipality or other governmental body within the state.

II. No plans and specifications shall be required whenever land is subdivided and the purpose of such subdivision is to correct or conform boundary lines or when land is exchanged between abutters and no building is contemplated on the exchanged land.

III. No plans and specifications shall be required for subdivision whenever land is proposed to be subdivided solely for the purpose of a bona fide gift of a lot or lots, and the person intending to subdivide the land certifies upon forms provided by the department that the proposed subdivision is a gift; provided that this limited exemption shall not relieve the donee of the lot, or lots, of the responsibility, and it shall be the responsibility of such donee to submit plans and specifications in accordance with this chapter in the event that such donee subsequently intends to (1) convey to others for consideration any such lot, or lots, or (2) intends to construct thereon a structure from which sewage or other waste will be discharged.

IV.(a) The repair or replacement in-kind of a sewage effluent disposal area shall qualify for a permit by rule, provided all of the following criteria are met:

(1) The existing system receives only domestic sewage.

(2) There is no increase in sewage loading proposed for the repaired or replacement system.

(3) The bottom of the bed is located no less than 24 inches above the seasonable high water table.

(4) The system is located 75 feet or more from an abutter's well unless there is a standard well release form recorded with the registry of deeds in accordance with RSA 485-A:30-b or there is an existing department waiver to the distance for the abutter's well.

(5) The system is located 75 feet or more from the owner's well unless there is an existing department waiver to the distance for the owner's well.

(6) The existing system received prior construction and operational approval from the department and the replacement or repaired system will conform to the provisions of such approval, provided the department may by rule require a minimum septic tank size of 1,000 gallons.

(7) The system is not within 75 feet of any surface water, water supply well, or very poorly drained soil unless authorized by the prior departmental approval described in subparagraph (6).

(8) No new waivers to the department's rules are requested.

(9) The system has not been previously repaired or replaced under a permit by rule in accordance with the provisions of this paragraph.

(b) Construction of the system may proceed upon the submission of an application to the department by a permitted designer under RSA 485-A:35 and receipt of the permit by rule from the department.

(c) The repaired or replacement system shall not be covered or placed in operation without final inspection and approval by an authorized agent of the department. All inspection by the department shall be accomplished within 7 business days after receipt of written notice from the installer that the system is ready for inspection. The installer shall provide the authorized agent of the department, at the time of the inspection, a copy of the previously approved plan bearing the state approval stamp and associated operational approval, and an existing conditions plan bearing the seal of the permitted designer performing work under the permit by rule.

(d) The applicant submitting the permit by rule application shall assume all liability and responsibility for the components of the design that are part of the system being repaired or replaced under the permit by rule.

(e) The installer constructing the system shall assume all liability and responsibility for the construction of the system components repaired or replaced under the permit by rule.

(f) For purposes of this paragraph, "in-kind" shall mean a repair or replacement of the effluent disposal area in strict accordance with what is shown on the previously approved plan.

HISTORY:

1989, 339:1, eff. Jan. 1, 1990. 1996, 228:106, eff. July 1, 1996. 2012, 174:2, eff. June 11, 2012.

Amendments

—2012.

The 2012 amendment added IV.

—1996.

Paragraph III: Substituted "department" for "division".

485-A:34. Soil Testing; Inspections.

I. The department shall require soil data describing soil types and their physical and related characteristics as exist in the proposed subdivision. Such soil data will consist of soils maps and charts as prepared by the U.S. Department of Agriculture, Natural Resources Conservation Service, or equivalent. The data provided by the soils map will supplement the information obtained by percolation tests and such other independent examination as the department may require to establish the adequacy of the proposed sewage or waste disposal facilities.

II. Lot sizes will be in accordance with the type of soil and its ability to absorb wastes without polluting water supplies or adjoining waters.

III. In all cases involving inspection of sewage or waste disposal systems in cities or towns which employ a full time health officer and/or building inspector, the department may delegate to such officer or inspector the responsibility for inspecting the proposed system as required under paragraph I of this section. In cities and towns which do not maintain full time health officers and/or building inspectors, the department may delegate the responsibility for such inspections to any local official deemed qualified by the department to fulfill the requirements of paragraph I of this section. All inspections delegated by the department under this paragraph to health officers, building inspectors or any other local officials shall be accomplished within 2 business days after receipt of written notification from the builder that such system is ready for inspection.

IV. The department may reject applications for septic tank disposal systems in those areas where there is already a high concentration of septic tanks on adjacent, contiguous or nearby areas or if the application is an obvious expansion, addition or annexation to an area which has already reached the maximum allowable concentration of sewage disposal through septic tanks and leaching systems.

HISTORY:

1989, 339:1. 1995, 206:2, eff. Aug. 11, 1995. 1996, 228:106, eff. July 1, 1996.

Amendments

—1996.

Substituted "department" for "division" wherever it appeared in pars. I, III and IV.

—1995.

Substituted "Natural Resources" for "Soil" following "Agriculture" in the second sentence.

485-A:35. Permit Eligibility; Exemption.

I.(a) All applications, plans, and specifications submitted in accordance with this chapter for subsurface sewage or waste disposal systems shall be prepared and signed by the individual who is directly responsible for them and who has a permit issued by the department to perform the work. The department shall issue a permit to any individual who applies to the department, pays a fee of $80, and demonstrates a sound working knowledge of the procedures and practices required in the site evaluation, design, and operation of subsurface sewage or waste disposal systems. The department shall require an oral or written examination or both to determine who may qualify for a permit. Permits shall be issued from January 1 and shall expire December 31 of every other year, subject to the grace periods specified in subparagraphs (c) and (d). Permits shall be renewable upon proper application, payment of a biennial permit fee of $80, and documentation of compliance with the continuing education requirement of subparagraph (b). A permit issued to any individual may be suspended, revoked or not renewed only for just cause and after the permit holder has had a full opportunity to be heard by the department. An appeal from a decision to revoke, suspend, or not renew a permit may be taken pursuant to RSA 541. All fees shall be deposited in the subsurface systems fund established in RSA 485-A:30, I-b.

(b) Permitted designers shall complete a minimum of 6 hours biennially of continuing education approved by the department. Any permitted designer who is also a permitted septic system installer under RSA 485-A:36 may fulfill the continuing education requirements for both permits with the same approved 6 hours of continuing education.

(c) A permitted designer who fails to file a complete application for renewal, the biennial permit fee, and documentation that the required continuing education has been completed with the department prior to the expiration of the permit shall pay an additional late renewal fee of $80 with the renewal application, biennial permit fee, and documentation, provided such fees, application, and documentation are filed with the department within 30 days of the permit expiration date.

(d) If the renewal application, biennial permit fee, late renewal fee, and documentation are not filed within 30 days of the permit expiration date, the permit shall be deemed suspended. The permit holder may request reinstatement of the permit within 60 days of the suspension by submitting a complete application for renewal, the biennial permit fee specified in subparagraph (a), the late renewal fee specified in subparagraph (c), documentation that the required continuing education has been completed, and a reinstatement fee of $80. If the individual does not request reinstatement within 60 days of the suspension, the permit shall be deemed void. Any individual whose permit has become void who wishes to obtain a designer's permit shall apply as for a new permit pursuant to subparagraph (a).

(e) No individual whose permit has been suspended or voided pursuant to subparagraph (d) shall submit any design to the department for a subsurface sewage or waste disposal system. Submittal of such a design after the designer's permit has been suspended or voided pursuant to subparagraph (d) shall constitute a violation of the provisions of this subdivision that is subject to the penalties specified in RSA 485-A:43.

II. Any person who desires to submit plans and specifications for a sewage or waste disposal system for the person's own domicile shall not be required to obtain a permit under this paragraph provided that the person attests to eligibility for this exemption in the application for construction approval. The commissioner shall adopt rules, prepared under the supervision of a professional engineer licensed to practice engineering in the state of New Hampshire, pursuant to RSA 541-A, relative to requiring a permit holder to be a licensed professional engineer with a civil or sanitary designation in order to submit applications for construction approval in certain complex situations. All fees collected pursuant to this section shall be deposited in the subsurface systems fund established in RSA 485-A:30, I-b.

HISTORY:
1989, 339:1. 1994, 312:1, eff. Aug. 7, 1994. 1996, 228:80, 106, eff. July 1, 1996. 2008, 349:4, eff. January 1, 2009. 2009, 144:44, eff. July 1, 2009. 2010, 342:1, 2, eff. September 18, 2010.

Codification.
Pursuant to 1989, 339:34, the amendment to former RSA 149-E:3, X(a) by 1989, 408:20, eff. Aug. 4, 1989, was incorporated in par. I of this section.

Amendments

—2010.
The 2010 amendment, in I(a), added "subject to the grace periods specified in subparagraphs (c) and (d)" in the fourth sentence and added "permit" following "biennial" in the fifth sentence; in I(b), substituted "6 hours biennially" for "3 hours annually" in the first sentence and added the second sentence; added I(c) through I(e); and made stylistic changes.

—2009.
The 2009 amendment added the last sentence of I(a) and substituted "section shall be deposited in the subsurface systems fund established in RSA 485-A:30, I-b" for "paragraph shall be deposited with the state treasurer as unrestricted revenue" in the last sentence of II.

—2008.
The 2008 amendment added designation I(a); in I(a), in the second sentence, substituted "$80" for "$40"; in the fourth sentence, substituted "every other" for "each" following "December 31 of"; and in the fifth sentence, substituted "payment of a biennial fee of $80, and documentation of compliance with the continuing education requirement of subparagraph (b)" for "and payment of an annual fee of $40" at the end; and added I(b).

—1996.
Paragraph I: Substituted "department" for "division" wherever it appeared.
Paragraph II: Substituted "the person's" for "his" preceding "own domicile" and "the person" for "he" preceding "attests to" and deleted "his" thereafter in the first sentence, and substituted "commissioner" for "division" in the second sentence.

—1994.
Paragraph II: In the second sentence, substituted "shall" for "may" following "division", inserted "prepared under the supervi-

sion of a professional engineer licensed to practice engineering in the state of New Hampshire" following "adopt rules", and substituted "licensed" for "registered" following "holder to be a".

485-A:36. System Installer Permit.

I.(a) No individual shall engage in the business of installing subsurface sewage or waste disposal systems under this subdivision without first obtaining an installer's permit from the department. The permit holder shall be responsible for installing the subsurface sewage or waste disposal system in strict accordance with the approved plan. The department shall issue an installer's permit to any individual who submits an application provided by the department, pays a fee of $80 and demonstrates a sound working knowledge of RSA 485-A:29–35 and the ability to read approved waste disposal plans. The department shall require an oral or written examination or both to determine who may qualify for an installer's permit. Permits shall be issued from January 1 and shall expire December 31 of every other year. Permits shall be renewable upon proper application, payment of a biennial permit fee of $80, and documentation of compliance with the continuing education requirement of subparagraph (b). The installer's permit may be suspended, revoked or not renewed for just cause, including, but not limited to, the installation of waste disposal systems in violation of this subdivision or the refusal by a permit holder to correct defective work. The department shall not suspend, revoke or refuse to renew a permit except for just cause until the permit holder has had an opportunity to be heard by the department. An appeal from such decision to revoke, suspend or not renew a permit may be taken pursuant to RSA 21-O:14. All fees shall be deposited in the subsurface systems fund established in RSA 485-A:30, I-b.

(b) Permitted installers shall complete a minimum of 6 hours biennially of continuing education approved by the department. Any permitted installer who is also a permitted designer under RSA 485-A:35 may fulfill the continuing education requirements for both permits with the same approved 6 hours of continuing education.

(c) A permitted installer who fails to file a complete application for renewal, the biennial permit fee, and documentation that the required continuing education has been completed with the department prior to the expiration of the permit shall pay an additional late renewal fee of $80 with the renewal application, biennial permit fee, and documentation, provided the fees, renewal application, and documentation are filed with the department within 30 days of the permit expiration date.

(d) If the renewal application, biennial permit fee, late renewal fee, and documentation are not filed within 30 days of the permit expiration date, the permit shall be deemed suspended. The permit holder may request reinstatement of the permit within 60 days of the suspension by submitting a complete application for renewal, the biennial permit fee specified in subparagraph (a), the late renewal fee specified in subparagraph (c), documentation that the required continuing education has been completed, and a reinstatement fee of $80. If the individual does not request reinstatement within 60 days of the suspension, the permit shall be deemed void. Any individual whose permit has become void who wishes to obtain an installer's permit shall apply as for a new permit pursuant to subparagraph (a).

(e) No individual whose permit has been suspended or voided pursuant to subparagraph (d) shall install any subsurface sewage or waste disposal system. Installation of such a system after the installer's permit has been suspended or voided pursuant to subparagraph (d) shall constitute a violation of the provisions of this subdivision that is subject to the penalties specified in RSA 485-A:43.

HISTORY:
1989, 339:1, eff. Jan. 1, 1990. 1996, 228:106, eff. July 1, 1996. 2008, 349:5, eff. January 1, 2009. 2009, 144:45, eff. July 1, 2009. 2010, 342:3, 4, eff. September 18, 2010.

Codification.
Pursuant to 1989, 339:34, the amendment to former RSA 149-E:3-a, I by 1989, 408:21, eff. Aug. 4, 1989, was incorporated in the text of this section.

Amendments

—2010.
The 2010 amendment, in I(a), in the second sentence, added "strict" and deleted "the intent of" preceding "the approved," deleted the former fifth sentence, which read: "Individuals who have been actively engaged in the business of installing systems for at least 12 months prior to January 1, 1980, shall not be required to submit to such examination, but shall be issued a permit upon filing an application and paying the initial fee, if application is made before June 30, 1980," and added "permit" following "biennial" in the sixth sentence; in I(b), substituted "6 hours biennially" for "3 hours annually" in the first sentence and added the second sentence; added I(c) through I(e); and made stylistic changes.

—2009.
The 2009 amendment substituted "in the subsurface systems fund established in RSA 485-A:30, I-b" for "with the state treasurer as unrestricted revenue" in the last sentence of I(a).

—2008.
The 2008 amendment added designation I(a); in I(a), in the third sentence, substituted "$80" for "$40"; in the sixth sentence, substi-

tuted "every other" for "each" following "December 31 of"; and in the seventh sentence, substituted "payment of a biennial fee of $80, and documentation of compliance with the continuing education requirement of subparagraph (b)" for "and payment of an annual fee of $40" at the end; and added I(b).

—1996.

Substituted "department" for "division" throughout the section.

485-A:37. Maintenance and Operation of Subsurface Septic Systems.

Any person who has installed or otherwise acquired a subsurface sewage or waste disposal system installed in accordance with the provisions of this subdivision is required to operate and maintain said system in such a manner as to prevent a nuisance or potential health hazard due to failure of the system. Failure to so operate and maintain shall be considered a violation of this chapter and shall be subject to the penalty as provided in RSA 485-A:43, IV. The department or its duly authorized agents are authorized to enter any and all premises at all reasonable hours for the purpose of inspecting and evaluating the maintenance and operating conditions of subsurface sewage or waste disposal facilities. As circumstances warrant, the department or its duly authorized agents are empowered to issue compliance orders in writing under the provisions of this section. Nothing in this section shall be construed to limit or modify the authority conferred upon the department or local health officers under the provisions of RSA 147 or upon local officials certified by the department under the provisions of RSA 485-A:42.

HISTORY:

1989, 339:1, eff. Jan. 1, 1990. 1996, 228:106, eff. July 1, 1996.

Amendments

—1996.

Substituted "department" for "division" throughout the section.

NOTES TO DECISIONS

1. Criminal violations

There was no merit to defendant's argument that RSA 485-A:37 did not allow the State to charge him with a misdemeanor because the exclusive penalty for a violation of that provision was civil forfeiture in accordance with RSA 485-A:43, IV. A violator of RSA 485-A:37 may be subject to both criminal and civil penalties. State v. Guay, 164 N.H. 696, 62 A.3d 831, 2013 N.H. LEXIS 33 (N.H. 2013).

485-A:38. Approval to Increase Load on a Sewage Disposal System.

I. Prior to expanding any structure or occupying any existing structure on a full-time basis, which would increase the load on a sewage disposal system, the owner of such structure shall submit an application for approval of the sewage disposal system to the department. Application for approval shall include one of the following:

(a) Evidence that the existing sewage disposal system meets the requirements of the department for the intended usage or the town's minimum standards for use or occupancy prescribed under RSA 48-A:11, whichever is more stringent.

(b) The design for a new system which meets the requirements of the department for the intended use or the town's minimum standards for use or occupancy, whichever is more stringent.

II. The fee for application under this section shall not exceed fees charged for new design applications.

II-a.(a) No construction or operational approval shall be required from the department prior to expanding, relocating, or replacing any structure that does not increase the load on a sewage disposal system, as long as all of the following conditions are met:

(1)(A) The lot is served by a sewage disposal system that received construction and operational approval from the department within 20 years of the date of the issuance of a building permit for the proposed expansion, relocation, or replacement; or

(B) The lot is 5 acres or more in size; or

(C) The lot is served by an off lot effluent disposal area.

(2) If the property is nonresidential, no waivers were granted in the construction or operational approval of any requirements for total wastewater lot loading, depth to groundwater, or horizontal distances to surface water, water supply systems, or very poorly drained soils.

(3) When applicable, the proposed expansion, relocation, or replacement complies with the requirements of the shoreland water quality protection act, RSA 483-B.

(b) An owner of a project that requires department approval to proceed because neither of the conditions of subparagraphs (a)(1)(A) or (B) are met, may either submit for approval a design for a new sewage disposal system or apply for a permit by rule for in-kind replacement under RSA 485-A:33, IV. Under either approach, once approval for the sewage disposal system is received from the department, work may commence on expanding, relocating, or replacing the structure. Construction of the sewage disposal system is not required to satisfy the requirements of this subparagraph.

III. The commissioner shall adopt rules under RSA 541-A requiring a person to comply with the provisions of paragraph I before taking any action which would increase the load on a sewage disposal system.

HISTORY:

1989, 339:1, eff. Jan. 1, 1990. 1996, 228:106, 110, eff. July 1, 1996. 2010, 342:5, eff. September 18, 2010. 2011, 224:411, eff. June 29, 2011. 2012, 147:1, eff. June 7, 2012. 2017, 238:3, eff. September 16, 2017.

Contingent 2012 amendment.

2012, 147:7, eff. June 7, 2012, provided in part, that if HB 1415 [ch. 174] of the 2012 legislative session becomes law, section 1 of this act shall take effect upon its passage and sections 2– 4 of this act shall not take effect. Pursuant to the terms of this provision RSA 485-A:38, II-a is set out above as amended by Ch. 147:1, eff. June 7, 2012.

Amendment Notes
The 2017 amendments to this section by Ch. 238 added II-a(a)(1)(C); and made a related change.

—2012.
The 2012 amendment added the II-a(a) designation; redesignated former II-a(a) through II-a(c) as II-a(a)(1)(A), II-a(a)(2), and II-a(a)(3); added II-a(a)(1)(B) added II-a(b); and made a related change.

—2011.
The 2011 amendment substituted "shoreland water quality" for "comprehensive shoreland" in II-a(c).

—2010.
The 2010 amendment added II-a.

—1996.
Paragraph I: Substituted "department" for "division" wherever it occurred.
Paragraph III: Substituted "commissioner" for "division".

485-A:39. Waterfront Property Sale; Site Assessment Study.

I. Prior to the execution of a purchase and sale agreement for any developed waterfront property using a septic disposal system, the owner of the property shall, at the owner's expense, engage a permitted subsurface sewer or waste disposal system designer to perform a site assessment study to determine if the site meets the current standards for septic disposal systems established by the department. The site assessment study shall include an on-site inspection. If the site assessment is not complete prior to the time that the buyer and seller enter into a purchase and sale contract, the contract shall be subject to the buyer's acceptance of the completed site assessment.

II. The site assessment study form shall become a part of the purchase and sale agreement.

III. The site assessment study form, with stated findings, shall be given to the buyer and the seller and receipt of the form shall be acknowledged in writing by the buyer and the seller.

IV. Failure of the seller or the seller's agent to notify the buyer of the findings or deliver the completed site assessment study form pursuant to paragraph III of this section shall be a violation and, notwithstanding RSA 651:2, shall be punishable by a fine not to exceed $500.

V. The site assessment study shall consist of 3 sections:

(a) Section A shall include the name, address, and telephone number of the seller and the seller's agent and the location and a brief description of the property, including the tax map reference and lot number.

(b) Section B shall include the lot size, slope, loading (based on the number of bedrooms in the structure), water source, soil type, and estimated

seasonal high water table information from U.S. Natural Resources Conservation Service maps. A space shall be included on the form for the permitted designer to write his assessment of the site for the current use of the system, based upon the criteria and information required in this subparagraph.

(c) Section C shall include information about the present septic disposal system, if available. If the installed system was approved by the department, a copy of the approval form, approval number and plan shall be attached to the site assessment study.

VI. The department shall design the site assessment form pursuant to paragraph V of this section. The commissioner shall adopt rules pursuant to RSA 541-A relative to the procedures for the availability and distribution of the form to interested parties.

VII. An assessment indicating that the site fails to meet any of the criteria established under this section shall not prohibit the sale of the property but shall be disclosed to the buyer as full and proper notice of the possible limitations of the site for a septic disposal system.

VIII. If the septic disposal system designer, during the course of a site assessment, discovers evidence that there is sewage discharge on the ground surface or directly into surface waters, the designer shall notify, in writing, the department and the local health officer, and shall include that information in the site assessment report.

HISTORY:
1989, 339:1. 1992, 278:2. 1995, 206:2, eff. Aug. 11, 1995. 1996, 228:81, 106, eff. July 1, 1996. 2007, 177:1, eff. August 17, 2007. 2008, 349:1, eff. January 1, 2009.

Amendments

—2008.
The 2008 amendment in I, in the first sentence, substituted "the owner's" for "his or her"; in III, added "and the seller" twice; in IV, substituted "the completed site assessment study form" for "approved plans of the septic disposal system"; deleted the former second paragraph of V(c); added VII and VIII.

—2007.
Paragraph I: Inserted "or her" following "property shall, at his" and added the third sentence.

—1996.
Substituted "department" for "division" in the first sentence of par. I, the second sentence of par. V(c) and the first sentence of par. VI and "commissioner" for "division" in the second sentence of par. V(c).

—1995.
Paragraph V(b): Substituted "Natural Resources" for "Soil" preceding "Conservation Service" in the first sentence.

—1992.
Paragraph I: In the first sentence substituted "the execution of a purchase and sale agreement for" for "offering for sale" following "prior to", "septic" for "sewage" following "property using a" and following "standards for" and "permitted subsurface sewer or waste" for "licensed sewage" following "engage a", and in the second

sentence substituted "shall include an on-site inspection" for "may be completed off-site" following "study".

Paragraph II: Substituted "purchase and sale" for "listing" preceding "agreement" and deleted "before the developed waterfront property may be offered for sale" thereafter.

Paragraph IV: Substituted "septic" for "sewage" preceding "disposal".

Paragraph V: Substituted "permitted" for "licensed" preceding "designer" in the second sentence of subpar. (b) and "septic" for "sewage" preceding "disposal" in the first sentence of subpar. (c) and in the concluding sentence.

NOTES TO DECISIONS

Construction

Seller's failure to strictly comply with this section did not entitle purchasers to rescission of contract for purchase of property. Gray v. First NH Banks, 138 N.H. 279, 640 A.2d 276, 1994 N.H. LEXIS 17 (N.H. 1994).

RESEARCH REFERENCES AND PRACTICE AIDS

Cross References.

Classification of crimes, see RSA 625:9.

Written notification of sewage disposal system requirements, see RSA 477:4-c.

New Hampshire Bar Journal.

For article, "Lex Loci," see N.H.B.J. 68 (1994).

485-A:40. Reconsideration and Appeal Procedure.

If any person submitting plans and specifications to the department for its approval is aggrieved or dissatisfied with its decision, he may file a motion for reconsideration and shall have a right of appeal from the decision of the department in the following manner:

I. Within 20 days after any decision of the department, any person whose rights may be directly affected may apply to the department for reconsideration of any matter determined by the department in its decision, specifying in the motion for reconsideration the grounds therefor, and the department may reconsider and revise its decision if in the opinion of the department good reason therefor is stated in said motion.

II. Such motion shall set forth fully every ground upon which it is claimed that the decision of the department is unlawful or unreasonable. No appeal from any decision of the department shall be taken unless the appellant shall have made application for reconsideration as provided in this section, and when such application shall have been made, no ground not set forth in such application shall be urged, relied on, or given any consideration by the court, unless the court for good cause shown shall allow the appellant to specify additional grounds.

III. Upon the filing of a motion for reconsideration, the department shall within 30 days either grant or deny the motion, and, at the same time, shall affirm, modify or reverse its decision.

IV. Within 30 days after the application for reconsideration is denied, or if the application is granted, then within 30 days after the decision on such reconsideration, the applicant may appeal by petition to the superior court.

V. Upon the hearing, the burden of proof shall be upon the party seeking to set aside the decision of the department to show that the same is unreasonable or unlawful, and all findings of the department upon all questions of fact properly before it shall be deemed to be prima facie lawful and reasonable; and the order or decision appealed from shall not be set aside or vacated, except for errors of law, unless the court is persuaded by the balance of probabilities, on the evidence before it, that the decision is unjust or unreasonable.

VI. Any person whose rights may be directly affected by said appeal may appear and become a party, or the court may order such persons to be joined as parties as justice may require.

VII. Upon the filing of an appeal, the clerk of court shall issue a summons requiring a certified copy of the record appealed from to be filed with the court. The filing of an appeal shall not suspend the decision appealed from, unless the court, on application and for good cause shown, shall grant a restraining order.

VIII. All evidence transferred by the department shall be, and all additional evidence received may be, considered by the court regardless of any technical rules which might have rendered the same inadmissible if originally offered in the trial of an action at law.

IX. The final judgment upon every appeal shall be a decree dismissing the appeal, or vacating the decision complained of in whole or in part, as the case may be; but in case such decision is wholly or partly vacated the court may also, in its discretion, remand the matter to the department for such further proceedings, not inconsistent with the decree, as justice may require.

X. An order of court to send up the record may be complied with by filing either the original papers or duly certified copies, or of such portions of such papers, as the order may specify, together with a certified statement of such other facts as show the grounds of the action appealed from.

XI. The court may take evidence or appoint a referee to take such evidence as it may direct and report the same with his findings of fact and conclusions of law.

XII. Costs shall not be allowed against the department unless it shall appear to the court that it acted with gross negligence, or in bad faith, or with malice in making the decision appealed from.

XIII. All proceedings under this chapter shall be entitled to a speedy hearing. If such hearing cannot be had within 30 days after the filing of the appeal, upon request of the appellant the matter shall be referred to a master.

HISTORY:

1989, 339:1, eff. Jan. 1, 1990. 1996, 228:106, eff. July 1, 1996. 2014, 204:30, eff. July 11, 2014.

Amendment Notes

—2014.

The 2014 amendment substituted "a summons" for "an order of notice" in the first sentence of VII.

—1996.

Substituted "department" for "division" throughout the section.

485-A:41. Rulemaking; Duties of the Commissioner.

The commissioner shall:

I. Exercise general supervision over the administration and enforcement of this subdivision.

II. Employ necessary personnel.

III. Prohibit construction of systems which would pollute the surface waters or groundwaters of the state, until an acceptable and practicable method exists which will prevent the pollution.

IV. Adopt rules, pursuant to RSA 541-A and after public hearing, relative to the implementation of this subdivision. The commissioner shall adopt rules relative to the circumstances under which the commissioner may grant a waiver of any rule, except that no waivers of rules relating to site loading or set-back distances to ground or surface waters shall be allowed for sewage or waste disposal systems on lots in subdivisions created after September 1, 1989. A waiver must be consistent with the intent of this subdivision and have a just result. In particular, an encroachment waiver shall meet the following criteria:

(a) The proposed waiver shall not encroach upon the right of the owner of abutting property to fully utilize his land, unless said property owner has granted consent in the form of a signed waiver or deeded easement; and

(b) Denial of the waiver would result in unnecessary hardship to the owner due to special characteristics of the property.

V. Adopt rules relative to the application for and granting of permits by rule for repair or replacement of certain sewage or waste disposal systems under RSA 485-A:33, IV.

HISTORY:

1989, 339:1, eff. Jan. 1, 1990. 1996, 228:82, 110, eff. July 1, 1996. 2012, 174:3, eff. June 11, 2012.

Codification.

Pursuant to 1989, 339:34, the amendment to former RSA 149-E:5, IV by 1989, 79:3, eff. July 30, 1989, was incorporated in par. IV of this section.

Contingent 2012 amendment.

2012, 147:7, eff. June 7, 2012, provided in part, that if HB 1415 [ch. 174] of the 2012 legislative session becomes law, section 1 of this act shall take effect upon its passage and sections 2– 4 of this act shall not take effect. Pursuant to the terms of this provision RSA 485-A:38, II-a is set out above as amended by Ch. 147:1, eff. June 7, 2012.

Amendments

—2012.

The 2012 amendment added V.

—1996.

Substituted "commissioner" for "division" in the section catchline, in the introductory paragraph and in the first sentence of par. IV and "the commissioner" for "it" preceding "may grant" in the second sentence in par. IV.

485-A:42. Enforcement.

I.(a) The department may issue an order to any person in violation of this chapter, of rules adopted under this chapter, or of any condition of a permit issued under this chapter.

(b) The department may require such remedial measures as are necessary to correct the violation.

(c) Such order may be appealed in accordance with RSA 21-O:14.

II. The written order issued under the provisions of paragraph I shall be recorded by the department in the registry of deeds for the county in which the property is situated and, upon recordation, the order shall run with the land; provided, however, that an appropriate description of the land involved including the accurate name of the land's owner shall be incorporated in the order. No fee shall be charged for recording such an administrative order; however, the fee for discharge of any such order shall be the same as for the discharge of a real estate lien.

III. Upon certification by the department, local officials are hereby authorized and fully empowered to exercise concurrent jurisdiction in the enforcement of this subdivision.

HISTORY:

1989, 339:1, eff. Jan. 1, 1990. 1996, 228:83, 106, eff. July 1, 1996.

Codification.

The amendment to former RSA 149-E:6 by 1989, 82:1, eff. June 30, 1989, was incorporated in the text of this section pursuant to 1989, 339:34; "division" was substituted for "division of water supply and pollution control" in pars. I(a), II and III in view of RSA 485-A:2, III, as added by 1989, 339:1; and "subdivision" was substituted for "chapter" at the end of par. III for purposes of conformity with 1989, 339:1.

Amendments

—1996.

Substituted "department" for "division" throughout the section and substituted "in accordance with RSA 21-O:14" for "to the water supply and pollution control council" following "appealed" in par. I(c).

485-A:43. Penalties.

I. Any person who shall violate any of the provisions of this subdivision or who shall knowingly fail, neglect or refuse to obey any order of the department or member or authorized agent of the department issued under the authority of this subdivision, or who shall knowingly make any misstatement of material fact for which said person is personally responsible in connection with an application for an approval pursuant to this subdivision shall be guilty of a misdemeanor if a natural person, or guilty of a felony if any other person.

II. Any person who knowingly produces any erroneous or fallacious data with regard to any application or plan submitted pursuant to this subdivision shall bear the full responsibility for same, and shall be guilty of a misdemeanor if a natural person, or guilty of a felony if any other person.

III. Notwithstanding any other penalty or fine for which liability is provided under this subdivision, any person may be liable to the state, in an action commenced in the name of the state, for a civil forfeiture of not more than $10,000 per day per violation for such violation, failure, neglect, refusal or any misstatement for which said person is personally responsible. Such forfeiture may be levied by the superior court in connection with actions for injunctive relief commenced pursuant to RSA 485-A:44. The proceeds of any civil forfeiture levied under this section shall be utilized in the enforcement of this subdivision. In determining a civil forfeiture, the court may take into consideration all relevant circumstances, including the degree of noncompliance, the extent of harm caused by the violation, the nature and persistence of the violation, the time and cost associated with the investigation by the state and the economic impact of the penalty on the liable person. The cost of corrective action shall not be considered in determining the civil forfeiture.

IV. Any person neglecting or refusing to comply with the provisions of RSA 485-A:37 shall be subject to a civil forfeiture not to exceed $1,000 for each day of neglect or refusal after notice as provided for in RSA 485-A:37.

V. The commissioner of environmental services, after notice and hearing pursuant to RSA 541-A, may impose an administrative fine not to exceed $2,000 for each offense upon any person who violates any provision of this subdivision including any rule adopted under the provisions of this chapter. Rehearings and appeals from a decision of the commissioner under this paragraph shall be in accordance with RSA 541. Any administrative fine imposed under this section shall not preclude the imposition of further penalties under this subdivision. The proceeds of administrative fines levied pursuant to this paragraph shall be deposited by the department in the general fund. The commissioner shall adopt rules, under RSA 541-A, relative to:

(a) A schedule of administrative fines which may be imposed under this paragraph for violations of this subdivision as provided above.

(b) Procedures for notice and hearing prior to the imposition of an administrative fine.

HISTORY:

1989, 339:1. 1995, 217:8, eff. Jan. 1, 1996. 1996, 228:106, eff. July 1, 1996. 2008, 169:1, eff. January 1, 2009.

Amendments

—2008.

The 2008 amendment substituted "$10,000 per day per violation" for "$5,000" preceding "for such violation" in the first sentence and added the fourth and fifth sentences.

—1996.

Substituted "department" for "division" throughout par. I and in the third sentence of the introductory paragraph of par. V.

—1995.

Paragraph V: Added "including any rule adopted under the provisions of this chapter" following "subdivision" in the first sentence and substituted "RSA 541" for "RSA 21-O:14" in the second sentence of the introductory paragraph and substituted "violations" for "violation" preceding "of this subdivision" and added "as provided above" thereafter in subpar. (a).

NOTES TO DECISIONS

Analysis

1. Construction
2. Criminal violations
3. Propriety of penalty

1. Construction

There is no conflict between a provision stating that violations of the sewage disposal systems subdivision are considered criminal acts, RSA 485-A:43, I, and a provision stating that a person may be subject to a civil fine for each day of noncompliance with a written Department of Environmental Services order, RSA 485-A:43, IV. State v. Guay, 164 N.H. 696, 62 A.3d 831, 2013 N.H. LEXIS 33 (N.H. 2013).

2. Criminal violations

There was no merit to defendant's argument that RSA 485-A:37 did not allow the State to charge him with a misdemeanor because the exclusive penalty for a violation of that provision was civil forfeiture in accordance with RSA 485-A:43, IV. A violator of RSA 485-A:37 may be subject to both criminal and civil penalties. State v. Guay, 164 N.H. 696, 62 A.3d 831, 2013 N.H. LEXIS 33 (N.H. 2013).

3. Propriety of penalty

Trial court properly fined respondents $5,000 under the Water Pollution Act, RSA 485-A:43, I, for their failure to obtain prior approval to construct a building from which waste would discharge, because the fine was based on the failure to obtain prior approval for the construction, not on disobedience of an order by the Department of Environmental Services. N.H. Dep't of Envtl. Servs. v. Marino, 155 N.H. 709, 928 A.2d 818, 2007 N.H. LEXIS 120 (N.H. 2007).

RESEARCH REFERENCES AND PRACTICE AIDS

Cross References.

Classification of crimes, see RSA 625:9.

Sentences, see RSA 651.

485-A:44. Injunction to Enforce.

I. On application of the department, the superior court or any justice of the court, in term time or in vacation, may enjoin any act in violation of this subdivision.

II. Municipalities may apply to a justice of the superior court for injunctive relief against existing or impending violations of this subdivision. The municipality shall give notice of any such action to the attorney general and the commissioner of environmental services, who may take such action as they deem necessary to ensure uniform statewide enforcement, including but not limited to joining the action, assuming sole prosecution of the action, or, as of right, dismissing the action without prejudice.

Such notice shall be given at least 30 days prior to the commencement of any such action, unless more immediate action is necessary to prevent irreparable environmental damage or other serious public harm, in which case such notice shall be given as soon as practicable, but in no event later than the date of commencement of the action. This paragraph shall not be construed to affect, in any manner, existing authority of municipalities to act based upon the provisions of other statutes or local ordinances.

HISTORY:
1989, 339:1. 1991, 340:5, eff. Jan. 1, 1992. 1996, 228:106, eff. July 1, 1996.

Amendments

—1996.
Paragraph I: Substituted "department" for "division".

—1991.
Designated the existing provisions of the section as par. I and added. II.

Winnipesaukee River Basin Control

RESEARCH REFERENCES AND PRACTICE AIDS

New Hampshire Code of Administrative Rules
Rules of the Department of Environmental Services—Water Supply and Pollution Control Division, Evn-Ws 1201.01 et seq., New Hampshire Code of Administrative Rules Annotated.

485-A:45. Authority to Acquire, Construct, and Operate.

I. The department is authorized and directed to acquire, plan, construct, and operate, to serve certain municipalities within the Winnipesaukee river basin (including, but not necessarily limited to Meredith, Laconia, Gilford, Belmont, Sanbornton, Tilton, Northfield, and Franklin) any and all sewage and waste disposal facilities (meaning only those facilities eligible for state aid) in accordance with basin and regional treatment needs consistent with federal and state requirements.

II. The word "construction" shall include all engineering services in addition to the construction of new sewage or waste treatment plants, pumping stations, and intercepting sewers; the altering, improving or adding to existing treatment plants, pumping stations, and intercepting sewers (except those intercepting sewers and facilities retained by municipalities); or any other associated work, or both, the intent being to include within the department area of responsibility all construction work considered eligible for state financial assistance under the provisions of RSA 486, and including any necessary land acquisition, easements and rights-of-way.

III. To achieve a high degree of reliability and to provide for efficient layout, construction and maintenance of pollution control facilities, the department is authorized to locate sewer and related facilities in all public roadways, whether owned or controlled by a municipality or the state subject to RSA 236:9.

IV. The department is also obligated to restore the public roads, when disturbed for the purpose indicated in paragraph III, to a condition acceptable to local and state highway authorities.

V. Nothing in this section shall be construed to impair or repeal the authority conferred upon municipalities, under RSA 149-I, to construct main drains and common sewers. Nothing in this section shall be construed to impair or repeal the authority conferred upon municipalities under RSA 147 to make and enforce regulations concerning disposal of wastes and abatement of nuisances. The municipalities served under this chapter may, by ordinance or regulation, increase the 100 foot distance contained in RSA 147:8 and RSA 147:11. Such regulations shall apply to the municipal sewerage system and to the regional facilities located within the municipality.

VI. Nothing contained in this section shall be construed to entitle municipalities to receive state aid in excess of their entitlement as provided for in connection with construction as defined in RSA 486.

VII. To produce maximum benefits with the least expenditure of federal, state, and local funds, the department, or any municipality served under this subdivision, is authorized, under terms mutually agreed upon, to accept full responsibility for the planning of sewerage projects involving a mixture of eligible and ineligible facilities as defined in RSA 486. The department and the particular municipality involved will bear their pro-rata share of the associated costs for the work performed under such an agreement.

HISTORY:
1989, 339:1, eff. Jan. 1, 1990. 1996, 228:106, eff. July 1, 1996.

Amendments

—1996.
Substituted "department" for "division" throughout the section.

NOTES TO DECISIONS

Cited:
Cited in Town of Tilton v. State, 137 N.H. 463, 629 A.2d 791, 1993 N.H. LEXIS 101 (1993).

485-A:46. Existing Disposal Systems.

Any future payments due from a municipality which has undertaken construction (or engaged in engineering study, planning or design), as outlined in RSA 485-A:45, since July 1, 1947, to pay for such construction, study, planning, or design, and the facility involved is acquired by the department, shall automatically become the obligation of the state, including engineering services and contract costs. With respect to payments for engineering services and contract costs in connection with contracts entered into after July 1, 1967, it is the intention of this section to obligate the state only if the contract giving rise to such obligations has been entered into pursuant to the provisions of RSA 485-A:4, XII.

HISTORY:

1989, 339:1, eff. Jan. 1, 1990. 1996, 228:106, eff. July 1, 1996.

Amendments

—1996.

Substituted "department" for "division" preceding "shall automatically" in the first sentence.

NOTES TO DECISIONS

Analysis

1. Obligation of towns
2. Indemnification of towns

1. Obligation of towns

Although a statute obligates the state to pay for engineering services and contract costs related to the construction of sewerage systems, it does not absolve towns of any initial obligation they might have under their own contracts or based on implied in law contract. Morgenroth & Assocs. v. Tilton, 121 N.H. 511, 431 A.2d 770, 1981 N.H. LEXIS 359 (N.H. 1981). (Decided under prior law.)

2. Indemnification of towns

A written contract cosigned by the New Hampshire Water Supply and Pollution Control Commission is a necessary prerequisite for a town to seek indemnification from the state under this section. Town of Tilton v. State, 137 N.H. 463, 629 A.2d 791, 1993 N.H. LEXIS 101 (N.H. 1993). (Decided under prior law.)

485-A:47. Administration.

To administer the provisions of this chapter and to perform such other related duties as may be required, the department of environmental services is designated as the agency to receive and utilize any federal or other aids which may at any time be made available in the interest of water pollution control in the basin. The department is empowered to hire consulting engineering firms for purposes of project design and to employ such professional, technical, clerical, accounting, or other staff or consulting personnel as are required to implement the provisions of this subdivision and to arrange for the orderly transfer of ownership and operation of existing pollution abatement facilities to the department on behalf of the state of New Hampshire within the limits of legislative appropriations. Any personnel (other than consultants) employed by the department shall be subject to the personnel laws of the state. This subdivision shall in no way impair or render null and void existing contracts between municipalities, contractors or other parties, or any of them, in connection with pollution control projects or sewerage, sewage or waste service contracts within the basin. Nothing in this subdivision shall be construed as prohibiting future sewerage or waste service contracts otherwise authorized by law between municipalities directly connected to the

regional facilities provided for by this subdivision and other persons, including but not limited to municipalities, served or to be served by such facilities but not directly connected to such facilities. All such future contracts, however, shall be submitted at least 60 days in advance of their effective dates to the department, which is empowered to disapprove the terms of any such future contract in whole or in part when in its judgment the efficient administration or the purposes of this subdivision would be adversely affected, and such contract shall not be valid to the extent it is disapproved. In any such contract, unless otherwise specifically provided in the contract, the person or persons served by such regional facility but not directly connected to such facility shall have strict responsibility for the accurate measurement of the amount of sewage or waste disposed of by such person or persons and shall be liable to the municipality directly connected to such regional facilities for the entire amount of sewage or waste, as measured, if any inaccuracy is in favor of such municipality, and for the actual amount of sewage or waste, as estimated, if any inaccuracy is in favor of such person or persons. The commissioner is authorized to adopt, pursuant to RSA 541-A and after public hearing, such rules as are necessary to implement the provisions of this subdivision.

HISTORY:

1989, 339:1, eff. Jan. 1, 1990. 1996, 228:84, eff. July 1, 1996.

Amendments

—1996.

Substituted "department" for "division" in the second, third and sixth sentences and "commissioner" for "division" in the eighth sentence.

485-A:48. Application of the Statutes.

All present powers, duties and functions conferred upon municipalities within the basin in connection with the planning, construction, financing and operation of sewage or waste treatment facilities (excepting common sewers and other collector facilities considered ineligible for state grants under the provisions of RSA 486), or both, as are contained in RSA 485, 485-A, 149-I and applicable statutes, are transferred to the department. Personnel of municipalities engaged in the operation of sewage or waste treatment facilities, or both, as referred to in this subdivision, shall be given an opportunity to become employees of the department (with all benefits previously accrued) upon the effective date of the transfer of the municipal sewage or waste treatment facilities, or both, to the department. In no case shall personnel accepting state employment, as provided under this subdivision, be paid less than the salary paid such individuals as of January 1, 1973, nor shall they suffer a loss or reduction in benefits associated with tenure of service. It shall be the responsibility of the municipality previously employing the individual to supplement such staff of

New Hampshire benefits if they are less than the employee might have received if his employment had continued uninterrupted with the municipality.

HISTORY:
1989, 339:1, eff. Jan. 1, 1990. 1996, 228:106, eff. July 1, 1996.

Revision note.
Substituted "RSA 485, 485-A, 149-I" for "RSA 485, 485-A, 252" in the first sentence in view of the recodification of the provisions of RSA 252 relating to sewers as RSA 149-I by 1981, 87:1, 2.

Substituted "state" for "staff" preceding "of New Hampshire" in the last sentence to correct an apparent typographical error.

Amendments

—1996.
Substituted "department" for "division" throughout the section.

485-A:49. Expenditures.

I. With the approval of the governor and council, the department may use state, federal or other funds accruing to the department and funds borrowed from the state water pollution control and drinking water revolving loan fund established under RSA 486:14 for the acquisition of existing sewage or waste treatment facilities, design and construction of new sewage or waste treatment facilities, alteration, improvement or additions to existing sewage or waste treatment facilities, pumping stations and intercepting sewers, inclusive of operation and maintenance of same; the terms operation and maintenance of treatment facilities shall include maintenance of all buildings, equipment, supplies, and administrative costs associated with the management of the treatment facilities, and for such other purposes as may be involved in the operation of an effective regional pollution control program. The department may purchase, take and hold for the state such materials, lands, easements and rights-of-way as may be required for the purposes of this subdivision. If the department is unable to purchase lands, easements or rights-of-way at what is deemed reasonable compensation, the department shall request the governor and council to appoint a commission to assess the damages sustained by the owner, and thereupon proceedings shall be conducted in the same manner and in accordance with provisions of RSA 230.

I-a. In addition to the uses set forth in paragraph I, and with the approval of the governor and council, the department may evaluate the most cost effective operation of such systems, including evaluating the cost effectiveness of alternative governance structures for the Winnipesaukee River basin control program under this subdivision. The department may not make any changes to the current governance structure unless specifically authorized by statute. The department may present any recommendations concerning alternative governance structures to the general court for consideration.

II. To provide funds for the municipal share of the costs involved pursuant to this subdivision, the state treasurer is authorized to borrow upon the credit of the state not exceeding the sum of $3,000,000 and for said purposes may issue bonds and notes in the name and on behalf of the state of New Hampshire in accordance with the provisions of RSA 6-A.

III. The payments of principal and interest on the bonds issued under paragraph II shall be made when due from the special fund established by RSA 485-A:50, VI.

HISTORY:
1989, 339:1, eff. Jan. 1, 1990. 1996, 228:106, eff. July 1, 1996. 2005, 117:1, eff. Aug. 14, 2005. 2016, 125:1, eff. July 19, 2016.

Amendment Notes
The 2016 amendments to this section by Ch. 125 added paragraph I-a.

—2005.
Paragraph I: Inserted "and funds borrowed from the state water pollution control and drinking water revolving loan fund established under RSA 486:14" in the first sentence.

—1996.
Paragraph I: Substituted "department" for "division" wherever it appeared.

485-A:50. Municipal Assessments.

I. The department shall annually, at the beginning of each fiscal year, assess each municipality served by the regional sewage disposal facilities provided for by this subdivision, a sum sufficient to recover its proportional share of the total in relation to the total costs estimated to be incurred during said fiscal year in treating, transporting and disposal of sewage of the communities served and those to be served; the proportional share of each community shall be determined by the procedure provided for in paragraph IV.

II. The department shall annually, at the beginning of each fiscal year, assess each municipality served or to be served by the regional sewage disposal facilities provided for by the provisions of this subdivision the costs estimated to be incurred during said fiscal year in administering this subdivision, plus a charge for amortization charges on such costs of all facilities amounting to 5 percent of the total amortization charges, meaning principal and interest, on such charges. The proportional share of each community's costs shall be determined by the procedure provided for in paragraph IV.

III. The respective share of the assessments made in paragraphs I and II shall be paid to the department by each municipality quarterly on July fifteenth, October fifteenth, January fifteenth, and April fifteenth of that fiscal year, except for capital cost recovery assessments which shall be paid annually on July fifteenth. After the close of each fiscal year, the department shall ascertain its actual total expenses in accordance with the foregoing provisions, and then shall adjust the assessment for the second quarterly payment of the new fiscal year for each such municipality served for any under-payment or over-payment by each such municipality served for the prior fiscal year.

IV. The assessments provided to be made by this section shall be made by taking into account the volume and strength of the industrial, domestic, commercial, and all other waste discharges treated or the estimated volume and strength of the industrial, domestic, commercial and all other waste discharges to be treated and techniques of treatment required. Proportional costs as determined by the department, associated with transporting raw and treated sewage through a major interceptor from a municipality at which it is generated or is to be generated to the point of treatment or discharge shall be allocated to the municipality which uses or will use the interceptor on the basis of volume and distance traveled or estimated volume and distance traveled. In determining said assessments for each municipality, the department shall abide by federal regulations which govern the allocation of costs and receipt of payments by industry for industrial discharges. Any operating and maintenance costs over and above what has been determined to be proportional by the department shall be an obligation of the state.

V. The municipality may recover charges assessed by means of user charges, connection fees, or such other techniques as may be utilized under state and local law, including sewage, sewerage, and waste service contracts, except that municipalities with industrial waste must abide by federal and state regulations which govern recovery of costs from said industries.

VI. All funds collected by the department by virtue of the assessments authorized under this section shall be paid to the state treasurer who shall keep the same in a special fund.

VII. Any municipality aggrieved or dissatisfied with any annual assessment levied against it under the provisions of this section may file a motion for reconsideration by the department control in the same manner and as provided in RSA 485-A:40.

VIII. The charges assessed by the department shall be made against the municipalities which are directly connected to the regional facilities provided for by this subsection and shall include:

(a) any sewage or waste generated within the municipality and transported to such regional facilities, and

(b) any sewage or waste generated outside the municipality and being transported through such municipality's sewage system. Such municipality may recover the charges assessed in accordance with paragraph V.

HISTORY:
1989, 339:1, eff. Jan. 1, 1990. 1996, 228:106, eff. July 1, 1996. 2007, 5:1, eff. July 1, 2007.

Revision note.
Substituted "this subdivision" for "this subsection" in the introductory clause of par. VIII to correct an error in the reference.

Amendments

—2007.
Paragraph III: Added "except for capital cost recovery assessment which shall be paid annually on July fifteenth" at the end of the first sentence and substituted "second" for "first" following "adjust the assessment for the" in the second sentence.

—1996.
Substituted "department" for "division" throughout the section.

485-A:51. Replacement Fund Established.

I. There is established a nonlapsing, revolving fund to provide capital for repair and replacement of major components of the water pollution control facilities administered under this subdivision which cannot be absorbed as regular budgetary items. The replacement fund is to be capitalized by contributions from the members served by the facilities based on each member's projected usage of the facilities.

II. The fund shall equal 5 percent of the equipment and other depreciable assets of the treatment facilities. The value of the equipment and other depreciable assets shall be computed every 5 years, beginning in 1990, and shall be based on current replacement costs.

III. Each member's share of the total fund shall be contributed over a period of 10 years after the initial establishment of the fund and shall be paid as a yearly surcharge to the member's operating charges. Thereafter, each member's surcharge shall be prorated as membership and design changes require.

IV. Once a member has fully funded its share of the replacement fund, the member shall make no further contributions until the fund is utilized for repair or replacement of a facility used by that member. Expenses for which the fund is used shall be proportionally charged against each member's contributions to the fund for the facilities utilizing the fund, which will subsequently be reimbursed by the member in successive years in addition to the member's yearly contribution to the fund, until the member's share of the fund is fully restored.

V. If a repair or replacement cost exceeds the value of the fund established for that particular facility, the repair cost shall be paid out of the portion of the fund established for other facilities, but reimbursement to the fund shall always be assessed back to members based on their projected usage of the facilities needing repair.

VI. As new facilities, if any, are added to the system, additional assessments shall be made to the members benefiting from these facilities, prorated on the basis of projected use.

VII. If a new member joins the system, the assessments shall be modified to reflect the new member's benefit from the facilities, and excess prior payments made by other members, if any, shall be credited to their accounts.

VIII. All contracts paid for using the fund shall be submitted to the governor and council for approval.

IX. This nonlapsing, revolving special purpose fund is continually appropriated to be used by the department in accordance with this subdivision. All moneys shall be deposited with the state treasurer who shall keep this money in a separate fund, notwithstanding RSA 6:12. The state treasurer shall invest the moneys deposited with him as provided by law. Interest received on investments made by the state treasurer shall also be credited to the fund. All such interest shall be added to each member's share of the fund based on each member's contribution to it.

HISTORY:

1989, 339:1, eff. Jan. 1, 1990. 1996, 228:106, eff. July 1, 1996.

Amendments

—1996.

Paragraph IX: Substituted "department" for "division" in the first sentence.

485-A:52. Advisory Board Established.

I. There is established a Winnipesaukee River advisory board consisting of one member, from each community, appointed by the board of selectmen of a town or the city council of a city involved. The term of office of each member shall be one year commencing July 1, 1972, and each member shall serve until his or her successor shall have been appointed. The advisory board shall annually elect a chairman by majority vote of its members, and the board shall meet at least quarterly upon the call of the chairman or at least 3 members of the board in order to consider matters properly coming before it for attention. The advisory board shall meet with the department at suitable intervals to review matters of mutual concern. An annual budget shall be submitted to the advisory board by the department, for review and comment, 60 days prior to the beginning of the new fiscal year. Members of the advisory board shall receive no per diem but shall be entitled to reimbursement for expenses including mileage when in the performance of duties required under this subdivision. Each municipality shall provide funds necessary to reimburse its members to the advisory board.

II. The advisory board shall make a recommendation to the governor and executive council on each request for a contract to plan, design, or construct capital improvements using moneys for expenditures under RSA 485-A:49. The department of environmental services shall include a letter from the advisory board to the governor and executive council documenting the decision and recommendations of the advisory board on such contract for the governor and executive council's consideration before approving or denying such contract.

HISTORY:

1989, 339:1, eff. Jan. 1, 1990. 1996, 228:106, eff. July 1, 1996. 2016, 104:1, eff. July 18, 2016.

Amendment Notes

The **2016 amendments to this section by Ch. 104**, added the I designation; added "or her" in the second sentence of paragraph I; and added paragraph II.

—1996.

Substituted "department" for "division" throughout the section.

485-A:53. Insurance.

The department shall purchase insurance, including extended coverage insurance, to protect the pollution control facilities administered under this subdivision against fire, vandalism, and malicious mischief. The cost of the insurance shall be included in the user fee. If the department determines that any of the foregoing insurance is unavailable or uneconomical, it may request the governor and council to waive the provisions of this section for the term of the coverage. Nothing in this section shall be construed as a waiver of the state's sovereign immunity regardless of the department's ability to procure the types of insurance described in this section.

HISTORY:

1989, 339:1, eff. Jan. 1, 1990. 1996, 228:106, eff. July 1, 1996. 2014, 146:1, eff. August 15, 2014. 2014, 327:69, eff. August 2, 2014.

Amendment Notes

—2014.

The 2014 amendment by Chapter 146, rewrote the section to the extent that a detailed comparison would be impracticable.

The 2014 amendment by Chapter 327, substituted "department of administrative services, division of procurement and support services" for "director of plant and property management" in the second sentence.

—1996.

Substituted "department" for "division" throughout the section.

485-A:54. Enforcement and Penalties.

I. The department may issue an order to any person in violation of this subdivision, a rule adopted under this subdivision, or any condition in any contract or permit issued or entered into under this subdivision. This order may require such remedial or corrective measures as may be necessary. Any person to whom such an order is directed may appeal in accordance with RSA 21-O:14.

II. If the department determines that the discharge to any state-owned treatment facility presents an imminent threat to the environment or to the operation of the treatment facility, the department may issue an order requiring such action as may be necessary to meet the emergency, or may take necessary action to block the public sewer to prevent the discharge of the waste into the treatment facility. Any order issued under this authority shall take effect immediately. A person to whom such an order is issued or any person affected by action taken by the department under this paragraph may appeal to the commissioner or designee for a hearing on such order or action, which shall be held within 2 working days after receipt of the request for the hearing. The person may appeal the decision on such hearing pursuant to RSA 21-O:14.

III. Any person who violates any of the provisions of this chapter, or any rule adopted or order issued under this subdivision, shall be subject to a civil penalty not to exceed $10,000 for each violation, or for each day of a continuing violation.

IV. Any violation of the provisions of this subdivision, or of any rule adopted or order issued under it, or of any condition in any permit issued or contract entered into under the authority of this subdivision, may be enjoined by the superior court upon application by the attorney general.

V. The commissioner of environmental services, after notice and hearing pursuant to RSA 541-A, may impose an administrative fine not to exceed $2,000 for each offense upon any person who violates any provision of this subdivision, any rule adopted under this subdivision, or any permit or contract entered into under the authority of this subdivision. Rehearings and appeals from a decision of the commissioner under this paragraph shall be in accordance with RSA 541. Any administrative fine imposed under this section shall not preclude the imposition of further penalties under this subdivision. The proceeds of administrative fines levied pursuant to this paragraph shall be deposited by the department in the replacement fund established pursuant to RSA 485-A:51. The commissioner shall adopt rules, under RSA 541-A, relative to:

(a) A schedule of administrative fines which may be imposed under this paragraph for violations of this chapter as provided above.

(b) Procedures for notice and hearing prior to the imposition of an administrative fine.

HISTORY:
1989, 339:1. 1995, 217:9, eff. Jan. 1, 1996. 1996, 228:85, 106, eff. July 1, 1996.

Amendments

—1996.
Paragraph I: Substituted "department" for "division" preceding "may issue" in the first sentence and "in accordance with RSA 21-O:14" for "to the water supply and pollution control council" following "may appeal" in the third sentence.
Paragraph II: Substituted "department" for "division" wherever it appeared, deleted "his" preceding "designee" in the third sentence, deleted the former fourth sentence, and deleted "to the water supply and pollution control council" preceding "pursuant to RSA" and substituted "21-O:14" for "21-O:7, IV" thereafter in the present fourth sentence.
Paragraph V: Substituted "department" for "division" in the fourth sentence of the introductory paragraph.

—1995.
Paragraph V: Substituted "RSA 541" for "RSA 21-O:14" in the second sentence of the introductory paragraph, and substituted "violations" for "violation" preceding "of this chapter" and added "as provided above" thereafter in subpar. (a).

Certain Household Cleansing Products Prohibited

485-A:55. Definitions.

In this subdivision:

I. "Household cleansing product" means any product, including but not limited to, soaps and detergents used for domestic cleaning purposes, including, but not limited to, the cleansing of fabric, dishes, food utensils and household premises.

II. "Phosphorus" means elemental phosphorus.

III. "Trace quantity" means an incidental amount of phosphorus which is not part of the household cleansing product formulation, is present either as a consequence of manufacturing, to assure product performance for purposes other than cleansing, or to assure container stability, and does not exceed 0.5 percent of the content of the product by weight, expressed as elemental phosphorus.

HISTORY:
1994, 303:1, eff. Jan. 1, 1995.

485-A:56. Products Prohibited.

No household cleansing products except those used for lead exposure hazard control purposes shall be distributed, sold or offered for sale in this state, which contain a phosphorus compound in concentrations in excess of a trace quantity.

HISTORY:
1994, 303:1, eff. Jan. 1, 1995. 1995, 306:7, eff. Aug. 20, 1995. 2009, 282:1, eff. July 1, 2010.

Amendments

—2009.
The 2009 amendment deleted "in dishwashers or" following "except those used."

—1995.
Inserted "or for lead exposure hazard control purposes" following "dishwashers".

485-A:57. Penalty.

Any person who violates the provisions of this subdivision shall be subject to a civil penalty not to exceed $50.

HISTORY:
1994, 303:1, eff. Jan. 1, 1995.

CHAPTER 489

INTEGRATED LAND DEVELOPMENT PERMIT

489:1. Purpose. [RSA 489 suspended temporarily, see suspension note below.]

This chapter is intended to:

I. Establish an integrated land development permit option that may be sought, at the discretion of the applicant, as an alternative to seeking one or more individual land development permits or approvals issued by the department of environmental services.

II. Provide a coordinated approach and holistic perspective in regulating land development activities to protect the quality and functions of New Hampshire's natural environment.

III. Establish an alternative project review and permitting process to improve communication and coordination between multiple organizations and entities involved in the permitting of proposed projects.

IV. Establish a structured pre-application process to provide enhanced guidance earlier in the project design process to facilitate compliance and improved environmental performance.

V. Encourage and facilitate implementation of environmentally superior projects.

VI. Recognize that the degree of relatedness of the affected programs presents a unique opportunity to achieve efficiencies and savings that are not possible to achieve by similar means within the other programs administered by the department.

HISTORY:
2013, 270:1, eff. July 1, 2017.

Suspension of RSA 489.
2017, 156:143, eff. July 1, 2017, provided that due to budgetary and staffing constraints, RSA 489, establishing a procedure to obtain an integrated land development permit from the department of environment services, is suspended for the biennium ending June 30, 2019.

Effective date.
2014, 156:1, eff. June 30, 2014, amended 2013, 270:7, I, to change the effective date of 2013, 270:1, 5, and 6 from Jan. 1, 2015 to July 1, 2017.

489:2. Definitions. [RSA 489 suspended temporarily, see suspension note below.]

In this chapter:

I. "Abutter" means any person who owns land immediately contiguous to the subject property or who owns flowage rights on such land. The term does not include the owner of any land that is separated by a public road or public waterway from the subject property or, in the absence of a public road or waterway, is more than ¼-mile from the limits of the proposed work. If any land that is immediately contiguous to the subject property is owned in whole or in part by the person who is proposing the work or is necessary to meet any frontage requirement, the term includes the person owning the next contiguous property.

II. "Affected programs" means the following programs implemented by the department:

(a) The terrain alteration program established under RSA 485-A:17 and rules adopted pursuant thereto;

(b) The subdivision and individual sewage disposal systems program established under RSA 485-A:29 through RSA 485-A:44 and rules adopted pursuant thereto;

(c) The wetlands program established under RSA 482-A and rules adopted pursuant thereto; and

(d) The shoreland water quality protection program established under RSA 483-B and rules adopted pursuant thereto.

III. "Applicant" means the person who initiates the application process for an integrated land development permit. If the applicant is not the owner of the property on which the project is proposed to occur, the applicant shall be authorized in writing by the property owner to undertake all actions and representations required under this chapter.

IV. "Department" means the department of environmental services.

V. "Integrated land development permit" means a single permit issued by the department in lieu of issuing separate permits or approvals under one or more of the affected programs.

VI. "Permittee" means a person who obtains an integrated land development permit under this chapter.

VII. "Subject property" means the property on which a project is proposed or, after issuance of a permit, is undertaken.

HISTORY:
2013, 270:1, eff. July 1, 2017.

Suspension of RSA 489.
2017, 156:143, eff. July 1, 2017, provided that due to budgetary and staffing constraints, RSA 489, establishing a procedure to obtain an integrated land development permit from the department of environment services, is suspended for the biennium ending June 30, 2019.

Effective date.
2014, 156:1, eff. June 30, 2014, amended 2013, 270:7, I, to change the effective date of 2013, 270:1, 5, and 6 from Jan. 1, 2015 to July 1, 2017.

489:3. Authorization. [RSA 489 suspended temporarily, see suspension note below.]

I. There is hereby established an integrated land

development permit, for which application may be made as an alternative to applying for separate, individual permits or approvals under the affected programs.

II. Municipalities may review materials, engage in discussions with the department, conduct independent site visits with the consent of the property owner and the applicant, if other than the property owner, and provide written comment to the department during any or all phases of the integrated land development permit process. Municipalities may attend site visits, attend meetings or participate in discussions between the applicant and the department in accordance with the following:

(a) Municipalities may participate in meetings or other discussions between the department and the applicant during the conceptual and pre-application phases of the integrated land development permit process under RSA 489:5 and RSA 489:6 with the consent of the applicant.

(b) Municipalities may participate in site visits conducted by state or federal regulatory agencies during the conceptual and pre-application phases of the integrated land development permit process under RSA 489:5 and RSA 489:6 with the consent of the property owner and the applicant, if other than the property owner.

(c) If the department concludes that it would promote the efficient and timely consideration of a final application under RSA 489:7, the department may invite the municipality in which the subject property is located to participate in meetings or other discussions between the department and the applicant or attend site visits conducted by state or federal regulatory agencies.

(d) To the extent practicable, site visits by municipalities for the purposes of commenting on a permit application or permit issued under this chapter shall be coordinated with entry upon the property by state or federal regulatory agencies under RSA 489:3, VI.

III. If administrative requirements or procedures contained in this chapter, or adopted by rule to execute this chapter, conflict with administrative requirements or procedures of any other statute or rule implemented by the department, the provisions under this chapter shall apply.

IV. The time limits prescribed in this chapter, or adopted by rule to execute this chapter, shall supersede any time limits provided in any other applicable provision of law.

V. Electronic communications and electronic document management may be employed to facilitate correspondence, application, notification, and coordination under this chapter.

VI. Submission of materials for the pre-application technical review under RSA 489:6, II or for final application under RSA 489:7 shall constitute express authorization by the property owner and the applicant, if other than the property owner, for the department and other participating regulatory

agencies, through their respective agents or employees, to enter upon the subject property for purposes of evaluating site conditions and the application made under this chapter at reasonable times and with reasonable notice except under exigent circumstances.

HISTORY:
2013, 270:1, eff. July 1, 2017.

Suspension of RSA 489.
2017, 156:143, eff. July 1, 2017, provided that due to budgetary and staffing constraints, RSA 489, establishing a procedure to obtain an integrated land development permit from the department of environment services, is suspended for the biennium ending June 30, 2019.

Effective date note.
2014, 156:1, eff. June 30, 2014, amended 2013, 270:7, I, to change the effective date of 2013, 270:1, 5, and 6 from Jan. 1, 2015 to July 1, 2017.

489:4. Applicability. [RSA 489 suspended temporarily, see suspension note below.]

I. Any person who wishes to conduct an activity requiring a permit or other approval from the department under 2 or more of the affected programs may choose to apply for an integrated land development permit from the department in lieu of all individual program permits or approvals otherwise required under the affected programs, subject to the following conditions and limitations:

(a) All permits or approvals otherwise required under the applicable affected programs shall be included in the application for an integrated land development permit and in any permit issued based on the application.

(b) No person shall be eligible under this chapter if the person is the subject of a state administrative, civil, or criminal enforcement action for violating this chapter or any of the affected programs at the time of initiating the application process.

(c) No person shall be eligible under this chapter if the person was the subject of a state administrative, civil, or criminal enforcement action for violating this chapter or any of the affected programs within the 5 years prior to initiating the application process, unless the action was withdrawn or overturned on appeal.

(d) No property shall be eligible under this chapter if the property is or has been the subject of an administrative enforcement action for violations of this chapter or any of the affected programs, unless the violations have been remediated or will be remediated as part of the proposed project and any outstanding fees, fines, and penalties assessed against the same person who owns the property at the time of the application have been paid in full.

(e) No property shall be eligible under this chapter without the prior consent of the attorney general if the property is, at the time of initiating the application process, or has been, within the 5 years prior to initiating the application process, the subject of a civil or criminal enforcement action for violations of this chapter or any of the affected programs. This subparagraph shall not apply to any action that was withdrawn or overturned on appeal.

(f) This chapter shall not apply if any of the work that is part of the project, other than preliminary site evaluation activities such as surveys or test pits not requiring a permit from the department, has been initiated or completed prior to the application process being initiated.

(g) This chapter shall not apply to permits for shoreline structures unless they are part of a larger project.

(h) This chapter shall not apply to emergency authorizations.

II. For projects that would otherwise require only a single permit from the department under the affected programs, the applicant may request a waiver of the requirement for 2 or more permits provided the project incorporates low-impact or minimum-impact design practices and the applicant demonstrates that the proposed project will achieve a superior overall environmental outcome in accordance with the requirements and procedures specified in RSA 489:9.

HISTORY:
2013, 270:1, eff. July 1, 2017.

Suspension of RSA 489.
2017, 156:143, eff. July 1, 2017, provided that due to budgetary and staffing constraints, RSA 489, establishing a procedure to obtain an integrated land development permit from the department of environment services, is suspended for the biennium ending June 30, 2019.

Effective date note.
2014, 156:1, eff. June 30, 2014, amended 2013, 270:7, I, to change the effective date of 2013, 270:1, 5, and 6 from Jan. 1, 2015 to July 1, 2017.

489:5. Conceptual Preliminary Discussions. [RSA 489 suspended temporarily, see suspension note below.]

Any person interested in pursuing an integrated land development permit may consult with the department regarding the applicable procedures and requirements. Applicants may request and participate in conceptual pre-application discussions with the department prior to initiating the formal pre-application technical review process under RSA 489:6. Such conceptual pre-application discussions shall not replace the formal pre-application technical review process.

HISTORY:
2013, 270:1, eff. July 1, 2017.

Suspension of RSA 489.
2017, 156:143, eff. July 1, 2017, provided that due to budgetary and staffing constraints, RSA 489, establishing a procedure to

obtain an integrated land development permit from the department of environment services, is suspended for the biennium ending June 30, 2019.

Effective date note.
2014, 156:1, eff. June 30, 2014, amended 2013, 270:7, I, to change the effective date of 2013, 270:1, 5, and 6 from Jan. 1, 2015 to July 1, 2017.

489:6. Pre-Application Technical Review. [RSA 489 suspended temporarily, see suspension note below.]

I. An applicant shall initiate the integrated land development permit process by conducting certain activities, as specified by the department in rules adopted under this chapter, in preparation for pre-application technical review by the department. These activities shall include the following:

(a) Inquiry or consultation with the department of natural and cultural resources's natural heritage bureau and the fish and game department;

(b) Notification of and provision of materials on the proposed project to the governing body, the planning department, the planning board, and conservation commission of the municipality or municipalities in which the proposed project is located;

(c) Notification of and provision of materials on the proposed project to the local river management advisory committee, when the project is in the corridor of a designated river or river segment under RSA 483;

(d) Notification of and consultation with federal regulatory entities, when applicable;

(e) Notification of, and, when requested, provision of materials on the proposed project to the New Hampshire division of historic resources;

(f) Assessment of site characteristics and location, as defined by the department in rules adopted under this chapter; and

(g) Other assessments, inquiries, notifications, and consultations as defined by the department in rules adopted under this chapter.

II. After conducting the activities required under paragraph I, the applicant shall submit to the department such materials as the department requires under rules adopted pursuant to RSA 541-A. The department may require the applicant to pay up to 30 percent of the expected final application fee under RSA 489:7, I to cover departmental costs associated with the pre-application technical review. Any payment made shall be applied towards the final application fee. Such payment shall not be refundable or transferable to another project should a final permit application not be submitted.

III. The applicant shall participate in a pre-application technical review with the department.

IV. As part of the pre-application technical review, the department shall review preliminary design plans, supporting information, and advisory input from state or federal entities notified or consulted pursuant to paragraph I and comments received from other persons notified pursuant to paragraph I to identify critical issues regarding site development and design, any requested waivers, and any mitigation that may be needed, and review the final permit application requirements with the applicant.

V. The department may invite any state or federal entities notified under paragraph I to participate in pre-application technical review discussions. Other persons or entities may be included at the request of the applicant.

VI. The pre-application technical review process shall not establish any presumption as to whether the department will approve the final application.

HISTORY:
2013, 270:1, eff. July 1, 2017. 2017, 156:14, eff. July 1, 2017.

Suspension of RSA 489.
2017, 156:143, eff. July 1, 2017, provided that due to budgetary and staffing constraints, RSA 489, establishing a procedure to obtain an integrated land development permit from the department of environment services, is suspended for the biennium ending June 30, 2019.

Effective date note.
2014, 156:1, eff. June 30, 2014, amended 2013, 270:7, I, to change the effective date of 2013, 270:1, 5, and 6 from Jan. 1, 2015 to July 1, 2017.

Amendment Notes
The 2017 amendments to this section by Ch. 156 substituted "natural and cultural resources" for "resources and economic development" in I(a).

489:7. Submission and Review of Final Application. [RSA 489 suspended temporarily, see suspension note below.]

I. Following the pre-application technical review, the applicant shall submit a complete application, as defined by the department in rules, together with the application fee, which shall be equal to the total of the permit fees specified in statute and in rules for each of the individual permits or approvals being replaced by the integrated land development permit, to the department. The proposed activities shall not be undertaken unless and until the applicant receives a permit from the department.

II. Within 14 days of receipt of the application, the department shall notify the applicant whether the application is complete or not. Incomplete applications shall not be accepted and shall be returned, along with the fee, to the applicant to be made complete and resubmitted to the department.

III. Concurrent with the submission of the final application to the department, the applicant shall:

(a) Provide a complete copy of the final application and all supporting materials, by certified mail or other delivery method that provides proof of receipt, to the municipality, or if applicable, municipalities in which the project is located and, when applicable, the local river management advisory committee or committees.

(b) Notify all abutters by certified mail or other delivery method that provides proof of receipt regarding the application. If any question arises as to whether all abutters were notified, the burden shall be on the applicant to show that notification was made.

IV. The department shall apply the technical criteria established in the affected programs.

V. The department may waive, in accordance with RSA 489:9, any technical criteria established by statute or rule under the affected programs, if such waiver is necessary to achieve a superior overall environmental outcome, or achieve an equivalent overall environmental outcome at reduced cost.

VI. Within 45 days of receiving a complete application, the department shall:

(a) Approve the application and issue a permit, which shall include such conditions as the department deems necessary to comply with this chapter or rules adopted under this chapter;

(b) Deny the application and issue written findings in support of the denial;

(c) Identify the need for and schedule a public hearing on the proposed project, and within 30 days of the public hearing approve or deny the application in accordance with subparagraph (a) or (b); or

(d) Extend the time for rendering a decision on the application for good cause and with the written agreement of the applicant.

VII. If the department fails to act within the applicable time frame established in this section, the applicant may ask the department to issue the permit by submitting a written request. If the applicant has previously agreed to accept communications from the department by electronic means, a request submitted electronically by the applicant shall constitute a written request.

(a) Within 14 days of the date of receipt of a written request from the applicant to issue the permit, the department shall:

(1) Approve the application, in whole or in part, and issue a permit; or

(2) Deny the application and issue written findings in support of the denial.

(b) If the department does not issue either a permit or a written denial within the 14-day period, the applicant shall be deemed to have a permit by default and may proceed with the project as presented in the application. The authorization provided by this subparagraph shall not relieve the applicant of complying with all requirements applicable to the project, including but not limited to requirements established in or under this chapter and any chapter relating to the applicable affected programs.

(c) Upon receipt of a written request from an applicant, the department shall issue written confirmation that the applicant has a permit by default pursuant to subparagraph (b), which authorizes the applicant to proceed with the project as presented in the application and requires the work to comply with all requirements applicable to the project, including but not limited to requirements established in or under this chapter and any chapter relating to the applicable affected programs.

VIII. Undertaking any activity authorized by a permit issued pursuant to VI(a), VII(a), or VII(c) shall constitute express authorization by the property owner and the permittee, if other than the property owner, for the department and other participating regulatory agencies, through their respective agents or employees, to enter upon the subject property for purposes of determining compliance with the permit and other applicable requirements at reasonable times and with reasonable notice except under exigent circumstances.

HISTORY:
2013, 270:1, eff. July 1, 2017.

Suspension of RSA 489.
2017, 156:143, eff. July 1, 2017, provided that due to budgetary and staffing constraints, RSA 489, establishing a procedure to obtain an integrated land development permit from the department of environment services, is suspended for the biennium ending June 30, 2019.

Effective date note.
2014, 156:1, eff. June 30, 2014, amended 2013, 270:7, I, to change the effective date of 2013, 270:1, 5, and 6 from Jan. 1, 2015 to July 1, 2017.

489:8.   Rulemaking. [RSA 489 suspended temporarily, see suspension note below.]

The commissioner of the department shall adopt rules under RSA 541-A relative to:

I. Requirements and procedures for the preapplication process and technical review, including requirements for notification of and coordination with municipalities, other state and federal agencies, local river management advisory committees, and other entities.

II. Application requirements and procedures for processing a final application for an integrated land development permit, including requirements for notification of and coordination with municipalities, other state and federal agencies, local river management advisory committees, and other entities.

III. Applicability of technical criteria of the affected program.

IV. Time extensions and duration of a permit, and procedures and requirements for amending a permit issued pursuant to this chapter.

V. Procedures and requirements for projects requiring a public hearing.

VI. Terms and conditions for permits issued under this chapter to ensure compliance with this chapter and affected programs.

HISTORY:
2013, 270:1, eff. July 1, 2017.

Suspension of RSA 489.
2017, 156:143, eff. July 1, 2017, provided that due to budgetary and staffing constraints, RSA 489, establishing a procedure to obtain an integrated land development permit from the department of environment services, is suspended for the biennium ending June 30, 2019.

Effective date note.
2014, 156:1, eff. June 30, 2014, amended 2013, 270:7, I, to change the effective date of 2013, 270:1, 5, and 6 from Jan. 1, 2015 to July 1, 2017.

489:9.   Waivers. [RSA 489 suspended temporarily, see suspension note below.]

I. No waiver from any affected program's requirement in rule or statute shall be granted unless the applicant requesting the waiver demonstrates that:

(a) There will be no substantial loss of wetland functions and values;

(b) Water quality will be protected to the maximum extent practicable and in compliance with the anti-degradation requirements of the federal Clean Water Act and departmental rules; and

(c) A superior overall environmental outcome will be achieved or an equivalent overall environmental outcome at reduced cost.

II. The demonstration required by paragraph I shall be made based on project design, mitigation, submission of modeling results, engineering calculations, relevant scientific studies, or such other documentation the applicant believes supports the requested waiver.

III. No waiver shall be granted if doing so results in a violation of any state statute or regulation outside those governing the affected programs, unless the statute or regulation expressly provides that the provisions may be waived.

IV. No waiver shall be granted if doing so results in a violation of any federal requirement, unless the federal requirement expressly provides that its provisions may be waived and the federal agency charged with enforcing the requirement agrees with the waiver.

V. Municipalities may adopt an innovative land use control ordinance pursuant to RSA 674:21, authorizing the planning board to allow a project that does not fully conform to the local zoning ordinance to proceed as approved by the department under this chapter, provided the planning board makes a finding that such a project meets the criteria of paragraph I.

HISTORY:
2013, 270:1, eff. July 1, 2017.

Suspension of RSA 489.
2017, 156:143, eff. July 1, 2017, provided that due to budgetary and staffing constraints, RSA 489, establishing a procedure to obtain an integrated land development permit from the department of environment services, is suspended for the biennium ending June 30, 2019.

Effective date note.
2014, 156:1, eff. June 30, 2014, amended 2013, 270:7, I, to change the effective date of 2013, 270:1, 5, and 6 from Jan. 1, 2015 to July 1, 2017.

489:10. Appeals. [RSA 489 suspended temporarily, see suspension note below.]

I. Any person aggrieved by a decision made under RSA 489:7, V, VI(a) or (b), or VII, and any person subject to an order of the department under RSA 489:11 who wishes to appeal shall, within 30 days of the decision, file a notice of appeal with the appeals clerk for a hearing before a joint water-wetland council described in paragraph II. At the time the notice of the appeal is filed, the person shall send a copy of the appeal to the commissioner. If the appeal is of a decision to issue a permit, the person shall also send a copy of the appeal to the permittee. The notice of appeal shall clearly state that it is being filed pursuant to this paragraph.

II. Upon receipt of a notice of appeal filed pursuant to paragraph I, the appeals clerk shall notify the chairperson of the water council established under RSA 21-O:7 and the chairperson of the wetlands council established under RSA 21-O:5-a. The chairperson shall each designate 4 members of their respective councils to sit with a hearing officer appointed under RSA 21-M:3, VIII as a joint council for purposes of the appeal. The interests represented by members of the joint council shall be as diverse as possible based on the council members available to be designated after any recusals are considered.

III. The appeal shall set forth fully every ground upon which it is claimed that the decision complained of is unlawful or unreasonable. Only those grounds set forth in the appeal shall be considered by the joint council.

IV. The joint council shall conduct an adjudicative proceedings as provided in RSA 21-M:3, IX and X, RSA 21-O:14, RSA 541-A, and rules to be adopted by both of the councils for appeals to be heard by the joint council. Until both of the councils have adopted the same rules, the rules of the wetlands council shall apply to any appeal. The burden of proof shall be on the party seeking to set aside the department's decision to show that the decision is unlawful or unreasonable. All findings of the department upon all questions of fact properly before it shall be prima facie lawful and reasonable.

V. If the appeal is of a decision to issue a permit, the permittee may appear and become a party to the appeal as a matter of right. Requests by any other person to intervene in any appeal shall be made and decided upon as provided in RSA 541-A:32.

VI. On appeal, the joint council may affirm the decision of the department or may remand to the department with a determination that the decision complained of is unlawful or unreasonable. In either case, the council shall specify the factual and legal basis for its determination and shall identify evidence in the record created before the council that supports its decision.

VII. Any party aggrieved by a decision of the joint council may appeal to the supreme court as specified in RSA 541.

VIII. In the case of a remand to the department by the joint council, the department shall consider the council's determination and may either reissue the subject decision or order or appeal as provided in paragraph VII.

HISTORY:
2013, 270:1, eff. July 1, 2017.

Suspension of RSA 489.
2017, 156:143, eff. July 1, 2017, provided that due to budgetary and staffing constraints, RSA 489, establishing a procedure to obtain an integrated land development permit from the department of environment services, is suspended for the biennium ending June 30, 2019.

Effective date note.
2014, 156:1, eff. June 30, 2014, amended 2013, 270:7, I, to change the effective date of 2013, 270:1, 5, and 6 from Jan. 1, 2015 to July 1, 2017.

489:11. Compliance. [RSA 489 suspended temporarily, see suspension note below.]

I. The following shall constitute noncompliance with this chapter:

(a) Failure to comply with this chapter or any rule adopted or permit issued under this chapter.

(b) Failure to comply with an order of the commissioner issued relative to this chapter or any rule adopted or permit issued under this chapter.

(c) Misrepresentation by any person of a material fact made in connection with any application filed under this chapter or any permit issued under this chapter.

II. The permittee shall be responsible for ensuring that all work done under the permit complies with the permit and all other applicable requirements. Any person who performs work under an integrated land development permit shall comply with the permit and all other applicable requirements.

III. The department may issue a written order to any person in noncompliance with this chapter as specified in paragraph I to cease any continuing noncompliance and to remediate or restore any land or water areas affected by the noncompliance.

IV. Any noncompliance with this chapter as specified in paragraph I may be enjoined by the superior court upon application of the attorney general.

V. Any person who knowingly fails to comply with this chapter as specified in paragraph I shall be subject to all remedies available under law in the applicable affected programs. For purposes of this paragraph, a permit issued under this chapter shall constitute a permit issued under each of the applicable affected programs.

HISTORY:
2013, 270:1, eff. July 1, 2017.

Suspension of RSA 489.
2017, 156:143, eff. July 1, 2017, provided that due to budgetary and staffing constraints, RSA 489, establishing a procedure to

obtain an integrated land development permit from the department of environment services, is suspended for the biennium ending June 30, 2019.

Effective date note.
2014, 156:1, eff. June 30, 2014, amended 2013, 270:7, I, to change the effective date of 2013, 270:1, 5, and 6 from Jan. 1, 2015 to July 1, 2017.

TITLE LXIV

PLANNING AND ZONING

Chapter
672. General Provisions
673. Local Land Use Boards
674. Local Land Use Planning and Regulatory Powers
675. Enactment and Adoption Procedures
676. Administrative and Enforcement Procedures
677. Rehearing and Appeal Procedures
678. Community Services and Care Planning Boards

Time period for modification of master plans and zoning ordinances to conform with RSA 672–677.

1983, 447:2, eff. Jan. 1, 1984, as amended by 1986, 73:1, eff. May 12, 1986, provided; "Each municipality shall have from January 1, 1984, until July 1, 1986, to make its master plan and its zoning ordinances conform with the relevant provisions of this act."

Terms of office and selection of members of planning boards, zoning boards of adjustment, building code boards of appeals, and historic district commissions.

1983, 447:3, eff. Jan. 1, 1984, provided:

"**I.** The terms of members of elected planning boards in office on the effective date of this act shall not be affected by this act. The members shall remain in office until the 1984 town election. At the 1984 town election, in any town whose elected planning board member's terms do not conform with the 3 year term established by this act, the town shall elect such members for such terms and the selectmen shall designate an ex officio member as may be necessary to bring the town's planning board into conformity with the provisions of this act. The town clerk, with the approval of the moderator, shall determine the terms to be filled at the 1984 town election and shall notify the existing planning board members accordingly. The vacancies determined to exist shall be filled by election of the voters at the 1984 town election in accordance with the provisions of this act.

"**II.** The terms of appointed members of planning boards, zoning boards of adjustment, and building code boards of appeals in office on the effective date of this act shall not be affected by this act. However, when the term of each member expires, each new member who is appointed shall be appointed for a term of 3 years by the appointing authority in order to comply with the provisions of this act.

"**III.** The terms of members of historic district commissions in office on the effective date of this act shall not be affected by this act."

NOTES TO DECISIONS

Review of zoning and planning disputes under 42 U.S.C.S. § 1983

Where the state offers a panoply of administrative and judicial remedies, litigants may not ordinarily obtain federal court review of local zoning and planning disputes by means of 42 U.S.C.S. § 1983. Raskiewicz v. New Boston, 1985-1 Trade Cas. (CCH) ¶6431, 754 F.2d 38, 1985 U.S. App. LEXIS 28974 (1st Cir. N.H.), cert. denied, 474 U.S. 845, 106 S. Ct. 135, 88 L. Ed. 2d 111, 1985 U.S. LEXIS 3587 (U.S. 1985).

RESEARCH REFERENCES AND PRACTICE AIDS

Cross References.

Acquisition, development and disposal of industrial land and facilities, see RSA 162-G.

Aid to municipalities for water pollution control, see RSA 486.

Airport zoning generally, see RSA 424.

Building and construction standards generally, see RSA 155-A, 155-B.

Condemnation of land for county uses, see RSA 26.

Condominiums, see RSA 356-B.

Conservation and preservation restrictions in conveyances of realty, see RSA 477:45 et seq.

Conservation commissions, see RSA 36-A.

Control of height of structures near airports, see RSA 422-B.

Council on resources and development, see RSA 162-C.

County powers generally, see RSA 23.

Current use taxation, see RSA 79-A.

Eminent domain procedure generally, see RSA 498-A.

Excavation and filling of wetlands, see RSA 483-A.

Hazardous waste facility fees, see RSA 147-D.

Hazardous waste facility review, see RSA 147-C.

Hazardous waste management generally, see RSA 147-A.

Historic preservation, see RSA 227-C.

Home rule powers of municipalities, see RSA 49-B.

Intermunicipal agreements generally, see RSA 53-A.

Interstate regional planning compact, see RSA 36-B.

Interstate water pollution control commission standards for sewage and waste treatment plant personnel, see RSA 484:22 et seq.

Land sales disclosure, see RSA 356-A.

Municipal central business service districts, see RSA 31:120 et seq.

Municipal economic development and revitalization districts, see RSA 162-K.

Municipal housing standards, see RSA 48-A.

New England Interstate Planning Compact, see RSA 163-A.

New England Interstate Water Control Compact, see RSA 484:17 et seq.

Northeastern Water and Related Land Resources Compact, see RSA 484.

Public recreation and park areas, see RSA 35-B.

Regulation of manufactured housing parks, see RSA 205-A.

Review of developments of regional impact, see RSA 36:54 et seq.

Rubbish and waste disposal generally, see RSA 147.

Sewage and waste disposal facilities compacts, see RSA 149-J, 149-K.

Sewage disposal systems, see RSA 485-A:29 et seq.

Siting of electric power plants and transmission lines, see RSA 162-F.

Siting of energy facilities generally, see RSA 162-H.

Solar skyspace easements, see RSA 477:49 et seq.

Solid waste management districts, see RSA 53-B.

Solid waste management generally, see RSA 149-M.

State development plan, see RSA 9-A.

Town powers generally, see RSA 31.

Unit ownership of real property, see RSA 479-A.

Water pollution control generally, see RSA 485-A.

Winnipesaukee river basin control, see RSA 485-A:45 et seq.

New Hampshire Code of Administrative Rules

Rules of the Department of Revenue Administration, Rev 101.01 et seq., New Hampshire Code of Administrative Rules Annotated.

Rules of the Department of Environmental Services, Dam Related Programs, Env-Wr 101.01 et seq., New Hampshire Code of Administrative Rules Annotated.

Rules of the Department of Environmental Services, Division of Water, Env-Ws 301.01 et seq., New Hampshire Code of Administrative Rules Annotated.

Rules of the Department of Environmental Services, Wetlands Programs, Env-Wt 101.01 et seq., New Hampshire Code of Administrative Rules Annotated.

New Hampshire Bar Journal.

For Attorney General article, "Department Of Justice's Transportation And Construction Bureau: Trains, Planes And Automobiles," see 45 N.H. B.J. 78 (Spring 2004).

For Article, "The New Zoning Variance Cases: Analyzing Unnecessary Hardship Under RSA 674:33," see 46 N.H. B.J. 40 (Fall 2005).

For Article, "Roads Revisited Creation And Termination Of Highways In New Hampshire - An Update," see , 46 N.H. B.J. 56 (Fall 2005).

For Article, "Unnecessary Hardship Under RSA 674:331(B)," see 46 N.H. B.J. 47 (Fall 2005).

CHAPTER 672
GENERAL PROVISIONS

Purpose

RESEARCH REFERENCES AND PRACTICE AIDS

New Hampshire Bar Journal.
For article, "An Overview of the New Hampshire Land Use Planning and Regulation Statutes, " see 34 N.H. B.J. 6 (June 1993).

Purpose

672:1. Declaration of Purpose.

The general court hereby finds and declares that:

I. Planning, zoning and related regulations have been and should continue to be the responsibility of municipal government;

II. Zoning, subdivision regulations and related regulations are a legislative tool that enables municipal government to meet more effectively the demands of evolving and growing communities;

III. Proper regulations enhance the public health, safety and general welfare and encourage the appropriate and wise use of land;

III-a. Proper regulations encourage energy efficient patterns of development, the use of solar energy, including adequate access to direct sunlight for solar energy uses, and the use of other renewable forms of energy, and energy conservation. Therefore, the installation of solar, wind, or other renewable energy systems or the building of structures that facilitate the collection of renewable energy shall not be unreasonably limited by use of municipal zoning powers or by the unreasonable interpretation of such powers except where necessary to protect the public health, safety, and welfare;

III-b. Agriculture makes vital and significant contributions to the food supply, the economy, the environment and the aesthetic features of the state of New Hampshire, and the tradition of using the land resource for agricultural production is an essential factor in providing for the favorable quality of life in the state. Natural features, terrain and the pattern of geography of the state frequently place agricultural land in close proximity to other forms of development and commonly in small parcels. Agricultural activities are a beneficial and worthwhile feature of the New Hampshire landscape. Agritourism, as defined in RSA 21:34-a, is undertaken by farmers to contribute to both the economic viability and the long-term sustainability of the primary agricultural activities of New Hampshire farms. Agricultural activities and agritourism shall not be unreasonably limited by use of municipal planning and zoning powers or by the unreasonable interpretation of such powers;

III-c. Forestry, when practiced in accordance with accepted silvicultural principles, constitutes a beneficial and desirable use of New Hampshire's forest resource. Forestry contributes greatly to the economy of the state through a vital forest products industry; and to the health of the state's forest and wildlife resources through sustained forest productivity, and through improvement of wildlife habitats. New Hampshire's forests are an essential component of the landscape and add immeasurably to the quality of life for the state's citizens. Because New Hampshire is a heavily forested state, forestry activities, including the harvest and transport of forest products, are often carried out in close proximity to populated areas. Further, the harvesting of timber often represents the only income that can be derived from property without resorting to development of the property for more intensive uses, and, pursuant to RSA 79-A:1, the state of New Hampshire has declared that it is in the public interest to encourage preservation of open space by conserving forest and other natural resources. Therefore, forestry activities, including the harvest and transport of forest products, shall not be unreasonably limited by use of municipal planning and zoning powers or by the unreasonable interpretation of such powers;

III-d. For purposes of paragraphs III-a, III-b, III-c, and III-e, "unreasonable interpretation" includes the failure of local land use authorities to recognize that agriculture and agritourism as defined in RSA 21:34-a, forestry, renewable energy systems, and commercial and recreational fisheries, when practiced in accordance with applicable laws and regulations, are traditional, fundamental and accessory uses of land throughout New Hampshire, and that a prohibition upon these uses cannot necessarily be inferred from the failure of an ordinance or regulation to address them;

III-e. All citizens of the state benefit from a balanced supply of housing which is affordable to persons and families of low and moderate income.

Establishment of housing which is decent, safe, sanitary and affordable to low and moderate income persons and families is in the best interests of each community and the state of New Hampshire, and serves a vital public need. Opportunity for development of such housing shall not be prohibited or unreasonably discouraged by use of municipal planning and zoning powers or by unreasonable interpretation of such powers;

III-f. New Hampshire commercial and recreational fisheries make vital and significant contributions to the food supply, the economy, the environment, and the aesthetic features of the state of New Hampshire, and the tradition of using marine resources for fisheries production is an essential factor in providing for economic stability and a favorable quality of life in the state. Many traditional commercial and recreational fisheries in New Hampshire's rivers and estuarine systems are located in close proximity to coastal development. Such fisheries are a beneficial and worthwhile feature of the New Hampshire landscape and tradition and should not be discouraged or eliminated by use of municipal planning and zoning powers or the unreasonable interpretation of such powers.

IV. The citizens of a municipality should be actively involved in directing the growth of their community;

V. The state should provide a workable framework for the fair and reasonable treatment of individuals;

V-a. The care of up to 6 full-time preschool children and 3 part-time school age children in the home of a child care provider makes a vital and significant contribution to the state's economy and the well-being of New Hampshire families. The care provided through home-based day care closely parallels the activities of any home with young children. Family based care, traditionally relied upon by New Hampshire families, should not be discouraged or eliminated by use of municipal planning and zoning powers or the unreasonable interpretation of such powers; and

VI. It is the policy of this state that competition and enterprise may be so displaced or limited by municipalities in the exercise of the powers and authority provided in this title as may be necessary to carry out the purposes of this title.

HISTORY:
1983, 447:1. 1985, 68:1. 335:3. 369:1. 1989, 42:1. 170:1. 1990, 174:1. 180:1, 2. 1991, 198:1, 2, eff. July 27, 1991. 2002, 73:1, eff. June 30, 2002. 2008, 299:3, eff. January 1, 2010 (see effective date note below). 357:2, 3, eff. July 11, 2009. 2016, 267:2, 3, eff. June 16, 2016.

Revision note.
Redesignated par. III-d, as added by 1990, 174:1, as par. III-e, pursuant to 1990, 174:2.

Effective date of amendments by 2008, 299:3.
2009, 157:1, eff. July 8, 2009, amended 2008, 299:4 to change the effective date of 2008, 299:3 from July 1, 2009 to January 1, 2010.

Amendment Notes
The **2016 amendments to this section by Ch. 267**, in III-b, rewrote the third sentence as the third and last sentences and added the fourth sentence; and added "and agritourism as defined in RSA 21:34-a" in III-d.

—2008.
The 2008 amendment by Chapter 299, substituted "shall not be prohibited or unreasonably discouraged" for "including so-called cluster development and the development of multi-family structures, should not be prohibited or discouraged" in the third sentence of III-e.
The 2008 amendment by Chapter 357, in III-a, in the second sentence, deleted "zoning ordinances should not unreasonably limit" preceding "the installation" and added "shall not be unreasonably limited by use of municipal zoning powers or by the unreasonable interpretation of such powers"; and in III(d), added "III-a" following "paragraphs" and added "renewable energy systems" following "agriculture, forestry".

—2002.
Paragraph III-a: Added the second sentence.

—1991.
Paragraph III-d: Deleted "and" preceding "III-c", inserted "and III-e" thereafter, deleted "and" preceding "forestry", inserted "and commercial and recreational fisheries" thereafter and made other minor stylistic changes.
Paragraph III-f: Added.

—1990.
Paragraph III-b: Chapter 180 substituted "shall not be unreasonably limited" for "should not be discouraged or eliminated" following "landscape and" in the third sentence.
Paragraph III-c: Chapter 180 rewrote the sixth sentence.
Paragraph III-d: Added by chs. 174 and 180.

—1989.
Paragraph III-c: Added by ch. 170.
Paragraph V: Chapter 42 deleted "and" following "individuals".
Paragraph V-a: Added by ch. 42.

—1985.
Paragraph III-a: Added by ch. 369.
Paragraph III-b: Added by ch. 335.
Paragraph IV: Chapter 68 deleted "and" following "community".
Paragraph V: Chapter 68 added "and" following "individuals".
Paragraph VI: Added by ch. 68.

Contingent 1985 amendment.
1985, 335:1 provided for amendment of this section. However, under the terms of 1985, 335:4, eff. July 1, 1985, the amendment did not become effective.

NOTES TO DECISIONS

1. Generally
RSA 674:17, I(i), RSA 672:1, III-b, RSA 672:1, III-d, and RSA 674:32-a do not support the contention that the legislature intended to require municipalities to allow "agritourism" within their borders; at most, they evince the legislature's general intent to support traditional agriculture and agricultural activities, and they demonstrate legislative intent to allow reasonable local regulation, not to preempt the entire field. Thus, they did not preempt a local ordinance. Forster v. Town of Henniker, 167 N.H. 745, 118 A.3d 1016, 2015 N.H. LEXIS 54 (N.H. 2015).

2. Effect on other provisions
RSA 674:17, I(i), RSA 672:1, III-b, RSA 672:1, III-d, and RSA 674:32-a do not support the contention that the legislature intended to require municipalities to allow "agritourism" within their borders; at most, they evince the legislature's general intent to support traditional agriculture and agricultural activities, and they demonstrate legislative intent to allow reasonable local regulation, not to preempt the entire field. Thus, they did not preempt a local

ordinance. Forster v. Town of Henniker, 167 N.H. 745, 118 A.3d 1016, 2015 N.H. LEXIS 54 (N.H. 2015).

Cited:
   Cited in Buskey v. Hanover, 133 N.H. 318, 577 A.2d 406, 1990 N.H. LEXIS 67 (1990); Caspersen v. Town of Lyme, 139 N.H. 637, 661 A.2d 759, 1995 N.H. LEXIS 70 (1995); Goldstein v. Town of Bedford, 154 N.H. 393, 910 A.2d 1158, 2006 N.H. LEXIS 173 (2006).

RESEARCH REFERENCES AND PRACTICE AIDS

Cross References.
   Acquisition of agricultural land development rights, see RSA 432:18 et seq.
   Conservation and preservation restrictions in conveyances of realty, see RSA 477:45 et seq.
   Definitions generally, see RSA 672:2 et seq.
   Home rule powers of municipalities, see RSA 49-B.
   Solar skyspace easements, see RSA 477:49 et seq.
   Town powers generally, see RSA 31.

New Hampshire Practice.
   15-2 N.H.P. Land Use Planning and Zoning § 2.15.
   15-2 N.H.P. Land Use Planning and Zoning § 2.16.
   15-14 N.H.P. Land Use Planning and Zoning § 14.06.
   15-18 N.H.P. Land Use Planning and Zoning § 18.02.

Words and Phrases Defined

672:2. Definition of Words and Phrases.

The following words and phrases when used in Title LXIV shall have the meanings given to them in this chapter.

HISTORY:
   1983, 447:1, eff. Jan. 1, 1984.

RESEARCH REFERENCES AND PRACTICE AIDS

References in text.
   Title LXIV, referred to in this section, is classified to Title 64 of LEXIS New Hampshire Revised Statutes Annotated, which is comprised of chapters 672–677.

672:3. Abutter.

"Abutter" means any person whose property is located in New Hampshire and adjoins or is directly across the street or stream from the land under consideration by the local land use board. For purposes of receiving testimony only, and not for purposes of notification, the term "abutter" shall include any person who is able to demonstrate that his land will be directly affected by the proposal under consideration. For purposes of receipt of notification by a municipality of a local land use board hearing, in the case of an abutting property being under a condominium or other collective form of ownership, the term abutter means the officers of the collective or association, as defined in RSA 356-B:3, XXIII. For purposes of receipt of notification by a municipality of a local land use board hearing, in the case of an abutting property being under a manufactured housing park form of ownership as defined in RSA 205-A:1, II, the term "abutter" includes the manufactured housing park owner and the tenants who

own manufactured housing which adjoins or is directly across the street or stream from the land under consideration by the local land use board.

HISTORY:
   1983, 447:1. 1986, 33:2, eff. June 28, 1986. 2002, 216:1, eff. July 15, 2002.

Amendments

—2002.
   Added the fourth sentence.

—1986.
   Added the third sentence.

NOTES TO DECISIONS

Cited:
   Cited in Hussey v. Barrington, 135 N.H. 227, 604 A.2d 82, 1992 N.H. LEXIS 3 (1992).

672:4. District Commissioners.

"District commissioners" means the board of commissioners of a village district or precinct.

HISTORY:
   1983, 447:1, eff. Jan. 1, 1984.

672:5. Ex Officio Member.

"Ex Officio member" means any member who holds office by virtue of an official position and who shall exercise all the powers of regular members of a local land use board.

HISTORY:
   1983, 447:1, eff. Jan. 1, 1984.

672:6. Local Governing Body.

"Local governing body" means, in addition to any other appropriate title:
   I. Board of selectmen in a town;
   II. City council or board of aldermen in a city;
   III. Village district commissioners in a village district; or
   IV. County commissioners in a county in which there are located unincorporated towns or unorganized places.

HISTORY:
   1983, 447:1. 1989, 266:7, eff. July 1, 1989.

Amendments

—1989.
   Made minor stylistic changes in pars. II and III and added par. IV.

672:7. Local Land Use Board.

"Local land use board" means a planning board, historic district commission, inspector of buildings, building code board of appeals, zoning board of adjustment, or other board or commission authorized under RSA 673 established by a local legislative body.

HISTORY:
1983, 447:1, eff. Jan. 1, 1984. 2010, 226:4, eff. August 27, 2010.

Amendments

—2010.
The 2010 amendment added "or other board or commission authorized under RSA 673" and made a related change.

672:8. Local Legislative Body.

"Local legislative body" means one of the following basic forms of government utilized by a municipality:
I. Council, whether city or town;
II. Mayor—council;
III. Mayor—board of aldermen;
IV. Village district or precinct;
V. Town meeting; or
VI. County convention.

HISTORY:
1983, 447:1. 1985, 103:18. 1989, 266:8, eff. July 1, 1989.

Revision note.
For purposes of conformity with style employed in LEXIS New Hampshire Revised Statutes Annotated, redesignated pars. (a)–(e) as pars. I–V.

Amendments

—1989.
Made minor stylistic changes in pars. IV and V and added par. VI.

—1985.
Paragraph IV: Deleted "excluding water and sewer precincts" following "precinct".

NOTES TO DECISIONS

Cited:
Cited in Storms v. Eaton, 131 N.H. 50, 549 A.2d 1208, 1988 N.H. LEXIS 87 (1988); Blue Jay Realty Trust v. Franklin, 132 N.H. 502, 567 A.2d 188, 1989 N.H. LEXIS 128 (1989).

672:9. Mayor.

"Mayor" means the chief executive officer of the municipality, whether the official designation of the office is mayor of a city, city or town manager, the board of selectmen of a town, the board of commissioners of a village district, the county commissioners of a county in which there are located unincorporated towns or unorganized places, or any other title or any official designated in the municipal charter to perform the duties of "mayor."

HISTORY:
1983, 447:1. 1989, 266:8. 1991, 377:3, eff. Aug. 31, 1991.

Amendments

—1991.
Added "or any official designated in the municipal charter to perform the duties of 'mayor' " following "title".

—1989.
Inserted "the county commissioners of a county in which there are located unincorporated towns or unorganized places" following "village district".

672:10. Municipality.

"Municipality" or "municipal" means, includes and relates to cities, towns, village districts, and counties in which there are located unincorporated towns or unorganized places.

HISTORY:
1983, 447:1. 1989, 266:8, eff. July 1, 1989.

Amendments

—1989.
Deleted "and" preceding "village districts" and added "and counties in which there are located unincorporated towns or unorganized places" thereafter.

RESEARCH REFERENCES AND PRACTICE AIDS

Cross References.
Town defined generally, see RSA 21:5.

672:11. Planning Board.

"Planning board" means and includes city, town, village district, and county planning boards, in counties which contain unincorporated towns or unorganized places, established under the provisions of RSA 673.

HISTORY:
1983, 447:1. 1989, 266:8, eff. July 1, 1989.

Amendments

—1989.
Deleted "and" preceding "village district" and inserted "and county" preceding "planning boards" and "in counties which contain unincorporated towns or unorganized places" thereafter.

672:12. Selectmen.

"Selectmen" means the board of selectmen of a town and the county commissioners of a county in which there are located unincorporated towns or unorganized places.

HISTORY:
1983, 447:1. 1989, 266:8, eff. July 1, 1989.

Amendments

—1989.
Added "and the county commissioners of a county in which there are located unincorporated towns or unorganized places" following "selectmen of a town".

RESEARCH REFERENCES AND PRACTICE AIDS

Cross References.
Selectmen defined generally, see RSA 21:28.

672:13. Street.

"Street" means, relates to and includes street, avenue, boulevard, road, lane, alley, viaduct, highway, freeway and other ways.

HISTORY:

1983, 447:1, eff. Jan. 1, 1984.

RESEARCH REFERENCES AND PRACTICE AIDS

Cross References.

Highway defined generally, see RSA 21:26.
Public way defined generally, see RSA 259:83.
Roadway defined generally, see RSA 259:92.
Way defined generally, see RSA 259:125.

672:14. Subdivision.

I. "Subdivision" means the division of the lot, tract, or parcel of land into 2 or more lots, plats, sites, or other divisions of land for the purpose, whether immediate or future, of sale, rent, lease, condominium conveyance or building development. It includes resubdivision and, when appropriate to the context, relates to the process of subdividing or to the land or territory subdivided.

II. The division of a parcel of land held in common and subsequently divided into parts among the several owners shall be deemed a subdivision under this title.

III. The grant of an easement in gross to a public utility for the purpose of placing and maintaining overhead and underground facilities necessary for its transmission or distribution network such as poles, wires, cable, conduit, manholes, repeaters and supporting apparatus, including any unstaffed structure which is less than 500 square feet, shall not be construed as a subdivision under this title, and shall not be deemed to create any new division of land for any other purpose.

IV. The rent, lease, development, or grant of an easement to a person for the purpose of placing and maintaining a wireless communications facility shall not be construed as a subdivision under this title, and shall not be deemed to create any new division of land for any other purpose. For purposes of this paragraph, "wireless communications facilities" means any towers, poles, antennas, or other unstaffed structure of less than 500 square feet intended for use in connection with licensed transmission or receipt of radio or television signals, or any other licensed spectrum-based transmissions or receptions. This paragraph shall not be deemed to affect other local zoning, site plan, or regulatory authority over wireless communications facilities.

HISTORY:

1983, 447:1. 1988, 75:1, eff. June 14, 1988. 1998, 299:1, 2, eff. June 1, 1999.

Amendments

—1998.

Paragraph III: Substituted "unstaffed structure" for "unmanned structure" and "500" for "200".

Paragraph IV: Added.

—1988.

Designated the first and second sentences as par. I, the third sentence as par. II and added par. III.

NOTES TO DECISIONS

"Subdivision"

Where property owners applied to town planning board to further subdivide lots that were previously subdivided, the town's planning board and zoning board of adjustment erred in denying the applications on the basis that owners did not adhere to the density requirements of the town's zoning ordinance and because they were not consistent with the original intent of the cluster subdivision approvals because (1) RSA 672:14, I provided that a resubdivision was included in the term "subdivision," and (2) because the specific density provisions of the local ordinance had been eliminated. Furthermore, inconsistency with the intent of the original subdivision was not a proper ground for denying the applications and the owners were entitled to have their new applications reviewed on their own merits under the applicable regulations, unconstrained by the prior subdivision approval. Feins v. Town of Wilmot, 154 N.H. 715, 919 A.2d 788, 2007 N.H. LEXIS 5 (N.H. 2007).

Definition of "subdivision" contained in subsection I was not intended to apply to conveyance and conversion of an existing apartment unit into a condominium. Bussiere v. Roberge, 142 N.H. 905, 714 A.2d 894, 1998 N.H. LEXIS 57 (N.H. 1998).

Term "subdivision" in RSA 674:35 authorizing municipal planning board to regulate subdivisions, means only the act of subdividing land; this section's definition of "subdivision" as "land or territory subdivided" is not encompassed within RSA 674:35. Lemm Dev. Corp. v. Bartlett, 133 N.H. 618, 580 A.2d 1082, 1990 N.H. LEXIS 114 (N.H. 1990).

A testator's division of property by devise did not fall within the definition of subdivision. In re Estate of Sayewich, 120 N.H. 237, 413 A.2d 581, 1980 N.H. LEXIS 266 (N.H. 1980). (Decided under prior law.)

Cited:

Cited in Plainfield v. Sanville, 125 N.H. 825, 485 A.2d 1052, 1984 N.H. LEXIS 318 (1984); Cohen v. Henniker, 134 N.H. 425, 593 A.2d 1145, 1991 N.H. LEXIS 78 (1991).

CHAPTER 673

LOCAL LAND USE BOARDS

Establishment of Boards

RESEARCH REFERENCES AND PRACTICE AIDS

Cross References.
Local land use board review of developments of regional impact, see RSA 36:54 et seq.
Ordinance, regulation and code administration and enforcement generally, see RSA 676.
Ordinance, regulation and code adoption procedures generally, see RSA 675.
Powers and duties of local land use boards generally, see RSA 674.
Rehearing and appeals procedures generally, see RSA 677.

New Hampshire Bar Journal.
For article, "An Overview of the New Hampshire Land Use Planning and Regulation Statutes," see 34 N.H. B.J. 6 (June 1993).

Establishment of Boards

673:1. Establishment of Local Land Use Boards.

I. Any local legislative body may establish a planning board, the members of which shall be residents of the municipality.

II. Any local legislative body may establish any or all of the following: a heritage commission, a historic district commission, an agricultural commission, and a housing commission.

III. Any local legislative body may provide for the appointment of an inspector of buildings. The local legislative body may fix the compensation for any inspector who is so appointed.

IV. Every zoning ordinance adopted by a local legislative body shall include provisions for the establishment of a zoning board of adjustment. Members of the zoning board of adjustment shall be either elected or appointed, subject to the provisions of RSA 673:3.

V. Every building code adopted by a local legislative body shall include provisions for the establishment of the position of a building inspector, who shall issue building permits, and for the establishment of a building code board of appeals. If no provision is made to establish a separate building code board of appeals, the ordinance shall designate the zoning board of adjustment to act as the building code board of appeals. If there is no zoning board of adjustment, the board of selectmen shall serve as the building code board of appeals.

HISTORY:
1983, 447:1. 1992, 64:5, eff. June 19, 1992. 2007, 266:2, eff. August 28, 2007. 2008, 391:2, eff. September 15, 2008. 2009, 286:1, eff. January 1, 2010.

Amendments

—2009.
The 2009 amendment added the second sentence of IV.

—2008.
The 2008 amendment in II, added "any or all of the following", substituted "an agricultural commission, and a housing commission" for "or both, and may establish an agricultural commission" and made stylistic changes.

—2007.
Paragraph II: Added "and may establish an agricultural commission" at the end.

—1992.
Paragraph II: Inserted "heritage commission" preceding "historic district commission" and added "or both" thereafter.

NOTES TO DECISIONS

Effect of failure to establish board of adjustment
The failure of a town, in its adoption of a zoning ordinance, to establish a board of adjustment rendered the ordinance invalid. Jaffrey v. Heffernan, 104 N.H. 249, 183 A.2d 246, 1962 N.H. LEXIS 61 (N.H. 1962). (Decided under former RSA 31:66.)

RESEARCH REFERENCES AND PRACTICE AIDS

Cross References.
Powers and duties of building code boards of appeals generally, see RSA 674:34.
Powers and duties of building inspectors generally, see RSA 676:11 et seq.
Powers and duties of heritage commissions generally, see RSA 674:44-b et seq.
Powers and duties of historic district commissions generally, see RSA 674:46 et seq.
Powers and duties of planning boards generally, see RSA 674:1 et seq.
Powers and duties of zoning boards of adjustment generally, see RSA 674:33.

Appointment and Terms of Local Land Use Board Members

RESEARCH REFERENCES AND PRACTICE AIDS

Cross References.
Designation of alternate members, see RSA 673:11.
Disqualification of members, see RSA 673:14.
Filling of vacancies, see RSA 673:12.
Removal of members, see RSA 673:13.

673:2. Planning Board.

I.(a) In cities, the planning board shall consist of 9 members:

(1) The mayor of the city, or with the approval of the local legislative body the mayor's designee, who shall be an ex officio member;

(2) An administrative official of the city selected by the mayor, who shall be an ex officio member;

(3) A member of the city council selected by the council, who shall be an ex officio member; and

(4) Six persons appointed by the mayor, if the mayor is an elected official, or such other method of appointment or election as shall be provided for by the local legislative body or municipal charter.

(b) Alternatively, the local legislative body in a city with a city council-city manager form of government may establish a planning board with membership as provided in paragraph I-a.

I-a. In cities with a city council-city manager form of government, the planning board may consist of the following 9 members:

(a) The city manager, or with the approval of the local legislative body the city manager's designee, who shall be an ex officio member;

(b) A member of the city council selected by the council, who shall be an ex officio member; and

(c) Seven persons appointed by the mayor, if the mayor is an elected official, or such other method of appointment or election as shall be provided for by the local legislative body or municipal charter.

I-b. In towns which operate under the town council form of government, the planning board shall consist of 7 or 9 members, as determined by the local legislative body or by the municipal charter. If the planning board shall consist of 9 members, the members shall be the persons listed in paragraph I. If the planning board shall consist of 7 members, the members shall be as follows:

(a) A member of the town council or administrative official of the town selected by the town council, who shall be an ex officio member; and

(b) Six persons appointed by the mayor, if the mayor is an elected official, or such other method of appointment or election as shall be provided for by the local legislative body or municipal charter.

II. In other towns, the planning board shall consist of 5 or 7 members as determined by the local legislative body. The membership shall be filled by one of the following procedures:

(a) The selectmen shall designate one selectman or administrative official of the town as an ex officio member and appoint 4 or 6 other persons who are residents of the town, as appropriate; or

(b) The local legislative body may decide, by majority vote at the town meeting, that planning board members shall be elected according to either the procedure in subparagraph (1) or in subparagraph (2). The official ballot shall be used on every referendum for the adoption of RSA 673:2, II(b)(1) or (2), and every subsequent rescission of such adoption pursuant to subparagraph

(c). The wording on the official ballot of any referendum for the adoption of RSA 673:2, II(b)(1) or (2) shall specifically state which procedure for electing planning board members is being voted upon. Following the majority vote at town meeting, planning board members shall be elected as follows:

(1) The selectmen shall choose one selectman or administrative official of the town as an ex officio member and the remaining planning board positions shall be filled at the next regular town election pursuant to RSA 669:17. Thereafter, a planning board member shall be elected for the term provided under RSA 673:5, II; or

(2) The selectmen shall choose one selectman or administrative official of the town as an ex officio member and the remaining planning board positions shall be filled on a staggered basis at the subsequent regular town elections pursuant to RSA 669:17 as the term of an appointed member expires, until each member of the board is an elected member. The maximum number of elections to occur annually shall be as provided in RSA 673:5, II. When each planning board member is an elected member, such member shall be elected for the term provided in RSA 673:5, II.

(c) A local legislative body which has voted to elect planning board members may, by majority vote at town meeting, decide to rescind that action and have the planning board appointed in the manner set forth in subparagraph (a). The vote to have planning board members so appointed shall take effect upon adoption by the town meeting, and the selectmen shall forthwith appoint members in accordance with RSA 673:5. The planning board shall, however, continue in existence, and the elected members in office at the time of the town meeting vote to appoint members may continue to serve until their successors are appointed and qualified.

III. In village districts, the planning board shall consist of either 5 or 7 members as determined by the village district meeting. The district commissioners shall:

(a) Designate one district commissioner or administrative official of the district as an ex officio member; and

(b) Appoint 4 or 6 other persons who are residents of the village district, as appropriate.

IV. In counties in which there are located unincorporated towns or unorganized places, the planning board shall consist of 5 or 9 members. The county commissioners shall recommend appointees to the planning board, and the appointees shall be approved by the county delegation. Planning board members shall be residents of the county, and shall be evenly distributed geographically throughout the county. The membership of the planning board shall be as follows:

(a) The chairperson of the board of county commissioners or designee shall be an ex officio member.

(b) A member of the county convention selected by the convention shall be an ex officio member.

(c) An administrative official of the county selected by the chairperson of the board of county commissioners shall be an ex officio member.

(d) Two or 6 persons appointed by the board of county commissioners and approved by the county convention.

(e) One or 3 alternates appointed by the board of county commissioners and approved by the county convention.

HISTORY:

1983, 447:1. 1987, 255:1. 1989, 266:9. 1991, 377:4. 1992, 89:1, 2. 1993, 69:1, eff. June 22, 1993. 1996, 42:1–4, eff. June 23, 1996. 181:1, eff. Aug. 2, 1996. 2000, 107:1, eff. July 7, 2000.

Amendments

—2000.

Designated the former introductory paragraph of par. I as present subpar. I(a), redesignated former subpars. I(a)–(d) as subpars. I(a)(1)–(4), and added subpar. (b), added new par. I-a, and redesignated former par. I-a as par. I-b.

—1996.

Paragraph I(a): Chapter 42 substituted "the mayor's" for "his" preceding "designee".

Paragraph I-a(a): Chapter 181 inserted "or administrative official of the town" preceding "selected by".

Paragraph II: Chapter 42 added the second sentence in subpar. (b).

Chapter 181 inserted "or administrative official of the town" preceding "as an ex officio" in subpars. (a), (b)(1) and (2).

Paragraph III(a): Chapter 181 inserted "or administrative official of the district" preceding "as an ex officio".

Paragraph IV(a): Chapter 42 substituted "chairperson" for "chairman" preceding "of the board" and deleted "his" preceding "designee".

Paragraph IV(c): Chapter 42 substituted "chairperson" for "chairman" preceding "of the board".

—1993.

Paragraph II(b): Rewritten to the extent that a detailed comparison would be impracticable.

—1992.

Paragraph I: Deleted "and in towns which operate under the town council form of government" following "cities" in the introductory paragraph and "or town" following "city" in subpars. (a)–(c).

Paragraph I-a: Added.

—1991.

Paragraph I(d): Substituted "or such other method of appointment or election as shall be provided for by the local legislative body or municipal charter" for "otherwise appointment shall be as provided for by the local legislative body" following "official".

—1989.

Paragraph IV: Added.

—1987.

Paragraph I(a): Inserted "or with the approval of the local legislative body his designee" following "town".

RESEARCH REFERENCES AND PRACTICE AIDS

Cross References.

Disqualification of members, see RSA 673:14.

Filling of vacancies, see RSA 673:12.

Removal of members, see RSA 673:13.

Terms of office of members, see RSA 673:5.

673:3. Zoning Board of Adjustment and Building Code Board of Appeals.

I. The zoning board of adjustment shall consist of 5 members. The members of the board shall either be elected in the manner prescribed by RSA 669, or appointed in a manner prescribed by the local legislative body. Each member of the board shall be a resident of the municipality in order to be appointed or elected.

II. Zoning board of adjustment members who are elected shall be elected for the term provided under RSA 673:5, II. A local legislative body which has previously provided for the appointment of zoning board of adjustment members may rescind that action by majority vote and choose to elect board members. The terms of appointed members of zoning boards of adjustment in municipalities in office on the effective date of an affirmative decision to elect such board members shall not be affected by the decision. However, when the term of each member expires, each new member shall be elected at the next regular municipal election for the term provided under RSA 673:5, II.

III. A local legislative body which has provided for the election of zoning board of adjustment members may rescind that action by majority vote, in which event members shall thereafter be appointed in a manner prescribed by the local legislative body. The elected board shall, however, continue in existence, and the elected members in office may continue to serve until their successors are appointed and qualified.

III-a. A local legislative body's decision to change from an elected to an appointed zoning board of adjustment, or from an appointed to an elected zoning board of adjustment, may be made without amending the zoning ordinance. In a town operating under the town meeting form of government, the decision may be made at any annual or special town meeting. If the town has adopted the official ballot for the election of town officers, the question may be, but is not required to be, placed on the official ballot. If the question is not placed on the official ballot, the question shall be placed in the warrant and shall be voted on as a separate article at the town meeting.

IV. The building code board of appeals shall consist of 3 or 5 members who shall be appointed in a manner prescribed by the local legislative body; provided, however, that an elected zoning board of adjustment may act as the building code board of appeals pursuant to RSA 673:1, V. Each member of the board shall be a resident of the municipality in order to be appointed.

HISTORY:

1983, 447:1. 1990, 71:1, eff. June 5, 1990. 2009, 286:2, eff. January 1, 2010.

Amendments

—2009.

The 2009 amendment added the second sentence of II; added "by majority vote" in the first sentence of III; and added III-a.

—1990.

Rewritten to the extent that a detailed comparison would be impracticable.

RESEARCH REFERENCES AND PRACTICE AIDS

Cross References.
Disqualification of members, see RSA 673:14.
Filling of vacancies, see RSA 673:12.
Removal of members, see RSA 673:13.
Terms of office of members, see RSA 673:5.

673:3-a. Training.

Within the first year of assuming office, a new member of a zoning board of adjustment or planning board may complete training offered by the office of strategic initiatives. The office of strategic initiatives may provide this training, which may be designed in a variety of formats including, but not limited to, web-based, distance learning, traditional classroom style, or self study.

HISTORY:

1986, 213:4, eff. Aug. 5, 1986. 1996, 42:5, eff. June 23, 1996. 2003, 319:9, eff. July 1, 2003. 2004, 257:44, eff. July 1, 2004. 2011, 224:121, eff. July 1, 2011. 2017, 156:64, eff. July 1, 2017.

Amendment Notes

The 2017 amendments to this section by Ch. 156 substituted "office of strategic initiatives" for "office of energy and planning" twice.

—2011.

The 2011 amendment, in the first sentence, substituted "the first year" for "6 months," "a new" for "for the first time, any non-ex-officio," "adjustment or planning" for "adjustment and the planning," and "complete training offered" for "at the member's option complete at least 6 hours of training for the member's respective position. The training shall be designed and furnished offered"; added the second sentence; and made a stylistic change.

—2004.

Substituted "office of energy and planning" for "office of state planning and energy programs" in the second sentence.

—2003.

Substituted "office of state planning and energy programs" for "office of state planning".

—1996.

Substituted "the member's" for "his" preceding "option" and "respective" in the first sentence.

673:4. Historic District Commission.

I. The historic district commission shall consist of not less than 3 members and no more than 7 members who shall be appointed in a manner as prescribed by the local legislative body.

II. Each historic district commission member shall be a resident of the city or town which establishes the district. One commission member shall be a member of the local governing body and one commission member may be a member of the planning board. Not more than 5 alternate members may be appointed. When an alternate sits in absence or disqualification of a regular member, the alternate shall have full voting powers. In determining each member's qualifications, the appointing authority shall take into consideration the appointee's demonstrated interest and ability to understand, appreciate and promote the purposes of the historic district commission.

III. Members of a historic district commission also may serve on other municipal boards and commissions, including but not limited to a conservation commission established under RSA 36-A, and a heritage commission established under RSA 673:4-a.

HISTORY:

1983, 447:1. 1995, 138:3, eff. July 23, 1995.

Amendments

—1995.

Paragraph I: Substituted "not less than 3 members and no more than 7" for "5 or 7" following "shall consist of".

Paragraph II: Substituted "local governing body" for "board of selectmen or the mayor of the municipality" preceding "and one" in the second sentence and added the third and fourth sentences.

Paragraph III: Added.

NOTES TO DECISIONS

Construction

RSA 674:45, RSA 674:46-a, and RSA 673:4, II do not speak to the legislature's intent regarding the standard of review to be applied to appeals before a zoning board of adjustment. Ouellette v. Town of Kingston, 157 N.H. 604, 956 A.2d 286, 2008 N.H. LEXIS 98 (N.H. 2008).

RESEARCH REFERENCES AND PRACTICE AIDS

Cross References.
Disqualification of members, see RSA 673:14.
Filling of vacancies, see RSA 673:12.
Removal of members, see RSA 673:13.
Terms of office of members, see RSA 673:5.

673:4-a. Heritage Commissions.

I. The heritage commission shall consist of not less than 3 members and no more than 7 members who shall be appointed in a manner as prescribed by the local legislative body.

II. Each heritage commission member shall be a resident of the city or town which establishes the commission. One commission member shall be a member of the local governing body. One commission member may be a member of the planning board. Not more than 5 alternate members may be appointed. When an alternate sits in absence or disqualification of a regular member, the alternate shall have full voting powers. If there is a historic district commission, one member of this commission shall be an ex officio member of the heritage commission. In determining each member's qualifications, the appointing authority shall take into consideration the appointee's demonstrated interest and ability to understand, appreciate and promote the purpose of the heritage commission.

III. Members of a heritage commission also may serve on other municipal boards and commissions, including but not limited to a conservation commission established under RSA 36-A, and a historic district commission established under RSA 673:4.

HISTORY:
1992, 64:6. 1995, 138:4, eff. July 23, 1995.

Revision note.
Substituted "boards" for "board" following "municipal" in par. III to correct a typographical error.

Amendments

—1995.
Rewritten to the extent that a detailed comparison would be impracticable.

RESEARCH REFERENCES AND PRACTICE AIDS

Cross References.
Heritage commissions generally, see RSA 674:44-a et seq.

673:4-b. Agricultural Commissions.

I. The agricultural commission shall consist of not less than 3 members and no more than 7 members who shall be appointed in a manner as prescribed by the local legislative body.

II. Each agricultural commission member shall be a resident of the city or town which establishes the commission. One commission member may be a member of the local governing body. One commission member may be a member of the planning board. Not more than 5 alternate members may be appointed. When an alternate sits in absence or disqualification of a regular member, the alternate shall have full voting powers. In determining each member's qualifications, the appointing authority shall take into consideration the appointee's demonstrated interest and ability to understand, appreciate, and promote the purpose of the agricultural commission.

III. Members of an agricultural commission also may serve on other municipal boards and commissions, including but not limited to a conservation commission established under RSA 36-A, a historic district commission established under RSA 674:46, or a heritage commission established under RSA 674:44-a.

HISTORY:
2007, 266:3, eff. August 28, 2007.

673:4-c. Housing Commissions.

I. The housing commission shall consist of not less than 3 members and no more than 7 members who shall be appointed in a manner as prescribed by the local legislative body.

II. Each housing commission member shall be a resident of the city or town which establishes the commission. One commission member may be a member of the local governing body. One commission member may be a member of the planning board. Not more than 5 alternate members may be appointed. When an alternate sits in absence or disqualification of a regular member, the alternate shall have full voting powers. In determining each member's qualifications, the appointing authority shall take into consideration the appointee's demonstrated interest and ability to understand, appreciate, and promote the purpose of the housing commission.

III. Members of a housing commission also may serve on other municipal boards and commissions, including but not limited to a conservation commission established under RSA 36-A, a historic district commission established under RSA 674:46, a heritage commission established under RSA 674:44-a, or an agriculture commission established under RSA 674:44-e.

HISTORY:
2008, 391:3, eff. September 15, 2008.

673:5. Terms of Local Land Use Board Members.

I.(a) Except as provided in subparagraph (b), the term of any ex officio member serving on a local land use board shall coincide with the term for that other office; except that the term of the administrative official appointed by the mayor shall terminate with the term of office of the mayor appointing the official, and that the term of the administrative official appointed by the town council, board of selectmen, or village district commissioners shall be for one year.

(b) A city or town council, board of selectmen, or the village district commissioners may determine that the city or town council member, the selectman member or the village district commission member shall be subject to a 4 month or an annual appointment under such conditions as it determines.

II. The term of an elected or appointed local land use board member shall be 3 years. The initial terms of members first appointed or elected to any local land use board shall be staggered so that no more than 3 appointments or elections occur annually in the case of a 7 or 9 member board and no more than 2 appointments or elections occur annually in the case of a 5 member board, except when required to fill vacancies.

III. The term of office for an appointed local land use board member shall begin on a date established by the appointing authority, or as soon thereafter as the member is qualified, and shall end 3 years after the date so established. If no successor has been appointed and qualified at the expiration of an appointed member's term, the member shall be entitled to remain in office until a successor has been appointed and qualified.

HISTORY:

1983, 447:1, eff. Jan. 1, 1984. 1996, 42:6, eff. June 23, 1996. 181:2, eff. Aug. 2, 1996. 2010, 226:3, eff. August 27, 2010.

Amendments

—2010.

The 2010 amendment added III.

—1996.

Paragraph I(a): Chapter 42 substituted "the official" for "him" following "mayor appointing".

Chapter 181 added "and that the term of the administrative official appointed by the town council, board of selectment, or village district commissioners shall be for one year" following "appointing the official".

Paragraph I(b): Chapter 181 inserted "a 4 month or an" preceding "annual appointment".

NOTES TO DECISIONS

Terms of ex officio members

The language of the statute to the effect that the terms of office of ex officio members of planning board should "correspond to their respective official tenures" was clear on its face in requiring that a selectman's term as planning board member was to conform to his term as selectman, and a board of selectmen violated the statute when they removed a selectman from a town planning board solely because he had served one year. Silva v. Botsch, 120 N.H. 600, 420 A.2d 301, 1980 N.H. LEXIS 366 (N.H. 1980). (Decided under former RSA 36:5.)

Because the statute required that a selectman's term on a planning board match, as nearly as possible, his term as a selectman and because the statute did not enumerate length of time served as a criterion for severance, the removal of a selectman from the planning board solely because he had served one year was a violation of the statute. Silva v. Botsch, 120 N.H. 600, 420 A.2d 301, 1980 N.H. LEXIS 366 (N.H. 1980). (Decided under former RSA 36:5.)

RESEARCH REFERENCES AND PRACTICE AIDS

Cross References.

Filling of vacancies, see RSA 673:12.

Removal of members, see RSA 673:13.

Terms of officers, see RSA 673:9.

673:6. Appointment, Number and Terms of Alternate Members.

I.(a) The local legislative body may provide for the appointment of not more than 5 alternate members to any appointed local land use board, who shall be appointed by the appointing authority. The terms of alternate members shall be 3 years.

(b) In a town which votes to elect its planning board members on a staggered basis according to the provisions of RSA 673:2, II(b)(2), alternate members of the planning board shall continue to be appointed according to the provisions of this paragraph until each member of the board is an elected member. Thereafter, the alternate planning board members shall be appointed according to the provisions of paragraph II.

II. An elected planning board may appoint 5 alternate members for a term of 3 years each, which shall be staggered in the same manner as elected members pursuant to RSA 673:5, II.

II-a. An elected zoning board of adjustment may appoint 5 alternate members for a term of 3 years each, which shall be staggered in the same manner as elected members pursuant to RSA 673:5, II.

III. The alternate for a city or town council member, selectman, or village district commission member shall be appointed by the respective council, board, or commission in the same manner and subject to the same qualifications as the city or town council member, selectman, or village district commission member under RSA 673:2. The terms of alternate members shall be the same as those of the respective members and may be in addition to the alternates provided for in paragraph I.

IV. Every alternate member appointed to a planning board under this section shall comply with the multiple membership requirements of RSA 673:7, I and II.

V. An alternate member of a local land use board may participate in meetings of the board as a nonvoting member pursuant to rules adopted under RSA 676:1.

HISTORY:

1983, 447:1. 1986, 29:1. 1987, 197:1. 1991, 176:1. 1993, 69:2, eff. June 22, 1993. 1996, 181:3, eff. Aug. 2, 1996. 217:1, eff. Aug. 9, 1996. 2010, 270:1, eff. July 6, 2010. 2017, 143:1, eff. August 15, 2017.

Amendment Notes

The 2017 amendments to this section by Ch. 143 added "in the same manner and subject to the same qualifications as the city or town council member, selectman, or village district commission member under RSA 673:2" in the first sentence of III.

—2010.

The 2010 amendment added V.

—1996.

Paragraphs II, II-a: Rewritten to the extent that a detailed comparison would be impracticable.

—1993.

Paragraph I: Designated the existing provisions of the paragraph as subpar. (a) and added subpar. (b).

—1991.

Paragraph II-a: added.

—1987.

Paragraph III: Substituted "appointed" for "provided for" following "shall be" in the first sentence and "those" for "that" preceding "of the respective members and" in the second sentence and "may" for "shall" thereafter.

—1986.

Paragraph I: Substituted "5" for "3" preceding "alternate" in the first sentence.

Contingent 1996 amendment.

1996, 181:3, provided for amendment of this section. However, under the terms of 1996, 181:4, eff. Aug. 2, 1996, the amendment did not become effective.

Cross References.
Designation of alternate members, see RSA 673:11.

673:7. Planning Board Members Serving on Other Local Boards.

I. In the case of towns, any 2 appointed or elected members of the planning board may also serve together on any other municipal board or commission, except that no more than one member of the planning board shall serve on the conservation commission, the local governing body, or a local land use board as defined in RSA 672:7.

II. In cities, appointed members shall not hold any other municipal office, except that:

(a) One of the appointed members may be a member of the zoning board of adjustment;

(b) Either one appointed member or one ex officio member may be a member of the conservation commission if one exists in the city; and

(c) Either one appointed member or one ex officio member may be a member of the heritage commission, the historic district commission, the agricultural commission, the housing commission, or all 4 if such commissions exist in the municipality.

III. In counties in which there are located unincorporated towns or unorganized places, the county commissioners shall determine which members of the planning board for those towns and places, if any, may serve on other municipal boards or commissions.

HISTORY:
1983, 447:1. 1989, 266:10. 1992, 64:7, eff. June 19, 1992. 2007, 266:4, eff. August 28, 2007. 2008, 391:4, eff. September 15, 2008. 2011, 190:1, eff. August 13, 2011.

Amendments

—2011.
The 2011 amendment, in I, added "any 2," added "together," substituted "except that no more than one member of the" for "provided that such multiple membership does not result in 2," and substituted "shall serve on the conservation commission, the local governing body, or a local land use board as defined in RSA 672:7" for "members serving on the same board or commission."

—2008.
The 2008 amendment in II(c), added "the housing commission", substituted "4" for "3" preceding "if such commissions" and "municipality" for "city" at the end; and made a related change.

—2007.
Paragraph II(c): Deleted "or" following "heritage commission" and substituted "or the agricultural commission, or all 3 if such commissions exist" for "or both, if such a commission exists".

—1992.
Paragraph II(c): Inserted "heritage commission, or the" preceding "historic" and substituted "or both, if such a commission" for "if one" preceding "exists".

—1989.
Paragraph III: Added.

Cross References.
Disqualification of members, see RSA 673:14.
Multiple membership of alternates, see RSA 673:6.

673:8. Organization.

Each local land use board shall elect its chairperson from the appointed or elected members and may create other offices as it deems necessary.

HISTORY:
1983, 447:1, eff. Jan. 1, 1984. 1996, 42:7, eff. June 23, 1996.

Amendments

—1996.
Substituted "chairperson" for "chairman" preceding "from the appointed".

Cross References.
Meetings, see RSA 673:10, 17.
Records, see RSA 673:17.
Staff and finances, see RSA 673:16.

673:9. Term of Chairperson and Officers.

I. The term of every officer and chairperson elected by a local land use board shall be one year. Both the chairperson and officers shall be eligible for reelection.

II. In the case of planning boards, an ex officio member shall not serve as chairperson.

HISTORY:
1983, 447:1, eff. Jan. 1, 1984. 1996, 42:8, eff. June 23, 1996.

Amendments

—1996.
Substituted "chairperson" for "chairman" wherever it appeared in the section.

Cross References.
Terms of office of members generally, see RSA 673:5.

General Provisions

Cross References.
Appointment and terms of board members generally, see RSA 673:2 et seq.

673:10. Scheduling of Meetings.

I. Meetings of the heritage commission, the historic district commission, the agricultural commission, the housing commission, the building code board of appeals, and the zoning board of adjustment shall be held at the call of the chairperson and at such other times as the board may determine.

II. The planning board shall hold at least one regular meeting in each month.

III. A majority of the membership of a local land use board shall constitute the quorum necessary in order to transact business at any meeting of a local land use board.

HISTORY:
1983, 447:1. 1992, 64:8, eff. June 19, 1992. 1996, 42:9, eff. June 23, 1996. 2007, 266:5, eff. August 28, 2007. 2008, 391:5, eff. September 15, 2008.

Amendments

—2008.
The 2008 amendment added "the housing commission" following "agricultural commission" and made a stylistic change in I.

—2007.
Paragraph I: Inserted "the agricultural commission" preceding "the building code".

—1996.
Paragraph I: Substituted "chairperson" for "chairman" following "call of the".

—1992.
Paragraph I: Inserted "heritage commission" preceding "historic".

RESEARCH REFERENCES AND PRACTICE AIDS

Cross References.
Public access to meetings, see RSA 673:17.

673:11. Designation of Alternate Members.

Whenever a regular member of a local land use board is absent or whenever a regular member disqualifies himself or herself, the chairperson shall designate an alternate, if one is present, to act in the absent member's place; except that only the alternate designated for the city or town council, board of selectmen, or village district commission member shall serve in place of that member.

HISTORY:
1983, 447:1, eff. Jan. 1, 1984. 1996, 42:10, eff. June 23, 1996.

Amendments

—1996.
Inserted "or herself" following "himself" and substituted "chairperson" for "chairman" preceding "shall designate".

NOTES TO DECISIONS

Failure to designate alternate members
On appeal of planning board decision approving a subdivision, claim concerning the board's failure to appoint alternates was properly dismissed where it was not raised within the 30-day period after the filing of the decision in the office of the planning board, as required by RSA 677:15. Frisella v. Farmington, 131 N.H. 78, 550 A.2d 102, 1988 N.H. LEXIS 94 (N.H. 1988).

RESEARCH REFERENCES AND PRACTICE AIDS

Cross References.
Appointment, number and terms of alternate members, see RSA 673:6.

Multiple memberships, see RSA 673:7.

673:12. Filling Vacancies in Membership.

Vacancies in the membership of a local land use board occurring other than through the expiration of a term of office shall be filled as follows:

I. For an elected member, by appointment by the remaining board members until the next regular municipal election at which time a successor shall be elected to either fill the unexpired term or start a new term, as appropriate.

II. For an appointed, ex officio, or alternate member, by the original appointing or designating authority, for the unexpired term.

III. The chairperson of the local land use board may designate an alternate member of the board to fill the vacancy temporarily until the vacancy is filled in the manner set forth in paragraph I or II. If the vacancy is for an ex officio member, the chairperson may only designate the person who has been appointed to serve as the alternate for the ex officio member.

HISTORY:
1983, 447:1, eff. Jan. 1, 1984. 2009, 114:1, eff. August 21, 2009.

Amendments

—2009.
The 2009 amendment added III.

NOTES TO DECISIONS

Filling of vacancy for elected member
Under the statute, which provided for the filling of a vacancy for an elected member of a planning board by selectmen until the next election, the town's election ballot notified the voters of three openings on the planning board, but did not mention a fourth opening, a vacancy on the board existed and the selectmen properly made an appointment to fill the vacancy. Derry v. Adams, 121 N.H. 473, 431 A.2d 766, 1981 N.H. LEXIS 354 (N.H. 1981). (Decided under former RSA 36:7.)

RESEARCH REFERENCES AND PRACTICE AIDS

Cross References.
Removal of members, see RSA 673:13.
Terms of office of members generally, see RSA 673:5.
Terms of officers, see RSA 673:9.

673:13. Removal of Members.

I. After public hearing, appointed members and alternate members of an appointed local land use board may be removed by the appointing authority upon written findings of inefficiency, neglect of duty, or malfeasance in office.

II. The board of selectmen may, for any cause enumerated in paragraph I, remove an elected member or alternate member after a public hearing.

III. The appointing authority or the planning board shall file with the city or town clerk, the village district clerk, or the clerk for the county commissioners, whichever is appropriate, a written statement of reasons for removal under this section.

IV. The council, selectmen, county commissioners with the approval of the county delegation, or district commissioners may for any cause enumerated in this section remove the members selected by them.

HISTORY:

1983, 447:1. 1989, 266:11, eff. July 1, 1989.

Amendments

—1989.

Paragraph III: Substituted "the" for "or" preceding "village district clerk" and inserted "or the clerk for the county commissioners" thereafter.

Paragraph IV: Inserted "county commissioners with the approval of the county delegation" following "selectmen".

NOTES TO DECISIONS

Malfeasance

Trial court erred in upholding city council's removal of a planning board official for acts alleged to constitute malfeasance in office, where the acts relied upon did not relate to the performance of the official's duties as a planning board member, and therefore did not fall within the scope of malfeasance under this section. Williams v. Dover, 130 N.H. 527, 543 A.2d 919, 1988 N.H. LEXIS 33 (N.H. 1988).

RESEARCH REFERENCES AND PRACTICE AIDS

Cross References.

Filling of vacancies, see RSA 673:12.

673:14. Disqualification of Member.

I. No member of a zoning board of adjustment, building code board of appeals, planning board, heritage commission, historic district commission, agricultural commission, or housing commission shall participate in deciding or shall sit upon the hearing of any question which the board is to decide in a judicial capacity if that member has a direct personal or pecuniary interest in the outcome which differs from the interest of other citizens, or if that member would be disqualified for any cause to act as a juror upon the trial of the same matter in any action at law. Reasons for disqualification do not include exemption from service as a juror or knowledge of the facts involved gained in the performance of the member's official duties.

II. When uncertainty arises as to the application of paragraph I to a board member in particular circumstances, the board shall, upon the request of that member or another member of the board, vote on the question of whether that member should be disqualified. Any such request and vote shall be made prior to or at the commencement of any required public hearing. Such a vote shall be advisory and non-binding, and may not be requested by persons other than board members, except as provided by local ordinance or by a procedural rule adopted under RSA 676:1.

III. If a member is disqualified or unable to act in any particular case pending before the board, the chairperson shall designate an alternate to act in the member's place, as provided in RSA 673:11.

HISTORY:

1983, 447:1. 1988, 26:1. 1992, 64:9, eff. June 19, 1992. 1996, 42:11, eff. June 23, 1996. 2007, 266:6, eff. August 28, 2007. 2008, 391:6, eff. September 15, 2008.

Amendments

—2008.

The 2008 amendment added "or housing commission" and made a related change in the first sentence of I.

—2007.

Paragraph I: Deleted "or" following "heritage commission" and inserted "or agricultural commission" following "historic district commission" in the first sentence.

—1996.

Paragraph III: Substituted "chairperson" for "chairman" preceding "shall designate" and "the member's" for "his" preceding "place".

—1992.

Paragraph I: Inserted "heritage commission" following "planning board" in the first sentence.

—1988.

Rewritten to the extent that a detailed comparison would be impracticable.

NOTES TO DECISIONS

Analysis

1. Construction
2. Disqualification not warranted
3. Effect of participation by disqualified member
4. Preservation for review

1. Construction

The statute does not place restrictions on who may object to the participation of board members; although plaintiffs were not statutorily prohibited from raising the issue, they failed to make a timely objection to board member's participation. Bayson Props. v. City of Lebanon, 150 N.H. 167, 834 A.2d 202, 2003 N.H. LEXIS 159 (N.H. 2003).

2. Disqualification not warranted

With respect to an application for an equitable waiver for a waterfront access easement over trustees' waterfront lot, the court rejected the trustees' argument that one of the zoning board of adjustment (ZBA) members should have recused herself under RSA 673:14, I and RSA 500-A:12 because she was a former employee of one of the owners who had originally created the easement. On its face, RSA 500-A:12 did not disqualify former employees per se, and the conclusion of the ZBA chairman that the other members had no concern about the alleged bias of the other member was supported by the record. Taylor v. Town of Wakefield, 158 N.H. 35, 959 A.2d 217, 2008 N.H. LEXIS 124 (N.H. 2008).

Trial court did not err in failing to find that planning board member should have recused himself or been disqualified for bias where the only allegation that concerned the member's alleged bias as to plaintiff's request to cut trees on a designated scenic road was that he moved to deny the request; his motion was not evidence of "prejudgment," but of judgment exercised at the appropriate time and place, nor was it evidence of bias. Webster v. Town of Candia, 146 N.H. 430, 778 A.2d 402, 2001 N.H. LEXIS 91 (N.H. 2001), amended, 2001 N.H. LEXIS 154 (N.H. Aug. 20, 2001).

A planning board member's discovery of obvious inconsistencies in submitted documents, and subsequent statement to an applicant explaining why such inconsistencies will preclude approval, does not show that the application has been prejudged so as to require member's disqualification. Dover v. Kimball, 136 N.H. 441, 616 A.2d 516, 1992 N.H. LEXIS 187 (N.H. 1992).

3. Effect of participation by disqualified member

Hearing on request for variance to add addition to county hospital was not rendered unfair, and decision of board was not made illegal, by reason of fact that a member of the board of adjustment worked in the county surplus food program. Sherman v. Brentwood, 112 N.H. 122, 290 A.2d 47, 1972 N.H. LEXIS 157 (N.H. 1972).

The fact that a disqualified member was present and acting as clerk was immaterial where he took no part in the deliberations or decisions. Gelinas v. Portsmouth, 97 N.H. 248, 85 A.2d 896, 1952 N.H. LEXIS 3 (N.H. 1952). (Decided under prior law.)

4. Preservation for review

Trustees timely raised the issue of disqualification of a zoning board of adjustment (ZBA) member. Although the trustees first raised the issue in their motion for rehearing, the issue was preserved for review because they raised it at the earliest possible time, having first learned of the member's potential conflict only after the ZBA voted on an application. Taylor v. Town of Wakefield, 158 N.H. 35, 959 A.2d 217, 2008 N.H. LEXIS 124 (N.H. 2008).

RESEARCH REFERENCES AND PRACTICE AIDS

Cross References.

Disqualification of member and appointment of alternate member of appeals board for appeals from decisions of commissioner of transportation, see RSA 21-L:14.

Disqualification of member and appointment of alternate member of railroad appeals board, see RSA 21-L:16.

Disqualifications of jurors generally, see RSA 500-A:12.

Multiple memberships, see RSA 673:7.

673:15. Power to Compel Witness Attendance and Administer Oaths.

The chairperson of the zoning board of adjustment or the chairperson of the building code board of appeals or, in the chairperson's absence, the acting chairperson may administer oaths. Whenever the board exercises its regulatory or quasi judicial powers it may, at its sole discretion, compel the attendance of witnesses. All expenses incurred under this section for compelling the attendance of a witness shall be paid by the party or parties requesting that a witness be compelled to attend a meeting of the board.

HISTORY:

1983, 447:1, eff. Jan. 1, 1984. 1996, 42:12, eff. June 23, 1996.

Amendments

—1996.

Substituted "chairperson" for "chairman" in three places and "the chairperson's" for "his" preceding "absence" in the first sentence.

RESEARCH REFERENCES AND PRACTICE AIDS

Cross References.

Administrative and enforcement procedures generally, see RSA 676.

Summoning witnesses generally, see RSA 516:1 et seq.

673:16. Staff; Finances.

I. Each local land use board may appoint such employees as it deems necessary for its work who shall be subject to the same employment rules as other corresponding civil employees of the municipality. Each board may also contract with planners, engineers, architects, and other consultants for such services as it may require. The expenditures of the board, exclusive of gifts, reimbursements, or amounts held pursuant to paragraph II, shall be within the amounts appropriated for the purpose by the local legislative body, which may provide such funds, equipment, and accommodations as it deems necessary or advisable for the board's work. Each board may accept and use gifts, grants, or contributions for the exercise of its functions, in accordance with procedures established for the expenditure of funds within the municipality.

II. Any fee which a local land use board, acting pursuant to this title, collects from an applicant to cover an expense lawfully imposed upon that applicant, including but not limited to the expense of notice, the expense of consultant services or investigative studies under RSA 676:4, I(g) or RSA 676:5, IV, or the implementation of conditions lawfully imposed as part of a conditional approval, may be paid out toward that expense without approval of the local legislative body. Such fees:

(a) Shall, whenever held by the municipality, be placed in the custody of the municipal treasurer, subject to the same investment limitations as for other municipal funds.

(b) Shall be paid out only for the purpose for which the expense was imposed upon the applicant.

(c) Shall be held in a separate, nonlapsing account, and not commingled with other municipal funds; provided, however, that such fees may be used to reimburse any account from which an amount has been paid out in anticipation of the receipt of said fees.

(d) Shall be paid out by the municipal treasurer only upon order of the local land use board or its designated agent for such purpose. This paragraph shall not apply to application, permit, or inspection fees which have been set by the local legislative body as part of an ordinance, or by the selectmen under RSA 41:9-a. Notwithstanding RSA 672:7, a building inspector shall not be considered a "local land use board" for purposes of this section.

HISTORY:

1983, 447:1. 1991, 377:5. 1992, 172:1, 2, eff. July 7, 1992. 2010, 303:2, eff. September 11, 2010.

Amendments

—2010.

The 2010 amendment added "or RSA 676:5, IV" in the first sentence of the introductory paragraph of II.

—1992.

Paragraph I: Deleted "or" following "gifts" and inserted "or amounts held pursuant to paragraph II" following "reimbursements" in the third sentence.

Paragraph II: Rewrote the introductory paragraph to the extent that a detailed comparison would be impracticable, substituted "shall be paid out" for "may be expended" preceding "only" and "the expense" for "it" preceding "was imposed" in subpar. (b), substituted "paid out" for "spent" preceding "in anticipation" in subpar. (c), and amended subpar. (d) generally.

—1991.
Designated the existing provisions of the section as par. I and added par. II.

RESEARCH REFERENCES AND PRACTICE AIDS

Cross References.
Municipal budgeting and finances generally, see RSA 32, 33.

New Hampshire Practice.
13-8 N.H.P. Local Government Law § 168.

673:17. Open Meetings; Records.

Each local land use board shall hold its meetings and maintain its records in accordance with RSA 91-A.

HISTORY:
1983, 447:1, eff. Jan. 1, 1984.

NOTES TO DECISIONS

Notice and hearing requirements
The fundamental purpose of the requirements for notice and hearing was to advise all affected parties of their opportunity to be heard in public meeting and to be apprised of the relief sought. Carter v. Nashua, 113 N.H. 407, 308 A.2d 847, 1973 N.H. LEXIS 285 (N.H. 1973). (Decided under prior law.)

A lack of compliance with the requirements that hearing be upon notice and open to the public would deprive a zoning board of adjustment of jurisdiction to grant a variance. Carter v. Nashua, 113 N.H. 407, 308 A.2d 847, 1973 N.H. LEXIS 285 (N.H. 1973). (Decided under prior law.)

Where notice of a second meeting of a zoning board of adjustment in the matter of a variance application was given 24 hours before the meeting instead of the 72-hour notice required by city ordinance, such failure was not sufficient to affect the board's jurisdiction over the matter, which it acquired by its compliance with all notice requirements for the first meeting. Carter v. Nashua, 113 N.H. 407, 308 A.2d 847, 1973 N.H. LEXIS 285 (N.H. 1973). (Decided under prior law.)

RESEARCH REFERENCES AND PRACTICE AIDS

Cross References.
Transfers of records upon abolition of local boards, see RSA 673:21, 22.

Abolition of Boards, Zoning Ordinances, or Building Codes

673:18. Abolishing Planning Board, Heritage Commission, Historic District Commission, Agricultural Commission, or Housing Commission.

I. The local legislative body of a city, of a county in which there are located unincorporated towns or unorganized places, or of a town operating under the town council form of government, shall determine the manner in which the planning board, the heri-

tage commission, the historic district commission, the agricultural commission, or the housing commission may be abolished.

II. In all other towns, upon a petition to abolish the planning board, the heritage commission, the historic district commission, the agricultural commission, or the housing commission, signed by 100 or more voters or $^1/_{10}$ of the registered voters in town, whichever number is less, the planning board, heritage commission, historic district commission, agricultural commission, or housing commission shall submit the proposal to the town or village district in the same manner prescribed in RSA 675:4, except that the question put to the voters shall be in substantially the following form: "Are you in favor of abolishing the planning board (heritage commission, historic district commission, agricultural commission, or housing commission) as proposed by petition of the voters of this town (village district)?"

HISTORY:
1983, 447:1. 1989, 266:12. 1992, 64:10, eff. June 19, 1992. 2007, 266:7, eff. August 28, 2007. 2008, 391:7, eff. September 15, 2008.

Amendments

—2008.
The 2008 amendment in the section heading, in I, and throughout in II, added "or housing commission" or variants and made related changes.

—2007.
Substituted "commission, historic district commission, or agricultural commission" for "commission or historic district commission" and "commission, the district commission, or agricultural commission" for "commission or the historic district commission" wherever it appeared throughout the section.

—1992.
Inserted "Heritage Commission" following "Planning Board" in the section catchline.
Paragraph I: Inserted "the heritage commission" following "planning board".
Paragraph II: Inserted "the heritage commission" following "abolish the planning board", "heritage commission" following "less, the planning board", "heritage commission, or" preceding "historic" in the parenthetical voter question and made other minor stylistic changes.

—1989.
Paragraph I: Inserted "of a county in which there are located unincorporated towns or unorganized places" following "city".

RESEARCH REFERENCES AND PRACTICE AIDS

Cross References.
Effect of abolition generally, see RSA 673:19, 20.
Elections generally, see RSA 652 et seq.
Establishment of board or commission, see RSA 673:1.
Home rule powers, see RSA 49-B.
Town elections, see RSA 39, 40, 669.
Transfer of documents of boards or commissions abolished, see RSA 673:21.
Village district elections, see RSA 39, 40, 670.

673:19. Effect of Abolishing Planning Boards.

Upon the effective date of the abolition of a planning board, all land use control activities in the municipality formerly performed by the planning board shall cease. Existing zoning ordinances shall remain in effect following the abolition date for a period not to exceed 2 years from the date of such action, but no amendment to a zoning ordinance requiring action by the former planning board shall be permitted.

HISTORY:
1983, 447:1, eff. Jan. 1, 1984.

RESEARCH REFERENCES AND PRACTICE AIDS

Cross References.
Transfer of records of abolished boards, see RSA 673:21.

673:20. Effect of Abolishing Heritage Commissions, Historic District Commissions, Agricultural Commissions, and Housing Commissions.

Upon the effective date of the abolition of a heritage commission, historic district commission, agricultural commission, or housing commission all the powers and duties of such commission shall cease.

HISTORY:
1983, 447:1. 1992, 64:11, eff. June 19, 1992. 2007, 266:8, eff. August 28, 2007. 2008, 391:8, eff. September 15, 2008.

Amendments

—2008.
The 2008 amendment in the section heading and in the section, added "and housing commission" or variant and made related changes.

—2007.
Deleted "and" following "heritage commissions" and added "and agricultural commissions" to the section heading; deleted "or" following "heritage commission" and inserted "or agricultural commission" following "historic dictrict commission".

—1992.
Inserted "Heritage Commissions and" preceding "Historic District" and substituted "Commissions" for "Commission" thereafter in the section catchline, and in the text of the section, inserted "heritage commission or" following "abolition of a", substituted "such" for "the" following "duties of" and deleted "designed to carry out the purpose of a historic district" preceding "shall cease".

RESEARCH REFERENCES AND PRACTICE AIDS

Cross References.
Transfer of records of abolished commissions, see RSA 673:21.

673:21. Transfer of Documents Upon Abolition of Planning Board, Heritage Commission, Historic District Commission, Agricultural Commission, and Housing Commission.

I. Whenever a heritage commission, historic district commission, agricultural commission, or housing commission is abolished, the records shall be transferred to the planning board. In a municipality where a planning board does not exist, the records shall be transferred to the city, town, or village

district clerk, or to the clerk for the county commissioners, whichever is appropriate.

II. Whenever a planning board is abolished, the records shall be transferred to the city or town clerk, to the clerk of the board of district commissioners, or to the clerk for the county commissioners, whichever is appropriate.

HISTORY:
1983, 447:1. 1989, 266:13. 1992, 64:12, eff. June 19, 1992. 2007, 266:9, eff. August 28, 2007. 2008, 391:9, eff. September 15, 2008.

Amendments

—2008.
The 2008 amendment in the section heading and in I, added "and housing commission" or variant and made related changes.

—2007.
Deleted "and" following "heritage commission" and added "and agricultural commission" to the section heading and in par. I deleted "or" following "heritage commission" and inserted "or agricultural commission" following "historic district commission" in the first sentence.

—1992.
Inserted "Heritage Commission" following "Planning Board" in the section catchline and "heritage commission or" preceding "historic" in the first sentence of par. I.

—1989.
Paragraph I: Inserted "or to the clerk for the county commissioners" preceding "whichever" in the second sentence.
Paragraph II: Deleted "or" following "city or town clerk" and inserted "or to the clerk for the county commissioners" preceding "whichever".

RESEARCH REFERENCES AND PRACTICE AIDS

Cross References.
Abolition of boards or commissions generally, see RSA 673:18.
Effect of abolition, see RSA 673:19, 20.

673:22. Transfer of Documents Upon Abolition of Zoning Ordinance or Building Code.

I. Whenever a zoning ordinance is abolished, the records of the zoning board of adjustment shall be transferred to the planning board.

II. Whenever a building code is abolished, the records of the building code board of appeals shall be transferred to the planning board.

HISTORY:
1983, 447:1, eff. Jan. 1, 1984.

CHAPTER 674

LOCAL LAND USE PLANNING AND REGULATORY POWERS

Master Plan

NOTES TO DECISIONS

Cited:
Cited in Soares v. Atkinson, 128 N.H. 350, 512 A.2d 436, 1986 N.H. LEXIS 298 (1986).

RESEARCH REFERENCES AND PRACTICE AIDS

Cross References.
Local land use boards generally, see RSA 673.
Local land use board review of development of regional impact, see RSA 36:54 et seq.
Ordinance, regulation and code administration and enforcement generally, see RSA 676.
Ordinance, regulation and code adoption procedures generally, see RSA 675.
Rehearing and appeals procedures generally, see RSA 677.
State development plan, see RSA 9-A.
Town powers generally, see RSA 31.

New Hampshire Bar Journal.
For article, "An Overview of the New Hampshire Land Use Planning and Regulation Statutes, " see 34 N.H. B.J. 6 (June 1993).
For Attorney General article, "Department Of Justice's Transportation And Construction Bureau: Trains, Planes And Automobiles," see 45 N.H. B.J. 78 (Spring 2004).
For article, "The New Zoning Variance Cases: Analyzing Unnecessary Hardship Under RSA 674:33," see 46 N.H. B.J. 40 (Fall 2005).
For article, "Unnecessary Hardship Under RSA 674:331(B)," see 46 N.H. B.J. 47 (Fall 2005).
For article, "Roads Revisited Creation And Termination Of Highways In New Hampshire – An Update," see 46 N.H. B.J. 56 (Fall 2005).

New Hampshire Practice.
15-29 N.H.P. Land Use Planning and Zoning § .29.18.

Master Plan

RESEARCH REFERENCES AND PRACTICE AIDS

Cross References.
Emergency temporary zoning and planning ordinances, see RSA 674:24 et seq.
Heritage commissions, see RSA 674:44-a et seq.
Historic districts, see RSA 674:45 et seq.
Manufactured housing regulation, see RSA 674:31 et seq.
Official municipal map, see RSA 674:9 et seq.
Site plan review, see RSA 674:43 et seq.
Subdivision regulation, see RSA 674:35 et seq.

674:1. Duties of the Planning Board.

I. It shall be the duty of every planning board established under RSA 673:1 to prepare and amend from time to time a master plan to guide the development of the municipality. A master plan may include consideration of any areas outside the boundaries of the municipality which in the judgment of the planning board bear a relation to or have an impact on the planning of the municipality. Every planning board shall from time to time update and amend the adopted master plan with funds appropriated for that purpose by the local legislative body. In preparing, amending, and updating the master plan:

(a) The planning board shall have responsibility for promoting interest in, and understanding of, the master plan of the municipality. In order to promote this interest and understanding, the planning board may publish and distribute copies of the master plan, or copies of any report relating to the master plan, and may employ such other means of publicity and education as it may deem advisable.

(b) The planning board shall also have authority to make any investigations, maps and reports, and recommendations which relate to the planning and development of the municipality.

II. The planning board may:

(a) From time to time report and recommend to the appropriate public officials and public agencies programs for the development of the municipality, programs for the erection of public structures, and programs for municipal improvements. Each program shall include recommendations for its financing. It shall be part of the planning board's duties to consult with and advise public officials and agencies, public utility companies, civic organizations, educational organizations, professional organizations, research organizations, and other organizations, and to consult with citizens, for the purposes of protecting or carrying out of the master plan as well as for making recommendations relating to the development of the municipality.

(b) Upon request advise the governing body as to whether proposed ordinances and bylaws regarding the maintenance and operation of stormwater systems under RSA 146-I:6, I-a are consistent with the master plan.

III. Members of the planning board, when duly authorized by the board as a whole, may attend municipal planning conferences or meetings, or hearings upon pending municipal planning legislation. The planning board may by majority vote authorize the payment of reasonable expenses incident to such attendance.

IV. The planning board, and its members, officers, and employees, in the performance of their functions may, by ordinance, be authorized to enter upon any land and make such examinations and surveys as are reasonably necessary and place and maintain necessary monuments and marks and, in the event consent for such entry is denied or not reasonably obtainable, to obtain an administrative inspection warrant under RSA 595-B.

V. The planning board may, from time to time, recommend to the local legislative body amendments of the zoning ordinance or zoning map or additions thereto.

VI. In general, the planning board may be given such powers by the municipality as may be necessary to enable it to fulfill its functions, promote municipal planning, or carry out the purposes of this title. Such powers shall not include regulating timber harvesting operations that are not part of a subdivision application or a development project subject to site plan review under this chapter.

HISTORY:

1983, 447:1. 1991, 231:12, eff. Aug. 9, 1991. 2011, 85:3, eff. July 15, 2011. 2015, 247:2, eff. September 11, 2015.

Amendment Notes

—2015.

The 2015 amendment substituted "civic organizations, educational organizations, professional organizations, research organizations" for "civic, educational, professional, research" in II(a); and added II(b).

—2011.

The 2011 amendment added the second sentence of VI.

—1991.

Paragraph IV: Added "and, in the event consent for such entry is denied or not reasonably obtainable, to obtain an administrative inspection warrant under RSA 595-B" following "marks".

NOTES TO DECISIONS

1 Generally

In absence of special grants of authority, the general function of a planning board was to prepare a master plan for development of the municipality and to investigate, advise, and recommend with respect to municipal planning. Kostreles v. Portsmouth, 104 N.H. 392, 187 A.2d 789, 1963 N.H. LEXIS 62 (N.H. 1963). (Decided under prior law.)

Cited:

Cited in Rancourt v. Barnstead, 129 N.H. 45, 523 A.2d 55, 1986 N.H. LEXIS 379 (1986); Treisman v. Bedford, 132 N.H. 54, 563 A.2d 786, 1989 N.H. LEXIS 75 (1989); Portsmouth Advocates v. Portsmouth, 133 N.H. 876, 587 A.2d 600, 1991 N.H. LEXIS 13 (1991); Dover v. Kimball, 136 N.H. 441, 616 A.2d 516, 1992 N.H. LEXIS 187 (1992); Caspersen v. Town of Lyme, 139 N.H. 637, 661 A.2d 759, 1995 N.H. LEXIS 70 (1995).

RESEARCH REFERENCES AND PRACTICE AIDS

Cross References.

Adoption and amendment of master plan, see RSA 674:6.
Preparation of master plan, see RSA 674:3.

New Hampshire Practice.

15-3 N.H.P. Land Use Planning and Zoning § 3.02.
15-26 N.H.P. Land Use Planning and Zoning § 26.03.
15-30 N.H.P. Land Use Planning and Zoning § 30.01.
15-31 N.H.P. Land Use Planning and Zoning § 31.01.
15-32 N.H.P. Land Use Planning and Zoning § 32.11.

674:2. Master Plan; Purpose and Description.

I. The purpose of the master plan is to set down as clearly and practically as possible the best and most appropriate future development of the area under the jurisdiction of the planning board, to aid the board in designing ordinances that result in preserving and enhancing the unique quality of life and culture of New Hampshire, and to guide the board in the performance of its other duties in a manner that achieves the principles of smart growth, sound planning, and wise resource protection.

II. The master plan shall be a set of statements and land use and development principles for the municipality with such accompanying maps, diagrams, charts and descriptions as to give legal standing to the implementation ordinances and other measures of the planning board. Each section of the master plan shall be consistent with the others in its implementation of the vision section. The master plan shall be a public record subject to the provisions of RSA 91-A. The master plan shall include, at a minimum, the following required sections:

(a) A vision section that serves to direct the other sections of the plan. This section shall contain a set of statements which articulate the desires of the citizens affected by the master plan, not only for their locality but for the region and the whole state. It shall contain a set of guiding principles and priorities to implement that vision.

(b) A land use section upon which all the following sections shall be based. This section shall translate the vision statements into physical terms. Based on a study of population, economic activity, and natural, historic, and cultural resources, it shall show existing conditions and the proposed location, extent, and intensity of future land use.

III. The master plan may also include the following sections:

(a) A transportation section which considers all pertinent modes of transportation and provides a framework for both adequate local needs and for coordination with regional and state transportation plans. Suggested items to be considered may include but are not limited to public transportation, park and ride facilities, and bicycle routes, or paths, or both.

(b) A community facilities section which identifies facilities to support the future land use pattern of subparagraph II(b), meets the projected needs of the community, and coordinates with other local governments' special districts and school districts, as well as with state and federal agencies that have multi-jurisdictional impacts.

(c) An economic development section which proposes actions to suit the community's economic goals, given its economic strengths and weaknesses in the region.

(d) A natural resources section which identifies and inventories any critical or sensitive areas or resources, not only those in the local community, but also those shared with abutting communities. This section, which may specifically include a water resources management and protection plan, shall provide a factual basis for any land development regulations that may be enacted to protect water resources and other identified natural areas. A key component in preparing this section is to identify any conflicts between other elements of the master plan and natural resources, as well as conflicts with plans of abutting communities. Nothing in this subparagraph shall be construed to permit municipalities to regulate surface or groundwater withdrawals that they are explicitly prohibited from regulating.

(e) A natural hazards section which documents the physical characteristics, severity, frequency, and extent of any potential natural hazards to the community. It should identify those elements of the built environment at risk from natural hazards as well as extent of current and future vulnerability that may result from current zoning and development policies.

(f) A recreation section which shows existing recreation areas and addresses future recreation needs.

(g) A utility and public service section analyzing the need for and showing the present and future general location of existing and anticipated public and private utilities, both local and regional, including telecommunications utilities, their supplies, and facilities for distribution and storage.

(h) A section which identifies cultural, archeological, and historic resources and protects them for rehabilitation or preservation from the impact of other land use tools such as land use regulations, housing, or transportation. Such section may encourage the preservation or restoration of stone walls, provided agricultural practices, as defined in RSA 21:34-a, are not impeded.

(i) A regional concern section, which describes the specific areas in the municipality of significant regional interest. These areas may include resources wholly contained within the municipality or bordering, or shared, or both, with neighboring municipalities. Items to be considered may include but are not limited to public facilities, natural resources, economic and housing potential, transportation, agriculture, and open space. The intent of this section is to promote regional awareness in managing growth while fulfilling the vision statements.

(j) A neighborhood plan section which focuses on a specific geographical area of local government that includes substantial residential development. This section is a part of the local master plan and shall be consistent with it. No neighborhood plan shall be adopted until a local master plan is adopted.

(k) A community design section to identify positive physical attributes in a municipality and provide for design goals and policies for planning in specific areas to guide private and public development.

(*l*) A housing section which assesses local housing conditions and projects future housing needs of residents of all levels of income and ages in the municipality and the region as identified in the regional housing needs assessment performed by the regional planning commission pursuant to RSA 36:47, II, and which integrates the availability of human services with other planning undertaken by the community.

(m) An implementation section, which is a long range action program of specific actions, time frames, allocation of responsibility for actions, description of land development regulations to be adopted, and procedures which the municipality may use to monitor and measure the effectiveness of each section of the plan.

(n) An energy section, which includes an analysis of energy and fuel resources, needs, scarcities, costs, and problems affecting the municipality and a statement of policy on the conservation of energy.

(*o*) A coastal management section which may address planning needs resulting from projected coastal property or habitat loss due to increased frequency of storm surge, flooding, and inundation.

HISTORY:

1983, 447:1. 1986, 167:2. 1988, 270:1. 1989, 339:28, eff. Jan. 1, 1990. 363:15, eff. Aug. 4, 1989. 2002, 178:2, eff. July 14, 2002. 2007, 40:1, eff. July 20, 2007. 2008, 269:1, eff. August 25, 2008. 2011, 224:118, eff. July 1, 2011. 2013, 76:1, eff. January 1, 2014. 189:1, eff. August 31, 2013. 202:1, eff. September 7, 2013.

Amendment Notes

—2013.

The 2013 amendment by Chapter 76, added "archeological" in the first sentence of III(h).

The 2013 amendment by Chapter 189, added III(*o*).

The 2013 amendment by Chapter 202, in III(d), in the second sentence, substituted "which may specifically include a water resources management and protection plan, shall provide" for "provides" and added "water resources and other identified" and added the last sentence.

—2011.

The 2011 amendment deleted the former last sentence of III(d), which read: "The natural resources section of the master plan should include a local water resources management and protection plan as specified in RSA 4-C:22."

—2008.

The 2008 amendment added III(n).

—2007.

Paragraph III(h): Added the second sentence.

—2002.

Rewritten to the extent that a detailed comparison would be impracticable.

—1989.

Paragraph VIII: Chapter 339 substituted "RSA 4-C:22" for "RSA 4:12-v" in the second sentence.

Paragraph VIII-a: Added by ch. 363.

—1988.

Paragraph III: Added "current and" preceding "future housing needs" and added "of residents of all levels of income of the municipality and of the region in which it is located, as identified in the regional housing needs assessment performed by the regional planning commission pursuant to RSA 36:47, II".

—1986.
Paragraph VIII: Added the second and third sentences.

NOTES TO DECISIONS

Scope of master plan
A master plan is merely a general guide to aid planning boards in making zoning decisions, and it need not and indeed cannot be particularly detailed in describing future land uses. Treisman v. Bedford, 132 N.H. 54, 563 A.2d 786, 1989 N.H. LEXIS 75 (N.H. 1989).

Cited:
Cited in Rancourt v. Barnstead, 129 N.H. 45, 523 A.2d 55, 1986 N.H. LEXIS 379 (1986); Portsmouth Advocates v. Portsmouth, 133 N.H. 876, 587 A.2d 600, 1991 N.H. LEXIS 13 (1991); Zukis v. Fitzwilliam, 135 N.H. 384, 604 A.2d 956, 1992 N.H. LEXIS 46 (1992); Quinlan v. Dover, 136 N.H. 226, 614 A.2d 1057, 1992 N.H. LEXIS 159 (1992).

RESEARCH REFERENCES AND PRACTICE AIDS

Cross References.
Adoption and amendment of master plan, see RSA 674:4.
Preparation of master plan, see RSA 674:3.

New Hampshire Practice.
15-3 N.H.P. Land Use Planning and Zoning § 3.02.
15-3 N.H.P. Land Use Planning and Zoning § 3.03.
15-3 N.H.P. Land Use Planning and Zoning § 3.04.
15-29 N.H.P. Land Use Planning and Zoning § 29.02.
15-36 N.H.P. Land Use Planning and Zoning § 36.20.

674:3. Master Plan Preparation.

I. In preparing, revising, or amending the master plan, the planning board may make surveys and studies, and may review data about the existing conditions, probable growth demands, and best design methods to prevent sprawl growth in the community and the region. The board may also consider the goals, policies, and guidelines of any regional or state plans, as well as those of abutting communities.

II. Revisions to the plan are recommended every 5 to 10 years.

III. During the preparation of the various sections of the master plan, the board shall inform the general public, the office of strategic initiatives, and regional planning commissions and solicit public comments regarding the future growth of the municipality in order to involve citizens in the preparation of the master plan in a way which is most appropriate for the municipality.

HISTORY:
1983, 447:1, eff. Jan. 1, 1984. 2002, 178:3, eff. July 14, 2002. 229:9, eff. July 1, 2002. 2003, 319:9, eff. July 1, 2003. 2004, 257:44, eff. July 1, 2004. 2017, 156:64, eff. July 1, 2017.

Amendment Notes
The 2017 amendments to this section by Ch. 156 substituted "office of strategic initiatives" for "office of energy and planning" in III.

—2004.
Paragraph III: Substituted "office of energy and planning" for "office of state planning and energy programs".

—2003.
Paragraph III: Substituted "office of state planning and energy programs" for "office of state planning".

—2002.
Chapter 229:9, eff. July 1, 2002, inserted "and the office of state planning and regional planning commissions" following "general public" in par. III.
Chapter 178:3, eff. July 14, 2002, rewrote pars. I–III.

NOTES TO DECISIONS

Cited:
Cited in Rancourt v. Barnstead, 129 N.H. 45, 523 A.2d 55, 1986 N.H. LEXIS 379 (1986).

RESEARCH REFERENCES AND PRACTICE AIDS

Cross References.
Contents of master plan generally, see RSA 674:2.
Duties of planning board as to master plan generally, see RSA 674:1.

New Hampshire Practice.
15-3 N.H.P. Land Use Planning and Zoning § 3.05.

674:4. Master Plan Adoption and Amendment.

The planning board may, according to the procedures required under RSA 675:6, adopt the master plan as a whole, or may adopt successive sections or parts of the plan. Sections or parts of the plan shall correspond with major geographical sections or divisions of the municipality, or with the functional elements of the plan, and may incorporate any amendment, extension, or addition to the plan.

HISTORY:
1983, 447:1, eff. Jan. 1, 1984.

NOTES TO DECISIONS

Cited:
Cited in Rancourt v. Barnstead, 129 N.H. 45, 523 A.2d 55, 1986 N.H. LEXIS 379 (1986); Zukis v. Fitzwilliam, 135 N.H. 384, 604 A.2d 956, 1992 N.H. LEXIS 46 (1992).

RESEARCH REFERENCES AND PRACTICE AIDS

Cross References.
Preparation of master plan, see RSA 674:3.

New Hampshire Practice.
15-3 N.H.P. Land Use Planning and Zoning § 3.06.
15-31 N.H.P. Land Use Planning and Zoning § 31.01.
15-35 N.H.P. Land Use Planning and Zoning § 35.17.

Capital Improvements Program

RESEARCH REFERENCES AND PRACTICE AIDS

Cross References.
Master plan generally, see RSA 674:1 et seq.
Municipal budgets and finance generally, see RSA 32– 34.

674:5. Authorization.

In a municipality where the planning board has adopted a master plan, the local legislative body may authorize the planning board to prepare and amend a recommended program of municipal capital improvement projects projected over a period of at least 6 years. As an alternative, the legislative body may authorize the governing body of a municipality to appoint a capital improvement program committee, which shall include at least one member of the planning board and may include but not be limited to other members of the planning board, the budget committee, or the town or city governing body, to prepare and amend a recommended program of municipal capital improvement projects projected over a period of at least 6 years. The capital improvements program may encompass major projects being currently undertaken or future projects to be undertaken with federal, state, county and other public funds. The sole purpose and effect of the capital improvements program shall be to aid the mayor or selectmen and the budget committee in their consideration of the annual budget.

HISTORY:

1983, 447:1, eff. Jan. 1, 1984. 2002, 90:1, eff. July 2, 2002.

Amendments

—2002.

Added the second sentence and inserted "or selectmen" following "mayor" in the fourth sentence.

NOTES TO DECISIONS

Construction and application

Other than its management tool capabilities, a capital improvements program has no part to play in review of subdivision applications presented to governmental authorities. Zukis v. Fitzwilliam, 135 N.H. 384, 604 A.2d 956, 1992 N.H. LEXIS 46 (N.H. 1992).

Cited:

Cited in Rancourt v. Barnstead, 129 N.H. 45, 523 A.2d 55, 1986 N.H. LEXIS 379 (1986).

RESEARCH REFERENCES AND PRACTICE AIDS

Cross References.

Consideration of program by mayor and budget committee, see RSA 674:8.

Preparation of program, see RSA 674:7.

New Hampshire Practice.

15-4 N.H.P. Land Use Planning and Zoning § 4.01.
15-5 N.H.P. Land Use Planning and Zoning § 5.09.
15-17 N.H.P. Land Use Planning and Zoning § 17.05.
15-26 N.H.P. Land Use Planning and Zoning § 26.03.
15-31 N.H.P. Land Use Planning and Zoning § 31.02.
16-2 N.H.P. Municipal Law & Taxation § 2.15.

674:6. Purpose and Description.

The capital improvements program shall classify projects according to the urgency and need for realization and shall recommend a time sequence for their implementation. The program may also contain the estimated cost of each project and indicate probable operating and maintenance costs and probable revenues, if any, as well as existing sources of funds or the need for additional sources of funds for the implementation and operation of each project. The program shall be based on information submitted by the departments and agencies of the municipality and shall take into account public facility needs indicated by the prospective development shown in the master plan of the municipality or as permitted by other municipal land use controls.

HISTORY:

1983, 447:1, eff. Jan. 1, 1984.

NOTES TO DECISIONS

Construction and application

Other than its management tool capabilities, a capital improvements program has no part to play in review of subdivision applications presented to governmental authorities. Zukis v. Fitzwilliam, 135 N.H. 384, 604 A.2d 956, 1992 N.H. LEXIS 46 (N.H. 1992).

RESEARCH REFERENCES AND PRACTICE AIDS

New Hampshire Practice.

15-4 N.H.P. Land Use Planning and Zoning § 4.02.
15-29 N.H.P. Land Use Planning and Zoning § 29.02.
16-2 N.H.P. Municipal Law & Taxation § 2.15.

674:7. Preparation.

I. In preparing the capital improvements program, the planning board or the capital improvement program committee shall confer, in a manner deemed appropriate by the board or the committee, with the mayor or the board of selectmen, or the chief fiscal officer, the budget committee, other municipal officials and agencies, the school board or boards, and shall review the recommendations of the master plan in relation to the proposed capital improvements program.

II. Whenever the planning board or the capital improvement program committee is authorized and directed to prepare a capital improvements program, every municipal department, authority or agency, and every affected school district board, department or agency, shall, upon request of the planning board or the capital improvement program committee, transmit to the board or committee a statement of all capital projects it proposes to undertake during the term of the program. The planning board or the capital improvement program committee shall study each proposed capital project, and shall advise and make recommendations to the department, authority, agency, or school district board, department or agency, concerning the relation of its project to the capital improvements program being prepared.

HISTORY:

1983, 447:1. 1995, 43:1, eff. July 2, 1995. 2002, 90:2, eff. July 2, 2002.

Amendments

—2002.

Paragraph I: Inserted "or the capital improvement program committee" preceding "shall confer" and "or the committee" preceding "with the mayor".

Paragraph II: Inserted "or the capital improvement program committee" following "planning board" in two places and "or committee" preceding "a statement" in the first sentence and "or the capital improvement program committee" preceding "shall study" in the second sentence.

—1995.

Paragraph II: Inserted "and every affected school district board, department or agency" preceding "shall, upon request" in the first sentence and deleted "or" following "authority" and inserted "or school district board, department or agency" preceding "concerning" in the second sentence.

RESEARCH REFERENCES AND PRACTICE AIDS

Cross References.
Authorization of program, see RSA 674:5.
Contents of program, see RSA 674:6.

New Hampshire Practice.
15-4 N.H.P. Land Use Planning and Zoning § 4.03.
16-2 N.H.P. Municipal Law & Taxation § 2.15.

674:8. Consideration by Mayor and Budget Committee.

Whenever the planning board or the capital improvement program committee has prepared a capital improvements program under RSA 674:7, it shall submit its recommendations for the current year to the mayor or selectmen and the budget committee, if one exists, for consideration as part of the annual budget.

HISTORY:
1983, 447:1, eff. Jan. 1, 1984. 2002, 90:3, eff. July 2, 2002.

Amendments

—2002.
Inserted "or the capital improvement program committee" following "planning board" and "or selectmen" following "mayor".

RESEARCH REFERENCES AND PRACTICE AIDS

Cross References.
Authorization of program, see RSA 674:5.
Purpose of program, see RSA 674:6.

New Hampshire Practice.
15-4 N.H.P. Land Use Planning and Zoning § 4.03.
16-2 N.H.P. Municipal Law & Taxation § 2.15.

Official Map of the Municipality

RESEARCH REFERENCES AND PRACTICE AIDS

Cross References.
City, town and village district highways, see RSA 231.
Highway regulations, see RSA 236.
Historic districts, see RSA 674:45 et seq.
Manufactured housing regulation, see RSA 674:31 et seq.
Master plan, see RSA 674:1 et seq.
Powers and duties of county commissioners as to highways generally, see RSA 232.
Site plan review, see RSA 674:43 et seq.
Subdivision regulation, see RSA 674:35 et seq.
Zoning generally, see RSA 674:16 et seq.

674:9. Mapping of Street Lines by Planning Board.

At any time after a planning board has adopted a master plan of the municipality which includes a major street plan or has progressed in its master planning to the stage of the making and adoption of a major street plan, the local legislative body may authorize the planning board to make or cause to be made from time to time surveys for the exact locating of the lines of new, extended, widened, or narrowed streets in the whole or in any portion of the municipality. The local legislative body may also empower the planning board to make and certify to the local legislative body, when completed, a plat of the area thus surveyed on which are indicated the locations of the lines recommended by the planning board as the planned or mapped lines of future streets, street extensions, street widenings, or street narrowings. The making or certifying of a plat by the planning board, under the authorization of the local legislative body, shall not in and of itself constitute or be deemed to constitute the opening or establishment of any street or the taking or acceptance of any land for street purposes.

HISTORY:
1983, 447:1, eff. Jan. 1, 1984.

RESEARCH REFERENCES AND PRACTICE AIDS

New Hampshire Bar Journal.
For article, "Roads Revisited: Creation and Termination of Highways in New Hampshire—An Update," see 46 N.H. B.J. 56 (Fall 2005).

New Hampshire Practice.
15-26 N.H.P. Land Use Planning and Zoning § 26.03.
15-31 N.H.P. Land Use Planning and Zoning § 31.03.

674:10. Establishment of Official Map.

After the planning board of any municipality has adopted a master plan which includes a major street plan, or has progressed in its master planning to the stage of the making and adoption of a major street plan, and has certified a copy of a major street plan to the local legislative body, as provided in RSA 674:9, the local legislative body is hereby empowered and authorized to establish an official map of the municipality showing the location of the exterior lines of streets of the whole or of any parts of the municipality up to that time existing, laid out and established by law as public streets, and may also show the location of the exterior lines of parks. The official map is to be deemed to be final and conclusive with respect to the location and width of streets and the location of parks shown thereon. The official map established under this section shall be established to conserve and promote the public health, safety, convenience or general welfare. The ordinance establishing or adopting the official map shall provide that a certificate, signed by the city or town clerk, the village district clerk, or other duly authorized recording official, giving notice that the municipality has established an official map, including the date of its establishment, shall be filed with the register of deeds of the county or counties in which the municipality is situated. Such certificates shall be accompanied by a certified copy of the official map as adopted or established. Whenever a municipality has established an official map and has filed a certificate to that effect, together with a copy of the official map, with the register of deeds for the county or counties in which the municipality is situated, then no plat of a subdivision of land within the municipality shall thereafter be filed or recorded at the office of the register of deeds until it has been approved by the planning board and such approval entered in writing on the plat by the chairperson or secretary of the planning board.

HISTORY:

1983, 447:1. 1995, 43:2, eff. July 2, 1995.

Amendments

—1995.

Substituted "chairperson" for "chairman" preceding "secretary" in the last sentence.

RESEARCH REFERENCES AND PRACTICE AIDS

Cross References.

Allowance of buildings and structures in mapped-street locations shown on official map, see RSA 674:12– 15.

Subdivision regulation generally, see RSA 674:35 et seq.

New Hampshire Practice.

15-31 N.H.P. Land Use Planning and Zoning § 31.03.

674:11. Amendments to Official Map.

The local legislative body is authorized and empowered, whenever and as often as it may deem it advisable or necessary for the public interest, to change or add to the official map of the municipality. Amendments may be made in order to establish the exterior lines of the new streets or parks, or to widen, extend, relocate, narrow, vacate, abandon, or close existing streets or parks, and to indicate the acceptance of, change of use, acquisition of land for, or sale or lease of any street or other public way, ground, place, property, or structure. No change shall become effective until after a public hearing has been held on the change, at which parties in interest and citizens shall have had an opportunity to be heard. Notice of the public hearing shall be given by publishing at least 10 days before the public hearing a notice of such hearing in a newspaper of general circulation in the municipality, and by posting a notice to the same effect at the city or town hall, or in whatever place other notices required by law in connection with municipal affairs are posted or customarily displayed. Before making such addition, amendment, or change, the local legislative body shall refer the matter to the planning board for a report. If the planning board does not make its

report within 30 days of such reference, it shall be deemed to have forfeited the right to further suspend action. In the event that the planning board disapproves the proposed addition, amendment, or change, the local legislative body shall not have the right to overrule the planning board's decision, unless by vote of not less than ⅔ of its entire membership in case of a city, or by majority vote of the legal voters present and voting at a regular or special town or district meeting in the case of a town or village district. Such additions, amendments, and changes when adopted shall become a part of the official map of the municipality and shall be deemed to be final and conclusive with respect to the location of the streets and parks shown on the official map. The locating, widening, narrowing, or closing, or the approval of locating, widening, narrowing, or closing, of streets and parks by the municipality under provisions of law other than those contained in this subdivision shall be deemed to be a change or addition to the official map and shall be subject to all the provisions of this subdivision.

HISTORY:

1983, 447:1, eff. Jan. 1, 1984.

674:12. Refusal of Permit.

A municipality which has established and recorded an official map, as provided in RSA 674:10, may for the purpose of preserving the integrity of such official map provide by ordinance that, from and after the time of such recording, no permit shall be issued for any building or structure, or part thereof, in the bed of or on any land located between the mapped lines of any street as shown or laid out on such official map, except as provided in RSA 674:13.

HISTORY:

1983, 447:1, eff. Jan. 1, 1984.

RESEARCH REFERENCES AND PRACTICE AIDS

Cross References.

Appeals from denial of permits, see RSA 674:13– 15.

674:13. Appeals Where There is a Zoning Ordinance.

I. Any zoning ordinance adopted pursuant to RSA 674:16 shall provide that the board of adjustment created under a local zoning ordinance and having the power to make variances or exceptions in zoning regulations shall have the further power, in specific cases and by vote of a majority of its members, upon an appeal filed with it by the owner of any such land, to grant a permit based on considerations of justice and equity for a building or structure, or part thereof, in a mapped-street location shown on the official map, in any case in which the board of adjustment finds, upon the evidence and arguments presented to it upon appeal:

(a) That the property of the appellant of which such mapped-street location forms a part will not yield a reasonable return to the owner unless such permit be granted; or

(b) That, balancing the interest of the municipality in preserving the integrity of the official map and in not increasing too greatly the cost of later opening such street, and the interest of the owner in the use and benefits of the owner's property, the grant of such permit is required by considerations of justice and equity.

II. In the event that the board of adjustment decides to authorize or issue a building permit in such case, it shall have the power to specify the exact location, ground area to be used or occupied, height, and other reasonable details and conditions of extent and character, and also the duration of the building, or part hereof, permitted. Such requirements shall be designed to promote the health, convenience, safety, or general welfare of and shall inure to the benefit of the municipality. The board of adjustment shall refuse a permit if the applicant will not be substantially damaged by placing the applicant's building outside the mapped-street location.

HISTORY:
1983, 447:1. 1995, 43:3, 4, eff. July 2, 1995.

Amendments

—1995.
Paragraph I(b): Substituted "the owner's" for "his" following "benefits of".
Paragraph II: Substituted "the applicant's" for "his" following "placing" in the third sentence.

RESEARCH REFERENCES AND PRACTICE AIDS

Cross References.
Appeals from denial of permits in municipalities having no zoning ordinances, see RSA 674:14.
Denial of permits generally, see RSA 674:12.
Hearings on appeals, see RSA 674:15.
Zoning generally, see RSA 674:16 et seq.

674:14. Appeals Where No Zoning Ordinance Exists.

In any municipality, other than a town, in which there is no zoning board of adjustment, the local legislative body, until such time as a board of adjustment may be appointed as a result of the adoption of a zoning ordinance, shall have the same powers as a board of adjustment to act, but only under the circumstances and in such special cases as are specified in RSA 674:13 and 674:41, and shall be subject to the same restrictions as apply to a board of adjustment. For this purpose, the local legislative body is hereby authorized to act as a discretionary administrative or quasi-judicial body. When so acting, it shall not sit as a legislative body but shall sit in a separate meeting for which separate minutes shall be kept. In any town or village district in which there is no board of adjustment, the local governing

body is hereby authorized to designate a board of appeals to be composed of 5 members, serving as such without compensation, which shall have the authority of and shall be subject to the same restrictions and regulations as apply to a zoning board of adjustment, but which shall have the power to act only under the circumstances and in such special cases as are specified herein and only until such time as a board of adjustment may be appointed as a result of the adoption of a zoning ordinance.

HISTORY:
1983, 447:1. 1988, 131:1, eff. June 19, 1988.

Amendments

—1988.
Substituted "governing body" for "legislative body" preceding "is hereby authorized" in the fourth sentence.

RESEARCH REFERENCES AND PRACTICE AIDS

Cross References.
Appeals from denial of permits generally, see RSA 674:13.
Denial of permits generally, see RSA 674:12.
Hearings on appeals, see RSA 674:15.
Zoning generally, see RSA 674:16 et seq.

674:15. Appeals; Public Hearing.

Before taking any action authorized in RSA 674:13, 674:14, and 674:41, the zoning board of adjustment, the legislative body, or the boards of appeal, according to whichever of them is designated by ordinance as the body to which appeals may be made, shall give a hearing at which parties in interest and others shall have an opportunity to be heard. Notice for a public hearing under this section shall be as provided in RSA 675:7.

HISTORY:
1983, 447:1, eff. Jan. 1, 1984.

RESEARCH REFERENCES AND PRACTICE AIDS

Cross References.
Appeals procedure generally, see RSA 674:13, 14.
Denial of permits generally, see RSA 674:12.

Zoning

NOTES TO DECISIONS

Analysis

1. Construction
2. Exercise of municipal power
3. Application

1. Construction
Under power delegated to municipalities to enact zoning ordinances to promote "the general welfare of the community," the term "community" includes the region of which the municipality is a part. Britton v. Chester, 134 N.H. 434, 595 A.2d 492, 1991 N.H. LEXIS 95 (N.H. 1991).

2. Exercise of municipal power

Ordinance which in effect wrongfully excluded development of low and moderate income housing constituted an invalid exercise of the municipality's power under enabling legislation delegating to the town the power to zone municipality to promote the general welfare of the community, which included not only the municipality itself, but the region in which it was located. Britton v. Chester, 134 N.H. 434, 595 A.2d 492, 1991 N.H. LEXIS 95 (N.H. 1991).

3. Application

Earth excavation regulations of a town zoning ordinance were not required to be adopted pursuant to this subdivision, since there were other specific enabling statutes for local earth excavation ordinances. Goffstown v. Thibeault, 129 N.H. 454, 529 A.2d 930, 1987 N.H. LEXIS 184 (N.H. 1987).

RESEARCH REFERENCES AND PRACTICE AIDS

Cross References.

Adoption of bylaws by towns generally, see RSA 31:39 et seq.
Adoption of ordinances and codes generally, see RSA 675.
Airport zoning generally, see RSA 424.
Building codes generally, see RSA 674:51 et seq.
Central business service districts, see RSA 31:120 et seq.
Economic development and revitalization districts, see RSA 162-K.
Emergency temporary zoning and planning ordinances, see RSA 674:24 et seq.
Historic district regulation, see RSA 674:45 et seq.
Site plan review regulations, see RSA 674:44.
Subdivision regulation, see RSA 674:35 et seq.

674:16. Grant of Power.

I. For the purpose of promoting the health, safety, or the general welfare of the community, the local legislative body of any city, town, or county in which there are located unincorporated towns or unorganized places is authorized to adopt or amend a zoning ordinance under the ordinance enactment procedures of RSA 675:2-5. The zoning ordinance shall be designed to regulate and restrict:

(a) The height, number of stories and size of buildings and other structures;

(b) Lot sizes, the percentage of a lot that may be occupied, and the size of yards, courts and other open spaces;

(c) The density of population in the municipality; and

(d) The location and use of buildings, structures and land used for business, industrial, residential, or other purposes.

II. The power to adopt a zoning ordinance under this subdivision expressly includes the power to adopt innovative land use controls which may include, but which are not limited to, the methods contained in RSA 674:21.

III. In its exercise of the powers granted under this subdivision, the local legislative body of a city, town, or county in which there are located unincorporated towns or unorganized places may regulate and control the timing of development as provided in RSA 674:22.

IV. Except as provided in RSA 424:5 or RSA 422-B or in any other provision of Title XXXIX, no city, town, or county in which there are located unincorporated towns or unorganized places shall adopt or amend a zoning ordinance or regulation with respect to antennas used exclusively in the amateur radio services that fails to conform to the limited federal preemption entitled Amateur Radio Preemption, 101 FCC 2nd 952 (1985) issued by the Federal Communications Commission.

V. In its exercise of the powers granted under this subdivision, the local legislative body of a city, town, or county in which there are located unincorporated towns or unorganized places may regulate and control accessory uses on private land. Unless specifically proscribed by local land use regulation, aircraft take offs and landings on private land by the owner of such land or by a person who resides on such land shall be considered a valid and permitted accessory use.

HISTORY:

1983, 447:1. 1985, 103:19. 1989, 266:14, 15. 1995, 176:1, eff. Aug. 4, 1995. 1996, 218:1, eff. Aug. 9, 1996.

Amendments

—1996.

Paragraph V: Added.

—1995.

Paragraph IV: Added.

—1989.

Paragraph I: Substituted "town, or county in which there are located unincorporated towns or unorganized places" for "or town" following "city" in the first sentence.

Paragraph III: Substituted "town, or county in which there are located unincorporated towns or unorganized places" for "or town" following "city".

—1985.

Paragraph IV: Repealed.

NOTES TO DECISIONS

Analysis

1. Constitutionality
2. Construction
3. Construction with other laws
4. Substantive Due Process
5. Equal protection
6. Facial Invalidity
7. Requirements regarding adoption of ordinances generally
8. Establishment of procedure for administration of ordinances
9. Regulation of particular matters—Lot size
10. —Aesthetic values
11. —Density of population
12. —Location of buildings
13. —Uses of buildings, structures, or land
14. —Rate of growth
15. —Aircraft takeoffs and landings

1. Constitutionality

The statute was a valid exercise of the police power. Sundeen v. Rogers, 83 N.H. 253, 141 A. 142, 1928 N.H. LEXIS 11 (N.H. 1928); Brady v. Keene, 90 N.H. 99, 4 A.2d 658, 1939 N.H. LEXIS 22 (N.H. 1939). (Decided under prior law.)

2. Construction

The statute granted localities broad authority to zone in order to promote public health, safety, morals and general welfare. Sanderson v. Greenland, 122 N.H. 1002, 453 A.2d 1285, 1982 N.H. LEXIS 511 (N.H. 1982). (Decided under prior law.)

3. Construction with other laws

The general police power delegated to a municipality pursuant to RSA 31:39 could not be used as a usual and expedient mechanism for effecting zoning regulations which would otherwise fall within the scope of RSA 31:60–89. Beck v. Raymond, 118 N.H. 793, 394 A.2d 847, 1978 N.H. LEXIS 296 (N.H. 1978)(Decided under prior law.)

4. Substantive Due Process

Application of city's zoning ordinance that banned correctional facilities to prohibit applicant from building halfway house that housed federal prisoners still serving out their sentences did not violate applicant's state constitutional right to substantive due process as the ordinance was rationally related to legitimate governmental interests, including concerns that the prisoners to be housed at a residential transition facility would either pose some threat to the surrounding community, engage in recidivism, exacerbate the city's perceived burden in accommodating a disproportionate share of social services or affect surrounding property values. Because the city could reasonably conceive these facts to be true, the ordinance served or could conceivably serve legitimate governmental interests. Cmty. Res. for Justice, Inc. v. City of Manchester, 154 N.H. 748, 917 A.2d 707, 2007 N.H. LEXIS 11 (N.H. 2007).

Town zoning ordinance, which provided that nonconforming uses that had been destroyed and were not rebuilt within a year had to comply with present zoning requirements, did not violate plaintiff's right to substantive due process as applied to her shed because the ordinance worked to reduce nonconforming uses by establishing a time limit on their reconstruction and the reduction and elimination of nonconforming uses was a legitimate purpose of zoning and so the ordinance's purpose of reducing nonconforming uses was a legitimate governmental interest. Furthermore, the ordinance bore a rational relationship to the legitimate goal since, by imposing a time limit on plaintiff's ability to rebuild her nonconforming shed, the provision reduced the possibility that she would reconstruct her nonconforming shed and increased the possibility that the shed, if rebuilt, would be rebuilt in compliance with the zoning ordinance and, as plaintiff did not rebuild her shed within a year, the efficacy of the time limitation was evident. McKenzie v. Town of Eaton Zoning Bd. of Adjustment, 154 N.H. 773, 917 A.2d 193, 2007 N.H. LEXIS 14 (N.H. 2007).

Trial court's ruling that Strafford, N.H., Zoning & Land Use Ordinances, Subdivision Regs., Non-Residential Site Plan Regs., & Bldg. Regs. ch. 1, § 4.1(F) was unconstitutional was vacated as it could not be determined what standard the trial court applied; the case was remanded for a rational basis review of a developer's substantive due process challenge. Boulders at Strafford, LLC v. Town of Strafford, 153 N.H. 633, 903 A.2d 1021, 2006 N.H. LEXIS 82 (N.H. 2006).

5. Equal protection

Intermediate scrutiny was the appropriate standard of review to be applied to applicant's equal protection challenge to application of zoning ordinance that banned correctional facilities to prohibit applicant from building halfway house. As the right to use and enjoy property is an important substantive right, the intermediate scrutiny test is used to review equal protection challenges to zoning ordinances that infringe upon this right. However, because the appellate court departed from its previous intermediate scrutiny standard and developed a new standard, the matter was remanded for further proceedings to apply the new standard. Cmty. Res. for Justice, Inc. v. City of Manchester, 154 N.H. 748, 917 A.2d 707, 2007 N.H. LEXIS 11 (N.H. 2007).

6. Facial Invalidity

Legislation may not be applied in a particular case if it is facially invalid and cannot constitutionally be applied in any case; thus, to succeed on its facial challenge to Strafford, N.H., Zoning & Land Use Ordinances, Subdivision Regs., Non-Residential Site Plan Regs., & Bldg. Regs. ch. 1, § 4.1(F), a developer had to prove that the ordinance was not rationally related to its intended purpose of protecting the wetlands, but there were many reasons besides scientific data that a town could posit to justify the zoning ordinance and any fair reason that could be assigned for bringing legislation within the town's purview might be sufficient to save it.

Boulders at Strafford, LLC v. Town of Strafford, 153 N.H. 633, 903 A.2d 1021, 2006 N.H. LEXIS 82 (N.H. 2006).

7. Requirements regarding adoption of ordinances generally

A town ordinance containing comprehensive regulations which sought to restrict the use of three areas of a town to single and two-family residential buildings, to regulate the use of buildings, the size and percentage of lots and indirectly to regulate the size of yards and other open spaces and the density of population, and which contemplated that permits would be granted for nonconforming uses, was a zoning ordinance which could not be legally enacted except in compliance with the statute authorizing zoning regulations and could not be justified under RSA 31:39. Bisson v. Milford, 109 N.H. 287, 249 A.2d 688, 1969 N.H. LEXIS 136 (N.H. 1969). (Decided under prior law.)

A town, in adopting a zoning ordinance, was required to comply with the provisions of the enabling statute both in its enactment, and its regulations, including provisions for its administration. Jaffrey v. Heffernan, 104 N.H. 249, 183 A.2d 246, 1962 N.H. LEXIS 61 (N.H. 1962). See also Bisson v. Milford, 109 N.H. 287, 249 A.2d 688, 1969 N.H. LEXIS 136 (N.H. 1969). (Decided under prior law.)

8. Establishment of procedure for administration of ordinances

In accordance with its power to pass zoning regulations and to establish a board of adjustment for the purpose of granting variances and exceptions from the terms of zoning ordinances, a municipality could prescribe reasonable procedures for the board to follow in order to carry out its purposes. Lavallee v. Britt, 118 N.H. 131, 383 A.2d 709, 1978 N.H. LEXIS 358 (N.H. 1978). (Decided under prior law.)

9. Regulation of particular matters—Lot size

The constitutionality of a zoning ordinance increasing minimum lot sizes could not be decided solely on the basis of whether the new sizes were necessary for health and safety, the test for zoning regulations being whether they had no rational tendency to promote the safety and general welfare of the community or to conserve property values throughout the municipality. Steel Hill Development, Inc. v. Sanbornton, 338 F. Supp. 301, 1972 U.S. Dist. LEXIS 15050 (D.N.H. 1972), aff'd, Steel Hill Dev., Inc. v. Sanbornton, 469 F.2d 956, 1972 U.S. App. LEXIS 6564 (1st Cir. 1972). (Decided under prior law.)

The proper test of the validity of an increase in minimum lot sizes was not just the size of the lot, or whether the immediate sale value for the intended purpose of property was depressed, but a balancing of the public objectives promoted by the restriction and the economic burden imposed on the owner of the restricted land. Steel Hill Development, Inc. v. Sanbornton, 338 F. Supp. 301, 1972 U.S. Dist. LEXIS 15050 (D.N.H. 1972), aff'd, Steel Hill Dev., Inc. v. Sanbornton, 469 F.2d 956, 1972 U.S. App. LEXIS 6564 (1st Cir. 1972). (Decided under prior law.)

10. —Aesthetic values

Municipalities may validly exercise zoning power solely to advance aesthetic values, since the preservation or enhancement of the visual environment may promote the general welfare. Asselin v. Town of Conway, 137 N.H. 368, 628 A.2d 247, 1993 N.H. LEXIS 89 (N.H. 1993).

11. —Density of population

Regulating and restricting the density of population were expressly delegated to a town in New Hampshire pursuant to this statute. Beck v. Raymond, 118 N.H. 793, 394 A.2d 847, 1978 N.H. LEXIS 296 (N.H. 1978). See also Durham v. White Enters., 115 N.H. 645, 348 A.2d 706, 1975 N.H. LEXIS 386 (N.H. 1975). (Decided under prior law.)

12. —Location of buildings

Adoption of ordinance requiring newly constructed buildings to be set back stated distance from public highway was within the general police powers of a town. Jaffrey v. Heffernan, 104 N.H. 249, 183 A.2d 246, 1962 N.H. LEXIS 61 (N.H. 1962). (Decided under prior law.)

13. —Uses of buildings, structures, or land

Trial court properly reversed the zoning adjustment board's decision that affirmed a zoning compliance officer's decision to prohibit the property owners from expanding the use of their seasonal residence to a year-round residence; ordinance drafters did not differentiate between seasonal and full-time residential occupancy and if they had at any point intended to do so, they had available the remedy of amending the ordinance pursuant to RSA 674:16, I , which they did not do. Severance v. Town of Epsom, 155 N.H. 359, 923 A.2d 1057, 2007 N.H. LEXIS 61 (N.H. 2007).

Municipalities were not authorized under their zoning powers to require the written consent of a certain percentage of abutting owners within a stated distance as a condition precedent to granting of extensions of nonconforming uses. A zoning ordinance was not discriminatory because it permitted the continuation of existing structures and conditions while the creation of new structures or conditions of the same type was prohibited. Ackley v. Nashua, 102 N.H. 551, 163 A.2d 6, 1960 N.H. LEXIS 78 (N.H. 1960).

A zoning ordinance was not discriminatory because it permitted the continuation of existing structures and conditions while the creation of new structures or conditions of the same type was prohibited. Stone v. Cray, 89 N.H. 483, 200 A. 517, 1938 N.H. LEXIS 60 (N.H. 1938). (Decided under prior law.)

14. —Rate of growth

The legislative body of any city or town was empowered to regulate and restrict density of population and size, location and use of buildings and land; this power necessarily implied the authority to direct and control population growth. Conway v. Stratham, 120 N.H. 257, 414 A.2d 539, 1980 N.H. LEXIS 269 (N.H. 1980). (Decided under prior law.)

When towns properly exercised the zoning power delegated to them by the legislature, they could adopt reasonable time controls on population growth. Beck v. Raymond, 118 N.H. 793, 394 A.2d 847, 1978 N.H. LEXIS 296 (N.H. 1978); Conway v. Stratham, 120 N.H. 257, 414 A.2d 539, 1980 N.H. LEXIS 269 (N.H. 1980). (Decided under prior law.)

A town's slow-growth ordinance did not improperly infringe upon the jurisdiction of town's planning board since the legislature, by granting growth control power to the town, necessarily limited the power of the planning board. Conway v. Stratham, 120 N.H. 257, 414 A.2d 539, 1980 N.H. LEXIS 269 (N.H. 1980). (Decided under prior law.)

The authority to enact land use regulations for the purpose of restricting growth was embodied in the power to zone. Beck v. Raymond, 118 N.H. 793, 394 A.2d 847, 1978 N.H. LEXIS 296 (N.H. 1978). (Decided under prior law.)

15. —Aircraft takeoffs and landings

Town's zoning ordinance did not violate RSA 674:16, V, by requiring landowners to obtain a special exception before using their land for aircraft takeoffs and landings. Like other valid and permitted accessory uses, aircraft takeoffs and landings could be regulated by requiring landowners to obtain a special exception, and such regulation comported with the constitutional right to use and enjoy one's property. Tonnesen v. Town of Gilmanton, 156 N.H. 813, 943 A.2d 782, 2008 N.H. LEXIS 30 (N.H. 2008).

Because zoning ordinance did not specifically refer to aircraft takeoffs and landings, but generally proscribed all uses not listed, defendants' use of their property for aircraft takeoffs and landings was a valid and permitted accessory use according to land use statute; neighbors' reliance on defeated amendments to ordinance that would have explicitly permitted aircraft takeoffs and landings was misplaced, because legislative history would not be consulted when language of ordinance was plain. Spengler v. Porter, 144 N.H. 163, 737 A.2d 1121, 1999 N.H. LEXIS 92 (N.H. 1999).

Amended land use statute was not unconstitutional as applied to neighbors abutting private airstrip, where neighbors made no factual allegations that would allow court to conclude that statute effected a taking of their property, or that statute discriminated in favor of airstrip owners; moreover, although neighbors alleged that misrepresentations made to legislators prior to passage of amendment rendered it unconstitutional, neighbors' petition failed to provide any legal theory to support relief sought. Spengler v. Porter, 144 N.H. 163, 737 A.2d 1121, 1999 N.H. LEXIS 92 (N.H. 1999).

Cited:

Cited in Soares v. Atkinson, 129 N.H. 313, 529 A.2d 867, 1987 N.H. LEXIS 223 (1987); Goffstown v. Thibeault, 129 N.H. 454, 529 A.2d 930, 1987 N.H. LEXIS 184 (1987); Treisman v. Bedford, 132 N.H. 54, 563 A.2d 786, 1989 N.H. LEXIS 75 (1989); Asselin v. Conway, 135 N.H. 576, 607 A.2d 132, 1992 N.H. LEXIS 83 (1992); Asselin v. Town of Conway, 137 N.H. 368, 628 A.2d 247, 1993 N.H. LEXIS 89 (1993); Hurley v. Town of Hollis, 143 N.H. 567, 729 A.2d 998, 1999 N.H. LEXIS 45 (1999); Simonsen v. Town of Derry, 145 N.H. 382, 765 A.2d 1033, 2000 N.H. LEXIS 73 (2000).

RESEARCH REFERENCES AND PRACTICE AIDS

Cross References.

Adoption of bylaws by towns generally, see RSA 31:39 et seq.

Applicability of ordinances, see RSA 674:19.

Authority of zoning board of adjustment as to appeals from proceedings for enforcement of zoning ordinances, see RSA 674:33.

Interim growth management regulations, see RSA 674:23.

New Hampshire Bar Journal.

For article, "The New Zoning Variance Cases: Analyzing Unnecessary Hardship Under RSA 674:33," see 46 N.H. B.J. 40 (Fall 2005).

For article, "Regional Economic Desegregation: *Britton v. Town of Chester*," see 33 N.H. B.J. 486 (1992).

New Hampshire Practice.

15-2 N.H.P. Land Use Planning and Zoning § 2.01.

15-3 N.H.P. Land Use Planning and Zoning § 3.03.

15-5 N.H.P. Land Use Planning and Zoning § 5.14.

15-7 N.H.P. Land Use Planning and Zoning § 7.14.

15-8 N.H.P. Land Use Planning and Zoning § 8.06.

15-12 N.H.P. Land Use Planning and Zoning § 12.03.

15-14 N.H.P. Land Use Planning and Zoning § 14.07.

15-15 N.H.P. Land Use Planning and Zoning § 15.02.

15-15 N.H.P. Land Use Planning and Zoning § 15.04.

15-15 N.H.P. Land Use Planning and Zoning § 15.07.

15-22 N.H.P. Land Use Planning and Zoning § 22.02.

15-24 N.H.P. Land Use Planning and Zoning § 24.12.

15-30 N.H.P. Land Use Planning and Zoning § 30.04.

15-35 N.H.P. Land Use Planning and Zoning § 35.15.

15-35 N.H.P. Land Use Planning and Zoning § 35.16.

References in text.

Title XXXIX, referred to in par. IV, is Title 39 of LEXIS New Hampshire Revised Statutes Annotated, which is comprised of chapters 422–424.

674:17. Purposes of Zoning Ordinances.

I. Every zoning ordinance shall be adopted in accordance with the requirements of RSA 674:18. Zoning ordinances shall be designed:

(a) To lessen congestion in the streets;

(b) To secure safety from fires, panic and other dangers;

(c) To promote health and the general welfare;

(d) To provide adequate light and air;

(e) To prevent the overcrowding of land;

(f) To avoid undue concentration of population;

(g) To facilitate the adequate provision of transportation, solid waste facilities, water, sewerage, schools, parks, child day care;

(h) To assure proper use of natural resources and other public requirements;

(i) To encourage the preservation of agricultural lands and buildings and the agricultural operations described in RSA 21:34-a supporting the agricultural lands and buildings; and

(j) To encourage the installation and use of solar, wind, or other renewable energy systems and protect access to energy sources by the regulation of orientation of streets, lots, and buildings; establishment of maximum building height, minimum set back requirements, and limitations on type, height, and placement of vegetation; and encouragement of the use of solar skyspace easements under RSA 477. Zoning ordinances may establish buffer zones or additional districts which overlap existing districts and may further regulate the planting and trimming of vegetation on public and private property to protect access to renewable energy systems.

II. Every zoning ordinance shall be made with reasonable consideration to, among other things, the character of the area involved and its peculiar suitability for particular uses, as well as with a view to conserving the value of buildings and encouraging the most appropriate use of land throughout the municipality.

III. Except as provided in RSA 424:5 or RSA 422-B or in any other provision of Title XXXIX, no city, town, or county in which there are located unincorporated towns or unorganized places shall adopt a zoning ordinance or regulation with respect to antennas used exclusively in the amateur radio service that fails to conform to the limited federal preemption entitled Amateur Radio Preemption, 101 FCC 2nd 952 (1985) issued by the Federal Communications Commission.

HISTORY:
1983, 447:1. 1989, 42:2. 1995, 176:2, eff. Aug. 4, 1995. 2000, 279:2, eff. July 1, 2001. 2002, 73:2, eff. June 30, 2002. 2011, 85:2, eff. July 15, 2011.

Amendments

—2011.
The 2011 amendment added "and the agricultural operations described in RSA 21:34-a supporting the agricultural lands and buildings" in I(i).

—2002.
Paragraph I: Made minor changes in phraseology in subpars. (h) and (i) and added subpar. (j).

—2000.
Paragraph I: Made minor stylistic changes in subpars. (g) and (h) and added subpar. (i).

—1995.
Paragraph III: Added.

—1989.
Paragraph I(g): Inserted "child day care" following "parks".

Purpose of 2000 amendment
2000, 279:1, eff. July 1, 2001, provided:
"The purpose of this act [which amended this section and added RSA 674:32-a– 674:32-c], is to clarify the requirements of RSA 672:1, III-b, that farming and agriculture, as defined in RSA 21:34-a, shall not be unreasonably limited by the use of municipal planning and zoning powers."

NOTES TO DECISIONS

Analysis

1. Generally
2. Construction
3. Validity of particular ordinances
4. Effect on other provisions

1. Generally
Property could be zoned not only to present conditions but also to the requirements of probable and desirable growth. Kimball v. Blanchard, 90 N.H. 298, 7 A.2d 394, 1939 N.H. LEXIS 64 (N.H. 1939); Edgewood Civic Club v. Blaisdell, 95 N.H. 244, 61 A.2d 517, 1948 N.H. LEXIS 228 (N.H. 1948). (Decided under prior law.)

2. Construction
This section does not restrict zoning ordinances to be designed only for fire safety. Therefore, fact that antenna structure might not be a fire hazard did not exempt it from height limitation in town zoning ordinance. Carnie v. Town of Richmond, 139 N.H. 21, 648 A.2d 205, 1994 N.H. LEXIS 99 (N.H. 1994).

3. Validity of particular ordinances
A town could restrict the density of occupancy of premises by a zoning regulation. Durham v. White Enters., 115 N.H. 645, 348 A.2d 706, 1975 N.H. LEXIS 386 (N.H. 1975). (Decided under prior law.)
A town could constitutionally restrict the density of occupancy of housing by unrelated persons while not restricting persons related by blood, marriage or adoption. Durham v. White Enters., 115 N.H. 645, 348 A.2d 706, 1975 N.H. LEXIS 386 (N.H. 1975). (Decided under prior law.)
Zoning as residential all properties in a town not zoned as commercial or industrial was valid where the bulk of the land in the town, apart from the sections zoned for business and industry, was rural, used primarily for farming and residential purposes, since it took into account the character of the area involved and its peculiar suitability for particular uses and encouraged the most appropriate use of land. Hudson v. Paradise, 101 N.H. 389, 143 A.2d 421, 1958 N.H. LEXIS 46 (N.H. 1958). (Decided under prior law.)
The fact that a city might have enacted special regulations for fire protection did not estop it from enacting zoning regulations with a view to securing safety from fire. Sullivan v. Anglo-American Inv. Trust, 89 N.H. 112, 193 A. 225, 1937 N.H. LEXIS 22 (N.H. 1937). (Decided under prior law.)
A zoning regulation requiring that auxiliary buildings, including garages, stables and the like, be placed upon the rear half of the lot was permissible. Sundeen v. Rogers, 83 N.H. 253, 141 A. 142, 1928 N.H. LEXIS 11 (N.H. 1928). (Decided under prior law.)

4. Effect on other provisions
RSA 674:17, I(i), RSA 672:1, III-b, RSA 672:1, III-d, and RSA 674:32-a do not support the contention that the legislature intended to require municipalities to allow "agritourism" within their borders; at most, they evince the legislature's general intent to support traditional agriculture and agricultural activities, and they demonstrate legislative intent to allow reasonable local regulation, not to preempt the entire field. Thus, they did not preempt a local ordinance. Forster v. Town of Henniker, 167 N.H. 745, 118 A.3d 1016, 2015 N.H. LEXIS 54 (N.H. 2015).

Cited:
Cited in Chesterfield v. Brooks, 126 N.H. 64, 489 A.2d 600, 1985 N.H. LEXIS 274 (1985); Treisman v. Bedford, 132 N.H. 54, 563 A.2d 786, 1989 N.H. LEXIS 75 (1989); Buskey v. Hanover, 133 N.H. 318, 577 A.2d 406, 1990 N.H. LEXIS 67 (1990); Asselin v. Town of Conway, 137 N.H. 368, 628 A.2d 247, 1993 N.H. LEXIS 89 (1993); Nine A, LLC v. Town of Chesterfield, 157 N.H. 361, 950 A.2d 197, 2008 N.H. LEXIS 71 (2008).

RESEARCH REFERENCES AND PRACTICE AIDS

Cross References.
Division of municipality into districts, see RSA 674:20.
Interim growth management regulations, see RSA 674:23.

Uses of innovative land controls, see RSA 674:21.

New Hampshire Practice.
15-2 N.H.P. Land Use Planning and Zoning § 2.01.
15-2 N.H.P. Land Use Planning and Zoning § 2.02.
15-2 N.H.P. Land Use Planning and Zoning § 2.11.
15-3 N.H.P. Land Use Planning and Zoning § 3.01.
15-17 N.H.P. Land Use Planning and Zoning § 17.02.
15-24 N.H.P. Land Use Planning and Zoning § 24.12.

References in text.
Title XXXIX, referred to in par. III, is Title 39 of LEXIS New Hampshire Revised Statutes Annotated, which is comprised of chapters 422–424.

674:18. Adoption of Zoning Ordinance.

The local legislative body may adopt a zoning ordinance under RSA 674:16 only after the planning board has adopted the mandatory sections of the master plan as described in RSA 674:2, I and II.

HISTORY:
1983, 447:1, eff. Jan. 1, 1984. 2002, 178:4, eff. July 14, 2002.

Amendments

—2002.
Substituted "mandatory sections" for "general statement of objectives and the land use section" preceding "of the master".

NOTES TO DECISIONS

Substantial compliance
Based on doctrine of substantial compliance, otherwise proper amendment to zoning ordinance would not be invalidated based on planning board's failure to certify its master plan. Treisman v. Bedford, 132 N.H. 54, 563 A.2d 786, 1989 N.H. LEXIS 75 (N.H. 1989).

Cited:
Cited in Hurley v. Town of Hollis, 143 N.H. 567, 729 A.2d 998, 1999 N.H. LEXIS 45 (1999).

RESEARCH REFERENCES AND PRACTICE AIDS

Cross References.
Growth management ordinances, see RSA 674:22, 23.
Innovative land use control ordinances, see RSA 674:21.

New Hampshire Practice.
15-2 N.H.P. Land Use Planning and Zoning § 2.02.
15-3 N.H.P. Land Use Planning and Zoning § 3.03.
15-3 N.H.P. Land Use Planning and Zoning § 3.04.

674:19. Applicability of Zoning Ordinance.

A zoning ordinance adopted under RSA 674:16 shall not apply to existing structures or to the existing use of any building. It shall apply to any alteration of a building for use for a purpose or in a manner which is substantially different from the use to which it was put before alteration.

HISTORY:
1983, 447:1, eff. Jan. 1, 1984.

NOTES TO DECISIONS

Analysis

1. Generally

2. Construction
3. Nonconforming uses
4. Ordinances in compliance
5. Changes in use
6. Particular cases

1. Generally
Nonconforming uses were protected by the statute as well as by the New Hampshire Constitution. Hampton v. Brust, 122 N.H. 463, 446 A.2d 458, 1982 N.H. LEXIS 375 (N.H. 1982). (Decided under prior law.)
The past use of land might create certain rights to a similar use in the future, and the statute protected an existing use not conforming to later ordinances. Flanagan v. Hollis, 112 N.H. 222, 293 A.2d 328, 1972 N.H. LEXIS 181 (N.H. 1972). (Decided under prior law.)

2. Construction
Signs were "structures" within the meaning of the provision of this section exempting "existing structures" from regulation through zoning ordinances. Dugas v. Conway, 125 N.H. 175, 480 A.2d 71, 1984 N.H. LEXIS 359 (N.H. 1984). (Decided under prior law.)

3. Nonconforming uses
The right to maintain nonconforming uses is meant to protect property owners from a retrospective application of zoning ordinances, so that property owners may continue using and enjoying their property when their uses were lawful prior to the enactment of a zoning ordinance. Town of Salem v. Wickson, 146 N.H. 328, 770 A.2d 1120, 2001 N.H. LEXIS 79 (N.H. 2001).
An established use of land is not disturbed by a subsequent land restriction; to qualify for such protection, a nonconforming use must lawfully exist at time restriction is adopted, and have continually existed since that time. Town of Seabrook v. Vachon Mgmt., Inc., 144 N.H. 660, 745 A.2d 1155, 2000 N.H. LEXIS 7 (N.H. 2000).
Well established policy of zoning law is to carefully limit enlargement and extension of nonconforming uses, and to reduce them to conformity as completely and rapidly as possible. Hurley v. Town of Hollis, 143 N.H. 567, 729 A.2d 998, 1999 N.H. LEXIS 45 (N.H. 1999).
Trial court did not err in concluding that use of theater for live performances was substantially different than use of theater to show movies, and that live entertainment was not a preexisting, nonconforming use of property. Conforti v. City of Manchester, 141 N.H. 78, 677 A.2d 147, 1996 N.H. LEXIS 52 (N.H. 1996).
A zoning ordinance does not apply to a pre-existing use unless that use is altered for a purpose or in a manner which is substantially different from the use to which it was put before alteration; when determining whether a nonconforming use is protected, the court will bear in mind that the creation of a nonconforming use depends upon the configuration of specific facts at a certain point in time and, therefore, in order to determine how much a nonconforming use may be expanded or changed, the court will look to the facts existing when the nonconforming use was created. Ray's Stateline Mkt. v. Town of Pelham, 140 N.H. 139, 665 A.2d 1068, 1995 N.H. LEXIS 111 (N.H. 1995).
A market owner was properly granted permits to move a coffee counter and to change two sign faces since a permit to build a new coffee counter would not result in a substantial change or an illegal expansion of the nonconforming use and the sign permit would not result in any appreciable effect on the neighborhood. Ray's Stateline Mkt. v. Town of Pelham, 140 N.H. 139, 665 A.2d 1068, 1995 N.H. LEXIS 111 (N.H. 1995).
The right to continue a previously lawful use of one's property after enactment of a zoning ordinance that prohibits such use is a vested right recognized by this section. New London Land Use Ass'n v. New London Zoning Bd. of Adjustment, 130 N.H. 510, 543 A.2d 1385, 1988 N.H. LEXIS 39 (N.H. 1988).
Nonconforming uses relate to conditions which exist prior to the time a zoning ordinance is passed. New London Land Use Ass'n v. New London Zoning Bd. of Adjustment, 130 N.H. 510, 543 A.2d 1385, 1988 N.H. LEXIS 39 (N.H. 1988).

4. Ordinances in compliance
Town clearly intended its zoning amendment to codify, not deviate from, existing law concerning expansion of nonconforming

uses, and superior court correctly applied this recognized standard in reviewing board's grant of special exception. Hurley v. Town of Hollis, 143 N.H. 567, 729 A.2d 998, 1999 N.H. LEXIS 45 (N.H. 1999).

A zoning ordinance would be construed to be consistent with the statute as limiting any "extension," "expansion," or "enlargement" of a nonconforming use and prohibiting its change to a "substantially different" nonconforming use. Ray's Stateline Mkt. v. Town of Pelham, 140 N.H. 139, 665 A.2d 1068, 1995 N.H. LEXIS 111 (N.H. 1995).

5. Changes in use

Because the general policy of zoning law is to carefully limit the extension and enlargement of nonconforming uses, provisions that permit the continuance of such uses are strictly construed, and the party asserting that a proposed use is not new or impermissible bears the burden of proof. Town of Salem v. Wickson, 146 N.H. 328, 770 A.2d 1120, 2001 N.H. LEXIS 79 (N.H. 2001).

An extension and enlargement that substantially changes the nature and purpose of a nonconforming use is impermissible. Town of Salem v. Wickson, 146 N.H. 328, 770 A.2d 1120, 2001 N.H. LEXIS 79 (N.H. 2001).

Considerations in determining whether there has been a substantial change in the nature or purpose of a preexisting nonconforming use are: (1) the extent the use in question reflects the nature and purpose of the prevailing nonconforming use; (2) whether the use at issue is merely a different manner of utilizing the same use or constitutes a use different in character, nature, and kind; and (3) whether the use will have a substantially different effect on the neighborhood. Town of Salem v. Wickson, 146 N.H. 328, 770 A.2d 1120, 2001 N.H. LEXIS 79 (N.H. 2001).

Where, at the time a zoning ordinance was enacted, the nature and purpose of a nonconforming use was for pig farming and the stockpiling of manure and earthen materials was incidental thereto, after the property owner abandoned pig farming, and started stockpiling material brought in from off-site, he changed the character and nature of that activity, and the trial court's finding that the nonconforming use had remained essentially unchanged was not supported by the evidence. Town of Salem v. Wickson, 146 N.H. 328, 770 A.2d 1120, 2001 N.H. LEXIS 79 (N.H. 2001).

Test for expansion of a nonconforming use, where expanded use is determined to be not "substantially different" from existing use, is a more restrictive test than that used to determine "changes of use" sufficient to trigger site plan review. Town of Seabrook v. Vachon Mgmt., Inc., 144 N.H. 660, 745 A.2d 1155, 2000 N.H. LEXIS 7 (N.H. 2000).

Change in use of leased unit, from a computer retail establishment to a venue for mud wrestling, was effected without required site plan approval and was thus illegal, and therefore the change in use was ineligible to later qualify as a lawful nonconforming use. Town of Seabrook v. Vachon Mgmt., Inc., 144 N.H. 660, 745 A.2d 1155, 2000 N.H. LEXIS 7 (N.H. 2000).

6. Particular cases

Trial court did not overstep its bounds by leaving only some of a planning board's parking limits intact. The board's decision to eliminate four of the proposed eight parking spaces brought the parking on the landowner's lot into compliance with the ordinance's requirement that all parking connect with a street or immediately to a driveway that afforded sufficient ingress and egress; the ordinance did not require the landowner to change his preexisting use of the lot to conform to the rest of the ordinance's parking space requirements. Dovaro 12 Atl., LLC v. Town of Hampton, 158 N.H. 222, 965 A.2d 1096, 2009 N.H. LEXIS 5 (N.H. 2009).

Trial court properly declined to find that converting seasonal apartments into year-round condominiums substantially changed or expanded a landowner's nonconforming use. The use of the lot for dwelling units even though the lot lacked sufficient parking to satisfy the zoning ordinance was the same regardless of whether the dwelling units were occupied seasonally or year-round; further, there was no evidence in the record that year-round occupancy of the units or year-round on-site parking would substantially affect the surrounding neighborhood. Dovaro 12 Atl., LLC v. Town of Hampton, 158 N.H. 222, 965 A.2d 1096, 2009 N.H. LEXIS 5 (N.H. 2009).

Court rejected a town's assertion that using off-site parking was part of a property owner's nonconforming use of the property. The trial court found that the tenants of the property—not the property owner—had secured off-site parking, and the town had not provided a record that demonstrated that it raised the issue of whether the record supported the finding in the trial court, thereby preserving it for review. Dovaro 12 Atl., LLC v. Town of Hampton, 158 N.H. 222, 965 A.2d 1096, 2009 N.H. LEXIS 5 (N.H. 2009).

A mere plan to reopen a store, a plan in no way implemented, was not an "existing use" within the meaning of the provision that zoning ordinances were not to apply to existing structures nor to the existing use of any building. Wunderlich v. Webster, 117 N.H. 283, 371 A.2d 1177, 1977 N.H. LEXIS 320 (N.H. 1977). (Decided under prior law.)

Since the legislature did not give towns authority to regulate existing structures, including large, off-premises signs, a town lacked the power to apply a zoning ordinance requiring removal of all existing nonconforming signs. Jackson v. Town & Country Motor Inn, 120 N.H. 699, 422 A.2d 1034, 1980 N.H. LEXIS 381 (N.H. 1980). (Decided under prior law.)

Cited:

Cited in Goffstown v. Thibeault, 129 N.H. 454, 529 A.2d 930, 1987 N.H. LEXIS 184 (1987); Blue Jay Realty Trust v. Franklin, 132 N.H. 502, 567 A.2d 188, 1989 N.H. LEXIS 128 (1989); Cohen v. Henniker, 134 N.H. 425, 593 A.2d 1145, 1991 N.H. LEXIS 78 (1991); Conforti v. City of Manchester, 141 N.H. 78, 677 A.2d 147, 1996 N.H. LEXIS 52 (1996); Peabody v. Town of Windham, 142 N.H. 488, 703 A.2d 886, 1997 N.H. LEXIS 121 (1997); N. Country Envtl. Servs. v. Town of Bethlehem, 146 N.H. 348, 772 A.2d 330, 2001 N.H. LEXIS 85 (2001).

RESEARCH REFERENCES AND PRACTICE AIDS

Cross References.

Authority to adopt or amend ordinances generally, see RSA 674:16.

Emergency temporary zoning and planning ordinance, see RSA 674:24 et seq.

Interim growth management ordinances, see RSA 674:23.

New Hampshire Bar Journal.

For article, "'Grandfathered'—The Law of Nonconforming Uses and Vested Rights," see 31 N.H. B.J. 17 (1990).

New Hampshire Practice.

14-20 N.H.P. Local Government Law § 750.

15-2 N.H.P. Land Use Planning and Zoning § 2.18.

15-3 N.H.P. Land Use Planning and Zoning § 3.01.

15-8 N.H.P. Land Use Planning and Zoning § 8.02.

15-8 N.H.P. Land Use Planning and Zoning § 8.06.

15-11 N.H.P. Land Use Planning and Zoning § 11.01.

15-29 N.H.P. Land Use Planning and Zoning § 29.03.

674:20. Districts.

In order to accomplish any or all of the purposes of a zoning ordinance enumerated under RSA 674:17, the local legislative body may divide the municipality into districts of a number, shape and area as may be deemed best suited to carry out the purposes of RSA 674:17. The local legislative body may regulate and restrict the erection, construction, reconstruction, alteration, repair, or use of buildings, structures, or land within each district which it creates. All regulations shall be uniform for each class or kind of buildings throughout each district, but the regulations in one district may differ from those in other districts.

HISTORY:

1983, 447:1, eff. Jan. 1, 1984.

NOTES TO DECISIONS

Analysis

1. Construction
2. Creation of districts
3. Standing

1. Construction

The provisions of the section were permissive rather than mandatory, and the establishment of a single district for zoning purposes would not for that reason alone invalidate a zoning ordinance. Plainfield v. Hood, 108 N.H. 502, 240 A.2d 60, 1968 N.H. LEXIS 200 (N.H. 1968). (Decided under prior law.)

2. Creation of districts

The fact that there was but one district did not invalidate a zoning ordinance. Gutoski v. Winchester, 114 N.H. 414, 322 A.2d 4, 1974 N.H. LEXIS 289 (N.H. 1974). (Decided under prior law.)

The proper zoning of an area as residential would not be affected by any invalid spot zoning of an adjoining area. Mater v. Dover, 97 N.H. 13, 79 A.2d 844, 1951 N.H. LEXIS 4 (N.H. 1951). (Decided under prior law.)

The requirement that a zoning regulation be made in accordance with a comprehensive plan required zoning to be by districts and not be individual pieces of property. Edgewood Civic Club v. Blaisdell, 95 N.H. 244, 61 A.2d 517, 1948 N.H. LEXIS 228 (N.H. 1948). (Decided under prior law.)

A zoning ordinance did not comply with the statute unless the classification was by districts and not by individual pieces of property. Kimball v. Blanchard, 90 N.H. 298, 7 A.2d 394, 1939 N.H. LEXIS 64 (N.H. 1939). (Decided under prior law.)

3. Standing

Merely alleging violations of New Hampshire's Equal Protection Clause and RSA 674:20 does not confer standing to challenge a zoning board of adjustment's decision under RSA 677:4. Thus, petitioner did not have standing when it asserted only that it had a right to ensure that all owners in a district "stood on an equal footing." Hannaford Bros. Co. v. Town of Bedford, 164 N.H. 764, 64 A.3d 951, 2013 N.H. LEXIS 41 (N.H. 2013).

RESEARCH REFERENCES AND PRACTICE AIDS

Cross References.
Authority to adopt or amend ordinances generally, see RSA 674:16.
Historic districts generally, see RSA 674:45 et seq.
Subdivisions generally, see RSA 674:35 et seq.

New Hampshire Practice.
15-2 N.H.P. Land Use Planning and Zoning § 2.01.
15-2 N.H.P. Land Use Planning and Zoning § 2.11.

674:21. Innovative Land Use Controls.

I. Innovative land use controls may include, but are not limited to:
    (a) Timing incentives.
    (b) Phased development.
    (c) Intensity and use incentive.
    (d) Transfer of density and development rights.
    (e) Planned unit development.
    (f) Cluster development.
    (g) Impact zoning.
    (h) Performance standards.
    (i) Flexible and discretionary zoning.
    (j) Environmental characteristics zoning.
    (k) Inclusionary zoning.
    (*l*) Impact fees.
    (m) Village plan alternative subdivision.
    (n) Integrated land development permit option.

II. An innovative land use control adopted under RSA 674:16 may be required when supported by the master plan and shall contain within it the standards which shall guide the person or board which administers the ordinance. An innovative land use control ordinance may provide for administration, including the granting of conditional or special use permits, by the planning board, board of selectmen, zoning board of adjustment, or such other person or board as the ordinance may designate. If the administration of the innovative provisions of the ordinance is not vested in the planning board, any proposal submitted under this section shall be reviewed by the planning board prior to final consideration by the administrator. In such a case, the planning board shall set forth its comments on the proposal in writing and the administrator shall, to the extent that the planning board's comments are not directly incorporated into its decision, set forth its findings and decisions on the planning board's comments.

III. Innovative land use controls must be adopted in accordance with RSA 675:1, II.

IV. As used in this section:
    (a) "Inclusionary zoning" means land use control regulations which provide a voluntary incentive or benefit to a property owner in order to induce the property owner to produce housing units which are affordable to persons or families of low and moderate income. Inclusionary zoning includes, but is not limited to, density bonuses, growth control exemptions, and a streamlined application process.
    (b) "Phased development" means a development, usually for large-scale projects, in which construction of public or private improvements proceeds in stages on a schedule over a period of years established in the subdivision or site plan approved by the planning board. In a phased development, the issuance of building permits in each phase is solely dependent on the completion of the prior phase and satisfaction of other conditions on the schedule approved by the planning board. Phased development does not include a general limit on the issuance of building permits or the granting of subdivision or site plan approval in the municipality, which may be accomplished only by a growth management ordinance under RSA 674:22 or a temporary moratorium or limitation under RSA 674:23.

V. As used in this section "impact fee" means a fee or assessment imposed upon development, including subdivision, building construction, or other land use change, in order to help meet the needs occasioned by that development for the construction or improvement of capital facilities owned or operated by the municipality, including and limited to water treatment and distribution facilities; wastewater treatment and disposal facilities; sanitary sewers; storm water, drainage and flood control facilities; municipal road systems and rights-of-way; municipal office facilities; public school facilities; the municipality's proportional share of capital facilities of a cooperative or regional school district of which the municipality is a member; public safety facilities; solid waste collection, transfer, recycling, processing, and disposal facilities; public library facilities; and public recreational facilities not including public open space. No later than July 1, 1993, all impact fee ordinances shall be subject to the following:

(a) The amount of any such fee shall be a proportional share of municipal capital improvement costs which is reasonably related to the capital needs created by the development, and to the benefits accruing to the development from the capital improvements financed by the fee. Upgrading of existing facilities and infrastructures, the need for which is not created by new development, shall not be paid for by impact fees.

(b) In order for a municipality to adopt an impact fee ordinance, it must have enacted a capital improvements program pursuant to RSA 674:5-7.

(c) Any impact fee shall be accounted for separately, shall be segregated from the municipality's general fund, may be spent upon order of the municipal governing body, shall be exempt from all provisions of RSA 32 relative to limitation and expenditure of town moneys, and shall be used solely for the capital improvements for which it was collected, or to recoup the cost of capital improvements made in anticipation of the needs which the fee was collected to meet.

(d) All impact fees imposed pursuant to this section shall be assessed at the time of planning board approval of a subdivision plat or site plan. When no planning board approval is required, or has been made prior to the adoption or amendment of the impact fee ordinance, impact fees shall be assessed prior to, or as a condition for, the issuance of a building permit or other appropriate permission to proceed with development. Impact fees shall be intended to reflect the effect of development upon municipal facilities at the time of the issuance of the building permit. Impact fees shall be collected at the time a certificate of occupancy is issued. If no certificate of occupancy is required, impact fees shall be collected when the development is ready for its intended use. Nothing in this subparagraph shall prevent the municipality and the assessed party from establishing an alternate, mutually acceptable schedule of payment of impact fees in effect at the time of subdivision plat or site plan approval by the planning board. If an alternate schedule of payment is established, municipalities may require developers to post bonds, issue letters of credit, accept liens, or otherwise provide suitable measures of security so as to guarantee future payment of the assessed impact fees.

(e) The ordinance shall establish reasonable times after which any portion of an impact fee which has not become encumbered or otherwise legally bound to be spent for the purpose for which it was collected shall be refunded, with any accrued interest. Whenever the calculation of an impact fee has been predicated upon some portion of capital improvement costs being borne by the municipality, a refund shall be made upon the failure of the legislative body to appropriate the municipality's share of the capital improvement costs within a reasonable time. The maximum time which shall be considered reasonable hereunder shall be 6 years.

(f) Unless otherwise specified in the ordinance, any decision under an impact fee ordinance may be appealed in the same manner provided by statute for appeals from the officer or board making that decision, as set forth in RSA 676:5, RSA 677:2-14, or RSA 677:15, respectively.

(g) The ordinance may also provide for a waiver process, including the criteria for the granting of such a waiver.

(h) The adoption of a growth management limitation or moratorium by a municipality shall not affect any development with respect to which an impact fee has been paid or assessed as part of the approval for that development.

(i) Neither the adoption of an impact fee ordinance, nor the failure to adopt such an ordinance, shall be deemed to affect existing authority of a planning board over subdivision or site plan review, except to the extent expressly stated in such an ordinance.

(j) The failure to adopt an impact fee ordinance shall not preclude a municipality from requiring developers to pay an exaction for the cost of off-site improvement needs determined by the planning board to be necessary for the occupancy of any portion of a development. For the purposes of this subparagraph, "off-site improvements" means those improvements that are necessitated by a development but which are located outside the boundaries of the property that is subject to a subdivision plat or site plan approval by the planning board. Such off-site improvements shall be limited to any necessary highway, drainage, and sewer and water upgrades pertinent to that development. The amount of any such exaction shall be a proportional share of municipal improvement costs not previously assessed against other developments, which is necessitated by the development, and which is reasonably related to the benefits accruing to the development from the improvements financed by the exaction. As an alternative to paying an exaction, the developer may elect to construct the necessary improvements, subject to bonding and timing conditions as may be reasonably required by the planning board. Any exaction imposed pursuant to this section shall be assessed at the time of planning board approval of the development necessitating an off-site improvement. Whenever the calculation of an exaction for an off-site improvement has been predicated upon some portion of the cost of that improvement being borne by the municipality, a refund of any collected exaction shall be made to the payor or payor's successor in interest upon the failure of the local legislative body to appropriate the municipality's share of that cost within 6 years from the date of collection. For the purposes of this subparagraph, failure of local legislative body to appropriate such funding or to construct any necessary off-site improvement shall not operate to prohibit an otherwise approved development.

(k) Revenue from impact fees imposed upon development and collected by a municipality under RSA 674:21, V for construction of or improvement to municipal road systems may be expended upon state highways within the municipality only for improvement costs that are related to the capital needs created by the development. Such improvements may include items such as, but not limited to, traffic signals and signage, turning lanes, additional travel lanes, and guard rails. No such improvements shall be constructed or installed without approval of the state department of transportation. In no event shall impact fees be used for any improvements to roads, bridges, or interchanges that are part of the interstate highway system. Nothing in RSA 674:21, V shall be construed as allowing or authorizing additional impact fees merely by virtue of having approved the expenditure of collected fee revenue for construction of or improvement of state highways, nor shall it be construed as allowing the adoption of new impact fees devoted to assessing impacts to state highways.

(*l*) No later than 60 days following the end of the fiscal year, any municipality having adopted an impact fee ordinance shall prepare a report listing all expenditures of impact fee revenue for the prior fiscal year, identifying the capital improvement project for which the fees were assessed and stating the dates upon which the fees were assessed and collected. The annual report shall enable the public to track the payment, expenditure, and status of the individually collected fees to determine whether said fees were expended, retained, or refunded.

VI.(a) In this section, "village plan alternative" means an optional land use control and subdivision regulation to provide a means of promoting a more efficient and cost effective method of land development. The village plan alternative's purpose is to encourage the preservation of open space wherever possible. The village plan alternative subdivision is meant to encourage beneficial consolidation of land development to permit the efficient layout of less costly to maintain roads, utilities, and other public and private infrastructures; to improve the ability of political subdivisions to provide more rapid and efficient delivery of public safety and school transportation services as community growth occurs; and finally, to provide owners of private property with a method for realizing the inherent development value of their real property in a manner conducive to the creation of substantial benefit to the environment and to the political subdivision's property tax base.

(b) An owner of record wishing to utilize the village plan alternative in the subdivision and development of a parcel of land, by locating the entire density permitted by the existing land use regulations of the political subdivision within which the property is located, on 20 percent or less of the entire parcel available for development, shall grant to the municipality within which the property is located, as a condition of approval, a recorded easement reserving the remaining land area of the entire, original lot, solely for agriculture, forestry, and conservation, or for public recreation. The recorded easement shall limit any new construction on the remainder lot to structures associated with farming operations, forest management operations, and conservation uses, and shall specify that the restrictions contained in the easement are enforceable by the municipality. Public recreational uses shall be subject to the written approval of those abutters whose property lies within the village plan alternative subdivision portion of the project at the time when such a public use is proposed.

(c) The submission and approval procedure for a village plan alternative subdivision shall be the same as that for a conventional subdivision. Existing zoning and subdivision regulations relating to emergency access, fire prevention, and public health and safety concerns including any setback requirement for wells, septic systems, or wetland requirement imposed by the department of environmental services shall apply to the developed portion of a village plan alternative subdivision, but lot size regulations and dimensional requirements having to do with frontage and setbacks measured from all new property lot lines, and lot size regulations, as well as density regulations, shall not apply.

(1) The total density of development within a village plan alternate subdivision shall not exceed the total potential development density permitted a conventional subdivision of the entire original lot unless provisions contained within the political subdivision's land use regulations provide a basis for increasing the permitted density of development within a village plan alternative subdivision.

(2) In no case shall a political subdivision impose lesser density requirements upon a village plan alternative subdivision than the density requirements imposed on a conventional subdivision.

(d) If the total area of a proposed village plan alternative subdivision including all roadways and improvements does not exceed 20 percent of the total land area of the undeveloped lot, and if the proposed subdivision incorporates the total sum of all proposed development as permitted by local regulation on the undeveloped lot, all existing and future dimensional requirements imposed by local regulation, including lot size, shall not apply to the proposed village plan alternative subdivision.

(e) The approving authority may increase, at existing property lines, the setback to new construction within a village plan alternative subdivision by up to 2 times the distance required by current zoning or subdivision regulations, subject to the provisions of subparagraph (c).

(f) Within a village plan alternative subdivision, the exterior wall construction of buildings shall meet or exceed the requirements for fire-rated construction described by the fire prevention and building codes being enforced by the state of New Hampshire at the date and time the property owner of record files a formal application for subdivision approval with the political subdivision having jurisdiction of the project. Exterior walls and openings of new buildings shall also conform to fire protective provisions of all other building codes in force in the political subdivision. Wherever building code or fire prevention code requirements for exterior wall construction appear to be in conflict, the more stringent building or fire prevention code requirements shall apply.

VII. In this section, "integrated land development permit option" means an optional land use control to allow a project to proceed, in whole or in part, as permitted by the department of environmental services under RSA 489.

HISTORY:

1983, 447:1. 1988, 149:1, 2. 1991, 283:1, 2. 1992, 42:1. 1994, 278:1, eff. Aug. 5, 1994. 2002, 236:1, 2, eff. July 16, 2002. 2004, 71:1, 2, eff. July 6, 2004. 199:2, eff. June 1, 2005. 199:3, eff. June 7, 2004. 2005, 61:1, 2, eff. July 22, 2005. 2008, 63:1, eff. July 20, 2008. 2012, 106:1, 2, eff. July 28, 2012. 2013, 270:5, 6, eff. July 1, 2017. 2015, 31:1, eff. July 6, 2015. 2016, 6:3, 4, eff. June 1, 2017.

Effective Date of 2013 amendment.

2014, 156:1, eff. June 30, 2014, amended 2013, 270:7, I, to change the effective date of 2013, 270:1, 5, and 6 from Jan. 1, 2015 to July 1, 2017.

Amendment Notes

The 2016 amendments to this section by Ch. 6 deleted former I(l), which read: "Accessory dwelling unit standards"; redesignated former I(m) through I(o) as I(l) through I(n); deleted former IV(b), which read: "'Accessory dwelling unit' means a second dwelling unit, attached or detached, which is permitted by a land use control regulation to be located on the same lot, plat, site, or other division of land as the permitted principal dwelling unit"; and redesignated former IV(c) as IV(b).

—2015.

The 2015 amendment added IV(c).

—2013.

The 2013 amendment added I(o) and VII.

—2012.

The 2012 amendment substituted "municipal" for "public" in the first sentence of the introductory language of V; added V(k) and V(l); and made a stylistic change.

—2008.

The 2008 amendment in VI(b), substituted "shall grant to the municipality" for "shall provide to the political subdivision" in the first sentence and added "and shall specify that the restrictions contained in the easement are enforceable by the municipality" in the second sentence.

—2005.

Paragraph VI(c)–(e): Rewritten to the extent that a detailed comparison would be impracticable.

Paragraph VI(f): Added.

—2004.

Paragraph I(d): Inserted "density and" preceding "development" by ch. 71.

Paragraph II: Inserted "may be required when supported by the master plan and" in the first sentence by ch. 71.

Paragraph V(d): Rewritten to the extent that a detailed comparison would be impracticable by ch. 199.

Paragraph V(j): Added by ch. 199.

—2002.

Paragraph I(n): Added.

Paragraph VI: Added.

—1994.

Paragraph V: Inserted "the municipality's proportional share of capital facilities of a cooperative or regional school district of which the municipality is a member" preceding "public safety" in the first sentence of the introductory paragraph.

—1992.

Paragraph V(i): Deleted the former first sentence.

—1991.

Paragraph I: Made minor changes in punctuation in subpars. (a)–(j), deleted "and" following "zoning" in subpar. (k), and added subpar. (m).

Paragraph V: Added.

—1988.

Paragraph I: Deleted "and" following "zoning" at the end of subpar. (i), made a minor stylistic change at the end of subpar. (j) and added subpars. (k) and (l).

Paragraph IV: Added.

NOTES TO DECISIONS

Analysis

1. Construction
2. Impact fees
3. Growth management ordinances

1. Construction

By any measure, the boundaries of a town's authority under RSA 674:21, I are not precisely drawn, but to say that the statute confers general authority incidental to shoreland protection to regulate personal boating and boat docking upon state-owned waters stretches its language beyond logic. It did not allow additional municipal regulation of a private dock. Lakeside Lodge, Inc. v. Town of New London, 158 N.H. 164, 960 A.2d 1268, 2008 N.H. LEXIS 140 (2008).

2. Impact fees

Trial court properly interpreted "refund" as it was used in the statute and concluded that a town was within its authority to enact an ordinance directing that any refund of impact fees be paid to the current property owner as opposed to the original developer.

Because petitioners no longer owned any of the properties for which they paid the impact fees at issue, they had no standing to seek a refund of the unencumbered fees. K.L.N. Constr. Co. v. Town of Pelham, 167 N.H. 180, 107 A.3d 658, 2014 N.H. LEXIS 143 (N.H. 2014).

Evidence supported the planning board's decision that the need for turnpike improvement, especially given its occasional flooding, was reasonably related to the developer's proposed development of property on the turnpike and, thus, the town could impose an impact fee on the developer pursuant to RSA 674:21, V(a). That evidence showed that the developer planned to replace the existing single-family residence on the developer's property and create four new residential lots, which would put more people at risk if the turnpike closed and justified having the developer bear some of the cost of the improvement even if the developer did not create the problem. Upton v. Town of Hopkinton, 157 N.H. 115, 945 A.2d 670, 2008 N.H. LEXIS 40 (N.H. 2008).

Ordinances that authorized local planning boards to adjust impact fees according to statistical models widely used in New Hampshire contained sufficient standards for adjustments so as to fall within the parameters of a statutory delegation of power. Caparco v. Town of Danville, 152 N.H. 722, 886 A.2d 1045, 2005 N.H. LEXIS 163 (N.H. 2005).

Because town had not enacted an impact fee ordinance, it lacked authority to condition site plan approval on zoning applicants' payment for off-site improvements. Simonsen v. Town of Derry, 145 N.H. 382, 765 A.2d 1033, 2000 N.H. LEXIS 73 (N.H. 2000).

3. Growth management ordinances

Supreme court reversed judgment that held town could not impose both impact fee and growth management ordinances on housing developer; under RSA 674:21, V(h) the growth management ordinance could be imposed since the impact fee had been neither paid nor assessed; neither the town's preliminary estimate of the impact fee nor its receiving an application in which fees were represented constituted a RSA 674:21, V(h) assessment. Monahan-Fortin Props. v. Town of Hudson, 148 N.H. 769, 813 A.2d 523, 2002 N.H. LEXIS 214 (N.H. 2002).

RESEARCH REFERENCES AND PRACTICE AIDS

Cross References.
Growth management ordinances, see RSA 674:22, 23.
Purposes of zoning ordinances generally, see RSA 674:17.
Subdivision regulation, see RSA 674:35 et seq.

New Hampshire Bar Journal.
For article, "Lex Loci: A Survey of New Hampshire Supreme Court Decisions," see 46 N.H. B.J. 52 (Winter 2006).
For article, "Municipal Exactions for Development in New Hampshire," see 34 N.H. B.J. 14 (June 1993).

New Hampshire Practice.
15-2 N.H.P. Land Use Planning and Zoning § 2.01.
15-4 N.H.P. Land Use Planning and Zoning § 4.02.
15-15 N.H.P. Land Use Planning and Zoning § 15.07.
15-17 N.H.P. Land Use Planning and Zoning § 17.02.
15-17 N.H.P. Land Use Planning and Zoning § 17.05.
15-18 N.H.P. Land Use Planning and Zoning § 18.01.
15-19 N.H.P. Land Use Planning and Zoning § 19.03.
15-22 N.H.P. Land Use Planning and Zoning § 22.02.
15-26 N.H.P. Land Use Planning and Zoning § 26.03.
15-31 N.H.P. Land Use Planning and Zoning § 31.05.

674:21-a. Development Restrictions Enforceable.

Any open space designation or other development restriction which is part of a cluster development, planned unit development, village plan alternative subdivision, or other proposal approved under innovative land use controls, or which is lawfully imposed by a local land use board as a condition of subdivision, site plan, variance, or other type of approval, and which has been filed in the records of the local land use board in accordance with its established procedure, shall be deemed to create a conservation restriction as defined in RSA 477:45, I, which shall run with the land, and shall be enforceable by the municipality, or by the owner of any property which would be specially damaged by the violation of such restriction, regardless of whether any deed or other instrument conveying such restriction has been executed or recorded. For purposes of this section, an applicant's statement of intent to restrict development, submitted with or contained in an application which is subsequently approved, shall be deemed a condition of the approval.

HISTORY:
1988, 149:3, eff. June 20, 1988. 2002, 236:3, eff. July 16, 2002.

Amendments

—2002.
Inserted "village plan alternative subdivision" following "planned unit development" near the beginning of the first sentence.

RESEARCH REFERENCES AND PRACTICE AIDS

New Hampshire Practice.
15-18 N.H.P. Land Use Planning and Zoning § 18.03.
15-32 N.H.P. Land Use Planning and Zoning § 32.11.
15-38 N.H.P. Land Use Planning and Zoning § 38.06.

674:22. Growth Management; Timing of Development.

I. The local legislative body may further exercise the powers granted under this subdivision to regulate and control the timing of development. Any ordinance imposing such a control may be adopted only after preparation and adoption by the planning board of a master plan and a capital improvement program and shall be based upon a growth management process intended to assess and balance community development needs and consider regional development needs.

II. The local legislative body may adopt a growth management ordinance under this section only if there is a demonstrated need to regulate the timing of development, based upon the municipality's lack of capacity to accommodate anticipated growth in the absence of such an ordinance. The need to regulate the timing of development shall be demonstrated by a study performed by or for the planning board or the governing body, or submitted with a petition of voters presented under RSA 675:4. The study shall be based on competent evidence and shall consider the municipality's projected growth rate and the municipality's need for additional services to accommodate such growth.

III. An ordinance adopted under this section shall include a termination date and shall restrict projected normal growth no more than is necessary to allow for orderly and good-faith development of municipal services. The planning board in a municipality that adopts such an ordinance shall promptly undertake development of a plan for the orderly and rational development of municipal services needed to accommodate anticipated normal growth; provided, however, that in a town that has established a capital improvement program committee under RSA 674:5, the plan shall be developed by that committee. The ordinance and the plan shall be evaluated by the planning board at least annually, to confirm that reasonable progress is being made to carry out the plan. The planning board shall report its findings to the legislative body in the municipality's annual report.

HISTORY:
1983, 447:1, eff. Jan. 1, 1984. 2008, 360:1, eff. July 11, 2008.

Revision note.
In the second sentence, inserted "plan" following "master" for purposes of clarity.

Amendments

—2008.
The 2008 amendment added designation I and added II and III.

Time Period for Modification of Existing Growth Management Ordinances.
2008, 360:3, eff. July 11, 2008, provided: "Each municipality that adopted a growth management ordinance under RSA 674:22 prior to the effective date of this act shall have until June 1, 2010 to amend its ordinance to conform to this act. If a municipality adopted an interim growth management ordinance under RSA 674:23 prior to the effective date of this act, that ordinance shall remain in effect until one year after its passage or until the municipality's next annual meeting, unless the ordinance prescribes an earlier expiration date, and unless a court of competent jurisdiction determines that the ordinance is illegal or is otherwise unenforceable."

NOTES TO DECISIONS

Analysis

1. Generally
2. Effect of master plan
3. Validity of particular ordinances or plans

1. Generally
This section and RSA 674:23 enable a municipality to adopt an ordinance providing for controlled growth after its planning board has adopted a master plan and a capital improvement program designed to assess and balance community and regional development needs. Rancourt v. Barnstead, 129 N.H. 45, 523 A.2d 55, 1986 N.H. LEXIS 379 (N.H. 1986).
Growth control ordinances are intended to regulate and control the timing of development, not the prevention of development. Stoney-Brook Dev. Corp. v. Fremont, 124 N.H. 583, 474 A.2d 561, 1984 N.H. LEXIS 348 (N.H. 1984). (Decided under prior law).

2. Effect of master plan
Comprehensive growth control planning assesses and balances the development concerns of the entire community, with less emphasis on the interests of any one particular landowner. Ettlingen Homes v. Town of Derry, 141 N.H. 296, 681 A.2d 97, 1996 N.H. LEXIS 93 (N.H. 1996).
A planning board may not apply a master plan itself to limit development; it may only apply ordinances adopted pursuant to this section or RSA 674:23 to regulate or control the timing of

development. Rancourt v. Barnstead, 129 N.H. 45, 523 A.2d 55, 1986 N.H. LEXIS 379 (N.H. 1986).
A municipal planning board cannot deny approval of a proposed subdivision on the basis of growth control rates set in a master plan without the municipality's first having enacted an ordinance providing for growth management or the board's having itself enacted a capital improvement program. Rancourt v. Barnstead, 129 N.H. 45, 523 A.2d 55, 1986 N.H. LEXIS 379 (N.H. 1986).

3. Validity of particular ordinances or plans
A zoning ordinance which required a minimum lot size of 50 acres in a mountain and forest district was not designed to regulate and control the timing of development in the town and, therefore, the statute was not applicable to the plaintiffs' challenge to the ordinance. Caspersen v. Town of Lyme, 139 N.H. 637, 661 A.2d 759, 1995 N.H. LEXIS 70 (N.H. 1995).
A growth rate of 3% in an article of a town zoning ordinance, enacted in 1975, which required that the number of building permits issued for new dwellings be limited annually to 3% of the number of dwellings in the town at the start of each calendar year, and which limited the number of permits to three per year for each developer or within a subdivision, was an arbitrary figure when it was selected in 1975 as the standard for limitation of new dwelling permits, and selection of an apparently arbitrary figure representing the growth rate at a particular point in time hardly constituted the assessment of community development needs and "careful study" contemplated by either the supreme court's decision in Beck v. Town of Raymond, 118 NH 793, 394 A.2d 847, 1978 N.H. LEXIS 296 (1978), or this section. Stoney-Brook Dev. Corp. v. Fremont, 124 N.H. 583, 474 A.2d 561, 1984 N.H. LEXIS 348 (N.H. 1984). (Decided under prior law).
Where a town's community plan, adopted in 1980, assumed a 3% growth rate that had been established in a zoning ordinance adopted in 1975, and where nothing in the record indicated that the community plan committee had made an independent determination that 3% would have been the growth rate unrestricted by the ordinance itself, the plan was invalid since the appropriateness of any particular growth restriction is premised on a determination of the normal growth rate. Stoney-Brook Dev. Corp. v. Fremont, 124 N.H. 583, 474 A.2d 561, 1984 N.H. LEXIS 348 (N.H. 1984). (Decided under prior law).
The record amply supported a master's finding that a town's comprehensive community plan was not a master plan or capital improvement program legally sufficient to support a growth control ordinance enacted pursuant to this section, and that the article of the town's zoning ordinance which required that the number of building permits issued for new dwellings be limited annually to 3% of the number of dwellings in the town at the start of each calendar year, and which limited the number of permits to three per year for each developer or within a subdivision, was illegal and unenforceable since the 3% growth rate was an arbitrary figure when it was selected in 1975 as the standard for the limitation of new dwelling building permits and did not constitute the assessment of community development needs and "careful study" contemplated by either the supreme court's decision in Beck v. Town of Raymond, 118 NH 793, 394 A.2d 847, 1978 N.H. LEXIS 296 (1978), or this section; since the community plan, adopted in 1980, perpetuated the growth rate at that arbitrary figure with no independent determination that 3% would have been the growth rate unrestricted by the ordinance itself; since the plan failed to address the ultimate objective of relaxing or ending growth controls and to articulate the means to accomplish that goal; and since it was unrealistic to suggest that limiting the town's growth indefinitely to 3% per year was guiding the town's growth, as expressed in its community plan, in a "reasonable, responsible and conscientious manner" when, by its own figures, the average growth in the seven abutting towns was almost double that growth rate. Stoney-Brook Dev. Corp. v. Fremont, 124 N.H. 583, 474 A.2d 561, 1984 N.H. LEXIS 348 (N.H. 1984). (Decided under prior law).

Cited:
Cited in Zukis v. Fitzwilliam, 135 N.H. 384, 604 A.2d 956, 1992 N.H. LEXIS 46 (1992); Quinlan v. Dover, 136 N.H. 226, 614 A.2d 1057, 1992 N.H. LEXIS 159 (1992).

RESEARCH REFERENCES AND PRACTICE AIDS

Cross References.

Authority to adopt or amend ordinances generally, see RSA 674:16.

Capital improvements programs generally, see RSA 674:5 et seq.

Innovative land use controls, see RSA 674:21.

Interim growth management ordinances, see RSA 674:23.

Master plans generally, see RSA 674:1 et seq.

New Hampshire Practice.

15-2 N.H.P. Land Use Planning and Zoning § 2.01.

15-3 N.H.P. Land Use Planning and Zoning § 3.04.

15-4 N.H.P. Land Use Planning and Zoning § 4.02.

15-14 N.H.P. Land Use Planning and Zoning § 14.03.

15-15 N.H.P. Land Use Planning and Zoning § 15.02.

15-15 N.H.P. Land Use Planning and Zoning § 15.04.

15-15 N.H.P. Land Use Planning and Zoning § 15.05.

15-15 N.H.P. Land Use Planning and Zoning § 15.06.

674:23. Temporary Moratoria and Limitations on Building Permits and the Approval of Subdivisions and Site Plans.

I. Upon recommendation of the planning board, the local legislative body may adopt or amend an ordinance establishing a moratorium or limitation on the issuance of building permits or the granting of subdivision or site plan approval for a definite term.

II. An ordinance may be adopted under this section in unusual circumstances that affect the ability of the municipality to provide adequate services and require prompt attention and to develop or alter a growth management process under RSA 674:22, a zoning ordinance, a master plan, or capital improvements program.

III. An ordinance under this section shall contain:

(a) A statement of the circumstances giving rise to the need for the moratorium or limitation.

(b) The planning board's written findings, on which subparagraph III(a) is based, which shall be included as an appendix to the ordinance.

(c) The term of the ordinance which shall not be more than one year.

(d) A list of the types or categories of development to which the ordinance applies.

(e) A description of the area of the municipality, if less than the entire municipality, to which the ordinance applies.

IV. An ordinance under this section shall be based on written findings by the planning board which:

(a) Describe the unusual circumstances that justify the ordinance.

(b) Recommend a course of action to correct or alleviate such circumstances.

V. An ordinance under this section may provide for the exemption from the moratorium or limitation of those types or categories of development that have minimal or no impact on the circumstances giving rise to the moratorium or limitation.

VI. An ordinance under this section may provide for a special exception or conditional use permit to allow development that has minimal or no impact on the circumstances giving rise to the moratorium or limitation.

VII. Additional ordinances may be adopted under this section only if they are based on circumstances that did not exist at the time of any prior ordinance. The authority to adopt ordinances under this section shall not be used to circumvent a municipality's need for a growth management ordinance under RSA 674:22.

HISTORY:

1983, 447:1. 1989, 266:16, eff. July 1, 1989. 1997, 15:1, eff. June 21, 1997. 2008, 360:2, eff. July 11, 2008.

Amendments

—2008.

The 2008 amendment rewrote the section to the extent that a detailed comparison would be impractical.

—1997.

Paragraph II(b): Substituted "90 days" for "45 days".

—1989.

Paragraph I: Substituted "town, or county in which there are located unincorporated towns or unorganized places" for "or town" following "program, a city".

Time Period for Modification of Existing Growth Management Ordinances.

2008, 360:3, eff. July 11, 2008, provided: "Each municipality that adopted a growth management ordinance under RSA 674:22 prior to the effective date of this act shall have until June 1, 2010 to amend its ordinance to conform to this act. If a municipality adopted an interim growth management ordinance under RSA 674:23 prior to the effective date of this act, that ordinance shall remain in effect until one year after its passage or until the municipality's next annual meeting, unless the ordinance prescribes an earlier expiration date, and unless a court of competent jurisdiction determines that the ordinance is illegal or is otherwise unenforceable."

NOTES TO DECISIONS

Analysis

1. Generally
2. Effect of master plan

1. Generally

A local interim growth management ordinance, which prohibited zoning and planning boards from formally accepting or acting upon any site plan applications creating a total of more than three lots for a one-year period was valid and not ultra vires where it was enacted pursuant to RSA 674:23, I and in accordance with the decision in Conway v. Stratham, 120 N.H. 257, 414 A.2d 539, 1980 N.H. LEXIS 269 (1980), which upheld the validity of a slow growth ordinance as a temporary measure, when it lasted for no more than one year towards the purpose of developing a comprehensive plan. Weare Land Use Ass'n v. Town of Weare, 153 N.H. 510, 899 A.2d 255, 2006 N.H. LEXIS 69 (N.H. 2006).

This section and RSA 674:22 enable a municipality to adopt an ordinance providing for controlled growth after its planning board has adopted a master plan and a capital improvement program designed to assess and balance community and regional development needs. Rancourt v. Barnstead, 129 N.H. 45, 523 A.2d 55, 1986 N.H. LEXIS 379 (N.H. 1986).

2. Effect of master plan

A planning board may not apply a master plan itself to limit development; it may only apply ordinances adopted pursuant to this section or RSA 674:22 to regulate or control the timing of development. Rancourt v. Barnstead, 129 N.H. 45, 523 A.2d 55, 1986 N.H. LEXIS 379 (N.H. 1986).

A municipal planning board cannot deny approval of a proposed subdivision on the basis of growth control rates set in a master plan without the municipality's first having enacted an ordinance providing for growth management or the board's having itself enacted a capital improvement program. Rancourt v. Barnstead, 129 N.H. 45, 523 A.2d 55, 1986 N.H. LEXIS 379 (N.H. 1986).

Cited:
Cited in Quinlan v. Dover, 136 N.H. 226, 614 A.2d 1057, 1992 N.H. LEXIS 159 (1992).

RESEARCH REFERENCES AND PRACTICE AIDS

Cross References.
Capital improvement programs generally, see RSA 674:5 et seq.
Emergency temporary zoning and planning ordinances, see RSA 674:24 et seq.
Master plans generally, see RSA 674:1 et seq.

New Hampshire Practice.
15-15 N.H.P. Land Use Planning and Zoning § 15.02.
15-15 N.H.P. Land Use Planning and Zoning § 15.03.
15-15 N.H.P. Land Use Planning and Zoning § 15.06.

Emergency Temporary Zoning and Planning Ordinances

NOTES TO DECISIONS

Analysis

1. Construction
2. Exercise of municipal power

1. Construction
Under power delegated to municipalities to enact zoning ordinances to promote "the general welfare of the community," the term "community" includes the region of which the municipality is a part. Britton v. Chester, 134 N.H. 434, 595 A.2d 492, 1991 N.H. LEXIS 95 (N.H. 1991).

2. Exercise of municipal power
Ordinance which in effect wrongfully excluded development of low and moderate income housing constituted an invalid exercise of the municipality's power under enabling legislation delegating to the town the power to zone municipality to promote the general welfare of the community, which included not only the municipality itself, but the region in which it was located. Britton v. Chester, 134 N.H. 434, 595 A.2d 492, 1991 N.H. LEXIS 95 (N.H. 1991).

RESEARCH REFERENCES AND PRACTICE AIDS

Cross References.
Procedure for enactment and adoption of ordinances and building codes generally, see RSA 675:1 et seq.
Procedure for enactment of emergency temporary zoning and planning ordinances in certain towns, see RSA 675:4-a.
Zoning generally, see RSA 674:16 et seq.

674:24. Definitions.

When used in this subdivision the following terms shall have the meanings given to them in this section:

I. "Frontage" means that portion of a lot bordering on a highway, street or right-of-way.

II. "Lot" means a parcel of land at least sufficient in size to meet the minimum requirements for use, coverage and area and to provide required yards and other open spaces. An undersize lot is permissible if it passes state standards for soil conditions and substantially meets the requirements here and if in existence on the date of adoption of this ordinance.

III. "Manufactured housing" means manufactured housing as defined by RSA 674:31.

IV. "Nonconforming" means use of land, building or premise which is not a use permitted by the provisions of this ordinance for the district in which such land, building or premise is situated.

V. "Permanent building" means any building resting upon a foundation or otherwise legally defined as "real estate".

VI. "Permanent resident" means an individual or family using any building continuously as a residence for a period of 6 months or more.

VII. "Right-of-way" means and includes all present and proposed town, state and federal highways and the land on either side of same as covered by statutes to determine the widths of rights-of-way.

VIII. "Setback" means the distance between the nearest portion of a building and a lot or right-of-way line, whichever is closer.

HISTORY:
1983, 447:1, eff. Jan. 1, 1984.

Revision note.
Paragraph III was revised, pursuant to the authority conferred by 1983, 447:4, for purposes of conformity with 1983, 230:5.

NOTES TO DECISIONS

Nonconforming use
Trial court erred in upholding zoning board of adjustment finding that mobile home park was a preexisting nonconforming use under this section where an interim zoning ordinance required a minimum density of one acre per site and mobile home park consisted of twenty-two sites on a single lot with 27.67 acres of developable land. Because the property constituted a single lot, it conformed to the density requirements of the ordinance and was therefore not a nonconforming use. Mudge v. Precinct of Haverhill Corner, 133 N.H. 881, 587 A.2d 603, 1991 N.H. LEXIS 10 (N.H. 1991).

RESEARCH REFERENCES AND PRACTICE AIDS

Cross References.
Definitions generally, see RSA 672.
State highways, see RSA 230.

New Hampshire Practice.
15-5 N.H.P. Land Use Planning and Zoning § 5.06.
15-29 N.H.P. Land Use Planning and Zoning § 29.16.

674:25. Districting Under Interim Zoning Ordinance.

For the purpose of regulating the use of land and the location and construction of buildings, any town adopting the provisions of an interim zoning ordinance shall be considered as one district with the following regulations and restrictions:

I. It shall be a district of residential agricultural use only. Business, commercial and industrial uses are prohibited in this district except as hereinafter provided.

II. Two apartments for permanent residents shall be the maximum allowable in any one given building.

III. Lots shall be at least one acre minimum in size, or larger, depending on soil and slope conditions, as may be suitable to sustain development according to state standards.

IV. There shall be observed the following setbacks in the construction of new buildings or in the relocation of existing ones:

(a) Minimum distance between any building and the edge of a right-of-way shall be 50 feet.

(b) Minimum distance from a lot's sidelines to any building shall be 30 feet; providing, however, that small detached accessory buildings may, as a special exception, be approved to within 15 feet of a lot line if the board of adjustment finds this would not be detrimental to the neighborhood.

(c) Minimum distance from a lot rearline to any building shall be 40 feet; providing, however, that small detached accessory buildings may, as a special exception, be approved to within 20 feet of a lot rearline, upon a finding of no detriment to the neighborhood.

(d) Maximum height of any building shall be 35 feet, with determination being the vertical distance from the average finished grade surrounding the building to a point midway between the highest and lowest points of the highest roof. Silos, barns and church towers are excepted, as are residential television and radio antennas.

(e) A deviation of 20 percent is allowed for side and rear setbacks in extenuating circumstances, as shall be recommended by the planning board or the selectmen if there is no planning board.

V. Home products and produce may be bought and sold and exposed for sale in this district.

VI. Hotels, motels and tourist homes may be maintained and operated, by special exception, provided that there be adequate parking and traffic provisions, that health standards be maintained, and that there be no detriment to the neighborhood.

VII. Private schools, nursing homes and sanitariums may be maintained by special exception, provided that there be adequate parking and traffic provisions, that health standards be maintained, and that there be no detriment to the neighborhood.

VIII. No building or set of buildings shall occupy more than 30 percent of its lot, nor shall it occupy more than 60 percent of its frontage if its front yard is less than 100 feet deep.

IX. No building, residence, or manufactured housing may be located anywhere in this district unless it meets all of the area and yard requirements of a residence in this district.

X. For the purpose of this ordinance, outdoor advertising shall be classified as commercial use and shall be permitted only if conforming to the following regulations:

(a) An outdoor sign shall not be larger than 6 square feet.

(b) It shall not be placed within 25 feet of a right-of-way nor within 150 feet of an intersection of a right-of-way unless affixed to a building and not extending beyond or above the same by more than 3 feet.

(c) Illumination shall be only by continuous nonflashing noncolored light.

(d) A permit for erection shall be procured from the building inspector, where present, and at the usual fee in accordance with the normal procedures in the community.

XI. Cluster development shall be permitted if the density does not exceed the provisions of paragraph III and if all other provisions of RSA 674:25–29 apply.

HISTORY:
1983, 447:1, eff. Jan. 1, 1984.

NOTES TO DECISIONS

Density
Trial court erred in overruling zoning board of adjustment determination that surface area of interior roads should not be included when calculating allowable density under this section. Mudge v. Precinct of Haverhill Corner, 133 N.H. 881, 587 A.2d 603, 1991 N.H. LEXIS 10 (N.H. 1991).

RESEARCH REFERENCES AND PRACTICE AIDS

Cross References.
Administration of ordinances, see RSA 674:29.
Districting of municipalities generally, see RSA 674:20.
Highways generally, see RSA 229 et seq.
Nonconforming properties and uses, see RSA 674:28.

New Hampshire Practice.
15-5 N.H.P. Land Use Planning and Zoning § 5.06.

674:26. Agricultural Use Under Interim Zoning Ordinance.

"Agricultural use" shall mean land used for agriculture, farming, dairying, pasturage, apiculture, horticulture, floriculture, silviculture and animal and poultry husbandry. Any such uses are permitted under an interim zoning ordinance except as restricted below:

I. The slaughtering of animals or poultry, except such as are raised for use of an owner or occupant; and the raising of animals or poultry or both for commercial purposes are permitted only as exceptions and subject to the following regulations:

(a) A lot shall be 8 acres or more in area.

(b) Each lot shall have at least 500 feet in frontage if adjacent to a right-of-way.

(c) A building for these purposes shall be placed at least 100 feet from any right-of-way.

(d) A building shall be located at least 200 feet from side or rear lines.

(e) Before approval by the board of adjustment, a public hearing shall be held with at least 15 days' notice of the time and place of the public hearing published in a paper of general circulation in the town or village district and with a legal notice thereof posted in at least 3 public places in the town or village district.

II. The proposed use shall not be approved if the board finds that it will cause hazard to health, property values or safety through fire, traffic, unsanitary conditions or through excessive noise, vibration, odor or other nuisance feature.

HISTORY:
1983, 447:1, eff. Jan. 1, 1984.

RESEARCH REFERENCES AND PRACTICE AIDS

Cross References.
Administration of ordinances, see RSA 674:29.
Commercial uses generally, see RSA 674:27.
Definitions generally, see RSA 674:24.
Permissible uses generally, see RSA 674:25.

New Hampshire Practice.
15-5 N.H.P. Land Use Planning and Zoning § 5.06.

674:27. Commercial Exceptions Under Interim Zoning Ordinance.

Business, commercial or industrial ventures other than those mentioned in RSA 674:25 or 674:26 may be given special exception by the board of adjustment upon submission and approval of a site plan; provided, however, that the following regulations and restrictions shall be observed:

I. No business, commercial or industrial venture or use shall be permitted which could cause any undue hazard to health, safety or property values or which is offensive to the public because of noise, vibration, excessive traffic, unsanitary conditions, noxious odor, smoke or other similar reason.

II. Sufficient acreage shall be included to allow the following setbacks:

(a) In the front, not less than 75 feet from a right-of-way to any building or parking lot having both an exit and an entrance and with grass or beautification in the buffer area.

(b) Side and rear: Not less than 50 feet from a building or parking lot to the lot line.

(c) Sufficient off-street parking to allow 300 square feet for each 3 anticipated patrons or employees on premises at the same time. In the case of service establishments, one car shall be deemed to contain 4 patrons.

III. On-premise advertising signs in connection with businesses receiving approval shall be exempt from the provisions of RSA 674:25, X and shall be considered as part of the application for commercial exception. They shall be limited to not more than 20 square feet in size and may be illuminated only by noncolored, nonflashing lights. Location may not be within any right-of-way nor within 150 feet of any intersection unless attached to a building.

IV. Before mining, excavation, or removal of soil, rock, sand or gravel or similar material, a special exception shall be received from the board of adjustment, subject to the usual fee permit. Excavation of earth shall be made in accordance with RSA 155-E.

V. All known abutters of any proposed business, commercial, or industrial site shall be notified by the board of adjustment by verified mail, as defined in RSA 451-C:1, VII, at least one week prior to any public hearing regarding the site. The names and addresses of the known abutters shall be supplied by the applicant on a plat plan to be submitted to the board of adjustment.

HISTORY:
1983, 447:1, eff. Jan. 1, 1984. 2017, 59:1, eff. August 1, 2017.

Amendment Notes
The 2017 amendment to this section by Ch. 59 substituted "by verified mail, as defined in RSA 451-C:1, VII" for "by certified mail" in the first sentence of V.

NOTES TO DECISIONS

Failure to obtain exception
Trial court improperly denied plaintiff's motion to vacate zoning board of adjustment's upholding of a building permit, where property owner failed to obtain a special exception for a commercial use of premises to be used for expansion of manufactured housing park. Mudge v. Precinct of Haverhill Corner, 133 N.H. 881, 587 A.2d 603, 1991 N.H. LEXIS 10 (N.H. 1991).

RESEARCH REFERENCES AND PRACTICE AIDS

Cross References.
Administration of ordinances, see RSA 674:29.
Agricultural uses generally, see RSA 674:26.
Permissible uses generally, see RSA 674:25.
Site plan review generally, see RSA 674:43, 44.

New Hampshire Practice.
15-5 N.H.P. Land Use Planning and Zoning § 5.06.

674:28. Nonconforming Buildings, Land, or Uses Under Interim Zoning Ordinance.

I. All nonconforming properties in active use when an interim ordinance is passed and adopted may continue indefinitely in their present use.

II. Any and all nonconforming property may be altered and expanded as the business and conditions warrant; providing, however, that any such expansion does not make any existing conforming structure nonconforming within the terms of the interim ordinance; nor shall such expansion bring any building within 35 feet of an abutter's building; nor shall the height exceed the limits as defined in RSA 674:25, IV(d); nor shall the use of such property be materially altered in purpose.

III. Any and all nonconforming property which is partially or totally destroyed by reason of obsolescence, fire or other act of God may be restored, remodeled and operated if done within 2 years; providing, however, that proximity to a lot line or right-of-way may be no nearer than the lesser of the original building and the setbacks defined in RSA

674:25, IV(a)–(c), and the height does not exceed the limits set forth in RSA 674:25, IV(d).

HISTORY:

1983, 447:1, eff. Jan. 1, 1984.

Revision note.

Substituted "RSA 674:25, IV(d)" for "RSA 674:25, IV, (d)" in pars. II and III and "RSA 674:25, IV(a)–(c)" for "RSA 674:25, IV, (a)–(c)" in par. III to conform reference to citation style employed in LEXIS New Hampshire Revised Statutes Annotated.

RESEARCH REFERENCES AND PRACTICE AIDS

Cross References.

Agricultural uses generally, see RSA 674:26.
Commercial uses generally, see RSA 674:27.
Permissible uses generally, see RSA 674:25.

New Hampshire Practice.

15-5 N.H.P. Land Use Planning and Zoning § 5.06.

674:29. Board of Adjustment and Administrative Provisions Under Interim Zoning Ordinance.

In any town in which an interim zoning ordinance has been adopted, and while it remains in effect, the board of selectmen shall be the appointing authority for the zoning board of adjustment and shall appoint the first such board forthwith, upon the adoption of interim zoning. Such board shall have all the powers and jurisdiction and be subject to all the duties, requirements and other provisions applicable to zoning boards of adjustment under RSA 673. The board of selectmen, if no building inspector exists, shall act jointly as the building inspector and administrative officer charged with enforcement and may issue building or use permits in the first instance if clearly permitted by law. The applicable provisions of RSA 677 shall govern motions for rehearing, appeals, enforcement, and interpretation. In addition to other remedies, any person convicted of violation of the provisions of RSA 674:25–29 by a court of competent jurisdiction shall be subject to a fine of not more than $50 for each offense. Each day the violation continues shall constitute a separate offense.

HISTORY:

1983, 447:1, eff. Jan. 1, 1984.

RESEARCH REFERENCES AND PRACTICE AIDS

Cross References.

Administration and enforcement of ordinances and building codes generally, see RSA 675.
Establishment and composition of zoning boards of adjustment generally, see RSA 673.
Powers of zoning boards of adjustment generally, see RSA 674:33.

New Hampshire Practice.

15-5 N.H.P. Land Use Planning and Zoning § 5.06.

674:30. Utility Structures.

Local ordinances, codes, and regulations enacted pursuant to this title shall apply to public utility structures, provided, however, that:

I. Notwithstanding the provisions of any such local ordinance, code, or regulation, a planning board, or its designee pursuant to paragraph II, upon application by a utility, may waive any requirement contained in an ordinance, code, or regulation for any unoccupied structure which is less than 200 square feet in area, which is necessary for the furnishing of utility service for the public health, safety, or general welfare, and for which the utility's siting options are limited by virtue of said structure being a physically integrated component of the utility's transmission or distribution apparatus. Any such waiver shall terminate, without further action by the planning board, if said structure ceases to be used for provisions of utility services.

II. The planning board may adopt regulations, pursuant to RSA 675:6 to ensure that such utility structures do not adversely affect the character of the area or create a hazard to the public. Such regulations may designate the building inspector, municipal engineer, road agent, or other official as agent of the planning board for purposes of this section. Notice shall be given by the planning board to abutters and the public, according to the procedures provided for in RSA 676:4, I(d), 10 days prior to any decision to be issued under such regulations. A hearing shall be held, if requested by the applicant or the abutters at any time prior to issuance of the decision, or if the board determines that a hearing is necessary. Notice of such hearing shall be given as provided in RSA 675:7, and no decision shall be issued until after the hearing.

III. A public utility which uses or proposes to use a structure which does not fit the criteria described in paragraph I, or fits those criteria and has been denied a waiver, or has been granted a waiver with conditions unacceptable to the utility when the waiver was applied for pursuant to paragraph I, may petition the public utilities commission to be exempted from the operation of any local ordinance, code, or regulation enacted under this title. The public utilities commission, following a public hearing, may grant such an exemption if it decides that the present or proposed situation of the structure in question is reasonably necessary for the convenience or welfare of the public and, if the purpose of the structure relates to water supply withdrawal, the exemption is recommended by the department of environmental services.

IV. Except for small power production facilities, as defined in RSA 362-A:1-a, X, and cogeneration facilities, as defined in RSA 362-A:1-a, I-c, owned and operated by a New Hampshire franchised utility, small power production facilities and cogeneration facilities shall not be considered to be public utilities under this section and may not petition the public utilities commission for an exemption from the operation of any regulation under this subdivision.

HISTORY:

1983, 447:1. 1986, 147:1. 1987, 152:1, eff. July 10, 1987. 1998, 124:5, eff. Aug. 1, 1998. 2006, 294:4, eff. August 14, 2006.

Amendments

—2006.
Paragraph IV: Substituted "I-c" for "I" preceding "owned and operated".

—1998.
Paragraph III: Added "and, if the purpose of the structure relates to water supply withdrawal, the exemption is recommended by the department of environmental services" following "welfare of the public" in the second sentence.

—1987.
Rewritten to the extent that a detailed comparison would be impracticable.

—1986.
Designated the existing provisions of the section as par. I and added par. II.

NOTES TO DECISIONS

Analysis

1. Construction
2. Attachment of conditions to exemption

1. Construction
The special provision in the statute relating to structures of public utilities was not to be construed as authorizing the regulation of governmental activities and uses, since public utilities uses have been commonly privately owned and operated. McGrath v. Manchester, 113 N.H. 355, 307 A.2d 830, 1973 N.H. LEXIS 273 (N.H. 1973). (Decided under prior law.)

2. Attachment of conditions to exemption
The public utilities commission could attach reasonable conditions in consideration of the interests of local residents when it granted a utility's petition for exemption from a zoning ordinance. Appeal of Milford Water Works, 126 N.H. 127, 489 A.2d 627, 1985 N.H. LEXIS 258 (N.H. 1985). (Decided under prior law.)

The public utilities commission had authority to condition its approval of an exemption from local zoning ordinances under its authority to consider the health and safety of local residents. Appeal of Milford Water Works, 126 N.H. 127, 489 A.2d 627, 1985 N.H. LEXIS 258 (N.H. 1985). (Decided under prior law.)

The public utilities commission acted within its authority, and rightfully considered the concerns of local residents, when it attached to its order granting a petition to exempt from local zoning ordinances structures related to a well project conditions which were designed to protect local residents against the possible adverse effects of wells on the ground water supply. Appeal of Milford Water Works, 126 N.H. 127, 489 A.2d 627, 1985 N.H. LEXIS 258 (N.H. 1985). (Decided under prior law.)

There was a reasonable basis in the record for finding that the public welfare and convenience required imposition, upon the grant of a petition for exemption of a well project from local zoning ordinances, of conditions designed to protect local residents against the possible adverse effects of the new wells on the ground water supply since, although expert testimony indicated that the effect of the well project on neighboring wells would be minimal, none of the experts stated that there would be no effect, and since there was testimony that other similar projects had caused depletion of neighboring wells. Appeal of Milford Water Works, 126 N.H. 127, 489 A.2d 627, 1985 N.H. LEXIS 258 (N.H. 1985). (Decided under prior law.)

Cited:
Cited in In re Public Serv. Co., 88 B.R. 521, 1988 Bankr. LEXIS 1030 (Bankr. D.N.H. 1988).

RESEARCH REFERENCES AND PRACTICE AIDS

Cross References.
Proceedings before public utilities commission generally, see RSA 365:8 et seq.

New Hampshire Practice.
13-15 N.H.P. Local Government Law § 510.

Manufactured Housing

RESEARCH REFERENCES AND PRACTICE AIDS

Cross References.
Modular building standards, see RSA 205-C.
Regulation of manufactured housing parks generally, see RSA 205-A.
Zoning generally, see RSA 674:16 et seq.

674:31. Definition.

As used in this subdivision, "manufactured housing" means any structure, transportable in one or more sections, which, in the traveling mode, is 8 body feet or more in width and 40 body feet or more in length, or when erected on site, is 320 square feet or more, and which is built on a permanent chassis and designed to be used as a dwelling with or without a permanent foundation when connected to required utilities, which include plumbing, heating and electrical heating systems contained therein. Manufactured housing as defined in this section shall not include presite built housing as defined in RSA 674:31-a.

HISTORY:
1983, 447:1. 1985, 104:1, eff. July 9, 1985.

Amendments

—1985.
Added the second sentence.

NOTES TO DECISIONS

Analysis

1. Construction
2. Construction with other law

1. Construction
Although a renter lived on an owner's property, which was not considered a "campground" under RSA 216-I:1, VII, the trial court did not reach the issue of whether the renter's camper/trailer was a "manufactured housing" unit within the meaning of RSA 205-A:1 and 674:31 before determining if the owner was a "landlord"; therefore, the owner's conviction under RSA 540-A:3, III had to be reversed and remanded for further proceedings. Comeau v. Vergato, 149 N.H. 508, 823 A.2d 764, 2003 N.H. LEXIS 74 (N.H. 2003).

2. Construction with other law
Debtors' mobile home was 14' x 80' and clearly fit within definition of manufactured housing. Therefore, it was real estate for purposes of federal bankruptcy law. In re Smith, 176 B.R. 298, 1994 Bankr. LEXIS 2099 (Bankr. D.N.H. 1994).

Cited:
Cited in Plainfield v. Sanville, 125 N.H. 825, 485 A.2d 1052, 1984 N.H. LEXIS 318 (1984); Chesterfield v. Brooks, 126 N.H. 64, 489 A.2d 600, 1985 N.H. LEXIS 274 (1985).

RESEARCH REFERENCES AND PRACTICE AIDS

New Hampshire Practice.
11-52 N.H.P. Probate Law & Procedure § 52-5.
15-13 N.H.P. Land Use Planning and Zoning § 13.02.

674:31-a. Definition; Presite Built Housing.

As used in this subdivision, "presite built housing" means any structure designed primarily for residential occupancy which is wholly or in substantial part made, fabricated, formed or assembled in off-site manufacturing facilities in conformance with the United States Department of Housing and Urban Development minimum property standards and local building codes, for installation, or assembly and installation, on the building site. For the purposes of this subdivision, presite built housing shall not include manufactured housing, as defined in RSA 674:31.

HISTORY:
1985, 104:2, eff. July 9, 1985.

674:32. Manufactured Housing.

I. Municipalities shall afford reasonable opportunities for the siting of manufactured housing, and a municipality shall not exclude manufactured housing completely from the municipality by regulation, zoning ordinance or by any other police power. A municipality which adopts land use control measures shall allow, in its sole discretion, manufactured housing to be located on individual lots in most, but not necessarily all, land areas in districts zoned to permit residential uses within the municipality, or in manufactured housing parks and subdivisions created for the placement of manufactured housing on individually owned lots in most, but not necessarily all, land areas in districts zoned to permit residential uses within the municipality, or in all 3 types of locations. Manufactured housing located on individual lots shall comply with lot size, frontage requirements, space limitations and other reasonable controls that conventional single family housing in the same district must meet. No special exception or special permit shall be required for manufactured housing located on individual lots or manufactured housing subdivisions unless such special exception or permit is required by the municipality for single family housing located on individual lots or in subdivisions. Municipalities permitting manufactured housing parks shall afford realistic opportunities for the development and expansion of manufactured housing parks. In order to provide such realistic opportunities, lot size and overall density requirements for manufactured housing parks shall be reasonable.

II. Notwithstanding paragraph I or any law or rule to the contrary, no zoning ordinance or bylaw shall prohibit an owner and occupier of a residence which has been damaged by fire or other disaster from placing a manufactured home on the lot of such residence and residing in such structure while the residence is being rebuilt. The period of such occupancy shall expire in 12 months from the placement of such structure or upon the issuance of a certificate of occupancy, whichever occurs first. Any such manufactured home shall be subject to state and local requirements relating to water supply and sewerage disposal. A manufactured home that is placed on a lot under this paragraph shall not attain the status of a vested nonconforming use.

HISTORY:
1983, 447:1. 1986, 91:2. 1987, 378:1. 1993, 158:1, eff. July 23, 1993.

Amendments

—1993.
Designated the existing provisions of the section as par. I and added par. II.

—1987.
Rewritten to the extent that a detailed comparison would be impracticable.

—1986.
Rewrote the first sentence and substituted "most" for "some" following "individual lots in" and "manufactured housing" for "mobile home" preceding "parks" and for "mobile homes" preceding "on individually owned lots" in the second sentence.

Legislative findings and purpose of 1986 amendment.
1986, 91:1, eff. July 18, 1986, provided:
"In the 1981 legislative session the general court passed chapter 406 relative to zoning of manufactured housing. In the declaration of purpose for that legislation, the general court acknowledged the need and right of individual citizens and families to decent, sanitary housing, and further recognized that the partial or total exclusion of manufactured housing would violate those rights. Since the passage of chapter 406 of the laws of 1981 housing costs have continued to increase substantially, thereby increasing the need for suitable moderately priced housing, such as manufactured housing. The general court reaffirms its findings that manufactured housing, when built in conformance with national codes, is almost indistinguishable from conventional site-built housing, and that the exclusion of manufactured housing is based upon outmoded perceptions. Since the passage of chapter 406, some municipalities across New Hampshire have failed to comply with chapter 406, or have complied by zoning in such a fashion as to relegate manufactured housing to zoning districts where land characteristics or costs effectively eliminate manufactured housing as an alternative to conventional site-built housing. It is the finding of this general court that some municipalities have misunderstood the intent of chapter 406 with the result that the original objective of the law has not been attained. It is the purpose of the general court that the passage of this act will ensure that the municipalities will exercise their authority to zone and regulate manufactured housing in such a manner that reasonable and realistic opportunities will exist for the placement of manufactured housing in all municipalities. To these ends, the purpose of this act is to:
"**I.** Impose an affirmative duty on municipalities to afford reasonable opportunities for manufactured housing;
"**II.** Require that manufactured housing on individual lots and in subdivisions be allowed in most, rather than some, zoning districts; or require that manufactured housing be allowed on individual lots in subdivisions and in manufactured housing parks; and
"**III.** Establish a date by which municipalities must be in compliance with RSA 674:32 or, if not in compliance, must allow manufactured housing in all residential areas within the municipality."

Time period for modification of municipal regulations, ordinances, etc.; effect of noncompliance with section —1987 amendment.
1987, 378:2, eff. May 26, 1987, provided:
"Every municipality which regulates manufactured housing by regulation, zoning ordinance, or by any other exercise of the police power shall be in compliance with the provisions of section 1 of this act by July 1, 1988. Any municipality which is not in compliance

with the provisions of section 1 of this act by July 1, 1988, shall permit manufactured housing in any area of the municipality in which other residential housing uses are permitted."

—1986 amendment.

1986, 91:3, eff. July 18, 1986, provided:

"Every municipality which regulates manufactured housing by regulation, zoning ordinance, or by any other exercise of the police power shall be in compliance with the provisions of section 2 of this act no later than June 1, 1987. Any municipality which is not in compliance with the provisions of section 2 of this act by June 1, 1987, shall allow manufactured housing in all residential areas within the municipality."

NOTES TO DECISIONS

Analysis

1. Validity of zoning ordinance
2. Failure to obtain exception
3. Grandfathered use

1. Validity of zoning ordinance

In a facial attack on a zoning ordinance, the case was remanded with instructions to the trial court to permit the plaintiffs to file a declaratory judgment petition setting forth specifically, clearly, and concisely their argument against the town's ordinance provisions regulating mobile homes. Delude v. Town of Amherst, 137 N.H. 361, 628 A.2d 251, 1993 N.H. LEXIS 90 (N.H. 1993).

Town ordinance prohibiting expansion of manufactured housing parks did not violate this section. Town was not a "municipality permitting manufactured housing parks" and thus was not subject to this section's requirement that municipalities afford opportunities for development and expansion of parks. Pope v. Hinsdale Planning Bd., 137 N.H. 233, 624 A.2d 1360, 1993 N.H. LEXIS 67 (N.H. 1993).

Requirement that mobile home parks obtain a special exception for a commercial use is valid and not violative of anti-exclusion protections of this section. Mudge v. Precinct of Haverhill Corner, 133 N.H. 881, 587 A.2d 603, 1991 N.H. LEXIS 10 (N.H. 1991).

Requirement of zoning ordinance that mobile home parks be limited to areas where city sewer and water is located was reasonable. Jensen's, Inc. v. Dover, 130 N.H. 761, 547 A.2d 277, 1988 N.H. LEXIS 60 (N.H. 1988).

Sufficient compliance with mandate of this section that areas be provided for the siting of manufactured housing was shown where mobile home parks were required to be located in R-40 zones and where vast majority of land areas zoned residential in a municipality were zoned R-40, with mobile homes permitted in subdivisions as of right and mobile home parks by special exception. Jensen's, Inc. v. Dover, 130 N.H. 761, 547 A.2d 277, 1988 N.H. LEXIS 60 (N.H. 1988).

Provision of zoning ordinance requiring a special exception and a finding, for a mobile home park, that it would not adversely affect overall land values, was permissible where the land value inquiry was reasonable, given the permitted density of nearly three times that of other residential development. Jensen's, Inc. v. Dover, 130 N.H. 761, 547 A.2d 277, 1988 N.H. LEXIS 60 (N.H. 1988).

A zoning ordinance which divided a town into two residential zones, and allowed mobile homes to be located in only one of the zones, complied with this section, which forbids total exclusion of such housing from a municipality, but affords wide discretion regarding its regulation. Chesterfield v. Brooks, 126 N.H. 64, 489 A.2d 600, 1985 N.H. LEXIS 274 (N.H. 1985). (Decided prior to 1986 amendment.)

Where town's zoning and mobile home ordinances did not clearly provide for individual ownership of lots upon which to place mobile homes, they failed to comply with the statute and were, therefore, invalid. Plainfield v. Sanville, 125 N.H. 825, 485 A.2d 1052, 1984 N.H. LEXIS 318 (N.H. 1984). (Decided under prior law.)

2. Failure to obtain exception

Trial court improperly denied plaintiff's motion to vacate zoning board of adjustment's upholding of a building permit, where property owner failed to obtain a special exception for a commercial use

of premises to be used for expansion of manufactured housing park. Mudge v. Precinct of Haverhill Corner, 133 N.H. 881, 587 A.2d 603, 1991 N.H. LEXIS 10 (N.H. 1991).

Manufactured housing parks are omitted from this section's exemption of manufactured housing from requirement that special exceptions to zoning ordinances be obtained by property owners. Mudge v. Precinct of Haverhill Corner, 133 N.H. 881, 587 A.2d 603, 1991 N.H. LEXIS 10 (N.H. 1991).

3. Grandfathered use

This section does not require a town to allow expansion of its existing manufactured housing parks. The goal of the legislature in enacting this section was to provide reasonable opportunities for the siting of manufactured housing, but not necessarily manufactured housing parks. Pope v. Hinsdale Planning Bd., 137 N.H. 233, 624 A.2d 1360, 1993 N.H. LEXIS 67 (N.H. 1993).

Cited:

Cited in Plaistow v. Nadeau, 126 N.H. 439, 493 A.2d 1158, 1985 N.H. LEXIS 320 (1985).

RESEARCH REFERENCES AND PRACTICE AIDS

New Hampshire Practice.

15-13 N.H.P. Land Use Planning and Zoning § 13.02.
15-14 N.H.P. Land Use Planning and Zoning § 14.05.

Agricultural Uses of Land

Purpose.

2000, 279:1, eff. July 1, 2001, provided:

"The purpose of this act [which enacted this subdivision and amended RSA 674:17], is to clarify the requirements of RSA 672:1, III-b, that farming and agriculture, as defined in RSA 21:34-a, shall not be unreasonably limited by the use of municipal planning and zoning powers."

674:32-a. Presumption.

In accordance with RSA 672:1, III-d, whenever agricultural activities are not explicitly addressed with respect to any zoning district or location, they shall be deemed to be permitted there, as either a primary or accessory use, so long as conducted in accordance with best management practices adopted by the commissioner of agriculture, markets, and food and with federal and state laws, regulations, and rules.

HISTORY:

2000, 279:3, eff. July 1, 2001.

NOTES TO DECISIONS

1. Effect on other provisions

RSA 674:17, I(i), RSA 672:1, III-b, RSA 672:1, III-d, and RSA 674:32-a do not support the contention that the legislature intended to require municipalities to allow "agritourism" within their borders; at most, they evince the legislature's general intent to support traditional agriculture and agricultural activities, and they demonstrate legislative intent to allow reasonable local regulation, not to preempt the entire field. Thus, they did not preempt a local ordinance. Forster v. Town of Henniker, 167 N.H. 745, 118 A.3d 1016, 2015 N.H. LEXIS 54 (N.H. 2015).

674:32-b. Existing Agricultural Uses.

Any agricultural use which exists pursuant to RSA 674:32-a may without restriction be expanded, altered to meet changing technology or markets, or changed to another agricultural use, as set forth in RSA 21:34-a, so long as any such expansion, alteration, or change complies with all federal and state laws, regulations, and rules, including best management practices adopted by the commissioner of agriculture, markets, and food; subject, however, to the following limitations:

I. Any new establishment, re-establishment after abandonment, or significant expansion of an operation involving the keeping of livestock, poultry, or other animals may be made subject to special exception, building permit, or other local land use board approval.

II. Any new establishment, re-establishment after abandonment, or significant expansion of a farm stand, retail operation, or other use involving on-site transactions with the public, including agritourism as defined in RSA 21:34-a, may be made subject to applicable special exception, building permit, or other local land use board approval and may be regulated to prevent traffic and parking from adversely impacting adjacent property, streets and sidewalks, or public safety.

HISTORY:
2000, 279:3, eff. July 1, 2001. 2016, 86:1, eff. July 18, 2016. 2016, 267:4, eff. June 16, 2016. 2016, 267:7, eff. July 18, 2016 at 12:01 a.m.

Amendment Notes
The 2016 amendments to this section by Ch. 86 substituted "re-establishment after abandonment" for "re-establishment after disuse" in paragraphs I and II.

The 2016 amendments to this section by Ch. 267:4, effective June 16, 2016, added "including agritourism as defined in RSA 21:34-a" in paragraph II.

The 2016 amendments to this section by Ch. 267:7, effective July 18, 2016 at 12:01 a.m., repealed and reenacted paragraph II.

674:32-c. Other General Provisions.

I. The tilling of soil and the growing and harvesting of crops and horticultural commodities, as a primary or accessory use, shall not be prohibited in any district.

II. Nothing in this subdivision shall exempt new, re-established, or expanded agricultural operations from generally applicable building and site requirements such as dimensional standards, setbacks, driveway and traffic regulations, parking requirements, noise, odor, or vibration restrictions or sign regulations; provided, however, that in circumstances where their literal application would effectively prohibit an agricultural use allowed by this subdivision, or would otherwise be unreasonable in the context of an agricultural use, the board of adjustment, building code board of appeals, or other applicable local board, after due notice and hearing, shall grant a waiver from such requirement to the extent necessary to reasonably permit the agricultural use, unless such waiver would have a demonstrated adverse effect on public health or safety, or the value of adjacent property. Such waiver shall

continue only as long as utilized for the permitted agricultural use.

III. Nothing in this subdivision shall apply to any aspect of an agricultural operation determined to be injurious to public health or safety under RSA 147. Nothing in this subdivision shall be deemed to modify or limit the duties and authority of the department of environmental services under RSA 485 or RSA 485-A or the commissioner of the department of agriculture, markets, and food under title XL.

IV. Nothing in this subdivision shall be deemed to affect the regulation of sludge or septage.

HISTORY:
2000, 279:3, eff. July 1, 2001.

RESEARCH REFERENCES AND PRACTICE AIDS

References in text.
Title XL, referred to in par. III, is classified to Title 40 of LEXIS New Hampshire Revised Statutes Annotated, which is comprised of chapters 425–437-a.

674:32-d. Agritourism Permitted.

Agritourism, as defined in RSA 21:34-a, shall not be prohibited on any property where the primary use is for agriculture, subject to RSA 674:32-b, II.

HISTORY:
2016, 267:5, eff. June 16, 2016.

Zoning Board of Adjustment and Building Code Board of Appeals

RESEARCH REFERENCES AND PRACTICE AIDS

Cross References.
Appointment and terms of members, see RSA 673:3 et seq.
Disqualification of members, see RSA 673:14.
Establishment of boards, see RSA 673:1.
Filling of vacancies, see RSA 673:12.
Meetings, see RSA 673:10, 15, 17.
Ordinance and code administration and enforcement generally, see RSA 676.
Ordinance and code adoption procedures generally, see RSA 675.
Rehearing and appeals procedures generally, see RSA 677.
Removal of members, see RSA 673:13.
Staff, see RSA 673:16.
Transfer of records of boards, see RSA 673:22.

674:33. Powers of Zoning Board of Adjustment.

I. The zoning board of adjustment shall have the power to:

(a) Hear and decide appeals if it is alleged there is error in any order, requirement, decision, or determination made by an administrative official in the enforcement of any zoning ordinance adopted pursuant to RSA 674:16; and

(b) Authorize, upon appeal in specific cases, a variance from the terms of the zoning ordinance if:

(1) The variance will not be contrary to the public interest;

(2) The spirit of the ordinance is observed;

(3) Substantial justice is done;

(4) The values of surrounding properties are not diminished; and

(5) Literal enforcement of the provisions of the ordinance would result in an unnecessary hardship.

(A) For purposes of this subparagraph, "unnecessary hardship" means that, owing to special conditions of the property that distinguish it from other properties in the area:

(i) No fair and substantial relationship exists between the general public purposes of the ordinance provision and the specific application of that provision to the property; and

(ii) The proposed use is a reasonable one.

(B) If the criteria in subparagraph (A) are not established, an unnecessary hardship will be deemed to exist if, and only if, owing to special conditions of the property that distinguish it from other properties in the area, the property cannot be reasonably used in strict conformance with the ordinance, and a variance is therefore necessary to enable a reasonable use of it.

The definition of "unnecessary hardship" set forth in subparagraph (5) shall apply whether the provision of the ordinance from which a variance is sought is a restriction on use, a dimensional or other limitation on a permitted use, or any other requirement of the ordinance.

I-a. Variances authorized under paragraph I shall be valid if exercised within 2 years from the date of final approval, or as further extended by local ordinance or by the zoning board of adjustment for good cause, provided that no such variance shall expire within 6 months after the resolution of a planning application filed in reliance upon the variance.

II. In exercising its powers under paragraph I, the zoning board of adjustment may reverse or affirm, wholly or in part, or may modify the order, requirement, decision, or determination appealed from and may make such order or decision as ought to be made and, to that end, shall have all the powers of the administrative official from whom the appeal is taken.

III. The concurring vote of 3 members of the board shall be necessary to reverse any action of the administrative official or to decide in favor of the applicant on any matter on which it is required to pass.

IV. A local zoning ordinance may provide that the zoning board of adjustment, in appropriate cases and subject to appropriate conditions and safeguards, make special exceptions to the terms of the ordinance. All special exceptions shall be made in harmony with the general purpose and intent of the zoning ordinance and shall be in accordance with

the general or specific rules contained in the ordinance. Special exceptions authorized under this paragraph shall be valid if exercised within 2 years from the date of final approval, or as further extended by local ordinance or by the zoning board of adjustment for good cause, provided that no such special exception shall expire within 6 months after the resolution of a planning application filed in reliance upon the special exception.

V. Notwithstanding subparagraph I(b), any zoning board of adjustment may grant a variance from the terms of a zoning ordinance without finding a hardship arising from the condition of a premises subject to the ordinance, when reasonable accommodations are necessary to allow a person or persons with a recognized physical disability to reside in or regularly use the premises, provided that:

(a) Any variance granted under this paragraph shall be in harmony with the general purpose and intent of the zoning ordinance.

(b) In granting any variance pursuant to this paragraph, the zoning board of adjustment may provide, in a finding included in the variance, that the variance shall survive only so long as the particular person has a continuing need to use the premises.

VI. The zoning board of adjustment shall not require submission of an application for or receipt of a permit or permits from other state or federal governmental bodies prior to accepting a submission for its review or rendering its decision.

VII. Neither a special exception nor a variance shall be required for a collocation or a modification of a personal wireless service facility, as defined in RSA 12-K:2.

HISTORY:

1983, 447:1. 1985, 103:20. 1987, 256:1, eff. July 17, 1987. 1998, 218:1, eff. Aug. 17, 1998. 2009, 307:6, eff. January 1, 2010. 2013, 93:1, 2, eff. August 19, 2013. 2013, 267:9, eff. September 22, 2013. 2013, 270:3, eff. September 22, 2013.

Contingent Renumbering.

2013, 267:13, eff. September 22, 2013, provided: "If SB 124-FN [ch. 270] of the 2013 regular legislative session becomes law, RSA 674:33, VI, as inserted by section 9 of this act, shall be renumbered as RSA 674:33, VII." Pursuant to the terms of this provision, RSA 674:33, VI, as added by 2013, 267:9 was renumbered to RSA 674:33, VII.

Amendment Notes

—2013.

The 2013 amendment by Chapter 93 added I-a and added the last sentence of IV.

The 2013 amendment by Chapter 267 added VII.

The 2013 amendment by Chapter 270 added VI.

—2009.

The 2009 amendment rewrote I(b) to the extent that a detailed comparison would be impracticable.

—1998.

Paragraph V: Added.

—1987.

Paragraph I(a): Substituted "of" for "thereof or" following "enforcement" and "to RSA 674:16" for "thereto" following "pursuant" and inserted "zoning" preceding "ordinance".

—1985.

Paragraph III: Substituted "on" for "or" preceding "any".

Severability of 2013 amendment.

2013, 267:12, eff. September 22, 2013, provided: "If any provision of this chapter or the application thereof to any person or circumstance is held invalid, such invalidity shall not affect other provisions or applications of the chapter which can be given effect without the invalid provision or application, and to that end the provisions of this chapter are declared to be severable."

Applicability of 2009 amendment.

2009, 307:7, eff. January 1, 2010, provided: "Section 6 [which amended this section by rewriting I(b)] of this act shall apply to any application or appeal for a variance that is filed on or after the effective date of this act."

Statement of Intent.

2009, 307:5, eff. January 1, 2010, provided: "The intent of section 6 [which amended this section by rewriting I(b)] of this act is to eliminate the separate "unnecessary hardship" standard for "area" variances, as established by the New Hampshire supreme court in the case of Boccia v. City of Portsmouth, 155 N.H. 84 (2004), and to provide that the unnecessary hardship standard shall be deemed satisfied, in both use and area variance cases, if the applicant meets the standards established in Simplex Technologies v. Town of Newington, 145 N.H. 727 (2001), as those standards have been interpreted by subsequent decisions of the supreme court. If the applicant fails to meet those standards, an unnecessary hardship shall be deemed to exist only if the applicant meets the standards prevailing prior to the Simplex decision, as exemplified by cases such as Governor's Island Club, Inc. v. Town of Gilford, 124 N.H. 126 (1983)."

NOTES TO DECISIONS

Analysis

I. Generally

1. Constitutional law.
2. Legislative intent.
3. Jurisdiction of board of adjustment.
4. Rules governing board of adjustment.
5. Failure to exhaust administrative remedy.
6. Authority of board of adjustment

II. Variances

10. Nature of variances.
11. Purposes of variances.
12. Ground for variances — Generally
13. —Unnecessary hardship
14. —Property values
15. Deliberations of board upon application for variance
16. Rendition of decision by board
17. Power of board as to granting of variances—Generally
18. —Attachment of conditions to variance

III. Special exceptions

19. Successive variance applications
30. Distinction between variances and special exceptions
31. Delegation of authority to make special exceptions to ordinances
32. Power of board as to special exceptions
33. Manufactured housing parks
34. Private docks
35. Remand by trial court
36. Standing to appeal
37. Appeal from planning board decision

I. Generally

1. Constitutional law.

Legislative power was not unconstitutionally conferred by empowering a board of adjustment to grant or refuse variances from compliance with the terms of a zoning ordinance. Sundeen v. Rogers, 83 N.H. 253, 141 A. 142, 1928 N.H. LEXIS 11 (N.H. 1928); Sundeen v. Rogers, 83 N.H. 253, 141 A. 142, 1928 N.H. LEXIS 11 (N.H. 1928). (Decided under prior law.)

2. Legislative intent.

This statute manifested a legislative intent to vest in a local board, whose members lived close to the circumstances and conditions, authority to determine the public need and the means of meeting it. Vannah v. Bedford, 111 N.H. 105, 276 A.2d 253, 1971 N.H. LEXIS 132 (1971), overruled in part, Cook v. Sanbornton, 118 N.H. 668, 392 A.2d 1201, 1978 N.H. LEXIS 267 (1978). (Decided under prior law.)

3. Jurisdiction of board of adjustment.

The jurisdiction of a town zoning board of adjustment related to the granting of special exceptions and variances and not to the consideration of orders by the selectmen, and, therefore, a zoning board had no jurisdiction to review an order of a board of town selectmen. Derry v. Simonsen, 117 N.H. 1010, 380 A.2d 1101, 1977 N.H. LEXIS 485 (N.H. 1977). (Decided under prior law.)

4. Rules governing board of adjustment.

In accordance with its power to pass zoning regulations and to establish a board of adjustment for the purpose of granting variances and exceptions from the terms of zoning ordinances, a municipality could prescribe reasonable procedures for the board to follow in order to carry out its purposes. Lavallee v. Britt, 118 N.H. 131, 383 A.2d 709, 1978 N.H. LEXIS 358 (N.H. 1978). (Decided under prior law.)

Pursuant to its power to pass zoning regulations and to establish a board of adjustment for the purpose of granting variances and exceptions from the terms of zoning ordinances, a municipality could impose, by municipal ordinance, a requirement that the board of adjustment record its findings or reasons for granting or refusing to grant a variance. Lavallee v. Britt, 118 N.H. 131, 383 A.2d 709, 1978 N.H. LEXIS 358 (N.H. 1978). (Decided under prior law.)

The statutory requirement that the board of adjustment adopt rules "in accordance with the provisions of the ordinances" contemplated such rules as related to procedure before the board, and the statutory command that they should conform to the ordinances did not mean that there must have been a provision in the ordinance therefor. Stone v. Cray, 89 N.H. 483, 200 A. 517, 1938 N.H. LEXIS 60 (N.H. 1938). (Decided under prior law.)

5. Failure to exhaust administrative remedy.

Homeowners' declaratory judgment action challenging the issuance of a building permit for an adjoining lot was properly dismissed because the homeowners failed to appeal the issuance of the permit to the local zoning board and thus they failed to exhaust their administrative remedies. McNamara v. Hersh, 157 N.H. 72, 945 A.2d 18, 2008 N.H. LEXIS 38 (N.H. 2008).

Zoning board of adjustment could review an appeal from a historic district commission de novo. RSA 674:33, II confers upon a zoning board of adjustment all the powers of the administrative official from whom the appeal is taken; when hearing and deciding an appeal, therefore, the board is authorized by statute to step into the shoes of the administrative official, the functional equivalent of de novo review. Ouellette v. Town of Kingston, 157 N.H. 604, 956 A.2d 286, 2008 N.H. LEXIS 98 (N.H. 2008).

Zoning board of adjustment may hear appeals de novo, based upon the broad powers granted to it by statute. Ouellette v. Town of Kingston, 157 N.H. 604, 956 A.2d 286, 2008 N.H. LEXIS 98 (N.H. 2008).

6. Authority of board of adjustment

Even assuming that an abutter's appeal challenged only whether the site qualified as a contractor's yard, the court could not conclude that by considering whether the use was potentially permitted under any other zoning classification, the zoning board of adjustment (ZBA) exceeded its statutory authority. By considering whether the proposed use was permitted under any zoning provision, the ZBA demonstrated its willingness to review petitioners' request for approval of the proposed use. Accurate Transp., Inc. v.

Town of Derry, 168 N.H. 108, 123 A.3d 263, 2015 N.H. LEXIS 81 (N.H. 2015).

II. Variances

10. Nature of variances.

A variance was in the nature of a waiver of the strict letter of a zoning ordinance without sacrifice to its spirit or purpose. New London v. Leskiewicz, 110 N.H. 462, 272 A.2d 856, 1970 N.H. LEXIS 200 (N.H. 1970). (Decided under prior law.)

11. Purposes of variances.

Variances were provided for by zoning statutes so that litigation of constitutional questions could be avoided and a speedy and adequate remedy afforded in cases where special conditions or exceptional environment presented such questions. Bouley v. Nashua, 106 N.H. 79, 205 A.2d 38, 1964 N.H. LEXIS 43 (N.H. 1964). (Decided under prior law.)

12. Ground for variances — Generally

In the absence of contrary legislative intent, contained in every variance application is the threshold question whether the applicant's proposed use of property requires a variance because the zoning board of adjustment (ZBA) will invariably consider this issue in deciding whether unnecessary hardship exists. Given the complexity of zoning regulation, the obligation of municipalities to provide assistance to all their citizens seeking approval under zoning ordinances, and the importance of the constitutional right to enjoy property, the New Hampshire Supreme Court cannot accept that the mere filing of a variance application limits the ZBA's or the superior court's consideration of whether the applicant's proposed use of property requires a variance in the first place. Bartlett v. City of Manchester, 164 N.H. 634, 62 A.3d 855, 2013 N.H. LEXIS 17 (N.H. 2013).

Remand for consideration of the factor of unnecessary hardship was required when the trial court improperly reversed the decision of a zoning board of adjustment (ZBA) granting a variance to erect parapet signs. The ZBA used the correct test to determine whether the public interest and spirit-of-the-ordinance factors were met, and there was evidence to support the ZBA's findings on these factors; the evidence supported the ZBA's finding that the general public would realize no appreciable gain from a denial of the parapet sign variance; and the assertion that the signs would have no effect on surrounding property values was uncontradicted. Harborside Assocs. v. Parade Residence Hotel, 162 N.H. 508, 34 A.3d 584, 2011 N.H. LEXIS 133 (N.H. 2011).

Trial court properly upheld the grant of a variance for the applicant, which operated a hotel, to erect marquee signs. Because the variance was to install signs on the building, it was proper to focus upon the building's size to determine whether special conditions existed; the evidence supported a finding that the building was unique because of its size; the applicant did not have to establish that its signs were "necessary" to its hotel operation; the unnecessary hardship test for obtaining an area variance was defunct; and in reaching its decision as to whether the signs would diminish property values, the zoning board was entitled to resolve conflicting evidence and credibility issues as well as to rely upon its own knowledge, experience and observations. Harborside Assocs. v. Parade Residence Hotel, 162 N.H. 508, 34 A.3d 584, 2011 N.H. LEXIS 133 (N.H. 2011).

In denying a variance that would replace a nonconforming building in a lake district with a nonconforming cluster development, a zoning board reasonably found the proposal to be contrary to the public interest and inconsistent with the spirit of the ordinance creating the district. The proposed development did not conform to acreage and frontage requirements of the district and contributed to lake-side congestion and over-development; moreover, the majority of the cluster would be on a six-acre parcel. Nine A, LLC v. Town of Chesterfield, 157 N.H. 361, 950 A.2d 197, 2008 N.H. LEXIS 71 (N.H. 2008).

The trial court did not err in ruling that variances to construct a wireless communications tower were consistent with the spirit of the ordinance, that the variances were not contrary to the public interest, and that substantial justice would be done in granting the variances. There was evidence that the tower: (1) would be reduced to 146 feet, would not have a light on its top, and would be screened

from view on the ground with vegetative buffer and disguised at the top as a pine tree; (2) would be located at a point farthest from abutting properties and would not generate noise, traffic, or odors; (3) would alleviate a significant gap in coverage and would limit the need for any further towers; and (4) was the only reasonable way to remedy an existing gap in coverage. Daniels v. Town of Londonderry, 157 N.H. 519, 953 A.2d 406, 2008 N.H. LEXIS 88 (N.H. 2008).

Where the zoning board of adjustment made no explicit findings on the RSA 674:33, I(b) variance factors in granting the variance to the applicant, it implicitly found that the factors were met in granting the variance; therefore, the trial court erred in finding that the requirements for a variance were not met since it could not make factual findings, but the board gave only cursory consideration to the variance issue, so a remand was necessary. Thomas v. Town of Hooksett, 153 N.H. 717, 903 A.2d 963, 2006 N.H. LEXIS 99 (N.H. 2006).

Where a zoning board specifically found that an owner had not satisfied two of the requirements under RSA 674:33, I(b) in the owner's application for a rehearing of the board's denial of a variance, the owner did not have to raise the conditions that were not specifically denied by the board; therefore, the trial court erred in interpreting RSA 677:3 as requiring the owner to raise all five conditions for a variance in an application for rehearing in order to preserve a right of appeal. Robinson v. Town of Hudson, 149 N.H. 255, 821 A.2d 959, 2003 N.H. LEXIS 33 (N.H. 2003).

Wrong legal standard was used to deny plaintiffs' request for a variance, where standard placed a higher burden on plaintiffs than was required by statute. Gray v. Seidel, 143 N.H. 327, 726 A.2d 1283, 1999 N.H. LEXIS 5 (N.H. 1999).

The statutory language authorizes a zoning board of appeals to attach reasonable conditions to variances granted "so that the spirit of the ordinance shall be observed and substantial justice done." Healey v. Town of New Durham Zoning Bd. of Adjustment, 140 N.H. 232, 665 A.2d 360, 1995 N.H. LEXIS 132 (N.H. 1995).

A variance was properly granted to allow a property owner to build a residence where (1) there was testimony that designing a house to fit on the property without a variance was "functionally not a reasonable thought," and (2) the property's slope, abundance of ledge, and remote location defeated the argument that there were uses for the property other than residential. Husnander v. Town of Barnstead, 139 N.H. 476, 660 A.2d 477, 1995 N.H. LEXIS 36 (N.H. 1995), overruled in part, Simplex Techs., Inc. v. Town of Newington, 145 N.H. 727, 766 A.2d 713, 2001 N.H. LEXIS 15 (N.H. 2001).

A zoning board of appeals is authorized to issue a variance from the terms of the zoning ordinance, provided that the variance is not contrary to the public interest, if, owing to special conditions, a literal enforcement of the provisions of the ordinance will result in unnecessary hardship, and so that the spirit of the ordinance will be observed and substantial justice done, and provided that the variance will not result in diminution of surrounding property values. Husnander v. Town of Barnstead, 139 N.H. 476, 660 A.2d 477, 1995 N.H. LEXIS 36 (N.H. 1995), overruled in part, Simplex Techs., Inc. v. Town of Newington, 145 N.H. 727, 766 A.2d 713, 2001 N.H. LEXIS 15 (N.H. 2001).

Party seeking zoning variance bears burden of establishing each of the requirements for a variance. Grey Rocks Land Trust v. Hebron, 136 N.H. 239, 614 A.2d 1048, 1992 N.H. LEXIS 162 (1992), overruled in part, Simplex Techs., Inc. v. Town of Newington, 145 N.H. 727, 766 A.2d 713, 2001 N.H. LEXIS 15 (2001), (overruled on other grounds, Simplex Techs., Inc. v. Town of Newington, 145 N.H. 727, 766 A.2d 713, 2001 N.H. LEXIS 15 (2001).)

To support a variance, it must have been found that no diminution in value of surrounding properties would be suffered; granting the permit would be of benefit to the public interest; denial of the permit would result in unnecessary hardship to the owner seeking it; granting the permit would do substantial justice; and the use would not be contrary to the spirit of the ordinance. Ouimette v. Somersworth, 119 N.H. 292, 402 A.2d 159, 1979 N.H. LEXIS 300 (N.H. 1979). (Decided under prior law.)

A variance could be granted if the requested use did not diminish the value of the surrounding properties, would benefit the public interest, denial would cause unnecessary hardship to the person seeking it and the use would not be contrary to the spirit of the ordinance. Alcorn v. Rochester Zoning Bd. of Adjustment, 114 N.H.

491, 322 A.2d 608, 1974 N.H. LEXIS 309 (N.H. 1974). (Decided under prior law.)

In order to support a variance it was necessary to have found that no diminution in value of surrounding properties would be suffered, that granting of the permit would be of benefit to the public interest, that its denial would result in unnecessary hardship to owner seeking it, that by granting permits substantial justice would be done, and that the use would not be contrary to the spirit of the ordinance. Gelinas v. Portsmouth, 97 N.H. 248, 85 A.2d 896, 1952 N.H. LEXIS 3 (N.H. 1952). (Decided under prior law.)

13. —Unnecessary hardship

In deciding whether a variance application satisfied the criterion of unnecessary hardship under RSA 674:33, I(b)(5), the trial court correctly determined that it had to consider the permissible uses of the property under the ordinance, including the accessory use provision. Thus, it had subject matter jurisdiction to consider accessory uses. Bartlett v. City of Manchester, 164 N.H. 634, 62 A.3d 855, 2013 N.H. LEXIS 17 (N.H. 2013).

Considerations of fairness, convenience, and policy require a defendant in a private nuisance suit to plead reliance on the accessory use doctrine. These considerations, however, do not warrant the imposition of an affirmative pleading requirement in the variance context where the zoning board of adjustment must consider what uses of a property are allowed before it can decide whether unnecessary hardship exists. Bartlett v. City of Manchester, 164 N.H. 634, 62 A.3d 855, 2013 N.H. LEXIS 17 (N.H. 2013).

Fact that petitioner's lot was larger than neighboring lots did not mean that limiting him to one dwelling on a three-acre lot constituted an unnecessary hardship under the variance statute. The zoning board of adjustment had considered both unnecessary hardship tests under the statute. Saviano v. Town of Atkinson, 2013 N.H. LEXIS 117 (N.H. Oct. 25, 2013).

By creating a lot that lacked sufficient frontage, petitioner's predecessor in title created the hardship for which petitioner now sought a variance; thus, it was proper to find that there was a self-created hardship under RSA 674:33, I(b). It was error, however, to make this finding of self-created hardship dispositive. Kwader v. Town of Chesterfield, 2011 N.H. LEXIS 45 (N.H. Mar. 21, 2011).

When an application to build a wireless telecommunications tower is designed to fill a significant gap in coverage, the suitability of a specific parcel of land for that purpose should be considered for purposes of determining hardship in relation to a variance; the fact that a proposed location is centrally located within the gap, has the correct topography, or is of an adequate size to effectively eliminate the gap in coverage may make it unique under the umbrella of the Telecommunications Act of 1996. Similarly, that there are no feasible alternatives to the proposed site may also make it unique; thus, although a parcel of land may be similar to the surrounding properties in terms of its general characteristics, it may still be "unique" for purposes of hardship when considered in light of the Act. Daniels v. Town of Londonderry, 157 N.H. 519, 953 A.2d 406, 2008 N.H. LEXIS 88 (N.H. 2008).

In reviewing a grant of variances to build a wireless communications tower, the trial court did not err in finding unnecessary hardship for both the use and area variances. There was evidence that the tower was necessary to fill a significant gap in coverage, that no reasonable alternatives would achieve similar coverage, and that the tower and its surrounding compound would not create noise or traffic. Daniels v. Town of Londonderry, 157 N.H. 519, 953 A.2d 406, 2008 N.H. LEXIS 88 (N.H. 2008).

There was no error in the trial court's failure to explicitly address each of the applicable factors in its order upholding a variance for a wireless telecommunications tower. The trial court accurately set forth the hardship standard for both use and area variances, noted relevant evidence before the zoning board of adjustment, and made generalized conclusions applicable to these factors; although a specific explanation of the evidence supporting its hardship findings was preferable, given the extensive record in the case, the trial court had adequately addressed the hardship standard. Daniels v. Town of Londonderry, 157 N.H. 519, 953 A.2d 406, 2008 N.H. LEXIS 88 (N.H. 2008).

In a zoning appeal wherein a trial court reversed a city's denial of an applicant's variance request to build a halfway house on the basis that it was a correctional facility that was not permitted within any of the city's zoning districts, the reviewing court reversed the trial court because no evidence existed in the record that demonstrated how the size and layout of the specific building proposed made the property particularly appropriate for the proposed use, no evidence demonstrated that the proposed site was unique, nor did the evidence reasonably support the trial court's conclusion that the applicant's property was burdened by the restriction in a manner that was distinct from similarly situated property. Thus, the applicant did not satisfy the first prong of the Simplex test to establish unnecessary hardship. Cmty. Res. for Justice, Inc. v. City of Manchester, 154 N.H. 748, 917 A.2d 707, 2007 N.H. LEXIS 11 (N.H. 2007).

When the unnecessary hardship prong of the variance test under RSA 674:33, I(b) is applied to use variances, a court applies Simplex Technologies v. Town of Newington, 145 N.H 727, 766 A.2d 713, 2001 N.H. LEXIS 15 (2001), but when the unnecessary hardship prong is applied to area variances, the factors that should be considered include: (1) whether an area variance is needed to enable the applicant's proposed use of the property given the special conditions of the property; and (2) whether the benefit sought by the applicant can be achieved by some other method reasonably feasible for the applicant to pursue, other than an area variance, and this second factor includes consideration of whether the variance is necessary to avoid an undue financial burden on the owner. Thus, remand was required where the record supported a finding that the variances granted to an intervenor by a city's zoning board of adjustment were needed to enable the proposed use of the property as a hotel, but where it was unclear whether there were reasonably feasible alternative methods to implement the proposed use, without undue financial burden to the landowner. Boccia v. City of Portsmouth, 151 N.H. 85, 855 A.2d 516, 2004 N.H. LEXIS 94 (N.H. 2004), superseded by statute as stated in Harborside Assocs. v. Parade Residence Hotel, 162 N.H. 508, 34 A.3d 584, 2011 N.H. LEXIS 133 (N.H. 2011), superseded by statute as stated in Hannaford Bros. Co. v. Town of Rindge, 2016 N.H. LEXIS 145 (N.H. May 12, 2016).

State supreme court reversed the superior court's judgment finding that property owners who owned a cabin by a lake were entitled to a variance from a local zoning ordinance so they could expand their cabin because the superior court did not address the factors which the supreme court established in its Boccia decision for determining unnecessary hardship in an area variance application. Shopland v. Town of Enfield, 151 N.H. 219, 855 A.2d 392, 2004 N.H. LEXIS 127 (N.H. 2004).

In order to establish an unnecessary hardship for variance purposes, an applicant needed to show that the zoning interfered with the reasonable use of the property, considering its unique setting in its environment; the evidence supported the grant of a variance to build a barn. Rancourt v. City of Manchester, 149 N.H. 51, 816 A.2d 1011, 2003 N.H. LEXIS 2 (N.H. 2003).

To establish unnecessary hardship, applicants for variances must prove: "(1) a zoning restriction as applied to their property interferes with their reasonable use of the property, considering the unique setting of the property in its environment; (2) no fair and substantial relationship exists between the general purposes of the zoning ordinance and the specific restriction on the property; and (3) the variance would not injure the public or private rights of others." Town of Plaistow Bd. of Selectmen v. Town of Plaistow Zoning Bd. of Adjustment, 146 N.H. 263, 769 A.2d 397, 2001 N.H. LEXIS 67 (N.H. 2001).

The Supreme Court of New Hampshire held that the court's definition of undue hardship had become too restrictive in light of the constitutional protections by which it must be tempered, i.e., the right to acquire, possess, and protect property under N.H. Const. pt. I, arts. 2, 12, and decided to depart from the restrictive approach that had defined unnecessary hardship and adopted an approach more considerate of the constitutional right to enjoy property. Henceforth, applicants for a variance could establish unnecessary hardship by proof that: (1) a zoning restriction as applied to their property interferes with their reasonable use of the property, considering the unique setting of the property in its environment; (2) no fair and substantial relationship exists between the general purposes of the zoning ordinance and the specific restriction on the property; and (3) the variance would not injure the public or private rights of others. Simplex Techs., Inc. v. Town of

Newington, 145 N.H. 727, 766 A.2d 713, 2001 N.H. LEXIS 15 (N.H. 2001).

Superior court erred by finding hardship necessary to sustain zoning board's award of a zoning variance to individual defendants to build two-car garage; finding that garage was necessary to keep defendant's car free from snow and ice, to enable defendant to make fast and unanticipated wintertime trips to the site of his job as an airline pilot called upon to make emergency flights, established nothing more than a need personal to the landowner, and did not satisfy condition that hardship be unique to applicant's parcel. Crossley v. Pelham, 133 N.H. 215, 578 A.2d 319, 1990 N.H. LEXIS 64 (N.H. 1990).

A variance from a municipal ordinance could be granted where, owing to special conditions, a literal enforcement of the provisions of the ordinance would result in an unnecessary hardship. Little v. Rye, 120 N.H. 533, 419 A.2d 396, 1980 N.H. LEXIS 347 (N.H. 1980). (Decided under prior law.)

Where applicant for zoning variance to erect an additional apartment building on property testified that his income from the existing apartments was sufficient to meet expenses and his reason for requesting the variance was to obtain a greater return on his investment, the court properly found that the town's board of adjustment had improperly granted a zoning variance since there was no evidence to demonstrate those "special conditions" which would distinguish applicant's property from other property and warrant a variance based upon unnecessary hardship. Rowe v. Salem, 119 N.H. 505, 403 A.2d 428, 1979 N.H. LEXIS 329 (N.H. 1979). (Decided under prior law.)

The criterion for unnecessary hardship to warrant the issuance of a zoning variance was not the uniqueness of the plight of the owner but the uniqueness of the land causing the plight. Rowe v. Salem, 119 N.H. 505, 403 A.2d 428, 1979 N.H. LEXIS 329 (N.H. 1979). (Decided under prior law.)

A "hardship" of the type needed for a zoning variance resulted only if use of the particular property was unduly restricted by the zoning ordinance because of special conditions unique to that property which distinguished it from all others similarly restricted. Ouimette v. Somersworth, 119 N.H. 292, 402 A.2d 159, 1979 N.H. LEXIS 300 (N.H. 1979). (Decided under prior law.)

Inability to use land for one particular purpose was irrelevant to whether a variance should be granted. Ouimette v. Somersworth, 119 N.H. 292, 402 A.2d 159, 1979 N.H. LEXIS 300 (N.H. 1979). (Decided under prior law.)

The language of the statute authorizing a zoning board of adjustment to grant variances did not distinguish between types of variances but instead required a showing of unnecessary hardship whenever an owner of property requested a variance. Ouimette v. Somersworth, 119 N.H. 292, 402 A.2d 159, 1979 N.H. LEXIS 300 (N.H. 1979). (Decided under prior law.)

To warrant the granting of a variance based upon a finding of unnecessary hardship there must have been something special about the applicant's property to distinguish it from other land in the same area with respect to its suitability for the use for which it was zoned. Carbonneau v. Exeter, 119 N.H. 259, 401 A.2d 675, 1979 N.H. LEXIS 289 (N.H. 1979). (Decided under prior law.)

A variance would be granted when special conditions created a situation in which strict enforcement of a zoning ordinance would result in unnecessary hardship for property owner. Rye v. McMahon, 117 N.H. 857, 379 A.2d 807, 1977 N.H. LEXIS 448 (N.H. 1977). (Decided under prior law.)

An unnecessary hardship was one suffered as the result of interference with the right to use property as one saw fit even though no public or private rights were injuriously affected by the use. Carter v. Nashua, 113 N.H. 407, 308 A.2d 847, 1973 N.H. LEXIS 285 (N.H. 1973). (Decided under prior law.)

Financial hardship did not alone warrant a variance, but if it was unduly oppressive because of conditions of the property distinguishing it from other properties similarly restricted it could constitute unnecessary hardship. Carter v. Nashua, 113 N.H. 407, 308 A.2d 847, 1973 N.H. LEXIS 285 (N.H. 1973). (Decided under prior law.)

A hardship resulted if a restriction upon use, when applied to a particular property, became arbitrary, confiscatory, or unduly oppressive because of conditions of the property distinguishing it from other properties similarly restricted. Vannah v. Bedford, 111 N.H. 105, 276 A.2d 253, 1971 N.H. LEXIS 132 (1971), overruled in part,

Cook v. Sanbornton, 118 N.H. 668, 392 A.2d 1201, 1978 N.H. LEXIS 267 (1978). (Decided under prior law.)

An unnecessary hardship was one suffered as the result of interference with the right to use property as the owner saw fit, although no public or private rights were injuriously affected thereby. Vannah v. Bedford, 111 N.H. 105, 276 A.2d 253, 1971 N.H. LEXIS 132 (1971), overruled in part, Cook v. Sanbornton, 118 N.H. 668, 392 A.2d 1201, 1978 N.H. LEXIS 267 (1978). (Decided under prior law.)

The unnecessary hardship referred to in the statute must have related to the owner and not to an option holder. Welch v. Nashua, 108 N.H. 92, 227 A.2d 600, 1967 N.H. LEXIS 128 (N.H. 1967). (Decided under prior law.)

The hardship referred to in the statute must have been one to whom the provision was designed to protect, and the statute was not designed to afford relief to a mere option holder of land as to which use variance was sought. Conery v. Nashua, 103 N.H. 16, 164 A.2d 247, 1960 N.H. LEXIS 3 (N.H. 1960). (Decided under prior law.)

Financial hardship in and of itself did not warrant the granting of a variance from the terms of a zoning ordinance. St. Onge v. Concord, 95 N.H. 306, 63 A.2d 221, 1949 N.H. LEXIS 158 (N.H. 1948). (Decided under prior law.)

A hardship within the meaning of the statute could result if the restriction upon use, when applied to a particular property, became arbitrary, confiscatory, or unduly oppressive because of conditions of the property distinguishing it from other properties similarly restricted. St. Onge v. Concord, 95 N.H. 306, 63 A.2d 221, 1949 N.H. LEXIS 158 (N.H. 1948). (Decided under prior law.)

14. —Property values

When a zoning board of appeals granted variances to construct a wireless communications tower, there was substantial evidence supporting its finding that there would be no loss of value to the surrounding properties, including the numerous studies submitted, the testimony of at least one appraiser, the lack of abatement requests in comparable areas, its own knowledge of the area, and personal observations made during simulated height tests. Daniels v. Town of Londonderry, 157 N.H. 519, 953 A.2d 406, 2008 N.H. LEXIS 88 (N.H. 2008).

15. Deliberations of board upon application for variance

In allowing an applicant variances to build a wireless telecommunications tower, a zoning board of adjustment properly considered the implications of the Telecommunications Act of 1996, which in certain circumstances could preempt local law. In doing so, the board had not allowed the Act to preempt its own findings regarding the variance criteria. Daniels v. Town of Londonderry, 157 N.H. 519, 953 A.2d 406, 2008 N.H. LEXIS 88 (N.H. 2008).

In arriving at a decision, the members of the board could consider their own knowledge concerning such factors as traffic conditions, surrounding uses, etc., resulting from their familiarity with the area involved. Vannah v. Bedford, 111 N.H. 105, 276 A.2d 253, 1971 N.H. LEXIS 132 (1971), overruled in part, Cook v. Sanbornton, 118 N.H. 668, 392 A.2d 1201, 1978 N.H. LEXIS 267 (1978). (Decided under prior law.)

The board of adjustment did not have to accept the conclusions of experts, but rather, could properly rely on its own knowledge of the area in which a variance was sought. Vannah v. Bedford, 111 N.H. 105, 276 A.2d 253, 1971 N.H. LEXIS 132 (1971), overruled in part, Cook v. Sanbornton, 118 N.H. 668, 392 A.2d 1201, 1978 N.H. LEXIS 267 (1978). (Decided under prior law.)

16. Rendition of decision by board

The duty of the board of adjustment to "make such order, or decision, as ought to be made" did not extend to the rendition of an advisory opinion, and was satisfied by a finding that a proposed use was not permissible. Perron v. Concord, 102 N.H. 32, 150 A.2d 403, 1959 N.H. LEXIS 11 (N.H. 1959). (Decided under prior law.)

17. Power of board as to granting of variances—Generally

A board's power to grant variances was not limited to slight variances. Carter v. Nashua, 113 N.H. 407, 308 A.2d 847, 1973 N.H. LEXIS 285 (N.H. 1973). (Decided under prior law.)

18. —Attachment of conditions to variance

While reaffirming its earlier ruling that the plaintiffs' construction business fell within the parameters of a nonconforming use, the zoning board of adjustment properly imposed conditions that (1) no paving materials or vehicles with residual paving materials were to be parked or repaired on the site, (2) equipment on site was limited to 10 pieces; and (3) none of the plaintiffs' vehicles larger than cars or pickup trucks could use the access road to the property. Peabody v. Town of Windham, 142 N.H. 488, 703 A.2d 886, 1997 N.H. LEXIS 121 (N.H. 1997).

A zoning board, considering an administrative appeal, may impose reasonable conditions to prevent improper expansions of nonconforming uses. Peabody v. Town of Windham, 142 N.H. 488, 703 A.2d 886, 1997 N.H. LEXIS 121 (N.H. 1997).

A claim that conditions attached to variance were ineffective was an ineffective attack upon a variance for the board of adjustment was not required to anticipate noncompliance or failure of proper public officials to insure that conditions would be met. Carter v. Nashua, 113 N.H. 407, 308 A.2d 847, 1973 N.H. LEXIS 285 (N.H. 1973). (Decided under prior law.)

The broad powers granted boards under the statute included the attachment of reasonable conditions necessary to observance of the spirit of pertinent ordinances, but the conditions were to relate to the use of the land, not the person who was to be using the land. Wentworth Hotel v. New Castle, 112 N.H. 21, 287 A.2d 615, 1972 N.H. LEXIS 135 (N.H. 1972). (Decided under prior law.)

A zoning variance condition requiring compliance with all ordinances and statutes and making all subsequently adopted ordinances applicable to the property would be interpreted as applying only to laws not infringing the vested rights of the party granted the variance and, as so interpreted, was valid. Wentworth Hotel v. New Castle, 112 N.H. 21, 287 A.2d 615, 1972 N.H. LEXIS 135 (N.H. 1972). (Decided under prior law.)

Conditions necessary to observance of the spirit of a zoning order could be attached to a variance. Vlahos Realty Co. v. Little Boar's Head Dist., 101 N.H. 460, 146 A.2d 257, 1958 N.H. LEXIS 63 (N.H. 1958). (Decided under prior law.)

While the statute contained no express provision permitting conditions to be attached to a variance, the board of adjustment was given broad powers and could make "such order, or decision, as ought to be made"; this language was inclusive enough to authorize the power to attach reasonable conditions to the granting of variances. Vlahos Realty Co. v. Little Boar's Head Dist., 101 N.H. 460, 146 A.2d 257, 1958 N.H. LEXIS 63 (N.H. 1958). (Decided under prior law.)

III. Special exceptions

19. Successive variance applications

It was error to decline to consider a 2009 variance application on the ground that circumstances had not changed sufficiently since an application in 1994 was denied. The case law interpreting former RSA 674:33, I(b) had changed significantly between 1994 and 2009, creating a reasonable possibility of a different outcome from that in 1994. Brandt Dev. Co. v. City of Somersworth, 162 N.H. 553, 34 A.3d 593, 2011 N.H. LEXIS 140 (N.H. 2011).

30. Distinction between variances and special exceptions

While in practice a sharp distinction between exceptions and variances may not in all cases be readily made, there is a major difference between the two: there is no necessity for a hardship to exist in order to qualify for a special exception. Stone v. Cray, 89 N.H. 483, 200 A. 517, 1938 N.H. LEXIS 60 (N.H. 1938); Burr v. Keene, 105 N.H. 228, 196 A.2d 63, 1963 N.H. LEXIS 54 (N.H. 1963). (Decided under prior law.)

A literal enforcement of an ordinance may be disregarded to permit a variance, while the conditions for an exception must be found in the ordinance and may not be varied. Stone v. Cray, 89 N.H. 483, 200 A. 517, 1938 N.H. LEXIS 60 (N.H. 1938). (Decided under prior law.)

31. Delegation of authority to make special exceptions to ordinances

Under state law, terms of a zoning ordinance and its self-described purposes establish the test for granting special excep-

tions. Town of Amherst v. Omnipoint Communs. Enters., Inc., 173 F.3d 9, 1999 U.S. App. LEXIS 6046 (1st Cir. N.H. 1999).

Earth excavation regulation of a town zoning ordinance did not conflict with paragraph IV of this section, vesting authority to grant exceptions in a board of adjustment, since the five listed categories of permissible earth removal activities in the ordinance, which were made subject to the selectmen's control, did not encompass earth removal for sale and were not therefore "exceptions" to the regulation's prohibition of earth removal for sale. Goffstown v. Thibeault, 129 N.H. 454, 529 A.2d 930, 1987 N.H. LEXIS 184 (N.H. 1987).

As this provision vested in the board of adjustment the power to "make special exceptions to the terms of the ordinance", an ordinance provision purporting to grant such power to a private association and the selectmen of the town, in addition to the board of adjustment, was an unlawful delegation of authority. Fernald v. Bassett, 107 N.H. 282, 220 A.2d 739, 1966 N.H. LEXIS 174 (N.H. 1966). (Decided under prior law.)

The delegation in a local ordinance of the authority to the municipal zoning board of adjustment to make special exceptions was defective where it failed to establish standards by which the board was to be governed in determining whether an exception should be made. Fernald v. Bassett, 107 N.H. 282, 220 A.2d 739, 1966 N.H. LEXIS 174 (N.H. 1966). (Decided under prior law.)

32. Power of board as to special exceptions

The zoning board of adjustment has authority under this section to grant special exceptions to zoning ordinance; however, it cannot waive that such special exceptions be obtained by property owners otherwise in violation of the ordinance. Mudge v. Precinct of Haverhill Corner, 133 N.H. 881, 587 A.2d 603, 1991 N.H. LEXIS 10 (N.H. 1991).

The terms of the ordinance are to define the cases or conditions in or upon which exceptions are allowable; the board's only function in respect to exceptions is to decide if the conditions exist which make the case an appropriate one. Stone v. Cray, 89 N.H. 483, 200 A. 517, 1938 N.H. LEXIS 60 (N.H. 1938). (Decided under prior law.)

Under the statutory provision relating to special exceptions, the ordinance was to declare when exceptions could be permitted; the language of the statute implied a denial of authority to the board to decide what conditions made an exception expedient. Stone v. Cray, 89 N.H. 483, 200 A. 517, 1938 N.H. LEXIS 60 (N.H. 1938). (Decided under prior law.)

The purpose and design of the statutory provision relating to the authority to make special exceptions was that only the ordinance could declare the exceptions, leaving it to the board of adjustment to decide their application in particular cases. Stone v. Cray, 89 N.H. 483, 200 A. 517, 1938 N.H. LEXIS 60 (N.H. 1938). (Decided under prior law.)

33. Manufactured housing parks

Manufactured housing parks are omitted from this section's exemption of manufactured housing from requirement that special exceptions to zoning ordinances be obtained by property owners. Mudge v. Precinct of Haverhill Corner, 133 N.H. 881, 587 A.2d 603, 1991 N.H. LEXIS 10 (N.H. 1991).

Trial court improperly denied plaintiff's motion to vacate zoning board of adjustment's upholding of a building permit, where property owner failed to obtain a special exception for a commercial use of premises to be used for expansion of manufactured housing park. Mudge v. Precinct of Haverhill Corner, 133 N.H. 881, 587 A.2d 603, 1991 N.H. LEXIS 10 (N.H. 1991).

34. Private docks

Although a zoning board of adjustment has broad authority to act under RSA 674:33, it acted ultra vires by imposing a six-user, six-boat limit upon the owner of a private dock. Lakeside Lodge, Inc. v. Town of New London, 158 N.H. 164, 960 A.2d 1268, 2008 N.H. LEXIS 140 (2008).

35. Remand by trial court

Although the trial court in a variance case had subject matter jurisdiction to consider the issue of accessory uses, it lacked a sufficient factual record to decide the accessory use issue. It should have remanded the case to the zoning board of adjustment to consider the issue in the first instance. Bartlett v. City of Manchester, 164 N.H. 634, 62 A.3d 855, 2013 N.H. LEXIS 17 (N.H. 2013).

36. Standing to appeal

Supermarket owner did not have standing under RSA 677:4 to appeal the grant of a variance to an applicant to construct a larger supermarket, as it was not a "person directly affected" under RSA 677:2. The fact that the zoning board of adjustment drew a comparison between petitioner's location and the applicant's location when considering the "spirit of the ordinance" under RSA 674:33, I(b) did not give petitioner more than a generalized interest in the outcome of the proceedings; furthermore, granting the variance did not make the applicant's competition unfair or illegal. Hannaford Bros. Co. v. Town of Bedford, 164 N.H. 764, 64 A.3d 951, 2013 N.H. LEXIS 41 (N.H. 2013).

37. Appeal from planning board decision

Although the caption and stated purpose of an abutter's appeal referenced only the code enforcement officer's determination that the proposed use of the property was permitted as a contractor's yard, the body of the appeal referred to, and challenged, actions taken by the planning board. Thus, given the broad authority of the zoning board of adjustment (ZBA) under RSA 674:33 and the content of the appeal itself, the ZBA did not err by finding that the abutter's appeal contained allegations relating to the planning board's decision and by then treating the appeal as an appeal of that decision. Accurate Transp., Inc. v. Town of Derry, 168 N.H. 108, 123 A.3d 263, 2015 N.H. LEXIS 81 (N.H. 2015).

Cited:

Cited in Saturley v. Hollis, Zoning Bd. of Adjustment, 129 N.H. 757, 533 A.2d 29, 1987 N.H. LEXIS 256 (1987); Margate Motel v. Gilford, 130 N.H. 91, 534 A.2d 717, 1987 N.H. LEXIS 272 (1987); Goslin v. Farmington, 132 N.H. 48, 561 A.2d 507, 1989 N.H. LEXIS 68 (1989); Korpi v. Peterborough, 135 N.H. 37, 599 A.2d 130, 1991 N.H. LEXIS 142 (1991); Olszak v. Town of New Hampton, 139 N.H. 723, 661 A.2d 768, 1995 N.H. LEXIS 81 (1995); Hurley v. Town of Hollis, 143 N.H. 567, 729 A.2d 998, 1999 N.H. LEXIS 45 (1999).

RESEARCH REFERENCES AND PRACTICE AIDS

New Hampshire Bar Journal.

For article, "A Brief History of Variance Standards for the Municipal Law Practitioner," see 48 N.H. B.J. 6 (Summer 2007).

For article, "The Federal Deficit Reduction Act of 2006: Errors to Cut Spending, Incentives to Enact New False Claims Acts," see 48 N.H. B.J. 6 (Summer 2007).

For article, "The New Zoning Variance Cases: Analyzing Unnecessary Hardship Under RSA 674:33," see 46 N.H. B.J. 40 (Fall 2005).

For article, "The New Zoning Variance Cases: Analyzing Unnecessary Hardship Under RSA 674:33," see 46 N.H. B.J. 40 (Fall 2005).

For article, "Unnecessary Hardship Under RSA 674:331(B)," see 46 N.H. B.J. 47 (Fall 2005).

New Hampshire Practice.

15-22 N.H.P. Land Use Planning and Zoning § 22.02A.

15-24 N.H.P. Land Use Planning and Zoning § 24.03.

15-24 N.H.P. Land Use Planning and Zoning § 24.16.

674:33-a. Equitable Waiver of Dimensional Requirement.

I. When a lot or other division of land, or structure thereupon, is discovered to be in violation of a physical layout or dimensional requirement imposed by a zoning ordinance enacted pursuant to RSA 674:16, the zoning board of adjustment shall, upon application by and with the burden of proof on the property owner, grant an equitable waiver from the requirement, if and only if the board makes all of the following findings:

(a) That the violation was not noticed or discovered by any owner, former owner, owner's agent or representative, or municipal official, until after a structure in violation had been substantially completed, or until after a lot or other division of land in violation had been subdivided by conveyance to a bona fide purchaser for value;

(b) That the violation was not an outcome of ignorance of the law or ordinance, failure to inquire, obfuscation, misrepresentation, or bad faith on the part of any owner, owner's agent or representative, but was instead caused by either a good faith error in measurement or calculation made by an owner or owner's agent, or by an error in ordinance interpretation or applicability made by a municipal official in the process of issuing a permit over which that official had authority;

(c) That the physical or dimensional violation does not constitute a public or private nuisance, nor diminish the value of other property in the area, nor interfere with or adversely affect any present or permissible future uses of any such property; and

(d) That due to the degree of past construction or investment made in ignorance of the facts constituting the violation, the cost of correction so far outweighs any public benefit to be gained, that it would be inequitable to require the violation to be corrected.

II. In lieu of the findings required by the board under subparagraphs I(a) and (b), the owner may demonstrate to the satisfaction of the board that the violation has existed for 10 years or more, and that no enforcement action, including written notice of violation, has been commenced against the violation during that time by the municipality or any person directly affected.

III. Application and hearing procedures for equitable waivers under this section shall be governed by RSA 676:5 through 7. Rehearings and appeals shall be governed by RSA 677:2 through 14.

IV. Waivers shall be granted under this section only from physical layout, mathematical or dimensional requirements, and not from use restrictions. An equitable waiver granted under this section shall not be construed as a nonconforming use, and shall not exempt future use, construction, reconstruction, or additions on the property from full compliance with the ordinance. This section shall not be construed to alter the principle that owners of land are bound by constructive knowledge of all applicable requirements. This section shall not be construed to impose upon municipal officials any duty to guarantee the correctness of plans reviewed by them or property inspected by them.

HISTORY:

1996, 226:4, eff. Jan. 1, 1997.

NOTES TO DECISIONS

Analysis

1. Construction
2. Particular cases

1. Construction

"Calculate" means to "ascertain by mathematical methods, compute," or "to answer or determine by mathematical processes." Viewed in the context of the entire subsection of RSA 674:33-a, I(b), the term "error in calculation" does not lend itself to an interpretation that includes an owner's misinterpretation of zoning ordinances; although an error interpreting a zoning ordinance by certain municipal officials is included in the statute, an owner's error in interpreting a zoning ordinance is not. Taylor v. Town of Wakefield, 158 N.H. 35, 959 A.2d 217, 2008 N.H. LEXIS 124 (N.H. 2008).

Use of the term "honest mistake" or "legitimate mistake" in describing the requirements of RSA 674:33-a, I(b) is overly broad. Certainly, innocent errors in measurement or calculation by an owner, or errors in ordinance interpretation or applicability made by certain municipal officials, may be honest or legitimate mistakes; however, the "legitimate mistake" standard encompasses more than the plain language of RSA 674:33-a, I(b). Taylor v. Town of Wakefield, 158 N.H. 35, 959 A.2d 217, 2008 N.H. LEXIS 124 (N.H. 2008).

Restriction on the construction of permanent buildings within a Wetlands and Watershed Protection overlay district was a use restriction and thus could not be waived under RSA 674:33-a. The waiver request was not made necessary by the physical characteristics of the lot, but by the district's unambiguous prohibition of permanent buildings within its boundaries; furthermore, the restriction prohibiting permanent buildings was enacted in order to protect the character of the surrounding area, thereby creating a use restriction. Schroeder v. Town of Windham, 158 N.H. 187, 965 A.2d 1081, 2008 N.H. LEXIS 143 (N.H. 2008).

2. Particular cases

It was error to grant an equitable waiver for a waterfront access easement under RSA 674:33-a, I(b). Any good faith error in interpreting or applying an ordinance was on the part of private parties, not that of a municipal official, and the record did not support a finding that an owner or owner's agent created an easement as a result of an error in measurement or calculation. Taylor v. Town of Wakefield, 158 N.H. 35, 959 A.2d 217, 2008 N.H. LEXIS 124 (N.H. 2008).

674:34. Powers of Building Code Board of Appeals.

The building code board of appeals shall hear and decide appeals of orders, decisions, or determinations made by the building official or fire official relative to the application and interpretation of the state building code or state fire code as defined in RSA 155-A:1. An application for appeal shall be based on a claim that the true intent of the code or the rules adopted thereunder have been incorrectly interpreted, the provisions of the code do not fully apply, or an equally good or better form of construction is proposed. The board shall have no authority to waive requirements of the state building code or the state fire code.

HISTORY:

1983, 447:1, eff. Jan. 1, 1984. 2012, 242:17, eff. June 18, 2012.

Amendments

—2012.

The 2012 amendment rewrote the section to the extent that a detailed comparison would be impracticable.

RESEARCH REFERENCES AND PRACTICE AIDS

Cross References.

Appeal from and review of building code boards of appeals decisions, see RSA 677:16.

Requirement and issuance of building permits generally, see RSA 676:11 et seq.

New Hampshire Practice.

15-19 N.H.P. Land Use Planning and Zoning § 19.03.
15-29 N.H.P. Land Use Planning and Zoning § 19.02.

Regulation of Subdivision of Land

NOTES TO DECISIONS

Constitutionality

The statute authorizing municipalities to enact ordinances regulating the subdivision of land to promote the orderly and planned growth of relatively undeveloped areas within the municipality is a proper exercise of the police power. Blevens v. Manchester, 103 N.H. 284, 170 A.2d 121, 1961 N.H. LEXIS 33 (N.H. 1961). (Decided under prior law.)

Cited:

Cited in Vachon v. New Durham Zoning Bd. of Adjustment, 131 N.H. 623, 557 A.2d 649, 1989 N.H. LEXIS 29 (1989).

RESEARCH REFERENCES AND PRACTICE AIDS

Cross References.

Building codes generally, see RSA 674:51 et seq.
Condominiums, see RSA 356-B.
Emergency temporary zoning and planning ordinances, see RSA 674:24 et seq.
Master plans generally, see RSA 674:1 et seq.
Official municipal maps generally, see RSA 674:9 et seq.
Site plan review, see RSA 674:43 et seq.
Unit ownership of real property, see RSA 479-A.
Zoning generally, see RSA 674:16 et seq.

674:35. Power to Regulate Subdivisions.

I. A municipality may by ordinance or resolution authorize the planning board to require preliminary review of subdivisions, and to approve or disapprove, in its discretion, plats, and to approve or disapprove plans showing the extent to which and the manner in which streets within subdivisions shall be graded and improved and to which streets water, sewer, and other utility mains, piping, connections, or facilities within subdivisions shall be installed. A municipality may by ordinance or resolution transfer authority to approve or disapprove plans showing the extent to which and the manner in which streets within subdivisions shall be graded and improved from the planning board to the governing body.

II. The planning board of a municipality shall have the authority to regulate the subdivision of land under the enactment procedures of RSA 675:6. The ordinance or resolution which authorizes the planning board to regulate the subdivision of land shall make it the duty of the city clerk, town clerk, clerk of district commissioners or other appropriate recording official to file with the register of deeds of the county in which the municipality is located a certificate of notice showing that the planning board has been so authorized, giving the date of such authorization.

III. The planning board shall not limit the number of building permits that may be issued except in accordance with an innovative land use control ordinance addressing timing incentives and phased development under RSA 674:21 and adopted under RSA 674:16; or an ordinance to regulate and control the timing of development, adopted under RSA 674:22; or an ordinance establishing a temporary moratorium or limitation on the issuance of building permits, adopted under RSA 674:23. This paragraph shall not be construed to limit the planning board's authority to deny a subdivision application on the basis that it is scattered or premature.

HISTORY:
1983, 447:1, eff. Jan. 1, 1984. 2004, 71:3, eff. July 6, 2004. 2005, 51:1, eff. July 22, 2005. 2009, 200:2, eff. September 13, 2009. 2014, 125:2, eff. August 15, 2014.

Amendment Notes

—2014.
The 2014 amendment, in I, deleted "other" preceding "facilities" in the first sentence and added the second sentence and made a stylistic change.

—2009.
The 2009 amendment substituted "establishing a temporary moratorium or limitation on the issuance of building permits" for "to regulate growth via interim regulation" in the first sentence of III.

—2005.
Paragraph III: Added.

—2004.
Paragraph I: Inserted "to require preliminary review of subdivisions, and" following "planning board".

NOTES TO DECISIONS

Analysis

1. Construction
2. Construction with other laws
3. Definition
4. Site plan review
5. Necessity for adoption of regulations
6. Conditions for approval of plans—Granting of easements
7. —Offsite improvements
8. Effect of zoning changes upon approved plots or plans
9. Conveyance without approval

1. Construction
This section grants the town planning board the power to regulate the act of subdividing but not the land that has been subdivided. Lemm Dev. Corp. v. Bartlett, 133 N.H. 618, 580 A.2d 1082, 1990 N.H. LEXIS 114 (N.H. 1990).

Town planning board's authority to enact subdivision controls is strictly confined to the terms of the enabling legislation. Lemm Dev. Corp. v. Bartlett, 133 N.H. 618, 580 A.2d 1082, 1990 N.H. LEXIS 114 (N.H. 1990).

Town planning board had no authority under its subdivision regulations to review or control corporation's planned construction of condominium amenities facility on subdivided land, where no division of ownership or physical division of the land was planned. Lemm Dev. Corp. v. Bartlett, 133 N.H. 618, 580 A.2d 1082, 1990 N.H. LEXIS 114 (N.H. 1990).

2. Construction with other laws
While it is the state which has the power to regulate access to state highways under RSA 236:13, a town may legitimately consider the impact that increased traffic may have upon the safety of an existing or proposed access in determining whether or not to grant approval of a subdivision plan. Diversified Properties v. Hopkinton Planning Bd., 125 N.H. 419, 480 A.2d 194, 1984 N.H. LEXIS 262 (N.H. 1984).

3. Definition
Term "subdivision" in this section means only the act of subdividing land; general zoning law provision in RSA 672:14 defining the "subdivision" as "land or territory subdivided" is not encompassed within this section. Lemm Dev. Corp. v. Bartlett, 133 N.H. 618, 580 A.2d 1082, 1990 N.H. LEXIS 114 (N.H. 1990).

4. Site plan review
To control the construction of condominium amenities facility on subdivided land, planning board must promulgate site plan review regulations. Lemm Dev. Corp. v. Bartlett, 133 N.H. 618, 580 A.2d 1082, 1990 N.H. LEXIS 114 (N.H. 1990).

5. Necessity for adoption of regulations
The statute authorized municipalities to grant their planning boards discretionary authority to approve or disapprove subdivision plans, but before a board could exercise that authority it was required to adopt subdivision regulations. Durant v. Dunbarton, 121 N.H. 352, 430 A.2d 140, 1981 N.H. LEXIS 318 (N.H. 1981). (Decided under prior law.)

6. Conditions for approval of plans—Granting of easements
A city planning board could not legally require a landowner, as a condition to approval of a site plan, to grant the city an easement ten feet wide on the edge of his property for highway purposes so that city could use it to widen the road in the future; any taking of such land would require just compensation. Robbins Auto Parts v. Laconia, 117 N.H. 235, 371 A.2d 1167, 1977 N.H. LEXIS 308 (N.H. 1977). (Decided under prior law.)

7. —Offsite improvements
Where a town planning board conditioned its approval of a developer's application for a subdivision on the developer's upgrading, at its own expense and to standards established by the town, of two roads leading to but located outside the proposed subdivision, and evidence indicated that traffic on the two roads, due to the proposed subdivision, would increase the hazard that an emergency would create, and that there must be improvement to the roads if the subdivision was fully developed, compelling the conclusion that, with respect to the criterion of safety, the proposed subdivision was premature, the town could legitimately condition its approval of the subdivision on the provision of improvements to the offsite access roads. Land/Vest Properties v. Plainfield, 117 N.H. 817, 379 A.2d 200, 1977 N.H. LEXIS 440 (N.H. 1977). (Decided under prior law.)

Where offsite improvements could properly be required of a subdivider by a town planning board, the subdivider could be compelled only to bear that portion of the cost which bore a rational nexus to the needs created by, and special benefits conferred upon, the subdivision. Land/Vest Properties v. Plainfield, 117 N.H. 817, 379 A.2d 200, 1977 N.H. LEXIS 440 (N.H. 1977). (Decided under prior law.)

8. Effect of zoning changes upon approved plots or plans
In the absence of a statute providing otherwise, final approval of a subdivision plot by a planning board under the statute did not place the lots beyond the authority of zoning changes. R.A. Vachon & Son v. Concord, 112 N.H. 107, 289 A.2d 646, 1972 N.H. LEXIS 153 (N.H. 1972). (Decided under prior law.)

9. Conveyance without approval
Trial court properly held that landowners owned a single parcel at the time they conveyed two lots separately to themselves without prior approval, thereby improperly subdividing their property. As early as 1961, the landowners and their predecessors had abolished the boundary line through their conduct. Town of Newbury v. Landrigan, 165 N.H. 236, 75 A.3d 1091, 2013 N.H. LEXIS 90 (N.H. 2013).

Cited:

Cited in Frisella v. Farmington, 131 N.H. 78, 550 A.2d 102, 1988 N.H. LEXIS 94 (1988); Morin v. Somersworth, 131 N.H. 253, 551 A.2d 527, 1988 N.H. LEXIS 109 (1988); New Eng. Brickmaster v. Salem, 133 N.H. 655, 582 A.2d 601, 1990 N.H. LEXIS 119 (1990); Blevens v. Town of Bow, 887 F. Supp. 38, 1994 U.S. Dist. LEXIS 14408 (D.N.H. 1994).

RESEARCH REFERENCES AND PRACTICE AIDS

Cross References.

Adoption of subdivision regulations, see RSA 674:36.
Approval and recording of plats, see RSA 674:37– 39.
Development on class V and VI highways, see RSA 674:41.
Effect of section upon existing laws, see RSA 674:42.
Street improvements generally, see RSA 674:40.

New Hampshire Bar Journal.

For article, "Roads Revisited: Creation and Termination of Highways in New Hampshire—An Update," see 46 N.H. B.J. 56 (Fall 2005).

New Hampshire Practice.

16-45 N.H.P. Municipal Law & Taxation § 45.02.
16-50 N.H.P. Municipal Law & Taxation § 50.06.

674:36. Subdivision Regulations.

I. Before the planning board exercises its powers under RSA 674:35, the planning board shall adopt subdivision regulations according to the procedures required by RSA 675:6.

II. The subdivision regulations which the planning board adopts may:

(a) Provide against such scattered or premature subdivision of land as would involve danger or injury to health, safety, or prosperity by reason of the lack of water supply, drainage, transportation, schools, fire protection, or other public services, or necessitate the excessive expenditure of public funds for the supply of such services;

(b) Provide for the harmonious development of the municipality and its environs;

(c) Require the proper arrangement and coordination of streets within subdivisions in relation to other existing or planned streets or with features of the official map of the municipality;

(d) Provide for open spaces of adequate proportions;

(e) Require suitably located streets of sufficient width to accommodate existing and prospective traffic and to afford adequate light, air, and access for firefighting apparatus and equipment to buildings, and be coordinated so as to compose a convenient system;

(f) Require, in proper cases, that plats showing new streets or narrowing or widening of such streets submitted to the planning board for approval shall show a park or parks suitably located for playground or other recreational purposes;

(g) Require that proposed parks shall be of reasonable size for neighborhood playgrounds or other recreational uses;

(h) Require that the land indicated on plats submitted to the planning board shall be of such character that it can be used for building purposes without danger to health;

(i) Prescribe minimum areas of lots so as to assure conformance with local zoning ordinances and to assure such additional areas as may be needed for each lot for on-site sanitary facilities;

(j) Include provisions which will tend to create conditions favorable to health, safety, convenience, or prosperity;

(k) Encourage the installation and use of solar, wind, or other renewable energy systems and protect access to energy sources by the regulation of orientation of streets, lots, and buildings; establishment of maximum building height, minimum set back requirements, and limitations on type, height, and placement of vegetation; and encouragement of the use of solar skyspace easements under RSA 477; and

(*l*) Provide for efficient and compact subdivision development which promotes retention and public usage of open space and wildlife habitat, by allowing for village plan alternative subdivision as defined in RSA 674:21, VI.

(m) Require innovative land use controls on lands when supported by the master plan.

(n) Include provision for waiver of any portion of the regulations. The basis for any waiver granted by the planning board shall be recorded in the minutes of the board. The planning board may only grant a waiver if the board finds, by majority vote, that:

(1) Strict conformity would pose an unnecessary hardship to the applicant and waiver would not be contrary to the spirit and intent of the regulations; or

(2) Specific circumstances relative to the subdivision, or conditions of the land in such subdivision, indicate that the waiver will properly carry out the spirit and intent of the regulations.

(*o*) As a condition of subdivision approval, where the subdivision requires an alteration of terrain permit under RSA 485-A:17, require that the applicant protect or document archeological resources in areas of archeological sensitivity that have been identified in the master plan in accordance with RSA 674:2, III(h).

III. The subdivision regulations of the planning board may stipulate, as a condition precedent to the approval of the plat, the extent to which and the manner in which streets shall be graded and improved and to which water, sewer, and other utility mains, piping, connections, or other facilities shall be installed. The regulations or practice of the planning board:

(a) May provide for the conditional approval of the plat before such improvements and installations have been constructed, but any such conditional approval shall not be entered upon the plat.

(b) Shall provide that, in lieu of the completion of street work and utility installations prior to the final approval of a plat, the planning board shall accept a performance bond, irrevocable letter of credit, or other type or types of security as shall be specified in the subdivision regulations; provided that in no event shall the exclusive form of security required by the planning board be in the form of cash or a passbook. As phases or portions of the secured improvements or installations are completed and approved by the planning board or its designee, the municipality shall partially release said security to the extent reasonably calculated to reflect the value of such completed improvements or installations. Cost escalation factors that are applied by the planning board to any bond or other security required under this section shall not exceed 10 percent per year. The planning board shall, within the limitations provided in this subparagraph, have the discretion to prescribe the type and amount of security, and specify a period for completion of the improvements and utilities to be expressed in the bond or other security, in order to secure to the municipality the actual construction and installation of such improvements and utilities. The municipality shall have the power to enforce such bonds or other securities by all appropriate legal and equitable remedies.

(c) May provide that in lieu of the completion of street work and utility installations prior to the final approval of the plat, the subdivision regulations may provide for an assessment or other method by which the municipality is put in an assured position to do said work and to make said alterations at the cost of the owners of the property within the subdivision.

IV. The planning board shall not require, or adopt any regulation requiring, the installation of a fire suppression sprinkler system in proposed one- or 2-family residences as a condition of approval for a local permit. Nothing in this paragraph shall prohibit a duly adopted regulation mandating a cistern, dry hydrant, fire pond, or other credible water source other than a fire suppression sprinkler system. Nothing in this paragraph shall prevent an applicant from offering to install fire suppression sprinkler systems in proposed one- or 2-family residences and, if the planning board accepts such offer, the installation of such systems shall be required and shall be enforceable as a condition of the approval. The applicant or the applicant's successor in interest may substitute another means of fire protection in lieu of the approved fire suppression sprinkler system provided that the planning board approves the substitution which approval shall not be unreasonably upheld or delayed.

HISTORY:
1983, 447:1. 1986, 200:2. 1988, 3:1, eff. April 19, 1988. 2002, 73:3, eff. June 30, 2002. 236:4, eff. July 16, 2002. 2004, 71:4, eff. July 6, 2004. 199:4, eff. June 7, 2004. 2009, 292:1, eff. September 29, 2009. 2011, 203:1, eff. July 1, 2011. 2013, 76:2, eff. January 1, 2014. 207:1, eff. September 8, 2013.

Revision note.
Made minor changes in punctuation at the end of par. II(j) and (k) in light of the amendment to this section by 2002, 236:4.

Amendment Notes

—2013.
The 2013 amendment by Chapter 76, added II(o).
The 2013 amendment by Chapter 207, added the last two sentences of IV.

—2011.
The 2011 amendment added IV.

—2009.
The 2009 amendment, in the introductory language of II(n), deleted "in such cases where, in the opinion of the planning board" at the end of the first sentence and added the second and third sentences; added the II(n)(1) designation; added II(n)(2); and made a related change.

—2004.
Paragraph II(m): Added by ch. 71.
Paragraph II(n): Added by ch. 199.

—2002.
Paragraph II: Chapter 73 made a minor change in phraseology in subpars. (i) and (j) and added subpar. (k).
Chapter 236 added subpar. (l).

—1988.
Paragraph III(b): Added "provided that in no event shall the exclusive form of security required by the planning board be in the form of cash or a passbook" following "regulations" at the end of the first sentence, added the second and third sentences, inserted "within the limitations provided in this subparagraph" following "planning board shall" and deleted "the bond or other security, require satisfactory evidence of the financial ability of any surety or financial institution to pay such bond or other type of" preceding "security, and specify" in the fourth sentence.

—1986.
Paragraph III: Rewritten to the extent that a detailed comparison would be impracticable.

NOTES TO DECISIONS

Analysis

1. Purpose
2. Construction
3. Construction with other laws
4. Access roads
5. Scope of authority
6. Scope of regulations—Generally
7. —Prevention of scattered or premature subdivision of land
8. —Arrangement and coordination of streets
9. —Open space and parks
10. —Lot size
11. Requirement of surety bonds

1. Purpose
This section serves to ensure that the town, through its planning board, retains control over its expenditures on the development, improvement, and maintenance of town services to new subdivisions. Stillwater Condominium Ass'n v. Town of Salem, 140 N.H. 505, 668 A.2d 38, 1995 N.H. LEXIS 177 (N.H. 1995).

2. Construction
The term "prosperity," as used in the statute, refers to a community's fiscal wellbeing, and not to an individual's financial interest and, therefore, the statute was not intended to protect owners of condominium units from financial harm caused by the developer's failure to construct a municipal water line extension. Stillwater Condominium Ass'n v. Town of Salem, 140 N.H. 505, 668 A.2d 38, 1995 N.H. LEXIS 177 (N.H. 1995).

3. Construction with other laws

Other than its management tool capabilities, a capital improvements program has no part to play in review of subdivision applications presented to governmental authorities. Zukis v. Fitzwilliam, 135 N.H. 384, 604 A.2d 956, 1992 N.H. LEXIS 46 (N.H. 1992).

While it is the state which has the power to regulate access to state highways under RSA 236:13, a town may legitimately consider the impact that increased traffic may have upon the safety of an existing or proposed access in determining whether or not to grant approval of a subdivision plan. Diversified Properties v. Hopkinton Planning Bd., 125 N.H. 419, 480 A.2d 194, 1984 N.H. LEXIS 262 (N.H. 1984).

Former RSA 36:19 (now covered by RSA 674:35) authorized municipalities to grant their planning boards discretionary authority to approve or disapprove subdivision plans, but before a board could exercise that authority it was required to adopt subdivision regulations. Durant v. Dunbarton, 121 N.H. 352, 430 A.2d 140, 1981 N.H. LEXIS 318 (N.H. 1981). (Decided under prior law.)

4. Access roads

Planning board may properly consider the present condition of access roads when ruling on a subdivision application, and if a hazard is created by the present level of development, it may find that future development is premature. Zukis v. Fitzwilliam, 135 N.H. 384, 604 A.2d 956, 1992 N.H. LEXIS 46 (N.H. 1992).

Trial court erred in ruling that preexisting inadequacy of access roads was not a valid basis for planning board's finding that proposed subdivision was premature, since exposing more households to risk that emergency vehicles would be unable to respond when their services were required would magnify existing hazard. Zukis v. Fitzwilliam, 135 N.H. 384, 604 A.2d 956, 1992 N.H. LEXIS 46 (N.H. 1992).

5. Scope of authority

Where a developer's conservation development subdivision (CDS) approved by a town board, contained a cul-de-sac that serviced seventeen lots, exceeding the 10-lot maximum of the town's subdivision regulations, and the record revealed that the board decided to waive the ten-lot requirement because it preferred the cul-de-sac configuration in the proposed CDS to the loop road configuration in the yield plan, the trial court erred in ruling that the waiver was reasonable under the circumstances, because there was no evidence that a loop road configuration would cause undue hardship or injustice to the developer, as required by RSA 674:36, II(n). Auger v. Town of Strafford, 156 N.H. 64, 931 A.2d 1213, 2007 N.H. LEXIS 142 (N.H. 2007).

Where a developer's yield plan associated with a conservation development subdivision depicted the location of the wetlands, but did not contain detailed information about the proposed disturbances and impact on those wetlands, the plan did not comply with applicable subdivision regulations, which required the plan to show all wetlands and proposed disturbances in sufficient detail so that the board could assess the impact, and to show that the proposed wetlands disturbance would be minimized in accordance with DES requirements. The trial court properly found that the yield plan did not comply with the subdivision regulations, but it improperly remanded the decision to the board to "obtain the information necessary" for determining whether the yield plan complied with the applicable regulations when it should have instead reversed the board's approval of the yield plan. Auger v. Town of Strafford, 156 N.H. 64, 931 A.2d 1213, 2007 N.H. LEXIS 142 (N.H. 2007).

Planning board's denial of subdivision proposal on grounds it was "premature" was plainly taken to control growth, and thus exceeded board's statutory authority under subdivision II(a) of this section. Ettlingen Homes v. Town of Derry, 141 N.H. 296, 681 A.2d 97, 1996 N.H. LEXIS 93 (N.H. 1996).

6. Scope of regulations—Generally

The scope of a municipality's subdivision regulations could be quite broad and generally could include provisions which would tend to create conditions favorable to health, safety, convenience or prosperity. Durant v. Dunbarton, 121 N.H. 352, 430 A.2d 140, 1981 N.H. LEXIS 318 (N.H. 1981). (Decided under prior law.)

Under the statute, delegation of a municipality's power to regulate subdivisions was quite broad, and the regulation of septic

---

tanks and sewerage systems fell within the purview of the statute. Durant v. Dunbarton, 121 N.H. 352, 430 A.2d 140, 1981 N.H. LEXIS 318 (N.H. 1981). (Decided under prior law.)

7. —Prevention of scattered or premature subdivision of land

Under the statute, a planning board could promulgate regulations which provided for consideration of off-site factors insofar as they rendered subdivisions "scattered or premature." Garipay v. Hanover, 116 N.H. 34, 351 A.2d 64, 1976 N.H. LEXIS 256 (N.H. 1976); Land/Vest Properties v. Plainfield, 117 N.H. 817, 379 A.2d 200, 1977 N.H. LEXIS 440 (N.H. 1977). (Decided under prior law.)

The authority of a planning board was not limited to a consideration of streets within a subdivision, but extended to off-site improvements and obligations necessitated by a proposed development, including improvement of a public road abutting the proposed subdivision. KBW, Inc. v. Bennington, 115 N.H. 392, 342 A.2d 653, 1975 N.H. LEXIS 319 (N.H. 1975); Land/Vest Properties v. Plainfield, 117 N.H. 817, 379 A.2d 200, 1977 N.H. LEXIS 440 (N.H. 1977). (Decided under prior law.)

Where a town planning board conditioned its approval of a developer's application for a subdivision on the developer's upgrading, at its own expense and to standards established by the town, of two roads leading to but located outside the proposed subdivision, and evidence indicated traffic on the two roads, due to the proposed subdivision, would increase the hazard that an emergency would create, and that there must be improvements to the roads if the subdivision was fully developed, compelling the conclusion that, with respect to the criterion of safety, the proposed subdivision was premature, the town could legitimately condition its approval of the subdivision on the provision of improvements to the off-site access roads. Land/Vest Properties v. Plainfield, 117 N.H. 817, 379 A.2d 200, 1977 N.H. LEXIS 440 (N.H. 1977). (Decided under prior law.)

8. —Arrangement and coordination of streets

The statute, which allowed planning boards to regulate the arrangement and coordination of streets within subdivisions in relation to other existing or planned streets, did not give municipalities control over access to state highways. J. E. D. Assocs. v. Sandown, 121 N.H. 317, 430 A.2d 129, 1981 N.H. LEXIS 332 (N.H. 1981). (Decided under prior law.)

9. —Open space and parks

A planning board could impose conditions, even though there had been compliance with the minimum lot size provisions contained in a zoning ordinance, when the conditions were necessary for "the harmonious development of the municipality and its environs" and for "open spaces of adequate proportion." Seabrook v. Tra-Sea Corp., 119 N.H. 937, 410 A.2d 240, 1979 N.H. LEXIS 424 (N.H. 1979). (Decided under prior law.)

The statute authorized planning boards to require open spaces of adequate proportion and parks of reasonable size in subdivisions. Patenaude v. Meredith, 118 N.H. 616, 392 A.2d 582, 1978 N.H. LEXIS 253 (N.H. 1978). (Decided under prior law.)

10. —Lot size

Town's requirement that lots have a certain minimum contiguous area for building purposes ensured that the lots had proper areas for drainage, conformed with the ordinances, and had sufficient areas for sanitary facilities; thus, Gilmanton, N.H., Subdivision Regulations § VI(C)(2), requiring a minimum lot size, served a legitimate land use purpose. Doyle v. Town of Gilmanton, 155 N.H. 733, 927 A.2d 1211, 2007 N.H. LEXIS 122 (N.H. 2007).

Though subdivision regulations could prescribe minimum lot areas, these prescriptions were required to conform to the local zoning ordinance. Seabrook v. Tra-Sea Corp., 119 N.H. 937, 410 A.2d 240, 1979 N.H. LEXIS 424 (N.H. 1979). (Decided under prior law.)

11. Requirement of surety bonds

The statute specifically vested jurisdiction to issue regulations governing performance bonds in the town planning board, and a regulation adopted by a board was defective where it purported to delegate to the town selectmen the authority to determine the amounts and conditions of any surety bonds. Levasseur v. Board of

Selectmen, 116 N.H. 340, 358 A.2d 665, 1976 N.H. LEXIS 349 (N.H. 1976). (Decided under prior law.)

Cited:

Cited in Cutting v. Wentworth, 126 N.H. 727, 497 A.2d 839, 1985 N.H. LEXIS 422 (1985); Mooney v. Laconia, 133 N.H. 30, 573 A.2d 447, 1990 N.H. LEXIS 31 (1990); K & P, Inc. v. Plaistow, 133 N.H. 283, 575 A.2d 804, 1990 N.H. LEXIS 50 (1990); State v. Wilson, 140 N.H. 44, 662 A.2d 954, 1995 N.H. LEXIS 91 (1995); Upton v. Town of Hopkinton, 157 N.H. 115, 945 A.2d 670, 2008 N.H. LEXIS 40 (2008).

RESEARCH REFERENCES AND PRACTICE AIDS

Cross References.

Development on class V and VI highways, see RSA 674:41.

Effect of uncompleted streets or utilities upon applications for building permits, see RSA 676:12.

Revocation of recorded subdivision plat approval, see RSA 676:4-a.

Street improvements generally, see RSA 674:40.

674:37. Recording of Plats.

After the certificate of notice referred to in RSA 674:35, II and the regulations referred to in RSA 674:36 have been filed with the appropriate recording officials, no plat shall be filed or recorded unless it is prepared and certified by a licensed land surveyor since July 1, 1981, or by a registered land surveyor between January 1, 1970 and June 30, 1981, and until it has been approved by the planning board and such approval has been endorsed in writing on the plat in such manner as the planning board may designate, except as provided in RSA 676:18, II and III and RSA 676:4, I(c). The filing or recording of a plat of a subdivision without the requisite approval of the planning board, or which has not been prepared and certified by a licensed land surveyor or by a registered land surveyor as provided in this section, shall be void.

HISTORY:

1983, 447:1. 1988, 233:1. 1990, 275:2. 1995, 303:2, eff. Jan. 1, 1996.

Revision note.

Substituted "of" for "or" preceding "notice" in the first sentence to correct a typographical error.

Amendments

—1995.

Inserted "since July 1, 1981, or by a registered land surveyor between January 1, 1970 and June 30, 1981" preceding "and until" in the first sentence and "or by a registered land surveyor as provided in this section" preceding "shall be void" in the second sentence.

—1990.

Added "and RSA 676:4, I(c)" following "RSA 676:18, II and III" in the first sentence.

—1988.

Substituted "RSA 674:36" for "674: 36" preceding "have been filed" and inserted "unless it is prepared and certified by a licensed land surveyor, and" following "filed or recorded" in the first sentence and inserted "or which has not been prepared and certified by a licensed land surveyor" preceding "shall be void" in the second sentence.

Applicability of 1990 amendment.

1990, 275:3, eff. June 27, 1990, provided that the amendment to this section by section 2 of the act shall be prospective only, and shall apply to any application submitted to and accepted as complete by the planning board on or after June 27, 1990.

RESEARCH REFERENCES AND PRACTICE AIDS

Cross References.

Development on class V and VI highways, see RSA 674:41.

Effect of approval of plats generally, see RSA 674:38, 39.

Revocation of recorded approval, see RSA 676:4-a.

Street improvements generally, see RSA 674:40.

674:37-a. Effect of Subdivision on Tax Assessment and Collection.

The collection of taxes with respect to land being subdivided shall be governed by the following provisions:

I. If approval of a subdivision plat has been granted on or before April 1 of a particular tax year, giving the owner a legal right to sell or transfer the lots, parcels or other divisions of land depicted on the plat without further approval or action by the municipality, then such lots or parcels shall for that tax year be assessed and appraised as separate estates pursuant to RSA 75:9, whether or not any such sale or transfer has actually occurred, and shall continue to be so assessed unless and until subdivision approval is revoked under RSA 676:4-a, or the parcels are merged pursuant to RSA 674:39-a.

II. If subdivision approval does not become final until after April 1, then all assessments, appraisals, and tax warrants for that property during that tax year shall pertain to the entire non-subdivided property as it was configured on April 1, notwithstanding any later sale or transfer of subdivided lots or parcels which may occur during that year.

III. When property has been assessed as a single parcel or estate in accordance with paragraph II, and some subdivided portion of that property is later sold or transferred prior to the payment of all taxes, interest, and costs due for that tax year, the municipality's tax lien shall remain in effect with respect to the entire property, and each lot or parcel transferred or retained shall remain obligated for the entire amount, and shall be subject to all procedures of RSA 80 until that amount is collected.

IV. In order to avoid the liability of subdivided lots or parcels for taxes due on the entire property as set forth in paragraph III, any person with a legal interest may, at the time of subdivision approval or any time thereafter, prepay all taxes to be assessed on the entire property for that tax year. If such prepayment is offered prior to the determination of the property's full tax obligation for that year, the collector shall notify the assessing officials, who shall make a reasonable jeopardy assessment in accordance with the provisions of RSA 76:10-a, and commit it to the collector. After full prepayment the tax collector shall upon request execute a statement identifying the subdivision plat, and stating that all real estate tax obligations for the tax year have been fulfilled with respect to the property shown on the plat. Such a statement may be recorded in the registry of deeds at the expense of the party requesting it.

V. Nothing in this section shall be construed to prevent the parties to a conveyance from making alternative provisions, through privately-held escrow or other means, for the allocation and satisfaction of tax obligations; provided, however, that the municipality shall not, with respect to property assessed as a single parcel or estate pursuant to paragraph II, be required to apportion taxes among subdivided lots, or to release any subdivided portion of such property from the municipality's tax lien unless and until the full tax obligation for the assessed property has been satisfied.

HISTORY:
  1998, 39:1, eff. Jan. 1, 1999.

RESEARCH REFERENCES AND PRACTICE AIDS

New Hampshire Practice.
  16-20 N.H.P. Municipal Law & Taxation § 20.05A.

674:38. Status of Plats Approved.

Every plat approved by the planning board shall, by virtue of the board's approval, be deemed to be an amendment of or an addition to or a detail of the official map. Every approved plat shall be a part of the official map. Approval of a plat shall not be deemed to constitute or result in an acceptance by the municipality or the public of the dedication of any street or other ground or open space shown upon the plat.

HISTORY:
  1983, 447:1, eff. Jan. 1, 1984.

RESEARCH REFERENCES AND PRACTICE AIDS

Cross References.
  Effect upon approved plats of subsequent changes in ordinances and regulations, see RSA 674:39.
  Master plans generally, see RSA 674:1 et seq.
  Official municipal maps generally, see RSA 674:9 et seq.
  Revocation of recorded approval, see RSA 676:4-a.

674:39. Five-Year Exemption.

I. Every subdivision plat approved by the planning board and properly recorded in the registry of deeds and every site plan approved by the planning board and properly recorded in the registry of deeds, if recording of site plans is required by the planning board or by local regulation, shall be exempt from all subsequent changes in subdivision regulations, site plan review regulations, impact fee ordinances, and zoning ordinances adopted by any city, town, or county in which there are located unincorporated towns or unorganized places, except those regulations and ordinances which expressly protect public

health standards, such as water quality and sewage treatment requirements, for a period of 5 years after the date of approval; provided that:

(a) Active and substantial development or building has begun on the site by the owner or the owner's successor in interest in accordance with the approved subdivision plat within 24 months after the date of approval, or in accordance with the terms of the approval, and, if a bond or other security to cover the costs of roads, drains, or sewers is required in connection with such approval, such bond or other security is posted with the city, town, or county in which there are located unincorporated towns or unorganized places, at the time of commencement of such development;

(b) Development remains in full compliance with the public health regulations and ordinances specified in this section; and

(c) At the time of approval and recording, the subdivision plat or site plan conforms to the subdivision regulations, site plan review regulations, and zoning ordinances then in effect at the location of such subdivision plat or site plan.

II. Once substantial completion of the improvements as shown on the subdivision plat or site plan has occurred in compliance with the approved subdivision plat or site plan or the terms of said approval or unless otherwise stipulated by the planning board, the rights of the owner or the owner's successor in interest shall vest and no subsequent changes in subdivision regulations, site plan regulations, or zoning ordinances, except impact fees adopted pursuant to RSA 674:21 and 675:2–4, shall operate to affect such improvements.

III. The planning board may, as part of its subdivision and site plan regulations or as a condition of subdivision plat or site plan approval, specify the threshold levels of work that shall constitute the following terms, with due regard to the scope and details of a particular project:

(a) "Substantial completion of the improvements as shown on the subdivision plat or site plan," for purposes of fulfilling paragraph II; and

(b) "Active and substantial development or building," for the purposes of fulfilling paragraph I.

IV. Failure of a planning board to specify by regulation or as a condition of subdivision plat or site plan approval what shall constitute "active and substantial development or building" shall entitle the subdivision plat or site plan approved by the planning board to the 5-year exemption described in paragraph I. The planning board may, for good cause, extend the 24-month period set forth in subparagraph I(a).

HISTORY:
  1983, 447:1. 1989, 266:17, 18. 1991, 331:1, 2. 1995, 43:5, eff. July 2, 1995. 291:7, 8, eff. Aug. 20, 1995. 2004, 199:1, eff. June 7, 2004. 2009, 93:1, eff. June 12, 2009. 2011, 215:1, eff. June 27, 2011.

Amendments

—2011.
  The 2011 amendment substituted "Five-Year" for "Four-Year" in

the section heading; substituted "5 years" for "4 years" in the introductory language of I; substituted "24 months" for "12 months" in I(a); in IV, substituted "5-year" for "4-year" in the first sentence and in the second sentence, substituted "24-month" for "12-month" and "subparagraph I(a)" for "paragraph I(a)"; and deleted former V, which read: "Notwithstanding the time limits established in paragraph I, every subdivision plat and site plan approved by the planning board on or after January 1, 2007 and prior to July 1, 2009 shall be allowed 36 months after the date of approval to achieve active and substantial development or building as described in subparagraph I(a) and every subdivision plat and site plan approved by the planning board on or after July 1, 2005 and prior to July 1, 2009 shall be allowed 6 years after the date of approval to achieve substantial completion of the improvements as described in paragraph II."

—2009.

The 2009 amendment added V.

—2004.

Rewritten to the extent that a detailed comparison would be impracticable.

—1995.

Chapter 43 substituted "the owner's" for "his" preceding "successor" in the introductory paragraph and in the first sentence of par. I.

Chapter 291 substituted "the" for "said" following "terms of" in par. I and added par. IV.

—1991.

Inserted "or site plan" following "every plat", "site plan review regulations" preceding "and zoning" and "or unless otherwise stipulated by the planning board" preceding "the rights" in the introductory paragraph and inserted "or site plan" preceding "conforms" and "site plan review regulations" preceding "and zoning" in par. III.

—1989.

Substituted "town, or county in which there are located unincorporated towns or unorganized places" for "or town" following "adopted by any city" in the introductory paragraph and following "posted with the city" in par. I.

Legislative purpose of 1991 amendment.

1991, 331:4, eff. Aug. 27, 1991, provided:

"The purpose of sections 1– 3 of this act [which amended this section and RSA 676:12] is to confirm and re-emphasize the intent of the general court at the time of the enactment of 1986, 229:3 and 1983, 447:1. Municipalities may not retroactively amend local land use regulations or zoning ordinances for the purpose of stopping proposed projects or developments while an application is under consideration by the municipality. This act shall not be interpreted as changing the intent of any provision of 1986, 229 or 1983, 447."

NOTES TO DECISIONS

Analysis

1. Applicability
2. "Substantial construction" standard
3. Change to site plan

1. Applicability

Developer's application for site plan approval was first subject to legal notice in July 2007, approximately eight months before a 2008 ordinance became effective; accordingly, pursuant to RSA 676:12, VI, the town's 2004 ordinance applied to the project. RSA 674:39, I, applied only to site plans that had been approved by the planning board and properly recorded in the registry of deeds, if local regulation required such recording. Ouellette v. Town of Kingston, 2010 N.H. LEXIS 199 (N.H. Dec. 17, 2010).

Where town ordinance was passed in March authorizing the adoption of a new impact fee schedule and a new fee schedule was approved in August of 2000, where plaintiff developer's first devel-

opment's approval was recorded before both the March passage of the first town ordinance and the August adoption of the new fees ordinance, it was exempt from the new fees under RSA 674:39; where developer's second development's approval was recorded after the March 2000, amendment, but before the board's adoption of the new fees, the amendment did not affect the developer's RSA 674:39 reliance on the fees existing when the second development's site plan approval was recorded and, as the developer began active or substantial development or building on the developments within 12 months of recording of approvals, it obtained a preliminary 4-year exemption (permanent when substantially completed) from zoning ordinances passed after site plan approval and recording, subject to certain RSA 674:39 exceptions. R.J. Moreau Cos. v. Town of Litchfield, 148 N.H. 773, 813 A.2d 527, 2002 N.H. LEXIS 213 (N.H. 2002).

This section, providing four-year exemption from lot size restrictions of recently enacted zoning ordinances, was inapplicable as to subdivision plat which was neither approved nor recorded. Chasse v. Candia, 132 N.H. 574, 567 A.2d 999, 1989 N.H. LEXIS 132 (N.H. 1989).

2. "Substantial construction" standard

Where Town of Hookset officials erroneously told the applicant that the building permit for the gas station would not be revoked under newly enacted zoning laws if the applicant obtained the permit within a year of when the litigation over approval of the gas station ended and if the applicant began building within six months of that, municipal estoppel did not require the reinstatement of the building permit where those statements turned out to be false; the applicant's reliance on the statements of the code enforcement officer and planning board member was not reasonable because a statute, former RSA 674:39, I (see now RSA 674:39, I(a)), required the applicant to begin active and substantial development of the property within one year in order to secure protection from zoning changes. Thomas v. Town of Hooksett, 153 N.H. 717, 903 A.2d 963, 2006 N.H. LEXIS 99 (N.H. 2006).

Where a developer expended a substantial amount of money on public improvements and constructed six houses, its work was enough to meet the "substantial construction" standard; its right to complete a project permanently vested. AWL Power, Inc. v. City of Rochester, 148 N.H. 603, 813 A.2d 517, 2002 N.H. LEXIS 178 (N.H. 2002).

3. Change to site plan

Any development pursuant to a site plan amendment that substantially changes the plan is, by definition, not "in accordance with the terms" of the original approval and, therefore, clearly does not fall within the protection of the exemption under RSA 674:39. Accordingly, seeing no ambiguity in RSA 674:39, the court declined to apply the administrative gloss doctrine. Harborside Assocs., L.P. v. City of Portsmouth, 163 N.H. 439, 42 A.3d 858, 2012 N.H. LEXIS 38 (2012).

While the terms of a site plan approval cannot sensibly be treated as absolute, as this would deprive developers of any flexibility to make even incidental changes, RSA 674:39 exempts from subsequent changes to zoning ordinances only amendments to approved site plans that do not alter the development to such an extent that it is no longer in accordance with the terms of the original approval; therefore, an amendment can no longer be said to be "in accordance" with the terms of a previously approved site plan if it substantially changes that plan. Whether an amendment constitutes a substantial change from the terms of the site plan's original approval necessarily turns upon the facts and circumstances of the particular case. Harborside Assocs., L.P. v. City of Portsmouth, 163 N.H. 439, 42 A.3d 858, 2012 N.H. LEXIS 38 (2012).

Trial court properly held that by seeking to replace a previously approved retail space with a conference center, the applicant presented a major change to its previously approved site plan, and therefore did not qualify for the exemption under RSA 674:39. A conference center was qualitatively different from retail space. Harborside Assocs., L.P. v. City of Portsmouth, 163 N.H. 439, 42 A.3d 858, 2012 N.H. LEXIS 38 (2012).

Cited:

Cited in Nottingham v. Bonser, 131 N.H. 120, 552 A.2d 58, 1988 N.H. LEXIS 108 (1988); Chasse v. Candia, 132 N.H. 574, 567 A.2d

999, 1989 N.H. LEXIS 132 (1989); Rall v. Town of Belmont, 138 N.H. 172, 635 A.2d 1368, 1993 N.H. LEXIS 185 (1993).

RESEARCH REFERENCES AND PRACTICE AIDS

Cross References.
Development on class V and VI highways, see RSA 674:41.
Effect of approval of plats generally, see RSA 674:38.
Recordation of plats in registry of deeds, see RSA 676:18.
Revocation of recorded approval, see RSA 676:4-a.
Street improvements generally, see RSA 674:40.

New Hampshire Bar Journal.
For article, "The Doctrine of Vested Rights—A Brief Survey," see 48 N.H. B.J. 18 (Autumn 2007).
For article, "'Grandfathered'—The Law of Nonconforming Uses and Vested Rights," see 31 N.H. B.J. 17 (1990).

New Hampshire Practice.
15-7 N.H.P. Land Use Planning and Zoning § 7.14.
15-11 N.H.P. Land Use Planning and Zoning § 11.05.
15-29 N.H.P. Land Use Planning and Zoning § 29.23.
15-30 N.H.P. Land Use Planning and Zoning § 30.11.

674:39-a. Voluntary Merger.

I. Any owner of 2 or more contiguous preexisting approved or subdivided lots or parcels who wishes to merge them for municipal regulation and taxation purposes may do so by applying to the planning board or its designee. Except as set forth in paragraphs II and III, all such requests shall be approved, and no public hearing or notice shall be required. No new survey plat need be recorded, but a notice of the merger, sufficient to identify the relevant parcels and endorsed in writing by the planning board or its designee, shall be filed for recording in the registry of deeds, and a copy mailed to the municipality's assessing officials. No such merged parcel shall thereafter be separately transferred without subdivision approval. No city, town, county, or village district may merge preexisting subdivided lots or parcels except upon the consent of the owner.

II. If there is any mortgage on any of the lots, the applicant shall give written notice to each mortgage holder at the time of the submission of the application. The written consent of each mortgage holder shall be required as a condition of approval of the merger, and shall be recorded with the notice of the merger pursuant to paragraph I. Upon recordation of the notice and each consent, the mortgage or mortgages shall be deemed by operation of law to apply to all lots involved in the merger. The municipality shall not be liable for any deficiency in the notice to mortgage holders.

III. No merger shall be approved that would create a violation of then-current ordinances or regulations.

HISTORY:
1995, 291:9, eff. Aug. 20, 1995. 2010, 345:1, eff. September 18, 2010. 2016, 327:1, eff. August 23, 2016.

Amendment Notes
The 2016 amendments to this section by Ch. 327 added the paragraph I designation; substituted "Except as set forth in para-graphs II and III" for "Except where such merger would create a violation of then-current ordinances or regulations" in the second sentence of paragraph I; and added paragraphs II and III.

—2010.
The 2010 amendment added the last sentence.

NOTES TO DECISIONS

Construction
Plain language of RSA 674:39-a, which governs voluntary merg-ers by owners of two or more parcels of land, gives property owners the right to merge contiguous lots, but nothing in its language precludes a town from automatically merging such lots pursuant to its zoning ordinance. Thus, nothing in RSA 674:39-a precludes a town from requiring the merger of contiguous, nonconforming lots in common ownership. Sutton v. Town of Gilford, 160 N.H. 43, 992 A.2d 709, 2010 N.H. LEXIS 24 (N.H. 2010).

674:39-aa. Restoration of Involuntarily Merged Lots.

I. In this section:
(a) "Involuntary merger" and "involuntarily merged" mean lots merged by municipal action for zoning, assessing, or taxation purposes without the consent of the owner.
(b) "Owner" means the person or entity that holds legal title to the lots in question, even if such person or entity did not hold legal title at the time of the involuntary merger.
(c) "Voluntary merger" and "voluntarily merged" mean a merger under RSA 674:39-a, or any overt action or conduct that indicates an owner regarded said lots as merged such as, but not limited to, abandoning a lot line.

II. Lots or parcels that were involuntarily merged prior to September 18, 2010 by a city, town, county, village district, or any other municipality, shall at the request of the owner, be restored to their pre-merger status and all zoning and tax maps shall be updated to identify the premerger boundaries of said lots or parcels as recorded at the appropriate regis-try of deeds, provided:
(a) The request is submitted to the governing body prior to December 31, 2021.
(b) No owner in the chain of title voluntarily merged his or her lots. If any owner in the chain of title voluntarily merged his or her lots, then all subsequent owners shall be estopped from re-questing restoration. The municipality shall have the burden of proof to show that any previous owner voluntarily merged his or her lots.

III. All decisions of the governing body may be appealed in accordance with the provisions of RSA 676.

IV. Any municipality may adopt local ordinances, including ordinances enacted prior to the effective date of this section, to restore previously merged properties that are less restrictive than the provi-sions in paragraph I and II.

V. The restoration of the lots to their premerger status shall not be deemed to cure any non-confor-mity with existing local land use ordinances.

VI. Municipalities shall post a notice informing residents that any involuntarily merged lots may be restored to premerger status upon the owner's request. Such notice shall be posted in a public place no later than January 1, 2012 and shall remain posted through December 31, 2016. Each municipality shall also publish the same or similar notice in its 2011 through 2015 annual reports.

HISTORY:

2011, 206:4, eff. July 24, 2011. 2016, 327:2, eff. August 23, 2016.

Amendment Notes

The 2016 amendments to this section by Ch. 327 substituted "December 31, 2021" for "December 31, 2016" in II(a).

NOTES TO DECISIONS

Analysis

1. Review
2. Voluntary merger

1. Review

New Hampshire Supreme Court does not construe the plain language of the statute governing restoration of involuntarily merged lots to alter the deferential standard of review applicable in zoning cases. Thus, on appeal from a finding that lots were voluntarily merged, the trial court did not err in applying the usual deferential standard of review to the zoning board of adjustment's decision. Roberts v. Town of Windham, 165 N.H. 186, 70 A.3d 489, 2013 N.H. LEXIS 85 (N.H. 2013).

2. Voluntary merger

Although neither a grantor's conveyance of four lots as one tract in a single deed nor did acquiescence to taxation as a single lot, standing alone, supported a finding of voluntary merger, the totality of the evidence supported a finding that the four lots were voluntarily merged. A garage on one lot was within two inches of another lot and faced that lot; it appeared that a bunkhouse and a cottage on different lots were to be used as part of a waterfront estate; and the prior owners had used one driveway to serve the multiple lots. Roberts v. Town of Windham, 165 N.H. 186, 70 A.3d 489, 2013 N.H. LEXIS 85 (N.H. 2013).

674:40. Improvements in Unapproved Streets.

I. A municipality which has established and recorded an official map, as provided in RSA 674:10, or has conferred upon a planning board platting jurisdiction in accordance with RSA 674:35 shall not thereafter accept, lay out, open, improve, grade, pave, or light any street or lay or authorize the laying of water mains, sewers, connections, or other facilities or utilities in any street, within any portion of the municipality unless such street:

(a) Has been accepted or opened as, or has otherwise received the legal status of, a public street prior to the conferring of platting jurisdiction upon the planning board; or

(b) Corresponds in its location and lines with a street shown on the official map, or with a street shown on a subdivision plat approved by the planning board, or with a street on a street plat made by and adopted by the board.

II. For the purposes of this section, the word "street" shall not mean or include a discontinued highway.

III. The local legislative body may, however, accept, locate and construct any street not shown on or not corresponding with a street on the official map or on an approved subdivision plat or an approved street plat, provided the ordinance or other measure for the accepting, locating, and construction of such street is first submitted to the planning board for its approval and:

(a) If approved by the board, be approved by a majority vote of those present and voting at a regular or special meeting of the local legislative body; or

(b) If disapproved by the planning board, be approved by not less than ⅔ of those present and voting at a regular or special meeting of the local legislative body.

IV. A street approved under paragraph III shall have the status of an approved street as though it had been originally shown on the official map or on a subdivision plat approved by the planning board or as though it had been originally platted by the planning board.

HISTORY:

1983, 447:1. 1989, 266:19, eff. July 1, 1989. 1998, 344:5, eff. Aug. 25, 1998.

Amendments

—1998.

Paragraph III(a): Substituted "those present and voting at a regular or special meeting" for "the entire membership" following "majority vote of".

Paragraph III(b): Rewritten to the extent that a detailed comparison would be impracticable.

—1989.

Paragraph III(b): Inserted "or of a county in which there are located unincorporated towns or unorganized places" preceding "or by majority".

RESEARCH REFERENCES AND PRACTICE AIDS

Cross References.

Approval and recording of plats, see RSA 674:37.
Development on class V and VI highways, see RSA 674:41.
Effect of approval of plats generally, see RSA 674:38, 39.
Master plans generally, see RSA 674:1 et seq.
Official municipal maps generally, see RSA 674:9 et seq.

New Hampshire Practice.

16-45 N.H.P. Municipal Law & Taxation § 45.02.

674:40-a. Delegation of Authority to Accept Dedicated Streets.

I. Notwithstanding RSA 674:40, a municipality with the town meeting form of government, which has conferred upon a planning board platting jurisdiction in accordance with RSA 674:35, may, by majority vote at an annual or special meeting, under an article in the warrant inserted by the local governing body, or by petition, delegate to the local governing body the authority to accept dedicated streets. Such a delegation may be rescinded by the municipality in the same manner.

II. If such a delegation is made, the local governing body may vote to accept any dedicated street only if the street corresponds in its location and lines with a street shown on a subdivision plat or site plan approved by the planning board, or on the official map, or on a street plat made and adopted by the board. A street which has not received such prior planning board approval shall not be accepted without a vote of the local legislative body pursuant to RSA 674:40, III.

III. The local governing body shall hold a public hearing on the proposed acceptance prior to taking action.

IV. A street accepted under this section shall have the status of a public highway under RSA 229:1. Such street shall be deemed a class V highway, subject to the municipality's duty of regular maintenance as set forth in RSA 231, unless otherwise designated pursuant to statute.

V. In this section, "dedicated street" means a street which has been dedicated to public use under the New Hampshire common law of dedication.

HISTORY:

1993, 80:1, eff. June 22, 1993.

Construction.

1993, 80:2, eff. June 22, 1993, provided that the provisions of section 1 of the act, which enacted this section, shall not be construed to affect the legal status of any street which was accepted by other means prior to June 22, 1993.

RESEARCH REFERENCES AND PRACTICE AIDS

New Hampshire Practice.

16-45 N.H.P. Municipal Law & Taxation § 45.02.

674:41. Erection of Buildings on Streets; Appeals.

I. From and after the time when a planning board shall expressly have been granted the authority to approve or disapprove plats by a municipality, as described in RSA 674:35, no building shall be erected on any lot within any part of the municipality nor shall a building permit be issued for the erection of a building unless the street giving access to the lot upon which such building is proposed to be placed:

(a) Shall have been accepted or opened as, or shall otherwise have received the legal status of, a class V or better highway prior to that time; or

(b) Corresponds in its location and lines with:

(1) A street shown on the official map; or

(2) A street on a subdivision plat approved by the planning board; or

(3) A street on a street plat made by and adopted by the planning board; or

(4) A street located and accepted by the local legislative body of the municipality, after submission to the planning board, and, in case of the planning board's disapproval, by the favorable vote required in RSA 674:40; or

(c) Is a class VI highway, provided that:

(1) The local governing body after review and comment by the planning board has voted to authorize the issuance of building permits for the erection of buildings on said class VI highway or a portion thereof; and

(2) The municipality neither assumes responsibility for maintenance of said class VI highway nor liability for any damages resulting from the use thereof; and

(3) Prior to the issuance of a building permit, the applicant shall produce evidence that notice of the limits of municipal responsibility and liability has been recorded in the county registry of deeds; or

(d) Is a private road, provided that:

(1) The local governing body, after review and comment by the planning board, has voted to authorize the issuance of building permits for the erection of buildings on said private road or portion thereof; and

(2) The municipality neither assumes responsibility for maintenance of said private roads nor liability for any damages resulting from the use thereof; and

(3) Prior to the issuance of a building permit, the applicant shall produce evidence that notice of the limits of municipal responsibility and liability has been recorded in the county registry of deeds for the lot for which the building permit is sought; or

(e) Is an existing street constructed prior to the effective date of this subparagraph and is shown on a subdivision plat that was approved by the local governing body or zoning board of adjustment before the municipality authorized the planning board to approve or disapprove subdivision plats in accordance with RSA 674:35, if one or more buildings have been erected on other lots on the same street.

II. Whenever the enforcement of the provisions of this section would entail practical difficulty or unnecessary hardship, and when the circumstances of the case do not require the building, structure or part thereof to be related to existing or proposed streets, the applicant for such permit may appeal from the decision of the administrative officer having charge of the issuance of permits to the zoning board of adjustment in any municipality which has adopted zoning regulations in accordance with RSA 674, or, in municipalities in which no board of adjustment exists, to the local legislative body, or to a board of appeals, whichever is appropriate, in accordance with RSA 674:14 and 674:15, including the requirement for a public hearing. In a municipality which does not require building permits, direct application may be made to the zoning board of adjustment, or the local legislative body, or the board of appeals for permission to erect the building. In passing on such appeal or application, the board of adjustment, local legislative body, or board of appeals may make any reasonable exception and shall have the power to authorize or issue a permit, subject to such conditions as it may impose, if the issuance of the permit or erection of the building would not tend to distort the official map or increase the difficulty of carrying out the master plan upon which it is based, and if erection of the building or issuance of the permit will not cause hardship to future purchasers or undue financial impact on the municipality. Any such decision made in this connection by a board of adjustment, local legislative body, or by a board of appeals pursuant to this section and RSA 674:14 and 674:15 shall be in writing, together with the reasons for the decision, and shall be subject to review in the manner described in RSA 677.

II-a. Municipalities may except any lot, including island lots for islands served exclusively by boats, from the requirements of paragraphs I and II by an affirmative vote of the local legislative body pursuant to RSA 675, first submitted to the planning board for its approval and:

(a) If approved by the board, approved by a majority of those present and voting at a regular or special meeting of the local legislative body; or

(b) If disapproved by the planning board, approved by not less than ⅔ of those present and voting at a regular or special meeting of the local legislative body.

III. This section shall supersede any less stringent local ordinance, code or regulation, and no existing lot or tract of land shall be exempted from the provisions of this section except in accordance with the procedures expressly set forth in this section. For purposes of paragraph I, "the street giving access to the lot" means a street or way abutting the lot and upon which the lot has frontage. It does not include a street from which the sole access to the lot is via a private easement or right-of-way, unless such easement or right-of-way also meets the criteria set forth in subparagraphs I(a), (b), (c), (d), or (e).

IV. In addition to the requirements for the erection of buildings in paragraph I and notwithstanding the exceptions provided in paragraph II, the planning board for a county in which there are located unincorporated towns or unorganized places shall require every building which is erected on leased land located within an unincorporated town or unorganized place to have a building permit. A building permit shall be required under this paragraph regardless of the proximity of the building to any street or highway. The county shall, by resolution, authorize the planning board to issue building permits under this paragraph.

HISTORY:
1983, 447:1. 1988, 131:2, 3. 1989, 266:20. 1995, 291:10, eff. Aug. 20, 1995. 1998, 344:6, eff. Aug. 25, 1998. 2002, 270:1, eff. July 17, 2002. 270:5, eff. April 17, 2002. 2004, 154:1, 2, eff. July 23, 2004. 2005, 226:1, 2, eff. Sept. 3, 2005.

Amendments

—2005.
Paragraph II-a: Inserted "any lot, including" preceding "island lots" and "pursuant to RSA 675" in the introductory paragraph.
Paragraph III: Substituted "subparagraphs I(a), (b), (c), (d), or (e)" for "subparagraphs I(a), (b), or (c)".

—2004.
Paragraph I(d)(3): Added "or" to the end of the paragraph.
Paragraph I(e): Added.

—2002.
Paragraph I(c)(3): Added "or" following "of deeds".
Paragraph I(d): Added.

—1998.
Paragraph II-a: Added.

—1995.
Paragraph III: Rewritten to the extent that a detailed comparison would be impracticable.

—1989.
Paragraph IV: Added.

—1988.
Paragraph II: Substituted "RSA 674:14 and 15" for "RSA 677" following "in accordance with" in the first sentence and preceding "shall be in writing" in the fourth sentence and made other minor stylistic changes.
Paragraph III: Added.

NOTES TO DECISIONS

Analysis

1. Purpose
2. Construction
3. Particular cases

1. Purpose
Purpose of provision of this section limiting erection of buildings on class VI highways, which applies with equal force to building permits and subdivision permits, is to provide against such scattered or premature subdivision as would necessitate excessive expenditure of public funds. Turco v. Barnstead, 136 N.H. 256, 615 A.2d 1237, 1992 N.H. LEXIS 164 (N.H. 1992).
Plaintiff landowners' subdivision request was not improperly denied by town, where this section, prohibiting building on class VI roads, applied to subdivision permits, and estoppel did not apply. Turco v. Barnstead, 136 N.H. 256, 615 A.2d 1237, 1992 N.H. LEXIS 164 (N.H. 1992).
Paragraph I of this section, prohibiting local planning boards from issuing building permits unless the street giving access to the lot qualifies as a class V or better highway, applies to all building permit applications, not just to subdivision applications. Vachon v. New Durham Zoning Bd. of Adjustment, 131 N.H. 623, 557 A.2d 649, 1989 N.H. LEXIS 29 (N.H. 1989).

2. Construction
In construing the statute, RSA 674:41, I(c) does not conflict with RSA 674:41, II. Rather, it simply sets forth the procedure to be followed by those applicants who cannot, choose not, or need not, demonstrate a practical difficulty or unnecessary hardship. Blagbrough Family Realty Trust v. A & T Forest Prods., 155 N.H. 29, 917 A.2d 1221, 2007 N.H. LEXIS 25 (N.H. 2007).
The provisions of this statute, prescribing that no building permit was to be issued unless the street had been accepted or had received the status of a public street, contemplated streets and highways as defined in former RSA 230:1 (now covered by RSA

229:1). Blevens v. Manchester, 103 N.H. 284, 170 A.2d 121, 1961 N.H. LEXIS 33 (N.H. 1961). (Decided under prior law.)

3. Particular cases

Because RSA 674:41, II and RSA 674:33, I(b) explicitly establish separate procedures for seeking exceptions to building permit requirements and seeking variances, petitioner needed to bring its variance application before the zoning board of adjustment in an action separate from its appeal to the trial court of the denial of its building permit application, and res judicata was inapplicable to petitioner's variance application. Merriam Farm, Inc. v. Town of Surry, 168 N.H. 197, 125 A.3d 362, 2015 N.H. LEXIS 103 (N.H. 2015).

Under the statute in effect when a public highway was discontinued in 1895, a town could not have made it a private road, and there was no evidence of an attempt to change its discontinued status. Thus, because the road was not private, it did not satisfy RSA 674:41, I(d), and a zoning board lawfully denied a building permit application. Russell Forest Mgmt., LLC v. Town of Henniker, 162 N.H. 141, 27 A.3d 651, 2011 N.H. LEXIS 81 (N.H. 2011).

As a private roadway was a street on a subdivision plat, which the town planning board had approved, RSA 674:41, I(b)(2) governed the subdivision building permits. Crowley v. Town of Loudon, 162 N.H. 768, 35 A.3d 597, 2011 N.H. LEXIS 176 (N.H. 2011).

As residents purchased their homes with notice that the town had limited responsibility and liability for a private roadway, and they failed to show a public need for the road, the trial court properly determined that there was no occasion for laying out the roadway as a public road pursuant to RSA 674:41, I(d) and 231:38, I. Crowley v. Town of Loudon, 162 N.H. 768, 35 A.3d 597, 2011 N.H. LEXIS 176 (N.H. 2011).

Cited:

Cited in Glick v. Ossipee, 130 N.H. 643, 547 A.2d 231, 1988 N.H. LEXIS 79 (1988); Hannigan v. City of Concord, 144 N.H. 68, 738 A.2d 1262, 1999 N.H. LEXIS 70 (1999).

RESEARCH REFERENCES AND PRACTICE AIDS

Cross References.
Approval and recording of plats, see RSA 674:37.
Effect of approval of plats generally, see RSA 674:38, 39.
Master plans generally, see RSA 674:1 et seq.
Official municipal maps generally, see RSA 674:9 et seq.
Requirement and issuance of building permits generally, see RSA 676:11 et seq.

New Hampshire Practice.
15-29 N.H.P. Land Use Planning and Zoning § 29.18.
16-55 N.H.P. Municipal Law & Taxation § 55.05A.

674:42. Status of Existing Platting Statutes.

After a planning board is granted platting jurisdiction by a municipality under RSA 674:35, the planning board's jurisdiction shall be exclusive, except to the extent that the municipality has transferred authority to approve or disapprove plans showing the extent to which and the manner in which streets within subdivisions shall be graded and improved from the planning board to the governing body pursuant to RSA 674:35, I. All statutory control over plats or subdivisions of land granted by other statutes shall be given effect to the extent that they are in harmony with the provisions of this title. The planning board shall have all statutory control over plats or subdivisions of land. Prior laws which are inconsistent with the powers granted to the planning board and the municipality under this title, and which have expressly by ordinance been adopted by a municipality and made available to a

planning board according to the provisions of this title, are hereby declared to have no application, force or effect so long as the powers conferred by this title shall continue to be exercised by a municipality.

HISTORY:

1983, 447:1, eff. Jan. 1, 1984. 2014, 125:3, eff. August 15, 2014.

Amendment Notes

—2014.
The 2014 amendment added "except to the extent that the municipality has transferred authority to approve or disapprove plans showing the extent to which and the manner in which streets within subdivisions shall be graded and improved from the planning board to the governing body pursuant to RSA 674:35, I" in the first sentence.

NOTES TO DECISIONS

Analysis

1. Generally
2. Public streets

1. Generally

Once a municipality created a planning board, that board had exclusive platting and subdivision jurisdiction; the city council retained no general concurrent jurisdiction. Ehrenberg v. Concord, 120 N.H. 656, 421 A.2d 128, 1980 N.H. LEXIS 373 (N.H. 1980). (Decided under prior law.)

2. Public streets

Since former RSA 36:24 expressly stated that approval of a subdivision plan by a planning board did not constitute acceptance of any street shown on the plan, a planning board had no power to avoid application of RSA 231:51, which released and discharged from all public servitude any street dedicated to public use which had not been open, built or used within 20 years of dedication, and this section could not preempt application of RSA 231:51 to a street never accepted by a municipality. Polizzo v. Hampton, 126 N.H. 398, 494 A.2d 254, 1985 N.H. LEXIS 342 (N.H. 1985). (Decided under prior law.)

RESEARCH REFERENCES AND PRACTICE AIDS

Cross References.
Effect of changes in regulations or ordinances upon approved plats, see RSA 674:39.

Site Plans

RESEARCH REFERENCES AND PRACTICE AIDS

Cross References.
Building codes generally, see RSA 674:51 et seq.
Condominiums generally, see RSA 356-B.
Historic preservation generally, see RSA 227-C.
Subdivision regulation generally, see RSA 674:35 et seq.
Unit ownership of real property, see RSA 479-A.
Zoning generally, see RSA 674:16 et seq.

674:43. Power to Review Site Plans.

I. A municipality, having adopted a zoning ordinance as provided in RSA 674:16, and where the planning board has adopted subdivision regulations as provided in RSA 674:36, may by ordinance or resolution further authorize the planning board to require preliminary review of site plans and to review and approve or disapprove site plans for the development or change or expansion of use of tracts for nonresidential uses or for multi-family dwelling units, which are defined as any structures containing more than 2 dwelling units, whether or not such development includes a subdivision or resubdivision of the site.

II. The ordinance or resolution which authorizes the planning board to review site plans shall make it the duty of the city clerk, town clerk, village district clerk or other appropriate recording official to file with the register of deeds of the county in which the municipality is situated a certificate of notice showing that the planning board has been so authorized, giving the date of such authorization.

III. The local legislative body of a municipality may by ordinance or resolution authorize the planning board to delegate its site review powers and duties in regard to minor site plans to a committee of technically qualified administrators chosen by the planning board from the departments of public works, engineering, community development, planning, or other similar departments in the municipality. The local legislative body may further stipulate that the committee members be residents of the municipality. This special site review committee may have final authority to approve or disapprove site plans reviewed by it, unless the local legislative body deems that final approval shall rest with the planning board, provided that the decision of the committee may be appealed to the full planning board so long as notice of appeal is filed within 20 days of the committee's decision. All provisions of RSA 676:4 shall apply to actions of the special site review committee, except that such a committee shall act to approve or disapprove within 60 days after submissions of applications, subject to extension or waiver as provided in RSA 676:4, I(f). If a municipality authorizes a site review committee in accordance with this paragraph, the planning board shall adopt or amend its regulations specifying application, acceptance and approval procedures and defining what size and kind of site plans may be reviewed by the site review committee prior to authorizing the committee.

IV. The local legislative body of a municipality may by ordinance or resolution establish thresholds based on the size of a project or a tract below which site plan review shall not be required. If a municipality establishes a size limit below which site plan review shall not be required, the planning board shall adopt or amend its regulations to clearly reflect that threshold. Nothing in this paragraph shall preclude the planning board from establishing such thresholds in the absence of action by the legislative body.

V. Site plan review shall not be required for a collocation or a modification of a personal wireless service facility, as defined in RSA 12-K:2.

HISTORY:
1983, 447:1. 1987, 256:2. 1988, 9:1. 1995, 303:3, eff. Jan. 1, 1996. 2005, 33:1, eff. July 9, 2005. 2013, 267:10, eff. September 22, 2013.

Amendment Notes

—2013.
The 2013 amendment added V.

—2005.
Paragraph I: Inserted "require preliminary review of site plans and to".

—1995.
Paragraph IV: Added.

—1988.
Paragraph III: Added.

—1987.
Paragraph I: Inserted "or change or expansion of use" following "site plans for the development".

Severability of 2013 amendment.
2013, 267:12, eff. September 22, 2013, provided: "If any provision of this chapter or the application thereof to any person or circumstance is held invalid, such invalidity shall not affect other provisions or applications of the chapter which can be given effect without the invalid provision or application, and to that end the provisions of this chapter are declared to be severable."

NOTES TO DECISIONS

Analysis

1. Construction with other laws
2. Scope of review
3. Imposition of conditions
4. Imposition of condition subsequent upon approval of application
5. Imposition of moratorium upon site development
6. Effect of zoning changes upon approved plans

1. Construction with other laws
Where an application for approval of a nonresidential use of land was approved subject to the fulfillment of certain conditions, a hearing was not necessary whenever the applicant submitted evidence that he had met a condition; subject to the time limitations imposed by former RSA 36:23, I(c) (now covered by RSA 676:4), governing procedures for approval of such applications, a planning board could wait until the applicant claimed to have fulfilled all conditions, and hold one hearing on all matters of compliance. Sklar Realty v. Merrimack, 125 N.H. 321, 480 A.2d 149, 1984 N.H. LEXIS 271 (N.H. 1984). (Decided under prior law.)
Site plan approvals under this statute were governed by former RSA 36:23 (now covered by RSA 676:4), which regulated the planning board's procedure on approval of plats. Carter v. Nashua, 116 N.H. 466, 362 A.2d 191, 1976 N.H. LEXIS 382 (1976), overruled in part, Weeks Restaurant Corp. v. City of Dover, 119 N.H. 541, 404 A.2d 294, 1979 N.H. LEXIS 349 (1979). (Decided under prior law.)

2. Scope of review
Court on appeal from rezoning decision rejected plaintiffs' argument that city council improperly relied on master plan without detailed evidence of physical characteristics of site; zoning ordinance did not require such specific site information, only planning board approval and public hearing were mandated, and site considerations were within province of planning board on site plan review. Quinlan v. Dover, 136 N.H. 226, 614 A.2d 1057, 1992 N.H. LEXIS 159 (N.H. 1992).

3. Imposition of conditions
Planning boards possess the authority to impose conditions in the site plan review process. Morin v. Somersworth, 131 N.H. 253, 551 A.2d 527, 1988 N.H. LEXIS 109 (N.H. 1988).

4. Imposition of condition subsequent upon approval of application
A planning board had authority to impose a condition subsequent upon approval of an application for nonresidential uses of land.

Sklar Realty v. Merrimack, 125 N.H. 321, 480 A.2d 149, 1984 N.H. LEXIS 271 (N.H. 1984). (Decided under prior law.)

5. Imposition of moratorium upon site development

When authorized by a municipality pursuant to the statute, a municipal planning board could pass upon site plans for development of land for nonresidential uses along a highway in accordance with regulations adopted by the board after notice and public hearing and consistent with an official map, but the planning board had no statutory authority to declare a blanket moratorium on site development pending completion of its planning of street changes and inclusion of proposed street changes in the official street map by city council enactment. Leda Lanes Realty v. Nashua, 112 N.H. 244, 293 A.2d 320, 1972 N.H. LEXIS 187 (N.H. 1972). (Decided under prior law.)

6. Effect of zoning changes upon approved plans

In the absence of a statute providing otherwise, final approval of a subdivision plat by the planning board under the statute did not place the lots beyond the authority of zoning changes. R.A. Vachon & Son v. Concord, 112 N.H. 107, 289 A.2d 646, 1972 N.H. LEXIS 153 (N.H. 1972). (Decided under prior law.)

Cited:

Cited in New Eng. Brickmaster v. Salem, 133 N.H. 655, 582 A.2d 601, 1990 N.H. LEXIS 119 (1990).

RESEARCH REFERENCES AND PRACTICE AIDS

Cross References.
Contents of regulations, see RSA 674:44.

New Hampshire Practice.
14-20 N.H.P. Local Government Law § 750.

674:44. Site Plan Review Regulations.

I. Before the planning board exercises its powers under RSA 674:43, it shall adopt site plan review regulations according to the procedures required by RSA 675:6.

II. The site plan review regulations which the planning board adopts may:

(a) Provide for the safe and attractive development or change or expansion of use of the site and guard against such conditions as would involve danger or injury to health, safety, or prosperity by reason of:

(1) Inadequate drainage or conditions conducive to flooding of the property or that of another;

(2) Inadequate protection for the quality of groundwater;

(3) Undesirable and preventable elements of pollution such as noise, smoke, soot, particulates, or any other discharge into the environment which might prove harmful to persons, structures, or adjacent properties; and

(4) Inadequate provision for fire safety, prevention, and control.

(b) Provide for the harmonious and aesthetically pleasing development of the municipality and its environs.

(c) Provide for open spaces and green spaces of adequate proportions.

(d) Require the proper arrangement and coordination of streets within the site in relation to other existing or planned streets or with features of the official map of the municipality;

(e) Require suitably located streets of sufficient width to accommodate existing and prospective traffic and to afford adequate light, air, and access for firefighting apparatus and equipment to buildings, and be coordinated so as to compose a convenient system;

(f) Require, in proper cases, that plats showing new streets or narrowing or widening of such streets be submitted to the planning board for approval;

(g) Require that the land indicated on plats submitted to the planning board shall be of such character that it can be used for building purposes without danger to health;

(h) Include such provisions as will tend to create conditions favorable for health, safety, convenience, and prosperity;

(i) Require innovative land use controls on lands when supported by the master plan; and

(j) Require preliminary review of site plans.

(k) As a condition of site plan approval, require that the applicant protect or document archeological resources in areas of archeological sensitivity that have been identified in the master plan in accordance with RSA 674:2, III(h).

III. The site plan review regulations which the planning board adopts shall:

(a) Provide the procedures which the board shall follow in reviewing site plans;

(b) Define the purposes of site plan review;

(c) Specify the general standards and requirements with which the proposed development shall comply, including appropriate reference to accepted codes and standards for construction;

(d) Include provisions for guarantees of performance, including bonds or other security; and

(e) Include provision for waiver of any portion of the regulations. The basis for any waiver granted by the planning board shall be recorded in the minutes of the board. The planning board may only grant a waiver if the board finds, by majority vote, that:

(1) Strict conformity would pose an unnecessary hardship to the applicant and waiver would not be contrary to the spirit and intent of the regulations; or

(2) Specific circumstances relative to the site plan, or conditions of the land in such site plan, indicate that the waiver will properly carry out the spirit and intent of the regulations.

IV. The site plan review regulations of the planning board may stipulate, as a condition precedent to the approval of the plat, the extent to which and the manner in which streets shall be graded and improved and to which water, sewer, and other utility mains, piping, connections, or other facilities shall be installed. The regulations or practice of the planning board:

(a) May provide for the conditional approval of the plat before such improvements and installations have been constructed, but any such conditional approval shall not be entered upon that plat.

(b) Shall provide that, in lieu of the completion of street work and utility installations prior to the final approval of a plat, the planning board shall accept a performance bond, irrevocable letter of credit, or other type or types of security as shall be specified in the site plan review regulations. The planning board shall have the discretion to prescribe the type and amount of the bond or other security, require satisfactory evidence of the financial ability of any surety or financial institution to pay such bond or other type of security, and specify a period for completion of the improvements and utilities to be expressed in the bond or other security, in order to secure to the municipality the actual construction and installation of such improvements and utilities. The municipality shall have the power to enforce such bonds or other securities by all appropriate legal and equitable remedies.

V. The planning board may, as part of its site plan review regulations, require an applicant to pay all costs for notification of abutters and may provide for the assessment of reasonable fees to cover the board's administrative expenses and costs of special investigation and the review of documents and other matters which may be required by particular applications.

HISTORY:

1983, 447:1. 1985, 103:21. 1986, 200:3. 1987, 256:3, eff. July 17, 1987. 2004, 71:5, eff. July 6, 2004. 2005, 33:2, eff. July 9, 2005. 2009, 292:2, eff. September 29, 2009. 2013, 76:3, eff. January 1, 2014.

Amendment Notes

—2013.

The 2013 amendment added II(k).

—2009.

The 2009 amendment, in the introductory language of III(e), deleted "in such cases where, in the opinion of the planning board" at the end of the first sentence and added the second and third sentences; added the III(e)(1) designation; added III(e)(2); and made a related change.

—2005.

Paragraph II: Added subpar. (j) and made minor stylistic changes in subpars. (g)–(i).

—2004.

Paragraph II(i): Added.

—1987.

Paragraph II(a): Inserted "or change or expansion of use" following "development" in the introductory clause.

—1986.

Paragraph IV: Rewritten to the extent that a detailed comparison would be impractical.

—1985.

Rewritten to the extent that a detailed comparison would be impractical.

NOTES TO DECISIONS

Analysis

1. Conditions
2. Definitions
3. Review of site plan
4. Necessity for adoption of regulations
5. Sufficiency of regulations
6. Contributions
7. Procedure
8. Waiver of regulations

1. Conditions

Local planning boards have authority to impose conditions upon the approval of a site plan. New Eng. Brickmaster v. Salem, 133 N.H. 655, 582 A.2d 601, 1990 N.H. LEXIS 119 (N.H. 1990).

2. Definitions

The term "streets" in this section refers to streets both on and off the site, and local planning boards are empowered to promulgate regulations which allow for the conditional approval of a site plan by requiring an applicant to contribute funds to the construction of off-site improvements bearing a rational nexus to the development. New Eng. Brickmaster v. Salem, 133 N.H. 655, 582 A.2d 601, 1990 N.H. LEXIS 119 (N.H. 1990).

3. Review of site plan

Court on appeal from rezoning decision rejected plaintiffs' argument that city council improperly relied on master plan without detailed evidence of physical characteristics of site; zoning ordinance did not require such specific site information, only planning board approval and public hearing were mandated, and site considerations were within province of planning board on site plan review. Quinlan v. Dover, 136 N.H. 226, 614 A.2d 1057, 1992 N.H. LEXIS 159 (N.H. 1992).

Requirement under subparagraph III(a) of this section, that local planning boards shall include "the procedures which the board shall follow in reviewing site plans," does not require that every detail relating to the actions of a planning board be spelled out. New Eng. Brickmaster v. Salem, 133 N.H. 655, 582 A.2d 601, 1990 N.H. LEXIS 119 (N.H. 1990).

4. Necessity for adoption of regulations

To control the construction of condominium amenities facility on subdivided land, planning board must promulgate site plan review regulations. Lemm Dev. Corp. v. Bartlett, 133 N.H. 618, 580 A.2d 1082, 1990 N.H. LEXIS 114 (N.H. 1990).

The statute, as amended by 1979, 455:3, and 1979, 455:4, the savings clause of the amendatory act, required that any planning board, even one that had been empowered by a zoning ordinance to review site plans before 1979, adopt specific site-plan review regulations prior to its exercise of site-plan review authority. Eddy Plaza Assocs. v. Concord, 122 N.H. 416, 445 A.2d 1106, 1982 N.H. LEXIS 362 (N.H. 1982). (Decided under prior law.)

Where rules and regulations embodied in a city zoning ordinance were inadequate to meet the requirements of the statute, the city planning board could not continue to exercise site-plan review authority until it adopted specific regulations as prescribed in the statute. Eddy Plaza Assocs. v. Concord, 122 N.H. 416, 445 A.2d 1106, 1982 N.H. LEXIS 362 (N.H. 1982). (Decided under prior law.)

5. Sufficiency of regulations

Rules and regulations embodied in a city zoning ordinance, which applied to the exercise of the planning board's site review powers relating to large-scale developments, were inadequate to meet the requirement of the statute, as amended in 1979, and the savings clause of the 1979 amendment, that any planning board adopt specific site-plan review regulations prior to its exercise of site-plan review authority where the "regulations" were a statement of general principles and guidelines from which regulations must still have been derived, the "regulations" were not self-implementing, and the "regulations" did not address the items required by the statute, such as notice and hearing requirements, and provisions relative to guarantees for performance, including bonds or other security. Eddy Plaza Assocs. v. Concord, 122 N.H. 416, 445 A.2d 1106, 1982 N.H. LEXIS 362 (N.H. 1982). (Decided under prior law.)

6. Contributions

In regard to the construction of subdivision, the legislature intended to authorize municipalities to recover fair contributions from subdividers of costs resulting from increased municipal services necessitated by changes to the land. New Eng. Brickmaster v. Salem, 133 N.H. 655, 582 A.2d 601, 1990 N.H. LEXIS 119 (N.H. 1990).

7. Procedure

Nothing in RSA 674:44, III(e), obligates a planning board to make specific findings of fact; rather, it simply requires that the basis of the board's decision be recorded in the minutes. The statute requires only that the underlying rationale of the planning board's decision to grant a waiver be adequately reflected in its minutes. Property Portfolio Group, LLC v. Town of Derry, 163 N.H. 754, 48 A.3d 937, 2012 N.H. LEXIS 84 (N.H. 2012).

In granting an applicant a waiver allowing it to move its dumpsters closer to its boundary with an adjacent landowner, the planning board's minutes under RSA 674:44, III(e), were adequate. The minutes demonstrated the board's concerns that complying with the setback would violate fire code requirements and pose safety risks, and would interfere with the applicant's use of a loading zone; the minutes further reflect the board's concern with whether the dumpsters would be adequately screened so as not to undermine the purpose of the setback. Property Portfolio Group, LLC v. Town of Derry, 163 N.H. 754, 48 A.3d 937, 2012 N.H. LEXIS 84 (N.H. 2012).

8. Waiver of regulations

Town planning board properly granted a waiver under RSA 674:44, III(e) allowing an applicant to move its dumpsters closer to its boundary. There was evidence that the setback caused unnecessary hardship, that the proposed location was the safest for the dumpsters, and that fencing and screening them would preserve the overall intent of the setback. Property Portfolio Group, LLC v. Town of Derry, 163 N.H. 754, 48 A.3d 937, 2012 N.H. LEXIS 84 (N.H. 2012).

Cited:

Cited in Morin v. Somersworth, 131 N.H. 253, 551 A.2d 527, 1988 N.H. LEXIS 109 (1988); Mooney v. Laconia, 133 N.H. 30, 573 A.2d 447, 1990 N.H. LEXIS 31 (1990); Lampert v. Town of Hudson, 136 N.H. 196, 612 A.2d 920, 1992 N.H. LEXIS 143 (1992); Town of Pelham v. Browning Ferris Indus., 141 N.H. 355, 683 A.2d 536, 1996 N.H. LEXIS 104 (1996); Town of Seabrook v. Vachon Mgmt., Inc., 144 N.H. 660, 745 A.2d 1155, 2000 N.H. LEXIS 7 (2000); Simonsen v. Town of Derry, 145 N.H. 382, 765 A.2d 1033, 2000 N.H. LEXIS 73 (2000); Bayson Props. v. City of Lebanon, 150 N.H. 167, 834 A.2d 202, 2003 N.H. LEXIS 159 (2003).

Heritage Commission

674:44-a. Heritage Commission.

A heritage commission may be established in accordance with RSA 673 for the proper recognition, use, and protection of resources, tangible or intangible, primarily man-made, that are valued for their historic, cultural, aesthetic, or community significance within their natural, built, or cultural contexts.

HISTORY:
1992, 64:2, eff. June 19, 1992.

674:44-b. Powers.

I. **Generally.** Heritage commissions shall have advisory and review authority, specifically, as follows:

(a) Survey and inventory all cultural resources.

(b) Conduct research and publish findings, including reports to establish the legal basis for a district and preparation of historic district ordinances within the municipality prior to its adoption or amendment as provided in RSA 675:6.

(c) Assist the planning board, as requested, in the development and review of those sections of the master plan which address cultural and historic resources.

(d) Advise, upon request, local agencies and other local boards in their review of requests on matters affecting or potentially affecting cultural and historic resources.

(e) Coordinate activities with appropriate service organizations and nonprofit groups.

(f) Publicize its activities.

(g) Hire consultants and contractors as needed.

(h) Receive gifts of money and property, both real and personal, in the name of the city or town, subject to the approval of the city council in a city or the board of selectmen in a town, such gifts to be managed and controlled by the commission for its proper purposes.

(i) Hold meetings and hearings necessary to carry out its duties.

II. **Property.** The commission may acquire, in the name of the town or city, subject to the approval of the local governing body, by gift, purchase, grant, bequest, devise, lease, or otherwise, a fee or lesser interest, development rights, covenant, or other contractual right, including conveyances with conditions, limitations, or reversions, as may be necessary to acquire, maintain, improve, protect, limit the future use of, or otherwise conserve and properly use the cultural resources of the city or town, and shall manage and control the same; provided, however, that the city, town, or commission shall not have the right to condemn property for these purposes.

III. **Historic District Commission.** Heritage commissions also may assume, if authorized by the local legislative body, the composition and duties of historic district commissions.

HISTORY:
1992, 64:2. 1993, 32:1, eff. June 7, 1993. 1995, 138:5, eff. July 23, 1995.

Amendments

—1995.
Paragraph II: Inserted "subject to the approval of the local governing body" following "town or city".

—1993.
Paragraph I(i): Added.

RESEARCH REFERENCES AND PRACTICE AIDS

Cross References.
Appointment and terms of heritage commission members, see RSA 673:4-a.

New Hampshire Practice.
15-35 N.H.P. Land Use Planning and Zoning § 35.17.

674:44-c. Separate Commissions.

A municipality may choose to maintain a separate and distinct heritage commission and historic district commission. In such cases, the heritage commission shall serve in an advisory capacity to the historic district commission as well as to the planning board and other local boards and residents.

HISTORY:
1992, 64:2, eff. June 19, 1992.

RESEARCH REFERENCES AND PRACTICE AIDS

New Hampshire Practice.
15-35 N.H.P. Land Use Planning and Zoning § 35.17.

674:44-d. Appropriations Authorized.

I. A town or city, having established a heritage commission under this subdivision, may appropriate money as deemed necessary to carry out its purposes. The whole or any part of money so appropriated in any year and any gifts of money received pursuant to RSA 674:44-b shall be placed in a heritage fund and allowed to accumulate from year to year. Money may be expended from such fund by the heritage commission for its purposes without further approval of the local legislative body.

II. The town treasurer, pursuant to RSA 41:29, shall have custody of all moneys in the heritage fund and shall pay out the same only upon order of the heritage commission. The disbursement of heritage funds shall be authorized by a majority of the heritage commission. Prior to the use of such funds for the purchase of any interest in real property, the heritage commission shall hold a public hearing with notice in accordance with RSA 675:7.

HISTORY:
1992, 64:2. 1993, 32:3, eff. June 7, 1993.

Amendments

—1993.
Paragraph I: Substituted "local legislative body" for "town meeting" at the end of the third sentence.

Agricultural Commission

674:44-e. Agricultural Commission.

An agricultural commission may be established in accordance with RSA 673 for the proper recognition, promotion, enhancement, encouragement, use, management, and protection of agriculture and agricultural resources, tangible or intangible, that are valued for their economic, aesthetic, cultural, historic, or community significance within their natural, built, or cultural contexts. The word "agriculture" shall include the entirety of RSA 21:34-a, which is the definition of farm, agriculture, and farming.

HISTORY:
2007, 266:1, eff. August 28, 2007.

NOTES TO DECISIONS

1. Effect
Even if using petitioner's Christmas tree farm as a venue for commercial weddings and similar events constituted "agritourism" for purposes of showing a permitted use, the plain meaning of RSA 21:34-a did not provide that they also constituted "agriculture," and RSA 674:44-e does not change the plain meaning of RSA 21:34-a. Forster v. Town of Henniker, 167 N.H. 745, 118 A.3d 1016, 2015 N.H. LEXIS 54 (N.H. 2015).

674:44-f. Powers.

Agricultural commissions shall have advisory and review authority and other duties as follows:
I. Survey and inventory all agricultural resources.
II. Conduct activities to recognize, promote, enhance, and encourage agriculture, agricultural resources, and agricultural-based economic opportunities.
III. Assist the planning board, as requested, in the development and review of those sections of the master plan which address agricultural resources.
IV. Advise, upon request, local agencies and other local boards in their review of requests on matters affecting or potentially affecting agricultural resources.
V. Coordinate activities with appropriate service organizations and nonprofit groups.
VI. Publicize and report its activities.
VII. Hire consultants and contractors as needed.
VIII. Receive gifts of money to assist in carrying out its purpose.
IX. Hold meetings and hearings necessary to carry out its duties.

HISTORY:
2007, 266:1, eff. August 28, 2007.

674:44-g. Appropriations Authorized.

I. A town or city, having established an agricultural commission under this subdivision, may appropriate money as deemed necessary to carry out its purposes. The whole or any part of money so appropriated in any year and any gifts of money received pursuant to RSA 674:44-f shall be placed in an agricultural fund and allowed to accumulate from year to year.

II. The town treasurer, pursuant to RSA 41:29, shall have custody of all moneys in the agricultural fund and shall pay out the same only upon order of the agricultural commission. The disbursement of agricultural funds shall be authorized by a majority of the agricultural commission. The use of such funds shall not be for the purchase of any interest in real property.

HISTORY:
2007, 266:1, eff. August 28, 2007.

Housing Commissions

674:44-h. Housing Commission.

A housing commission may be established in accordance with RSA 673 for the proper recognition, promotion, enhancement, encouragement, and development of a balanced and diverse supply of housing to meet the economic, social, and physical needs of the municipality and its residents, viewed in the context of the region within which the municipality is situated. The establishment of a housing commission shall in no way limit a municipality's authority relative to a housing authority under RSA 203.

HISTORY:
2008, 391:10, eff. September 15, 2008.

674:44-i. Powers.

I. Housing commissions shall have authority to:
  (a) Conduct a housing needs assessment, which may be done in cooperation with the regional housing needs assessment compiled by the regional planning commission under RSA 36:47, II.
  (b) Conduct activities to recognize, promote, enhance, and encourage the development of housing, particularly affordable and workforce housing.
  (c) Assist the planning board, as requested, in the development and review of those sections of the master plan which address housing, and those sections of the zoning ordinance, subdivision regulations, and site plan regulations that address housing or otherwise have the potential to affect the cost or availability of housing.
  (d) Advise, upon request, local agencies and other local boards in their review of requests on matters affecting or potentially affecting housing resources.
  (e) Coordinate activities with appropriate service organizations and nonprofit groups.
  (f) Publicize and report its activities.
  (g) Hire consultants and contractors.

  (h) Receive gifts of money and property, both real and personal, in the name of the city or town, to assist in carrying out the purpose of this section.
  (i) Hold meetings and hearings necessary to carry out its duties.
II. The commission may acquire real property, in the name of the town or city, subject to the approval of the local governing body, by gift, purchase, grant, bequest, devise, lease, development rights, covenant, or other contractual right, including conveyances with conditions, limitations, or reversions, as may be necessary to maintain, improve, protect, limit the future use of, or otherwise conserve and properly use the affordable housing of the city or town, and shall manage and control the same; provided, however, that the city, town, or commission shall not have the right to condemn property for these purposes. The commission shall also have the right to dispose of property so acquired, subject to the approval of the local governing body. Prior to the use of such funds for the purchase of any interest in real property, the housing commission shall hold a public hearing with notice in accordance with RSA 675:7.

HISTORY:
2008, 391:10, eff. September 15, 2008.

674:44-j. Appropriations Authorized.

I. A town or city, having established a housing commission under this subdivision, may appropriate money to the housing commission as necessary to carry out its purposes. The whole or any part of money so appropriated in any year and any gifts of money received under RSA 674:44-i shall be placed in a housing fund and allowed to accumulate from year to year.

II. The town treasurer, pursuant to RSA 41:29, shall have custody of all moneys in the housing fund and shall pay out the same only upon order of the housing commission. The disbursement of housing funds shall be authorized by a majority of the housing commission.

HISTORY:
2008, 391:10, eff. September 15, 2008.

Historic Districts

RESEARCH REFERENCES AND PRACTICE AIDS

Cross References.
  Abolition of historic district commissions, see RSA 673:20.
  Appointment and terms of members of historic district commissions generally, see RSA 673:4 et seq.
  Establishment of historic district commissions, see RSA 673:1.
  Filling of vacancies on commissions, see RSA 673:12.
  Heritage commission, see RSA 674:44-a et seq.
  Historic preservation generally, see RSA 227-C.
  Meetings of commissions, see RSA 673:10, 15, 17.
  Ordinance administration and enforcement generally, see RSA 676.

Ordinance adoption procedures generally, see RSA 675.
Rehearing and appeals procedures generally, see RSA 677.
Removal of members of commissions, see RSA 673:13.
Staff, see RSA 673:16.
Transfer of records of commissions, see RSA 673:21.
Zoning generally, see RSA 674:16 et seq.

674:45. Purposes.

The preservation of cultural resources, and particularly of structures and places of historic, architectural and community value is hereby declared to be a public purpose. The heritage of the municipality will be safeguarded by:

I. Preserving districts in the municipality which reflect elements of its cultural, social, economic, political, community and architectural history;

II. Conserving property values in such districts;

III. Fostering civic beauty;

IV. Strengthening the local economy; and

V. Promoting the use of historic districts for the education, pleasure and welfare of the citizens of the municipality.

HISTORY:

1983, 447:1. 1992, 64:13, 14, eff. June 19, 1992.

Amendments

—1992.

Inserted "cultural resources, and particularly of" preceding "structures", deleted "and" preceding "architectural" and inserted "and community" thereafter in the first sentence of the introductory paragraph.

Paragraph I: Substituted "districts" for "a district" following "preserving", "reflect" for "reflects" preceding "elements" and inserted "community" following "political".

Paragraph II: Substituted "districts" for "district" following "values in such".

Paragraph V: Substituted "historic districts" for "a historic district" preceding "for the education".

NOTES TO DECISIONS

Construction

RSA 674:45, RSA 674:46-a, and RSA 673:4, II do not speak to the legislature's intent regarding the standard of review to be applied to appeals before a zoning board of adjustment. Ouellette v. Town of Kingston, 157 N.H. 604, 956 A.2d 286, 2008 N.H. LEXIS 98 (N.H. 2008).

The statements of purpose in the statute did not impose a burden of proof on any party when a historic district commission considered proposed changes within a historic district. Hanrahan v. Portsmouth, 119 N.H. 944, 409 A.2d 1336, 1979 N.H. LEXIS 425 (N.H. 1979), limited, Ouellette v. Town of Kingston, 157 N.H. 604, 956 A.2d 286, 2008 N.H. LEXIS 98 (N.H. 2008). (Decided under prior law.)

Cited:

Cited in Chesterfield v. Brooks, 126 N.H. 64, 489 A.2d 600, 1985 N.H. LEXIS 274 (1985); Victorian Realty Group v. Nashua, 130 N.H. 60, 534 A.2d 381, 1987 N.H. LEXIS 278 (1987); Portsmouth Advocates v. Portsmouth, 133 N.H. 876, 587 A.2d 600, 1991 N.H. LEXIS 13 (1991).

RESEARCH REFERENCES AND PRACTICE AIDS

New Hampshire Practice.

15-35 N.H.P. Land Use Planning and Zoning § 35.01.

674:46. Authority Granted.

For the purpose of this subdivision, the local legislative body of any city, town, or county in which there are located unincorporated towns or unorganized places shall have the authority, by ordinance, to establish, change, lay out and define historic districts. Within the district, the municipality is empowered to regulate the construction, alteration, repair, moving, demolition or use of such structures and places.

HISTORY:

1983, 447:1. 1985, 103:22. 1989, 266:21, eff. July 1, 1989.

Amendments

—1989.

Substituted "town, or county in which there are located unincorporated towns or unorganized places" for "or town" following "city" in the first sentence.

—1985.

Inserted "by ordinance" following "authority" in the first sentence, made other minor stylistic changes in that sentence and deleted the third and fourth sentences.

NOTES TO DECISIONS

Construction with other laws

City council was not prohibited from rezoning boundary between two historic districts by requirement of RSA 674:46-a that all historic districts and regulations be compatible with master plan and zoning ordinances of the city, town or county in which they exist; RSA 674:46-a was directed toward local historic district commissions and not municipality's legislative body. Portsmouth Advocates v. Portsmouth, 133 N.H. 876, 587 A.2d 600, 1991 N.H. LEXIS 13 (N.H. 1991).

674:46-a. Powers and Duties of the Historic District Commission.

I. For the purpose of establishing a legal basis for the district, the historic district commission may perform research and prepare the content of the historic district ordinance prior to its adoption or amendment as provided in RSA 675:2. In cases in which a municipality chooses to have both a heritage commission and a historic district commission, the historic district commission may request assistance from the heritage commission in performing research and preparing the content of the historic district ordinance.

II. The historic district commission may adopt and amend regulations in the manner provided in RSA 675:6.

III. The historic district commission shall be responsible for administering the ordinance and regulations within the historic district as provided in RSA 676:8–10.

IV. All districts and regulations shall be compatible with the master plan and zoning ordinance of the city, town, or county in which they exist.

V. The historic district commission may assume, if authorized by the local legislative body, the composition and duties of heritage commissions.

HISTORY:

1985, 103:23. 1989, 266:22. 1992, 64:15. 1993, 32:2, eff. June 7, 1993.

Amendments

—1993.

Paragraph V: Added.

—1992.

Paragraph I: Added the second sentence.

—1989.

Paragraph IV: Deleted "or" preceding "town" and inserted "or county" thereafter.

NOTES TO DECISIONS

Analysis

1. Construction
2. Construction with other laws

1. Construction

RSA 674:45, RSA 674:46-a, and RSA 673:4, II do not speak to the legislature's intent regarding the standard of review to be applied to appeals before a zoning board of adjustment. Ouellette v. Town of Kingston, 157 N.H. 604, 956 A.2d 286, 2008 N.H. LEXIS 98 (N.H. 2008).

2. Construction with other laws

City council was not prohibited from rezoning boundary between two historic districts by this section, which was directed toward local historic district commissions and not toward municipality's legislative body. Portsmouth Advocates v. Portsmouth, 133 N.H. 876, 587 A.2d 600, 1991 N.H. LEXIS 13 (N.H. 1991).

RESEARCH REFERENCES AND PRACTICE AIDS

Cross References.

Master plan generally, see RSA 674:1 et seq.
Zoning ordinances generally, see RSA 674:16 et seq.

674:47. Abolition of Historic Districts.

I. Except as provided in paragraph II, any district established pursuant to the provisions of this subdivision may be abolished in the following manner: Upon petition of 25 voters, the historic district commission shall hold 2 public hearings at least 15 days apart on the proposal to abolish the historic district, at which hearings citizens shall have an opportunity to be heard. Notice for each public hearing shall be as provided in RSA 675:7. Following the above public hearings, the proposal to abolish a historic district shall be presented for insertion in the warrant of a regular or special town meeting as provided in RSA 39:3. The historic district shall be abolished upon a vote of ⅔ of the members of the local legislative body present and voting.

II. In counties in which there are located unincorporated towns or unorganized places, the local legislative body shall determine the manner in which any district established pursuant to the provisions of this subdivision may be abolished for those unincorporated towns and unorganized places.

HISTORY:

1983, 447:1. 1989, 266:23, eff. July 1, 1989.

Amendments

—1989.

Designated the existing provisions of the section as par. I, added "except as provided in paragraph II" preceding "any district" in the first sentence of that paragraph, and added par. II.

RESEARCH REFERENCES AND PRACTICE AIDS

Cross References.

Abolition of historic district commissions, see RSA 673:18, 20, 21.

674:48. Interpretation.

Nothing in this subdivision shall be construed to prevent ordinary maintenance or repair of any structure or place within any historic district nor to prevent the construction, alteration, repair, moving or demolition of any structure under a permit issued by the building inspector or other duly delegated authority prior to the establishment of any historic district.

HISTORY:

1983, 447:1, eff. Jan. 1, 1984.

674:49. Enforcement.

The enforcement of the provisions of this subdivision shall be made through the zoning ordinance of the municipality. Any local legislative body which has established a historic district commission under RSA 673 shall include provisions for the enforcement of the commission's administrative decisions in the zoning ordinance of the municipality.

HISTORY:

1983, 447:1, eff. Jan. 1, 1984.

RESEARCH REFERENCES AND PRACTICE AIDS

Cross References.

Administration and enforcement of ordinances generally, see RSA 676.

New Hampshire Practice.

15-35 N.H.P. Land Use Planning and Zoning § 35.13.

674:50. Remedies for Violations.

In case of the violation of any ordinance or regulation made under the authority conferred by this subdivision, the historic district commission, in addition to other remedies, may institute any appropriate action or proceedings to prevent, restrain, correct or abate such violation.

HISTORY:

1983, 447:1, eff. Jan. 1, 1984.

RESEARCH REFERENCES AND PRACTICE AIDS

Cross References.

Penalties and remedies generally, see RSA 676:15 et seq.

New Hampshire Practice.
15-35 N.H.P. Land Use Planning and Zoning § 35.13.

Building Codes

RESEARCH REFERENCES AND PRACTICE AIDS

Cross References.
Appointment and terms of members of building code boards of appeals, see RSA 673:3 et seq.
Building and construction standards generally, see RSA 155-A, 155-B.
Code administration and enforcement generally, see RSA 676.
Code adoption procedures generally, see RSA 675.
Disqualification of members of boards, see RSA 673:14.
Establishment of building code boards of appeals, see RSA 673:1.
Filling of vacancies on boards, see RSA 673:12.
Housing standards, see RSA 48-A.
Meetings of boards, see RSA 673:10, 15, 17.
Modular building standards, see RSA 205-C.
Powers of building code boards of appeals generally, see RSA 674:34.
Rehearing and appeals procedures generally, see RSA 677.
Removal of members of boards, see RSA 673:13.
Staff, see RSA 673:16.
Transfer of records of boards, see RSA 673:22.

New Hampshire Practice.
15-35 N.H.P. Land Use Planning and Zoning § 35.13.

674:51. Power to Amend State Building Code and Establish Enforcement Procedures.

The state building code established in RSA 155-A shall be effective in all towns and cities in the state and shall be enforced as provided in RSA 155-A:7. In addition, towns and cities shall have the following authority:

I. The local legislative body may enact as an ordinance or adopt, pursuant to the procedures of RSA 675:2–4, additional provisions of the state building code for the construction, remodeling, and maintenance of all buildings and structures in the municipality, provided that such additional regulations are not less stringent than the requirements of the state building code. The local legislative body may also enact a process for the enforcement of the state building code and any additional regulations thereto, and the provisions of a nationally recognized code that are not included in and are not inconsistent with the state building code. Any local enforcement process adopted prior to the effective date of this paragraph shall remain in effect unless it conflicts with the state building code or is amended or repealed by the municipality.

II. Any such ordinance adopted under paragraph I by a local legislative body shall be submitted to the state building code review board for informational purposes.

III. The local ordinance or amendment adopted according to the provisions of paragraph I shall include, at a minimum, the following provisions:

(a) The date of first enactment of any building code regulations in the municipality and of each subsequent amendment thereto.

(b) Provision for the establishment of a building code board of appeals as provided in RSA 673:1, V; 673:3, IV; and 673:5.

(c) Provision for the establishment of the position of building inspector as provided in RSA 673:1, V. The building inspector shall have the authority to issue building permits as provided in RSA 676:11–13 and any certificates of occupancy as enacted pursuant to paragraph III, and to perform inspections as may be necessary to assure compliance with the local building code.

(d) A schedule of fees, or a provision authorizing the governing body to establish fees, to be charged for building permits, inspections, and for any certificate of occupancy enacted pursuant to paragraph III.

IV. The regulations adopted pursuant to paragraph I may include a requirement for a certificate of occupancy to be issued prior to the use or occupancy of any building or structure that is erected or remodeled, or undergoes a change or expansion of use, subsequent to the effective date of such requirement.

V. No municipality or local land use board as defined in RSA 672:7 shall adopt any ordinance, regulation, code, or administrative practice requiring the installation of automatic fire suppression sprinklers in any new or existing detached one- or 2-family dwelling unit in a structure used only for residential purposes. Notwithstanding any provision of law to the contrary, no municipality or local land use board shall enforce any existing ordinance, regulation, code, or administrative practice requiring the installation or use of automatic fire suppression sprinklers in any manufactured housing unit as defined in RSA 674:31 situated in a manufactured housing park as defined in RSA 205-A:1, II. Nothing in this paragraph shall affect the ability of an applicant for a local land use permit to include the installation of fire suppression sprinklers pursuant to RSA 674:36, IV, or affect the validity or enforceability of such inclusion.

HISTORY:
1983, 447:1. 1989, 70:1. 1990, 71:3, eff. June 5, 1990. 2002, 8:10, eff. April 17, 2002. 2003, 245:7, eff. July 14, 2003. 2008, 38:1, eff. July 11, 2008. 2011, 269:1, eff. July 1, 2011. 2013, 207:2, eff. September 8, 2013.

Amendments

—2013.
The 2013 amendment added the last sentence of V.

—2011.
The 2011 amendment added par. V.

—2008.
The 2008 amendment added the introductory language.

—2003.
Paragraph I: Added the third sentence.

—2002.

Rewritten to the extent that a detailed comparison would be impracticable.

—1990.

Subparagraph II(b): Substituted "673:3, IV" for "673:3, II".

—1989.

Rewritten to the extent that a detailed comparison would be impracticable.

Effect of 1989 amendment on existing local building codes.

1989, 70:3, eff. June 18, 1989, provided that any local building code enacted or amended by a municipality in accordance with existing law prior to June 18, 1989, shall remain in effect until it is amended or repealed; and, provided further, that any local building code enacted or amended by a municipality after June 18, 1989, shall be in conformance with the provisions of this section, as amended by 1989, 70:1.

RESEARCH REFERENCES AND PRACTICE AIDS

New Hampshire Practice.

13 N.H.P. Local Government Law §§ 13, 14, 307.

14 N.H.P. Local Government Law §§ 900, 950.

674:51-a. Local Adoption of Building Codes by Reference.

In addition to the local powers under RSA 674:51 a municipality may adopt by reference any of the codes promulgated by the International Code Conference which are not included in the state building code under RSA 155-A.

HISTORY:

2003, 245:8, eff. July 14, 2003.

674:52. Power to Adopt Building Codes by Reference. [Repealed.]

[Repealed 2002, 8:12, II, eff. September 14, 2002.]

Former section(s).

Former RSA 674:52, which was derived from 1983, 447:1; 1989, 70:2, 266:24; 1997, 44:9; and 2000, 195:1 related to local adoption of building codes by reference.

RESEARCH REFERENCES AND PRACTICE AIDS

New Hampshire Practice.

14-24 N.H.P. Local Government Law §§ 900, 910, 950.

Authority to Order Building Vacated

674:52-a. Ordering Building Vacated.

I. The building inspector shall have the authority to order occupants to vacate a building, structure, or other premises if the inspector determines, based on reasonable information and belief, that there is imminent danger of failure or collapse, or the condition of such premises otherwise constitutes a clear and imminent danger to the life or safety of occupants or other persons and that protection of life or safety requires vacating the premises. Such an order shall be subject to the procedures of RSA 147:16-a, which shall supersede inconsistent provisions contained in any local code or code adopted by reference.

II. The provisions of paragraph I shall not apply to a residence which is occupied by the owner and his or her immediate family, unless the condition of such premises constitutes a clear and imminent danger to the life or health of persons other than the occupant or occupants.

HISTORY:

1998, 318:3, eff. Aug. 25, 1998.

RESEARCH REFERENCES AND PRACTICE AIDS

New Hampshire Practice.

13-8 N.H.P. Local Government Law § 174.

Land Affected by Municipal Boundaries

674:53. Land Affected by Municipal Boundaries.

I. An owner of contiguous land which is located in more than one municipality may treat a municipal boundary line as an existing boundary between lots, tracts, sites or other divisions of land for purposes of this title unless the existing or proposed use of land or arrangement of structures in one of the municipalities requires and is dependent upon land or improvements located in the other municipality or municipalities in order to fulfill the land use ordinances or regulations of the first municipality with respect to such matters as lot size, density, frontage, uses or accessory uses, set-backs or access, or in order to comply with applicable state or federal regulations.

II. Upon receipt of an application for a permit or approval under this title for the subdivision, development, change of use of, or erection or alteration of any structure upon any lot, tract, site or other division of land whose boundary or portion thereof is a municipal boundary line, or whose sole street access or sole maintained street access is via a private road or class IV, V, or VI highway located in an adjoining municipality, the municipality receiving the application shall inquire in writing to the appropriate administrative officials in the adjoining municipality or municipalities as to the existence of facts or regulations which, under paragraphs I, III, or IV of this section or otherwise, would preclude or affect such subdivision, development, construction, or change of use. Response shall be made to such inquiries within the period provided by this title for approval or disapproval of the underlying application. A response which invokes an ordinance or regulation of such adjoining municipality may be appealed in that adjoining municipality in the same manner as any other administrative decision. An adjoining municipality in which is located an existing private road or class VI highway that serves as an applicant's sole means of fulfilling the street access requirements under RSA 674:41 shall have the same regulatory powers under that statute with respect to that road or highway as if the proposed building or development were located within that same municipality.

III. An owner of contiguous land in more than one municipality may treat such contiguous land as a single lot, tract, site, or other division of land for purposes of this title, notwithstanding the municipal boundary line, provided that:

(a) All uses of land, buildings, or structures shall comply with the regulations or ordinances of the municipality in which they are located.

(b) When an owner has fulfilled or proposes to fulfill the requirements of one municipality, through the inclusion of land or improvements located in an adjoining municipality, such owner or the owner's successors shall not thereafter use that land or those improvements in a manner such that those requirements of the first municipality are no longer fulfilled. This paragraph may be enforced by the municipality whose requirements are to be fulfilled.

IV. No plat or plan showing land or streets in more than one municipality in the state shall be deemed approved for purposes of this title unless it has been approved by the planning boards of all included municipalities in which the planning board has been granted authority over approval of that type of plat or plan. In addition, no plat or plan showing land whose sole street access or sole maintained street access is or is planned to be via a private road or class IV, V, or VI highway located in an adjoining municipality shall be deemed approved for purposes of this title unless it has been approved by the planning board, if any, of that adjoining municipality, provided however that the sole issue which may be addressed or regulated by the adjoining municipality shall be the adequacy of such street access, and the impact of the proposal upon it.

V. With respect to a proposal for the use of contiguous land in more than one municipality:

(a) The fact that a lot, tract, or site straddles a municipal boundary, or that the requirements of one municipality are proposed to be fulfilled by the use of land or improvements in an adjoining municipality, shall not be the sole grounds for disapproval of any application.

(b) A planning board may waive or vary its regulations with respect to access or interior roads in order to provide better harmony with the regulations of an adjoining municipality, whenever strict compliance would be unreasonable in light of the overall design of a proposal.

VI. When local land use boards from more than one municipality have jurisdiction over a proposed use, subdivision, or development of property:

(a) The applicant may petition the respective local land use boards of each such municipality to proceed with the application on a joint basis, and

upon such petition, joint hearings or meetings shall be held throughout the application process. However, each board may meet separately to confer and take final action upon the application, but may not condition final approval upon the receipt of information not previously requested at a joint hearing or meeting.

(b) Not less than a quorum of each involved land use board shall attend the joint hearing or meeting, and the members who attend the joint hearing or meeting shall have the authority of the full board over that application. In the alternative, the full board may attend the joint hearing or meeting. Each land use board shall be responsible for rendering a decision on the subject matter within its jurisdiction.

(c) The board members present at such a joint meeting or hearing shall select an interim chairperson from among such members, who shall prescribe rules of procedure, subject to alteration by the members present, but consistent with RSA 676.

VII. Whenever a subdivision plat or site plan submitted to a planning board includes land whose only maintained public highway access to the Class I and II highway system is via a Class IV or V highway maintained by another municipality in the state, the local governing body and planning board, if any, of that other municipality shall be deemed "abutters" for purposes of notice under RSA 676:4. A planning board may, by regulation, set forth additional circumstances in which notice to adjoining municipalities is required. A planning board, in determining whether an application satisfies its regulations, may consider the effect of the proposal on adjoining municipalities.

HISTORY:

1989, 381:1. 1995, 43:6, 7, eff. July 2, 1995. 1998, 57:1, 2, eff. July 11, 1998.

Amendments

—1998.

Paragraph II: Rewritten to the extent that a detailed comparison would be impracticable.

Paragraph IV: Added the last sentence.

—1995.

Paragraph III(b): Substituted "the owner's" for "his" preceding "successors" in the first sentence.

Paragraph VI(c): Substituted "chairperson" for "chairman" following "select an interim".

NOTES TO DECISIONS

Construction

Decision of a city's zoning board of adjustment that denied a landowner's request for a permit to engage in an apartment expansion involving two parcels, with one parcel lying within the city's boundaries, and the other adjoining parcel lying within a town's boundaries was wrongly upheld as RSA 674:53, II prohibited the city from treating the parcels as separate. Churchill Realty Trust v. Dover Zoning Bd. of Adjustment, 156 N.H. 667, 941 A.2d 584, 2008 N.H. LEXIS 2 (N.H. 2008).

RESEARCH REFERENCES AND PRACTICE AIDS

New Hampshire Practice.
15-29 N.H.P. Land Use Planning and Zoning § 29.12.

Governmental Use of Property

Amendments

—1998.
1998, 281:1, eff. Aug. 25, 1998, deleted "Notification to Municipalities of" preceding "Governmental" in the subdivision heading.

674:54. Governmental Land Uses.

I. In this section, "governmental use" means a use, construction, or development of land owned or occupied, or proposed to be owned or occupied, by the state, university system, the community college system of New Hampshire, or by a county, town, city, school district, or village district, or any of their agents, for any public purpose which is statutorily or traditionally governmental in nature.

II. The state, university system, community college system of New Hampshire, county, town, city, school district, or village district shall give written notification to the governing body and planning board, if such exists, of a municipality of any proposed governmental use of property within its jurisdiction, which constitutes a substantial change in use or a substantial new use. Written notification shall contain plans, specifications, explanations of proposed changes available at the time, a statement of the governmental nature of the use as set forth in paragraph I, and a proposed construction schedule. Such notification shall be provided at least 60 days prior to the beginning of construction. Either the governing body or planning board of the municipality may conduct a public hearing relative to the proposed governmental use. Any such hearing shall be held within 30 days after receipt of notice by the governing body or planning board. A representative of the governmental entity which provided notice shall be available to present the plans, specifications, and construction schedule, and to provide explanations. The governing body or planning board may issue nonbinding written comments relative to conformity or nonconformity of the proposal with normally applicable land use regulations to the sponsor of the governmental use within 30 days after the hearing.

II-a. Any use, construction, or development of land occurring on governmentally owned or occupied land, but which is not a governmental use as defined in paragraph I, shall be fully subject to local land use regulations.

II-b. The construction and operation of any solid waste disposal facility on land owned or occupied by any city or town within another city or town shall be subject to local land use regulations to the same extent as if the land were owned and occupied by a private entity. Nothing in this paragraph shall affect the construction and operation of a solid waste facility on land owned by a solid waste management district formed under RSA 53-A or RSA 53-B or any combination of municipalities authorized by an act of the general court, if the land is located within a city or town that is part of the district.

III. This section shall not apply to:

(a) The layout or construction of public highways of any class, or to the distribution lines or transmission apparatus of governmental utilities, provided that the erection of a highway or utility easement across a parcel of land, shall not, in and of itself, be deemed to subdivide the remaining land into 2 or more lots or sites for conveyance for development purposes in the absence of subdivision approval under this title. For purposes of this subparagraph, "transmission apparatus" shall not include wireless communication facilities.

(b) The erection, installation, or maintenance of poles, structures, conduits and cables, or wires in, under, or across any public highways under RSA 231, or licenses or leases for telecommunication facilities in, under, or across railroad rights of way. For purposes of this subparagraph, "structures" shall not include wireless communications facilities.

IV. In the event of exigent circumstances where the delay entailed by compliance with this section would endanger public health or safety, the governor may declare a governmental use exempt from the requirements of this section.

HISTORY:
1996, 262:1, eff. Aug. 9, 1996. 1998, 281:2, eff. Aug. 25, 1998. 2007, 29:1, eff. May 14, 2007. 361:32, eff. July 17, 2007.

Amendments

—2007.
Paragraph I: Chapter 361 inserted "the community college system of New Hampshire" following "university system".
Paragraph II: Chapter 361 inserted "community college system of New Hampshire" following "university system" in the first sentence.
Paragraph II-b: Added by ch. 29.

—1998.
Rewrote pars. II and III and added pars. II-a and IV.

Wetlands

674:55. Wetlands.

Wherever the term "wetlands," whether singular or plural, is used in regulations and ordinances adopted pursuant to this chapter, such term shall be given the meaning in RSA 482-A:2, X and the delineation of wetlands for purposes of such regulations and ordinances shall be as prescribed in rules adopted under RSA 482-A. Nothing in this subdivision shall be construed to limit the powers otherwise granted under this chapter for municipalities to plan land use and enact regulations based on consideration of environmental characteristics, vegetation, wildlife habit, open space, drainage, potential for flooding, and protection of natural resources, including critical or sensitive areas or resources and groundwater. In the context of such authority, municipalities may define and delineate resources or environmental characteristics, such as wet soils or areas, and shoreline or buffer areas, in a manner different from the common meaning and delineation of wetlands required herein.

HISTORY:
2004, 243:2, eff. July 1, 2005.

Flood Hazards

Amendments

—2009.
The 2009 amendment by 2009, 181:1, eff. July 13, 2009, rewrote the subdivision heading, which formerly read: "Floodplains."

674:56. Flood Hazards.

I. Municipalities may adopt floodplain ordinances as part of their enrollment in the National Flood Insurance Program. Such ordinances shall be adopted pursuant to the authority granted under RSA 674:16 and 17, and shall be adopted and amended pursuant to the procedures in RSA 675 for the adoption and amendment of zoning ordinances. Municipalities may adopt floodplain ordinances either as an amendment to an existing zoning ordinance or as a separate ordinance. A municipality which adopts a floodplain ordinance which is separate from its zoning ordinance or without otherwise having adopted a zoning ordinance, shall observe all legal and procedural requirements for the floodplain ordinance that would be required for a zoning ordinance, including the creation of a board of adjustment. If a municipality has adopted a zoning ordinance either before or after the adoption of a floodplain ordinance, the board of adjustment shall be the same for both ordinances.

II.(a) Municipalities may adopt fluvial erosion hazard ordinances. Such ordinances shall be adopted pursuant to the authority granted under RSA 674:16 and 17, and shall be adopted and amended pursuant to the procedures in RSA 675 for the adoption and amendment of zoning ordinances. Municipalities may adopt fluvial erosion hazard ordinances either as an amendment to an existing zoning ordinance or as a separate ordinance. A municipality which adopts a fluvial erosion hazard ordinance which is separate from its zoning ordinance or without otherwise having adopted a zoning ordinance, shall observe all legal and procedural requirements for the fluvial erosion hazard ordinance that would be required for a zoning ordinance, including the creation of a board of adjustment. If a municipality has adopted a zoning ordinance either before or after the adoption of a floodplain ordinance, the board of adjustment shall be the same for both ordinances.

(b) Any fluvial erosion hazard zoning shall be based on delineation of zones consistent with any fluvial erosion hazard protocols established by the department of environmental services in effect on the date of its adoption. If the planning board of a municipality proposes to adopt, by ordinance or amendment, a fluvial erosion hazard ordinance or an amendment to a fluvial erosion hazard ordinance, the board shall, prior to determining the final form of the ordinance or amendment under RSA 675:2 or RSA 675:3, submit to the department of environmental services a map of all fluvial erosion hazard zones. The department shall review the map and advise the board within 30 days whether the map and zones are consistent with department protocols. The department's comments, if any, shall be advisory only.

HISTORY:
2006, 176:2, eff. May 25, 2006. 2009, 181:2, eff. July 13, 2009.

Amendments

—2009.
The 2009 amendment rewrote the section heading, which formerly read: "Floodplain Ordinances"; added the I designation; and added II.

Intent.
2006, 176:1, eff. May 25, 2006, provided: "The intent of this act [which enacted this subdivision] is to clarify the authority of municipalities to adopt floodplain ordinances pursuant to enrolling in the National Flood Insurance Program, to enable the adoption of flood insurance rate map amendments by resolution of the local governing body, and to ratify the past actions of municipalities in adopting local floodplain ordinances and maps. The general court recognizes that municipalities that fail to adopt amendments to the flood insurance rate maps as required for their participation in the National Flood Insurance Program risk suspension from that program by the federal government."

Ratification of Previously Adopted Floodplain Ordinances.
2006, 176:3, eff May 25, 2006, provided:
"The following municipalities and political subdivisions have previously adopted floodplain ordinances and are enrolled in the National Flood Insurance Program (NFIP). The general court hereby ratifies the following previously adopted floodplain ordinances as legal:
"Municipality: Acworth, Albany, Allenstown, Alstead, Alton, Amherst, Andover, Antrim, Ashland, Auburn, Barnstead, Barrington, Bartlett, Bath, Bedford, Belmont, Bennington, Berlin, Bethlehem, Boscawen, Bow, Bradford, Brentwood, Bridgewater, Bristol, Brookfield, Brookline, Campton, Canaan, Canterbury, Carroll, Charlestown, Chester, Chesterfield, Chichester, Claremont, Colebrook, Columbia, Concord, Conway, Cornish, Dalton, Danbury, Danville, Deerfield, Deering, Derry, Dover, Dummer, Dunbarton, Durham, East Kingston, Easton, Enfield, Epping, Epsom, Errol, Exeter, Farmington, Fitzwilliam, Francestown, Franconia, Franklin, Freedom, Fremont, Gilford, Gilsum, Goffstown, Gorham, Goshen, Grantham, Greenfield, Greenland, Greenville, Groton, Hampstead, Hampton, Hampton Falls, Hancock, Hanover, Hart's Location, Haverhill, Hebron, Henniker, Hill, Hillsborough, Hinsdale, Holderness, Hollis, Hooksett, Hopkinton, Hudson, Jackson, Jaffrey, Jefferson, Keene, Kingston, Laconia, Lancaster, Lebanon, Lee, Lincoln, Lisbon, Litchfield, Littleton, Londonderry, Loudon, Lyme, Madison, Manchester, Marlborough, Marlow, Mason, Meredith, Merrimack, Middleton, Milan, Milford, Milton, Moultonborough, Nashua, New Boston, New Castle, New Durham, New Hampton, New Ipswich, New London, Newbury, Newfields, Newmarket, Newport, North Hampton, Northfield, Northumberland, Northwood, Nottingham, Orford, Ossipee, Pelham, Pembroke, Peterborough, Piermont, Pittsfield, Plainfield, Plaistow, Plymouth, Portsmouth,

Raymond, Rindge, Rochester, Rollinsford, Roxbury, Rye, Salem, Salisbury, Sanbornton, Sandown, Sandwich, Seabrook, Seabrook Beach Village District, Shelburne, Somersworth, South Hampton, Stark, Stewartstown, Strafford, Stratford, Stratham, Sugar Hill, Sullivan, Sunapee, Sutton, Swanzey, Tamworth, Thornton, Tilton, Troy, Tuftonboro, Wakefield, Walpole, Warner, Warren, Waterville Valley, Weare, Webster, Wentworth, Westmoreland, Whitefield, Wilmot, Wilton, Winchester, Windham, Wolfeboro, and Woodstock."

674:57. Flood Insurance Rate Maps.

In a municipality which has enrolled in the National Flood Insurance Program (NFIP), special flood hazard areas shall be as designated on flood insurance rate maps issued by the Federal Emergency Management Agency. Amendments to the flood insurance rate maps shall apply to local floodplain ordinances upon their adoption by resolution of the local governing body of a municipality and shall require no further action by the local legislative body. Map amendments are subject to appeal by owners and lessees of affected real property under 44 C.F.R. 67.5.

HISTORY:
2006, 176:2, eff. May 25, 2006.

Workforce Housing

674:58. Definitions.

In this subdivision:

I. "Affordable" means housing with combined rental and utility costs or combined mortgage loan debt services, property taxes, and required insurance that do not exceed 30 percent of a household's gross annual income.

II. "Multi-family housing" for the purpose of workforce housing developments, means a building or structure containing 5 or more dwelling units, each designed for occupancy by an individual household.

III. "Reasonable and realistic opportunities for the development of workforce housing" means opportunities to develop economically viable workforce housing within the framework of a municipality's ordinances and regulations adopted pursuant to this chapter and consistent with RSA 672:1, III-e. The collective impact of all such ordinances and regulations on a proposal for the development of workforce housing shall be considered in determining whether opportunities for the development of workforce housing are reasonable and realistic. If the ordinances and regulations of a municipality make feasible the development of sufficient workforce housing to satisfy the municipality's obligation under RSA 674:59, and such development is not unduly inhibited by natural features, the municipality shall not be in violation of its obligation under RSA 674:59 by virtue of economic conditions beyond the control of the municipality that affect the economic viability of workforce housing development.

IV. "Workforce housing" means housing which is intended for sale and which is affordable to a household with an income of no more than 100 percent of the median income for a 4-person household for the metropolitan area or county in which the housing is located as published annually by the United States Department of Housing and Urban Development. "Workforce housing" also means rental housing which is affordable to a household with an income of no more than 60 percent of the median income for a 3-person household for the metropolitan area or county in which the housing is located as published annually by the United States Department of Housing and Urban Development. Housing developments that exclude minor children from more than 20 percent of the units, or in which more than 50 percent of the dwelling units have fewer than two bedrooms, shall not constitute workforce housing for the purposes of this subdivision.

HISTORY:
2008, 299:2, eff. January 1, 2010 (see effective date note below)

Effective date of amendments by 2008, 299:2.
2009, 157:1, eff. July 8, 2009, amended 2008, 299:4 to change the effective date of 2008, 299:1 and 299:2 from July 1, 2009 to January 1, 2010.

Findings and Statement of Purpose—2008 enactment.
2008, 299:1, eff. January 1, 2010 (see effective date note), provided:
"**I.** The state of New Hampshire is experiencing a shortage of housing that is affordable to working households. This housing shortage poses a threat to the state's economic growth, presents a barrier to the expansion of the state's labor force, undermines state efforts to foster a productive and self-reliant workforce, and adversely affects the ability of many communities to host new businesses.
"**II.** Achieving a balanced supply of housing, which requires increasing the supply of workforce housing, serves a statewide public interest, and constitutes an urgent and compelling public policy goal.
"**III.** The purpose of this act is to clarify the requirements of Britton v. Chester (134 N.H. 439 (1991)) and to provide additional guidance for complying with those requirements to local officials and the public.
"**IV.** Section 2 of this act is intended to provide the maximum feasible flexibility to municipalities in exercising the zoning powers under RSA 674 consistent with their obligation to provide reasonable opportunities for the development of workforce housing, and is not intended to create a system of statewide land use regulation or a statewide zoning process."

674:59. Workforce Housing Opportunities.

I. In every municipality that exercises the power to adopt land use ordinances and regulations, such ordinances and regulations shall provide reasonable and realistic opportunities for the development of workforce housing, including rental multi-family housing. In order to provide such opportunities, lot size and overall density requirements for workforce housing shall be reasonable. A municipality that adopts land use ordinances and regulations shall allow workforce housing to be located in a majority, but not necessarily all, of the land area that is zoned to permit residential uses within the municipality. Such a municipality shall have the discretion to determine what land areas are appropriate to meet this obligation. This obligation may be satisfied by the adoption of inclusionary zoning as defined in RSA 674:21, IV(a). This paragraph shall not be construed to require a municipality to allow for the development of multifamily housing in a majority of its land zoned to permit residential uses.

II. A municipality shall not fulfill the requirements of this section by adopting voluntary inclusionary zoning provisions that rely on inducements that render workforce housing developments economically unviable.

III. A municipality's existing housing stock shall be taken into consideration in determining its compliance with this section. If a municipality's existing housing stock is sufficient to accommodate its fair share of the current and reasonably foreseeable regional need for such housing, the municipality shall be deemed to be in compliance with this subdivision and RSA 672:1, III-e.

IV. Paragraph I shall not be construed to require municipalities to allow workforce housing that does not meet reasonable standards or conditions of approval related to environmental protection, water supply, sanitary disposal, traffic safety, and fire and life safety protection.

HISTORY:
2008, 299:2, eff. January 1, 2010 (see effective date note below)

Effective date of amendments by 2008, 299:2.
2009, 157:1, eff. July 8, 2009, amended 2008, 299:4 to change the effective date of 2008, 299:2 from July 1, 2009 to January 1, 2010.

674:60. Procedure.

I. Any person who applies to a land use board for approval of a development that is intended to qualify as workforce housing under this subdivision shall file a written statement of such intent as part of the application. The failure to file such a statement shall constitute a waiver of the applicant's rights under RSA 674:61, but shall not preclude an appeal under other applicable laws. In any appeal where the applicant has failed to file the statement required by this paragraph, the applicant shall not be entitled to a judgment on appeal that allows construction of the proposed development, or otherwise permits the proposed workforce housing development to proceed despite its nonconformance with the municipality's ordinances or regulations.

II. If a land use board approves an application to develop workforce housing subject to conditions or restrictions, it shall notify the applicant in writing of such conditions and restrictions and give the applicant an opportunity to establish the cost of complying with the conditions and restrictions and the effect of compliance on the economic viability of the proposed development. The board's notice to the applicant of the conditions and restrictions shall constitute a conditional approval solely for the purpose of complying with the requirements of RSA 676:4, I(c)(1). It shall not constitute a final decision for any other purpose, including the commencement of any applicable appeal period.

III. Upon receiving notice of conditions and restrictions under paragraph II, the applicant may submit evidence to establish the cost of complying with the conditions and restrictions and the effect on economic viability within the period directed by the board, which shall not be less than 30 days.

(a) Upon receipt of such evidence from the applicant, the board shall allow the applicant to review the evidence at the board's next meeting for which 10 days' notice can be given, and shall give written notice of the meeting to the applicant at least 10 days in advance. At such meeting, the board may also receive and consider evidence from other sources.

(b) The board may affirm, alter, or rescind any or all of the conditions or restrictions of approval after such meeting.

(c) Subject to subparagraph (d), the board shall not issue its final decision on the application before such meeting, unless the applicant fails to submit the required evidence within the period designated by the board, in which case it may issue its final decision any time after the expiration of the period.

(d) If an applicant notifies the board in writing at any time that the applicant accepts the conditions and restrictions of approval, the board may issue its final decision without further action under this paragraph.

IV. A municipality may require that an applicant record restrictive covenants acceptable to the land use board that the workforce housing may not be rented to or sold to any household whose income is greater than that specified in RSA 674:58, IV. The covenant shall be for the term specified in the regulations of the land use board. The municipality may adopt regulations to insure compliance with the covenants, which regulations may include requirements for the monitoring of the project by the municipality or by a suitable third party agency qualified to carry out such requirements, including but not limited to requiring the production of annual income verification for renters and non-owner occupiers. The land use board may consider the existence of recorded covenants or income qualification and occupancy criteria as satisfying the purpose of this paragraph if such covenants or criteria are administered by a state or federal entity.

HISTORY:
2008, 299:2, eff. January 1, 2010 (see effective date note below). 2010, 150:1, eff. June 14, 2010.

Effective date of amendments by 2008, 299:2.
2009, 157:1, eff. July 8, 2009, amended 2008, 299:4 to change the effective date of 2008, 299:2 from July 1, 2009 to January 1, 2010.

Amendments

—2010.
The 2010 amendment added IV.

674:61. Appeals.

I. Any person who has filed the written notice required by RSA 674:60, and whose application to develop workforce housing is denied or is approved with conditions or restrictions which have a substantial adverse effect on the viability of the proposed workforce housing development may appeal the municipal action to the superior court under RSA 677:4 or RSA 677:15 seeking permission to develop the proposed workforce housing. The petition to the court shall set forth how the denial is due to the municipality's failure to comply with the workforce housing requirements of RSA 674:59 or how the conditions or restrictions of approval otherwise violate such requirements.

II. A hearing on the merits of the appeal shall be held within 6 months of the date on which the action was filed unless counsel for the parties agree to a later date, or the court so orders for good cause. If the court determines that it will be unable to meet this requirement, at the request of either party it shall promptly appoint a referee to hear the appeal within 6 months. Referees shall be impartial, and shall be chosen on the basis of qualifications and experience in planning and zoning law.

III. In the event the decision of the court or referee grants the petitioner a judgment that allows construction of the proposed development or otherwise orders that the proposed development may proceed despite its nonconformance with local regulations, conditions, or restrictions, the court or referee shall direct the parties to negotiate in good faith over assurances that the project will be maintained for the long term as workforce housing. The court or referee shall retain jurisdiction and upon motion of either party affirming that negotiations are deadlocked, the court or referee shall hold a further hearing on the appropriate term and form of use restrictions to be applied to the project.

HISTORY:
2008, 299:2, eff. January 1, 2010 (see effective date note below)

Effective date of amendments by 2008, 299:2.
2009, 157:1, eff. July 8, 2009, amended 2008, 299:4 to change the effective date of 2008, 299:2 from July 1, 2009 to January 1, 2010.

Small Wind Energy Systems

674:62. Definitions.

In this subdivision:

I. "Small wind energy system" means a wind energy conversion system consisting of a wind turbine, a tower, and associated control or conversion electronics, which has a rated capacity of not more than 100 kilowatts and which will be used in the first instance for onsite consumption.

II. "System height" means the height above grade of the tower plus the wind generator.

III. "Tower height" means the height above grade of the fixed portion of the tower, excluding the wind generator.

IV. "Wind generator" means blades and associated mechanical and electrical conversion components mounted on top of the tower.

HISTORY:
2008, 357:1, eff. July 11, 2009. 2010, 143:5, eff. August 13, 2010.

Amendments

—2010.
The 2010 amendment, in I, substituted "of not more than 100 kilowatts" for "consistent with the net metering specifications of RSA 362-A:9" and "in the first instance" for "primarily."

674:63. Municipal Regulations of Small Wind Energy Systems.

Ordinances or regulations adopted by municipalities to regulate the installation and operation of small wind energy systems shall not unreasonably limit such installations or unreasonably hinder the performance of such installations. Unreasonable limits or hindrances to performance shall include the following:

I. Prohibiting small wind energy systems in all districts within the municipality.

II. Restricting tower height or system height through application of a generic ordinance or regulation on height that does not specifically address allowable tower height or system height of a small wind energy system.

III. Requiring a setback from property boundaries for a tower greater than 150 percent of the system height. In a municipality that does not adopt specific setback requirements for small wind energy systems, any small wind energy system shall be set back from the nearest property boundary a distance at least equal to 150 percent of the system height; provided, however, that this requirement may be modified by the zoning board of adjustment upon application in an individual case if the applicant establishes the conditions for a variance under this chapter.

IV. Setting a noise level limit lower than 55 decibels, as measured at the site property line, or not allowing for limit overages during short-term events such as utility outages and severe wind storms.

V. Setting electrical or structural design criteria that exceed applicable state, federal, or international building or electrical codes or laws.

HISTORY:
2008, 357:1, eff. July 11, 2009.

674:64. Aviation Requirements.

Small wind energy systems shall be built to comply with all applicable Federal Aviation Administration requirements, including 14 C.F.R. part 77, subpart B regarding installations close to airports, and the airport zoning regulations adopted under RSA 424:5.

HISTORY:
2008, 357:1, eff. July 11, 2009.

674:65. Abandonment.

A small wind energy system that is out-of-service for a continuous 12-month period shall be deemed abandoned. The planning board administrator may issue a notice of abandonment to the owner of an abandoned small wind energy system. The owner shall have the right to respond to the notice of abandonment within 30 days from the receipt date. The planning board shall withdraw the notice of abandonment and notify the owner that the notice has been withdrawn if the owner provides the planning board with information demonstrating the small wind energy system has not been abandoned. If the small wind energy system is determined to be abandoned, the owner of the small wind energy system shall remove the wind generator from the tower at the owner's sole expense within 3 months of receipt of notice of abandonment. If the owner fails to remove the wind generator from the tower, the administrator may pursue a legal action to have the wind generator removed at the owner's expense.

HISTORY:
2008, 357:1, eff. July 11, 2009.

674:66. Abutter and Regional Notification.

I.(a) A municipal building inspector shall notify all abutters by verified mail, as defined in RSA 451-C:1, VII, upon application for a building permit to construct a small wind energy system. Abutters shall be afforded a 30-day comment period prior to the issuance of a building permit. An appeal may be made to the building code board of appeals pursuant to RSA 674:34 or to the zoning board of adjustment pursuant to RSA 676:5, as may be appropriate.

(b) The cost of abutter notification shall be borne by the applicant.

(c) The building inspector shall provide notice of the application for a building permit to the local governing body.

II. The building inspector, acting as a local land use board pursuant to RSA 672:7, shall review an application for a small wind energy system pursuant to RSA 36:56 to determine whether it is a development of regional impact, as defined in RSA 36:55. If the building inspector determines that the proposal has the potential for regional impact, he or she shall follow the procedures set forth in RSA 36:57, IV.

HISTORY:
2008, 357:1, eff. July 11, 2009. 2017, 59:2, eff. August 1, 2017.

Amendment Notes
The **2017 amendment to this section by Ch. 59** substituted "by verified mail, as defined in RSA 451-C:1, VII" for "by certified mail" in the first sentence of I(a).

Traditional Commercial and Recreational Fishing Protection Act

HISTORY:
2015, 236:2, eff. September 11, 2015.

674:67. Definitions.

In this subdivision:

I. "Commercial fishing operation" means any type of activity conducted on land, requiring the location or storage of commercial fishing equipment such as fishing vessels, fishing gear, docks, piers, loading areas, landing areas, and cold storage facilities, including any activity necessary to prepare finfish or shellfish for refrigeration, conducted by any person licensed to take, possess, land, or transport, on the waters of New Hampshire, any marine species by any method for the purpose of sale. Commercial fishing operation shall not include operations with the sole or primary function of processing seafood.

II. "Recreational fishing operation" means a party or charter boat that takes paying passengers for recreational fishing in coastal waters.

HISTORY:
2015, 236:2, eff. September 11, 2015.

674:68. Protection of Commercial and Recreational Fishing Operations.

No commercial or recreational fishing operation shall be declared a public or private nuisance solely because of a change in ownership or a change in the character of the property in or around the locality of the operation.

HISTORY:
2015, 236:2, eff. September 11, 2015.

674:69. Local Ordinances Prohibited.

No local legislative body shall adopt any ordinance that declares any commercial or recreational fishing operation to be a nuisance solely because it is a commercial or recreational fishing operation, or any zoning ordinance that unreasonably burdens or forces the closure of any commercial or recreational fishing operation, including any fishing operation conducted as a home occupation. Nothing in this subdivision shall prevent a local government from regulating commercial and recreational fishing operations, including by requiring the use of methods, structures, or appliances where such use will prevent, ameliorate, or remove conditions which create or may create a nuisance.

HISTORY:
2015, 236:2, eff. September 11, 2015.

674:70. Construction of Subdivision.

This subdivision shall not be construed to permit an existing commercial or recreational fishing operation to change to a larger operation with regard to emitting more noise or odor, where such change violates local ordinances or regulations or creates a nuisance.

HISTORY:
2015, 236:2, eff. September 11, 2015.

Accessory Dwelling Units

HISTORY:
2016, 6:2, eff. June 1, 2017.

674:71. Definition.

As used in this subdivision, "accessory dwelling unit" means a residential living unit that is within or attached to a single-family dwelling, and that provides independent living facilities for one or more persons, including provisions for sleeping, eating, cooking, and sanitation on the same parcel of land as the principal dwelling unit it accompanies.

2016, 6:2, eff. June 1, 2017.

674:72. Accessory Dwelling Units.

I. A municipality that adopts a zoning ordinance pursuant to the authority granted in this chapter shall allow accessory dwelling units as a matter of right or by either conditional use permit pursuant to RSA 674:21 or by special exception, in all zoning districts that permit single-family dwellings. One accessory dwelling unit shall be allowed without additional requirements for lot size, frontage, space limitations, or other controls beyond what would be required for a single-family dwelling without an accessory dwelling unit. The municipality is not required to allow more than one accessory dwelling unit for any single-family dwelling. The municipality may prohibit accessory dwelling units associated with multiple single-family dwellings attached to each other such as townhouses, and with manufactured housing as defined in RSA 674:31. Subsequent condominium conveyance of any accessory dwelling unit separate from that of the principal dwelling unit shall be prohibited, notwithstanding the provisions of RSA 356-B:5, unless allowed by the municipality.

II. If a zoning ordinance contains no provisions pertaining to accessory dwelling units, then one accessory dwelling unit shall be deemed a permitted accessory use, as a matter of right, to any single-family dwelling in the municipality, and no municipal permits or conditions shall be required other than a building permit, if necessary.

III. An interior door shall be provided between the principal dwelling unit and the accessory dwelling unit, but a municipality shall not require that it remain unlocked.

IV. Any municipal regulation applicable to single-family dwellings shall also apply to the combination of a principal dwelling unit and an accessory dwelling unit including, but not limited to lot coverage standards and standards for maximum occupancy per bedroom consistent with policy adopted by the United States Department of Housing and Urban Development. A municipality may require adequate parking to accommodate an accessory dwelling unit.

V. The applicant for a permit to construct an accessory dwelling unit shall make adequate provisions for water supply and sewage disposal for the accessory dwelling unit in accordance with RSA 485-A:38, but separate systems shall not be required for the principal and accessory dwelling units. In order to comply with this paragraph and prior to constructing an accessory dwelling unit, an application for approval for a sewage disposal system shall be submitted in accordance with RSA 485-A as applicable. The approved sewage disposal system shall be installed if the existing system has not received construction approval and approval to operate under current rules or predecessor rules, or the system fails or otherwise needs to be repaired or replaced.

VI. A municipality may require owner occupancy of one of the dwelling units, but it shall not specify which unit the owner must occupy. A municipality may require that the owner demonstrate that one of the units is his or her principal place of residence, and the municipality may establish reasonable regulations to enforce such a requirement.

VII. A municipality may establish standards for accessory dwelling units for the purpose of maintaining the aesthetic continuity with the principal dwelling unit as a single-family dwelling. A municipality may also establish minimum and maximum sizes for an accessory dwelling unit, provided that size may not be restricted to less than 750 square feet.

VIII. A municipality may not require a familial relationship between the occupants of an accessory dwelling unit and the occupants of a principal dwelling unit.

IX. A municipality may not limit an accessory dwelling unit to only one bedroom.

X. An accessory dwelling unit may be deemed a unit of workforce housing for purposes of satisfying the municipality's obligation under RSA 674:59 if the unit meets the criteria in RSA 674:58, IV for rental units.

HISTORY:
2016, 6:2, eff. June 1, 2017. 2017, 89:1, eff. June 5, 2017. 2017, 238:4, eff. September 16, 2017.

Amendment Notes
The 2017 amendments to this section by Ch. 89 added the last two sentences of I.

The **2017 amendments to this section by Ch. 238** added the last two sentences of V.

674:73. Detached Accessory Dwelling Units.

A municipality is not required to but may permit detached accessory dwelling units. Detached accessory dwelling units shall comply with the requirements of, and any municipal ordinances or regulations adopted pursuant to, RSA 674:72, IV through IX. If a municipality allows detached accessory dwelling units, it may require an increased lot size.

2016, 6:2, eff. June 1, 2017.

CHAPTER 675

ENACTMENT AND ADOPTION PROCEDURES

General Provisions

Section
675:1. General Requirements.

Zoning Ordinance, Historic District Ordinance and Building Code Enactment Procedures

675:2. Method of Enactment in Cities and Towns Operating Under Town Council Form of Government.
675:3. Method of Enactment in Certain Towns and Village Districts.
675:4. Method of Enactment by Petition.
675:4-a. Adoption of Emergency Temporary Zoning and Planning Ordinance in Certain Towns.
675:5. Zoning Ordinance Protest Petition.
675:6. Method of Adoption.
675:7. Notice Requirements for Public Hearing.
675:8. Filing of Zoning Ordinances, Historic District Ordinances, Building Codes, Subdivision Regulations, Site Plan Review Regulations, and Amendments.
675:9. Place for Filing Documents; Reporting of Adoptions or Amendments.

RESEARCH REFERENCES AND PRACTICE AIDS

Cross References.
Administration and enforcement of ordinances, regulations and codes generally, see RSA 676.
Adoption of bylaws by towns generally, see RSA 31:39 et seq.
Bylaw defined, see RSA 21:45.
Definitions generally, see RSA 672:2 et seq.
Local land use boards generally, see RSA 673.
Local land use planning and regulatory powers generally, see RSA 674.
Rehearing and appeals procedures generally, see RSA 677.

New Hampshire Bar Journal.
For article, "An Overview of the New Hampshire Land Use Planning and Regulation Statutes, " see 34 N.H. B.J. 6 (June 1993).

New Hampshire Practice.
13-11 N.H.P. Local Government Law § 200.
15-5 N.H.P. Land Use Planning and Zoning §§ 5.01, et seq.

General Provisions

675:1. General Requirements.

I. The following shall be adopted under RSA 675:6:

(a) Every master plan or amendment to a master plan proposed under RSA 674:1;
(b) Subdivision regulations proposed under RSA 674:35;
(c) Site plan review regulations proposed under RSA 674:44; and
(d) Historic district regulations proposed under RSA 674:46-a.
II. Zoning ordinances proposed under RSA 674:16, historic district ordinances proposed under RSA 674:46 and building codes proposed under RSA 674:51 shall be adopted in accordance with the procedures required under RSA 675:2–5.
III. If an official map is established, it shall be established according to the procedures required under RSA 674:10.

HISTORY:
1983, 447:1. 1985, 103:24, eff. Jan. 1, 1986.

Amendments

—1985.
Paragraph I(b): Deleted "and" following "RSA 674:35".
Paragraph I(c): Added "and" following "RSA 674:44".
Paragraph I(d): Added.
Paragraph II: Inserted "historic district ordinances proposed under RSA 674:46" following "RSA 674:16".
Paragraph III: Substituted "RSA 674:10" for "RSA 674:9" at the end of the paragraph.

RESEARCH REFERENCES AND PRACTICE AIDS

Cross References.
Adoption and amendment of master plan generally, see RSA 674:4.
Adoption of emergency temporary zoning and planning ordinances in certain towns, see RSA 675:4-a.
Adoption of innovative land use controls, see RSA 674:21.
Emergency temporary zoning and planning ordinances generally, see RSA 674:24 et seq.

New Hampshire Practice.
15-15 N.H.P. Land Use Planning and Zoning § 15.07.

Zoning Ordinance, Historic District Ordinance and Building Code Enactment Procedures

RESEARCH REFERENCES AND PRACTICE AIDS

Cross References.
Building codes generally, see RSA 674:51 et seq.
Emergency temporary zoning and planning ordinances generally, see RSA 674:24 et seq.
Filling of zoning ordinances, historic district ordinances or building codes, see RSA 675:8, 9.
Historic district ordinances generally, see RSA 674:45 et seq.
Master plans generally, see RSA 674:1 et seq.
Official municipal maps generally, see RSA 674:9 et seq.
Site plan review regulations generally, see RSA 674:43 et seq.
Subdivision regulations generally, see RSA 674:35 et seq.
Zoning ordinances generally, see RSA 674:16 et seq.

675:2. Method of Enactment in Cities and Towns Operating Under Town Council Form of Government.

I. In cities or in towns operating under the town

council form of government, and in counties in which there are located unincorporated towns or unorganized places, the local legislative body shall determine the manner in which a zoning ordinance, historic district ordinance, or a building code is established and amended; provided, however, that any question concerning the establishment and amendment of a zoning ordinance, historic district ordinance, or a building code may be placed on a ballot separate from the ballot used to elect city or town officers. The planning board shall forward to the town clerk all proposed amendments to a zoning ordinance, historic district ordinance, or building code not later than the fifth Tuesday prior to the date for electing city or town officers.

II. No zoning ordinance, historic district ordinance, or building code shall be established or amended until after a public hearing is held in accordance with the procedures required under RSA 675:7 on the proposed zoning ordinance, historic district ordinance, building code or amendment.

HISTORY:

1983, 447:1. 1985, 103:24. 266:1. 1989, 266:25. 1990, 54:1, eff. June 5, 1990.

Amendments

—1990.

Paragraph I: Added the second sentence.

—1989.

Paragraph I: Inserted "and in counties in which there are located unincorporated towns or unorganized places" following "government".

—1985.

Paragraph I: Rewritten by ch. 266 to the extent that a detailed comparison would be impracticable.

Paragraph II: Chapter 103 inserted "historic district ordinance" following "zoning ordinance" wherever it appeared.

Rescinded 1985, 103 amendment.

1985, 103:24 provided for amendment of pars. I and II, effective Jan. 1, 1986. However, 1985, 266:4, eff. Aug. 6, 1985, declared the amendment to par. I made by 1985, 103:24 to be null and void.

NOTES TO DECISIONS

Analysis

1. Purpose of hearings
2. Sufficiency of notice
3. Cure of defects
4. Validity of particular enactments

1. Purpose of hearings

The purpose of public hearings was to insure that the current views of local residents would be taken into account by the council when it considered enactment of a proposed ordinance. Bosse v. Portsmouth, 107 N.H. 523, 226 A.2d 99, 1967 N.H. LEXIS 212 (N.H. 1967). (Decided under prior law.)

2. Sufficiency of notice

While there was no specific statutory requirement that the description of the zones be published, a notice would have been meaningless unless it included some reference to the area involved sufficient to give the reader reasonable warning that his interest might be affected. Schadlick v. Concord, 108 N.H. 319, 234 A.2d 523, 1967 N.H. LEXIS 179 (N.H. 1967). (Decided under prior law.)

3. Cure of defects

A legislative act legalizing the votes and proceedings of a number of town meetings was ineffective to cure the invalidity of a zoning amendment adopted without compliance with the notice provision. Olson v. Litchfield, 112 N.H. 261, 296 A.2d 470, 1972 N.H. LEXIS 191 (N.H. 1972); Calawa v. Litchfield, 112 N.H. 263, 296 A.2d 124, 1972 N.H. LEXIS 193 (N.H. 1972). (Decided under prior law.)

4. Validity of particular enactments

A city's adoption of former RSA 156:3-a (now covered by RSA 676:12), allowing building permits to be withheld pending zoning changes, was not subject to the public hearing requirements needed to enact zoning ordinances since former RSA 156:3-a was not a zoning ordinance. Socha v. Manchester, 126 N.H. 289, 490 A.2d 794, 1985 N.H. LEXIS 297 (N.H. 1985). (Decided under prior law.)

Cited:

Cited in Bedford Residents Group v. Bedford, 130 N.H. 632, 547 A.2d 225, 1988 N.H. LEXIS 65 (1988).

RESEARCH REFERENCES AND PRACTICE AIDS

Cross References.

Enactment of zoning ordinances, historic district ordinances and building codes pursuant to petition of voters, see RSA 675:4.

Enactment of zoning ordinances, historic district ordinances or building codes by towns not operating under town council form of government and village districts, see RSA 675:3.

675:3. Method of Enactment in Certain Towns and Village Districts.

I. Any town not operating under the town council form of government, or any village district which is specifically authorized by law to enact a zoning ordinance, shall establish and amend a zoning ordinance, historic district ordinance, or building code upon the affirmative vote by ballot of a majority of the legal voters present and voting on the day of the meeting, as provided in paragraph VII. Any proposed zoning ordinance, as submitted by a planning board or any amendment to an existing zoning ordinance as proposed by a planning board, board of selectmen or village district commission shall be submitted to the voters of a town or village district in the manner prescribed in this section.

II. No zoning ordinance, historic district ordinance, or building code shall be established or amended at a town or village district meeting until after the planning board holds at least one public hearing on the proposed ordinance, code or amendment. Notice for the time and place of each public hearing shall be the same as that provided in RSA 675:7.

III. After the public hearing the planning board shall, by vote, determine the final form of the ordinance, amendment, or amendments to be presented to the town or village district, which ordinance or amendment may include editorial revisions and textual modifications resulting from the proceedings of that hearing.

IV. An additional public hearing shall be held if the proposal is substantively altered by the planning board after public hearing. Subsequent public hearings shall be held at least 14 days after the prior public hearing and with the notice provided in RSA 675:7.

V. Official copies of the final proposal to adopt or amend the zoning ordinance, historic district ordinance, or building code shall be placed on file and made available to the public at the town or village clerk's office not later than the fifth Tuesday prior to the date when action is to be taken. An official copy of the proposal shall be on display for the voters at the meeting place on the date of the meeting.

VI. Each village district must be specifically authorized to zone by the legislature.

VII. If the town or village district has adopted an official ballot for the election of its respective officers, the issue as to the adoption of the proposed ordinance, building code, or amendment shall be presented to the voters of the town or village district by having the town or village district clerk prepare an official ballot separate from the official ballot used to elect town or village district officers which shall include the following question, or by including the following question on the official ballot as prepared by the town or village district clerk:

"Are you in favor of the adoption of the zoning ordinance, historic district ordinance, or building code (or amendment to the existing town (village district) zoning ordinance, historic district ordinance, or building code) as proposed by the planning board?" In the event that there shall be more than a single proposed amendment to be submitted to the voters at any given meeting, the issue as to the several amendments shall be put in the following manner: "Are you in favor of the adoption of Amendment No. _____ as proposed by the planning board for the town (village district) zoning ordinance (historic district ordinance or building code) as follows: (Here insert topical description of substance of amendment.)?" If such action is to be taken at a meeting other than the one at which officers are to be elected, the clerk shall prepare a special ballot containing the question or questions above stated, and the meeting shall open not later than noon and shall remain open at least 8 hours. If such action is to be taken at a meeting in a town or village district which has not adopted an official ballot, the clerk may prepare a special ballot likewise separate from the ballot used to elect town or village district officers for the use of voters in voting on the question. If a majority of the voters present and voting on any question as herein provided shall vote in the affirmative, the ordinance or amendment thereto shall be declared to have been adopted. When submitting any question to the voters under this section, there shall be 2 squares printed after the question, one with the word "yes" beside it and another with the word "no" beside it.

VIII. If an amendment is submitted by the selectmen or village district commissioners, the ballot shall so indicate. A notation on the ballot stating the planning board's approval or disapproval shall immediately follow the question's description.

IX. The method for amending a zoning ordinance, historic district ordinance or building code, as set forth in this section, may also be utilized to repeal such ordinance or code. The ballot question shall use the word "repeal" in place of the words "adoption" or "amendment."

HISTORY:
1983, 447:1. 1985, 103:24. 266:2. 1990, 54:2, eff. June 5, 1990. 1996, 43:1, eff. June 23, 1996.

Amendments

—1996.
Paragraph IX: Added.

—1990.
Paragraph V: Substituted "not later than the fifth Tuesday" for "4 weeks" following "office" in the first sentence.

—1985.
Paragraph I: Chapter 103 inserted "historic district ordinance" preceding "or building code" in the first sentence and added the second sentence.
Paragraphs II and V: Chapter 103 inserted "historic district ordinance" preceding "or building code" in the first sentence.
Paragraph VII: Rewritten by ch. 266 to the extent that a detailed comparison would be impracticable.
Paragraph VIII: Added by ch. 103.

Rescinded 1985 amendment.
1985, 103:24 provided for amendment of pars. I, II, V and VII, reenactment of pars. III, IV and V without changes and addition of par. VIII, effective Jan. 1, 1986. However, 1985, 266:4, eff. Aug. 6, 1985, declared the amendment to par. VII made by 1985, 103:24 to be null and void.

NOTES TO DECISIONS

Analysis

1. Constitutionality
2. Applicability of procedure
3. Notice and hearing
4. Records of meeting of planning board
5. Submission of amendments to voters

1. Constitutionality
The submission of a zoning ordinance to the voters under the statute was not an unconstitutional exercise of legislative power by referendum, and the provisions for hearings before the planning board and the restriction of the voters to consideration of only those changes as were proposed was not a delegation of legislative power to the board, but a valid limitation upon the power of the town. Cutter v. Durham, 109 N.H. 33, 241 A.2d 216, 1968 N.H. LEXIS 109 (N.H. 1968). (Decided under prior law.)

2. Applicability of procedure
Where RSA 675:3, VII and RSA 675:4, I pertained to ballots, not warrant articles, and the trial court conflated warrant articles and ballots, the trial court misapprehended the relevant statutes and the matter had to be remanded for further consideration. Lower Bartlett Water Precinct v. Murnik, 150 N.H. 690, 845 A.2d 1245, 2004 N.H. LEXIS 55 (N.H. 2004).

Whether or not a particular law was a zoning measure subject to the prerequisites for the enactment of such an ordinance under the statute or was an expression of some other phase of the police power, not so subject, was to be determined by the nature and purpose of the particular enactment. Piper v. Meredith, 110 N.H. 291, 266 A.2d 103, 1970 N.H. LEXIS 156 (N.H. 1970). (Decided under prior law.)

An ordinance establishing a height and setback limitation for buildings in a portion of a town came within the police powers of

RSA 31:39 and did not have to be adopted under the provisions of this statute. Piper v. Meredith, 110 N.H. 291, 266 A.2d 103, 1970 N.H. LEXIS 156 (N.H. 1970). (Decided under prior law.)

3. Notice and hearing

The provision for public hearing in this statute required a hearing before the legislative body. Towle v. Nashua, 106 N.H. 394, 212 A.2d 204, 1965 N.H. LEXIS 177 (N.H. 1965). (Decided under prior law.)

4. Records of meeting of planning board

The statute did not require that minutes of the meeting of the planning board be kept, and the lack of precise records of the board did not invalidate the action taken at a town meeting. Collins v. Derry, 109 N.H. 470, 256 A.2d 654, 1969 N.H. LEXIS 181 (N.H. 1969). (Decided under prior law.)

5. Submission of amendments to voters

The "single subject" rule is applicable to RSA 675:3 and a proposed amendment that includes changes to multiple sections of an ordinance is proper so long as the sections sought to be changed are reasonably germane to the subject of the amendment. Handley v. Town of Hooksett, 147 N.H. 184, 785 A.2d 399, 2001 N.H. LEXIS 192 (N.H. 2001).

The requirements of the statute were met when all amendments to a zoning ordinance were printed and distributed to all voters, the amendments and the town zoning map were available from the town clerk, and copies of the amendments were displayed in the town. Hampton v. Brust, 122 N.H. 463, 446 A.2d 458, 1982 N.H. LEXIS 375 (N.H. 1982). (Decided under prior law.)

The provision requiring the planning board to determine the final form in which a proposed amendment was to be presented to the voters, and allowing editorial revisions and textual modifications after a second public hearing, could not be interpreted to allow substantive changes, since such changes would violate the spirit of the statute, the entire purpose of which was to allow the public to participate in the process of amending zoning ordinances. Hampton v. Brust, 122 N.H. 463, 446 A.2d 458, 1982 N.H. LEXIS 375 (N.H. 1982). (Decided under prior law.)

No substantial amendments could be included in a proposed zoning ordinance after a second public hearing unless an additional third hearing was held because the public must have had an opportunity to discuss the ordinance before it voted. Hampton v. Brust, 122 N.H. 463, 446 A.2d 458, 1982 N.H. LEXIS 375 (N.H. 1982). (Decided under prior law.)

Where the town planning board added a second sentence to a proposed zoning ordinance defining a penny arcade, after a second public hearing had been held and before the amendment was presented to the voters for approval, the changes made after the second hearing were not editorial revisions or textual modifications permitted by the statute, and the ordinance was void and unenforceable, not having been validly enacted, even though it was submitted to and approved by the voters, since a third hearing had not been held after the planning board added the second sentence. Hampton v. Brust, 122 N.H. 463, 446 A.2d 458, 1982 N.H. LEXIS 375 (N.H. 1982). (Decided under prior law.)

There was compliance with the statute and the voters were given adequate notice of the proposal on which they were to vote where, although notice of the second public hearing contained only the changes in the original proposal set forth in the notice for the first public hearing and did not contain all the amendments that were being proposed, all amendments to be acted upon were printed in a town report and distributed to all voters, the amendments and the zoning map were on file and copies were available at the town clerk's office two weeks prior to the town meeting, and copies of the amendments were posted in each polling booth and displayed in other places in the town hall. Collins v. Derry, 109 N.H. 470, 256 A.2d 654, 1969 N.H. LEXIS 181 (N.H. 1969). (Decided under prior law.)

Cited:

Cited in Rall v. Town of Belmont, 138 N.H. 172, 635 A.2d 1368, 1993 N.H. LEXIS 185 (1993).

OPINIONS OF THE ATTORNEY GENERAL

Analysis

1. Notice and hearing
2. Submission of amendments to voters

1. Notice and hearing

Zoning amendments accepted by a planning board were to be fully and legally noticed to inform the public, and if additional amendments were to be considered after the hearing, there were to be further hearings at which such amendments would be considered before they were placed on the ballot. 1 N.H.Op.A.G. 162. (Decided under prior law.)

2. Submission of amendments to voters

There was nothing in the statute which required all amendments to a zoning ordinance to be presented as one package; therefore, amendments could be submitted to the voters separately. 1 N.H.Op.A.G. 157. (Decided under prior law.)

RESEARCH REFERENCES AND PRACTICE AIDS

Cross References.

Enactment of zoning ordinances, historic district ordinances or building codes by cities and towns operating under town council form of government, see RSA 675:2.

Enactment of zoning ordinances, historic district ordinances or building codes pursuant to petition of voters, see RSA 675:4.

Filing of zoning ordinances, historic district ordinances or building codes, see RSA 675:8, 9.

New Hampshire Practice.

13-9 N.H.P. Local Government Law § 200.

15-5 N.H.P. Land Use Planning and Zoning § 5.16.

675:4. Method of Enactment by Petition.

I. Twenty-five or more voters may petition for an amendment to a zoning ordinance, historic district ordinance, or a building code. Petitioned amendments shall be voted only at the annual town or village district meeting. A petition to amend a zoning ordinance, historic district ordinance, or a building code shall be submitted to the board of selectmen or the village district commissioners during the period between 120 and 90 days prior to the annual town or village district meeting. The petition shall be in correct warrant article form, as determined by the selectmen or village district commissioners, to amend the zoning ordinance, historic district ordinance, or building code. The selectmen or the village district commissioners shall submit the petitions to the planning board in a timely manner.

II. The planning board at its first regular meeting following the petition period shall set the date of the public hearing for each petitioned amendment which is received and shall hold a public hearing on each petitioned amendment. Notice for the time and place of the public hearing shall be the same as that provided in RSA 675:7.

III. Each petitioned amendment shall be placed on a ballot which may be separate from the ballot used to elect town or village district officers. A notation on the ballot stating the planning board's approval or disapproval shall immediately follow the question's description. Any petitioned question receiving an affirmative vote of a majority of the legal voters present and voting shall be adopted, except as provided in RSA 675:5. The planning board shall forward to the town or village district clerk all proposed amendments to a zoning ordinance, historic district ordinance, or building code under this section not later than the fifth Tuesday prior to the date for electing town or village district officers.

IV. The town or village district clerk shall include each question on a petitioned amendment on the appropriate official or special ballot, or separate official ballot, in the same manner as provided in paragraph III and in RSA 675:3, VII.

V. The method for amending a zoning ordinance, historic district ordinance or building code, as set forth in this section, may also be utilized to repeal such ordinance or code. The ballot question shall use the word "repeal" in place of the word "amendment."

HISTORY:

1983, 447:1. 1985, 103:24. 266:3. 1990, 54:3, eff. June 5, 1990. 1996, 43:2, eff. June 23, 1996.

Amendments

—1996.
Paragraph V: Added.

—1990.
Paragraph III: Added the fourth sentence.

—1985.
Paragraph I: Chapter 103 inserted "historic district ordinance" following "zoning ordinance" in the first, second and third sentences.
Paragraph III: Chapter 266 added "which may be separate from the ballot used to elect town or village district officers" following "ballot" at the end of the first sentence.
Paragraph IV: Chapter 266 inserted "or separate official ballot" preceding "in the same manner as provided in" and "paragraph III and in" thereafter.

Rescinded 1985, 103 amendment.
1985, 103:24 provided for amendment of par. I and reenactment of pars. II–IV without changes, effective Jan. 1, 1986. However, 1985, 266:4, eff. Aug. 6, 1985, declared the amendments to pars. III and IV purportedly made by 1985, 103:24 to be null and void.

NOTES TO DECISIONS

Analysis

1. Construction with other laws
2. Notice and hearing
3. Petition for repeal

1. Construction with other laws
RSA 39:2, requiring that town selectmen include in the town meeting warrant all subject matter to be considered at the meeting, and this statute, empowering selectmen to determine whether a petition for a zoning amendment was in correct form, did not require that petitions be submitted to the selectmen before submission to the planning board; the petition was to be submitted, but only after the planning board had completed its part in the amending process. Board of Selectmen v. Planning Bd., 118 N.H. 150, 383 A.2d 1122, 1978 N.H. LEXIS 362 (N.H. 1978). (Decided under prior law.)

2. Notice and hearing
Under the terms of the statute, the date from which time is to be reckoned is the date of the town meeting, and the days prior to the

meeting date are to be counted not counting the date of the meeting. Miller v. Town of Tilton, 139 N.H. 429, 655 A.2d 409, 1995 N.H. LEXIS 24 (N.H. 1995).

3. Petition for repeal
Where RSA 675:3, VII and RSA 675:4, I pertained to ballots, not warrant articles, and the trial court conflated warrant articles and ballots, the trial court misapprehended the relevant statutes and the matter had to be remanded for further consideration. Lower Bartlett Water Precinct v. Murnik, 150 N.H. 690, 845 A.2d 1245, 2004 N.H. LEXIS 55 (N.H. 2004).

RESEARCH REFERENCES AND PRACTICE AIDS

Cross References.
Enactment of zoning ordinances, historic district ordinances or building codes generally, see RSA 675:2, 3.
Filing of zoning ordinances, historic district ordinances or building codes, see RSA 675:8, 9.
Warrants for town meetings generally, see RSA 39.

New Hampshire Practice.
15-5 N.H.P. Land Use Planning and Zoning § 5.16.
15-15 N.H.P. Land Use Planning and Zoning § 15.05.

675:4-a. Adoption of Emergency Temporary Zoning and Planning Ordinance in Certain Towns.

I. In any town which does not have a planning board, as provided by RSA 674, or a zoning ordinance, as provided in this subdivision, or in any town which has a planning board, but which does not have in effect a zoning ordinance, the selectmen, upon recommendation of the planning board, or upon written application to them for this purpose signed by 5 percent of the voters of the town, shall call a special town meeting, warning the same as provided by law, to act upon the following question: "Shall the town adopt the provisions of RSA 674:24–29 entitled 'Emergency Temporary Zoning and Planning Ordinance'? "

II. The provisions of RSA 675 relating to method of enactment shall not apply; provided, however, that there shall be a public hearing, with notice as provided in RSA 675:7, not more than 7 calendar days before the proposed special town meeting. There shall be reasonable opportunity for debate of such question at such town meeting before balloting commences. Voting shall be by ballot, with the use of the checklist used at the most recent annual meeting plus any new registrations, and the polls shall remain open at least 2 hours after debate has ended for the casting of ballots. If the question in paragraph I receives affirmative votes amounting at least to a majority of those present and voting, the provisions of RSA 674:24–29 shall take effect forthwith in the town and shall remain in effect until 2 annual town meetings shall have been held or the voters of the town consider a zoning ordinance as provided for by this chapter, whichever period of time is the lesser.

III. If no zoning ordinance has been considered and no zoning ordinance under the applicable provisions of this chapter has been proposed for action by the time of the second such annual town meeting, the selectmen shall include in the warrant for such meeting the following proposal to be put as a question to be voted upon by ballot after discussion: To see if the town will vote to continue for one additional year the temporary zoning ordinance enacted under the provisions of RSA 674:24–29. If a majority of those present and voting on said article vote in the affirmative, the provisions of RSA 674:24–29 shall remain in effect in the town for one year from the date of such meeting. If a majority of those present and voting on the article vote in the negative, the provisions of RSA 674:24–29 shall cease to be in effect.

HISTORY:
1985, 103:24, eff. Jan. 1, 1986.

RESEARCH REFERENCES AND PRACTICE AIDS

Cross References.
Filing of zoning ordinances, historic district ordinances or building codes, see RSA 675:8, 9.
Warnings of town meetings generally, see RSA 39.

675:5. Zoning Ordinance Protest Petition.

I. Zoning regulations, restrictions and boundaries may from time to time be amended or repealed.

I-a. A favorable vote of ⅔ of all the members of the legislative body present and voting shall be required to act upon any amendment or repeal in the case of a protest against such zoning change signed by either:

(a) The owners of 20 percent of the area of the lots included in such proposed change; or

(b) The owners of 20 percent of the area within 100 feet immediately adjacent to the area affected by the change or across a street from such area.

I-b. Paragraph I-a shall apply only to amendments which alter the boundary locations separating previously defined zoning districts, or to amendments which alter the regulations or restrictions of an area not larger than ⅓ of the land area within the municipality.

I-c. The area of streets, commons, or land owned by a governmental entity shall not be included in any calculation under this section.

II. In order to have any protest considered pursuant to paragraph I-a:

(a) The owners signing the petition shall identify themselves on the petition by name and address, and by address of the property involved, or by lot and map number, or by whatever other means is used within the town or village district to identify the land in question, so that the selectmen or commissioners may identify such owners as interested and affected parties; and

(b) The signed protest petition shall be submitted to the selectmen or village district commissioners at least 7 days prior to the town or village district meeting; provided, however, that each protest petition shall apply to only one article on

the warrant. A notice of receipt of the protest petition shall be posted at the polling place, and the moderator shall announce at the opening of the town meeting that a protest petition has been received.

HISTORY:
1983, 447:1. 1985, 103:24. 1989, 44:1–3, eff. June 11, 1989.

Amendments

—1989.
Paragraph I: Deleted the second sentence.
Paragraphs I-a–I-c: Added.
Paragraph II: Substituted "paragraph I-a" for "paragraph I" in the introductory clause.

—1985.
Paragraph I: Rewritten to the extent that a detailed comparison would be impracticable.

NOTES TO DECISIONS

Analysis

1. Generally
2. Protests—Persons who may file protests
3. —Signature of petition
4. —Filing
5. —Determination of validity of protest petition
6. Approval of change by members of legislative body
7. Effect of noncompliance with statutory procedures
8. Cure of defects in proceedings

1. Generally
Preexisting land use regulations were not so comprehensive as to acquire the status of de facto zoning and, therefore, a town properly enacted a zoning ordinance by a simple majority, rather than a two-thirds majority; the preexisting regulations included a mobile home and trailer park ordinance, a sign ordinance, a town beach bylaw, a building permit ordinance, excavation regulations, driveway access regulations, a floodplain ordinance, and a large institutional land ordinance. Caspersen v. Town of Lyme, 139 N.H. 637, 661 A.2d 759, 1995 N.H. LEXIS 70 (N.H. 1995).
Amendments and changes must have been reasonable and in the public interest. Edgewood Civic Club v. Blaisdell, 95 N.H. 244, 61 A.2d 517, 1948 N.H. LEXIS 228 (N.H. 1948). (Decided under prior law.)
The power to amend a zoning ordinance was not unlimited, but must have been exercised reasonably. Brady v. Keene, 90 N.H. 99, 4 A.2d 658, 1939 N.H. LEXIS 22 (N.H. 1939). (Decided under prior law.)

2. Protests—Persons who may file protests
By its plain terms, RSA 675:5, I-a encompasses all land within 100 feet of an area subject to the change by a zoning amendment regardless of whether it is within the same municipality and RSA 675:5, II(a) does not limit protest petitions to owners of land within the municipality in which the petition is filed; in addition, the town's tax maps are more than sufficient to determine whether a protest petition meets the threshold of community support required by RSA 675:5, I-a. Smagula v. Town of Hooksett, 149 N.H. 784, 834 A.2d 333, 2003 N.H. LEXIS 125 (N.H. 2003).
Where a proposed amendment would rezone from residential to general business use a single tract adjoining a general business district fronting upon a public highway, the statute could properly be interpreted to require protest by the owners of twenty percent of the area extending one hundred feet from the area to be rezoned on all sides except the frontage adjoining the business district on the highway. Towle v. Nashua, 106 N.H. 394, 212 A.2d 204, 1965 N.H. LEXIS 177 (N.H. 1965). (Decided under prior law.)

3. —Signature of petition
Superior court properly determined that protest petition failed to satisfy requirements of this section and therefore did not require a

two-thirds vote for passage of zoning amendment where petition did not contain signatures of the owners of 20 percent of the land adjacent to or across the street from area to be rezoned. Treisman v. Bedford, 132 N.H. 54, 563 A.2d 786, 1989 N.H. LEXIS 75 (N.H. 1989).

Where land was owned by joint tenants, the signature of just one of them on the petition was sufficient. Disco v. Board of Selectmen, 115 N.H. 609, 347 A.2d 451, 1975 N.H. LEXIS 375 (N.H. 1975). (Decided under prior law.)

Withdrawal of a name from the protest petition two days after tabulation of the votes was not permissible. Disco v. Board of Selectmen, 115 N.H. 609, 347 A.2d 451, 1975 N.H. LEXIS 375 (N.H. 1975). (Decided under prior law.)

Property owned by trusts, partnerships and cotenants did not have to be represented by the signatures of all the parties having an interest in the properties where those not signing authorized a signing in their behalf. Alton v. Fisher, 114 N.H. 359, 320 A.2d 653, 1974 N.H. LEXIS 278 (N.H. 1974). (Decided under prior law.)

4. —Filing

Protests against a proposed amendment of the zoning ordinance were to be filed with the board of aldermen. Towle v. Nashua, 106 N.H. 394, 212 A.2d 204, 1965 N.H. LEXIS 177 (N.H. 1965). (Decided under prior law.)

5. —Determination of validity of protest petition

RSA 675:5 does not mandate a determination of the validity of a protest petition prior to voting. Handley v. Town of Hooksett, 147 N.H. 184, 785 A.2d 399, 2001 N.H. LEXIS 192 (N.H. 2001). (Decided under prior law.)

6. Approval of change by members of legislative body

The purpose of the requirement that two-thirds of all members of the legislative body of the municipality present and voting adopt a zoning change after a valid protest had been filed was to confer an added protection to property owners against unwanted or ill-considered changes. Disco v. Board of Selectmen, 115 N.H. 609, 347 A.2d 451, 1975 N.H. LEXIS 375 (N.H. 1975). (Decided under prior law.)

In the case of a protest, a vote of two-thirds of all the members of the legislative body present and voting was required for adoption, and that statutory requirement controlled over the provisions of a local ordinance. Cutter v. Durham, 109 N.H. 33, 241 A.2d 216, 1968 N.H. LEXIS 109 (N.H. 1968). (Decided under prior law.)

7. Effect of noncompliance with statutory procedures

Since minor deviations from or technical violations of a statutory procedure could be excused if there had been substantial compliance, a town's demurrer to a plaintiff-protestor's petition for injunctive relief arising out of the adoption of a zoning ordinance amendment was properly overruled where the plaintiff established a basis upon which the relief could be granted by pleading substantial compliance. Bourgeois v. Bedford, 120 N.H. 145, 412 A.2d 1021, 1980 N.H. LEXIS 247 (N.H. 1980). (Decided under prior law.)

8. Cure of defects in proceedings

An act of the state legislature legalizing, ratifying and confirming votes and proceedings of a town meeting could not override a lawful vote of the townspeople defeating a proposed amendment and was without legal effect to make a valid enactment an amendment declared by the moderator to have passed and to be in effect even though it did not receive a two-thirds favorable vote. Drown v. Hudson, 112 N.H. 386, 296 A.2d 897, 1972 N.H. LEXIS 225 (N.H. 1972). (Decided under prior law.)

Cited:

Cited in Blue Jay Realty Trust v. Franklin, 132 N.H. 502, 567 A.2d 188, 1989 N.H. LEXIS 128 (1989); Real Estate Planners v. Newmarket, 134 N.H. 696, 597 A.2d 78, 1991 N.H. LEXIS 125 (1991).

RESEARCH REFERENCES AND PRACTICE AIDS

New Hampshire Practice.

15-5 N.H.P. Land Use Planning and Zoning § 5.11.

675:6. Method of Adoption.

Every local master plan, subdivision regulation, site plan review regulation and historic district regulation referred to in this title shall be adopted or amended by the planning board or historic district commission, as appropriate, in the following manner:

I. The board or commission, as appropriate, shall hold a public hearing prior to adoption or amendment. Notice for the time and place of the hearing shall be as provided in RSA 675:7.

II. The board or commission, as appropriate, may adopt or amend the master plan or regulation upon completion of the public hearing by an affirmative vote of a majority of its members.

III. No master plan, regulation, amendment or exception adopted under this section shall be legal or have any force and effect until copies of it are certified by a majority of the board or commission and filed with the city clerk, town clerk, or clerk for the county commissioners.

IV. The historic district commission may adopt or amend regulations only after the commission has held a public hearing within the district. Notice for the time and place shall be as provided in RSA 675:7. The adopted regulations shall be certified by a majority of the historic district commission members and filed with the city clerk, town clerk, or clerk for the county commissioners.

HISTORY:

1983, 447:1. 1985, 103:24. 1989, 266:26, eff. July 1, 1989.

Amendments

—1989.

Paragraph III: Substituted "clerk, town clerk, or clerk for the county commissioners" for "or town clerk" following "city".

Paragraph IV: Substituted "clerk, town clerk, or clerk for the county commissioners" for "or town clerk" following "city" in the second sentence.

—1985.

Rewritten to the extent that a detailed comparison would be impracticable.

NOTES TO DECISIONS

Analysis

1. Construction
2. Uncertified master plan

1. Construction

Because certification and filing of proposed amendment to subdivision regulations had not taken place, amendment was not yet effective, and planning board was thus not entitled to decline jurisdiction over plaintiff's subdivision application for failure to comply with amendment. Rallis v. Town of Hampton Planning Bd., 146 N.H. 18, 766 A.2d 281, 2001 N.H. LEXIS 20 (N.H. 2001).

2. Uncertified master plan

Master plan adopted by town planning board but not certified by the board before filing with the town clerk did not meet all requirements necessary to give the plan legal effect. Treisman v. Bedford, 132 N.H. 54, 563 A.2d 786, 1989 N.H. LEXIS 75 (N.H. 1989).

Based on doctrine of substantial compliance, otherwise proper amendment to zoning ordinance would not be invalidated based on planning board's failure to certify its master plan. Treisman v. Bedford, 132 N.H. 54, 563 A.2d 786, 1989 N.H. LEXIS 75 (N.H. 1989).

Cited:
Cited in Frisella v. Farmington, 131 N.H. 78, 550 A.2d 102, 1988 N.H. LEXIS 94 (1988); New Eng. Brickmaster v. Salem, 133 N.H. 655, 582 A.2d 601, 1990 N.H. LEXIS 119 (1990); Rall v. Town of Belmont, 138 N.H. 172, 635 A.2d 1368, 1993 N.H. LEXIS 185 (1993).

RESEARCH REFERENCES AND PRACTICE AIDS

Cross References.
Filing of master plans, subdivision regulations, site plan review regulations, and historic district regulations, see RSA 675:8, 9.

675:7. Notice Requirements for Public Hearing.

I. Notice shall be given for the time and place of each public hearing held under RSA 675:2-4 and RSA 675:6 at least 10 calendar days before the hearing. The notice required under this section shall not include the day notice is posted or the day of the public hearing. Notice of each public hearing shall be published in a paper of general circulation in the municipality and shall be posted in at least 2 public places. Any person owning property in the municipality may request notice of all public hearings on proposed amendments to the zoning ordinance, and the municipality shall provide notice, at no cost to the person, electronically or by first class mail.

I-a. If a proposed amendment to a zoning ordinance would change a boundary of a zoning district and the change would affect 100 or fewer properties, notice of a public hearing on the amendment shall be sent by first class mail to the owners of each affected property. If a proposed amendment to a zoning ordinance would change the minimum lot sizes or the permitted uses in a zoning district that includes 100 or fewer properties, notice of a public hearing on the amendment shall be sent by first class mail to the owner of each property in the district. Notice by mail shall be sent to the address used for mailing local property tax bills, provided that a good faith effort and substantial compliance shall satisfy the notice by mail requirements of this paragraph.

I-b. In the case of a petitioned zoning amendment as authorized in RSA 675:4, the petitioners shall be responsible for the cost of notice by mail under paragraph I-a. If the full cost of notice is not paid at the time of submission, the municipality shall inform the voter whose name appears first on the petition of the cost of notice within 5 business days, and the balance shall be paid within another 5 business days. If full payment is not made and received within 5 business days, the selectmen or village district commissioners may, in their discretion, decide to accept or decline the petition for submission. Failure by the municipality to inform

the responsible person of the cost of notice shall be deemed a waiver of the payment requirement.

II. The full text of the proposed master plan, zoning ordinance, building code, subdivision regulation, site plan review regulation and historic district regulation, ordinance, or amendment need not be included in the notice if an adequate statement describing the proposal and designating the place where the proposal is on file for public inspection is stated in the notice. The notice of a hearing on a proposed amendment to a zoning ordinance to be sent electronically or by first class mail shall include a statement describing, to the greatest extent practicable and in easily understood language, the proposed changes to the zoning ordinance, the areas affected, and any other information calculated to improve public understanding of the proposal.

HISTORY:
1983, 447:1. 1985, 103:24, eff. Jan. 1, 1986. 2014, 161:8, eff. July 10, 2014. 2017, 231:1, eff. September 16, 2017.

Amendment Notes
The 2017 amendments to this section by Ch. 231 added the I-a designation; deleted the former last sentence of I-a, which read: "Petitioned amendments as authorized in RSA 675:4 shall not be subject to notification by mail requirements"; and added I-b.

—2014.
The 2014 amendment added the fourth through last sentences of I and added the second sentence of II.

—1985.
Paragraph II: Inserted "subdivision regulation, site plan review regulation and historic district regulation, ordinance" following "building code", substituted "proposal" for "proposed master plan, zoning ordinance, building code, or amendment" preceding "is on file for public inspection is" and "stated in" for "attached to" thereafter.

NOTES TO DECISIONS

Analysis

1. Constructive notice
2. Sufficiency of notice

1. Constructive notice
While property owners who might be affected by a zoning amendment need not be afforded actual notice of a proposed zoning change, they must be afforded constructive notice sufficient to inform the public of the essence and scope of the zoning regulation under consideration. Bedford Residents Group v. Bedford, 130 N.H. 632, 547 A.2d 225, 1988 N.H. LEXIS 65 (N.H. 1988).

Publication and posting of documents that indicated planning board would be considering zoning amendments, and further stated that copies of the proposed amendments were on file for public inspection, was not sufficient notice to property owners who might be affected by zoning amendments, since notice did not satisfy requirements of this section for constructive notice because it did not contain even essential information to alert interested parties of the change under consideration. Bedford Residents Group v. Bedford, 130 N.H. 632, 547 A.2d 225, 1988 N.H. LEXIS 65 (N.H. 1988).

2. Sufficiency of notice
Notice was sufficient where it alerted readers that height, area, or bulk regulations pertaining to one-family or two-family zoning districts might be changed, and accurately noted that such a change would promote consistency between those two districts, and also directed readers to city clerk's office for copies of amendments.

Bradley v. City of Manchester, 141 N.H. 329, 682 A.2d 1194, 1996 N.H. LEXIS 100 (N.H. 1996).

675:8. Filing of Zoning Ordinances, Historic District Ordinances, Building Codes, Subdivision Regulations, Site Plan Review Regulations, and Amendments.

All zoning ordinances, historic district ordinances, building codes, subdivision regulations, site plan review regulations, historic district regulations and their amendments shall be placed on file with the city, town, or village district clerk, or, in the case of unincorporated towns or unorganized places, with the clerk for the county commissioners for public inspection.

HISTORY:
1983, 447:1. 1985, 103:24. 1989, 266:27, eff. July 1, 1989.

Amendments

—1989.
Inserted "or, in the case of unincorporated towns or unorganized places, with the clerk for the county commissioners" preceding "for public inspection".

—1985.
Inserted "historic district ordinances" following "zoning ordinances" and "historic district regulations" preceding "and their".

RESEARCH REFERENCES AND PRACTICE AIDS

Cross References.
Filing of ordinances, codes, regulations and amendments with office of state planning, see RSA 675:9.

New Hampshire Practice.
15-5 N.H.P. Land Use Planning and Zoning § 5.13.
15-29 N.H.P. Land Use Planning and Zoning § 29.22.

675:9. Place for Filing Documents; Reporting of Adoptions or Amendments.

A copy of each master plan, zoning ordinance, historic district ordinance, capital improvement plan, building code, subdivision regulation, historic district regulation, site plan review regulation or amendment which is adopted by a municipality shall be placed in a central file with the office of strategic initiatives; provided, however, that failure to file these documents or amendments with the office of strategic initiatives shall not affect the validity of the document. Every municipality which adopts a master plan, zoning ordinance, historic district ordinance, capital improvement plan, building code, subdivision regulation or site plan review regulation or amendment thereto, shall inform the office of strategic initiatives of such adoption or amendment. The office of strategic initiatives is hereby authorized to gather this information by way of an annual survey of the municipalities or other such means as may be deemed appropriate. The office of strategic initiatives shall periodically create lists and reports of the information gathered for use by the municipalities and the general public.

HISTORY:
1983, 447:1. 1985, 103:24. 1987, 50:1. 1989, 266:28, eff. July 1, 1989. 2002, 8:12, III, eff. Sept. 14, 2002. 2003, 319:9, eff. July 1, 2003. 2004, 257:44, eff. July 1, 2004. 2011, 224:122, eff. July 1, 2011. 2017, 156:64, eff. July 1, 2017.

Amendment Notes
The 2017 amendments to this section by Ch. 156 substituted "office of strategic initiatives" for "office of energy and planning" throughout the section.

—2011.
The 2011 amendment rewrote the section to the extent that a detailed comparison would be impracticable.

—2004.
Paragraph I: Substituted "office of energy and planning" for "office of state planning and energy programs".

—2003.
Paragraph I: Substituted "office of state planning and energy programs" for "office of state planning".

—2002.
Paragraph II: Repealed.

—1989.
Paragraph II: Inserted "or a county" preceding "adopts".

—1987.
Paragraph I: Inserted "capital improvement plan" preceding "building code".

—1985.
Paragraph I: Inserted "historic district ordinance" preceding "building code, subdivision regulation" and "historic district regulation" thereafter.

RESEARCH REFERENCES AND PRACTICE AIDS

Cross References.
Filing of ordinances, codes, regulations and amendments with municipal clerks, see RSA 675:8.

CHAPTER 676

ADMINISTRATIVE AND ENFORCEMENT PROCEDURES

Revision of organization of chapter.
1987, 256:4, eff. July 17, 1987, amended this chapter by adding the subdivision heading preceding RSA 676:5.

RESEARCH REFERENCES AND PRACTICE AIDS

Cross References.
Local land use boards generally, see RSA 673.
Ordinance, regulation and code adoption procedures generally, see RSA 675.
Rehearing and appeal procedures generally, see RSA 677.

New Hampshire Bar Journal.
For article, "An Overview of the New Hampshire Land Use Planning and Regulation Statutes, " see 34 N.H. B.J. 6 (June 1993).

New Hampshire Practice.
15-28 N.H.P. Land Use Planning and Zoning § 28.08.

General Provisions

676:1. Method of Adopting Rules of Procedure.

Every local land use board shall adopt rules of procedure concerning the method of conducting its business. Rules of procedure shall be adopted at a regular meeting of the board and shall be placed on file with city, town, village district clerk, or clerk for the county commissioners for public inspection. The rules of procedure shall include when and how an alternate may participate in meetings of the land use board.

HISTORY:
1983, 447:1. 1989, 266:29, eff. July 1, 1989. 2010, 270:2, eff. July 6, 2010.

Amendments

—2010.
The 2010 amendment added the last sentence and made a stylistic change.

—1989.
Deleted "or" preceding "village" and inserted "or clerk for the county commissioners" preceding "for public inspection" in the second sentence.

NOTES TO DECISIONS

Cited:
Cited in Cardinal Dev. Corp. v. Town of Winchester Zoning Bd. of Adjustment, 157 N.H. 710, 958 A.2d 996, 2008 N.H. LEXIS 114 (2008).

RESEARCH REFERENCES AND PRACTICE AIDS

Cross References.
Meetings and records of boards generally, see RSA 673:10, 17.

676:2. Joint Meetings and Hearings.

I. An applicant seeking a local permit may petition 2 or more land use boards to hold a joint meeting or hearing when the subject matter of the requested permit is within the responsibilities of those land use boards. Each board shall adopt rules of procedure relative to joint meetings and hearings, and each board shall have the authority on its own initiative to request a joint meeting. Each land use board shall have the discretion as to whether or not to hold a joint meeting with any other land use board. The planning board chair shall chair joint meetings unless the planning board is not involved with the subject matter of the requested permit. In that situation, the appropriate agencies which are involved shall determine which board shall be in charge.

II. Procedures for joint meetings or hearings relating to testimony, notice of hearings, and filing of decisions shall be consistent with the procedures established by this chapter for individual boards.

III. Every local land use board shall be responsible for rendering a decision on the subject matter which is within its jurisdiction.

HISTORY:
1983, 447:1, eff. Jan. 1, 1984.

RESEARCH REFERENCES AND PRACTICE AIDS

Cross References.
Adoption of rules of procedure generally, see RSA 676:1.
Issuance of decision generally, see RSA 676:3.
Meetings and records of boards generally, see RSA 673:10, 17.
Powers of boards as to administration of oaths and compulsion of attendance of witnesses generally, see RSA 673:15.

676:3. Issuance of Decision.

I. The local land use board shall issue a final written decision which either approves or disapproves an application for a local permit and make a copy of the decision available to the applicant. If the application is not approved, the board shall provide the applicant with written reasons for the disapproval. If the application is approved with conditions, the board shall include in the written decision a detailed description of all conditions necessary to obtain final approval.

II. Whenever a local land use board votes to approve or disapprove an application or deny a motion for rehearing, the minutes of the meeting at which such vote is taken, including the written decision containing the reasons therefor and all conditions of approval, shall be placed on file in the board's office and shall be made available for public inspection within 5 business days of such vote. Boards in towns that do not have an office of the board that has regular business hours shall file copies of their decisions with the town clerk.

III. Whenever a plat is recorded to memorialize an approval issued by a local land use board, the final written decision, including all conditions of approval, shall be recorded with or on the plat.

HISTORY:

1983, 447:1, eff. Jan. 1, 1984. 2000, 144:1, eff. Jan. 1, 2001. 2009, 266:1, eff. September 14, 2009.

Amendments

—2009.

The 2009 amendment, in I, added "and make a copy of the decision available to the applicant" at the end of the first sentence and added the third sentence; in the first sentence of II, added "and all conditions of approval" and substituted "5 business days" for "144 hours"; and added III.

—2000.

Paragraph II: Rewritten to the extent that a detailed comparison would be impracticable.

Nullification of 2009 amendment.

2009, 266:5, eff. September 14, 2009, provided that the amendment to this section by 2009, 49:2, would not take effect.

RESEARCH REFERENCES AND PRACTICE AIDS

Cross References.

Issuance of decisions in cases involving joint meetings or hearings, see RSA 676:2.

Maintenance of records of boards generally, see RSA 673:17.

Planning Board

RESEARCH REFERENCES AND PRACTICE AIDS

Cross References.

Master plans generally, see RSA 675:1 et seq.

Official municipal maps generally, see RSA 674:9 et seq.

Site plan review regulations generally, see RSA 674:43 et seq.

Subdivision regulation generally, see RSA 674:35 et seq.

Zoning ordinances generally, see RSA 674:16 et seq.

676:4. Board's Procedures on Plats.

I. The procedures to be followed by the planning board when considering or acting upon a plat or application submitted to it for approval under this title shall be as set forth in the board's subdivision regulations, subject to the following requirements:

(a) An application for approval filed with the planning board under this title, other than an application for subdivision approval, shall be sub-ject to the minimum requirements set forth in this section and shall be governed by the procedures set forth in the subdivision regulations, unless the planning board by regulation specifies other procedures for that type of application.

(b) The planning board shall specify by regulation what constitutes a completed application sufficient to invoke jurisdiction to obtain approval. A completed application means that sufficient information is included or submitted to allow the board to proceed with consideration and to make an informed decision. A completed application sufficient to invoke jurisdiction of the board shall be submitted to and accepted by the board only at a public meeting of the board, with notice as provided in subparagraph (d). An application shall not be considered incomplete solely because it is dependent upon the submission of an application to or the issuance of permits or approvals from other state or federal governmental bodies; however, the planning board may condition approval upon the receipt of such permits or approvals in accordance with subparagraph (i). The applicant shall file the application with the board or its agent at least 21 days prior to the meeting at which the application will be accepted. The application shall include the names and addresses of the applicant, all holders of conservation, preservation, or agricultural preservation restrictions as defined in RSA 477:45, and all abutters as indicated in the town records for incorporated towns or county records for unincorporated towns or unorganized places not more than 5 days before the day of filing. Abutters shall also be identified on any plat submitted to the board. The application shall also include the name and business address of every engineer, architect, land surveyor, or soil scientist whose professional seal appears on any plat submitted to the board.

(c)(1) The board shall, at the next regular meeting or within 30 days following the delivery of the application, for which notice can be given in accordance with the requirements of subparagraph (b), determine if a submitted application is complete according to the board's regulation and shall vote upon its acceptance. Upon determination by the board that a submitted application is incomplete according to the board's regulations, the board shall notify the applicant of the determination in accordance with RSA 676:3, which shall describe the information, procedure, or other requirement necessary for the application to be complete. Upon determination by the board that a submitted application is complete according to the board's regulations, the board shall begin formal consideration and shall act to approve, conditionally approve as provided in subparagraph (i), or disapprove within 65 days, subject to extension or waiver as provided in subparagraph (f). Upon failure of the board to approve, conditionally approve, or disapprove the application, the selectmen or city council shall, upon request of the applicant, immediately issue an order directing the board to act on the application within 30 days. If the planning board does not act on the application within that 30-day time period, then within 40 days of the issuance of the order, the selectmen or city council shall certify on the applicant's application that the plat is approved pursuant to this paragraph, unless within those 40 days the selectmen or city council has identified in writing some specific subdivision regulation or zoning or other ordinance provision with which the application does not comply. Such a certification, citing this paragraph, shall constitute final approval for all purposes including filing and recording under RSA 674:37 and 676:18, and court review under RSA 677:15.

(2) Failure of the selectmen or city council to issue an order to the planning board under subparagraph (1), or to certify approval of the plat upon the planning board's failure to comply with the order, shall constitute grounds for the superior court, upon petition of the applicant, to issue an order approving the application if the court determines that the proposal complies with existing subdivision regulations and zoning or other ordinances. If the court determines that the failure of the selectmen or the city council to act was not justified, the court may order the municipality to pay the applicant's reasonable costs, including attorney's fees, incurred in securing such order.

(d)(1) Notice to the applicant, holders of conservation, preservation, or agricultural preservation restrictions, abutters, and the public shall be given as follows: The planning board shall notify the abutters, the applicant, holders of conservation, preservation, or agricultural preservation restrictions, and every engineer, architect, land surveyor, or soil scientist whose professional seal appears on any plat submitted to the board by verified mail, as defined in RSA 451-C:1, VII, of the date upon which the application will be formally submitted to the board. Notice shall be mailed at least 10 days prior to submission. Notice to the general public shall also be given at the same time by posting or publication as required by the subdivision regulations. The notice shall include a general description of the proposal which is the subject of the application and shall identify the applicant and the location of the proposal. For any public hearing on the application, the same notice as required for notice of submission of the application shall be given. If notice of public hearing has been included in the notice of submission or any prior notice, additional notice of that hearing is not required nor shall additional notice be required of an adjourned session of a hearing

with proper notice if the date, time, and place of the adjourned session was made known at the prior hearing. All costs of notice, whether mailed, posted, or published, shall be paid in advance by the applicant. Failure to pay such costs shall constitute valid grounds for the planning board to terminate further consideration and to disapprove the plat without a public hearing.

(2) For those proposals in which any structure or proposed building site will be within 500 feet of the top of the bank of any lake, pond, river, or stream, the planning board shall also notify the department of environmental services by first class mail at the same time that notice is provided to abutters, cost to be paid in advance by the applicant consistent with subparagraph (d)(1). The sole purpose of notification to the department shall be to provide information to the department for dam hazard classification. This requirement shall not confer upon the department the status of an abutter. Failure by the municipality to notify the department shall not be considered a defect of notice.

(e) Except as provided in this section, no application may be denied or approved without a public hearing on the application. At the hearing, any applicant, abutter, holder of conservation, preservation, or agricultural preservation restriction, or any person with a direct interest in the matter may testify in person or in writing. Other persons may testify as permitted by the subdivision regulations or the board at each hearing. Public hearings shall not be required, unless specified by the subdivision regulations, when the board is considering or acting upon:

(1) Minor lot line adjustments or boundary agreements which do not create buildable lots, except that notice to abutters and holders of conservation, preservation, or agricultural preservation restrictions shall be given prior to approval of the application in accordance with subparagraph (d) and any abutter or holder of conservation, preservation, or agricultural preservation restrictions may be heard on the application upon request; or

(2) Disapprovals of applications based upon failure of the applicant to supply information required by the regulations, including identification of abutters or holders of conservation, preservation, or agricultural preservation restrictions; or failure to meet reasonable deadlines established by the board; or failure to pay costs of notice or other fees required by the board.

(f) The planning board may apply to the selectmen or city council for an extension not to exceed an additional 90 days before acting to approve or disapprove an application. The applicant may waive the requirement for planning board action within the time periods specified in subparagraph

(c) and consent to such extension as may be mutually agreeable.

(g) Reasonable fees in addition to fees for notice under subparagraph (d) may be imposed by the board to cover its administrative expenses and costs of special investigative studies, review of documents and other matters which may be required by particular applications.

(h) In case of disapproval of any application submitted to the planning board, the ground for such disapproval shall be adequately stated upon the records of the planning board.

(i) A planning board may grant conditional approval of a plat or application, which approval shall become final without further public hearing, upon certification to the board by its designee or based upon evidence submitted by the applicant of satisfactory compliance with the conditions imposed. Such conditions may include a statement notifying the applicant that an approval is conditioned upon the receipt of state or federal permits relating to a project, however, a planning board may not refuse to process an application solely for lack of said permits. Final approval of a plat or application may occur in the foregoing manner only when the conditions are:

(1) Minor plan changes whether or not imposed by the board as a result of a public hearing, compliance with which is administrative and which does not involve discretionary judgment; or

(2) Conditions which are in themselves administrative and which involve no discretionary judgment on the part of the board; or

(3) Conditions with regard to the applicant's possession of permits and approvals granted by other boards or agencies or approvals granted by other boards or agencies, including state and federal permits.

All conditions not specified within this subparagraph as minor, administrative, or relating to issuance of other approvals shall require a hearing, and notice as provided in subparagraph I(d), except that additional notice shall not be required of an adjourned session of a hearing with proper notice if the date, time, and place of the adjourned session were made known at the prior hearing.

II. A planning board may provide for preliminary review of applications and plats by specific regulations subject to the following:

(a) **Preliminary Conceptual Consultation Phase.** The regulations shall define the limits of preliminary conceptual consultation which shall be directed at review of the basic concept of the proposal and suggestions which might be of assistance in resolving problems with meeting requirements during final consideration. Such consultation shall not bind either the applicant or the board and statements made by planning board members shall not be the basis for disqualifying said members or invalidating any action taken.

The board and the applicant may discuss proposals in conceptual form only and in general terms such as desirability of types of development and proposals under the master plan. Such discussion may occur without the necessity of giving formal public notice as required under subparagraph I(d), but such discussions may occur only at formal meetings of the board.

(b) **Design review phase.** The board or its designee may engage in nonbinding discussions with the applicant beyond conceptual and general discussions which involve more specific design and engineering details; provided, however, that the design review phase may proceed only after identification of and notice to abutters, holders of conservation, preservation, or agricultural preservation restrictions, and the general public as required by subparagraph I(d). The board may establish reasonable rules of procedure relating to the design review process, including submission requirements. At a public meeting, the board may determine that the design review process of an application has ended and shall inform the applicant in writing within 10 days of such determination. Statements made by planning board members shall not be the basis for disqualifying said members or invalidating any action taken.

(c) Preliminary review shall be separate and apart from formal consideration under paragraph I, and the time limits for acting under subparagraph I(c) shall not apply until formal application is submitted under subparagraph I(b).

III. A planning board may, by adopting regulations, provide for an expedited review and approval for proposals involving minor subdivisions which create not more than 3 lots for building development purposes or for proposals which do not involve creation of lots for building development purposes. Such expedited review may allow submission and approval at one or more board meetings, but no application may be approved without the full notice to the abutters, holders of conservation, preservation, or agricultural preservation restrictions, and public required under subparagraph I(d). A hearing, with notice as provided in subparagraph I(d), shall be held if requested by the applicant, abutters, or holders of conservation, preservation, or agricultural preservation restrictions any time prior to approval or disapproval or if the planning board determines to hold a hearing.

IV. Jurisdiction of the courts to review procedural aspects of planning board decisions and actions shall be limited to consideration of compliance with applicable provisions of the constitution, statutes and regulations. The procedural requirements specified in this section are intended to provide fair and reasonable treatment for all parties and persons. The planning board's procedures shall not be subjected to strict scrutiny for technical compliance. Procedural defects shall result in the reversal of a planning board's actions by judicial action only when such defects create serious impairment of opportunity for notice and participation.

HISTORY:

1983, 447:1. 1985, 159:1. 1986, 57:1, 2. 229:1, 2. 1989, 266:30. 1990, 275:1. 1995, 117:1, 2, eff. July 15, 1995. 1997, 142:1–4, eff. Aug. 8, 1997. 249:1, eff. Aug. 18, 1997. 1998, 274:1, eff. Aug. 25, 1998. 2004, 71:6, eff. July 6, 2004. 2005, 33:3, 4, eff. July 9, 2005. 2008, 229:2, eff. August 19, 2008. 2009, 31:2, 3, eff. July 14, 2009. 2010, 39:1, 2, eff. July 17, 2010. 2011, 164:1, 2, eff. August 13, 2011. 2013, 270:2, eff. September 22, 2013. 2016, 81:1, eff. July 18, 2016. 2017, 59:3, eff. August 1, 2017.

Amendment Notes

The 2017 amendment to this section by Ch. 59 substituted "by verified mail, as defined in RSA 451-C:1, VII" for "by certified mail" in the first sentence of I(d)(1).

The 2016 amendments to this section by Ch. 81 substituted "at least 21 days" for "at least 15 days" in the fifth sentence of I(b).

—2013.

The 2013 amendment, in the fourth sentence of I(b), added "submission of an application to or the" and "state or federal."

—2011.

The 2011 amendment deleted the former last sentence of I(b), which read: "Since construction of any structure near streams or rivers downstream of a dam can increase the hazard classification of the dam established by the department of environmental services, the application shall identify the nearest dam upstream and include the name and address of the dam owners"; added the I(d)(1) designation; in I(d)(1), deleted "upstream dam owners, the department of environmental services dam bureau" following "restrictions, abutters" in the first sentence and deleted the former second sentence, which read: "For those proposals near rivers and streams and downstream of a dam, the planning board shall also notify the owners of the upstream dam and the department of environmental services dam bureau by certified mail"; and added I(d)(2).

—2010.

The 2010 amendment added the fourth sentence of I(b); added the second sentence of the introductory language of I(i); added "including state and federal permits" in I(i)(3); and substituted "conditions not specified within this subparagraph as minor, administrative, or relating to issuance of other approvals" for "other conditions" in the concluding language of I(i).

—2009.

The 2009 amendment added the last sentence of I(b) and in I(d), added "upstream dam owners, the department of environmental services dam bureau" in the first sentence and added the second sentence.

—2008.

The 2008 amendment added the second and third sentences of II(b).

—2005.

Paragraph II: Substituted "preliminary" for "preapplication" in the introductory paragraph and in subpar. (c).

—2004.

Paragraph II(c): Deleted the former first sentence.

—1998.

Paragraph I(c)(1): Rewritten to the extent that a detailed comparison would be impracticable.

—1997.

Paragraph I(b): Inserted "all holders of conservation, preservation, or agricultural preservation restrictions as defined in RSA 477:45" in the fifth sentence.

Paragraph I(c)(1): Substituted "receipt" for "submission" preceding "of the completed application" and added "by the board or its designee" thereafter in the first sentence, added the second sentence, and substituted "receipt of the completed application by the board or its designee" for "submission" following "90 days after" in the third sentence.

Paragraph I(d): Inserted "holders of conservation, preservation, or agricultural preservation restrictions" in two places in the first sentence.

Paragraph I(e): Rewritten to the extent that a detailed comparison would be impracticable.

Paragraph II(b): Inserted "holders of conservation, preservation, or agricultural preservation restrictions" following "abutters" in the first sentence.

Paragraph III: Inserted "holders of conservation, preservation, or agricultural preservation restrictions" in the second and third sentences and made a minor stylistic change in the third sentence.

—1995.

Paragraph I(b): Added the seventh sentence.

Paragraph I(d): Deleted "and" following "notify the abutters" and inserted "and every engineer, architect, land surveyor, or soil scientist whose professional seal appears on any plat submitted to the board" preceding "by certified" in the first sentence.

—1990.

Paragraph I(c): Rewritten to the extent that a detailed comparison would be impracticable.

—1989.

Paragraph I(b): Substituted "the town records for incorporated towns or county records for unincorporated towns or unorganized places" for "town records" preceding "not more than 5 days" in the fifth sentence.

—1986.

Paragraph I(c): Chapter 57:2 inserted "conditionally approve as provided in subparagraph (i)" following "approve" in the second sentence and "conditionally approve" following "approve" in the third sentence.

Paragraph I(i) added by ch. 57:1.

Chapter 229:1 deleted "conditionally approved" following "approval of a plat or application" in the introductory clause and "conditions and" preceding "minor plan changes" in clause (1) of the second sentence, substituted "whether or not" for "or conditions or minor plan changes" preceding "imposed by the board" in clause (1) of the second sentence, and rewrote the third sentence.

Paragraph II: Amended generally by ch. 229:2.

—1985.

Paragraph I(d): Deleted "return receipt requested" following "mail" in the first sentence.

Applicability of 1990 amendment.

1990, 275:3, eff. June 27, 1990, provided that the amendment to this section by section 1 of the act shall be prospective only and shall apply to any application submitted to and accepted as complete by the planning board on or after June 27, 1990.

NOTES TO DECISIONS

Analysis

1. Construction with other laws
2. Applicability
3. Authority of board
4. Preliminary discussions
5. Submission of application
6. Completeness of application
7. Time for action on application—Generally
8. —Effect of revision of application
9. Proceedings upon failure of board to act on application within limitation period
10. Hearings
11. Applicant's right to speak
12. Statement of reasons for denial of application
13. Procedure upon disapproval of application
14. Accepting jurisdiction of site plan application

15. Successive applications

1. Construction with other laws

Site plan approvals under former RSA 36:19-a (now covered by RSA 674:43) were governed by this statute regulating the board's procedure for approval of plats. Carter v. Nashua, 116 N.H. 466, 362 A.2d 191, 1976 N.H. LEXIS 382 (1976), overruled in part, Weeks Restaurant Corp. v. City of Dover, 119 N.H. 541, 404 A.2d 294, 1979 N.H. LEXIS 349 (1979). (Decided under prior law.)

2. Applicability

Plaintiff abutter's claim that trial court had jurisdiction to review procedural aspects of a town planning board's decision granting approval to applicant's site plan determination under RSA 676:4, IV was improper as that provision does not address the process by which one may appeal a planning board decision. RSA 676:4, IV must be read in conjunction with RSA 677:15, which describes that process and requires that such appeal be brought within thirty-days of the planning board's decision. Because plaintiff failed to file its appeal within the thirty-day window, the superior court had no jurisdiction over the appeal. Prop. Portfolio Group, LLC v. Town of Derry, 154 N.H. 610, 913 A.2d 750, 2006 N.H. LEXIS 206 (N.H. 2006).

3. Authority of board

Local planning boards have authority to impose conditions upon the approval of a site plan. New Eng. Brickmaster v. Salem, 133 N.H. 655, 582 A.2d 601, 1990 N.H. LEXIS 119 (N.H. 1990).

The statute provided no power for a planning board to enact a subdivision regulation that required automatic approval of an application for a subdivision. Davis v. Barrington, 127 N.H. 202, 497 A.2d 1232, 1985 N.H. LEXIS 387 (N.H. 1985). (Decided under prior law.)

4. Preliminary discussions

Planning board is not bound to give final approval to a project based solely upon preliminary discussions, but must act reasonably in both preliminary and formal stages of review. Batakis v. Belmont, 135 N.H. 595, 607 A.2d 956, 1992 N.H. LEXIS 88 (N.H. 1992).

This section specifically recognizes the need for allowing planning board to separate non-binding consultations from formal review of completed applications. Batakis v. Belmont, 135 N.H. 595, 607 A.2d 956, 1992 N.H. LEXIS 88 (N.H. 1992).

5. Submission of application

Where a landowner submitted a plat at a planning board meeting, the plat did not meet the requirement that lot sizes be shown in square feet, the board refused to accept the plat and the landowner took it away to have the required information added, the plat had not been submitted within the meaning of the statute for purposes of the provision requiring approval or disapproval of the application within 90 days after submission. Allard v. Thalheimer, 116 N.H. 299, 358 A.2d 395, 1976 N.H. LEXIS 336 (N.H. 1976). (Decided under prior law.)

6. Completeness of application

Where a subdivision application was not complete in terms of compliance with an ordinance that included a subdivision checklist, the jurisdiction of the planning board could not be invoked and the board was free not to accept the application for consideration. DHB, Inc. v. Town of Pembroke, 152 N.H. 314, 876 A.2d 206, 2005 N.H. LEXIS 99 (N.H. 2005).

Plaintiff's subdivision application was sufficiently complete for planning board to exercise jurisdiction over it, and fact that plaintiff offered to revise or redesign his plans to satisfy various planning board concerns, after submitting a completed application, did not render his application incomplete for jurisdictional purposes. Rallis v. Town of Hampton Planning Bd., 146 N.H. 18, 766 A.2d 281, 2001 N.H. LEXIS 20 (N.H. 2001).

7. Time for action on application—Generally

The statute clearly stated that a town planning board had ninety days to act on any plat submitted to it and was required to state its reason for disapproval upon the record, and if an applicant's filing was improper in form, the board had ninety days to disapprove it and was required to state that reason on the record. Savage v. Rye,

120 N.H. 409, 415 A.2d 873, 1980 N.H. LEXIS 303 (N.H. 1980). (Decided under prior law.)

8. —Effect of revision of application

Revision of a plan subsequent to its submission with an application for subdivision approval could result in a new filing date for purposes of the statutory provision requiring a town planning board to approve or disapprove of a subdivision within ninety days of submission of the application. Savage v. Rye, 120 N.H. 409, 415 A.2d 873, 1980 N.H. LEXIS 303 (N.H. 1980). (Decided under prior law.)

9. Proceedings upon failure of board to act on application within limitation period

A master properly refused to order approval of a subdivision application as a matter of law because of a planning board's failure to act within the time prescribed by local regulation, since, under the statute, there was no right to automatic approval. Davis v. Barrington, 127 N.H. 202, 497 A.2d 1232, 1985 N.H. LEXIS 387 (N.H. 1985). (Decided under prior law.)

Where a town planning board failed to approve or disapprove a subdivision application within ninety days of submission of the application, the town was required to certify this failure on the plan, thereby allowing the applicant to record the subdivision plan at the registry of deeds without written endorsement by the planning board. Savage v. Rye, 120 N.H. 409, 415 A.2d 873, 1980 N.H. LEXIS 303 (N.H. 1980). (Decided under prior law.)

10. Hearings

Where a landowner submitted a site plan for nonresidential use of land to the town zoning board of adjustment and applied for a special exception to the zoning ordinance, the board voted to preliminarily approve the application subject to eleven conditions; and an abutting landowner was not given notice of or an opportunity to be heard at a subsequent compliance hearing, at which the board found that all the conditions had been satisfied and signed the site plan, the failure to allow testimony from the abutting landowner on the issue of compliance with the conditions was a serious impairment of the opportunity for participation under this section, for which reversal was the only effective remedy. Sklar Realty v. Merrimack, 125 N.H. 321, 480 A.2d 149, 1984 N.H. LEXIS 271 (N.H. 1984). (Decided under prior law.)

11. Applicant's right to speak

By its plain language, a public meeting was not the same as a hearing mandated by statute; therefore, a subdivision approval applicant whose application had not been accepted did not have a right to speak at a public meeting that was held on the matter. DHB, Inc. v. Town of Pembroke, 152 N.H. 314, 876 A.2d 206, 2005 N.H. LEXIS 99 (N.H. 2005).

12. Statement of reasons for denial of application

In denying a subdivision application, a planning board did not fail to provide an adequate record under RSA 676:4, I(h). The board agreed that its secretary's recitation described its reasons for denial; based on this, the trial court properly found that the board denied the application based on aesthetics, safety concerns, and environmental concerns. Ltd. Editions Props., Inc. v. Town of Hebron, 162 N.H. 488, 34 A.3d 688, 2011 N.H. LEXIS 131 (N.H. 2011).

Planning board's casting separate votes on each of seven criteria with respect to a project as a whole, without providing reasons, explanations or findings directed to adversely affected wetland areas or buffer zones, was not an adequate statement for the grounds of disapproval of a special use permit necessary to comply with RSA 676:4, I(h). Because the board's minutes did not satisfy RSA 676:4, I(h), the record supported the ruling to vacate and remand. Motorsports Holdings, Llc v. Town of Tamworth, 160 N.H. 95, 993 A.2d 189, 2010 N.H. LEXIS 31 (2010).

Letter from a planning board denying a landowner's site plan application was sufficient to start the time for appeal running where the letter discussed three reasons for denial and also enclosed a copy of the minutes of the meeting. Route 12 Books & Video v. Town of Troy, 149 N.H. 569, 825 A.2d 493, 2003 N.H. LEXIS 79 (N.H. 2003).

Certified record, including minutes of three lengthy public hearings, coupled with a detailed letter sent to the applicant for site plan approval of a shooting range, providing multiple reasons for denial of the application, were adequate to apprise the applicant of planning board's reasons for such denial. Star Vector Corp. v. Town of Windham, 146 N.H. 490, 776 A.2d 138, 2001 N.H. LEXIS 102 (N.H. 2001).

Purpose of requirement that planning board state adequate reasons on the record for its denial of an application is to insure that the developer receives written reasons for the disapproval, and that a record of the board's reasoning exists so that the decision may be reviewed on appeal. K & P, Inc. v. Plaistow, 133 N.H. 283, 575 A.2d 804, 1990 N.H. LEXIS 50 (N.H. 1990).

Requirement that planning board state adequate reasons on the record for its denial of an application may be satisfied by a letter from the board to the applicant, together with minutes of board meetings. K & P, Inc. v. Plaistow, 133 N.H. 283, 575 A.2d 804, 1990 N.H. LEXIS 50 (N.H. 1990).

13. Procedure upon disapproval of application

Subdividers were to receive written reasons for a planning board's disapproval of subdivision plans submitted to the board, and a written record, not limited to the minutes of the planning board meeting, was to exist so that a reviewing authority could hold the board accountable. Patenaude v. Meredith, 118 N.H. 616, 392 A.2d 582, 1978 N.H. LEXIS 253 (N.H. 1978). (Decided under prior law.)

Planning boards were not required to reiterate their reasons for disapproval of a resubmitted plan that contained the same fundamental defect that proved fatal to the original plan. Patenaude v. Meredith, 118 N.H. 616, 392 A.2d 582, 1978 N.H. LEXIS 253 (N.H. 1978). (Decided under prior law.)

Letters from planning boards notifying developers of the reasons for plan disapproval met the statutory requirements and were "records" within the meaning of the statute. Patenaude v. Meredith, 118 N.H. 616, 392 A.2d 582, 1978 N.H. LEXIS 253 (N.H. 1978). (Decided under prior law.)

Where the planning board wrote a landowner that it would approve the plat if one lot was increased to the minimum size, and the letter stated that eight other lots were under consideration and demanded an "affirmative response" to the problem of the undersized lot, the board's letter constituted disapproval under the statute. Allard v. Thalheimer, 116 N.H. 299, 358 A.2d 395, 1976 N.H. LEXIS 336 (N.H. 1976). (Decided under prior law.)

14. Accepting jurisdiction of site plan application

Appeal to a zoning board of adjustment (ZBA) was timely under RSA 676:5, III because by merely accepting jurisdiction of the site plan application on June 19 under RSA 676:4, the planning board made no decision regarding zoning compliance; it was not until its August 21 meeting, when it voted to approve the application, that the planning board rendered a zoning determination that was appealable to the ZBA. Accurate Transp., Inc. v. Town of Derry, 168 N.H. 108, 123 A.3d 263, 2015 N.H. LEXIS 81 (N.H. 2015).

15. Successive applications

Board's refusal to consider the second site plan application was proper because the subsequent application doctrine applied in the planning board context, and the board reasonably concluded that the modified application was not materially different from the initial site plan application. CBDA Dev. v. Town of Thornton, 168 N.H. 715, 137 A.3d 1107, 2016 N.H. LEXIS 34 (N.H. 2016).

Cited:

Cited in Real Estate Planners v. Newmarket, 134 N.H. 696, 597 A.2d 78, 1991 N.H. LEXIS 125 (1991).

RESEARCH REFERENCES AND PRACTICE AIDS

Cross References.
Appeals to boards of adjustment, see RSA 676:5 et seq.
Conservation restriction assessment, see RSA 79-B.
Rehearing and appeal procedures generally, see RSA 677.
Soil conservation and farmland preservation, see RSA 432.

New Hampshire Practice.
15-11 N.H.P. Land Use Planning and Zoning § 11.04.
15-28 N.H.P. Land Use Planning and Zoning § 28.02.
15-29 N.H.P. Land Use Planning and Zoning § 29.23.
15-32 N.H.P. Land Use Planning and Zoning § 32.02.
15-32 N.H.P. Land Use Planning and Zoning § 32.12.
15-32 N.H.P. Land Use Planning and Zoning § 32.18.

676:4-a. Revocation of Recorded Approval.

I. A subdivision plat, street plat, site plan or other approval which has been filed with the appropriate recording official under RSA 674:37 may not be revoked, in whole or in part, by the planning board, except pursuant to this section, and only under the following circumstances:

(a) At the request of, or by agreement with, the applicant or the applicant's successor in interest.

(b) When the applicant or successor in interest to the applicant has performed work, erected a structure or structures, or established a use of land, which fails to conform to the statements, plans or specifications upon which the approval was based, or has materially violated any requirement or condition of such approval.

(c) When the applicant or successor in interest to the applicant has failed to perform any condition of the approval within a reasonable time specified in the approval, or, if no such time is specified, within the time periods specified in RSA 674:39.

(d) When the time periods specified in RSA 674:39 have elapsed without any vesting of rights as set forth therein, and the plat, plan or other approval no longer conforms to applicable ordinances or regulations.

(e) When the applicant or successor in interest to the applicant has failed to provide for the continuation of adequate security as provided by RSA 674:36, III(b) and 674:44, III(d) until such time as the work secured thereby has been completed.

II. Prior to recording any revocation under this section, the planning board shall give notice, as provided by RSA 676:4, I(d), to the public, the applicant or the applicant's successor in interest, and all abutters and holders of conservation, preservation, or agricultural preservation restrictions. The notice shall include the board's reasons for the revocation. A hearing with notice as provided in RSA 676:4, I(d) shall be held at the request of any party receiving such notice, submitted within 30 days of receiving such notice, or if the planning board determines to hold a hearing.

III. A declaration of revocation, dated and endorsed in writing by the planning board, and containing reference to the recording information for the plat, plan, or other approval being revoked, shall be filed for recording with the register of deeds, no sooner than 30 days after written notification of the revocation is served on the applicant or the applicant's successor in interest, in person or by verified mail, as defined in RSA 451-C:1, VII, or 30 days after any public hearing, whichever is later. If only part of an approval is revoked, that portion of land subject to revocation shall be clearly identified in the declaration. The declaration shall be recorded under the same name or names as was the original approval, as well as the names of subsequent owners, if any, of the land or part thereof subject to revocation, as identified by the municipality.

IV. A revocation under this section may be appealed pursuant to RSA 677:15. Nothing in this section shall affect the municipality's ability, either before or after such a revocation, to pursue other remedies or penalties as set forth in RSA 676:15–17.

HISTORY:
1991, 237:1, eff. Aug. 9, 1991. 1997, 142:5, eff. Aug. 8, 1997. 2017, 59:4, eff. August 1, 2017.

Amendment Notes
The 2017 amendment to this section by Ch. 59 substituted "by verified mail, as defined in RSA 451-C:1, VII" for "by certified mail" in the first sentence of III.

—1997.
Paragraph II: Added "and holders of conservation, preservation, or agricultural preservation restrictions" at the end of the first sentence.

NOTES TO DECISIONS

Analysis

1. Due process
2. Practice and procedure

1. Due process
Planning board's decision to revoke site plan approval for soccer facility was not erroneous as a matter of law or unsupported by record, where town communicated with land owners by letter no less than eight times regarding alleged violations of site plan conditions, and record revealed a recurring pattern of complaints and alleged violations, followed by hearings before board and promises of remedial action by land owners. Brewster v. Town of Amherst, 144 N.H. 364, 742 A.2d 121, 1999 N.H. LEXIS 122 (N.H. 1999).

2. Practice and procedure
Although neither initial site plan revocation, nor unsubstantiated complaints by abutters contained in record, were appropriate factors for planning board to consider in determining materiality of violations in subsequent revocation determination, board was entitled, once it found that subsequent violations were material, to consider prior violations in determining appropriate sanction or penalty for noncompliance with material conditions. Brewster v. Town of Amherst, 144 N.H. 364, 742 A.2d 121, 1999 N.H. LEXIS 122 (N.H. 1999).

676:4-b. Third Party Review and Inspection.

I. A planning board reviewing a subdivision plat, site plan, or other land use application may require the applicant to reimburse the board for expenses reasonably incurred by obtaining third party review and consultation during the review process, provided that the review and consultation does not substantially replicate a review and consultation obtained by the zoning board of adjustment. The applicant may request the planning board choose a different third party consultant and the request may include the name of a preferred consultant. The planning board shall exercise reasonable discretion to determine whether the request is warranted. When such a request is granted by the planning board, the 65-day period for the board's action on an application stated in RSA 676:4, I(c)(1) shall be extended 45 days to provide the board adequate time to identify a different consultant.

II. A planning board approval of a subdivision plat, site plan, or other land use application may require the applicant to reimburse the board for expenses reasonably incurred by obtaining third party inspection during the construction process.

III. A planning board retaining services under paragraph I or II shall require detailed invoices with reasonable task descriptions for services rendered. Upon request of the applicant, the planning board shall promptly provide a reasonably detailed accounting of expenses, or corresponding escrow deductions, with copies of supporting documentation.

IV. A person retained as a third party inspector during the construction process shall observe, record, and promptly report to the planning board or appropriate municipal authority and applicant or applicant's successor in interest any perceived construction defect or deviation from the terms of the approval or approved project plans.

V. Any person who becomes aware of a failure by a third party inspector to report properly and promptly a construction defect or deviation from the terms of the approval or approved project plans, may file a written complaint to the joint board established under RSA 310-A:1 for possible peer review or disciplinary action.

HISTORY:
2009, 73:1, eff. August 8, 2009. 2010, 303:3, eff. September 11, 2010. 2015, 126:1, eff. August 8, 2015.

Amendment Notes

—2015.
The 2015 amendment added second through last sentences of paragraph I.

—2010.
The 2010 amendment added "provided that the review and consultation does not substantially replicate a review and consultation obtained by the zoning board of adjustment" in I.

Zoning Board of Adjustment

676:5. Appeals to Board of Adjustment.

I. Appeals to the board of adjustment concerning any matter within the board's powers as set forth in RSA 674:33 may be taken by any person aggrieved or by any officer, department, board, or bureau of the municipality affected by any decision of the administrative officer. Such appeal shall be taken within a reasonable time, as provided by the rules of the board, by filing with the officer from whom the appeal is taken and with the board a notice of appeal specifying the grounds thereof. The officer from whom the appeal is taken shall forthwith transmit to the board all the papers constituting the record upon which the action appealed from was taken.

II. For the purposes of this section:

(a) The "administrative officer" means any official or board who, in that municipality, has responsibility for issuing permits or certificates under the ordinance, or for enforcing the ordinance, and may include a building inspector, board of selectmen, or other official or board with such responsibility.

(b) A "decision of the administrative officer" includes any decision involving construction, interpretation or application of the terms of the ordinance. It does not include a discretionary decision to commence formal or informal enforcement proceedings, but does include any construction, interpretation or application of the terms of the ordinance which is implicated in such enforcement proceedings.

III. If, in the exercise of subdivision or site plan review, the planning board makes any decision or determination which is based upon the terms of the zoning ordinance, or upon any construction, interpretation, or application of the zoning ordinance, which would be appealable to the board of adjustment if it had been made by the administrative officer, then such decision may be appealed to the board of adjustment under this section; provided, however, that if the zoning ordinance contains an innovative land use control adopted pursuant to RSA 674:21 which delegates administration, including the granting of conditional or special use permits, to the planning board, then the planning board's decision made pursuant to that delegation cannot be appealed to the board of adjustment, but may be appealed to the superior court as provided by RSA 677:15.

IV. The board of adjustment may impose reasonable fees to cover its administrative expenses and costs of special investigative studies, review of documents, and other matters which may be required by particular appeals or applications.

V.(a) A board of adjustment reviewing a land use application may require the applicant to reimburse the board for expenses reasonably incurred by obtaining third party review and consultation during the review process, provided that the review and consultation does not substantially replicate a review and consultation obtained by the planning board.

(b) A board of adjustment retaining services under subparagraph (a) shall require detailed invoices with reasonable task descriptions for services rendered. Upon request of the applicant, the board of adjustment shall promptly provide a reasonably detailed accounting of expenses, or corresponding escrow deductions, with copies of supporting documentation.

HISTORY:

1983, 447:1. 1987, 256:5. 1989, 69:1. 1991, 231:13. 1995, 243:1, eff. Jan. 1, 1996. 2010, 303:1, eff. September 11, 2010.

Amendments

—2010.
The 2010 amendment added IV and V.

—1995.
Paragraph III: Deleted "the board states" preceding "is based" and "solely" thereafter.

—1991.
Paragraph III: Added.

—1989.
Designated the existing provisions of the section as par. I and added par. II.

—1987.
Inserted "concerning any matter within the board's powers as set forth in RSA 674:33" following "board of adjustment" in the first sentence.

NOTES TO DECISIONS

Analysis

1. Generally
2. Construction
3. Jurisdiction of court
4. Legislative intent
5. Standing
6. Time limitation
7. Reviewability of issues
8. Decision of administrative officer

1. Generally
The provision for administrative review precluded resort to the courts before seeking such review. Carrick v. Langtry, 99 N.H. 251, 108 A.2d 546, 1954 N.H. LEXIS 61 (N.H. 1954). (Decided under prior law.)

2. Construction
RSA 677:15, I, and RSA 676:5, III, together create two separate appeal processes when a planning board decision is based upon both zoning and planning issues; while the statutes allow a party to appeal planning issues associated with a plat or subdivision directly to the superior court, they also provide for an initial layer of review at the local level for decisions involving the interpretation or application of a zoning ordinance. The legislature has provided this initial layer of review to ensure uniform application of local zoning laws., and the overall policy and purpose sought to be advanced by this statutory scheme is best served by interpreting RSA 676:5, III to mean that a planning board decision about a zoning ordinance is ripe and appealable to the zoning board of adjustment (ZBA) when such a decision is made. Atwater v. Town of Plainfield, 160 N.H. 503, 8 A.3d 159, 2010 N.H. LEXIS 80 (N.H. 2010).

Nothing in the plain language of RSA 677:15, I, or RSA 676:5, III, requires that the planning board first complete its consideration of the planning issues involved in a site plan review, or that the applicant satisfy the conditions imposed on a site plan application prior to the zoning board considering the zoning issues on appeal. Atwater v. Town of Plainfield, 160 N.H. 503, 8 A.3d 159, 2010 N.H. LEXIS 80 (N.H. 2010).

There is no indication either in case law or in RSA 676:5, III, that the parties must wait for final approval of the site plan before they bring an appeal to the zoning board of adjustment challenging the planning board's interpretation or application of a zoning ordinance. Atwater v. Town of Plainfield, 160 N.H. 503, 8 A.3d 159, 2010 N.H. LEXIS 80 (N.H. 2010).

Mere fact that an individual is a taxpaying resident of a town does not give that individual standing to seek mandamus relief requiring the town to enforce its zoning ordinances. Pursuant to RSA 676:5, 677:2, 677:4, an individual can seek relief before a zoning board of appeals or in the courts with regard to a zoning officer's decision only if the individual is an "aggrieved person," which requires a showing that he or she has some direct, definite interest in the outcome of the zoning decision itself, and the mere fact that an individual lives and/or pays taxes to a town, does not, by itself, give that individual a direct, definite interest in town zoning decisions. Goldstein v. Town of Bedford, 154 N.H. 393, 910 A.2d 1158, 2006 N.H. LEXIS 173 (N.H. 2006).

Petitioners had actual or constructive notice of issuance of building permit, as well as respondent's construction activities, and their decision to wait for fifty-five days to file their appeal did not constitute filing within a reasonable time. Tausanovitch v. Town of Lyme, 143 N.H. 144, 722 A.2d 914, 1998 N.H. LEXIS 81 (N.H. 1998).

3. Jurisdiction of court

Decisions or determinations appealable under RSA 676:5, III are "final," for purposes of ripeness for appellate review, when made, and do not contemplate additional action on the part of the town, but conclusively determine the applicable issue at the planning board level; they are immediately appealable to the zoning board of adjustment under RSA 676:5, III, and further to the superior court, subject to the requirement of a prior application for rehearing under RSA 677:2 and RSA 677:3, I. Accordingly, there was no merit to the argument that the trial court lacked subject matter jurisdiction because a planning board decision was not final. Saunders v. Town of Kingston, 160 N.H. 560, 8 A.3d 89, 2010 N.H. LEXIS 87 (N.H. 2010).

Homeowners' declaratory judgment action challenging the issuance of a building permit for an adjoining lot was properly dismissed because the homeowners failed to appeal the issuance of the permit to the local zoning board and thus they failed to exhaust their administrative remedies. McNamara v. Hersh, 157 N.H. 72, 945 A.2d 18, 2008 N.H. LEXIS 38 (N.H. 2008).

Although an applicant for site plan approval had a right to expect the town to assist with the application process, instead of failing to respond to the applicant's communications, the issue was moot; the trial court had lacked jurisdiction over the applicant's appeal from the planning board's action application of its site plan review rules, because of the applicant's failure to seek review within 30 days, and it lacked jurisdiction over the applicant's appeal from the planning board's application of zoning regulations because, in the absence of a ruling by the zoning board of adjustment, there was nothing to appeal from to the trial court. Route 12 Books & Video v. Town of Troy, 149 N.H. 569, 825 A.2d 493, 2003 N.H. LEXIS 79 (N.H. 2003).

Landowners were required to seek zoning adjustment board review of a planning board's decision to apply only an architectural design review to a parking lot application, and failure to seek board review resulted in the reviewing court's lacking jurisdiction to consider the landowners' appeals. Heartz v. City of Concord, 148 N.H. 325, 808 A.2d 76, 2002 N.H. LEXIS 131 (N.H. 2002).

4. Legislative intent

Where the legislature did not intend to grant standing to request a rehearing to all municipal boards that could initiate an appeal, a town conservation commission lacked standing to request a rehearing or to appeal a zoning board decision. Hooksett Conservation Comm'n v. Hooksett Zoning Bd. of Adjustment, 149 N.H. 63, 816 A.2d 948, 2003 N.H. LEXIS 5 (N.H. 2003).

5. Standing

Residents who were non-abutters lacked standing under RSA 676:5, I, to appeal a planning board's major subdivision and site plan approvals to the zoning board of adjustment. Close proximity alone did not establish a direct, definite interest; although converting an existing building into a four-unit condominium presumably would cause some increase in traffic and noise and affect the preservation of open space, the residents had not shown direct injury to themselves; and only one resident had participated in the planning board proceedings. Golf Course Investors of NH, LLC v. Town of Jaffrey, 161 N.H. 675, 20 A.3d 846, 2011 N.H. LEXIS 48 (2011).

Superior court properly dismissed the mandamus petition filed by a town resident, seeking to require the town to enforce its zoning ordinances, because the resident was not an "aggrieved person," which was required for him to have standing under RSA 676:5, I, 677:2, 677:4, to seek administrative review of a zoning officer's decision or to seek judicial review of actions taken by the town's zoning board of adjustment. The mere fact that the resident lived in, and paid taxes to, the town did not give him a direct, definite interest in the zoning decision that he challenged, which pertained to permits obtained by a third party with regard to his nonconforming lots. Goldstein v. Town of Bedford, 154 N.H. 393, 910 A.2d 1158, 2006 N.H. LEXIS 173 (N.H. 2006).

6. Time limitation

Appeal to a zoning board of adjustment (ZBA) was timely under RSA 676:5, III because by merely accepting jurisdiction of the site plan application on June 19 under RSA 676:4, the planning board made no decision regarding zoning compliance; it was not until its August 21 meeting, when it voted to approve the application, that the planning board rendered a zoning determination that was appealable to the ZBA. Accurate Transp., Inc. v. Town of Derry, 168 N.H. 108, 123 A.3d 263, 2015 N.H. LEXIS 81 (N.H. 2015).

RSA 676:5, III, when read with RSA 677:15, I, meant that a planning board decision about a zoning ordinance was ripe and appealable to a zoning board of adjustment when such a decision was made. Thus, petitioners' appeal period under RSA 676:5 began to run with the planning board's conditional approval of an application for site plan review. Atwater v. Town of Plainfield, 160 N.H. 503, 8 A.3d 159, 2010 N.H. LEXIS 80 (N.H. 2010).

7. Reviewability of issues

Petitioners' motion for reconsideration filed with a zoning board of adjustment (ZBA) did not challenge the ZBA's conclusion that the length of an appeal period was fifteen days or raise petitioner's estoppel issue. Therefore, the trial court did not err when it declined to consider these arguments. Atwater v. Town of Plainfield, 160 N.H. 503, 8 A.3d 159, 2010 N.H. LEXIS 80 (N.H. 2010).

To the extent that petitioners argued that they had "good cause" to raise the issue of the length of an appeal period in the trial court despite the fact that the issue was not raised with the zoning board of adjustment (ZBA), the court found this argument unpersuasive. Petitioners had not challenged the representation that the ZBA's rules of procedure were available for public inspection, nor had they asserted that they ever requested a copy of the rules of procedure from the town or that they at any point went to the town clerk's office and asked to see the rules of procedure. Atwater v. Town of Plainfield, 160 N.H. 503, 8 A.3d 159, 2010 N.H. LEXIS 80 (N.H. 2010).

8. Decision of administrative officer

RSA 676:5, II(b) defines "decision of the administrative officer" that is appealable to the zoning board of adjustment to be, in part, "any decision involving construction, interpretation or application of the terms of the ordinance." The code enforcement officer, however, never made such a "decision" here, but simply opined that the proposed use was permitted and thus preliminarily approved the use before petitioners filed a formal site plan application with the planning board; his recommendation was not binding as it was ultimately for the planning board to decide whether the proposed use was permitted. Accurate Transp., Inc. v. Town of Derry, 168 N.H. 108, 123 A.3d 263, 2015 N.H. LEXIS 81 (N.H. 2015).

Cited:

Cited in Doggett v. Town of N. Hampton Zoning Bd. of Adjustment, 138 N.H. 744, 645 A.2d 673, 1994 N.H. LEXIS 97 (1994); Babiarz v. Town of Grafton, 155 N.H. 757, 930 A.2d 395, 2007 N.H. LEXIS 127 (2007).

RESEARCH REFERENCES AND PRACTICE AIDS

Cross References.
   Effect of appeals, see RSA 676:6.
   Hearings before boards of adjustment, see RSA 676:7.
   Powers of boards of adjustment generally, see RSA 674:33.
   Rehearings and appeals procedures generally, see RSA 677.

New Hampshire Bar Journal.
   For article, "Lex Loci: A Survey of New Hampshire Supreme Court Decisions," see 47 N.H. B.J. 44 (Winter 2007).

New Hampshire Practice.
   15-22 N.H.P. Land Use Planning and Zoning § 22.02.
   15-29 N.H.P. Land Use Planning and Zoning § 29.07.

15-33 N.H.P. Land Use Planning and Zoning § 33.01.

676:6. Effect of Appeal to Board.

The effect of an appeal to the board shall be to maintain the status quo. An appeal of the issuance of any permit or certificate shall be deemed to suspend such permit or certificate, and no construction, alteration, or change of use which is contingent upon it shall be commenced. An appeal of any order or other enforcement action shall stay all proceedings under the action appealed from unless the officer from whom the appeal is taken certifies to the board of adjustment, after notice of appeal shall have been filed with such officer, that, by reason of facts stated in the certificate, a stay would, in the officer's opinion, cause imminent peril to life, health, safety, property, or the environment. In such case, the proceedings shall not be stayed otherwise than by a restraining order which may be granted by the board or by the superior court on notice to the officer from whom the appeal is taken and cause shown.

HISTORY:
1983, 447:1. 1995, 243:2, eff. Jan. 1, 1996.

Amendments

—1995.
Rewritten to the extent that a detailed comparison would be impracticable.

—1985.
Paragraph I(a): Deleted "return receipt requested" following "mail" in the first sentence.

RESEARCH REFERENCES AND PRACTICE AIDS

Cross References.
Appeals procedure generally, see RSA 676:5.

New Hampshire Practice.
15-25 N.H.P. Land Use Planning and Zoning § 25.10.

676:7. Public Hearing; Notice.

I. Prior to exercising its appeals powers, the board of adjustment shall hold a public hearing. Notice of the public hearing shall be given as follows:

(a) The appellant and every abutter and holder of conservation, preservation, or agricultural preservation restrictions shall be notified of the hearing by verified mail, as defined in RSA 451-C:1, VII, stating the time and place of the hearing, and such notice shall be given not less than 5 days before the date fixed for the hearing of the appeal. The board shall hear all abutters and holders of conservation, preservation, or agricultural preservation restrictions desiring to submit testimony and all nonabutters who can demonstrate that they are affected directly by the proposal under consideration. The board may hear such other persons as it deems appropriate.

(b) A public notice of the hearing shall be placed in a newspaper of general circulation in the area not less than 5 days before the date fixed for the hearing of the appeal.

II. The public hearing shall be held within 30 days of the receipt of the notice of appeal.

III. Any party may appear in person or by the party's agent or attorney at the hearing of an appeal.

IV. The cost of notice, whether mailed, posted, or published, shall be paid in advance by the applicant. Failure to pay such costs shall constitute valid grounds for the board to terminate further consideration and to deny the appeal without public hearing.

V. If the board of adjustment finds that it cannot conclude the public hearing within the time available, it may vote to continue the hearing to a specified time and place with no additional notice required.

HISTORY:
1983, 447:1. 1985, 159:2, eff. July 26, 1985. 1996, 226:1, eff. Jan. 1, 1997. 1997, 142:6, eff. Aug. 8, 1997. 2017, 4:1, eff. May 30, 2017. 2017, 59:5, eff. August 1, 2017.

Amendment Notes
The 2017 amendments to this section by Ch. 4 added V.
The 2017 amendment to this section by Ch. 59 substituted "by verified mail, as defined in RSA 451-C:1, VII" for "by certified mail" in the first sentence of I(a).

—1997.
Paragraph I(a): Inserted "and holder of conservation, preservation, or agricultural preservation restrictions" in the first sentence and "and holders of conservation, preservation, or agricultural preservation restrictions" in the second sentence.

—1996.
Paragraph III: Substituted "the party's" for "his" preceding "agent".

—1985.
Paragraph I(a): Deleted "return receipt requested" following "mail" in the first sentence.

NOTES TO DECISIONS

Analysis

1. Application
2. Conditions precedent to hearing
3. Effect of failure to hold timely hearing

1. Application
Where 1987 hearing on landowner's request for variance was conducted without jurisdiction because all abutters had not received notice, and in 1989 zoning board of adjustment ordered landowner to reapply for variance because of lack of notice, 1989 hearing on variance was a new hearing calling for a fresh decision. Hussey v. Barrington, 135 N.H. 227, 604 A.2d 82, 1992 N.H. LEXIS 3 (N.H. 1992).

2. Conditions precedent to hearing
The absence of any statutory provision specifically authorizing the making of consent of property owners a condition precedent to a hearing for a variance did not preclude a city from imposing such a condition. Robwood Advertising Assocs. v. Nashua, 102 N.H. 215, 153 A.2d 787, 1959 N.H. LEXIS 49 (N.H. 1959). (Decided under prior law.)

3. Effect of failure to hold timely hearing
A party was not entitled to have a variance granted as a matter of law because a zoning board of adjustment had violated the time

requirement of the statute by failing to hold a hearing on the application for a variance within thirty days after the application was filed; the legislature had not seen fit to provide that a zoning board's failure to comply with the statute would constitute approval of an application for a variance submitted to it. Barry v. Amherst, 121 N.H. 335, 430 A.2d 132, 1981 N.H. LEXIS 314 (N.H. 1981). (Decided under prior law.)

RESEARCH REFERENCES AND PRACTICE AIDS

Cross References.
Powers of boards of adjustment generally, see RSA 674:33.

Historic District Commission

RESEARCH REFERENCES AND PRACTICE AIDS

Cross References.
Building codes generally, see RSA 674:51 et seq.
Building permits generally, see RSA 676:11 et seq.
Historic districts generally, see RSA 674:45 et seq.
Protection of New Hampshire heritage landmarks from development, see RSA 227-C:24 et seq.

676:8. Issuing Approval for Building Permits.

The historic district commission shall review applications for building permits within the historic district for their impact on the historic district and its objectives by:

I. Requesting reports and recommendations regarding the feasibility of the applicant's proposal from the planning board, fire chief, building inspector, health officer and other administrative officials who may possess information concerning the impact of the proposal on the historic district.

II. Seeking advice from professional, educational, cultural or other groups or persons as may be deemed necessary for the determination of a reasonable decision.

III. Filing with the building inspector or other duly delegated authority either a certificate of approval or a notice of disapproval following the review and determination of the application.

HISTORY:
1983, 447:1, eff. Jan. 1, 1984.

NOTES TO DECISIONS

Basis for decision of commission
The statute placed on the commission the duty to reach a reasoned decision. Hanrahan v. Portsmouth, 119 N.H. 944, 409 A.2d 1336, 1979 N.H. LEXIS 425 (N.H. 1979), limited, Ouellette v. Town of Kingston, 157 N.H. 604, 956 A.2d 286, 2008 N.H. LEXIS 98 (N.H. 2008). (Decided under prior law.)
The statute imposed a duty on district commissions to make a group assessment of information that was more than the mere personal opinion of one or more members. Hanrahan v. Portsmouth, 119 N.H. 944, 409 A.2d 1336, 1979 N.H. LEXIS 425 (N.H. 1979), limited, Ouellette v. Town of Kingston, 157 N.H. 604, 956 A.2d 286, 2008 N.H. LEXIS 98 (N.H. 2008). (Decided under prior law.)

RESEARCH REFERENCES AND PRACTICE AIDS

Cross References.
Issuance of certificate of approval or notice of disapproval, see RSA 676:9.

Powers and duties of historic district commission generally, see RSA 674:46-a.

676:9. Procedure for Approval of Building Permits.

I. The historic commission district shall file a certificate of approval or a notice of disapproval pursuant to RSA 676:8, III within 45 days after the filing of the application for the certificate, unless the applicant agrees to a longer period of time.

II. No building permit shall be issued until a certificate of approval has been filed with the building inspector; but, in the case of disapproval, notice of disapproval shall be binding upon the building inspector or other duly delegated authority, and no permit shall be issued.

III. Failure to file the certificate within the specified period of time shall constitute approval by the commission.

HISTORY:
1983, 447:1, eff. Jan. 1, 1984.

676:10. Enforcement by Historic District Commission.

I. In municipalities which have established one or more historic districts pursuant to RSA 674:46, but which have no local zoning ordinances, the historic district commission shall have within the bounds of the historic district all the authority, powers and duties prescribed in this chapter for planning boards insofar as such authority, powers and duties are within the intent of the historic district commission's grant of power. In such municipalities, the requirement of conformity with the local zoning ordinance, as provided in RSA 674:46, shall not apply.

II. In municipalities which do not have a planning board, the requirements of RSA 674:46 and 676:6 relating to conformity with the master plan and the requirement of RSA 673:4 that one member of the commission may be a planning board member shall not apply.

III. In municipalities which do not have a building inspector, the certificate of approval of the commission, as provided in RSA 676:8, III, shall be the equivalent of a building permit. In municipalities which do not have a zoning board of adjustment, motions for rehearing and appeals from decisions of the historic district commission shall be governed by the provisions of RSA 677, insofar as applicable.

HISTORY:
1983, 447:1, eff. Jan. 1, 1984.

RESEARCH REFERENCES AND PRACTICE AIDS

Cross References.
Powers and duties of historic district commissions generally, see RSA 674:46-a.
Powers and duties of planning boards generally, see RSA 676:4 et seq.

Building Permits

RESEARCH REFERENCES AND PRACTICE AIDS

Cross References.
Building codes generally, see RSA 674:51 et seq.
Powers of building code boards of appeals generally, see RSA 674:34.
Zoning ordinances generally, see RSA 674:16 et seq.

676:11. Building Permits Required.

After a municipality has adopted a building code, any person who intends to erect or remodel any building in the municipality shall submit the plans to the building inspector for the building inspector's examination and approval prior to commencement of the planned construction.

HISTORY:
1983, 447:1, eff. Jan. 1, 1984. 1996, 226:2, eff. Jan. 1, 1997.

Amendments

—1996.
Substituted "the building inspector's" for "his" preceding "examination".

676:12. Building Permits to be Withheld in Certain Cases.

I. The building inspector shall not issue any building permit within the 120 days prior to the annual or special town or village district meeting if:

(a) Application for such permit is made after the first legal notice of proposed changes in the building code or zoning ordinance has been posted pursuant to the provisions of RSA 675:7; and

(b) The proposed changes in the building code or the zoning ordinance would, if adopted, justify refusal of such permit.

II. After final action has been taken on the proposed changes in the building code or zoning ordinance, the building inspector shall issue or refuse to issue a permit which has been held in abeyance under this section pursuant to a final action under this section.

III. The provisions of paragraph I shall not be applicable in a city or in a county in which there are located unincorporated towns or unorganized places unless the governing body of the city or the county votes by majority vote to be subject to the provisions of such paragraph.

IV. The building inspector may be authorized by the local legislative body to issue a temporary occupancy permit not to exceed 30 days, which may be extended at the discretion of the building inspector.

V. No building permit shall be denied on the grounds of uncompleted streets or utilities when the construction of such streets or utilities has been secured to the municipality by a bond or other security approved by the planning board pursuant to RSA 674:36, III or RSA 674:44, IV; provided, however, that on land which is part of a subdivision plat or site plan, no building shall be used or occupied prior to the completion of required streets and utilities, except upon such terms as the planning board may have authorized as part of its decision approving the plat or site plan.

VI. The provisions of paragraph I shall not apply to any plat or application which has been the subject of notice by the planning board pursuant to RSA 676:4, I(d) prior to the first legal notice of a proposed change in a building code or zoning ordinance or any amendment thereto. No proposed subdivision or site plan review or zoning ordinance or amendment thereto shall affect a plat or application which has been the subject of notice by the planning board pursuant to RSA 676:4, I(d) so long as said plat or application was the subject of notice prior to the first legal notice of said change or amendment. The provisions of this paragraph shall also apply to proposals submitted to a planning board for design review pursuant to RSA 676:4, II(b), provided that a formal application is filed with the planning board within 12 months of the end of the design review process.

HISTORY:
1983, 447:1. 1986, 200:1. 229:3. 1989, 266:31. 1991, 331:3, eff. Aug. 27, 1991. 2003, 134:1, eff. Aug. 13, 2003. 2006, 285:1, eff. August 14, 2006. 2008, 229:1, eff. August 19, 2008.

Amendments

—2008.
The 2008 amendment added "also" following "this paragraph shall" in the third sentence of VI.

—2006.
Paragraph VI: In the first sentence, substituted "the subject of notice" for "formally accepted" and "which has been the subject of notice" preceding "by the planning board pursuant to RSA 676:4" and substituted "I(d)" for "I(b)", substituted "the subject of notice" for "accepted", and added the second sentence.

—2003.
Rewritten to the extent that a detailed comparison would be impracticable.

—1991.
Paragraph V: Substituted "or zoning ordinance" for "regulation" following "review" in the second sentence.

—1989.
Paragraph II: Inserted "or in a county in which there are located unincorporated towns or unorganized places" preceding "unless" and "or the county" preceding "votes by majority".

—1986.
Paragraph IV: Added by ch. 200.
Paragraph V: Added by ch. 229.

Legislative purpose of 1991 amendment.
1991, 331:4, eff. Aug. 27, 1991, provided:
"The purpose of sections 1– 3 of this act [which amended this section and RSA 674:39] is to confirm and re-emphasize the intent of the general court at the time of the enactment of 1986, 229:3 and 1983, 447:1. Municipalities may not retroactively amend local land use regulations or zoning ordinances for the purpose of stopping proposed projects or developments while an application is under consideration by the municipality. This act shall not be interpreted as changing the intent of any provisions of 1986, 229 or 1983, 447."

NOTES TO DECISIONS

Analysis

1. Purpose
2. Application of section
3. Procedure for adoption of section

1. Purpose

The purpose of the statute allowing building permits to be withheld pending proposed zoning changes was not land use regulation, but rather enhancement of the effectiveness of the zoning process by preventing landowners from adopting property uses inconsistent with proposed zoning changes during the zoning deliberation process. Socha v. Manchester, 126 N.H. 289, 490 A.2d 794, 1985 N.H. LEXIS 297 (N.H. 1985). (Decided under prior law.)

2. Application of section

Developer's application for site plan approval was first subject to legal notice in July 2007, approximately eight months before a 2008 ordinance became effective; accordingly, pursuant to RSA 676:12, VI, the town's 2004 ordinance applied to the project. RSA 676:39, I, applied only to site plans that had been approved by the planning board and properly recorded in the registry of deeds, if local regulation required such recording. Ouellette v. Town of Kingston, 2010 N.H. LEXIS 199 (N.H. Dec. 17, 2010).

Purpose of former RSA 676:12, V (see now 676:12,VI for similar provisions) was to protect a zoning application from any regulatory amendments passed while application was under formal consideration, and since plaintiff's subdivision application had not yet been accepted by planning board, RSA 676:12, V could not be relied upon by board to deny jurisdiction over plaintiff's application. Rallis v. Town of Hampton Planning Bd., 146 N.H. 18, 766 A.2d 281, 2001 N.H. LEXIS 20 (N.H. 2001).

Former version of this section extended grandfather protection to subdivision applicants from certain proposed and adopted land use regulations. However, the 1988 version of this section only provided protection from subdivision and site plan review regulations, not from zoning ordinances. Rall v. Town of Belmont, 138 N.H. 172, 635 A.2d 1368, 1993 N.H. LEXIS 185 (N.H. 1993).

3. Procedure for adoption of section

A city's adoption of the statute allowing building permits to be withheld pending zoning changes did not operate as a zoning ordinance where zoning deliberations did not extend beyond a reasonable time; therefore, the adoption of the statute was not subject to the public hearing requirements of former RSA 31:63 (now covered by RSA 675:2) needed to enact zoning ordinances. Socha v. Manchester, 126 N.H. 289, 490 A.2d 794, 1985 N.H. LEXIS 297 (N.H. 1985). (Decided under prior law.)

Cited:

Cited in Real Estate Planners v. Newmarket, 134 N.H. 696, 597 A.2d 78, 1991 N.H. LEXIS 125 (1991); State v. Roy, 138 N.H. 97, 635 A.2d 486, 1993 N.H. LEXIS 166 (1993).

RESEARCH REFERENCES AND PRACTICE AIDS

New Hampshire Bar Journal.

For article, "'Grandfathered'—The Law of Nonconforming Uses and Vested Rights," see 31 N.H. B.J. 17 (1990).

New Hampshire Practice.

15-7 N.H.P. Land Use Planning and Zoning § 7.14.
15-11 N.H.P. Land Use Planning and Zoning § 11.04.
15-28 N.H.P. Land Use Planning and Zoning § 28.02.
15-29 N.H.P. Land Use Planning and Zoning § 29.23.
15-32 N.H.P. Land Use Planning and Zoning § 32.02.

676:13. Building Permits Restricted.

I. The building inspector shall not issue any building or occupancy permit for any proposed construction, remodeling, or maintenance which will not comply with any or all zoning ordinances, building codes, or planning board regulations which are in effect.

II. If any building inspector is prosecuted for violation of RSA 643:1 and found guilty of issuing any permit contrary to the provisions of this section, it shall be prima facie evidence that the building inspector has knowingly refrained from performing a duty imposed on the building inspector by law.

III. The building inspector shall adopt a form or set of standards specifying the minimum contents of a completed application for any building permit. Upon the submission of a completed application, the building inspector shall act to approve or deny a building permit within 30 days; provided, however, that nonresidential applications or residential applications encompassing more than 10 dwelling units shall be approved or denied within 60 days.

IV. The time for the building inspector to act upon building permits for collocation applications and modification applications for personal wireless service facilities shall be governed by RSA 12-K:10. In the event that the form or set of standards for a building permit application conflicts with any of the limitations under RSA 12-K:11 for a collocation application or a modification application for a personal wireless service facility, the limitations in RSA 12-K:11 shall control.

HISTORY:

1983, 447:1. 1986, 150:1, eff. July 26, 1986. 1996, 226:3, eff. Jan. 1, 1997. 2013, 267:11, eff. September 22, 2013.

Amendment Notes

—2013.

The 2013 amendment added IV.

—1996.

Paragraph II: Substituted "the building inspector" for "he" preceding "has knowingly" and "the building inspector" for "him" preceding "by law".

—1986.

Paragraph III: Added.

Severability of 2013 amendment.

2013, 267:12, eff. September 22, 2013, provided: "If any provision of this chapter or the application thereof to any person or circumstance is held invalid, such invalidity shall not affect other provisions or applications of the chapter which can be given effect without the invalid provision or application, and to that end the provisions of this chapter are declared to be severable."

RESEARCH REFERENCES AND PRACTICE AIDS

Cross References.

Penalties for violations of title generally, see RSA 676:17.

New Hampshire Trial Bar News.

For article, "Presumptions in New Hampshire Law—A Guide Through the Impenetrable Jungle (Part 1)," see 10 N.H. Trial Bar News 55, 60 (Winter 1990).

Local Conflicts of Law

676:14. Determination of Which Local Ordinance Takes Precedence.

Whenever a local land use ordinance is enacted or a regulation is adopted which differs from the authority of an existing ordinance or other regulation, the provision which imposes the greater restriction or higher standard shall be controlling.

HISTORY:
1983, 447:1, eff. Jan. 1, 1984.

Penalties and Remedies

RESEARCH REFERENCES AND PRACTICE AIDS

Cross References.
Fines for violations of RSA 674:25– 29, see RSA 674:29.
Remedies for violations of historic district ordinances or regulations generally, see RSA 674:50.

676:15. Injunctive Relief.

In case any building or structure or part thereof is or is proposed to be erected, constructed, altered, or reconstructed, or any land is or is proposed to be used in violation of this title or of any local ordinance, code, or regulation adopted under this title, or of any provision or specification of an application, plat, or plan approved by, or any requirement or condition of a permit or decision issued by, any local administrator or land use board acting under the authority of this title, the building inspector or other official with authority to enforce the provisions of this title or any local ordinance, code, or regulation adopted under this title, or the owner of any adjacent or neighboring property who would be specially damaged by such violation may, in addition to other remedies provided by law, institute injunction, mandamus, abatement, or any other appropriate action or proceeding to prevent, enjoin, abate, or remove such unlawful erection, construction, alteration, or reconstruction.

HISTORY:
1983, 447:1. 1988, 19:5, eff. Jan. 1, 1989.

Amendments

—1988.
Rewritten to the extent that a detailed comparison would be impracticable.

NOTES TO DECISIONS

Standing
Private landowners who sought relief from alleged zoning violation had standing, where evidence showed that the landowners were specially damaged by the alleged violation. Barton v. H.D. Riders Motorcycle Club, 131 N.H. 60, 550 A.2d 91, 1988 N.H. LEXIS 89 (N.H. 1988).

Cited:
Cited in White v. Francoeur, 138 N.H. 307, 638 A.2d 1250, 1994 N.H. LEXIS 27 (1994); Miner v. A & C Tire Co., 146 N.H. 631, 776 A.2d 1286, 2001 N.H. LEXIS 124 (2001).

RESEARCH REFERENCES AND PRACTICE AIDS

Cross References.
Recovery of costs and attorney's fees in actions under section, see RSA 676:17.
Requirement of bond in actions under section, see RSA 676:17.

676:16. Penalties for Transferring Lots in Unapproved Subdivisions.

Any owner, or agent of the owner, of any land located within a subdivision in a municipality that has adopted subdivision regulations who transfers or sells any land before a plat of the subdivision has been approved by the planning board and filed with the appropriate recording official under RSA 674:35, II, shall forfeit and pay a civil penalty of $1,000 for each lot or parcel so transferred or sold; and the description by metes and bounds in the instrument of transfer or other document used in the process of selling or transferring shall not exempt the transaction from such penalties. The municipality may enjoin a transfer or sale which violates the provisions of this section and may recover the penalty imposed by civil action. In any action to recover a penalty, the prevailing party may recover reasonable court costs and attorney's fees as may be ordered by the court.

HISTORY:
1983, 447:1, eff. Jan. 1, 1984. 1997, 92:3, eff. Jan. 1, 1998.

Amendments

—1997.
Substituted "$1,000" for "$500" in the first sentence.

NOTES TO DECISIONS

Analysis

1. Conveyance in violation of a subdivision plat
2. Attorney fees
3. Conveyance without planning board approval

1. Conveyance in violation of a subdivision plat
A conveyance in violation of a subdivision plat is not void. White v. Francoeur, 138 N.H. 307, 638 A.2d 1250, 1994 N.H. LEXIS 27 (N.H. 1994).

2. Attorney fees
Where trial court ruled that defendant had violated this section, it had the power to grant attorney's fees to plaintiff, and it was not required to make a finding of bad faith before awarding attorney's fees. Town of Windham v. Lawrence Sav. Bank, 146 N.H. 517, 776 A.2d 730, 2001 N.H. LEXIS 109 (N.H. 2001).
Where trial court ruled that defendant had violated this section, it did not abuse its discretion in declining to award attorney's fees based on its consideration of a number of factors including: (1) whether plaintiff town alleged that defendant acted in bad faith; (2) the relative merits of the parties' positions; and (3) the true purpose of the litigation. Town of Windham v. Lawrence Sav. Bank, 146 N.H. 517, 776 A.2d 730, 2001 N.H. LEXIS 109 (N.H. 2001).

3. Conveyance without planning board approval

Trial court properly held that landowners owned a single parcel at the time they conveyed two lots separately to themselves without prior approval, thereby improperly subdividing their property. As early as 1961, the landowners and their predecessors had abolished the boundary line through their conduct. Town of Newbury v. Landrigan, 165 N.H. 236, 75 A.3d 1091, 2013 N.H. LEXIS 90 (N.H. 2013).

Where expandable lands were not separated from other lands by a road or any boundary except that which the developer established when he submitted land to a condominium, and, further, planning board approved a plan that designated the expandable land as a single parcel and never treated the phases of development or the expandable lands as distinct parcels, therefore, conveyance of a portion of the expandable land as a separate lot prior to receiving planning board subdivision approval was in violation of this section. Town of Windham v. Lawrence Sav. Bank, 146 N.H. 517, 776 A.2d 730, 2001 N.H. LEXIS 109 (N.H. 2001).

Cited:

Cited in Erin Food Servs. v. Derry Motel, 131 N.H. 353, 553 A.2d 304, 1988 N.H. LEXIS 136 (1988); Dover v. Kimball, 136 N.H. 441, 616 A.2d 516, 1992 N.H. LEXIS 187 (1992).

RESEARCH REFERENCES AND PRACTICE AIDS

Cross References.
Filing or recording by registers of deeds of unapproved subdivision plats, see RSA 676:18.
Fines and penalties generally, see RSA 676:17.
Injunctions generally, see RSA 676:15.

New Hampshire Practice.
15-29 N.H.P. Land Use Planning and Zoning § 29.24.

676:17. Fines and Penalties; Second Offense.

I. Any person who violates any of the provisions of this title, or any local ordinance, code, or regulation adopted under this title, or any provision or specification of any application, plat, or plan approved by, or any requirement or condition of a permit or decision issued by, any local administrator or land use board acting under the authority of this title shall be guilty of a misdemeanor if a natural person, or guilty of a felony if any other person; and shall be subject to a civil penalty of $275 for the first offense, and $550 for subsequent offenses, for each day that such violation is found to continue after the conviction date or after the date on which the violator receives written notice from the municipality that the violator is in violation, whichever is earlier. Each day that a violation continues shall be a separate offense.

II. In any legal action brought by a municipality to enforce, by way of injunctive relief as provided by RSA 676:15 or otherwise, any local ordinance, code or regulation adopted under this title, or to enforce any planning board, zoning board of adjustment or building code board of appeals decision made pursuant to this title, or to seek the payment of any fine levied under paragraph I, the municipality shall recover its costs and reasonable attorney's fees actually expended in pursuing the legal action if it is found to be a prevailing party in the action. For the purposes of this paragraph, recoverable costs shall include all out-of-pocket expenses actually incurred, including but not limited to, inspection fees, expert fees and investigatory expenses.

III. If any violation of a local ordinance, code or regulation, or any violation of a planning board, zoning board of adjustment or building code board of appeals decision, results in the expenditure of public funds by a municipality which are not reimbursed under paragraph II, the court in its discretion may order, as an additional civil penalty, that a violator make restitution to the municipality for such funds so expended.

IV. The superior court may, upon a petition filed by a municipality and after notice and a preliminary hearing as in the case of prejudgment attachments under RSA 511-A, require an alleged violator to post a bond with the court to secure payment of any penalty or remedy or the performance of any injunctive relief which may be ordered or both. At the hearing, the burden shall be on the municipality to show that there is a strong likelihood that it will prevail on the merits, that the penalties or remedies sought are reasonably likely to be awarded by the court in an amount consistent with the bond sought, and that the bond represents the amount of the projected expense of compliance with the injunctive relief sought.

V. The building inspector or other local official with the authority to enforce the provisions of this title or any local ordinance, code, or regulation adopted under this title may commence an action under paragraph I either in the district court pursuant to RSA 502-A:11-a, or in the superior court. The prosecuting official in the official's discretion may, prior to or at the time of arraignment, charge the offense as a violation, and in such cases the penalties to be imposed by the court shall be limited to those provided for a violation under RSA 651:2 and the civil penalty provided in subparagraph I(b) of this section. The provisions of this section shall supersede any inconsistent local penalty provision.

HISTORY:
1983, 447:1. 1985, 103:25. 210:4. 1988, 19:6, 7, eff. Jan. 1, 1989. 1996, 226:5, 6, eff. Jan. 1, 1997. 1997, 92:4, 5, eff. Jan. 1, 1998. 2004, 242:1, eff. Jan. 1, 2005. 2006, 101:1, eff. January 1, 2007. 2009, 173:1, eff. September 11, 2009.

Amendments

—2009.
The 2009 amendment added the second sentence of I and made stylistic changes.

—2006.
Paragraph I: Substituted "of $275" for "not to exceed $275".

—2004.
Paragraph I: Rewritten to the extent that a detailed comparison would be impracticable.
Paragraph II: Substituted "shall recover" for "may recover" in the first sentence.

—1997.
Paragraph I(b): Substituted "$275" for "$100".
Paragraph V: Substituted "subparagraph I(b)" for "subparagraph I(a)" in the second sentence.

—1996.

Paragraph I(b): Substituted "the violator" for "he" following "municipality that".

Paragraph V: Substituted "the official's" for "his" preceding "discretion" in the second sentence.

—1988.

Paragraph I: Rewritten to the extent that a detailed comparison would be impracticable.

Paragraph V: Added.

—1985.

Rewritten by chs. 103 and 210 to the extent that a detailed comparison would be impracticable.

Contingent 1985 amendment.

1985, 210:2 provided for amendment of this section. However, under the terms of 1985, 210:3, the amendment did not become effective.

Applicability of 1985 amendment.

1985, 210:3, provided that this section, as amended by 1985, 210, would apply to all actions filed after 12:01 a.m. Jan. 1, 1986.

NOTES TO DECISIONS

Analysis

1. Constitutionality
2. Construction
3. Notice of violation
4. Attorney's fees
5. Penalty

1. Constitutionality

Trial court did not abuse its discretion by imposing $14,650 in fines and awarding town $6,000 in attorney's fees against property owners who agreed to move two mobile homes by June 15, 1993, but who did not move second mobile home until July 1997. Town of Nottingham v. Newman, 147 N.H. 131, 785 A.2d 891, 2001 N.H. LEXIS 184 (N.H. 2001).

2. Construction

Under the plain meaning of RSA 676:17, I, the civil penalty imposed is $275 per day "for the first offense" and $550 per day "for subsequent offenses"; when RSA 676:17, I, is read as a whole, the word "offense" refers to the violation(s) for which "the violator receives written notice from the municipality that the violator is in violation." Here, because a town issued only one notice of violation to respondents, only a "first offense" was at issue, and respondents were subject to a penalty of $275 for each of the 200 days of this offense. Town of Atkinson v. Realty Trust, 164 N.H. 62, 53 A.3d 561, 2012 N.H. LEXIS 108 (2012).

RSA 676:17, II, does not contain any language that would remove a zoning enforcement action from the realm of "civil proceedings" to which N.H. Super. Ct. R. 87 applies. No finding of bad faith is required under RSA 676:17, and the New Hampshire Supreme Court refuses to add language that the legislature did not see fit to include. City of Portsmouth v. Boyle, 160 N.H. 534, 8 A.3d 37, 2010 N.H. LEXIS 77 (N.H. 2010).

In practical terms, RSA 676:17 does not conflict with N.H. Super. Ct. R. 87 87 and, therefore, the two can be construed harmoniously. Accordingly, RSA 676:17 does not prevent a trial court from awarding costs under Rule 87 absent a finding that the municipality acted in bad faith. City of Portsmouth v. Boyle, 160 N.H. 534, 8 A.3d 37, 2010 N.H. LEXIS 77 (N.H. 2010).

When a trustee prevailed in a city's zoning enforcement action against him, the trial court properly awarded the trustee costs under N.H. Super. Ct. R. 87. RSA 676:17, II, did not prevent such an award; the rule applied to equity cases and the city was engaged in an equitable action when it requested injunctive relief and penalties; the rule did not require a finding of bad faith; and the trial court had carefully analyzed the trustee's requests for costs, granting some and denying others. City of Portsmouth v. Boyle, 160 N.H. 534, 8 A.3d 37, 2010 N.H. LEXIS 77 (N.H. 2010).

Daily civil penalty imposed on a property owner for a non-conforming shed was unlawful where the continuing violation of RSA 676:17, I was a single offense rather than daily separate offenses, and the amount of the penalty exceeded the jurisdictional limit of the trial court under RSA 502-A:14, II. Town of Amherst v. Gilroy, 157 N.H. 275, 950 A.2d 193, 2008 N.H. LEXIS 63 (N.H. 2008), superseded by statute as stated in Town of Bartlett v. Furlong, 168 N.H. 171, 124 A.3d 221, 2015 N.H. LEXIS 97 (N.H. 2015).

"Shall be subject to" clause granted the trial court the authority to impose the statutory penalties set forth in RSA 676:17, I(b) rather than the obligation to impose such penalties. Thus, RSA 676:17, I(b) granted the trial court the authority to determine whether or not to impose a penalty and the amount of the penalty should it choose to impose one, and the city's argument that imposition of a statutory penalty was mandatory was rejected. City of Rochester v. Corpening, 153 N.H. 571, 907 A.2d 383, 2006 N.H. LEXIS 73 (N.H. 2006).

3. Notice of violation

Developer could not be fined with civil penalties under this section unless given reasonable written notice that he was in fact in violation of a town ordinance, and mere reference to RSA chapter 310-A—the licensing statute applicable to architects, engineers, and land surveyors—in town's cease and desist order was not sufficient notice. Town of Swanzey v. Liebeler, 140 N.H. 760, 674 A.2d 968, 1996 N.H. LEXIS 26 (N.H. 1996), superseded by statute as stated in Bennett v. Town of Hampstead, 157 N.H. 477, 953 A.2d 388, 2008 N.H. LEXIS 84 (N.H. 2008).

4. Attorney's fees

Because it was unclear as to the extent to which an award of attorney's fees in favor of a town was improperly based upon excavation that might have been conducted incidental to construction of an otherwise permitted building, the court vacated the award and remanded the case for the trial court to revisit the fee issue after determining the extent to which the owner excavated incidental to constructing a building. Town of Carroll v. Rines, 164 N.H. 523, 62 A.3d 733, 2013 N.H. LEXIS 4 (N.H. 2012).

Given the evident purpose of RSA 676:17, II, which is to mandate an award of reasonable attorney's fees to a prevailing municipality, when a municipal attorney is paid under a retainer agreement, the phrase "actually expended" means the amount of the retainer that has been depleted because of the attorney's work on the enforcement action. Accordingly, it was error to hold that a town was not entitled to attorney's fees because its attorney had been paid under a retainer agreement. Town of Atkinson v. Realty Trust, 164 N.H. 62, 53 A.3d 561, 2012 N.H. LEXIS 108 (2012).

In awarding fees under RSA 676:17, II, it was within the trial court's discretion to accept town counsel's conservative estimate of the time he spent on the issues upon which the town prevailed as opposed to the claims it nonsuited. Even without this estimate, it was within the trial court's discretion, given its involvement in the ongoing proceedings, to find that the time claimed to have been spent on the successful issues was reasonable. Town of Barrington v. Townsend, 164 N.H. 241, 55 A.3d 952, 2012 N.H. LEXIS 133 (N.H. 2012).

In awarding fees under RSA 676:17, II, the trial court was not required to specifically find that counsel's hourly rate was reasonable, but whether the overall fee charged was reasonable. Town of Barrington v. Townsend, 164 N.H. 241, 55 A.3d 952, 2012 N.H. LEXIS 133 (N.H. 2012).

RSA 155-E:10 provides only for discretionary fee awards. To construe this statute as providing for mandatory fee awards by incorporation of RSA 676:17 would override the express provision for discretionary awards, in contravention of legislative intent. Bedard v. Town of Alexandria, 159 N.H. 740, 992 A.2d 607, 2010 N.H. LEXIS 13 (N.H. 2010).

By amending RSA 676:17, II to use the words "shall recover," the legislature removed discretion in awarding attorney fees from the trial court. RSA 676:17, II now mandates that in any legal action brought by a municipality to enforce an ordinance, code, regulation, or zoning board decision in which the municipality is found to be a prevailing party in the action, the municipality is entitled to recover reasonable attorney's fees actually expended in pursuing that action. Bennett v. Town of Hampstead, 157 N.H. 477, 953 A.2d 388, 2008 N.H. LEXIS 84 (N.H. 2008).

There was no merit to landowners' claim that an award of attorney's fees to a town in a zoning enforcement action under RSA 676:17, II violated their procedural due process rights. A letter sent to the landowners before the town filed its action not only informed them of the possibility that they might have to pay attorney's fees, but also cited the statute upon which the town had authority to request such fees; moreover, every person was presumed to know the law, and the statute clearly provided for a prevailing town to receive attorney's fees. Bennett v. Town of Hampstead, 157 N.H. 477, 953 A.2d 388, 2008 N.H. LEXIS 84 (N.H. 2008).

Where town sought civil penalties against developer, it was reasonable for him to challenge the basis for imposing them, and since litigation was not unreasonably prolonged by developer's conduct, trial court correctly denied award of attorney's fees to town. Town of Swanzey v. Liebeler, 140 N.H. 760, 674 A.2d 968, 1996 N.H. LEXIS 26 (N.H. 1996), superseded by statute as stated in Bennett v. Town of Hampstead, 157 N.H. 477, 953 A.2d 388, 2008 N.H. LEXIS 84 (N.H. 2008).

Town was not entitled to award of attorney's fees and costs, where its enforcement action was a de minimis portion of its case and trial court's findings did not support an award of fees and costs under subdivision II of this section. White v. Francoeur, 138 N.H. 307, 638 A.2d 1250, 1994 N.H. LEXIS 27 (N.H. 1994).

5. Penalty

Trial court did not err in imposing a penalty of $344,025 upon defendant because the amendment to RSA 676:17, I stating that "each day that a violation continues shall be a separate offense" was remedial and did not change defendant's substantive rights. The only consequence of the amendment was that the town was relieved of the need to transfer the case to superior court if it wanted to collect more than $25,000, while defendant was always subject to the same penalties for the violations he committed. Town of Bartlett v. Furlong, 168 N.H. 171, 124 A.3d 221, 2015 N.H. LEXIS 97 (N.H. 2015).

RESEARCH REFERENCES AND PRACTICE AIDS

Cross References.
Classification of crimes, see RSA 625:9.
Sentences, see RSA 651.

New Hampshire Practice.
14-24 N.H.P. Local Government Law § 900.
14-24 N.H.P. Local Government Law § 920.
14-24 N.H.P. Local Government Law § 925.
14-24 N.H.P. Local Government Law § 981.
15-7 N.H.P. Land Use Planning and Zoning § 7.07.
15-7 N.H.P. Land Use Planning and Zoning § 7.13.
15-7 N.H.P. Land Use Planning and Zoning § 7.19.
15-29 N.H.P. Land Use Planning and Zoning § 29.24.

676:17-a. Cease and Desist Orders.

The building inspector, code enforcement officer, zoning administrator or other official designated as an enforcement authority by ordinance or resolution of the local legislative body may issue a cease and desist order against any violation of this title, any local ordinance, code or regulation adopted under this title, or any provision or specification of an application, plat, or plan approved by, or any requirement or condition of a permit or decision issued by, any local administrator or land use board acting under the authority of this title, subject to the following:

I. The order shall state, in writing:

(a) The precise regulation, provision, specification or condition which is being violated.

(b) The facts constituting the violation, including the date of any inspection from which these facts were ascertained.

(c) The corrective action required, including a reasonable time within which such action shall be taken.

(d) A statement that a motion for summary enforcement of the order shall be made to the court of the district in which the property is situated unless such corrective action is taken within the time provided, or unless an answer is filed within 20 days, as provided in paragraph V.

(e) A statement that failure to either take the corrective action, or to file an answer, may result in corrective action being taken by the municipality, and that if this occurs the municipality's costs shall constitute a lien against the real estate, enforceable in the same manner as real estate taxes, including possible loss of the property if not paid.

II. The order shall be served upon the record owner of the property or the record owner's agent, and upon the person to whom taxes are assessed for the property, if other than the owner, and upon any occupying tenant of the property, and upon any other person known by the enforcing officer to exercise control over the premises in violation, and upon all persons holding mortgages upon such property as recorded in the office of the register of deeds, in the same manner provided for service of a summons in a civil action in district court. Personal service may be made by a sheriff, deputy sheriff, local police officer, or constable. If the owner is unknown or cannot be found, the order shall be served by posting it upon the property and by 4 weeks' publication in a newspaper in general circulation in the municipality.

III. Upon service of the order, the owner or the owner's agent, occupying tenant or the tenant's agent, or any other person who is engaged in development, construction, excavation, or other changes of the land or buildings on the land shall cease immediately such activities, if so provided in the order, until such time as judgment is rendered under paragraphs VI or VII. Failure to cease such activity shall constitute a separate violation of this title in addition to the violation cited in the order, unless such order is annulled as provided in paragraph VII.

IV. A copy of the order with proof of service shall be filed with clerk of the district court of the district in which the property is located not fewer than 5 days prior to the filing of a motion to enforce under paragraph VI.

V. Within 20 days after the date of service, any person upon whom the order is served may serve an answer in the manner provided for the service of an answer in a civil action, specifically denying such facts in the order as are in dispute.

VI. If no answer is served, the enforcement official may move the court for the enforcement of the order. If such a motion is made the court may, upon the presentation of such evidence as it may require, affirm or modify the order and enter judgment accordingly, fixing a time after which the governing body may proceed with the enforcement of the order. The clerk of the court shall mail a copy of the judgment to all persons upon whom the original order was served.

VII. If an answer is filed and served as provided in paragraph V, further proceedings in the action shall be governed by the rules of the district court. If the order is sustained following trial, the court shall enter judgment and shall fix a time within which the corrective action shall be taken, in compliance with the order as originally filed, or as modified by the court. If the order is not sustained, it shall be annulled and set aside. If it appears to the court that the order was frivolous, was commenced in bad faith, or was not based upon information and belief formed after reasonable inquiry or was not well-grounded in fact, then the court shall order the defendant's costs and reasonable attorneys fees to be paid by the municipality. The clerk of the court shall mail a copy of the judgment to the persons upon whom the original order was served.

VIII. If a judgment is not complied with in the time prescribed, the local governing body may cause the corrective action to be taken as set forth in the judgment. The cost to the municipality of taking such corrective action together with its other expenses as provided in paragraph IX, shall be a lien against the real estate on which the violation occurred, which shall continue for 18 months from the date upon which the expense account is allowed by the court, as provided in paragraph IX.

IX. The municipality shall keep an accurate account of the expenses incurred in carrying out the order and of all other expenses in connection with its enforcement, including but not limited to filing fees, service fees, publication fees, the expense of searching the registry of deeds to identify mortgages, witness and expert fees, attorneys fees and traveling expenses. The court shall examine, correct if necessary, and allow the expense account. The municipal governing body, by majority vote, may commit the expense account to the collector of taxes, in which case the mayor, as defined by RSA 672:9, shall direct the expense account, together with a warrant under the mayor's hand and seal, to the municipal tax collector, requiring the tax collector to collect the same from the person to whom real estate taxes are assessed for the premises upon which such corrective action was taken, and to pay the amount so collected to the municipal treasurer. Within 30 days after the receipt of such warrant, the collector shall send a bill as provided in RSA 76:11. Interest as provided in RSA 76:13 shall be charged on any amount not paid within 30 days after the bill is mailed. The collector shall have the same rights and remedies as in the collection of taxes, as provided in RSA 80.

X. A party aggrieved by the judgment of the district court may appeal, within 15 days after the rendering of such judgment, to the superior court.

XI. The remedy provided in this section is supplementary to other enforcement remedies provided by this chapter or local ordinance. At the discretion of the local enforcement official, an action to enforce a cease and desist order under this section may be joined with an action under RSA 676:17, I, and the cease and desist order shall constitute the written notice under RSA 676:17, I(b).

HISTORY:

1991, 328:1, eff. June 28, 1991. 1996, 226:7, 8, eff. Jan. 1, 1997. 1997, 79:1, eff. Jan. 1, 1998.

Amendments

—1997.

Paragraph II: Added the second sentence.

—1996.

Paragraph II: Substituted "the record owner's" for "his" preceding "agent" in the first sentence.

Paragraph III: Substituted "the owner's" for "his" preceding "agent, occupying tenant or" and substituted "the tenant's" for "his" thereafter.

Paragraph IX: Substituted "the mayor's" for "his" preceding "hand and seal" and "the tax collector" for "him" following "requiring" in the third sentence.

NOTES TO DECISIONS

Attorney fees

Corporation was entitled to attorney's fees and costs under RSA 676:17-a, VII, where a trial court vacated a cease and desist order entered by a town against the corporation's co-generation facility; the town had no authority to issue the order as the field of air quality control had been preempted by the State under RSA ch. 125-C. Bio Energy, LLC v. Town of Hopkinton, 153 N.H. 145, 891 A.2d 509, 2005 N.H. LEXIS 188 (N.H. 2005).

RESEARCH REFERENCES AND PRACTICE AIDS

New Hampshire Practice.

14-26 N.H.P. Local Government Law § 981.

15-16 N.H.P. Land Use Planning and Zoning § 16.06.

676:17-b. Local Land Use Citations; Pleas by Mail.

A building inspector or other local official with authority to prosecute an offense within the scope of RSA 676:17, and who, prior to or at the time of serving the summons, elects, pursuant to RSA 676:17, V, to charge the offense as a violation, may issue and serve upon the defendant, in addition to the summons, a local land use citation as set forth in this section. The defendant receiving such a citation may plead guilty or nolo contendere by mail by entering that plea as provided herein. If such a plea is accepted by the court, the defendant shall not be required to appear personally or by counsel; otherwise the defendant shall appear as directed by the court. The following procedure shall be used:

I. No local land use citation as set forth in this section shall be served unless the defendant has first been given written notice of the violation by the municipality. If the notice involves or includes a decision which may be appealed to the zoning board of adjustment pursuant to RSA 676:5, or to the building code board of appeals pursuant to RSA 674:34, such notice to the building code board of appeals pursuant to RSA 674:34, such notice shall set forth a reasonable period, as provided by the rules of the respective board, in no case less than 7 days, within which such appeal shall be filed after receipt of the written notice, and the citation shall not be served until after the end of such period. If such an appeal is filed, further proceedings shall be governed by RSA 676:6.

II. The local land use citation shall contain:

(a) The caption: "Local Land Use Citation, Town (City) of _____".

(b) The name of the offender, and address if known to the prosecuting official.

(c) The statute, code, ordinance, regulation, provision, specification, requirement or condition the offender is charged with violating.

(d) The act or circumstances constituting the violation.

(e) The place of the violation.

(f) The date upon which the offender received written notice of the violation by the municipality.

(g) The time and date upon which the violation was witnessed subsequent to such written notice.

(h) The amount of the civil penalty as set forth in RSA 676:17, I, which is payable by the offender for each day the violation continued subsequent to such written notice, up to a maximum of 5 days' violation charged in one citation.

(i) Instructions informing the defendant that the defendant may answer the citation by mail or may personally appear in court upon the date on the summons, and instructing the defendant how to enter a plea by mail, together with either the amount of the penalty specified in the citation, or a request for a trial.

(j) The address of the clerk of the district court, where the plea by mail may be entered.

(k) A warning to the defendant that failure to respond to the citation on or before the date on the summons may result in the defendant's arrest as provided in paragraph V.

(l) The signature of the prosecuting official.

III. Defendants who are issued a summons and local land use citation and who wish to plead guilty or nolo contendere shall enter their plea on the summons and return it with payment of the civil penalty, as set forth in the citation, to the clerk of the court prior to the arraignment date, or shall appear in court on the date of arraignment.

IV. Civil penalties collected by the district court under this section shall be remitted to the municipality issuing the citation. Whenever a defendant (a) does not enter a plea by mail prior to the arraignment day or does not appear personally or by counsel on or before that date or move for a continuance; or (b) otherwise fails to appear for a scheduled court appearance in connection with a summons for any offense, the defendant shall be defaulted and the court shall determine what the civil penalty would be upon a plea of guilty or nolo contendere and shall impose an administrative processing fee in addition to the civil penalty. Such fee shall be the same as the administrative processing fee under RSA 502-A:19-b, and shall be retained by the court for the benefit of the state.

V. The court may, in its discretion, issue a bench warrant for the arrest of any defendant who:

(a) Is defaulted in accordance with the provisions of paragraph IV of this section;

(b) Fails to pay a fine or other penalty imposed in connection with a conviction under this title which a court has determined the defendant is able to pay, or issues a bad check in payment of a fine or other penalty; or

(c) Fails to comply with a similar order on any matter within the court's discretion.

VI. For cause, the court in its discretion may refuse to accept a plea by mail and may impose a fine or penalty other than that stated in the local land use citation. The court may order the defendant to appear personally in court for the disposition of the defendant's case.

VII. The prosecuting official may serve additional local land use citations, without giving additional written notice or appeal opportunity under paragraph I, if the facts or circumstances constituting the violation continue beyond the date or dates of any prior citation. A plea of guilty or nolo contendere to the prior citation shall not affect the rights of the defendant with respect to a subsequent citation.

VIII. Forms and rules for the local land use citation and summons shall be developed and adopted by the New Hampshire supreme court.

IX. This section is not intended in any way to abrogate other enforcement actions or remedies in the district or superior court pursuant to this title, nor to require written notice as a prerequisite to other types of actions or remedies under this title.

HISTORY:
1991, 374:2, eff. Jan. 1, 1992. 1996, 226:9–13, eff. Jan. 1, 1997. 2014, 291:3, eff. September 26, 2014.

Revision note.
This section, which was originally enacted as RSA 676:17-a by 1991, 374:2, was redesignated as RSA 676:17-b pursuant to 1991, 374:3.

Substituted "paragraph V" for "paragraph IV" in par. II(k) to correct an error in the reference.

Amendment Notes

—2014.
The 2014 amendment substituted "RSA 676:17, I" for "RSA 676:17, I(b)" in II(h).

—1996.
Substituted "the defendant" for "he" preceding "shall appear" in the third sentence of the introductory paragraph.

Paragraph II(i): Substituted "the defendant" for "he" preceding "may answer".

Paragraph II(k): Substituted "the defendant's" for "his" preceding "arrest".

Paragraph V(b): Substituted "the defendant" for "he" following "has determined".

Paragraph VI: Substituted "the defendant's" for "his" following "disposition of" in the second sentence.

RESEARCH REFERENCES AND PRACTICE AIDS

New Hampshire Practice.
15-7 N.H.P. Land Use Planning and Zoning § 7.06.

676:18. Register of Deeds.

I. A register of deeds who files or records a plat of a subdivision without the approval of a planning board shall be guilty of a misdemeanor.

II. Notwithstanding the provisions of paragraph I, the register of deeds shall accept for recording a plat prepared and certified by a licensed land surveyor or by a former registered land surveyor if such plat bears a certificate by a licensed or registered land surveyor that this survey plat is not a subdivision pursuant to this title and that the lines of streets and ways shown are those of public or private streets or ways already established and that no new ways are shown. The recording of any such plat shall not relieve any owner from compliance with the provisions of this chapter.

II-a. Notwithstanding the provisions of paragraph I or II, the register of deeds may accept for recording a plat without the licensed land surveyor's seal if such plat was in existence on December 31, 1969, or if the plat has been incorporated into deeds or other instruments recorded before town zoning ordinances or planning board subdivision regulations, or both, became effective in that particular town.

III. The certificate by a licensed land surveyor shall be in the following form:

"I certify that this survey plat is not a subdivision pursuant to this title and that the lines of streets and ways shown are those of public or private streets or ways already established and that no new ways are shown."

Date: _____

_____
Licensed Land Surveyor

SEAL

IV. Prior to recording any plat in the registry of deeds, the surveyor shall file, for information purposes only, a copy of the survey with the town planning board.

V. All decisions of the district, superior, and supreme courts, which affect property boundaries, shall be recorded by the register of deeds in the registry of deeds for the county in which the site is situated, and, upon recordation, such decision shall run with the land. Subsequent to any probate court decision creating divisions of land, a survey plat shall be prepared by a licensed land surveyor, which, if approved by the probate court, shall be recorded, along with the court's decision, at the registry of deeds without local planning board approval. The recording of such decision or plat, however, shall not be deemed to authorize any transfer or development of the property in violation of any applicable local land use regulations adopted pursuant to this title.

HISTORY:
1983, 447:1. 1985, 103:26. 1988, 233:2. 1989, 120:1, 2. 1990, 64:1, 2. 1995, 303:4, 5, eff. Jan. 1, 1996.

Amendments

—1995.
Amended pars. II and III generally.

—1990.
Paragraph II-a: Substituted "licensed" for "registered" preceding "land surveyor's", "was" for "has been" preceding "in existence", "on December 31, 1969" for "since December 31, 1958" thereafter, "or" for "and" following "ordinances" and inserted "or both" following "regulations".

Paragraph V: Inserted "and" preceding "supreme", deleted "and probate" thereafter and made a minor change in punctuation in the first sentence, rewrote the second sentence and added the third sentence.

—1989.
Paragraphs II-a and V: Added.

—1988.
Paragraph II: Substituted "a plat prepared and certified by a licensed land surveyor if such plat bears" preceding "a certificate by a" and substituted "licensed" for "registered" thereafter in the first sentence.

—1985.
Paragraph IV: Added.

NOTES TO DECISIONS

Cited:
Cited in Dover v. Kimball, 136 N.H. 441, 616 A.2d 516, 1992 N.H. LEXIS 187 (1992).

RESEARCH REFERENCES AND PRACTICE AIDS

Cross References.
Classification of crimes, see RSA 625:9.
Sentences, see RSA 651.
Transfers or sales of land prior to approval of subdivision plats, see RSA 676:16.

New Hampshire Practice.
16-20 N.H.P. Municipal Law & Taxation § 20.05.

676:19. Penalties. [Repealed.]

[Repealed 1985, 103:27, eff. Jan. 1, 1986.]

Former section(s).
Former RSA 676:19, which was derived from 1983, 447:1, related to penalties for violations of ordinances, codes or regulations adopted pursuant to this title. See now RSA 676:17.

CHAPTER 677
REHEARING AND APPEAL PROCEDURES

NOTES TO DECISIONS

Cited:
Cited in Vachon v. New Durham Zoning Bd. of Adjustment, 131 N.H. 623, 557 A.2d 649, 1989 N.H. LEXIS 29 (1989); Blue Jay Realty Trust v. Franklin, 132 N.H. 502, 567 A.2d 188, 1989 N.H. LEXIS 128 (1989); Allen v. Wetlands Bd., 133 N.H. 379, 577 A.2d 92, 1990 N.H. LEXIS 71 (1990).

RESEARCH REFERENCES AND PRACTICE AIDS

Cross References.
Local land use boards generally, see RSA 673.
Local land use planning and regulatory powers generally, see RSA 674.
Ordinance, regulation and code administration and enforcement generally, see RSA 676.
Ordinance, regulation and code adoption procedure generally, see RSA 675.
Rehearings and appeals generally, see RSA 541.

New Hampshire Bar Journal.
For article, "An Overview of the New Hampshire Land Use Planning and Regulation Statutes, " see 34 N.H. B.J. 6 (June 1993).

For article, "The New Zoning Variance Cases: Analyzing Unnecessary Hardship Under RSA 674:33," see 46 N.H. B.J. 40 (Fall 2005).
For article, "Unnecessary Hardship Under RSA 674:331(B)," see 46 N.H. B.J. 47 (Fall 2005).

General Provisions

677:1. Procedure.

Whenever a person or a municipality seeks a rehearing on or an appeal of a zoning-related order or decision, the procedures enacted under this chapter shall be followed.

HISTORY:
1983, 447:1, eff. Jan. 1, 1984.

Rehearing Procedures Before Board of Adjustment, Board of Appeals and Local Legislative Body

Revision note.
Inserted "Board of Appeals" following "Board of Adjustment" in the subdivision heading for purposes of conformity with RSA 677:2 and 677:3, as amended by 1988, 131:4, 5, eff. June 19, 1988.

RESEARCH REFERENCES AND PRACTICE AIDS

Cross References.
Appeals from decisions of historic district cimmissions exercising powers of boards of adjustment, see RSA 676:10.
Appeals to boards of adjustment, see RSA 676:5– 7.
Ordinance, regulation and code enactment generally, see RSA 675.
Powers of zoning boards adjustment generally, see RSA 674:33.
Rehearings of decisions of historic district commission, see RSA 677:17 et seq.
Zoning ordinances generally, see RSA 674:16 et seq.

677:2. Motion for Rehearing of Board of Adjustment, Board of Appeals, and Local Legislative Body Decisions.

Within 30 days after any order or decision of the zoning board of adjustment, or any decision of the local legislative body or a board of appeals in regard to its zoning, the selectmen, any party to the action or proceedings, or any person directly affected thereby may apply for a rehearing in respect to any matter determined in the action or proceeding, or covered or included in the order, specifying in the motion for rehearing the ground therefor; and the board of adjustment, a board of appeals, or the local legislative body, may grant such rehearing if in its opinion good reason therefor is stated in the motion. This 30-day time period shall be counted in calendar days beginning with the date following the date upon which the board voted to approve or disapprove the application in accordance with RSA 21:35; provided however, that if the moving party shows that the minutes of the meeting at which such vote was taken, including the written decision, were not filed within 5 business days after the vote pursuant to RSA 676:3, II, the person applying for the rehearing shall have the right to amend the motion for rehearing, including the grounds therefor, within 30 days after the date on which the written decision was actually filed. If the decision complained against is that made by a town meeting, the application for rehearing shall be made to the board of selectmen, and, upon receipt of such application, the board of selectmen shall hold a rehearing within 30 days after receipt of the petition. Following the rehearing, if in the judgment of the selectmen the protest warrants action, the selectmen shall call a special town meeting.

HISTORY:

1983, 447:1. 1988, 131:4. 1994, 116:1, eff. July 10, 1994. 1995, 243:3, eff. Jan. 1, 1996. 2000, 144:2, eff. Jan. 1, 2001. 2005, 105:1, eff. Aug. 14, 2005. 2009, 266:2, eff. September 14, 2009.

Amendments

—2009.

The 2009 amendment substituted "5 business days after" for "144 hours of" in the second sentence.

—2005.

Inserted "following the date" preceding "upon which the board voted" and "in accordance with RSA 21:35" following "application" in the second sentence.

—2000.

Rewritten to the extent that a detailed comparison would be impracticable.

—1995.

Inserted "has been filed and first becomes available for public inspection in the office of the respective board or body or of its clerk or secretary" preceding "the selectmen" in the first sentence.

—1994.

Added the second sentence.

—1988.

Inserted "Board of Appeals" following "Board of Adjustment" in the section catchline, "or a board of appeals" following "legislative body" and "a board of appeals" following "the board of adjustment" in the first sentence.

Nullification of 2009 amendment.

2009, 266:5, eff. September 14, 2009, provided that the amendment to this section by 2009, 49:3, would not take effect.

NOTES TO DECISIONS

Analysis

1. Generally
2. Application
3. Request for rehearing
4. Persons entitled to request rehearing
5. Requirements of motion for rehearing
6. Amendment of motion for rehearing
7. Motion for rehearing as basis for appeal
8. Timeliness of motion

1. Generally

In the interest of finality of decisions by zoning boards, rehearings were not to be lightly granted. Griauzde v. Nashua, 103 N.H. 468, 174 A.2d 432, 1961 N.H. LEXIS 68 (N.H. 1961). (Decided under prior law.)

2. Application

Affirmative defense of illegality, asserted by developers who signed promissory note, was not barred by appeal provisions of this section and RSA 677:4. Questions of ordinance's legality and ultimately the binding effect of promissory note were not questions of administrative action under these sections, but affirmative defenses relating to underlying legality of legislative action. City of Portsmouth v. Schlesinger, 140 N.H. 733, 672 A.2d 712, 1996 N.H. LEXIS 17 (N.H. 1996).

In challenge to validity of zoning amendments by petition for declaratory judgment, this section does not apply, and failure to pursue rehearing is no bar to direct relief. Blue Jay Realty Trust v. City of Franklin, 132 N.H. 502, 567 A.2d 188, 1989 N.H. LEXIS 128 (N.H. 1989).

3. Request for rehearing

Where a zoning board of adjustment denied a property owner's motion for rehearing on her variance application, the owner was not required by RSA 677:2 et seq., to file a second motion for rehearing to preserve for appeal new issues, findings, or rulings first raised by the board's denial order. McDonald v. Town of Effingham Zoning Bd. of Adjustment, 152 N.H. 171, 872 A.2d 1018, 2005 N.H. LEXIS 68 (N.H. 2005).

There is no statutory requirement that a request for rehearing on a zoning board of adjustment decision come only after a formal vote of the board of selectmen, thus, a town manager could file a rehearing request with the authorization of a majority of the selectmen. Town of Plaistow Bd. of Selectmen v. Town of Plaistow Zoning Bd. of Adjustment, 146 N.H. 263, 769 A.2d 397, 2001 N.H. LEXIS 67 (N.H. 2001).

4. Persons entitled to request rehearing

Supermarket owner did not have standing under RSA 677:4 to appeal the grant of a variance to an applicant to construct a larger supermarket, as it was not a "person directly affected" under RSA 677:2. The fact that the zoning board of adjustment drew a comparison between petitioner's location and the applicant's location when considering the "spirit of the ordinance" under RSA 674:33, I(b) did not give petitioner more than a generalized interest in the outcome of the proceedings; furthermore, granting the variance did not make the applicant's competition unfair or illegal. Hannaford Bros. Co. v. Town of Bedford, 164 N.H. 764, 64 A.3d 951, 2013 N.H. LEXIS 41 (N.H. 2013).

Mere fact that an individual is a taxpaying resident of a town does not give that individual standing to seek mandamus relief requiring the town to enforce its zoning ordinances. Pursuant to RSA 676:5, 677:2, 677:4, an individual can seek relief before a zoning board of appeals or in the courts with regard to a zoning officer's decision only if the individual is an "aggrieved person," which requires a showing that he or she has some direct, definite interest in the outcome of the zoning decision itself, and the mere fact that an individual lives and/or pays taxes to a town, does not, by itself, give that individual a direct, definite interest in town zoning decisions. Goldstein v. Town of Bedford, 154 N.H. 393, 910 A.2d 1158, 2006 N.H. LEXIS 173 (N.H. 2006).

Superior court properly dismissed the mandamus petition filed by a town resident, seeking to require the town to enforce its zoning ordinances, because the resident was not an "aggrieved person," which was required for him to have standing under RSA 677:4 to seek judicial review of actions taken by the town's zoning board of adjustment. The mere fact that the resident lived in, and paid taxes to, the town did not give him a direct, definite interest in the zoning decision that he challenged, which pertained to permits obtained by a third party with regard to his nonconforming lots. Goldstein v. Town of Bedford, 154 N.H. 393, 910 A.2d 1158, 2006 N.H. LEXIS 173 (N.H. 2006).

Where the applicant sought permission to build a gas station, the challengers to the applicant would have been a competing gas station, and the challengers' property was located within 1,000 feet of the applicant's property and within a groundwater conservation district, under which circumstances the amended zoning code barred new gas stations, the challengers had standing under RSA 677:4 to appeal the decision of the zoning board of adjustment, as the challengers were directly affected by the proceedings pursuant to RSA 677:2. Thomas v. Town of Hooksett, 153 N.H. 717, 903 A.2d 963, 2006 N.H. LEXIS 99 (N.H. 2006).

The citizens of a city were "directly affected" by the action of a zoning board and were thus entitled to move for rehearing and to appeal, at least to the extent that their appeal questioned whether an amendment to a zoning ordinance was validly adopted. Towle v. Nashua, 106 N.H. 394, 212 A.2d 204, 1965 N.H. LEXIS 177 (N.H. 1965). (Decided under prior law.)

5. Requirements of motion for rehearing

The requirement of former RSA 31:75 (now covered by RSA 677:3) that a party moving for rehearing before a zoning board of adjustment specify in the motion the grounds upon which a rehearing was sought, and the provision that no ground not set forth in the motion could be considered by the superior court on appeal from the board, did not give the moving party the right to control the scope of the proceeding on rehearing; rather, it was intended to ensure that the board had the first opportunity to pass upon errors which it might have made in the first hearing. Fisher v. Boscawen, 121 N.H. 438, 431 A.2d 131, 1981 N.H. LEXIS 348 (N.H. 1981). (Decided under prior law.)

Compliance with the requirement that a rehearing be applied for within 20 days was mandatory, and failure to comply could not be waived by the board of adjustment. Keene v. Zoning Bd. of Adjustment, 114 N.H. 744, 329 A.2d 141, 1974 N.H. LEXIS 364 (N.H. 1974). (Decided under prior law.)

Failure to file a motion for rehearing satisfying the requirements of this statute and former RSA 31:75 (now covered by RSA 677:3) by motion seasonably filed, setting forth "every ground" upon which the plaintiffs claimed the order of the board of adjustment was unlawful or unreasonable, precluded maintenance of their pending appeal. Dipietro v. Nashua, 109 N.H. 174, 246 A.2d 695, 1968 N.H. LEXIS 149 (N.H. 1968). (Decided under prior law.)

6. Amendment of motion for rehearing

Where a motion for rehearing as originally filed was insufficient, it was not subject to amendment by supplemental filing after the twenty-day limitation had expired. Dipietro v. Nashua, 109 N.H. 174, 246 A.2d 695, 1968 N.H. LEXIS 149 (N.H. 1968). (Decided under prior law.)

7. Motion for rehearing as basis for appeal

The filing of an application for rehearing on the decision of a zoning board of adjustment was a precondition of appeal to the court by an aggrieved person. Shaw v. Manchester, 118 N.H. 158, 384 A.2d 491, 1978 N.H. LEXIS 364 (N.H. 1978). But see Metzger v. Brentwood, 115 N.H. 287, 343 A.2d 24, 1975 N.H. LEXIS 289 (N.H. 1975). (Decided under prior law.)

The statutory scheme for zoning in this state was geared to the proposition that the board of adjustment would have a first opportunity to correct any action it had taken, if correction was necessary, before an appeal to the court was filed; thus a party could not appeal the decision of a board of adjustment to the superior court without first applying for a rehearing before the board under this statute. Bourassa v. Keene, 108 N.H. 261, 234 A.2d 112, 1967 N.H. LEXIS 168 (N.H. 1967). (Decided under prior law.)

8. Timeliness of motion

Under RSA 677:2, a motion for rehearing may be filed within 30 days after any order or decision and the 30-day time period shall be counted in calendar days beginning with the date following the date upon which the zoning board of adjustment voted to approve or disapprove the application. "Any order or decision" is not limited to a written order or decision, and a "vote to approve or disapprove the application" is not limited to a memorialization of a vote which provides reasoning for the decision. Bosonetto v. Town of Richmond, 163 N.H. 736, 48 A.3d 973, 2012 N.H. LEXIS 87 (N.H. 2012).

Pursuant to the plain language of RSA 677:2, the 30-day period to file a motion for rehearing began to run the day after the zoning board of adjustment disapproved an application by a vote on an oral motion. Accordingly, a property owner's appeal was properly dismissed under RSA 677:3 on the ground that the motion for rehearing was untimely. Bosonetto v. Town of Richmond, 163 N.H. 736, 48 A.3d 973, 2012 N.H. LEXIS 87 (N.H. 2012).

Town was not equitably estopped from raising the issue of the timeliness of petitioner's motion for rehearing of a zoning board of adjustment decision under RSA 677:2. Although the instructions provided to petitioner were incorrect, there was no evidence that

they were created specifically for him, and the instructions warned readers against solely relying upon them; moreover, a party could not assert equitable estoppel to avoid the application of a statute, the law did not favor application of estoppel against municipalities, the misstatement here was one of law, and permitting estoppel would permit the trial court to assume jurisdiction contrary to the present court's prior holdings that failure to timely move for rehearing divested a trial court of subject matter jurisdiction under RSA 677:3. Bosonetto v. Town of Richmond, 163 N.H. 736, 48 A.3d 973, 2012 N.H. LEXIS 87 (N.H. 2012).

Although the statute does not specifically state that the window for applying for rehearing under RSA 677:2 closes when the zoning board of adjustment (ZBA) closes for business on the thirtieth day, such a requirement is a matter of common sense absent any ZBA procedural rule allowing after-hours filing. Accordingly, a landowner's motion for rehearing was untimely because it was faxed to the ZBA after the close of business and thus was not filed until the next day; thus, the trial court properly dismissed the landowner's appeal for lack of jurisdiction. Cardinal Dev. Corp. v. Town of Winchester Zoning Bd. of Adjustment, 157 N.H. 710, 958 A.2d 996, 2008 N.H. LEXIS 114 (N.H. 2008).

New Hampshire Supreme Court's holding that the window for applying for rehearing under RSA 677:2 closes when a zoning board of adjustment closes for business on the thirtieth day does not prevent zoning boards of adjustment from adopting rules permitting after-hours filing. Cardinal Dev. Corp. v. Town of Winchester Zoning Bd. of Adjustment, 157 N.H. 710, 958 A.2d 996, 2008 N.H. LEXIS 114 (N.H. 2008).

Zoning board of adjustment (ZBA) was not equitably estopped from asserting the untimeliness of a landowner's motion for rehearing. There was no evidence that its land use assistant had the authority to either accept a filing on behalf of the ZBA after the close of business or to waive the 30-day period for moving for rehearing; even assuming that the assistant assured the landowner's counsel that the fax would be retrieved later in the evening, a municipal agent's unauthorized conduct could not estop a municipality. Cardinal Dev. Corp. v. Town of Winchester Zoning Bd. of Adjustment, 157 N.H. 710, 958 A.2d 996, 2008 N.H. LEXIS 114 (N.H. 2008).

Language of RSA 677:2 is unambiguous and provides that the 30-day time period for filing a motion for a rehearing of a zoning board's decision begins to run on the date of the decision. Because a variance applicant filed his motion for a rehearing 33 days after the date of the board's vote, the motion was not timely filed. Pelletier v. City of Manchester, 150 N.H. 687, 844 A.2d 484, 2004 N.H. LEXIS 54 (N.H. 2004).

Because RSA 21:35 provides that the general rule for computing a time period does not apply if the statute in question specifically states a contrary rule, the general rule of computing a time period by excluding the first day from which a period is to be determined does not apply to RSA 677:2, which specifically states that the time period for filing a motion for a rehearing of a zoning board's decision begins to run on the date of a zoning board's vote. Pelletier v. City of Manchester, 150 N.H. 687, 844 A.2d 484, 2004 N.H. LEXIS 54 (N.H. 2004).

Where the date that a zoning board of adjustment denied an owner's variance was included in calculating the time for an appeal under RSA 677:2, the owner's appeal was due 30 days later on a Friday; because the appeal was filed on the following Monday, it was properly dismissed as untimely under RSA 677:3. Ireland v. Town of Candia, 151 N.H. 69, 851 A.2d 630, 2004 N.H. LEXIS 90 (N.H. 2004).

Where zoning board of adjustment erroneously waived appeal period rule to hear an appeal from grant of building permit on the merits, defendant was not required to move for rehearing under this section prior to seeking summary judgment in supreme court; issue of timeliness was jurisdictional and could be raised at any time. Daniel v. B & J Realty, 134 N.H. 174, 589 A.2d 998, 1991 N.H. LEXIS 43 (N.H. 1991).

Cited:

Cited in Bedford Residents Group v. Bedford, 130 N.H. 632, 547 A.2d 225, 1988 N.H. LEXIS 65 (1988); McGovern v. Manchester, 130 N.H. 628, 546 A.2d 1057, 1988 N.H. LEXIS 54 (1988); Hussey v. Barrington, 135 N.H. 227, 604 A.2d 82, 1992 N.H. LEXIS 3 (1992); City of Portsmouth v. Schlesinger, 57 F.3d 12, 1995 U.S.

App. LEXIS 14582 (1st Cir. N.H. 1995); Bourne v. Town of Madison, 494 F. Supp. 2d 80, 2007 U.S. Dist. LEXIS 47625 (D.N.H. 2007).

RESEARCH REFERENCES AND PRACTICE AIDS

New Hampshire Practice.
14-26 N.H.P. Local Government Law § 973.
15-7 N.H.P. Land Use Planning and Zoning § 7.15.
15-22 N.H.P. Land Use Planning and Zoning § 22.02A.

677:3. Rehearing by Board of Adjustment, Board of Appeals, or Local Legislative Body.

I. A motion for rehearing made under RSA 677:2 shall set forth fully every ground upon which it is claimed that the decision or order complained of is unlawful or unreasonable. No appeal from any order or decision of the zoning board of adjustment, a board of appeals, or the local legislative body shall be taken unless the appellant shall have made application for rehearing as provided in RSA 677:2; and, when such application shall have been made, no ground not set forth in the application shall be urged, relied on, or given any consideration by a court unless the court for good cause shown shall allow the appellant to specify additional grounds.

II. Upon the filing of a motion for a rehearing, the board of adjustment, a board of appeals, or the local legislative body shall within 30 days either grant or deny the application, or suspend the order or decision complained of pending further consideration. Any order of suspension may be upon such terms and conditions as the board of adjustment, a board of appeals, or the local legislative body may prescribe. If the motion for rehearing is against a decision of the local legislative body and if the selectmen, as provided in RSA 677:2, shall have called a special town meeting within 25 days from the receipt of an application for a rehearing, the town shall grant or deny the same or suspend the order or decision complained of pending further consideration; and any order of suspension may be upon such terms and conditions as the town may prescribe.

HISTORY:
1983, 447:1. 1988, 131:5. 1994, 116:2, eff. July 10, 1994.

Amendments

—1994.
Paragraph II: Substituted "30" for "10" preceding "days" in the first sentence.

—1988.
Inserted "Board of Appeals" following "Board of Adjustment" in the section catchline.
Paragraph I: Inserted "a board of appeals" following "board of adjustment" in the second sentence.
Paragraph II: Inserted "a board of appeals" following "board of adjustment" in the first and second sentences.

NOTES TO DECISIONS

Analysis

1. Purpose of requirement of motion for rehearing

2. Failure to move for rehearing
3. Grounds for rehearing
4. Timeliness of appeal
5. Motion for rehearing as basis for appeal
6. Procedure on rehearing
7. Motion to reconsider
8. Failure to exhaust administrative remedies
9. Timeliness of motion for rehearing
10. Jurisdiction

1. Purpose of requirement of motion for rehearing
The rule requiring exhaustion of administrative remedies before appealing to the courts, embodied in this statute, was based on the reasonable policies of encouraging the exercising of administrative expertise, preserving agency autonomy and promoting judicial efficiency. Metzger v. Brentwood, 115 N.H. 287, 343 A.2d 24, 1975 N.H. LEXIS 289 (N.H. 1975). (Decided under former RSA 31:75.)
Where the issue before a zoning board of adjustment was a narrow legal one, rigid adherence to the provision of this section requiring an application for a rehearing prior to appealing to the superior court was not necessary. Metzger v. Brentwood, 115 N.H. 287, 343 A.2d 24, 1975 N.H. LEXIS 289 (N.H. 1975). (Decided under former RSA 31:75.)

2. Failure to move for rehearing
Where a zoning board of adjustment denied a property owner's motion for rehearing on her variance application, the owner was not required by RSA 677:2 et seq., to file a second motion for rehearing to preserve for appeal new issues, findings, or rulings first raised by the board's denial order. McDonald v. Town of Effingham Zoning Bd. of Adjustment, 152 N.H. 171, 872 A.2d 1018, 2005 N.H. LEXIS 68 (N.H. 2005).
Superior court correctly dismissed plaintiff's appeal contesting special exceptions granted by zoning board of adjustment, where plaintiff failed to file a motion for rehearing and thus its appeal did not satisfy statutory prerequisites. Mountain Valley Mall Assocs. v. Municipality of Conway, 144 N.H. 642, 745 A.2d 481, 2000 N.H. LEXIS 1 (N.H. 2000).

3. Grounds for rehearing
Trial court's refusal to consider the property owner's vagueness argument concerning a cost condition imposed on the property owner's property as a condition of the property owner being able to obtain a requested variance was not error and the state supreme court would not review that claim for the first time on the property owner's appeal; the property owner was required to, but did not, raise that argument in the motion for rehearing that the property owner filed before the zoning board of appeals. Robinson v. Town of Hudson, 154 N.H. 563, 914 A.2d 239, 2006 N.H. LEXIS 200 (N.H. 2006).
Where a zoning board specifically found that an owner had not satisfied two of the requirements under RSA 674:33, I(b) in the owner's application for a rehearing of the board's denial of a variance, the owner did not have to raise the conditions that were not specifically denied by the board; therefore, the trial court erred in interpreting RSA 677:3 as requiring the owner to raise all five conditions for a variance in an application for rehearing in order to preserve a right of appeal. Robinson v. Town of Hudson, 149 N.H. 255, 821 A.2d 959, 2003 N.H. LEXIS 33 (N.H. 2003).
Where plaintiff referenced and attached to its request for rehearing the planning board's memorandum, which listed three specific grounds for a rehearing, the trial court correctly found that incorporation of the memorandum adequately set forth grounds for the rehearing. Town of Plaistow Bd. of Selectmen v. Town of Plaistow Zoning Bd. of Adjustment, 146 N.H. 263, 769 A.2d 397, 2001 N.H. LEXIS 67 (N.H. 2001).
The requirement that a party moving for rehearing before a zoning board of adjustment was to specify in the motion the grounds upon which a rehearing was sought, and the provision that no ground not set forth in the motion could be considered by the superior court on appeal from the board, did not give the moving party the right to control the scope of the proceeding on rehearing; rather, it was intended to ensure that the board had the first opportunity to pass upon errors which it might have made in the first hearing. Fisher v. Boscawen, 121 N.H. 438, 431 A.2d 131, 1981 N.H. LEXIS 348 (N.H. 1981). (Decided under former RSA 31:75.)

The temporary unavailability of the minutes of testimony at a zoning board hearing did not relieve plaintiffs of the necessity of stating the ground of motion for rehearing as they attended the hearing and the nature of the evidence presented must have been ascertainable by counsel retained after the hearing. Dipietro v. Nashua, 109 N.H. 174, 246 A.2d 695, 1968 N.H. LEXIS 149 (N.H. 1968). (Decided under former RSA 31:75.)

4. Timeliness of appeal

Where the date that a zoning board of adjustment denied an owner's variance was included in calculating the time for an appeal under RSA 677:2, the owner's appeal was due 30 days later on a Friday; because the appeal was filed on the following Monday, it was properly dismissed as untimely under RSA 677:3. Ireland v. Town of Candia, 151 N.H. 69, 851 A.2d 630, 2004 N.H. LEXIS 90 (N.H. 2004).

5. Motion for rehearing as basis for appeal

The statute required an aggrieved party to file a new motion for rehearing that raised any new issues that were thrust upon the appealing party where a procedural decision was reversed, and the board then issued a decision on the merits consistent with the procedural result, and the aggrieved party remained the same, but following the decision upon rehearing, it was aggrieved by a substantive issue rather than a procedural issue; to hold otherwise would deny the board an opportunity to correct its errors and would limit the court to consideration of the errors alleged in the original rehearing motion. Dziama v. City of Portsmouth, 140 N.H. 542, 669 A.2d 217, 1995 N.H. LEXIS 185 (N.H. 1995).

In light of the plaintiff's reasonable reliance upon a prior case, the court's holding requiring an aggrieved party to file a new motion for rehearing in certain circumstances would be enforced prospectively only and the plaintiff would be permitted additional time in which to move for rehearing before the board. Dziama v. City of Portsmouth, 140 N.H. 542, 669 A.2d 217, 1995 N.H. LEXIS 185 (N.H. 1995).

The filing of an application for rehearing on the decision of a zoning board of adjustment was a precondition of appeal to the court by an aggrieved person. Shaw v. Manchester, 118 N.H. 158, 384 A.2d 491, 1978 N.H. LEXIS 364 (N.H. 1978). (Decided under former RSA 31:75.)

It could not be successfully claimed, where a board of adjustment denied a petition without notice or hearing and took no action on the motion for rehearing, that the matter was never before the board and the board took no proper action and that, therefore, there could be no appeal to superior court and the court could not remand to the board. Smith v. Nutter, 113 N.H. 58, 301 A.2d 90, 1973 N.H. LEXIS 200 (N.H. 1973). (Decided under former RSA 31:75.)

6. Procedure on rehearing

The zoning board of adjustment rehearing process was designed to afford a board an opportunity to correct its own mistakes before appeal to the courts, and a board which denied an application for a special exception, stating its reason, could, upon rehearing, decide that such reason was erroneous and proceed to consider the application again and deny it for another reason. Fisher v. Boscawen, 121 N.H. 438, 431 A.2d 131, 1981 N.H. LEXIS 348 (N.H. 1981). (Decided under former RSA 31:76.)

Where a zoning board of adjustment denied an application for a special exception on the stated ground that it could not approve the application in the absence of approval of the site by the planning board, and, at a rehearing, decided its ground for denial was erroneous and that planning board approval was not a prerequisite to zoning board of adjustment approval, the zoning board of adjustment was free on the rehearing to consider the application on its merits. Fisher v. Boscawen, 121 N.H. 438, 431 A.2d 131, 1981 N.H. LEXIS 348 (N.H. 1981). (Decided under former RSA 31:76.)

7. Motion to reconsider

Zoning board of adjustment has the inherent authority to reconsider a decision to deny a request for rehearing, upon its own motion or at the request of a party to the proceeding, within the 30-day appeal period established by RSA 677:4. 74 Cox St., LLC v. City of Nashua, 156 N.H. 228, 931 A.2d 1194, 2007 N.H. LEXIS 163 (N.H. 2007).

8. Failure to exhaust administrative remedies

Homeowners' declaratory judgment action challenging the issuance of a building permit for an adjoining lot was properly dismissed because the homeowners failed to appeal the issuance of the permit to the local zoning board and thus they failed to exhaust their administrative remedies. McNamara v. Hersh, 157 N.H. 72, 945 A.2d 18, 2008 N.H. LEXIS 38 (N.H. 2008).

9. Timeliness of motion for rehearing

Pursuant to the plain language of RSA 677:2, the 30-day period to file a motion for rehearing began to run the day after the zoning board of adjustment disapproved an application by a vote on an oral motion. Accordingly, a property owner's appeal was properly dismissed under RSA 677:3 on the ground that the motion for rehearing was untimely. Bosonetto v. Town of Richmond, 163 N.H. 736, 48 A.3d 973, 2012 N.H. LEXIS 87 (N.H. 2012).

Town was not equitably estopped from raising the issue of the timeliness of petitioner's motion for rehearing of a zoning board of adjustment decision under RSA 677:2. Although the instructions provided to petitioner were incorrect, there was no evidence that they were created specifically for him, and the instructions warned readers against solely relying upon them; moreover, a party could not assert equitable estoppel to avoid the application of a statute, the law did not favor application of estoppel against municipalities, the misstatement here was one of law, and permitting estoppel would permit the trial court to assume jurisdiction contrary to the present court's prior holdings that failure to timely move for rehearing divested a trial court of subject matter jurisdiction under RSA 677:3. Bosonetto v. Town of Richmond, 163 N.H. 736, 48 A.3d 973, 2012 N.H. LEXIS 87 (N.H. 2012).

Although the statute does not specifically state that the window for applying for rehearing under RSA 677:2 closes when the zoning board of adjustment (ZBA) closes for business on the thirtieth day, such a requirement is a matter of common sense absent any ZBA procedural rule allowing after-hours filing. Accordingly, a landowner's motion for rehearing was untimely because it was faxed to the ZBA after the close of business and thus was not filed until the next day; thus, the trial court properly dismissed the landowner's appeal for lack of jurisdiction. Cardinal Dev. Corp. v. Town of Winchester Zoning Bd. of Adjustment, 157 N.H. 710, 958 A.2d 996, 2008 N.H. LEXIS 114 (N.H. 2008).

10. Jurisdiction

Insofar as a selectboard maintained that the issue of whether a sign was an off-premise sign was raised for the first time before the superior court, it was mistaken, as the selectboard itself had raised the issue in its motion for rehearing before the zoning board of adjustment. Accordingly, the trial court had subject matter jurisdiction to consider initially whether the sign was, in fact, an off-premise sign. Town of Bartlett Bd. of Selectmen v. Town of Bartlett Zoning Bd. of Adjustment, 164 N.H. 757, 64 A.3d 984, 2013 N.H. LEXIS 38 (N.H. 2013).

Cited:

Cited in Bedford Residents Group v. Bedford, 130 N.H. 632, 547 A.2d 225, 1988 N.H. LEXIS 65 (1988); Blue Jay Realty Trust v. Franklin, 132 N.H. 502, 567 A.2d 188, 1989 N.H. LEXIS 128 (1989); Granite State Minerals v. Portsmouth, 134 N.H. 408, 593 A.2d 1142, 1991 N.H. LEXIS 80 (1991); Prime Fin. Group v. Masters, 141 N.H. 33, 676 A.2d 528, 1996 N.H. LEXIS 43 (1996); NBAC Corp. v. Town of Weare, 147 N.H. 328, 786 A.2d 867, 2001 N.H. LEXIS 219 (2001).

RESEARCH REFERENCES AND PRACTICE AIDS

New Hampshire Bar Journal.

For article, "Lex Loci: A Survey of New Hampshire Supreme Court Decisions," see 47 N.H. B.J. 46 (Spring 2006).

Appeal and Court Review of Board of Adjustment and Local Legislative Body Decisions

RESEARCH REFERENCES AND PRACTICE AIDS

Cross References.

Appeal and review of building code boards of appeals decisions, see RSA 677:16.

Appeal and review of planning board decisions, see RSA 677:15.

Appeal of historic district commission decisions, see RSA 677:17 et seq.

Ordinance, regulation and code enactment generally, see RSA 675.

Procedure for rehearings, see RSA 677:2, 3.

Powers of zoning boards of adjustment generally, see RSA 674:33.

Zoning ordinances generally, see RSA 674:16 et seq.

677:4. Appeal from Decision on Motion for Rehearing.

Any person aggrieved by any order or decision of the zoning board of adjustment or any decision of the local legislative body may apply, by petition, to the superior court within 30 days after the date upon which the board voted to deny the motion for rehearing; provided however, that if the petitioner shows that the minutes of the meeting at which such vote was taken, including the written decision, were not filed within 5 business days after the vote pursuant to RSA 676:3, II, the petitioner shall have the right to amend the petition within 30 days after the date on which the written decision was actually filed. The petition shall set forth that such decision or order is illegal or unreasonable, in whole or in part, and shall specify the grounds upon which the decision or order is claimed to be illegal or unreasonable. For purposes of this section, "person aggrieved" includes any party entitled to request a rehearing under RSA 677:2.

HISTORY:

1983, 447:1. 1994, 116:3, eff. July 10, 1994. 1995, 243:4, eff. Jan. 1, 1996. 1996, 43:3, eff. June 23, 1996. 2000, 144:3, eff. Jan. 1, 2001. 2009, 266:3, eff. September 14, 2009.

Amendments

—2009.

The 2009 amendment substituted "5 business days after" for "144 hours of" in the first sentence.

—2000.

Rewritten to the extent that a detailed comparison would be impracticable.

—1996.

Added the third sentence.

—1995.

Inserted "by petition" following "body may apply" and substituted "filed and first becomes available for public inspection in the office of the respective board or body or of its clerk or secretary" for "recorded, by petition" preceding "setting forth" in the first sentence and substituted "filing" for "recording" following "the date of" in the second sentence.

—1994.

Added the second sentence.

Nullification of 2009 amendment.

2009, 266:5, eff. September 14, 2009, provided that the amendment to this section by 2009, 49:4, would not take effect.

NOTES TO DECISIONS

Analysis

1. Jurisdiction

2. Applicability
3. Conflict of laws
4. Standing to appeal
5. Prior law
6. Prerequisite for appeal
7. Filing of appeal
8. Statement of grounds for appeal
9. Notification of other parties of filing of appeal—Generally
10. Continuance pending notification of appeal
11. Motion to reconsider

1. Jurisdiction

Where a zoning board of adjustment denied a property owner's motion for rehearing on her variance application, the owner was not required by RSA 677:2 et seq., to file a second motion for rehearing to preserve for appeal new issues, findings, or rulings first raised by the board's denial order. McDonald v. Town of Effingham Zoning Bd. of Adjustment, 152 N.H. 171, 872 A.2d 1018, 2005 N.H. LEXIS 68 (N.H. 2005).

Superior court in zoning appeal correctly declined to address propriety of zoning board of adjustment's decision; since plaintiff filed its direct appeal under RSA 677:15, rather than RSA 677:4, superior court lacked jurisdiction beyond evaluating decision of planning board. Mountain Valley Mall Assocs. v. Municipality of Conway, 144 N.H. 642, 745 A.2d 481, 2000 N.H. LEXIS 1 (N.H. 2000).

Superior court erred by exercising its jurisdiction under this section to review town selectmen's decision to revoke a building permit. Storms v. Eaton, 131 N.H. 50, 549 A.2d 1208, 1988 N.H. LEXIS 87 (N.H. 1988).

2. Applicability

Affirmative defense of illegality, asserted by developers who signed promissory note, was not barred by appeal provisions of this section and RSA 677:2. Questions of ordinance's legality and ultimately the binding effect of promissory note were not questions of administrative action under these sections, but affirmative defenses relating to underlying legality of legislative action. City of Portsmouth v. Schlesinger, 140 N.H. 733, 672 A.2d 712, 1996 N.H. LEXIS 17 (N.H. 1996).

Superior court erroneously dismissed petition for declaratory judgment and injunctive relief, challenging validity of amendments to zoning ordinance, based on 30-day requirement of this section. Blue Jay Realty Trust v. City of Franklin, 132 N.H. 502, 567 A.2d 188, 1989 N.H. LEXIS 128 (N.H. 1989).

3. Conflict of laws

Second suit provision of RSA 508:10 applied to zoning board of adjustment appeal brought pursuant to this section. Since defendants' voluntary nonsuit in their appeal was not a judgment on the merits, RSA 508:10 authorized defendants to revive their appeal if revival would not be manifestly unjust to opposing party. Town of Plaistow v. Riddle, 141 N.H. 307, 681 A.2d 650, 1996 N.H. LEXIS 94 (N.H. 1996).

Provisions of "second suit" statute set forth in RSA 508:10 applied to appeals originally brought in superior court pursuant to this section. Doggett v. Town of North Hampton Zoning Bd. of Adjustment, 138 N.H. 744, 645 A.2d 673, 1994 N.H. LEXIS 97 (N.H. 1994).

4. Standing to appeal

Supermarket owner did not have standing under RSA 677:4 to appeal the grant of a variance to an applicant to construct a larger supermarket, as it was not a "person directly affected" under RSA 677:2. The fact that the zoning board of adjustment drew a comparison between petitioner's location and the applicant's location when considering the "spirit of the ordinance" under RSA 674:33, I(b) did not give petitioner more than a generalized interest in the outcome of the proceedings; furthermore, granting the variance did not make the applicant's competition unfair or illegal. Hannaford Bros. Co. v. Town of Bedford, 164 N.H. 764, 64 A.3d 951, 2013 N.H. LEXIS 41 (N.H. 2013).

Merely alleging violations of New Hampshire's Equal Protection Clause and RSA 674:20 does not confer standing to challenge a zoning board of adjustment's decision under RSA 677:4. Thus, petitioner did not have standing when it asserted only that it had a right to ensure that all owners in a district "stood on an equal footing." Hannaford Bros. Co. v. Town of Bedford, 164 N.H. 764, 64 A.3d 951, 2013 N.H. LEXIS 41 (N.H. 2013).

Indefinite concern with possible "future action" did not give petitioner standing to appeal the grant of a variance. Hannaford Bros. Co. v. Town of Bedford, 164 N.H. 764, 64 A.3d 951, 2013 N.H. LEXIS 41 (N.H. 2013).

Mere fact that an individual is a taxpaying resident of a town does not give that individual standing to seek mandamus relief requiring the town to enforce its zoning ordinances. Pursuant to RSA 676:5, RSA 677:2, RSA 677:4, an individual can seek relief before a zoning board of appeals or in the courts with regard to a zoning officer's decision only if the individual is an "aggrieved person," which requires a showing that he or she has some direct, definite interest in the outcome of the zoning decision itself, and the mere fact that an individual lives and/or pays taxes to a town, does not, by itself, give that individual a direct, definite interest in town zoning decisions. Goldstein v. Town of Bedford, 154 N.H. 393, 910 A.2d 1158, 2006 N.H. LEXIS 173 (N.H. 2006).

Superior court properly dismissed the mandamus petition filed by a town resident, seeking to require the town to enforce its zoning ordinances, because the resident was not an "aggrieved person," which was required for him to have standing under RSA 677:4 to seek judicial review of actions taken by the town's zoning board of adjustment. The mere fact that the resident lived in, and paid taxes to, the town did not give him a direct, definite interest in the zoning decision that he challenged, which pertained to permits obtained by a third party with regard to his nonconforming lots. Goldstein v. Town of Bedford, 154 N.H. 393, 910 A.2d 1158, 2006 N.H. LEXIS 173 (N.H. 2006).

Where the applicant sought permission to build a gas station, the challengers to the applicant would have been a competing gas station, and the challengers' property was located within 1,000 feet of the applicant's property and within a groundwater conservation district, under which circumstances the amended zoning code barred new gas stations, the challengers had standing under RSA 677:4 to appeal the decision of the zoning board of adjustment, as the challengers were directly affected by the proceedings pursuant to RSA 677:2. Thomas v. Town of Hooksett, 153 N.H. 717, 903 A.2d 963, 2006 N.H. LEXIS 99 (N.H. 2006).

Where the legislature did not intend to grant standing to request a rehearing to all municipal boards that could initiate an appeal, a town conservation commission lacked standing to request a rehearing or to appeal a zoning board decision. Hooksett Conservation Comm'n v. Hooksett Zoning Bd. of Adjustment, 149 N.H. 63, 816 A.2d 948, 2003 N.H. LEXIS 5 (N.H. 2003).

Aggrievement is found when the appellant shows a direct definite interest in the outcome of the proceedings; the existence of this interest, and the resultant standing to appeal, is a factual determination in each case. Caspersen v. Town of Lyme, 139 N.H. 637, 661 A.2d 759, 1995 N.H. LEXIS 70 (N.H. 1995).

The plaintiffs did not have a sufficient interest in contesting the effect of a zoning ordinance on the availability of low- or moderate-income housing so as to be aggrieved by the alleged exclusionary effect of the ordinance where they admitted that they were not in the construction business and had no present or future intention to provide low- or moderate-income housing on their own land. Caspersen v. Town of Lyme, 139 N.H. 637, 661 A.2d 759, 1995 N.H. LEXIS 70 (N.H. 1995).

The plaintiffs' properties were too remote from a proposed hospital addition, which was to house an exercise and rehabilitation center open to both patients and the public, to be sufficiently affected by the zoning board of appeal's decision so as to confer standing, as the only adverse impact that might be felt by the plaintiffs as a result of the decision was that of increased competition with their businesses. Nautilus of Exeter v. Town of Exeter, 139 N.H. 450, 656 A.2d 407, 1995 N.H. LEXIS 28 (N.H. 1995).

Persons entitled to protest by reason of ownership of property in, or adjoining, or across from, an area sought to be rezoned could be regarded as having a direct pecuniary interest in the change and, as such, to be entitled to review. Towle v. Nashua, 106 N.H. 394, 212 A.2d 204, 1965 N.H. LEXIS 177 (N.H. 1965). (Decided under prior law.)

5. Prior law

Prior to the 1949 amendment, the provision for an appeal from the city government to the superior court was held to confer the same right of appeal as that granted from the board of adjustment (Scott v. Davis, 94 NH 35, 45 A2d 654, 1946 N.H. LEXIS 137 (1946)). The right of appeal was analogous to the award of a new trial by which the previous verdict is entirely set aside and the case heard anew (Scott v. Davis, 94 NH 35, 45 A2d 654, 1946 N.H. LEXIS 137 (1946); Vogel v. Board of Adjustment for City of Manchester, 92 NH 195, 27 A2d 105, 1942 N.H. LEXIS 55 (1942)) and the appellate court heard the case like an original action Vogel v. Board of Adjustment for City of Manchester, 92 NH 195, 27 A2d 105, 1942 N.H. LEXIS 55 (1942)) and could substitute its judgment for that of either the city government or board of adjustment (Scott v. Davis, 94 N.H. 35, 45 A.2d 654, 1946 N.H. LEXIS 137 (N.H. 1946).

6. Prerequisite for appeal

Homeowners' declaratory judgment action challenging the issuance of a building permit for an adjoining lot was properly dismissed because the homeowners failed to appeal the issuance of the permit to the local zoning board and thus they failed to exhaust their administrative remedies. McNamara v. Hersh, 157 N.H. 72, 945 A.2d 18, 2008 N.H. LEXIS 38 (N.H. 2008).

The filing of an application for rehearing on a decision of a zoning board of adjustment was a precondition of appeal to the court by an aggrieved person. Shaw v. Manchester, 118 N.H. 158, 384 A.2d 491, 1978 N.H. LEXIS 364 (N.H. 1978). (Decided under prior law.)

Under the statutory scheme for zoning, an application for a variance was to be first directed to the zoning board of adjustment, and the superior court only had jurisdiction to hear appeals from decisions of the zoning board of adjustment. Derry v. Simonsen, 117 N.H. 1010, 380 A.2d 1101, 1977 N.H. LEXIS 485 (N.H. 1977). (Decided under prior law.)

The statutory scheme for zoning in this state was geared to the proposition that the board of adjustment was to have a first opportunity to correct any action it had taken, if correction was necessary, before an appeal to the court was filed; thus a party could not appeal the decision of a board of adjustment to the superior court without first applying for a rehearing before the board under former RSA 31:74 (now covered by RSA 677:2). Bourassa v. Keene, 108 N.H. 261, 234 A.2d 112, 1967 N.H. LEXIS 168 (N.H. 1967). (Decided under prior law.)

The statutory scheme for zoning contemplated that the parties were to exhaust their administrative remedies prior to the court appeal. Bourassa v. Keene, 108 N.H. 261, 234 A.2d 112, 1967 N.H. LEXIS 168 (N.H. 1967). (Decided under prior law.)

7. Filing of appeal

Under the plain language of RSA 21:35, II, if the thirty-day filing deadline set forth in RSA 677:4 falls on a weekend or legal holiday, the deadline is extended to the next business day. Thus, a filing was timely when the 30-day deadline fell on Saturday, February 5, because the deadline was extended until Monday, February 7. Trefethen v. Town of Derry, 164 N.H. 754, 64 A.3d 959, 2013 N.H. LEXIS 39 (N.H. 2013).

Notwithstanding N.H. Super. Ct. R. 12(1), the plain language of RSA 677:4 does not allow for filing an appeal beyond 30 days when the thirtieth day falls on a Saturday. Compliance with the 30-day filing deadline was a necessary prerequisite to establishing jurisdiction; thus, petitioners could not rely upon Rule 12(1) to establish jurisdiction that did not exist in the first instance, and although under the common law a terminal day that fell on a Sunday was to be excluded from a computation, there was no comparable principle as to Saturdays. Radziewicz v. Town of Hudson, 159 N.H. 313, 982 A.2d 415, 2009 N.H. LEXIS 117 (N.H. 2009).

Where a zoning board of adjustment denied a realty company's request for a variance and special exception for construction on November 3, 1975, but later granted the variance and special exception on January 5, 1976, after the realty company had filed a timely motion for rehearing, and the plaintiff properly applied for a rehearing on January 12, 1976, but was notified by board on January 20, 1976, that the hearing of January 5, 1976, was a rehearing and that his next move was to appeal to the superior court, the plaintiff was an aggrieved party as a result of the January 5, 1976, order and the board's notification to him amounted to denial of a rehearing, at which time the limit on appeal began to run, so that his appeal to the superior court on February 10, 1976, was timely as being within 30 days from the day action complained of had been recorded. Shaw v. Manchester, 118

N.H. 158, 384 A.2d 491, 1978 N.H. LEXIS 364 (N.H. 1978). (Decided under prior law.)

An appeal was untimely where it was not filed within thirty days after the action of the board of adjustment was recorded, and lack of written notice was no defense as such notice was not required by statute. Salmonsen v. Rindge, 113 N.H. 46, 299 A.2d 926, 1973 N.H. LEXIS 196 (N.H. 1973). (Decided under prior law.)

Under the statute, in order to transfer the cause to the superior court, an appellant was required to do no more than to seasonably file the appeal. Kelley v. Hopkinton Village Precinct, 108 N.H. 206, 231 A.2d 269, 1967 N.H. LEXIS 155 (N.H. 1967). (Decided under prior law.)

8. Statement of grounds for appeal

Plaintiffs did not comply with RSA 677:4 and meet their burden under RSA 677:6 by merely citing ordinance provisions and claiming that the planning board violated them. Saunders v. Town of Kingston, 160 N.H. 560, 8 A.3d 89, 2010 N.H. LEXIS 87 (N.H. 2010).

The filing of a document entitled "Appeal from Board of Adjustment" did not alone constitute compliance with the statute for this so-called appeal failed to claim that the board of adjustment decision was illegal, unjust or unreasonable and failed to specify any grounds for an appeal. Derry v. Diorio, 113 N.H. 375, 308 A.2d 523, 1973 N.H. LEXIS 279 (N.H. 1973). (Decided under prior law.)

9. Notification of other parties of filing of appeal—Generally

This statute and former RSA 31:78 and RSA 31:79 (now covered by RSA 677:6 and RSA 677:7) imposed no requirement of notice to any party in advance of filing of an appeal. Kelley v. Hopkinton Village Precinct, 108 N.H. 206, 231 A.2d 269, 1967 N.H. LEXIS 155 (N.H. 1967). (Decided under prior law.)

Upon the seasonable filing of an appeal under the statute, the superior court was vested with jurisdiction of the subject matter, and the fact that the order of notice first issued was erroneously directed to the wrong party did not operate to divest the court's jurisdiction, even though proper notice remained to be given. Kelley v. Hopkinton Village Precinct, 108 N.H. 206, 231 A.2d 269, 1967 N.H. LEXIS 155 (N.H. 1967). (Decided under prior law.)

10. Continuance pending notification of appeal

The provisions of RSA 514:3, relating to continuances pending notification of a party of an action, applied to an appeal under this statute. Kelley v. Hopkinton Village Precinct, 108 N.H. 206, 231 A.2d 269, 1967 N.H. LEXIS 155 (N.H. 1967). (Decided under prior law.)

11. Motion to reconsider

Zoning board of adjustment has the inherent authority to reconsider a decision to deny a request for rehearing, upon its own motion or at the request of a party to the proceeding, within the 30-day appeal period established by RSA 677:4. 74 Cox St., LLC v. City of Nashua, 156 N.H. 228, 931 A.2d 1194, 2007 N.H. LEXIS 163 (N.H. 2007).

Cited:

Cited in Narbonne v. Rye, 130 N.H. 70, 534 A.2d 388, 1987 N.H. LEXIS 271 (1987); Margate Motel v. Gilford, 130 N.H. 91, 534 A.2d 717, 1987 N.H. LEXIS 272 (1987); New London Land Use Ass'n v. New London Zoning Bd. of Adjustment, 130 N.H. 510, 543 A.2d 1385, 1988 N.H. LEXIS 39 (1988); McGovern v. Manchester, 130 N.H. 628, 546 A.2d 1057, 1988 N.H. LEXIS 54 (1988); Jensen's, Inc. v. Dover, 130 N.H. 761, 547 A.2d 277, 1988 N.H. LEXIS 60 (1988); Crossley v. Pelham, 133 N.H. 215, 578 A.2d 319, 1990 N.H. LEXIS 64 (1990); Bow School Dist. v. Quentin W., 750 F. Supp. 546, 1990 U.S. Dist. LEXIS 15500 (D.N.H. 1990); Allen v. Wetlands Bd., 133 N.H. 379, 577 A.2d 92, 1990 N.H. LEXIS 71 (1990); Portsmouth Advocates v. Portsmouth, 133 N.H. 876, 587 A.2d 600, 1991 N.H. LEXIS 13 (1991); Korpi v. Peterborough, 135 N.H. 37, 599 A.2d 130, 1991 N.H. LEXIS 142 (1991); Quinlan v. Dover, 136 N.H. 226, 614 A.2d 1057, 1992 N.H. LEXIS 159 (1992); Grey Rocks Land Trust v. Hebron, 136 N.H. 239, 614 A.2d 1048, 1992 N.H. LEXIS 162 (1992); Asselin v. Town of Conway, 137 N.H. 368, 628 A.2d 247, 1993 N.H. LEXIS 89 (1993); Nestor v. Town of Meredith Zoning Bd. of Adjustment, 138 N.H. 632, 644 A.2d 548, 1994 N.H. LEXIS 77 (1994); Carnie v. Town of Richmond, 139 N.H. 21, 648 A.2d 205,

1994 N.H. LEXIS 99 (1994); City of Portsmouth v. Schlesinger, 57 F.3d 12, 1995 U.S. App. LEXIS 14582 (1st Cir. N.H. 1995); Husnander v. Town of Barnstead, 139 N.H. 476, 660 A.2d 477, 1995 N.H. LEXIS 36 (1995); Ray's Stateline Mkt. v. Town of Pelham, 140 N.H. 139, 665 A.2d 1068, 1995 N.H. LEXIS 111 (1995); Conforti v. City of Manchester, 141 N.H. 78, 677 A.2d 147, 1996 N.H. LEXIS 52 (1996); Bourne v. Town of Madison, 494 F. Supp. 2d 80, 2007 U.S. Dist. LEXIS 47625 (D.N.H. 2007).

RESEARCH REFERENCES AND PRACTICE AIDS

Cross References.
Effect of filing of appeal, see RSA 677:9.
Furnishing of record on appeal, see RSA 677:12.
Issuance of order of notice by clerk of court, see RSA 677:8.
Joinder of parties, see RSA 677:7.

New Hampshire Bar Journal.
For article, "Lex Loci: A Survey of New Hampshire Supreme Court Decisions," see 47 N.H. B.J. 46 (Spring 2006).

New Hampshire Practice.
14-26 N.H.P. Local Government Law § 973.
15-14 N.H.P. Land Use Planning and Zoning § 14.08.

677:5. Priority.

Any hearing by the superior court upon an appeal under RSA 677:4 shall be given priority on the court calendar.

HISTORY:
1983, 447:1, eff. Jan. 1, 1984.

RESEARCH REFERENCES AND PRACTICE AIDS

New Hampshire Court Rules Annotated
Docketing of cases for trial generally, see Rules 10 and 11, Rules of the Superior Court, New Hampshire Court Rules Annotated.

677:6. Burden of Proof.

In an appeal to the court, the burden of proof shall be upon the party seeking to set aside any order or decision of the zoning board of adjustment or any decision of the local legislative body to show that the order or decision is unlawful or unreasonable. All findings of the zoning board of adjustment or the local legislative body upon all questions of fact properly before the court shall be prima facie lawful and reasonable. The order or decision appealed from shall not be set aside or vacated, except for errors of law, unless the court is persuaded by the balance of probabilities, on the evidence before it, that said order or decision is unreasonable.

HISTORY:
1983, 447:1, eff. Jan. 1, 1984.

NOTES TO DECISIONS

Analysis

1. Prior law
2. Nature of proceedings generally
3. Presumptions
4. Standard of review
5. Particular cases
6. Remand to zoning board of adjustment

1. Prior law

On an appeal from the decision of the city government in a zoning case, the burden of proof in the superior court remained upon the party who had the burden of proving a public need for the amendment of the zoning ordinance. Scott v. Davis, 94 N.H. 35, 45 A.2d 654, 1946 N.H. LEXIS 137 (N.H. 1946). (Decided under prior law.)

2. Nature of proceedings generally

Under the statute additional evidence could be introduced in superior court, but there was no trial de novo. Beaudoin v. Rye Beach Village Dist., 116 N.H. 768, 369 A.2d 618, 1976 N.H. LEXIS 466 (1976), overruled in part, Cook v. Sanbornton, 118 N.H. 668, 392 A.2d 1201, 1978 N.H. LEXIS 267 (1978). (Decided under prior law.)

The decision of the board of adjustment was deemed on appeal to be prima facie lawful and reasonable upon all questions of fact before the board and could not be upset on appeal, except for errors of law, unless the court was persuaded by the balance of probabilities that the decision was unjust or unreasonable; although the court could receive additional evidence on the appeal, the decision of the board could not be overturned except for the foregoing reasons, and there was no trial de novo. Glidden v. Nottingham, 109 N.H. 134, 244 A.2d 430, 1968 N.H. LEXIS 137 (N.H. 1968). (Decided under prior law.)

There was no trial de novo before the court under the statute. Gelinas v. Portsmouth, 97 N.H. 248, 85 A.2d 896, 1952 N.H. LEXIS 3 (N.H. 1952); Conery v. Nashua, 103 N.H. 16, 164 A.2d 247, 1960 N.H. LEXIS 3 (N.H. 1960); H I K Corp. v. Manchester, 103 N.H. 378, 172 A.2d 368, 1961 N.H. LEXIS 55 (N.H. 1961). (Decided under prior law.)

3. Presumptions

A statutory presumption exists that a zoning board's findings are prima facie lawful and reasonable, and they may be set aside only when a court is persuaded by the balance of probabilities, on the evidence before it, that said order or decision is unlawful or unreasonable. Korpi v. Peterborough, 135 N.H. 37, 599 A.2d 130, 1991 N.H. LEXIS 142 (N.H. 1991).

A presumption exists that zoning board's findings are prima facie lawful and reasonable, and they may be set aside only when a court is persuaded by the balance of probabilities, on the evidence before it, that said order or decision is unreasonable. Rowe v. North Hampton, 131 N.H. 424, 553 A.2d 1331, 1989 N.H. LEXIS 5 (N.H. 1989).

All findings of a zoning board of adjustment, upon all questions of fact properly before it, were deemed to be prima facie lawful and reasonable, and the decision appealed from could not be set aside, except for errors of law, unless the court was persuaded, by a balance of probabilities, on the evidence before it, that the decision was unreasonable. Biggs v. Sandwich, 124 N.H. 421, 470 A.2d 928, 1984 N.H. LEXIS 211 (N.H. 1984). (Decided under prior law.)

The factual findings of a zoning board of adjustment were deemed prima facie lawful and reasonable on appeal. Richardson v. Salisbury, 123 N.H. 93, 455 A.2d 1059, 1983 N.H. LEXIS 231 (N.H. 1983). (Decided under prior law.)

All findings of the zoning board were deemed prima facie reasonable and lawful. Barrington E. Cluster I Unit Owners' Ass'n v. Barrington, 121 N.H. 627, 433 A.2d 1266, 1981 N.H. LEXIS 385 (N.H. 1981). (Decided under prior law.)

In a zoning appeal, there was a statutory presumption that all findings of a zoning board of adjustment were prima facie lawful and reasonable. Pappas v. Manchester Zoning Bd. of Adjustment, 117 N.H. 622, 376 A.2d 885, 1977 N.H. LEXIS 395 (N.H. 1977). (Decided under prior law.)

Where a question presented on appeal was a question of law, the court was not bound by the conclusions of the zoning board. Gratton v. Pellegrino, 115 N.H. 619, 348 A.2d 349, 1975 N.H. LEXIS 379 (N.H. 1975). (Decided under prior law.)

4. Standard of review

State supreme court affirmed the trial court's decision that affirmed the decision of the zoning board of appeals; the trial court had to treat the factual findings of the zoning board of appeals as prima facie lawful and reasonable, and, under that standard, the findings that the cost and liability decisions that the zoning board

of appeals imposed on the property owner of record in order to obtain a requested variance were neither arbitrary nor unreasonable. Robinson v. Town of Hudson, 154 N.H. 563, 914 A.2d 239, 2006 N.H. LEXIS 200 (N.H. 2006).

Regardless of whether the trial court correctly reviewed a planning board's decision denying site approval under RSA 677:15 or incorrectly reviewed it under RSA 677:6, the provision applicable to appeals from zoning board decisions, the standard of review was the same, and the trial court properly found no legal error and sufficient evidence supporting the planning board's determination that a proposed site plan for a neighborhood shopping center failed to comply with landscaping and buffer zone regulations; there was no denial of due process or equal protection to the owner and developer, because the denial was without prejudice to submission of complying plans, and because a statute regarding disqualification of board members did not preclude them from raising the issue before the board. Bayson Props. v. City of Lebanon, 150 N.H. 167, 834 A.2d 202, 2003 N.H. LEXIS 159 (N.H. 2003).

Superior court was not to set aside or vacate the decision of a zoning board of adjustment except for errors of law, unless the court was persuaded by the balance of probabilities, on the evidence before it, that the order or decision was unreasonable; the evidence supported the grant of a variance to build a barn where the applicants showed an unnecessary hardship in that the zoning interfered with the reasonable use of the property, considering its unique setting in its environment. Rancourt v. City of Manchester, 149 N.H. 51, 816 A.2d 1011, 2003 N.H. LEXIS 2 (N.H. 2003).

Construction of terms of a zoning ordinance is a question of law, upon which court is not bound by interpretations of zoning board. Sundberg v. Greenville Bd. of Adjustment, 144 N.H. 341, 740 A.2d 1068, 1999 N.H. LEXIS 119 (N.H. 1999).

Trial court's decision is limited to determination of whether, on balance of probabilities, decision of board was unlawful or unreasonable. Bartlett v. Town of Kingston, 142 N.H. 702, 708 A.2d 60, 1998 N.H. LEXIS 21 (N.H. 1998).

When construing zoning appeals, the superior court must treat all findings of the zoning board of appeals as prima facie lawful. Dube v. Town of Hudson, 140 N.H. 135, 663 A.2d 626, 1995 N.H. LEXIS 113 (N.H. 1995).

When construing zoning appeals, the order or decision appealed from must not be set aside or vacated, except for errors of law, unless the court is persuaded by the balance of probabilities, on the evidence before it, that the order or decision is unreasonable. Dube v. Town of Hudson, 140 N.H. 135, 663 A.2d 626, 1995 N.H. LEXIS 113 (N.H. 1995).

A zoning board's decision is subject to limited judicial review, and the appealing party must show that the decision is unlawful or unreasonable. Labrecque v. Salem, 128 N.H. 455, 514 A.2d 829, 1986 N.H. LEXIS 314 (N.H. 1986). (Decided under prior law.)

A zoning board's decision is subject to limited judicial review, and the appealing party must show that the decision is unlawful or unreasonable. Labrecque v. Salem, 128 N.H. 455, 514 A.2d 829, 1986 N.H. LEXIS 314 (N.H. 1986). (Decided under prior law.)

The statute did not impose an absolute requirement that the board's decision be erroneous as a matter of law before a trial judge could change it; the court was required only to inquire whether there was such error when it was not persuaded by the balance of the probabilities, on the evidence before it, that said order or decision was unjust or unreasonable. Cook v. Sanbornton, 118 N.H. 668, 392 A.2d 1201, 1978 N.H. LEXIS 267 (N.H. 1978). See also Ouimette v. Somersworth, 119 N.H. 292, 402 A.2d 159, 1979 N.H. LEXIS 300 (N.H. 1979); Associated Home Utils. v. Bedford, 120 N.H. 812, 424 A.2d 186, 1980 N.H. LEXIS 395 (N.H. 1980); Belanger v. Nashua, 121 N.H. 389, 430 A.2d 166, 1981 N.H. LEXIS 328 (N.H. 1981); Colby v. Rye, 122 N.H. 991, 453 A.2d 1270, 1982 N.H. LEXIS 507 (N.H. 1982); Richardson v. Salisbury, 123 N.H. 93, 455 A.2d 1059, 1983 N.H. LEXIS 231 (N.H. 1983). (Decided under prior law.)

A court could not substitute its judgment for that of zoning board of adjustment; on appeal from an order, the order could not be set aside or vacated except for errors of law, unless the court was persuaded by the balance of probabilities that the order or decision was unjust or unreasonable. Pappas v. Manchester Zoning Bd. of Adjustment, 117 N.H. 622, 376 A.2d 885, 1977 N.H. LEXIS 395 (N.H. 1977). (Decided under prior law.)

Whether an appeal could be sustained depended on whether the record before the board, together with such other evidence as might have been received by the court, persuaded the court that the order of the board was unjust or unreasonable. H I K Corp. v. Manchester, 103 N.H. 378, 172 A.2d 368, 1961 N.H. LEXIS 55 (N.H. 1961). (Decided under prior law.)

5. Particular cases

New Hampshire Supreme Court does not construe the plain language of the statute governing restoration of involuntarily merged lots to alter the deferential standard of review applicable in zoning cases. Thus, on appeal from a finding that lots were voluntarily merged, the trial court did not err in applying the usual deferential standard of review to the zoning board of adjustment's decision. Roberts v. Town of Windham, 165 N.H. 186, 70 A.3d 489, 2013 N.H. LEXIS 85 (N.H. 2013).

Plaintiffs did not comply with RSA 677:4 and meet their burden under RSA 677:6 by merely citing ordinance provisions and claiming that the planning board violated them. Saunders v. Town of Kingston, 160 N.H. 560, 8 A.3d 89, 2010 N.H. LEXIS 87 (N.H. 2010).

Denial by a town zoning board of adjustment of a request for a special exception was properly vacated by a trial court upon a determination that the board's decision was unreasonable after a proper balancing of the probabilities based upon the evidence with respect to construction of a road that would go over a Wetlands Conservation District and in the vicinity of a vernal pool; the property owner and another provided expert testimony that there would be no negative impact from the road, whereas evidence for the town provided merely general knowledge about wetlands conservation. Cont'l Paving, Inc. v. Town of Litchfield, 158 N.H. 570, 969 A.2d 467, 2009 N.H. LEXIS 42 (N.H. 2009).

Where property owners applied to town planning board to further subdivide lots that were previously subdivided, the town's planning board and zoning board of adjustment erred in denying the applications on the basis that owners did not adhere to the density requirements of the town's zoning ordinance and because they were not consistent with the original intent of the cluster subdivision approvals because (1) RSA 672:14(I) provided that a resubdivision was included in the term "subdivision," and (2) because the specific density provisions of the local ordinance had been eliminated. Furthermore, inconsistency with the intent of the original subdivision was not a proper ground for denying the applications and the owners were entitled to have their new applications reviewed on their own merits under the applicable regulations, unconstrained by the prior subdivision approval. Feins v. Town of Wilmot, 154 N.H. 715, 919 A.2d 788, 2007 N.H. LEXIS 5 (N.H. 2007).

In a zoning appeal wherein a trial court reversed a city's denial of an applicant's variance request to build a halfway house on the basis that it was a correctional facility that was not permitted within any of the city's zoning districts, the reviewing court reversed the trial court because no evidence existed in the record that demonstrated how the size and layout of the specific building proposed made the property particularly appropriate for the proposed use, no evidence demonstrated that the proposed site was unique, nor did the evidence reasonably support the trial court's conclusion that the applicant's property was burdened by the restriction in a manner that was distinct from similarly situated property. Thus, the applicant did not satisfy the first prong of the Simplex test to establish unnecessary hardship. Cmty. Res. for Justice, Inc. v. City of Manchester, 154 N.H. 748, 917 A.2d 707, 2007 N.H. LEXIS 11 (N.H. 2007).

6. Remand to zoning board of adjustment

Nothing in the plain language of RSA 677:6, RSA 677:10, RSA 677:13 or RSA 677:11 or in the New Hampshire case law prevented a superior court from remanding a matter to a Zoning Board of Adjustment for clarification based on the preexisting record. However, the remand was not an opportunity for any party to enlarge the record or to introduce new evidence. Kalil v. Town of Dummer Zoning Bd. of Adjustment, 155 N.H. 307, 922 A.2d 672, 2007 N.H. LEXIS 57 (N.H. 2007).

Cited:

Cited in Chester Rod & Gun Club, Inc. v. Town of Chester, 152 N.H. 577, 883 A.2d 1034, 2005 N.H. LEXIS 137 (2005); Nadeau v.

Durham, 129 N.H. 663, 531 A.2d 335, 1987 N.H. LEXIS 230 (1987); Saturley v. Hollis, Zoning Bd. of Adjustment, 129 N.H. 757, 533 A.2d 29, 1987 N.H. LEXIS 256 (1987); Narbonne v. Rye, 130 N.H. 70, 534 A.2d 388, 1987 N.H. LEXIS 271 (1987); Margate Motel v. Gilford, 130 N.H. 91, 534 A.2d 717, 1987 N.H. LEXIS 272 (1987); Goslin v. Farmington, 132 N.H. 48, 561 A.2d 507, 1989 N.H. LEXIS 68 (1989); Peter Christian's, Inc. v. Hanover, 132 N.H. 677, 569 A.2d 758, 1990 N.H. LEXIS 7 (1990); Lake Sunapee Protective Ass'n v. New Hampshire Wetlands Bd., 133 N.H. 98, 574 A.2d 1368, 1990 N.H. LEXIS 38 (1990); Crossley v. Pelham, 133 N.H. 215, 578 A.2d 319, 1990 N.H. LEXIS 64 (1990); Bow School Dist. v. Quentin W., 750 F. Supp. 546, 1990 U.S. Dist. LEXIS 15500 (D.N.H. 1990); Portsmouth Advocates v. Portsmouth, 133 N.H. 876, 587 A.2d 600, 1991 N.H. LEXIS 13 (1991); Daniel v. B & J Realty, 134 N.H. 174, 589 A.2d 998, 1991 N.H. LEXIS 43 (1991); Quinlan v. Dover, 136 N.H. 226, 614 A.2d 1057, 1992 N.H. LEXIS 159 (1992); Grey Rocks Land Trust v. Hebron, 136 N.H. 239, 614 A.2d 1048, 1992 N.H. LEXIS 162 (1992); Ray's Stateline Mkt. v. Town of Pelham, 140 N.H. 139, 665 A.2d 1068, 1995 N.H. LEXIS 111 (1995); Peabody v. Town of Windham, 142 N.H. 488, 703 A.2d 886, 1997 N.H. LEXIS 121 (1997); Gray v. Seidel, 143 N.H. 327, 726 A.2d 1283, 1999 N.H. LEXIS 5 (1999); Mountain Valley Mall Assocs. v. Municipality of Conway, 144 N.H. 642, 745 A.2d 481, 2000 N.H. LEXIS 1 (2000); Heron Cove Ass'n v. DVMD Holdings, Inc., 146 N.H. 211, 769 A.2d 373, 2001 N.H. LEXIS 60 (2001); Cosseboom v. Town of Epsom, 146 N.H. 311, 771 A.2d 565, 2001 N.H. LEXIS 76 (2001); Hynes v. Hale, 146 N.H. 533, 776 A.2d 722, 2001 N.H. LEXIS 111 (2001); NBAC Corp. v. Town of Weare, 147 N.H. 328, 786 A.2d 867, 2001 N.H. LEXIS 219 (2001); Golf Course Investors of NH, LLC v. Town of Jaffrey, 161 N.H. 675, 20 A.3d 846, 2011 N.H. LEXIS 48 (2011).

RESEARCH REFERENCES AND PRACTICE AIDS

Cross References.
Evidence considered on appeal, see RSA 677:10.
Hearing on appeal, see RSA 677:13.

New Hampshire Trial Bar News.
For article, "Presumptions in New Hampshire Law—A Guide Through the Impenetrable Jungle (Part 1)," see 10 N.H. Trial Bar News 55, 60 (Winter 1990).

677:7. Parties in Interest.

Any person whose rights may be directly affected by the outcome of the appeal may appear and become a party, or the court may order such persons to be joined as parties as justice may require.

HISTORY:
1983, 447:1, eff. Jan. 1, 1984.

NOTES TO DECISIONS

Parties to appeal
In an appeal from the decision of a zoning board of adjustment, the municipality, rather than its board of adjustment, was the proper party defendant. Kelley v. Hopkinton Village Precinct, 108 N.H. 206, 231 A.2d 269, 1967 N.H. LEXIS 155 (N.H. 1967). (Decided under prior law.)

Members of the board of adjustment were not proper parties to an appeal from a decision of the board. Kearney v. Hazelton, 84 N.H. 228, 149 A. 78, 1930 N.H. LEXIS 68 (N.H. 1930). (Decided under prior law.)

RESEARCH REFERENCES AND PRACTICE AIDS

Cross References.
Right of appeal generally, see RSA 677:4.

677:8. Filing Certified Record.

Upon the filing of an appeal, the clerk of court

shall issue a summons requiring a certified copy of the record appealed from to be filed with the court.

HISTORY:
    1983, 447:1, eff. Jan. 1, 1984. 2014, 204:45, eff. July 11, 2014.

Amendment Notes

—2014.
    The 2014 amendment substituted "a summons" for "an order of notice."

NOTES TO DECISIONS

Effect of failure to require certification of record
    Where there was sufficient evidence presented at trial from which the court could reasonably and fully decide the issues before it, the trial court did not commit reversible error in not requiring the board of adjustment to certify a copy of its record to the court. Johnston v. Exeter, 121 N.H. 938, 436 A.2d 1147, 1981 N.H. LEXIS 433 (N.H. 1981). (Decided under prior law.)

RESEARCH REFERENCES AND PRACTICE AIDS

Cross References.
    Evidence considered on appeal, see RSA 677:10.
    Filing of appeal, see RSA 677:4.
    Furnishing of record on appeal, see RSA 677:12.
    Hearings on appeal, see RSA 667:13.

677:9. Restraining Order.

The filing of an appeal shall not stay any enforcement proceedings upon the decision appealed from, and shall not have the effect of suspending the decision of the zoning board of adjustment or local legislative body. However, the court, on application and notice, for good cause shown, may grant a restraining order.

HISTORY:
    1983, 447:1. 1995, 243:5, eff. Jan. 1, 1996.

Revision note.
    Substituted "for" for "on" preceding "good cause".

Amendments

—1995.
    Rewrote the first sentence.

RESEARCH REFERENCES AND PRACTICE AIDS

Cross References.
    Filing of appeal, see RSA 677:4.

New Hampshire Court Rules Annotated
    Granting of injunctions and restraining orders generally, see Rules 161– 163, Rules of the Superior Court, New Hampshire Court Rules Annotated.

677:10. Evidence; How Considered.

All evidence transferred by the zoning board of adjustment or the local legislative body shall be, and all additional evidence received may be, considered by the court regardless of any technical rule which might have rendered the evidence inadmissible if originally offered in the trial of an action at law.

HISTORY:
    1983, 447:1, eff. Jan. 1, 1984.

NOTES TO DECISIONS

Analysis

1. Generally
2. Purpose
3. Consideration of evidence not presented to board of adjustment
4. Admissibility of testimony of members of board of adjustment

1. Generally
    Technical rules of evidence did not apply to the admission of evidence in appeals from zoning boards of adjustment. Levesque v. Hudson, 106 N.H. 470, 214 A.2d 553, 1965 N.H. LEXIS 192 (1965), overruled in part, Winslow v. Holderness Planning Bd., 125 N.H. 262, 480 A.2d 114, 1984 N.H. LEXIS 281 (1984). (Decided under prior law.)

2. Purpose
    Purpose of this section is not to afford a trial de novo but rather to assist the court in evaluating the action of the board. Lake Sunapee Protective Ass'n v. New Hampshire Wetlands Bd., 133 N.H. 98, 574 A.2d 1368, 1990 N.H. LEXIS 38 (N.H. 1990).
    The purpose of this statute was not to afford the appealing party a trial de novo, which was no longer available, but rather to assist the court in evaluating the action of the board where the record was incomplete, even though the evidence itself was not presented at the hearing before the board. Sweeney v. Dover, 108 N.H. 307, 234 A.2d 521, 1967 N.H. LEXIS 176 (1967), overruled in part, Cook v. Sanbornton, 118 N.H. 668, 392 A.2d 1201, 1978 N.H. LEXIS 267 (1978). (Decided under prior law.)

3. Consideration of evidence not presented to board of adjustment
    Nothing in the plain language of RSA 677:6, RSA 677:10, RSA 677:13 or RSA 677:11 or in the New Hampshire case law prevented a superior court from remanding a matter to a Zoning Board of Adjustment for clarification based on the preexisting record. However, the remand was not an opportunity for any party to enlarge the record or to introduce new evidence. Kalil v. Town of Dummer Zoning Bd. of Adjustment, 155 N.H. 307, 922 A.2d 672, 2007 N.H. LEXIS 57 (N.H. 2007).
    Under this section, if the record of the evidence before the board is either incomplete or nonexistent, a party may present further evidence to the trial court; the additional evidence may be taken into consideration even though it was not before the board. Lake Sunapee Protective Ass'n v. New Hampshire Wetlands Bd., 133 N.H. 98, 574 A.2d 1368, 1990 N.H. LEXIS 38 (N.H. 1990).
    To the extent the record of evidence before the zoning board of adjustment was incomplete or nonexistent, an aggrieved party could avail himself of this statute and former RSA 31:85 (now covered by RSA 677:13) and present evidence to the trial court; such additional evidence could be taken into consideration even though it was not before the board. Pappas v. Manchester Zoning Bd. of Adjustment, 117 N.H. 622, 376 A.2d 885, 1977 N.H. LEXIS 395 (N.H. 1977). (Decided under prior law.)
    In an appeal from a board of adjustment, the superior court was authorized under this statute and former RSA 31:85 (now covered by RSA 677:13) to receive evidence in addition to that presented before the board. Conery v. Nashua, 103 N.H. 16, 164 A.2d 247, 1960 N.H. LEXIS 3 (N.H. 1960). (Decided under prior law.)

4. Admissibility of testimony of members of board of adjustment
    The trial court did not abuse its discretion in allowing the chairman of a board of adjustment to testify as to matters not set forth in the minutes of the board meeting relating to the matter on appeal where the minutes were not contradicted, ambiguities were clarified and matters not shown by the bare minutes were brought to the court's attention. Alcorn v. Rochester Zoning Bd. of Adjustment, 114 N.H. 491, 322 A.2d 608, 1974 N.H. LEXIS 309 (N.H. 1974). (Decided under prior law.)

It was discretionary with the superior court to admit testimony of members of the board of adjustment as experts. Plourde v. Zoning Bd. of Adjustment, 93 N.H. 376, 42 A.2d 736, 1945 N.H. LEXIS 137 (N.H. 1945); Gelinas v. Portsmouth, 97 N.H. 248, 85 A.2d 896, 1952 N.H. LEXIS 3 (N.H. 1952). (Decided under prior law.)

Cited:

Cited in Peter Christian's, Inc. v. Hanover, 132 N.H. 677, 569 A.2d 758, 1990 N.H. LEXIS 7 (1990); Estabrooks v. Jefferson, 134 N.H. 367, 592 A.2d 1154, 1991 N.H. LEXIS 67 (1991); Robinson v. Town of Hudson, 149 N.H. 255, 821 A.2d 959, 2003 N.H. LEXIS 33 (2003).

RESEARCH REFERENCES AND PRACTICE AIDS

Cross References.
Burden of proof on appeal generally, see RSA 677:6.
Furnishing of record on appeal, see RSA 677:8, 12.
Hearings on appeal, see RSA 677:13.

New Hampshire Court Rules Annotated
Admissibility of evidence generally, see Rules of Evidence, New Hampshire Court Rules Annotated.

New Hampshire Practice.
15-25 N.H.P. Land Use Planning and Zoning § 25.09.

677:11. Judgment.

The final judgment upon every appeal shall be a decree dismissing the appeal, or vacating the order or decision complained of in whole or in part, as the case may be; but, in case such order or decision is wholly or partly vacated, the court may also, in its discretion, remand the matter to the zoning board of adjustment or local legislative body for such further proceedings, not inconsistent with the decree, as justice may require.

HISTORY:
1983, 447:1, eff. Jan. 1, 1984.

NOTES TO DECISIONS

Analysis

1. Modification of order of zoning board
2. Remand

1. Modification of order of zoning board
The authority of the superior court with respect to zoning appeals did not extend to modification of the order of the zoning board. Perron v. Concord, 102 N.H. 32, 150 A.2d 403, 1959 N.H. LEXIS 11 (N.H. 1959). (Decided under prior law.)

2. Remand
Nothing in the plain language of RSA 677:6, RSA 677:10, RSA 677:13 or RSA 677:11 or in the New Hampshire case law prevented a superior court from remanding a matter to a Zoning Board of Adjustment for clarification based on the preexisting record. However, the remand was not an opportunity for any party to enlarge the record or to introduce new evidence. Kalil v. Town of Dummer Zoning Bd. of Adjustment, 155 N.H. 307, 922 A.2d 672, 2007 N.H. LEXIS 57 (N.H. 2007).

RESEARCH REFERENCES AND PRACTICE AIDS

Cross References.
Allowance of costs of appeal, see RSA 677:14.

677:12. Appeals to Court: Certifying Record.

An order of court to send up the record may be complied with by filing either the original papers or duly certified copies thereof, or of such portions thereof as the order may specify, together with a certified statement of such other facts as show the grounds of the action appealed from.

HISTORY:
1983, 447:1, eff. Jan. 1, 1984.

RESEARCH REFERENCES AND PRACTICE AIDS

Cross References.
Filing of appeal, see RSA 677:4.
Issuance of order of notice by clerk of court, see RSA 677:8.

677:13. Hearing.

The court may take evidence or appoint a referee to take such evidence as it may direct and report the same with the referee's findings of fact and conclusions of law.

HISTORY:
1983, 447:1. 1995, 243:6, eff. Jan. 1, 1996.

Amendments

—1995.
Substituted "the referee's" for "his" preceding "findings".

NOTES TO DECISIONS

Consideration of evidence not presented to board of adjustment
Nothing in the plain language of RSA 677:6, RSA 677:10, RSA 677:13 or RSA 677:11 or in the New Hampshire case law prevented a superior court from remanding a matter to a Zoning Board of Adjustment for clarification based on the preexisting record. However, the remand was not an opportunity for any party to enlarge the record or to introduce new evidence. Kalil v. Town of Dummer Zoning Bd. of Adjustment, 155 N.H. 307, 922 A.2d 672, 2007 N.H. LEXIS 57 (N.H. 2007).

To the extent the record before the zoning board of adjustment was incomplete or nonexistent, an aggrieved party could avail himself of former RSA 31:82 (now covered by RSA 677:10) and this statute and present evidence to the trial court; such additional evidence could be taken into consideration even though it was not before the board. Pappas v. Manchester Zoning Bd. of Adjustment, 117 N.H. 622, 376 A.2d 885, 1977 N.H. LEXIS 395 (N.H. 1977). (Decided under prior law.)

In an appeal from a board of adjustment, the superior court was authorized under former RSA 31:82 (now covered by RSA 677:10) and this statute to receive evidence in addition to that presented before the board. Conery v. Nashua, 103 N.H. 16, 164 A.2d 247, 1960 N.H. LEXIS 3 (N.H. 1960). (Decided under prior law.)

Cited:
Cited in Rowe v. North Hampton, 131 N.H. 424, 553 A.2d 1331, 1989 N.H. LEXIS 5 (1989); Estabrooks v. Jefferson, 134 N.H. 367, 592 A.2d 1154, 1991 N.H. LEXIS 67 (1991).

RESEARCH REFERENCES AND PRACTICE AIDS

Cross References.
Burden of proof on appeal, see RSA 677:6.
Evidence considered on appeal, see RSA 677:10.

New Hampshire Court Rules Annotated

Appointment of and proceedings before referees, see Rules 81–85-A, Rules of the Superior Court, New Hampshire Court Rules Annotated.

677:14. Costs.

Costs shall not be allowed against the municipality unless it shall appear to the court that the zoning board of adjustment acted in bad faith or with malice or gross negligence in making the decision appealed from.

HISTORY:

1983, 447:1, eff. Jan. 1, 1984.

RESEARCH REFERENCES AND PRACTICE AIDS

Cross References.

Judgment on appeal generally, see RSA 677:11.

Appeal and Court Review of Planning Board Decisions

RESEARCH REFERENCES AND PRACTICE AIDS

Cross References.

Appeal and review of building code boards of appeals decisions, see RSA 677:16 et seq.

Appeal and review of decisions of local legislative bodies and boards of adjustment, see RSA 677:4 et seq.

Appeals of historic district commission decisions, see RSA 677:17 et seq.

Powers of planning boards generally, see RSA 674:1 et seq., 674:5 et seq., 674:9 et seq., 674:35 et seq., 674:43 et seq.

Procedure for consideration by planning boards of plats or applications for subdivisions, see RSA 676:4.

677:15. Court Review.

I. Any persons aggrieved by any decision of the planning board concerning a plat or subdivision may present to the superior court a petition, duly verified, setting forth that such decision is illegal or unreasonable in whole or in part and specifying the grounds upon which the same is claimed to be illegal or unreasonable. Such petition shall be presented to the court within 30 days after the date upon which the board voted to approve or disapprove the application; provided however, that if the petitioner shows that the minutes of the meeting at which such vote was taken, including the written decision, were not filed within 5 business days after the vote pursuant to RSA 676:3, II, the petitioner shall have the right to amend the petition within 30 days after the date on which the written decision was actually filed. This paragraph shall not apply to planning board decisions appealable to the board of adjustment pursuant to RSA 676:5, III. The 30-day time period shall be counted in calendar days beginning with the date following the date upon which the planning board voted to approve or disapprove the application, in accordance with RSA 21:35.

I-a.(a) If an aggrieved party desires to appeal a decision of the planning board, and if any of the matters to be appealed are appealable to the board of adjustment under RSA 676:5, III, such matters shall be appealed to the board of adjustment before any appeal is taken to the superior court under this section. If any party appeals any part of the planning board's decision to the superior court before all matters appealed to the board of adjustment have been resolved, the court shall stay the appeal until resolution of such matters. After the final resolution of all such matters appealed to the board of adjustment, any aggrieved party may appeal to the superior court, by petition, any or all matters concerning the subdivision or site plan decided by the planning board or the board of adjustment. The petition shall be presented to the superior court within 30 days after the board of adjustment's denial of a motion for rehearing under RSA 677:3, subject to the provisions of paragraph I.

(b) If, upon an appeal to the superior court under this section, the court determines, on its own motion within 30 days after delivery of proof of service of process upon the defendants, or on motion of any party made within the same period, that any matters contained in the appeal should have been appealed to the board of adjustment under RSA 676:5, III, the court shall issue an order to that effect, and shall stay proceedings on any remaining matters until final resolution of all matters before the board of adjustment. Upon such a determination by the superior court, the party who brought the appeal shall have 30 days to present such matters to the board of adjustment under RSA 676:5, III. Except as provided in this paragraph, no matter contained in the appeal shall be dismissed on the basis that it should have been appealed to the board of adjustment under RSA 676:5, III.

II. Upon presentation of such petition, the court may allow a certiorari order directed to the planning board to review such decision and shall prescribe therein the time within which return thereto shall be made and served upon the petitioner's attorney, which shall not be less than 10 days and may be extended by the court. The allowance of the order shall stay proceedings upon the decision appealed from. The planning board shall not be required to return the original papers acted upon by it; but it shall be sufficient to return certified or sworn copies thereof, or of such portions thereof as may be called for by such order. The return shall concisely set forth such other facts as may be pertinent and material to show the grounds of the decision appealed from and shall be verified.

III. If, upon the hearing, it shall appear to the court that testimony is necessary for the proper disposition of the matter, it may take evidence or appoint a referee to take such evidence as it may direct and report the same to the court with the referee's findings of fact and conclusion of law, which shall constitute a part of the proceedings upon which the determination of the court shall be made.

IV. The court shall give any hearing under this section priority on the court calendar.

V. The court may reverse or affirm, wholly or partly, or may modify the decision brought up for review when there is an error of law or when the court is persuaded by the balance of probabilities, on the evidence before it, that said decision is unreasonable. Costs shall not be allowed against the municipality unless it shall appear to the court that the planning board acted in bad faith or with malice in making the decision appealed from.

HISTORY:

1983, 447:1. 1991, 231:14. 1995, 243:7, 8, eff. Jan. 1, 1996. 2000, 144:4, eff. Jan. 1, 2001. 2005, 105:2, eff. Aug. 14, 2005. 2009, 266:4, eff. September 14, 2009. 2013, 179:1, eff. August 31, 2013.

Amendment Notes

—2013.

The 2013 amendment added I-a.

—2009.

The 2009 amendment substituted "5 business days after" for "144 hours of" in the second sentence of I.

—2005.

Paragraph I: Added the last sentence.

—2000.

Paragraph I: Rewrote the second sentence.

—1995.

Paragraph I: Substituted "decision of the planning board has been filed and first becomes available for public inspection" for "filing of the decision" preceding "in the office" and added "or of its clerk or secretary" at the end of the second sentence.

Paragraph III: Substituted "the referee's" for "his" preceding "findings".

—1991.

Paragraph I: Added the third sentence.

Nullification of 2009 amendment.

2009, 266:5, eff. September 14, 2009, provided that the amendment to this section by 2009, 49:5, would not take effect.

NOTES TO DECISIONS

Analysis

1. Construction
2. Application
3. Jurisdiction
4. Persons entitled to review
5. Decisions subject to review
6. Time limitation
7. Verification requirement
8. Evidence
9. Standard of review
10. Proceedings upon receipt of petition by court

1. Construction

RSA 677:15, I, and RSA 676:5, III, together create two separate appeal processes when a planning board decision is based upon both zoning and planning issues; while the statutes allow a party to appeal planning issues associated with a plat or subdivision directly to the superior court, they also provide for an initial layer of review at the local level for decisions involving the interpretation or application of a zoning ordinance. The legislature has provided this initial layer of review to ensure uniform application of local zoning laws., and the overall policy and purpose sought to be advanced by this statutory scheme is best served by interpreting RSA 676:5, III to mean that a planning board decision about a zoning ordinance is ripe and appealable to the zoning board of adjustment (ZBA) when such a decision is made. Atwater v. Town of Plainfield, 160 N.H. 503, 8 A.3d 159, 2010 N.H. LEXIS 80 (N.H. 2010).

Nothing in the plain language of RSA 677:15, I, or RSA 676:5, III, requires that the planning board first complete its consideration of the planning issues involved in a site plan review, or that the applicant satisfy the conditions imposed on a site plan application prior to the zoning board considering the zoning issues on appeal. Atwater v. Town of Plainfield, 160 N.H. 503, 8 A.3d 159, 2010 N.H. LEXIS 80 (N.H. 2010).

Letter from town counsel, advising landowners of planning board's position on consolidation of lots, was not a "decision" of the planning board concerning subdivision, and appeal was therefore not required within thirty days. Blevens v. Town of Bow, 146 N.H. 67, 767 A.2d 446, 2001 N.H. LEXIS 32 (N.H. 2001).

2. Application

Where property owners applied to town planning board to further subdivide lots that were previously subdivided, the town's planning board and zoning board of adjustment erred in denying the applications on the basis that owners did not adhere to the density requirements of the town's zoning ordinance and because they were not consistent with the original intent of the cluster subdivision approvals because (1) RSA 672:14(I) provided that a resubdivision was included in the term "subdivision," and (2) because the specific density provisions of the local ordinance had been eliminated. Furthermore, inconsistency with the intent of the original subdivision was not a proper ground for denying the applications and the owners were entitled to have their new applications reviewed on their own merits under the applicable regulations, unconstrained by the prior subdivision approval. Feins v. Town of Wilmot, 154 N.H. 715, 919 A.2d 788, 2007 N.H. LEXIS 5 (N.H. 2007).

Trial court erred in finding, pursuant to RSA 677:15, that the decision of a town planning board to deny a developer's special use permit for failing to address the extent of impact in wetland buffer areas was unlawful and unreasonable. It was neither unlawful nor unreasonable for the board to require the developers to establish that the design and construction of the proposed subdivision road would minimize detrimental impact upon the wetlands buffer and that no feasible alternative design would have a less detrimental impact. Cherry v. Town of Hampton Falls, 150 N.H. 720, 846 A.2d 508, 2004 N.H. LEXIS 63 (N.H. 2004).

City satisfied its constitutional burden of assisting a developer seeking site plan approval where the city provided rigorous review, input, hearings, opportunity for public comment, and the opportunity to file evidence on the final day of the hearings; therefore, a trial court erred in finding that the city's planning board incorrectly denied the developer's site plan application. Richmond Co. v. City of Concord, 149 N.H. 312, 821 A.2d 1059, 2003 N.H. LEXIS 43 (N.H. 2003).

The plaintiffs' properties were too remote from a proposed hospital addition, which was to house an exercise and rehabilitation center open to both patients and the public, to be sufficiently affected by a zoning board of appeal's decision so as to confer standing. The only adverse impact that might be felt by the plaintiffs as a result of the decision was that of increased competition with their businesses. Nautilus of Exeter v. Town of Exeter, 139 N.H. 450, 656 A.2d 407, 1995 N.H. LEXIS 28 (N.H. 1995).

This section authorizes trial court review of planning board decisions and grants the court discretion to hear additional evidence, and to reverse, affirm, or modify unreasonable decisions. Dumont v. Town of Wolfeboro, 137 N.H. 1, 622 A.2d 1238, 1993 N.H. LEXIS 28 (N.H. 1993).

Superior court erred in reversing planning board's decision approving subdivision lot with restrictions as to location of septic system and buildings, where board's decision replaced an earlier decision approving lot on contingency that study be conducted; board's review of its own decision pursuant to stipulation was analogous to review on rehearing or reconsideration, and board had opportunity to affirm, reject or modify its earlier decision. Deer Leap Assocs. v. Windham, 136 N.H. 555, 618 A.2d 837, 1992 N.H. LEXIS 207 (N.H. 1992).

3. Jurisdiction

As plaintiffs filed their appeal of a town planning board's approval of a company's site plan application within 30 days, jurisdiction was established pursuant to RSA 677:15, I; the fact that the town, as the proper party-defendant, was not joined until after that time did not affect the established jurisdiction. Atwater v. Town of Plainfield, 156 N.H. 265, 931 A.2d 1220, 2007 N.H. LEXIS 171 (N.H. 2007).

Because an abutter filed its appeal five months after a planning board approved an application for site plan determination, its appeal was untimely under RSA 677:15,I and, thus, the trial court did not err when it ruled that it lacked jurisdiction to decide the appeal. Prop. Portfolio Group, LLC v. Town of Derry, 154 N.H. 610, 913 A.2d 750, 2006 N.H. LEXIS 206 (N.H. 2006).

Review of a planning board's refusal to accept an application was proper despite the fact that in the absence of an accepted application, it could not be approved or denied; the trial court could properly treat the appeal as a certiorari petition, and exercise jurisdiction in that way. DHB, Inc. v. Town of Pembroke, 152 N.H. 314, 876 A.2d 206, 2005 N.H. LEXIS 99 (N.H. 2005).

Landowners were required to seek zoning adjustment board review of a planning board's decision to apply only an architectural design review to a parking lot application, and failure to seek board review resulted in the reviewing court's lacking jurisdiction to consider the landowners' appeals. Heartz v. City of Concord, 148 N.H. 325, 808 A.2d 76, 2002 N.H. LEXIS 131 (N.H. 2002).

Superior court in zoning appeal correctly declined to address propriety of zoning board of adjustment's decision; since plaintiff filed its direct appeal under RSA 677:15, rather than RSA 677:4, superior court lacked jurisdiction beyond evaluating decision of planning board. Mountain Valley Mall Assocs. v. Municipality of Conway, 144 N.H. 642, 745 A.2d 481, 2000 N.H. LEXIS 1 (N.H. 2000).

4. Persons entitled to review

Based upon an application of the Weeks Restaurant Corp. v. City of Dover, 119 N.H. 541, 545, 404 A.2d 294; 1979 N.H. LEXIS 349 (1979) factors, standing to appeal a town planning board's decision to grant a special use permit was conferred upon owners of a condominium unit as a matter of law because the facts showed that: (1) the owners' unit was near the parcel for which the permit was granted; (2) the proposed change was a significant one; and (3) the owners had participated actively in the planning board hearing. Johnson v. Town of Wolfeboro Planning Bd., 157 N.H. 94, 945 A.2d 13, 2008 N.H. LEXIS 37 (N.H. 2008).

Where a subdivision applicant petitioned for review of a decision of a town's planning board, the petition was dismissed for lack of standing because: (1) the applicant no longer had standing as a contract vendee since all the contracts relied upon for standing were no longer in effect; and (2) the applicant's speculative interest in the property, the applicant's investments in the subdivision application, and the effect on remedies in a separate suit against the property owner did not provide standing. Joyce v. Town of Weare, 156 N.H. 526, 937 A.2d 919, 2007 N.H. LEXIS 217 (N.H. 2007).

Despite the fact that neither of two property owners challenging a decision of a planning board approving a subdivision owned property abutting it, where one of them owned property across a public highway from the proposed subdivision and the other owned a right of way across it, with which the approved plan would interfere, where both property owners alleged that increased traffic and noise would reduce their enjoyment of their respective properties, and where they had participated in the hearings before the planning board, they had standing to seek certiorari for review of the planning board decision. Price v. Planning Bd. of Keene, 120 N.H. 481, 417 A.2d 997, 1980 N.H. LEXIS 328 (N.H. 1980). (Decided under prior law.)

Whether a party had a sufficient interest in the outcome of a planning board or zoning board proceeding to have standing was a factual determination in each case, and the trial court in making its determination could consider factors such as the proximity of plaintiff's property to the site for which approval was sought, the type of change proposed, the immediacy of injury claimed, and plaintiff's participation in the administrative hearings. Hancock v. Concord, 114 N.H. 404, 322 A.2d 605, 1974 N.H. LEXIS 287 (1974), overruled in part, Weeks Restaurant Corp. v. City of Dover, 119 N.H. 541, 404 A.2d 294, 1979 N.H. LEXIS 349 (1979). (Decided under prior law.)

Nonabutters could appeal from planning board decisions under the statute provided they had a definite interest in the outcome. Hancock v. Concord, 114 N.H. 404, 322 A.2d 605, 1974 N.H. LEXIS 287 (1974), overruled in part, Weeks Restaurant Corp. v. City of Dover, 119 N.H. 541, 404 A.2d 294, 1979 N.H. LEXIS 349 (1979). (Decided under prior law.)

5. Decisions subject to review

A decision of a town planning board denying a developer's request for a waiver of certain subdivision requirements, which was claimed to be unreasonable, was a decision of the planning board concerning a subdivision permit, and, therefore, the superior court could consider the developer's petition for review of the planning board's denial of the waiver pursuant to the criteria set forth in the statute. Hinsdale v. Emerson, 122 N.H. 931, 453 A.2d 1249, 1982 N.H. LEXIS 494 (N.H. 1982). (Decided under prior law.)

A town planning board's conditional approval of a preliminary layout of a subdivision was not a decision of the planning board subject to review where the conditional approval was not a final order, did not create any substantive rights, did not constitute approval of the final plat, did not require the board to give final approval and did not authorize any construction or development. Totty v. Grantham Planning Bd., 120 N.H. 388, 415 A.2d 687, 1980 N.H. LEXIS 299 (N.H. 1980). (Decided under prior law.)

6. Time limitation

There is no indication from the plain language of RSA 677:15, I, that the legislature intended to exempt all planning board decisions, save those approving or disapproving applications, from the thirty-day appeal requirement of RSA 677:15, I. Collden Corp. v. Town of Wolfeboro, 159 N.H. 747, 993 A.2d 184, 2010 N.H. LEXIS 15 (N.H. 2010).

Planning board's 2004 decision that its approval for a subdivision had expired was a final decision subject to the time restrictions of RSA 677:15, I. There was no indication from the plain language of RSA 677:15, I, that the statute's 30-day period for appeals applied only to planning board decisions approving or disapproving applications, and to permit the developer to bring its municipal estoppel claim over three years after the planning board's decision would circumvent the purposes of RSA 677:15, I, which provided for deference to the decisions of local land use bodies, finality for those whose interests were affected by such decisions, and speedy appeals. Collden Corp. v. Town of Wolfeboro, 159 N.H. 747, 993 A.2d 184, 2010 N.H. LEXIS 15 (N.H. 2010).

New Hampshire Supreme Court has held that a plaintiff who chooses to initiate a declaratory judgment action to challenge the validity of a zoning ordinance may do so after the expiration of the applicable statutory appeal period; this is because when the issue in an appeal involves a question of law rather than a question of the exercise of administrative discretion, administrative remedies need not always be exhausted. However, the court has never expanded this line of cases to challenges to planning board decisions, and it declines to do so. Collden Corp. v. Town of Wolfeboro, 159 N.H. 747, 993 A.2d 184, 2010 N.H. LEXIS 15 (N.H. 2010).

RSA 676:5, III, when read with RSA 677:15, I, meant that a planning board decision about a zoning ordinance was ripe and appealable to a zoning board of adjustment when such a decision was made. Thus, petitioners' appeal period under RSA 676:5 began to run with the planning board's conditional approval of an application for site plan review. Atwater v. Town of Plainfield, 160 N.H. 503, 8 A.3d 159, 2010 N.H. LEXIS 80 (N.H. 2010).

Town planning board's decision with respect to a site plan determination was a final appealable decision for purposes of RSA 677:15 where, despite the fact that the applicant for site plan determination submitted the official planning board forms for the application after the fact, the record showed that the proposal submitted before the hearing, which was sufficiently publicized to abutters and the public, functioned as an application and the proposal came in response to the town's request for proposals and met the requirements of that request. Procedural defects shall result in the reversal of a planning board's actions by judicial action only when such defects create serious impairment of opportunity for notice and participation; by approving the application for site plan determination and, therefore, waiving site plan review, the planning board followed the expedited procedure for site plan determination set forth in the applicable regulations and, thus, the proposal was an application upon which a valid final decision could be made and appealed. Prop. Portfolio Group, LLC v. Town of Derry, 154 N.H. 610, 913 A.2d 750, 2006 N.H. LEXIS 206 (N.H. 2006).

Town planning board's decision granting approval of applicant's site plan determination with conditions constituted a final decision that was appealable to the superior court under RSA 677:15, I as the conditions were not conditions precedent, which contemplate additional action on the part of the town and, thus, cannot constitute final approval, but were actually conditions subsequent, which do not delay approval; the "condition" for approval in this case was not required to be fulfilled before any renovation commenced, and, thus, was a condition subsequent, not a condition precedent. Furthermore, within the context of the site plan determination process, what the applicant received from the planning board was an approval; had the planning board intended that the applicant go through the rigors of site plan review, it would have denied the application for site plan determination. Prop. Portfolio Group, LLC v. Town of Derry, 154 N.H. 610, 913 A.2d 750, 2006 N.H. LEXIS 206 (N.H. 2006).

Although an applicant for site plan approval had a right to expect the town to assist with the application process, instead of failing to respond to the applicant's communications, the issue was moot; the trial court had lacked jurisdiction over the applicant's appeal from the planning board's action application of its site plan review rules, because of the applicant's failure to seek review within 30 days, and it lacked jurisdiction over the applicant's appeal from the planning board's application of zoning regulations because, in the absence of a ruling by the zoning board of adjustment, there was nothing to appeal to the trial court. Route 12 Books & Video v. Town of Troy, 149 N.H. 569, 825 A.2d 493, 2003 N.H. LEXIS 79 (N.H. 2003).

The triggering event for the start of the appeal period is the filing of the signed notice of action. K & J Assocs. v. City of Lebanon, 142 N.H. 331, 703 A.2d 253, 1997 N.H. LEXIS 99 (N.H. 1997).

Because the plaintiffs failed to appeal the planning board's decision within the 30-day period prescribed by this section, subject matter jurisdiction was never conferred upon the superior court, which remained powerless to grant the plaintiffs' petition for certiorari. Dermody v. Town of Gilford Planning Bd., 137 N.H. 294, 627 A.2d 570, 1993 N.H. LEXIS 71 (N.H. 1993).

J. E. D. Assocs. v. Atkinson, 121 N.H. 581, 432 A.2d 12, 1981 N.H. LEXIS 367 (1981) is overruled to the extent it may be read to hold unqualifiedly that a constitutional objection to a property disposition required by planning board regulation need not be litigated by appeal brought within 30-day period provided by paragraph I of this section. Auburn v. McEvoy, 131 N.H. 383, 553 A.2d 317, 1988 N.H. LEXIS 129 (N.H. 1988).

On appeal of planning board decision approving a subdivision, claim concerning the board's failure to appoint alternates was properly dismissed where it was not raised within the 30-day period after the filing of the decision in the office of the planning board. Frisella v. Farmington, 131 N.H. 78, 550 A.2d 102, 1988 N.H. LEXIS 94 (N.H. 1988).

7. Verification requirement

Verification requirement in statute governing review of planning board decisions was not a jurisdictional prerequisite, and thus zoning applicants' failure to verify petition did not divest trial court of subject matter jurisdiction. Simonsen v. Town of Derry, 145 N.H. 382, 765 A.2d 1033, 2000 N.H. LEXIS 73 (N.H. 2000).

8. Evidence

Trial court did not err in finding a planning board's decision denying a subdivision application to be reasonable under RSA 677:15, V. The record supported the board's concerns about, among other things, the potential for significant and lasting damage occurring during the construction process, and further evinced the applicant's failure to adequately alleviate those concerns. Ltd. Editions Props., Inc. v. Town of Hebron, 162 N.H. 488, 34 A.3d 688, 2011 N.H. LEXIS 131 (N.H. 2011).

There was no abuse of discretion in a trial court's decision, on review of a planning board's decision to limit the height of a flagpole it would allow a dealership to erect at its site, not to allow the dealership to offer an affidavit in evidence that would supplement the evidence already before the trial court; the dealership simply failed to sustain its burden of showing that concerns about factors such as noise and lighting were unreasonable bases for the board's

decisions. Summa Humma Enters., LLC v. Town of Tilton, 151 N.H. 75, 849 A.2d 146, 2004 N.H. LEXIS 93 (N.H. 2004).

Although paragraph III of this section refers to a hearing, it does not require the court to conduct one to determine if additional evidence is necessary. Webster v. Town of Candia, 146 N.H. 430, 778 A.2d 402, 2001 N.H. LEXIS 91 (N.H. 2001), amended, 2001 N.H. LEXIS 154 (N.H. Aug. 20, 2001); Sanderson v. Town of Candia, 146 N.H. 598, 787 A.2d 167, 2001 N.H. LEXIS 116 (N.H. 2001).

Where trial court had before it the certified record of planning board proceedings and the pleadings in the instant case as well as those in plaintiff's related cases, it was not an abuse of discretion for the trial court not to admit additional evidence. Webster v. Town of Candia, 146 N.H. 430, 778 A.2d 402, 2001 N.H. LEXIS 91 (N.H. 2001), amended, 2001 N.H. LEXIS 154 (N.H. Aug. 20, 2001).

Where the trial court was presented with a voluminous certified record, including audiotapes, a multitude of pleadings and memoranda, and found that the record accurately reflected proposed testimony, it did not abuse its discretion when it precluded live testimony of an expert witness and failed to review videotapes of planning board proceedings. Star Vector Corp. v. Town of Windham, 146 N.H. 490, 776 A.2d 138, 2001 N.H. LEXIS 102 (N.H. 2001).

Legislature's use of phrase "may take evidence" indicated that appellant was not entitled to a full evidentiary hearing in zoning appeal; rather, it was court's prerogative to determine whether admission of further evidence would advance justice or judicial economy. Mountain Valley Mall Assocs. v. Municipality of Conway, 144 N.H. 642, 745 A.2d 481, 2000 N.H. LEXIS 1 (N.H. 2000).

The practical effect of the statute providing for court review of planning board decisions was to broaden the scope of review by way of certiorari by granting to the superior court discretion to receive and to consider additional evidence when it was deemed necessary. Price v. Planning Bd. of Keene, 120 N.H. 481, 417 A.2d 997, 1980 N.H. LEXIS 328 (N.H. 1980). (Decided under prior law.)

The court did not abuse its discretion by not allowing a full evidentiary hearing on a petition for certiorari to review a planning board's decision approving a subdivision where the trial court had the record of proceedings before the board, as well as the arguments of counsel, before it and, given the nature of the issues involved, the court could well have concluded that receiving further evidence would not advance justice or judicial economy. Price v. Planning Bd. of Keene, 120 N.H. 481, 417 A.2d 997, 1980 N.H. LEXIS 328 (N.H. 1980). (Decided under prior law.)

9. Standard of review

Regardless of whether the trial court correctly reviewed a planning board's decision denying site approval under RSA 677:15 or incorrectly reviewed it under RSA 677:6, the provision applicable to appeals from zoning board decisions, the standard of review was the same, and the trial court properly found no legal error and sufficient evidence supporting the planning board's determination that a proposed site plan for a neighborhood shopping center failed to comply with landscaping and buffer zone regulations; there was no denial of due process or equal protection to the owner and developer, because the denial was without prejudice to submission of complying plans, and because a statute regarding disqualification of board members did not preclude them from raising the issue before the board. Bayson Props. v. City of Lebanon, 150 N.H. 167, 834 A.2d 202, 2003 N.H. LEXIS 159 (N.H. 2003).

When reviewing superior court's disposition of appeals from planning board, supreme court will uphold trial court unless its decision is not supported by evidence or is legally erroneous. Mountain Valley Mall Assocs. v. Municipality of Conway, 144 N.H. 642, 745 A.2d 481, 2000 N.H. LEXIS 1 (N.H. 2000).

Superior court's decision on review of planning board action will not be overturned unless unsupported by evidence or legally erroneous. Deer Leap Assocs. v. Windham, 136 N.H. 555, 618 A.2d 837, 1992 N.H. LEXIS 207 (N.H. 1992).

A decision of a planning board could not be set aside by the superior court unless there was an error of law or unless the court was persuaded, by the balance of probabilities, on the evidence before it, that the decision was unreasonable. Durant v. Dunbarton, 121 N.H. 352, 430 A.2d 140, 1981 N.H. LEXIS 318 (N.H. 1981). (Decided under prior law.)

10. Proceedings upon receipt of petition by court

Under the statute, a justice of the superior court was required to review the petition to determine whether a certiorari order should issue. Price v. Planning Bd. of Keene, 120 N.H. 481, 417 A.2d 997, 1980 N.H. LEXIS 328 (N.H. 1980). (Decided under prior law.)

It was for the trial court to determine from the petition, together with any other pleadings, whether a certiorari order should issue. Price v. Planning Bd. of Keene, 120 N.H. 481, 417 A.2d 997, 1980 N.H. LEXIS 328 (N.H. 1980). (Decided under prior law.)

Under the statute, a certiorari order to a planning board directed the board to forward its record to the superior court. Price v. Planning Bd. of Keene, 120 N.H. 481, 417 A.2d 997, 1980 N.H. LEXIS 328 (N.H. 1980). (Decided under prior law.)

Under the statute, the superior court was not provided with authority to order what amounted to a rehearing; the review mentioned was to be performed by the court subsequent to its decision that a certiorari order should issue. Price v. Planning Bd. of Keene, 120 N.H. 481, 417 A.2d 997, 1980 N.H. LEXIS 328 (N.H. 1980). (Decided under prior law.)

An order of notice from the superior court to a planning board, directing the board to reconsider its opinion regarding intervenors' subdivision, was erroneous, since the statute required review by the court itself subsequent to its decision that a certiorari order should issue; because the board declined to review or reconsider its opinion, the error was harmless. Price v. Planning Bd. of Keene, 120 N.H. 481, 417 A.2d 997, 1980 N.H. LEXIS 328 (N.H. 1980). (Decided under prior law.)

Cited:

Cited in Cutting v. Wentworth, 126 N.H. 727, 497 A.2d 839, 1985 N.H. LEXIS 422 (1985); Rancourt v. Barnstead, 129 N.H. 45, 523 A.2d 55, 1986 N.H. LEXIS 379 (1986); Nadeau v. Durham, 129 N.H. 663, 531 A.2d 335, 1987 N.H. LEXIS 230 (1987); Victorian Realty Group v. Nashua, 130 N.H. 60, 534 A.2d 381, 1987 N.H. LEXIS 278 (1987); Bedford Residents Group v. Bedford, 130 N.H. 632, 547 A.2d 225, 1988 N.H. LEXIS 65 (1988); Morin v. Somersworth, 131 N.H. 253, 551 A.2d 527, 1988 N.H. LEXIS 109 (1988); Condos E. Corp. v. Conway, 132 N.H. 431, 566 A.2d 1136, 1989 N.H. LEXIS 121 (1989); Quality Discount Mkt. Corp. v. Laconia Planning Bd., 132 N.H. 734, 571 A.2d 271, 1990 N.H. LEXIS 18 (1990); K & P, Inc. v. Plaistow, 133 N.H. 283, 575 A.2d 804, 1990 N.H. LEXIS 50 (1990); Bow School Dist. v. Quentin W., 750 F. Supp. 546, 1990 U.S. Dist. LEXIS 15500 (D.N.H. 1990); Ossipee Auto Parts v. Ossipee Planning Bd., 134 N.H. 401, 593 A.2d 241, 1991 N.H. LEXIS 74 (1991); Zukis v. Fitzwilliam, 135 N.H. 384, 604 A.2d 956, 1992 N.H. LEXIS 46 (1992); Batakis v. Belmont, 135 N.H. 595, 607 A.2d 956, 1992 N.H. LEXIS 88 (1992); Lampert v. Town of Hudson, 136 N.H. 196, 612 A.2d 920, 1992 N.H. LEXIS 143 (1992); Smith v. Wolfeboro, 136 N.H. 337, 615 A.2d 1252, 1992 N.H. LEXIS 176 (1992); State v. Roy, 138 N.H. 97, 635 A.2d 486, 1993 N.H. LEXIS 166 (1993); White v. Francoeur, 138 N.H. 307, 638 A.2d 1250, 1994 N.H. LEXIS 27 (1994); Blevens v. Town of Bow, 887 F. Supp. 38, 1994 U.S. Dist. LEXIS 14408 (D.N.H. 1994); K & J Assocs. v. City of Lebanon, 142 N.H. 331, 703 A.2d 253, 1997 N.H. LEXIS 99 (1997); Heron Cove Ass'n v. DVMD Holdings, Inc., 146 N.H. 211, 769 A.2d 373, 2001 N.H. LEXIS 60 (2001); NBAC Corp. v. Town of Weare, 147 N.H. 328, 786 A.2d 867, 2001 N.H. LEXIS 219 (2001); AWL Power, Inc. v. City of Rochester, 148 N.H. 603, 813 A.2d 517, 2002 N.H. LEXIS 178 (2002); R.J. Moreau Cos. v. Town of Litchfield, 148 N.H. 773, 813 A.2d 527, 2002 N.H. LEXIS 213 (2002); Monahan-Fortin Props. v. Town of Hudson, 148 N.H. 769, 813 A.2d 523, 2002 N.H. LEXIS 214 (2002).

NOTES TO UNPUBLISHED DECISIONS

1. Time limitation

Unpublished decision: Once the 30-day statutory deadline under RSA § 677:15 for appealing the site-plan approval came and went, the planning board was without legal authority to reconsider its approval of the plaintiffs' site plan. Thus, its agreement not to do so in the consent decree fell well short of being a material change in the parties' legal relationship resulting from the litigation; rather, the plaintiffs' victory was merely the sort of technical or de minimis success that was insufficient to establish prevailing-party status for an award of attorney's fees and costs under 42 U.S.C.S. § 1988. Signs for Jesus v. Town of Chichester, 2011 U.S. Dist. LEXIS 103430 (D.N.H. Sept. 13, 2011).

RESEARCH REFERENCES AND PRACTICE AIDS

New Hampshire Court Rules Annotated

Appointment of and proceedings before referees, see Rules 81–85-A, Rules of the Superior Court, New Hampshire Court Rules Annotated.

Docketing of cases for trial generally, see Rules 10 and 11, Rules of the Superior Court, New Hampshire Court Rules Annotated.

New Hampshire Practice.

4-7 N.H.P. Civil Practice & Procedure § 7.23.
15-14 N.H.P. Land Use Planning and Zoning § 14.08.
15-25 N.H.P. Land Use Planning and Zoning § 25.10.
15-32 N.H.P. Land Use Planning and Zoning § 32.02.
15-33 N.H.P. Land Use Planning and Zoning § 33.01.
15-33 N.H.P. Land Use Planning and Zoning § 33.02.
15-33 N.H.P. Land Use Planning and Zoning § 33.03.
15-33 N.H.P. Land Use Planning and Zoning § 33.06.
15-33 N.H.P. Land Use Planning and Zoning § 33.08.

Appeal and Court Review of Building Code Board of Appeals Decisions

RESEARCH REFERENCES AND PRACTICE AIDS

Cross References.

Administration and enforcement of building codes generally, see RSA 676:11 et seq.

Appeal and review of decisions of local legislative bodies and boards of adjustment, see RSA 677:4 et seq.

Appeal of historic district commission decisions, see RSA 677:17 et seq.

Building codes generally, se RSA 674:51 et seq.

Powers of building code boards of appeals generally, see RSA 674:34.

677:16. Court Review.

Any person aggrieved by a decision of the designated building code board of appeals may appeal the decision to the superior court for the county, and said court shall make such orders as justice may require.

HISTORY:

1983, 447:1, eff. Jan. 1, 1984.

NOTES TO DECISIONS

Cited:

Cited in R.J. Moreau Cos. v. Town of Litchfield, 148 N.H. 773, 813 A.2d 527, 2002 N.H. LEXIS 213 (2002).

Rehearing and Appeal of Historic District Commission Decisions

RESEARCH REFERENCES AND PRACTICE AIDS

Cross References.

Administrative and enforcement powers of historic district commissions generally, see RSA 676:8 et seq.

Appeal and review of building code boards of appeals decisions, see RSA 677:16 et seq.

Appeals and review of decisions of local legislative bodies and boards of adjustment, see RSA 677:4 et seq.

Appeals from decisions of historic district commissions exercising powers of boards of adjustment, see RSA 676:10.

Historic districts and historic district commissions generally, see RSA 674:45 et seq.

677:17. Appeal When Zoning Ordinance Exists.

Any person or persons jointly or severally aggrieved by a decision of the historic district commission shall have the right to appeal that decision to the zoning board of adjustment in accordance with the provisions of RSA 676:5 and RSA 677:1–14.

HISTORY:
1983, 447:1. 1987, 256:6, eff. July 17, 1987.

Amendments

—1987.
Inserted "RSA 676:5 and" preceding "RSA 677:1– 14".

RESEARCH REFERENCES AND PRACTICE AIDS

New Hampshire Practice.
15-19 N.H.P. Land Use Planning and Zoning § 19.03.

677:18. Appeal When No Zoning Ordinance Exists.

In municipalities which do not have a zoning board of adjustment, motions for rehearing and appeals from decisions of the historic district commission shall be governed by the applicable provisions of RSA 677:1–14.

HISTORY:
1983, 447:1, eff. Jan. 1, 1984.

RESEARCH REFERENCES AND PRACTICE AIDS

Cross References.
Rehearings and appeals from historic district commission decisions generally, see RSA 676:10.

Invalid Ordinances

677:19. Subsequent Amendment.

Whenever an appeal to the superior court is initiated under this chapter and the court finds that the ordinance, or section thereof, upon which the board of adjustment, board of appeals, or local legislative body based its decision was invalid at the time such appeal was initiated, or that the application should have been approved but the ordinance was amended to prohibit the type of project applied for during the pendency of the appeal, notwithstanding the fact that the ordinance may have been amended to remove the invalidity subsequent to the initiation of the appeal or that the type of project applied for is no longer permitted, as the case may be, the court shall, upon request of the petitioner, issue an order approving the application, provided that the court finds the application complies with valid zoning and subdivision regulations existing at the time of the application.

HISTORY:
1989, 381:2, eff. Aug. 4, 1989.

RESEARCH REFERENCES AND PRACTICE AIDS

New Hampshire Practice.
15-16 N.H.P. Land Use Planning and Zoning § 16.04.
15-25 N.H.P. Land Use Planning and Zoning § 25.09.

CHAPTER 678
COMMUNITY SERVICES AND CARE PLANNING BOARDS

678:1. Declaration of Purpose and Findings.

The general court hereby finds and declares that:

I. New Hampshire has a rich history of neighbors helping neighbors and residents of municipalities actively participating and organizing themselves to take care of their fellow residents and improve their communities. It also serves the public good and general welfare for the state to support, maintain, and strengthen these locally-based practices and traditions.

II. There is a critical need for the proper and continuous assessment of the community service needs of all residents and the development of local plans, projects, support systems, and other mechanisms to enhance the public health, prosperity, quality of life, safety, and general welfare of all citizens.

HISTORY:
2008, 20:1, eff. July 11, 2008.

678:2. Definitions.

In this chapter:

I. "Board" means a community services and care planning board established under this chapter.

II. "Community services master plan" or "CSMP" means an assessment of the availability, adequacy, and accessibility of the human services systems in each community and shall include the following elements:

(a) A list and description of the specific community assets and programs in existence to serve and support citizens of all ages and abilities;

(b) An analysis of specific improvements to community assets and programs, in priority order that the board recommends be made over the next 5 years and the specific issues these improvements address. These improvements shall be as measurable as possible and include consideration of improvements to all health and human services provided to residents and funded all or in part by the state and other public sources;

(c) The community assets available and needed to achieve each improvement, the most important barriers that must be overcome to achieve each improvement, and an assessment of the feasibility and cost of achieving each improvement;

(d) An overall strategy and problem-solving approach and process for achieving the improvements and a description of the rationale for using these strategies; and

(e) A 5-year plan of action with annual updates as required, which follow the strategy to achieve the improvements. These action steps shall include describing each step, establishing measurable objectives and benchmarks for achieving each step, setting up timelines and the process and methods for achieving each step, and identifying the agencies and persons responsible for accomplishing each step.

III. "Community services" means all the health and social services and supports provided and available to residents in a municipality including those provided by charitable, for profit, and proprietary providers; individuals and groups; and agencies and other providers funded in all or part by the department of health and human services or other state, county, and governmental entities.

IV. "Community well-being index" means an aggregate measure consisting of individual measures of specific aspects of the physical and social well-being of all residents of a municipality that is adopted by the board for use in its annual assessment and state of the community report and to develop its CSMP. The index may include measures of the health of residents and their quality of health care; the quality of housing and prevalence of homelessness; the sense of community and belonging, as measured by participation in community events and decisions; successful mobility; safe and well-managed schools; volunteering and other contributions by residents to the community and their neighbors; children and youth thriving and transitioning successfully into adulthood; youth and adults avoiding dangerous and risky behaviors; elders and residents with disabilities living in dignity and included in community life; the breadth and vitality of community activities, institutions, traditions, and celebrations; shared vision and common purpose; and commitment to building community for the future and ensuring that fellow residents get the care they need.

HISTORY:
2008, 20:1, eff. July 11, 2008.

678:3. Establishment of Community Services and Care Planning Boards.

I. The legislative body of any municipality may establish a community services and care planning board.

II. The community services and care planning board shall consist of no fewer than 3 and no more than 9 members who shall be residents of the municipality, and appointed in a manner as prescribed by the legislative body of the municipality.

III. No more than 5 alternate members may be appointed. When an alternate sits in the absence or the disqualification of a regular member, the alternate shall have full voting powers. Members of a community services and care planning board may also serve on other municipal boards and commissions, including a conservation commission established under RSA 36-A, a historic district commission established under RSA 673:4, or a heritage commission established under RSA 673:4-a.

HISTORY:
2008, 20:1, eff. July 11, 2008.

678:4. Duties of the Board.

I. It shall be the duty of every board established under RSA 678:3 to prepare and amend from time to time a CSMP to guide the development of community services and support systems and the provision of health and social services and community supports to residents that affect community well-being. A CSMP may include consideration of any areas outside the boundaries of the municipality which in the judgment of the board bear a relationship to or have an impact on the planning of the municipality. Every board shall update and amend the adopted CSMP with funds appropriated for that purpose by the local legislative body. In preparing, amending, and updating the master plan:

(a) The board shall have responsibility for promoting interest in, and understanding of, the CSMP of the municipality. In order to promote this interest and understanding, the board may publish and distribute copies of the community services master plan, or copies of any report relating to the community services master plan, hold public forums and meetings, and employ such other means of publicity and education as it deems advisable.

(b) The board shall also have authority to make any inventories of community assets, investigations of community social issues, evaluations of the availability and accessibility of health and social services and support systems, and necessary recommendations.

II. It shall be the duty of every board established under RSA 678:3 to prepare an annual state of the community report which shall be included in the municipality's annual report. The report shall include the community well-being index as defined in

RSA 678:2, IV and information explaining all its components, how it was devised, and any other sections the board deems necessary to describe and explain the social services and support systems of the municipality and trends in the municipality.

III. The board may report and recommend to the appropriate public officials and public agencies programs for the development, protection, and improvement of the social services and support systems of the municipality. Each program shall include recommendations for its financing. The board may consult with and advise public officials and agencies; health and human services providers and funders; civic and charitable groups, networks, and associations; schools; educational, professional, advocacy, and research groups; and other organizations. The board may also consult with citizens, for the purposes of implementing the CSMP and making recommendations for developing the social services and support systems of the municipality.

IV. Members of the board, when duly authorized by the board as a whole, may attend planning conferences or meetings, or hearings upon pending municipal planning legislation. The board may by majority vote authorize the payment of reasonable expenses incident to such attendance.

V. The board may recommend to the governing body amendments or additions to local ordinances, services, and programs to improve the community's social services and support systems.

VI. In general, the board may be given such powers by the municipality as are necessary to enable the board to fulfill its functions.

HISTORY:
2008, 20:1, eff. July 11, 2008.

678:5. Terms of Board Members.

Terms of board members shall be 3 years, except that all vacancies shall be filled for the unexpired term. In the first year of a community services and care planning board's existence, members shall be appointed to the following terms: at least one member to a one-year term, at least one member to a 2-year term, and at least one member to a 3-year term.

HISTORY:
2008, 20:1, eff. July 11, 2008.

678:6. Abolishment of Board.

I. The local legislative body of a city, of a county in which there are located unincorporated towns or unorganized places, or of a town operating under the town council form of government, shall determine the manner in which the board may be abolished.

II. In all other towns, upon a petition to abolish the board, signed by 100 or more voters or $1/10$ of the registered voters in town, whichever number is less, the board shall submit the proposal to the town or village district in the same manner prescribed in RSA 675:4.

III. The question put to the voters shall be in substantially the following form: "Are you in favor of abolishing the community services and care planning board as proposed by petition of the voters of this town (village district)?"

HISTORY:
2008, 20:1, eff. July 11, 2008.

678:7. Transfer of Documents Upon Abolition of Board.

If the board is abolished, the records shall be transferred to the city or town clerk.

HISTORY:
2008, 20:1, eff. July 11, 2008.

APPENDIX OF RELATED LAWS

The statutes listed below relate to the performance of planning and land use regulation by municipalities in New Hampshire. Since they are employed by local officials less frequently than those statutes set out in the body of the pamphlet, they have been summarized rather than reproduced in full. The text of these statutes, accompanied by related notes and annotations, appears in LEXIS New Hampshire Revised Statutes Annotated.

RSA
CHAPTER

12-E   Mining and Reclamation, 12-E:1–12-E:14

This chapter provides for a procedure governing mining and prospecting permits; specifies operator duties during mining and reclamation; and provides emergency authority to halt such operations.

32   Municipal Budget Law, 32:1–32:26

This chapter authorizes the establishment of the local budget committee and describes their duties.

34   Capital Reserve Funds for Cities, 34:1–34:16

This chapter authorizes the establishment of reserve funds by cities for capital improvements.

35   Capital Reserve Funds of Counties, Towns, Districts, and Water Departments, 35:1–35:18

This chapter authorizes the establishment of reserve funds by municipalities for capital improvements.

35-B   Public Recreation and Parks, 35-B:1–35-B:7

This chapter allows municipalities to acquire and administer park land. It authorizes the appointment of a recreation or park commission and establishes their organizational procedures.

36-B   Interstate Regional Planning Compact, 36-B:1–36-B:2

This chapter provides that the Office of State Planning and/or a regional planning commission may negotiate with adjacent states for interstate regional planning services. Articles of a compact agreement are presented.

48-A   Housing Standards, 48-A:1–48-A:15

This chapter authorizes the governing body of any municipality to correct dwellings that are unfit for human habitation due to dilapidation, lack of maintenance, etc. Ordinances, codes and bylaws may be adopted to establish a three-member board to administer provisions and specific standards that qualify a structure as being habitable or unfit.

49-B   Home Rule—Municipal Charters, 49-B:1–49-B:13

This chapter authorizes municipalities to select one of five forms of local government and to legally establish, by charter, the selected governmental form.

49-C   Local Option—City Charters, 49-C:1–49-C:34

This chapter enables municipalities to draft city charters within the framework of part I, article 39 of the New Hampshire constitution.

49-D   Local Option—Town Charters, 49-D:1–49-D:5

This chapter provides for optional forms of town government that municipalities may adopt pursuant to part I, article 39 of the New Hampshire constitution and RSA 49-B.

52   Village Districts, 52:1–52:26

This chapter authorizes the establishment of village districts or precincts for the purposes listed in RSA 52:1. Administration procedures, powers and duties are also described.

79-A   Current Use Taxation, 79-A:1–79-A:26

This chapter establishes an administrative framework that allows managed open space land to be taxed at rates lower than those accorded to the lands highest and best use.

79-D   Discretionary Preservation Easements, 79-D:1–79-D:14

This chapter allows a property owner to convey a discretionary preservation easement of an historic agricultural structure which provides one or more demonstrated public benefits to the municipality in which the structure is located. The bill contains special taxation provisions for historic agricultural structures subject to a discretionary preservation easement.

126   Commission to Study Environmentally-Triggered Chronic Illness, 126-A:73

This section establishes a commission to study environmentally-triggered chronic illness.

147   Nuisances; Toilets; Drains; Expectoration; Rubbish and Waste, 147:1–147:58

These sections set forth the responsibilities and administrative procedures associated with municipal health officers.

149-J   New Hampshire-Vermont Interstate Sewage and Waste Disposal Facilities Compact, 149-J:1

This chapter authorizes cooperative agreements and sets procedures and conditions to govern intergovernmental agreements.

149-K   New Hampshire-Massachusetts Interstate Sewage and Waste Disposal Facilities Compact, 149-K:1

This chapter authorizes cooperative agreements and sets procedures and conditions to govern intergovernmental agreements.

149-M   Solid Waste Management, 149-M:1–149-M:60

This chapter is administered by the Division of Waste Management of the Department of Environmental Services. The Division is responsible for review of district plans; regulation of the storage, transfer, treatment, processing and disposal of solid waste, including administration of a permit system; investigations; hearings, and other activities contributing to orderly management. Rules may be written and adopted by the Division of Waste Management. Towns are required to participate in district planning.

155   Factories, Tenements, Schoolhouses, and Places of Public Accommodation, Resort or Assembly, 155:1–155:78

These sections provide that town and village districts may make bylaws for public structures to insure health and safety. The bylaws shall conform to the life safety code, as promulgated by the State Fire Marshal.

155-B   Hazardous and Dilapidated Buildings, 155-B:1–155-B:15

These sections provide municipalities with the administrative process for repair or removal of hazardous buildings.

155-D   **Energy Conservation in New Building Construction, 155-D:1–155-D:10**

This chapter establishes a statewide energy conservation code for all new buildings or structures/additions designed primarily for human occupancy. The "New Hampshire Code for Energy Conservation in New Building Construction" is administered by local building officials or by the Public Utilities Commission where no building official exists.

162-G   **Acquisition, Development and Disposal of Industrial Land and Facilities, 162-G:1–162-G:17**

This chapter authorizes cities to encourage industrial development by acquiring and marketing land, issuing bonds for project costs, establishing an Industrial Development Authority, and other activities which promote industrial development.

162-H   **Energy Facility Evaluation, Siting, Construction and Operation, 162-H:1–162-H:22**

This chapter establishes the Site Evaluation Committee and outlines procedures for the review, approval, monitoring and enforcement of compliance in the planning, siting, construction and operation of energy facilities.

162-K   **Municipal Economic Development and Revitalization Districts, 162-K:1–162-K:15**

Through adoption of this chapter. municipalities may establish one or more development districts to improve commercial development, employment, open space relief and other facilities which benefit their economy. Establishment procedures, financing options, and administrative requirements are described.

204-C   **Housing Finance Authority, 204-C:1–204-C:87**

These sections establish the Housing Finance Authority as a separate, nonprofit organization not associated with state government. A nine-member Housing Finance Board is established (appointed by the Governor) to appoint an Executive Director and oversee responsibilities. Authority and administrative guidelines are provided. RSA 204-A and 204-B are repealed.

205-A   **Regulation of Manufactured Housing Parks, 205-A:1–205-A:31**

This chapter establishes administrative rules concerning business relationships between the manufactured housing park owner/operator and the manufactured housing owner/lessee, rules governing health and safety conditions, and rules governing notification of tenants prior to sales of housing parks. A nine-member Board of Manufactured Housing is established to hear and determine matters involving manufactured housing park rules.

231-A   **Municipal Trails, 231-A:1—231A:8**

This chapter authorizes municipalities to reclassify Highways as municipal trails, designate public trail use restrictions, and acquire or discontinue trails.

310-A   **Joint Board of Licensure and Certification, 310-A:1–310-A:97, 310-A:140–310-A:160, 310-A:182–310-A:221, 310-A:202–310-A:221**

License requirements are established for the practice of engineering, architectural design, surveying, soil science, landscape architecture, and home inspection in the state. Administration procedures for application, qualifications, fees, violations, hearings, renewals, and disciplinary actions are presented. A joint board is formed to meet quarterly for administrative purposes.

319-C   **Electricians, 319-C:1–319-C:15**

This chapter establishes a registration requirement for individuals performing electrical installation work.

An Electricians' Board is formed to evaluate applicants, issue licenses to qualified practitioners, and conduct other administrative duties.

356-A   **Land Sales Full Disclosure Act, 356-A:1–356-A:22**

This chapter establishes a registration requirement for subdivisions of 16 lots or greater, administered by the Consumer Protection and Antitrust Bureau of the Division of Public Protection of the Department of Justice.

356-B   **Condominium Act, 356-B:1–356-B:70**

This chapter is administered by the Consumer Protection and Antitrust Bureau of the Division of Public Protection of the Department of Justice. The statutes establish legal guidelines for the creation, sale and management of condominium property. RSA 356-B:5 provides the statutory framework within which municipalities may regulate condominium developments. Specific provisions for condominium conversion/development must be cited in local subdivision regulations for applicable review.

432   **Acquisition of Agricultural Land Development Rights, 432:18–432:31-a**

These sections authorize the establishment of an Agricultural Lands Preservation Committee to administer funds for the acquisition of development rights associated with land suitable for agricultural use.

477   **Solar Skyspace Easements, 477:49–477:52**

These sections authorize the establishment of and provide a form for the creation of a solar skyspace easement.

479-A   **Unit Ownership of Real Property, 479-A:1–479-A:28**

This chapter sets forth the guidelines for single unit ownership within multiunit developments (condominiums). It enables the establishment of a Board of Directors to administer bylaws governing the various properties in the development.

482-A   **Fill and Dredge in Wetlands, 482-A:1–482-A:15-a**

These sections establish the Wetlands Board to oversee fill and dredging activity in the states. The sections authorize the Wetlands Board to review, hold hearings, and approve or disapprove applications for filling or dredging activity. Three copies of the application must be sent to the town or city clerk who, in turn, distributes them to the Board of Selectmen/Mayor or City Manager, Planning Board, and Conservation Commission.

485-A   **Dredging (Terrain Alteration), 485-A:17**

This section requires individuals proposing to dredge, excavate, place fill, mine, transport forest products or undertake construction in or on border of the surface waters of the state and individuals proposing to significantly alter the characteristic of the terrain to submit detailed plans of the activity to the Division of Water Supply and Pollution Control of the Department of Environmental Services.

Sewage Disposal Systems, 485-A:29–485-A:44

These sections require the submission to, and approval of plans by, the Division of Water Supply and Pollution Control of the Department of Environmental Services in order to protect water supplies, and to prevent pollution in the surface waters of the State. They also set forth procedures and penalties.

669   **Town Elections, 669:1–669:75**

This chapter establishes procedures for the election of local officials, including elected planning board and budget committee members.

670   **Village District Elections, 670:1–670:12**

This chapter establishes procedures for the election of
village district officers.

Index

BUILDING CODES —Cont'd
State building code —Cont'd
Review board —Cont'd
Appeal of decisions of the state board for licensing plumbers, 155-A:11-a.
Appeals from decisions of board, 155-A:12.
State funded buildings, 155-A:13.
Vacating buildings.
Authority to order building vacated, 674:52-a.

BUILDING PERMITS.
Historic districts.
Commissions, 676:8, 676:9.
Issuance.
Building inspector, duties, 676:12.
Restrictions, 676:13.
Required, 676:11.
State building code, 155-A:4.
Withholding.
Building inspector, duties, 676:12.

BURDEN OF PROOF.
Sewage disposal systems.
Plans and specifications.
Reconsideration of department decision on, 485-A:40.

C

CAMPGROUNDS.
Recreation camp safety generally, 485-A:23 to 485-A:25-g.

CAPITAL IMPROVEMENTS PROGRAMS.
Authority, 674:5.
Contents, requirements, 674:6.
Planning board, duties, 674:5.
Preparation, 674:7.
Statement of purpose, 674:6.
Submission to mayor and budget committee, 674:8.

CEASE AND DESIST ORDERS.
Issuance, 676:17-a.
Water pollution.
Environmental services department, 485-A:22.
Wetlands, 482-A:14-a.

CITATIONS.
Issuance, 676:17-b.

CITIES.
Bond issues.
Municipal economic development and revitalization districts, 162-K:8.
Building codes, 47:22 to 47:27.
Amendment, 47:23.
Examination by public, 47:25.
Exceptions to provisions, 47:24.
Hearing on, 47:26.
Manufactured housing, 47:22-a, 47:22-b.
Penalties for violations, 47:24.
Power to adopt, 47:22.
Community revitalization tax relief incentive, 79-E:1 to 79-E:14.
Conservation commissions, 36-A:1 to 36-A:6.
Economic development.
Municipal economic development and revitalization districts, 162-K:1 to 162-K:15.
See MUNICIPAL ECONOMIC DEVELOPMENT AND REVITALIZATION DISTRICTS.
Elections.
Interfering with voters.
City bylaws and ordinances as to, 47:17.
Local election reporting requirements.
City bylaws and ordinances as to, 47:17.
Energy efficiency and clean energy districts, 53-F:1 to 53-F:8.
See ENERGY EFFICIENCY AND CLEAN ENERGY DISTRICTS.

CITIES —Cont'd
Flood insurance.
National flood insurance program.
Floodplain ordinances.
Adoption as part of, 674:56, 674:57.
Fluoride introduced into municipal water supply.
Public hearing, approval by voters, 485:14 to 485:14-b.
Highways.
City, town and village district highways.
See HIGHWAYS.
Immunities.
Municipal executives, 31:104.
National flood insurance program.
Floodplain ordinances.
Adoption as part of, 674:56, 674:57.
Nonprofit corporations.
Municipal records storage and management, 31:132, 31:133.
Off highway recreational vehicles.
Bylaws or ordinances regulating, 215-A:15.
Office of strategic initiatives.
Regional and municipal assistance, 4-C:7 to 4-C:10.
Contact point, 4-C:10.
Coordination, 4-C:9.
Establishment of program, 4-C:7.
Responsibilities, 4-C:8.
Revolving funds, 4-C:9-a.
Oil refineries.
Local option for siting in cities, 47:27.
Ordinances.
Building codes, 47:22 to 47:27.
Generally, 47:17.
Local regulation excavations, 155-E:1 to 155-E:11.
Notice and publication, 47:18.
Validity of municipal legislation, 31:126 to 31:131.
Police.
Bylaws and ordinances to regulate, 47:17.
Property taxes.
Community revitalization tax relief incentive, 79-E:1 to 79-E:14.
Farm structures and land under farm structures.
Municipal adoption of provisions, 79-F:2.
Public utilities.
Water and/or sewer utility districts, 31:134 to 31:149.
Records.
Municipal records storage and management.
Nonprofit corporations, 31:132, 31:133.
Reports.
Elections.
Local election reporting requirements.
City bylaws and ordinances as to, 47:17.
Shoreland protection.
Municipal authority, 483-B:8.
Exemptions from provisions, 483-B:12.
Shoreland water quality protection.
Office of strategic initiatives.
Assistance to municipalities, 483-B:16.
Special assessments districts, 52-A:1 to 52-A:12.
Appropriation methods, 52-A:6.
Assessment and collection, 52-A:7.
Authority to establish, 52-A:2.
Bonds and other indebtedness, 52-A:9.
Definitions, 52-A:1.
Dissolution, 52-A:12.
Establishment, 52-A:5.
Initiation procedures, 52-A:4.
Lien priority, 52-A:10.
Requirements, 52-A:3.
Special assessment fund, 52-A:11.
Use of proceeds, 52-A:8.
Taxation.
Tax maps, 31:95-a.
Validity of municipal legislation, 31:126 to 31:131.
Water and/or sewer utility districts, 31:134 to 31:149.
Water pollution control.
Municipal responsibility, 485-A:5-b.

HIGHWAYS —Cont'd
City, town and village district highways —Cont'd
Liability of municipalities, 231:93.
Danger signs, 231:91.
Notice of insufficiency, 231:90.
Standard of care, 231:92.
Right of ways, conditional layout of, 231:28.
Scenic roads.
Designation, 231:157, 231:158.
Street names and markers.
Changes, 231:133.
Names, 231:133.
Signs, 231:133.
Corridor protection, 230-A:1 to 230-A:19.
Acquisitions, 230-A:12.
Agreements, intergovernmental, 230-A:18.
Amendments, 230-A:13.
Appeal, 230-A:5.
Damages, 230-A:10.
Definitions, 230-A:1.
Effects, 230-A:7.
Federal law compliance, 230-A:19.
Hearing, 230-A:4.
Intergovernmental agreements, 230-A:18.
Land use permits, relations to other, 230-A:8.
Layout, 230-A:2.
Local law compliance, 230-A:19.
Municipalities, 230-A:17.
Notice of hearing, 230-A:3.
Payment of damages, 230-A:10.
Permit application, 230-A:9.
Remedies, 230-A:16.
Restrictions, 230-A:11.
Return, 230-A:6.
State law compliance, 230-A:19.
Tender of damages, 230-A:10.
Termination of corridor, 230-A:14.
Notification, 230-A:15.
Driveways, 236:13.
Excavations.
Local permits, exemption, 155-E:2.
Regulations.
Penalties for violating, 236:14.
State highways.
Classes, 229:5.
Construction.
Limitation, 230:6.
County commissioners, roads laid out by, 229:6.
Courts of common pleas, roads laid out by, 229:6.
Defined, 229:1.
Reconstruction, limitation of, 230:6.
Telecommunications-related uses of state highway system, 228:31-a.
Village districts.
Powers and duties, 52:3-a.
Water supply and waterworks.
Private.
Restrictions on highway construction, 485:9.

HIKING TRAILS.
Water pollution.
Terrain alteration permits.
Exemptions, 485-A:17.

HISTORIC DISTRICT COMMISSIONS.
Abolition.
Authority, 673:18.
Effect, 673:20.
Transfer of documents, 673:21.
Accounts and accounting, 673:16.
Approvals.
Building permits, 676:8, 676:9.
Chairpersons.
Oaths, administering, 673:15.
Powers, 673:15.
Term of office, 673:9.
Court review of local decisions, 677:17, 677:18.

HISTORIC DISTRICT COMMISSIONS —Cont'd
Decisions, 676:3.
Employees, 673:16.
Enforcement of law, 676:10.
Establishment, 673:1.
Hearings.
Joint hearings, 676:2.
Meetings, 673:10.
Joint meetings, 676:2.
Members.
Alternate members, 673:6, 673:11.
Appointment, 673:4.
Disqualification, 673:14.
Removal from office, 673:13.
Term of office, 673:5.
Open meetings, 673:17.
Organization, 673:8.
Powers and duties, 674:46-a.
Procedural rules.
Adoption, 676:1.
Purpose, 674:45.
Recordkeeping, 673:17.
Vacancies in office, 673:12.

HISTORIC DISTRICTS.
Abolition procedure, 674:47.
Enforcement of law, 674:49.
Establishment, 674:46.
Nonconforming structures.
Construction and interpretation, 674:48.
Ordinances.
Amendment, 675:5.
Filing.
Place for filing, 675:9.
Reports, 675:9.
Requirements, generally, 675:8.
General requirements, 675:1.
Interim ordinances, 675:4-a.
Petition, 675:4.
Public hearing, requirements, 675:6, 675:7.
Repeal, 675:5.
Town and village districts, 675:3.
Town council form of government, 675:2.
Violations of law, 674:50.

HOME INSPECTORS.
Board of home inspectors.
Appeal of board decisions, 155-A:11-a.

HOUSEHOLD CLEANSING PRODUCTS.
Prohibition of certain products, 485-A:56.
Definitions, 485-A:55.
Penalties, 485-A:57.

HOUSING.
Commissions.
See HOUSING COMMISSIONS.
Drug-free zones.
Public housing authority property.
City bylaws and ordinances as to, 47:17.
Manufactured housing.
Prefabricated homes, warranties, 205-B:1 to 205-B:4.
Regulation of manufactured housing parks.
Definitions, 205-A:1.
Prefabricated homes.
Warranties on, 205-B:1 to 205-B:4.
Presite built homes.
Warranties on, 205-B:1 to 205-B:4.
Workforce housing, 674:58 to 674:61.

HOUSING COMMISSIONS.
Abolishing.
Effect, 673:20.
Procedure, 673:18.
Transfer of documents, 673:21.
Appropriations, 674:44-j.
Disqualification of members, 673:14.
Establishment, 673:1, 674:44-h.
Generally, 673:4-c.

Topical Statute Index